VIRGIL'S AENEID

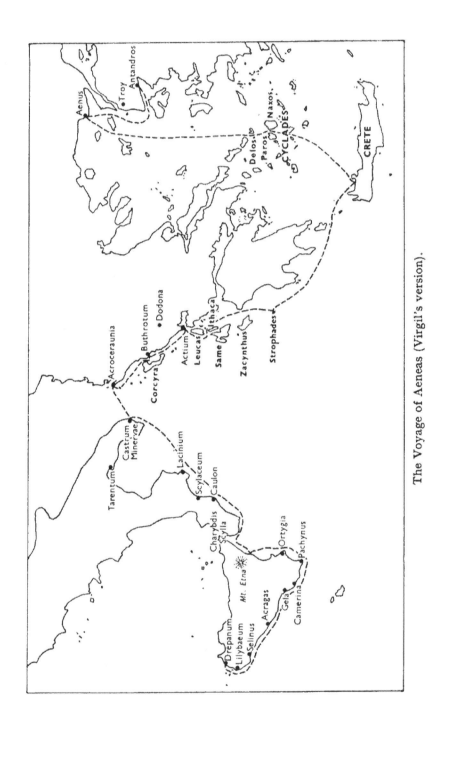

The Voyage of Aeneas (Virgil's version).

VIRGIL'S AENEID
Complete
Books I-XII

With an Introduction, Latin text and Notes
by
R. DERYCK WILLIAMS

Edited by
Giles Laurén

SOPHRON IMPRIMIT

ISBN 10: 0985081163
ISBN 13: 978-0985081164

Cover: The Cumae Virgil
Back cover: *Virgil reading to Augustus, Octavia.*
by Jean-Baptiste Wicar. Art Institute of Chicago.

Design by Sophron

Editor's Note

When Virgil set out to write the *Aeneid* he intended to write a founding mythology for the Roman people to commemorate their unification and achievements under Augustus. In the first six books of the *Aeneid* he demonstrates that the Latin language combined with Roman invention could rival Homer and in the latter six books he seeks to demonstrate that the Romans have even surpassed the Greeks by realising their Stoic ideals. Whereas the Greek hero Odysseus returned home much as he was when he left it, a classical hero, Virgil's parallel Roman hero, Aeneas, undergoes quite similar trials and arrives in Italy a new, improved man. He has attained the Stoic sophrosyne of the then ideal Roman. This is a major advance in Western Civilization.

It is puzzling to note the exaggerated interest in the first six books of the *Aeneid* since late classical days and wonder what part the Church had to play in this truncation. Was the Church perhaps jealous of the last six books because they displayed a Pagan society that valued *pietas*?

The Pharr edition of Virgil has long proved its value as a vocabulary builder and introduction to Roman poetry. Had it been a complete *Aeneid* this present edition might never have been produced, but the absence of the last six Books makes it useless for teaching the *Aeneid* as a foundation text for Western Civilization. At the other extreme, the twelve volume Oxford series has the disadvantages of expense and cumbersomeness.

In view of Virgil's intent the need for a complete, one volume, annotated and affordable *Aeneid* seems universally acknowledged. To limit one's study to selections from the first six Books is to defeat Virgil's purpose and can only be excused because of the size of the work and the constraints of classroom hours. Even so, if the *Aeneid* must be taught from selections, some of the selections should come from the last six books if the student is to understand Virgil's significance. The present edition includes an Introduction to the entire work, individual Book introductions and text summaries throughout that allow the reader to quickly follow the arguments of the sections not being prepared.

Dante, Spencer, Milton, Shakespeare, Byron, Shelley and Tennyson all borrowed heavily from Virgil. Indeed, it may be asked how well one can appreciate English literature without a knowledge of Virgil?

The history of critical Virgilian scholarship begins somewhere in the 1st. century B.C. and extends into an indeterminate future. The choice of basing this edition of the Aeneid on the work of R. D. Williams was determined by his profound familiarity with the entire spectrum of Virgilian scholarship, a point acknowledged by even his critics. Further, whenever Williams considers a textual note incomplete he includes a reference for deeper exploration. For this editor, to hear him cite the ancient sources like Quintilian, Macrobius and Servius along with the Neo Latinists such as de la Cerda, Scalinger and Bentley, and the moderns such as Conington, Page, Fairclough and Austin and bring them all together, gives the reader a certain sense of the timeless appeal of the *Aeneid*. This edition further serves as a provocative introduction to the delightful conundrums of classical source text, grammar, and meaning confronting any burgeoning classicist or curious reader.

Williams' Latin text of the *Aeneid* is the best presently available and is likely to remain so for many years to come. In part, because his notes offer clearly reasoned arguments as to why he favoured one reading of a previous editor over an alternative reading by another editor and he always cites the MSS sources. The reader, supplied with the alternatives, is thus informed and free to disagree and choose an alternative reading.

Williams's generation was that of the scholars whose notes went far beyond questions of grammar and included such ancillary information in their notes as historical events, mythology, religious and philosophical influences, poetic forms, points on Roman culture and then current objectives and intentions along with standard grammar explanations, word meanings and origins and a good deal of literary criticism and explanation. Many examples of parallels in English verse from Spencer, Milton and Shakespeare are cited to illustrate Virgil's legacy.

One of Williams' contemporaries wondered where he found the time to annotate all of the *Aeneid* and it is evident that his work was done under the pressure of a heavy schedule. Much of the work of this editor has been 'sharpening' notes and punctuation written in haste.

The Notes have been recast as footnotes such that the cited note appears on the same page as the annotated passage. Each note is referenced both by footnote number and by line number to give the reader two means to reading the text. Each sentence is signalled by a capital letter in acknowledgement of 2000 years of advances in punctuation. A Glossary of largely poetical terms has been added and the Index now covers all twelve Books. The two maps will be found useful.

Williams makes it clear that poetry is always a work in progress. How can a poem ever be finished, perfect? Isn't there always a word or phrase that will improve it? Aren't these the thoughts that ran through the minds of earlier editors and scribes? As Virgil well knew, there can be no perfect *Aeneid* text.

This edition of the *Aeneid* aspires to offer the best possible text combined with the best possible notes in a one volume edition at the best possible price in an ongoing attempt to encourage classical studies and provide a convenient text for the general reader

All criticisms, suggestions and especially corrections will be warmly received at [███████.███] and considered for later printings of this POD text.

Sacramento, Giles Laurén

liberdux@comcast.net

ROBERT DERYCK WILLIAMS, the son of a solicitor, was born in Hall Green, Birmingham on November 27, 1917 and educated at King Edward's School where he won a state scholarship and major open scholarship in classics to St. John's College, Cambridge. At St. John's he took a first in both parts of the Classical Tripos and won both the Samuel Nunn Exhibition and the Graves Prize.

During WWII he served in Persia and the Middle East as an officer in the RAF special duties branch.

He was appointed to the department of classics at Reading University in 1945, where he began a life-long career as teacher, tutor, researcher and supervisor of higher degree students. He was appointed Professor of Classics in 1979 and retired in 1983.

During his tenure at Reading he was much in demand as a speaker and regularly visited universities abroad, teaching at Chicago, Pennsylvania, Victoria British Columbia, Ottawa, Canberra, Perth, Melbourne and Otago. He was an outstanding lecturer and teacher; his lectures, particularly on his favourite poet, Virgil, were marked by enthusiasm, humanity, and a splendid delivery, especially of quotations both in Latin and in translation.

He made Virgil his life's work and was the obvious choice to produce a pamphlet reviewing contemporary Virgil studies for the Classical Association, for which he produced supplements at intervals. Over his career he helped to increase the poet's accessibility to school and university students as well as the general reader.

His 1967 *Virgil*, first of the *Greece and Rome Surveys*, set a high standard. In 1982, he was commissioned with T. S. Pattie to produce a commemorative work, *Virgil: His Poetry Throughout the Ages,* for the British Library's bimillennary exhibition. Other publications include *Aeneas and the Roman Hero;* a chapter on eighteenth and nineteenth century attitudes to Virgil in D. R. Dudley's collection of essays; a chapter on the *Aeneid* in the *Cambridge History of Classical Literature* and a noteworthy commentary on C. Day Lewis's translation of the *Aeneid.*

Before he died, Williams submitted the manuscript of a book on Virgil for the general reader.

Long a mainstay, he was president of the Virgil Society in 1975 and president of the Classical Association in 1981.

He was a keen cricketer in his youth and he excelled at squash which he played at a high standard until his 65th birthday.

His wife, Grace, predeceased him in 1979. There were three daughters of the marriage. He died in Reading on July 9, 1986 aged 68.

ACKNOWLEDGMENTS

My grateful thanks to Susan Patricia Melia and Professor Peter Kruschwitz, Humanities / Classics Department, Reading University, for their kind assistance in locating biographical material about R. D. Williams. Also to James J. Murphy and Craig Kallendorf for their sustaining encouragement. Especial thanks are due to Mark Riley for his continuous support, advice, assistance and encouragement throughout.

Contents

Preface   x

Introduction   xii

1. Life and Works of Virgil   xii
2. Virgil and Augustus   xiii
3. The Legend of Aeneas   xiii
4. Sources of the Aeneid   xiv
5. Synopsis of the Aeneid   xv
6. Structure and Themes   xvi
7. Virgil's Hexameter   xx
8. Manuscripts of the Aeneid and Ancient Commentators   xxi
9. Differences of Text   xxii
10. Bibliography   xxvii
BOOK 1   1
BOOK 2   49
BOOK 3   94
BOOK 4   144
BOOK 5   191
BOOK 6   245
BOOK 7   298
BOOK 8   348
BOOK 9   389
BOOK 10   431
BOOK 11   484
BOOK 12   534
Index to the Notes   594
Glossary   603

Preface

No commentary on the whole *Aeneid* (except Mackail's highly selective commentary, 1930) has appeared in English since T. E. Page's exemplary edition of 1894-1900. Page was one of the most perceptive commentators Virgil has ever had, a man almost always in tune with the poet (except for his Victorian views on *Aeneid* 4), and familiar with him not through card-indexes but through constant reading of Latin literature. In seventy years our approaches to poetry have changed and our knowledge of the ancient world has been enlarged in many ways, and the times call for a new commentary in a more modern idiom.

The present edition is intended to be suitable for the upper forms of schools and for universities, and I hope that it will also be useful for more advanced scholars. It is designed on a scale which requires brevity and immediate relevance to the text; the fuller type of exposition to be found in the Clarendon Press editions of individual books is therefore precluded, but I have always tried to be concise rather than omissive. I have not hesitated to explain relatively simple questions of diction, metre, and construction, but I have aimed above all to interpret the poetic methods and intentions of the *Aeneid*, and to explain not only what Virgil says but how he says it and why he says it in the particular way which he chooses. I have quite frequently quoted imitations and similarities of diction from English poets, especially from Spenser and Milton, because this can illuminate the literary impact of the Virgilian passage.

I have established a new text, and in the Introduction I have listed its points of difference from Sir Roger Mynors's recent Oxford Text (1969), and from its predecessor (Hirtzel, 1900). I have discussed all such instances, and others where there is any significant doubt about the text, in the note on the passage in question. I have not thought it necessary to include an *apparatus criticus*, as the salient features of the evidence which have led me to adopt a particular reading are outlined in the notes, and fuller details are easily available for those who require them in the apparatus of Mynors or Hirtzel (or Sabbadini or Goelzer and Durand; see Bibliography).

I have refrained from overloading the commentary with the names of scholars who have helped me towards my interpretations, but I am of course enormously indebted, directly or indirectly, to an almost countless number of Virgilian commentators and critics, of whom I mention here Servius, Heyne, Conington, Henry, Page, Lejay, Mackail, Conway, Austin. I owe a very special debt to T. R. Glover, who taught me in my undergraduate years to begin to appreciate the poetry of Virgil.

I am most grateful for help in the preparation of my commentary to Mr P. T. Eden, Professor E. Laughton, Mr. A. G. Lee, Mr. F. Robertson, Professor W. J. N. Rudd; I am particularly indebted to Mr. E. L. Harrison, who has read and improved the first draft of the whole of the work. Finally I gratefully acknowledge the kind permission of the Delegates of the Clarendon Press for me to use in an abridged form the material of my commentaries on *Aeneid* 5 and *Aeneid* 3, published by the Clarendon Press in 1960 and 1962 respectively.

Reading, February 1971

R. D. WILLIAMS

Introduction

Publius Vergilius[2] Maro was born on October 15th 70 B.C., of peasant stock, at a village called Andes near Mantua, in Northern Italy in the area of the River Po. Here he spent his childhood on his father's farm, living a countryman's life and learning to love the beauties of the north Italian landscape. He was educated at Cremona, Milan and then at Rome; we know that for a time he studied with the Epicurean Siro. During his youth he met some of the men who were destined to play prominent parts in public life, and through his poetry he met more (Pollio, Gallus, Varus, Octavian himself); he became an important member of the literary court circle under Maecenas, and though he himself took no part in military or political life, he was on close terms with those who did, and was thus in constant touch with national problems and aspirations.

His earliest poems[3] were the *Eclogues*, a collection of ten pastoral poems written during the period 42-37 B.C., and published in 37 B.C. From the first and ninth of these it seems that he was involved in the confiscation of property in the Mantua area during the resettlement of the veterans of the civil wars; at all events he did not return to live in the north, but spent the rest of his life in Campania, at Nola or Naples. Here from 37-30 B.C. he composed the *Georgics*, a poetic account (dedicated to Maecenas) of Italian farming which bears full witness to his personal knowledge of the countryside, its crops, its animals, its farmers, and of his deep love for rural Italy, as well as of his mastery of the Latin hexameter.

During all this time Virgil had been preparing[4] himself to undertake an epic poem, the peak of literary aspiration, and in 30 B.C. he began to compose the *Aeneid*, a poem to express Rome's national greatness and destiny by means of the story of her legendary origins. By 19 B.C. the *Aeneid* was virtually complete,[5] but Virgil decided to give it a further three years' revision, and set out on a voyage to Greece to give himself local colour for the parts he meant to modify. Early in his travels he fell ill of a fever, and was forced to return to Italy; he died at Brundisium within a few days of landing. He left

---

1 The main ancient sources (apart from the poems themselves) are to be found in the lives by Servius and by Aelius Donatus (the latter sometimes attributed to Suetonius); these are published in the O.C.T. *Vitae Vergilianae Antiquae* (ed. C. Hardie, 1954). See also Mackail's *Aeneid,* Intro, pp. xxiiif., W. F. Jackson Knight, *Roman Vergil* II chap, ii, and the introduction to E. de Saint-Denis' Budé *Eclogues* (1942).

2 Strictly his name in English should be spelled Vergil, but the spelling Virgil has been traditional for so long that it seems inappropriate to abandon it.

3 There exist a number of minor poems attributed to Virgil, collected under the title of the *Appendix Vergiliana.* Very few of these are likely to be genuine works of Virgil.

4 See *Ecl.* 6.3-5, *Geo.* 3.16f.; Servius tells us of a project to write on the Alban kings, and Donatus that Virgil began a Roman theme but finding his material uncongenial resumed pastoral poetry.

5 It has some fifty incomplete lines and some stop-gap passages, and clearly was undergoing continuous revision and rewriting, but it is in no real sense unfinished.

instructions that the *Aeneid* should be burnt, but Augustus countermanded them and had the poem published posthumously.

2. *VIRGIL AND AUGUSTUS*

When Virgil was born, Cisalpine Gaul (the name of the area of northern Italy around the river Po) was not yet part of Roman Italy. Parts of the province did not gain Roman citizenship until 49 B.C., and it was not finally incorporated into Italy until 42 B.C. Catullus too was born in this area, and it is possible that the deeply felt and 'romantic' sensitivity which the two poets have in common is partly due to their environment. During Virgil's early manhood Italy was ravaged by the civil wars between Caesar and Pompey, and subsequently by those between Antony and Octavian on the one side and Brutus and Cassius on the other; finally there was the conflict between Antony and Octavian (the future emperor Augustus).[1] When Augustus finally defeated Antony and Cleopatra at the battle of Actium in 31 B.C., Virgil and his contemporaries had indeed experienced so much of the suffering involved in civil war that their intense longing for peace and stability is easily understood.[2] This was what it seemed that Augustus could offer;[3] with the restoration of morality and religion[4] the new Golden Age of the *pax Romana* could be inaugurated. In the public sector optimism prevailed and hopes were high; Virgil's personal friends included many who had a large part to play in directing events. What wonder that he was inspired to portray the hopes of peace and concord at last after seemingly endless discord? When we are told, as we often have been since antiquity in one form of phraseology or another, that Augustus 'imposed' upon Virgil the composition of his epic, we may reply that this is true to approximately the same extent as that Virgil imposed upon Augustus the political, social and religious reforms which he inaugurated. The truth is that there were very many people at this time, including Virgil and Augustus, who felt that only by a return to the religion and patriotic virtues of the past could Rome recapture her true identity. The emperor embodied these ideas in political and administrative procedures, and the poet embodied them in the *Aeneid*.

3. *THE LEGEND OF AENEAS*

It is possible to isolate a number of reasons for Virgil's choice of the Aeneas legend as his subject for an epic poem. It satisfied his first requirement, which was that the theme should be national (in a way that Valerius Flaccus' *Argonautica* or Statius' *Thebaid* could not be), and yet it avoided the inflexibility of a historical subject (like Lucan's *Pharsalia* or Silius' *Punica*) or annalistic treatment (like Ennius' *Annales*). By using the legendary story of the very first settlement in Italy which led ultimately to the foundation of Rome, Virgil could constantly relate distant events to his own time, partly by adumbration of Roman mores in the character of Aeneas, and

---

1 For a vivid account of this period see R. Syme, *The Roman Revolution,* Oxford, 1939.

2 Cf. *Ecl.* 4, *Geo.* 1.498f., Hor. *Epod.* 7 and 16.

3 Cf. Prop. 4.6.37 *mundi servator.*

4 See Livy 3.20.5, Hor. *Odes* 3.6.1f. for the misfortune brought by neglecting religion.

of Roman customs and festivals in describing their origins (the method of aetiology), and partly by prophecies, visions and imaginary pictures of future events (as on Aeneas' shield). In particular he could glorify the origins of Rome by relating them to an antique past, and especially magnify the Julian *gens* of Augustus. At the same time his subject was contemporary with the *Iliad* and the *Odyssey*, and could contain elements from the fabulous and distant world of the *Odyssey* (as in Book 3), as well as specific retelling of the Homeric stories (as of *Odyssey* 5-8 in *Aeneid* 1 and *Iliad* 22 in *Aeneid* 12).

The legend itself[1] was of great antiquity in Virgil's time, but it was also very flexible and varied (like our own King Arthur legend before Malory). Strong traces of a Trojan foundation in the west are found from the sixth century onwards, and by the third century the story of the Trojan foundation of Rome was strongly established, for example in Timaeus, Lycophron and Naevius. A comparison with the beginning of Livy 1 and with the first book of Dionysius of Halicarnassus shows the very large extent to which Virgil could vary the legend to achieve his own poetic purposes. The story of Aeneas and Dido for example (though probably already in Naevius' epic poem) played no part comparable with that which Virgil has given it; the second visit to Sicily (and the consequent funeral celebrations for Anchises) was Virgil's own; and the arrangement of the relationship between Latinus, Turnus, Mezentius, Evander was very different in other versions than Virgil's. The legend then was important, well-known, national, but of such a kind that Virgil could re-arrange its episodes and universalise it in his own special poetic way.

4. SOURCES OF THE AENEID

We have seen that a primary source for the composition of the Aeneid was Virgil's enthusiasm for Rome and her future destiny; an equally important source was the literature of the past, especially the spell which the poems of Homer[2] had cast upon Virgil. Here was a Greek panorama of the human experience which Virgil could try to rival for the Romans; here was a framework into which he could set his own thoughts. The *Iliad* and the *Odyssey* offered a method of presenting heroic behaviour which Virgil could adapt to a more complex society. He could use the structure, the episodes, the divine machinery, the similes, the very phraseology, in order to create something quite new in ethos and tone, something that would be as relevant to the Roman world as Homer was to the Greeks. By taking the Aeneas legend as the subject for his national poem he could not only adumbrate Roman values and ways of life through the story of the first founder of the Roman people, but he could also keep the closest possible link with Homer's world; for Aeneas was a contemporary of Achilles and Odysseus, a member of the heroic age who has to step out into a new civilisation, and from being the last Trojan become the first Roman.

Homer was by far the most important literary influence on Virgil, but there were others of great importance. The tragedies of fifth-century Athens deeply

---

1 See my OUP Ed. of *Aeneid* 3, pp. 7f.

2 See Brooks Otis, *Virgil* (passim); W. S. Anderson, *T.A. Ph.A.*, 1957, pp. 17f.; R. D. Williams, *Phoenix*, 1963, pp. 266f. The parallel passages have been tabulated in full by G. N. Knauer, *Die Aeneis und Homer*, Gottingen 1964.

influenced Virgil's account of the fall of Troy, and especially of the fate of Dido and of Turnus. Apollonius of Rhodes had shown how a love motif, sensitively and intensely presented as in lyric or elegy, could be incorporated into epic, and Virgil's fourth *Aeneid* owes (for all its differences) a good deal to him. Of the Romans Ennius had adapted the Greek hexameter to the Latin language and portrayed the character of early Rome in many a memorable passage, and Virgil frequently echoes his phrases. Lucretius had shown how the hexameter could be used majestically and with vivid imagery. Catullus in his sixty-fourth poem used a delicate and sensitive rhythm to convey the pathos of desertion, and is recalled often in the fourth *Aeneid*, and elsewhere in passages of special tenderness. Virgil is unique in his ability to appreciate and recreate moods of contrasting and indeed contradictory kinds: Ennius and Catullus were poles apart, yet Virgil could respond to what each was seeking to portray. The *Aeneid* is a poem founded firmly on the real life of Augustan Rome, yet it seeks enlightenment for its deepest problems from literature of every kind. It is indeed a brilliant personal synthesis of the human situation as it had been seen through many different eyes.

5. SYNOPSIS OF THE AENEID

The *Aeneid* tells the story of how Aeneas escaped from Troy when it was destroyed by the Greeks, and under a divine mission sailed west to found a new city which Fate had decreed should rule the world.

Book 1. The poem begins as the Trojans, after seven years of wanderings, are leaving Sicily for Italy, the place of their promised city. But Juno arouses a storm and they are driven off course to Carthage. Here they are hospitably welcomed by the queen Dido. Through the scheming of Venus Dido falls in love with Aeneas and at a banquet asks to hear the story of his wanderings.

Books 2 and 3. These books are a recounting for Dido of Aeneas' adventures prior to the action of Book 1. The second book is intense and tragic, concerned with the events of one single night, the night of Troy's destruction. The third book is slow-moving, conveying the weary endurance of years of voyaging to reach the 'ever-receding shores' of Italy.

Book 4. The story of the love of Dido and Aeneas is continued. Jupiter sends Mercury to order Aeneas to leave Carthage in order to fulfil his divine mission to found Rome, and he immediately realises that he must sacrifice his love for Dido to his national and religious duty. He attempts to explain to Dido why he has to leave her, but she accepts no explanation and, as the Trojans depart, in frenzy and despair she kills herself.

Book 5. The Trojans return to Sicily and celebrate funeral games for Aeneas' father Anchises who had died there a year earlier. Juno causes the Trojan women to set fire to the ships, but the fire is quenched by Jupiter. On the last stage of the journey the helmsman Palinurus is swept overboard by the god Sleep.

Book 6. The Trojans reach Italy at Cumae, and Aeneas descends with the Sibyl to the underworld in order to consult the ghost of his father Anchises. The future heroes of Roman history pass in a pageant before him, and he returns to the upper world strengthened in resolution.

Book 7. The Trojans reach the Tiber, and are hospitably welcomed by King Latinus, who recognises that Aeneas is the stranger referred to in an oracle as the destined husband of his daughter Lavinia. She is already betrothed to Turnus the Rutulian, and Juno again intervenes to ensure that Turnus will fight the Trojans. War breaks out, and the book ends with a catalogue of the Italian forces assisting Turnus.

Book 8. Aeneas visits Evander, an Arcadian living at Pallanteum on the site of Rome, to seek help. Evander sends his son Pallas at the head of a contingent of Arcadians. Venus has a new shield made for her son Aeneas, and the book ends with a description of the pictures from Roman history depicted on the shield — a reminder before the general outbreak of hostilities of why Aeneas has to fight this war against Turnus, and what depends on it.

Book 9. In the absence of Aeneas the Rutulian Turnus achieves great deeds. The sally from the Trojan camp by Nisus and Euryalus ends in their death, and Turnus breaks into the Trojan camp, but in his pride and hubris he omits to open the gates so his forces can join him, and has to escape by jumping into the Tiber.

Book 10. Aeneas returns with Pallas and the fighting continues. Turnus seeks out Pallas and kills him, arrogantly boasting over him and stripping off his sword-belt. Aeneas in violent anger and guilt rages over the battlefield, and kills many of his opponents, including Lausus, young son of Mezentius, and Mezentius himself.

Book 11. The funeral for Pallas is described; a truce is made for burial of the dead, but shortly the fighting is resumed, and the heroic deeds and death of the Italian warrior-maiden Camilla are described.

Book 12. A single combat is arranged between Turnus and Aeneas; but the truce is broken and Aeneas is wounded. The scene shifts to Olympus where the discord is settled on the divine plane when Juno accepts defeat on condition that the Italians shall be the dominant partners in the Trojan-Italian stock from which the Romans will be born. Aeneas pursues Turnus as Achilles had pursued Hector, and wounds him. Turnus begs for mercy, but Aeneas, seeing the sword belt of Pallas on Turnus' shoulder, kills him in vengeance.

The subsequent events, between the death of Turnus at the end of the *Aeneid* (twelfth century B.C.) and the foundation of Rome itself (eighth century B.C.), are foretold in Jupiter's prophecy (*Aen.* 1.266f.). Aeneas founds Lavinium; after three years his son Ascanius succeeds him and rules for thirty years in Lavinium before transferring the settlement to Alba Longa. Here the Alban kings (*Aen.* 6.760f.) rule for 300 years until Romulus, grandson of Numitor, founds Rome (traditional date 753 B.C.).

6. STRUCTURE AND THEMES[1]

The structure of the *Aeneid* is elaborately organised, as is essential for an epic poem (in the words of Dr Johnson 'whoever purposes, as it is expressed in Milton, "to build the lofty rhyme" must first acquaint himself with the law

---

1 See the introductory note to the commentary on each book for a brief literary analysis of the individual books.

of poetic architecture, and take care that his edifice be solid as well as beautiful'). The *Aeneid* may be viewed as two halves, an Odyssean and an Iliadic half; equally it may be viewed as three thirds, the tragedy of Dido, the Roman centre, the tragedy of Turnus. Individual books act as blocks to give symmetry or contrast: thus the third and fifth books are relatively calm and unemotional, serving to vary the intensity of the second, fourth, and sixth books.

Again, there are balances between the two halves; the seventh book reiterates the hostility of Juno which motivates the action of the first book; the eighth book gives the first glimpse of Rome as the second book had given the last glimpse of Troy; the tenth book has in the death of Pallas something of the intense feeling of tragedy which colours the whole fourth book. The death of Turnus at the end of Book 12 recalls the sense of bewilderment caused by the prophecy of Marcellus' death at the end of Book 6. This description of structural organisation could be prolonged, but we must always remind ourselves that in a poem the structure is a servant of the themes.

The themes of the *Aeneid* are perhaps best considered as the exploration of various tensions. Here I shall present three.[1] Firstly there is a powerful tension between the primary subject of the poem, Rome's greatness, and the pathos of human suffering which exists in spite of, or even because of, Rome's greatness. The element of pathos is so obvious to all readers of Virgil, and has been so strongly stressed in the last hundred years of Virgilian criticism, that it is necessary to emphasise the other polarity, the optimistic note of Rome's greatness. The poem is first and foremost about Rome's mission, about the restoration of the Golden Age which can be achieved under Augustus. This was what the ancient critics thought the poem was about, and so did the English eighteenth century,[2] and they were not wrong. Consider the proud certainty of Jupiter's prophecy to Venus in Book I (278-9, 291): 'To these I set no bounds in space or time; I have given them rule without end' . . . 'Then shall the rough generations be softened into peace Or the pageant of Roman heroes in Book 6, ending with Anchises' claim (851-3) that the Romans will rule the peoples with their government, give them peace and civilisation, spare the conquered and suppress the arrogant. Consider the description of Aeneas' shield in Book 8 (626f.), where the concepts of military success leading to a settled and religious way of life are powerfully conveyed; or the final promise of Jupiter to Juno in Book 12 (834f.) that the Romans, inheriting the qualities of the Italians, will surpass all others in *pietas* (devotion to the gods and service to men). There should not be, indeed cannot be, any doubt that Virgil's public voice was sincerely optimistic. But side by side with his public voice is the private voice, expressing deep concern for the lonely individual who does not fit into these cosmic schemes. The fulfilment of the Roman mission requires the sacrifice of Dido and the destruction of Turnus and countless other warriors; it seems to require in Aeneas himself a rejection

---

1 For a fuller account see my article in *Antichthon*, 1967, pp. 29f.

2 For Servius the poem's intention was 'to imitate Homer and praise Augustus through his ancestors'. Dryden says 'he concluded it to be in the interest of his country to be so governed; to infuse an awful respect into the people towards such a prince; by that respect to confirm their obedience to him, and by that obedience to make them happy. This was the moral of his divine poem.'

of love (for Dido) and mercy (for Turnus). It involves the opposition of Juno and all the suffering which she can cause: 'why do the heavenly powers feel such anger?' (*Aen.* 1.11). We may call this private voice a Catullan voice, set in tension with the strong vigorous attitude of an Ennius or a Livy. The conflict involves Virgil in a question which permits of no clear answer, and it could be (though this is pure conjecture) that his failure to find an answer, his failure to justify Rome on all counts, led to his dying wish that the poem should be burned. In two ways he approaches an answer: the first is that 'it was so great a task to found the Roman race' (*Aen.* 1.33), and only through great suffering can greatness be achieved; and the second is that (as we see in Book 6) in some way imperfectly understood, indeed only faintly glimpsed, the life to come may set aright and compensate the seemingly senseless suffering of this world. But when all is said Virgil has no real answer. It is a measure of his greatness as a poet that he has posed and explored the question in so many of its aspects, always honestly and without pretence or specious simplification.

The second tension is that between the Homeric world to which Aeneas belongs and the Roman world which he has to inaugurate. The poem unfolds on a double time-scale: Aeneas belongs to the heroic age, yet he also has to be a proto-Augustan. Virgil's problem is to depict a new kind of hero, a hero for an age no longer 'heroic'. Patently the qualities of an Achilles will not suit the founder of Rome; some no doubt will (bravery, resolution and so on), but others not (like impetuosity, proud self-confidence, concern for self). Aeneas has to find out which of his heroic qualities to preserve and which to let go, and it is because he is trying to find out that he does not 'cut a figure' as Achilles does. There is something splendid and larger than life about the man who, like Achilles, always knows what is expected and required of him and acts accordingly; there is something much more human in the man who ponders, worries, negotiates, but such a man does not perhaps command our emulation or our wonder in the same way. This is one reason why the character of Aeneas has been frequently criticised[1] (i.e. because he is insufficiently 'heroic'), and why Turnus (an entirely 'heroic' character) has seemed to many more convincing. And there is a further aspect of this criticism: Aeneas is by no means entirely successful in realising this new concept of heroism. Basically this is a social type of heroism, concerned with the group rather than the individual (how much we admire Odysseus, man of many resources, for getting safely back to Ithaca, but he did not succeed in bringing any of his comrades safely back with him). It is based on *pietas*, an attitude of responsibility towards gods and men, an attitude which may involve the subjugation of individual passions (like the desire for glorious death at Troy, or the love of Dido) to the demands of duty. In the outcome Aeneas is not totally able or even totally willing to achieve this degree of self-denial; he forgets his mission in order to stay with Dido until Jupiter intervenes, and he is sometimes overcome by elements of irrational passion

---

1 Another reason, discussed later in this section, is that his relationship with the gods makes him seem to some to be lacking in free-will.

(*furor*) within himself or as manifested by others. On the battlefield he tries for the most part to behave humanely, and there is a real contrast between him (as he fights only because war is forced upon him) and Turnus, the warrior of heroic type (who fights because he enjoys it and is good at it). But on three occasions at least Aeneas becomes exactly like Turnus; after the death of Pallas (10.510f.), after he has himself been wounded (12.441f.), and at the very end of the poem. Here, when Turnus begs for mercy, we expect Aeneas to grant it; but he sees the belt of Pallas on Turnus' shoulder and in a fit of fury and a lust for vengeance he kills him. If we remember the circumstances of the death of Pallas (10.441f.), we easily understand why Aeneas feels himself justified, but the fact remains that at the last moment Aeneas is no different from the old heroic type he is supposed to be superseding. Nothing could have been easier for Virgil than to avoid this dilemma. Instead of being wounded in battle Turnus could have been killed, but he wanted his readers to be involved in the dilemma. How righteous is righteous anger? Are we glad that Aeneas yields to it?

The third tension is between the world of men and the world of gods. Virgil inherited from Homer the supernatural machinery of Olympian deities, and in certain ways uses it as Homer had done, for example, to initiate action on the human plane, and to diversify the familiar human scene with glimpses of an imagined world. This visual aspect of another world beyond the clouds is one that figures very largely in the *Aeneid*; the sheer pictorial beauty of shapes which the human eye cannot see forms a great part of Virgil's imagery. Think of Juno, proud queen of heaven, stately and forbidding; of Neptune with his trident and retinue of sea-deities calming the storm; of Iris descending on the path of the rainbow; of Mercury with his winged sandals and his wand winging his way to Mt. Atlas; of Jupiter with his serene nod of supreme authority; this is the material of myth painted on canvas and which Virgil seeks to capture in words.

There is one special respect in which Virgil's concept of supernatural powers differed from Homer's, and this is the idea that fate and Jupiter are working out their far-reaching purpose for the benefit of mankind. Aeneas is *fato profugus* (*Aen*. 1.2). It is a concept greatly influenced by Roman Stoicism,[1] and it introduces a theme of human endeavour to achieve what the gods wish, a theme dominant throughout Aeneas' actions. Aeneas accepts a divine mission, and to the extent of his human ability devotes himself to it. Often it seems that the task is too great for his human frailty, but in moments of despair and crisis he receives help and strength from the supernatural world which enables him to continue. This does not mean that he is without freewill; it means that Virgil is exploring the meaning of his profound conviction that man does not live in this world alone. In the memorable words of Cicero, as he expounds the Stoic attitude (*Tusc*. 1.118): *Non enim temere nec fortuito sati et creati sumus, sed profecto fuit quaedam vis quae generi consuleret humano* . . . 'For we were not born and brought into this world blindly or by chance, but there existed surely a power to look after mortal men . . .' For

---

1 See Arnold, *Roman Stoicism*, p.80 & p.199.

Virgil as for Cicero there existed a divine power which guided and directed those capable of receiving its instructions; the character of Aeneas is to be interpreted in the Light of his Stoic endeavours, often imperfectly realised, to understand and to follow the will of this divine power.

7. VIRGIL'S HEXAMETER

The metrical movement[1] of Virgil's hexameter, the sheer word-music, has always been acclaimed even by those who would deny him much else,[2] and Virgil's achievement is very justly summarised in Tennyson's famous line 'Wielder of the stateliest measure ever moulded by the lips of man'. Here attention may be drawn to three aspects of Virgil's mastery.

First of all, Virgil more than any other Latin poet was able to exploit the possibility of interplay between sentence endings and line endings. In his predecessors generally speaking the line was the sentence unit; it had been relatively rare for a sentence to end elsewhere than at a line ending. Virgil in the Latin hexameter, like Milton in English blank verse, made new use of the kinds of emphasis available through run-on words, mid-line pauses, staccato short sentences. The result of this is not only an extra force in particular places, but an enormous increase in the variety of narrative movement, so that the hexameter can retain the reader's attention (as it could not have if used as in Catullus 64) over thousands of lines.[3]

Secondly Virgil achieved the variety he needed by the continued use, but within strict control, of metrical abnormalities and licences used by his predecessors. He occupies a middle place between the freedom or mannerisms of Ennius, Lucretius, Catullus and the disappearance of almost all irregularities in Ovid and afterwards. Earlier poetry is recalled by monosyllabic endings, lengthening in arsis, hyper-metric elisions, hiatus, spondaic fifth feet, unusual caesurae; but these features are employed rarely, and often with deliberate effect. Examples may be studied by use of the index under the heading 'metre'.

Thirdly Virgil understood and exploited more than any other Latin poet the two rhythms which were inherent in his metre ever since Ennius had employed the quantitative hexameter (taken from the Greeks) for the more strongly stressed Latin language. The result of this was to impose on the normal stress pronunciation of Latin an artificial scheme of scansion according to long and short syllables; and the effect was to make possible at every point coincidence or conflict of these two rhythms.[4] The quantitative pattern called for a metrical ictus, or beat, at the beginning of each foot of the hexameter; the natural stress accent[5] on each word could occur in the same

---

1 For methods of scansion see Huxley's edition of *Georgia* 1 and 4 (London, 1963) and Maguinness' edition of *Aeneid* 12 (London, 1953). For aesthetic appreciation see also L. P. Wilkinson, *Golden Latin Artistry*, Cambridge, 1963.

2 Cf. Coleridge's famous question: 'If you take from Virgil his diction and metre, what do you leave him'?

3 For illustrations see the indexes to my OUP Ed.s of *Aeneid* 3 and 5 under the heading of 'metre'.

4 On this see especially W. F. Jackson Knight, *Accentual Symmetry in Vergil* (Oxford, 1939), and *Roman Vergil* I pp. 292f., as well as Wilkinson (cited above).

5 The rules for the Latin stress accent are very easy, being almost exactly the same as English: thus if the last syllable but one is long it takes the stress (*amóris, condúntur*), otherwise the stress is on the last syllable but two (*cármina, carmínibus*).

place as the ictus or not, according to choice. Clearly the interplay of these rhythms can be used for aesthetic effects of various kinds: in Virgil's

$$\acute{} \; - \quad \acute{} \; \cup \; \cup \quad \acute{} \; \cup \; \cup \quad \acute{} \cup \cup \; \acute{} \quad \cup \quad \cup \quad \acute{} \; \cup$$

spargens | umida | mella so|porife|rumque pa|paver   (4.48(

the total coincidence of the two rhythms gives a peaceful and drowsy line, while in

$$- \; \acute{} \; - \quad \acute{} \; - \; \acute{} \quad - \; - \quad \acute{} \; \cup \cup \quad \acute{} \; -$$

appa|rent ra|ri nan|tes in | gurgite | vasto   (1.118)

the conflict in the first four feet (especially with the spondaic movement) gives a feeling of struggle. These are extreme examples; Virgil's mastery is to be seen in the controlled use of these two rhythms throughout his poem, and it is this interplay of ictus and accent (or, as it equally is, of word pattern within the metrical structure) which perhaps more than any other single feature makes 'the stateliest measure'.

Using these technical devices, and many others (like the interplay of spondees and dactyls, the subtle music of alliteration and assonance, the variation of the Catullan patterned line for description with vigorous and fast-moving rhythms for narrative) Virgil was able to an extraordinary degree to make the sound suit the sense. The boxing-match in Book 5 is violent and excessive in metrical rhythm as well as in meaning; the last speech of Dido to Aeneas is vehement in movement as well as diction; the scene as Aeneas enters the underworld is ghostly in sound as well as sense. In the last analysis it is the range of metrical movement, as it is the range of mood and emotion, which triumphantly sustains the epic theme.

8. MANUSCRIPTS OF THE AENEID AND ANCIENT COMMENTATORS

The text of Virgil has been preserved far better than that of any other Latin poet. We possess manuscripts in capital letters from the fourth and fifth century, as well as many citations in ancient authors such as Seneca, Quintilian, Aulus Gellius and the invaluable commentary of Servius (c. a.d. 400). Ninth-century MSS (the date of our earliest testimony for very many authors) abound for Virgil, and the recent collation of a dozen of these by Mynors for his Oxford Text (1969) has served to confirm the enormous reliability of our capital MSS. In most cases of doubt about the text in Virgil the choice is between variants already existing by the fifth century; the number of places in which our fifth century testimony has to be rejected is very small indeed.

The following are the chief MSS:

M (Mediceus), fifth century, complete for the *Aeneid.*

P (Palatinus), fourth or fifth century, containing about nine-tenths of the Aeneid.

R (Romanus), fifth century, containing about four-fifths of the Aeneid, less reliable than M and P. (The missing portions of P and R can be restored with fair confidence by ninth century MSS which are closely related to them: γ

(Gudianus) for P, and a (Bernensis) for R). In addition there are four other much more fragmentary capital MSS:

F (Vaticanus), fourth century, with illustrations, containing about a fifth of the Aeneid.

V (Veronensis), fifth century, containing about an eighth of the Aeneid.

G (Sangallensis), fifth century, only small fragments.

A (Augusteus), fragments of the Georgics, and four lines of the Aeneid (now lost, but known from a transcription).

The commentary of Servius (edited Thilo and Hagen, 1878-1902, and edit. Harvard, 1946-65 for Aen. i-v) is of the utmost importance in establishing the text as well as explaining it. The commentary exists in two versions, a shorter and a longer (called Servius auct. or Servius Dan.); the relationship between these two has not yet been established, and I have not differentiated between them in this edition. One of the outstanding merits of the commentary from the point of view of Virgil's text is the preservation of the views and readings of earlier grammarians like Probus, Asper, Aelius Donatus.

The Saturnalia of Macrobius (c. a.d. 400) contains very large numbers of citations from Virgil, and is of value (though less so than Servius) for the text as well as for its explanation.

The commentary of Tiberius Claudius Donatus (c. a.d. 400) is of far less value, concerned as it is with paraphrase rather than explanation, and with verbose expositions of the moral significance of the Aeneid.

9. DIFFERENCES OF TEXT

I give here a list of differences of text between this edition and those of Hirtzel (O.C.T., 1900) and Mynors (O.C.T., 1969), omitting minor points of orthography and punctuation and the following misprints in Mynors: 2.326 omnis, 4.91-2 tara . . . caiibus, 5.146 immisis, 6.581 flumine 11.321 amicitae, 11.350 cum, 12.416 hic, 12.874. possim.

Aen.	*Williams*	*Hirtzel*	*Mynors*
1.1a-d	om.	habet	om.
1.2	Laviniaque	Laviniaque	Laviniaque
1.193	humo	humi	humi
1.224	despiciens	dispiciens	despiciens
1.343	agri	agri	auri
1.374	componat	componet	componet
1.427	theatri	theatris	theatris
1.429	alta	alta	apta
1.455	inter	intra	inter
1.599	exhaustis	exhaustis	exhaustos
1.604	iustitiae	iustitia	iustitiae
1.708	pictis.	pictis.	pictis
2.37	subiectisve	subiectisque	subiectisque
2.114	scitantem	scitatum	scitatum
2.349	audendi	audendi	audentem
2.392	Androgeo	Androgeo	Androgei

2.433	vices Danaum	vices, Danaum	vices, Danaum
2.567-88	*habet*	*habet*	*secludit*
2.569	clara	clara	claram
2.572	Danaum poenam	poenas Danaum	Danaum poenam
2.584	nec habet	nec habet	habet haec
2.587	flammae	flammae	†famam
2.616	nimbo	limbo	nimbo
2.691	augurium	augurium	auxilium
2.727	ex agmine	ex agmine	examine
2-739	lassa	lassa	lapsa

2.778	hinc comitem
	    asportare
		hinc comitem
		    asportare
			comitem hinc
			    portare

3.125-6	Naxon, Olearon, Paron	-urn, -um, -um	-on, -on, -on
3.127	concita	consita	concita
3.360	tripoda ae Clarii	tripodas, Clarii	tripodas Clarii et
3.416	ferunt; cum	ferunt, cum	ferunt, cum
3.465	ac secto	sectoque	ac secto
3.535	dimittunt	dimittunt	demittunt
3.673	intremuere	contremuere	intremuere

3.684	Scyllam atque
	    Charybdim
		S. atque C.	Scyllamque
			    Charybdinque

3.685	inter, utramque	inter utramque	inter, utrimque
3.686	teneant	teneant	teneam
4.25	adigat	abigat	adigat
4.54	incensum	impenso	impenso
4.427	cineres	cineres	cinerem
4.540	ratibusve	ratibusque	ratibusve
4.559	iuventa	iuventae	iuventa

4.573	'praecipites
	    vigilate
		praecipitis:
		    'vigilate
			praecipitis:
			    'vigilate

4.593	diripientque	deripientque	diripientque
4.614	haeret,	haeret:	haeret,
4.641	celerabat	celebrabat	celebrabat
4.646	rogos	gradus	rogos
5.29	demittere	demittere	dimittere
5.112	talenta	talentum	talenta
5.162	cursum	gressum	cursum
5.238	porriciam	proiciam	proiciam
5.279	nixantem	nexantem	nexantem
5.317	signant	signant.	signant,
5.326	ambiguumve	ambiguumque	ambiguumque
5.349	pueri,	pueri	pueri
5.486	ponit	dicit	dicit
5.505	timuitque	timuitque	micuitque
5.512	atra	alta	atra
5.520	contorsit	contorsit	contendit
5.551	discedere	discedere	decedere
5.649	quis	quis	qui
5.768	nomen	numen	numen
5-776	porricit	proicit	proicit
5.777-8	778 *post* 777	778 *post* 777	777 *post* 778

5.825	tenent	tenent	tenet
5.851	caelo	caelo	caeli
6.122	totiens –	totiens.	totiens.
6.122	Thesea magnum	Thesea, magnum	Thesea, magnum
6.141	quis	qui	quis
6.177	sepulcri	sepulcro	sepulcro (?)
6.193	agnovit	agnoscit	agnovit
6.203	gemina	geminae	gemina
6.255	lumina	lumina	limina
6.383	terrae	terra	terra
6.427	flentes in	flentes, in	flentes, in
6.433	consilium	concilium	consilium
6.438	trastique … unda	tristisque… undae	tristisque.., undae
6.475	concussus	concussus	percussus
6.495	vidit	vidit	videt et
6.505	Rhoeteo	Rhoeteo	Rhoeteo in
6.524	amovet	amovet	emovet
5.561	plangor ad auras	clangor ad auris	plangor ad auras
6.586	flammas	flammam	flammas
6.602	quos	quo *post lacunam*	quos
6.609	aut	aut	et
6.658	lauris	lauri	lauris
6.664	aliquos	alios	aliquos
6.724	terras	terram	terras
6.731	noxia corpora	corpora noxia	noxia corpora
6.742-3	igni. quisque	igni – quisque	igni (quisque
6.744	tenemus donec	tenemus – donec	tenemus), donec
6.827	prementur	premuntur	prementur
6.852	pacique	pacisque	pacique
6.882-3	rumpas! tu	rumpas, tu	rumpas, tu
6.900	litore	litore	limite
7.37	tempora rerum	tempora, rerum	tempora, rerum
7.129	exsiliis	exitiis	exitiis
7.307	Lapithis … Calydone	Lapithis … Calydone	Lapithas … Calydona
7.307	merente	merente	merentem
7.358	nata	natae	natae
7.363	an	at	at
7.410	Acrisionacis	Acrisioneis	Acrisioneis
7.430	arma	arma	arva
7.486	lati	late	late
7.528	ponto	vento	vento
7.543	conversa	†convexa†	conversa
7.571	levavit	levabat	levabat
7.586	pelagi	pelagi	pelago
7.638	frementis	frementis	trementis
7.684	pascis	pascit	pascis

7.695	Aequosque	aequosque	Aequosque
7.703	ex agmine	ex agmine	examine
7.737	tenebat	tenebat	premebat
7.757	vulnere	vulnera	vulnera
8.75	tenet	tenet	tenent
8.90	celerant rumore	celerant. rumore	celerant rumore
8.108	tacitos	tacitis	tacitos
8.205	furiis	furis	furis
8.211	raptos	raptos	raptor
3.223	oculi	oculi	oculis
3.270	sacri.	sacri.	sacri
3.506	Tarchon	Tarcho	Tarchon
3.512	fata indulgent	fata indulgent	fatum indulget
3.519	nomine	munere	nomine
3.533	poscor Olympo.	poscor. Olympo	poscor Olympo.
3.566	tunc	tum	tunc
3.588	in medio	in medio	it medio
9.68	aequum	aequor	aequum
9.85	*habet*	*secludit*	*habet*
9.102	qualis	quales	qualis
9.130	exspectans	exspectant	exspectant
9.132	gentis	gentes	gentes
9.146	qui	quis	qui
9.151	*secludit*	*secludit*	*habet*
9.208	nec fas; non ita	nec fas, non: ita	nec fas; non ita
9.214	si qua Fortuna	si qua id Fortuna	si qua id Fortuna
9.243	fallet	fallit	fallit
9.287	pericli	pericli est	pericli
9.305	Cnosius	Gnosius	Cnosius
9.349	purpuream vomit	purpureum: vomit	purpuream vomit
9.363	*habet*	*secludit*	*habet*
9.380	abitum	abitum	aditum
9.402	torquet	torquens	torquet
9.403	Lunam et sic	Lunam sic	Lunam et sic
9.429-30	*post* amicum *orat.fin.*	*post* testor *orat.fin.*	*post* amicum *orat.fin.*
9.432	transabiit	transabiit	transadigit
9.456	plenos spumanti	plenos spumanti	pleno spumantis
9.463	cogit	cogit	cogunt
9.464	suos	suas	suos
9.486	te tua funere	te, tua funera.	te tua funere
9.514	iuvat	iuvat	iuvet

9.579	infixa est	adfixa est	infixa est
	alte lateri	lateri manus	alte lateri
9.623	intendit	intendit	contendit
9.646	forma	formam	forma
9.679	Liquetia	liquentia	liquentia
9.724	magna	multa	multa
9.782	quae iam	quae iam	quaeve
9.789	pugnae	pugna	pugna
9.810	iubae capiti	iubae, capiti	iubae, capiti
10.24	fossae	fossas	fossae
10.72	nostra	nostri	nostra
10.186	Cunare	†Cinyre†	Cunare
10.237	horrentis	ardentis	horrentis
10.238	tenet	tenet	tenent
10.280	ipse viris	ipse, viri	ipse viris
10.281	referto	referte	referto
10.293	proram	proram	proras
10.303	vadis,	vadi	vadis,
10.316-	- sacrum casus . . .	sacrum: casus . .	sacrum: casus...
17	quod licuit parvo.	quo licuit parvo?	quo licuit parvo?
10.363	intulerat	impulerat	intulerat
10.366	aquis	quis	aquis
10.378	petamus	petemus	petamus
10.381	vellit magno	magno vellit	vellit magno
10.384	super occupat	superoccupat	super occupat
10.390	arvis	agris	arvis
10.512	tempus versis	versis tempus	tempus versis
10.661-64	*ordine tradito*	661-2 *post* 663-4	661-2 *post* 663-4
10.673	quosne	quosne	quosque
10.704	genitore	genitori	genitore
10.710	pascit	pastus	pascit
10.712	propiusve	propiusque	propiusve
10.714-18	714-6 *post* 717-8	*ordine tradito*	714-6 *post* 717-8
10.727	incumbens	accumbens	incumbens
10.742	quae	quae	quem
10.754	insignis	insignis	insidiis
10.760	hinc Venus	hinc Venus	hic Venus
10.850	exsilium	exitium	exitium
10.862	cruenta	cruenta	cruenti
11.151	voci	vocis	voci
11.152	petenti	parenti	parenti
11.173	armis	armis	arvis
11.356	iungas	firmes	iungas
11.378	semper, Drance	Drance, semper	semper, Drance

11.404	*secludit*	*secludit*	*habet*
11.466	firmet. . . capessat	firmet. . . capessat	firment . . . capessant
11.614	ingenti	ingentem	ingenti
11.654	derigit	dirigit	derigit
11.688	redargueret	redarguerit	redarguerit
11.821	fida...quae	fidam . . . ,quae	fida . . . quae
11.830	relinquens	relinquunt	relinquens
12.24	agris	agris	arvis
12.35	Thybrina	Tiberina	Thybrina
12.104	atque	atque	aut
12.154	profudit	profudit	profundit
12.218	non viribus acquis	[non viribus acquis]	non viribus acquos
12.221	pubentesque	tabentesque	pubentesque
12.232	fatalesque	fatalesque	fatalisque
12.310	clauduntur	clauduntur	conduntur
12.371	frementem;	frementem,	frementem
12.423	nullo	nulla	nullo
12.470	relinquit	relinquit	reliquit
12.541	acris	acrei	acrei
12.605	floros	floros	flavos
12.641	ne nostrum	nostrum ne	ne nostrum
12.648	inscia	nescia	inscia
12.714	miscentur	miscentur	miscetur
12.893	clausumve	clausumve	clausumque
12.899	illud	illud	illum
12.904	manus	manus	manu
12.930	supplexque	supplexque	supplex

10. BIBLIOGRAPHY

(The entries are listed in chronological order. For fuller information see *Greece and Rome, New Surveys in the Classics No. 1: Virgil by* R. D. Williams, 1967).

(a) *Texts*

Ribbeck (1859-68); Hirtzel (O.C.T., 1900); Goelzer and Durand (Budé, 1925-36); Janell (Teubner, 1930); Sabbadini (Rome, 1930), reprinted with minor alterations by Castiglioni (Corpus Paravianum, 1945-52); Mynors (O.C.T.,1969).

(b) *Commentaries*

Servius (ed. Thilo and Hagen, 1878-1902 and *edit. Harvard., Aen.* i-v, 1946-65); Heyne-Wagner (fourth ed. 1830-41); James Henry, *Aeneidea* (1873-92); Conington-Nettleship-Haverfield (1858-98); T. E. Page (1894-1900) Plessis-Lejay (1919); J. W. Mackail *(Aeneid* with full Intro. and very brief commentary, 1930). *Separate books:* Conway *Aen.* i (1935); Austin, *Aen.* ii (1964); Williams, *Aen.* iii (1962); Austin, *Aen.* iv (1955); Pease, *Aen.* iv (1935); Williams, *Aen.* v

(1960); Norden, *Aen.* vi (third ed. 1926); Butler, *Aen.* vi (1920); Fletcher, *Aen.* vi (1941); Maguinness. *Aen.* xii (1953).

c) *Translations*

Dryden (1697), Mackail (1908), Fairclough (Loeb, second ed. 1934-5), Day Lewis (1952), Jackson Knight 1955).

d) *Literary criticism, etc.*

C. A. Sainte-Beuve, *Étude sur Virgile* (Paris, 1857).

W. Y. Sellar, *The Roman Poets of the Augustan Age: Virgil (Oxford, 1877; third ed. 1897).*

R. Heinze, *Virgils epische Technik* (Leipzig, 1903; third ed.1915).

T. R. Glover, *Virgil* (London, 1904; seventh ed. 1942).

C. Bailey, *Religion in Virgil* (Oxford, 1935).

W. F. Jackson Knight, *Roman Vergil* (London, 1944; second ed. 1966).

T. S. Eliot, *What is a Classic?* (London, 1945).

C. M. Bowra, *From Virgil to Milton* (London, 1945).

V. Pöschl, *Die Dichtkünst Virgils: Bild und Symbol in der Aeneis* (Innsbruck, 1950, trans. Seligson, Michigan, 1962).

J. Perret, *Virgile, l'homme et l'oeuvre* (Paris, 1952; second ed. 1965).

Brooks Otis, *Virgil: a Study in Civilized Poetry* (Oxford, 1963).

L. P. Wilkinson, *Golden Latin Artistry* (Cambridge, 1963).

A. Parry, *The Two voices of Virgil's Aeneid (Arion* ii, 1963, pp. 66f.).

M. C. J. Putnam, *The Poetry of the Aeneid* (Harvard, 1965).

Steele Commager (ed.), *Twentieth Century Views: Virgil* (New Jersey, 1966).

F. Klingner, *Virgil: Bucolica, Georgica, Aeneis* (Zurich, 1967).

R. D. Williams, *Virgil (Greece and Rome, New Surveys in the Classics No. 1,* Oxford, 1967).

K. Quinn, *Virgil's Aeneid; a Critical Description* (London, 1968).

W. S. Anderson, *The Art of the Aeneid* (New Jersey, 1969).

D. R. Dudley (ed.), 'Virgil' (*Studies in Latin Literature and its influence,* London, 1969).

W. A. Camps, *An introduction to Virgil's Aeneid* (Cambridge, 1969).

BOOK 1

Introductory note

The first book of the *Aeneid* presents in a variety of ways many aspects of the main subject matter of the whole poem, its tensions, its problems, its methods of expression, its levels of meaning. Virgil's relationship with Homer is put before us at the very beginning of the poem (see note on 1f.), and is particularly evident throughout this book: more than three-quarters of the material corresponds closely with the episode and incident of *Odyssey* 5-8, with occasional elements from elsewhere in the *Odyssey* (see my article in *Phoenix*, 1963, pp. 267f.). The only parts without an Odyssean parallel are those concerned with the gods (12-33, 257-96, 657-94). Virgil invites us to see in Aeneas a new Odysseus, often in similar situations, but in vital ways profoundly different. Odysseus was trying to get back home to Ithaca to resume the life he had left; Aeneas had to leave behind his old way of life and found a new type of civilisation which would lead eventually to the world-rule of the Roman Empire. Virgil explores to what extent such a man would have the same qualities as the heroic Odysseus, and to what extent different qualities.

The non-Odyssean element in the book, that which is special to Aeneas and Rome, is the note of mission, of fate, of the will of Jupiter for the world. This is introduced in the second line (*fato profugus*), is implicit throughout Aeneas' endeavours to struggle onwards to his destined goal (summarised in line 33), and is sonorously and serenely expressed by Jupiter to Venus (see note on 223f.). It is a mission to bring peace and civilisation to all men, and the nobility of its concept never quite fades from Virgil's mind even when he explores the unhappiness and disaster attendant upon it in the story of Aeneas and the history of Rome.

In tension with the will of Jupiter is the hostility of Juno; this is set before us in the prologue before the action starts (12f.), and linked with her support for Carthage. As well as this historical element of opposition, she represents more generally the forces of hostile circumstance, the 'slings and arrows of outrageous fortune' which seem to prevent human achievement even when it is deserved and in accordance with the will of providence. Throughout the poem Juno tries to prevent Aeneas from achieving what he is called on to achieve, and when at the end of Book 12 she is reconciled she has already caused such suffering as to justify Virgil's question (line 11) *tantaene animis caelestibus irae?*

The character of Aeneas is outlined (see note on 81f., 305f.); in the invocation he is spoken of as *insignem pietate virum,* and we see in him an honest and honourable endeavour to shoulder his immense social, religious, and military obligations. But he is a new type of hero, an 'unheroic' type. His strength is limited, his resolution sometimes frail; he gropes his way forward through darkness and uncertainty. We are never sure, as the poem develops, whether he will succeed.

The mythology and pictorial symbolism in which Virgil delighted is greatly to the fore in this book (see note on 34f.). First Juno, then Aeolus, then Neptune — these are all visualised and described in the strange and romantic colours of another world of existence from our own. They play their part in the intellectual development of the poem; they can be rationalised, and seen to portray aspects of the cosmic scene. But the reader of Virgil is not justified in letting their symbolic value replace the visual beauty and terror of these preternatural shapes from a world of poetic imagination.

Finally Book 1 begins the story of Dido (see note on 494f.). There is a most marked contrast with the tragic tones of Book 4, as we hear from Venus the impressive description of her bravery, meet her administering her city, a queenly figure whose beauty is enhanced by her qualities of leadership, listen to her greeting Aeneas and promising help. Only at the end of the book, when Venus and Cupid scheme to entrap her, do we become aware of the first undertones of disaster.

1-33. Virgil's statement of the theme of the poem is followed by the invocation to the Muse and by the mention of Carthage, Juno's beloved city. In her fear for Carthage and her hatred of the Trojans she has for long years kept the Trojans away from their promised home in Latium. So great a task it was to found the Roman race.

[1]Arma[2] virumque cano, Troiae qui primus ab oris[3]
Italiam[4] fato[5] profugus Laviniaque[6] venit
litora, multum ille et terris iactatus et alto[7]

---

1 1f. In the opening sections Virgil places before us many of the leading themes of the poem. That the *Aeneid* is to be a Roman continuation of Homer's *Iliad* and *Odyssey* is already suggested in the opening words *arma* (*Iliad*) *virumque* (*Odyssey*); the Roman element follows immediately (*fato profugus, dum conderet urbem*); and the movement of the poem from Troy to Rome, from Homer's heroic age to Virgil's Augustan Age, is anticipated in the structure of the long relative clause beginning with *Troiae* and ending with *Romae*.

The nature of the Roman mission decreed by fate is partly defined in the phrases *dum conderet urbem* and *inferretque deos Latio*. Aeneas is fated to found a new city to replace burnt Troy, a city rich in men, to establish and spread a new civilisation; and he must do it with proper reverence for the gods. This concept of Rome's destiny is finely summed up in Horace (*Odes* 3.6.5) *dis te minorem quod geris, imperas.*

Another major theme is the hostility of Juno, mentioned in line 4 as the reason for Aeneas' long sufferings, and presented in the invocation as the major problem of the poem. Aeneas is characterised as accepting his social and religious responsibilities (*insignem pietate virum*) and yet a victim of Juno's persecution. Two reasons are given for this persecution: first Juno's support for Carthage (see note on 15-16), Rome's great rival for Mediterranean supremacy (this is a constant undertone in the story of Dido); and second, her mythological hostility to the Trojans because of the judgment of Paris, and her jealousy of Ganymede. To these explicit statements we may add a symbolic interpretation of Juno; that she represents the forces of hostile circumstances (like the storm she causes) which involve otherwise inexplicable suffering and distress. Thus paradoxically the project which fate directs becomes most difficult to accomplish: *tantae molis erat Romanam condere gentern.*

2 **arma virumque**: the first word, indicating war as the subject matter of the poem, challenges a comparison with Homer's *Iliad;* the second challenges comparison with the *Odyssey,* of which the opening words are ανδρα μοι εννεπε, Μουσα. . . . 'Sing, Muse, of the man who. . .'. Throughout the *Aeneid* Virgil sets his Roman theme in tension with the heroic world of Homer; Aeneas has to leave the old world and enter the new.

3 1. The following four lines are quoted by Donatus and Servius as having been removed from the beginning of the *Aeneid* by Varius and Tucca, posthumous editors of the poem:

Ille ego, qui quondam gracili modulatus avena

carmen, et egressus silvis vicina coegi

ut quamvis avido parerent arva colono,

gratum opus agricolis, at nunc horrentia Martis

arma virumque cano . . .

'I am he who once tuned my song on a slender pipe, and then leaving the woods made the nearby fields obey the husbandman however greedy, a work to win favour with farmers; but now I sing of the bristling arms of Mars and the man . . .'

These lines refer autobiographically to the *Eclogues* and the *Georgia.* They are not in any of the major MSS, and it is certain that they should be omitted. They were likely written long after Virgil by some proud owner of a text of the *Aeneid;* just possibly Virgil himself wrote them, but if so decided against using them. That the Romans thought the poem began with the words *arma virumque* is explicitly attested as early as Ovid (*Trist.* 2.534), and frequently afterwards. The matter is discussed in full by R. G. Austin, *C.Q.* 1968, 107f.

4 2. **Italiam**: accusative of motion towards (like *litora*), quite common in Virgil without the preposition which prose would require (cf. 512). The first vowel is long (*contra naturam,* says Servius); in the adjective *Italus* it is short or long according to the requirement of scansion. Similarly the quantity of the *a* of *Lavinius, Lavinium, Lavinia* varies; see note on 258.

5 **fato profugus:** here Virgil indicates the difference between Aeneas and Odysseus. Odysseus, the resourceful individual, overcomes temptation and danger in order to return to his former life in Ithaca; Aeneas on the other hand has a mission laid upon him by fate, to found a new city in a place he will be shown, and to establish a new way of life which the gods destine for a future civilised world.

6 **Laviniaque:** this is the adjective of Lavinium, the name of Aeneas' first settlement in Latium. The second *i* is treated as a consonant, see note on 2.16. Some MSS have *Lavinaque* (cf. Prop. 2.34.64), but cf. *Aen.* 4.236.

7 3. 'much harassed indeed both on land and sea'; the phrase is in apposition to the subject of the relative clause, and *ille* reiterates the subject (like *o γε* in Hom. *Od.* 1.4). Servius comments that *ille* is redundant, and gives us a choice between metrical necessity or a certain impressiveness; cf. 5.457.

vi superum,[1] saevae memorem Iunonis ob iram,
multa[2] quoque et bello passus, dum[3] conderet urbem   5
inferretque[4] deos Latio;[5] genus unde Latinum
Albanique[6] patres atque altae[7] moenia Romae.[8]
    Musa, mihi causas memora, quo[9] numine laeso
quidve dolens regina deum tot volvere casus
insignem[10] pietate virum, tot adire labores   10
impulerit. Tantaene[11] animis caelestibus irae?
    Urbs antiqua fuit (Tyrii tenuere coloni)
Karthago,[12] Italiam[13] contra Tiberinaque longe
ostia, dives opum[14] studiisque asperrima belli,
quam Iuno fertur terris[15] magis omnibus unam   15

---

1 4. **superum:** this genitive form is an archaism, used by Virgil with a limited number of words (*deum, divum, virum, socium,* and often proper names, *Danaum, Argivum, Pelasgum,* etc.).

The opposition of Juno is emphasised very strongly in the opening section; cf. lines 9f., 15f., 36f., and see note on 1f.

2 5. This phrase refers particularly to the second half of the *Aeneid;* line 3 refers mainly to the first half.

3 **dum conderet:** 'until he could establish'; the use of the subjunctive indicates the purpose of his endurance, cf. *Aen.* 10.800.

4 6. **inferretque deos Latio:** the shade of Hector had entrusted the Penates of Troy to Aeneas, and it was a major factor in his destiny to establish a continuity of religious worship between Troy and Rome. Ovid coins the splendid adjective *penatiger* for Aeneas.

5 **Latio:** dative of motion towards, very common in Virgil with compound verbs, cf. 377, 616.

6 7. **Albanique patres:** after the death of Aeneas his son Ascanius moved the new settlement from Lavinium to Alba Longa where his people remained for 300 years (lines 267f — cf. the Alban kings in 6.760f.), until Romulus founded Rome.

7 **altae moenia Romae:** the rhythm (a single word filling the fourth foot) is not very common in Virgil (e.g. in line 1 he does not write *qui Troiae*), and is employed mainly for special effect, particularly to round off a paragraph, as here. This is one of the features discussed by W. F. J. Knight, *Accentual Symmetry in Vergil,* Oxford, 1939.

8 8-11. Notice that in his invocation Virgil asks the Muse not for the story (as Homer does) but for the reasons behind the story, particularly the reasons why the powers of heaven allow or cause such suffering as is involved in the story of Aeneas, especially when he is *insignis pietate.*

9 8. **quo numine laeso:** 'through what slight to her divinity.' The phrase is terse; as a direct question it would be *quod numen laesum est?,* 'what aspect of her divinity was harmed?' It is also possible, as Servius says, that *quo* is ablative of manner, corresponding to *in quo, in qua causa.* Compare the phrase lèse-majesté.

10 10. **insignem pietate virum:** the quality of *pietas,* which gives Aeneas his epithet of *pietas,* indicates that he accepted the responsibility placed upon him by his position as destined leader of Trojans and saviour of Troy's religion, as well as the ordinary social responsibilities towards family and friends.

11 11. **tantaene . . . irae?:** 'can there be such anger in the hearts of gods?' in Milton's words (*P.L.* 6.788) 'In heav'nly Spirits could such perverseness dwell?' This is the question which the *Aeneid* explores, 'to justify the ways of God to men'; Virgil unlike Milton finds only groping and imperfect answers.

12 13. Notice the juxtaposition of *Karthago* and *Italiam*; the thought of the Punic Wars would for a Roman reader underlie the whole section about Carthage. The legend of the foundation of Carthage by Dido fleeing from Tyre does not occur in prose versions of the Aeneas story; see note on 297f.

13 13-14. **Italiam ... ostia:** 'facing Italy and the mouth of the Tiber far off'. *Contra* governs *Italiam* as well as *ostia:* this postposition of disyllabic prepositions is common in Virgil; cf. 32. Carthage is 'facing' in the sense that there is open sea between Carthage and Ostia, with Sicily to the east and Sardinia to the west of the direct line.

14 14. **opum:** a Greek genitive, variously called 'respect' or 'sphere in which', whose Latin use is extended by Virgil and Horace; cf. 343, 441, and 2.22.

15 15-16. 'and it is said that Juno loved this land uniquely beyond all others; even Samos came second'. Samos, a feminine word, was an island in the Aegean which had a famous temple to Juno, the Heraeum; cf. Herod. 3.60, Cic. *Verr.* 2.4.71, Ov. *Met.* 8.220-1. Juno's special association with Carthage was due to her identification with the goddess Tanit, the supreme Carthaginian deity.

posthabita coluisse Samo:[1] hic illius arma,
hic currus fuit; hoc regnum dea gentibus esse,
si qua fata sinant, iam tum tenditque[2] fovetque.
Progeniem sed[3] enim Troiano a sanguine duci[4]
audierat Tyrias olim[5] quae verteret arces;   20
hinc populum late regem belloque superbum
venturum excidio[6] Libyae; sic[7] volvere Parcas.
Id metuens veterisque memor Saturnia[8] belli,
prima quod ad Troiam pro caris gesserat Argis[9]
(necdum etiam causae irarum saevique dolores   25
exciderant animo; manet alta[10] mente repostum
iudicium Paridis spretaeque[11] iniuria formae
et genus[12] invisum et rapti[13] Ganymedis honores) —
his accensa super[14] iactatos aequore toto
Troas, reliquias[15] Danaum atque immitis Achilli,[16]   30
arcebat longe Latio, multosque per annos
errabant acti fatis maria omnia circum.

---

1 16. **Samo: hic**: notice the hiatus at the caesura, cf. *Aen.* 5.735.

2 18. **tenditque fovetque**: 'intends and nurtures' Carthage to be capital of the peoples. The two disparate verbs coalesce in sense to govern an accusative and infinitive construction, as after some phrase like *propter intentum amorem studet*.

3 19. **sed enim**: 'but indeed', the archaic force of *enim*, cf. *Aen.* 2.164, 5.395.

4 **duci**: 'was being established', a vivid use of the present referring to the future, suggesting that the Roman mission was sure to be fulfilled.

5 20. **olim**: 'one day', cf. 203, 234, 289. The reference here to the Punic wars of the third and second centuries B.C. is evident.

6 22. **excidio**: equivalent to *ad excidium*, a rather extended use of the dative of purpose; cf. 299.

7 **sic volvere Parcas**: 'thus the Fates ordained'. The three Parcae were Clotho, Lachesis and Atropos; the image in *volvere* is from spinning, or perhaps unrolling a volume.

8 23. **Saturnia**: a constant epithet of Juno, daughter of Saturnus.

9 24. This line refers to the Trojan war in which Juno had earlier (*prima*) opposed the Trojans on behalf of the Greeks: she is Argive Hera in Homer (*Il.* 4.8). *Argi* is the form Virgil uses for the city of Argos. It is possible that *prima* here suggests that Juno was the foremost supporter of the Greeks, but see Conway's note ad loc.

10 26. **alta mente repostum**: 'stored deep in her heart'; *repostum* is a contracted form (syncope) for *repositum*.

11 27. **spretaeque iniuria formae**: 'the wrong done to her in the slighting of her beauty'; *spretae formae* is a genitive of definition, indicating the nature of the wrong. Paris, named to decide the relative beauties of Juno, Minerva and Venus, awarded the prize of a golden apple to Venus. This element of mythology, along with Juno's jealousy of Ganymede (mentioned in the next line) may seem a secondary reason for her hostility than her support of Carthage. The importance of mythology in the *Aeneid* should not be underestimated (see note on 34f.).

12 28. **genus invisum**: Juno hated the Trojan race because it descended from Dardanus, a son of Jupiter by Electra.

13 **rapti Ganymedis honores**: 'the privileges of stolen Ganymede'. Jupiter, enamoured of the beauty of the Trojan prince Ganymede, caused him to be snatched up from earth by an eagle to be his cupbearer in heaven; cf. *Aen.* 5.252f.

14 29. **super**: best taken with *his*, 'angered over this' (cf. *Geo.* 4.559), rather than adverbial, 'angered by this as well'.

15 30. **reliquias Danaum**: 'remnants left by the Greeks', cf. line 598, 3.87. The Greeks are very frequently called *Danai*, from Danaus the founder of Argos. The first syllable of *reliquias* is scanned long; cf. *religio*. According to Servius Virgil spelled the word with a double *l*, but the main MSS give only a single *l*.

16 **Achilli**: fifth declension form of the genitive; cf. 220 and 207.

Tantae molis erat Romanam condere gentem.[1]

34-80. As the Trojans are sailing from Sicily on the last stage of their voyage to Italy Juno intervenes to stop them. She goes to Aeolus, king of the winds, and urges him to stir up a storm and wreck the Trojans. He agrees to do so.

[2]Vix[3] e conspectu Siculae telluris in altum[4]
vela dabant laeti et spumas[5] salis aere ruebant,   35
cum[6] Iuno[7] aeternum servans[8] sub pectore vulnus
haec secum: 'mene[9] incepto desistere victam
nec posse Italia[10] Teucrorum[11] avertere regem?

---

1 33. 'A matter of such toil was it to found the Roman race'; *molis* is genitive of description used predicatively. The line is tremendously emphatic, separated and isolated as it is at the end of the preliminary section, and it summarises the theme of the *Aeneid.* Donatus drily comments: 'magna enim sine magno labore condi non possunt'.

2 34f. The theme of Juno's hostility, which has dominated the introductory section of the poem, continues as the major feature in the beginning of the narrative. The storm symbolises her opposition as she uses the powers of nature to frustrate the Trojan destiny; in Book 7 she reiterates her intense enmity, this time using fiends from the Hades as her instruments.
The planning of the storm is presented in rich mythology, coloured with all the available beauty, majesty, and terror of Greco-Roman myth. This supernatural atmosphere is deliberately evoked throughout the *Aeneid;* the gods and demigods, nymphs and preternatural beings, play a large part in Virgil's poetic imagination, and must not be rationalised away. They certainly sometimes symbolise ideas, intellectual concepts, but they also exist in their own right, vivid visual creatures of another plane of existence, visions of a world transcending the mortal condition of the human race. Virgil tries to make a synthesis of the real and the visionary; the storm here, for instance, begins with mythology (Juno and Aeolus), becomes a naturalistic description of a hyperbolical kind (great waves and sand-banks), and ends again with mythology (Neptune and his retinue calming the waves). As the narrative begins, it is immediately evident that Virgil is following the events of *Odyssey* 5, where we first meet Odysseus on the island of Calypso. As Odysseus sets out on his raft, Poseidon angrily soliloquises and raises a storm, as Juno does here; the cave of Aeolus switches to *Odyssey* 10; with the storm and the reactions of Aeneas we return to *Odyssey* 5. On this revisit the Introduction.

3 **vix e conspectu**: these words go together; the Trojans were hardly out of sight of Sicily (round which they had sailed on the last stage of their journey to Italy).

4 34. Virgil does not begin his narrative at the beginning of Aeneas' voyage, but when it seems near its end (cf. Hor. *A.P.* 148, where Homer is commended for similarly plunging *in medias res*). In this way the prominence already given to Juno in the prologue can be emphasised by her immediate appearance in the narrative; and the visit to Carthage and Dido becomes imminent. The events which occurred before the point at which Virgil's narrative starts are told by Aeneas to Dido in Books 2 and 3.

5 35. **spumas salis aere ruebant**: 'were churning the foam of the salt sea with their bronze-beaked ships'; for *aere* cf. *Aen.* 10. 214 and 223 *aeratae . . . prorae,* for *ruere* cf. 85. The phrase is a good example of how Latin 'poetic diction' differed from prose; both *sal* and *aes* here are instances of metonymy, and this use of *ruere* (a favourite word of Virgil) is not found in prose.

6 36-7. **cum .. . secum**: supply a verb like *loquitur* or *volutat* (50); cf. 76. The 'inverted' *cum* construction is very frequent in Virgil; it makes the sentence virtually two sentences ('they were sailing along . . . and then all of a sudden . . .'), and it is one of the ways in which Virgil avoids the subordination characteristic of Latin prose style. *Cum* with the pluperfect subjunctive, which would be found several times on almost any page of Caesar or Livy, does not occur in the *Aeneid* at all.

7 36f. Compare Hom. *Od.* 5.284f where Poseidon angrily soliloquises and raises a storm to wreck Odysseus.

8 36. **servans sub pectore**: 'nursing deep in her heart'.

9 37. **mene** . . . **victam**: 'am I, defeated, giving up my plans?' The construction is akin to the accusative and infinitive of exclamation: some phrase like 'who could believe that. . .?' is understood to govern the oratio obliqua. The enclitic *-ne* makes the phrase into a rhetorical question; cf. 97f.

10 38. **Italia**: like *incepto* in the previous line, this is ablative of separation; in prose *desistere* can take this ablative without a preposition, but *avertere* would require a preposition. Case usages which dispense with a preposition are characteristic of poetic style; cf. lines 2 and 6.

11 **Teucrorum**: the Trojans are frequently called *Teucri* or *Dardanidae.* According to one version of the legend Teucer was succeeded by Dardanus as king of Troy, and according to another Dardanus was the original founder; see note on 3.167-8.

Quippe[1] vetor fatis. Pallasne exurere classem
Argivum atque ipsos potuit summergere ponto   40
unius ob noxam et furias Aiacis Oilei?[2]
Ipsa[3] Iovis rapidum iaculata e nubibus ignem
disiecitque[4] rates evertitque aequora ventis,
illum exspirantem transfixo pectore flammas[5]
turbine corripuit scopuloque infixit acuto;   45
ast[6] ego, quae divum[7] incedo[8] regina Iovisque
et soror[9] et coniunx, una cum gente tot annos
bella gero. Et quisquam[10] numen Iunonis adorat[11]
praeterea aut supplex aris imponet honorem?'[12]
  Talia flammato[13] secum dea corde volutans   50
nimborum in patriam, loca feta furentibus Austris,[14]
Aeoliam venit. Hic vasto rex Aeolus[15] antro

---

1 39. **quippe vetor fatis:** 'but of course I am prevented by the fates', an ironical use of *quippe*, cf. *Aen.* 4.218. Juno is aware (cf. 18) that the fates are against her: nevertheless she has power to scheme against them and thereby delay them. For all the dominance of the idea of fate in the *Aeneid*, Virgil is very far from being a fatalist; it needs the actions of men to bring to fruition the intention of fate, and there are supernatural powers working both for and against fate.

2 41. 'because of the frenzied crime of a single man, Ajax son of Oileus'. Ajax is so called to differentiate him from the more famous Ajax, son of Telamon. The word scans Oilei, with synizesis (slurring) of the *e* with the *i*; cf. *Ilionei* (120). The story is that Pallas Athena was angered because Ajax had violated Cassandra in her temple (cf. 2.403f., 6.840), and took vengeance upon him and his companions by setting the Greek fleet on fire with a thunderbolt and sinking it in a storm as it was returning home past Euboea (cf. Eur. *Tro.* 77f., Ov. *Met.* 13.410f., and for a somewhat different version Hom. *Od.* 4.499f).

3 42. **ipsa:** i.e. Athena was allowed to use the thunderbolt herself (cf. Aesch. *Eum.* 827, Eur. *Tro.* 80); Juno has to work with help from Aeolus.

4 43. **-que ... -que:** 'both . . . and,' a feature of epic style not found in normal prose usage.

5 44-5. 'and as Ajax's breath turned to fire from his pierced lungs she snatched him up in a whirlwind and impaled him on a jagged cliff'; cf. Milton *P.L.* 2.180-2 'caught in a fierie Tempest shall be hurld / each on his rock transfixt, the sport and prey / of racking whirlwinds.' Note how the spondees of line 44 give way in 45 to the dactylic movement of Athena's action.

6 46. **ast:** an archaic form of *at*, used by Virgil a score of times.

7 **divum:** this genitive form is also an archaism, see note on 4.

8 **incedo:** this word contributes much to the majesty of the line: Servius says *proprie est nobilium personarum*. Cf. Shakespeare, *Tempest* 4.1.101-2 'Great Juno comes; I know her by her gait', and lines 405, 497.

9 47. **et soror et coniunx:** Juno and Jupiter were children of Saturnus, cf. Hes. *Theog.* 454f.

10 48. **quisquam:** this pronoun, which is used in negative sentences, emphasises the negative answer expected to the rhetorical question.

11 48-9. **adorat . . . imponet:** the first verb is a vivid use of the present for the future to express indignation (made clear by *praeterea = postea*, cf. *Geo.* 4.502); in the second clause Juno uses the expected future. Some minor MSS have changed to *imponit* to make the balance which Virgil wants to avoid.

12 49. **honorem:** 'offerings', a frequent use, cf. line 632.

13 50. **flammato . . . corde:** 'in burning anger'. The Romans were very fond of metaphors from fire (cf. *accensa*, 29).

14 51. 'the land of the storm-clouds, a place teeming with raging winds': *Austris* (south winds) is used for the winds in general, especially in their stormier aspects.

15 52f. King Aeolus in Homer (*Od.* 10.1f.) ruled the floating island of Aeolia, home of the winds (identified with the blustery and volcanic Lipari islands, between Italy and Sicily). He is a very minor deity in Virgil, much dependent on Juno (76f.). Virgil has used his gusty island as a subject for fine mythological imagery of a highly pictorial kind, in which the descriptive words are reinforced with strong metrical effects: the slow spondees of the long words in 53, as the winds groan and struggle, are released by the two quick dactyls of *imperio premit;* the very marked alliteration in the spondaic movement of 55-6 (*i, m, c*); the dactyls of the imagined escape (first halves of 58-59); the final reassertion of the alliteration of *m* in 61.

luctantis ventos tempestatesque sonoras
imperio premit ac vinclis[1] et carcere frenat.
Illi indignantes magno cum murmure montis[2]   55
circum claustra fremunt; celsa sedet Aeolus arce
sceptra tenens mollitque animos[3] et temperat iras;
ni faciat, maria ac terras caelumque profundum
quippe ferant rapidi secum verrantque[4] per auras.
Sed pater omnipotens speluncis abdidit atris   60
hoc metuens molemque[5] et montis insuper altos
imposuit, regemque dedit qui foedere[6] certo
et premere et laxas[7] sciret dare iussus habenas.
Ad quem tum Iuno supplex his vocibus usa est:
    'Aeole, namque[8] tibi divum[9] pater atque hominum rex   65
et mulcere[10] dedit fluctus et tollere vento,
gens inimica mihi Tyrrhenum[11] navigat aequor
Ilium in Italiam portans victosque[12] penatis:
incute vim ventis summersasque obrue puppis,[13]
aut age diversos et disice[14] corpora ponto.   70
[15]Sunt mihi bis septem praestanti corpore Nymphae,

---

1 54. **vinclis et carcere:** hendiadys, 'within the confines of their cell'; with the metaphor *frenat* (taken up again in 63) *carcere* perhaps gets an overtone of its meaning from the starting barrier on a racecourse.

2 55f. Cf. Lucr. 6.189f., especially 197 (of winds imprisoned in a thundercloud) *magno indignantur murmure clausi.* Servius rightly says that *montis* should be taken with *murmure,* not with *claustra;* cf. 245.

3 57. **animos:** 'passions', perhaps with some play on the Greek word for wind, ανεμος, connected etymologically with *animus.*

4 59. Cf. Lucr. 1.2 77f.; *verrere,* 'sweep', is transitive.

5 61. **molemque et montis . . . altos:** an oft quoted example of hendiadys — 'massive high mountains'.

6 62. **foedere certo:** 'under fixed rules', imposed by Jupiter; cf. *iussus* in the next line

7 63. 'who would know how to hold tight the reins and how to let them go slack when instructed to do so.' *Sciret* is final subjunctive; its use with the infinitive in the sense of 'know how to . . .' is regular in prose. *Laxas dare* is equivalent to *laxare;* see Conway ad loc. for Virgil's fondness for periphrases with *dare.*

8 65. **namque:** the ellipsis (I speak to you, for to you . . .) is not uncommon in apostrophe, cf. lines 198 and 731, and Hom. *Il.* 7.328.

9 **divum pater atque hominum rex:** the phrase is from Ennius (*Ann.* 175), and with its monosyllabic ending has an archaic and formulaic sound.

10 66. **mulcere dedit:** the infinitive in this sense is poetic, not uncommon in Virgil; cf. 79, 319, 523, and my note on 5.247-8 (OUP Ed.). Compare also 357, 527-8. The line is based on Hom. *Od.* 10.21-2.

11 67. **Tyrrhenum navigat aequor:** i.e. the sea nearest to Rome; Juno means they are nearly there. *Aequor* is accusative of extent of space, common after words of travelling; cf. 524.

12 68. **victosque penatis:** see note on 6.

13 69. 'strike violence into your winds: overwhelm and sink their ships'. The first phrase is very powerful ('goad them to fury'); cf. Enn. *Ann.* 512 *dictis Romanis incutit iram.*

14 70. **disice:** compounds of *iacio* are normally spelled without the consonantal *i,* but it is pronounced and affects the scansion.

15 71f. The bribe is reminiscent of Hom. *Il.* 14.267f., where Hera offers to the god Sleep one of her Graces in marriage. The mythological account of the storm is here given a touch of the baroque, in the Ovidian manner. Servius is concerned about the morality of the passage, as Aeolus was married; he offers four different defences, of which perhaps the nicest is *quod ex priori coniuge improbos filios Aeolus habuerit.*

quarum quae forma pulcherrima Deiopea,[1]
conubio[2] iungam stabili propriamque[3] dicabo,[4]
omnis ut tecum meritis pro talibus annos
exigat et pulchra faciat te prole parentem.'   75

    [5]Aeolus haec contra: 'tuus, o regina, quid optes
explorare labor; mihi iussa capessere fas est.
Tu mihi quodcumque[6] hoc regni, tu sceptra Iovemque
concilias,[7] tu das[8] epulis accumbere divum
nimborumque[9] facis tempestatumque potentem.'   80

    81-123. Aeolus causes the storm to begin; Aeneas is panic-stricken, and prays for death. The ships are buffeted, and that of Orontes sinks.

    [10]Haec ubi dicta, cavum conversa cuspide montem[11]
impulit in latus; ac venti velut[12] agmine facto,
qua data porta, ruunt et terras turbine perflant.

---

1 72. **Deiopea**: she is one of Cyrene's attendants in *Geo.* 4.343; the polysyllabic ending is not uncommon with proper names. The word is in the nominative because it is in the relative clause grammatically; cf. 573.

2 **conubio**: the scansion of this word varies, *conubia* in the plural, but here *conubio* (rather than *conubjo*); see Austin on *Aen.* 4.126.

3 **propriamque dicabo**: formulaic words: 'I will pronounce her your own'.

4 73. This line is again used by Juno, goddess of marriage, in 4.126, where she suggests that she will give Dido in marriage to Aeneas.

5 76f. Aeolus' reply is formal and deferential — it is yours to consider what you desire and mine to take your orders. Servius explains that Juno in her capacity of queen of the air (*physica allegoria*) has special power over Aeolus.

6 78. **quodcumque hoc regni**: 'all this my little kingdom', cf. Lucr. 2.16 *hoc aevi quodcumque est* ('all this our little life').

7 79. **concilias**: the verb is here used with two different constructions, first with two impersonal objects (= 'procure') and then with a personal object (= 'make favourable'). Translate: 'it is you, none other, who give me all this my little kingdom, my power, Jupiter's favour'.

8 **das ... accumbere**: see note on 66.

9 80. **nimborumque ... potentem**: the genitive with *potens* is common in Livy and the poets, cf. *Aen.* 3.528.

10 81f. Virgil here very closely follows the description of the storm in *Odyssey* 5, colouring it with the hyperbole of Roman rhetoric and the clashing and sonorous word-music of his hexameter. As a piece of verbal painting it far surpasses the more extravagant storm scenes of later Roman poets (Ovid, *Tr. 1.2, Met.* 11.474f., Lucan 5.597f., Stat. *Th.* 5.361f, Val. Fl. 1.608f.). The first appearance of Aeneas in the poem is also modelled on *Odyssey* 5; his reactions to the storm and his speech are like those of Odysseus. Two points are important here: one is that Aeneas has much in common with Odysseus initially, but he must learn over what follows of the poem to leave the heroic world behind and enter a Roman world; and the second is that Virgil wishes to show us at the outset Aeneas' human frailty. Though he has fate to support him, he must himself by his own endeavours achieve his mission (this paradox is absolutely central to the significance of the *Aeneid*), and his strength is hardly sufficient for the difficulty of the task. As Conway says: 'It is a mistake to suppose that Virgil meant to portray Aeneas as faultless.' It is because of his human faults and failings that his achievements compel our interest. Aeneas has often been criticised as an instrument, a paragon, an abstraction, all of which he patently is not; he could much more justly be criticised as insufficiently sublime and virtuous, too human, too weak. But Virgil's conception of the human situation was such that for him true heroism did not lie in overblown, supremely self confident attitudes, but in the uncertain and wavering quest for what seemed right.
The sound effects are very marked in this passage: there is alliteration of *c*, then *v*, then *t*, and the rhythm of the beginning of 82 (with diaeresis after each of the first two feet) is unusual in Virgil and compels the attention; cf. 116, and Ennius *Ann.* 551-2 *nam me gravis impetus Orci / percutit in latus*.

11 81-2. 'he reversed his spear and struck it against the side of the hollow mountain', thus causing the *claustra* to open up.

12 82. **velut agmine facto**: 'as if in armed array,' cf. *Geo.* 4.167 (of a swarm of bees).

9

Incubuere[1] mari totumque a sedibus imis
una[2] Eurusque Notusque ruunt[3] creberque procellis   85
Africus,[4] et vastos volvunt ad litora fluctus;
insequitur clamorque virum stridorque rudentum.
Eripiunt subito nubes caelumque diemque
Teucrorum[5] ex oculis; ponto nox incubat[6] atra.
Intonuere poli et crebris micat ignibus aether   90
praesentemque viris intentant omnia mortem.[7]
Extemplo[8] Aeneae solvuntur frigore membra;
ingemit et duplicis[9] tendens ad sidera palmas
talia voce refert: [10]'o terque quaterque beati,
quis ante ora patrum Troiae sub moenibus altis[11]   95
contigit oppetere! O Danaum fortissime gentis
Tydide![12] Mene[13] Iliacis occumbere campis
non potuisse tuaque animam hanc effundere dextra,
saevus[14] ubi Aeacidae telo iacet Hector, ubi ingens

---

1 84. **incubuere mari**: 'now they have swooped down on the ocean;' for this use of the 'instantaneous' perfect cf. line 90, and *Geo.* 1.330f. Cf. Tennyson's phrase (of the winds) 'leaning upon the ridged sea.' Henry draws attention to the energy depicted by the four verbs *incubuere, insequitur, eripiunt, intonuere,* each containing an intensive particle, beginning a line, and preceding its subject.

2 85-6. These lines are taken from Homer's storm in *Odyssey* 5 (295f.) συν δ Ευπος τε Νοτος τ επεσον, Ζεφυπος τε δυσαης, / και βοπεης αιθπηγενετης, μεγα κυμα κυλινδων.

3 **ruunt**: transitive, 'upheave the whole ocean', a favourite word of Virgil's, both transitively (cf. 35) and intransitively (83).

4 **Africus**: the southwest wind, cf. Hor. *Odes* 1.1. 15.

5 88-9. Again from *Odyssey* 5 (293-4) συν δε νεφεεσσι καλυψε / γαιαν ομου και ποντον, ορωρελ δ ουρανοθεν νυξ. Cf. also *Aen.* 3. 198f. 89.

6 89. **incubat**: 'broods over', cf. *Geo.* 2.507.

7 91. 'the whole scene threatens them with instant death:' a magnificently sonorous line, where the solemn alliteration of *n* and *m* is strengthened by the slow spondees and the coincidence of accent and ictus in the fourth foot for the first time since line 83. Compare Cat. 64.187 *omnia sunt deserta, ostentant omnia letum.* On *viris* (meaning little more than *eis*) Mackail has a good note.

8 92. 'Immediately Aeneas' limbs were numbed in cold fear;' again Virgil follows *Odyssey* 5 (297) και τοτ Οδυσσηος λυτο γουνατα και φιλον ητορ. This is Aeneas' first appearance in the poem, and his reactions indicate his human frailty; the hero of the *Aeneid* is not sublimely strong or possessed of super-human resolution. His task often seems too heavy for him, but although he sometimes despairs he does not give up.

9 93. **duplicis**: a formal way of saying 'both', appropriate in the formal situation of prayer.

10 94f. Aeneas' first words are taken from *Odyssey* 5.306f. τρις μακαρεσ Δαναοι και τετρακις οι τοτ ολοντο. . . . Aeneas' behaviour in Book 2 shows this desire for the heroic death, but in the rest of the poem he has to learn that his life is not his to throw away, but that it must be used in the service of his destiny.

11 95-6. **quis . . . contigit oppetere**: 'those whose fortune it was to die'; *quis* is a less common alternative form for *quibus*; *oppetere mortem* is a normal prose usage, and *oppetere* is used absolutely in this sense by the poets and in post-Augustan prose.

12 97. **Tydide**: Greek vocative — long *e* — of the patronymic *Tydides,* son of Tydeus (Diomedes). Aeneas was almost killed in single combat against him (*Il.* 5.297f.).

13 97-8. **mene ... occumbere . . . non potuisse**: 'why could I not have fallen?' the same construction as in 37.

14 99. 'where fierce Hector lies low beneath the spear of Aeacides'. *Saevus* seems at first a strange adjective for Aeneas to apply to Hector, but its point here is that for all Hector's fierceness in war he was killed when Aeneas was not. Aeacides refers to Achilles, son of Peleus, son of Aeacus. *Telo iacet* is elliptical, equivalent in sense to *telo necatus iacet;* Aeneas sees the past flash before his eyes.

Sarpedon,[1] ubi tot Simois[2] correpta sub undis   100
scuta virum galeasque et fortia corpora volvit!'
    [3]Talia iactanti stridens Aquilone procella
velum adversa ferit, fluctusque ad sidera tollit.
Franguntur remi, tum prora[4] avertit et undis
dat latus, insequitur cumulo[5] praeruptus aquae mons.   105
Hi summo in fluctu pendent; [6]his unda dehiscens
terram inter fluctus aperit, furit aestus harenis.
Tris[7] Notus abreptas in saxa latentia torquet
(saxa vocant Itali mediis quae in fluctibus[8] Aras,
dorsum immane mari summo), tris Eurus ab alto   110
in brevia[9] et syrtis urget, miserabile visu,
inliditque vadis atque aggere cingit harenae.[10]
Unam, quae Lycios fidumque vehebat Oronten,
ipsius[11] ante oculos ingens a[12] vertice pontus
in puppim ferit; [13]excutitur pronusque magister   115

---

1 100. **Sarpedon**: though Zeus wished to save him (*Aen.* 10.470f.), he was killed by Patroclus (*Il.* 16.638f.).

2 100-1. 'where Simois has seized and sweeps beneath its waters the shields and helmets and brave bodies of so many warriors'. Cf. Hom. *Il.* 12.22f., and for the phraseology cf. *Aen.* 8.538f. Simois and Xanthus (also called Scamander) were the rivers of Troy; cf. 473, 618. Notice the fourth foot rhythm for the paragraph ending; see note on 7.

3 102-3. 'As he wildly spoke these words, a howling northerly storm struck full against the sails'; *iactanti* ('for him speaking') is a kind of ethic dative, in the loosest possible grammatical relationship with the sentence, cf. *Aen.* 2.713; *iactare* (often used with words like *minas*) suggests wildness, cf. *Aen.* 2.588, 768.

4 104. **prora avertit**: *avertit* is intransitive, cf. 402. Failure to see this has led the chief MSS to read *proram,* but to supply *procella* as the subject is intolerably harsh.

5 105. 'a sheer massive mountain of water came on them'; for *cumulo,* ablative of manner, literally 'in a mass', cf. *Aen.* 2.498. The rhythm is deliberately dislocated by the monosyllabic ending; see my note on 5.481 (OUP Ed.). Day Lewis renders the effect with 'a precipice of sea hung'.

6 106-7. 'Some hang on the wave's crest; some see the billow ebb back and reveal the sea-bed between the waves; the wild water is aswirl with sand'. The high rhetorical and hyperbolical style reaches its acme here, but even in a grandiose passage of this kind Virgil (unlike Ovid, *Tr.* 1.2 or Lucan, 5.597f.), prefers to stop short of the grotesque. *Hi* and *his* refer to men still on board their ships.

7 108. **tris**: alternative accusative form of *tres,* understand *naves.*

8 109. Suspicion has been cast on this line as an interpolation, but the MSS have it and Quintilian (8.2.14) quotes it (as well he might) as an example of unnatural word order — the prose order would be *saxa quae in mediis fluctibus (latentia) Itali Aras vocant.* The reference evidently is to rocks sometimes visible 'as a huge ridge on the sea's surface' and at other times hidden (cf. *Aen.* 5.125f.)

9 111. **in brevia et syrtis**: 'into the shallows and the sandbanks'; *brevia* is like the Greek τα βραχεα, *syrtis* has particular application to the famous Syrtes off the coast of Africa (4.41).

10 112. This is a splendid final picture of their fate, static after wild movement, again with the special rhythmic effect in the fourth foot, see note on 7.

11 114. **ipsius**: i.e. Aeneas.

12 **a vertice**: 'from high above', cf. *Geo.* 2.310, *Aen.* 5.444, and *Od.* 5.313 κατ ακρης.

13 115f. 'the helmsman was hurled out, and fell headfirst down into the sea; while the wave whirled the ship and turned it round three times where it was, and the devouring eddy swallowed it in the ocean'. From 6.334 it seems that Orontes' helmsman was called Leucaspis. Notice the metrical effect of *volvitur in caput;* cf. 82. Ribbeck emended *illam* to *aliam* to account for the twenty ships (only 19 are accounted for in the text); it is worth reading Henry's vigorous denunciation of this emendation (*Aeneidea,* i.xxf.).

volvitur in caput, ast illam ter fluctus ibidem
torquet agens circum et rapidus vorat aequore vertex.
Apparent rari nantes in ¹gurgite vasto,
arma virum² tabulaeque et Troia gaza per undas.
Iam validam Ilionei³ navem, iam fortis Achatae,   120
et qua vectus Abas, et qua grandaevus Aletes,
vicit hiems; ⁴laxis laterum compagibus omnes
accipiunt inimicum imbrem rimisque fatiscunt.

> *124-56. Neptune intervenes, angrily rebukes the winds, and calms the storm.*

Interea magno misceri⁵ murmure pontum
emissamque hiemem sensit Neptunus et⁶ imis   125
stagna refusa vadis, graviter commotus; et alto⁷
prospiciens summa placidum⁸ caput extulit unda.
Disiectam Aeneae toto videt aequore classem,
fluctibus oppressos Troas caelique⁹ ruina;
nec latuere doli fratrem Iunonis¹⁰ et irae.   130
Eurum ad se Zephyrumque vocat, dehinc¹¹ talia fatur:
   'Tantane vos generis¹² tenuit fiducia vestri?
Iam caelum terramque meo sine numine,¹³ venti,
miscere et tantas audetis tollere moles?¹⁴

---

1 118. 'Here and there men appear, swimming in the expanse of ocean'; a very remarkable line of spondaic movement (following the dactyls of 117), with word accent clashing with ictus.

2 119. Supply *apparent* again: 'and the heroes' armour is seen, and planks, and Troy's treasure in the ocean'. The adjective *Troius* is a dactyl, the noun *Troia* (95) a trochee.

3 120. For the scansion of *Ilionei* see note on 41; Ilioneus is Aeneas' spokesman at 521f. and 7.212f.; Achates is Aeneas' righthand man (e.g. 312), a very colourless figure. Abas and Aletes in the next line are less important.

4 122-3. 'through the weakened fastenings of their hulls they all take in the deadly water, and gape at the seams'; for *imber,* often used in this sense by Lucretius, Servius quotes Ennius (*Ann.* 497-8) *ratibusque fremebat / imber Neptuni.*

5 124. **misceri**: a favourite word with Virgil to denote turmoil, often (as here) used with alliteration of *m* in adjacent words; cf. 4.160.

6 125-6. **et imis stagna refusa vadis**: 'and that the still waters were upheaved from the sea's bottom'; *stagna* refers to the water at the bottom of the ocean which even if comparatively shallow (*vadis*) would still normally be calm.

7 126-7. **alto prospiciens**: 'gazing out over the deep', for the ablative cf. 181.

8 127. **placidum caput**: although Neptune is very angry (*graviter commotus*) at this interference in his kingdom, the god's countenance is always serene.

9 129. **caelique ruina**: 'the falling heavens', a rhetorically exaggerated phrase comparable with *Geo.* 1.324 *ruit arduus aether.*

10 130. Juno was daughter of Saturnus (23); his three sons (Jupiter, Neptune, Pluto) divided the world between them by lot; cf. 139, and Hom. *Il.* 15.187f.

11 131. **dehinc**: sometimes an iambus in Virgil, sometimes (as here and in 256) a single syllable.

12 132. **generis**... **fiducia**: 'confidence in your ancestry'; according to Hesiod (*Theog.* 378f.) the winds were born of the Titan Astraeus and the goddess Eos.

13 133. **numine**: 'divine authority', cf. line 8.

14 134. **moles**: 'confusion', cf. *Aen.* 5.790, where Venus uses the word to refer to this storm.

Quos[1] ego — sed motos praestat componere fluctus;　　　　135
post[2] mihi non simili poena commissa luetis.
Maturate fugam regique haec dicite vestro:
non illi imperium pelagi saevumque tridentem,
sed mihi sorte datum. Tenet ille immania saxa,
vestras,[3] Eure, domos; illa[4] se iactet in aula　　　　140
Aeolus et clauso ventorum carcere regnet.'
　　Sic ait et dicto citius tumida aequora placat
collectasque[5] fugat nubes solemque reducit.
Cymothoe[6] simul et Triton adnixus acuto
detrudunt navis scopulo; levat ipse tridenti　　　　145
et vastas aperit syrtis et temperat aequor
atque rotis summas levibus perlabitur undas.
Ac[7] veluti magno in populo cum saepe coorta est
seditio saevitque animis ignobile vulgus,
iamque faces et saxa volant, furor[8] arma ministrat;　　　　150
tum, pietate gravem ac meritis si[9] forte virum quem
conspexere, silent arrectisque auribus astant;
ille regit dictis animos et pectora mulcet:
sic cunctus pelagi cecidit fragor, aequora postquam

---

1 135. **quos ego:** these two pronouns, with the sentence left incomplete (aposiopesis), show the power of an inflected language to convey meaning by case endings. This picture of Neptune calming the storm has often been a subject for painters, and is sometimes known as the *Quos ego* scene.

2 136. 'Later, I promise you, you will pay for what you have done with a very different punishment', i.e. not just words. This seems more natural than to take *non simili* as meaning that the punishment will more than fit the crime.

3 140. **vestras, Eure, domos:** he speaks to them all (*vestras*), but particularises one of them in the vocative; cf. *Aen.* 9.525.

4 140-1. Notice the emphasis on the first words in the clauses, *illa* and *clauso;* the jussive subjunctives are limited by the condition imposed by these first words. Day Lewis renders the contemptuous tone with: 'Let Aeolus be king of that castle'.

5 143. **collectas:**'gathered'.

6 144f. The description of the nymph Cymothoe ('wave-runner'), the sea-god Triton, and Neptune himself with his trident rescuing the ships is extremely pictorial; cf. Hom. *Il.* 13.23f., and *Aen.* 5.819f.

148f. This first simile in the poem is extremely striking because it illustrates the world of nature from the world of human behaviour. Much more often similes operate the other way round: cf. Hom. *Il.* 2.144f. where the assembly is moved like the waves of the sea or the corn in a windy field; Cicero often speaks of the storms and waves of political life, and cf. Scipio's words in Livy 28.27.11. Like a number of Virgilian similes, this one contains elements which link up not only with the immediate context, but with wide aspects of the narrative as a whole: the word *furor* (150) is the element in human behaviour which seems to be responsible for folly and sin (cf. 294), while the quality of *pietas* (151) is that through which Aeneas seeks to inaugurate a better world order; moreover the control exercised by the wise and responsible statesman depicted here (*regit,* 153) anticipates in miniature the mission of Rome, *regere imperio populos* (see Otis, *Virgil,* pp. 221f., 229, and Pöschl, *The Art of Vergil,* pp. 20f.). The violence and storms of passion are more easily calmed here by Neptune than in the *Aeneid* by Aeneas or in Virgil's world by the Romans.

7 148. **ac veluti . . . cum saepe**: 'just as often happens when in a crowded assembly . . .'; the misplacement of *saepe* seems to be idiomatic, cf. Lucr. 3.913, *Aen.* 5.273, 527. Some take *magna in populo* to mean 'in a great nation', but this seems less likely.

8 150. **furor arma ministrat:** cf. Milton *P.L.* 6.635 'Rage prompted them at length, and found them arms'.

9 151f. 'then if it happens that they look upon someone respected for his public devotion and services, they fall silent, and stand still listening intently...'. For *si . . . virum quem* cf. 181; with an enclitic the monosyllabic ending to the hexameter is hardly felt. It is suggested that Virgil may have had Cato in mind; cf. Plut. *Cat. Min.* 44.3-4.

13

prospiciens genitor caeloque invectus aperto   155
flectit equos curruque[1] volans dat lora secundo.

> *157-222. The Trojans land in Africa after the storm. Aeneas*
> *reconnoitres, and shoots seven stags. He heartens his men*
> *and they feast, saddened by the apparent loss of thirteen of*
> *their twenty ships.*

Defessi Aeneadae[2] quae proxima litora cursu
contendunt petere, et Libyae vertuntur ad oras.
Est[3] in secessu longo locus: insula portum[4]
efficit obiectu laterum, quibus omnis ab alto   160
frangitur inque sinus scindit sese unda reductos.
Hinc atque hinc vastae rupes geminique[5] minantur[6]
in caelum scopuli, quorum sub vertice late
aequora tuta silent; tum[7] silvis scaena coruscis
desuper, horrentique atrum nemus imminet umbra.   165
Fronte[8] sub adversa scopulis pendentibus antrum,
intus aquae dulces vivoque[9] sedilia saxo,
Nympharum domus. Hic fessas non vincula navis[10]
ulla tenent, unco non alligat ancora morsu.
Huc septem[11] Aeneas collectis navibus omni   170
ex numero subit; ac magno telluris amore
egressi optata potiuntur Troes[12] harena

---

1 156. 'and flying onwards gave free rein to his willing chariot'; *curru* is dative, cf. 257, 476.

2 157. **Aeneadae**: the followers of Aeneas, the proto-Romans; cf. Lucr. 1.1 *Aeneadum genetrix* (of Venus, Aeneas' mother). The people are called after their leader; Conway compares *Thesidae* (Athenians) in *Geo.* 2.383.

3 159f. This imaginary description of a harbour is based on Homer's description of the harbour of Ithaca (*Od.* 13.96f); all its parts occur there except the island. It is a full scale rhetorical description (ecphrasis), with *est. . . locus* picked up by *huc* (170); cf. 441f., and Austin on *Aen.* 4.480f., 483.

4 159-161. 'an island makes a harbour with the barrier of its edges, for all the waves from the open sea break on it and part into receding ripples'. The meaning of the last phrase (which occurs also in *Geo.* 4.420) is not certain, but the version given seems better than the alternative — "part into the sheltered creeks'.

5 162f. Cf. the harbour of Castrum Minervae in 3.535f *gemino dimittunt bracchia muro / turriti scopuli.*

6 162. **minantur:** Servius says *eminent*, and compares 4.88-9 *minaeque / murorum ingentes;* he adds *ita est ut quae eminent minari videantur.*

7 164f. 'then there is a background of waving trees above, and a dark wood looming high with its sinister shadows'; *tum* means further backwards and upwards as you look from the harbour; *scaena (Geo.* 3.24) is the backdrop which closes in the whole picture (429). Cf. Milton, *P.L.* 4.137f.

8 166. **fronte sub adversa:** i.e. at the head of the bay, facing the entrance with its island, and flanked by the cliffs and woods just described.

9 167. **vivoque sedilia saxo:** 'seats in the natural rock', cf. Ov. *Met.* 5.317. This cave of the Nymphs is based on Hom. *Od.* 12.317f. as well as 13.103f.

10 168-9. The diction is very far indeed from that of prose; the 'weary' ships, the anchor with its 'hooked bite' (cf. *Aen.* 6.3 f. *dente tenaci / ancora*).

11 170. **septem:** he had twenty (line 381) to start with.

12 172. **Troes:** Greek nominative plural with short final syllable, cf. 468, 500.

et sale[1] tabentis artus in litore ponunt.
Ac primum silici[2] scintillam excudit Achates
suscepitque[3] ignem foliis atque arida circum   175
nutrimenta dedit rapuitque in fomite flammam.
Tum Cererem[4] corruptam undis Cerealiaque arma[5]
expediunt fessi rerum,[6] frugesque receptas
et torrere parant flammis et frangere saxo.

    Aeneas scopulum interea conscendit, et omnem   180
prospectum late pelago[7] petit, Anthea[8] si quem
iactatum vento videat Phrygiasque biremis
aut Capyn aut celsis in puppibus arma[9] Caici.
Navem[10] in conspectu nullam, tris litore cervos
prospicit errantis; hos tota armenta sequuntur   185
a tergo et longum per vallis pascitur agmen.
Constitit hic arcumque manu celerisque sagittas
corripuit, fidus quae tela gerebat Achates,
ductoresque ipsos primum capita[11] alta ferentis
cornibus arboreis sternit, tum vulgus[12] et omnem   190
miscet[13] agens telis nemora inter frondea turbam;
nec prius absistit quam septem ingentia victor[14]

---

1 173. **sale tabentis**: 'drenched with salt water'.

2 174. **silici**: ablative, cf. *capiti*, 7.668. For the sense cf. 6.6f.

3 175-6. 'and caught the fire in leaves and put dry kindling around, and got a flame going in brushwood'. For *rapere* of things catching fire cf. Ov. *Met.* 3.374, Lucan 3.684; Virgil has here varied the construction to mean that Achates 'caught' the flame in the brushwood. There seems no parallel for the suggestion that *rapuit* here means 'fanned'.

4 177. **Cererem**: 'corn', metonymy of the goddess for her attribute; cf. 701, and *Bacchus* in 215.

5 **Cerealiaque arma**: i.e. grinding mills, kneading troughs, etc.

6 178. **rerum**: cf. 12.589 *trepidi rerum*, Hor. *Odes* 2.6.7 *lasso maris;* it is a Greek genitive of cause (origin), 'wearied from. . .'.

7 181. **pelago**: 'over the sea', cf. 126.

8 181-2. **Anthea si quem . . . videat**: 'if he could see some sign of Antheus'; the condition is of the *'si forte'* type, meaning 'in the hope that', cf. 578 and 2.136. *Anthea* is Greek accusative; *quem (= aliquem)* is here used strangely, but cf. 2.81-2 *aliquod. . . nomen Palamedis,* 'any mention of the name of Palamedes', and Ov. *Met.* 9.8-9 *nomine si qua suo fando pervenit ad aures / Deianira tuas, Met.* 15.497 *aliquem Hippolytum.* It is not unlike the colloquial use of *nullus: nullum Anthea vidit* would be 'he saw no sign of Antheus'.

9 183. **arma**: i.e. armour displayed on the ship's prow, cf. *Aen.* 10.80.

10 184f. The episode of the shooting of the stags is based on *Od.* 10.158f. (cf. perhaps also 9.154f, where Odysseus shoots a stag and takes it back to his comrades in the ship. The passage is presented in accordance with the heroic tradition, but is not one of Virgil's most successful adaptations of Homer.

11 189-90. **capita . . . arboreis**: 'as they held their heads high with their branching antlers'; for *arboreis* cf. *Ecl.* 7.30 *ramosa . . . cornua cervi.*

12 190-1. **vulgus et omnem . . . turbam**: 'the rest of them, the whole crowd', cf. Enn. *Frag. Inc.* 15 *avium vulgus,* Lucr. 2.921 *praeter vulgum turbamque animantum, Geo.* 3.469.

13 191. **miscet**: 'threw into confusion', cf. 124.

14 192. **victor**: 'triumphantly', continuing the military phrases of the previous line, but rather exaggerated.

corpora fundat[1] humo[2] et numerum cum navibus aequet.
Hinc portum petit et socios partitur in omnis.
Vina bonus quae deinde[3] cadis onerarat Acestes[4]   195
litore Trinacrio[5] dederatque abeuntibus heros[6]
dividit, et dictis maerentia pectora mulcet:
  'O[7] socii (neque enim[8] ignari sumus ante malorum),
o passi[9] graviora, dabit deus his quoque finem.
Vos[10] et Scyllaeam rabiem penitusque[11] sonantis   200
accestis[12] scopulos, vos et Cyclopia saxa
experti: revocate animos maestumque timorem
mittite; forsan et haec olim[13] meminisse iuvabit.
Per varios casus, per tot discrimina rerum
tendimus in Latium, sedes ubi fata quietas   205
ostendunt; illic fas[14] regna resurgere Troiae.
Durate, et vosmet rebus servate secundis.'

---

1 193. **fundat**: the subjunctive is used to express purpose, cf. 473.

2 **humo**: 'to the ground', cf. *Geo.* 2.460, *Aen.* 9.214. It is however very possible that Servius and some inferior MSS are right with *humi*.

3 195. **deinde**: Virgil is fond of postponing *deinde;* see Conway's note, and cf. *Aen.* 3.609. This is however his most striking example of the usage, and it gives a curiously dislocated effect.

4 **Acestes**: the Sicilian king from whom the Trojans had just come, and whom they revisit in Book 5; Segesta was called after him.

5 196. **Trinacrio**: Sicily was called Trinacria from its triangular shape, see note on 3.384.

6 **heros**: this word should certainly be taken with Acestes, subject of *dederat,* not with Aeneas, subject of *dividit.* It means in heroic (i.e. generous, chivalrous) fashion; for its position cf. *dea* in 412.

7 198f. Aeneas' speech is based on that of Odysseus in Hom. *Od.* 12.208f. Macrobius regards Aeneas' speech as *locupletior* than Odysseus'; and Conway draws attention to the emphasis in Homer on Odysseus' own prowess, in Virgil on Aeneas' trust in the gods and in his men's courage.

8 198. Cf. Hom. *Od.* 12.208 Ω φιλοι ου γαρ πω τι κακων αδαημονες ειμεν. For *enim* see note on 65; *ante* goes with *sumus,* 'we have not before now been unacquainted with suffering', rather than with *malorum* in the Greek sense of των πριν κακων.

9 199. **o passi graviora**: Cf. Hom. *Od.* 20.18 τετλαθι δη, κραδιν, και κυντερον αλλο ποτ ετλης, and Hor. *Odes* 1.7.30-1 *o fortes peioraque passi / mecum saepe viri,*

10 200. In *Aen.* 3.420f Helenus describes to the Trojans the danger of Scylla and Charybdis, and warns them to keep away; in 3.558f. their escape from this peril is described. *Rabiem* probably refers especially to the dogs associated with Scylla (Lucr. 5.892 *rabidis canibus succincta,* of Scylla); so does *penitusque sonantis scopulos,* cf. 3.432 *caeruleis canibus resonantia saxa.* Immediately after their escape from Scylla (3.569f) the Trojans come to Etna and the home of the Cyclops, where they land and narrowly escape from Polyphemus and his fellows. These two incidents are among the most marked similarities with the *Odyssey;* cf. *Od.* 12.73f. and 222f., *Od.* 9.106f.

11 200. **penitusque**: probably with *sonantis,* 'sounding deep within', (cf. *Aen.* 6.59) rather than with *accestis,* 'approached right up to'.

12 201. **accestis**: syncope for *accessistis,* a mark of archaising style; cf. *Aen.* 4.606.

13 203. Again this recalls Odysseus' speech in *Od.* 12 (212) και που τωνδε μνησεσθαι οιω. Virgil emphasises the idea of pleasure in looking back at dangers overcome. *Olim* means 'one day', cf. 20, 234, 289; *forsan* with the indicative is common in poetry.

14 206. **fas**: the laws of heaven permit it, as Aeneas had learned from oracles during his journey (e.g. 3.94f., 154f., 376f.). These had told him of Italy, of Cumae, and of a river past Circe's isle where he would find rest from his toils; the actual word *Latium* had not been used, but no reader of Virgil need feel any great disquiet on that account.

Talia voce refert curisque ingentibus aeger[1]
spem vultu simulat, premit altum corde dolorem.
Illi se praedae accingunt dapibusque futuris:[2]   210
tergora diripiunt costis et viscera nudant;
pars in frusta secant veribusque trementia figunt,
litore aëna locant alii flammasque ministrant.
Tum victu revocant viris, fusique per herbam
implentur veteris Bacchi[3] pinguisque ferinae.   215
Postquam exempta[4] fames epulis mensaeque remotae,
amissos longo socios sermone requirunt,[5]
spemque metumque inter dubii,[6] seu vivere credant
sive extrema pati nec[7] iam exaudire vocatos.
Praecipue pius[8] Aeneas nunc acris Oronti,[9]   220
nunc Amyci casum gemit et crudelia secum
fata Lyci fortemque Gyan[10] fortemque Cloanthum.

---

1 208-9. It is typical of Virgil's method of character drawing for him to comment as narrator on the events or statements of the story; cf. for example 4.331-2 (*curam . . .premebat*), 4.393f. Line 209 is imitated by Dryden, *Annus Mirabilis* 73 'His face spake hope, while deep his sorrows flow'.

2 210f. This elaborate description of the preparation for a feast is very much in the Homeric style; cf. *Il.* 1.459f.

3 215. 'they take their fill of old wine and rich venison'; the genitive is less common than the ablative after *implentur,* and helps to emphasise the Greek tone of the passage. For *Bacchus* (wine) cf. *Ceres* (corn) in 177.

4 216-17. This is imitated from Hom. *Od.* 12.308-9, except for *mensaeque remotae,* which refers to the Roman custom at the conclusion of a meal (cf. 723).

5 217. **requirunt**: like *desiderant,* 'they lament the loss of'; cf. *quaerere* in *Aen.* 5.814.

6 218. 'Hovering between hope and fear, not knowing whether to believe that they still live. . .'. *Dubii* governs both *inter* and the *seu . . . sive* clauses; for *seu* in an indirect question cf. *Aen.* 2.739.

7 219. **nec iam exaudire vocatos**: 'can no longer hear when called', a reference to the Roman custom of *conclamatio* at death, the calling by name before hope is finally abandoned.

8 220. **pius**: here with reference to his responsibility as leader, see note on 10.

9 **Oronti**: fifth declension form, see note on 30.

10 222. Gyas and Cloanthus are two of the competitors in the boat race in Book 5.

223-96. Venus complains to Jupiter that the promise of Aeneas' destiny is not being fulfilled. He replies that it will be fulfilled, and outlines the glory awaiting the Roman people and their mission to civilise the world.

[1]Et iam[2] finis erat, cum Iuppiter aethere summo
despiciens mare velivolum[3] terrasque iacentis
litoraque et latos populos, sic[4] vertice caeli   225
constitit et Libyae defixit lumina regnis.
Atque illum talis[5] iactantem pectore curas
tristior[6] et lacrimis oculos[7] suffusa nitentis
adloquitur Venus: 'o qui res hominumque deumque
aeternis regis imperiis et fulmine terres,   230
quid meus[8] Aeneas in te committere tantum,
quid Troes potuere, quibus tot funera passis[9]
cunctus ob Italiam terrarum clauditur orbis?
Certe hinc[10] Romanos olim volventibus annis,
hinc fore ductores, revocato[11] a sanguine Teucri,   235
qui mare, qui terras omnis dicione tenerent,

---

1 223f. The scene in heaven is based to begin with on the complaints by Thetis to Zeus in Hom. *Il.* 1.495f, and of Athena to Zeus in *Od.* 5.5f. But it differs entirely from Homer in the emphasis laid both by Venus and by Jupiter on the mission of the storm tossed hero in the context of world history. Venus knows that world empire has been promised (934f.), and Jupiter majestically confirms it, elaborating in serene tones the radiantly optimistic picture of the new Golden Age. We have been invited so far in this book to think of Aeneas as a second Odysseus; now we are shown how he is to be different. Odysseus succeeds as a brilliantly resourceful individual; Aeneas must succeed as the leader of his people.

The prophecy of Jupiter outlines the Roman mission, first conquest and then civilisation and peace; and it gives an impetus to the poem which lifts it on to a level above the individual actions of the human characters. It shines through the dark places, and provides a partial answer to the problems of human suffering with which the *Aeneid* is so preoccupied. Without it the events of (say) Book 4 or Book 12 would seem like the senseless suffering of a blind world; with it there is a reason for the suffering, even if it does not satisfy us. The world order, which seems here so desirable, cannot be achieved without suffering and sacrifice, and as the poem explores these sacrifices, the reader must remember why they have to be made. We must not be unmindful of Jupiter's speech when Aeneas has to face the problems which it involves.

2 223. **Et iam finis erat**: 'and now all was ended', a curious transition, vaguely and majestically suggesting that when the mortals had fallen to sleep the king of the gods disposes the affairs with which they had exhausted themselves.

3 224. 'looking down on the sail-winged sea and the outspread lands'; *velivolus* is a most vivid epithet, used by Ennius and Lucretius to describe ships. See note on 3.544.

4 225. **sic**: used somewhat redundantly (cf. the Greek ουτως), here to emphasise the picture of Jupiter looking down over all the peoples and while thus occupied (*sicut erat*) suddenly stopping and fixing his eyes on Libya; cf. *Aen.* 7.668.

5 227. **talis**: i.e. the thoughts caused by what he saw there.

6 228. **tristior**: the comparative signifies 'unusually sad', not with her usual serenity.

7 **oculos suffusa nitentis:** 'her bright eyes brimming', the retained accusative construction of which Virgil is fond, based partly on imitation of the Greek middle voice, and partly on the Greek accusative of respect (see note on 320); cf. 481, 561, 579, 658, 713, *Aen.* 12.64f. *lacrimis . . . perfusa genas*, and my note on *Aen.* 5.135 (OUP Ed.).

8 231. **meus**: used emotionally, a mother speaking of her son; cf. *Aen.* 2.522.

9 232-3. 'that when they have suffered such great losses the whole expanse of the world is closed to them because of Italy', i.e. to prevent their reaching Italy, Juno persecutes them wherever they are.

10 234. **hinc**: 'from them'; cf. line 6.

11 235. **revocato a sanguine Teucri:** 'from the restored line of Teucer', restored after the destruction of Troy; for the Trojan king Teucer see note on 38.

pollicitus.[1] Quae[2] te, genitor, sententia vertit?
Hoc[3] equidem occasum Troiae tristisque ruinas
solabar fatis[4] contraria fata rependens;
nunc eadem fortuna viros tot casibus actos   240
insequitur. Quem das finem, rex magne, laborum?
Antenor[5] potuit mediis elapsus Achivis
Illyricos penetrare sinus atque intima tutus
regna Liburnorum et fontem superare[6] Timavi,
unde per ora novem vasto cum murmure montis[7]   245
it mare proruptum et pelago premit arva sonanti.
Hic tamen ille urbem Patavi sedesque locavit
Teucrorum et genti nomen dedit armaque[8] fixit
Troia, nunc placida[9] compostus pace quiescit:
nos, tua progenies, caeli quibus adnuis[10] arcem,   250
navibus (infandum!) amissis unius ob iram
prodimur atque Italis longe disiungimur oris.
Hic pietatis honos?[11] Sic nos in sceptra reponis?'
    Olli[12] subridens hominum sator atque deorum

---

1 237. **pollicitus:** understand *es*; cf. 202 *experti* (*estis*), 5.687.

2 **quae . . . vertit:** 'what thought has changed your mind?', a variation on the commoner phrase *cur sententiam mutavisti?*

3 238-9. **hoc . . . solabar:** 'with this I consoled myself for . . .'; this use of *solari* is not uncommon in Virgil, cf. *Geo.* 1.293, *Aen.* 949.

4 239. **fatis . .. rependens:** 'balancing one fate against another (its opposite);' according to Servius the metaphor is financial. For the phraseology cf. *Aen.* 7.293f. *fatis contraria nostris / fata Phrygum.*

5 242f. The story of Antenor (an important Trojan in Homer, e.g. *Il.* 7.347f) is told in Livy 1.1; he led a party of Trojans to the area of Venice, and called the place Troia — thus he would pass Liburnia and Illyricum (near the head of the Adriatic on the east side) and the river Timavus, right at the head, to reach Patavium, modern Padua near Venice, on the west side. *Penetrare intima regna* merely means that he sailed past this remote northern area of the Adriatic (Livy 1.1 *intimum Adriatici maris sinum*); there is no reason to think that he travelled overland into the hinterland.

6 244. **superare:** a nautical term, according to Servius; cf. *Aen.* 3.698, Livy 31.22 *superare Sunium.*

7 445-6. The intention of Venus is to build up a formidable picture of the difficulties which Antenor was allowed to overcome; the floods of the Timavus are not strictly relevant to people sailing past by sea. *Mare* and *pelago* are used hyperbolically of the river's flood; for *proruptum* 'bursting forth' cf. *Aen.* 7.459, Lucr. 6.436. Henry has a long geographical note on the peculiarities of the Timavus.

8 248. **armaque fixit:** cf. *Aen.* 3.287; the armour would be hung up and dedicated in a temple.

9 249. 'now settled in quiet rest he is at peace'; this does not mean that he is dead, but that all his difficulties are over; cf. Enn. *Ann.* 375 *nunc senio confectus quiescit* and for *compositus* Ov. *Am.* 1.4.53. Venus' point is that Antenor has achieved peace after the successful foundation of his city, in contrast with Aeneas whose frustrations and perils seem to know no end.

10 250. Venus identifies herself with Aeneas; for *adnuis* cf. *Atn.* 12.187. Aeneas, like Romulus, was supposed to have become a god after death.

11 253. 'Is this the reward for devotion? Is this how you restore us to empire?' Venus' first question recalls the invocation to the poem (10-11), and summarises the nature of the problem which Virgil explores. Cf. Milton, *P.L.* 11.452 'Is Pietie thus and pure Devotion paid?'

12 254. **olli:** archaic for *illi*, quite frequent in Virgil as in Ennius.

vultu, quo caelum tempestatesque[1] serenat,   255
oscula libavit natae, dehinc talia fatur:
'parce[2] metu, Cytherea,[3] manent immota tuorum
fata tibi;[4] cernes urbem et promissa Lavini[5]
moenia sublimemque feres ad sidera caeli
magnanimum Aenean; neque me sententia vertit.   260
Hic tibi (fabor enim, quando haec te cura remordet,
longius, et volvens[6] fatorum arcana movebo)
bellum ingens geret Italia populosque ferocis[7]
contundet moresque viris et moenia ponet,
tertia dum Latio regnantem viderit aestas,[8]   265
ternaque transierint Rutulis hiberna subactis.
At puer Ascanius,[9] cui nunc cognomen Iulo[10]
additur (Ilus erat, dum res stetit Ilia regno),
triginta[11] magnos volvendis[12] mensibus orbis
imperio explebit, regnumque ab sede Lavini   270
transferet, et Longam multa vi muniet Albam.[13]
Hic iam ter[14] centum totos regnabitur annos

---

1 255-6. 'with the countenance (i.e. expression) with which he makes the heavens and the changing skies turn sunny he lightly kissed his daughter's lips'; cf. Enn. *Ann.* 457-8 *Iuppiter hic risit, tempestatesque serenae / riserunt omnes risu Iovis omnipotentis,* where *tempestates* means weather rather than storms.

2 257. **parce metu**: 'spare your fear', i.e. cease to be afraid; cf. *Aen.* 2.534 *nec voci iraeque pepercit. Metu* is dative, cf. 156.

3 **Cytherea**: a frequent epithet of Venus, from the seat of her worship in Cythera (680), an island just south of Greece.

4 258. **tibi**: ethic dative, cf. 463, and note on 102-3.

5 **Lavini**: Aeneas' first settlement, see note on 2. Notice the variation of scansion from *Laviniaque* in line 2; cf. *Italia* and *Italus* (2.109), *Sychaeus* (343, 348), *Sidonius* (446, 678), *Eous* (489, 2.417), *Diana* (499, 3.681), *Orion* (535, 3.517), *Sicania* and *Sicanos* (557, 5.24). For a full discussion see my note on 5.571 (OUP Ed.).

6 262. **volvens . . . movebo**: 'I will unroll and bring to light the secrets of the book of fate'; *volvens* is a metaphor from unrolling a book, cf. 22; for *movebo* cf. Hor. *Odes* 3.7.20.

7 263-4. Jupiter states the two elements in Aeneas' mission; first to conquer, and then to civilise (for *mores* cf. *Aen.* 6.852 *pacique imponere morem*). Compare 4.230f. *Italiam regeret. . . ac totum sub leges mitteret orbem. Moenia* suggests the settled life of city dwellers.

8 265-6. These lines refer obliquely to the death (or disappearance from the earth) of Aeneas, three years after the *Aeneid* comes to its end. The word *hiberna* is generally taken to mean that the Trojans remained in their camp for these three years; but it is more likely to be a Virgilian variation for *hiemes.*

9 267-8. Virgil uses the Roman form Iulus nearly as often as the Greek name Ascanius for Aeneas' son. The etymological connexion with Ilium (Troy) is taken a step further in line 288 to connect it with the Julian *gens*. Both Julius Caesar and Augustus were interested in emphasising the alleged Trojan origins of their family; cf. Hor. *Sat.* 2.5.62f. For Virgil's fondness for etymology of this kind cf. 5.117f., 7.706f., and see my note on 5.117f. (OUP Ed.).

10 267. **Iulo**: the dative agreeing with *cui* is a more common idiom than the nominative in apposition with the subject.

11 269. 'thirty great cycles as the months roll by'. The chronology is three years of rule for Iulus in Lavinium and Alba Longa, three hundred for his successors in Alba Longa; thus the gap in time (between the fall of Troy early in the twelfth century and the foundation of Rome in the middle of the eighth) is more or less explained.

12 **volvendis**: the gerundive supplies the place of the present participle passive, cf. *Aen.* 9.7, Enn. *Ann.* 531 *clamor . . . volvendus,* Lucr. 5.1276 *volvenda aetas.*

13 271. Some of the kings of Alba Longa are described in the pageant of Roman heroes in 6.760f.

14 272. **ter centum totos . . . annos**: 'full 300 years'.

20

gente[1] sub Hectorea, donec regina sacerdos[2]
Marte gravis geminam partu dabit Ilia prolem.
Inde lupae[3] fulvo nutricis tegmine laetus   275
Romulus excipiet gentem et Mavortia[4] condet
moenia Romanosque suo de nomine dicet.
His[5] ego nec metas rerum nec tempora pono:
imperium sine fine dedi. Quin[6] aspera Iuno,
quae mare nunc terrasque metu[7] caelumque fatigat,   280
consilia[8] in melius referet, mecumque fovebit
Romanos, rerum[9] dominos gentemque togatam.
Sic placitum. Veniet lustris labentibus aetas
cum domus Assaraci[10] Pthiam[11] clarasque Mycenas
servitio premet ac victis dominabitur Argis.   285
Nascetur pulchra Troianus origine Caesar,[12]
imperium Oceano, famam qui terminet astris,
Iulius, a magno demissum nomen Iulo.
Hunc tu olim caelo spoliis[13] Orientis onustum

---

1 273. **gente sub Hectorea**: there is strong emotional significance in this reference to Troy's great champion who did not survive Troy; cf. 5.190, 12.440.

2 273-7. This is the most famous part of the Roman legend: the name Ilia, an alternative for Rhea Silvia, the mother by Mars of Romulus and Remus, has obvious connexions with Troy (Ilium).

3 275. The picture of the she-wolf suckling the twins Romulus and Remus (when they were washed ashore after having been set adrift on the Tiber by the wicked Amulius; Livy 1.3.10f.) was a most familiar aspect of Roman legendary history; Virgil makes it the first picture on Aeneas' shield (8.630f.). Propertius (4.10.20) describes Romulus as wearing a wolfskin helmet.

4 276. **Mavortia**: an older form of *Martia* (Mavors = Mars), cf. *Aen.* 3.13.

5 278-9. 'For them I set no bounds in space or time: I have given them rule without end'. These are sonorous and unforgettable phrases: the proud certainty of Roman imperial rule must have had a profound patriotic impact on Virgil's readers.

6 279. **quin**: 'indeed', like the fuller form *quin etiam,* cf. *Aen.* 6.115.

7 280. **metu ... fatigat**: 'is harassing and alarming' (cf. *Aen.* 11.401) rather than 'is harassing because alarmed'.

8 281. **consilia in melius referet**: cf. *Aen.* 12.807f., Hor. *Odes* 3.3.17f.

9 282. **rerum dominos gentemque togatam**: 'lords of the world, a people wearing the toga'; i.e. warriors first, and then men of peace, the *toga* being the garment worn by civilians — cf. Cicero's famous phrase *cedant arma togae.*

10 284. **Assaracus**: grandfather of Anchises, cf. *Aen.* 6.650.

11 284-5. The reference to the defeat of Greece (it became a Roman province in the second century B.C.) is expressed in terms appropriate to the time of the Trojan war (cf. 6.836f). Pthia was the home of Achilles, Mycenae of Agamemnon; Argos as well as being a generic term for Greece was specifically the home of Diomedes.

12 286. **Caesar**: it is much disputed whether this is Julius Caesar or Augustus. Servius gives the former, and Conway argues strongly for this view. But it seems to me that the context, with its tremendous buildup leading to this final tableau, must refer not to any precursor of the restored Golden Age, but to the man thought to have actually restored it (6.791f.). Two other arguments seem to add additional weight in favour of Augustus: (i) the word Caesar elsewhere in the poem is used of Augustus, and on the one occasion when Julius Caesar is certainly referred to (6.834f.) it is in a context of sorrow; (ii) the references to the spoils of the east (the battle of Actium, 8.678f., see next note) is more appropriate to Augustus than to Julius Caesar, and the references to the closing of the gates of war (closed by Augustus in 29 B.C.. and again in 25 B.C.) and to the end of civil war (lines 292, 294) surely refer to Augustus. With Servius' interpretation the word *tum* has to take us from Julius Caesar to Augustus.

13 289. **spoliis Orientis**: cf. *Aen.* 8.687-8 (of Antony at Actium) *Aegyptum virisque Orientis et ultima secum / Bactra vehit, Geo.* 2.171f., 4.560f.

accipies secura;[1] vocabitur hic[2] quoque votis.   290
Aspera tum positis mitescent saecula bellis:[3]
cana[4] Fides et Vesta, Remo[5] cum fratre Quirinus
iura dabunt; dirae ferro et compagibus artis
claudentur Belli portae;[6] Furor[7] impius intus
saeva sedens super arma et centum vinctus aënis   295
post tergum nodis fremet horridus ore cruento.'[8]

297-304. Jupiter sends Mercury to tell Dido to receive the Trojans hospitably.

[9]Haec ait et Maia[10] genitum demittit ab alto,
ut terrae utque novae[11] pateant Karthaginis arces
hospitio Teucris, ne fati[12] nescia Dido
finibus arceret.[13] Volat ille per aera[14] magnum   300

---

1 290. Notice the unusual rhythm, with no strong caesura in the third or fourth foot. *Secura* means 'anxious no more'; Juno will no longer be in opposition.

2 **hic quoque:** as well as Aeneas. The poets were ready to promise deification to Augustus (*Geo.* 1.24f., Hor. *Odes* 3.3.11f., 3.5.2f.); Julius had already been deified.

3 291f. This is the fullest expression of that vision which is gradually revealed to Aeneas over the course of the poem; it is this very vision, however dimly seen, which enables him to persist through suffering and discouragement, weariness and misfortune towards his ultimate destiny. See note on 223f.

4 292. **cana Fides et Vesta:** *fides* was a word very highly valued in Roman moral beliefs; Livy tells (1.21.4) that Numa established the worship and the first temple of Fides; cf. Hor. *Carm. Saec.* 57. She is called *cana* because she is one of the original old-fashioned virtues of the *mos maiorum* (cf. *cana Vesta,* 5.744). Similarly Vesta, goddess of the hearth, often associated with the Lares and Penates, personifies traditional family ties (*Geo.* 1.498).

5 **Remo cum fratre Quirinus**: Quirinus is also used of Romulus in *Aen.* 6.859. The killing of Remus by Romulus is used as a symbol of the beginning of civil war in Rome; cf. Hor. *Epod.* 7, esp. 17f.; a very forceful protest against the folly of civil war (cf. also *Epod.* 16, *Geo.* 1.498f.).

6 294. The gates of war were those of Janus' temple; there is a full description of them in *Aen.* 7.607 f. Cf. Enn. *Ann.* 266-7 *postquam Discordia taetra / Belli ferratos postes portasque refregit.* They were closed in 29 B.C. (for the first time since 235), and again in 25 B.C.

7 **Furor impius:** here is personified the quality of mad strife seen especially in civil war, in which *pietas* was especially profaned (Hor. *Epod.* 16.9). For the importance of *furor* and *pietas* in the *Aeneid* see note on 148f. The picture of *Furor impius* is said by Servius to be based on a painting by Apelles, (Pliny *N.H.* 35 93) which Augustus placed in his own forum; it certainly makes a most powerful visual impact. Cf. Spenser *F.Q.,* 2.4.15 (Guyon taming Furor).

8 296. Notice the effect of a single word filling the fourth foot to round-off a paragraph; cr. 7 and 101.

9 297f. The visit of Aeneas to Carthage and his meeting with Dido was not in the prose version of the legend (as told by Dionysius, for instance); it was ruled out by chronological considerations, as Carthage was certainly not founded until three or four centuries after the time of Aeneas. There are various traces of early versions of a Dido story without Aeneas, and there is some reason to think that Naevius in his *Bellum Punicum* (late third century B.C.) first brought them together (see Pease's introduction to Book 4). But it is certain that the scope and extent of the Aeneas-Dido story is Virgil's own.

10 297. **Maia genitum**: Mercury was the son of Maia, daughter of Atlas, cf. *Aen.* 4.258.

11 298. **novae . . . Karthaginis:** (see also 366) according to Servius the word Carthage in Punic meant *Nova Civitas,* so that Virgil here is using *novus* to point to the etymology; see note on 267-8.

12 299. **fati nescia**: Dido was of course ignorant of the fates. This phrase does not mean that she was told of them (indeed when she was told in Book 4 she was completely unconvinced), but that Jupiter took action to aid the progress of the fates. Page has an interesting note on fate and free-will.

13 300. **arceret**: the different sequence from *pateant* indicates that while the former clause gives Jupiter's instructions, the latter is added as an explanation.

14 **aera**: a few Greek third-declension nouns have their Latin accusative in -*a*, e.g., *aethera, cratera, aegida, lampada,* and a number of proper names.

remigio[1] alarum ac Libyae citus astitit oris.

Et iam iussa facit, ponuntque ferocia Poeni

corda volente deo; in primis regina quietum

accipit in Teucros animum mentemque benignam.

305-417. Aeneas meets his mother Venus, disguised as a huntress. She tells him the history of Dido and Carthage, and when she asks him for his story, he complains bitterly of his ill fortune. She replies that his companions will return safely, and disappears after hiding him and Achates in a cloud.

[2]At pius[3] Aeneas per noctem plurima volvens,   305

ut primum lux alma data est, [4]exire locosque

Explorare novos, quas vento accesserit oras,

qui teneant (nam inculta videt[5]), hominesne feraene,

quaerere constituit sociisque exacta[6] referre.

Classem in convexo[7] nemorum sub rupe cavata   310

arboribus clausam circum atque horrentibus umbris

occulit; ipse uno graditur comitatus Achate

bina manu lato crispans[8] hastilia ferro.

Cui mater media sese tulit obvia silva[9]

virginis os habitumque gerens et virginis arma   315

---

1 301. **remigio alarum:** 'on the oarage of his wings', i.e. with wings for oars, cf. *Aen.* 6.19. The metaphor occurs in Aeschylus (*Agam.* 52), and was used by Lucretius (6.743). Cf. Milton, *P.L.* 7.438f. 'The swan with arched neck / between her white wings mantling proudly, rows / her state with oaric feet'.

2 305f. The narrative here, quite often based on *Odyssey* 6 and 7, is very fast-moving and filled with event and fact. It is in marked contrast with the slow and sonorous movement of the previous eighty lines. In it we hear the story of Dido, recounted by Venus in a way which immediately elicits sympathy and admiration (see note on 364). Her fortunes have been in many ways similar to those of Aeneas, with the one great difference that she has already founded her city.

In Aeneas' reply to Venus' questions (372f.) we see the effects upon him of the strain of seven years wandering and danger. He is angry and resentful at this latest misfortune, and Virgil shows that it is only by a narrow margin that he has been able so far to conquer his anxieties and human frailties, and to continue on with his mission. He is not yet (or ever to be) the stern, hard, self-sufficient man held out by the Stoics as their ideal (see note on 384-5). We are partly prepared for and ready to understand, the failure in self-discipline and devotion to duty which leads him to stay on in Carthage long after he should have renewed his pursuit of the ever-receding shores of Italy, and produces a situation of tragedy for which he must bear much of the onus.

3 305. **pius Aeneas:** see note on 220. Here the nature of his responsibility is stressed by the description of his sleeplessness. Servius says 'decet enim pro cunctis regem esse sollicitum'.

4 306f. The construction is *constituit exire locosque explorare novos, quaerere quas oras accesserit. . . .*

5 308. **videt:** the last syllable is lengthened in arsis, i.e. by the ictus (beat) at the beginning of the foot, cf. 478, 651, 668. See Austin's note on *Aen.* 4.64.

6 309. **exacta:** 'what he had achieved' (cf. *Aen.* 6.637), here with the sense of 'what he had found out' (as in Hor. *Sat.* 2.4.36).

7 310. **convexo:** 'arch'; this adjective used in the neuter as a noun is much more common in the plural (e.g. *Aen.* 4.451).

8 313. 'grasping two broad-bladed spears that quivered in his hand'; *crispans* does not mean 'brandishing' here or in 12.165, where this line occurs again.

9 314f. Virgil is following Homer *Od.* 7.19f., where the disguised Athena meets Odysseus (cf. also *Od.* 13.221f.); he conflates this episode with parts of the story of Nausicaa and Odysseus in *Odyssey* 6.

Spartanae,[1] vel qualis equos Threissa fatigat[2]
Harpalyce volucremque fuga praevertitur[3] Hebrum.[4]
Namque umeris de[5] more habilem[6] suspenderat arcum
venatrix dederatque[7] comam diffundere ventis,
nuda[8] genu nodoque[9] sinus collecta fluentis.   320
Ac prior 'heus', inquit, 'iuvenes, monstrate,[10] mearum
vidistis si quam hic errantem[11] forte sororum
succinctam pharetra et maculosae tegmine lyncis,
aut spumantis apri cursum clamore prementem.'

   Sic Venus, et Veneris contra sic filius orsus: 325
'nulla tuarum audita mihi neque visa sororum,
o quam te memorem, virgo? Namque haud tibi vultus
mortalis, nec vox hominem[12] sonat; o, dea certe
(an Phoebi soror?[13] An Nympharum sanguinis una?),
sis felix nostrumque leves, quaecumque,[14] laborem   330
et quo sub caelo tandem, quibus orbis in oris
iactemur doceas; [15]ignari hominumque locorumque
erramus vento huc vastis et fluctibus acti.

---

1 316f. Spartan maidens were well known for their physical toughness in hunting and the like; Harpalyce from Thrace devoted herself to the wild life of the woods (like Virgil's Camilla).

2 316. **fatigat**: 'outlasts', wearies them out by racing them.

3 317. **praevertitur**: 'outstrips'. Elsewhere Virgil uses the active form (7.807, 12.345); here the object is governed by the prepositional force of *prae-*.

4 **Hebrum**: a river in Thrace. The emendation *Eurum* (the east wind) has found some support, but all the MSS and Servius attest *Hebrum,* and so does Silius (2.73f.).

5 318. **de more**: 'in the proper style', explained by *venatrix.*

6 **habilem**: 'ready', i.e. of suitable size and well adjusted, cf. *Aen.* 9.305.

7 319. For this use of *dederat* see note on 66.

8 320. **nuda genu**: Greek accusative of respect, found once in Lucretius (3.489), common in Virgil especially with parts of the body; cf. 589 and 5.97 *nigrantis terga iuvencos* with my note there (OUP Ed.). See also note on 228.

9 **nodoque sinus collecta fluentis**: 'with her flowing garments secured by a knot,' literally 'having secured the flowing folds of her garments'; for the retained accusative see on 228, and cf. Ov. *Fast.* 1.407 *illa super suras tunicam collecta. . . .*

10 321-2. **monstrate ... vidistis si quam**: 'if you have seen any . . . show me where'; *si* here introduces a true condition, not an indirect question.

11 322-4. **errantem ... aut... prementem**: 'roaming around ... or chasing'. Some commentators have found difficulty with *aut* (and have therefore suggested that it might link *lyncis* with *apri*), but the two proper activities of a huntsman are *either* roaming around in search of prey (Servius for *errantem* rightly says *investigantem*) *or* chasing it.

12 328. **hominem sonat**: 'sound mortal', an extended use of the adverbial or cognate accusative (*humanum sonat*): cf. Pers. 3.21 *sonat vitium* ('rings false'). Compare Spenser *F.Q.* 2.3.33 'O Goddesse (for such I thee take to bee) / For neither doth thy face terrestrial shew, / Nor voyce sound mortall. . .'

13 329. The sister of Phoebus is Diana the huntress; if not Diana, Aeneas says, then surely one of her Nymphs (Oreades, 500). So spoke Odysseus to Nausicaa, *Od.* 6.149f.

14 330. **quaecumque**: in apposition with the subject: 'lighten our suffering, whoever you are'.

15 332. There are two unusual elisions in this line — the long final vowel of *ignari* before the short first syllable of *hominumque;* and the hypermetric elision of *locorumque* before *erramus* in the next line (cf. 448 and my note on *Aen.* 5.422 (OUP Ed.). The effect here is to suggest the catch in his voice as he speaks these words of despair (cf. the effect of indignation in 4.629).

Multa[1] tibi ante aras nostra cadet hostia dextra.'
    TumVenus: 'haud equidem tali me dignor honore;   335
virginibus[2] Tyriis mos est gestare pharetram
purpureoque alte suras vincire coturno.[3]
Punica regna vides, Tyrios et Agenoris[4] urbem;
sed[5] fines Libyci, genus intractabile bello.
Imperium[6] Dido Tyria regit urbe profecta,   340
germanum fugiens. [7]Longa est iniuria, longae
ambages; sed summa sequar fastigia rerum.
Huic coniunx Sychaeus[8] erat, ditissimus[9] agri
Phoenicum, et magno miserae[10] dilectus amore,
cui pater intactam dederat primisque[11] iugarat   345
ominibus. Sed regna Tyri germanus habebat
Pygmalion,[12] scelere ante alios immanior omnis.
Quos inter medius venit furor. Ille Sychaeum
impius[13] ante aras atque auri caecus amore
clam ferro incautum superat, securus[14] amorum   350
germanae; [15]factumque diu celavit et aegram
multa malus simulans vana spe lusit amantem.
Ipsa sed in somnis inhumati venit imago

---

1 334. **multa ... hostia**: 'many a victim'; for the singular cf. Hor. *Odes* 1.5.1 *multa . . . rosa ,Geo.* 1.187.

2 336. **virginibus Tyriis**: by implication Venus suggests that she is one.

3 337. Cf. *Ecl.* 7.32 (of Diana) *puniceo stabis suras evincta coturno;* evidently the type of *coturnus* (a high boot secured with bands) worn by hunters was brightly coloured.

4 338. **Agenor**: one of Dido's ancestors in Tyre.

5 339. **sed fines Libyci**: 'but the territory around is Libyan' (i.e. the surrounds of Carthage, in contrast to the city and the area immediately around it) — cf. 367f., 563f.

6 340. **imperium Dido .. . regit**: 'Dido is in command'; for the cognate accusative cf. Ov. *Pont.* 3.3.61. Servius tells us that Elissa was Dido's original Phoenician name (Virgil uses it in the oblique cases), but that she was called Dido (= *virago*, 'Heroine') after she had killed herself rather than break her vows by marrying an African suitor (this is the early form of her story before it was linked, perhaps by Naevius, with the Aeneas legend; see note on 297f.).

7 341-2. 'It is a long story of crime, a long involved story, but I will go through the main outlines of the events'. *Fastigia* is a rare variant for *capita.*

8 343. **Sychaeus**: Servius says his Punic name was Sicarbas; in Virgil's Latinised form the quantity of the *y* varies, cf. 348. See note on 258.

9 **ditissimus agri**: for the genitive see on 14; there seems no need for the emendation *auri.*

10 344. **miserae dilectus**: cf. *Aen.* 4.31 *dilecta sorori.*

11 345-6. **primisque . . . ominibus**: 'and had joined her to him in this her first marriage ceremony;' *primis* repeats the idea of *intactam.*

12 347. **Pygmalion**: the other Pygmalion, who fell in love with the statue he had made, was also of the royal house of Tyre.

13 349. **impius**: mainly with reference to the religious transgression (*ante aras*), but also including the family crime of killing his brother-in-law.

14 350-1. **securus amorum germanae**: 'caring nothing for his sister's love', cf. *Aen.* 7.304 and (a little differently) 10.326. The plural *amores* in the sense 'love' (cf. *Aen.* 4.28, 5.334) occurs in prose as well as poetry.

15 351-2. 'wickedly making up many false stories he deceived the distraught bride with vain hope'.

coniugis ora modis attollens pallida miris;[1]
crudelis aras traiectaque pectora ferro   355
nudavit,[2] caecumque domus[3] scelus omne retexit.
Tum celerare[4] fugam patriaque excedere suadet
auxiliumque[5] viae veteres tellure[6] recludit
thesauros, ignotum argenti pondus et auri.
[7]His commota fugam Dido sociosque parabat.   360
Conveniunt quibus aut odium[8] crudele tyranni
aut metus acer erat; navis, quae forte paratae,[9]
corripiunt onerantque auro. Portantur avari
Pygmalionis opes pelago; dux[10] femina facti.
Devenere locos ubi nunc ingentia cernes   365
moenia surgentemque novae Karthaginis arcem,
mercatique[11] solum, facti de nomine Byrsam,[12]
taurino quantum possent circumdare tergo.
Sed vos qui tandem? Quibus aut venistis ab oris?
Quove tenetis iter?' Quaerenti talibus[13] ille   370
suspirans imoque trahens a pectore vocem:
    'O dea, si prima repetens ab origine pergam

---

1 354. 'lifting his face to look at her, strangely pale'; cf. Lucr. 1.123 *simulacra modis pallentia miris,* a phrase used by Virgil in *Geo.* 1.477.

2 356. **nudavit... retexit**: *nudavit* is probably visual (he brought before her eyes in her dream) and *retexit* oral (revealed by telling her).

3 **domus**: 'of the family', cf. *Aen.* 3.97.

4 357. **celerare**: the infinitive with *suadere* is common in Virgil, cf. 3.363 and note on 527-8; so with *hortari* (2.33), *imperare* (7.36), and *instimulare* (4.576).

5 358. **auxiliumque viae**: in apposition to *thesauros,* 'to help the voyage'.

6 **tellure recludit**: in her dream Dido sees Sychaeus 'unearthing' the treasure for her; cf. *Geo.* 2.423.

7 360f. The narrative, which has been fast-moving throughout, moves to its climax at great speed, with short sentences and many main verbs. This kind of writing is in marked contrast with the descriptive, reflective tone which Virgil is especially associated with. It is this command of variety in narrative movement which maintains the impetus of the *Aeneid* through its twelve books. Contrast poem 64 of Catullus.

8 361. **odium crudele tyranni**: i.e. *odium crudelis tyranni,* says Servius (transferred epithet). This is partly true, but a transferred epithet should also make sense before it is transferred (see Conway ad loc.); so here they felt cruel hatred of a tyrant, the cruelty of the tyrant made their reaction cruel.

9 362-4. Servius suggests that there are here traces of a story according to which Pygmalion sent ships carrying gold to go trading for corn, and Dido's party seized these ships.

10 364. **dux femina facti**: the character of Dido as shown in the rest of Book 1 was in every way equal to facing danger and assuming authority. Her ability to establish her city and administer it causes the Trojans to admire and envy her. Thus her abdication of her queenly responsibilities and qualities in Book 4 is all the more tragic.

11 367. **mercatique**. supply *sunt;* the omission of the verb 'to be' is not very common where, as here, the effect is to suggest a subordinate clause.

12 **Byrsa**: this is the Greek word for a bull's hide; the legend is that the hide was cut into one very long thin strip. The story perhaps arose from the fact that Byrsa was, according to Strabo, the Carthaginian word for their citadel.

13 370. **talibus**: supply *verbis,* cf. 410, 559.

et vacet[1] annalis nostrorum audire laborum,
ante diem clauso componat Vesper Olympo.[2]
Nos Troia antiqua, [3]si vestras forte per auris   375
Troiae nomen iit, diversa per aequora vectos
forte[4] sua Libycis tempestas appulit oris.
Sum[5] pius Aeneas, raptos qui ex hoste penatis[6]
classe veho mecum, fama super aethera notus;
Italiam quaero patriam[7], et genus ab Iove summo.   380
Bis denis Phrygium conscendi[8] navibus aequor,
matre dea[9] monstrante viam data fata secutus;
vix septem convulsae undis Euroque supersunt.[10]
Ipse ignotus, egens, Libyae deserta peragro,
Europa atque Asia pulsus.' Nec plura querentem   385
passa Venus medio sic interfata dolore est:

---

1 373. **vacet:** 'if you had time'.

2 374. 'Before I could finish, the evening star would close up Olympus and lay the day to rest'. *Ante* is adverbial (= *antea*); for *diem . . . componat* cf. 135, *Geo.* 4.189, *Ecl.* 9.52 *cantando . . . condere soles; clauso . . . Olympo* refers to the gates of heaven (*Geo.* 3.261). I have with some doubt preferred *componat* to *componet;* the major MSS are divided, and as the tendency would be for scribes to regularise the condition, most editors adopt *componet,* quoting Hor. *Odes* 3.3.7-8. But there a special rhetorical effect is achieved by the irregularity; here there would be nothing but a feeling of awkwardness.

3 375-6. Notice the irony, reinforced by repetition — from Troy, if you happen ever to have heard of it, Troy it's called.

4 377. **forte sua:**'by its caprice'.

5 378. **sum pius Aeneas:** much indignant ink has been spilled on this phrase. It is based on Odysseus' introduction of himself, *Od.* 9.19-20 ειμ Οδυαευς Γαερτιαδης, ος πασι δολοισιν / ανθρωποιοι μελω, και μευ κλεος ουρανον ικει ('I am Odysseus son of Laertes who am known among all men for my subtle resources, and my fame reaches the heavens'.) The second half of line 379 is a translation of the Homer passage. Exception is taken to Aeneas' use of the epithet *pius* of himself, but it seems to me that it is used here with tremendous power, implying 'and is this what I get for it?' (*hic pietatis honos? as* Venus said to Jupiter, 253). This accords with the rest of what Aeneas says as he lists the reasons why he might expect fate to deal less unkindly with him and launches into bitter complaints about what has happened to him and his people. Henry has a superbly vigorous note on the passage beginning: "Charles James Fox, in a letter to his friend Trotter, having first observed: 'Though the detached parts of the *Aeneid* appear to me to be equal to anything, the story and characters appear more faulty every time I read it. My chief objection (I mean that to the character of Aeneas) is of course not so much felt in the first three books; but afterwards he is always either insipid or odious; sometimes excites interest against him, and never for him;' adds in a postscript and by way of example: "Even in the first book Aeneas says: *sum pius Aeneas. ..*" and inquires "Can you bear this?". Trotter's answer not having come down to us, I beg leave to answer for him, Yes; why not? Why not as well as any other announcement of a person's real name, rank, dignity, and quality? Why not as well as. . .etc. etc." Servius puts it more briefly: *non est hoc loco arrogantia, sed indicium.*

6 **penatis:** see note on 6.

7 380. **patriam:** the meaning is 'to be my fatherland' rather than 'which is already my fatherland', with reference to Dardanus' origins there (cf. 3.167f.).

'and my ancestry comes from Jupiter the highest'; Aeneas says this again in 6.123. The phrase comes in abruptly here, but perhaps intentionally so, to express Aeneas' angry indignation. Most commentators take *genus* as a second object for *quaero* — 'I seek Italy and a posterity descended from Jupiter'.

8 381. **conscendi ... aequor:** *contendere* (*navem* or *in navem*) is the regular term for 'to embark'; here the normal phrase is given an unexpected construction with the object *aequor,* adding the notion of going up from the shore to the sea; cf. *deferri* (e.g. 5.57) for sailing into harbour.

9 382. **matre dea:** perhaps with a touch of rebuke; the irony of the situation is exploited. For Venus' help at Troy cf. 2.610f.; it has often been remarked that Apollo, not Venus, looks after Aeneas in Book 3. Servius gets round this difficulty by quoting Varro to the effect that Venus' star guided him to Latium (cf. 2.801f.).

10 384-5. Aeneas' last words are a fine climax to his protests (again echoing what Venus herself had said to Jupiter, 233), and the word *querentem* summarises the content of his speech. He is very far from being the perfect Stoic; see G. M. Bowra, *Greece and Rome* 1933-4, pp. 8f., and M. W. Edwards, *Phoenix* 1960, pp. 151f.

'Quisquis[1] es, haud, credo, [2]invisus caelestibus auras
vitalis carpis, Tyriam qui[3] adveneris urbem.
Perge modo atque hinc te reginae ad limina perfer.
Namque tibi reduces socios classemque relatam   390
nuntio et in tutum versis[4] Aquilonibus actam,
ni[5] frustra augurium vani docuere parentes.
Aspice bis senos laetantis agmine cycnos,[6]
aetheria quos lapsa plaga Iovis ales aperto
turbabat caelo; [7]nunc terras ordine longo   395
aut capere aut captas iam despectare videntur:
ut reduces illi ludunt stridentibus alis
et coetu cinxere[8] polum cantusque dedere,
haud aliter puppesque tuae pubesque tuorum
aut portum[9] tenet aut pleno subit ostia velo.   400
Perge modo et, qua te ducit via, derige gressum.'
     [10]Dixit et avertens rosea cervice refulsit,
ambrosiaeque comae divinum vertice odorem
spiravere; pedes vestis defluxit ad imos,
et vera incessu patuit dea. Ille ubi matrem   405
agnovit tali fugientem est voce secutus:

---

1 387. **quisquis es:** a cruel touch of irony, as Venus affects not to be aware of the names Troy or Aeneas.

2 387f. Cf. *Od.* 6.240f. where Nausicaa says to her maidens that she thinks Odysseus has come to Phaeacia in accordance with the will of the gods.

3 388. **qui adveneris:** causal subjunctive, implying that the Tyrians will receive him kindly.

4 391. **versis Aquilonibus:** 'by a shift of the wind'.

5 392. 'unless my parents have deceived me and taught me augury without any success'.

6 393. For a similar omen cf. *Aen.* 12.247f., where an eagle (*fulvus Iovis ales*) seizes a swan but is forced to relinquish its prey by the other swans. Here the twelve swans correspond to Aeneas' twelve lost ships (the thirteenth, that of Orontes, is known to be sunk). The swans are particularly appropriate for this omen, because they were sacred to Venus.

7 395-6. 'now they can be seen in long line either settling on the ground or looking down where others have settled'; this is the best sense that can be made from *captas*, rather better than 'looking down on where they have decided to settle'. Another possibility is that the swans have been scattered out to sea, and now they are either reaching the shore, or have reached it and are looking down at it for a place to settle. Ribbeck's conjecture *capsos* (a scarce word meaning an enclosure for animals) is one of the most ingenious and most unlikely in the long history of emendation.

8 398. 'and have circled the sky in formation, and have given song', i.e. they seem to fill the sky because they are flying low and close together, as opposed to the scattered specks when the eagle was chasing them. The perfect tenses in this line convey single actions compared with the longer lasting *ludunt* in the previous line.

9 400. **portum tenet:** 'has reached harbour,' to correspond with *capere*, as *subit* corresponds with *despectare*. Mackail's explanation of *tenet* ('is making for') destroys this correspondence, and would be unnatural Latin.

10 402f. 'as she turned away a radiance shone from her rosy-flushed neck, and her immortal locks breathed from her head a perfume divine; her garments were unloosed to cover her feet, and as she went her true divinity was clear to see'. For *avertens* cf. 104; for line 403 cf. Hom. *Il.* 1.529; *defluxit* refers to the unloosing of the knot which had tied-up her clothes when she was a huntress; for *incessu* cf. line 46 and for *vera patuit dea* cf. *Aen.* 2.591 *confessa deam.* The hiatus after *dea* (405) is of a kind not found elsewhere in the *Aeneid;* it serves to emphasise the word *dea* and the long pause after the brilliant description of her.

'quid natum totiens, [1]crudelis tu quoque, falsis
ludis imaginibus? Cur dextrae iungere dextram
non datur ac veras audire et reddere voces?'
Talibus incusat gressumque ad moenia tendit.[2]   410
At Venus obscuro[3] gradientis aere saepsit,
et multo nebulae circum dea fudit amictu,
cernere ne quis eos neu quis contingere posset
molirive[4] moram aut veniendi poscere causas.
Ipsa Paphum[5] sublimis abit sedesque revisit   415
laeta suas, ubi templum illi, centumque Sabaeo[6]
ture calent arae sertisque recentibus halant.

> *418-493. Aeneas and Achates marvel at the size and activity
> of the newly established town of Carthage. They come to the
> temple of Juno, where they see on the walls pictures of
> events in the Trojan war; Aeneas is heartened by this, and
> studies them one after the other, reminding himself of the
> triumphs and reverses of the war.*

[7]Corripuere[8] viam interea, qua semita monstrat.

---

1 407f. The pathos of these lines is very marked. We are reminded that after the death of Anchises Aeneas has no family comfort, he cannot even embrace his goddess mother and his son is too young yet to help. In *crudelis tu quoque* he summarises his despair.

2 410. Notice the typically Virgilian coordination of two short clauses: in English we should say 'With these words of protest he turned. . .'.

3 411f. In Hom. *Od.* 7.14f. (and 13.189f.) Odysseus is concealed in a cloud by Athena; the tmesis of *circumfudit* is perhaps suggested by *Od.* 13.189 περι γαρ θεος ηερα χευε for the position of *dea* cf. 692.

4 414. **molirive moram:** 'engineer delay', cf. *Geo.* 1.871; *moliri* has here the idea of creating an obstacle as well as making with effort (424). It is a favourite word with Virgil.

5 415. **Paphum:** seat of her worship in Cyprus, cf. *Aen.* 10.51.

6 416-17. **Sabaeo ture:** from Arabia, cf. *Geo.* 1.57.

7 418f. This is a quiet piece of narrative leading up to the appearance of Dido and sketching in the background to the Trojans' voyage by means of the pictures on Juno's temple. It is based on events in *Odyssey* 7 and 8; Aeneas marvels at Carthage as Odysseus had at Phacacia (7.43f.); the splendour of the temple of Juno is described in terms which recall Alcinous' palace (7.84f.); the pictures of past events, and Aeneas' tears at recalling them, are reminiscent of Demodocus' song of the Trojan war and Odysseus'tears (8.73f., 86).

The description of the pictures is a fully developed ecphrasis. This term is used for two kinds of descriptive passage, firstly that of natural scenery (like the harbour, lines 159f., where see note); and secondly that of works of art, like Achilles' shield in Homer (*Il.* 18.478f.), imitated by Virgil in *Aen.* 8.625f., or the carved cup in Theoc. 1.27f., or the coverlet in Catullus 64.50f. Compare the pictures on Apollo's temple in *Aen.* 6.20f., and see my note on *Aen.* 5.254f. (OUP Ed.). Cf. Chaucer, *House of Fame* 119f., and *Knight's Tale* 1060f.; Shakespeare, *Rape of Lucrece,* 1366f.

The pictures here are evidently paintings on the walls of the temple (anachronistic for the heroic age). They are arranged in pairs: (i) the Greeks flee, the Trojans flee; (ii) death of Rhesus, death of Troilus; (iii) supplication by the Trojan women, supplication by Priam; (iv) Memnon's Eastern armies, Penthesilea's Amazons. Aeneas himself is depicted between the third and fourth pairs of pictures, and throughout Virgil shows us these pictures through the eye of the beholder. The descriptive passage is made integral with the poem by the insight which it gives us into how Aeneas has been affected by these events of his past — *quaeque ipse miserrima vidi / et quorum pars magna fui,* 2.5-6 — and how he continues affected. We understand better what he and his friends have suffered; we are given a preview of the tragic descriptions of Book 2. We are shown the ruthless cruelty of the Greek invaders, particularly of Achilles, and the unfolding of the doom of Troy; the oracles about Rhesus and Troilus (see notes on 469f., 474f.), the hostility of Pallas, the death of their champion Hector. For further discussion see my article in *C.Q.* 1960, pp. 145f.

8 418. **corripuere viam**: 'they hastened along their way', a poetic use of the verb, cf. *Geo.* 3.104, *Aen.* 5.145, 316, 6.634. *Rapidus* is related to *rapere.*

Iamque ascendebant collem, qui[1] plurimus urbi
imminet adversasque aspectat desuper arces.   420
Miratur molem Aeneas, magalia[2] quondam,
miratur portas strepitumque et strata[3] viarum.
Instant ardentes Tyrii: pars ducere[4] muros
molirique[5] arcem et manibus subvolvere[6] saxa,
pars optare locum tecto[7] et[8] concludere sulco;   425
iura magistratusque legunt sanctumque senatum.
Hic portus alii effodiunt; hic alta[9] theatri
fundamenta locant alii, immanisque columnas
rupibus excidunt, scaenis decora alta[10] futuris.
[11]Qualis[12] apes aestate nova per florea rura   430
exercet sub sole labor, cum gentis[13] adultos
educunt fetus, aut cum liquentia mella
stipant[14] et dulci distendunt nectare cellas,
aut onera accipiunt venientum, aut agmine facto
ignavum[15] fucos pecus a praesepibus arcent;   435
fervet[16] opus redolentque thymo fragrantia mella.
'O fortunati, quorum iam moenia surgunt!'[17]

---

1 419-20. **qui plurimus urbi imminet**: 'which looms large over the city'; for *plurimus* cf. *Geo.* 3.52, *Aen.* 6.659.

2 421. **magalia**: 'huts', a Carthaginian word.

3 422. **strata viarum**: 'the paved streets'; the phrase is from Lucretius (1.315, 4.415). For the poetic use of neuter adjectives followed by a genitive see my note on 5.695 (OUP Ed.). Compare especially *Aen.* 2.332, 6.633.

4 **ducere**: historic infinitive, like the four following verbs; this seems better than punctuating so that the infinitives depend on *instant* (as in *Aen.* 2.627). *Ducere* is normal Latin for building walls or long structures (Livy 7.23.5).

5 424. **molirique**: 'toil at', cf. *Aen.* 3.6, 132.

6 **subvolvere**: 'roll up'; the word is found only here.

7 425. **tecto**: 'for a building' cf. *Aen.* 3.109 *optavitque locum regno.*

8 **et concludere sulco**: 'enclosing it with a furrow', a reference to the Roman method of marking out the site for the walls of a city (*Aen.* 5.755), transferred here to the site of a building.

9 427-8. **alta theatri fundamenta locant alii**: the MSS vary between *alta* and *lata, theatri* and *theatris* (Servius attests the singular) and *locant* and *petunt.*

10 429. **alta**: Mynors prints Bentley's conjecture *apta,* to avoid the repetition with 427, but the Romans were less sensitive to this kind of repetition than we are; see my note on 5.254 (OUP Ed.).

11 430f. The simile is based on phrases and whole lines used in *Geo.* 4.162-9. Virgil uses bee similes again in 6.707f, 12.587f., Cf. Hom. *Il.* 2.87f., Milton, *P.L.* 1.768f.

12 430-1. **qualis . . . labor**: 'like the busy activity which seizes the bees. ..'

13 431-2. **gentis ... fetus**: 'pour forth their populous youth about the hive' (Milton, *P.L.* 1.770).

14 433. 'and fill to bursting the honeycomb cells with the sweet nectar', a variation of the previous phrase.

15 435. **ignavum fucos pecus**: 'the drones, an idle tribe'; for the word order (with *fucos* in apposition between the noun and its adjective) cf. *Ecl.* 1.57 *raucae tua cura palumbes; Geo.* 4.246 *dirum tineae genus.*

16 436. **fervet opus**: cf. *Aen.* 4.407 (of ants) *opere omnis semita fervet.*

17 437. This line summarises Aeneas' frustrated longing during seven years of wandering to begin to build his city; cf. his words to Helenus in 3.493f.

Aeneas ait et fastigia suspicit[1] urbis.
Infert se saeptus nebula (mirabile dictu)
per medios, miscetque[2] viris neque cernitur ulli.[3]   440
    Lucus in urbe fuit media, laetissimus[4] umbrae,
quo primum iactati undis et turbine Poeni
effodere loco signum,[5] quod regia Iuno
monstrarat, caput acris equi; sic[6] nam fore bello
egregiam et facilem[7] victu per saecula gentem.   445
Hic templum Iunoni ingens Sidonia[8] Dido
condebat, donis[9] opulentum et numine divae,
aerea cui gradibus surgebant[10] limina [11]nexaeque[12]
aere trabes, foribus cardo stridebat[13] aenis.
Hoc[14] primum in luco nova[15] res oblata timorem[16]   450
leniit, hic primum Aeneas sperare salutem
ausus et adflictis melius confidere rebus.

---

1 438. **suspicit**: 'looks up at', having presumably now come down from the hill.

2 440. **miscetque viris**: it is better to supply *se* from the previous line than to regard *miscet* as intransitive (cf. 104).

3 **ulli**: the dative of the agent is used much more freely in poetry than prose; cf. (e.g.) 326, 344, 494.

4 441. **laetissimus umbrae**: 'very rich in shade'; most MSS have *umbra*, but *umbrae* is attested by Probus, and Servius quotes Sallust *frugum pabulique laetus ager.* For the genitive cf. 14 and 343.

5 443. **signum**: Servius tells the story: when Dido and her followers fled from Tyre they received an oracle from Juno whereafter which they dug in the ground on the site selected for their new city. They found an ox's head, but as this indicated servitude, they moved to another site and this time found a horse's head, token of victory in war as well as of peaceful prosperity (*facilem victu*); cf. *Aen.* 3.539f. The coins of Carthage often showed a horse's head. Conington points out that the horse's head was to the Carthaginians what the white sow was to Aeneas.

6 444-5. **sic nam fore . . . gentem:** the *oratio obliqua* reports Juno's oracle.

7 445. **facilem victu**: 'prosperous in their way of life', an unusual phrase extended from the more natural usage of *Geo.* 2.460 *fundit humo facilem victum iustissima tellus.* These two Carthaginian attributes, military power and wealth, were coupled in the first mention of Carthage (14).

8 446. **Sidonia:** this epithet is used several times of Dido (Virgil uses Tyre and Sidon interchangeably); the quantity of the *o* is sometimes long, sometimes short (678): see note on 258.

9 447. **donis . . . divae:** 'rich with offerings and the presence of the goddess'; the zeugma is striking, although *numen* no doubt implies a statue.

10 448. 'Its bronze threshold towered high above the steps'; this use of *surgere* is mainly poetic, cf. *Geo.* 3.29, *Aen.* 10.476.

11 **nexaeque:** hypermetric elision, see note on 332.

12 448-9. **nexaeque aere trabes:** Servius reported an alternative *nixaeque* ('the beams rested on bronze', cf. Hom. *Od.* 7.83), but we get a better meaning with the MSS reading *nexaeque*: 'the beams (which form the frame for the door) are bound in with bronze' — i.e. the wooden framework of the door is joined together and decorated with bronze.

13 449. **stridebat:** a normal word for a heavy door on its hinges (*Aen.* 6.573, 7.613).

14 450-1. Notice the very powerful repetition of *hoc primum . . hic primum*; Virgil prepares the scene for his description of the pictures (and for Aeneas' subsequent stay in Carthage) with great emphasis.

15 450. **nova res oblata:** 'a strange sight that met his eyes'.

16 **timorem**: Aeneas has not been not wholly convinced by Venus' promises and instructions; in particular he is not confident that the Carthaginians will be friendly. This is why he is so heartened (463) to find the pictures of the Trojan war which indicate the city of a civilised people, ready to be moved to pity by suffering.

Namque sub ingenti lustrat dum[1] singula templo
reginam opperiens, [2]dum quae fortuna sit urbi
artificumque manus inter se operumque laborem   455
miratur, videt Iliacas ex[3] ordine pugnas
bellaque iam fama totum vulgata per orbem,
Atridas[4] Priamumque et saevum ambobus Achiliem.
Constitit et lacrimans 'quis[5] iam locus' inquit 'Achate,
quae regio in terris nostri non plena laboris?   460
En[6] Priamus. [7]Sunt hic etiam sua praemia laudi,
sunt lacrimae rerum et mentem mortalia tangunt.
Solve metus; [8]feret haec aliquam tibi fama salutem.'
Sic ait atque animum[9] pictura pascit inani
multa gemens, largoque umectat[10] flumine vultum.   465
Namque videbat[11] uti bellantes Pergama[12] circum
hac fugerent Grai, premeret Troiana iuventus,
hac[13] Phryges, instaret curru cristatus Achilles.

---

1 453. 'For while he was looking around at everything, in the shadow of the huge temple'; the postposition of *dum* after its verb *lustrat* is an artificiality characteristic of poetic diction. There are about 80 instances in the *Aeneid* of such a reversal of prose order.

2 454-6. 'while he marvelled at the city's prosperity and the harmonious handiwork of the several artists and the work that had gone into these achievements'; for *manus* cf. *Aen.* 12.210, Prop 3.21.30, Milton, *P.R.* 4.59 'carv'd work, the hand of fam'd Artificers', and for *operumque laborem* line 507 and *Geo.* 2.155. *Inter se* (working together) is used in a condensed sense also in *Aen.* 2.454, 4.193, 8.452; *intra se* (with *miratur*, 'inwardly marvels') is read by a ninth century MS, but *secum* is Virgil's normal phrase for 'inwardly'.

3 456. **ex ordine**: i.e. there was a series of panels along the wall.

4 458. **Atridas:** Agamemnon and Menelaus. Achilles was fierce towards them (as well as towards Priam) because of his anger against Agamemnon, which led to his withdrawal from the fighting (Hom. *Il.* 1).

5 459. **quis iam locus**: the adjective *quis* is much less common in prose than *qui*, but is preferred by Virgil, cf. 615.

6 461. **En Priamus**: this probably refers to the picture described at greater length in 483-7, where Priam goes to Achilles and beseeches him to return the body of Hector (*Il.* 24.471f.). The rest of this line and the next have some specific reference to Priam: he gained glory and won sympathy by daring to approach Achilles, and this is appreciated by the Carthaginians who have made a picture of the scene.

7 461-2. 'here too there are due rewards for glory, here too there are tears for human happenings and mortal sufferings touch the heart'. *Sua* is in the sense of *propria* ('glory has its own reward'); it is used freely in this sense by the poets even where it does not refer to the subject, cf. *Aen.* 3.469. *Rerum* is an extended objective genitive (cf. *Aen.* 2.704) helped also by phrases like *fessi rerum* (178); the meaning of the word is simply 'happenings', like 204, 229, 452. Line 462 is often detached from its context and quoted to summarise the note of pathos in the *Aeneid*; there is no harm in this provided that it is understood that the meaning is 'people are sympathetic', not 'the world is full of sorrows, is a vale of tears'.

8 463. The meaning is 'we need not fear — the Carthaginians know of our sufferings and evidently are people who feel pity and sympathy'; see note on 450 (*timorem*). *Tibi* is ethic dative; cf. 258.

9 464. **animum pictura pascit inani**: 'he fed his thoughts on the lifeless picture', cf. *Geo.* 2.285.

10 465. **umectat**: cf. Lucr. 1.920. For *flumen* cf. our 'flood of tears'.

11 466f. For an analysis of the pictures see note on 418f.

12 466. **Pergama**: the citadel of Troy, frequent for Troy itself (cf. 651); the word also occurs in the singular *Pergamum*, but not in hexameter poetry.

13 **468. hac Phryges**: 'in another direction the Trojans were in flight': *Phryges* is Greek nominative plural with short final syllable.

Nec procul hinc Rhesi[1] niveis tentoria velis
agnoscit lacrimans, primo[2] quae prodita somno   470
Tydides multa vastabat caede cruentus,
ardentisque avertit equos in castra prius quam
pabula gustassent[3] Troiae Xanthumque[4] bibissent.
Parte alia fugiens amissis[5] Troilus[6] armis,
infelix puer atque impar[7] congressus Achilli,   475
fertur[8] equis curruque haeret resupinus inani,
lora tenens tamen; huic cervixque comaeque trahuntur
per terram, et versa pulvis inscribitur hasta.
Interea ad templum non aequae Palladis ibant[9]
crinibus Iliades passis peplumque ferebant   480
suppliciter, tristes et tunsae[10] pectora palmis;
diva solo fixos oculos aversa tenebat.
Ter circum Iliacos raptaverat[11] Hectora muros
exanimumque auro corpus vendebat Achilles.
Tum vero ingentem gemitum dat pectore ab imo,   485
ut spolia, ut currus, utque ipsum corpus amici

---

1 469f. The story of Rhesus' death is told in *Iliad* 10 and in Euripides' *Rhesus*; he was a Thracian who came to help the Trojans, and Diomedes (*Tydides,* 471). Odysseus made a night attack on his camp immediately after his arrival, killing him and many of his followers. There was an oracle (this is not in Homer or Euripides) that if his horses cropped the grass of Troy and drank from the river Xanthus Troy would not fall; hence the Greek attack and the removal of the horses to the Greek camp.

2 470. **primo . . . prodita somno**: 'taken by surprise as soon as they slept'. Servius gives two explanations: either when sleep is deepest, or on their first night; both ideas are present. Henry has an excellent note on this.

3 473. **gustassent**: 'could have tasted', for the subjunctive implying purpose ('in order that they might not have tasted') cf. line 193 and *Geo.* 3.469.

4 **Xanthum**: one of Troy's rivers, see note on 100-1.

5 474. **amissis . . . armis**: i.e. he is caught without his armour on, all he has is the spear (see below) which he has been using as a goad.

6 474f. Virgil is following the Greek tradition that Troilus, the young son of Priam, was ambushed by Achilles when unarmed; again there was an oracle about the fate of Troy (as with Rhesus), namely that if Troilus had lived to the age of twenty, Troy would not have been taken (Plautus, *Bacch.* 953f.); see my article in *C.Q.* 1960, 145f., for a detailed discussion of this passage.

7 475. **impar congressus Achilli**: 'who was no match for Achilles when he met him in battle'; the dative with words like *congredi* (cf. *certare*) is mainly poetic, cf. 493.

8 476-8. 'was dragged along by his horses, and fallen backwards was entangled with the empty chariot, still grasping the reins in spite of all; his neck and hair were being dragged along the ground, and the dust was scored by his reversed spear'. For *fertur equis* cf. *Geo.* 1.514; *curru* is dative, cf. 156. *Lora tenens tamen* indicates that he is wounded, but still clings on in the hope of yet controlling his horses; the unusual diaeresis after the second foot serves to emphasise *tamen. Versa hasta* means that the spear, which he had been using reversed as a goad (cf. 9.609f.), now trails on the ground; it does not refer (as some commentators think) to the spear of Achilles with which Troilus was transfixed. The final syllable of *pulvis* is lengthened in arsis (see note on 308); it may have been long in early Latin (Enn. *Ann.* 28a).

9 479. The picture of the Trojan women beseeching the hostile goddess Pallas and taking a robe (*peplum*) as an offering is based on Hom. *Il.* 6.297f.

10 481. **tunsae**: 'beating', see note on 228

11 483f. The picture of Achilles receiving a ransom from Priam for Hector's body (*Il.* 24.502f.) is prefixed by a reference to what had happened previously to the body (note the pluperfect tense, *raptaverat*). In Homer Achilles dragged Hector's body around Patroclus' tomb; Virgil follows a later Greek version (Eur. *Andr.* 107f.) which emphasises even more the cruelty of Achilles.

tendentemque manus Priamum conspexit inermis.
Se quoque principibus permixtum agnovit Achivis,[1]
Eoasque acies et nigri Memnonis[2] arma.
Ducit Amazonidum[3] lunatis[4] agmina peltis   490
Penthesilea furens mediisque in milibus ardet
aurea subnectens[5] exsertae cingula mammae
bellatrix, audetque viris concurrere virgo.

> *494-656. Dido comes to the temple, and while she is attending to the city's affairs, Aeneas' lost companions approach. Ilioneus on their behalf asks for help, which she readily grants. Aeneas then comes forth from the cloud and gratefully expresses his thanks. She is amazed to find that so famous a hero has come to her kingdom, and proclaims sacrifices and a feast. Aeneas for his part sends Achates to bring presents.*

[6]Haec dum Dardanio[7] Aeneae miranda videntur,
dum stupet obtutuque haeret defixus in uno,   495
regina ad templum, forma pulcherrima Dido,
incessit[8] magna iuvenum stipante caterva.

---

1 488. Aeneas' recognition of himself fighting against the Greek leaders (cf. *Il.* 20.332f.) relates the pictures to the story, as did his personal reactions to the picture of Hector (485f.).

2 489. Memnon the Aethiopian (son of Aurora — Eos — 751; his followers are called Eastern, *Eoas*) belongs to the post-Iliad period of the Trojan war, after the death of Hector.

3 490f. Penthesilea, queen of the Amazons, also came to Troy near the end of the war; she as well as Memnon figured largely in the cyclic epic *Aethiopis,* and their exploits are described by Quintus of Smyrna (fourth century A.D.). Penthesilea is a prototype of Virgil's Camilla. Amazons are mentioned in Hom. *Il.* 3.189.

4 490. **lunatis . .. peltis**: crescent-shaped shields, of the Amazons again in 11.663.

5 492. 'in the act of buckling her golden girdle beneath her naked breast'. *Subnectens* must refer to the action of the picture (see Mackail); Servius' explanation *subnexa habens* cannot be right.

6 494f. In this very idyllic scene the characters of Aeneas and Dido are presented most sympathetically. The tributes paid to Aeneas by Ilioneus when he is unaware of his presence give a picture of a king held in admiration and affection by his men; and Dido is beautiful, altogether queenly in her attributes, and at the same time modest and sympathetic. Throughout we see indirectly the effect each has on the other.
The growing expectation for Dido's appearance has been developed long before she appears in the narrative, by Jupiter's instructions to Mercury, by Venus' telling Aeneas of her story (see note on 364), by the pictures she had had painted on Juno's temple. When she appears she is like Diana in beauty; she is intent on the welfare of her people; she is kind and generous to Ilioneus; she is filled with admiration for Aeneas; and she ends her speech to him with words which indicate to the reader the bond of sympathy, humanity, and mutual understanding likely to exist between her and Aeneas: *me quoque per multos similis fortuna labores . . .* (628). It is a happy start to a tragic tale.

7 494. **Dardanio Aeneae:** dative of agent (with *videntur*), cf. 440. The epithet *Dardanius* is used here because Aeneas' emotions are due to the Trojan scenes he has been gazing at.

8 497. **incessit:** of Juno in 46, of Venus in 405.

Qualis[1] in Eurotae[2] ripis aut per iuga Cynthi
exercet Diana choros, quam mille secutae
hinc atque hinc glomerantur Oreades; illa pharetram   500
fert umero gradiensque deas supereminet omnis
(Latonae tacitum pertemptant[3] gaudia pectus):
talis erat Dido, talem se laeta ferebat
per medios instans operi regnisque futuris.
Tum foribus divae, [4]media testudine templi,   505
saepta armis solioque alte subnixa resedit.
Iura dabat legesque viris, operumque laborem
partibus aequabat iustis aut sorte trahebat:
cum subito Aeneas concursu accedere magno
Anthea Sergestumque videt fortemque Cloanthum   510
Teucrorumque alios, ater quos aequore turbo
dispulerat penitusque[5] alias avexerat oras.
Obstipuit simul ipse, simul percussus Achates
laetitiaque metuque; avidi coniungere[6] dextras
ardebant, sed res[7] animos incognita turbat.   515
Dissimulant[8] et nube cava speculantur amicti
quae fortuna viris, classem quo litore linquant,
quid veniant; cunctis nam lecti navibus ibant

---

1 498f. The simile is based (like the simile in Ap. Rh. 3.876f.) on Hom. *Od.* 6.102f. where Nausicaa is compared with Artemis; Aulus Gellius (9.9) records Probus' hostile criticisms of Virgil's adaptation, particularly to the effect that the comparison is much more appropriate to Nausicaa dancing among her maidens than to Dido giving instructions to her people. This is certainly true, but the Virgilian simile — as so often — aims at setting up implications, half defined penumbrae of meaning, at substituting for Homeric clarity a density of associations which reaches forward and backwards into the narrative. Here we reach backwards towards the disguised Venus who seemed to Aeneas (329) like Diana, and forward to the simile in 4.143f. where Aeneas is like Apollo on the ridges of Cynthus; and we see Dido not only as the composed queen of her people which the narrative presents, but also possessed of the joyful beauty and vivacity of a goddess dancing. See also note on 502, and Pöschl, *The Art of Vergil,* pp. 60f.

2 498-502. Eurotas was the river on which Sparta stood (cf. 316), Cynthus a ridge in Delos (where Latona gave birth to Apollo and Diana), cf. 4.147; *Oreades* (Greek plural with short *-es*) are mountain nymphs. *Diana* elsewhere has a short first syllable; see note on 258.

3 502. 'joy thrills the silent heart of Latona;' as her mother watches, she is proud of her daughter's beauty. This line (based on Hom. *Od.* 6.106) is said to be irrelevant in Virgil's simile, but it surely conveys the effect which Dido has upon those watching her, particularly Aeneas. For *pertemptant* cf. *Aen.* 5.828, *Geo.* 3.250.

4 505-6. 'Then by the goddess's doors, beneath the centre of the temple's vault, escorted by warriors, and positioned high up on her throne she took her seat'. *Foribus divae* refers to the inner sanctuary of the goddess, where her statue would be; cf. *Geo.* 3.16 *in medio mihi Caesar erit templumque tenebit. Testudo* is an architectural term for an arch or vault. The Roman senate often met in a temple.

5 512. 'and had driven away to far distant shores'; for *penitus* cf. 536, *Ecl.* 1.66; *alias* means elsewhere from where Aeneas landed; for the accusative *oras* cf. 553 and see note on 2.

6 514-15. **coniungere . . . ardebant:** the infinitive with *ardere* is mainly poetic, cf. 581.

7 515. **res . . . incognita:** 'the uncertainty of the situation', i.e. they do not know what has happened or how they will be received by the Carthaginians.

8 416. **dissimulant:** 'they conceal their eagerness (Page),' rather than 'they remain in hiding'.

orantes veniam[1] et templum clamore petebant.

Postquam introgressi et coram data copia fandi,   520
maximus[2] Ilioneus placido sic pectore coepit;
'o regina, novam cui condere[3] Iuppiter urbem
iustitiaque dedit gentis[4] frenare superbas,
Troes te miseri, ventis maria[5] omnia vecti,
oramus: prohibe infandos a navibus ignis,   525
parce pio generi et propius[6] res aspice nostras.
Non nos aut ferro Libycos populare[7] penatis
venimus, aut raptas ad litora vertere praedas;
non ea vis animo nec tanta superbia victis.[8]
Est locus, [9]Hesperiam Grai cognomine dicunt,   530
terra antiqua, potens armis atque ubere[10] glaebae;
Oenotri[11] coluere viri; nunc fama minores
Italiam[12] dixisse ducis de nomine gentem.
Hic cursus fuit,[13]
Cum subito adsurgens fluctu nimbosus Orion[14]   535
in[15] vada caeca tulit penitusque procacibus Austris

---

1 519. **veniam:** 'favour', cf. *Aen.* 4.435, 11.101; the word does not necessarily mean pardon.

2 521. **maximus Ilioneus**: their 'elder statesman', who is also the spokesman to King Latinus in 7.212f.

3 522-3. **condere . . . dedit:** 'has allowed to found', see note on 66.

4 523. **gentis frenare superbas:** he refers to the barbarians without Dido's city (339, 439f.).

5 524. **maria:** accusative of extent of space, cf. 67.

6 526. **propius:** from nearer, i.e. 'more favourably', cf. *Aen.* 8.78, Tac. *Ann.* 13.57.

7 527-8. **populare . . . venimus;** infinitive of purpose; cf. *Aen.* 3.4-5 *quaerere . . . agimur* (with my note, OUP Ed.) and compare notes on 66, 357, 704. The greatly extended use by the poets of the infinitive was made possible partly as a revival of early Latin usage (there are fairly frequent instances in Plautus — e.g. *missa sum ludere*) which had died out in prose in favour of more cumbersome methods of expression, and partly by Greek influence.
It is a brief and economical way of expressing the relationship of two clauses (compare *ad penatis populandos,* or *penatium populandorum causa*).

8 529. 'Conquered people do not have such violence nor such pride in their hearts'; the sentence is not two separate clauses.

9 530-3. These four lines are repeated in 3.163-6. For line 530 cf. Enn. *Ann.* 23 *est locus Hesperiam quam mortales perhibebant;* for the parenthetical construction (Servius says *deest 'quam'*) cf. line 12. *Hesperia* means the Western Land, and is used frequently by Virgil of Italy.

10 531. **ubere:** 'fertility', cf. 3.95, and Homer's ουθαρ αρουρης (*Il.*9.141).

11 532. **Oenotri**: first applied to the inhabitants of S. Italy, and then by the poets to the Italians generally; Aristotle (*Pol.* 7.9.2) relates a tradition that a king of the Oenotrians called Italus gave his name to the country. Others made Italus a Sicilian, and Servius mentions a derivation from the Greek word for a calf (ιταλος, Latin *vitulus*); cf. Aul. Gell. 11.1.1.

12 533. **Italiam dixisse ... gentem**: 'have called their nation Italy', a variation on the expected 'have called their land Italy'.

13 534. This is the first of rather more than fifty 'half-lines' in the *Aeneid*, cf. 560, 636. They are an indication of incomplete revision, not a deliberate metrical device; see my note (OUP Ed.) on 5.294.

14 535. The setting of Orion in the autumn was associated with storms (*Aen.* 7.719, Hor. *Odes* 1.28.21, 3.27.18, *Epod.* 10.10); thus the constellation itself was regarded as hostile to sailors (cf. *Aen.* 4.52, Hor. *Epod.* 15.7 *nautis infestus Orion*), and here is used by metonymy for the storm it causes. For *adsurgens fluctu* of a storm cf. *Geo.* 2.160. It is impossible to believe (as many commentators suggest) that *adsurgens* also means the rising of the constellation. The first vowel of *Orion* varies in quantity; see note on 258.

15 536-8. 'and scattered us afar with its fierce south winds over waves and barriers of rock as the ocean mastered us'.

perque undas superante salo perque invia saxa
dispulit; huc pauci vestris adnavimus oris.
Quod genus hoc hominum? Quaeve hunc tam barbara morem
permittit patria? Hospitio[1] prohibemur harenae;   540
bella cient primaque vetant consistere terra.
Si genus humanum et mortalia temnitis arma,
at sperate[2] deos memores fandi atque nefandi.
Rex erat Aeneas nobis, [3]quo[4] iustior alter
nec pietate fuit, nec bello maior et armis.   545
Quem si fata virum servant, si vescitur[5] aura
aetheria neque adhuc crudelibus occubat umbris,[6]
non metus, officio nec[7] te certasse priorem
paeniteat: sunt et Siculis[8] regionibus urbes
armaque, Troianoque a sanguine clarus Acestes.   550
Quassatam ventis liceat subducere classem
et silvis[9] aptare trabes et stringere remos,
si datur [10]Italiam sociis et rege recepto
tendere, ut Italiam laeti Latiumque petamus;
sin absumpta salus, et te, pater optime Teucrum,   555
pontus habet Libyae nec[11] spes iam restat Iuli,
at freta Sicaniae saltem sedesque paratas,
unde huc advecti, regemque petamus Acesten.'
Talibus Ilioncus; cuncti simul ore fremebant
Dardanidae.   560

---

1 540. **hospitio ... haxenae**: 'the welcome of the shore', which shipwrecked sailors have a right to expect. Servius quotes Cicero, *Pro Rosc.* 72 *quid est tarn commune quam . . . litus eiectis*?

2 543. A magnificent line, made specially memorable by the use of *sperate,* almost in the sense of *respicere* 'have a thought for', 'expect action from'; it is much extended from the fairly common poetic sense of 'expect (but not hope)' as in *Aen.* 2.658, 4.419, 11.275. For *fandi atque nefandi* 'right and wrong', cf. Cat. 64.405, Livy 10.41.3

3 544f. The tribute by Ilioncus to his (supposedly) absent leader conveys to the reader a perhaps warmer picture of Aeneas than the direct narrative references to his *pietas;* line 555 especially is an indication of the affection in which Aeneas was clearly held.

4 544-5. The order is *quo alter nec pietate iustior fuit nec bello et armis maior.* Others supply *nec* before *iustior* and take *pietate* with *maior.*

5 546. **vescitur aura:** a Lucretian phrase, cf. Lucr. 5.857.

6 547. **umbris**: 'land of darkness'; for this local meaning cf. *Aen.* 6.461.

7 548-9. 'nor would you regret taking the initiative in a contest of kindness'; *nec . . .paeniteat* is potential, rather than equivalent to *ne paeniteat* as in *Ecl.* 2.34, 10.17, where the meaning is different.

8 549f. He means that they have resources in Sicily also with which they can repay kindness, in addition to what they have with them; for Acestes see note on 195.

9 552. 'to prepare planks in your woods and trim timber for oars'; cf. *Aen.* 4.399, 5.753.

10 553-4. the order is *ut Italiam, si datur . . . tendere, laeti. . . petamus. Italiam* is accusative of motion towards, see note on 2 and cf. *Aen.* 6.696.

11 556. **nec spes iam restat Iuli:** 'our hopes of Iulus are gone', i.e. the hope placed in him as Aeneas' heir; cf. 4.274.

Tum breviter Dido vultum[1] demissa profatur:
'solvite corde metum, Teucri, secludite[2] curas.
Res dura et regni novitas me talia cogunt[3]
moliri et late finis custode[4] tueri.
Quis genus Aeneadum,[5] quis Troiae nesciat urbem,   565
virtutesque virosque aut tanti incendia belli?
Non obtunsa[6] adeo gestamus pectora Poeni,
nec tam aversus equos Tyria Sol iungit ab urbe.
Seu vos Hesperiam magnam Saturniaque[7] arva
sive Erycis[8] finis regemque optatis Acesten,   570
auxilio tutos dimittam opibusque iuvabo.
Vultis et his mecum pariter considere regnis?
Urbem[9] quam statuo, vestra est; subducite navis;
Tros[10] Tyriusque mihi nullo discrimine agetur.
Atque utinam rex ipse noto compulsus eodem   575
adforet Aeneas! Equidem per litora certos[11]
dimittam et Libyae lustrare extrema iubebo,
si[12] quibus eiectus silvis aut urbibus errat.'
    His animum[13] arrecti dictis et fortis Achates
et pater Aeneas iamdudum erumpere[14] nubem   580

---

1 561. **vultum demissa**: 'lowering her eyes'; for the middle use of *demissa* see note on 228.

2 562. **secludite curas**: 'cast your cares aside'; Servius says *pro 'excludite'*.

3 563. 'harsh necessity and the newness of my kingdom . . .'; she fears the hostile people of the neighbourhood as well as the possibility of attack from Tyre by her brother.

4 564. **custode**: singular for plural, common in prose with *miles, eques, hostis* and national names (*Romanus, Poenus*, etc.); cf. *Aen.* 9.380.

5 565. **Aeneadum**: cf. 157 — Dido takes up Ilioneus' words *rex erat Aeneas nobis* (544). For the form of the genitive see note on 3.21.

6 567. **obtunsa**: 'unfeeling', so as to be indifferent to what we hear about; the next line explains that they are not so far away from the civilised world (from the path of the Sun, cf. *Aen.* 6.796 *extra anni solisque vias*), not so benighted, as not to hear about such great events,

7 569. **Saturniaque arva**: the golden age in Latium was under Saturnus' rule (*Ecl.* 4.6); Latium was said to be so-called because Saturnus hid there (*latuit*) when deposed by Jupiter (cf. *Aen.* 8.319f).

8 570. Eryx was a half-brother of Aeneas who gave his name to the well known town and mountain in Sicily; see note on 5.24.

9 573. **urbem quam statuo, vestra est**: this is a very striking example of the attraction of the antecedent to the case of the relative, or perhaps it is better to say of the antecedent being treated as if taken into the relative clause (cf. 7a): *quam urbem statuo, ea vestra est*. It has an archaic sound to it, cf. Ter. *Eun.* 653.

10 574. 'Trojans and Tyrians will be treated by me with no distinction (equally)'; the phrase is very unusual, and acts as a passive for *agam de Troianis et Tyriis nullo discrimine*. The singular *agetur* emphasises the unity of the two subjects. Nonius quotes the line with *habetur*, but this is no improvement.

11 576. **certos**: 'reliable men'.

12 578. 'if by chance he has been cast ashore and is wandering in any woods or towns'; for the elliptical condition ('in the hope that')cf. 181.

13 579. **animum arrecti**: 'their hearts excited'; *animum* is retained accusative, see note on 228.

14 580. **erumpere**: 'burst out of, unusual in this transitive sense, cf. the commoner *evadere* (5.689), *exire* (5.438).

38

ardebant. Prior Aenean compellat Achates;
'nate dea, quae nunc animo sententia surgit?
Omnia tuta vides, classem sociosque receptos.
Unus abest, medio in fluctu quem vidimus ipsi[1]
summersum; dictis respondent cetera matris'.   585
Vix ea fatus erat cum circumfusa repente
scindit se nubes et in aethera purgat[2] apertum.
Restitit[3] Aeneas claraque in luce refulsit
os[4] umerosque deo similis; [5]namque ipsa decoram
caesariem nato genetrix lumenque iuventae   590
purpureum et laetos oculis adflarat honores:
quale[6] manus addunt ebori decus, aut ubi flavo
argentum Pariusve[7] lapis circumdatur auro.
Tum sic reginam adloquitur cunctisque repente
improvisus ait: 'coram, quem quaeritis, adsum,   595
Troius Aeneas, Libycis ereptus ab undis.
O sola[8] infandos Troiae miserata labores,
quae nos, reliquias[9] Danaum, terraeque marisque
omnibus exhaustis[10] iam casibus, omnium[11] egenos,
urbe[12], domo socias, grates persolvere dignas   600
non opis est nostrae, Dido, nec quidquid[13] ubique est
gentis Dardaniae, magnum quae sparsa per orbem.

---

1 584. i.e. Orontes (113f.).

2 587. **purgat:** supply *se*, 'dispersed', cf. Lucr. 4.341.

3 588. **restitit:** 'stood there'; Virgil conveys a statuesque picture of Aeneas as the cloud cleared away.

4 589. **os umerosque**: accusative of respect, as in 579.

5 589f. 'for his mother herself had breathed upon her son and given him beautiful flowing locks and the radiant glow of youth and a happy brightness in his eyes.' The passage is based on *Od.* 6.229f. (= *Od.* 23.156f.) where Athena beautifies Odysseus.

6 592f. The Homeric simile (*Od.* 6.232f.) compares the beautification of Odysseus with the overlaying of silver with gold, a single vivid image; Virgil, as is his way, elaborates by adding marble to Homer's picture, and giving a new image of decorated ivory; cf. *Aen.* 12.67f, and generally 10.134f.

7 593. **Pariusve lapis:** marble, cf. Hor. *Odes* 1.19.6, *Aen.* 3.126, 6.471.

8 597. **sola:** it is the first friendly welcome he has received from a foreign people.

9 598. **reliquias Danaum:** cf. 30.

10 599. **exhaustis:** most MSS have *exhaustos*, but *exhaurire casus* is the more Virgilian usage, cf. 4.14, 10.57.

11 **omnium:** this form occurs only here in Virgil, and such an elision in the fifth foot is very striking; it occurs otherwise only with the word *Ilium* (e.g. 6.64).

12 600. **urbe domo socias:** 'give us a share in your city, your home'.

13 601-2. 'is not in our power, nor in the power of any of the Trojan people anywhere'. The phrase *quidquid... gentis* takes the place of a genitive after *opis*, equivalent to *nec totius gentis Troianae*. The neuter pronoun followed by a genitive is a favourite turn with Catullus (e.g. 3.2 *quantum est hominum venustiorum*).

Di tibi, [1]si qua pios respectant numina, si quid
usquam iustitiae est, et mens sibi conscia recti
praemia digna ferant. Quae te tam laeta tulerunt[2]   605
saecula? Qui tanti talem genuere parentes?
In freta dum fluvii current, dum montibus umbrae[3]
lustrabunt convexa, polus dum sidera pascet,
semper honos nomenque tuum laudesque manebunt,[4]
quae me cumque vocant terrae.' [5]Sic fatus amicum   610
Ilionea[6] petit dextra laevaque Serestum,
post alios, fortemque Gyan fortemque Cloanthum.

    Obstipuit primo[7] aspectu Sidonia Dido,
casu deinde viri tanto, et sic ore locuta est:
'quis te, nate dea, per tanta pericula casus   615
insequitur? Quae vis immanibus[8] applicat oris?
Tune ille Aeneas quem Dardanio[9] Anchisae
alma Venus Phrygii genuit Simoentis[10] ad undam?
Atque equidem Teucrum[11] memini Sidona[12] venire
finibus expulsum patriis, nova regna petentem   620
auxilio Beli; genitor tum Belus opimam

---

1 603-5. 'May the gods (if there are any powers who have thought for the good, if there is any justice anywhere) and your own inner knowledge that you have done right bring you worthy rewards.' That this is the correct way of taking the phrases is shown by *Aen.* 9.252f.: *quae vobis, quae digna, viri, pro laudibus istis / praemia posse rear solvi? pulcherrima primum / di moresque dabunt vestri.* Many commentators take *mens. . . recti* as a second subject of *usquam est,* but this is impossible with the reading *iustitiae* and very difficult with *iustitia.* I have preferred the reading of the rest of the MSS (*iustitiae*) against *iustitia* (first hand in *M*) partly because the genitive following the neuter pronoun accords well with 601-2 *quidquid... gentis,* and partly because the turn *iustitia est aliquid* (cf. Ov. *Met.* 6.542-3 *si numina divum sunt aliquid,* Prop. 4.7.1 *sunt aliquid manes*)'does not seem Virgilian. For *si qua* in the sense 'as surely as there are' Page (whose note on this passage is first rate) compares *Aen.* 3.433f.

2 605f. The extravagant compliments are based on Hom. *Od.* 6.154f.

3 607-8. 'as long as shadows move on the mountain slopes, as long as the heavens feed the stars'; for the first phrase cf. Hor. *Odes* 3.6.41-2 *sol ubi montium / mutaret umbras,* and for *convexa* cf. 310. The second phrase is from Lucr. 1.231 (cf. 5.525) *unde aether sidera pascit;* cf. Sen. *N.Q.* 7.20.2.

4 609. This line occurs in *Ecl.* 5.78 (Daphnis will be famous as long as fishes swim and bees feed on thyme).

5 610. There is an irony in these closing words; it is the call of Italy in Book 4 which leads to Dido's desertion and death.

6 611. **Ilionea:** this *-ea* accusative ending is a transliteration of the Homeric form.

7 613. **primo aspectu:** 'at the first sight of him'. This is the same sense as if *primo* were an adverb.

8 616. **immanibus applicat oris:** 'drives you to these savage shores'; *applicare navem* is the technical term for bringing in a ship to land.

9 617. **Dardanio Anchisae:** the spondee in the fifth foot, with hiatus, gives a rhythmic effect that is very unusual in Latin (in Homer hiatus and spondaic fifth feet are frequent): it is used in the *Aeneid* five times, always with names; cf. 3.74, 7.631, 9.647, 11.31.

10 618. **Simoentis:** one of Troy's rivers, see note on 100-1. Servius tells us that goddesses and nymphs gave birth by the banks of rivers or in woods.

11 619. The story is that the Greek Teucer, brother of Ajax, on his return from the Trojan war to Salamis, was forced to leave his home; he founded a new Salamis in Cyprus (Hor. *Odes* 1.7.21f.). There seems no source before Virgil for his having gone to Sidon to get help from Dido's father Belus who was waging a successful war in Cyprus.

12 **Sidona:** Greek accusative, motion towards.

vastabat Cyprum et victor dicione tenebat.
Tempore iam ex illo casus mihi cognitus[1] urbis
Troianae nomenque tuum regesque Pelasgi.
Ipse[2] hostis Teucros insigni laude ferebat   625
seque ortum antiqua Teucrorum a stirpe volebat.
Quare agite, o tectis, iuvenes, succedite nostris.
Me quoque per multos similis fortuna labores
iactatam hac demum voluit consistere terra.
Non[3] ignara mali miseris succurrere disco.'   630
Sic memorat; simul Aenean in regia ducit
tecta, simul divum templis indicit[4] honorem.
Nec minus interea sociis ad litora mittit
viginti tauros, magnorum horrentia centum[5]
terga suum, pinguis centum cum matribus agnos,   635
munera laetitiamque dii.[6]
At domus interior regali splendida luxu
instruitur, mediisque parant convivia tectis:
arte laboratae vestes[7] ostroque superbo,
ingens[8] argentum mensis, caelataque[9] in auro   640
fortia facta patrum, series[10] longissima rerum
per tot ducta viros antiqua ab origine gentis.
　　Aeneas (neque enim patrius consistere mentem
passus amor) rapidum ad navis praemittit Achaten,

---

1 623f. Dido heard of the Trojan war from Teucer who told her both about the Greeks (Pelasgi) and their enemies the Trojans; he had praised the latter highly, and bearing the same name as they did (*Teucri*) wanted it to be thought that he was descended from the same ancestry (as indeed he was, through his mother Hesione).

2 625. **ipse hostis:** probably Teucer himself, rather than the Greeks generally.

3 630. A famous line of which the meaning is 'I am not unacquainted with suffering and I am learning how to help the unhappy (now that I am in a position to do so).' Some argue, following Servius, that *non* goes with the whole line: 'I am not, as someone inexperienced, learning ... (I don't have to learn)', but this seems wholly unlikely.

4 632. **indicit honorem:** 'proclaimed sacrifices' in honour of the safety of Aeneas.

5 634-5. 'a hundred bristling backs of great boars', i.e. 'a hundred great bristly-backed boars'.

6 636. **dii:** all the MSS have *dei,* but Aulus Gellius (9.14.8) read *dii* and explained it as a genitive of *dies,* quoting various parallel (*acii, specii,* etc.); the meaning thus is 'the day's joyful gifts', in apposition to the previous lines. If *dei* is read, the reference is to Bacchus and the joy of wine (cf. 734 *laetitiae Bacchus dator*). This is attractive, but it seems to me that the coordination with the previous lines, if this were an extra item, would be harsh. The choice of reading here is very difficult to make, especially as the half-line may indicate that Virgil had not completed what he wanted to say, but the balance inclines towards *dii.*

7 639. Supply *sunt;* cf. 703 and 4.131. The *vestes* are coverlets for the couches (*Geo.* a.464), and we are reminded of Cat. 64, of which line 637 is a reminiscence (Cat. 64.46).

8 640. **ingens argentum:** 'a vast quantity of silver', rather than 'massive pieces of silver', cf. phrases like *ingens pecunia* (Cicero).

9 **caelataque in auro**: these embossed decorations would be on golden plate; the phrase does not refer to inlaid gold on the silver plate just mentioned.

10 641-2. 'a long series of exploits extending through the lives of their many heroes from the distant beginning of their race'.

Ascanio ferat[1] haec ipsumque ad moenia ducat;   645
omnis in Ascanio cari[2] stat[3] cura parentis.
Munera praeterea Iliacis erepta ruinis
ferre iubet, pallam[4] signis auroque rigentem
et circumtextum croceo velamen[5] acantho,
ornatus Argivae Helenae,[6] quos illa Mycenis,   650
Pergama[7] cum peteret inconcessosque hymenaeos,
extulerat, matris[8] Ledae mirabile donum;
praeterea sceptrum, Ilione[9] quod gesserat olim,
maxima natarum Priami, colloque monile
bacatum,[10] et duplicem[11] gemmis auroque coronam.   655
Haec celerans iter ad navis tendebat Achates.

---

1 645. **ferat:** jussive subjunctive in parataxis, cf. *Aen.* 4.289.

2 646. **cari:** 'loving', an unusual active use of the word; cf. *Aen.* 11.215.

3 **stat:** 'was always, lay always' (Conway), who explains that it is a slightly stronger form of assertion than *est* and compares Lucr. 2.181 *tanta stat praedita culpa.*

4 648. **pallam:** a long robe, here decorated with golden embroidery (Lucr. 5.1428), and therefore stiff.

5 649. **velamen:** the veil is bordered with yellow acanthus, a common type of floral design. The stylised leaf of the acanthus was used as part of the decoration of Corinthian capitals.

6 650. Helen's epithet 'Argive' is from Homer (*Il.* 2.161); *Mycenis* is used in a general sense to mean the realm of Greece — specifically Helen was from Sparta where she was the wife of Menelaus; cf. *Aen.* 2.577-8 (of Helen) *scilicet haec Spartam incolumis patriasque Mycenas / aspiciet?*

7 651. Pergama is Troy (466); the unlawful marriage is with Paris. For the lengthening of the last syllable of *peteret* see note on 308; for the polysyllabic ending with a Greek word cf. (e.g.) *elephanto* (3.464), *cyparissi* (3.680), *hyacinthi* (11.69).

8 652. **matris Ledae:** Helen was the daughter of Leda by Jupiter in the guise of a swan; cf. *Aen.* 7.364.

9 653. Ilione, the eldest of Priam's daughters, is not mentioned in Homer. According to a later legend she became the wife of Polymnestor of Thrace.

10 655. **bacatum:** 'of pearls', a rare word from *baca*, a berry or thing shaped like a berry, quite often a pearl.

11 **duplicem ... coronam:** this seems to be a crown encircled by two bands of gold and gems (cf. *Aen.* 5.251).

657-94. Venus intervenes by instructing Cupid to disguise himself as Ascanius and make Dido fall in love with Aeneas. She spirits Ascanius away.

[1]At Cytherea[2] novas artis, nova pectore versat

consilia, ut faciem mutatus et ora Cupido

pro dulci Ascanio veniat, donisque furentem

incendat reginam atque ossibus implicet ignem.   660

Quippe domum timet[3] ambiguam[4] Tyriosque bilinguis,

urit[5] atrox Iuno et sub noctem cura recursat.

Ergo his aligerum dictis adfatur Amorem:[6]

'nate, meae vires, [7]mea magna potentia, solus,

nate, patris summi qui tela Typhoea temnis,   665

ad te confugio et supplex tua numina posco.

Frater[8] ut[9] Aeneas pelago tuus omnia circum

litora iactetur[10] odiis Iunonis acerbae,

nota tibi, et nostro doluisti saepe dolore.

Nunc Phoenissa tenet Dido blandisque moratur   670

---

1 657f. The scheming intervention of Venus is Hellenistic in tone, based on the trickery devised by Hera and Athena in Apollonius Rhodius 3.6f., where they persuade Aphrodite to cause her son Eros to shoot his love-arrows at Medea. The tone of the passage in Apollonius is mocking and the behaviour of the goddesses frivolous and cruel. Virgil has modified and dignified his picture of the goddess of Love (for Venus was much more than a Roman Aphrodite), but elements of cruelty remain, and Venus shows an irresponsible pleasure in what to her is the subtle use of her great power. Here she is no longer *alma Venus, Venus Genetrix,* great mother of Aeneas and Rome, but a moderate version of 'laughter-loving Aphrodite' (cf. 8.370f.), a personification of the tyranny of love which led Virgil to exclaim (4.412) *improbe Amor, quid non mortalia pectora cogis*! Venus' motivation, apart from her desire to exercise her special power, is here very weak; Dido is already showing hospitality to Aeneas, and the outcome of the goddess's schemes is to delay Aeneas and nearly cause the abandonment of his mission. As far as Dido is concerned, Venus shows the ruthless recklessness for her human enemies which is seen so often among the gods and goddesses of Ovid's *Metamorphoses.* The divine machinery of the *Aeneid* generally suggests the care of providence for humans (albeit very imperfectly understood), but here and there come flashes of primitive cruelty and wanton exercise of power.

2 657-60. 'But the Cytherean goddess turned over in her mind fresh devices and fresh plans, to make Cupid change his appearance and aspect and come instead of sweet Ascanius, and fire the queen to passion with his gifts and instil the flames of love into her innermost being.' Notice the use of the adjective *novus* to introduce not merely a change in the narrative events, but a change of mood from the idyllic first meeting of Dido and Aeneas to the sombre and threatening undertones of disaster; cf. 5.603f., the transition from the happy celebration of the games to the firing of the Trojan ships. Venus is called *Cytherea* from her island (680); *faciem* and *ora* are retained accusatives (see note on 228); *furentem* is proleptic.

3 661. **timet**: cf. Juno's taunt to Venus in 4.96f. that she is frightened and therefore suspicious of Carthage.

4 **ambiguam ... bilinguis**: *ambiguam* is 'untrustworthy', (*esse ambigua fide,* Livy 6.2.3), and *bilinguis* is 'double-tongued', 'treacherous', as several times in Plautus. The two phrases combine to suggest the proverbial bad faith of Carthage, *Punica fides*.

5 662. **urit atrox Iuno**: 'the image of cruel Juno chafes her'.

6 663. Cupid is frequently depicted in art with wings (cf. Prop. 2.12.5); the compound *aliger* does not occur before Virgil.

7 664-5. Cupid symbolises the power of Venus; pictures of him breaking or trampling on the thunderbolt occur on coins. The thunderbolt is called *tela Typhoea* because Jupiter used it against the giant Typhoeus (Typhon), burning him to ashes (Aesch. *P.V.* 358f.). I have punctuated so that *solus* goes with *qui*, as Servius recommends: in this way the *qui* clause comes is more apposite, and *mea magna potentia* is much better without *solus*.

8 667. **frater**: Ovid (*Her.* 7) twice makes play with the relationship of the half-brothers Aeneas and Cupid.

9 667-8. **ut... iactetur**: indirect question, 'you know how he is storm-tossed'; the plural *nota* (these are things known to you) is much less normal than *notum*, and influenced by Greek.

10 668. **iactetur**: for the lengthening of the final syllable in arsis see note on 308. All the major MSS, except the first hand of *F,* have *iacteturque*, which heals the metre but makes no sense.

vocibus, et vereor[1] quo se Iunonia vertant
hospitia: haud tanto cessabit cardine rerum.
Quocirca capere ante dolis et cingere flamma[2]
reginam meditor, ne[3] quo se numine mutet,
sed magno Aeneae mecum[4] teneatur amore.   675
Qua facere id possis nostram nunc accipe mentem:
regius accitu cari genitoris ad urbem
Sidoniam puer ire parat, mea maxima cura,
dona ferens pelago[5] et flammis restantia Troiae;
hunc ego sopitum[6] somno super[7] alta Cythera 680
aut super Idalium sacrata sede recondam,
ne qua scire dolos mediusve occurrere possit.
Tu faciem illius noctem[8] non amplius unam
falle[9] dolo et notos pueri[10] puer indue vultus,
ut, cum[11] te gremio accipiet laetissima Dido 685
regalis inter mensas laticemque[12] Lyaeum,
cum dabit amplexus atque oscula dulcia figet,
occultum inspires ignem fallasque[13] veneno.'
Paret Amor dictis carae genetricis, et alas
exuit et gressu gaudens incedit Iuli.   690
At Venus Ascanio placidam per membra quietem

---

1 671-2. **vereor . . . hospitia:** 'I fear the outcome of this hospitality inspired by Juno; she will not be inactive at such a critical time.' Venus presumably is afraid that Carthaginian friendliness will turn out to be a plot to destroy the Trojans. It was Jupiter, not Juno, who made Dido welcome the Trojans, but Venus naturally assumes that Juno as patron goddess of Carthage is active. The metaphorical use of *cardo* (hinge, hence critical time, turning point) does not occur before Virgil; Statius imitates it with *fatorum in cardine summo* (*Theb.* 10.853). Cf. Sir Winston Churchill's 'The Hinge of Fate'.

2 673. Conway well remarks on the military metaphors and the 'cruel play on the literal and metaphorical meaning of *flamma*' characteristic of Venus, 'whose affection, even for her son, never knows where to stop and does more harm than good'.

3 674. **ne quo se numine mutet:** 'so that she may not change her mind because of any divine influence', i.e. that of Juno.

4 675. **mecum teneatur:** 'be kept on my side', continuing the military metaphor of 673.

5 679. **pelago . . . Troiae:** 'which have survived from the sea and the flames of Troy'; the nouns are probably ablative, rather than dative as after *superesse*.

6 680f. Notice the hissing of the *s*'s, as Venus gleefully unfolds her plot.

7 680-1. **super... Idalium:** *super* is used because Venus' sacred groves would be in high inaccessible places; Cythera, the island off So. Greece, gave Venus one of her most frequent epithets (657); Idalium — also Idalia, 693 — was in Cyprus.

8 683. **noctem non amplius unam:** this paratactic construction (one night, not more) is quite common in prose.

9 684.. **falle:** a very strange use, 'impersonate' or 'counterfeit' his appearance, cf. *mentiri* in *Ecl.* 4.42.

10 **pueri puer:** a repetition common in Greek, cf. *Aen.* 3.329, 4.83, 5.569, 10.600.

11 685-8. The accretion of subordinate clauses (*ut, cum . . ., cum*) is very unusual in Virgil, and here deliberately used to lead up to the climax in 688.

12 686. **laticemque Lyaeum:** high-flown poetic diction for wine; Lyaeus (cf. *Aen.* 458) is the Greek equivalent for Liber (Bacchus the 'releaser' of cares). It is here used as an adjective, see Conway ad loc. and cf. *Aen.* 4.552.

13 688. **fallasque veneno:** 'poison her unobserved', picking up the idea of *occultum*, cf. *Aen.* 7.350. *Venenum* is said to be derived originally from *Venus* ('love-charm'); for this use cf. Prop. 2.12.19.

inrigat,[1] et fotum gremio dea tollit in altos
Idaliae lucos, [2]ubi mollis amaracus illum
floribus et dulci aspirans complectitur umbra.

> *695-756. Cupid disguised as Ascanius arrives, and the banquet begins. Dido is captivated by his charm. After a song by the minstrel, she asks Aeneas to tell the story of his seven-years' wanderings.*

[3]Iamque ibat dicto parens et dona Cupido   695
regia portabat Tyriis duce laetus Achate.
Cum[4] venit, aulaeis iam se regina superbis
aurea composuit sponda mediamque locavit;
iam pater Aeneas et iam Troiana iuventus
conveniunt, stratoque super discumbitur[5] ostro.   700
Dant[6] manibus famuli lymphas Cereremque[7] canistris
expediunt tonsisque[8] ferunt mantelia villis.
Quinquaginta[9] intus famulae, quibus ordine longam[10]
cura[11] penum struere et flammis adolere penatis;
centum aliae totidemque pares aetate ministri,   705
qui dapibus mensas onerent et pocula ponant.
Nec non et Tyrii per limma laeta frequentes

---

1 692. **inrigat:** the metaphor is from channels of water refreshing the land; cf. Lucr. 4.907-8 *somnus per membra quietem / inriget,* and for the same verb with a different construction cf. *Aen.* 3.511.

2 693-4. 'where soft marjoram breathes its fragrance over him and wraps him round with its blossoms and sweet shade'. Cf. Cat. 61.6-7 (addressing Hymenaeus) *cinge tempora floribus / suave olentis amaraci;* the flower was connected with love and is appropriate for Venus (Lucr. 4.1179).

3 695f. The joyful mood of the banquet has undertones of impending misfortune as Virgil takes the reader beyond the narrative (712, 718, 749) and enables him to appreciate the tragic irony of Dido's happy words of welcome (731f.). The reader is invited, as all through Book 4, to consider the interrelation of divine and human causation, the tension between the myth of Cupid and the psychology of Dido. It would be a great mistake to think of Dido as powerless to resist the divine plan; immutable circumstances encompass her which she can accept or resist. These circumstances are not her's to dispute, but her reaction to them is. At each point in the narrative the decision is hers.

4 697f. 'When he got there the queen had already taken her position amidst the gorgeous tapestries, placing herself in the centre, on a golden couch.' *Aulaeis* refers to the curtains or draperies decorating the hall (Hor. *Odes* 3.29.15); the ablative is used very loosely, as a sort of ablative of attendant circumstances. *Sponda* is a couch on which banqueters reclined, as Queen and hostess Dido has her couch in the centre. *Aurea* (ablative) is scanned as a spondee by synizesis (slurring) of the *e*, cf. 726.

5 700. 'and they all take their places on couches with purple coverlets'; *discumbitur* is impersonal passive.

6 701f. The description of the banquet is based on Hom. *Od.* 1.136f. with considerable elaboration; cf. also *Geo.* 4.376f.

7 *Cererem*:'bread', see note on 177.

8 702. **tonsisque . . . villis:** 'bring serviettes of smooth nap', (literally 'shorn'); the same words occur in *Geo.* 4.377.

9 703. Supply *sunt,* as in 705; cf. 639.

10 703-4. 'whose task it was to prepare in due order the long feast, and to honour the household gods with blazing fires'. The fifty servants *intus* ('in the kitchen') are contrasted with the two hundred waiters (705); the reading *longam* is discussed as an alternative to *longo* (read by all the MSS) by Aulus Gellius (4.1.15), and the grammarian Charisius cites it. *Flammis adolere penatis* is a good example of elevated poetic style avoiding the commonplace ('keep a good fire going').

11 704. **cura . . . struere:** the use of the infinitive following a noun is frequent in the poets; cf. *Aen.* 2.10 (with Page's note) and see note on 527-8.

convenere, toris iussi discumbere pictis.
Mirantur dona Aeneae, mirantur Iulum,
flagrantisque[1] dei vultus simulataque verba,   710
pallamque et pictum croceo velamen acantho.[2]
Praecipue infelix,[3] pesti devota futurae,
expleri[4] mentem nequit ardescitque[5] tuendo
Phoenissa, et pariter puero donisque movetur.
ille ubi complexu Aeneae colloque pependit   715
et magnum falsi[6] implevit genitoris amorem,
reginam petit. [7]Haec oculis,[8] haec pectore toto
haeret et interdum gremio fovet inscia Dido
insidat quantus miserae deus. At memor[9] ille
matris Acidaliae paulatim abolere[10] Sychaeum   720
incipit et vivo temptat praevertere amore[11]
iam pridem resides animos desuetaque corda.
    [12]Postquam prima quies epulis mensaeque remotae,
crateras magnos statuunt et vina[13] coronant.
Fit[14] strepitus tectis vocemque[15] per ampla volutant   725

---

1 710. 'the radiant face of the god and his dissembling words'; *flagrantis,* as Servius says, because he was a god; *simulata* means 'spoken as if by Ascanius'.

2 711. These are the presents brought from the Trojan ships; see 648-9.

3 712. This is the first of many anticipatory comments in Virgil's own person on the narrative of Dido's fate: 'unhappy Dido, doomed to disaster'; cf. 718-19, 749, 4.68, 169f. In 4.450, 529, 596 the epithet *infelix* has ceased to be anticipatory, and has become actual.

4 713. **expleri mentem nequit:** 'cannot satisfy her heart', a middle use of *expleri* with a retained accusative; see note on 228, and cf. *Aen.* 8.265.

5 **ardescitque tuendo:** cf. Cat. 64.91f. (of Ariadne falling in love with Theseus), a poem which Virgil several times recalls in memorable passages of Book 4, e.g. 305, 316, 657-8.

6 716. **falsi ... genitoris:** 'of the deluded father'.

7 717. The sentence ending after the second foot is unusual and throws great weight on the sinister verb *petit.*

8 717-19. 'her gaze and all her thoughts were riveted upon him; now and then she held him on her lap; poor Dido, she did not know that an all-powerful god sat there'. The emphasis on *deus* at the sentence ending at a bucolic diaeresis is very powerful.

9 719-20. **memor ... Acidaliae:** 'mindful (of the instructions) of his Acidalian mother'. This epithet of Venus is said by Servius to come from a spring in Boeotia where the Graces, attendants of Venus, used to bathe.

10 720. **abolere Sychaeum:** 'efface the memory of Sychaeus'; cf. line 343.

11 721-2. 'tries to capture with living love her long-slumbering affection and oblivious heart'; for Dido love was a thing of the past, epitomised in her memory of Sychaeus.

12 723. Cf. 216.

13 724. **vina coronant:** the same phrase in *Aen.* 7.147, cf. also *Geo.* 2.528 *cratera coronant.* In *Aen.* 3.525-6 there is the phrase *cratera corona induit,* which suggests that Virgil has altered the meaning of Homer's κρητῆρας επεστεψαντο ποτοιο (e.g. *Od.* 1.148) from 'filling to the brim' to literally crowning with leaves or flowers.

14 725. **fit strepitus tectis:** 'a clamour arises in the hall'. This is the reading of the best MSS; others have *it,* a reading known to Servius. With *it, tectis* would be dative: 'sucto the roof', cf. *Aen.* 5.451 *it clamor caelo.* But the parallel with 730 seems decisive.

15 **vocemque ... volutant:** 'and they send their words echoing', cf. *Aen.* 5.149, 10.98.

atria; dependent lychni laquearibus[1] aureis
incensi et noctem flammis funalia[2] vincunt.
Hic regina gravem gemmis auroque poposcit
implevitque mero pateram, quam[3] Belus et omnes[4]
a Belo soliti; tum facta silentia tectis: 730
'Iuppiter, hospitibus[5] nam te dare iura loquuntur,
hunc laetum[6] Tyriisque diem Troiaque profectis
esse velis, nostrosque huius meminisse minores.
Adsit laetitiae Bacchus dator et bona Iuno;
et vos o coetum,[7] Tyrii, celebrate faventes.'   735
Dixit et in mensam[8] laticum libavit honorem
primaque, libato,[9] summo[10] tenus attigit ore;
tum Bitiae dedit increpitans;[11] ille impiger hausit[12]
spumantem pateram et pleno se proluit auro;[13]
post alii proceres. Cithara[14] crinitus Iopas   740
personat aurata, docuit quem maximus Atlas.

---

1 726. 'lamps hang from the golden panelled ceilings'; cf. Lucr. 5.295f. *Laquearia* means panelled ceilings rather than chains hanging from the ceilings, as Conway holds. For the scansion of *aureis* cf. 698.

2 727. **funalia**: torches of waxed rope (*funis*).

3 729. **quam**: supply *implere*; cf. *Aen.* 9.300.

4 729-30. **omnes a Belo**: if this means (as it probably does) 'everyone from the time of Belus' or 'everyone descended from Belus', then Belus cannot be Dido's father (621), but must be the early founder of the Tyrian dynasty (cf. Carthaginian names like Hanni*bal*, Hasdru*bal*). But it is possible that it means 'all the guests in turn after Belus'; cf. Plaut. *Most.* 347, *Pers.* 771.

5 731. One of Jupiter's epithets was *Hospitalis;* Alcinous when entertaining Odysseus (*Od.* 7.179f.) pours a libation to Zeus. For *nam* see note on 65.

6 732f. The tragic irony in Dido's prayer (*laetum, meminisse minores, bona Iuno*) is very powerful.

7 735. **coetum . . . celebrate faventes**: 'attend our gathering with good will', cf. for *coetum* Cat. 64.33, for *celebrate faventes Aen.* 8.173.

8 736. in **mensam** . . . **honorem**: 'she poured in libation an offering of the wine on to the table', cf. *Aen.* 8.279. For *laticum* cf. 686 (singular), *Geo.* 3.509 (plural).

9 737. **libato**: ablative absolute of one word, cf. *auspicato, impetrato.*

10 **summo** . . . **ore**: 'put it just lightly to her lips'; for *tenus* cf. *Aen.* 2.553.

11 738. **increpitans**: normally rendered 'with a challenge', though the word elsewhere always has a connotation of blame. Henry's note on the passage leads him to the conclusion that as the word must mean blame, and as Bitias has done nothing blameworthy, Dido must be blaming the wine. It seems perhaps more likely that as Bitias politely waits for her to drink it down, she hands it on impatiently (cf. *Aen.* 3.454, *Geo.* 4.138), jestingly rebuking him for thinking she would drink it (Servius says: *et verecundiam reginae ostendit, et morem Romanum; nam apud maiores nostros feminae non utebantur vino, nisi sacrorum causa certis diebus*).

12 738-9. 'He promptly drained the foaming bowl and soaked himself in its brimming gold'; the vigorous language brings a note of comedy to relieve the undertone of impending tragedy.

13 739. **auro**: Henry neatly comments 'The expression *auro* . . . seems sufficiently strange to us, to whom the expression *glass* . . . does not. . . seem in the least degree strange.'

14 740-1. The minstrel sings at the banquet, as Demodocus sings three times at Alcinous' banquet (*Od.* 8). The mythical giant Atlas was vaguely connected with physical philosophy, and as his mountain was in Africa he is a suitable tutor for Iopas.

Hic canit[1] errantem lunam solisque[2] labores,
unde hominum genus et pecudes, unde imber et ignes,
Arcturum pluviasque Hyadas geminosque Triones;[3]
quid tantum Oceano properent se tingere soles   745
hiberni, vel quae tardis mora[4] noctibus obstet.
ingeminant[5] plausu Tyrii, Troesque sequuntur.
Nec non et vario noctem sermone trahebat
infelix Dido longumque[6] bibebat amorem,
multa super Priamo rogitans, super Hectore multa;   750
nunc quibus Aurorae venisset filius armis,[7]
nunc quales Diomedis[8] equi, nunc quantus Achilles.
'Immo age et a prima die, hospes, origine nobis
insidias' inquit 'Danaum casusque tuorum
erroresque tuos; nam te iam septima[9] portat   755
omnibus errantem terris et fluctibus aestas.

---

1 742f. The subject of Iopas' song is partly based on Ap. Rh. 1.496f., where Orpheus sings of heaven and earth, stars and moon, rivers and mountains, and is reminiscent of Silenus' song in *Ecl.* 6; but above all it recalls *Geo.* 2.477f. (phrases and two whole lines are the same), a passage in which Virgil expresses his wish to be like Lucretius and understand the nature of things.

2 742. **solisque labores**: i.e. eclipses (*lunaeque labores* in *Geo.* 2.478).

3 744. This line is repeated in *Aen.* 3.516. Arcturus (the Bear Watcher) is a bright star near the Great Bear; Hyades are the 'rainers', as Virgil indicates with his epithet *pluvias* (see note on 267-8); they rose at the time of the spring rains. The twin Triones are Ursa Major and Ursa Minor; the seven stars of Ursa Major (the Plough) gave the word *septentriones* for 'north'.

4 746. **mora . . . obstet**: i.e. what stops them from ending sooner in the winter.

5 747. **ingeminant plausu**: 'applaud again and again', Virgil uses *ingeminate* both transitively and intransitively.

6 749. **longumque bibebat amorem**: 'drank deep draughts of love', deep and therefore lasting, cf. *Aen.* 3.487.

7 751. The reference is to Memnon, see note on 489; Dido is thinking of all the questions she can.

8 752. Aeneas had met both Diomedes (97) and Achilles (*Il.* 20.160f.) in single combat.

9 755-6. 'for it is now the seventh summer that carries you in your wanderings over all the lands and seas'. Dido shows that she knows already (from Teucer) how long it is since Troy fell. The words *septima . . . aestas* are also used by Beroe a year later in 5.626, which suggests that the ritual number seven was in Virgil's mind, and that he had not yet revised the *Aeneid* for chronological inconsistencies.

BOOK 2

Introductory note

Few if any of the stories of antiquity have captured the imagination more than the tale of the wooden horse and the fall of Troy. For the Greeks it was a tale of triumph in which the tragedy of the victims might sometimes overshadow the joy of the conquerors (as in Euripides); for Virgil it was a tale of doom and disaster which was the prelude to a new dawn: 'Ilion falling, Rome arising'. *Aeneid* 2 is in itself almost wholly tragic and dark, with only rare flashes of hope; but within the whole poem the darkness is seen as the night which preceded the dawn of Roman civilization. There is a symmetrical balance of position with Book 8, the book of Aeneas at the site of Rome.

The similarity of *Aeneid* 2 to Greek tragedy has often been discussed; probably Virgil knew Sophocles' tragedies (now lost) called *Sinon* and *Laocoon,* and there are echoes from the *Troades* and the *Hecuba* of Euripides. Certain formal resemblances to Greek tragedy can be observed; for example the account of Laocoon's death reminds us of a messenger's speech; invocations and reflections by the poet (e.g. 241-2, 402) are reminiscent of a chorus; Creusa appears at the end as *dea ex machina.* But this aspect of the book should not be exaggerated: Virgil had no intention of grafting a piece in tragic form on to the epic narrative. The main resemblance is not really formal, but consists partly of the unity and completeness of the plot within the book, and partly of the intensity of tragic pathos. The contrast with the discursive narrative of diverse events in the far less intense atmosphere of *Aeneid* 3 is very marked.

The book is made up of three episodes of roughly equal length: the story of the wooden horse (1-249); the sack of the city and the death of Priam (250-558); the fortunes of Aeneas and his family (559-804). Of these the middle section is the most intense; the first sets the scene for the disaster in vigorous and vivid description, and the last shows how the general catastrophe affected the one family upon whose escape the fortunes of Rome depended.

In this book Aeneas appears as a heroic and impetuous warrior, determined to do all that courage can and when, in spite of courage, all is lost, to court death in battle, to make the heroic gesture. Gradually he has to learn that this is not enough; that the responsibilities which he bears go beyond the satisfaction of his personal honour. At the first sight of the burning of Troy he rushes madly to battle: *arma amens capio; nec sat rationis in armis ... furor iraque mentem praecipitat, pulchrumque mori succurrit in armis . . . moriamur et in media arma ruamus.* Like wolves he and his followers go into battle; he invokes the ashes of Troy to witness that he made no effort to save his own life, that he exposed himself to every danger. Later he is restrained by Venus from killing Helen, and reminded of his responsibilities towards his own family; when his father refuses to go Aeneas again falls into despair and is on the point of rushing out to seek death. Again a divine intervention is necessary to prevent him. Finally at the loss of Creusa he plunges into the burning city without regard for personal safety, and is restrained only by the supernatural vision of his wife. Only at the end of the book, when the prophecy of Hector's ghost is repeated by Creusa, does Aeneas begin to understand that not only Troy but the whole heroic age must be left behind, and a new way learned. The vision of Creusa is the prelude to the long lessons of the years of wanderings and battles in Latium, as the divine plan is increasingly revealed. As she speaks her last words to him the jagged confusions of human emotions in this time of catastrophe are balanced by the prospect of long years and other destinies. What seems so terrible in an immediate and personal context as to destroy the individual is now seen in the wider context of history, as a part of the destiny of nations. For Aeneas the solution must not be to cast himself into the flames which are consuming the past and the present, but to build a life for the future out of the ruins.

1-56. Aeneas begins his story, and tells of the discovery of the wooden horse on the beach and of the different opinions among the Trojans about the best thing to do. Laocoon vehemently urges its destruction.

¹Conticuere omnes intentique² ora tenebant.

Inde toro³ pater Aeneas sic orsus ab alto:

'infandum,⁴ regina, iubes renovare dolorem,

Troianas ut⁵ opes et lamentabile regnum

eruerint Danai, ⁶quaeque ipse miserrima vidi   5

et quorum pars magna fui. Quis talia fando

Myrmidonum⁷ Dolopumve aut duri miles Ulixi

temperet a lacrimis? Et iam nox umida caelo

---

1 1f. Aeneas begins his story to Dido in words heavy with sorrow and tragic memory; the scars of suffering are by no means healed. For the first quarter of the book there is nothing tragic; the account is fast paced and factual, but with an undercurrent of impending doom, *fata Troiana*. The narrative begins immediately, without preamble, with the story of the horse, and in a passage of intense irony Aeneas describes the joy of the Trojans when they think that the Greeks have at last gone away. Some however are suspicious about the horse, and the speech of Laocoon has a desperate urgency, with diction and vocal imagery of an unusually exaggerated kind; the tension is released as Aeneas' closing reflexion takes us for a moment away from the events he is describing to the unchangeable sequel in history: *Troiaque nunc staret, Priamique arx alta maneres.*

2 1. **intentique ora tenebant**: 'in rapt attention kept their gaze still', cf. *Aen.* 7.250, 8.520; Servius says '*aut ora intuebantur loquentis, aut immobiles vultus habebant*', of which the second is probably correct. Another possibility is the meaning 'kept quiet', cf. *Geo.* 4-483, but this adds less to the rest of the line.

3 2. **toro**: the couch on which he was reclining at the banquet.

4 3f. Notice how these lines are filled with expressions of sorrow: *infandum . . . dolorem, lamentabile* (a most sonorous word), *miserrima, quis . . . temperet a lacrimis*. So Odysseus (*Od.* 9.12f.) begins his story to Alcinous with emphasis on the sufferings which he is asked to recall.

5 4-5. **ut . . . eruerint**: 'how they overthrew', indirect question dependent on the notion of 'telling' in *renovare dolorem.*

6 5-6. 'dreadful things which I saw myself, and in which I was myself greatly involved'.

7 7. The Myrmidons were Achilles' special soldiers, and the Dolopians, also from Thessaly, were specially associated with Achilles' son Pyrrhus. Ulysses (Odysseus) is a particularly hateful character from the Trojan point of view, unscrupulous and cruel (44, 261); Sinon purposely speaks about him (90, 125, 164) in Trojan terms. See W. B. Stanford's fascinating book *The Ulysses Theme.* For the genitive form *Ulixi*, always used by Virgil, cf. 90, 436, 3.273, 613, 691 and note on 1.30 *Achilli.*

praecipitat[1] suadentque cadentia sidera somnos.
Sed si tantus amor[2] casus cognoscere nostros   10
et breviter Troiae supremum audire laborem,
quamquam animus meminisse horret luctuque refugit,[3]
incipiam. Fracti bello fatisque repulsi
ductores Danaum tot iam labentibus annis
instar[4] montis equum[5] divina[6] Palladis arte   15
aedificant,[7] sectaque intexunt abiete[8] costas;
votum[9] pro reditu simulant; ea fama vagatur.
Huc delecta[10] virum sortiti corpora furtim
includunt caeco[11] lateri penitusque cavernas
ingentis uterumque[12] armato milite complent.   20
    Est in[13] conspectu Tenedos, notissima fama
insula, dives[14] opum Priami dum regna manebant,
nunc[15] tantum sinus et statio male fida carinis:
huc se provecti deserto in litore condunt.

---

1 9. **praecipitat**: intransitive, 'is speeding from the sky', i.e. has passed its mid course. *Cadentia* means that in the night sky one constellation after another is seen to set, or perhaps is used more loosely of the stars growing pale at first dawn (cf. *Aen.* 8.59). Notice the lilting rhythm with no strong caesura to follow the trochee in the third foot, and the rhyme of -*dent*-.

2 10. **amor . . . cognoscere**: poetic use of the infinitive, see note on 1.704.

3 12. **refugit**: perfect, 'has recoiled'.

4 15. **instar montis**: 'the size of a mountain'; the word *instar* (here in apposition to *equum*) is a neuter noun, meaning 'equivalent (weight)', and its most common usage is with the genitive, meaning 'as big as', 'like'; cf. Cic. *Att.* 10.4.1 (*epistola*) *quae voluminis instarerat*, and *Aen.* 3.637, 7.707.

5 15f. For a brilliant account of the Trojan Horse in art and literature see R. G. Austin, *J. R. S.* 1959, pp. 16-25, summarised in his edition of Book 2, pages 34-6. It is mentioned three times in the *Odyssey* as a familiar story, and figured in cyclic epic (*Ilias Parva* and *Iliupersis*). It was a frequent subject in Roman drama (Livius Andronicus and Naevius both wrote an *Equus Troianus*), and it can be seen from an amusing passage in Plautus (*Bacch.* 925f., 987f.) how very well known it was.

6 **divina Palladis arte**: the horse was Ulysses' idea, and Epeos (264) made it with the help of the goddess Athena (Hom. *Od.* 8.493 τον Επειος εποιησεν ουν Αθηνη; cf. Eur. *Tro.* 10).

7 16. **aedificant . . . intexunt**: metaphors used in shipbuilding; *castas* are the 'ribs' of the structure.

8 **abiete**: the *i* is treated as a consonant, making the word a dactyl, cf. *ariete* (492), *parietibus* (442). The material of which the horse is made (pine here, cf. 258) is later said by Sinon to be maple (112); this may be taken as a sign either of lack of revision or of lack of special interest in carpentry. The word *robur*, when used of the horse in 186, 230, 260, has the general sense of 'wood' rather than its specific meaning 'oak'.

9 17. 'they pretend that it is a votive offering for their return; that is the story spread around'. *Votum* is a noun rather than (as Servius suggests) a verb.

10 18. **delecta... corpora:** 'selecting picked men'. *Corpora virum* is a periphrasis for *viri* with the idea, as Conington says, of so many bodies filling up the space.

11 19. **caeco lateri**: 'into its dark side', in prose *in caecum latus*. The dative of motion towards is common in Virgil especially with compound verbs; see Page ad loc, line 85 and cf. 9.729 *incluserit urbi*.

12 20. **uterum**: its womb, cf. 38, 52, *alvus* in 51, and *feta armis* in 238. The metaphor was traditional, cf. Eur. *Tro.* 11, Enn. *Scen.* 76-7 *gravidus armatis equus, / qui suo partu ardua perdat Pergama.*

13 21. **in conspectu**: 'in sight of Troy'; Tenedos was a few miles off the coast.

14 22. **dives opum**: the same phrase in *Aen.* 1,14.

15 23. 'now just a curve of coastline, and a treacherous landfall for ships'; it is often said that this line is a comment by Virgil, not in the person of Aeneas, but when *nos* follows so closely this is inconceivable. Aeneas refers to the deterioration of the famous harbour during the war, and his words help to explain why the Trojans so readily assumed that the Greeks had sailed away.

Nos[1] abiisse rati et vento petiisse Mycenas.   25
Ergo omnis longo[2] solvit se Teucria luctu:
panduntur portae, iuvat ire et Dorica castra
desertosque videre locos litusque relictum:
hic Dolopum manus, hic saevus tendebat[3] Achilles;
classibus hic locus, hic acie certare solebant.   30
Pars stupet[4] innuptae donum exitiale Minervae
et molem mirantur equi; primusque Thymoetes
duci intra muros hortatur[5] et arce locari,
sive[6] dolo seu iam Troiae sic fata ferebant.
At Capys,[7] et quorum melior sententia menti,   35
aut pelago Danaum insidias suspectaque dona[8]
praecipitare iubent subiectisve[9] urere flammis,
aut[10] terebrare cavas uteri et temptare latebras.
Scinditur incertum studia in contraria vulgus.
    Primus ibi ante omnis magna comitante caterva   40
Laocoon[11] ardens summa decurrit ab arce,
et procul 'o miseri, quae tanta insania, cives?
Creditis avectos hostis? Aut ulla putatis
dona carere [12]dolis Danaum? Sic notus Ulixes?

---

1 25. 'we thought — gone, sailed on the wind for Mycenae'; observe the staccato effect of the omission of *sumus* (cf. 651) and *eos*.

2 26. This is a very memorable line, simple in diction, slow, monotonous with dissyllables, with patterned alliteration of *s* and *l* — it is like a long deep sigh of relief.

3 29-30. These lines express the thoughts in the minds of the Trojans as they visit the Greek camp. *Tendebat* means 'had his tent', (understand *tentoria*), a normal military phrase; cf. *Aen.* 8.605. Servius says *classibus* refers to the cavalry, and Mackail follows him; but no reader would take it in this way unless prevented from understanding it to mean 'fleet' by something in the context. Here a mention of the Greek fleet, so prominent a feature of the Trojan landscape for ten years, is extremely appropriate.

4 31. 'Some gaze in amazement at the fatal gift to the maiden goddess Minerva'; Hyginus (*Fab.* 108) says the inscription on the horse was *Danai Minervae dono dant*.

5 33. **hortatur:** for the infinitive after *hortari* cf. 74 and see note on 1.357 (*suadere*).

6 34. **sive dolo**: Servius tells a story that Thymoetes' wife and son were put to death by Priam; hence Thymoetes had cause for treachery.

7 35. **Capys**: he was one of those who came with Aeneas, cf. 1.183, 10.145; he gave his name to Capua.

8 36f. In Hom. *Od.* 8.507f. the Trojans debate whether to break the horse open, throw it from a cliff, or accept it.

9 37. **subiectisve**: our MSS all have *-que*, but Servius reports that some early MSS had *-ve*. There are many instances (see Austin's note for references) where *-que* is used when *-ve* would seem more natural; on the other hand *-ve* a nd *-que* are constantly confused in the MSS, and in this instance *-que* seems to me unacceptable, even allowing that the first *aut* clause links two methods of destruction as opposed to the idea in the second *aut* clause (investigation).

10 38. 'or to pierce and explore the hollow recesses of its belly'.

11 41f. Laocoon figures in the epic cycle (*Iliupersis*), and there was a tragedy by Sophocles called *Laocoon*. He was a son of Priam and priest of Apollo (see note on 201). In the general tradition of the fall of Troy his part was subordinate to that of Cassandra, and it seems certain that it is an innovation by Virgil to make him the central character. For further and full discussion see Austin's edition of Book 2, pp. 44-5, and 94-9.

12 44. Our attention is compelled by the alliteration of *d*, leading to the summary: 'is this all you've learned about Ulysses?' Laocoon does not have knowledge that Ulysses was the originator of the idea of the horse, but he ascribes plots and trickery of all description as likely to come from that source.

Aut hoc inclusi ligno occultantur Achivi.[1]   45
Aut haec in nostros fabricata est machina muros,
inspectura domos venturaque desuper urbi,
aut aliquis latet error;[2] equo ne credite, Teucri.
Quidquid id est, timeo[3] Danaos et dona ferentis.'
Sic fatus validis ingentem viribus hastam   50
in latus inque feri[4] curvam[5] compagibus alvum
contorsit. Stetit illa tremens, uteroque recusso
insonuere cavae gemitumque dedere cavernae.[6]
Et,[7] si fata deum, si mens non laeva fuisset,
impulerat ferro Argolicas foedare latebras,   55
Troiaque nunc staret, Priamique arx alta maneres.

---

1 45f. Laocoon makes two precise suggestions: the first (which is correct) is that the horse contains Greek warriors, the second is that it is a kind of scaling ladder by which the walls can be breached. If neither of these is correct, he says, there is some (other) trick behind it.

2 48. **error:** 'deception', cf. Livy 22.1.3.

3 49. **timeo Danaos et dona ferentis:** from the time of Donatus this phrase has become a proverbial expression with its meaning slightly twisted. Laocoon here says: 'I fear the Greeks even when they are making offerings', that is to say religious offerings to Minerva, a goddess of Troy.

4 51. **feri:** of a horse at 5.818, of a tame stag in 7.489.

5 **curvam compagibus:** a favourite Virgilian ablative, where *curvis compagibus* would be more normal; cf. 208, 765 and Mackail's Appendix A in his edition.

6 53. The assonance of this line, intended to convey the reverberation caused by the quivering spear, is most remarkable, mainly because of the trochaic caesurae and the rhyme of *-ere, -ae*.

7 54f. 'and if the fates of the gods and their intentions had not been against us, he would have prevailed on us to despoil with steel the Greek hiding place, and Troy would now be standing, and lofty citadel of Priam you would yet survive'. For *mens deum* cf. 170, *Geo.* 4.220, Ov. *Met.* 15.137: some take the phrase to refer to the Trojans' minds (cf. *Ecl.* 1.16), but this gives an unbalanced sentence. For *impulerat* (the indicative used vividly in a past unfulfilled condition) cf. *Geo.* 2.133, Hor. *Odes* 2.17.28. For *staret* some MSS have *stares,* but the change from third person narrative to second-person apostrophe in the parallel clauses is very effective.

57-199. A group of Trojan shepherds bring in the Greek Sinon, who has allowed himself to be captured in order to persuade the Trojans to take the wooden horse into the city. He tells his story of deceit, pretending that he was about to be put to death by Greeks, but made his escape and is now throwing himself on the Trojans' mercy. The Trojans pity him and release his fetters; Sinon completes his story, telling them that the horse is a religious offering in atonement for the stolen Palladium, and that if they take it into Troy the defeat of the Greeks is certain.

[1]Ecce, manus[2] iuvenem interea post terga revinctum
pastores magno ad regem clamore trahebant
Dardanidae,[3] qui se ignotum venientibus ultro,
hoc[4] ipsum ut strueret Troiamque aperiret Achivis,   60
obtulerat, fidens animi[5] atque in utrumque paratus,
seu[6] versare dolos seu certae occumbere morti.
Undique visendi studio Troiana iuventus
circumfusa ruit certantque inludere capto.
Accipe[7] nunc Danaum insidias et crimine ab uno   65
disce omnis.
Namque ut conspectu in medio turbatus, inermis,
constitit atque oculis Phrygia agmina circumspexit,[8]
'heu, quae me tellus' inquit 'quae me aequora possunt
accipere? Aut quid iam misero mihi denique restat,   70

---

1 The story of Sinon, like that of Laocoon, occurs in the epic cycle (not in Homer), and there was a tragedy by Sophocles called *Sinon*. Virgil's version is probably the first from a Trojan point of view. There are marked similarities with the Achaemenides episode in 3.588f.; see Mackail's edition, Appendix B. Sinon (a parallel to Tarquin in treachery) is among the Trojan pictures which Lucrece sees in Shakespeare's *Rape of Lucrece* (1501f.).

'At last she sees a wretched image bound,

That piteous looks to Phrygian shepherds lent . . .'

Two points stand out in Virgil's brilliant treatment of this episode; first the contrast between the guile and cold deception of Sinon and the warm hearts of the Trojans who are moved to pity; and secondly the masterly rhetoric which Sinon commands in all its moods, despair, subtlety, humility, anger, appeals to pity. Austin in his commentary summarises Sinon's speech with the words: 'Cicero would have enjoyed reading it, and would have recognised its quality'.

2 57. **mantis**: retained accusative, see note on 210.

3 59. **Dardanidae**: noun (cf. 72) in apposition with *pastores*.

4 60. **hoc ipsum**: i.e. to be brought to the king, so that he could tell his false story.

5 61. **animi**: 'in heart', 'in courage', genitive of 'sphere in which', (not locative); see my note on 5.202 *furens animi* (OUP Ed.).

6 62. 'either to weave his web of lies or to meet certain death'; the first alternative is if he succeeded in getting himself taken to the king, the second is if the shepherds decided to kill him as soon as they found him.

7 65-6. 'Now listen to the treachery of the Greeks, and from one act of crime comprehend it all'; with *omnis* understand *insidias* (rather than *Danaos*). This is in direct reply to Dido's request (1.754) *die . . . insidias Danaum;* Aeneas now says he will give one example for all, the last one. For the half-line see note on 1.534; the others in this book are 233, 346, 468, 614, 623, 640, 720, 767, 787.

8 68. **circumspexit**: Virgil (unlike Catullus) rarely has a spondee in the fifth foot (35 instances altogether, mostly with Greek words, compared with 30 in the four hundred lines of Catullus 64); here it has a most marked aesthetic effect, conveying the slow hopelessness of Sinon's gaze. For further metrical references see my note on 5.320 (OUP Ed.).

cui neque apud Danaos usquam locus, et super ipsi
Dardanidae infensi poenas cum sanguine poscunt?'
Quo[1] gemitu conversi animi compressus et omnis
impetus. Hortamur fari quo sanguine cretus,[2]
quidve[3] ferat; memoret[4] quae sit fiducia capto.   75
[Ille haec deposita tandem formidine fatur:][5]
    'Cuncta equidem tibi, rex, fuerit[6] quodcumque, fatebor
vera,' inquit; 'neque me Argolica de gente negabo.
Hoc primum; nec, [7]si miserum Fortuna Sinonem
finxit, vanum etiam mendacemque improba finget.   80
Fando aliquod[8] si forte tuas pervenit ad auris
Belidae[9] nomen Palamedis et incluta fama
gloria, quem falsa[10] sub proditione Pelasgi
insontem[11] infando indicio, quia bella vetabat,
demisere neci, nunc cassum[12] lumine lugent: 85
illi me comitem et consanguinitate propinquum[13]
pauper in arma pater primis huc misit ab annis.[14]

---

1 73. 'At his words of anguish our feelings changed, and all menacing gestures ceased'; the contrast of Trojan friendliness with Greek ruthlessness is very marked. Donatus says 'bonitatem Troianorum vult Aeneas ostendere', Taubmann 'tribuit poeta ubique pietatem simplicita temque animi Troianis'.

2 74. **cretus:** sc. *sit,* passive participle of *cresco* with active meaning; cf. *Aen.* 3.608, 4.191.

3 75. **quidve ferat:** 'what information he is bringing'; cf. *Aen.* 10.150.

4 **memoret quae sit fiducia capto:** 'let him say what he relies on as a captive'; Sinon has indicated that he has no place now among the Greeks, so the Trojans ask him what grounds he has for thinking they will wish to receive him: 'What is the prisoner's case, what has he to say for himself?' (Henry, quoting Tac. *Ann.* 3.11). This seems the best interpretation of a difficult passage; another of Servius' suggestions is 'let him remember what a captive must depend on', i.e. telling the truth, but this seems impossible for *memoret.*

5 76. This line (the same as 3.612) is not in the chief MSS, is not appropriate here with *inquit* following, and should therefore be omitted.

6 77. **fuerit quodcumque**: 'come what may'.

7 79-80. 'and if Fortune has made Sinon unhappy, she shall not also, tyrant though she may be, make him false and untruthful'. For *improba* cf. 356, *Aen.* 4.412 *improbe Amor.*

8 81-2. **aliquod . . . nomen**: 'any mention of the name', cf. *Aen.* 1.181 *Anthea si quem* ('any sign of Antheus') and Ov. *Met.* 9.8, 15.497.

9 82. **Belidae . . . Palamedis**: the story first occurs in cyclic epic (*Cypria*), and Euripides wrote a tragedy called *Palamedes;* cf. also Eur. *Orest.* 432f., and Cic. *De Off.* 3.97-8. Ulysses, angry because Palamedes had uncovered the trick by which he had tried to avoid going to Troy, forged a letter in which Palamedes promised to betray the Greeks, and hid gold in his tent. Palamedes was put to death. The suggestion that Palamedes 'forbad the war' (84) may be added by Virgil to make Sinon's speech more persuasive. *Belides* is derived from Belus, father of Danaus and Aegyptus, not the same as Dido's ancestor (1.621, 729); Virgil lengthens the *i* of the patronymic as if it were from Beleus (cf.104).

10 83. **falsa sub proditione**: 'under a false accusation of betrayal', (so Servius), a curiously compressed phrase; Conington thinks it means 'under a false information', but as the story concerned betrayal of the Greeks we would expect that idea here.

11 84. The alliteration of *in-* and the elisions are highly emphatic.

12 85. **cassum lumine**: 'deprived of the light', cf. Lucr. 5.719, *Aen.* 11.104.

13 86. The main clause begins here: 'it was to him that my father sent me as a companion and a relative by blood'; *et* rather unusually links *comitem* which is predicative and *propinquum* which is attributive.

14 87. Compare what Achaemenides says in 3.614-15.

Dum stabat regno incolumis regumque[1] vigebat
conciliis, et nos aliquod nomenque decusque
gessimus. Invidia postquam pellacis[2] Ulixi   90
(haud ignota loquor) superis[3] concessit ab oris,
adflictus vitam in tenebris luctuque trahebam
et easum insontis mecum indignabar amici.
Nec tacui demens et me, fors[4] si qua tulisset,
si patrios umquam remeassem victor ad Argos,   95
promisi ultorem et verbis odia aspera movi.
Hinc mihi prima mali[5] labes, hinc semper Ulixes
criminibus terrere[6] novis, hinc spargere voces
in[7] vulgum ambiguas[8] et quaerere[9] conscius arma.
Nec requievit enim[10] donec Calchante[11] ministro —   100
sed[12] quid ego haec autem nequiquam ingrata revolvo,
quidve moror? Si omnis uno ordine habetis Achivos,
idque audire sat est, iamdudum[13] sumite poenas:
hoc Ithacus[14] velit et magno mercentur Atridae.'[15]
    Tum vero ardemus[16] scitari et quaerere causas,   105

---

1 88. **regno incolumis**. Palamedes was one of the *reges*.

2 90. **pellacis**: the word is not found elsewhere before the fourth century; the very rare noun *pellacia* occurs in Lucr. 2.559 (= 5.1004) *placidi pellacia ponti*. The verb *pellicere* ('entice') is fairly common. Some MSS have *fallacis*, which seems like a gloss or an easier reading substituted.

3 91. **superis concessit ab oris:** 'departed from the shores of life', a phrase in high epic style, in keeping with the rhetorical eloquence which Sinon commands.

4 94. **fors si qua tulisset:** 'if any chance brought it about'; cf. line 34, 11.345. *Tulisset* is reported future perfect; cf. 136, 189, 756.

5 97. **mali labes:** 'slip towards disaster'; Servius says *ruinam significat,* a *'lapsu',* and Justin (17.1.5) imitates the passage and takes it in this way: *haec prima mali labes, hoc initium impendentis ruinae fuit.* Cf. also Lucr. 2.1145 *dabunt labem putrisque ruinas.* In *Aen.* 6.746, in the only other place where Virgil uses the word *labes,* it has its other meaning, 'stain', which is not inconceivable here.

6 98. **terrere:** historic infinitive, frequent in Virgil, cf. 132, 169, 685, here used for repeated action (cf. *Aen.* 4422).

7 99. **in vulgum:** the masculine is much rarer than the neuter form;cf. Lucr. 2.921.

8 **ambiguas**: 'double-edged'.

9 **quaerere conscius arma**: 'he sought assistance for his conspiracy against me'; *conscius* is literally 'as a conspirator', 'with deliberate intent'. *Arma* is vague, anything he could use for his purpose, suspicion, hostility: Servius says *arma sunt instrumenta cuius libet rei.*

10 100. **enim:** an archaic usage meaning 'indeed', cf. line 164 and 6.317.

11 **Calchante ministro**: the sentence is broken off, left unfinished by aposiopesis. Calchas was the chief Greek seer at Troy, cf.Hom.*Il.* 1.68f.

12 101. **sed . . . autem:** a colloquialism, only found elsewhere in comedy, helping to convey the change of tone as he comes to the end of his speech.

13 103. 'and it's enough to hear that name, then exact now the overdue punishment'; *iamdudum* with the imperative is an elliptical way of combining past and future (take it now, you should have long ago), cf. Sen. *Ep. Mor.* 84.14 *relinque ista iamdudum,* Ov. *Met.* 11.482.

14 104. **Ithacus**: with some contempt, describing Ulysses without mentioning his name; cf. 122.

15 **Atridae:** the sons of Atreus, Agamemnon and Menelaus, cf. 415, 500 and *Aen.* 1.458.

16 105. **ardemus scitari:** for the infinitive cf. 316 and *Aen.* 1.515, 4.281.

ignari scelerum tantorum artisque Pelasgae.
Prosequitur pavitans et ficto pectore fatur:
   [1]Saepe fugam Danai Troia cupiere relicta
moliri et longo fessi discedere bello;
fecissentque[2] utinam! Saepe illos aspera ponti   110
interclusit hiems et terruit Auster euntis.
Praecipue cum iam hic trabibus contextus[3] acernis
staret equus, toto sonuerunt aethere nimbi.
Suspensi Eurypylum scitantem[4] oracula Phoebi
mittimus, isque adytis haec tristia dicta reportat: 115
"sanguine placastis ventos et virgine caesa,[5]
cum primum Iliacas, Danai, venistis ad oras:
sanguine quaerendi reditus animaque[6] litandum
Argolica." Vulgi quae vox ut venit ad auris,
obstipuere animi gelidusque per ima cucurrit   120
ossa tremor, cui[7] fata parent, quem poscat Apollo.
Hic Ithacus vatem magno Calchanta tumultu
protrahit in medios; quae[8] sint ea numina divum
flagitat. [9]Et mihi iam multi crudele canebant
artificis scelus, et taciti ventura videbant.   125
Bis quinos silet ille dies tectusque[10] recusat
prodere voce sua quemquam aut opponere morti.
Vix tandem, magnis Ithaci clamoribus actus,

---

1 108. 'Sinon begins with casual simplicity, almost as if he were telling a bedtime story' (Austin). Austin's detailed comments on the rhetorical trickery of Sinon's speeches are vivid and penetrating.

2 110. **fecissentque utinam:** 'if only they had done it', cf. *Aen.* 3.615.

3 112. **contextus acernis:** see note on 16.

4 114. **scitantem:** Servius says *id est scitaturum*, 'to consult'; *M2* and some other MSS have the *supine scitatum*, but *scitantem* seems acceptable as an extension of phrases like *mittere auxilium orantes*. Eurypylus is mentioned in Hom. *Il.* 2.736.

5 116. The reference is to the sacrifice of Iphigenia at Aulis; cf. Lucr. 1.84f.

6 118-19. **animaque litandum Argolica:** 'favour must be won with a Greek life'; *litare* is a ritual word, meaning to obtain favour by sacrificing. Notice the emphatic position of *Argolica*.

7 121. **cui fata parent**: '(as they wondered) for whom they were to prepare death, who it was that Apollo demanded'; the indirect question is loosely linked to the previous sentence, cf. *Aen.* 12.718f. This is the interpretation which Servius gives (*cui praeparent mortem*) and the deliberative question fits well with the gerundives of 118: 'you must sacrifice — whom then are we to sacrifice?' For *fata parare* cf. 132. Others take *fata* as nominative 'for whom the fates are preparing' but the absence of an object is very strange. Others again accept the conjecture *paret*, making Apollo the subject.

8 123-4. **quae . . . flagitat**: 'he demands to know what these indications of the divine will mean';cf. *Aen.* 3.359f.

9 124-5. 'And now many of them were beginning to prophesy for me the cruel crime of that schemer, and silently were foreseeing the future'. *Canere* is in the sense of foretelling by prophecy; *taciti* means, as Austin points out, that Sinon's friends brooded over what they saw coming to him; perhaps it also implies that they did not speak out or take action.

10 126. **tectus:** 'shut up in his tent', cf. *Aen.* 7.600.

composito[1] rumpit[2] vocem et me destinat arae.
adsensere omnes et, quae sibi quisque timebat,   130
unius in miseri exitium conversa tulere.[3]
Iamque dies infanda aderat; mihi sacra parari[4]
et salsae[5] fruges et circum tempora vittae.
Eripui, fateor, leto me et vincula rupi,
limosoque lacu per noctem obscurus in ulva   135
delitui dum[6] vela darent, si forte dedissent.
Nec mihi iam patriam antiquam spes ulla videndi[7]
nec dulcis natos exoptatumque parentem,
quos[8] illi fors et poenas ob nostra reposcent
effugia, et culpam hanc miserorum morte piabunt.   140
Quod[9] te per superos et conscia numina veri,
per[10] si qua est quae restet adhuc mortalibus usquam
intemerata fides, oro, miserere laborum
tantorum, miserere animi non digna ferentis.'
    His lacrimis vitam damus et miserescimus ultro.[11]   145
Ipse viro primus manicas atque arta levari
vincla iubet Priamus dictisque ita fatur amicis:
'quisquis es, [12]amissos hinc iam obliviscere Graios;
noster eris. Mihique haec edissere vera roganti:
quo molem hanc immanis equi statuere? Quis auctor?   150
Quidve petunt? Quae religio? Aut quae[13] machina belli?'

---

1 129. **composito:** 'in accordance with the' agreement' (*ex pacta,* Servius); cf. *composita hora,* at the agreed hour.

2 **rupit vocem:** 'broke into words', broke silence; cf. *Aen.* 3.246, 4.553, 11.377. The phrase is based on the Greek ρηξαι φωνην.

3 131. **tulere:** 'accepted', in the sense of *aequo animo tulerunt.*

4 132. **parari:** historic infinitive, see note on 98.

5 133. **salsae fruges:** 'salted corn' (*mola salsa*), frequent in sacrificial offerings; cf. *Aen.* 12.173.

6 136. 'I lay hidden waiting for them to set sail, if only they would'; in *dum darent* the subject expresses his purpose in waiting, cf. *Aen.* 1.5. The conditional clause is of the special type, often with *forte,* where the if clause is not the protasis to the expressed main clause, and conveys an idea of purpose or hope; cf. *Aen.* 1.181, 578 and especially 2.756. *Dedissent* is reported future perfect, cf. 94; the thought in his mind is 'if only they will go'.

7 137f. Sinon comes to his peroration in the well known oratorical style, with an appeal for pity (*miseratio*).

8 139. 'from whom perhaps they will even exact a penalty for my escape'; *quos* and *poenas* are accusatives after *reposcere* (cf. *Aen.* 7.606); *fors* is adverbial, probably archaic, equivalent to *forsit, forsitan,* cf. 5.232, and for *fors et* 11.50.

9 141. **quod:** as in *quod si,* literally 'with regard to which', cf. *Aen.* 6.363.

10 142-3. 'by any faith which anywhere still remains uncorrupted among men'; the whole clause acts as object to the preposition *per,* cf. *Aen.* 6.459.

11 145. **ultro:** the commonest meaning of this word is 'first, of one's own accord' (59, 193, 279, 372); here the shade of meaning is 'beyond what might be expected' (*Aen.* 5.55), 'into the bargain' (Austin). See Page's excellent note ad loc.

12 148. 'whoever you are, from now forget the Greeks you have lost'.

13 151. **quae ... belli:** 'what is its religious purpose, or what kind of military machine is it?' These are the two possible meanings of the horse which were debated by the Trojans before Sinon came. For the long first syllable of *religio* cf. 188, 365, 715, and *Aen.* 1.30 (*reliquias*).

Dixerat. Ille dolis instructus et arte Pelasga
sustulit exutas vinclis ad sidera palmas:
'vos, aeterni[1] ignes, et non violabile vestrum
testor numen,' ait, 'vos arae ensesque nefandi,   155
quos fugi, vittaeque deum, quas hostia gessi:
fas mihi Graiorum sacrata resolvere iura,
fas odisse viros atque omnia ferre sub auras,
si qua tegunt; teneor patriae nec legibus ullis.
Tu modo promissis maneas servataque serves[2]   160
Troia fidem, si vera feram, si magna rependam.
Omnis spes Danaum et coepti fiducia belli
Palladis auxiliis semper stetit. [3]Impius ex quo
Tydides sed enim scelerumque inventor Ulixes,
fatale adgressi sacrato avellere templo   165
Palladium[4] caesis summae custodibus arcis,
corripuere sacram effigiem manibusque cruentis
virgineas ausi[5] divae contingere vittas,
ex illo fluere[6] ac retro sublapsa referri
spes Danaum, fractae vires, aversa deae[7] mens.   170
Nec dubiis ea[8] signa dedit Tritonia[9] monstris.
Vix[10] positum castris simulacrum: arsere coruscae
luminibus flammae arrectis, salsusque per artus
sudor iit, terque ipsa solo [11](mirabile dictu)
emicuit parmamque ferens hastamque trementem.   175

---

1 154. **aeterni ignes**: i.e. the heavenly bodies.

2 160-1. The apostrophe to Troy, rather than the Trojans, adds to the rhetorical effect; *magnificentius*, says Servius.

3 163-4. 'But indeed from the time when the godless son of Tydeus along with Ulysses, the deviser of sin . . .' *Ex quo* is picked up by *ex illo* after an unusually long series of subordinate clauses. For *sed enim* cf. *Aen.* 1.19, 6.28 and note on 100. Diomedes, son of Tydeus, is called *impius* with reference to this particular crime, but perhaps also (as Servius says) because he had fought against gods (Hom. *Il.* 5.330f.); for the hostile attitude to Ulysses see note on 7, and particularly 125 and 6.529 *hortator scelerum*.

4 166. **Palladium**: the story of the sacred image of the maiden goddess Pallas Athena, on which the safety of Troy depended (*fatale*), goes back to cyclic epic (it is not in Homer). According to one version it was a false Palladium which the Greeks stole, and the real one was brought from Troy to Rome by Aeneas; according to another Aeneas recovered it from Diomedes after the fall of Troy. For a full account see Austin's note on 163.

5 168. **ausi**: understand *sunt;* the parallelism with *corripuere* prevents possible ambiguity in this long sentence.

6 169. **fluere . . . referri**: historic infinitives, cf. 98; for the last part of the line cf. *Geo.* 1.200.

7 170. **deae mens**: the monosyllabic ending is unusual and emphatic; see note on 1.105, and cf. 250, 355.

8 171. **ea signa**: 'signs of it', i.e. her hostility, a frequent Latin idiom, cf. *Aen.* 7.595 has poenas = harum rerum poenas.

9 **Tritonia**: a frequent epithet of Pallas (615, cf. 226), apparently from an obscure lake Tritonis in Africa near which she was said to have been born or first alighted on earth after her birth (Lucan 9.354).

10 172. **vix positum . . . arsere**: *vix positum est cum arsere*, one of the types of parataxis of which Virgil was fond, cf. 692, 3.90.

11 174-5. The meaning is that apart from the miraculous behaviour of the image (flashing eyes, salt sweat), an apparition of Pallas herself was three times seen.

Extemplo temptanda fuga canit aequora Calchas,
nec posse Argolicis exscindi Pergama telis
omina ni repetant Argis numenque reducant[1]
quod pelago et curvis secum avexere carinis.
Et[2] nunc quod patrias vento petiere Mycenas,   180
arma deosque parant comites pelagoque[3] remenso
improvisi aderunt; ita digerit omina Calchas.
Hanc pro Palladio moniti, pro numine laeso
effigiem statuere, nefas quae triste piaret.
Hanc[4] tamen immensam Calchas attollere molem   185
roboribus textis caeloque[5] educere iussit,
ne recipi portis aut duci in moenia posset,
neu populum antiqua[6] sub religione tueri.
Nam si vestra manus violasset[7] dona Minervae,
tum magnum exitium (quod di prius omen in[8] ipsum   190
convertant!) Priami imperio Phrygibusque futurum;
sin manibus vestris vestram ascendisset in urbem,
ultro Asiam magno Pelopea[9] ad moenia bello
venturam, et nostros ea fata manere nepotes.'
    Talibus insidiis periurique arte Sinonis[10]   195
credita res, captique dolis lacrimisque coactis[11]
quos neque Tydides[12] nec Larisaeus Achilles,

---

1 178-9. 'unless they seek new omens in Argos, and bring back the deity (which they have now taken away with them over the sea in their curved ships)'. Lines 177-8 are what Calchas said; line 179 is Sinon's comment. Conington's version of 179 (the divine favour which they originally brought away with them from Greece) has been followed by some, but is improbable.

2 180. **et nunc quod**: a rather loose and colloquial opening to a sentence, 'as to the fact that', found sometimes in Cicero's letters, and cf. Lucr. 4.885, Cat. 83.4. Translate 'The reason why they have gone ... is because they are preparing. . .'.

3 181. **pelagoque remenso**: 'when they have travelled back again over the sea'; cf. *Aen.* 5.25 *remetior astra,* and for the passive sense 3.143.

4 185. **hanc tamen**: slightly disjointed, still referring to the horse, the *hanc effigiem* of the previous sentence. The connexion seems to be: 'they have made this horse to expiate their crime, but Calchas said it had to be of enormous size, so that it could not be taken into Troy'.

5 186. **caeloque**: dative of motion towards, cf. 688, 6.178.

6 188. **antiqua sub religione**: so that it could not take the place of the Palladium (183), and save Troy from destruction.

7 189. **violasset**: reported future perfect, cf. 94.

8 190. **in ipsum**: on Calchas himself.

9 193-4. 'Then Asia would herself in mighty warfare come to the walls of Pelops, and that fate awaited our descendants'; cf. *Aen.* 11.286. Pelops (who gave his name to the Peloponnese) was grandfather of Agamemnon. The prophecy came true when the Trojan-Romans conquered Greece; cf. 1.283f., 6.836f.

10 195. Cf. Shakespeare, *Rape of Lucrece,* 1548f. 'Look, look, how listening Priam wets his eyes, / To see those borrow'd tears that Sinon sheds . . .'

11 196. **coacti**: 'forced', cf. Ov. *Met.* 6.628, Juv. 13.133 *vexare oculos umore coacto.*

12 197. Diomedes and Achilles are linked also in 1.752; Achilles came from Pthia in Thessaly, near Larissa.

non anni domuere decem, non mille[1] carinae.

199-249. At this point a terrible portent occurs: twin serpents from the sea seize Laocoon and his two sons and kill them. The Trojans regard this as a final indication that the horse must not be harmed, and amidst scenes of rejoicing they take it inside Troy.

[2]Hic aliud maius miseris multoque tremendum[3]
obicitur magis atque improvida pectora turbat.   200
Laocoon,[4] ductus Neptuno sorte sacerdos,
sollemnis taurum ingentem mactabat ad aras.[5]
Ecce autem gemini a Tenedo[6] tranquiila per alta[7]
(horresco referens) immensis orbibus angues
incumbunt[8] pelago pariterque ad litora tendunt;   205
pectora quorum inter fluctus arrecta iubaeque[9]
sanguineae superant undas, pars cetera pontum
pone legit sinuatque[10] immensa volumine terga.
Fit sonitus[11] spumante salo; iamque arva tenebant

---

1 198. The 'thousand ships' (cf. 9.148) goes back to Aesch. *Agam.* 45. The actual number in Homer's catalogue has been counted as 1186, 'but', Austin asks, 'could Helen's face have launched 1186 ships?'

2 The story of the death of Laocoon is told in a passage of great immediacy and power, and has always been one of the best known parts of the *Aeneid.* The description of the snakes is vivid and terrifying, and effects of rhythm and sound are used throughout with the utmost skill to reinforce the meaning of the words; but perhaps the main impact is the remorseless inevitability of doom. We are reminded of a messenger's speech in Greek tragedy (e.g. Eur. *Hipp.* 1210f.), when events are described which are too full of horror to be presented on the stage.

The passage was used by Lessing (*Laocoon,* 1766), as a basis for his famous discussion of the difference between the techniques of poetry and the fine arts. The marble group of Laocoon and his two sons (now in the Vatican), dating probably from the second half of the first century B.C., was regarded by Pliny (*Nat. Hist.* 36.37) as surpassing all other works of painting or sculpture; it is possible that Virgil knew it, or knew a painting from which it derived. For a full appreciation of the passage, and a discussion of the source material and the variations in the Laocoon legend, see R. G. Austin, *J.R.S.* 1959, p. 20 and his note (with full bibliography) on *Aen.* 2.199-227.

3 199-200. 'Then another thing happened to shake the unhappy Trojans, much more significant and much more terrifying, confusing our blind wits'; the alliteration is marked, and the unusual position of *magis* is very emphatic.

4 201. Laocoon in the general tradition was a priest of Apollo: see note on 41f. and 199f. Servius explains that the priest of Neptune had been killed and Laocoon was appointed to his duties. The metonymy *ductus sorte* (= *factus sorte ducta*) is not uncommon; cf. Cic. *Rep.* 1.51.

5 202. The altars are presumably on the shore, cf. *Aen.* 3.21.

6 203. The snakes come from the direction of Tenedos because that is the direction from which the Greek fleet is to come (cf. 21f.). Henry draws attention to the parallels between the serpents and the fleet, from their red crests corresponding with the flame signal (256) to their reception by Athena corresponding with her part in Troy's destruction (615).

7 203-4. Notice how the separation of *angues* from its adjective *gemini* by a series of descriptive phrases gives tension to the sentence.

8 205. **incumbunt pelago:** 'breast the sea'; *pelaga* is dative, cf. *Aen.* 1.84.

9 206. **iubaeque:** the crests on their heads give a dragon-like effect to the serpents; Pliny (*N.H.* 11.122) firmly says *draconum cristas qui viderit, non reperitur,* and Livy (43.13.4) mentions such a thing as a prodigy. Page quotes Milton, *P.L.* 7.496f. (of the serpent) 'with brazen Eyes / and hairie Mane terrific'.

10 208. **sinuatque . . . terga:** 'arches its enormous length in coils'; *sinuo* is always transitive, cf. *Geo.* 3.192 and Ov. *Met.* 3.42.

11 209-11. The alliteration, especially of *s,* is very powerful, and the description is brought to an end with a patterned line of gruesome finality. For other snake descriptions in Virgil cf. 379f, 471f, *Geo.* 2.153f., 3.425f., *Aen.* 5.84f., 273f.

ardentisque oculos[1] suffecti sanguine et igni   210
sibila lambebant linguis vibrantibus ora.
Diffugimus[2] visu exsangues. Illi agmine certo
Laocoonta petunt; et primum parva duorum
corpora natorum serpens amplexus uterque
implicat et miseros morsu depascitur artus;   215
post ipsum auxilio subeuntem ac tela ferentem
corripiunt spirisque ligant ingentibus; [3]et iam
bis medium amplexi, bis collo[4] squamea circum
terga dati superant capite et cervicibus altis.
Ille simul manibus tendit divellere nodos   220
perfusus[5] sanie vittas atroque veneno,
clamores simul horrendos ad sidera tollit:
qualis[6] mugitus, fugit cum saucius aram
taurus et incertam[7] excussit cervice securim.
At[8] gemini lapsu delubra ad summa dracones   225
effugiunt saevaeque[9] petunt Tritonidis arcem,
sub pedibusque deae clipeique sub orbe teguntur.
Tum vero tremefacta novus per pectora cunctis
insinuat pavor, et scelus expendisse merentem
Laocoonta ferunt, sacrum qui cuspide robur   230
laeserit et tergo[10] sceleratam intorserit hastam.
Ducendum ad sedes[11] simulacrum orandaque divae

---

1 210. 'their gleaming eyes shot with blood and fire'; *oculos* is retained accusative (here after a verb with a middle meaning), cf. 57, 219, 221, 273, 275, 393, 511, 629, 721 and note on 1.228 *oculos suffusa. Suffecti* is rare in this sense, cf. Val. Fl. 2.105 *maculis suffecta genas.*

2 212-13. Notice how after the lingering descriptive passage the two staccato short sentences convey the rapidity of the events. For *agmine* cf. *Aen.* 5.90, *Geo.* 3.423, and note on 782.

3 217. The unusual pause after the fifth foot, and the double monosyllable at the line ending, compel the attention for the statuesque description of the next two lines.

4 218-19. **collo squamea circum terga dati**: 'entwining their scaly bodies round his neck'; for the tmesis of *circumdati* cf. 792, for its construction cf. 510, and for the middle use cf. *cingitur* in 511.

5 221. **perfusus . . . vittas**: retained accusative with a passive meaning in the verb, see note on 210.

6 223. **qualis mugitus, fugit cum**: 'like the bellowing when a bull has escaped . . .'; the full construction would be *tales clamores tollit qualis est mugitus. . . .* The comparison, apart from its main point of resemblance (cries of agony), conveys with intense irony that Laocoon is now become the sacrificial victim (202).

7 224. **incertam**: 'ill-aimed'.

8 225. **at**: the particle of transition conveys that the struggle is over, and leaves the death of Laocoon un-narrated.

9 226. **saevaeque . . . Tritonidis**: i.e. Athena, see note on 171. For *saeva* cf. 1.479, the picture of the Trojan women supplicating the hostile Athena.

10 231. **tergo**: poetic dative of motion towards after the compound. *intorserit*, 'hurled at', cf. 236. 240. *Intorserit* (like *laeserit*) is causal subjunctive.

11 232. With *sedes* understand *divae* (i.e. *Minervae*); the word *simulacrum* is here applied to the horse (cf. 172, of the Palladium).

numina conclamant.

Dividimus muros[1] et moenia pandimus urbis.

Accingunt[2] omnes operi [3]pedibusque rotarum[4]   235

subiciunt lapsus, et stuppea vincula collo

intendunt: scandit fatalis machina muros

feta[5] armis. Pueri circum innuptaeque puellae

sacra canunt funemque manu contingere gaudent;

illa subit mediaeque minans inlabitur urbi.   240

O patria, o divum domus Ilium et incluta bello[6]

moenia Dardanidum![7] Quater ipso in limine portae

substitit atque utero sonitum quater arma dedere;

instamus tamen immemores caecique furore

et monstrum[8] infelix sacrata sistimus arce.   245

Tunc etiam fatis aperit Cassandra futuris[9]

ora dei iussu non umquam credita Teucris.

Nos delubra deum miseri, quibus ultimus esset[10]

ille dies, festa velamus fronde per urbem.

> *250-67. Night falls; the Trojans sleep. The Greek fleet leaves Tenedos, and Sinon receiving a fire signal from them opens the horse. The Greeks hidden in it come out, kill the Trojan sentries, and open the gates of Troy to their companions.*

[11]Vertitur interea caelum et ruit Oceano nox[12]   250

involvens umbra magna terramque polumque

---

1 234. **muros . . . moenia**: *muros* are the city walls which they breach by the gate, and *moenia* the buildings within.

2 235. **accingunt**: intransitive, used reflexively; cf. *Aen.* 1.104.

3 235f. For descriptions of the entry of the horse cf. Eur. *Tro.* 511f., *Hec.* 905f., Plaut. *Bacch.* 933f. Notice the very short clauses, with eight main verbs in six lines, to convey the relentless movement of the action.

4 235-7. 'and put rollers under its feet and secure hemp ropes tightly on its neck'; *lapsus rotarum* (literally 'the glidings of wheels') is a very ornate phrase, cf. *remigium alarum* (1.301).

5 238. **feta armis**: for the metaphor see note on 20.

6 241f. Aeneas' invocation is based on Enn. *Scen.* 92f. *o pater, o patria: o Priami domus . . . .*

7 242. **Dardanidum**: for the form of the genitive see note on 3.21.

8 245. Observe how the finality of this line is achieved by slow spondees, alliteration of *s,* use of the powerful word *monstrum,* and juxtaposition of the conflicting religious terms *infelix* and *sacrata.*

9 246-7. Once again, and for the last time, Cassandra prophesies misfortune, and once again is disbelieved. *Fatis . . . futuris* is dative of purpose, a condensed turn for *fatis futuris canendis; credita* agrees with *ora,* not *Cassandra.*

10 248. **esset**: for *futurus esset;* the subjunctive is causal after *miseri quibus* (cf. 231).

11 After the slow moving and reflective final lines describing the entry of the horse within the walls of Troy, the narrative now becomes very rapid. The whole of the book so far has been concerned with whether or not the Trojans will bring the horse into their city; now that they have done so, the immediate and tragic consequences are compressed into just a few lines.

12 250. 'Meanwhile the heavens revolved and night sped up from the Ocean'; the first phrase is from Ennius, *Ann.* 211, the second from Hom. *Od.* 5.294 ορωρει δ ουρανοθεν νυξ the Homeric rhythm is also imitated.

Myrmidonumque[1] dolos; fusi per moenia Teucri
conticuere; sopor fessos complectitur artus.
Et iam Argiva phalanx instructis navibus ibat
a Tenedo tacitae[2] per amica silentia lunae   255
litora nota petens, [3]flammas cum regia puppis
extulerat,[4] fatisque deum defensus iniquis[5]
inclusos utero Danaos et pinea furtim
laxat claustra Sinon. Illos patefactus ad auras
reddit equus, laetique cavo se[6] robore promunt   260
Thessandrus[7] Sthenelusque duces et dirus Ulixes,
demissum lapsi per funem, Acamasque Thoasque
Pelidesque[8] Neoptolemus primusque[9] Machaon
et Menelaus et ipse doli fabricator Epeos.
Invadunt urbem somno vinoque sepultam;   265
caeduntur vigiles, portisque patentibus omnis[10]
accipiunt socios atque agmina conscia iungunt.

---

1 252. **Myrmidonumque**: see note on 7; here the word is used generally for the Greeks.

2 255. 'in the friendly silence of the quiet moon', i.e. in the still of night advantageous for their purpose. Some commentators have argued that *tacita* means 'not visible', as *luna silens* is used of the night before the new moon (cf. Cato *De Agr.* 29); but the descriptive impact of the phrase is like Catullus' *quam sidera multa, cum tacet nox* (7.7; cf. *Geo.* 1.247), or Coleridge's 'quietly shining to the quiet moon'. It is evident in line 340 that the moon is shining; for further references see Austin's note ad loc.

3 256f. The tradition of the fire-signal varied; according to some versions Sinon sent a signal to Agamemnon, and in 6.517 Helen gives a signal to the Greeks (to show them the way after landing). Virgil's account here is appropriately vivid for a narrative centred on Troy; the reader pictures himself in Troy, not in the Greek ships.

4 257. **extulerat**: the tense is strange and has led some editors to think that the construction is *ibat cum extulerat*, 'they were proceeding after Agamemnon had given the sign', an unacceptably weak sense. *Extulerat* like *laxat* is in the inverted *cum* clause: 'they were proceeding when suddenly Agamemnon had given the signal and Sinon is releasing the Greeks. . .'.

5 **iniquis**: i.e. to Troy, cf. 54.

6 260. **se . . . promunt**: 'get themselves out'; the word is not used reflexively before Virgil. Austin says 'the Greeks cheerfully decant themselves from the Horse's depths'.

7 261f. The men in the horse are in groups of three, each containing one of the leading G reek generals — Ulysses, Neoptolemus, Menelaus. Thessandrus was a son of Polynices, Sthenelus a close friend of Diomedes, Acamas a son of Theseus, Thoas a Homeric hero (*Il.* 2.638f.), Machaon a surgeon, Epeos, as Virgil tells us (cf. Hom. *Od.* 8.493), the maker of the horse which Ulysses had invented.

8 263. **Pelidesque Neoptolemus**: Neoptolemus (Pyrrhus) was the son of Achilles, and grandson of Peleus; his prominent part in the story is told in lines 469f.

9 **primusque Machaon**: *primus* is strange, but presumably means 'chieftain', cf. *Il.* 11.506; it does not mean that he was first to come out (being mentioned seventh), nor that he was a leading surgeon.

10 266-7. Notice how the fourth foot coincidence in 266 prepares for the even more decisive coincidence (diaeresis before and after a dactyl) of 267; see note on 1.7.

268-97. The ghost of Hector appears to Aeneas, and tells him that he must escape from Troy, taking with him Troy's sacred emblems and the Penates.

[1]Tempus erat quo prima quies mortalibus aegris
incipit et dono divum gratissima serpit.
In somnis, ecce, ante oculos maestissimus Hector   270
visus adesse[2] mihi largosque effundere fletus,
raptatus bigis ut quondam, aterque cruento[3]
pulvere perque pedes traiectus[4] lora tumentis.
Ei mihi, qualis erat,[5] quantum mutatus ab illo
Hectore qui redit[6] exuvias[7] indutus Achilli[8]   275
vel Danaum Phrygios iaculatus puppibiis ignis!
Squalentem barbam et concretos sanguine crinis
vulneraque illa gerens, quae circum plurima muros
accepit patrios. Ultro flens ipse videbar
compellare virum et maestas expromere voces: 280

---

1 268f. Here for the first time in the book Aeneas himself enters his story. The passage is one of the most forceful in the *Aeneid*, with its contrast between the happy sleep of Aeneas, freed at last from anxiety because he believes that the Greeks have gone, and the terse statements of doom which he receives from Hector's ghost. The reversal of events is total: Aeneas believes that the long ordeal is over; Hector tells him that there is no chance whatever of Troy's survival. The themes of the *Aeneid* are briefly set out: the imminent destruction of Troy, the impossibility of its defence; the responsibility of Aeneas for rescuing from the ashes the gods of his city and founding a new home for them. Thus that he should escape when so many died is seen to be a divine destiny, a duty to be accepted, not an act of cowardice. In the course of the book he still shows signs of courting the noble death, and still feels impelled to defend himself for having escaped with his life (431f.), but Hector's words mark the first stage in the transformation of Aeneas from a Trojan warrior to an instrument of fate.

The dream vision is a favourite Virgilian technique for the amalgamation of past, present, and future; it is often used (like prophecies) to emphasise the connexion of the divine plan with human action. This is among the most memorable because it also contains psychological elements of the dreamworld (like Dido's dream in 4.465f.); the confusion of Aeneas and his inability to recall past events. The lonely, sad apparition of Hector, combine to produce an effect of a supernatural world outside the natural. For other prophetic dreams and visions cf. that of the Penates in 3.147f, of Mercury in 4.265f., 556f., of Anchises in 5.722f., of Tiberinus in 8.31f.

2 271. Cf. Lucr. 1.125f. (Ennius' vision of Homer) *speciem lacrimas effundere salsas / coepisse;* Enn. *Ann.* 6 visits *Homerus adesse poeta.*

3 272. 'as he was in days gone by when dragged behind the chariot'; cf. Hom. *Il.* 22.396f., Enn. *Scen.* 101. Austin points out that Dido must have thought of the picture of Hector on the walls of her temple to Juno (1.483). For the ghost still showing the wounds of life cf. *Aen.* 1.353f. (Sychaeus), 6.494f. (Deiphobus), and Tac. *Ann.* 1.65 (Quintilius Varus). The tradition of the dragging of Hector's body round the walls is post-Homeric; see note on 1.483f.

4 273. **traiectus lora**: 'pierced with thongs'. The accusative *lora* is a remarkable instance of a retained accusative (see note on a 10) with a passive verb (*traicere lora per pedes, so traiectus lora per pedes*) where there is no middle idea (as in 275) nor any idea of accusative of respect (as in 221). The nearest parallel in Virgil is *Ecl.* 3.106 (*flores*) *inscripti nomina regum.*

5 274-5. 'Ah me, what a sight! How different indeed from that other Hector who came back wearing the trophies of Achilles, or after hurling Trojan firebrands on the Greek ships.' Servius tells us that the first phrase is from Ennius (*Ann.* 7). Compare Ov. *Met.* 6.273 and Milton, *P.L.* 1.84-5 'But o how fall'n! how chang'd / From him, who in the happy Realms of Light. . . .' Achilles lent his armour to Patroclus, and Hector captured it when he killed Patroclus (*Il.* 17.194f.) The Trojan attack on the Greek ships which they almost set on fire is described in *Il.* 15; also *Il.* 22.374.

6 275. **redit**: the present tense is used very vividly to indicate Aeneas' remembrance of the earlier event side by side with the present vision.

7 **exuvias indutus**: retained accusative after the middle use of *indutus* ('having put on'); cf. 393, 721-2 and note on 210.

8 **Achilli**: for the form of the genitive cf. 7 and note on 1.30. Contrast line476 (*Achillis*). 277-8. 'with matted beard, hair clotted with blood, and those wounds, those many wounds he received around the walls of his native city'. Cf. Hom. *Il.* 22.367f.

'o[1] lux Dardaniae, spes o fidissima Teucrum,
quae tantae tenuere morae? Quibus Hector ab oris
exspectate[2] venis? Ut[3] te post multa tuorum
funera, post varios hominumque urbisque labores
defessi aspicimus! Quae causa indigna serenos   285
foedavit vultus? Aut cur haec vulnera cerno?'
Ille nihil, nec me quaerentem vana moratur,[4]
sed graviter gemitus imo de pectore ducens,
'heu[5] fuge, nate dea, teque his' ait 'eripe flammis.
Hostis habet muros; ruit alto[6] a culmine Troia.   290
Sat patriae Priamoque datum: si Pergama dextra
defendi possent, etiam hac defensa fuissent.
Sacra suosque tibi commendat Troia penatis;[7]
hos cape fatorum comites, his moenia quaere
magna[8] pererrato statues quae denique ponto.'   295
Sic ait et manibus vittas Vestamque potentem[9]
aeternumque adytis effert penetralibus ignem.

> *298-317. Aeneas awakes, climbs to the roof of his father's house, sees the scenes of destruction all around him and wildly prepares to rush to the battle.*

Diverso[10] interea miscentur moenia luctu,
et magis atque magis, quamquam secreta parentis[11]
Anchisae domus arboribusque obtecta recessit,   300

---

1 281f. Aeneas' words have the inconsequential nature of a dream: in reality he knew only too well the manner of Hector's death. In his dream he remembers only that Hector has recently been absent from the Trojan ranks, and in phrases of intense pathos asks him why. Macrobius (*Sat.* 6.2.18) quotes a passage from Ennius (*Scen.* 72f.) *o lux Troiae, germane Hector, / quid ita cum tuo lacerato corpore / miser es, aut qui te sic respectantibus / tractavere nobis?*

2 283. **exspectate**: vocative, agreeing with *Hector;* the sense is somewhat predicative, cf. *Aen.* 12.947.

3 **ut**: with *aspicimus,* equivalent to 'how gladly', cf *Aen.* 8.154f.

4 287. **moratur**: 'heed', cf. *Aen.* 5.400.

5 289f. Hector's speech justifies the flight of Aeneas from Troy, which in certain traditions had been regarded as a coward's way out. He begins by giving precise instructions; Aeneas is to escape; and he follows with the reasons. First, Troy cannot be saved, all that could be done has been done; secondly, Aeneas has a destiny to fulfil in taking Troy's gods to a new home over the sea. Servius' comments stress that Hector shows Aeneas' flight to be *utile, necessarium* and *honestum.*

6 290. **alto a culmine**: 'from its topmost heights', the Greek κατ ακρης (*Il.* 13.772); cf. 603.

7 293. **penatis**: cf. *Aen.* 1.6 *inferretque deos Latio,* with the note there, and 3.148f.

8 295. 'for them seek a city, which in the end you shall establish, a mighty city, when you have wandered over the ocean's width'; cf. *Aen.* 3.159 f. *Magna* belongs rather to the relative clause than to the main clause.

9 296-7. These are the *sacra* of 293; Vesta, the goddess of the hearth, is very closely linked with the Penates, cf. 5.744, 9.258f. For the undying fire on her altar at Rome cf. Ov. *Fast.* 6.297.

10 298. **diverso . . . luctu:** 'the city was a turmoil of grief everywhere'; Virgil is very fond of *misceri* to describe confusion, cf. 329, 487, 1.124, 12.445.

11 299-300. 'although the house of my father Anchises was in a remote part, set back and screened by trees'.

clarescunt sonitus armorumque ingruit[1] horror.
Excutior somno et summi fastigia tecti
ascensu[2] supero atque arrectis auribus asto:
in segetem veluti cum flamma furentibus Austris[3]
incidit, aut rapidus montano flumine torrens   305
sternit agros, sternit sata laeta boumque labores
praecipitisque trahit silvas; stupet inscius[4] alto
accipiens sonitum saxi de vertice pastor.
Tum vero manifesta fides,[5] Danaumque patescunt
insidiae. Iam Deiphobi[6] dedit ampla ruinam   310
Volcano[7] superante domus, iam proximus ardet
Ucalegon;[8] Sigea[9] igni freta lata relucent.
Exoritur clamorque virum clangorque tubarum.
Arma amens capio; nec sat rationis in armis,[10]
sed glomerare[11] manum bello et concurrere in arcem   315
cum sociis ardent animi; furor iraque mentem
praecipitat, pulchrumque[12] mori succurrit in armis.

---

1 301. **ingruit**: 'advanced upon us', cf. *Aen*, 8.535.

2 303. **ascensu supero**: 'climbed onto', cf. *Aen.* 6.676.

3 304f. The main point of the comparison in this brilliant simile is that Aeneas and the shepherd both helplessly watch and listen from a height while destruction occurs all round. The Homeric simile on which it is based (*Il.* 4.452f.) compares a battle scene with two rivers meeting, while a shepherd listens from the mountains; Virgil has taken the detail of the shepherd from Homer and made it central in his picture. For the comparison with both fire and flood cf. *Aen.* 12.521f. and for flood cf. also 496f., Hor. *Odes* 3.29.33f., 4.14.25f., Spenser, *F.Q.*, 2.11.18.

4 307. **inscius**: 'bewildered', almost 'helpless'; it was a situation which he had not known before.

5 309. **fides**: 'the proof', cf. *Aen.* 3.375; or perhaps with bitter sarcasm 'the trustworthiness of the Greeks', i.e. their perfidy.

6 310. The Trojan Deiphobus, who had married Helen after the death of Paris, appears to Aeneas in the underworld (6.494f.).

7 **311. Volcano**: the name of the fire-god is used by metonymy for fire, cf. Ceres, Bacchus, etc.

8 312. **Ucalegon**: a well known example of metonymy for *domus Ucalegonis* (cf. Hor. *Sat.* 1.5.71-2); Horace (*Ep.* 1.18.84) alludes to this passage, and so does Juvenal (3.199). Ucalegon was one of Priam's friends (Hom. *Il.* 3.148).

9 **Sigea . . . relucent**: Sigeum was a promontory near Troy, cf. *Aen.* 7.294. The phrase is imitated by Dryden, *Annus Mirabilis* 231 (of the Fire of London): 'A key of fire ran all along the shore, / And lighten'd all the river with the blaze'.

10 314f. In these lines Aeneas shows the typical characteristics of the Homeric hero courting a brave death: thoughts of valour drive out *ratio*, and he is a victim of *furor* and *ira*. This wild and impetuous attitude is one he has to try to learn to conquer as he leaves the Homeric world and journeys towards a different way of life; but his success in conquering it is intermittent and imperfect.

11 315. **glomerare manum bello**: 'to mass together a group for fighting'. *Glomerare* is a favourite word with Virgil; for this sense cf. 9.792.

12 317. 'my thoughts were of the glory of death in battle'; *pulchrum* (*esse*) *mori in armis* is the subject of *succurrit* (= *subit*). For the thought cf. Hor. *Odes* 3.2.13 *dulce et decorum est pro patria mori*.

318-69. Panthus, priest of Apollo, arrives at Anchises' house and tells him that the city is lost. With a few companions Aeneas goes into battle.

Ecce autem telis Panthus[1] elapsus Achivum,
Panthus Othryades, arcis[2] Phoebique sacerdos,
sacra manu victosque deos[3] parvumque[4] nepotem   320
ipse trahit cursuque amens ad limina[5] tendit.
'Quo[6] res summa loco, Panthu? Quam[7] prendimus arcem?'
Vix ea fatus eram gemitu cum talia reddit:
'venit summa dies et ineluctabile tempus[8]
Dardaniae. Fuimus[9] Troes, fuit Ilium et ingens   325
gloria Teucrorum; ferus omnia[10] Iuppiter Argos
transtulit;[11] incensa Danai dominantur in urbe.
Arduus armatos mediis in moenibus astans
fundit equus victorque Sinon incendia[12] miscet
insultans.[13] Portis alii bipatentibus[14] adsunt,   330
milia quot magnis umquam venere Mycenis;

---

1 318. **Panthus:** the word is contracted from Panthoos in the Greek style and has a long *u* in the nominative and in Virgil's vocative form *Panthu* (322). Servius tells us how Panthus, the son of Othryas, had been captured from Delphi, brought to Troy, and made priest of Apollo by Priam. He is mentioned in Hom. *Il*.3.146.

2 319. **arcis Phoebique:** i.e. of the temple of Apollo on the citadel.

3 320-1. The verb *trahit* applies strictly only to the third of its objects; to the first two supply from it a verb like *portat. Sacra* are the emblems of which Hector had spoken; *deos* refers to images of the gods, especially of the Penates; cf. 293.

4 320. **parvumque nepotem:** we hear no more of Panthus' little grandchild. Austin's comment is excellent: 'he is a pathetic prolepsis, as it were, of Iulus'.

5 321. **limina:** i.e. Anchises' house, which Aeneas is just leaving.

6 322. **quo ... loco:** 'Where is the decisive battle?' For the meaning of *res summa* cf. Livy 23.49.8 *ibi rem summam agi cernentes.* Others take *quo . . . loco* to be metaphorical — 'in what condition', (so Austin, comparing *Aen.* 9.723, Hor. *Epist.* 1.12.25); others again take *res summa* as equivalent to *respublica* ('how is our country?'), but this is very unlikely. Aeneas eagerly and rapidly asks which way to go to join the last stand; the slow and hopeless reply of Panthus is in very strong contrast.

7 **quam . . . arcem:** 'what strong point are we holding'; *arx* is used in its widest sense, referring not specifically to the citadel, but to any point which could be held; *prendimus* is probably perfect, literally 'have we taken?'

8 324. The movement of the line reflects Panthus' hopelessness; the slow spondee filling the first foot, the sonorous adjective of inevitability *ineluctabile* (not found before Virgil, cf. *Aen.* 8.334), and the assonance of long *e*, combine to produce a memorable opening to Panthus' speech comparable with the splendid lines of Homer (*Il.* 6.448f.) εσσεται ημαρ .... Macrobius (*Sat.* 5.1.9) quotes this passage as an example of *copiosissime dicere,* and continues *quis fons quis torrens quod mare tot fluctibus quot hic verbis inundavit?*

9 325. **fuimus:** 'have been', i.e. are no more; the perfect tense conveys that all is over. Cf. *Aen.* 7413 *sed fortuna fuit,* Prop. 2.8.10 *altaque Troia fuit.* Dryden imitates the construction in *All for Love* (5.1.75f.): 'O horror, horror! / Egypt has been; our latest hour is come!'

10 326-7. **omnia . . . Argos transtulit:** 'has handed over everything we had to Argos', cf. Hor. *Odes* 3.29.51 (*Fortuna*) *transmutat incertos honores. Argos* is accusative plural of motion towards.

11 327-8. Notice the alliteration of pairs of words, adding to the emphasis of the words themselves.

12 329. **incendia miscet:** 'hurls firebrands all around'; for *miscere* cf. 298.

13 330. **insultans:** 'mocking us'; the emphatic position of this word conveys the irony of the Trojans now suffering at the hands of the prisoner they had treated kindly.

14 **bipatentibus:** 'double' gates (cf. Enn. *Ann.* 61, *Aen.* 10.5), emphasising that both halves are flung wide open.

obsedere alii telis angusta[1] viarum
oppositis; stat ferri acies[2] mucrone corusco
stricta, parata neci; vix primi proelia temptant
portarum vigiles et caeco Marte resistunt.'			335
Talibus Othryadae dictis et numine[3] divum
in flammas et in arma feror, quo tristis Erinys,[4]
quo fremitus vocat et sublatus ad aethera clamor.
Addunt se socios Rhipeus et maximus armis
Epytus, oblati per lunam, Hypanisque Dymasque			340
et lateri adglomerant[5] nostro, iuvenisque Coroebus
Mygdonides — illis ad Troiam forte diebus
venerat insano Cassandrae incensus amore
et gener[6] auxilium Priamo Phrygibusque ferebat,
infelix qui non sponsae praecepta furentis			345
audierit![7]
Quos ubi confertos audere[8] in proelia vidi,
incipio super[9] his: 'iuvenes, fortissima frustra
pectora, si[10] vobis audendi extrema cupido
certa sequi, quae sit rebus fortuna videtis:			350
excessere[11] omnes adytis arisque relictis
di quibus imperium hoc steterat; succurritis urbi
incensae; moriamur[12] et in media arma ruamus.

---

1 332. **angusta viarum**: cf. *strata viarum* (t .422, where see note), and line 725.

2 333. 'a steel line of flashing blades unsheathed stands ready to slaughter us'; for *acies* cf. *Aen*. 6.291. The ablative of description *mucrone corusco* acts almost as a compound adjective with *acies;* see Mackail's edition of the *Aeneid,* Appendix A.

3 336. **numine divum**: Panthus as the priest of Apollo expresses the will of the gods, and Aeneas hearing that they intend the destruction of Troy rushes madly out to sell his life dearly (353-4).

4 337. **Erinys**: the Greek Fury (573, 7.447), the personification of the force leading to destruction.

5 341. **adglomerant**: the word is transitive, and *se* is to be supplied from 339, cf. *Aen*. 1.440.
Coroebus, son of Mygdon king of Phrygia, is first mentioned in Eur. *Rhes*. 539; Virgil has given him the part of Othryoneus in Homer *Il*. 13.363f. who came late (*illis . . . diebus*) to Troy to help the Trojans in the hope of marrying Cassandra (246).

6 344. **gener**: 'would-be son-in-law', cf. *Ecl*. 8.18.

7 346. **audierit**: causal subjunctive. The incomplete line conveys most poignantly a sense of frustration and pathos, and would have been very difficult to complete effectively in revision, but it cannot be regarded as a deliberate device; see note on 1.534.

8 347. **audere in proelia**: a very unusual phrase, cf. Stat. *Th*. 1.439. Gronovius' conjecture *ardere* is attractive.

9 348. **super**: adverbial; his speech is intended to add to their existing enthusiasm, cf. 355 *furor additus;* compare *Aen*. 10.556, 11.685. With *his* supply *dictis.*

10 349-50. **si vobis . . . sequi**: 'if your enthusiasm to put all to the hazard is resolved to follow me'. Some MSS have *audentem* — 'if your enthusiasm is resolved to follow me as I put all to the hazard'. Neither is wholly satisfactory and the passage might well have been revised; the emendations carry little conviction.

11 351-2. **excessere . . . di**: cf. Tac. *Hist*. 5.13 (the siege of Jerusalem) *audita maior humana vox, excedere deos*. See Austin ad loc. for the *evocatio deorum* at the destruction of a city.

12 353. **moriamur ... ruamus**: a famous example of the grammarians' hysteron proteron. Page rightly points out the inadequacy of this explanation; see also my note on *Aen*. 5.316 (OUP Ed.). The more important verb is put first, and the impact of the sentence is 'Let us die, and let us do so by rushing into battle'. Notice the absence of strong caesurae, and the assonance of *a* and *r.*

Una[1] salus victis nullam sperare salutem.'
Sic animis iuvenum furor additus. Inde, [2]lupi[3] ceu   355
raptores atra in nebula, quos improba[4] ventris
exegit caecos rabies catulique relicti
faucibus exspectant siccis, per tela, per hostis
vadimus haud dubiam in mortem mediaeque[5] tenemus
urbis iter; nox atra cava[6] circumvolat umbra.   360
Quis cladem illius noctis, quis funera fando
explicet aut possit lacrimis aequare labores?
Urbs antiqua ruit multos dominata per annos;[7]
plurima perque vias sternuntur inertia[8] passim
corpora perque domos et religiosa[9] deorum   365
limina. Nec soli poenas dant sanguine Teucri;
quondam[10] etiam victis redit in praecordia virtus
victoresque cadunt Danai. Crudelis ubique
luctus, ubique pavor[11] et plurima mortis imago.

370-401. The Greek Androgens mistakes the Trojans for Greeks; he and his followers are killed and the Trojans disguise themselves in Greek armour.

Primus se Danaum magna comitante caterva   370
Androgeos[12] offert nobis, socia agmina credens
inscius, atque ultro verbis compellat amicis
'festinate, viri! nam quae tam sera moratur

---

1 354. The gnomic line (*sententia*) is of a kind not very common in Virgil, but frequent in Lucan and the Silver Age; cf. Stat. *Th.* 10.493 *est ubi dat vires nimius timor.*

2 355f. Wolf similes occur several times in Homer; there are three others in the *Aeneid*, two of them applied to Turnus (9.59f. 9.565f., 11.809f.). The effect here is to reinforce the concept of *furor*, and to suggest the wild and violent anger of the Trojans in this moment of the final destruction of their city.

3 355. **lupi ceu:** the unusual word order and line ending suggest the Homeric λυκοι ως.

4 356. **improba:** 'irresistible', cf. 80 with note, and 9.62.

5 359-60. **mediaeque . . . iter:** 'the road through the centre of the city', possessive genitive, cf. *Aen.* 9.391f.

6 360. **cava:** 'enfolding', cf. *Aen.* 1.516, 6.866.

7 363. The simplicity and finality of this line makes it one of the most memorable of the whole poem — 'in one sad night consum'd and throwen down' (Spenser, *F.Q.* 3.9.39). Austin compares Livy 1.29.6.

8 364. **inertia:** 'unmoving', i.e. lifeless, rather than 'helpless'.

9 365. **religiosa:** for the long first syllable see note on 151.

10 367. **quondam:** 'sometimes', cf. 416, 7.378.

11 369. **pavor:** for the lengthening of the final syllable (which in this case was long in early Latin) in arsis cf. 411, 563 and see note on 1.308. Notice the rhythm of the paragraph ending (cf. 267), and for the phraseology cf. Tac. *Hist.* 3.28 *omni imagine mortium.*

12 371. **Androgeos:** the name of a Greek not otherwise known; it was also the name of Minos' son (6.20). Notice the long final syllable (the Greek Attic second declension) and the Greek genitive *Androgeo* (392).

segnities? Alii rapiunt[1] incensa feruntque
Pergama: vos celsis nunc primum a navibus itis?'   375
Dixit, et extemplo (neque enim responsa dabantur
fida satis) sensit[2] medios delapsus in hostis.
Obstipuit retroque pedem cum voce repressit.
Improvisum[3] aspris[4] veluti qui sentibus anguem
pressit humi nitens[5] trepidusque repente refugit   380
attollentem iras et caerula colla[6] tumentem,
haud secus Androgeos visu tremefactus abibat.[7]
Inruimus densis[8] et circumfundimur armis,
ignarosque loci passim et formidine captos
sternimus; aspirat[9] primo Fortuna labori.   385
Atque hic successu exsultans animisque Coroebus
'o socii, qua prima' inquit 'Fortuna salutis
monstrat iter, quaque ostendit se dextra, sequamur:
mutemus clipeos Danaumque insignia nobis
aptemus. [10]Dolus an virtus, quis in hoste requirat?   390
Arnia dabunt ipsi.' Sic fatus deinde comantem[11]
Androgeo[12] galeam clipeique[13] insigne decorum
induitur[14] laterique Argivum accommodat ensem.
Hoc Rhipeus, hoc ipse[15] Dymas omnisque iuventus

---

1 374. **rapiunt. . . feruntque**: cf. the Greek phrase for plundering, αγειν και φεριν.

2 377. **sensit . . . delapus**: *sentio* with a participle (instead of accusative and infinitive) is an unparalleled imitation of the normal Greek construction after such verbs; Austin quotes Milton, *P.L.* 9.792 'and knew not eating death'. Instances such as *Geo.* 2.510 *gaudent perfusi sanguine fratrum* (cited by commentators) are quite normal Latin.

3 379f. The simile is an elaborate reworking of Hom. *Il.* 3.32f. where Paris draws back from the battle like a man who has seen a snake. Virgil has characteristically varied and decorated his original, especially in adding a description of the snake (381).

4 379. **aspris**: a very rare syncope for *asperis*, cf. the common cases of *periclum, repostus*, etc.

5 380-1. Notice the sound effects: the slowness of *nitens* ('treading on it') followed by the very rapid dactyls with trochaic caesurae, and the rhyme in the descriptive line which after the action of 380 focusses on the picture of the snake (for which cf. *Geo.* 3.421). *Attollentem iras* combines the ideas of rousing up its anger and lifting its angry head.

6 381. **colla**: Greek accusative of respect, see note on 1.320.

7 382. **abibat**: 'was trying to escape'. Servius says 'bene imperfecto usus est, non enim abiit'.

8 383. **densis . . . armis**: 'and we surround him with our massed weapons'; *circumfundimur* is middle, or reflexive, cf. 401.

9 385. **aspirat**: 'smiles on'; the metaphor is from a favouring breeze, cf. *Aen.* 9.525, Ov. *Met.* 1.3.

10 390. The staccato phrasing (for *utrum dolus sit an virtus*) is in keeping with the rest of Coroebus' rapid words.

11 391. For postponed *deinde* cf. *Aen.* 1.195; compare *tum* in 5.382.

12 392. **Androgeo**: genitive, see note on 3 71.

13 **clipeique . . . decorum**: 'the handsome device of his shield', i.e. his shield with its handsome device. *Insigne* is used as a noun, cf. *Aen.* 7.657 *insigne paternum*, Livy 29.25.11.

14 393. **induitur**: middle, see note on 275. Servius explains that the shield is 'put on' by inserting the hand through the straps; cf. 672.

15 394. **ipse**: the word is somewhat redundant, but the view reported by Servius that the passage should be punctuated so that *ipse* = *Aeneas* is quite impossible.

laeta facit: spoliis se quisque recentibus armat.   395
Vadimus immixti Danais haud[1] numine nostro
multaque per caecam congressi proelia noctem
conserimus, multos Danaum demittimus Orco.[2]
Diffugiunt alii ad navis et litora cursu
fida petunt; [3]pars ingentem formidine turpi   400
scandunt rursus equum et nota conduntur in alvo.

> *402-52. Coroebus sees Cassandra being dragged away into captivity and tries to save her; in the fighting which follows many of Aeneas' companions are killed. Aeneas with two friends finds himself near Priam's palace which is on the point of capture.*

[4]Heu[5] nihil invitis fas quemquam fidere divis![6]
Ecce trahebatur passis Priameia virgo
crinibus a templo Cassandra adytisque Minervae
ad caelum tendens ardentia lumina[7] frustra,   405
lumina, nam teneras arcebant vincula palmas.
Non tulit hanc speciem furiata mente Coroebus
et sese medium iniecit periturus in agmen.
Consequimur cuncti et densis incurrimus armis.
Hic primum ex alto delubri[8] culmine telis   410

---

1 396. **haud numine nostro**: 'protected by gods not our own'; almost 'under false colours'.

2 398. **Orco**: for the dative cf. 85 and 5.691-2 *morti / ... demitte.*

3 400-1. The concept of Greeks rushing back again into the wooden horse is most unconvincing; it is rare for Virgil to indulge in hyperbolical conceits of the kind beloved by many Silver Age writers.

4 402f. This passage affords under close analysis an example of a relatively unrevised section of the poem; it contains some exceptionally fine writing and some imperfections that would doubtless have undergone revision. The pathos of the picture of Cassandra and the devotion of Coroebus (403-8) is superbly done, and so is the sad account of the deaths of Aeneas' comrades, especially Rhipeus and Panthus, followed by Aeneas' magnificent outburst of emotion (424-34). The linking passages are less successful: line 409 is repetitive of 383; the recognition of the disguised Trojans (413f., 422f.) is somewhat unclear in narration; the simile (416f.) is of a conventional kind, made memorable only by its superb word-music. Lines 434-6 add detail which is less relevant than is usually the case; 436 is awkwardly expressed; the sentence in 438-41 is syntactically clumsy; the use of *has* in 450 is strange. The contrast with the high polish of the previous parts of this book serves to emphasise the extraordinary skill and uniform perfection to which Virgil aspired in the workmanship of his fully revised work. This does not of course imply that the relatively unrevised parts of the poem (among which the second half of Book 2 is clearly to be counted) are inferior in their high poetic qualities; they do however lack the touch here and there which would have brought them up to the level of finish which the *Georgics* have and most of the *Aeneid* has, the quality of never nodding (*aequalitas*) which Quintilian praises (10.1.86).

5 402. 'Alas, nobody may put any trust in the gods when they are hostile', i.e. the gods have decided on the destruction of Troy, and so the success of Aeneas and his followers cannot last.

6 403f. For the story of how Ajax son of Oileus violated the temple of Athena (226) by dragging off her priestess Cassandra see note on 1.41.

7 405-6. **lumina frustra, lumina:** for the use of repetition to achieve pathos (perhaps a specially Alexandrian feature of style) cf. *Aen.* 6.495-6 *lacerum crudeliter ora, / ora manusque ambas, Aen.* 10.821-2 *at vera ut vultum vidit morientis et ora, / ora modis Anchisiades pallentia miris, Aen.* 12.546-7 *domus alta sub Ida, / Lyrnesi domus alta, solo Laurente sepulcrum.* Austin quotes Milton, *Lycidas* 'But O the heavy change now thou art gone, / now thou art gone, and never must return'.

8 410. **delubri:** i.e. of Athena's temple.

nostrorum obruimur[1] oriturque miserrima caedes
armorum[2] facie et Graiarum errore iubarum.
Tum[3] Danai gemitu atque ereptae virginis ira
undique collecti invadunt, acerrimus Aiax[4]
et gemini Atridae Dolopumque exercitus omnis;   415
adversi rupto[5] ceu quondam turbine venti[6]
confligunt, Zephyrusque Notusque et laetus Eois
Eurus equis; stridunt silvae saevitque tridenti
spumeus atque imo Nereus[7] ciet aequora fundo.
Illi etiam, si quos obscura nocte per umbram   420
fudimus insidiis totaque agitavimus urbe,
apparent; primi[8] clipeos mentitaque[9] tela
agnoscunt atque ora[10] sono discordia signant.
Ilicet[11] obruimur numero, primusque Coroebus
Penelei dextra divae armipotentis[12] ad aram   425
procumbit; cadit et Rhipeus, iustissimus unus
qui fuit in Teucris et servantissimus aequi
(dis[13] aliter visum); pereunt Hypanisque Dymasque

---

1 411. **obruimur:** for the lengthening of the final syllable in arsis before the caesura see note on 369.

2 412. 'from (because of) the appearance of our armour and the confusion caused by our Greek plumes'.

3 413. 'Then the Greeks shouting in frustration and angry at the maiden's rescue . . .'; we may assume from this the initial success of Coroebus in rescuing Cassandra. For *gemitu* cf. *Aen.* 3.664; for *ereptae virginis* (objective genitive) cf. Livy 37.51.6 *ira provinciae ereptae.*

4 414-15. Ajax son of Oileus is here referred to; see note on 403f. The mention of the Atridae, Menelaus and Agamemnon, is significant because Cassandra became Agamemnon's slave-girl. For *Dolopes* see note on 7.

5 416. **rupto . . . turbine:** 'when a whirlwind breaks', cf. *Geo.* 3.428.

6 416f. The simile of winds meeting is based on Hom. *Il.* 9.4f.; the passage is also reminiscent of the storm description in *Aen.* 1.82f.

7 418-19. The alliteration of *s* is very heavy, and the postponement of the subject (Nereus); cf. *Aen.* 7.464f. adds to the elaborate effect. Here the lesser sea-god is given Neptune's trident.

8 422. **primi:** this is difficult (because the Trojans have already been attacked, 413f.), and has given rise to suggested transpositions (420-3 to follow 412) and even to acceptance of *P's* reading *Priami.* It is best to take it to mean that these men were the first to be able to explain the confusion.

9 **mentitaque tela**: 'quae nos Graecos esse mentiebantur' (Servius).

10 423. **ora . . . signant:** 'they observe that our speech sounds different'; the epic convention in Virgil as in Homer (a necessary one) is that the Trojans and the Greeks speak the same language, but in a situation like this the more likely idea of different languages is an easily acceptable inconsistency. For *signant = discernunt* cf. perhaps *Aen.* 5.317.

11 424. **ilicet**: 'instantly', cf. 758.

12 425. Athena is often called *armipotens;* cf. *Aen.* 11.483.

13 428. **dis aliter visum**: this is a Stoic formula, here used very elliptically — you might have thought he would therefore have been spared, but the gods willed otherwise; cf. Sen. *Ep. Mot.* 98.4-5 where the good Stoic is urged to say when disaster befalls *dis aliter visum est,* or better still *di melius.* For Virgil the Stoic formula left the problem unanswered.

confixi a sociis; nec te tua plurima, [1]Panthu,
labentem pietas nec Apollinis infula texit.   430
Iliaci cineres et flamma extrema meorum,
testor, in occasu vestro nec tela nec ullas
vitavisse[2] vices Danaum, et, si fata fuissent
ut caderem, meruisse manu. Divellimur inde,
Iphitus et Pelias mecum (quorum Iphitus aevo   435
iam gravior, Pelias et[3] vulnere tardus Ulixi),
protinus ad sedes Priami clamore vocati.
Hic[4] vero ingentem pugnam ceu cetera nusquam
bella forent, nulli[5] tota morerentur in urbe,
sic Martem indomitum Danaosque ad tecta mentis   440
cernimus obsessumque[6] acta testudine limen.
Haerent[7] parietibus[8] scalae postisque sub ipsos
nituntur gradibus clipeosque ad[9] tela sinistris
protecti obiciunt, prensant fastigia dextris.
Dardanidae contra turris ac tota[10] domorum   445
culmina convellunt; his se, quando ultima cernunt,
extrema iam in morte parant defendere telis,
auratasque trabes, veterum decora[11] alta parentum,
devolvunt; alii strictis mucronibus imas
obsedere fores, has servant agmine denso.   450

---

1 429f. The pathos builds up in this little cameo; the apostrophe to Panthus emphasises it, and what claims he had on the favour of the gods; the alliteration of *p* and the present participle (bringing the actuality of the scene to the reader) add to the effect. Cf. *Aen.* 9.327-8. Thus the emotional pitch is raised in readiness for Aeneas' outburst as he invokes his burning city, again emphasised and made memorable by alliteration (of *c, m, v, f, m*), especially in the strange phrase *flamma extrema meorum* ('the final fire that engulfed my people'). The word *occasus* (several times used by Cicero in this sense, cf. also *Aen.* 1.238) carries powerful emotional overtones.

2 433. **vitavisse vices Danaum**: for the omission of the subject *me* cf. *Aen.* 6.352. *Vices Danaum* should be taken together 'hazards from the Greeks', vicissitudes of battle; it is a powerful and unexpected phrase made easier by the preceding *tela*. It is most unlikely that *Danaum* should be taken with *manu*, as in the punctuation of Mynors, Hirtzel and others.

3 436. **et**: the meaning, awkwardly expressed, is that Iphitus was disabled by old age and Pelias also disabled with a wound from Ulysses.

4 438f. This is an unrefined sentence with *sic* breaking the run of the syntax; the passage from 434-51 lacks its *ultima manus* (see note on 402f.).

5 439. **nulli**: rare in the plural, cf. *Geo.* 2.10.

6 441. **obsessumque . . . limen**: 'the entrance to the palace besieged by a tortoise formation'; *testudo* refers probably to the cover of shields held over the head rather than the siege engine later developed and given this name; cf. *Aen.* 9.505.

7 442f. The arrangement of the scenes of battle is chiastic: the Greeks attack the gates (441), and others climb the walls (442-4); the Trojans defend the walls (445-9) and the gates (449-50).

8 442. **parietibus**: the first syllable is lengthened by the treatment of the following *i* as a *j*; see note on 16.

9 443. **ad tela**: most MSS have *ac tela*, but *ad* was preferred by Servius ('id est, contra tela'), and *clipeosque ac tela* make an odd pair for *sinistris*.

10 445. **tota**: most MSS have *tecta*, but this would be a feeble adjective for *culmina*.

11 448. **decora alta**: cf. *Aen.* 1.429. Some MSS have *ilia* (cf. 503), but *alta* is better with *devolvunt*; cf. also Stat. *Th.* 5.424.

Instaurati[1] animi regis succurrere tectis
auxilioque levare viros vimque addere victis.

> *453-505. Aeneas gets on to the roof of Priam's palace by means of a back entrance, and joins in dislodging a tower on to the besiegers. But they still come on, and Pyrrhus breaches the gates; the Greeks pour into the palace and massacre the Trojans.*

[2]Limen erat caecaeque fores et pervius usus[3]
tectorum inter se Priami, postesque relicti
a tergo, infelix qua se, dum regna manebant,   455
saepius Andromache ferre incomitata solebat
ad[4] soceros et avo puerum Astyanacta[5] trahebat.
Evado[6] ad summi fastigia culminis, unde
tela manu miseri iactabant inrita Teucri.
Turrim[7] in praecipiti stantem summisque sub astra   460
eductam tectis, unde omnis Troia videri[8]
et Danaum solitae naves et Achaica castra,
adgressi ferro circum, qua[9] summa labantis
iuncturas tabulata dabant, convellimus altis
sedibus impulimusque; [10]ea lapsa repente ruinam   465
cum sonitu trahit et Danaum super agmina late

---

1 451. **instaurati animi**: 'my courage revived'; the following infinitives are after the idea of desire (*rursus ardebam*) conveyed by the phrase.

2 453-505. Here the narrative moves to an elevated pitch of horror, preparatory to the climax in the death of Priam. Domestic touches are interwoven in the military narrative (455f., 483f., 489f., 501f.), and the picture of Pyrrhus in his insolent power is drawn in the most compelling colours (469f, 479f., especially 491f. *instat vi patria Pyrrhus,* 499f. *furentem caede Neoptolemum*). By arranging his narrative so that Aeneas climbs to the roof to join the defenders Virgil is able to make Aeneas' eyewitness narrative of the horror within (of which he was a powerless spectator) well imaged and detailed.

3 453-5. 'There was an entrance, a hidden gate and a through passage linking the parts of Priam's palace together, a remote doorway in the rear. . .'. For *usus* Servius says verbum iuris (i.e. right-of-way); Currie compares (*G. and R.* 1959, p. 165) 'Crooked Usage', a street in Chelsea. For the doorway in the rear cf. Hom. *Od.* 22.126f., Hor. *Epist.* 1.5.31 *atria servantem postico falle clientem.* Evidently Hector and Andromache lived in a part of Priam's palace, and Andromache could make her way privately from the women's quarters by this postern gate and passage from Hector's part into Priam's.

4 457. **ad soceros:** 'to her parents-in-law', i.e. Priam and Hecuba; cf. Ov. *Met.* 3.132 *soceri tibi Marsque Venusque.*

5 **Astyanacta:** Greek accusative. The farewell scene between Hector and his wife and son in Hom. *Il.* 6.402f. is well known; Hector called his son Scamandrius, but everyone else called him Astyanax, prince of the city; cf. *Aen.* 3.482f. Virgil does not refer to his fate at the sack of Troy (he was hurled from the walls to his death), but the reader's knowledge of it adds to the pathos of this passage.

6 458. **evado:** the transition is rather abrupt; Servius says rightly *hac evado,* i.e. Aeneas gets to the roof by means of the back entrance and an inner stairway.

7 460f. Notice the long separation of the accusative *turrim* from its verbs *adgressi, convellimus, impulimusque*; it is interesting that Servius found it necessary to tell his readers 'et est ordo: turrim convellimus'.

8 461. **videri:** supply *solita est;* the tower was a regularly used observation point.

9 463-4. **qua . . . dabant:** 'where the top stories offered joints that would give way'; i.e. at the point where the tower joined the walls from which it rose. Cf. Juv. 10.105f.

10 465. Notice the imitative rhythm: the dactylic feet, the elision at the caesura, the absence of any further masculine caesura, the trochaic breaks in fourth and fifth foot (cf. 380). The effect continues in the following dactylic line, and the 'run-on' verb *incidit.*

incidit. Ast alii subeunt, nec saxa nec ullum
telorum interea cessat genus.

    Vestibulum ante ipsum primoque in limine Pyrrhus[1]
exsultat[2] telis[3] et luce coruscus aëna;   470
qualis[4] ubi in lucem coluber mala[5] gramina pastus,
frigida sub terra tumidum quem bruma tegebat,
nunc, positis novus exuviis nitidusque iuventa,
lubrica convolvit sublato pectore terga
arduus ad solem, et linguis micat ore trisulcis.   475
Una ingens Periphas[6] et equorum agitator Achillis,
armiger Automedon, una omnis Scyria pubes
succedunt tecto et flammas ad culmina iactant.
Ipse inter primos correpta dura bipenni
limina perrumpit postisque a cardine vellit   480
aeratos; [7]iamque excisa trabe firma cavavit
robora et ingentem lato dedit ore fenestram.
Apparet[8] domus intus et atria longa patescunt;
apparent Priami et veterum penetralia regum,

---

1 469. Pyrrhus (also called Neoptolemus, cf. 263) was the son of Achilles; his name means in Greek 'red-haired', and the following line, with its description of light and glitter, hints at the etymology. The end of his story is mentioned in *Aen.* 3.295f.

2 470. **exsultat**: 'prances'; Virgil's choice of word perhaps causes an association with the form of dance known as the Pyrrhic (Eur. *Andr.* 1135f., Plato *Laws* 815a, Pliny *N. H.* 7.204).

3 **telis . . . aëna**: 'fiery in his flashing bronze armour'; cf. Hom. *Il.* 13.341, and cf. Tennyson's phrases in *The Princess* (5.39) 'sheathing splendours and the golden scale / of harness, issued in the sun'.

4 471f. In essence Virgil's simile is based on the idea of shimmering light, note the emphatic position of *in lucem,* coming from the scales of the snake with its old slough (*exuviae*) cast off, but he has added to it the motion of the sinister danger which Pyrrhus presents; observe the Homeric phrase *mala gramina pastus* (βεβρωκὼς κακὰ φαρμακ, *Il.* 22.94) and the description of the snake's fangs (475). Perhaps too we may connect the renewed snake (*novus*) with the renewal of Achilles in Neoptolemus (which in Greek means 'new war'). Spenser imitates the simile (*F.Q.* 4.3.23):
So fresh he seemed and so fierce in sight;
Like as a Snake, whom wearie winters teene
Hath worne to nought, now feeling sommers might,
Casts off his ragged skin and freshly doth him dight.
Lines 473 and 475 are from *Geo.* 3.437 and 439; line 474 from *Geo.* 3.426; for other snake descriptions see on 209-11, and for an excellent account of snake imagery in Book 2 see B. M. W. Knox, *A. J.P.* 1950, pp. 379f.

5 471. **mala gramina pastus**: 'that has fed on evil plants'; for the accusative cf. *Geo.* 3.314, 4.181.

6 476-7. Periphas is an obscure name taken from Homer (*Il.* 5.842); Automedon, the charioteer of Achilles, now armour bearer to his son, is frequently referred to. Pyrrhus was born to Achilles and Deidamia while Achilles was in the island of Scyros, hence *Scyria pubes.*

7 481-2. The previous lines had described Pyrrhus' general assault on the gates, as he tried to break through them with an axe and to tear the posts from their sockets (which is achieved in 492-3); now specifically we hear that he made a hole in the gates by knocking out one of the planks, making a wide, gaping (*lato ore*) opening in them.

8 483-4. The rhythm of line 483 is haunting, with its absence of main caesura in third or fourth foot (cf. 12.619); the repetition *apparet, apparent* at the beginning of both lines and both sentences draws the attention arrestingly to this repugnant military profanation of the domestic city.

armatosque[1] vident stantis in limine primo.   485
At[2] domus interior gemitu[3] miseroque tumultu
miscetur, penitusque[4] cavae plangoribus aedes
femineis ululant; ferit aurea[5] sidera clamor.
Tum pavidae tectis matres ingentibus errant
amplexaeque tenent postis atque oscula figunt.   490
Instat vi[6] patria Pyrrhus; nec claustra nec ipsi
custodes sufferre valent; labat ariete[7] crebro
ianua, et emoti[8] procumbunt cardine postes.
Fit via vi; rumpunt[9] aditus primosque trucidant
immissi Danai et late loca milite complent.   495
Non sic, [10]aggeribus ruptis cum spumeus amnis
exiit oppositasque evicit gurgite moles,
fertur in arva furens cumulo[11] camposque per omnis
cum stabulis armenta trahit. Vidi[12] ipse furentem
caede Neoptolemum geminosque in limine Atridas,   500
vidi Hecubam centumque[13] nurus Priamumque per aras
sanguine foedantem quos ipse sacraverat ignis.
Quinquaginta illi thalami, spes ampla nepotum,
barbarico[14] postes auro spoliisque superbi
procubuere; tenent Danai qua deficit ignis.   505

---

1 485. **armatosque vident**: this is generally taken to mean 'they (the Greeks) see armed men', i.e. the Trojans inside on guard (449, 492); but the imagery of the previous lines requires that the subject of *vident* should be the Trojans inside, Priam and those around him.

2 486f. Servius says this passage is based on the destruction of Alba Longa (i.e. in Ennius: cf. also Livy 1.29).

3 486-7. **gemitu . . . miscetur:** 'is in an uproar of groans and pitiful confusion'; for *miscetur* see note on 298.

4 487-8. **penitusque . . . ululant**: 'and throughout their length and breadth the echoing halls are shrill with the cries of women'; *cavae* ('hollow') helps to produce the effect of the noise, cf. 53. For *ululant* cf. *Aen.* 4.667f., a similar passage describing the scene in Dido's palace when her death was discovered.

5 488. **aurea**: consider the contrast between the beauty of the stars in the heavens and the horror of the earthly scene.

6 491. **vi patria**: cf. *Aen.* 3.326 *stirpis Achilleae fastus;* Pyrrhus has the violence and arrogance of his father Achilles.

7 492. **ariete**: for the scansion see note on 16.

8 493. **emoti . . . postes**: 'the gates, wrenched from their sockets, fall flat'; see Page's note ad loc. for a full account of how these *postes* (part of the gates) were attached by pivots to the *limen* and to the lintel.

9 494. **rumpunt:** 'force', cf. *Aen.* 10.372f. *ferro rumpenda per hostis / est via.*

10 496f. The simile is based on Hom. *Il.* 5.87f.; see also note on 304f. The idea of *reckless* destruction is made prominent by the repetition in the narrative (*furentem*, 499) of *furens* in the simile (498).

11 498. **cumulo:** cf. *Aen.* 1.105.

12 499-501. The repetition (*vidi ipse. . . vidi*) strengthens the pathos and the antithesis between the attackers (Pyrrhus, Menelaus, Agamemnon) and the victims (Hecuba, Priam); cf. Enn. *Scen.* 94f. (referred to on 241f.) *vidi ego te adstantem ope barbarica. . . .*

13 501. **centumque nurus**: i.e. fifty daughters and fifty daughters-in-law (503; cf. *Il.* 6.243f., 24.495f. for Priam's fifty sons). *Nurus* is frequent in Ovid to mean young women generally, e.g. *Met.* 3.529.

14 504. **barbarico . . . auro:** i.e. Eastern gold, cf. *Aen.* 8.685 and the passage from Ennius quoted on 499-501.

506-58. Aeneas tells the story of the death of Priam. The old king had put on his armour and was on his way to meet death at the hands of the enemy when Hecuba prevailed on him to seek sanctuary with her and her daughters at the altar. One of his sons, Polites, had been wounded by Pyrrhus and came running, pursued by Pyrrhus, to the altar, where he fell dead before his father's eyes. Priam's angry outburst is answered by a sword-thrust, and the old king of Troy lies dead.

[1]Forsitan et Priami fuerint quae fata requiras.[2]

Urbis uti captae casum convulsaque vidit

limina tectorum et medium in penetralibus hostem,

arma[3] diu senior desueta trementibus aevo

circumdat nequiquam umeris et inutile ferrum   510

cingitur,[4] ac densos fertur moriturus in hostis.

Aedibus in mediis nudoque sub aetheris axe

ingens ara[5] fuit iuxtaque veterrima laurus

incumbens arae atque umbra complexa penatis.

Hic Hecuba et natae nequiquam altaria circum,   515

praecipites[6] atra ceu tempestate columbae,

condensae et divum amplexae simulacra sedebant.

Ipsum autem sumptis Priamum iuvenalibus armis

ut vidit, 'quae mens tam dira, miserrime coniunx,

impulit his cingi telis? Aut[7] quo ruis? 'Inquit.   520

'Non tali auxilio nec defensoribus[8] istis

---

1 506f. Here the contrast between the violent insolence of the young invader Pyrrhus and the helpless old king and his family is intense and horrifying. The pathos of the domestic scene between Priam and Hecuba is followed by the appearance of Pyrrhus exulting in bloodshed (*ardens insequitur*); the outraged protest of Priam is answered in coldly insolent and sarcastic phrases and Pyrrhus' arrogant *nunc morere* is promptly and heartlessly accomplished. The passage ends by transferring the perspective from the immediate and particularised bloodshed to the long vista of history, where Priam is no longer a brave helpless old man but the symbol of Troy's dead past, the nameless headless corpse who once had been king of Asia's proudest city.
For discussion of the various versions from which Virgil has built his picture of Priam's death see note on 554f.

2 506. After the finality of the previous line, in which the hopelessness of total collapse is conveyed, Aeneas resumes by recounting Priam's death with a line of poignant simplicity, quite without the elaboration of sorrow with which he introduced his story at the beginning of the book.

3 509f. 'he vainly put on those shoulders unsteady with age the armour which in his late years had long been unused, and he fastened round him the sword which he could no longer manage, and moved towards the thick of the enemy to meet death'.

4 511. **cingitur**: used in a middle sense, see notes on 218-19 and 275, and cf. *Aen.* 4.493.

5 513f. The altar to Zeus Herceus (Hom. *Il.* 24.306, Eur. *Tro.* 483. Sen. *Ag.* 448), in the centre of the open courtyard, is here given a Roman aspect by the mention of the Penates.

6 516. For the simile cf. Eur. *Andr.* 1140f. *Praecipites* is elliptical, 'driven headlong'.

7 520. **aut**: this usage, found often in Plautus, merely introduces another question not necessarily alternative to the first; cf. 595 and *Geo.* 4.324.

8 521-2. Hecuba probably means that the situation does not permit of armed resistance (*defensoribus = telis*) and would not even if Hector were alive; possibly however Servius is right in thinking that the second sentence is left incomplete with an ellipsis of words like *Troiam servare posset*.

tempus eget; non, si ipse meus nunc adforet Hector.
Huc tandem concede; haec ara tuebitur omnis,
aut moriere simul.' Sic ore effata recepit
ad sese et sacra longaevum in sede locavit.   525
    Ecce autem elapsus Pyrrhi de caede Polites, [1]
unus natorum Priami, per tela, per hostis
porticibus longis fugit et vacua[2] atria lustrat
saucius. Illum ardens infesto[3] vulnere Pyrrhus
insequitur, iam iamque manu tenet[4] et premit hasta.   530
Ut tandem ante oculos evasit et ora parentum,
concidit ac multo vitam cum sanguine fudit.
hic Priamus, quamquam in media iam morte tenetur,
non tamen abstinuit nec voci iraeque pepercit:
'at tibi pro scelere,' exclamat, 'pro talibus ausis   535
di, si qua est caelo pietas[5] quae talia curet,
persolvant grates dignas et praemia reddant
debita, qui nati coram[6] me cernere letum
fecisti et patrios foedasti funere vultus.
At non ille, satum[7] quo te mentiris, Achilles   540
talis in hoste fuit Priamo; sed iura[8] fidemque
supplicis erubuit corpusque exsangue sepulcro
reddidit Hectoreum meque in mea regna remisit.'
Sic fatus[9] senior telumque imbelle sine[10] ictu
coniecit, rauco quod protinus aere repulsum,   545

---

1 526. Polites, Priam's son, is mentioned several times in Homer, e.g. *Il.* 2.791.

2 528. **vacua atria:** Polites runs across a part of the palace not yet filled by men fighting.

3 529. **infesto vulnere**: 'with weapon poised to kill'; cf. *Aen.* 7.533 for *vulnus* in the sense *telum vulniferum*.

4 530. Notice the vehement rhythm of the two pyrrhic verbs *tenet, premit*, the second causing a conflict of accent with ictus in the fifth foot. The paratactic construction is typically Virgilian: 'is on the point of catching him as he presses close upon him with his spear'. For *iam iamque* cf. *Aen.* 12.754.

5 536f. For the *pietas* of the gods cf. *Aen.*4.382, 5.688f.

6 538-9. 'who made me see my son's death with my own eyes'; *coram* is adverbial. For *facere* with the infinitive cf. Enn. *Ann.* 452 and Lucr. 3.301.

7 540. **satum quo te mentiris**: 'whose son you lyingly claim to be', because you show none of his better qualities. Homer tells in *Iliad* 24 of how Priam visited Achilles in his tent to plead for the return of Hector's body; Achilles granted the request and Priam returned safely back to Troy.

8 541-2. **iura . . . erubuit:** 'he had respect for the rights of a suppliant's trust'; the use of *erubesco* with a direct object (= *erubescendo servavit)* is very striking; cf. Prop. 3.14.20 *fratres erubuisse deos* and compare *palleo* in Hor. *Odes* 3.27.27f. *pontum mediasque fraudes / palluit audax.*

9 544. **fatus:** supply *est,* as with *repulsum* in the next line; the effect is rapid and staccato.

10 544. **sine ictu**: without power to penetrate.

et summo[1] clipei nequiquam umbone pependit.
Cui Pyrrhus: 'referes ergo haec et nuntius ibis[2]
Pelidae genitori. Illi mea tristia facta
degeneremque Neoptolemum narrare memento.[3]
Nunc morere.' Hoc dicens altaria ad ipsa trementem[4]   550
traxit et in multo lapsantem sanguine nati,
implicuitque comam laeva, dextraque coruscum[5]
extulit ac lateri[6] capulo[7] tenus abdidit ensem.
Haec[8] finis Priami[9] fatorum, hic exitus illum
sorte tulit Troiam incensam et prolapsa videntem   555
Pergama, tot[10] quondam populis terrisque superbum
regnatorem Asiae. [11]Iacet ingens litore truncus,
avulsumque umeris caput et sine nomine corpus.

*559-66. The death of Priam makes Aeneas think of his own
family; he looks round for support, but is alone.*

[12]At me tum[13] primum saevus circumstetit horror.

---

1 546. **summo ... umbone:** 'from the surface of the shield's boss'; the very end of the spear just pierces the outside of the shield sufficiently to hang there by its point.

2 547-8. 'So then you shall report this and go to tell the tale to my father Pelides', i.e. in the underworld; for *Pelides* see note on 263.

3 549. Pyrrhus refers ironically to lines 540-1. *Memento* is sarcastic: 'be sure you don't forget to tell him that Neoptolemus disgraces his father's name'.

4 550. **trementem**: 'non formidine sed aetate' (Servius).

5 552-3. **coruscum . . . ensem:** emphasis is put on the flash of the sword through the division of adjective and noun by the two verbs; cf. 470f.

6 553. **lateri**: *in latus;* the dative with *abdere* (the ablative is much more usual) depicts the moment of striking.

7 **capulo tenus**: for the preposition *tenus* following the ablative which it governs (its normal construction) cf. *hactenus, quatenus,* and *Aen.* 3.427.

8 554f. The tradition of the murder of Priam by Pyrrhus is not mentioned in Homer when Odysseus tells Achilles of his son's exploits (*Od.* 11.505f.). It was in cyclic epic, and occurs in Euripides (*Hec.* 23f., *Tro.* 16f., 481f.) and vases depict Pyrrhus killing Priam at the altars. The different version, according to which Pyrrhus killed him at Achilles' tomb on the shore, is referred to in 557; Servius quotes Pacuvius for this version, and suggests that Virgil uses it to allude to the death of Pompey, murdered on the shore of Egypt (Lucan 8.667f.). Certainly no Roman could read lines 557-8 without thinking of Pompey; and equally certainly Virgil has achieved by his strange conflation of two contrasting versions an astonishing effect of lasting desolation succeeding the immediate horror of destruction.

9 554-5. Some modern editors punctuate after *Priami,* so that *fatorum* goes with *sorte,* but this is very abrupt, and *sorte* can stand by itself meaning 'by the decree of fate', cf. *Aen.* 10.501.

10 556-7. **tot. . . Asiae:** 'once the proud ruler of Asia, proud indeed with all those countless peoples and lands'; cf. 363 and Spenser *F.Q.*, 3.9.39 'and of all Asie bore the soveraigne crowne'. *Regnatorem* is perhaps best taken in apposition to *ilium* (Priam), though it is possible to take it with *Pergama.*

11 557-8. The final picture is one of awful desolation; as his city burns to ashes the proud ruler becomes a mutilated, nameless corpse. Cf. Shelley's *Ozymandias:* 'Nothing beside remains. Round the decay / of that colossal wreck, boundless and bare / the lone and level sands stretch far away'.

12 559-66. This short passage marks the transition from the middle section of the book (the destruction of Troy culminating in the death of Priam) to the final section which is concerned with Aeneas' own family. The tale of public disintegration alters to a tale of private concern.

13 559. **tum primum**: the shock of realisation which comes to Aeneas now for the first time is that the calamity not only affects him as an heroic warrior, but also involves the safety and lives of his family, his father Anchises (the same age as Priam), his wife Creusa, and their little son Iulus.

Obstipui; subiit cari genitoris imago,   560

ut regem aequaevum crudeli vulnere vidi

vitam exhalantem; [1]subiit deserta Creusa[2]

et direpta domus[3] et parvi casus Iuli.

Respicio[4] et quae sit me circum copia lustro.

Deseruere omnes defessi, et corpora saltu   565

ad terram misere aut ignibus aegra dedere.

567-87. Aeneas catches sight of Helen hiding at the temple of Vesta; fury blazes up in him and he thinks of avenging his burning city by killing her.

[5]Iamque adeo super[6] unus eram, cum limina Vestae

servantem et tacitam secreta in sede latentem

Tyndarida[7] aspicio; dant clara incendia lucem

erranti[8] passimque oculos per cuncta ferenti.   570

Illa sibi infestos eversa ob Pergama Teucros

et Danaum poenam et deserti coniugis iras

praemetuens, Troiae et patriae communis[9] Erinys,

abdiderat sese atque aris invisa sedebat.

Exarsere ignes animo; subit[10] ira cadentem   575

---

1 562-3. 'there came to my mind the thought of Creusa left alone, my house plundered, the fate of little Iulus'.

2 562. For the different forms of the legend about Aeneas' wife (whose name was Eurydice in the earlier versions) see note on 730f.

3 563. **domus**: the final syllable is lengthened in arsis, see note on 369.

4 564. 'I turned my head and looked round to see what support was at hand', i.e. on the walls, helping the defence. He finds none; they have all jumped off or been engulfed in the flames.

5 567f. This passage (567-87 and the transitional line 588) is not given by the major manuscripts of Virgil and survives because it is quoted in Servius' commentary. Servius says that it was a passage written by Virgil but removed by the editors of the *Aeneid*, Varius and Tucca. Its authenticity has long been disputed, but it is highly likely that the passage is Virgilian (see Austin's commentary pp. 217f.) and it is equally clear that Virgil was not satisfied with it (which may well have been apparent, perhaps through indications in the margins of the manuscript, to the editors who deleted it). There are difficulties in the language (especially 584f.) and the account of Helen's fear (571f.) contradicts the story that she was in concert with the Greeks in 6.515f. What is particularly interesting is that Virgil's concept of the character of Aeneas, of the frenzied despair to which he had given way, was such that he could present his hero thus. Even in the second half of the poem, after Aeneas has learned much about how to restrain impetuous emotions, we often find him (especially in Book 10 and at the end of 12) yielding to moods of violence. It is possible that Virgil deleted the passage because he could not on second thoughts allow his hero to speak of killing a woman; but his first thoughts had allowed it, and should remind us that the efforts of Aeneas in the poem to control violence in himself and others meet with only very imperfect success. Aeneas is a man of violence who tries hard to learn a better way.

6 567-9. **super unus eram cum . . . aspicio**: 'I was the only one left when suddenly I saw'; *super eram* is separated by tmesis, cf. *Ecl.* 6.6. The transition is a little abrupt, the sense being 'I had just realised I was alone when . . .'

7 569. **Tyndarida**: Greek accusative, 'daughter of Tyndareus', i.e. Helen.

8 570. **erranti**: sc. *mihi* — presumably Aeneas is looking for the best way of getting through to Anchises' house.

9 573. **communis Erinys**: a fine phrase: Helen is the personification of destruction (Aesch. *Agam.* 689f, 749) both for Greece and Troy. Lucan imitates the phrase in 10.59 (of Cleopatra) *Latii feralis Erinys*. On the possible contradiction with the passage in Book 6 where Helen seems to be on good terms with the Greeks see on 567f. For *Erinys* see note on 337.

10 575-6. **subit ira . . . ulcisci**: for the poetic use of the infinitive cf. *Aen.* 9.757 and see note on 1.704.

ulcisci patriam et sceleratas[1] sumere poenas.
'Scilicet haec Spartam[2] incolumis patriasque Mycenas
aspiciet, partoque ibit regina triumpho,
coniugiumque domumque patris[3] natosque[4] videbit
Iliadum turba et Phrygiis comitata ministris?   580
Occiderit[5] ferro Priamus? Troia arserit igni?
Dardanium totiens sudarit sanguine litus?
Non ita. Namque etsi nullum memorabile nomen
[6]feminea in poena est nec[7] habet victoria laudem,
exstinxisse nefas[8] tamen et sumpsisse merentis[9]   585
laudabor poenas, animumque explesse iuvabit
ultricis[10] flammae et cineres satiasse meorum.'

> *588-623. Venus appears to Aeneas and rebukes him, telling him to think instead of the safety of his family. She reveals to him the giant shapes of gods and goddesses working the destruction of Troy.*

[11]Talia iactabam[12] et furiata mente ferebar,
cum[13] mihi se, non ante oculis tam ciara, videndam

---

1 576. **sceleratas sumere poenas**: a much disputed phrase, but it probably should be understood in the sense which it naturally bears, namely 'to exact a punishment wicked to inflict'. It would be a strange Virgilian experiment in language if we had to extract the meaning 'punishment for her crime'; 'criminal punishment' means something quite different from 'punishment for crime'. Aeneas as he tells his story realises now that to have killed a woman at an altar would have been *sceleratum*. But he goes on to describe (585-6) how his blind anger had made the deed seem at the time a praiseworthy act.

2 577. **Spartam ... Mycenas**: Sparta was the home of her husband Menelaus, Mycenae is a generalised term for Greece (cf. 1.650).

3 579. **patris**: the MSS of Servius read *patres,* which requires the sense of *parentis* (cf. 457), but the rhythm of the line is against this.

4 **natosque**: Helen had a daughter Hermione and (according to some) a son Nicostratus, but the phrase may be very general.

5 581-2. The future perfects in the rhetorical questions convey the idea 'all this has been so, and shall I do nothing about it?'; cf. *Aen.* 4.591.

6 584-7. The text here is extremely uncertain, because the passage was clearly unfinished.

7 584. **nec habet**: this is an emendation for *habet haec,* which can hardly stand because of *tamen*; cf. Eur. *Orest.* 1133 (Pylades on the idea of murdering Helen) δυσκλεης αν ην φονοσ, and *Aen.* 11.790f. See Austin's discussion of the difficulties in his notes ad loc. and his article in *C.Q.* 1961, 185f.

8 585. **nefas**: the abstract word is used meaning *nefariam feminam*, like *coniugium* for *coniugem* in 579; cf. Stat. *Th.* 7.514.

9 **merentis**: accusative plural with *poenas* rather than genitive singular; see note on 576. It is a very strange phrase and *merenti,* read by one MS, may be right.

10 587. **ultricis flammae**: 'the fire of vengeance'*; flammae* is a late correction of the senseless *famam* or *fatnae* of the MSS. It gives a strange phrase and an unparalleled genitive after *explesse*, and it must be said that the text here cannot be established with anything approaching certainty.

11 588f. The supernatural vision which Venus allows Aeneas to see is one of the finest passages in the poem, and gives the fullest scope for Virgil's imaginative and pictorial powers. All through the *Aeneid* Virgil is fascinated by the possibilities of describing poetically the visual aspect of a supernatural world beyond human sight, and this is perhaps the most brilliant, most majestic and most awe-inspiring of all his 'gleams of a remoter world'.

12 588. **iactabam**: 'I was wildly saying', cf. *Aen.* 1.102.

13 589f. Observe how the inverted *cum* clause, which itself compels attention to sudden action, is given special power by the postponement of the subject *alma parens* to the very end.

obtulit et pura per noctem in luce refulsit 590
alma parens, confessa[1] deam qualisque[2] videri
caelicolis et quanta solet, dextraque prehensum
continuit roseoque haec insuper addidit ore:
'nate, quis indomitas[3] tantus dolor excitat iras?
Quid furis aut quonam[4] nostri tibi cura recessit? 595
Non prius aspicies ubi fessum aetate parentem
liqueris Anchisen, superet[5] coniunxne Creusa
Ascaniusque puer? Quos[6] omnis undique Graiae
circum[7] errant acies et, ni mea cura resistat,
iam flammae tulerint inimicus et hauserit ensis. 600
Non tibi[8] Tyndaridis[9] facies invisa Lacaenae[10]
culpatusve[11] Paris, divum inclementia, divum,[12]
has evertit opes sternitque a culmine Troiam.
Aspice (namque omnem, [13]quae nunc obducta tuenti
mortalis hebetat visus tibi et umida circum 605
caligat, nubem eripiam; tu ne qua parentis
iussa time neu praeceptis parere recusa):
hic, ubi disiectas moles avulsaque saxis
saxa vides, mixtoque undantem pulvere fumum,

---

1 591. **confessa deam**: 'revealing her divinity'; cf. the description of Venus in 1.405 *et vera incessu patuit dea,* and for the abstract meaning of *deum* cf. Ov. *Met.* 12.601 *fassusque deum.* Mackail quotes Dryden's 'assumes the god'.

2 591-2. **qualisque . . . solet**: 'in appearance and stature the same as she is when the gods see her'; except when disguised as mortals the gods were thought of as larger than humans.

3 594-5. Venus uses phrases (*indomitae irae, quid furis*) which relate Aeneas' wild and violent reactions towards Helen to the forces of passion and frenzy which he so often encounters in others throughout the poem.

4 595. **quonam ... recessit**: 'wherever has your love for us gone?' By *nostri* Venus means the family.

5 597. **superet coniunxne**: for postponed *-ne,* which is rare, cf. Hor. *Epist.* 2.2.65; for *superare* meaning survive cf. 643.

6 598. **quos omnis**: governed by *circum* in the next line.

7 599-600. 'if my care were not preventing it, the flames would already have taken them off and the enemy sword drunk their blood'; the condition is made more vivid by the use of primary tenses as in 6.292f. For *tulerint = abstulerint* cf. 555; for *haurire* in this sense cf. *Aen.* 10.314.

8 601. **tibi**: 'I tell you', ethic dative, cf. *Aen.* 1.258.

9 **Tyndaridis ... Lacaenae**: Helen of Sparta, see note on 569, and cf. *Aen.* 6.511.

10 601f. The construction is: it is not the beauty of Helen, nor the wickedness of Paris, *but* the merciless gods who are responsible for the destruction. For the thought cf. Hom. *Il.* 3.164.

11 602. **culpatusve**: 'wicked', a usage of the word not found before Virgil; cf. Stat. *Ach.* 1.23 (Paris) *culpatum relegebat iter.*

12 **divum ... divum**: Venus' indignation finds expression in the repetition of the responsible agents, Juno in particular with Jupiter acquiescing.

13 604-6. 'Look — for I will remove all the cloud which now veils your vision and dims your mortal sight, misty and dark all around you.' The idea is based on Hom. *Il.* 5.127 where Athena speaks in similar tones to Diomedes; Virgil has elaborated it into a majestic and preternatural vision of giant powers at work.

Neptunus[1] muros magnoque emota tridenti   610
fundamenta quatit totamque a sedibus urbem
eruit. Hic Iuno[2] Scaeas[3] saevissima portas
prima tenet sociumque furens a navibus agmen
ferro accincta vocat.
Iam summas arces Tritonia,[4] respice, Pallas   615
insedit nimbo[5] effulgens et Gorgone saeva.
Ipse pater Danais animos virisque secundas
sufficit, ipse deos in Dardana suscitat arma.
Eripe,[6] nate, fugam finemque impone labori.
Nusquam abero et tutum patrio te limine sistam.'   620
Dixerat et spissis noctis se condidit umbris.
Apparent[7] dirae facies inimicaque Troiae
numina magna deum.

> *624-633. Aeneas now realises that Troy's hour of destruction
> has come, like the final fall of a tree beneath the woodman's
> axe. He makes his way home.*

Tum vero omne mihi visum considere in ignis
Ilium et ex imo verti Neptunia Troia;   625

---

1 610. **Neptunus**: here in his capacity as Poseidon the Earth-shaker (Ενοσιχθων); his hostility was due to his having been cheated by Laomedon of his promised reward when he and Apollo had built the walls of Troy (hence *Neptunia Troia*, 625); cf. *Aen.* 5.810-11.

2 612. **Juno**: her hostility to Troy (which beleaguers the Trojan exiles throughout) was explained at the beginning of the poem (see note on 1.1f.); it was due to her love for Carthage (which the Trojan-Romans would destroy), her anger at the judgment of Paris against her, and the favour of Jupiter for the Trojan Ganymede.

3 **Scaeas**: the most famous gates of Troy, said to be so called because they were on the west, i.e. the left hand side (σκαιος) looking north; cf. *Aen.* 3.351. Thus facing the Greek camp.

4 615. **Tritonia . . . Pallas**: see note on 171. As the chief goddess of the Greeks she is naturally to be found in the forefront of the destruction of Troy, in spite of having a temple on the citadel there (165f.).

5 616. **nimbo . . . saeva**: 'flashing out from a storm-cloud, a terrifying figure with her Gorgon shield'; against the backdrop of darkness appears the terrible radiance of Athena. Servius took *nimbus* to mean the divine halo which surrounds goddesses, but Henry demolished this unnatural meaning for *nimbus*. Servius also mentions the reading *limbus* ('radiant with her bordered robe', cf. *Aen.* 4.137); but this metonymy is most unnatural. It is possible to take *saeva* as ablative, but this gives less good balance. Athena's shield bore the head of the Gorgon Medusa, decapitated by Perseus; cf. *Aen.* 8.437-8.

6 619. **eripe . . . fugam:** Servius paraphrases *eripe* with *accelera, raptim fac*. Venus here echoes Hector's instructions in 289, where see note.

7 622-3. 'There appear before me terrible shapes, and the mighty powers of divinities hostile to Troy': the half-line (see note on 1.534), with its sonorous assonance, is majestic and awe-inspiring.

ac[1] veluti[2] summis antiquam in montibus ornum
cum ferro[3] accisam crebrisque bipennibus instant
eruere agricolae certatim; illa usque minatur
et tremefacta comam concusso vertice nutat,
vulneribus donec paulatim evicta supremum[4]   630
congemuit traxitque[5] iugis avulsa ruinam.
Descendo ac [6]ducente deo[7] flammam inter et hostis
expedior: dant tela locum flammaeque recedunt.

> *634-670. Aeneas reaches home, but Anchises refuses to leave. Aeneas in despair prepares to court death again by rushing out against the Greeks.*

[8]Atque ubi iam patriae perventum ad limina sedis
antiquasque domos, genitor, quem tollere in altos   635
optabam primum montis primumque petebam,
abnegat[9] excisa vitam producere Troia

---

1 626f. The simile is based on Hom. *Il.* 4.482f. (cf. Ap. Rh. 4.1682f.). It is admirably imitated by Spenser, *F.Q.* 1.8.22:
> as an aged tree,

High growing on the top of rocky clift,
Whose hartstrings with keene Steele nigh hewen be,
The mightie trunck halfe rent, with ragged rift
Doth roll adowne the rocks, and fall with fearefull drift.

The points of comparison in Virgil's simile are (i) the ash, like Troy, is old; (ii) like Troy it is mighty; (iii) like Troy it has resisted for some time. The effect of the simile is tremendous: it marks the actual moment of Troy's destruction and it gives a certain distance and inevitability to the events which until now Aeneas could not accept. He has felt till now that he ought to have been able to prevent the chopping down of the tree of Troy: now he sees it as a *fait accompli.*

2 626. **ac veluti**: 'and it was as when', cf. *Aen.* 4.402f, 6.707f., for this elliptical manner of introducing a simile.

3 627-9. 'when it has been hacked at with the steel of blow after blow of the axes and the farmers eagerly vie with each other to bring it down; it looks like falling all the time and as its leafy boughs shiver, and its lofty top is shaken, it sways to and fro'. Notice the personification (not unusual with trees and frequent in the *Georgics*) of *coma* and *vertex, vulneribus* and *congemuit. Comam* is retained accusative, see note on 210.

4 630. **supremum**: adverbial accusative, cf. 693, 3.68.

5 631. **traxitque . . . ruinam:** 'torn away from the hill top crashed to the ground all its length', cf. Cat. 64.105f., Ov. *Met.* 8.776. For *trahere ruinam* cf. 465-6, 8.192. There is no need to feel difficulty over *avulsa* applied to a tree cut down; the image is of a great mass displaced from its surrounds.

6 632. Notice the sudden quiet tone after the finality of Troy's fall, emphasised by the alliteration of *d.* Much has been written about the uncertainty of Aeneas' movements in this passage; most readers will have assumed that before now he had come down off the roof. This line would fit well after 566, and it is quite clear that 567-631 had not been finally fitted into the sequence of the narrative.

7 **deo**: some MSS read *dea,* but Servius and Macrobius support *deo;* the concept of divinity may be masculine even when applied to a goddess, as with the Greek θεός.

8 634f. The first appearance of Anchises in the poem shows a helpless old man whose useful years are long past (647); as yet he knows nothing of the future destiny of his son, and the transformation in him when the divine intention is revealed by the signs from heaven is very remarkable. From the useless old man he is transfigured into the intrepid companion and counsellor of Aeneas; he plays a dominant role in *Aeneid* 3 (see note on 3.1f.). Aeneas' filial devotion to him is shown very plainly in this passage (cf. *primum . . . primum,* 636, and lines 657-8).

At this setback to his plan for escape Aeneas lapses again into the wild frenzy and despair which have previously been a marked feature of his character in this book. He longs for death (655); he prepares to make the ultimate heroic gesture and throw his life away (668-70). He has not yet understood that his destiny imposes upon him the obligation of survival.

9 637. **abnegat . . . producere**: for the construction cf. *Geo.* 3.456, *Aen.* 4.428.

exsiliumque pati. 'Vos o, quibus integer[1] aevi
sanguis,' ait, 'solidaeque suo stant robore vires,
vos agitate[2] fugam.   640
Me si caelicolae voluissent ducere vitam,
has mihi servassent sedes. [3]Satis una superque
vidimus excidia et captae superavimus urbi.
Sic[4] o sic positum adfati discedite corpus.
Ipse[5] manu mortem inveniam; miserebitur hostis   645
exuviasque petet. Facilis[6] iactura sepulcri.
Iam pridem invisus divis et inutilis annos
demoror, ex quo me divum[7] pater atque hominum rex
fulminis adflavit ventis et contigit igni.'[8]

   Talia perstabat memorans fixusque manebat.   650
Nos contra effusi[9] lacrimis coniunxque[10] Creusa
Ascaniusque omnisque domus, ne vertere secum
cuncta pater fatoque[11] urgenti incumbere vellet.
Abnegat inceptoque[12] et sedibus haeret in isdem.
Rursus[13] in arma feror mortemque miserrimus opto.   655
Nam quod consilium aut quae iam fortuna dabatur?
'Mene efferre pedem, genitor, te posse relicto
sperasti tantumque nefas patrio excidit ore?

---

1 638. **integer aevi**: genitive of respect, see note on 1.14 and compare 5.73 *aevi maturus*. Cf. Enn. *Scen.* 414 *deos aevi integros*.

2 640. **agitate fugam**: Servius is probably right in saying that the meaning is 'consider'; others take it as equivalent to *agite* ('take flight').

3 642-3. 'it is enough and more than enough that I have seen one destruction and survived my city when it was captured'; Anchises refers to the sack of Troy by Hercules when Laomedon cheated him of the promise of his famous horses; cf. *Aen.* 8.290f. *Excidia* is a poetic plural, which accounts for the rare use of *una* in the plural.

4 644. 'Speak to me your last words as I now am, as I now am composed as if in death, and depart'; Anchises adopts an attitude as though already dead and asks for the final valediction customary at death (cf. *Aen.* 9.483f.)

5 645. **ipse manu mortem inveniam**: 'I myself will find death by my own acts'; i.e. by rushing upon the enemy. Some MSS have *manum morti*, 'a hand to kill me', but the wide meaning of the ablative *manu* to reinforce *ipse* is very much in Virgil's style; cf. 3.372, 5.499.

6 646. **facilis iactura sepulcri**: this is, as it is meant to be, a very startling sentiment in view of the importance attached in the ancient world to burial. Anchises minimises a situation which Aeneas could not possibly accept: he tries to convince his son that when the last farewells have been duly spoken all will be well.

7 648. **divum . . . rex**: a reminiscence of Ennius, cf. *Aen.* 1.65.

8 649. The story was that Anchises boasted of Venus' love for him, for which Jupiter resolved to punish him with a thunderbolt; Venus however diverted it so that he was scorched but not killed.

9 651. **effusi lacrimis**: a bold and exciting phrase; instead of 'we shed floods of tears' Virgil says 'we were flooded in tears', i.e. we dissolved into tears; the *ne* clause depends on the idea of fear or prayer in this phrase.

10 **coniunxque Creusa**: -*que* means 'both'; the nouns are all in partial apposition to *nos*.

11 653. **fatoque urgenti incumbere**: 'add his weight to the burden of our fate', cf. Livy 3.16.5.

12 654. **inceptoque . . . isdem**: 'he stayed firm in his intention and in the palace where he was', a slight zeugma.

13 655. Notice the fierce alliteration of *r* in this frenzied decision of Aeneas.

Si nihii ex tanta superis placet urbe relinqui,

et sedet hoc[1] animo perituraeque addere Troiae   660

teque tuosque iuvat, patet isti ianua leto,

iamque aderit multo Priami de sanguine Pyrrhus,

natum ante ora patris,[2] patrem qui obtruncat ad aras.

Hoc[3] erat, alma parens, quod me per tela, per ignis

eripis, ut mediis hostem in penetralibus utque   665

Ascanium patremque meum iuxtaque Creusam

alterum in alterius mactatos sanguine cernam?

Arma, viri, ferte arma; vocat lux ultima victos.

Reddite me Danais; sinite[4] instaurata revisam

proelia. Numquam[5] omnes hodie moriemur inulti.'   670

> *671-729. As Creusa begs Aeneas not to leave them, a tongue of fire suddenly plays around Iulus' head. Anchises asks for confirmation of the omen, and following thunder on the left a shooting star is seen. Anchises now declares himself ready to leave and Aeneas sets forth carrying his father on his shoulders and leading his little son by the hand; Creusa follows behind.*

[6]Hinc ferro accingor rursus clipeoque sinistram

insertabam aptans meque extra tecta ferebam.

Ecce autem complexa pedes in limine coniunx

haerebat, parvumque patri tendebat Iulum:

'si periturus abis, et nos rape in omnia tecum;   675

sin aliquam expertus[7] sumptis spem ponis in armis,

hanc primum tutare domum. Cui parvus Iulus,

cui pater et coniunx quondam[8] tua dicta relinquor?'

---

1 660. **hoc:** the neuter singular has a long syllable (though the vowel is short) because of its origin *hod-ce;* cf. 664, 703.

2 663. Observe the rare variation in metrical treatment within the same line of *patris, patrem;* cf. Hor. *Odes* 1.32.11.

3 664. **hoc erat. . . quod:** 'was this why', literally 'that you are saving me was (for) this, was it, that I should see. . .?' *Hoc* is the predicate to the *quod* clause, and is explained by the *ut* clause. For the idiomatic use of *erat* cf. *Aen.* 7.128.

4 669. **sinite . . . revisam:** the jussive subjunctive is used in parataxis with *sino,* which in prose takes the accusative and infinitive; cf. *Aen.* 5.163, 71 7.

5 670. **numquam:** rather colloquial, cf. *Ecl.* 3.49 *numquam hodie effugies.*

6 671f. The transformation of Anchises from dejection to joy after the divine signs is total and immediate (see note on 634f.); similarly Aeneas is transformed from the frenzied warrior to the man of destiny. The transformation is symbolised in the last four lines of the passage; previously he had known no fear as he felt in his despair that he had nothing to lose, but now, as he leads his family and his people out to safety, every breeze and every sound terrifies him.

The tableau of departure: Anchises on Aeneas' shoulder, little Iulus holding his hand, Creusa following behind, was already well-known in art long before Virgil, and after him continued to be illustrated constantly in sculpture, painting, illuminated manuscripts and on coins (see Austin's note on 708 for some references).

7 676. **expertus:** 'from what you know of the situation'.

8 678. **quondam:** anticipatory, 'I who was once your wife (but shall soon be your widow)'.

Talia vociferans gemitu tectum omne replebat,
cum subitum dictuque oritur mirabile monstrum.   680
Namque manus[1] inter maestorumque ora parentum
ecce[2] levis summo de vertice visus Iuli
fundere lumen apex, tactuque innoxia mollis
lambere flamma comas et circum tempora pasci.
Nos[3] pavidi trepidare metu crinemque flagrantem   685
excutere et sanctos restinguere fontibus ignis.
At pater Anchises[4] oculos ad sidera laetus
extulit et caelo palmas cum voce tetendit:
'Iuppiter omnipotens, precibus si flecteris ullis,
aspice nos, hoc[5] tantum, et si pietate[6] meremur,   690
da deinde augurium,[7] pater, atque haec omina firma.'
   Vix ea fatus erat senior, subitoque fragore
intonuit laevum,[8] et de caelo lapsa per umbras
stella[9] facem ducens multa cum luce cucurrit.
Illam summa super labentem culmina tecti   695
cernimus Idaea claram[10] se condere silva
signantemque vias; [11]tum longo limite sulcus
dat lucem et late circum loca sulphure fumant.

---

1 681f. **manus . . . parentum**: 'in between the embracing arms and faces of his grief-stricken parents'. The phrase is very precisely pictorial: Creusa on her knees is holding Iulus out towards Aeneas (674), who puts out his arms to take him.

2 682-3. 'a thin tongue of flame was to be seen, radiating its light from the very top of Iulus' head'; the omen is reminiscent of the story of the flames surrounding the head of the infant Servius Tullius, marking him out as destined for kingship (Livy 1.39.1) compare also the flames on Lavinia's head in *Aen.* 7.71f. Servius draws attention to the meaning of *apex* as part of the headdress of a priest (e.g. *Aen.* 8.664) but for the meaning 'tongue of flame' cf. Ov. *Fast.* 6.636, and see K. Quinn, *Virgil's Aeneid,* pp.388-9.

3 685f. The historic infinitives (cf. 98) convey rapid action; *excutere* means that they tried to extinguish the flames by shaking out Ascanius' hair.

4 687. Anchises is often seen in Book 3 as the man especially able to interpret divine signs; he was said to have received this gift from Venus, cf. Enn. *Ann.* 18-9.

5 690. **hoc tantum**: 'just this', parenthetical, cf. 79.

6 **pietate**: notice the key word of the poem here used as the basis for Anchises' claim for divine help.

7 691. 'give us an augury now, father, and confirm this omen'; the MSS read *auxilium* but Probus (on *Ecl.* 6.31) read *augurium* a Sendrvius' explanation of the rest of the line shows that he read it. Anchises means that he has taken the flame as an omen sent spontaneously (*oblativum*); another one sent in response to prayer (*impetrativum*) will confirm the divine intention. For *deinde* (next, immediately in the future) cf. *Aen.* 4.561.

8 693. **laevum**: adverbial accusative, cf. 630; for the left as favourable in Roman augury cf. *Aen.* 9.631 and Cic. *Div.* 2.82. In Greek augury the right was favourable.

9 694. **Stella facem ducens**: 'a star leaving a trail of light', i.e. a shooting star; compare the simile of a shooting star in *Aen.* 5.527f., and cf. *Geo.* 1.365f., Lucr. 2.206f. *nocturnasque faces caeli sublime volantis / nonne vides longos flammarum ducere tractus?*

10 696-7. **claram ... signantemque** vias 'brilliant and leaving the trace of its path'; the parallel with *Aen.* 5.526 *signavitque viam flammis* suggests that this is the meaning here, rather than (as Servius and others say) 'pointing out the way' (cf. Ap. Rh. 4.294f.). For Mt. Ida in the Troad cf. 801.

11 697-8. 'after that its path still shone out in a long trail, and all the place for miles around was smoky with sulphur-fumes', i.e. after the star had disappeared (*tum*) the signs of its passage remained.

Hic vero victus genitor se[1] tollit ad auras
adfaturque deos et sanctum sidus adorat.   700
'Iam iam nulla mora est; sequor et qua ducitis adsum,
di patrii; servate domum, servate nepotem.
Vestrum hoc augurium, vestroque[2] in numine Troia est.
Cedo equidem nec, nate, tibi comes ire recuso.'
Dixerat ille, et iam per moenia clarior ignis   705
auditur, propiusque aestus incendia volvunt.
'Ergo age, care pater, cervici[3] imponere nostrae;
ipse subibo umeris nec me labor iste gravabit;
quo res cumque cadent, unum et commune periclum,
una salus ambobus erit. Mihi parvus Iulus   710
sit comes, et longe[4] servet vestigia coniunx.
Vos, famuli, quae dicam animis[5] advertite vestris.
Est urbe egressis[6] tumulus templumque vetustum
desertae[7] Cereris, iuxtaque antiqua cupressus
religione patrum multos servata per annos;   715
hanc ex diverso sedem veniemus in unam.
Tu,[8] genitor, cape sacra manu patriosque penatis;
me bello e tanto digressum et caede recenti
attrectare nefas, donec me flumine vivo
abluero.'   720
Haec fatus latos umeros[9] subiectaque colla
veste super fulvique insternor pelle leonis,
succedoque oneri; dextrae se parvus Iulus
implicuit sequiturque patrem non passibus aequis;

---

1 699. **se tollit ad auras**: the picture is of the hitherto dejected Anchises rising to his full height and flinging his arms high in joy.

2 703. **vestroque in numine**: 'under your protection', cf. 396 and 9.247.

3 707. **cervici imponere nostrae**: 'put yourself on my shoulders'; *imponere* is the passive imperative with a middle sense, and *cervici* the common poetic use of the dative for *in cervicem*.

4 711. **longe servet**: 'follow at a distance'. This part of Aeneas' plan leads to misfortune; Servius attempts to save Aeneas from blame by explaining *longe* as *valde*, but this is impossible.

5 712. **animis advertite vestris**: notice the variation on the prose phrase *animadvertere; animis* is dative, cf. 707.

6 713. **egressis**: for the dative cf. *Aen.* 1.102.

7 714. **desertae**: it is very difficult here to choose between various possibilities: (i) the temple is derelict (because of the war, or its replacement by another, or some other cause); (ii) Ceres was worshipped in remote places, as the rustic deity of earth; (iii) the temple was in commemoration of Proserpina, Ceres' lost daughter. The last would fit best with the cypress, the tree of mourning.

8 717. Now that Anchises has been persuaded to leave, Aeneas' thoughts return to Hector's instructions (293).

9 721-2. **umeros . . . insternor**: retained accusative after a passive verb with a middle sense; see note on 275. *Super* is adverbial, and *veste et pelle* hendiadys — 'with the covering of a skin'.

pone[1] subit coniunx. Ferimur per opaca[2] locorum,   725
et me, quem dudum non ulla iniecta movebant
tela neque adverso glomerati ex[3] agmine Grai,
nunc omnes terrent aurae, sonus excitat omnis
suspensum et pariter comitique onerique timentem.

> *730-95. Just as they are reaching safety the noise of the enemy is heard, and in the confusion Creusa is lost. Aeneas retraces his steps, wildly shouting his wife's name; then there appears to him a supernatural phantom of her, and she bids him depart on his destined journey, leaving her in the care of the goddess Cybele.*

[4]Iamque propinquabam portis omnemque videbar   730
evasisse[5] viam, subito cum creber[6] ad auris
visus adesse pedum sonitus, genitorque per umbram
prospiciens 'nate' exclamat 'fuge, nate; propinquant.
Ardentis clipeos atque aera micantia cerno.'
Hic mihi nescio quod trepido male[7] numen amicum   735
confusam eripuit mentem. Namque avia[8] cursu
dum sequor et nota excedo regione viarum,
heu misero[9] coniunx fatone erepta Creusa[10]

---

1 725. **pone**: cf. *Geo.* 4.487 *pone sequens*. The word has an archaic flavour.

2 **opaca locorum**: 'the darkness of the way', cf. 332.

3 727. **ex agmine**: Housman's *exagmine* (= *examine*) here and in 7.703 is accepted by Mackail and Mynors, but Virgil does not elsewhere use *examen* of people.

4 730f. This tremendous passage shows signs of incomplete finish: (half-lines, 767, 787; lines repeated elsewhere, 774-5, 792-4; perhaps the inconsistency of 781-2 with *Aen.* 3.7 (where see note). It may serve as a reminder that what Virgil did not achieve in the *Aeneid* because of his premature death is insignificant compared with what he did.
The tension between Aeneas' personal grief and the necessity for him to accept the will of the gods for Troy has been a dominant aspect of this book. Here it reaches its superb climax as his wild sorrow and reckless despair is countered by the serene appearance of Creusa's phantom, telling him that these things do not happen unless the gods will it so — *non haec sine numine divum eveniunt.*
Virgil has used the conflicting versions of the tradition for his own purposes. In some sources Aeneas' wife was called Eurydice, and it was only later that Priam's daughter Creusa was fitted to this role. Again in early sources Aeneas' wife accompanied him into exile; Virgil needed the version which could bring the story of the burning of Troy to this terrifying and yet comforting climax. The story of the loss of another Eurydice, which he had told in *Georgics* 4, adds to the poignancy and pathos here, and brings into relief the happier ending. For a full discussion of the sources see Austin's note on 795.

5 731. **evasisse**: 'got through', cf. *Aen.* 12.907.

6 731-2. **creber ... pedum sonitus**: 'the sound of many feet'; notice the imitative rhythm of the dactyls, and the elliptical construction of *ad auris (veniens) adesse.*

7 735. **male ... amicum**: *inimicum*, cf. 23, *Geo.* 1.105 *male pinguis harenae.*

8 736. **avia**: 'byways'; the adjective *avius* is used in the neuter plural as a noun, cf. *Aen.* 9.58.

9 738. **misero**: dative after *erepia* with *mihi* understood.

10 738f. 'alas, the tragedy of it, my wife Creusa — was it by fate that she was taken from me and stopped? Or did she lose the way or tired out pause for rest? I cannot tell — but I never saw her again.' The disjunctive style is used very appropriately for Aeneas' confused emotions in the face of this loss for which he was primarily responsible. There has been doubt among the commentators about how to take 738-9, but the balancing positions of *-ne* make it clear that Aeneas asks (i) was it by fate that she was snatched off and stopped coming with us or (ii) was it due to her own frailty, in losing her way or giving up through weariness?

substitit, erravitne via seu lassa[1] resedit,

incertum; nec post oculis est reddita nostris.[2]   740

Nec prius amissam respexi animumve reflexi

quam tumulum antiquae Cereris sedemque sacratam

venimus: hic demum collectis omnibus una

defuit, et comites natumque virumque fefellit.[3]

Quem non incusavi amens hominumque deorumque,[4]   745

aut quid in eversa vidi crudelius urbe?

Ascanium Anchisenque patrem Teucrosque penatis

commendo sociis et curva valle recondo;

ipse urbem repeto et cingor fulgentibus armis.

Stat[5] casus renovare omnis omnemque reverti   750

per Troiam et rursus caput obiectare periclis.

Principio muros obscuraque limina portae,[6]

qua gressum extuleram, repeto et vestigia retro

observata sequor per noctem et lumine[7] lustro:

horror ubique animo, simul ipsa silentia terrent.   755

Inde domum, si forte pedem, si forte tulisset,[8]

me refero: inruerant Danai et tectum omne tenebant.

Ilicet ignis edax summa ad fastigia vento

volvitur; exsuperant flammae, furit aestus ad auras.

Procedo et Priami sedes arcemque reviso: 760

et iam porticibus vacuis Iunonis[9] asylo

custodes lecti Phoenix[10] et dirus Ulixes

praedam adservabant. Huc undique Troia gaza

incensis erepta adytis, mensaeque deorum

crateresque auro solidi, captivaque vestis   765

---

1 739. **lassa**: Austin has an excellent note on the deliberate use here of this 'more homely' alternative to *fessus*. *M* has *lapsa*, which Mynors accepts.

2 740. We are irresistibly reminded here of the end of the story of Eurydice in *Geo.* 4.500f.

3 744. **fefellit**: 'was missing, to the despair of. . . .'; this is a very intense use of the word, combining the ideas of her absence having been unnoticed till then and of her disappointing the hopes of her friends who were expecting her; cf. *Aen.* 4.17.

4 745. The line is made memorable by its two striking elisions, the second hyper-metric (cf. *Aen.* 1.332).

5 750. **stat . . . renovare**: 'my firm purpose is to risk again . . .'; cf. *Aen.* 12.678.

6 752. **portae**: the city gate by which he had got out, cf. 730.

7 754. **lumine lustro**: 'scan them with intent gaze', cf. *Aen.* 8.153 *totum lustrabat lumine corpus.*

8 756. A poignant and unforgettable line: 'if only, if only she has gone there'. For the *si forte* type of condition cf. 136; *tulisset* is reported future perfect after the historic present *refero* (I went home thinking 'if only I shall find she has gone there').

9 761f. The sanctuary of Juno is evidently on the citadel; Austin calls attention to the irony of the place for helpless suppliants being used as a dumping-ground for loot.

10 762f. **Phoenix**: tutor of Achilles, leader of the embassy to him in Hom. *Il.* 9.

congeritur. Pueri et pavidae longo ordine matres
stant circum.
Ausus quin etiam voces iactare per umbram
implevi clamore vias, maestusque Creusam
nequiquam ingeminans iterumque iterumque vocavi.   770
Quaerenti et tectis urbis sine fine ruenti[1]
infelix[2] simulacrum[3] atque ipsius umbra Creusae
visa mihi ante oculos et nota maior imago.
Obstipui, steteruntque[4] comae et vox faucibus haesit.[5]
Tum sic adfari et curas his demere dictis: 775
'quid tantum insano iuvat indulgere dolori,
o dulcis coniunx? Non[6] haec sine numine divum
eveniunt; nec te hinc comitem asportare Creusam
fas[7] aut ille sinit superi regnator Olympi.
Longa[8] tibi exsilia et vastum maris aequor arandum,   780
et terram Hesperiam venies, [9]ubi Lydius[10] arva
inter opima virum leni[11] fluit agmine Thybris.
Illic res laetae regnumque et regia[12] coniunx
parta tibi; lacrimas dilectae pelle Creusae.[13]
Non ego Myrmidonum[14] sedes Dolopumve superbas   785
aspiciam aut Grais servitum[15] matribus ibo,

---

1 771f. The final scene of Aeneas' search is introduced with a slowing of movement, emphasised by the rhyme of *quaerenti* and *ruenti,* and the assonance of *i* and *o*. The words *ipsius umbra Creusae* are quoted by St. Augustine (*Conf.* 1.13) when he speaks of the fascination Virgil exercised upon him in his boyhood.

2 772. **infelix**: as Servius says, *mihi non sibi.*

3 772-3. The words *simulacrum, umbra, nota maior imago* most impressively build up a picture of a supernatural apparition (cf. 591 and Ov. *Fast.* 2.503, of the ghost of Romulus, *pulcher et humano maior*).

4 774. **steteruntque**: notice the short *e* of *-erunt,* is rarely used by Virgil (cf. 3.681, 10.334); he greatly prefers the perfect ending *-ere.*

5 774-5. Both these lines occur elsewhere, 774 in 3.48, 775 in 3.153, 8.35. It is perhaps better to supply *visa* to govern the infinitives in 775 rather than (as most do) to regard them as historic.

6 777-8. **non haec . . . eveniunt:** this is the lesson of the book which Aeneas has been (understandably) so slow to learn.

7 779. **fas:** 'the laws of heaven', i.e. fate, cf. *Aen.* 6.438, *Geo.* 1.269. Supply *sinit* rather than *est. Ille* is formulaic, cf. *Aen.* 7.558.

8 780. The elliptical construction; suppling *obeunda sunt* to *exsilia* gives an impression of oracular style.

9 781f. This is the first indication to Aeneas of the site of the new settlement which Hector's ghost had foretold (294-5). Hesperia means the western land, and was commonly applied to Italy (1.530).

10 781-2. 'Where the Lydian Tiber flows with smooth sweep through the fertile fields of the people'; the point of *virum* is that Aeneas' destined home is already peopled by the Italians who will contribute so much to the future race of Rome. The river Tiber is called *Lydius* because much of its course was through the land of the Etruscans (*Geo.* 1.499), a people thought to have originated in Lydia in Asia Minor (*Aen.* 8.479, Herod. 1.94).

11 782. **leni fluit agmine:** from Ennius (*Ann.* 173).

12 783. **regia coniunx:** i.e. Lavinia; notice that Aeneas does not conceal this part of the prophesy from Dido.

13 784. **Creusae:** objective genitive, 'tears for. . ', cf. *Aen.* 1.462.

14 785. **Myrmidonum . . . Dolopumve:** see note on line 7.

15 786. **servitum:** supine, rare in elevated poetry, and adding a domestic touch here to Creusa's words to her husband.

Dardanis[1] et divae Veneris nurus;
sed me magna[2] deum genetrix his detinet oris.
Iamque vale et nati[3] serva communis amorem.'
Haec ubi dicta[4] dedit, lacrimantem et multa volentem   790
dicere deseruit, tenuisque recessit in auras.
Ter conatus ibi collo[5] dare bracchia circum;
ter frustra comprensa manus effugit imago,
par levibus ventis volucrique simillima somno.
Sic[6] demum socios consumpta nocte reviso.   795

> *796-804. Aeneas returns to the rest of his family and finds their number augmented by other refugees. The morning star rises and as dawn breaks Aeneas sets off for the mountains.*

Atque hic ingentem comitum adfluxisse novorum
invenio admirans numerum, matresque virosque,
collectam[7] exsilio pubem, miserabile vulgus.
Undique convenere animis opibusque parati[8]
in quascumque velim pelago deducere[9] terras.   800
Iamque[10] iugis summae surgebat Lucifer Idae
ducebatque diem, Danaique obsessa tenebant
limina portarum, [11]nec spes opis ulla dabatur.
Cessi et sublato montis genitore petivi.

---

1 787. **Dardanis:** 'a woman of Dardanus' line'; Dardanus was the founder of the dynasty of Priam, Creusa's father.

2 788. **magna deum genetrix:** Cybele, whose main seat of worship was in the Troad (3.111, 6.784, 9.80f.).

3 789. **nati . . . amorem:** 'cherish your love for our son'; these final words are the only touch of pathos in Creusa's serene explanation of what has happened to her.

4 790-1. These phrases, emphasised by the heavy alliteration of *d* and *t,* are again reminiscent of Eurydice in *Geo.* 4 (499f.); cf. 740.

5 792f. 'Three times then I tried to put my arms round her neck; three times the phantom vainly clasped escaped my grasp, like the light winds and very like a winged dream.' These three lines are translated from Hom. *Od.* 11.206f., and occur again in *Aen.* 6.700f., where Aeneas tries to embrace the ghost of his father Anchises.

6 795. **sic demum:** 'and so it was that at last. . .'; the tragic tale is ended.

7 798. **collectam exsilio pubem:** 'a band assembled for exile'; *exsilio* is dative of purpose, cf. *Aen.* 1.22. There is much bitterness in these words: *pubes collecta* would normally have some different purpose than exile; the truth is revealed in the appositional phrase, *miserabile vulgus.*

8 799-800. **parati in quascumque:** there is an ellipsis after *parati* of a verb like *proficisci.*

9 800. **deducere:** the technical phrase for founding a colony.

10 801f. Observe the symbolism of the new dawn after Troy's dark night of disaster; notice too that Lucifer, the morning star, is the planet Venus. Varro records a tradition that Venus guided her son to Latium by means of her star; cf. 1.382.

11 803-4. Once again, for the last time, Aeneas stresses that there was no hope left of staying in Troy; so he yields to fate and departs carrying his father to the mountains.

BOOK 3

Introductory note

After the intense tragedy of the second book, Book 3 provides a relaxation of tension, a diminution of emotional involvement on the part of the reader. Its function is in many ways comparable with that of the fifth book, to provide a breathing space between two books of great dramatic power. Most of this book is written in an objective style; there is, for example, only one simile, and only in the passage concerning Andromache does Virgil aim at the pathos elsewhere so characteristic of him. The movement is diffuse and expansive, rather than concentrated and intense. Emotionally in this book we rest; intellectually, however, our interest is maintained in the unfolding of the major themes of the poem.

The story of the wanderings of Aeneas clearly offers a possible Virgilian Odyssey. In a number of places Virgil does indeed attempt to recapture the otherworldly atmosphere of strange adventures which were so familiar to him from *Odyssey* 9-12: the episode of the Harpies is partly based on *Odyssey* 12 (see note on 209f.); Aeneas comes in sight of Scylla and Charybdis (see note on 420f.); and above all the encounter with the Cyclops (see note on 617) is reminiscent of *Odyssey* 9. The fantastic world of Homeric folktale had indeed cast its spell over Virgil. But essentially the voyage of Aeneas is different from that of Odysseus; it is set in the real world of the Roman Mediterranean, and the many episodes are given coherence by the progressive revelation to Aeneas of the end which he is seeking. Through oracles from Apollo or his prophets Aeneas gradually learns more and more of his future city and its destiny.

Virgil's arrangement of his material for the seven-year journey is very carefully contrived, with variations of length and interest in the different stages, and a comparison with the account of Dionysius of Halicarnassus shows the ways in which he has avoided the danger of a dull catalogue of landfalls and departures (for a full account of this see the introduction to my OUP Ed.). The journey may best be divided into three groups of three: in the Aegean (Thrace, Delos, Crete); in Greece (Strophades, Actium, Buthrotum); in Italy and Sicily (Castrum Minervae, Etna, voyage round Sicily). The variety of mood and intention in these stages is very considerable: Thrace is grim, terrifying; Delos heartening and exciting; Crete plague-ridden and perilous; the Strophades weird and fearsome; Actium wholly Roman and aetiological; Buthrotum prophetic; Castrum Minervae (the first landing in Italy) at once hopeful and full of foreboding over future wars; Etna and Polyphemus grandiose, rhetorical, baroque; and lastly the passage round Sicily provides a quiet, concluding fulfilment to the voyage.

Three especial themes in the book should be emphasised. The first is the sense of toil and weariness as the Trojan exiles wander from place to place over the unending seas; the suffering and endurance called for seems almost intolerable, and is an indispensable prelude to explain the weakness and weariness of Aeneas which leads him to stay with Dido when he should be pressing onwards towards Italy. The second is the progressive revelation to

94

the Trojans, mainly through Apollo, of their destiny and future glory, expressed in proud patriotic terms (97f., 158f., 462). The third is the part played by Anchises in guiding and advising his son, especially in religious matters, towards the understanding and achievement of his mission. Aeneas learns from his father many of the things which he must teach his own son, and his son's sons, so that the city of Rome will be founded aright on the moral and religious principles which the gods ordain for the future capital of the world. Aeneas must leave the heroic world of Troy and enter the world of Rome's imperial destiny; he must leave the dead past and enter the unborn future.

1-12. After the destruction of Troy Aeneas and his companions build a fleet, and at the beginning of summer set sail for unknown lands.

^{1}Postquam res^2 Asiae Priamique evertere gentem
immeritam^3 visum superis, ceciditque superbum
Ilium et omnis humo^4 fumat Neptunia^5 Troia,
diversa^6 exsilia et desertas^7 quaerere^8 terras
auguriis agimur divum, classemque sub^9 ipsa   5
Antandro et Phrygiae molimur^{10} montibus Idae,
incerti^{11} quo fata ferant, ubi sistere^{12} detur,
contrahimusque viros. ^{13}Vix prima inceperat aestas
et pater Anchises dare fatis vela iubebat,
litora cum patriae lacrimans portusque relinquo   10

1 1f. The short opening paragraph links the new narrative with what went before by means of a brief backward glance (as at the beginning of Book 5). There is very strong emphasis in these lines, as indeed throughout the book, on the divine background to the human action (2 *visum superis;* 5 *auguriis divum;* 7 *quo fata ferant;* 9 *dare fatis vela;* 12 *cum . . .penatibus et magnis dis*). The mention of Anchises' instructions in line 9 prepares the way for the important part to be played in this book by Aeneas' father in helping and advising his son (102f., 263f., 472f., 610f.); the honour in which he is held reflects the importance of the father-son relationship in Roman family life. Aeneas always received from Anchises the help and guidance which he himself was to give to Iulus.

2 1. **res Asiae**: 'the kingdom of Asia', cf. *Aen.* 8.471 *res Troiae.* Priam is called *regnatorem Asiae* in 2.557.

3 2. **immeritum**: a final protest against the divine decision (*visum superis*) to destroy Troy.

4 3. **humo fumat**: 'was a flattened smoking ruin'; notice the change in tense: Troy had fallen and was still smoking as Aeneas began his departure.

5 **Neptunia Troia**: see note on 2.610.

6 4. **diversa exsilia**: 'a far-off place of exile' (so Servius) rather than 'different places of exile'; cf. 2.780 *longa tibi exsilia.*

7 **desertas ... terras**: 'empty lands', in contrast with the flourishing civilisation which they formerly knew.

8 4-5. **quaerere . . . agimur**: for the final use of the infinitive cf. 682-3 and note on 527-8.

9 5-6. **sub ipsa Antandro**: 'just by Antandros', a town in the Troad on the other side of Mt. Ida from Troy.

10 6. **molimur**: 'toil at building', cf. 132.

11 7. **incerti**: throughout the early part of Book 3 the Trojans are ignorant of the whereabouts of their destined city, in spite of Creusa's prophecy in 2.781f. where Hesperia and the Tiber were named. This is one of a number of minor inconsistencies which Book 3 contains; see the Intro. to my OUP Ed. of Book 3, pp. 19f.

12 **sistere**: 'to stop' (= *consistere*), cf. *Geo.* 1.479.

13 8-10. 'Scarcely had early summer begun —— and father Anchises was urging us to entrust our ships to the fates — when I set sail. . . .'; line 9 is slightly parenthetical. The burning of Troy was traditionally placed in the late winter or early spring.

et campos ubi Troia fuit.[1] Feror exsul in altum
cum sociis natoque penatibus[2] et magnis dis.[3]

> *13-18. Aeneas sails to Thrace, and begins to build a city there.*

[4]Terra[5] procul vastis colitur Mavortia[6] campis
(Thraces[7] arant) acri quondam regnata[8] Lycurgo,
hospitium[9] antiquum Troiae sociique penates   15
dum fortuna fuit. Feror huc et litore curvo
moenia prima loco fatis[10] ingressus iniquis
Aeneadasque[11] meo nomen de nomine fingo.

---

1 11. **fuit:** 'once stood', (was and is not); cf. *Aen.* 2.325.

2 12. **penatibus et magnis dis:** cf. 2.293f. (Hector's instructions to Aeneas to take the *penates* with him). It is uncertain whether the *magni di* were the *penates* (as Varro says) or different deities; it seems best to regard the phrase as broadening the meaning of *penates* by associating them with the public cult and such allied deities as Vesta and the Lares.

3 12. This line is a reminiscence of Ennius (*Ann. 201 dono, ducite, doque volentibus cum magnis dis*). The unusual rhythm of the trochaic caesura in the third foot without a main caesura in the fourth, the spondaic fifth foot, and the monosyllabic ending all echo Virgil's source and would remind the Roman readers at this important point in the narrative of their first national hexameter poet. The line ending is used again in *Aen.* 8.679 in the picture on Aeneas' shield of Augustus leading the Italians to battle.

4 13f. Aeneas' visit to Thrace was well established in the legend (Livy 1.1-4); Virgil has added to it from poetic sources the story of Polydorus and its macabre sequel.

5 13. **terra procul. .. colitur:** 'there lies at a distance a land. . . .'; *procul* does not necessarily imply a very great distance. *Colitur* is used in a general sense, 'is inhabited', 'is known of, 'exists', cf. 73.

6 **Mavortia:** Thrace had very strong associations with Ares and Mars, cf. line 35, *Geo.* 4.462 *Rhesi Mavortia tellus.*

7 14. **Thraces arant:** for the parenthetical syntax, quite common in Virgil, cf. *Aen.* 1.12; for the final short syllable of the Greek nominative plural *Thraces* cf. *Cyclopes* (644).

8 **regnata Lycurgo:** the intransitive verb *regnare* is here used in the passive as if it were transitive on the analogy of *regere;* cf. *Aen.* 6.793. *Lycurgo* is dative of the agent, cf. 275. Lycurgus resisted the introduction of the worship of Dionysus into Thrace.

9 15. **hospitium:** 'place of friendship', cf. 61.

10 17. **fatis ingressus iniquis:** this anticipates the narrative, and prepares the reader for the grim sequel.

11 18. The people of this new town are to be called Aeneadae; Virgil is not specific about the name of the town itself, perhaps because the legend varied (there was a town called Aenus at the mouth of the Hebrus, associated with Polydorus, Pliny, *Nat. Hist.* 4.43, and also a town Aenia in Chalcidice said to have been founded by Aeneas). For the aetiological association of place names with the Aeneas legend cf. Pergamum (133), Chaonia (335) and note on 1.267-8 (Iulus and Ilium).

19-68. As Aeneas tears up some myrtle and cornel shoots in order to wreathe the altars, drops of blood come from the broken stems. Then a cry is heard from beneath the earth, and the voice of Polydorus tells Aeneas that the shoots have grown from the spears which transfixed him when he was murdered after being sent to Thrace. Aeneas calls a council, and the Trojans decide to leave; funeral rites for Polydorus are prepared.

[1]Sacra Dionaeae[2] matri divisque[3] ferebam

auspicibus coeptorum operum, superoque nitentem 20

caelicolum[4] regi mactabam in litore taurum.

Forte fuit iuxta tumulus, quo[5] cornea summo

virgulta et densis hastilibus horrida myrtus.

Accessi viridemque ab humo convellere silvam[6]

conatus, ramis tegerem[7] ut frondentibus aras, 25

horrendum et dictu video mirabile monstrum.

---

1 19f. The grim, strange story of Polydorus and the drops of blood trickling from the myrtle shoots is not found before Virgil; no trace exists in the very varied tradition about him of this sequel to his death. Moreover there is no reason to think that Polydorus played any part in the Aeneas legend before Virgil,

although as we have seen (see note on 13f.) Aeneas' visit to Thrace was part of the normal tradition.

The introduction of the supernatural sequel to Polydorus' death may of course be due to some lost source of Virgil, but it seems more likely that it was Virgil's own invention, based upon such folklore as the spear thrown by Romulus on to the Palatine, which took root and grew into a tree, or the stories of Dryads or Hamadryads, the nymphs who lived in trees and were sometimes physically identified with them, so that an injury to the tree caused them injury; cf. Ap. Rh. 2.476f., Ov. *Met.* 8.738f., and Shelley's lines on the Woodman '... killing the tall treen / the soul of whom, by Nature's gentle law, / was each a Wood nymph.'Virgil's story was imitated by Dante (*Inf.* 13) and Spenser (*F.Q..* 1.2.30f.):

And thinking of those braunches greene to frame

A girlond for her dainty forehead fit

He pluckt a bough; out of whose rift there came

Small drops of gory bloud, that trickled downe the same.

Therewith a piteous yelling voyce was heard,

Crying, O spare with guilty hands to teare

My tender sides in this rough rynd embard,

But fly, ah fly far hence away. . . .

It remains to ask why Virgil has introduced into the Aeneas legend this altered version of the story of Polydorus. It is intended to make us feel that the long voyage which ends in the foundation of Rome begins in missteps, tragedy, horror, and despair. It is an episode of primitive folklore, and in it Aeneas receives his first omen of the voyage, a grim and unhappy one. It serves to emphasise the atmosphere of gloom and sorrow in which Aeneas, still a 'ghost of Troy' rather than yet 'father of Rome', sets out from his destroyed homeland. See C. S. Lewis, *A Preface to Paradise Lost,* chap. vi.

2 19. **Dionaeae:** Venus has this epithet (cf. *Ecl.* 9.47) as daughter of Dione, child of Oceanus and Tethys.

3 19-20. **divisque ... operum:** 'and to the gods who give their favour to new undertakings'; Servius specifies Jupiter, Apollo and Bacchus. For *auspicibus* cf. *Aen.* 4.45; here of course the hoped for favour was not forthcoming.

4 21. **caelicolum:** archaic form of the genitive plural of the first declension, cf. 1.565 *Aeneadum* and line 550 *Graiugenum.*

5 22-3. **quo ... myrtus:** 'on the top of which grew cornel shrubs and a bristling thicket of myrtle-shoots'; for the omission of the verb to be in a descriptive passage cf. 216f., 533f., 618f. Myrtle and cornel were used for making spears, cf. *Geo.* 2.447-8; the word *hostile* is here used of the spiky growth of the tree, but with a forward reference to its real meaning ('spear'), cf. 46. *Horrida* is frequent in this sense of 'bristling', cf. *Aen.* 10.178, 11.601-2, and Milton's 'horrid arms', 'horrent arms'.

6 24. **silvam:** 'undergrowth', cf. *Geo.* 1.76, 152.

7 25. **tegerem ut:** the conjunction is preceded by its verb only in poetry; cf. 473 for a striking instance.

Nam ¹quae prima solo ruptis radicibus arbos
vellitur, huic atro liquuntur sanguine guttae
et terram tabo maculant. Mihi frigidus horror
membra quatit gelidusque² coit formidine sanguis.   30
Rursus et alterius lentum³ convellere⁴ vimen
insequor et causas penitus temptare latentis;
ater et alterius sequitur de cortice sanguis.
Multa movens animo Nymphas⁵ venerabar agrestis
Gradivumque⁶ patrem, Geticis⁷ qui praesidet arvis,   35
rite ⁸secundarent visus omenque levarent.
Tertia sed postquam maiore hastilia nisu
adgredior genibusque adversae obluctor harenae
(eloquar an sileam?) gemitus lacrimabilis⁹ imo
auditur tumulo et vox¹⁰ reddita fertur ad auris: 40
'quid miserum, Aenea, laceras? Iam parce sepulto,
parce pias¹¹ scelerare manus. ¹²Non me tibi Troia
externum tulit aut cruor hic de stipite manat.
Heu fuge crudelis terras, fuge litus avarum:
nam Polydorus¹³ ego. ¹⁴Hic confixum ferrea texit   45
telorum seges et iaculis increvit acutis.'
tum vero ancipiti mentem¹⁵ formidine pressus

---

1 27-8. 'For when the first sapling was torn out of the ground, its roots severed, there came oozing from it drops of black blood. . .' The antecedent for *quae* (*arbori*) is taken into the relative clause; cf. 94. The dative *huic* (prose would have *ab hoc*) is a poetic extension of the dative of the thing concerned in an action; *mihi* in the next line is a much more normal example of this construction.

2 30. **gelidusque . . . sanguis:** 'and my blood curdles, frozen with fear'; cf. 259, *Aen.* 10.452.

3 31. **lentum:** 'tough', 'springy', cf. *Geo.* 4.34.

4 31-2. **convellere . . . insequor:** for the extended poetic use of the infinitive see note on 4-5. The analogy is with verbs like *instare, pergere;* there is no other instance of the infinitive with *insequi*.

5 34. **Nymphas:** i.e. Hamadryads, see note on 19f.

6 35. **Gradivumque patrem:** this is a name of Mars (line 13); cf. *Aen.* 10.542.

7 **Geticis**: the Getae lived in Thrace, cf. *Geo.* 3.462.

8 36. 'that they would duly give a favourable issue to what I had seen, and lighten the omen'. The construction is an indirect petition after the idea of *orans* which is present in *venerabar*. Aeneas realises that what he has just witnessed is clearly an omen, and apparently a bad one, and he prays that it may be changed to good.

9 39. **lacrimabilis:** probably 'piteous' rather than 'tearful'; cf. *Aen.* 7.604 *lacrimabile bellum*.

10 40. **vox reddita:** 'an answering cry', cf. *Aen.* 7.95.

11 42. **pias:** Aeneas' own epithet, here with reference to religious obligations and common nationality.

12 42-3. 'I am no stranger to you, for Troy gave me birth; and this welling blood is not coming from wood.' For the use of *aut* with the negative carried forward to its clause cf. 162. Only the words *externum* and *de stipite* are affected by the negative.

13 45. **Polydorus**: the details of the story are told in 49f.; for Virgil's sources see note on 19f.

14 45-6. 'Here was I transfixed, here an iron crop of weapons covered me over, and grew up with pointed shafts', i.e. the volley of spears which pinned him to the ground took root and grew into myrtle and cornel shoots. The metaphor of *ferrea seges* is one of which Virgil was fond; cf. 7.526, 12.663.

15 47. **mentem . . . pressus**: 'overwhelmed in mind'; for the retained accusative *mentem* cf. 65, 81, 428, and note on 1.228.

obstipui steteruntque comae et vox faucibus haesit.[1]

  [2]Hunc Polydorum[3] auri quondam cum pondere magno
infelix Priamus furtim mandarat alendum   50
Threicio[4] regi, cum iam diffideret armis
Dardaniae cingique urbem obsidione videret.
Ille, ut opes fractae Teucrum et Fortuna recessit,
res Agamemnonias victriciaque arma secutus
fas[5] omne abrumpit: Polydorum obtruncat, et auro[6]   55
vi potitur. Quid[7] non mortalia pectora cogis,
auri sacra[8] fames! Postquam pavor ossa reliquit,
delectos[9] populi ad proceres primumque parentem
monstra deum refero, et quae sit sententia posco.
Omnibus idem animus, scelerata excedere terra,[10]   60
linqui pollutum[11] hospitium et dare[12] classibus Austros.
Ergo instauramus[13] Polydoro funus, et ingens
aggeritur tumulo[14] tellus; stant[15] manibus arae,
caeruleis maestae vittis atraque cupresso,
et circum Iliades crinem[16] de more solutae;   65
inferimus tepido spumantia [17]cymbia lacte

---

1 48. This line is found also at 2.774; for the form *steterunt* see note there.

2 49-57. The insertion of this narrative of past events to explain the present is perfectly natural when we remember that Aeneas is recounting the story to Dido; what he did not know at the time he now does know, so that he can tell the complete story. The transition back to the main narrative (56-7) by means of the exclamation against the corrupting power of gold would have special significance for Dido, as Pygmalion had murdered her husband Sychaeus for gold.

3 49f. This part of the story of Polydorus (who was Priam's youngest son) is quite closely modelled on Euripides' *Hecuba* (10f., 716f., 781-2).

4 51. **Threicio regi**: Polymestor, who had married Iliona, one of Priam's daughters.

5 55. **fas omne abrumpit**: 'broke all his sacred obligations', i.e. kinship,hospitality and good faith.

6 55-6. Notice the staccato effect of the short phrases which conclude the narrative about Polymestor.

7 56-7. **quid ... fames!**: for the phraseology cf. *Aen.* 4.412 *improbe Amor, quid non mortalia pectora cogis*! Pliny (*Nat. Hist.* 33.6) refers to Virgil's phrase in a passage decrying luxury.

8 57. **sacra**: 'accursed'. The phrase *sacer esto* occurs in the Twelve Tables, and probably by Virgil's time this meaning had an archaic flavour; cf. *Geo.* 3.566.

9 58-9. Aeneas' language here has something of the formality of the Roman senate; he is most anxious to follow the correct procedure in the face of this trial.

10 60-1. The infinitives are in apposition to *idem animus (est)*; the variation (active, passive, active) is unusual.

11 61. **pollutum hospitium**: 'this place where friendship had been desecrated': see line 15 and cf. *Aen.* 7.467 *polluta pace*.

12 **dare classibus Austros**: 'to give the fleet its winds', a personification of the impatient fleet.

13 62. **instauramus**: 'we renew'; in a sense Polydorus was already buried (lines 22, 41), but the appropriate rites had not been performed.

14 63. **tumulo**: 'on the mound', the one referred to in line 22.

15 **stant manibus arae**: 'altars are set up in honour of his shade'; cf. line 305 (Hector) and 5.48 (Anchises), and Bailey, *Religion in Virgil*, pp. 259f., 290f.

16 65. **crinem ... solutae**: for the retained accusative see note on 47.

17 66. For the offerings given cf. *Aen.* 5.77f.; the spirit was supposed to partake of them. For *cymbia* ('cups') cf. *Aen.* 5.267; Servius says they were boat-shaped (*cumba*).

sanguinis et sacri pateras, animamque[1] sepulcro
condimus et magna supremum voce ciemus.[2]

69-83. The Trojans sail to Delos, the sacred island of Apollo, and are hospitably received by Anius.

[3]Inde ubi prima fides pelago, placataque venti
dant maria et lenis[4] crepitans vocat Auster[5] in altum,   70
deducunt socii navis et litora complent.
Provehimur portu terraeque urbesque recedunt.
Sacra mari colitur[6] medio gratissima tellus
Nereidum[7] matri et Neptuno[8] Aegaeo,
quam[9] pius arquitenens[10] oras et litora circum   75
errantem[11] Mycono[12] e celsa Gyaroque revinxit,

---

1 67-8. **animamque ... condimus:** 'we lay his spirit to rest in its tomb'. Previously it has been restless and disturbed; now it receives due burial and peace; cf. *Aen.* 6.152.

2 68. To call on the ghost of the dead man for the last time was a regular procedure at Roman funerals; cf. *Aen.* 2.644, 6.231, 506.

3 69f. The visit to Delos occurs also in Dionysius' version (1.50) of Aeneas' wanderings. It was a very suitable episode for Virgil to include, partly because of its attractive literary associations (75-6), but mainly because Delos above all places offered the best setting for prophecy and the revelation of the purpose of the Trojan voyage; the theme which provides a unifying motif throughout this book.
This second episode of Aeneas' voyage provides a strong contrast in mood with the sorrow and gloom of the opening movement of the book; after four preliminary lines describing the departure it continues with an attractive picture of the famous island and concludes with calm and serene phrases describing the arrival at the harbour and the meeting with Anius, an old friend of Anchises.

4 70. **lenis crepitans:** for the adjective used adverbially with a present participle (not a prose usage) cf. *Aen.* 5.764. *Crepitans* ('rustling') is unusual and colourful in this context.

5 **Auster:** Delos is south of Thrace; the geographical direction of winds is not to be pressed in the poets (Servius says 'auster autem qui vis ventus').

6 73-4. 'There is a sacred land lying in the midst of sea, dearly loved by the mother of the Nereids'. For *colitur* cf. 13; the mother of the Nereids (sea-nymphs) was Doris, wife of Nereus.

7 74. The rhythm of this line (which also occurs in *Ciris* 474) is Greek, and contains several features which are unusual in Latin: there is a hiatus after *matri* and another after *Neptuno,* the fifth foot is spondaic and it is preceded by a spondaic fourth foot, a curious rhythm. See note on 1.617.

8 **Neptuno Aegaeo:** the epithet refers primarily to the Aegean sea in which Delos is situated, but also suggests Aegae, the place of Poseidon's palace in Homer (*Il.* 13.21f.).

9 75-6. 'it used to float around from coast to coast until the Archer god in due gratitude fixed it firmly to lofty Myconos and Gyarus'. Apollo is called *pius* because he fulfilled his obligations to the island that had sheltered his mother Latona (Leto) from Juno's wrath when she gave birth to him and Diana. Throughout antiquity Delos was regarded as one of the main seats of Apollo; cf. Hom. *Od.* 6.162f., Hor. *Odes* 3.4.60f., *Aen.* 4.144. The arrival of Aeneas at Delos is the subject of one of Claude Lorrain's classical landscapes (in the National Gallery); Keats has a fine description of Apollo's island in *Hyperion,* Book III, beginning:
Chief isle of the embowered Cyclades,
Rejoice, O Delos, with thine olives green
And poplars, and lawn-shading palms, and beech,
In which the Zephyr breathes the loudest song,
And hazels thick, dark-stemm'd beneath the shade;
Apollo is once more the golden theme.

10 75. **arquitenens**: this compound adjective (cf. 544 *Palladis armisonae*) has a Homeric ring (αργυροτοξος, κλυτοτοξος, υοξοφορος); it is found in Latin as early as Naevius.

11 76. **errantem:** compare the floating island of Aeolia (Hom. *Od.* 10.1f.), and the stories of the Planctae and Symplegades ('wandering', 'clashing' rocks). The legend that Delos was once a floating island is found first in Pindar (quoted in Strabo 10.485); cf. also Callimachus (*Hymn. Del.* 35f.), Prop. 4.6.27f., Ov. *Met.* 6.333-4, and Spenser *F.Q.*, 2.12.13.

12 **Mycono e celsa Gyaroque**: these two islands, adjacent to Delos, are coupled in Stat. *Th.* 3.438, an imitation of this passage.

immotamque coli dedit[1] et contemnere[2] ventos.
Huc feror, haec fessos[3] tuto placidissima portu
accipit; egressi veneramur Apollinis urbem.
Rex Anius,[4] rex idem hominum Phoebique sacerdos,   80
vittis et sacra redimitus tempora[5] lauro[6]
occurrit; veterem Anchisen agnovit amicum.
Iungimus hospitio dextras et tecta subimus.

> *84-120. At Delos Aeneas prays to Apollo for guidance, and receives an oracular response bidding the Trojans to seek out their 'ancient mother'. Anchises interprets this as the island of Crete, and they prepare to set out.*

[7]Templa dei saxo venerabar structa vetusto:
'da propriam,[8] Thymbraee,[9] domum; da moenia fessis   85
et genus et mansuram urbem; [10]serva altera Troiae
Pergama, reliquias[11] Danaum atque immitis Achilli.
Quem sequimur?[12] Quove ire iubes? Ubi ponere sedes?
Da, pater, augurium[13] atque animis inlabere nostris.'
Vix ea fatus eram: tremere omnia visa repente,[14]   90

---

1 77. **dedit**: 'granted'; for the poetic use with the infinitive, see note on 1.66.

2 **contemnere ventos**: because when it floated, it was at the mercy of the winds; cf. Pliny's description (*Ep.* 8.20.6f.) of the little floating islands on Lake Vadimon.

3 78. **fessos**: a key word in this book; notice how early in the wanderings it is used. The Trojans are weary exiles, struggling onwards, from the first stages of their pilgrimage.

4 80f. Like the Roman kings, Anius combined the offices of *rex* and *sacerdos;* cf. Ov. *Met.* 13.632f. According to Servius (on *Aen.* 8.158) Anchises had visited Anius before the Trojan war.

5 81. **tempora**: retained accusative, see note on 47.

6 **lauro**: Apollo's tree (91); cf. Ov. *Met.* 1.452f.

7 84f. In Thrace, the first stage of his journey, Aeneas received an omen and a supernatural revelation to tell him that he was not to make his home there. Now at the oracle of Apollo in Delos he receives the first positive indication during his voyage of where his goal lies. The oracle is delivered by the god himself (line 99), not through an intermediary priestess; the personal guidance given by Apollo to the Trojan exiles is thus stressed.

The directions of Apollo (which are misinterpreted by Anchises, see note on 94-8) are concluded with a brief statement of the glorious future awaiting the house of Aeneas, a prophecy reiterated by the Penates (158f.). Such prophecies form a bright pattern within the *Aeneid* as a foil to the darker tones of toil and suffering. Compare especially Jupiter's speech in *Aen.* 1.257f., the oracle to Latinus (7.96f.), the speech of Tiberinus (8.36f.), and Jupiter's final speech in 12.830f. The same prophetic effect is achieved by the vision of Roman heroes in 6.756f., and the description of Aeneas' shield (8.625f.).

8 85. **propriam**: 'to be our own', i.e. lasting, permanent; cf. 167 and *mansuram* in the following line.

9 85. **Thymbraee**: this epithet of Apollo (cf. *Geo.* 4.323) derives from Thymbra in the Troad, where Apollo had a well-known temple.

10 86-7. 'keep safe Troy's other citadel, the remnant left by the Greeks and cruel Achilles.' *Pergama* was the citadel of Troy, the real one has been destroyed and Aeneas and his followers are now symbolically the only 'citadel' left; cf. 8.37, and the Greek proverb: 'Men, not walls, make a city'. (Thuc. 7.77.7).

11 87. **reliquias . . . Achilli**: cf. *Aen.* 1.30, and Spenser *F.Q.* 3.9.41, 'and with a remnant did to sea repaire'.

12 88. **sequimur**: the indicative is sometimes used vividly instead of the subjunctive in what is equivalent to a deliberative question; cf. 367.

13 89. **augurium**: an omen as an indication of the divine will; cf. *Aen.* 2.691.

14 90. The paratactic construction, *vix ea fatus eram (cum)* (or *et*) *tremere omnia visa sunt,* and the dactylic movement help to convey the immediacy of the response.

liminaque[1] laurusque dei, totusque moveri
mons[2] circum et mugire adytis cortina[3] reclusis.
Summissi petimus terram et vox fertur ad auris:
'Dardanidae duri,[4] [5]quae vos a stirpe parentum[6]
prima tulit tellus, eadem vos ubere[7] laeto   95
accipiet reduces. Antiquam[8] exquirite matrem.
hic[9] domus Aeneae cunctis dominabitur oris
et nati natorum et qui nascentur ab illis.'
Haec Phoebus; mixtoque ingens exorta tumultu
laetitia, et cuncti quae sint ea moenia quaerunt,   100
quo Phoebus vocet errantis iubeatque reverti.
Tum[10] genitor veterum volvens[11] monimenta virorum
'audite, o proceres,' ait 'et spes discite vestras.
Creta[12] Iovis magni medio iacet insula ponto,
mons[13] Idaeus ubi[14] et gentis cunabula nostrae.   105
Centum[15] urbes habitant magnas, uberrima regna,
maximus[16] unde pater, si rite audita recordor,

---

1 91. **liminaque laurusque**: the lengthening in arsis of the first *-que* is in imitation of Homeric lengthening of τε; all 16 instances of this in Virgil are before a double consonant except this one and *Aen.* 12.363. See also note on 1.308.

2 92. **mons**: Mount Cynthus, cf. *Aen.* 4.147.

3 **cortina**: cf. *Aen.* 6.347. The word means a rounded vessel; in an oracular shrine it was placed on the sacred tripod. The word *mugire* is associated with supernatural happenings in 4.490, 6.256.

4 94. **duri**: the word stresses the virtues of toughness and endurance which the Trojan exiles, and later the Romans, were called upon to display in adverse circumstances.

5 94-8. The riddling oracle is taken by Anchises to refer to Crete, the homeland of the Trojan king Teucer; in fact Italy is meant, the original home of Dardanus (see note on 167-8).

6 94-5. Notice the heavy alliteration of *d*, giving an archaic impressiveness for the beginning of the oracle, and the emphatic effect of putting the relative clause first (with the antecedent *tellus* taken into it; cf. 27) and resuming it with *eadem*.

7 95. **ubere laeto**: 'in her loving bosom'. Both words have a double meaning, applicable to *mater* and *tellus*. *Uber* means the mother's breast or the earth's fertility; *laetus* can mean the mother's joy or the fruitfulness of the land.

8 96. **antiquam . . . matrem**: personification of the 'mother' country is natural and frequent in all literature; cf. *Geo.* a. 173-4, *Aen.* 7.762, and Mother Earth in the story of Brutus and the Tarquins, or Deucalion and Pyrrha.

9 97-8. These lines are based on Hom. *Il.* 20.307-8 where Poseidon prophesies that Aeneas will rule the Trojans, and his sons's sons and those who come thereafter; Virgil has widened the area of rule to the whole world.

10 102f. Notice that it is to Anchises that the interpretation of the oracle is left; see note on 1f.

11 102. **volvens monimenta**: 'pondering the traditions'; the meaning of *monimenta* (information which they left) is defined on 107.

12 104. Crete was Jupiter's island because he was born and brought up there by the nymphs (*Geo.* 4.149f.). See also on 111f.

13 105. **mons Idaeus**: Mt. Ida in Crete gave its name to Mt. Ida in theTroad (112).

14 **ubi**: the conjunction is postponed (cf. 25), and the verb *est* omitted.

15 106. For Crete's hundred cities cf. Hom. *Il.* 2.649, Hor. *Odes* 3.27.33f.; *uberrima regna* picks up *ubere laeto* in 95.

16 107. **maximus . . . pater**: 'first ancestor'; *maximus* is used in the sense of *maximus natu*.

Teucrus[1] Rhoeteas[2] primum est advectus in oras,
optavitque locum regno. Nondum Ilium et arces[3]
Pergameae steterant;[4] habitabant vallibus imis.　　　110
Hinc[5] mater cultrix[6] Cybeli Corybantiaque aera
Idaeumque nemus,[7] hinc fida[8] silentia sacris,
et iuncti currum dominae subiere leones.[9]
Ergo agite et divum ducunt qua[10] iussa sequamur:
placemus ventos et Cnosia[11] regna petamus.　　　115
nec longo distant cursu: modo[12] Iuppiter adsit,
tertia lux classem Cretaeis sistet in oris.'
Sic fatus meritos[13] aris mactavit honores,
taurum Neptuno,[14] taurum tibi, pulcher Apollo,
nigram[15] Hiemi pecudem, Zephyris felicibus albam.　　　120

121-34. The Trojans sail from Delos to Crete, where they
land and begin to build a town called Pergamum.

[16]Fama volat pulsum regnis cessisse paternis

---

1 108. **Teucrus:** the Latin form is much more commonly *Teucer.* Anchises, having missed the clue in *Dardanidae duri* is following the version of the legend according to which Teucer had arrived in Troy from Crete before Dardanus came from Italy (Apollod. 3.12.1). As it turns out however (167f.) the correct version is the one which gave priority to Dardanus.

2 **Rhoeteas:** Rhoeteum was a promontory near Troy, cf. *Aen.* 6.505.

3 109-10. Virgil is closely following Homer's lines about Dardanus founding Troy (*Il.* 20.216f.).

4 110. **steterant:** 'had come into existence'.

5 111f. 'From here came the mother who dwells on Mt. Cybelus, and the cymbals of the Corybants and our grove of Ida; from here came the custom of obedient silence at the rites, and yoked lions bowed their necks beneath the chariot of the queen'. The goddess here described is Cybele or Cybebe, the *Magna Mater,* the Berecynthian mother (*Aen.* 6.784f.) whose rites were introduced into Rome from Phrygia at the end of the third century B.C. She is invoked by Aeneas in *Aen.* 7.139, 10.252; she had taken Creusa into her care on the last night of Troy (2.788f.); it is at her prayer that Jupiter turns the Trojans ships into nymphs (9.82f.). Cf. Catullus' brilliant description of her worship (poem 63), and Lucr. 2.600f., Ov. *Fast.* 4.179f. Her cult in Phrygia was influenced by the cult of Rhea in Crete, and the clashing of cymbals in her worship by the Corybantes was linked with the legend of the Curetes in Dicte drowning the cries of the infant Jupiter (Lucr. 2.633f) when Saturn was hunting for him.

6 111. **cultrix Cybeli:** for *cultrix* cf. *Geo.* 1.14. Some MSS read *Cybele,* the goddess's name, but this leaves *cultrix* without construction.

7 112. **nemus:** the last syllable is lengthened in arsis, see note on 2.369.

8 **fida silentia sacris**: this associates Cybele with Demeter, another personification of the concept of the Mother goddess, whose initiation ceremonies at Eleusis were never to be divulged; cf. Hor. *Odes* 3.2.25f.

9 113. The lions which draw the chariot of Cybele (Cat. 63.76f., *Aen.* 10.253) probably symbolise her power over untamed nature.

10 114. Notice how the postposition of *qua* puts emphasis on the words which precede it, an emphasis strengthened by the alliteration of *d.*

11 115. **Cnosia regna:** the kingdom of Cnossos, chief town of King Minos' Crete.

12 116. **modo Iuppiter adsit:** 'only let Jupiter be favourable', the paratactic equivalent of *dummodo,* 'provided that'.

13 118. **meritos . . .honores:** 'the offerings called for', 'deserved' by the occasion. For *honores* cf. 264, 547.

14 119. Neptune and Apollo were the gods with whom the description of the Delos episode began (74f.); the sacrifices due to them conclude the Trojan visit to the island.

15 120. The black victim is for the potentially hostile deity, the white one for the potentially propitious (*felix*).

16 121f. The visit to Crete does not occur in other extant versions of the Aeneas legend. By including Crete Virgil has been able to enrich his story with all the associations between Crete and Troy mentioned by Anchises (104f.),and especially to give a setting for a new prophecy of the future glory of Rome and the Trojans (154f.).

Idomenea[1] ducem, desertaque litora Cretae,
hoste[2] vacare domum sedesque astare[3] relictas.
Linquimus Ortygiae[4] portus pelagoque volamus
bacchatamque[5] iugis Naxon[6] viridemque Donusam,   125
Olearon niveamque[7] Paron sparsasque per aequor
Cycladas,[8] et crebris legimus[9] freta concita[10] terris.
Nauticus[11] exoritur vario certamine clamor:
hortantur socii Cretam[12] proavosque petamus.
Prosequitur surgens a puppi ventus euntis,   130
et tandem antiquis Curetum[13] adlabimur oris.
Ergo avidus muros optatae[14] molior[15] urbis
Pergameamque[16] voco, et laetam cognomine gentem
hortor[17] amare[18] focos arcemque[19] attollere tectis.

---

1 122. **Idomenea**: this is the Homeric form of the Greek accusative, cf. *Aen.* 1.611 (*Ilionea*). Idomeneus of Crete was one of the main Greek chieftains in the war against Troy (Hom. *Il.* 13.210f.). Servius tells the story of how on his return from Troy Idomeneus was caught in a storm, and vowed that if he were saved he would sacrifice the first thing he saw on landing. This was his son; when he fulfilled his vow a pestilence came on the land, and he was driven out. He went to the land of the Sallentini in Calabria and founded a state there (line 400); cf. also *Aen.* 11.264-5. Mozart's *Idomeneo* is based on this story.

2 123. **hoste vacare domum**: 'here was a home for us unoccupied by the enemy', or possibly 'his palace was empty of our enemy'.

3 **astare**: 'were standing ready', cf. *Aen.* 2.303.

4 124. **Ortygiae**: a name of Delos, meaning 'Quail-island'; various stories survive in explanation of the name, for instance that Latona's sister, Asteria, was turned into a quail to avoid the love of Jupiter.

5 125. **bacchatamque iugis Naxon**: 'Naxos that holds Bacchic revel on its mountains'; *bacchata* is generally explained as passive in meaning ('revelled upon', cf. *Geo.* 2.487), but this makes *iugis* very awkward; an active meaning such as that given in the translation is normal of persons (*Aen.* 4.301), and here the personification of the island is quite natural.

6 125f. These islands of the Cyclades are all close to Delos, to the south.

7 126. **niveamque Paron**: the white marble of Paros was famous, (*Geo.* 3.34, *Aen.* 1.593).

8 127. Cycladas: notice the short final vowel of the Greek declension; cf. *tripodas* (360), *lebetas* (466), *Hyadas* (516), *Cyclopas* (647), and compare note on 14.

9 **legimus freta**: 'thread the straits' (Fairclough); cf. 706.

10 **concita**: 'made rough by'; Servius rightly explains that the sea is naturally more disturbed near land. Cf. Tac. *Agr.* 10.6, and for the rough waters around the Cyclades cf. Hor. *Odes* 1.14.19f., Livy 36.43.1. A few inferior MSS read *consita*, 'planted with', 'strewn with'.

11 128. **nauticus . . . clamor**: 'the shouts of the sailors', doubtless including the calling of the time by the bo'sun (*celeuma*), but conveying also the general hubbub of the happy crew (*socii*).

12 129. **Cretam . . . petamus**: perhaps the actual words of the sailors, in *oratio recta*, rather than indirect command.

13 131. **Curetum**: see note on 111.

14 132. **optatae**: 'longed for', cf. 509, not here 'chosen'.

15 **molior**: cf. line 6 and *Aen.* 1.424.

16 133. **Pergameam**: adjective agreeing with *urbem*, understood from the previous line. Cf. 349f. for calling new places by old names. Velleius and Pliny mention a town Pergamum in Crete.

17 134. **hortor amare**: poetic use of the infinitive of indirect command, as also in 144, 608-9. See note on 4-5.

18 **amare focos**: 'to cherish their homes'; *focos* has something of the sense of *penates*.

19 **arcemque attollere tectis**: 'to raise the citadel high with buildings', cf. *Aen.* 2.185f.

135-91. As the Trojans busy themselves with building their new home in Crete, a pestilence suddenly attacks them. Anchises suggests that they should return to Delos to consult the oracle again, but a vision of the Penates appears to Aeneas at night, telling him that it is in Hesperia, now called Italia, that he is to found his destined city. Anchises recognises his error in interpreting the oracle of Apollo, and the Trojans leave Crete.

¹Iamque² fere sicco subductae litore puppes;   135
conubiis arvisque novis operata³ iuventus;
iura domosque dabam; ⁴subito cum tabida membris
corrupto caeli tractu miserandaque venit
arboribusque satisque lues et letifer⁵ annus.
Linquebant⁶ dulcis animas aut aegra trahebant   140
corpora; tum sterilis⁷ exurere⁸ Sirius⁹ agros,
arebant herbae et victum¹⁰ seges aegra negabat.
Rursus¹¹ ad oraclum¹² Ortygiae Phoebumque remenso¹³
hortatur pater ire mari veniamque precari,
quam¹⁴ fessis¹⁵ finem rebus ferat, unde laborum   145
temptare auxilium iubeat, quo vertere cursus.

---

1 135f. Notice the sudden change of mood, from confidence to misfortune (contrast 69f.). The alternation of hope and gloom is characteristic of this book, as the Trojans struggle on towards their goal (as indeed it is characteristic of the whole *Aeneid;* cf. especially the last sections of Book 6 and Book 12). The mood changes again at 147f., where the heartening prophecy of the Penates is described in a passage of remarkable visual impact. Dreams and visions play a major part in the pattern of the *Aeneid,* emphasising the contrast of the divine plan with the human action, often occurring at moments when Aeneas is near despair or mishap; see notes on 84f. and 2.268f.

2 135. **Iamque fere . . . cum:** the first two words indicate a description of the present situation (*subductae sunt, operata est, dabam*), and prepare us for an alteration to it, which is given in the inverted *cum* clause; cf. *Aen.* 5.327f.

3 136. **operata:** 'were occupied with', cf. Liv. 4.60.2; the word probably includes an idea of the religious ceremonies involved, cf. *Geo.* 1.339.

4 137-9. 'when suddenly the expanse of the air was infected and upon our bodies there came a corrupting pestilence, pitiable to see; upon the trees and the crops too it came, a pestilence and a season of death'. The buildup of the words in this sentence cannot be rendered in English without repetition; new points are added in the Latin as the sentence unfolds about its single main verb. For the phraseology cf. *Geo.* 3.478f, Lucr. 6.1090f.

5 139. **letifer annus:** *letifer* is a poetic word (cf. Cat. 64.394); for *annus* = 'season' cf. *Aen.*6.311.

6 140. 'Men gave up the sweet breath of life'; the subject of *linquebant* is unexpressed as in 106, 110. The unexpected use of *linquere* is a variation on phrases like *linquebant lumina vitae* (Lucr. 5.989). Notice the very heavy assonance of *-ebant.*

7 141. **sterilis:** a clear example of the proleptic use of an adjective; 'burnt them so that they became barren'.

8 **exurere:** historic infinitive, cf. 666-7.

9 **Sirius**: the Dog-star, associated commonly with heat and fever, cf. *Geo.* 2.353, *Aen.* 10.273.

10 142. **victum . . . negabat:** 'the diseased crop gave no sustenance', cf. *Geo.* 1.149.

11 143f. This passage is similar to the situation in Hom. *Il.* 1.59f. where Achilles urges the Greeks to consult the priests in order to seek out the cause of Apollo's anger as shown in the plague he has sent.

12 143. **oraclum**: syncope for *oraculum,* which is unmanageable in hexameters; cf. *periclis* (711).

13 143-4. **remenso . . . mari**: 'sailing back again', cf. *Aen.* 2.181.

14 145f. The indirect questions are dependent on the idea of 'asking' conveyed in the previous lines; cf. *Aen* 2.651f.

15 145. **fessis . . . ferat**: the alliteration of *f*, and the vivid phrase *fessae res*, add to the intensity of the prayer.

[1]Nox erat et terris animalia somnus habebat:[2]
effigies sacrae divum Phrygiique Penates,
quos mecum ab Troia mediisque ex ignibus urbis
extuleram, visi ante oculos astare iacentis   150
in[3] somnis multo manifesti lumine,[4] qua se
plena per insertas fundebat luna fenestras;[5]
tum sic adfari et curas his demere dictis:
'quod[6] tibi delato Ortygiam dicturus Apollo est,
hic canit et tua nos en ultro ad limina mittit.   155
Nos[7] te Dardania incensa tuaque arma secuti,
nos tumidum sub te permensi classibus aequor,
idem venturos tollemus in astra nepotes
imperiumque urbi dabimus. [8]Tu moenia magnis
magna para longumque fugae ne linque laborem.   160
Mutandae sedes. [9]Non haec tibi litora suasit
Delius aut Cretae[10] iussit considere Apollo.
est locus, Hesperiam Grai cognomine dicunt,[11]
terra antiqua, potens armis atque ubere glaebae;
Oenotri coluere viri; nunc fama minores   165
Italiam dixisse ducis de nomine gentem:

---

1 148f. For the significance of this vision see note on 135f. It comes to Aeneas in sleep (151), the natural light sleep when visions can be seen, not the deep sleep (*sopor,* 173) in which unreal dreams and figments of the imagination occur.

2 148. 'The sacred images of the gods, the Phrygian Penates'; *effigies* means the actual images which Aeneas is carrying with him (cf. *Aen.* 2.293): the Penates appear to him in the form in which he knows them. *Effigies . . . Phrygiique Penates* is a hendiadys, cf. *Aen.* 1.54, 61.

3 151. **in somnis**: a frequent poetic plural, cf. *Aen.* 4.560.

4 151-2. 'very clear in bright light, where the full moon came pouring in through the open windows'. The meaning of *insertas* is much disputed. I incline to accept one of the suggestions of Servius — 'un-shuttered' — as making the best sense; the word would then be a Virgilian coinage making a negative adjective from the participle of *sero.* Other suggestions are 'latticed' (also Servius, perhaps rightly), 'inset' (an uninteresting epithet, to say the least), and 'translucent' (hardly possible from the Latin).

5 153. This line occurs also in 2.775 and 8.35; it is best to understand the infinitives as dependent on *visi* rather than as historic infinitives.

6 154-5. Apollo takes the initiative (*ultro*) without waiting for Aeneas to return to Delos (*Ortygia*). Observe the rhetorical case of the tense usage, much more vivid than 'what he would have told you'.

7 156-9. Notice how the antithesis of *tua nos* (155) is continued in these lines, and resumed in the subject *idem.* Impressiveness is sought by very simple devices of diction, for the prophecy of Roman greatness see note on 84f., and cf. especially *Aen.* 1.278f.

8 159-60. The alliteration here is very marked, first of *m* and then of *l*, reinforced by the -ng-, -gn-, -nqu- sounds. This, along with the repetition of *magnus,* continues the feeling of impressiveness secured by obvious art. The phraseology is reminiscent of Hector's words in 2.294-5 *his moenia quaere / magna. . . .*

9 161-2. 'It was not these shores which Delian Apollo urged you to seek, nor did he bid you make your settlement in Crete'. For *non* continued by *aut* cf. 42-3. Observe the interwoven order; *Delius Apollo* is the subject of both clauses, though the adjective is in one clause and the noun in the other.

10 162. **Cretae**: the locative of *Creta* is most unusual.

11 163-6. These lines occur in exactly the same form in 1.530-3, where see notes.

hae[1] nobis propriae sedes, hinc Dardanus[2] ortus
Iasiusque pater, genus a quo principe nostrum.
Surge age et haec laetus longaevo dicta parenti
haud dubitanda refer: Corythum[3] terrasque requirat   170
Ausonias;[4] Dictaea[5] negat tibi Iuppiter arva.'
Talibus attonitus visis et voce deorum
(nec[6] sopor illud erat, sed coram agnoscere vultus
velatasque comas praesentiaque ora videbar;
tum gelidus toto manabat corpore sudor)[7]   175
corripio e stratis corpus tendoque supinas[8]
ad caelum cum voce manus et munera[9] libo
intemerata focis. Perfecto laetus honore
Anchisen facio certum remque ordine pando.
Agnovit[10] prolem ambiguam geminosque parentis,   180
seque novo veterum deceptum errore locorum.
Tum memorat: 'nate, Iliacis[11] exercite fatis,
sola mihi talis casus Cassandra[12] canebat.
Nunc repeto haec generi portendere[13] debita nostro
et saepe Hesperiam, saepe Itala regna vocare.   185
Sed quis ad Hesperiae[14] venturos litora Teucros

---

1 167-8. The three clauses are all without a main verb; the effect is an oracular brevity.

2 167-8. One of the most frequent epithets of the Trojans is *Dardanidae*. One Latin version of the story was that the brothers Iasius and Dardanus set out from Italy to make a settlement abroad, and Dardanus went to Troy and Iasius to Samothrace. But in another version (*Aen.* 7.207f.) Dardanus is said to have gone both to Samothrace and Troy. For Dardanus and Teucer as founders of Troy see note on 108; cf. also 8.134 *Dardanus Iliacae primus pater urbis et auctor.*

3 170. **Corythum**: Corythus and Electra were the parents of Iasius and Dardanus (Dardanus, however, was born of Electra by Jupiter). The city bearing Corythus' name was identified with Cortona, north of Trasimene; cf. *Aen.* 7.209.

4 171. **Ausonias**: this very common word meaning Italian is cognate with *Aurunci,* a people of central Italy.

5 **Dictaea**: Dicte was the mountain in Crete where Jupiter was born (cf. 104).

6 173. **nec sopor illud erat**: 'nor was that an empty dream'; Virgil is following the distinction made in Hom. *Od.* 19.547 between πναρ and υπαρ (see note on 148f.). Cf. also *Aen.* 8.42, 10.642.

7 175. Cf. Enn. *Ann.* 418 *tunc timido manat ex omni corpore sudor.*

8 176f. Sacrifices are made after a supernatural vision also at 5.743f., 8.68f.

9 177-8. **munera ... focis**:' I offer pure sacrifice at the hearths'; for *libare* cf. 303, 354. *Intemerata* (not found before Virgil) means that there is no violation of the required ritual.

10 180-1. 'He recognised that our people were of double ancestry, of twofold parentage, and that he had been deceived by a new mistake about ancient lands'; both Dardanus and Teucer were *parentis.*

11 182. **Iliacis ... fatis**: 'hard-pressed by Trojan destiny'. The same phrase is used by the shade of Anchises to Aeneas in 5.725. The ill-fortune of Troy was proverbial, cf. 6.62. The word *exercite* suggests Stoic terminology; in some ways (but not all) Aeneas is like a Stoic undergoing his tests.

12 183. **Cassandra**: cf. 2.246f., 10.67f.; it was fated that because she had spurned Apollo her prophecies should be disbelieved.

13 184. The subject (*Cassandram*) of the infinitive *portendere* is omitted; cf. 144, 146, 472. *Portendere* reports the imperfect indicative; cf. *Aen.* 1.619.

14 186. Notice the strong rhetorical emphasis on the word *Hesperiae,* repeated from the previous line in the same position of the line; cf. 253-4.

crederet?[1] Aut quem tum vates Cassandra moveret?
Cedamus Phoebo et moniti meliora sequamur.'
Sic ait, et cuncti dicto paremus ovantes.
hanc quoque deserimus sedem paucisque[2] relictis   190
vela damus vastumque cava[3] trabe currimus[4] aequor.

   192-208. The Trojans endure a great storm at sea for three
   days and nights, and on the fourth day reach the Strophades.

Postquam altum tenuere rates nec iam amplius ullae[5]
apparent terrae, caelum undique et undique pontus,
tum mihi caeruleus[6] supra caput astitit imber
noctem hiememque ferens, et[7] inhorruit unda tenebris.   195
Continuo venti volvunt mare magnaque surgunt
aequora, dispersi iactamur gurgite vasto;
involvere diem nimbi et nox umida caelum
abstulit,[8] ingeminant[9] abruptis nubibus ignes.
Excutimur cursu et caecis[10] erramus in undis.   200
ipse[11] diem noctemque negat[12] discernere caelo
nec[13] meminisse[14] viae media Palinurus[15] in unda.
Tris[16] adeo incertos[17] caeca caligine soles
erramus pelago, totidem sine sidere noctes.

---

1 187. **crederet ... moveret**: past potential subjunctives: 'who would have believed.. . ?

2 190. **paucisque relictis**: thus Virgil accounts for the existing town of Pergamum in Crete.

3 191. **cava trabe**: the metonymy of *trabs* for *navis* (cf. *Aen.* 4.566) is common from Ennius onwards.

4 **currimus aequor**: accusative of extent of space, cf. *Aen.* 1.67.

5 192-5. These lines, which are modelled on Hom. *Od.* 12.403-6 (= 14.301-4), are almost exactly repeated in *Aen.* 5.8-11.

6 194. **caeruleus . . . imber**: 'a black storm-cloud'; for *caeruleus* of dark colour cf. 64.

7 195. **et inhorruit . . . tenebris**: 'and the waves grew rough under its dark onset'. For *inhorruit* cf. Pacuvius *ap.* Cic. *De Div.* 1.24 *inhorrtscit mare, tenebrae conduplicantur,* and *Geo.* 1.314, *Aen.* 10.711; compare also Cat. 64.269, and line 285 of this book where (as here) a dactylic rhythm is used for the surge of the sea.

8 199. **abstulit**: 'took from us', 'hid', cf. *Aen* 1.88.

9 **ingeminant ... ignes**: 'the clouds are rent, and the lightning redoubles its fury'; cf. Ov. *Fast.* 2.495.

10 200. The violence of being 'hurled off course' is reflected by the harsh alliteration of *c*; *caecis* means 'unseen, dangerous', cf. 706.

11 201-2. Notice the interlaced order with *ipse* in one clause and *Palinurus* in the next; cf. 161-2.

12 201. **negat discernere:** the reflexive subject of the infinitive is omitted, cf. 603 and *Geo.* 2.234; the phrase is equivalent to *negat se posse discernere.*

13 202. **nec**: *negate* is sometimes followed by a redundantly negative coordinating word; cf. Cic. *Acad.* 2.79.

14 **meminisse**: a rather unexpected word, apparently meaning 'recognize, keep reckoning of'; in the darkness he has no navigational aid from the sky, or from landmarks.

15 **Palinurus**: the chief helmsman of the Trojans (cf. 513); his story is told at the end of Book 5, and in 6.347f.

16 203. **tris adeo . . . soles:** 'for three long days'; *adeo* intensifies *tris*, cf. *Aen.* 7.629.

17 **incertos ... caligine**: 'obscured in black darkness'; *incertos* means there was *nihil certum,* both literally and metaphorically.

Quarto terra die[1] primum se attollere tandem   205
visa, aperire procul montis ac volvere fumum.
Vela[2] cadunt, remis insurgimus; haud mora, nautae
adnixi torquent spumas et caerula verrunt.[3]

> *209-77. The Trojans land on the Strophades, kill some cattle*
> *for a meal, and are at once attacked by the Harpies, half*
> *human monsters who pollute their food. Aeneas and his men*
> *drive them off, and Celaeno, oldest of the Harpies, in a*
> *hostile prophecy proclaims that the Trojans will not found*
> *their city until hunger has made them eat their tables. They*
> *set sail and after passing Ithaca land at Leucate.*

Servatum[4] ex undis Strophadum[5] me litora primum
excipiunt. [6]Strophades Graio stant nomine dictae   210
insulae[7] Ionio[8] in magno, quas dira[9] Celaeno

---

1 205-6. 'Only on the fourth day did we at long last see land rising up, revealing mountains far off and curling smoke'; for *aperire* cf. 275.

2 207. **vela cadunt:** 'down come the sails', i.e. the yardarm to which the sails were attached is taken down (cf. 549) so that they can bring the ships into land by rowing.

3 208. The same line occurs in 4.583; cf. also line 290, Enn. *Ann.* 384, Spenser, *F.Q.* 2.12.10 'with his stiffe oares did brush the sea so strong'. For *caerula* (the neuter of the adjective used as a noun) cf. 315, 434.

4 209f. The episode of the Harpies is partly based on Apollonius (2.178f., esp. 262f.), the tale of how the two sons of Boreas drove the Harpies away from Phineus; there are also some marked points of similarity with the theft of the cattle of the Sun-god by Odysseus' companions (Hom. *Od.* 12.260f.).
This episode and the episode of Achaemenides (588f.) are the two major mythological adventure stories which Virgil includes in the wanderings of Aeneas; there is also the brief account of Scylla and Charybdis (554f.). They serve to give variety and add an element of mystery and fantasy to the national and quasi-historical atmosphere of most of the voyage. In tone and mood they do not harmonize with the rest of this book; they are Odyssean rather than Roman; and yet like a touch of baroque on an simple building they give a irrational pleasure. They are handled differently: the Achaemenides story is elaborated into a piece of grandiose and hyperbolic writing, but the story of Harpies depends on the rapid and direct narrative of strange, fantastic events. A link with the main theme is achieved by Celaeno's prophecy about the tables, a very old feature of the legend which Virgil was the first to attribute to the Harpies (see note on 256f.). The main effect of this passage is to bring the reader away from the mood of hope which the previous episode has encouraged into an atmosphere of hostility, gloom and misfortune; we see the Trojans again as exiles wandering over a vastness of sea, very far from their promised home.

5 209. **Strophadum:** these are small islands to the west of the Peloponnese; they did not figure in the Aeneas legend before Virgil.

6 210-11. 'They are islands set in the wide Ionian sea, called by their Greek name Strophades'. *Stant* is used in its geographical sense, cf. *Aen.* 8.233 and our 'London stands on the Thames'. Virgil here refers to the derivation of Strophades from the Greek στρεφεσθαι ('turn'), because in one version of the story the sons of Boreas were here turned back by the goddess Iris from their pursuit of the Harpies (Ap. Rh. 2.296f.).

7 211. **insulae Ionio:** a remarkable instance of the shortening of a diphthong in hiatus after the Greek style ;cf. *Geo.* 1.437, 4.461, *Aen.* 5.261.

8 **Ionio in magno:** the Ionian sea was the southern part of the Adriatic; *Ionium* is used as a noun (*mare* being understood), cf. 'the Atlantic'.

9 211-12. **dira Celaeno Harpyiaeque:** in Homer the Harpies are personifications of storm-winds ('Snatchers', from αρπαξειν), cf. *Od.* 1.241, 14.371, 20.61-78. Their names (Swiftfoot, Whirlwind, Swiftwing; Hom. *Il.* 16.150, Hes. *Theog.* 267) are appropriate for storm winds, and so is Celaeno (κελαινος, 'dark'), a name which is not found before Virgil. They are represented as birds with the faces of women, and are often associated with the Sirens and with the Furies (cf. 252). The concept of Harpies as foul and disgusting creatures came later, and was especially associated with the story of how Zeus sent them to torment Phineus by snatching his food from him and polluting what remained (Ap. Rh, 2.178f.). When the Argonauts passed his home in Bithynia he appealed to them for help, and the sons of Boreas (Calais and Zetes) drove the Harpies away and would have killed them had not Iris intervened, promising that they would never torment Phineus again. There is a full description of the Snatchers in William Morris, *The Life and Death of Jason*, 5.229f.; cf. also Dante, *Inf.* 13.10f.; Milton, *PL.* 2.596f. ('harpy-footed Furies'), *P.R.* 2.401f., 'Both Table and Provision vanished quite / with sound of Harpies' wings and Talons heard'. In *The Tempest* (3.3) Ariel enters 'like a harpy; claps his wings upon the table; and, with a quaint device, the banquet vanishes'.

Harpyiaeque[1] colunt aliae, Phineia postquam
clausa domus mensasque metu liquere priores.
Tristius[2] haud illis monstrum, nec saevior ulla
pestis et ira deum Stygiis sese extulit undis.   215
Virginei volucrum vultus, foedissima ventris
proluvies uncaeque manus et pallida semper[3]
ora fame.[4]
Huc ubi delati portus intravimus, ecce
laeta[5] boum passim campis armenta videmus[6]   220
caprigenumque[7] pecus nullo custode per herbas.
Inruimus ferro et divos ipsumque vocamus
in[8] partem praedamque Iovem; tum litore curvo
exstruimusque[9] toros dapibusque epulamur opimis.
At subitae horrifico lapsu de montibus adsunt   225
Harpyiae et magnis quatiunt clangoribus[10] alas,
diripiuntque dapes contactuque omnia foedant
immundo; tum[11] vox taetrum dira inter odorem.
Rursum[12] in secessu longo sub rupe cavata
[arboribus clausam circum atque horrentibus umbris][13]   230
instruimus mensas arisque reponimus ignem;[14]
rursum ex[15] diverso caeli caecisque latebris

---

1 212. **Harpyiae**: the word scans as three long syllables, the middle syllable being the Greek diphthong υι.

2 214-15. 'There never arose from the waters of Styx any more horrid abomination than these, nor any more savage plague sent by the angry gods'. *Monstrum* indicates a supernatural horror (cf. 658, 4.181, 8.198); *ira deum* is explanatory of *pestis*. The Harpies have a place at the entrance to the underworld in 6.289.

3 217-18. The perpetual hunger of the Harpies gives special point to Celaeno's prophecy in 256 about the Trojans eating their tables because of *dira fames*.

4 118. For the incomplete line, see note on 1.534; the others in this book are 316, 340, 470, 527, 640, 661.

5 220. **laeta**: 'sleek': Servius says *pinguia*.

6 220. This is reminiscent of the forbidden cattle of the Sun-god in Hom. *Od.* 12.261f., 353f.

7 221. **caprigenum**: a striking adjective of an archaic type; Macrobius (*Sat.* 6.5.14) cites instances from Pacuvius and Accius, and there is an instance in Cicero's verse (*caprigeni pecoris custos*).

8 223. **in partem praedamque**: 'to share the spoil', a good example of hendiadys, cf. *Aen.* 1.54.

9 224. For *-que . . . -que* ('both . . . and') cf. 91. The couches are 'built up' from turf, leaves, etc.; cf. *Aen.* 11.66. *Epulari* is very rare with the ablative ('feast on', like *vesci*); cf. *Geo.* 2.537.

10 226. **clangoribus:** a strange and vivid word applied to the noise of their wings; Day Lewis well renders 'hoarse vibration of wingbeats'. Servius cannot be right in applying it to their cries because of *tum vox* in 228.

11 228. **tum vox . . . odorem:** cf. Lucr. 3.581. Notice the omission of *est* or *fit*; the whole phrase has a strange rhythm.

12 229f. **rursum . . . rursum**: this archaic form of *rursus* occurs in Virgil only here and once in the *Georgics*.

13 230. This verse occurs at *Aen.* 1.311, where *clausam* is grammatical, as here it is not. Probably some early scribe or reader of Virgil remembered it and inserted it here in his copy.

14 231. Notice the emphasis on the religious associations of the banquet ;cf. 222f.

15 232. **ex diverso caeli**: 'from a different quarter of the sky'. The neuter of *diversus* is used as a noun, cf. *Aen.* 2.716, and see note on 1.422.

turba sonans praedam pedibus circumvolat uncis,
polluit ore dapes. [1]Sociis tunc arma capessant
edico, et dira bellum cum gente gerendum.   235
Hand secus ac iussi[2] faciunt tectosque[3] per herbam
disponunt ensis et scuta latentia condunt.
Ergo ubi delapsae sonitum per curva dedere
litora, dat signum specula Misenus[4] ab alta
aere cavo. Invadunt socii et nova[5] proelia temptant,   240
obscenas[6] pelagi[7] ferro foedare volucris.
Sed[8] neque vim plumis ullam nec vulnera tergo
accipiunt, celerique fuga sub sidera lapsae
semesam[9] praedam et vestigia foeda relinquunt.
una in praecelsa[10] consedit rupe [11]Celaeno,[12]   245
infelix[13] vates, rumpitque[14] hanc pectore vocem:
'bellum[15] etiam pro caede boum stratisque iuvencis,
Laomedontiadae, [16] bellumne inferre paratis
et patrio Harpyias insontis pellere regno?
Accipite ergo animis atque haec mea figite dicta,   250
quae Phoebo pater omnipotens, mihi Phoebus Apollo

---

1 234-5. Notice the variation of construction with *edico:* first the jussive subjunctive in parataxis (cf. 456f.), and then the accusative with the gerundive.

2 236. **iussi:** supply *sunt,* cf. 561.

3 236-7. **tectos . . . latentia:** both epithets are predicative: 'they put their swords out of sight and hide their shields from view'.

4 239. Misenus has been posted as a lookout and now gives the alarm on his trumpet; the story of his death is told in *Aen.* 6.162f.

5 240. **nova:** 'strange','weird'.

6 241. **obscenas:** a very strong word, cf. 262, 367, *Aen.* 4.455.

7 **pelagi:** the parentage of the Harpies varied considerably in legend; Servius recounts a version which made them children of Sea and Earth.

8 242-3. The invulnerability of the Harpies (*accipiunt* = feel) is not mentioned elsewhere; compare, however, the brazen feathers of the Stymphalian birds (Hercules' sixth labour).

9 244. **semesam:** = *semiesam,* cf. *semustum* (578).

10 245. **praecelsa:** a rare variant for *excelsus.* Virgil is fond of the intensifying *prae;* cf. *praepinguis* (698), *praedives, praedurus, praedulcis, praevalidus.*

11 **Celaeno:** see note on 211-12, and cf. Spenser, *F.Q.* 2.7.23 where Celaeno is a bird of ill-omen at the entrance to Mammon's cave:
Whiles sad Celeno, sitting on a clift,
A song of bale and bitter sorrow sings . . .

12 245-6. These lines have a very vivid visual impact; notice too how the spondaic rhythm slows the movement for the grim prophecy.

13 246. **infelix vates:** 'prophetess of doom', cf. *F.Q.* 2.12.36, 'The hellish Harpies, prophets of sad destiny'.

14 **rumpitque . . . vocem:** 'and breaks out with this cry'. This unusual poetic sense of *rumpere* is first found in Virgil; see note on *Aen.* 2.129.

15 247-8. 'War as well, is it? You are ready to wage war, are you, in return for the slaughter of our cattle and the killing of our heifers?' *Pro* is used ironically; some recompense would be expected, instead of one wrong heaped on another.

16 248. **Laomedontiadae:** the epithet has implications of treachery (cf. *Geo.* 1.502, *Aen.* 4.542); the early Trojan king Laomedon cheated the gods of the promised reward for building the walls of Troy (Hor. *Odes* 3.3.21f.).

praedixit, vobis Furiarum[1] ego maxima pando.
Italiam cursu petitis ventisque vocatis:
ibitis Italiam[2] portusque intrare licebit.
Sed non ante datam[3] cingetis moenibus urbem   255
quam [4]vos dira fames nostraeque[5] iniuria caedis
ambesas[6] subigat malis absumere mensas.'
Dixit, et in silvam pennis ablata refugit.
at sociis subita gelidus[7] formidine sanguis
deriguit: [8]cecidere animi, nec iam amplius armis,   260
sed votis precibusque iubent exposcere pacem,
sive deae seu sint[9] dirae obscenaeque volucres.
Et pater Anchises[10] passis[11] de litore palmis
numina magna vocat meritosque[12] indicit honores:
'di, prohibete minas; di, talem avertite casum   265
et placidi[13] servate pios.'[14] Tum litore funem
deripere excussosque[15] iubet laxare rudentis.
Tendunt vela Noti: fugimus spumantibus undis

---

1 252. **Furiarum ego maxima**: the Harpies are commonly identified with the Furies; the phrase *Furiarum maxima* is used in *Aen.* 6.605 of the Fury, who is engaged in the harpy-like activity of preventing the damned from reaching the food spread out before them.

2 254. The repetition of *Italiam* helps to build up the tension in this line of mocking irony before the resolution of tension in *sed non. . . .*

3 255. **datam**: even Celaeno must admit that the city is promised; cf. 501.

4 256f. 'until terrible hunger and the wrong you have done in trying to kill us compel you to gnaw at your tables, and chew them up in your mouths.'
The prophecy is fulfilled in *Aen.* 7.109f., when the Trojans immediately after landing in Italy make a meal of *poma agrestia* laid out on thin platters of bread (*Cereale solum*). The meal is insufficient, so they eat the platters too, and Iulus cries *'Heus etiam mensas consumimus'*, upon which Aeneas recognizes the omen and recalls the prophecy, wrongly attributing it to Anchises. Virgil was the first to attribute it to Celaeno, and it is indeed suited to the strange and fabulous world of the perpetually famished Harpies; for the sources of the story see note on 7.107f.

5 256. **nostraeque iniuria caedis**: for the genitive of definition ('wrong consisting of. . .') cf. *Aen.* 1.27 and line 604. The word *caedes* is here used with rhetorical exaggeration of the unsuccessful attempt to slaughter the Harpies.

6 257. **ambesas**: 'eaten round', 'gnawed round the edge', a uncommon word; cf. *Aen.* 5.752.

7 259-60. cf. line 30; *gelidus* here as there is predicative. *Deriguit* means 'curdled', like *coit* in 30. The word is nowhere else used in this sense.

8 260-1. There is a quite marked zeugma here; the sense is *turn iam armis petere salutem sed exposcendo pacem.*

9 262. **sint**: subjunctive as part of the *iubent* construction.

10 263. Notice how Anchises takes the initiative; see note on 1f.

11 **passis**: *pandere* does not occur elsewhere in Virgil with *palmas;* his usual phrase is *tendere palmas.*

12 264. **meritosque . . . honores**: 'proclaims due sacrifices', cf. 118. *Indicere* is a formal and solemn word, cf. *Aen.* 1.632.

13 266. **placidi**: 'graciously', cf. *Aen.* 4.578.

14 **pios**: the keyword of the poem, see note on 42 and cf. *Aen.* 1.526.

15 267. **excussosque . . . rudentis**: 'to free and let out the sheets'. The previous phrase refers to the mooring rope; this phrase refers to the ropes attached to the lower corners of the sails, which would be paid out according to the angle required with the wind.

qua cursum ventusque gubernatorque vocabat.[1]
Iam [2]medio apparet fluctu nemorosa[3] Zacynthos   270
Dulichiumque Sameque et Neritos ardua saxis.
Effugimus scopulos Ithacae, Laertia[4] regna,
et [5]terram altricem saevi exsecramur Ulixi.[6]
Mox [7]et Leucatae nimbosa cacumina montis
et formidatus nautis[8] aperitur[9] Apollo.[10]   275
Hunc petimus fessi et parvae[11] succedimus urbi;
ancora de prora iacitur, stant litore puppes.

> *278-93. The Trojans make offerings and celebrate games at
> Actium; Aeneas dedicates a shield to Apollo, and they sail
> on again to Buthrotum.*

[12]Ergo insperata[13] tandem tellure potiti
lustramurque[14] Iovi votisque incendimus aras,

---

1 269. Virgil imitates Hom. *Od.* 11.10 την δ ανεμος τε κυβερνητης τ ιθυνε, using *-que...-que* (see note on 91) and the Greek trochaic caesura in the third foot without a strong caesura in the fourth foot, an unusual Latin rhythm which here gives an effect of speed.

2 270-1. The first three names are from Homer *Od.* 9.24, all places near Ithaca. Neritos surely derives from Homer's Mt. Nerito on Ithaca (*Od.* 9.22, *Il.* 2.632), but clearly Virgil thinks of it as an island.

3 270. **nemorosa Zacynthos:** Homer's υληεσσα Ζακυνθος (*Od.* 9.24), hence the licence of the short *a* before the double consonant z.

4 272. **Laertia regna:** *Laertius* is an adjective from Laertes, Odysseus' father.

5 273. Notice the vehemence of this line, reinforced by the spondaic movement with two heavy elisions. The Virgilian Ulysses (*dirus Ulixes, scelerum inventor*) is an unpleasant character, very different from the Homeric Odysseus; see note on 2.7.

6 **Ulixi:** for the genitive form see note on 2.7

7 274f. In the tradition of Aeneas' voyage as given by Dionysius (1.50.3-4) the Trojans stopped and built temples at Zacynthus, Leucas, and Actium. Virgil, wishing to avoid sameness of episodes, brings them past Zacynthus and then combines Leucas and Actium into a single stage without reconciling the geographical facts. Leucate, with its well known temple to Apollo was a notoriously dangerous promontory on the southern tip of the island of Leucas; Actium, some thirty or forty miles further north, also had a temple to Apollo recently restored by Augustus in honour of his victory (Suet. *Aug.* 18, *Aen.* 8.704). Cf. *Aen.* 8.677 where Leucate is mentioned as the scene of the battle of Actium, and for further geographical discussion see R. B. Lloyd, *A.J. Ph.*, 1954, pp. 292f.

8 275. **nautis:** dative of agent, cf. 14.

9 **aperitur:** 'is revealed to view', cf. 205-6.

10 **Apollo:** the name of the god stands for his temple, a common metonymy; cf. 552.

11 276. **parvae ... urbi:** i.e. the little town which Augustus had recently enlarged into Nicopolis; for elaboration of this kind of effect cf. Aeneas' visit (8.337f.) to Evander's simple dwelling on the site of Rome.

12 278f. Actium, like Zacynthus and Leucas, was one of the places in this area which figured in the Aeneas legend (Dion. 1.50.4). Virgil has put special emphasis on Actium by transferring there the games associated in the legend with Zacynthus, thus linking the past with the present by giving a prototype for Augustus' great Actian games (see note on 280). This aetiological intention is the more noticeable because this is the only one of the episodes on the way to Italy which does not contain prophecy or some other indication of progression towards the ultimate goal; it stands out as an Augustan episode in the midst of Aeneas' voyage.

13 278. **insperata:** because they have been sailing through Greek seas and have just passed the most dangerous area of all, the islands around Ithaca (282-3).

14 279. 'we perform the rituals of purification to Jupiter, and make the altars blaze with our offerings': *lustramur* is here middle ('we purify ourselves'), see note on 405.

Actiaque[1] Iliacis celebramus litora ludis.   280
Exercent[2] patrias oleo labente palaestras
nudati socii: iuvat evasisse[3] tot urbes
Argolicas mediosque fugam tenuisse per hostis.
Interea[4] magnum sol circumvolvitur annum
et glacialis hiems Aquilonibus asperat undas;   285
aere[5] cavo clipeum, magni gestamen[6] Abantis,[7]
postibus adversis figo et rem[8] carmine signo:
AENEAS HAEC DE DANAIS VICTORIBVS ARMA.[9]
Linquere tum portus iubeo et considere transtris.
Certatim socii feriunt mare et aequora verrunt.   290
Protinus aerias[10] Phaeacum abscondimus[11] arces
litoraque Epiri legimus[12] portuque[13] subimus
Chaonio[14] et celsam Buthroti accedimus urbem.

---

1 280. **Actia:** the poetic form of *Actiacus*, the adjective of Actirm, the name of the promontory off which Augustus defeated Antony and Cleopatra in 31 B.C. The temple to Apollo was restored and enlarged, and Augustus instituted at Nicopolis, the site of his camp, a large scale festival called the Actian games. They were modelled on the great Greek festivals, and the extended account in *Aeneid* 5 of the anniversary games for Anchises is clearly associated with the revived interest in this type of athletic competition which Augustus stimulated; see the Intro. to my *Aeneid* 5 (OUP), pp. xf.

2 281. **exercent patrias ... palaestras:** 'engage in their traditional wrestling bouts'; for *exercere* cf. *Aen.* 4.87.

3 282. **evasisse:** 'to have avoided'; the transitive use is quite common in poetry, cf. *Geo.* 4.485, *Aen.* 5.689.

4 284. 'Meanwhile the sun rolls on through the great circle of the year', an ornate poetic expression for the passage of time as winter comes on (285). The accusative *annum* is governed by the preposition in the verb.

5 286. **aere cavo clipeum:** 'a shield of curved bronze', i.e. made concave by beating, cf. *Aen.* 10.784.

6 **gestamen:** 'accoutrement', that which is carried, cf. *Aen.* 7.246.

7 **Abantis:** Servius suggests that Abas was one of the Greek party whose armour the Trojans captured during the sack of the city (*Aen.* 2.389f.). The dedication of enemy spoils suggests the trophies which Augustus dedicated after his victory at Actium.

8 287. **rem carmine signo:** 'I commemorate the event with a verse', i.e. an inscription, cf. *Ecl.* 5.42.

9 288. In Latin inscriptions the verb *dat* or *dedicat* is frequently abbreviated or omitted. The phrase here is rather elliptical, as *de* depends on some understood verb like *erepta*. Notice the irony of the inscription with *victoribus* where *victis* would be expected.

10 291. **aērias Phaeacum . . . arces:** 'the cloud-capped towers of the Phaeacians', a mysterious and haunting phrase. The fairyland of the Phaeacians, ruled by King Alcinous, was the last of all the places visited by Odysseus; by the time of Apollonius (4.991f.) it was definitely localised at Corcyra.

11 **abscondimus:** 'we lose from view', a most remarkable use of the word, imitated by Seneca (*Ep. Mor.* 70.2) and Claudian (*R.P.* 3.140). Servius says it was a nautical technical term.

12 292. **legimus:** 'skirt', cf. 706.

13 **portu:** dative, cf. 541, 692.

14 293. **Chaonio:** the name of a part of Epirus (cf. 334-5) where Buthrotum was a town on the coast.

294-355. At Buthrotum the Trojans hear that Helenus, son of Priam, is ruling over part of Pyrrhus' kingdom and is married to Andromache. Aeneas meets Andromache as she is making offerings at the empty tomb of Hector. She tells the story of her misfortunes since the fall of Troy, and Helenus approaches and welcomes the Trojans hospitably.

[1]Hic incredibilis rerum fama occupat[2] auris,
Priamiden[3] Helenum Graias regnare per urbis   295
coniugio[4] Aeacidae[5] Pyrrhi sceptrisque potitum,
et[6] patrio Andromachen iterum cessisse marito.
Obstipui, miroque[7] incensum pectus amore
compellare[8] virum et casus cognoscere tantos.
Progredior portu classis et litora linquens,   300
sollemnis[9] cum forte dapes et tristia dona[10]
ante urbem in luco falsi[11] Simoentis ad undam
libabat[12] cineri Andromache manisque vocabat

---

1 294f. The visit of the Trojans to Buthrotum was well established in the tradition of the legend, but the introduction of Andromache seems to be a Virgilian innovation. She figured, of course, very largely in other stories which would be familiar to Virgil especially perhaps from Euripides' *Andromache* and *Troades,* and Virgil's introduction of her here raises the level of emotional intensity in a book which otherwise has little of the sensitive pathos which we so frequently find elsewhere in the *Aeneid.*

This long episode is constructed in three scenes: the arrival, the prophecy of Helenus, and the departure. The long central prophecy (see note on 374f.) is sedate and factual, combining reminiscence of literary sources with emphasis on religious ritual, and making little demand on the emotions. It is framed by the two scenes about Andromache, both of them full of pathos and sympathy which become particularly marked in the final scene (488-91). Only here in the whole book do we see the Trojans in contact with human society (except for the very brief mention of Anius and the meeting with the castaway Achaemenides).

2 294- **occupat auris**: 'strikes our ears', 'comes on our startled ears', a vivid use of the word.

3 295. **Priamiden Helenum**: the Trojan Helenus, one of the sons of Priam, appears a number of times in the *Iliad;* he is the best of augurs (*Il.* 6.76). Cf. Ov. *Met.* 15.436f. for his prophecy to Aeneas of Rome's greatness.

4 296. **coniugio**: 'the bride', abstract for concrete, cf. *Aen.* 2.579.

5 296. **Aeacidae Pyrrhi**: Pyrrhus or Neoptolemus, son of Achilles, was the great-grandson of Aeacus. The story about Pyrrhus and Helenus (see Servius' note on 2.166) was as follows. At the fall of Troy Helenus and Andromache became captives of Pyrrhus. Helenus with his prophetic powers foresaw that the sea voyage for the Greeks would be fraught with reverses, and urged Pyrrhus to return home by land. This he did, accompanied by Helenus and Andromache; and when he died (see note on 332) he left to Helenus in gratitude a share of his kingdom, and Andromache for wife.

6 297. 'and that Andromache had passed to a husband of her own race again', i.e. a Trojan (she originally came from Thebe in Asia Minor, but the reference here is to her as former wife to Hector).

7 298. **miro . . . amore**: the strong phrase suggests the overwhelming longing of the exile to meet his old friend.

8 299. **compellare**: for the infinitive dependent on the noun *amor* cf. *Aen.* 2.10 and line 670 (*potestas*).

300f. 'I set out from the harbour, leaving behind me the ships on the shore, as it chanced just at a time when Andromache was making her libation to the dead, a libation of ritual feasts and gifts of sorrow, in front of the city in a grove by the stream which the exiles pretended was Simois. She was calling Hector's ghost to visit his tomb, a cenotaph of green turf where she had consecrated twin altars, there to shed her tears'.

The construction of the sentence is elaborate, with a gradual compounding of phrases before the verb and then the subject, and then very late in the sentence the key word *Hectoreum.*

9 301. **sollemnis**: 'ritual', 'regularly performed'.

10 301f. The pouring of libations and the offering of food at *inferiae* for the dead was normal; cf. 66 and *Aen.* 5.77f. For the invocation of the dead cf. *Aen.* 5.98, 6.506.

11 302. **falsi Simoentis**: i.e. this river was called Simois after the real Simois in Troy (cf. *Aen.* 1.100).

12 303. **libabat:cf.** 177-8.

Hectoreum ad tumulum, viridi[1] quem caespite inanem
et geminas, causam[2] lacrimis, sacraverat aras.   305
Ut me conspexit venientem et Troia[3] circum
arma amens vidit, magnis[4] exterrita monstris
deriguit visu in medio, calor ossa reliquit;
labitur[5] et longo[6] vix tandem tempore fatur:
'verane[7] te facies, verus mihi nuntius adfers,   310
nate dea? Vivisne? Aut, si lux alma recessit,
Hector ubi est?' Dixit, lacrimasque effudit et omnem
implevit clamore locum. [8]Vix pauca furenti
subicio et raris turbatus vocibus hisco:
'vivo equidem vitamque extrema per omnia duco;   315
ne dubita, nam vera vides.
Heu! Quis te casus deiectam[9] coniuge tanto
excipit, aut quae digna satis fortuna revisit,
Hectoris Andromache? Pyrrhin[10] conubia[11] servas?'
Deiecit vultum et demissa voce locuta est: 320
'o felix [12]una ante alias Priameia virgo,
hostilem ad tumulum Troiae sub moenibus altis
iussa mori, quae sortitus[13] non pertulit ullos
nec victoris heri[14] tetigit captiva cubile!

---

1 304. **viridi quem caespite**: the impact of this part of the sentence is given by the individual phrases taken in their order; the effect is achieved by a certain loosening of the syntax. The tomb was of green turf, it was a cenotaph, (an empty tomb or monument to honour a person or group of people whose remains are elsewhere) Andromache had dedicated twin altars there.

2 305. **causam lacrimis**: the tomb with its altars 'causes' Andromache's tears because here her sorrow has its focal point.

3 306-7. **Troia circum arma**: probably 'Trojan warriors accompanying me' (as they were, 347) rather than 'the Trojan armour I was wearing'.

4 307. **magnis ... monstris**: 'a marvel so incredible', it seems supernatural, unreal, to Andromache. The poetic plural *monstra* is of the type where the plural adds impressiveness, as *templa, sceptra*, etc.

5 309. **labitur**: 'she falls', i.e. faints, cf. *Aen.* 11.818.

6 **longo ... tempore**: the ablative is probably by analogy with the common *longo post tempore*.

7 310-12. Andromache can hardly credit Aeneas's presence in person; she half believes he is a phantom, come in response to her invocations at Hector's tomb; why has he come instead of Hector?

8 313-14. 'Hardly could I make this brief reply to her distraught words, in my confusion stammering these broken phrases'; *hiscere* occurs only here in Virgil, cf. *hiare* in the same sense in *Aen.* 6.493.

9 317. **deiectam coniuge tanto**: 'bereaved of your noble husband'; the use of *deiectus* is similar to that in *spe deiectus*, etc. Notice the slow spondees here.

10 319. **Pyrrhin**: for*Pyrrhine*, cf. *Aen.* 6.779, 12.797.

11 **conubia servas**: an extension of such phrases as *promissum servare, amicitiam servare*, cf. *Aen.* 2.789.

12 321f. Andromache contrasts her fate with that of Priam's daughter Polyxena, who was sacrificed on the tomb of Achilles; cf. Eur. *Hec.* 218f., Ov. *Met.* 13.439f. For the form of the sentence cf. *Aen.* 1.94f, 5.623f.

13 323. **sortitus**: the Greeks drew lots for their prisoners after the fall of Troy (Eur. *Tro.* 235f.).

14 324. **heri**: *herus* (*erus*) is a common word in comedy, but it is quite rare in epic and the high style; Andromache's use of the everyday word emphasises her anger and contempt.

Nos patria incensa diversa per aequora vectae   325
stirpis Achilleae fastus iuvenemque superbum
servitio[1] enixae tulimus; qui deinde secutus
Ledaeam[2] Hermionen Lacedaemoniosque hymenaeos
me[3] famulo famulamque Heleno transmisit[4] habendam.
Ast illum ereptae magno flammatus amore   330
coniugis[5] et scelerum[6] furiis agitatus Orestes
excipit[7] incautum patriasque obtruncat ad aras.
Morte Neoptolemi regnorum reddita[8] cessit
pars Heleno, [9]qui Chaonios cognomine campos
Chaoniamque omnem Troiano a Chaone dixit,   335
Pergamaque[10] Iliacamque iugis hanc addidit arcem.
Sed tibi qui cursum venti, quae fata dedere?[11]
Aut quisnam ignarum nostris deus appulit oris?
Quid puer Ascanius? Superatne[12] et vescitur aura?
quem tibi iam Troia —[13]   340
ecqua tamen[14] puero est amissae[15] cura parentis?

---

1 327. **servitio enixae:** 'bringing forth a child in slavery', cf. Eur. *Andr.* 24f. The child was Molossus, ancestor of the Molossian kings of Epirus.

2 328. **Ledaeam Hermionen:** Hermione was the daughter of Helen and Menelaus, Helen the daughter of Leda (*Aen.* 1.652). We hear in Homer (*Od.* 4.3f.) of the arrangements for the marriage of Hermione and Pyrrhus: in Euripides' *Andromache* she is married to him only to leave him for Orestes.

3 329. 'handed me over into the possession of Helenus, a slave to a slave'; for the repetition in the Greek style cf. *Aen.* 1.684, 5.569. The coordinating -*que* is not necessary grammatically, and so adds fuller emphasis; cf. *Aen.* 5.447, 12.289.

4 **transmisit habendam:** the phrase is scornful, suggesting the transfer of property.

5 331. **coniugis:** Orestes' intended bride, cf. *Aen.* 2.344 (*gener*).

6 **scelerum furiis agitatus:** 'hounded by the madness of his crimes', cf. *Aen.* 4.471. The story of how Orestes killed his mother Clytemnestra to avenge his father and of his subsequent madness induced by the Furies was a very well known one in Roman drama and art; see Austin on *Aen.* 4.469f.

7 332. **excipit:** 'caught', a usage common in hunting terminology, cf. *Ecl.* 3.18.
Pyrrhus was killed in Apollo's temple at Delphi (Eur. *Or.* 1653f.), and Servius explains *patrias* by referring to a tradition that Pyrrhus had set up an altar to his father Achilles in this temple. Thus Pyrrhus in a sense undergoes what he had inflicted on Polites and Priam (*Aen.* 2.526f., esp. 663).

8 333. **reddita cessit:** 'was duly bequeathed and passed'; the compound *re-* in *reddere* does not always mean 'back', but may indicate 'appropriately', cf. *Aen.* 4.392. 5.386.

9 334-5. 'who called the plains by the name Chaonian, and the whole area Chaonia after Chaon of Troy'. The etymological association (see note on 18) seems to be Virgil's own; Chaon is not heard of elsewhere, and the general tradition about the Chaonians was that they were so called before the Trojan war.

10 336. 'and set this our Pergama and this Ilian citadel upon their hills'; for the reuse of Trojan names in Epirus cf. 302, 349f.

11 337-8. Notice the emphasis on divine motivation; although Andromache does not know, she puts her questions so as to lead to the answer of Roman destiny.

12 339. **superatne:** 'is he still alive?'; cf. *Aen.* 2.567, 643.

13 340. This is the only half-line in the *Aeneid* where the sense is incomplete. It is very difficult to see what was in Virgil's mind when he wrote these four words; all we can say is that he began some thought which he could not bring into the form in which he wanted it, and he left it there and went on.

14 341. **tamen:** the force of this is very obscure, and in view of the uncertainty of the intended meaning of the previous line must remain so.

15 **amissae cura parentis:** i.e. Creusa. Virgil does not tell us how Andromache knew that Creusa had been lost.

Ecquid in antiquam virtutem animosque virilis
et pater Aeneas et avunculus excitat Hector?'[1]
Talia fundebat lacrimans longosque ciebat
incassum fletus, cum sese a moenibus heros   345
Priamides multis Helenus comitantibus adfert,
agnoscitque suos laetusque ad limina ducit,
et multum[2] lacrimas verba inter singula fundit.
Procedo[3] et parvam Troiam simulataque[4] magnis
Pergama et arentem Xanthi cognomine rivum   350
agnosco, Scaeaeque amplector limina portae.
Nec non et Teucri socia simul urbe fruuntur.
Illos porticibus rex[5] accipiebat in amplis:
aulai[6] medio libabant[7] pocula Bacchi
impositis auro dapibus, paterasque tenebant.   355

> *356-73. Aeneas consults Helenus about his voyage and Celaeno's threat. Helenus takes him to the temple and begins his prophecy.*

Iamque dies alterque dies processit, et aurae
vela vocant tumidoque inflatur carbasus austro:
his vatem adgredior dictis ac talia quaeso:
'Troiugena,[8] interpres divum, qui numina Phoebi,
qui tripoda[9] ac Clarii laurus, [10]qui sidera sentis   360
et volucrum linguas et praepetis omina pennae,

---

1 343. This line is repeated in 12.440. Creusa, Aeneas' wife, was Hector's sister.

2 348. **multum lacrimas**: *P* has *lacrimans,* and Servius knew the reading, but pointed out that we need *lacrimas* as the object of *fundit.* The adverbial use of *multum* is common enough (*Aen.* 6.481, 11.49), but its use here is strange. It is very likely that in revision Virgil would have recast this line.

3 349-51. Helenus has called his town by the names of his old city; it is a little Troy, with a citadel called Pergama, a copy of mighty Pergama, with a dried up river called Xanthus; very different from the whirling Xanthus of Troy (Hom. *Il.* 20.73), and with a Scaean gate, called after the west gate of Troy (*Aen.* 2.612).

4 349. **simulataque magnis:** literally 'made like the mighty Pergama', cf. Ov. *Met.* 13.721, Cic. *Ad Att.* 9.8.2.

5 353f. The king receives the Trojans in the colonnades around the *aula,* in the centre of which is the altar.

6 354. **aulai**: this archaic disyllabic form of the genitive ending and found in Ennius, is used very frequently by Lucretius (169 times), but occurs only four times in Virgil (*Aen.* 6.747, 7.464, 9.26) and not at all in Ovid or Silver Age epic.

7 354. **libabant pocula Bacchi**: 'they poured in libation the juice of wine'; for the metonymy of *Bacchus* for *vinum* cf. *Aen.* 1.215.

8 359. **Troiugena**: 'Trojan born', cf. *Aen.* 8.117, 12.626 and compare *Graiugena* (550).

9 360. **tripoda ac Clarii laurus**: *tripoda ac* is Mackail's emendation for *tripodas,* which gives a harsh asyndeton. Others read *tripodas Clarii et,* found in some late MSS. The priestesses of Apollo's shrine at Delphi gave their prophecies from their position on the sacred tripod, their hair crowned with laurel; cf. 81, 92 and Lucr. 1.739. Apollo's epithet *Clarius* is from his worship at Claros near Colophon.

10 360-1. Here Aeneas refers to various methods of divination, first astrology, and then augury from the cries or flight of birds; cf. *Aen.* 10.175f. Astrology was much discussed by the Romans, but is rarely mentioned in the *Aeneid,* never at length. For signs from birds cf. *Ecl.* 9.14f., *Aen.* 1.393f., 12.244f. The word *praepes* is a strange one; as a technical term in augury it indicated 'high', and 'propitious', but it came to be used in a much wider sense in poetry, simply meaning 'winged', 'flying'.

fare age [1](namque omnis cursum mihi prospera dixit
religio, et cuncti suaserunt numine divi
Italiam petere et terras temptare repostas;[2]
sola novum dictuque nefas Harpyia Celaeno   365
prodigium canit et tristis denuntiat iras
obscenamque famem) quae prima pericula vito?[3]
Quidve sequens tantos possim[4] superare labores?'
Hic[5] Helenus caesis primum de more iuvencis
exorat pacem divum vittasque[6] resolvit   370
sacrati capitis, meque ad tua limina, Phoebe,
ipse manu multo[7] suspensum numine ducit,
atque haec deinde canit divino ex ore sacerdos:

---

1 362-3. 'for all the divine signs have spoken to me of my journey in favourable terms'. The reference is to the various signs and oracles which Aeneas has already received, such as the prophecies by Apollo and the Penates, and the signs given to Anchises in Book 2. For the strange phrase *omnis religio* cf. *Aen.* 12.182 and *fas omne* (5.800).

2 364. **repostas**: 'remote', syncope for *repositas*, cf. *Aen.* 1.26.

3 367. **vito**: for the indicative in a deliberative question cf. 88.

4 368. **possim**: potential, *sequins* having the sense of *si sequar.*

5 369. **hic**: 'at this', cf. *Aen.* 2.699, 735.

6 370. **vittasque resolvit**: the garlands were removed before the oracular trance, so that the hair fell loose and no hindrance might prevent the abandonment of the person to the gods; cf. *Aen.* 6.48.

7 372. **multo suspensum numine**: 'tensely anxious in the manifold presence of deity', cf. *Aen.* 2.114, 729.

*374-463. Helenus makes his prophecy, telling the Trojans
that they still have far to go; they will know that they have
reached the site of their city by the sign of the white sow.
There is no need to fear Celaeno's threat. They must beware
of the eastern coast of Italy, and after sacrificing in the
prescribed manner must sail on round Sicily, thus avoiding
Scylla and Charybdis. Above all they must make constant
prayer and sacrifice to Juno. They must then land at Cumae
to consult the Sibyl; she will tell them of the wars to be
fought in Italy.*

[1]"Nate dea (nam te maioribus[2] ire per altum

auspiciis manifesta fides,[3] sic fata[4] deum[5] rex   375

sortitur volvitque vices, is vertitur ordo),

pauca tibi e multis, quo tutior hospita[6] lustres

aequora et Ausonio possis considere portu,

expediam dictis: prohibent nam cetera Parcae

scire Helenum farique vetat Saturnia Iuno.   380

Principio Italiam, quam tu iam rere[7] propinquam

vicinosque, ignare, paras invadere portus,

longa[8] procul longis via dividit invia terris.

---

1 374f. Just as the visit to Buthrotum forms a centrepiece for the events of Book 3, so the long speech of Helenus is the central feature of this visit. It is by far the longest piece of prophecy about the voyage of Aeneas and may be compared with Circe's prophecy to Odysseus in Hom. *Od.* 12.37-141, and with that of Phineus in Ap. Rh. 2.311f.

The speech is delivered in oracular style, that is to say it is admonitory, emphatic, directly didactic; its effects are not subtle or sophisticated, and the level of emotional tension is not high. It contrasts very markedly in this with the passages about Andromache which precede and follow it. There are lines with very obvious rhetorical effects, especially those involving repetition (383, 412, 433f.), and alliteration is frequent (375-6, 424-8, 455-9). The metrical movement does not have Virgil's usual variety of cadence and is in somewhat reminiscent of his predecessors. For fuller discussion see my OUP Ed. ad loc.

Virgil is able to choose which events of the voyage Helenus should reveal by telling us (377f.) that Juno permits him to reveal only part of the future (cf. Ap. Rh. 3.311f.). Thus he omits mention of Polyphemus, the death of Anchises, the storm which drives the Trojans to Carthage, the visit to Carthage, the return visit to Sicily with the burning of the ships and the death of Palinurus, the visit to the underworld. Helenus' speech is largely concerned with divine signs, propitiation of deities, consultation of oracles. In three places Helenus dwells on his theme at some length: the method of sacrificing, Scylla and Charybdis, the Sibylline oracle. The first and third of these have direct reference to contemporary Roman religion, the second is inspired by Circe's prophecy in Homer. We see Virgil here, as often elsewhere, melding reminiscence of Homer with Roman aetiology.

2 374-5. **maioribus . . . auspiciis**: a technical term of religion, cf. Cic. *DeRep.* 2.26.

3 375. **fides**: 'proof', cf. *Aen.* 2.309.

4 375-6. 'thus does the king of the gods apportion the fates and turn the wheel of change, this is the sequence of the cycle of events'; notice how oracular impressiveness is built up by the accumulation of phrases of similar meaning. For *volvit* cf. *Aen.* 1.22, for *vertitur Aen.* 2.250.

5 375. **deum rex**: the monosyllabic ending, reminiscent of Ennius, contributes to an archaic effect, cf. line 12 and *Aen.* 1.65..

6 377-8. **hospita lustres aequora**: 'traverse the waters that will receive you'. *Hospita* is neuter plural as though from *hospitus* ('receiving', 'welcoming'), an adjective of *hospes* whose existence is suggested by the feminine singular *hospita* (539).

7 381. **rere propinquam**: Italy was in fact near, but not the part of it to which Aeneas had to sail. For *rere* = *reris* cf. *Aen.* 7.437.

8 383. 'a long pathless path with long coastlines lies between you and Italy'; for *dividit* cf. *Aen.* 12.44f. The line has a very oracular ring about it, with the oxymoron of *via invia* and the obvious device in the repetition of *longus*, and it is emphasised by the assonance of *i*, the rhyme at the caesura and line ending, and the coincidence of words with feet in the second half.

Ante[1] et Trinacria[2] lentandus[3] remus in unda
et salis[4] Ausonii lustrandum navibus aequor   385
infernique[5] lacus Aeaeaeque[6] insula Circae,[7]
quam tuta possis urbem componere terra.
Signa[8] tibi dicam, tu[9] condita mente teneto:
cum[10] tibi sollicito secreti[11] ad fluminis undam
litoreis[12] ingens inventa sub ilicibus sus[13]   390
triginta[14] capitum fetus enixa iacebit,
alba solo recubans, albi[15] circum ubera nati,
is locus urbis erit, requies ea certa laborum.
Nec[16] tu mensarum morsus horresce futuros:[17]
fata viam invenient aderitque vocatus Apollo.   395
Has autem terras [18]Italique hanc litoris oram,

---

1 384-7. **ante ... quam ... possis**: cf. 255f. for *ante ... quam* with the subjunctive of futurity.

2 384. **Trinacria ... in unda**: Sicily was called Trinacria (cf. 429, 554) because of its triangular shape with its three promontories; the supposed derivation was τρεις ακραι. The Homeric form of the word was Thrinacia ('trident island').

3 **lentandus remus**: 'you must bend the oar'; the verb, which is unusual and poetic, refers to the 'give' of an oar in the water due to its slight pliancy, cf. Cat. 64.183. There is also an overtone of struggle and effort involved.

4 385. **salis Ausonii**: the meaning is the sea to the southwest of Italy, commonly called the Tyrrhenian sea; the epithet is used to link with Ausonia as Aeneas' promised land (378).

5 386. **infernique lacus**: cf. 441f. with note.

6 **Aeaeaeque insula Circae**: after leaving Cumae and calling at Caieta Aeneas passed the island of the enchantress Circe (*Aen.* 7.10f.), half-way between Cumae and the mouth of the Tiber. Circe's island Aeaea in Homer is in the East (*Od.* 12.3-4);later tradition placed her in the West (Hes. *Theog.* 1011f., Ap. Rh. 3.311f.), but she always had strong associations with the Black Sea area and the magic of Colchis. See note on *Aen.* 7.10-11.

7 386. The nominatives in this line require some verb to be supplied from *lustrandum*, e.g. *adeunda sunt*.

8 388. **signa**: 'signs', i.e. indications by which they will know they have reached the correct place (cf. *Aen.* 1.443).

9 **tu ... teneto**: the phrase is reminiscent of Homeric formulae (συ δ ενι φρεσι βαλλεο σ αιν, ου δε συνθεο θυηω). Notice the conglomeration of *t*'s, and the formal ring of this form of the imperative, suitable for the didactic style (Virgil uses it often in the *Georgics*).

10 389f. The legend of the portent of the sow is found (with considerable variations) in the Aeneas saga from an early stage; cf. Lycophr. 1.255f., and my OUP Ed. ad loc. for full discussion. The prophecy is repeated by Tiberinus (8.43f.), and its fulfilment described in 8.81f. Helenus refers the portent to the site of Aeneas' new city (presumably Lavinium); Tiberinus adds that it indicates the foundation of Alba in thirty years' time.
It is possible that there is a connexion between this Trojan legend and the Latin word *troia* (French *truie*) meaning a sow (though *troia* is not found before the eighth century). This would give an etymological association comparable with that of the *lusus Troiae* (where *Troia* is perhaps connected with an Etruscan word meaning 'maze-like movements'; see note on *Aen.* 5.545f.).

11 389. **secreti**: 'remote', emphasising the idea of distance and also contrasting the later fame of the Tiber with its present obscurity, cf. *Aen.* 5.83.

12 **litoreis**: *litus* is not commonly used of a river bank; cf. *Ecl.* 5.83.

13 390. Notice the monosyllabic ending (see note on 375); here the effect is, as Page says, one of 'archaic simplicity and rudeness'. The line is marked by strong assonance of *i*.

14 391. 'delivered of a litter of thirty young'; for *enixa* cf. 327, for *caput* ('head' of cattle) cf. *Aen.* 5.61f.

15 392. **albi ... nati**: a parenthetical insertion into the sentence (understand *erunt*), typical of Virgil's fondness for parataxis; cf. 14.

16 394. **nec ... horresce**: *nec* is commonly used in verse, and sometimes in prose, for *neve* (Geo. 2.96).

17 394f. This refers to Celaeno's prophecy (see note on 256f.), which was the immediate cause of Aeneas' inquiries (365f.).

18 396. After his introductory statements about the length of the voyage, and the sign of arrival, Helenus begins to outline the events of the voyage.

proxima quae nostri perfunditur aequoris aestu,
effuge; cuncta malis[1] habitantur moenia Grais.
Hic et Narycii[2] posuerunt moenia Locri,
et Sallentinos[3] obsedit milite[4] campos   400
Lyctius[5] Idomeneus; [6]hic illa ducis Meliboei
parva Philoctetae subnixa[7] Petelia muro.
Quin[8] ubi transmissae steterint[9] trans aequora classes[10]
et positis aris iam vota in litore solves,
purpureo velare[11] comas adopertus amictu,[12]   405
ne qua inter sanctos ignis in[13] honore deorum
hostilis facies occurrat et omina turbet.
Hunc socii morem sacrorum, hunc ipse teneto;
hac casti maneant in religione nepotes.
Ast ubi digressum Siculae te admoverit orae   410
ventus, et angusti[14] rarescent claustra Pelori,
laeva tibi tellus et longo laeva[15] petantur

---

1 398. **malis . . . Grais**: dative of agent. The epithet *malis* is natural in the mouth of a Trojan after the sack of Troy. Virgil allows himself some degree of anachronism in describing the part of the world known in his times as *Magna Graecia,* which the Greeks did not colonise till long after the fall of Troy.

2 399. **Narycii. . . Locri**: Narycium (*Geo.* 2.438) was a town of the Locri who lived near Euboea. The story went that they were shipwrecked on their return from Troy with Ajax son of Oileus (*Aen.* 1.40f.), and some made their way to Southern Italy.

3 400. **Sallentinos . . . campos**: in Calabria, the part of Italy nearest to Epirus.

4 **milite**: 'soldiery', 'soldiers', a frequent use of the collective singular.

5 401. **Lyctius Idomeneus**: Lyctos was a town in the east of Crete (*Ecl.* 5.72); for Idomeneus see note on 122. The last syllable of his name is a diphthong, as in Greek.

6 401-2. Petelia lay on the coast between the Sallentini and the Locri; the name is presumably connected with the old Latin word *petilus,* 'thin', 'small', so that *parva* is an etymological epithet (see note on 693). Philoctetes, who came from Meliboea in Thessaly, was said in one version of the legend about him to have fled from his home to Southern Italy where he founded Petelia and Crimissa (Lycophr. 911f.).

7 402. **subnixa**: 'resting on', cf. *Aen.* 1.506; (he word here includes the nuance of 'defended by'.

8 403. **quin**: the use of *quin* (= *quin etiam*) adds an extra point with strong emphasis.

9 **steterint**: 'are anchored', a nautical use of the verb, cf. 277.

10 403f. Helenus here indicates by implication rather than direct instruction that the Trojans will land in Italy when they first sight it, and after paying their vows will proceed to Sicily (cf. 521-50).

11 **velare**: imperative passive, used in a middle sense, cf. 279, 509, 545.

12 405. It was a Roman custom to cover the head during sacrifice; the Greeks did not do so (cf. Lucr. 5.1198f., Ov. *Fast.* 3.363). Virgil is very fond of this sort of aetiological reference to the origins of customs familiar in his time; cf. 443 and *Aen.* 5.596f. (*lusus Troiae*), and see note on 18.

13 406-7. The veiled head prevented the sight of ill-omen, as the formula *favete lingua* prevented the hearing of ill-omen.

14 411. **angusti . . . Pelori**: 'the headlands of the narrow strait of Pelorus begin to show space between them'. This is a very remarkable use of *rarescere;* the nearest parallel seems to be Tac. *Germ.* 30 *colles paulatim rarescunt* (the hills gradually thin out, become less frequent). Pelorus was the promontory at the northeast tip of Sicily, cf. 687; evidently here it gives its name to the Straits of Messina.

15 412. **laeva . . . laeva**: the repetition is in the emphatic style of an oracle (cf. 383), and the line is also made to sound impressive by the pattern of alliteration of *l* and *t.*

aequora circuitu; dextrum[1] fuge litus et undas.
haec[2] loca vi quondam et vasta convulsa ruina
(tantum[3] aevi longinqua valet mutare vetustas)   415
dissiluisse ferunt; [4]cum protinus utraque tellus
una foret, venit medio vi pontus et undis
Hesperium [5]Siculo latus abscidit, arvaque et urbes
litore diductas angusto interluit aestu.
Dextrum[6] Scylla latus, laevum implacata[7] Charybdis   420
obsidet, [8]atque imo barathri[9] ter gurgite vastos
sorbet in[10] abruptum fluctus rursusque sub auras
erigit alternos, et sidera verberat[11] unda.
At Scyllam [12]caecis cohibet spelunca latebris[13]

---

1 413. **dextrum . . . litus**: as soon as the Trojans come west of the toe of Italy they must strike leftwards across to Sicily in spite of the long detour round the island; they must not follow Italy round to the right, which would involve the passage of the Straits of Messina.

2 414f. The Romans believed, rightly, that Sicily was once joined to Italy; cf. Pliny *N.H.* 2.204, Ov. *Met.* 15.290. The name Rhegium is connected with ρηγνυναι ('break off').

3 415. 'such great changes can be brought about by the long process of time past'; in the context the phrase does not mean that things gradually change, but that in the long process of the ages major changes occur (in this case, suddenly).

4 416-17. 'when the two countries were one unbroken stretch, the sea came mightily in the midst'. Most editors punctuate so that the *cum* phrase goes with what precedes; I have followed Mackail's punctuation, which gives a more forceful and more idiomatically Latin order. For *protinus* ('straight on') cf. *Ecl.* 1.13, *Aen.* 10.340.

5 418-19. 'and separated the lands and cities from each other by a coastline, and flowed between them in a narrow tideway.' For *interluere* cf. *Aen.* 7.717, and in general cf. Lucretius' description of the Straits of Messina (1.720-1).

6 420f. Scylla, the monster with six necks, and Charybdis, the whirlpool, are described in Hom. *Od.* 12.73f., 222f. Virgil recalls some Homeric features, but his Scylla is different (see note on 424f.). By Virgil's time Scylla and Charybdis were traditionally situated in the Straits of Messina (Ap. Rh. 4.789f., Lucr. 1.722); the Italian promontory still preserves the name Scilla. Ovid (*Met.* 13.900f.) tells the story of how Scylla, because of the enmity of Circe, was transformed first into a monster and then into a rock; in *Met.* 13.730f., he closely follows this passage in Virgil. Spenser (*F.Q.* 2.12.3-8) uses Scylla and Charybdis allegorically in his Rocke of Vile Reproch and Gulfe of Greedinesse.

7 420. **implacata**: a rare word, an alternative form for *implacabilis*, found only here and in Ov. *Met.* 8.845.

8 421-3. 'and three times with the deep whirlpool of her abyss does she suck down the mighty billows of the sea into a fathomless depth, and each time she hurls them up again to the heavens and lashes the stars with the spray'. Virgil is following Homer *Od.* 12.105-6 and 235f. The meaning of *ter* is that Charybdis produces this effect three times in quick succession each day at a particular point in the tide; she probably was thought of as being able to influence the tide, so as to go into motion whenever a ship drew near. In mythology she was a *femina voracissima*, born of Neptune and Earth, who stole the cattle of Hercules and was struck by Jupiter's thunderbolt and hurled into the sea. In her new home she preserved her ancient characteristics.

9 421. **barathri**: 'abyss' of land or sea, often used of the underworld (Lucr. 3.966, *Aen.* 8.245). Virgil's phraseology here is very similar to Cat. 68.107f. *tanto te absorbens vertice amoris / aestus in abruptum detulerat barathrum.*

10 422. **in abruptum**: the neuter of the participle is used as a noun; cf. *Aen.* 12.687 and Milton, *P.L.* 2.408f. 'Upborne with indefatigable wings / over the vast abrupt'.

11 423. **verberat**: cf. *Aen.* 5.377 and Shakespeare, *Othello* 2.1.12 'The chidden billow seems to pelt the clouds'. The hyperbole is emphasised by the rhythm, with words coinciding with feet in the second half of the line.

12 424f. In Homer (*Od.* 12.85f.) Scylla is described as a monster with twelve feet and six necks, hidden in a cave to her middle, and hanging out her necks to fish for dolphins and sea dogs. She has a voice like a newborn hound; this seems to be the origin of the later version, which Virgil follows, that she had wolves or dogs below the waist. Her name was connected etymologically with σκυλλειν ('tear', 'rend') and σκυλαξ ('a young hound'). Cf. *Ecl.* 6.75, Lucr. 5.892, Ov. *Met.* 13.730f., 14.63f.; in *Aen.* 6.286 *Scyllae biformes* are among the monsters at the entrance of Hell. Spenser's Errour (*F.Q.* 1.1.13-15) is based on Scylla, and so is Milton's description of Sin (*P.L.* 2.650f.). 'About her middle round / a cry of Hell Hounds never ceasing barkd / with wide Cerberean mouths full loud, and rung / a hideous Peal... .'

13 424-8. The assonance and the alliteration in the description of Scylla is very marked indeed, so that the exaggerated sound effects fit the gruesome monster.

ora[1] exsertantem et navis in saxa trahentem.   425
Prima[2] hominis facies et pulchro pectore virgo
pube[3] tenus, postrema immani corpore pistrix
delphinum caudas utero commissa[4] luporum.
Praestat Trinacrii metas lustrare Pachyni[5]
cessantem, longos et circumflectere cursus,   430
quam semel informem vasto vidisse sub antro
Scyllam et caeruleis[6] canibus resonantia saxa.[7]
Praeterea, si qua est Heleno prudentia vati,
si qua fides, animum si veris implet Apollo,
unum illud tibi, nate dea, proque[8] omnibus unum   435
praedicam et repetens iterumque iterumque monebo,
Iunonis magnae primum prece numen adora,[9]
Iunoni cane[10] vota libens dominamque potentem
supplicibus supera[11] donis: sic denique victor
Trinacria finis[12] Italos mittere relicta.   440
Huc [13]ubi delatus Cumaeam accesseris urbem
divinosque lacus et Averna sonantia silvis,
insanam[14] vatem aspicies, quae rupe[15] sub ima

---

1 425. **ora exsertantem**: cf. Hom. *Od.* 12.94, 251f. Notice how Virgil has exaggerated Homer's picture by making Scylla drag the ships on to the rocks after seizing her prey. *Exsertare* (the frequentative form of *exserere:* 'always darting out') is a very rare word.

2 426f. 'Her upper part is of human shape: she is a fair-bosomed maiden down to the waist, but below she is a sea-monster of frightful appearance, with a belly of wolves ending in the tails of dolphins'.

3 427. **pube tenus:** the preposition *tenus* follows its noun and takes the genitive or (more commonly) the ablative; cf. 1.737, 2.553.

4 428. **commissa**: the passive participle is used in a middle sense (literally 'joining the tails of dolphins on to a belly of wolves'); see note on 47. For the word cf. Ov. *Met.* 12.472f. (of a Centaur) *latus eruit hasta / qua vir equo commissus erat.*

5 429-30. Pachynus (or Pachynum) is the south-eastern promontory of Sicily; cf. 699. For *Trinacrii* see note on 384; *meta* is a metaphor from the turning point in a stadium. Observe the emphasis thrown on *longos* by the postposition of *et*, and the very spondaic movement.

6 432. **caeruleis . . . saxa**: Scylla's dogs (see note on 424f.) are the colour of the sea, cf. *Aen.* 5.819; for the rocks cf. *Aen.* 1.200f.

7 433f. The emphasis which Helenus achieves here is extreme, first by means of the use of his own name, then by repetition (*si, unum, iterum, Iunoni*).

8 435. **proque omnibus unum**: 'and one thing to outweigh all the rest', a much stronger way of saying *ante omnia.*

9 437. Notice the great emphasis on propitiating the hostility of Juno; see intro. to Book 1, and compare *Aen.* 8.60f.

10 438. **cane vota libens**: 'gladly chant prayers', cf. 546f.

11 439. **supera** : 'win over', cf. *Aen.* 8.61.

12 440. **finis Italos mittere**: 'you will be sent to the shores of Italy'; the passive form 'you will be sent' rather than 'you will come' puts emphasis on the divine guidance.

13 441f. The events here prophesied are fulfilled at the beginning of Book 6. The lakes near Cumae are the Lucrine and Avernian lakes, which in Virgil's time were joined (*Geo.* 2.161f.); the latter of course was the one particularly associated with the underworld.

14 443. **insanam vatem**: the Sibyl of Cumae, Apollo's priestess. Her frenzy is described in *Aen.* 6.46f., 77f. The collection of her oracles known as the Sibylline books played a very considerable part in Roman religion (cf. *Ecl.* 4); during Augustus' reign they were transferred to the temple of Apollo on the Palatine.

15 **rupe sub ima**: 'deep in a rocky cave', cf. *Aen.* 6.42f.

fata canit foliisque[1] notas et nomina mandat.
Quaecumque in foliis descripsit carmina virgo   445
digerit[2] in numerum atque antro seclusa relinquit:
illa manent immota locis neque ab ordine cedunt.
Verum eadem, verso tenuis cum cardine ventus
impuiit et teneras turbavit ianua frondes,
numquam deinde cavo volitantia prendere saxo[3]   450
nec revocare situs aut iungere carmina curat.
inconsulti[4] abeunt sedemque odere Sibyllae.
Hic[5] tibi ne qua morae fuerint dispendia tanti,
quamvis increpitent socii et vi cursus in altum
vela vocet, possisque sinus[6] implere secundos,   455
quin adeas vatem precibusque oracula poscas[7]
ipsa canat vocemque volens atque ora resolvat.
Illa tibi Italiae populos venturaque bella[8]
et quo quemque modo fugiasque[9] ferasque laborem
expediet, cursusque dabit venerata secundos.   460
Haec sunt quae nostra liceat te voce moneri.
Vade [10]age et ingentem factis fer ad aethera Troiam.'

463-505. Helenus bestows presents upon the Trojans, and gives his last instructions. Andromache adds her gifts to Ascanius in memory of Astyanax. Aeneas bids them farewell and promises eternal friendship between their two cities.

Quae postquam vates sic ore effatus amico est,

---

1 444. **foliisque . . . mandat**: 'and writes down marks and words on leaves', cf. *Geo.* 3.158. Servius quotes Varro to the effect that the Sibyl wrote on palm leaves.

2 446. **digerit in numerum**: 'she arranges in order', i.e. she writes a phrase or two on a particular leaf, and for the consecutive understanding of her prophecies it is essential that the leaves should be in order.

3 450f. Cf. Shakespeare, *Titus Andr.* 4.1.104f. 'The angry northern wind / will blow these sands like Sibyl's leaves abroad, / and where's your lesson then?'

4 452. 'Men depart without receiving advice, and hate the abode of the Sibyl'; for the vague subject cf. 110. The meaning of *inconsultus* is very unusual; it generally means either 'without being consulted' or 'not having taken counsel, rash'.

5 453-6. 'Here do not let any thoughts of the loss of time have such weight with you ... as to prevent you from approaching the priestess'. *Morae dispendia* is an unusual phrase, literally 'the expenditure of delay'.

6 455. **sinus implere secundos:** 'make your canvas billow before the wind'; *secundus* is transferred from its common association with *ventus* to the sails affected by a favouring wind.

7 456-7. **poscas ... canat**: *canat* is jussive subjunctive in parataxis with *poscas;* cf. Aeneas' actual words to the Sibyl (*Aen.* 6.76) *ipsa canas oro.*

8 458f. In *Aen.* 6.83f. the Sibyl briefly prophesies the events in Italy, and Anchises (*Aen.* 6.890f.) gives details; line 459 is repeated in the third person in 6.892.

9 459. **fugiasque ferasque**: indirect deliberative questions.

10 462. 'Onwards then and make Troy mighty by your deeds, and raise her to the skies'. *Ingentem factis* is proleptic, and very emphatic because at the moment of Helenus' words Troy was a ruin, and the Trojans a small band of exiles.

dona dehinc auro gravia[1] ac secto[2] elephanto
imperat ad navis ferri, stipatque carinis   465
ingens argentum Dodonaeosque[3] lebetas,
loricam[4] consertam hamis auroque trilicem,
et conum[5] insignis galeae cristasque comantis,
arma[6] Neoptolemi. Sunt[7] et sua dona parenti.
Addit[8] equos, additque duces,[9]   470
remigium[10] supplet, socios simu! Instruit armis.
    Interea classem velis aptare iubebat
Anchises,[11] fieret vento mora ne qua ferenti.[12]
Quem Phoebi interpres multo compellat honore:
'coniugio, Anchisa,[13] Veneris dignate[14] superbo,   475
cura[15] deum, bis[16] Pergameis erepte ruinis,
ecce[17] tibi Ausoniae tellus: hanc[18] arripe velis.
Et[19] tamen hanc pelago praeterlabare[20] necesse est:

---

1 464. **gravia ac secto elephanto:** I now accept with some uncertainty Schaper's emendation for *gravia sectoque elephanto* given by all the MSS and by Servius. The MSS reading involves the lengthening of the short final vowel of *gravia,* and although this can be paralleled in Ennius (e.g. *Ann.* 147) there is no certain instance in Virgil (except for final *-que*). The corruption can be accounted for by the insertion of *-que* to eliminate the hiatus, and the consequent dropping of *ac*.

2 464. **secto elephanto:** for the hiatus in this position cf. 1.617; for the polysyllabic ending see note on 1.651.

3 466. **Dodonaeosque lebetas:** bronze cauldrons were hung from branches in the famous shrine of Jupiter at Dodona. Dodona was not far from Buthrotum, and some forms of the legend connected Helenus with Dodona.

4 467. 'a breast-plate interwoven with chain and triple meshed in gold', i.e. a coat of mail; cf. *Aen.* 5.259f.

5 468. 'a superb helmet with flowing plumes set at its apex', literally 'the apex (*conum*) and flowing plumes of a superb helmet'. Attention is concentrated on the plume in its setting rather than on the whole helmet, and something of the logic of the sentence is sacrificed.

6 469. **arma Neoptolemi:** i.e. Helenus had been bequeathed these possessions by Neoptolemus, see note on 296.

7 **sunt . . . parenti:** these are special gifts of honour for Anchises; for *sua* cf. *Aen.* 1.461.

8 470. The half-line, which is of a stopgap nature, suggests that this is an unrevised passage, an impression which is strengthened by the absence of subtlety in the rhythm of 465-7 and the fact that 467 occurs in *Aen.* 5.259 in very similar form.

9 **duces:** 'pilots' to guide the fleet.

10 471. 'he makes up the complement of oarsmen, and also fits out the crew with equipment', i.e. to replace the men lost or left behind in Crete. Cf. Livy 26.39.7, *Aen.* 8.80.

11 472f. Notice how Anchises plays the leading part in organising; see note on 1f.

12 473. **ferenti:** 'following', cf. *Aen.* 4.430.

13 475. **Anchisa:** the normal Latin vocative of such Greek words is in long *-e,* but the influence of vocatives such as *Aenea* led to some variation.

14 **dignate:** 'thought worthy of; *dignari* is used passively several times in Cicero.

15 476. **cura deum:** 'beloved of the gods', cf. *Aen.* 10.132.

16 **bis . . . minis :** see note on *Aen.* 2.642-3.

17 477. **ecce tibi:** 'look'; *tibi* is ethic dative, cf. *Aen.* 5.419. Helenus points in the direction of Italy, across the short sea road.

18 **hanc arripe velis:** 'make for it under full sail'; *ampere* has here a strong element of its cognate word *rapidus,* cf. *Aen.* 9.13, 10.298.

19 478. Helenus repeats the warning he has given earlier (381f.).

20 **praeterlabare:** jussive subjunctive in parataxis with *necesse est,* quite a common construction (cf. 234-5, 456-7). The accusative *hanc* is governed by the preposition in the verb; cf. 688 and *Aen.* 6.874.

Ausoniae [1]pars illa procul quam pandit[2] Apollo.
Vade,' ait 'o felix nati[3] pietate. Quid ultra   480
provehor[4] et fando surgentis demoror Austros?'
Nec minus Andromache[5] digressu maesta supremo
fert picturatas[6] auri subtemine[7] vestis
et Phrygiam Ascanio chlamydem (nec[8] cedit honore)
textilibusque onerat donis, ac talia fatur   485
'accipe et haec, [9]manuum tibi quae monimenta mearum
sint, puer, et longum Andromachae testentur amorem,
coniugis Hectoreae. Cape dona extrema tuorum,
o mihi [10]sola mei super[11] Astyanactis imago.
Sic [12]oculos, sic ille manus, sic ora ferebat;   490
et nunc aequali tecum pubesceret aevo.'
Hos ego digrediens lacrimis adfabar obortis:
'vivite felices, quibus est fortuna peracta[13]
iam sua: [14]nos alia ex aliis in fata vocamur.
Vobis parta quies: nullum maris aequor arandum, [15]   495
arva neque Ausoniae semper [16]cedentia retro
quaerenda. Effigiem[17] Xanthi Troiamque videtis

---

1 479. The very heavy alliteration of *p* gives an oracular emphasis to the line.

2 **pandit**: 'reveals' (in his oracular response through Helenus); cf. 252.

3 480. **nati pietate**: the often stressed quality of Aeneas is here given special emphasis by the most unusual rhythm of a heavy stop in the fifth foot.

4 481. **provehor**: 'go on' speaking, cf. Cic. *Dom.* 32.

5 482f. It was of Hector that Andromache spoke when she met Aeneas (310f.); it is of their son Astyanax that she speaks now as she says goodbye.

6 483. **picturatas**: a rare word, not found before Virgil, nor often afterwards (cf. Stat. *Th.* 6.58).

7 **subtemine**: this word, sometimes spelled *subtegmine*, refers to the golden thread which is either woven into the yarn to make the picture, or embroidered on it.

8 484. **nec cedit honore**: 'nor does she fall short in honouring the guests'. With *cedit* understand the dative *Helena*; Helenus had paid due honour to his departing guests by his gifts and his speech, and Andromache does likewise. Some MSS read the dative *honori,* and Servius preferred this.

9 486. The alliteration of *m* and the assonance of final *-um, -em* are very marked, reflecting the controlled sadness of her words.

10 489. 'for you are the only picture I have left now of my Astyanax'; for Andromache's son Astyanax see note on 2.457.

11 **super**: the adverb is used adjectivally, almost equivalent to *superstes* or *quae superest.*

12 490-1. 'he had the same look in his eyes, the same gestures, the same expression as you have, and he would now have,been the same age as you, growing up to manhood'; cf. Hom. *Od.* 4.149f. (Telemachus' resemblance to Odysseus).

13 493f. We are reminded of Aeneas' words at Carthage, *O fortunati quorum iam moenia surgunt* (*Aen.* 1.437).

14 494. **sua**: the word is used non-reflexively (cf. 469), and its reference to the second person makes the statement very general. Page well says, 'The speaker places those he is addressing among a class of men, viz. those whose toils are over. Every man has his destiny (*fortuna sua*) to work out, and, until it is worked out, he cannot rest.'

15 495. Aeneas recalls Creusa's words to him in 2.780 *longa tibi exsilia et vastum maris aequor arandum.*

16 496. For the 'ever receding' land of Italy cf. *Aen.* 5.629 *Italiam sequimur fugientem,* 6.61.

17 497. **effigiem Xanthi Troiamque**: for the new settlement with the old names cf. 349-51.

quam vestrae fecere manus, melioribus[1], opto,
auspiciis, et quae fuerit minus obvia Grais.
Si quando Thybrim[2] vicinaque Thybridis arva   500
intraro gentique meae data moenia cernam,
cognatas[3] urbes olim populosque propinquos,
Epiro[4] Hesperiam (quibus idem Dardanus auctor
atque idem casus), unam faciemus utramque
Troiam animis: maneat nostros ea cura nepotes.'   505

> *506-47. After leaving Buthrotum the Trojans sail to Acroceraunia. Here they spend the night; they set off early next day and sight Italy. They land at Castrum Minervae, and Anchises interprets the sight of four white horses as an omen both of peace and of war. They make offerings to Juno and re-embark.*

[5]Provehimur pelago vicina[6] Ceraunia iuxta,
unde iter[7] Italiam cursusque brevissimus undis.
Sol[8] ruit interea et montes umbrantur opaci.
Sternimur[9] optatae gremio[10] telluris ad undam
sortiti[11] remos passimque in litore sicco   510
corpora curamus; fessos[12] sopor inrigat artus.

---

1 498-9. **melioribus . . . Grais**: 'under better auspices, I trust, and less likely to be exposed to the Greeks'; *fuerit* is perfect subjunctive expressing a wish with *opto*.

2 500. **Thybrim . . . Thybridis**: Virgil prefers the Greek form *Thybris* to the Latin *Tiberis*. Aeneas knows of the Tiber as his goal from Creusa's prophecy in *Aen.* 2.782.

3 502f. 'then one day we will make these cities of kinsmen, these neighbouring peoples of ours, Hesperia and Epirus (each of us have the same Dardanus as our first founder, the same fortunes); we will make both our peoples into one Troy in spirit; this is a prospect for which our descendants must strive'. The sentence is complicated, particularly in the reiteration of the object (*cognatas urbes populosque, propinquos*) by *utramque*, which stands for *utrosque*, assimilated to *Troiam*.

4 503. **Epiro Hesperiam**: *Hesperiam* is in apposition to *populosque*: 'neighbouring peoples, Hesperia to Epirus'. Servius and some MSS read *Hesperia*, in which case both *Epiro* and *Hesperia* would be local ablative.

5 506f. The Trojans now sail north past the Ceraunian mountains towards Acroceraunia, the point for the shortest sea-passage to Italy; cf. *Geo.* 1.332, Hor. *Odes* 1.3.20. Virgil has not adopted the general tradition (Dion. Hal. 1.51.2) that the Trojans crossed from Onchesmus, a place considerably south of Acroceraunia, because the name was connected with a version of the tradition according to which Anchises died there.
After the ponderous account of the stay at Buthrotum the narrative speed changes, and events follow one another rapidly. There is a feeling of urgency now that the Trojans have come at last into the part of the world which is to be their home.

6 506. **vicina Ceraunia iuxta**: the disyllabic preposition is postponed, as often in poetry, cf. 75.

7 507. **iter Italiam**: the accusative of motion towards without a preposition is used here after the verbal notion in the noun *iter*; cf. *Aen.* 6.542.

8 508. **sol ruit**: an unusual phrase, meaning not necessarily 'the sun set', but 'the sun sped on its course'; cf. *Aen.* 10.256f.

9 509. **sternimur**: middle in sense, 'we throw ourselves down', cf. *Geo.* 4.432.

10 **gremio**: cf. Lucr. 1.251 *ingremium matris terrai, Aen.* 5.31.

11 510. **sortiti remos**: 'after we had allotted the order of rowing', cf. Ap. Rh. 1.358, 395, Prop. 3.21.12. The reference is to the allocation of places at the oars for the next day's rowing; it is done in advance so that a timely start can be made.

12 511. **fessos . . . artus**: 'slumber flows through our weary limbs'. The metaphor is from channels of water refreshing the land; it is not only the dampness of sleep but its diffusing power which is pictured metaphorically. Cf. *Aen.* 5.857, and (with a different construction of *inrigare*) *Aen.* 1.691f.

Necdum[1] orbem medium Nox[2] Horis acta subibat:
haud[3] segnis strato surgit Palinurus et omnis
explorat ventos atque auribus aera captat;
sidera cuncta notat tacito labentia caelo,[4]   515
Arcturum pluviasque Hyadas geminosque Triones,[5]
armatumque auro circumspicit[6] Oriona.[7]
Postquam [8]cuncta videt caelo constare sereno,
dat clarum e puppi signum: nos castra movemus
temptamusque viam et velorum[9] pandimus alas.   520
    Iamque rubescebat[10] stellis[11] Aurora fugatis
cum procul obscuros collis humilemque[12] videmus
Italiam.[13] Italiam primus conclamat Achates,
Italiam laeto socii clamore salutant.
Tum pater Anchises magnum cratera[14] corona[15]   525
induit implevitque mero, divosque vocavit
stans celsa in puppi:
'di maris et terrae tempestatumque potentes,[16]
ferte viam vento facilem et spirate secundi.'

---

1 512f. 'Not yet was Night, drawn by the Hours, reaching the mid-point of her circuit (when) Palinurus rose. . .'. The juxtaposition of these two clauses without subordination is characteristic of Virgil's paratactic style, cf. 358.

2 512. **Nox Horis acta:** Night is drawn in her chariot (cf. *Aen.* 5.721) across the sky by the Hours. The personified Hours play a large part in Greek literature; in Homer they guard the gates of heaven and roll back the clouds (*Il.* 5.749f., 8.393f.), and they occur very frequently in Pindar and afterwards as personifications of the seasons. They figure less prominently in Latin literature, generally as personifications of the divisions of day or night, as here; cf. Ov. *Fast.* 1.125, *Met.* 2.26, 118. Compare Milton, *P.L.* 6.2f. 'Morn, / wak't by the circling Hours, with rosie hand / unbarrd the gates of Light.'

3 513-14. 'tests for all the winds, and tries to feel the breeze blowing in his ears', i.e. he turns his head so as to feel (or hear) the direction of the wind as it blows into one ear or the other; a much more reliable method than wetting a finger and holding it up.

4 515f. Compare the description of Odysseus watching the stars as he guides his raft (Hom. *Od.* 5.271f.).

5 516. This line is repeated from *Aen.* 1.744, where see note.

6 517. **circumspicit**: 'looks round and sees', because Orion, unlike the other constellations mentioned, is in the southern part of the sky. Orion the hunter is 'armed with gold' because his belt and sword are formed by two lines of stars.

7 **Oriona:** Greek accusative, cf. *cratera* (525). For the spondaic fifth foot cf. 549 and see note on 2.68.

8 518. 'when he saw that all the signs were favourable in the cloudless sky'; i.e. no sign of bad weather, no *stellis acies obtunsa* (*Geo.* 1.395). The use of *constare* is like the common use in the phrase *ratio constat*.

9 520. **velorum** . . . **alas:** compare *volare* in 124, and *Aen.* 1.224 *mare velivolum.*

10 521. **rubescebat:** the word is not found before Virgil; cf. *Aen.* 7.25.

11 **stellis ... fugatis**: cf. Hor. *Odes* 3.21.24 *dum rediens fugat astra Phoebus, Aen.* 5.42, and the beginning of FitzGerald's Omar Khayyam: 'Awake, for Morning in the Bowl of Night / has flung the Stone that puts the Stars to flight'.

12 522. **humilem:** land sighted far off, even when hilly, appears as a smudge on the horizon. The words *obscurus* and *humilis* here are purely visual, but perhaps they may also suggest the contrast of the humble present with the glorious future.

13 523-4. The threefold repetition of the word *Italiam* gives the dramatic emphasis required, with a suggestion also of the word passing from lip to lip. The heavy pause in line 523 after the elision of the run-on word gives rhythmical emphasis to reinforce the emphasis of diction.

14 525. **cratera**: Greek accusative, cf. 517.

15 525-6. **corona induit**: i.e. a crown of leaves or the like is put around the wine cup; see note on 1.724, and cf. Tib. 2.5.98.

16 528. **potentes:** the genitive with *potens* is common in Livy and the poets, cf. *Aen.* 1.80.

Crebrescunt[1] optatae aurae portusque patescit 530
iam propior, [2]templumque apparet in arce Minervae.
Vela[3] legunt socii et proras ad litora torquent.
Portus[4] ab euroo fluctu curvatus in arcum,
obiectae salsa spumant aspergine cautes,
ipse latet: [5]gemino dimittunt bracchia muro 535
turriti scopuli refugitque ab litore templum.
Quattuor hic, primum[6] omen, equos in gramine vidi
tondentis campum late, candore nivali.
Et pater Anchises 'beltum, o terra[7] hospita, portas:
bello armantur[8] equi, bellum haec armenta minantur. 540
Sed tamen idem olim[9] curru succedere sueti
quadripedes et frena iugo concordia ferre:
spes[10] et pacis' ait. Tum numina sancta precamur
Palladis[11] armisonae, quae prima accepit ovantis,
et[12] capita ante[13] aras Phrygio velamur amictu, 545
praeceptisque[14] Heleni, dederat quae maxima, rite

---

1 530. **crebrescunt:** 'freshen', cf. *Aen.* 5.764.

2 531. This is the site of Castrum Minervae in Calabria, where the temple was a well-known landmark (Strabo 6.281).

3 532. **vela legunt:** 'furl the sails', cf. *Geo.* 1.373. The Trojans now begin to row, the normal method of approaching or leaving harbour. Although they know that this is not the part of Italy where they are to stay, they land to perform the rites Helenus had instructed them to pay (403f.).

4 533-5. 'There is a harbour shaped like a bow curving away from the waves which the East winds drive; the rocky breakwaters foam with salt spray but the harbour itself is safe behind them'. For the use of *ab* cf. 570. Notice the alliteration of *s*, imitative of the sea; cf. *Aen.* 5.866.

5 535-6. 'the tower-like cliffs extend their arms to form two walls, and the temple shelters back from the shore'. For the 'arms' cf. Ov. *Met.* 11.229f.; for *gemino muro* cf. *Aen.* 1.162f. The word *refugitque* adds a little touch of personification.

6 537. **primum omen:** on arrival in Italy the Trojans would naturally be looking for anything which could be interpreted as an omen, and the first feature to present itself is the sign of the four horses. Compare the sign of the horse's head revealed to the Carthaginian settlers (*Aen.* 1.442f.). The four white horses suggest a Roman triumphal procession; cf. Livy 5.23.5, Prop. 4.1.32, Ov. *A.A.* 1.214.

7 539. **terra hospita:** 'land of our sojourn', see note on 377-8.

8 540. **armantur . . . armenta minantur:** the assonance is extremely marked, and coupled with the threefold repetition of *bellum* makes Anchises' speech sound formal and oracular. There seems to be an etymological connexion intended between *armari* and *armenta* (see note on 693); for *armenta* of horses cf. *Geo.* 3.129, *Aen.* 11.494.

9 541. **olim:** 'sometimes', an archaic use surviving in poetry, cf. *Aen.* 5.125.

10 543. 'there is hope of peace too'; i.e. as well as expectation of war first. This symbolises the entire vision of the Roman mission: first war against the proud, then civilisation for the subdued peoples.

11 544. **Palladis armisonae:** Minerva, to whose temple they have come, is here given her Greek name and an epithet associating her with her martial aspects (cf. *Aen.*) 1.483). The adjective *armisonus* seems to have been coined by Virgil; for other striking compound adjectives (which Virgil uses sparingly) cf. 75, 221, 553, and for further discussion see my note ad loc. (OUP Ed.).

12 545f. The Trojans now obey the instructions given by Helenus (403f.); for *capita vetamur* see note on 405, and on 1.228.

13 545. **ante aras:** these are not the altars of the temple, but those which Aeneas has set up on the shore (cf. 404).

14 546-7. 'and in accordance with the instructions upon which Helenus had especially insisted we duly offer sacrifice, as we had been bidden, to Juno of Argos.' The causal ablative *praeceptis* is in a loose syntactical relationship to the sentence. Juno is here called *Argiva* (cf. 1.24) to stress her association with the Greeks in whose territory the Trojans have temporarily landed. For *adolere* cf. *Ecl.* 8.65, Ov. *Met.* 8.740.

Iunoni Argivae iussos adolemus honores.

> *548-87. The Trojans sail across the bay of Tarentum, escape Scylla and Charybdis, and approach the Sicilian coast near Mt. Etna. They pass a night of fear in the shadow of the volcano.*

[1]Haud mora, continuo perfectis ordine votis
cornua[2] velatarum obvertimus antemnarum,
Graiugenumque[3] domos suspectaque linquimus arva.   550
Hinc[4] sinus Herculei[5] (si vera est fama) Tarenti
cernitur, attollit se diva[6] Lacinia contra,
Caulonisque arces et navifragum[7] Scylaceum.
Tum procul e[8] fluctu Trinacria[9] cernitur Aetna,
et [10]gemitum ingentem pelagi pulsataque saxa   555
audimus longe fractasque[11] ad litora voces,

---

1 548f. After the rapid narrative of the previous section Virgil now changes the movement again, as he comes to a part of the poem which is concerned with descriptions of terror and power on the grand scale. The first indication of this is the mention of Etna far off (554); then Scylla and Charybdis are described in the high rhetorical style before the full-scale portrayal of the mighty volcano (571f.). The mood is thus established for the grandiose rhetoric of the story of Polyphemus.

2 549. 'we turn the ends of the sail-covered yards towards the sea'. The yard (*antemna*) was the name of the crosspiece fixed across the mast to which the sail was attached; sometimes it would consist of two pieces joined at the centre, and therefore the plural *antemnae* is commonly used. *Cornua* was the technical term for the two ends of the yard, cf. *Aen.* 5.832, Ov. *Met.* 11.482-3. The meaning is that the sailors of each ship hoist and adjust the yard with the attached sail; it would have been lowered when the sails were furled (532).

The rhythm of this line is very unusual; it has no caesura at all except that made by elision in the third foot, and consequently ictus and accent coincide throughout. The fifth foot is spondaic, which is rare in Virgil and generally occurs when a Greek word is involved; see note on 2.68. The rhyme of *velatarum . . . antemnarum* is also very striking. There does not seem to be any correspondence of the rhythm with the sense; it appears that Virgil has used a line of unusual sound-effects simply for variety.

3 550. **Graiugenum**: genitive, see note on 21; for the formation of the word cf. *Troiugena*, 359.

4 551f. Aeneas is now sailing across the Gulf of Tarentum from the 'heel' to the 'toe' of Italy; Lacinium is the promontory on the far side of the gulf, and Caulon (Caulonia) and Scylaceum are further on, in reverse order. There is a certain amount of anachronism in the use of these names; see note on 398.

5 551. **Herculei . . . Tarenti**: there were many different accounts of the foundation of Tarentum, as Virgil's *si vera est fama* suggests. One of the famous towns in this area (Heraclea) bore Hercules' name, and he was particularly associated with the nearby town of Croton (Ov. *Met.* 15.12f.). In the legend he returned to Greece by this route after killing the cattle of Geryon in Spain.

6 552. **diva Lacinia**: 'the Lacinian goddess', i.e. the temple of the Lacinian goddess, Juno; for the metonymy cf. 275. This temple of Juno at Lacinium was very famous; cf. Cic. *De Div.* 1.48, Livy 24.3.3. According to Dionysius (1.51.3) Aeneas landed here and sacrificed to Juno; Virgil has avoided undue repetition of landings and departures by placing the sacrifices to Juno at the previous landing at Castrum Minervae.

7 553. **navifragum**: a rarer variant of *naufragus*.

8 554. **e fluctu**: dependent on the idea of *apparere* in the verb *cernitur*.

9 **Trinacria ... Aetna**: *Trinacrius* is an epithet of Sicily, cf. 384; Etna is described in 571f, where see notes.

10 555. 'the mighty groaning of the sea as it dashed against the rocks'; the two phrases form a single complex image. For *gemitus* with inanimate subjects cf. 577, *Aen.* 5.806.

11 556. **fractasque . . . voces**: 'and the voice of the breakers reverberating on the shore'. This is a very unusual use of *voces*, more so than in English (cf. Wordsworth's 'Two voices are there; one is of the sea . . .', and Psalm 93.3 'The floods have lifted up their voice'). Two considerations have led Virgil towards this vivid phrase; the first that a much easier personification of the sea has already been made with the word *gemitus*, and the second that musical instruments, particularly the bugle, have a 'voice' in Latin (*Aen.* 7.519, Ov. *Met.* 1.338). The meaning of *fractae* (cf. *Geo.* 4.72) is generally taken as 'intermittent', but it is perhaps better to refer it to the pulsating or reverberating effect of a noise low in pitch. There is probably also a suggestion of the idea of 'breaking' waves; cf. *Aen.* 1.161, 10.291. I have tried to convey these two converging streams of meaning in my translation by rendering *fractae* twice.

exsultantque [1]vada atque aestu miscentur harenae.
Et pater Anchises 'nimirum hic illa Charybdis:[2]
hos Helenus scopulos, haec saxa horrenda canebat.
Eripite,[3] o socii, pariterque insurgite remis.'   560
haud [4]minus ac iussi faciunt, primusque rudentem[5]
contorsit Iaevas proram Palinurus ad undas;
laevam cuncta cohors[6] remis ventisque petivit.
tollimur [7]in caelum curvato[8] gurgite, et idem[9]
subducta ad manis[10] imos desedimus[11] unda.   565
Ter scopuli clamorem[12] inter cava saxa dedere,
ter spumam elisam[13] et rorantia[14] vidimus astra.
Interea fessos ventus[15] cum sole reliquit,
ignarique viae Cyclopum[16] adlabimur oris.
        Portus[17] ab accessu ventorum immotus et ingens   570

---

1 557. 'the waters seethe and the sand swirls in the surge'; cf. Hom. *Od.* 12.240f. (Charybdis) and for *exsultant Aen.* 7.464.

2 558-9. Cf. Helenus' words in 420f.

3 560. **Eripite:** the omission of the object (*nos*) is natural in excited speech.

4 561f. Palinurus' ship takes the lead in the dangerous situation, as in *Aen.* 5.833f.

5 561-2. **rudentem ... proram:** 'groaning prow'. For the verb cf. *Aen.* 7.16, 8.248; it is not normally applied to inanimate subjects, but cf. the personifications in 555-6 and 566.

6 563. **cohors:** 'company'; the word is mainly poetic in this wide sense, cf. *Aen.* 10.328, 11.500.

7 564f. Compare the rhetorical and hyperbolical description of storm waves in *Aen.* 1.106f., Ov. *Tr.* 1.2.l9f., and Shakespeare, *Othello*, 2.1.190f.
And let the labouring bark climb hills of seas
Olympus-high, and duck again as low
As hell's from heaven.

8 564. **curvato gurgite:** 'on the arching billow', cf. Hom. *Od.* 11.244, *Geo.* 4.361.

9 **idem:** the reiteration of the subject by means of this word seems to hold them for a moment on the summit of the wave.

10 565. **manis imos:** *manes* here means 'the abode of the shades', cf. *Geo.* 1.243, *Aen.* 4.387.

11 **desedimus:** 'instantaneous' perfect (from *desidere*); cf. *Aen* 1.84.

12 566. **clamorem:** this word, like *gemitus* (555), *voces* (556), *rudens* (561) is rarely applied to inanimate things. It makes us think of the monster Charybdis as well as of the whirlpool.

13 567. **elisam:** 'forced out', an unexpected use of the word, perhaps with the overtone of the 'shattered' wave (Lucan 9.339). We might say 'the splintered spray'.

14 **rorantia:** the hyperbole has disturbed some commentators, but it is surely wholly in keeping with the rest of the superbly exaggerated picture of Charybdis' whirlpool. Page well quotes *Othello* 2.1.13f.:
The wind-shak'd surge, with high and monstrous mane,
Seems to cast water on the burning bear
And quench the guards of the ever-fixed pole.

15 568. **ventus cum sole reliquit:** 'the sun set and the wind forsook us'; a change of wind often occurs at dawn or sunset.

16 569. **Cyclopum:** see note on 617. By Virgil's time they had long been localised in the area of Mt. Etna; cf. Eur. *Cycl.* 20f., Callim. *Hymn.* 3.46f., *Aen.* 8.416f. The volcanic rocks in the sea off Mt. Etna are today called Scogli dei Ciclopi.

17 570-1. 'There is a harbour away from the reach of the winds, undisturbed and spacious in itself, but close to it Etna thunders in terrifying eruptions'. Compare Homer's description of the harbour on the island near the land of the Cyclopes (*Od.* 9.136f.). For *ruinae* ('falling material') cf. *Aen.* 1.129, Hor. *Odes* 3.3.8.

ipse: [1]sed horrificis iuxta tonat Aetna ruinis,
interdumque[2] atram[3] prorumpit ad aethera nubem
turbine fumantem piceo et candente favilla,
attollitque globos[4] flammarum et sidera lambit,
interdum[5] scopulos avulsaque viscera montis   575
erigit eructans, liquefactaque saxa sub auras
cum gemitu glomerat fundoque exaestuat imo.
Fama[6] est Enceladi semustum[7] fulmine corpus
urgeri mole hac, ingentemque insuper Aetnam
impositam ruptis[8] flammam exspirare caminis,   580
et fessum quotiens mutet[9] latus, intremere[10] omnem
murmure Trinacriam et caelum[11] subtexere fumo.

---

1 571f. In his description of Etna Virgil writes in the grand style of hyperbole. There has so far been little of this kind of writing in *Aeneid* 3; here Virgil has introduced the heightened style by lines 564-9, and now he lays on his colours very thickly. For this he was criticised by Favorinus (Aul. Gell. 17.10), who compares Pindar's description (*Pyth.* 1.21f.) to the disadvantage of Virgil, mainly because he found the powerful effect at which Virgil aims altogether overpowering.

Lucretius discusses the eruption of Etna in 6.639f. (cf. also 1.722f.); he was imitated by the author of the didactic poem called *Aetna.* Pliny's accounts of the eruption of Vesuvius (*Ep.* 6.16 and 20) may be compared, though they are more detailed and specific. There are some vividly descriptive passages in Arnold's *Empedodes on Etna,* Act II, and Spenser has a fine simile referring to the dragon with which the Red Cross Knight fought (*F.Q.* 1.11.44):

As burning Aetna from his boyling stew
Doth belch out flames, and rockes in peeces broke,
And ragged ribs of mountaines molten new,
Enwrapt in coleblacke clouds and filthy smoke,
That all the land with stench, and heaven with horror choke.

2 572f. The two *interdum* clauses are particularised descriptions of the general picture in line 571: the first of them describes the more visual aspects of flame and smoke, and the second the active features of an eruption.

3 572. **atram . . . nubem:** 'shoots a burst of cloudy blackness up to the heavens'. The transitive use of *prorumpere* is scarce, and not precisely paralleled. It is based on the passive used in the sense of the intransitive active, e.g. Lucr. 6.436, *Aen.* 1.246, 7.459. passage Cf. *rumpere* in 246.

4 574. **globos flammarum:** cf. *Geo.* 1.472f. *undantem ruptis fornacibus Aetnam, / flammarumque globos liquefactaque volvere saxa,* a passage which Virgil re-echoes in 576, 580.

5 575f. 'sometimes it belches forth and hurls high rocks torn from the living body of the mountain, and with a groan brings up balls of molten rock to the surface, bubbling up and boiling from its very foundations'. The phrase *avulsaque viscera* is explanatory of *scopulos,* a kind of hendiadys; for the metaphorical use of *viscera* cf. Ov. *Met.* 1.138 and compare Milton, *P.L.* 1.233f. 'thundring Etna, whose combustible / and fuelled entrails thence conceiving fire / sublim'd with mineral fury, aid the winds. . . .' For *eructans* cf. *Aen.* 6.297 and Milton, *P.L.* 1.670f. 'There stood a Hill not far, whose griesly top / belchd fire and rouling smoke'. For *glomerare* cf. *Aen.* 2.315, 4.155, 6.311. Notice the pattern of alliteration and assonance in these powerfully descriptive lines: initial *e,* the *-ac-* sounds in *lique factaque saxa,* initial *g.*

6 578f. Enceladus was one of the Giants who rebelled against Jupiter (*Aen.* 4.179, Hor. *Odes* 3.4.56). His fate was to be struck down by Jupiter's thunderbolt, and according to the most common version of the legend he was buried under Mt. Inarime, and it was Typhoeus (Typhon) who was buried under Etna. In Virgil's version the punishments are reversed; cf. also *Aen.* 9.716.

7 578. **semustum:** for this spelling (*semi, ustum*) cf. 244.

8 580. **ruptis . . . caminis:** 'as its furnaces burst open'; the meaning is that the furnaces of Etna cannot contain the flames of the thunderbolt which are issuing from Enceladus' burning body; cf. *Aen.* 1.44.

9 581. **mutet latus:** 'changes position'.

10 **intremere omnem:** the rhythm here is most unusual, with the marked conflict of accent and ictus in the fifth foot; clearly Virgil intends by this dislocation of the rhythm to reflect the violence of the earthquake. Note also the powerful alliteration of *m* in this line and the next.

11 582. **caelum subtexere fumo:** 'veils the sky with smoke'; the metaphor is weaving something beneath an object overhead, hence concealing it; cf. Lucr. 5.466, 6.482.

Noctem[1] illam tecti silvis immania[2] monstra
perferimus, nec quae sonitum det causa videmus.
Nam neque erant astrorum ignes nec[3] lucidus aethra   585
siderea polus, obscuro sed nubila caelo,
et lunam in nimbo nox[4] intempesta tenebat.

> *588-654. The Trojans meet an emaciated castaway, who appeals to them for help. He tells them that he is Achaemenides, left behind on the island by Ulysses after his encounter with the Cyclops Polyphemus.*

[5]Postera iamque dies primo[6] surgebat Eoo
umentemque Aurora polo dimoverat umbram,
cum[7] subito e silvis macie confecta suprema   590
ignoti nova forma viri miserandaque cultu
procedit supplexque manus ad litora tendit.
respicimus.[8] Dira[9] inluvies immissaque barba,

---

1 583. **noctem illam:** 'all through that night'; observe how the alliteration of *m* continues through this slow menacing spondaic line.

2 **immania monstra** 'terrifying horrors'; the word *monstra* has an aura of the supernatural, cf. 26, 307.

3 585-6. **nec lucidus aethra siderea polus:** 'nor were the heavens bright with starry radiance'; *aethra* is a rare and vivid word which Servius well defines as *splendor aetheris*. Cf. Enn. *Ann.* 435, Lucr. 6.467, *Aen.* 12.247.

4 587. **nox intempesta:** 'timeless night', the dead of night when time seems to stand still. The phrase is used by Ennius (*Ann.* 102, 167) and Lucretius (5.986); cf. also *Geo.* 1.247, *Aen.* 12.846. Notice how the fear and dread of the passage is finalised in this spondaic line with most subtle alliteration of *n, m, t.*

5 588f. The episode about Achaemenides and Polyphemus did not figure in the Aeneas legend, and indeed Achaemenides is not heard of before Virgil; it seems very probable that Virgil invented this part of his story. Its purpose is to introduce a reworking of Homer's story about the Cyclops; Odyssean touches have already occurred in this book with the Harpies (partly based on an Odyssean episode, see note on 209f.), Phaeacia (291), Circe (386), Scylla and Charybdis (420f.). But this is a far more sustained and direct attempt to bring Aeneas into the world of Homer.
There are many indications that Virgil was not satisfied with the episode; there are signs of imperfect finish (621, 640, 661, 669, 684f.), and the marked similarities between Achaemenides and Sinon (*Aen.* 2.57f.) suggest that when Virgil was writing the second book he used this passage as a quarry, intending to recast or remove it later on; see Mackail's edition, Appendix B. We may conjecture that as the *Aeneid* progressed Aeneas became to Virgil a less legendary figure, more Roman, more historical, less Odyssean.
But while Virgil may have felt uncertain whether the episode was a proper part of the fabric of the poem, we may still admire it as a patch piece of brilliant colours. It is a passage of rhetorical and grandiose writing, detached from the immediate world of human experience, and capable of being handled in sonorous and grandiloquent hyperbole. This was the kind of writing which the Silver Age loved; Virgil uses it far less often, but we should beware of thinking that it was alien to him. The boxing match in *Aeneid* 5 is another such episode. Ovid was evidently much impressed by the story of Achaemenides, and tells it at length in a recast version (*Met.* 14.160f.).

6 588. **primo . . . Eoo:** 'with the first appearance of the morning star'. The adjective *Eous* (eastern) is here used as a noun; cf. *Geo.* 1.288, *Aen.* 11.4.

7 590-1. 'in the last stages of exhaustion and emaciation, the extraordinary figure of a man unknown to us, most pitiable in aspect... .' *Nova* suggests that the Trojans had seen nothing like this degree of wretchedness before; the strangeness of the picture is emphasised by the abstract turn of the subject (*forma viri procedit* instead of *vir procedit*). Compare the castaway Ben Gunn in *Treasure Island:* 'unlike any man that I had ever seen . . . yet a man it was'.

8 593. **respicimus:** 'we stared at him'; for this meaning of fixing the eyes upon something cf. *Aen.* 2.615, 7.454. The very brief sentence helps to convey the drama of the events.

9 593-5. 'His squalor was terrible to see, his beard unkempt, his clothing held together with briars; yet in all else he was a Greek, and had in days gone by been sent to Troy in the service of his country.' The descriptive passage is given impetus by the omission of the main verbs.

consertum tegimen spinis: at[1] cetera Graius,
et[2] quondam patriis ad Troiam missus in armis.   595
Isque ubi Dardanios habitus et Troia vidit
arma procul, paulum aspectu conterritus haesit
continuitque gradum; mox sese ad litora praeceps
cum fletu precibusque tulit: 'per sidera testor,
per superos atque hoc caeli spirabile[3] lumen,   600
tollite[4] me, Teucri; quascumque[5] abducite terras:
hoc sat. [6]Erit scio me[7] Danais e classibus unum[8]
et bello Iliacos fateor[9] petiisse penatis.
Pro quo, si sceleris tanta est iniuria nostri,
spargite[10] me in fluctus vastoque immergite ponto;   605
si pereo,[11] hominum manibus periisse iuvabit.'
Dixerat[12] et genua amplexus genibusque volutans
haerebat. [13]Qui sit fari, quo[14] sanguine cretus,
hortamur, quae deinde[15] agitet fortuna fateri.
Ipse[16] pater dextram Anchises haud multa moratus   610

---

1 594. **at cetera Graius:** the expression here is elliptical; the thought is that in some respects he was unidentifiable (because of his wretched plight), but in others, which Virgil does not specify, he could be recognised as Greek. After the ten years siege the Trojans could recognise a Greek when they saw one even thus changed. *Cetera* is the Greek accusative of respect; cf. *Aen.* 4.558, 9.656.

2 595. This line seems to anticipate the narrative rather strangely, but if we remember that Aeneas is telling the story to Dido such an anticipation is acceptable.

3 600. **spirabile lumen:** 'the light of life which we breathe', a strange and haunting innovation, based on the normal use of *spirabilis* applied to the air; cf. Ov. *Met.* 14.175 (of Achaemenides) *lumen vitale,* and for an analogous image *Geo.* 3.340 *cum primae lucem pecudes hausere.*

4 601. **tollite me:** 'take me on board', cf. *Aen.* 6.370.

5 **quascumque ... terras:** accusative of motion towards, cf. 254. For *quascumque* ('any at all') cf. 654 and 682.

6 602. **scio:** only with *scio* (*Ecl.* 8.43) and *nescio* (fairly often) does Virgil scan as short the final *-o* of a verb. In the Silver Age this scansion became much more common. In a few disyllabic words (other than verbs) the short final *-o* is normal (iambic shortening); e.g. *duo* (623), *ego, modo, cito.*

7 **me ... unum:** 'that I am one of the men from the Greek fleet'.

8 602-3. Compare Sinon's words in *Aen.* 2.77f.

9 603. **fateor ... petiisse:** for the omission of the reflexive subject of the infinitive cf. 201.

10 605. **spargite me in fluctus:** the phrase is elliptical for *dilacerate meum corpus et spargite;* cf. the fuller expression in *Aen.* 4.600f.

11 606. **pereo, hominum:** there is hiatus between these two words; a special effect is achieved here as the natural pause after *pereo* is accentuated while he stays for a moment on the grim word, and emphasis is put on *hominum,* the key word of his speech.

12 607-8. 'He spoke, and clasping our knees, grovelling at our knees, he clung to us.' The phrases express Achaemenides' intense emotion; they contrast with the calmness of the following lines as the Trojans reassure him. *Volutans* is unusual in this intransitive usage; cf. Ov. *Am.* 3.6.45.

13 608-9. Again we are reminded of the story of Sinon (*Aen.* 2.74f.).

14 608. **quo sanguine cretus:** 'of what parentage he comes'; for the past participle of *crescere* (= *natus*) cf. *Aen.* 2.74, 4.191.

15 609. **deinde:** to be taken with *hortamur fateri:* for the postposition of *deinde* cf. *Aen.* 1.195.

16 610f. Compare Priam's reception of Sinon, *Aen.* 2.146f. Notice how Anchises (not Aeneas) takes the initiative; see note on 1f.

dat iuveni atque animum praesenti[1] pignore firmat.
Ille haec deposita tandem formidine fatur:
'sum[2] patria ex Ithaca, comes infelicis[3] Ulixi,
nomine Achaemenides,[4] Troiam genitore Adamasto[5]
paupere (mansissetque utinam fortuna!) profectus.   615
Hic me, dum trepidi crudelia[6] limina linquunt,
immemores [7]socii vasto Cyclopis[8] in antro
deseruere. [9]Domus[10] sanie dapibusque cruentis,
intus opaca, ingens. Ipse arduus, altaque pulsat[11]
sidera (di talem terris avertite pestem!)   620
Nec[12] visu facilis nec dictu adfabilis ulli;
visceribus miserorum et sanguine vescitur atro.
Vidi[13] egomet duo de numero cum corpora nostro[14]

---

1 611. **praesenti pignore**: 'with a ready sign of friendship', i.e. the offering of his hand.

2 613f. Achaemenides' first words immediately take us into the world of Homer's *Odyssey* with the mention of Odysseus' home Ithaca and then of Odysseus (Ulysses) himself. Achaemenides begins quietly and formally with information about himself; then the parenthesis of 615 leads into the heightened tone and sustained hyperbole of the description of Polyphemus.

3 613. **infelicis**: an unexpected epithet (echoed in 691); Servius wanted it to mean 'accursed', but the word in Virgil when applied to humans always has a strong suggestion of sympathy. It is perhaps an echo of καμμορος, used a number of times by Homer of Odysseus, and it puts the emphasis on the toils which Odysseus endured.

4 614. **Achaemenides**: nothing is known of him before Virgil; see note on 588f.

5 614-15. 'and because my father Adamastus was poor — and if only such poverty had remained my lot in life — I went away to Troy'. Cf. Sinon's words in *Aen.* 2.87. By *fortuna* he means his humble lot as son of a poor man, infinitely preferable to his present plight.

6 616. **crudelia limina**: by saying 'cruel entrance' rather than 'cruel cave' or the like Virgil reminds us of the part of Homer's story which Achaemenides does not tell, how Odysseus and his companions got out past the blinded Cyclops waiting at the entrance to the cave by clinging under the sheep as they went out to graze.

7 617. The strong assonance of *o* begins the series of striking sound effects in this powerful descriptive passage.

8 **Cyclopis**: the Cyclopes in Homer (*Od.* 9.106f.) were a race of savage one-eyed giants, shepherds by occupation (cf. 657). Chief among them was Polyphemus, who is often (as here) simply called Cyclops. Virgil's version here follows Homer, with no reference to post-Homeric features like the forging of thunderbolts in their cave (*Aen.* 8.418f.), or the half-pathetic amorous Polyphemus who loved Galatea (*Theoc.* 11, Ov. *Met.* 13.749f.).
For the history of the Polyphemus legend, and other stories analogous to it, see Frazer's Loeb edition of Apollodorus, Appendix 13, and D. L. Page, *The Homeric Odyssey*, chap. 1; one of the best known is the story of the great black giant in the third voyage of Sindbad the Sailor.

9 618. The very marked sense pause after the second foot trochee is unusual and striking, it is reinforced by the alliteration of *d*, the absence of a main verb, and the very unusual syntax.

10 **domus . . . cruentis**: the ablatives of description have a most abrupt impact because the words are not of the qualitative kind normally used in this construction; the syntax produces an effect of violence and strangeness which is appropriate to the subject matter.

11 619. This is another remarkable line, composed very largely of descriptive adjectives, with the verb again unexpressed, and marked assonance of initial *i* and *a*.

12 621. 'not easy to look upon, nor would anyone dare to speak to him'; Macrobius (*Sat.* 6.1.55) quotes a line from Accius as Virgil's source: *quem neque tueri contra nec adfari queas.*
This self-contained line is the climax of the description; its finality is emphasised by the unusual degree of correspondence of ictus and accent in the middle of the line.

13 623. **vidi egomet. . . cum**: 'with my own eyes I watched while . . .', a much less common construction than *vidi frangentem*. Notice how the suspense is built up in this sentence as clause follows clause before the verb *frangeret*.

14 623f. Virgil here follows Homer quite closely (*Od.* 9.280f.), except that in Homer it is not until the second night that Odysseus blinds Polyphemus, by which time he has eaten six of his men.

prensa manu magna medio resupinus in antro
frangeret ad saxum, sanieque aspersa natarent[1]   625
limina; vidi atro cum membra fluentia tabo
manderet[2] et tepidi tremerent sub dentibus artus —
haud impune quidem, nec talia passus Ulixes
oblitusve sui est Ithacus discrimine tanto.
Nam simul[3] expletus dapibus vinoque sepultus   630
cervicem[4] inflexam posuit, iacuitque per antrum
immensus saniem eructans et frusta cruento[5]
per somnum commixta mero, nos magna precati
numina sortitique[6] vices una undique circum
fundimur, et telo lumen terebramus acuto[7]   635
ingens quod[8] torva solum sub fronte latebat,
Argolici[9] clipei aut Phoebeae[10] lampadis instar,
et tandem laeti sociorum ulciscimur umbras.
Sed fugite, o miseri, fugite atque ab litore funem
rumpite.[11]   640
Nam qualis quantusque[12] cavo Polyphemus in antro
lanigeras[13] claudit pecudes atque ubera pressat,
centum alii curva haec habitant ad litora vulgo
infandi Cyclopes[14] et altis montibus errant.

---

1 625. **natarent:** cf. Cic. *Phil.* 2.105 *natabant pavimenta vino, Geo.* 1.372.

2 627. Notice the alliteration of *t* and *d* in this gruesome line, which is an elaboration of Hom. *Od.* 9.292f.

3 630. **simul:** = *simul ac,* cf. *Ecl.* 4.26f., *Geo.* 4.232f.

4 631-2. 'he laid his lolling head down to sleep, stretched out on the floor of the cave in all his mighty bulk'; cf. Hom. *Od.* 9.372 and *Aen.* 6.422f.

5 632-3. Virgil here is virtually translating Hom. *Od.* 9.373-4; cf. also Ov. *Met.* 14.211f. where also the word *frusta* ('fragments') is used.

6 634. **sortitique vices:** 'drawing lots for our parts'; cf. 376 and Hom. *Od.* 9.331.

7 635f. Homer (*Od.* 9375-94) has a much longer description of the blinding of Polyphemus. Great emphasis is put on Virgil's favourite word *ingens* by its position at the end of its clause and the beginning of the line.

8 636. **quod ... latebat:** 'his only eye, deep-set in his savage brow'; for *latere* in this sense cf. Cic. *N.D.* 2.143.

9 637. **Argolici clipei:** the 'Greek shield' was the large round type commonly used by the Greeks (and by the Romans), said to have been invented by the sons of Abas of Argos; cf. 286.

10 **Phoebeae lampadis instar:** 'like the lamp of Phoebus', i.e. the sun (cf. Ov. *Met.* 13.853); compare *Aen.* 4.6. *For instar* cf. *Aen.* 2.15.

11 640. **rumpite:** a much stronger word than the normal *solvite,* expressing urgency (cf. 667). The incomplete lines here and at 661 are among indications that the passage had not been finally revised; see note on 588f.

12 641f. **qualis quantusque ... centum alii:** 'there are a hundred others of like appearance and size as Polyphemus. . . .' For *qualis quantusque* cf. *Aen.* 2.591f.

13 642. **lanigeras:** for the colourful compound adjective cf. Enn. *Sat.* 66, *Geo.* 3.287. The description of the pastoral way of life of the Cyclopes strongly recalls Homer (cf. *Od.* 9.187f., 237f.).

14 644. **Cyclopes:** this is the Greek form of the nominative plural with a short final syllable; cf. the accusative *Cyclopas* (647), and see note on 127. This line has a trochaic caesura in the third foot without a strong caesura in the fourth, a rhythm used by Virgil only rarely and for special effect; see note on 269. Here it emphasises the powerful words *infandi Cyclopes.*

Tertia iam ¹lunae se cornua lumine complent 645
cum vitam in silvis inter deserta ferarum
lustra² domosque traho, vastosque ab rupe Cyclopas³
prospicio⁴ sonitumque pedum vocemque tremesco.
Victum infelicem, ⁵bacas lapidosaque corna,
dant rami, et vulsis pascunt radicibus herbae. 650
Omnia conlustrans hanc primum ad litora classem
conspexi venientem. ⁶Huic me, quaecumque fuisset,
addixi: satis est gentem effugisse nefandam.
Vos animam hanc potius quocumque absumite leto.'

> *655-91. The blinded Polyphemus and his fellow Cyclopes appear. Taking Achaemenides with them the Trojans set sail with all speed, and as the wind is from the north they succeed in avoiding Scylla and Charybdis and they sail southwards along the coast of Sicily.*

⁷Vix⁸ ea fatus erat summo cum monte videmus 655
ipsum inter pecudes vasta se mole moventem
pastorem Polyphemum et litora nota petentem,
monstrum horrendum, informe, ingens, cui lumen ademptum.
Trunca manum pinus regit et vestigia firmat;
lanigerae comitantur oves; ea sola⁹ voluptas 660

---

1 645-7. 'The horns of the moon are now filling with light for the third time while I have been dragging out my days', or more idiomatically 'since I first began to drag out. . .'. For this rare use of *cum* (= *cum interea*) cf. *Aen.* 5.627f., 10.665, Prop. 2.20.21f.

2 647. **lustra**: 'dens', cf. *Geo.* 2.471, *Aen.* 4.151.

3 647. **Cyclopas**: the first syllable here is left short (contrast 644 and the other instances of the word in this book); for the Greek accusative see note on 127.

4 647-8. 'looking out for the monstrous Cyclopes from a rock'; he is hiding in the woods and from time to time climbs to a point of vantage to look for a ship and observe his enemies.

5 649-50. 'The trees afford me a wretched existence on berries and stony cornels, and the vegetation keeps me alive on the roots I pull up.' *Cornum (Geo.* 2.34) is a sort of wild plum; this is Henry's comment on the cornel tree: 'Its oblong, red, shining berries, consisting of little more than a mere membrane carrying a large and hard stone, are sold in the streets of the Italian towns. "Bad enough food for a hungry man!" said I to myself, as I spat out some I had bought in Bassano, and tasted for the sake of Achaemenides.'

6 652-3. 'To these ships, whatever they might be, I gave myself. *Addicere* is a legal word, 'to make over'; *addictus* means a bondsman. *Fuisset* is a reported future perfect; *addixi* contains a meaning like *vovi me in potestate futurum.*

7 655-8. In this passage Virgil very deliberately and obviously makes the sound and movement of the lines match the sense. It is appropriate for a description of the giant Polyphemus that the effects should be heavy and immediately apparent (cf. 424-8), not subtle and haunting as so often elsewhere in Virgil. Alliteration of *m* is noticeable from the beginning, developing into a marked assonance of *-urn* and *-em* sounds; there is rhyme at the line endings of 656-7 (see Austin's note on *Aen.* 4.55); the elisions of 657 (over the caesura) and 658 (the first three words all elided) are very noticeable, in the latter case with spondaic movement, asyndeton and accumulation of adjectives (cf. *Aen.* 4.181 for a less exaggerated effect). We are reminded of Pope's well-known lines (*Essay on Criticism,* 370-1):
When Ajax strives some rock's vast weight to throw,
The line too labours, and the words move slow.

8 655f. For Polyphemus see note on 617; for the whole episode see note on 588f.

9 660-1. There is a touch of pathos here, reinforced by the similar sound of *sola* and *solamen;* cf. Hom. *Od.* 9.447f.

solamenque mali.[1]
Postquam altos tetigit fluctus et ad aequora venit,
luminis effossi fluidum lavit[2] inde[3] cruorem
dentibus infrendens gemitu, graditurque per aequor
iam medium, necdum fluctus latera ardua tinxit.   665
Nos procul inde fugam[4] trepidi celerare recepto
supplice sic merito tacitique incidere funem,
vertimus et proni certantibus aequora remis.
Sensit,[5] et ad sonitum vocis[6] vestigia torsit.
Verum ubi nulla datur dextra[7] adfectare potestas   670
nec potis[8] Ionios fluctus[9] aequare sequendo,
clamorem[10] immensum tollit, quo pontus et omnes
intremuere undae, penitusque[11] exterrita tellus
Italiae curvisque immugiit[12] Aetna cavernis.
At genus e silvis Cyclopum et montibus altis   675
excitum ruit ad portus et litora complent.
cemimus[13] astantis nequiquam[14] lumine[15] torvo
Aetnaeos fratres caelo capita alta ferentis,

---

1 661. This incomplete line is completed in some MSS with *de collo fistula pendet,* but as some of the primary MSS omit, there is immediately a strong case for exclusion.

2 663. **lavit:** archaic third conjugation form; cf. *Geo.* 3.221, 359, *Aen.* 10.727 and contrast *Aen.* 6.219, 12.722.

3 **inde:** 'from it' (i.e. the water); we should say 'he bathed his eye in it'.

4 666f. The description of flight is reminiscent of the escape of Odysseus (*Od.* 9.471f.). The dactylic rhythm and the use of historic infinitives help to convey speed.

5 669. Notice the absence of the subject of *sensit:* Polyphemus is so much in our minds that when the narrative returns to him it is not necessary to name him again.

6 **vocis:** this is strange in view of *taciti* (667), and maybe a further indication that this passage was unrevised. It cannot mean the sound of the oars, as Servius suggests, and it seems best to take it to refer to the shouting of time by the bo'sun. The contradiction with *taciti* is not insuperable; they keep quiet until they are confident that they are out of range.

7 670. **dextra adfectare potestas:** 'chance of clutching at us with his hand'; for *potestas* with the infinitive cf. *Aen.* 7.591 and compare line 299. *Adfectare* is strangely used, perhaps by extension of phrases like *adfectare imperium;* he has no chance of 'aiming at' the ship with a grab.

8 671. **potis:** a word with rather an archaic flavour (*potis est = potest*) used only three times in Virgil.

9 **fluctus aequare sequendo:** probably this means that Polyphemus could not keep up with the speed of the ships which the waves, whipped up by the wind, gave them (cf. *Aen.* 10.248); the other possibility is that Polyphemus was getting out of his depth.

10 672f. Polyphemus' cry, and the appearance of the other Cyclopes, is based on Hom. *Od.* 9.395f.; Virgil has greatly extended the 'pathetic fallacy' of the reaction of personified Nature.

11 673. **penitusque:** 'deep within', i.e. far inland.

12 674. **immugiit:** not found before Virgil, cf. *Aen.* 11.38. For *mugire* of the earth cf. *Aen.* 4.490, 6.256 and compare line 92. Cf. Milton, *P.L.* 2.788-9 'Hell trembl'd at the hideous Name, and sigh'd / from all her Caves, and back resounded "Death!" '

13 677-81. This is one of the most striking pieces of visual imagery in Virgil; every word is telling as he builds up the massive and eerie picture of these giant figures thronging the shore. The simile (679f.) is the only one in Book 3.

14 677. **nequiquam:** 'frustrated', because Aeneas' ships are out of range.

15 **lumine torvo:** 'each with a single glaring eye'; they are all one-eyed, like Polyphemus.

concilium horrendum: quales[1] cum vertice[2] celso
aeriae[3] quercus aut coniferae[4] cyparissi 680
constiterunt,[5] silva alta Iovis[6] lucusve Dianae.
Praecipitis metus acer agit quocumque[7] rudentis[8]
excutere et ventis intendere vela secundis.
Contra[9] iussa monent Heleni, Scyllam atque Charybdim
inter, utramque viam leti discrimine parvo, 685
ni teneant cursus; certum est dare lintea retro.
Ecce autem Boreas angusta ab sede Pelori[10]
missus adest: vivo[11] praetervehor ostia saxo
Pantagiae[12] Megarosque[13] sinus Thapsumque iacentem.
Talia monstrabat relegens[14] errata retrorsus 690
litora Achaemenides, comes infelicis Ulixi.

---

1 679-81. **quales cum ... constiterunt**: 'like oaks standing there'; for this method of introducing a simile cf. *Aen.* 8.622.

2 679. **vertice celso**: 'with their high tops' (cf. *Aen.* 9.679f.) rather than 'on a high mountain peak'.

3 680. **aeriae**: a very poetic word; cf. line 291 and Tennyson's 'the aerial poplar'.

4 **coniferae**: again a colourful word, which is not found elsewhere till the third century.

5 681. **constiterunt**: for the scansion see note on 2.774; the perfect of *consistere* is similar in meaning to the present of *stare*.

6 **Iovis ... Dianae**: Jupiter had a famous oak grove at Dodona, and Diana the huntress was naturally associated with woods, and in her person as Hecate of the underworld is connected with cypresses, the trees of death.

7 682. **quocumque**: 'in any direction' (cf. 601, 654) i.e. which ever way the wind will blow them fastest. They get a south wind, which drives them towards Scylla and Charybdis, but all is well when it suddenly changes to north (687).

8 682. **rudentis excutere**: see note on 267; for the infinitive see note on 4-5.

9 684-6. I have discussed the difficulties of these three lines fully in my OUP Ed.; I do not think that any interpretation or emendation of them (see Mynors's *app. crit.*) produces a sentence which would have satisfied Virgil. They represent jottings of metrical phrases which would have been shaped later into a final version. As they stand in the MSS and as I have printed them the best meaning that can be extracted is 'On the other hand the instructions of Helenus bid them not to hold their course between Scylla and Charybdis (a way which on both sides is only a hairsbreadth from death)'. *Ni* is equivalent to *ne; teneant* is strangely third person where we would expect *teneamus*. For *leti discrimine parvo* cf. *Aen.* 9.143, 10.511.

10 687. For the narrow straits of Pelorus cf. 411.

11 688. **vivo ... saxo**: 'of natural rock', cf. *Aen.* 1.167.

12 689. In this line and in the last section of the book Virgil makes great use of the poetic possibilities of proper names of places (as Milton often does). The places mentioned here are on the east coast of Sicily, in the order in which they would be reached going southwards.

13 **Megarosque sinus**: i.e. the bay of Megara Hyblaea. The normal adjective is *Megaricus;* cf. 280, 401.

14 690-1. **relegens errata retrorsus litora**: 'skirting again in the opposite direction the coasts of his previous wanderings', i.e. with Odysseus when he came north from the land of the Lotus Eaters. For the passive use of the intransitive verb *errare* cf. *Aen.* 2.895.

692-718. The Trojans continue to sail round Sicily, finally reaching Drepanum where Anchises dies. From there, Aeneas tells Dido, they were driven by a storm to Carthage; and so he ends the tale of his wanderings.

¹Sicanio ²praetenta³ sinu iacet insula contra
Plemyrium undosum;⁴ nomen dixere priores
Ortygiam.⁵ Alpheum⁶ fama est huc Elidis amnem
occultas egisse vias subter mare, qui nunc⁷   695
ore,⁸ Arethusa, tuo Siculis confunditur undis.
Iussi numina magna loci veneramur, et inde
exsupero⁹ praepingue solum stagnantis¹⁰ Helori.
hinc¹¹ altas cautes proiectaque saxa Pachyni¹²
radimus,¹³ et fatis numquam¹⁴ concessa moveri   700
apparet Camerina¹⁵ procul campique Geloi,¹⁶

---

1 692f. In this final section of the book Virgil brings us away from the fabulous world of the Cyclopes back to the real world of the voyage of Rome's first founder. He does it by a kind of catalogue, consisting of very short descriptions of some of the most famous places of Sicily; it is reminiscent of Hellenistic descriptions of places, origins and etymologies such as we find, for example, in Apollonius. It ends the book with a sort of diminuendo.

2 692-4. 'There lies an island fronting a Sicilian bay, over against wave-beaten Plemyrium; the ancients called it Ortygia'. Virgil is describing the bay of Syracuse; Plemyrium is the headland at the south, and Ortygia is an island on the north side of the bay.

3 692. **praetenta:** literally 'spread in front of; *sinu* is dative, cf. 292. Compare *Aen.* 6.60 *praetentaque Syrtibus arva.*

4 693. **undosum:** a very clear instance of an etymological adjective, 'translating' the Greek word Plemyrium (πλημυρις, the tide). See note on 1.267-8, and cf. 698, 703.

5 694. Ortygiam: this was also a name of Delos (line 124). The name here is probably due to the association with Diana, who was born on Delos and connected with the Arethusa story (see next note).

6 694f. The river Alpheus in South Greece (Elis) passes underground a number of times in its course; hence the story about its underwater passage from Greece to Sicily. The legend was that the river-god Alpheus pursued the nymph Arethusa, and Diana changed her into a fountain; whereupon Alpheus followed her under the sea, and united his waters with hers in Ortygia. Cf. *Ecl.* 10.1f., Shelley's *Arethusa,* and Milton, *Arcades,* 28f:
Of famous Arcady ye are, and sprung
Of that renowned flood, so often sung,
Divine Alpheus, who by secret sluse
Stole under Seas to meet his Arethuse.

7 695. The rhythm of the line ending is harsh and unusual; cf. *Aen.* 5.731 with my note there (OUP Ed.) for full discussion.

8 696. **ore ... tuo**: cf. *Aen.* 1.245; the construction is ablative of means ('by way of).

9 698. **exsupero**: 'I sail past', an unusual sense; the singular after the plural *veneramur* is a little harsh, as is the number of heavy consonants in the line.

10 **stagnantis Helori:** another etymological adjective (see note on 693); ελος is the Greek word for marsh.

11 699. **hinc:** 'after that', a variant on *inde* (697).

12 **Pachyni:** the southeastern tip of Sicily, cf. 429.

13 700. **radimus:** 'skirt', a metaphor from grazing the turning point in a race; cf. *Aen.* 5.170, 7.10.

14 **numquam concessa moveri:** 'not allowed ever to be disturbed'; the construction here is analogous to Virgil's quite frequent use of *dare* with the infinitive (cf. 77), though it is more striking in this passive form.

15 701. **Camerina:** about fifty miles west of Pachynus, on the south coast of Sicily. Servius tells the story that when the nearby marsh (which was also called Camerina) was causing a pestilence, the inhabitants of the town consulted the oracle to ask whether they should drain the marsh, and were told not to do so in a response which became a Greek proverb: 'Don't move Camerina; it is better not moved.' They ignored the oracle and drained the marsh, with the result that the town was sacked by enemy forces who approached over the land where the marsh had been.

16 701-2. The town of Gela took its name from the river Gelas; the long *a* in its scansion is unusual and perhaps helped by the following *fl-. Immanis* should be taken with *fluvii,* referring to the terrible winter torrent of the river.

immanisque Gela fluvii cognomine dicta.[1]
Arduus[2] inde Acragas ostentat maxima longe
moenia, magnanimum[3] quondam[4] generator[5] equorum;
teque datis linquo ventis, palmosa[6] Selinus,   705
et vada dura lego saxis Lilybeia[7] caecis.
Hinc[8] Drepani[9] me portus et inlaetabilis ora
accipit. [10]Hic pelagi tot tempestatibus actus[11]
heu, genitorem, omnis curae casusque levamen,
amitto Anchisen. Hic me, pater[12] optime, fessum   710
deseris, heu, tantis nequiquam erepte[13] periclis!
Nec vates Helenus, cum multa horrenda moneret,
hos mihi praedixit luctus, non dira Celaeno.
Hic [14]labor extremus, longarum haec meta[15] viarum;

---

1 703f. Servius here comments on the anachronism of the description of all these places, and finds special fault with it because it is put in the mouth of Aeneas.

2 703. **arduus . . . Acragas**: *arduus* (steep, Greek ακρος) is a clear etymological epithet; see note on 693. This famous and important town, which the Romans called Agrigentum, was about halfway along the southern coast of Sicily.

3 704. **magnanimum**: this is the only adjective with which Virgil employs the old genitive form in *-urn* (cf. *Geo.* 4.476, *Aen.* 6.307), except perhaps *omnigenum* in *Aen.* 8.698.

4 **quondam:** 'once'; the anachronism here, in the mouth of Aeneas, seems very harsh, but the meaning 'one day (destined to be)' is wholly inappropriate.

5 **generator equorum:** a number of Pindar's odes honour victors in the chariot race who came from Agrigentum; Pliny (*N.H.* 8.155) tells of the tombs of horses there.

6 705. **palmosa Selinus:** Selinus (on the south west coast) is a third declension word with long *-us* (genitive *Selinuntis*). *Palmosa* is generally taken to mean 'famous for its palm trees', but it is more likely to mean 'conferring the victor's palm', because the plant σελινον (selinon), a kind of parsley, which figured on the coins of Selinus, was one of the plants used for the victor's crown, especially at the Isthmian games. Thus we have another etymological epithet (see note on 693).

7 706. **Lilybaeum:** the western extremity of the south coast of Sicily. Virgil emphasises the forbidding nature of the place, cruel with its hidden rocks, to prepare for the harsh blow of fate described in the following lines.

8 707. Observe the very unusual rhythm of this remarkable line, with a trochaic caesura in the third foot and no caesura in the fourth; cf. *Aen.* 5.781, 12.619.

9 **Drepani inlaetabilis ora:** Drepanum is on the west coast of Sicily, not far from Eryx; its shore is *inlaetabilis* (a rare word) because of the death of Anchises.

10 708f. The place of Anchises' death varied very considerably in different versions of the legend: Servius says 'bene hic subtrahitur, ne parum decoro amori intersit', and certainly Virgil could not have conceived Book 4 in its present form, with Aeneas staying with Dido forgetful of fate, if Anchises had still been alive. Moreover, by placing the death of Anchises at this stage, Virgil has motivated the second visit to Sicily (in Book 5), which seems to have been original in his version, and is able to give a narrative of the religious ceremonies and games on the anniversary of Anchises' death in the part of the poem where there is proper room for them.

11 708-10. The tension is held all through this sentence: first *hic* reiterating *hinc,* then the clause in apposition to the subject, the sigh of *heu,* the object of the verb followed by a pause caused by an unusually placed elision, a phrase in apposition to the object, and then at last the verb and the reiterated object.

12 710. **pater optime:** the apostrophe here is much more than a rhetorical or metrical device (contrast 696); the expectation of emotion has already been built up, and so the apostrophe may be used to reinforce it, cf. *Aen.* 4.408f.

13 711. **erepte:** this use of the vocative of the past participle is a favourite with Virgil; cf. *Aen.* 2.283.

14 714-15. Virgil uses his favourite threefold repetition (*hic . . . haec . . . hinc*) to close the speech; cf. 408-9.

15 714. **meta:** 'the end'; the word means the turning point at either end of a racecourse (cf. 429), and hence can mean the finish of a race as well as the turning points during the race; cf. *Aen.* 10.472, 12.546. Aeneas omits mention of the storm which drove him to Carthage after leaving Sicily because it has already been described to Dido (*Aen.* 1.535f.), and he pays her the compliment of implying that now they have reached Carthage their trials are over.

hinc me digressum vestris deus appulit oris.'   715
    [1]Sic pater Aeneas intentis omnibus unus
fata[2] renarrabat divum cursusque docebat.
Conticuit[3] tandem factoque hic fine quievit.

---

1 716-18. The phrases *intentis omnibus* and *conticuit tandem* remind us of the start of his story at the beginning of Book 2.

2 717. **fata renarrabat divum:** 'recited the destiny sent by heaven', cf. *Aen.* 2.54. The force of *re-* is not that he told the story for the second time, but that he went through (this time in words) the events again.

3 718. Notice the pattern of alliteration, *c, q,* and *f*. Page comments on the contrast of the momentary stillness and repose here both with the adventures just told and with the opening words of Book 4.

BOOK 4

Introductory Note

The story of Dido's tragedy has always been the best known part of the *Aeneid* (Ov. *Trist.* 2.533f., cf. Her. 7; Macrob. *Sat.* 5.17.4f.). It was a favoured theme in twelfth century French romances; in Chaucer's *House of Fame* it has twice as much space as the rest of the *Aeneid;* Marlowe's *Dido, Queen of Carthage* is among the most familiar dramas on the subject, and the operas of Purcell and Berlioz are well known. It has been said that Dido is the only character created by a Roman poet to pass into world literature. Far more often than not Dido has been sympathetically portrayed.

Virgil's sources for the legend of Dido were very varied. There are traces in the Greek historian Timaeus (third century B.C.) of the story of her flight to Libya, and she figured (as did Aeneas) in Naevius' *Bellum Punicum* (late third century).The prose writers of the Aeneas legend, such as Virgil's contemporaries Livy and Dionysius, naturally make no mention of a visit by Aeneas to Dido, because the chronology would not permit of it: Carthage was not founded until several centuries after the time of Aeneas. What is certain is that Virgil's detailed treatment of Aeneas' visit to Dido in Carthage is largely original.

Certain heroines in literature were available as models for Virgil, but here again we find that his treatment of Dido is profoundly different from any of his sources. The gentle Nausicaa in Homer (*Od.* 6) has nothing in common with the tormented Dido; Dido is closer in situation to the Homeric witches, Circe and Calypso, both of whom are obstacles to Odysseus on his homeward voyage. But they are supernatural figures who do not arouse our pity, as Dido most certainly does. Apollonius Rhodius' Medea in *Arg.* 3 presented Virgil with certain ideas (see note on 1f., 166f., 474f., 588-9) and with the concept of describing love in an epic poem in the tone of elegy or lyric; but Apollonius' Medea is a young girl, excited, confused, uncertain, while Dido is a mature queen well aware of the issues involved. Finally the Ariadne of Catullus 64, deserted by Theseus, had a marked effect on Virgil's poetry, especially in passages of pathos (see note on 296f., 657-8), but the sadness and loneliness of Ariadne is something quite different from the tragic sublimity of Dido.

Indeed the word tragic is wholly appropriate for Dido in this book. We know much less about Aeneas' feelings here, only a touch now and then to tell of the love he must sacrifice (see note on 279f.); it is Dido who holds the stage and in many ways she resembles the tragic figures of Greek drama (see note on 296f., 450f., 630f. and K. Quinn, *Latin Explorations,* pp. 29f.) more than her predecessors in epic or epyllion. She falls indeed from prosperity and success to utter disaster; the contrast between the capable, beautiful and wholly admirable queen in Book 1 and the terrifying personification of hatred and vengeance which she becomes in the second half of Book 4 is truly the stuff of the great Greek tragedies (one thinks especially of Euripides' Phaedra or Medea).

The basis of the tragedy is that Dido gives up everything for her love for Aeneas; she allows the span of her abilities and excellencies and interests to narrow to this one object, so that when she finds it is unattainable she has left herself with nothing. Carthage has come to a halt (86f.) and Anna is right when she says in the last scene (682-3) that Dido has brought to destruction not only herself but the people of Carthage. Dido has burnt all her bridges and her pride can know no retreat; she utterly refuses to understand Aeneas' arguments about his duty (see note on 331f.), because in her eyes personal considerations override everything else. She has allowed herself to be drawn into a position from which she can find no way back; she has allowed herself to become enmeshed in a net of circumstances. Whether she could have resisted successfully had she tried we do not know; all we know is what happened when she yielded.

The element of pathos in the first half of the book as Dido allows herself to be swept on is very great; and in the second half it persists, intermingled with a feeling of horror and terror as she becomes no longer a queen, no longer a woman, but a stylised and archetypal fury of vengeance (see note on 362f., 584f.). The tragedy is that she should have been driven, or should have driven herself, to a point where her human qualities are entirely submerged in a sweeping torrent of frenzy, hatred and despair. Near the end of the book, in her final speech, both these aspects (pathos and hatred) are present; lines 651-8 show us the generous queen brought piteously to tragic disaster, the unhappy woman for whom St. Augustine and many since shed tears. But in her very last words (659-62) we see again her frantic desire for vengeance; she cannot now have it in life, but in death she must and will. This is the Dido whose anger still burns in the underworld when Aeneas meets her, and who is no more moved by his words than if she were flint or Marpesian rock (6.471). What has brought her to destruction and turned her heart to flint? Her own faults, folly, pride? Or the force of uncontrollable events, the pressure of hostile circumstances too powerful to resist? Or both?

1-55. Dido is consumed with love for Aeneas, and tells her sister Anna that had she not firmly resolved after Sychaeus' death not to marry again she might have yielded. Anna in reply enumerates the advantages of marriage with Aeneas, and Dido is persuaded.

¹At² regina gravi iamdudum saucia³ cura

vulnus⁴ alit venis et caeco⁵ carpitur igni.

Multa⁶ viri virtus animo multusque recursat

gentis honos; haerent infixi pectore vultus

verbaque, nec placidam membris dat cura quietem.   5

Postera⁷ Phoebea lustrabat lampade terras

umentemque Aurora polo dimoverat umbram,

cum sic unanimam⁸ adloquitur male⁹ sana sororem:

'Anna soror, quae¹⁰ me suspensam insomnia terrent!

Quis¹¹ novus hic nostris successit sedibus¹² hospes,   10

---

1 1f. The opening section of the book concentrates on Dido and her love for Aeneas. During the Trojan story of Books 2 and 3 the reader has hardly been conscious of the listening Dido, but now the theme of the end of Book 1 is resumed and kept in the foreground. The note is one of foreboding; imagery of fire, illness, wounding, frenzy, madness is constant throughout this section and the next (*saucia, vulnus, carpitur igni, male sana, flammavit, furentem, flamma, vulnus, uritur, furens, demens, pestis* and finally (101) *ardet amaxns Dido traitque per ossa furorem*).

There are some reminiscences of Catullus' Ariadne (Cat. 64), and many of Apollonius' Medea (*Argonautica* 3), and Virgil's intimate portrayal of the lover's anguished heart owes much to both. But his Dido is of a different dimension from either of these; we have seen her in Book 1 as a proud queen, a woman of outstanding abilities and achievements, so that her agony, uncertainty, and final despair is far more tragic.

The part played by Anna is structurally not unlike that of Medea's sister Chalciope in Apollonius, though the differences are great, especially in that Medea does not tell Chalciope of her true emotions. We may also compare the nurse or confidante in Greek tragedy; Anna's persuasive speech, full of rhetorical devices to lead Dido to the course Anna knows she wants to take, is somewhat similar to that of the nurse to Phaedra in Euripides' *Hippolytus*, 433f. Its persuasive intention is wholly and immediately successful, so that Dido who had sworn that the earth should swallow her up before she violated *pudor* (27) now can accept that her duty towards Carthage's future as well as her personal inclinations justify her in violating it (55).

2 1. **At regina:** the beginning of the book focusses on Dido, and these two words recur at decisive moments in the book, i.e. 296 and 504.

3 **saucia cura:** the imagery of love's wound (cf. *vulnus,* line 2) is frequent throughout this section (cf. especially the simile in 69f.); *cura* in this sense of the anxious suffering of the lover is frequent in poetry, cf. 394, *Aen.* 6.444, and Cat. 64.250 *multiplices animo volvebat saucia curas;* this is the first of many reminiscences of Catullus' Ariadne.

4 2. **vulnus alit venis:** 'nourishes the wound with her life-blood' ; i.e. keeps the wound unhealed, cf. 67.

5 **caeco carpitur igni:** 'is consumed by a fire she keeps hidden'; cf. Medea in Apollonius 3.296 in whose heart 'deadly love burned secretly' (cf. also 3.286, 'Love's arrow blazed in her heart like fire'). For *carpere* in this sense, 'destroy, consume', cf. Prop. 3.5.3 and line 32.

6 3f. Notice that Dido, herself a queen, is moved by the qualities of Aeneas as well as his personal appearance; contrast the fine description of Medea in Ap. Rh. 3.453f. where her memories and thoughts of her beloved Jason are entirely visual.

7 6. 'The next day's dawn was moving over the earth with Phoebus' torch'. Notice the interwoven order of *postera . . . Aurora,* and for the phrase *Phoebea lampas* (the sun) cf. *Aen.* 3.637.

8 8. **unanimam . . . sororem:** 'her loving sister'. Anna was in Naevius' version of the story, and in Virgil corresponds to some extent with Chalciope, Medea's sister in Apollonius; see note on 1f.

9 **male sana:** 'barely sane', cf. *Aen.* 2.23.

10 9. **quae ... terrent:** 'oh, the dreams which frighten my distracted heart'; a translation of Medea's words in Ap. Rh. 3.636. Servius knew a reading *terret,* in which case *insomnia* would mean sleeplessness, but the parallel with Apollonius is decisive, and cf. *Aen.* 6.896.

11 10. **quis:** like *quae* in the previous line and *quam* in the next, this is exclamatory (= *qualis*); cf. 47 and *Aen.* 6.771.

12 **sedibus hospes:** cf. Cat. 64.176.

quem sese ore ferens, [1]quam forti pectore et armis!

Credo equidem, nec vana fides, genus[2] esse deorum.

Degeneres[3] animos timor arguit. Heu, quibus ille

iactatus fatis! Quae bella exhausta canebat!

Si mihi non animo fixum immotumque sederet   15

ne cui me vinclo vellem sociare iugali,

postquam primus amor deceptam[4] morte fefellit;

si non pertaesum thalami[5] taedaeque fuisset,

huic uni forsan[6] potui succumbere culpae.[7]

Anna, fatebor enim, miseri post fata Sychaei   20

coniugis et sparsos[8] fraterna caede penatis

solus hic inflexit sensus animumque[9] labantem

impulit. Agnosco veteris vestigia flammae.

Sed mihi vel tellus optem[10] prius ima dehiscat

vel pater omnipotens adigat[11] me fulmine ad umbras,   25

pallentis umbras Erebo[12] noctemque profundam,

ante, pudor,[13] quam te violo aut tua iura resolvo.

Ille[14] meos, primus qui me sibi iunxit, amores

abstulit; ille habeat secum servetque sepulcro.'

---

1 11. 'what distinction he has in his looks, what courage and martial prowess'; cf. *Aen.* 3.490. Austin supports the view that *armis* means 'shoulders' (from *armus*, cf. 11.644, 12.433), but in an ambiguity of this kind the reader naturally takes the more normal meaning (cf. 1.545) unless the context prevents it. Servius has a good remark on this line: 'et bene virtutis commemoratione excusat supra dictam pulchritudinis laudem.'

2 12. Dido indeed knows that he is of divine descent; cf. *Aen.* 1.617.

3 13. **degeneres**: probably 'degenerate' (with reference to *genus* in the previous line) rather than 'not of divine birth'. The fearlessness of Aeneas has appeared from his narrative in Books 2 and 3, to which Dido refers in the following phrases.

4 17. **deceptam morte fefellit**: 'cheated and deceived me by his death', i.e. frustrated my hopes of long lasting happiness; the word *deceptus* is frequent on tombstones, for *fefellit* cf. *Aen.* 2.744. The death of Dido's husband Sychaeus at the hands of her brother Pygmalion was briefly described in *Aen.* 1.343f.

5 18. **thalami taedaeque**: 'the bridal chamber and marriage torch', frequent synonyms for marriage, cf. 339, 550.

6 19. **forsan potui**: 'perhaps I could have. . . .' The indicative of *possum* is normal to express past potential sentences. In prose, however, the subjunctive would be used after *forsan*.

7 **culpae**: here Dido herself recognizes that to break her oath of loyalty to Sychaeus would be a fault or error; later (172) Virgil's narrative tells us the same. The word (like the Greek hamartia) does not *necessarily* carry strong moral condemnation; the extent to which it does must be determined from the context.

8 21. **sparsos . . . penatis**: 'the bespattering of my household gods with blood shed by my brother'; cf. Cat. 64.181.

9 22-3. **animumque labantem impulit**: 'moved my wavering heart'; *labantem* is consequential upon *inflexit sensus*, and need not be taken predicatively.

10 24. **optem . . . dehiscat**: 'I would wish that the earth should gape open'; the paratactic subjunctive with *optare* is quite common.

11 25. **adigat**: cf. *Aen.* 6.594; *abigat* is read by *F* and some modern editors (cf. *Aen.* 11.261).

12 26. **Erebo**: this (local ablative) is the reading of the majority of the good MSS against the rather easier *Erebi* of others; for *Erebus* (the underworld) cf. 510.

13 27. **pudor**: here 'conscience' (cf. 55); she had promised Sychaeus' ashes (552) that she would be loyal to his memory by not marrying again. In Rome the goddess Pudicitia was worshipped only by *matronae univirae*, and *univira* is frequent on tombstones.

14 28-29. Notice the emphatic metrical features (reinforcing the balancing *ille . . . ille*): the run-on word *abstulit* with assonance (*amores abstulit*), and the strong alliteration of *s*.

Sic effata sinum¹ lacrimis implevit obortis.   30
    Anna refert: 'o luce magis dilecta sorori,
solane perpetua maerens carpere² iuventa
nec dulcis natos Veneris³ nec praemia noris?
Id cinerem aut manis credis curare sepultos?
Esto, aegram⁴ nulli quondam flexere mariti,   35
non⁵ Libyae, non ante Tyro; despectus Iarbas⁶
ductoresque alii, quos Africa terra triumphis
dives alit: placitone⁷ etiam pugnabis amori?
Nec⁸ venit in mentem quorum consederis arvis?
Hinc Gaetulae⁹ urbes, genus insuperabile bello,   40
et Numidae infreni¹⁰ cingunt et inhospita Syrtis;
hinc¹¹ deserta siti regio lateque furentes
Barcaci. Quid bella Tyro surgentia dicam¹²
germanique minas?¹³
Dis equidem auspicibus reor et Iunone¹⁴ secunda   45
hunc cursum Iliacas vento tenuisse carinas.
Quam tu urbem, soror, hanc cernes, quae surgere regna
coniugio tali! Teucrum comitantibus armis
Punica¹⁵ se quantis attollet gloria rebus!

---

1 30. **sinum**: her bosom, cf. Ap. Rh. 3.804.

2 32. 'will you waste away in loneliness and grief all through your youth?'; for *carpere* (future passive) cf. line 2; by *iuventa* Anna means that Dido is still of marriageable age.

3 33. **Veneris nec**: *nec* is postponed, cf. 124.

4 35-8. Notice the antithesis between *aegram* and *placitone:* Anna says 'I grant that no would-be husbands have moved you in your desolation up to now, but surely you won't resist a love which you want?'.

5 36. **non Libyae ... Tyro:** 'not in Libya, nor before that in Tyre'; the cases are unusual, *Libyae* being locative when one would expect *Libya,* and *Tyro* ablative of place where instead of the locative *Tyri.* Servius' alternative, 'suitors of Libya or Tyre', is less likely.

6 **Iarbas**: an African king, cf. 196f. According to one version of the legend (Justin 18.6) Dido committed suicide to escape marriage with him.

7 38. **placitone . . . amori**: 'a pleasing love' (cf. Ov. *Am.* 2.4.18); for the dative see note on 1.475.

8 39. Dido herself (*Aen.* 1.563-4) had told the Trojans about her need to defend her kingdom against local attack. Anna knows the kind of argument that will sway her.

9 40-1. The Gaetulae and Numidae were peoples to the south and west of Carthage; Syrtis was the name of the famous quicksands with their hinterland to the southeast (cf. *Aen.* 1.111).

10 41. **infreni**: 'riding without bridles' (cf. *Aen.* 10.750), doubtless also containing the metaphorical meaning of 'wild'.

11 42. **hinc deserta siti regio**: 'on this side is an area deserted because of drought', i.e. to the south and southeast, where the Barcaei lived their nomadic life. Barca was the name of the family to which Hasdrubal and Hannibal belonged.

12 43-4. Anna refers to the danger of attack from Dido's brother Pygmalion from whom she had fled; cf. line 325.

13 44. For the half-line see note on 1.534; others in this book are 361, 400, 503, 516.

14 45. **Iunone secunda**: Anna mentions Juno as the chief goddess of Carthage (1.15), and also as goddess of marriage (line 166).

15 49. 'with what mighty achievements will Punic glory soar'. Notice the irony of the suggestion that Carthage will grow great by assimilating Rome.

Tu modo posce deos veniam, sacrisque[1] litatis   50
indulge hospitio causasque innecte morandi,
dum pelago desaevit hiems et aquosus[2] Orion,
quassataeque rates, [3]dum non tractabile caelum.'
His dictis incensum[4] animum flammavit amore
spemque dedit dubiae menti solvitque[5] pudorem.   55

> *56-89. Dido makes sacrifices to win the gods' favour. In her frenzied state she is like a deer shot by a hunter's arrow; she cannot forget her love, and the building of her city is neglected.*

[6]Principio delubra adeunt pacemque[7] per aras
exquirunt; mactant lectas de more bidentis[8]
legiferae Cereri[9] Phoeboque patrique Lyaeo,
Iunoni[10] ante omnis, cui vincla iugalia curae.
Ipsa tenens dextra pateram pulcherrima Dido[11]   60
candentis vaccae media inter cornua fundit,[12]
aut ante[13] ora deum pinguis spatiatur[14] ad aras,
instauratque[15] diem donis, pecudumque reclusis
pectoribus[16] inhians spirantia consulit exta.

---

1 50. **sacrisque litatis**: 'when favourable sacrifices have been obtained'; see note on 2.118-9, and Prop. 4.1.24.

2 52. **aquosus Orion**: the setting of Orion in the autumn was associated with storms; see note on 1.535.

3 53. 'while the ships are still damaged, and the weather is impossible'; cf. *Geo.* 1.211.

4 54. **incensum**: a few MSS have *impenso* ('with great love', cf. Lucr. 5.964) and both readings were known to Servius, but *impensus* in this sense does not occur elsewhere in Virgil, and *amore* fits better with *incensum;* Anna heaps fuel on the fire, she does not light the fire.

5 55. **solvitque pudorem**: 'broke the bonds of conscience'; notice how easily Dido is persuaded to reject her oath to Sychaeus (24f.). In Glover's words 'To resolve to win the love of Aeneas is no wrong thought or action, but to attempt it against her conscience is the first step towards shame.'

6 56f. The picture of Dido's frenzied love, given in the opening lines of the book, is now even more vividly painted. Her propitiatory sacrifices are fully described and the situation seems hopeful, but first in a personal intervention into the narrative (65-7), and then in a memorable simile Virgil presents again the undertones of impending tragedy. We return to the narrative, and Dido's frenzy is reflected in the emotional distraction of her behaviour; this was in part evident to those present (she stops in mid-sentence, she hangs on his lips) but the reader is also taken behind the scenes and sees her alone, unhappy, trying to console herself by memory and imagination. Finally, her utter preoccupation with her love, to the exclusion of all else, is explicitly stated.

7 56. **pacem**: 'divine approval', cf. *Geo.* 4.535, *Aen.* 3.370.

8 57. **bidentis:** sheep in their second year have two prominent teeth; Henry's note on the subject is well worth reading.

9 58. These three deities, Ceres, Apollo, Bacchus, are invoked probably as being especially concerned with the foundation of cities. Ceres is called *legifera* because the discovery of corn was associated with the beginnings of settled life, cf. *Geo.* 1.7 f., Ov. *Met.* 5.343 *prima dedit leges.* For *Lyaeus* cf. *Aen.* 1.686.

10 59. **Iunoni**: see note on 45.

11 60f. For the detailed description of sacrifices (a frequent feature in the *Aeneid*) cf. especially *Aen.* 6.243f.

12 61. **fundit**: supply as object *pateram* from the previous line, in the sense of *vinum de patera.*

13 62. **ante ora deum**: i.e. in front of the images of the gods.

14 **spatiatur** a solemn ritual word; cf. *incessit* of Dido leading her procession in *Aen.* 1.497.

15 63. **instauratque**: 'renews' i.e. 'inaugurates afresh', cf. line 145 and *Aen.* 3.62.

16 64. **pectoribus:** for the lengthening in arsis of the final syllable see Austin ad loc. and cf. lines 146 and 322.

Heu,[1] vatum ignarae mentes! Quid vota furentem,   65
quid delubra iuvant? Est[2] mollis[3] flamma medullas
interea et tacitum vivit sub pectore vulnus.
Uritur infelix[4] Dido totaque vagatur
urbe furens,[5] qualis coniecta cerva sagitta,
quam procul incautam nemora[6] inter Cresia fixit   70
pastor agens telis liquitque volatile ferrum
nescius: illa fuga silvas saltusque peragrat
Dictaeos; haeret[7] lateri letalis harundo.
Nunc media Aenean secum per moenia ducit
Sidoniasque[8] ostentat opes urbemque paratam,[9]   75
incipit effari mediaque in voce resistit;
nunc eadem[10] labente die convivia quaerit,
Iliacosque iterum demens audire[11] labores
exposcit pendetque[12] iterum narrantis ab ore.
Post ubi digressi, [13]lumenque obscura vicissim   80
luna premit suadentque cadentia sidera somnos,

---

1 65. The poet intervenes in his narrative to comment on it; cf. lines 169f., 412 and especially *Aen.* 10.501f. *nescia mens hominum.* . . . The implication here is that the priests imagine that the sacred rites which they prescribe and interpret will ensure Dido's happiness, unaware as they are of the destructive nature of Dido's frenzied love (*furentem*), unaware that her 'wound' is not being cured.

2 66. **est:** contracted form for *edit*, cf. *Aen.* 5.683. This phrase and the next are reminiscent of the first two lines of the book; no change has been effected by the sacrifices.

3 **mollis:** accusative plural, cf. Cat. 45.16 *mollibus in medullis.*

4 68. **infelix:** cf. *Aen.* 1.712, 749 and in this book lines 450, 529, 596; the undertone of impending tragedy is made more and more clear.

5 69f. This wonderful simile well illustrates how Virgil can use traditional epic machinery of Homer in a new way. The actual point of comparison is in the wounded deer rushing wildly about; the additional details in the simile relate to the themes of the story and point forward as well as backwards, indirectly anticipating the events and involving the reader in a half-knowledge of the future as well as a recollection of the past. Dido, the hunted and helpless victim, has been caught *incauta;* this is a word of grim association, often suggesting resultant tragedy (*Aen.* 3.333, 10.812). The arrow of love has not yet caused death, but will do so and cannot be dislodged (73). And finally the hunting shepherd is unaware of having shot his victim, as Aeneas is unaware of the disastrous effect of the love he has caused. As Austin points out, the contrast between the emphatic run-on word *nescius* and the following *illa* adds to the unconscious cruelty. See further Otis, *Virgil,* pp. 72f., Pöschl, *The Art of Vergil,* pp. 80f.

6 70. **nemora inter Cresia:** archery is particularly associated with Crete, cf. *Aen.* 5.306. For Mt. Dicte (73) in Crete cf. *Aen.* 3.171.

7 73. Notice the pattern of alliteration at the close of the simile: *haer-, l, l, har-.*

8 75. **Sidonias:** Virgil uses *Tyrius* and *Sidonius* interchangeably to refer to Dido's original home in Tyre.

9 **paratam:** notice the significance of this word; Dido can show Aeneas that she has already done what he yet has to do; cf. *Aen.* 1.437 *o fortunati quorum iam moenia surgunt.*

10 77. **eadem:** a repetition of the banquet at which some days earlier Aeneas had recounted his story.

11 78-9. **audire . . . exposcit:** poetic infinitive, cf. *Aen.* 9.193 and see note on 1.527-8.

12 79. **pendetque . . . ab ore:** cf. Ariadne in Cat. 64.69f.

13 80-1. The sun has long since set; now the dim moon in turn sets, and the constellations one after another. The last phrase is repeated from *Aen.* 2.9 where see note.

sola domo maeret vacua stratisque[1] relictis
incubat. Illum absens absentem[2] auditque videtque,
aut gremio Ascanium[3] genitoris imagine capta
detinet, infandum si fallere[4] possit amorem.   85
Non[5] coeptae adsurgunt turres, non arma iuventus
exercet portusve aut propugnacula bello
tuta parant: [6]pendent opera interrupta minaeque
murorum ingentes aequataque machina caelo.

> *90-128. In Olympus the goddesses Juno and Venus converse about the mortal scene. Juno, hoping to prevent the establishment of the Trojan race in Italy, proposes an alliance between Trojans and Carthaginians. Venus agrees if Jupiter can be persuaded (as she knows he cannot), and Juno plans that Dido and Aeneas shall seek shelter from a storm in the same Cave, and that here she will join them in marriage.*

[7]Quam simul ac tali persensit peste[8] teneri   90
cara Iovis coniunx nec famam obstare furori,
talibus adgreditur Venerem Saturnia[9] dictis:

---

1 82. **stratisque relictis**: the reference (as Servius saw) is to the couch on which Aeneas had reclined at the banquet (Ov. *Met.* 5.34).

2 83. **absens absentem**: the Greek type of repetition is very emphatic, cf. *Aen.* 1.684, 10.600.

3 84. Dido recalls in imagination the events of the day (cf. Ap. Rh. 3.453f.), hearing and seeing Aeneas, holding Ascanius in her lap; the words *absens absentem* extend to this line too.

4 85. 'if thus she could solace a love beyond words'; *fallere* literally is 'deceive', i.e. seem to satisfy. For the Greek form of the conditional sentence ('in the hope that') see note on 1.181-2.

5 86f. This passage is vitally important as indicating quite specifically that Dido has now abdicated the queenly responsibilities which she had been performing with such success before Aeneas came (1.423f., 507f.). Notice how the slow spondaic movement reflects the lack of activity.

6 88-9. 'all building stops and the mighty threatening walls and the structures that tower sky high are idle'; the metrical effects are noticeable here, with the elision of *opera* after the third foot, the pause in the fifth foot, and the assonance of *aequataque machina*. *Minae* probably is general ('threatening walls', cf. *Aen.* 1.162), but it might more specifically mean (as Servius says) 'pinnacles of the walls'. *Machina*, as Servius saw and as is shown by a passage in Val. Fl. 6.383, means 'structure', not 'machinery' (cranes, scaffolding, or the like); the former meaning is an extension of the Lucretian phrase *machina mundi*, while the latter would be inappropriate with the verbs *pendent interrupta*. Virgil uses the word elsewhere only of the Trojan horse (2.46 etc.).

7 90f. The ruthless and malicious scheming of the goddesses is here shown at its most blatant. Juno's desire is clearly to frustrate the foundation of Rome by keeping Aeneas at Carthage, and to this end she uses on Venus all her powers of irony and persuasion. Venus' intentions are much less clear; presumably she is confident, in the light of what Jupiter had foretold of the future (1.257f.) that Juno's plans will be frustrated, so that it gives her pleasure to appear to support them, and thus score over her divine adversary. As for Dido, neither goddess sees her as more than an instrument to use in the pursuit of their own policies. The portrayal of the goddesses here owes something to the beginning of Apollonius 3, where Hera and Athena go to Aphrodite for help in their schemes; and we are reminded of Venus' intervention in *Aen.* 1.657f., where see note.

8 90. **peste**: the word has been used already (in an anticipatory context) of Dido's love, *Aen.* 1.712; cf. its use by Catullus in his prayer to be released from the cruel disease of his love for Lesbia, 76.20.

9 92. **Saturnia**: Juno, daughter of Saturnus, cf. 1.23.

'egregiam[1] vero laudem et spolia ampla refertis
tuque puerque tuus, magnum et memorabile numen,
una dolo divum si femina victa duorum est.   95
Nec me adeo fallit veritam te moenia nostra[2]
suspectas habuisse domos Karthaginis altae.
Sed[3] quis erit modus, aut quo nunc certamine tanto?
Quin[4] potius pacem aeternam pactosque hymenaeos
exercemus? Habes tota quod mente petisti: 100
ardet amans Dido traxitque per ossa furorem.[5]
Communem hunc ergo populum paribusque regamus[6]
auspiciis; liceat Phrygio servire marito
dotalisque tuae Tyrios permittere dextrae.'
    Olli (sensit enim simulata[7] mente locutam,[8]   105
quo[9] regnum Italiae Libycas averteret oras)
sic contra est ingressa Venus: 'quis talia demens
abnuat aut tecum malit contendere bello —
si[10] modo quod memoras factum fortuna sequatur?
Sed[11] fatis incerta feror, si Iuppiter unam   110
esse velit Tyriis urbem Troiaque profectis,
miscerive probet populos aut foedera iungi.

---

1 93-5. 'Glittering indeed is the glory and piled high the booty which you come back with, you and your boy, mighty and memorable is your majesty indeed, if one woman is brought low by the trickery of two gods.' Juno's opening phrases are sarcastic in the highest degree, with the ironical adjective placed first (cf. 6.523), the military metaphor applied to a goddess whose battles were not real ones, the derogatory *tuque puerque tuus* (Cupid), and the rhetorical antithesis of two against one, gods against a mortal woman. *Numen* is in loose apposition to *tuque puerque tuus*, cf. Ov. *Met.* 4.452, and for *memorabile numen* Ov. *Met.* 4.416-17. The reading *nomen*, found in some late MSS, is very attractive; cf. *Aen.* 2.583.

2 96f. Cf. *Aen.* 1.661f., for Venus' fear of Carthage.

3 98. 'But what will be the end of it, or what do you now hope to get with all this opposition?' With *quo* ('whither') understand some verb like *tendis* ('what is your object'); *certamine tanto* is ablative of means.

4 99-100. **quin . . . exercemus?**: 'Why don't we rather work out. . .?'; this use of *quin* is from colloquial speech, cf. 547. *Exercere* is extended from its normal use in phrases like *odium exercere, amores exercere*.

5 101. Cf. *Aen.* 1.675; Juno says that Venus' plan for Dido to fall in love with Aeneas is more than fulfilled, she is on fire with frenzied passion; for *trahere* cf. Ov. *Met.* 4.675.

6 102-3. 'So let us rule this people together, with equal authority'; cf. *Aen.* 7.256-7. Juno then proceeds to forms of words which make concessions: *servire, permittere*. For Juno to propose that the Carthaginians should be a dowry for the hated leader of the Trojans rightly arouses Venus' suspicions; in 12.819f. Juno is only reconciled to the Trojans on the condition that in their intermarriage with the Italians they shall be the recessive partner.

7 105. **simulata mente**: 'with pretended purpose', i.e. as if she were really interested in a union between the Trojans and Carthaginians, whereas in fact her only purpose is to keep the Trojans from settling in Italy (*Aen.* 1.19f.).

8 **locutam**: for the omission of the pronoun *eam* see note on 383.

9 106. 'so that she might divert the kingdom of Italy to Libyan shores'. *Quo* introduces a final clause (= *ut eo modo*); *oras* is accusative of motion towards.

10 109. **si modo . . . fortuna sequatur**: 'provided that success will follow . . .', but, as she goes on to say, she has doubts.

11 110. **sed ... feror, si:** 'but I am tossed in doubt because of the fates, uncertain whether. . . .'; *fatis* is causal ablative dependent on the phrase *incerta feror* (= *fatis distrahor*). The next two lines depend on *si* (= *num*), and all three clauses refer to the same option: 'whether he wishes one city, or *approves* mingling or treaties'. Venus in fact knows very well that he does not.

Tu coniunx, tibi fas animum temptare precando.
Perge, sequar.' Tum sic excepit regia Iuno:
'mecum erit iste labor. [1]Nunc qua ratione quod instat   115
confieri possit, paucis (adverte) docebo.
Venatum Aeneas unaque miserrima Dido
in nemus ire parant, ubi primos crastinus ortus
extulerit Titan[2] radiisque[3] retexerit orbem.
His ego nigrantem commixta grandine nimbum,   120
dum trepidant alae[4] saltusque indagine cingunt,
desuper infundam et tonitru caelum omne ciebo.
Diffugient comites et nocte tegentur opaca:
speluncam Dido dux et[5] Troianus eandem
devenient. Adero et, tua si mihi certa voluntas,   125
conubio iungam stabili propriamque dicabo.[6]
Hic[7] hymenaeus erit.' [8]Non adversata petenti
adnuit atque dolis risit Cytherea repertis.

> *129-172. Dido and her Carthaginians, accompanied by
> Aeneas and the Trojans, ride out for the hunt. In the midst of
> the joyful scene Juno sends a storm, and Dido and Aeneas
> shelter in the same cave. The powers of Nature seem to
> perform the ritual of a wedding ceremony, and Dido now
> considers herself to be married to Aeneas.*

[9]Oceanum interea surgens Aurora reliquit.
It portis iubare[10] exorto delecta iuventus,   130

---

1 115-16. Notice the matter-of-fact prosaic diction; Juno speaks of how to deal with an item on the agenda.

2 119. **Titan:** the sun, child of the Titan Hyperion, cf. *Aen.* 6.725.

3 **radiisque retexerit orbem:** 'reveals the world with his rays' cf. *Aen.* 5.65, the same phrase, 9.461.

4 121. **alae:** the groups of horsemen (132), excitedly active (*trepidant*) in closing in on the wild animals with a cordon (*indagine*).

5 124. The postponed *et* seems to link the two unsuspecting subjects more closely.

6 126. This line, characteristic of Juno's power as *pronuba,* is repeated from *Aen.* 1.73, where see notes.

7 127. **hic hymenaeus erit:** 'this shall be their wedding'; this Greek word is elsewhere plural in Virgil, but cf. Cat. 66.11.

8 127-8. 'The Cytherean goddess did not oppose her request, but nodded agreement and smiled at having seen through her trickery'. For Venus' epithet *Cythtrea* cf. *Aen.* 1.257; her smile here reminds us of Homer's 'laughter-loving Aphrodite', and especially of her malicious pleasure in herself tricking people (cf. Hor. *Odes* 3.27.67 *perfidum ridens Venus*). *Dolis . . . repertis* might mean 'at the trickery Juno had devised', but the words refer better to Venus' perception of Juno's deceit (105).

9 129f. In this passage the contrast between joy and gloom is total. The hunt is described in the most radiant and brilliant colours; it is full of movement, excitement and splendour. The beauty of Dido's appearance is fully described (137f.), while Aeneas for his part is no less majestic than Apollo (143f.). The young Ascanius enjoys every moment of the chase.
The fulfilment of Juno's plans is introduced in menacing lines (160f.), with sinister repetition of the words of her speech to Venus (161, 165). The primeval and elemental forces of Nature and the supernatural enact a ceremony which corresponds in a daemonic way to the real events of a marriage. Dido is deluded by these cosmic manifestations, and the poet interrupts his narrative to reflect on the inevitable sequence of events now set in train.

10 130. **iubare exorto:** 'when the sun's rays appeared'; for the singular use of *iubar* cf. Ov. *Met.* 7.663 *iubar aureus extulerat Sol.*

retia rara, plagae, lato venabula ferro,[1]
Massylique[2] ruunt equites et odora[3] canum vis.
Reginam thalamo cunctantem ad limina primi
Poenorum exspectant, ostroque insignis et auro
stat [4]sonipes ac frena ferox spumantia mandit.   135
Tandem progreditur magna stipante caterva
Sidoniam[5] picto chlamydem circumdata limbo;
cui pharetra ex auro, crines[6] nodantur in aurum,
aurea purpuream subnectit fibula vestem.
Nec non et Phrygii comites et laetus Iulus   140
incedunt. Ipse ante alios pulcherrimus omnis
infert se socium Aeneas atque agmina[7] iungit.
Qualis[8] ubi hibernam[9] Lyciam Xanthique fluenta
deserit ac Delum maternam invisit Apollo
instauratque choros, mixtique altaria circum   145
Cretesque[10] Dryopesque fremunt pictique Agathyrsi:
ipse iugis Cynthi[11] graditur mollique fluentem
fronde premit crinem[12] fingens atque implicat auro,
tela sonant umeris: haud[13] illo segnior ibat
Aeneas, tantum egregio decus enitet ore.   150

---

1 131. The omission of the verb 'to be' is striking here; cf. *Aen.* 1.639, 3.618. Possibly a verb may be supplied by zeugma from *ruunt* or *it;* in this case cf. Hor. *Epist.* 1.6.58. *Retia rara* are wide-meshed nets, *plagae* are smaller nets; cf. Hor. *Epod.* 2.32f.

2 132. **Massyli:** an African people to the west of Carthage, cf. 483, *Aen.* 6.60.

3 132. **odora canum vis:** literally 'the keen-scented power of dogs', i.e. keen-scented strong dogs. The type of phrase is Homeric (cf. *Il.* 11.690, 23.720) and is found in Lucretius with *canum* (4.681, 6.1222); it is particularly remarkable here because of the archaic type of monosyllabic ending (cf. *Aen.* 1.65 and Austin's full note on this passage) and the innovated meaning of *odorus*.

4 135. Notice the strong alliteration and assonance *(s, f, man-)* to add emphasis to the fine colourful picture.

5 137. 'wearing a Sidonian cloak with embroidered border'; *chlamydem* is a retained accusative with the passive verb used in a middle sense, see note on 1.228 and cf. 216-17, 493, 509, 518, 589-90, 644, 659.

6 138. **crines nodantur in aurum:** 'her hair was fastened with (on to) a golden clasp'; for a similar three-fold repetition of 'golden' in a descriptive passage cf. *Aen.* 7.278-9, 8.659-71, 11.774-6.

7 142. **agmina iungit:** 'joins his troop with hers', cf. *Aen.* 2.267.

8 143f. The comparison of Aeneas with Apollo is primarily concerned with beauty and majesty; secondly with hunting and archery; and thirdly is reminiscent of the comparison of Dido with Diana in 1.498f with which there are several similarities *(exercet . . . choros, per iuga Cynthi, mille secutae, pharetram fert umero, gradiens)*. In Apollonius Jason is compared with Apollo (1.307f.).

9 143. **hibernam Lyciam:** 'Lycia in winter'; Servius tells us that Apollo was said to give oracles during the winter months in southern Asia Minor at Patara in Lycia (through which a river called Xanthus flowed, not to be confused with Troy's Xanthus), and during the summer in Delos, where he was born (see note on 3.75-6); cf. Hor. *Odes* 3.4.60f.

10 146. **Cretesque Dryopesque:** notice the lengthening in arsis of the first *-que;* see note on 3.91. This and the quadri-syllabic ending give a Greek touch to the metre, to correspond with the Greek names. The peoples mentioned come from widely separated parts; the Dryopes from North Greece and the Agathyrsi from Scythia.

11 147. **Cynthi:** the highest hill of Delos, cf. *Aen.* 1.498.

12 148. **premit crinem fingens:** 'shapes and secures his locks', cf. *Aen.* 6.80.

13 149-50. Aeneas is compared with Apollo first in the composure and majesty of his movements *(haud segnior ibat)*, and second in his beauty *(tantum decus)*.

Postquam altos ventum in montis atque invia lustra,
ecce ferae saxi deiectae[1] vertice caprae
decurrere iugis; alia de parte patentis
transmittunt[2] cursu campos atque agmina cervi
pulverulenta fuga glomerant[3] montisque relinquunt.   155
At puer Ascanius mediis in vallibus acri
gaudet equo iamque hos cursu, iam praeterit illos,
spumantemque dari pecora[4] inter inertia votis
optat aprum, aut fulvum descendere monte leonem.
   Interea magno misceri murmure caelum[5]   160
incipit, insequitur commixta grandine nimbus,
et Tyrii comites passim et Troiana iuventus
Dardaniusque[6] nepos Veneris diversa per agros
tecta[7] metu petiere; ruunt de montibus amnes.
Speluncam Dido dux et Troianus eandem   165
deveniunt. [8]Prima et Tellus et pronuba Iuno
dant signum; fulsere ignes et conscius aether
conubiis, summoque ulularunt vertice Nymphae.
Ille dies primus leti primusque malorum
causafuit; [9]neque enim specie famave movetur   170

---

1 152. **deiectae**: 'dislodged', frightened by the hunters.

2 154. **transmittunt**: 'cross', cf. Cic. *Fin.* 5.87, Lucr. 2.330, *Aen.* 6.313; the subject of this clause as of the next is *cervi*.

3 155. **glomerant**: 'mass', cf. *Aen.* 1.500, 2.315.

4 158. **pecora inter inertia**: 'in among all these timid creatures', cf. *Aen.* 9.730. The hunt is depicted on the Low Ham mosaic (see *J.R.S.* 1946, p. 142).

5 160. Observe how the movement changes from the joyful hunting scene by means of the slow rhythm of spondees and the menacing alliteration of *m*. For *misceri*, suggesting disturbance, see note on 1.124. Notice too how closely the following lines correspond with Juno's speech (lines 120f.), especially the crucial line 165 (= 124). This passage is imitated by Spenser, *F.Q.*, 1.1.6-7.

6 163. **Dardaniusque nepos Veneris**: i.e. Ascanius, Venus' Trojan grandson.

7 169f. Notice how Virgil here intervenes in his narrative, partly to anticipate the results of the action (169-70), partly to reveal its effect on Dido (esp. 172).

8 166f. The marriage in a cave is reminiscent of the marriage of Jason and Medea in Ap. Rh. 4.1130f., but the difference is profound. In Apollonius the occasion is a happy one, a real marriage; in Virgil the elemental powers of nature and supernatural divinities conspire to produce a parody of a wedding, a hallucination by which the unhappy Dido is deceived. *Dant signum* refers generally to the inauguration of the ceremony, here performed by Mother Earth, the oldest of divinities, and Juno in her special capacity as goddess of marriage. The 'lightning flashes' (*fulsere ignes*) seem to Dido to be the wedding torches; the ether 'witnesses' the marriage, and the nymphs sing the wedding song. Milton (*P.L.* 9.782f., cf. also 1000f.), put the imagery of this passage to a different use:
'Earth felt the wound, and Nature from her seate
Sighing through all her Works gave signs of woe,
That all was lost'.

9 170. Supply *iam* to the first clause: Dido is no longer affected by appearances or reputation, nor does she any longer think of a hidden love.

nec iam furtivum Dido meditatur amorem: coniugium vocat, hoc
praetexit nomine culpam.[1]

> *173-218. The terrifying figure of Rumour is described; she
> spreads abroad in malicious terms the story of the love of
> Dido and Aeneas. Finally she goes to King Iarbas, Dido's
> suitor; angered beyond measure he asks Jupiter if he is
> aware of so disgraceful a situation, or whether his worship
> is vain.*

[2]Extemplo Libyae magnas it Fama per urbes,
Fama, malum qua non aliud velocius ullum:
mobilitate[3] viget virisque adquirit eundo,   175
parva metu primo, [4]mox sese attollit in auras
ingrediturque solo et caput inter nubila condit.[5]
Illam Terra parens ira[6] inritata deorum
extremam, ut perhibent, Coeo[7] Enceladoque sororem
progenuit pedibus celerem et pernicibus alis,   180
monstrum[8] horrendum, ingens, cui quot sunt corpore plumae,[9]

---

1 172. 'She calls it marriage, and under this name she cloaks her sin'; for *praetexere* cf. 500,for *culpa* cf. 19. For Dido's belief that it was marriage cf. lines 316, 324, 496; for Aeneas' denial cf. lines 338-9.

2 173f. The personification of Rumour occurs as early as Homer (*Od.* 24.413f.; cf. Hesiod, *Works* 761f. where she is a goddess); the detail of Virgil's picture incorporates some memorable phrases from Homer's personified Strife (*Il.* 4.442-3; see note on 176-7), but is very greatly enlarged and elaborated. The style of description is grandiose and rhetorical, in some ways baroque, and it has met with disapproval from many commentators. But this is a style of writing which Virgil enjoyed (cf. for example Polyphemus in Book 3 and the boxing match in Book 5 — and, rather differently, Atlas in this book, 246f.); and it is used here to vary the pathos and intensity of the developing human tragedy by transporting the reader to a world of imagination, to a dimension of nonhuman imagery.
Among the imitations of this passage mention should be made of Ovid, *Met.* 12.41f.; Chaucer, *House of Fame,* 3.266f.; Pope, *Temple of Fame,* 258f.:
When on the goddess first I cast my sight,
Scarce seem'd her stature of a cubit's height;
But swell'd to larger size, the more I gazed,
Till to the roof her towering front she raised . . .
Such was her form, as ancient bards have told,
Wings raise her arms, and wings her feet infold;
A thousand busy tongues the goddess hears,
And thousand open eyes, and thousand listening ears.

3 175. **mobilitate viget:** 'she thrives on speed'; other creatures weaken the faster they go, but Rumour gets stronger. For the phrases cf. Lucr. 6.340f. (of a thunderbolt).

4 176-7. This is a close imitation of Hom. *Il.* 4.442-3, where personified Strife is described, small at first but then her head reaches the heavens while she walks on the earth; Virgil has added the notion of Rumour being timid at first while she is small.

5 177. This line is repeated in *Aen.* 10.767; Pease has a long note on hyperbole, and quotes Ben Jonson 'As her brow the clouds invade / Her feet do strike the ground'.

6 178. **ira inritata deorum:** 'provoked by her anger against the gods', because they exterminated her children, the Giants and the Titans (Ap. Rh. 2.39f., Hor. *Odes* 3.4.73f.).

7 179. Coeus (*Geo.* 1.279) was a Titan and Enceladus (*Aen.* 3.578) a Giant; both were destroyed by Jupiter. Mother Earth then bore one last child, Fama, to be their sister and take vengeance on gods and men with her evil tongue.

8 181. **monstrum horrendum ingens:** a reminiscence of the description of the Cyclops in 3.658.

9 181-3. 'for every feather on her body there is a watchful eye beneath (astonishing to tell) — and she has as many tongues, too, as many shouting mouths, as many pricked-up ears'. Compare the hundred-eyed monster Argus, whose eyes became the rings on the tail of Juno's peacock.

tot vigiles oculi subter (mirabile dictu),
tot linguae, totidem ora sonant, tot subrigit auris.
Nocte volat caeli[1] medio terraeque per umbram
stridens,[2] nec dulci declinat lumina somno;   185
luce sedet custos[3] aut summi culmine tecti
turribus aut altis, et magnas territat urbes,
tam[4] ficti pravique tenax quam nuntia veri.
Haec tum multiplici populos sermone replebat
gaudens, et pariter facta atque infecta canebat: 190
venisse[5] Aenean Troiano sanguine cretum,[6]
cui se pulchra viro dignetur iungere Dido;
nunc hiemem inter se luxu, quam[7] longa, fovere
regnorum[8] immemores turpique cupidine captos.
Haec passim dea foeda virum[9] diffundit in ora.   195
Protinus ad regem cursus detorquet Iarban[10]
incenditque animum dictis atque aggerat iras.

    Hic Hammone[11] satus rapta Garamantide nympha
templa Iovi centum latis immania regnis,
centum aras posuit vigilemque sacraverat ignem,   200
excubias[12] divum aetemas, [13]pecudumque cruore
pingue solum et variis florentia limina sertis.

---

1 184. **caeli medio terraeque:** 'between earth and sky', cf. Ov. *Met.* 12.39f., and for the construction *Aen.* 9.230.

2 185. **stridens:** notice the effect of -the 'run-on' spondaic word filling the first foot, a rare rhythm (cf. 190 and 562). Very strong emphasis is thus put on the descriptive participle. *Stridens* is similarly placed in *Aen.* 9.419, 12.859 (referring to an arrow).

3 186. **custos:** 'watching', so as to miss nothing.

4 188. 'as persistent a messenger of what is false and distorted as of the truth', cf. *facta atque infecta canebat* (190).

5 191f. The accusative and infinitive reports Rumour's story; it is not wholly untrue in itself, but it is phrased in malicious terms, calculated to anger Iarbas.

6 191. **cretum:** 'born of', cf. *Aen.* 2.74.

7 193. 'now they enjoy the winter, all its length, in dalliance together'; for *quam longa* cf. *Aen.* 8.86, for *hiemem fovere* (a striking phrase, literally 'keep the winter warm') cf. *Geo.* 4.43 and compare Val. Fl. 8.371. Some take *hiemem* as accusative of duration of time, with *fovere inter se* meaning 'enjoy each other's company' (cf. *Aen.* 1.718), but this seems less likely.

8 194. **regnorum immemores:** this is indeed true of both of them (cf. 86f., 225).

9 195. **virum diffundit in ora:** 'spread abroad on to men's lips', i.e. caused them to pass on the rumours.

10 196. **Iarban:** see note on 36; Austin well comments how Virgil has drawn a subtle picture of primitive mentality in this fierce barbarian despot. Iarbas plays a large part in Marlowe's *Dido, Queen of Carthage.*

11 198. Iarbas is the son of Jupiter Hammon (or Ammon); this was the epithet of Jupiter in Africa, presumably indicating that an original local god Hammon was identified by the Romans with their Jupiter. For his famous African oracle (in the land of the Garamantes) cf. Lucan 9.511f.; for the Garamantes cf. also *Aen.* 6.794. The name of Iarbas' mother, the nymph ravished by Jupiter, is not known. *Satus* ('son of') is mainly poetic, cf. *Aen.* 2.540, 5.424.

12 201. **excubias divum aeternas:** 'as the ever-lasting sentinel of the gods', in apposition to *vigilem ignem.*

13 201-2. It seems best to supply *erat* to the clauses, cf. 131; it is however possible to regard the nouns as accusative after some verbal notion taken by zeugma from *sacraverat.*

Isque amens animi[1] et rumore accensus amaro
dicitur ante aras media[2] inter numina divum
multa Iovem manibus supplex orasse supinis: 205
'Iuppiter omnipotens, cui nunc[3] Maurusia[4] pictis
gens epulata toris Lenacum[5] libat honorem,
aspicis haec? An te, genitor, cum fulmina torques
nequiquam horremus, [6]caecique in nubibus ignes
terrificant animos et inania murmura miscent?   210
Femina,[7] quae nostris errans in finibus urbem
exiguam pretio posuit, cui litus arandum[8]
cuique loci leges dedimus, conubia nostra
reppulit ac dominum[9] Aenean in regna recepit.
Et [10]nunc ille Paris cum semiviro comitatu,   215
Maconia mentum[11] mitra crinemque madentem
subnexus, rapto potitur: nos munera tempiis
quippe[12] tuis ferimus famamque fovemus inanem.'

1 203. **animi:** 'in mind', genitive not locative; cf. 300, 529 and see note on 2.61.

2 204. **media inter numina divum**: 'surrounded by the encompassing divinity of the gods', a strong phrase; cf. *Aen.* 1.447.

3 206. **nunc**: because Iarbas had introduced the worship which had not existed before.

4 **Maurusia:** 'Moorish', a general word for African, not here specific for Mauretania (cf. Hor. *Odes* 2.6.3-4).

5 207. **Lenaeum libat honorem:** 'pours in libation offerings of wine'; cf. *Aen.* 1736, and for *Lenaeus* (god of the wine-press) cf. *Geo.* 2.4.

6 209-10. Notice the emphasis on the first word in each clause:'is it in vain? . . . are the lightnings aimless? . . . are the noises purposeless?'

7 211f. Notice the building irony and disgust, first *femina* (he expects to dictate to women), then *nostris in finibus* (*my* land), *errans* (she was a homeless exile), *exiguam* (a tiny city, nothing like mine)*, pretio* (I sold her the site; notice the alliteration of *p* here), *litus arandum* (I gave her a barren bit of sand to plough), *loci leges* (and conditions of tenure). Iarbas performed all these acts of charity for a helpless exile, and what happens? *Conubia nostra reppulit:* 'she has rejected my offer of marriage'.

8 212. For the foundation of Carthage cf. *Aen.* 1.365f and compare Marlowe, *Dido, Queen of Carthage,* 4.2.12-13, 'Where, straying in our borders up and down, / She crav'd a hide of ground to build a town'.

9 214. **dominum**: here contemptuous, 'as lord and master', because she seems to Iarbas to be in a wholly dependent position.

10 215f. This powerful expression of contempt for the Trojans may be compared especially with Numanus the Rutulian's speech in 9.598f., particularly 617f. where they are taunted with being Phrygian women, not Phrygian men; and with Turnus' words in 12.97f., where he refers to Aeneas as *semivir Phryx,* with crimped hair dripping with myrrh. For the taunt that Aeneas is another Paris (abducting another Helen) cf. *Aen.* 7.321, 363, 9.138f. The quadri-syllabic ending *comitatu* (see note on 1.651) reinforces the unRoman tone of the line.

11 216-17. 'his chin and oiled locks tied up with a Maconian bonnet'; there is extremely heavy alliteration of *m. Maeonius* (cf. 8.499) means Phrygian or Lydian, *mitra* was a foreign type of headdress worn especially by women (Cat. 64.63, Juv. 3.66, cf. *Aen.* 9.616). *Mentum crinemque subnexus* is an example of the retained accusative construction (cf. 137), *subnexus* having a middle force. The major MSS read *subnixus* ('supporting'), but *subnexus* is a more appropriate word (cf. *Geo.* 3.167, *Aen.* 10.138) and the palaeographical confusion is a very easy one.

12 218. **quippe**: highly sarcastic (= *scilicet),* cf. *Aen.* 1.39.
The alliteration of *f* is startling in the extreme; it is generally avoided by the poets (cf. Quint. 12.10.29 for unfavourable comments about the sound of *f),* and here it gives a violent scorn to Iarbas' closing words.

219-237. Jupiter tells Mercury to convey a message to Aeneas, reminding him of his destiny, and ordering him to sail away from Carthage.

[1]Talibus orantem dictis arasque tenentem
audiit Omnipotens, oculosque ad moenia torsit   220
regia et oblitos famae melioris amantis.
Tum sic Mercurium[2] adloquitur[3] ac talia mandat:
'vade age, nate, voca Zephyros et labere pennis
Dardaniumque ducem, Tyria Karthagine qui nunc
exspectat[4] fatisque[5] datas non respicit urbes,   225
adloquere et celeris defer mea dicta per auras.
Non illum nobis genetrix[6] pulcherrima talem
promisit Graiumque ideo bis[7] vindicat[8] armis;
sed fore qui gravidam imperiis belloque frementem
Italiam regeret, genus alto a sanguine Teucri[9]   230
proderet, ac totum sub leges mitteret orbem.
Si nulla[10] accendit tantarum gloria rerum
nec super[11] ipse sua molitur laude laborem,
Ascanione pater[12] Romanas invidet arces?
Quid struit? [13]Aut qua spe inimica in gente moratur   235

---

1 219f. The intervention of Jupiter is reminiscent of that of Zeus in Hom. *Od.* 5.28f., where he sends Hermes to order Calypso to let Odysseus go; but the difference is very marked. The message from Jupiter is to Aeneas personally, stating powerfully the reasons why he must leave; it is an action directed at the conscience of Aeneas. Aeneas must remember his divine mission, and he then is in a position to act accordingly; it is not necessary to release him (as it is with Odysseus) from a situation which he cannot overcome. We are justified to some extent in rationalising the action of Jupiter and Mercury as the promptings of Aeneas' conscience; the vision of Mercury speaks to him as an inner voice, persuading him towards what he knows is the right course. But if we accept this psychological undertone to the narrative we must not lose sight of the terms in which Virgil presents it; the king of the gods gives his instructions, his messenger flies through the breezes, finds Aeneas, speaks to him and vanishes again back beyond the clouds. The supernatural, however much we rationalise it, is presented in the most powerful images.

2 222. Mercury is Jupiter's personal messenger, as in 1.297; cf. Hermes in Hom. *Od.* 5.28f.

3 **adloquitur**: the final syllable is lengthened in arsis, see note on 1.308 and cf. line 64.

4 225. **exspectat**: 'delays', a very unusual usage in the sense of *moratur, deterit tempus* (Servius). Housman conjectured *Hesperiam*, but the ablative *Karthagine* requires a verb; in any case the innovated shade of meaning is perfectly acceptable.

5 **fatisque datas**: the theme of the city granted by fate runs through the *Aeneid*, cf. for example 1.258, 3.255, 11.112.

6 227f. 'It was not such a man as this that his beautiful mother promised us, therefore twice rescuing him from Greek warfare; but that he would be one who would rule Italy teeming with empire and clamourous with war, who would produce a people of the noble blood of Teucer, and bring all the world beneath the sway of laws.' This is one of the finest expressions in the poem of the Roman mission; first to conquer in war, and then to bring laws and civilisation. Compare Jupiter's speech in 1.263f., Anchises' in 6.847f., Jupiter's in 12.838f.; for the fulfilment under Augustus cf. *Geo.* 4.561f., *victorque volentis / per populos dat iura.*

7 228. **bis**: once from Diomedes (Hom. *Il.* 5.311f.) and once from burning Troy (*Aen.* 2.589f.).

8 **vindicat:** for the present tense (she is his rescuer), cf. 549 and *Aen.* 8.141, 9.266.

9 230. **Teucri**: for Teucer, ancestor of the Trojans, see note on 1.38.

10 232. **nulla**: 'not at all', literally 'no glory', an idiomatic expression, cf. *Aen.* 6.405.

11 233. 'and he does not shoulder the task for his own fame'; *super* is used (as Servius says) in the sense of *pro,* like the Greek ὑπέρ.

12 234. **pater:** we would say in English 'does he grudge his son Ascanius. . .?'; for the destiny of Ascanius cf. *Aen.* 1.267f.

13 235. Notice the hiatus at the caesura; cf. *Aen.* :.16, and see Austin's full discussion in his note on this line.

nec prolem[1] Ausoniam et Lavinia[2] respicit arva?
Naviget! Haec[3] summa est, hic nostri nuntius esto.'

238-278. Mercury puts on his winged sandals, takes his wand, and flies down to earth, alighting first on Mt. Atlas. When he reaches Carthage he finds Aeneas busy with the enlargement of Carthage, and angrily delivers Jupiter's message, telling him to think of his destiny and that of Ascanius in Italy. The message delivered, Mercury vanishes.

[4]Dixerat. Ille patris magni parere parabat
imperio; et primum pedibus talaria[5] nectit
aurea, quae sublimem alis sive aequora supra   240
seu terram rapido pariter cum flamine portant.
Tum virgam[6] capit: hac animas ille evocat Orco
pallentis, alias sub Tartara tristia mittit,
dat somnos adimitque, [7]et lumina morte resignat.
Illa[8] fretus agit ventos et turbida tranat[9]   245
nubila. Iamque volans apicem ct latera ardua cernit
Atlantis duri caelum qui vertice fulcit,

---

1 236. **prolem Ausoniam:** his offspring will be Italian (cf. 3.171) as well as Trojan (230), because of the fusion of the races; cf. 6.756-7.

2 **Lavinia . . . arva:** for *Lavinius*, the adjective of Lavinium, Aeneas' first settlement in Italy, cf. 1.2.

3 237. 'Let him sail — this is the long and short of it, let this be my message'. The other possible meaning, 'be my messenger of this decree', seems less natural.

4 238f. The account of Mercury's journey is vividly descriptive, and has the same sort of function in the variety of narrative tone as the description of Rumour (see note on 173f.). Colour and shape from another world is painted for us on Virgil's canvas. Mercury himself is depicted in words as he was so often in visual art, with his golden winged sandals, his wand. This passage is reminiscent of Homer (*Od.* 5.44f.) and so is the end of the description when Mercury swoops down like a bird wheeling around the rock pools on the shore.

Into the description of Mercury is inset a strange and memorable picture of Atlas, at once a mountain and a giant. The passage is ornate, baroque, even in some sense grotesque; it has come in for harsh criticism from most commentators, mainly on the ground that a poet should know whether he is describing a mountain or a man. The ambiguity is subtle: in 246-7 with *apicem* and *latera* and *duri* (hard or enduring) and *vertice* there is nothing inappropriate for a mountain, which is what the reader is expecting to be described; yet all the words could apply to a man. With *caput* in 249 we see the mountain changing, with *umeros, mento senis, horrida barba* it has indeed changed. Those who have seen the giant profile of Idris in the changing shadows of Cader Idris will respond to what Virgil attempts here.

5 239. **talaria:** these are the famous winged sandals, or perhaps more precisely anklets (line 259), of Mercury (Hermes); cf. Hom. *Od.* 5.44f. (= *Il.* 24.340f.), a passage which Virgil closely follows. Statius (*Th.* 1.303f.) has a variation on the Virgilian theme; Milton's description of Raphael's flight (*P.L.* 5.266f.) ends 'Like Maia's son he stood, / and shook his Plumes, that Heav'nly fragrance filld / the circuit wide'.

6 242. **virgam:** 'his wand', i.e. the *caduceus* (ραβδος); for Hermes as ψυχοπομπος, guide of the dead, cf. Hom. *Od.* 24.1f. where he conducts the souls of the suitors down to the underworld.

7 244. The first phrase is from Homer (Hermes puts to sleep or awakens anyone he wishes); the second, which is not, elaborates *adimitque,* and means 'unseals the eyes in death', so that the ghosts can see. For *resignare* cf. Hor. *Epist.* 1.7.9; Conington compares Statius' use (*Th.* 3.129) of *signare* (sealing the eyes of the dead). In Roman ritual the eyes were closed by relatives at death (*Aen.* 9.487) and opened again on the pyre (Pliny, *N.H.* 11.150).

8 245. **illa fretus agit ventos:** 'using this he drives the winds'; the image appears to be that of a charioteer with a whip.

9 **tranat:** 'flies through' cf. Lucr. 4.177, *Aen.* 10.265, and compare *Aen.* 6.16.

Atlantis,[1] cinctum adsidue cui nubibus atris[2]
piniferum caput et vento pulsatur ct imbri,
nix umeros infusa tegit, tum[3] flumina mento   250
praecipitant[4] senis, et glacie riget horrida barba.
Hic primum paribus[5] nitens Cyllenius[6] alis
constitit; hinc toto praeceps se corpore ad undas
misit avi[7] similis, quae circum litora, circum
piscosos scopulos humilis volat aequora iuxta.   255
Haud aliter terras inter caelumque volabat
litus[8] harenosum ad Libyae, ventosque secabat
materno veniens ab avo Cyllenia proles.[9]
Ut primum alatis[10] tetigit magalia[11] plantis,
Aenean fundantem[12] arces ac tecta novantem   260
conspicit. Atque[13] illi stellatus iaspide[14] fulva
ensis erat Tyrioque ardebat murice laena[15]
demissa ex umeris, dives[16] quae munera Dido
fecerat, et tenui telas[17] discreverat auro.

---

1 247. **Atlantis:** for the mixed picture of man and mountain see note on 238f., and compare Ov. *Met.* 4.657f.; for Atlas cf. also lines 481-2 and *Aen.* 1.741, 6.706f. The Titan Atlas was condemned to support the heavens on his shoulders; he was identified with Mt. Atlas in N. Africa.

2 248-51. 'whose pine-covered head, for ever veiled in dark clouds, is assailed by wind and rain alike; a mantle of snow conceals his shoulders; then streams rush down from the old man's chin, and his bristling beard is stiff with ice'.

3 250. **tum:** used in enumerations to mean the next thing one notices, cf. *Aen.* 1.164.

4 251. **praecipitant:** used intransitively, cf. line 565 and *Aen.* 2.9.

5 252. **paribus nitens . . . alis:** 'poised on balanced wings'; for *nitens* cf. Ov. *Pont.* 2.7.27, for *paribus alis* cf. *Aen.* 5.657.

6 **Cyllenius:** Mercury was born on Mt. Cyllene in Arcadia (*Aen.* 8.139).

7 254. **avi similis:** again the detail is taken from Homer (*Od.* 5.51f., where Hermes is like the cormorant speeding low over the waves in quest of fish).

8 257. **litus harenosum ad Libyae:** the major MSS have *ao* (*P*) and *at* (*M*) for *ad*, but there are no grounds for omitting it as some editors do. For the position of the preposition cf. line 671, *Aen.* 6.58 *corpus in Aeacidae*, 7.234, 9.643.

9 258. A frigid line, with learned Alexandrian allusiveness; Maia, Mercury's mother, was the daughter of Atlas.

10 259. **alatis . . . plantis:** cf. Shakespeare, *King John*, 4.2.174 'Be Mercury, set feathers to thy heels', and Keats, *Endymion*, 4.331 'foot-feather'd Mercury'.

11 **magalia:** 'huts', a Carthaginian word (1.421).

12 260. **fundantem . . . novantem:** 'establishing fortifications and building new dwelling places'; the rhyme reinforces the emphasis on Aeneas' activities, which should be taking place, in Italy on his own behalf, not in Carthage on Dido's.

13 261. **atque:** 'yes, and...', a further reason for Mercury's displeasure; Aeneas is not only acting as Dido's architect (in Conington's phrase), but his dress and accoutrements are in luxurious eastern style. Thoughts of Mark Antony and Cleopatra may have entered the mind of the Roman reader.

14 **iaspide:** a Greek word denoting the precious stone jasper; it scans *iaspide*. It is probably the hilt of the sword rather than the scabbard that is be-starred with jasper.

15 262. **laena:** a thick outer cloak which would look particularly splendid in bright colours (Juv. 3.283).

16 263-4. **dives . . . fecerat:** 'a gift which rich Dido had made', i.e. a rich gift, as befitted a rich giver. *Munera* is poetic plural, adding impressiveness.

17 264. **telas discreverat:** 'had interwoven the texture'; *discreverat* is literally 'separated'.

Continuo invadit:[1] 'tu[2] nunc Karthaginis altae   265
fundamenta locas pulchramque uxorius[3] urbem
exstruis, heu regni rerumque oblite[4] tuarum?
Ipse[5] deum tibi me claro demittit Olympo
regnator, caelum et terras qui numine torquet;
ipse [6]haec ferre iubet celeris mandata per auras: 270
quid struis? Aut qua spe Libycis[7] teris otia terris?
Si te nulla movet tantarum gloria rerum
[nec super ipse tua moliris laude laborem,][8]
Ascanium surgentem et spes[9] heredis Iuli
respice, cui regnum Italiae Romanaque tellus   275
debetur.' Tali Cyllenius ore locutus
mortalis visus medio sermone reliquit
et procul in tenuem ex oculis evanuit[10] auram.

> *279-95. Aeneas is aghast and immediately decides to leave.*
> *He is now faced with the bitter prospect of trying to explain*
> *to Dido as best he can why he must leave the land and the*
> *woman he loves.*

[11]At vero [12]Aeneas aspectu obmutuit amens,
arrectaeque horrore comae et vox faucibus haesit.   280

---

1 265. **invadit**: 'he attacks him', a powerful word rarely used of speech, cf. Tac. *Ann.* 6.4.

2 **tu nunc**: notice the anger of the monosyllables before anything specific is said: you of all people, now of all times.

3 266. **uxorius**: 'under a wife's sway', very contemptuous, cf. Hor. *Odes* 1.2.19-20.

4 267. **oblite**: Virgil is very fond of attracting the predicate into the vocative, cf. *Aen.* 2.283.

5 268. **ipse deum tibi me**: notice the juxtaposition of the three pronouns representing the three actors in this drama, Jupiter himself, you, me. *Deum* is archaic genitive for *deorum,* as often.

6 270f. Much of Mercury's speech is repeated from Jupiter's; this is a very frequent feature of Homeric epic, but more unusual in Virgil. Here it is employed to bring home to the reader by reiteration the gravity of Aeneas' negligence.

7 271. **Libycis teris otia terris**: Mercury rewords the second half of line 235 by substituting *Libycis . . . terris* for *inimica in gente* (which Aeneas would not have understood and might have disputed), and intensifying *moratur* into *teris otia.* Notice the resultant disappearance of Jupiter's hiatus, and the introduction of the assonance of *ter.*

8 273. This line (an interpolation suggested by 233) is not in the major MSS, and should be omitted.

9 274. **spes heredis Iuli**: 'the hopes placed in your heir Iulus'; the genitive is probably objective (cf. 1.556, 6.364) rather than subjective ('the hopes Iulus has'). To call Aeneas' son Ascanius and Iulus in the same line emphasises the second name and draws the reader's attention to his destiny as the founder of the Julian line (see note on 1.267-8).

10 278. 'and vanished from sight far away into thin air'; a fine line on which Austin comments (with regard to the elision of *tenuem*) 'the syllable vanishes, just as the god does'. The line is repeated in 9.658 (of Apollo).

11 279f. In this brief passage, for the first time in the book, our attention is turned upon the feelings of Aeneas; so far Dido has occupied the stage. There is no wavering about his decision, no question in his mind of how he should react to this conflict between duty and love; he decides instantly and overwhelmingly for duty. It is only after the decision that we see into his mind and emotions as he tries to decide how best to explain to Dido that his love for her (see note on 291) must yield to his duty. He is a lonely figure amidst his rejoicing Trojans, and there is great irony and pathos in the description of his desperate efforts to decide how to approach her, for in the suite she is totally unable to understand his motivation, and in his attempted explanation (333f.) there is nothing either *mollis* (293) or *dexter* (294).

12 279. Notice the very marked assonance of initial *a*, (picked up at the beginning of each of the next three lines, and continued in the three after that) which seems to reinforce the powerful imagery and diction used to describe Aeneas' aghast amazement.

Ardet abire[1] fuga dulcisque relinquere terras,[2]
attonitus tanto monitu imperioque deorum.
Heu quid agat? [3]Quo nunc reginam ambire furentem
audeat adfatu? Quae prima exordia sumat?
Atque[4] animum nunc huc celerem nunc dividit illuc   285
in partisque rapit varias perque omnia versat.
Haec alternanti potior sententia visa est:
Mnesthea[5] Sergestumque vocat fortemque Serestum,
classem aptent[6] taciti sociosque ad litora cogant,
arma[7] parent et quae rebus[8] sit causa novandis   290
dissimulent; sese interea, quando optima[9] Dido
nesciat[10] et tantos rumpi non speret amores,
temptaturum aditus et quae mollissima fandi
tempora, quis rebus dexter modus. Ocius omnes
imperio laeti[11] parent et iussa facessunt.   295

---

1 **ambire**: 'approach', 'try to win over', *blanditiis circumvenire* (Servius); cf. *Aen.* 7.333, Hor. *Odes* 1.355.

2 281-2. These lines clearly express the conflict of love and duty in Aeneas, and his immediate recognition of guilt and decision for duty: Dido's country is *dulcis,* but he has received his mandate from heaven, and so is on fire to go, *ardet abire.* For *ardet* with the infinitive (a mainly poetical use) cf. *Aen.* 1.515.

3 283. Notice how the deliberative questions involve the reader in Aeneas' dilemma; cf. *Aen.* 9.399.

4 285-6. 'and he shoots his swift thoughts one way and another, rapidly directing them towards all kinds of aspects, turning them through all possibilities'; these lines, which are repeated in 8.20-1, are based on Homer's διανδιχα μερμηριξεν (e.g. *Il.* 1.189). Tennyson has 'this way and that dividing the swift mind.' The next line too is Homeric, e.g. *Il.* 2.5.

5 288. **Mnesthea**: Greek accusative. These men are captains of Aeneas' ships, cf. 5.1 16f., 1.510, 1.611.

6 289. **aptent**: this and the following verbs are jussive subjunctives, reporting Aeneas' orders which in direct speech would be imperatives.

7 290. **arma**: 'tackle', a nautical technical term (compare 299), cf. *Aen.* 5.15, 6.353. Servius and others take it to mean 'weapons', in case of a Carthaginian attack, but it seems unlikely that Aeneas is thinking along such lines.

8 **rebus . . . novandis**: 'for the change of plan'.

9 291. **optima Dido**: notice that the phrase is in oratio obliqua, reporting the words of Aeneas. It refers to the respect and gratitude which Aeneas feels towards Dido for her queenly qualities and gracious reception of the Trojans, while *tantos . . . amores* in the next line defines their relationship more personally. That Aeneas was in love with Dido is made very clear by Virgil (cf. also 221, 332, and especially 395); but he has now decided irrevocably to sacrifice his love for his mission.

10 293-4. 'he would look for a way of approaching her and try to find the kindest occasion for telling her, the right method for the purpose.' For the phraseology cf. Dido's words to Anna in 423.

11 295. **laeti**: the contrast between the enthusiastic Trojans, joyful to be on their way again, and the unhappy plight of Aeneas is very poignant.

296-330. Dido senses that Aeneas is preparing to leave; she becomes distraught like a Bacchanal, and then appeals to him in a speech of despair, reproach, and intense pathos.

[1]At[2] regina dolos (quis fallere possit amantem?)
praesensit,[3] motusque excepit prima futuros
omnia[4] tuta timens. Eadem[5] impia Fama furenti
detulit armari classem cursumque parari.
saevit inops animi totamque incensa per urbem   300
bacchatur, [6]qualis commotis[7] excita sacris
Thyias,[8] ubi audito stimulant trieterica Baccho[9]
orgia nocturnusque vocat clamore Cithaeron.
Tandem his Aenean compellat vocibus ultro:[10]
'dissimulare etiam sperasti, perfide,[11] tantum   305
posse nefas tacitusque mea decedere terra?[12]
Nec te noster amor nec te data[13] dextera quondam

---

1 296f. The series of three speeches of which this is the first relates the story of Dido and Aeneas closely to a Greek tragedy; we are reminded for example of the conflict of wills between Medea and Jason in Euripides' *Medea* (446f.), and the simile of 301f. brings the action into relationship with the tragic event of Euripides' *Bacchae*. There are other important literary sources too: the Medea of Apollonius (e.g. 4.355f.) and the Ariadne of Catullus 64. The influence of Catullus is especially marked in the pathos of the speech (see notes on 316, 327f.) but Dido's tragic plight is at a higher level of intensity. The pathos is deepened by the enormous contrast between her present helplessness and her past greatness and dignity; and the tragedy is the more terrible because of its inevitability. We know that her pleas, however moving, cannot possibly win Aeneas over because he is not free to be won.

2 296. **At regina**: see note on line 1.

3 297. Dido sensed Aeneas' plans before he came to tell her (*praesensit,* felt a 'presentiment') and first of anyone caught wind of the intended departure (one might have expected one of her subjects to see the preparations beginning, and rush to tell her, but Rumour gets there first). For *excipere* cf. Livy 2.4.5; for the general idea cf. the imitations in Ov. *Met.* 4.68, Val. Fl. 8.410f.

4 298. **omnia tuta timens**: 'anxious even when all seemed safe', not, with Henry, 'because everything seemed too quiet'; cf. Ov. *Met.* 7.47. Dido's conscience makes her uneasy (see Austin's notes on 297 and 298).

5 **eadem impia Fama**: 'it was that same evil Rumour . . .'; *eadem* refers back to 173f., *impia* to 174. Some take *eadem* as accusative plural, but this is unnatural.

6 301f. The simile, in which Dido is compared with a Bacchante (*Thyias*) wildly revelling on Mt. Cithaeron in Boeotia in honour of the god Bacchus, is of the utmost importance in the development of Dido's frenzy; it marks the point at which she begins to lose control of her actions, becomes 'possessed'. The nature of her frenzy has been stressed often indeed in this book (see note on 1f.) and the words *furenti* (298), *saevit inops animi,* *incensa* (300) reinforce what we know already. But the Bacchic simile goes much deeper, suggesting wild, uncontrolled behaviour and potential destruction; Virgil uses such a simile again to describe Amata (7.385f.) after she has been maddened by the fiend Allecto; (cf. also 10.41). The imagery (which is very dense) recalls Euripides' *Bacchae,* where the action takes place near Mt. Cithaeron; the feeling of impending tragedy is thus strengthened.

7 301. **commotis . . . sacris**: 'by the brandishing of the sacred emblems'; cf. Hor. *Odes* 1.18.11f.

8 302. **Thyias**: the epithet derives from θύειν, 'to rage'; the *-yi-* is a diphthong, and the word scans as a trochee.

9 302f. 'when the biennial rites arouse her as the Bacchic cry is heard, and Cithaeron calls her at night with its noise'. For *trieterica,* every three years by Roman inclusive reckoning, every two years for ours, cf. Ov. *Rem.* 593, *Met.* 6.587. *Audito . . . Baccho* means when the Bacchic cry (*euhoe Bacche,* 7.389) was heard, rather than when the god Bacchus was heard.

10 304. **ultro**: 'first', i.e. before he could speak to her.

11 305. The use of *perfide* is the first of a number of reminiscences of Ariadne's speech to Theseus in Cat. 64.132f. Notice the anger with which Dido begins, reflected in the hissing *s*'s as well as in the diction of the opening words; but her anger quickly gives way to entreaty.

12 306. For the omission of the reflexive subject (of *posse*) cf. *Aen.* 2.432-3.

13 307. **data dextera**: 'the pledge given', an indefinite phrase, which probably in the context with *amor* refers to the 'marriage' in the cave.

nec moritura[1] tenet crudeli funere Dido?

Quin etiam hiberno[2] moliris[3] sidere classem

et mediis properas Aquilonibus ire per altum,   310

crudelis? [4]Quid, si non arva aliena domosque

ignotas peteres, et Troia antiqua maneret,

Troia per undosum peteretur classibus aequor?

Mene fugis? [5]Per ego has lacrimas dextramque tuam te

(quando aliud mihi iam miserae nihil ipsa reliqui),   315

per conubia nostra, per inceptos hymenaeos,[6]

si bene quid de te merui, fuit aut tibi quicquam

dulce meum, miserere domus[7] labentis et istam,

oro, si quis adhuc precibus locus, exue mentem.

Te[8] propter Libycae gentes Nomadumque tyranni   320

odere, infensi[9] Tyrii; te propter eundem

exstinctus[10] pudor et, qua sola sidera adibam,

fama prior. Cui[11] me moribundam deseris, — hospes[12]

(hoc solum nomen quoniam de coniuge restat)?

---

1 308. **moritura:** the word is ambiguous; Aeneas doubtless takes it with reference to the danger from Dido's rejected suitors (cf. 323, 325f.) but the reader suspects another implication.

2 309. **hiberno . . . , sidere**: 'in the season of winter'; the metonymy of *sidus* for *tempestas* is common in certain contexts, cf. *Geo.* 1.1.

3 **moliris . . . classem**: 'are you busied with your fleet'; the verb is a favourite with Virgil, cf. 233 and *Aen.* 3.6.

4 311f. Dido says that Aeneas would not even set out for Troy (if it still existed) in such conditions; how then can he think of leaving for an unknown destination?

5 314f. Dido turns from the logic of the preceding lines to an appeal to pure pity; the simple words *mene fugis?* (do you want so much to get away from me?) convey strong pathos, which is continued by the broken word order normal with a prayer (cf. *Aen.* 12.56), the jerky hexameter ending of the pronouns *tuam te*, and the long accumulation of clauses before the main verb *miserere*.

6 316. A very clear imitation of Catullus' Ariadne (64.141) *sed conubia laeta, sed optatos hymenaeos*, the more noticeable because of the Greek type of rhythm with no main caesura and a quadri-syllabic ending. The nouns are synonyms, and *inceptos* means, as often, 'entered upon'; there is no implication, as some commentators suggest, that Dido thinks the wedding is incomplete.

7 318. **domus labentis:** 'a house destined for disaster'; Dido turns the emphasis from herself to her dynasty (cf. *Aen.* 12.59), hoping in this way to add an extra point to her argument, a point which she elaborates at length in the next lines.

8 320. **te propter**: 'because of *you*'; the postposition of *propter* is not common and here causes strong emphasis on *te*. Dido refers to the hostility of local tribes whose rulers she had rejected as suitors (36); presumably they accepted this when her plea was loyalty to the dead Sychaeus, but not when they were rejected in favour of a living Trojan.

9 321. **infensi Tyrii**: 'my Tyrians hate me', referring to her Carthaginian subjects. This is a new touch, not previously referred to, and it adds greatly here to Dido's plea of loneliness (cf. Eur. *Med.* 506f.); she had said nothing to Aeneas about the disapproval of her people while things went well between them.

10 322-3. 'my honour is lost and my one-time reputation, my only hope of reaching the stars'. For *pudor* see note on 27; she has been disloyal to Sychaeus, has not kept faith with him, and this as she now looks back could have been the one great achievement of her life. Compare Odysseus' words to his faithful Penelope (*Od.* 19.108) where he says that her reputation has reached the broad heavens; and Shakespeare, *Richard II*, 1.1.1 77f. 'The purest treasure mortal times afford / is spotless reputation; that away, / men are but gilded loam or painted clay.'

11 323. **cui**: 'to what' rather than 'to whom', cf. *Aen.* 2.678.

12 **hospes:** 'visitor'; this is what she called him in line 10, now it is all she can call the man who she had thought was her husband. Servius tells us that Virgil's voice showed great emotion when he read these lines to Augustus.

Quid[1] moror? An mea Pygmalion[2] dum moenia frater 325
destruat aut captam ducat Gaetulus Iarbas?
Saltem[3] si qua mihi de te suscepta fuisset
ante fugam suboles, si quis mihi parvulus aula
luderet Aeneas, qui te tamen ore referret,
non equidem omnino capta ac deserta viderer.' 330

> *331-61. Aeneas, because of Jupiter's commands, keeps his love hidden and replies coldly and formally. He ends by telling Dido of Mercury's appearance to him with instructions from heaven; he is therefore leaving her for Italy not of his own free will.*

[4]Dixerat. Ille Iovis monitis immota tenebat
lumina et obnixus curam sub corde premebat.[5]
Tandem pauca[6] refert: 'ego[7] te, quae plurima fando
enumerare vales, numquam, regina, negabo

---

1 325. **quid moror?:** 'why should I keep on?', i.e. 'what have I got to look forward to?'. She lists the unacceptable alternatives, leaving the implied answer, 'only death'.

2 325-6. For Pygmalion cf. 44, for Iarbas cf 36.

3 327f. 'At least if I had taken in my arms a child by you before you left, if a darling little Aeneas were playing in my palace, whose looks would remind me of you in spite of everything, then I would not indeed feel so utterly cheated and forlorn'. This is an appeal which, in Page's words, 'would move a stone'; it does move Aeneas, but it cannot change his resolution (331-2). Nowhere else in the *Aeneid* (or in epic) is such immediacy of feeling presented in this way. *Parvulus* is the only example of a diminutive adjective in the *Aeneid;* epic requires a type of diction which precludes the homely and intimate. We are reminded irresistibly of the diminutives of the private poetry of Catullus, and especially of Cat. 61.209f., *Torquatus volo parvulus.* . . . The fame of this astonishingly un-epic phrase is testified by Juvenal (5.138) in a passage of characteristic cynicism.
Notice the use made of the particles *saltem* (a spondaic word filling the first foot, see note on 185) and *tamen* (cf. 396). Notice too the 'more than pluperfect' of the unfulfilled condition (*suscepta fuisset*). For *capta = decepta* cf. *Aen.* 1.673, 2.196; for *deserta* cf. Ariadne in Cat. 64.57.

4 331f. Page (ad loc), in oft-quoted words, says 'Not all Virgil's art can make the figure of Aeneas here appear other than despicable'; he adds a cross reference to his introduction where he says 'To an appeal which would move a stone Aeneas replies with the cold and formal rhetoric of an attorney'. The second of these statements is largely true; the first is not. Virgil has taken the utmost care to convey the reasons why Aeneas' reply is cold; it is (331-2) because he knows he must not yield and therefore he smothers his love and his emotions. He endeavours to use logical and persuasive arguments to put his case (Servius points out some of the rhetorical devices, reminiscent of a *controversia*), honestly believing that Dido will see that he has no option. The tragedy is that neither of the lovers can understand the other's point of view. When all is said between them they are further apart than they were before. When Aeneas makes his final statement about Mercury he seems to be certain that Dido will see that he must obey; but she sees nothing except her own untenable predicament. Everything to her is personal between herself and Aeneas; she accepts no other considerations, indeed understands none. Aeneas' speech to her is indeed 'cold and formal', but Virgil has shown us very clearly that this is not because he feels no emotions but because he has decided that he must subdue them. Many readers of this speech would have wished it otherwise; but as it stands it is in full accord with Aeneas' acceptance of the almost intolerably heavy burden of duty. For further discussion see Austin's excellent note ad loc.

5 332. 'and with a great effort kept his love hidden in his heart'; for *curam* see note on line 1. Virgil has immediately given the reason why Aeneas' reply cannot be gentle; because of his divine instructions he does not meet her eyes and he stifles the anguish (cf. *Aen.* 1.209) which his love for Dido causes him. Notice how the phrases are coupled by the rhyme at the line-endings. These two lines must be kept firmly in mind as we read the deliberately cold and unemotional words which follow.

6 333. **pauca:** the speech is not in fact particularly short, but it contains little out of all that might have been said had Aeneas felt free to speak openly.

7 **ego te:** 'the two persons concerned face each other syntactically, as it were' (Austin).

promeritam, nec[1] me meminisse pigebit Elissae[2]   335
dum memor ipse mei, dum spiritus hos regit artus.
Pro[3] re pauca loquar. [4]Neque ego hanc abscondere[5] furto
speravi (ne finge) fugam, nec coniugis umquam
praetendi taedas aut haec in foedera veni.
Me si fata meis paterentur ducere vitam   340
auspiciis et sponte mea componere curas,
urbem Troianam primum dulcisque meorum
reliquias colerem[6], Priami tecta alta manerent,
et recidiva manu[7] posuissem Pergama victis.
Sed nunc Italiam magnam Gryneus[8] Apollo,   345
Italiam Lyciae iussere capessere tortes;
hic[9] amor, haec patria est. Si te Karthaginis arces
Phoenissam[10] Libycaeque aspectus detinet urbis,
quae[11] tandem Ausonia Teucros considere terra
invidia est? Et nos fas extera quaerere regna.   350
Me patris Anchisae, [12]quotiens umentibus umbris
nox operit terras, quotiens astra ignea surgunt,

---

1 335-6. 'and I shall never regret the memory of Elissa, as long as I have memory of myself and life rules these limbs'. The statement seems cold to the modern reader, but from a Stoic point of view (which Aeneas as a pious man should accept) it is rebellious, it shows failure to subdue personal wishes; Aeneas from this point of view should indeed have regretted the memory of his lapse from duty.

2 335. **Elissae**: this is Dido's original Phoenician name (see note on 1.340), used again in line 610 and *Aen.* 5.3 (always in the genitive; the name *Dido* is not used in the oblique cases). It does not seem that there is any difference other than metrical preference in the use of the two names.

3 337. **pro re pauca loquar**: 'I will speak briefly for my case'; these are very cold and formal words, as in a law court, deliberately chosen to prevent emotion from mastering his tongue.

4 337-9. Both these statements are true (he did not intend to go away secretly, nor did he propose marriage; Dido's interpretation of the events of the cave was entirely her own); but their plain and brutal truth is not likely to comfort Dido. Notice the insistent spondees of 339.

5 337-8. **abscondere . . . speravi**: for the present infinitive with *spero* cf. *Aen.* 5.18 and compare 425-6, *Aen.* 11.503.

6 343. **colerem**: 'I would be looking after'; Aeneas' behaviour in Book 2 justifies this claim; he was reluctant to accept the divine instructions that he should leave Troy. By *Priami tecta alia manerent* Aeneas does not mean that he could have saved it from the Greeks, but that he would have rebuilt it and it would be existing now, still called Priam's palace though Priam was dead.

7 344. 'and I would myself (*manu*) have founded a re-born Pergama for the conquered'; after the Greek destruction he would have rebuilt Troy if he had been free to do so. Some early versions of the legend said that he did stay in Troy and did restore it.

8 345. **Gryneus Apollo**: there was a wood sacred to Apollo at Grynium in Lydia; we have not previously heard of a prophecy associated with Grynium, nor of these *Lyciae sortes* (for Apollo's oracle in Lycia see note on 143); it was the Penates in Crete (3.166) who, interpreting Apollo's previous oracle at Delos, first revealed to Aeneas the name Italy. It is probable therefore that Aeneas refers to this oracle, giving Apollo two of his familiar epithets without meaning that the oracle was given in these places; less likely is the possibility that messages reached Aeneas from these places before he left the Troad.

9 347. **hic amor, haec patria est**: 'this is my love, this is my homeland'; the attraction of gender is normal. Aeneas is not free to yield to personal feelings of love (307); Italy has to be his love.

10 348. **Phoenissam**: a Phoenician (from Tyre); cf. *Aen.* 1.670, 714.

11 349-50. **quae . . . invidia**: 'why begrudge. . .?'; for the infinitive after a noun see note on 1.704.

12 351f. This is another fact from the past (cf. 345) of which we have not previously heard; it is referred to again in 6.695f. Mackail points out the psychological insight with which Virgil portrays Aeneas here; he remembers things pointing in the same direction as Mercury's instructions though they had little impact on him at the time.

admonet in somnis et turbida[1] terret imago;
me puer Ascanius capitisque[2] iniuria cari,[3]
quem regno Hesperiae fraudo et fatalibus[4] arvis.   355
Nunc[5] etiam interpres divum Iove missus ab ipso
(testor utrumque[6] caput) celeris mandata per auras
detulit: ipse deum manifesto in lumine vidi
intrantem muros vocemque his auribus hausi.[7]
Desine[8] meque tuis incendere teque querelis;   360
Italiam non sponte sequor.'

*362-92. Dido in reply assails her lover with angry hatred
and scorn; she rejects his arguments utterly and calls down
curses upon him. Finally she prays for vengeance and the
knowledge of vengeance.*

[9]Talia dicentem iamdudum aversa[10] tuetur
huc illuc volvens oculos totumque[11] pererrat
luminibus[12] tacitis et sic accensa profatur:

---

1 353. **turbida:** 'agitated', cf. *Aen.* 6.694 *quam metui. . .* and 695 *tua tristis imago.*

2 354. **capitisque iniuria cari**: 'the wrong being done to one so dear'; the genitive is objective. For the use of *caput* cf. 613, Hor. *Odes* 1.24.2

3 354f. A verb like *movet* has to be supplied from the sense of the previous line. Aeneas here restates the message he received from Mercury (274f.).

4 355. **fatalibus arvis**: 'fated fields', his by destiny; cf. *Aen.* 582.

5 356f. This is the fact which Aeneas feels sure must convince Dido. Notice the way it is constructed: *nunc etiam* (there is something else which has just happened); *interpres divum Iove missus ab ipso* (what could be more conclusive?); *testor utrumque caput* (and I swear that it did happen); *mandata* (specific instructions, no option is given, no question of trying to interpret the meaning); *ipse* (I saw him in person); *manifesto in lumine* (in clear light, it was no vague dream); *intrantem muros* (he didn't suddenly appear, I watched him arrive); *vocemque his auribus hausi* (and I heard his words with my own ears). After this Aeneas feels no further arguments are needed, and he concludes simply: 'so don't prolong our agony; I am forced to go.' How little it all meant to Dido is shown by her mockery of these words (377f.).

6 357. **utrumque caput**: his own and Dido's (cf. Ov. *Her.* 3.107, Ap. Rh. 3.151).

7 359. **hausi**: an unusual usage, cf. *Aen.* 6.559, 12.26, Livy 27.51.1. The metaphor is the same as with *bibere* (*Hor. Odes* 2. 13-32).

8 360-1. 'Stop making us both emotional by your pleas; I go to Italy not of my own free will'. Pease quotes Rand's excellent phrases: 'These last words resume in brief compass the elements of the tragedy that confronts Aeneas: *Italiam* , his mission; *non sponte,* his love; *sequor,* his resolution'. It is hard to imagine how Virgil would have completed this half-line; 'four words thus left rugged and abrupt' (Page).

9 362f. Charles James Fox, quoted by Henry, said of this passage 'on the whole' perhaps the finest thing in all poetry'. Dido's speech has something in common with the words of Medea in Euripides (*Med.* 465f.) and in Apollonius (4.355f.) but Virgil has used the resources of Latin rhetoric and hexameter technique to make it into something quite different.
The contrast with Dido's previous speech is very marked. There she had pleaded with Aeneas in words of intense pathos; here she has given up all hope of prevailing upon him, and with this realisation she changes into an archetypal symbol of hatred and revenge. Communication with her as an ordinary human being is no longer possible; what she has suffered has changed her into a kind of fury of vengeance. We feel the inevitability of the kind of frenzied progression towards disaster which is so familiar in Greek tragedy. This speech is highly rhetorical, frighteningly remote from the give-and-take of human behaviour; the frustration of hopes and pride has led to an elaborately formalised and grandiose concentration of all the hatred of her outraged heart.

10 362. **aversa tuetur**: 'she had been watching him without looking at him', a very striking paradox where the literal meaning ('askance') merges with the metaphorical meaning; she rejects his every word. Similarly her ghost rejects him (*aversa*) in *Aen.* 6.469.

11 363. **totumque pererrat**: 'scanning him up and down'; there is no parallel for this use of *pererrare* with a personal object. Aeneas no longer seems human to Dido.

12 364. **luminibus tacitis**: 'with expressionless eyes', cf. Ov. *Am.* 2.5.17 *non oculi tacuere tui* ('your eyes spoke to me').

'nec[1] tibi diva parens generis nec Dardanus auctor,   365

perfide, sed duris genuit te cautibus horrens

Caucasus Hyrcanaeque[2] admorunt[3] ubera tigres.

Nam[4] quid dissimulo aut quae me ad maiora reservo?

Num[5] fletu ingemuit nostro? Num lumina flexit?

Num lacrimas victus dedit aut miseratus amantem est?   370

Quae[6] quibus anteferam? Iam iam nec maxima Iuno

nec[7] Saturnius haec oculis pater aspicit aequis.

Nusquam tuta fides.[8] Eiectum litore, egentem

excepi et regni demens in parte locavi.

Amissam classem, [9]socios a morte reduxi   375

(heu[10] furiis incensa feror!): [11]nunc augur Apollo,

nunc Lyciae sortes, nunc et Iove missus ab ipso

interpres divum fert horrida iussa per auras.

Scilicet[12] is superis labor est, ea cura quietos

sollicitat. Neque te teneo neque dicta refello: 380

---

1 365f. Dido's opening words are a rhetorical commonplace; she has nothing from the heart to say to Aeneas now, and she has recourse to a formally elaborate imprecation. Invective based on parentage goes back to Homer (*Il.* 16.33f.); cf. also Eur. *Bacc.* 987f., Cat. 60.1f., 64.154f., and the many parallels given by Pease (ad loc). Here there is particular point in the reversal of what Dido had earlier said in her very first words to Aeneas (1.615f.), where she had asked if he was in very truth the one who was born of Venus to Anchises (*tune ille Aeneas . . .*); compare also her words to Anna in line 12. Now she denies it all, she has been duped by treachery (*perfide,* repeated from 305).

2 367. 'and Hyrcanian tigresses gave you suck'; Hyrcania was an area near the Caucasus Mts. and the Caspian Sea. Cf. Shakespeare, 3 *Henry VI*, 1.4.154-5. 'But you are more inhuman, more inexorable, / O ten times more, than tigers of Hyrcania'.

3 **admorunt**: contracted for *admoverunt.*

4 368. 'For why should I pretend, or for what more crucial moment hold myself back?' Notice the staccato rhetorical questions in this line and the next three. The vivid indicative is used for the deliberative subjunctive (cf. 534 and *Aen.* 3.88). Dido feels that she has been finally rejected, and there is therefore no reason why she should not speak her true feelings; the possibility of pleading is gone.

5 369f. The tricolon with anaphora of *num* is in the highest rhetorical style, and the distancing of her words by the use of the third person is a cold and formal indication of the distance that now separates the lovers.

6 371. **quae quibus anteferam?**: 'what shall I say first, what second?' (literally 'what shall I prefer to what?'). This rhetorical question could come from a Ciceronian speech. Servius gives it the rhetorical tag 'amphibolia' and explains that it suggests that *omnia et paria et magna sunt.*

7 372. **nec Saturnius**: the diaeresis after the second foot gives a most unusual rhythm (cf. 385); the epithet (which is frequent for Juno) is not used elsewhere in Virgil for Jupiter.

8 373f. 'He was shipwrecked on my shore, destitute, and I took him in . . .'. Notice the alliteration of *e,* the asyndeton, and the unusual pause in the fifth foot.

9 375f. As the fires of frenzy burn hotter in Dido her words become more disjointed: to *amissam classem* we must supply from *a morte reduxi* some verb like *servavi,* and the tricolon introduced by repeated *nunc* has no verb for the first two nouns.

10 376. **heu furiis incensa feror**: 'oh I am whirled by the furies on winds of fire'; cf. *Aen.* 12.946.

11 376f. Dido now mocks Aeneas' words (345, 346, 356-7), and the slight variation (*horrida iussa* for *mandate*) increases the sarcasm by the use of an adjective in which she does not believe.

12 379f. As Dido's overwhelming anger and scorn overcome her, the metre becomes agitated and violent through the almost total conflict of accent and ictus in this and the following four lines. The sarcastic word *scilicet* and the hissing of *s*'s are pointers for the bitterness of her words about the gods; both *labor* and *sollicitat* are ironical as applied to the gods, and her statement immediately associates her with Epicurean ideas; the word *quietus* is used by Lucretius of the Epicurean deities (e.g. 6.73). Dido is not prepared to believe that anyone should sacrifice his personal life to requirements supposed to be imposed by the gods. It is a conflict between belief in a man-centred universe and belief in a divinely controlled world.

i,[1] sequere Italiam ventis, pete regna per undas.
Spero[2] equidem mediis, si quid pia numina possunt,
supplicia hausurum[3] scopulis et nomine Dido
saepe vocaturum. [4]Sequar atris ignibus absens
et, cum frigida mors anima[5] seduxerit artus,   385
omnibus umbra locis adero. Dabis, improbe, poenas.
Audiam et haec[6] manis veniet mihi fama sub imos.'
His medium[7] dictis sermonem abrumpit et auras
aegra fugit[8] seque ex oculis avertit et aufert,
linquens multa metu cunctantem et multa parantem 390
dicere. Suscipiunt famulae conlapsaque membra
marmoreo referunt thalamo stratisque reponunt.

> *393-415. Aeneas, in spite of his longing to comfort Dido, returns to the fleet. The Trojans make their preparations for departure. Dido in her misery determines to make one further appeal to Aeneas through her sister Anna.*

At pius[9] Aeneas, quamquam lenire dolentem

---

1 381. **i, sequere**: the rhetorical device (often *i nunc*) is called *permissio*. The first phrase of this line echoes 361, the second 350.

2 382f. 'I hope, indeed I hope, if the righteous deities have any power, that you will drain the cup of punishment on rocks in mid-ocean, and often call on the name of Dido'. The word order, with the wide separation of *mediis . . . scopulis* seems to emphasise the hoped for isolation of her shipwrecked lover, far from human aid. The parenthesis bitterly recalls Aeneas' promise to Dido in 1.603f., and the use of the epithet *pius* against Aeneas is full of irony. Dido's use of her own name adds pathos; cf. 308, 596 and Catullus' frequent use of his own name in his lyrics.

3 383. **hausurum:** for the omission of the pronoun (*te*) cf. 105, 493.

4 384f. At the middle of this line the conflict of accent and ictus changes to coincidence, which continues at the beginning of the next two lines: the effect is to convey a kind of deliberateness (emphasised by sonorous alliteration of *m* and *n*), as Dido collects herself for her final measured curse. In two places the coincidence is very marked; the fourth foot of this line consisting of a single spondee (for full discussion of this see my note on *Aen.* 5.116, OUP Ed.); and the second foot of the next line consisting of a single dactyl.

The diction contains elements of ambiguity and foreboding. In *atris ignibus* the primary meaning is the murky torches of the Furies (cf. 7.456); Dido, like Medea in Ap. Rh. 4.386, will be a fiend of vengeance. But there is also (as Servius saw) a hint at the flames of her funeral pyre (cf. lines 661-2). Similarly the reference to her death may suggest, though she does not say so, that it will be the means of her vengeance. Finally the vagueness of *umbra* makes her threat broader; her soul will be in the underworld (387), but visions, phantoms, memories of her will always and everywhere haunt Aeneas.

5 385. **anima seduxerit artus**: 'has severed body from soul', an unusual phrase (called hypallage by Servius because *animam artubus* would be more normal).

6 387. **haec . . . imos:** 'the report of it will reach me deep in the underworld'; for the local meaning of *manes,* 'place of the shades', cf. *Geo.* 1.243. Dido's bloodcurdling speech concludes with the expression of her distraught desire for vengeance and also for the knowledge that she has achieved it.

7 388. **medium ... sermonem**: cf. line 277; the meaning is not that the speech is unfinished but that no opportunity is given for reply.

8 389. 'leaving him frightened, deeply uncertain, rehearsing many answers'; notice the rhyme of *-antem,* indicating the dinning insistence in Aeneas' mind.

9 393. **pius Aeneas:** some commentators have here failed to understand the significance Virgil has put into the use of the epithet. Page, for example, says (intro. p. xix) 'Virgil . . begins the next paragraph quite placidly *at pius Aeneas. . .*! How the man who wrote the lines placed in Dido's mouth could immediately afterwards speak of 'the good Aeneas etc.' is one of the puzzles of literature'. But the only possible defence for Aeneas' actions is his *pietas;* in any other capacity than as man of destiny he should have stayed; *pietas* is why he must leave, and Virgil wants us to know this. It may be that many (presumably including Page) would wish that *pietas* had not prevailed, but it is utterly wrong to object to being told that it has done so.

We might translate 'But Aeneas, because of duty . . . .' For further discussion see Austin's excellent note ad loc.

solando cupit et dictis avertere curas,

multa gemens magnoque[1] animum labefactus amore   395

iussa[2] tamen divum exsequitur classemque revisit.

Tum[3] vero Teucri incumbunt et litore celsas

deducunt toto navis. Natat[4] uncta carina,

frondentisque ferunt remos[5] et robora silvis

infabricata fugae studio.   400

Migrantis cernas[6] totaque ex urbe ruentis:

ac velut[7] ingentem formicae farris acervum[8]

cum populant hiemis memores tectoque reponunt,

it[9] nigrum campis agmen praedamque per herbas

convectant calle angusto; pars grandia[10] trudunt   405

obnixae frumenta umeris, pars agmina cogunt[11]

castigantque moras, opere omnis semita fervet.

Quis tibi tum,[12] Dido, cernenti talia sensus,

quosve dabas gemitus, cum litora fervere[13] late

prospiceres arce ex summa, totumque videres   410

misceri[14] ante oculos tantis clamoribus aequor!

---

1 395. **magnoque ... amore**: 'shaken to the heart by his great love'; the nature of the conflict in Aeneas is once more powerfully emphasised. For the construction of *animum* see note on 137, and cf. *Aen*. 3.47 *mentem formidine pressus*.

2 396. **iussa tamen divum**: the Stoic, in times of personal sorrow, consoled himself with the formula *dis aliter visum* (the will of the gods was otherwise). This is what Aeneas has to do.

3 397. Once again, as in 294-5, Virgil stresses the joy of the Trojans in contrast to the sorrow of Aeneas.

4 398. **natat uncta carina**: 'the vessel shiny with pitch goes afloat'; the use of the singular here gives a sudden picture of one of the many ships as it is launched. For *natat* cf. Cat. 4.3, *Aen*. 8.93.

5 399f. 'and they bring oars with leaves still on and unshaped logs from the woods in their eagerness to depart'; i.e. the branches for oars and the logs, for general repairs during the voyage, are brought on board untrimmed; for the phrases cf. *Aen*. 1.552.

6 401. **cernas**: 'you could have seen them'; for the second person, and for the use of the vivid present, cf. *Aen*. 8.691.

7 402. **ac velut**: for the. elliptical way of introducing a simile ('and it was as when') cf. *Aen*. 2.626, 6.707.

8 402f. The simile is very typically Virgilian, reminiscent of the poet of the *Georgics* (cf. especially *Geo*. 1.185-6); compare the bee similes in *Aen*. 1.430f., 6.707f., 12.587f. Apart from one example in Apollonius (4.1452f., where ants are mentioned briefly along with flies) this is the only simile in Greek or Latin epic concerned with ants. The main point of comparison, of course, is bustle and busy movement, but there is an important subsidiary point, namely smallness and distance. We are invited to see the Trojans as Dido saw them from her palace, tiny, far off, remote from her now.

9 404. **it . . . agmen**: from Ennius, who according to Servius applied the phrase to elephants. Virgil gives a most attractive mock grandeur to the world of the ants; notice the spondaic movement of this line and the next two, conveying the mighty effort involved.

10 405. **grandia:** a splendid touch; compare the description of the mouse from a mouse's point of view in *Geo*. 1.181-2.

11 406. **cogunt:** 'marshal', a military term, cf. Tac. *Hist*. 2.68 *agminis coactores;* this kind of personification is frequent with the bees in *Geo*. 4 (e.g. 67f., 82f.).

12 408. 'What were your feelings, Dido, then, when you saw all this?' The apostrophe here is enormously effective; the personal involvement of the poet with Dido's tragic plight is such that his direct address to her seems natural and real rather than rhetorical; compare *Aen*. 3.710.

13 409. **fervere:** notice the third conjugation form (cf. 567), fairly frequent in the poets but rather remarkable here after *fervet* (407). Compare also *fulgere* (*Aen*. 6.826), *stridere* (*Geo*. 4.556).

14 411. **misceri . . . tantis clamoribus**: 'a confusion of shouting and noise'; for this use of *misceri* cf. 160.

Improbe[1] Amor, quid non mortalia pectora cogis!
Ire iterum in lacrimas, iterum temptare precando
cogitur et supplex animos summittere amori,
ne quid inexpertum frustra[2] moritura relinquat.   415

> *416-49. Dido begs Anna to make a further appeal to Aeneas,*
> *asking him to wait for favourable weather before he*
> *departs; she asks just for time to accustom herself to her*
> *sorrow. But Aeneas is resolute, like an oak tree buffeted by*
> *the gales but not overthrown.*

[3]Anna, vides[4] toto properari litore circum:
undique convenere; vocat iam carbasus auras,
puppibus et laeti nautae imposuere coronas.
Hunc ego si[5] potui tantum sperare[6] dolorem,
et perferre, soror, potero. Miserae hoc tamen unum[7]   420
exsequere, Anna,[8] mihi; solam nam perfidus ille
te colere,[9] arcanos etiam tibi credere sensus;
sola viri mollis aditus et tempora noras:[10]
i, soror, atque hostem[11] supplex adfare superbum:

---

1 412. 'Tyrant love, to what do you not drive mortal hearts?' Virgil follows his moving apostrophe to Dido with a different kind of subjective intrusion into the narrative, a reflexion on what has happened to his characters (cf. 3.56-7). The line is based on Ap. Rh. 4.445 (cf. 3.297) when Medea purposes to kill her brother so that she can escape with her lover, and the poet reflects on the cruelty of love. Virgil's epithet *improbus* implies excess (cf. *Aen.* 2.80 and see Austin on 4.386). Dido is like the slave of an all-powerful tyrant, under a compulsion which she cannot or will not resist.

2 415. **frustra moritura:** 'and go to her death in vain', i.e. she has resolved to die if she finds no way of keeping Aeneas, so she must first try every way to keep him.

3 416f. Dido's last plea, made through Anna, makes the pathos of her situation even more apparent as she relents from the implacable anger of her last speech; and the dilemma of Aeneas is once again presented with intense insight. The simile of the oak tree is preceded by phrases of tension; *nullis ille movetur fletibus ... aut voces ullas tractabilis audit . . . fata obstant . . . placidasque viri deus obstruit auris.* The pressure on the oak tree is violent; *Alpini Boreae nunc hinc nunc flatibus illinc eruere inter se certant. . . it stridor. . . consternunt terram frondes . . . concusso stipite;* and so with Aeneas; *tunditur . . . persentit curas.* The final unforgettable line: *mens immota manet, lacrimae volvuntur inanes* summarises the conflict and its resolution more poignantly than Aeneas' own summary *Italiam non sponte sequor* (361), but to exactly the same effect.

4 **416. vides . . . circum:** 'you see the bustle going on around all along the shore'; *properari* is impersonal passive, *circum* is an adverb. Some editors punctuate so that *circum* goes with the next line, this is highly improbable, as is well argued by Henry.

5 419. **si potui:** 'if I was able'; the surface meaning is *(si = siquidem)* 'as surely as I was able': Anna understands Dido to mean that she had expected it, and will endure it. But *si* may also be taken ironically: 'if I could have expected it (but I could not), then, as is not the case, I shall be able also to bear it'; cf. Hor. *Odes* 3.5.31f.

6 419. **sperare:** 'expect', as in 292, *Aen.* 11.275.

7 420-1. 'But perform for me, Anna, in my misery, this one favour'. The dislocation of rhythm at the line ending (see Austin ad loc.) expresses something of Dido's agitation.

8 421f. Servius reports from Varro a version of the tradition according to which it was Anna with whom Aeneas fell in love; the suggestion here of a close relationship between them may be a trace of that view.

9 422. **colere:** the historic infinitive is here used for repeated or continuous action, cf. *Aen.* 2.98, 11.822.

10 423. **noras:** notice the past tense (*noveras*); in spite of the new appeal she is to make, Dido subconsciously puts Aeneas in the past. The phraseology of the line is reminiscent of 293 where Aeneas has to approach Dido as best he can; now the situation is reversed.

11 424. These are measured and chilling words: Aeneas has changed from *coniunx* to *hospes* (323) and now to *hostis;* he has conquered and in the pride of his victory can only be addressed in suppliant tones. Dido torments herself with words she had never thought to speak to anyone.

non ego cum Danais Troianam exscindere[1] gentem[2]   425
Aulide iuravi classemve ad Pergama misi,
nec patris Anchisae cineres manisve revelli:
cur mea dicta negat[3] duras demittere in auris?
Quo ruit? Extremum hoc miserae det munus amanti:
exspectet facilemque fugam ventosque ferentis.   430
Non iam coniugium antiquum, quod prodidit, oro,
nec pulchro[4] ut Latio careat regnumque relinquat:[5]
tempus inane peto, requiem spatiumque furori,
dum mea me victam doceat fortuna dolere.
Extremam hanc oro veniam[6] (miserere sororis),   435
quam[7] mihi cum dederit cumulatam morte remittam.'
　　Talibus orabat, talisque miserrima fletus
fertque[8] refertque soror. Sed nullis ille movetur
fletibus, aut voces ullas tractabilis[9] audit;
fata obstant placidasque viri deus[10] obstruit auris.   440

---

1 425-6. **exscindere . . . iuravi**: for the construction see note on 337-8.

2 425f. Dido begins rhetorically (Quint. 9.2.39 calls this figure *aversio*) by enumerating acts which would have justified Aeneas in refusing to hear her, acts of which she is innocent: she was not an ally of the Greeks when they gathered at Aulis in N. Greece (Hom. *Il.* 2.303) to sail against Troy; nor has she committed sacrilege against the grave of Anchises. The second of these statements is strange: Servius relates a vague story about a tradition that Diomedes did in fact profane Anchises' grave, and it has been suggested that Dido recalls in a confused way Aeneas' words of 351-3; but it seems best to regard it as a thought which Dido wildly throws out as she seeks for imaginary and heinous crimes which she has not committed.

3 428. **negat . . . demittere**: for the infinitive with *negare* in the sense of 'refuse' cf. *Geo.* 2.215-16, 3.207-8, and compare *Aen.* 2.637. For *demittere* cf. Livy 34.50.2.

4 432. The irony of *pulchro* (cf. 266) is reinforced by its position before the word introducing its clause (*ut*); notice the alliteration of *r* and *q* in the last two words.

5 433-4. 'I want just time, a respite and a breathing space for my madness, till my fate can teach my vanquished heart how to grieve'. By *tempus inane* she means that the time would be useless to her for any other purpose than gradually to heal her wound; there was nothing she could do with it, it was mere time.

6 435. **veniam:** 'favour', as often, cf. *Aen.* 1.519.

7 436. 'and when he has granted it to me, I will pay it back with interest when I die'. The last phrase is purposely ambiguous, indeed obscure: Anna presumably understands it to be a vague reference to some intended benevolence (perhaps she will take back her threat of haunting him), but the reader (prepared for Dido's tragic intention, 415) visualises Dido paying back Aeneas' loan of time at the price of her death. This will be her gift in return for his: cf. *Ecl.* 8.59f., *praeceps aerii specula de montis in undas / deferar; extremum hoc munus morientis habeto.* For *dederit* (so the best MSS) Servius read *dederis*, which destroys the ambiguity in the next phrase. *Cumulatam* is a financial metaphor, 'with interest' (Livy 2.23.6, Cic. *Phil.* 14.30); for *remittam* in this sense cf. *Aen.* 11.359.

8 438. **fertque refertque:** 'took and took again', cf. *Aen.* 12.866.

9 439. **tractabilis:** 'sympathetically', literally 'able to be dealt with', cf. line 53 and Suet. *Aug.* 65 *Agrippam nihilo tractabiliorem.*

10 440. 'The fates stand in the way, and the god blocks his kindly mortal ears'. The juxtaposition of *viri* and *deus* expresses in little the essence of the matter: personally as a man he would have listened, but as an instrument of destiny he cannot. For the sense of *placidas* cf. *Aen.* 7.194, 11.251, Ov. *Pont.* 1.2.127, Stat. *Th.* 5.732. Others take it proleptically; 'so that they were unmoved, tranquil', but this is inappropriate for *placidas* and far less significant in the context. See Pearce in *C.R.* 1968, p. 13.

Ac[1] velut[2] annoso[3] validam cum robore quercum
Alpini[4] Boreae nunc hinc nunc fiatibus illinc
eruere inter se certant; it stridor, et altae
consternunt terram concusso stipite frondes;
ipsa[5] haeret scopulis et quantum vertice ad auras   445
aetherias, tantum radice in Tartara tendit:
haud secus adsiduis hinc atque hinc vocibus heros
tunditur, et magno persentit pectore curas;
mens immota manet, lacrimae[6] volvuntur inanes.

450-73. Dido now resolves on death, and is confirmed in her resolution by terrible portents and the memory of ancient prophecies. She has nightmare dreams of Aeneas pursuing her, and of her utter desolation; she is like Pentheus or Orestes hounded by the Furies.

[7]Tum vero infelix fatis[8] exterrita Dido   450
mortem orat; taedet caeli[9] convexa tueri.
Quo magis inceptum peragat lucemque relinquat,
vidit, turicremis[10] cum dona imponeret aris,
(horrendum dictu) latices[11] nigrescere sacros

---

1 441f. The simile, which is developed at unusual length, gives a magnificent image of resolution which is assailed but not overthrown: the tree is fully grown, strong, deeply rooted, and though it creaks in the gales and its trunk is shaken so that its leaves fall, it remains firmly fixed in its place. Virgil has very greatly developed his sources (Hom. *Il.* 12.131f., 16.765f.; cf. also Cat. 64.105f.); he has applied to mental strength what is generally an image of physical strength. Dryden imitates the passage (*Annus Mirabilis* 61) 'All bare, like some old Oak which tempests beat, / He stands, and sees below his scatter'd leaves'.

2 441. **ac velut... cum**: 'and just as when . . .'; this time *ac* has its own clause introduced by *haud secus* (447); contrast 402.

3 **annoso validam ... robore**: 'mighty with the strength of years', cf. *Aen.* 6.282, 10.766.

4 442. **Alpini Boreae**: the localisation in N. Italy suggests Virgil's persona] experience.

5 445f. 'but itself, it holds firmly to its rocks, reaching as far with its roots towards Tartarus as it does with its topmost branches towards the breezes of heaven'; *ipsa* contrasts the immovable tree with its falling leaves. The words *quantum . . . tendit* are repeated from *Geo.* 2.291-2.

6 449. 'his purpose remains unmoved, the tears fall in vain'. Whose tears? Servius says those of Aeneas (so Augustine, *C.D.* 9.4), maintaining that this phrase corresponds with the falling leaves of the tree (an unlikely reason), but adds that others think they are Dido's and Anna's too. The fact is that Virgil has not said whose tears; by not specifying he widens the area of sorrow, generalises this particular conflict into the universal conflict of pity with duty. For *lacrimae inanes* cf. *Aen.* 10.465; for the Stoic attitude (not unfeeling but resolute) cf. Sen. *Dial.* 1.2.2, *Ep. Mor.* 9.3.

7 450f. The narrative now becomes laden with death. Dido is encompassed with ghastly and supernatural horrors; portents of which she does not speak even to Anna, supernatural voices in the dead of night, dinning memories of ancient prophecies, nightmares of terror and desolation. The theme of Greek tragedy — *thus quos vult perdere dementat prius* — is powerfully predominant and given absolutely explicit statement in the double simile (469f.) where Dido is compared with Pentheus and Orestes, two of the most famous tragic heroes of the Greek stage.

8 450. **fatis exterrita**: 'distraught by doom'; she now sees no way out from the fate she has settled for herself.

9 451. **caeli convexa**: 'the vaults of heaven', cf. *Aen.* 6.241, Cic. *Arat.* 314 *convexum caeli.*

10 453. **turicremis**: 'incense-burning', a vivid compound adjective, cf. Lucr. 2.353; see note on 3.544.

11 454. **latices ... sacros**: 'holy water'; Servius thought that *Latices* was the same as *vina* in the next line. This is possible, but it seems more likely that Virgil is describing two different aspects of the portent.

fusaque in obcenum[1] se vertere vina cruorem.   455

Hoc visum nulli, non ipsi effata sorori.

Praeterea fuit in tectis de marmore[2] templum

coniugis antiqui, miro quod honore colebat,

velleribus[3] niveis et festa fronde revinctum:

hinc exaudiri voces et verba vocantis   460

visa viri, nox cum terras obscura teneret,

solaque[4] culminibus ferali carmine bubo

saepe queri et longas in fletum ducere voces;

multaque praeterea vatum praedicta priorum[5]

terribili monitu horrificant. [6]Agit ipse furentem[7]   465

in somnis ferus[8] Aeneas, semperque relinqui

sola sibi, semper longam incomitata videtur

ire viam et Tyrios deserta quaerere terra,

[9]Eumenidum[10] veluti demens videt agmina[11] Pentheus

et solem geminum et duplices se ostendere Thebas,   470

---

1 455. **obscenum**: 'loathsome', one of the very strongest words available; cf. *Aen.* 3.241, and especially *Geo.* 1.470 where the word occurs in the list of horrible omens and portents at Julius Caesar's death.

2 457f. For the marble shrine dedicated to Sychaeus cf. Ov. *Her.* 7.99f.; for the custom cf. Cic. *Verr.* 2.4.4 and Servius' note on *Aen.* 6.152.

3 460f. 'From the shrine she thought she heard sounds, the words of her husband calling her'; notice the eerie alliteration of *v*.

4 462f. 'and the lonely owl often moaning on rooftops with its ill-boding song, prolonging its drawn-out hooting into a wail'; the assonance of the long vowels imitates the uncanny sound. For the ill-omened owl cf. *Aen.* 12.862f., Ov. *Ibis* 223-4, *Met.* 5.549f., and for more examples Pease's monumental note ad loc. Compare Shakespeare, *Macbeth* 2.2.4-5 'It was the owl that shriek'd, the fatal bellman, / which gives the stern'st goodnight'; and for *queri* Gray's *Elegy* 10 'The moping owl does to the moon complain'.

5 464. **priorum**: 'of olden days'; Dido recalls far-off prophecies which she had ignored at the time. The reading in some MSS, *piorum,* known to Servius, is much inferior.

6 465. The clash of word accent with ictus in this line conveys agitation; in each of the first four feet the word accent is on the second syllable of a dactyl.

7 465f. Dido's dream is a reflexion of her state of mind (cf. Medea's dream in Ap. Rh. 3.616f.); this is rare in dream descriptions, which generally are used for prophecy or revelation (see note on 2.268f.). There is an other-worldly terror about her dream; she is being pursued, she is all alone on an endless road, she cannot find any friends (cf. 320). In this respect it resembles Ilia's dream in Ennius (*Ann.* 39f.); the nearest parallel in the *Aeneid* is 12.908f.

8 466. **ferus**: Aeneas as proud enemy (424) becomes in Dido's dream a hunter pursuing a terrified quarry.

9 469f. The doubled simile illustrates Dido's frenzy, and relates her very specifically with the heroes of Greek tragedies: first she is compared with the demented Pentheus (King of Thebes) of Euripides' *Bacchae,* driven to tragic madness by Dionysus so that he sees two suns in the sky, two cities of Thebes (Eur. *Bacch.* 918-19); and secondly with Orestes, son of Agamemnon, as portrayed in Aeschylus' *Eumenides,* when after having killed his mother Clytemnestra to avenge her murder of his father he is pursued by the ghost of his mother and the Furies. There were many Roman tragedies on these subjects, by Accius, Pacuvius and others.

10 469. **Eumenidum**: the Greek euphemism ('kindly ones') for the Furies; cf. *Aen.* 6.250, 280, 375. They do not normally figure in the Pentheus legend, being replaced by the avenging Bacchic women, but Pease refers to a Pompeian wall painting of Pentheus with Furies in the background. The phrase *ultrices Dirae* (473) refers also to them; cf. 610, 8.701, 12.845, 869.

11 469. **agmina**: cf. *Aen.* 6.572 of the Fury Tisiphone, *vocat agmina saeva sororum.*

aut Agamemnonius scaenis[1] agitatus Orestes,
armatam[2] facibus matrem et serpentibus atris
cum fugit ultricesque sedent in limine Dirae.

> *474-503. Dido takes the decision to commit suicide, and deceives Anna into assisting her plans by pretending that she has found magic means of freeing herself from her love. A pyre is to be built to burn the relics of Aeneas. Anna, not suspecting the real purpose of the pyre, performs Dido's orders.*

[3]Ergo ubi concepit[4] furias evicta dolore
decrevitque mori, tempus secum ipsa modumque   475
exigit,[5] et maestam dictis adgressa sororem
consilium[6] vultu tegit ac spem fronte screnat:
'inveni, germana, viam (gratare[7] sorori)
quae mihi reddat eum vel eo me solvat amantem.[8]
Oceani finem iuxta solemque cadentem   480
ultimus Aethiopum[9] locus est, ubi maximus Atlas
axem umero torquet stellis ardentibus aptum:[10]
hinc mihi Massylae[11] gentis monstrata sacerdos,

---

1 471. **scaenis agitatus**: 'hounded on the stage'; notice that the comparison is not merely with the story of a Greek tragedy, but with its actual performance on the stage. Page oddly maintains that 'the introduction of the word *scaenis* is an error; it suggests unreality'. But it is a masterstroke designed to associate Dido's tragic plight with that of the heroes of Greek tragedy, not merely with the legends about them, but with the presentation of these legends as tragedy. There is no more 'unreality' about Greek tragedy than there is about Virgil's *Aeneid.*

2 472. Torches and snakes are the emblems of the avenging Furies which Clytemnestra here carries (cf. Allecto in *Aen.* 7.346, 456).

3 474f. The recourse of Dido to magic identifies her more closely with Medea, especially the Medea of Apollonius (see notes on 484-5, 489f.). Her reluctance to be driven to this expedient (493) reinforces the feeling of foreboding and horror which develops throughout this episode and the next. The Roman attitude to magic is well summed up by Servius: *cum multa sacra Romani susciperent, semper magica damnarunt.* For full discussion of magic see Pease's notes on 479, 493 and Austin's note on 498.

4 474. **concepit furias**: 'caught the madness', cf. Cat. 64.92, Ov. *Met.* 2.640.

5 476. **exigit**: 'she pondered', 'went through', cf. Ov. *Met.* 10.587.

6 477. 'she concealed her plan with her expression, and made hope shine out on her face'; the second phrase is a very remarkable innovation, imitated by Silius (11.367). Compare the more natural use of *serenat* in *Aen.* 1.255, and for the meaning *Aen.* 1.209.

7 478. **gratare sorori**: there is a grim contrast with 435.

8 479. The use of *is* in oblique cases is generally avoided by the epic poets (see Austin ad loc.), and here the double use in the same line conveys contempt; he is not worth naming.

9 481. **Aethiopum**: this is a reference to the western Aethiopians (Hom. *Il.* 1.423, *Od.* 1.23-4).

10 482. The line (repeated in *Aen.* 6.797) is adapted from Ennius (*Ann.* 159, 339); *aptum* means 'fitted with', i.e. 'studded with'.

11 483. 'A priestess of Massylian race coming from there has been pointed out to me': for the Massyli, west of Carthage, see note on 132; *hinc* depends on *sacerdos* with some notion like *profecta.*

Hesperidum[1] templi custos, epulasque draconi
quae dabat et sacros servabat in arbore ramos,   485
spargens umida mella soporiferumque papaver.[2]
Haec se carminibus promittit solvere[3] mentes
quas velit, ast aliis[4] duras immittere curas,
sistere[5] aquam fluviis et vertere sidera retro,
nocturnosque movet manis: mugire[6] videbis   490
sub pedibus terram et descendere montibus ornos.
Testor, cara, deos et te, germana, tuumque
dulce caput, magicas[7] invitam accingier artis.
Tu secreta pyram tecto[8] interiore sub auras
erige, et arma[9] viri thalamo quae fixa reliquit   495
impius[10] exuviasque omnis lectumque[11] iugalem,
quo perii, super imponas: [12]abolere nefandi
cuncta viri monimenta iuvat monstratque sacerdos.'
Haec effata silet, pallor simul occupat ora.
Non tamen Anna novis[13] praetexere funera sacris   500

---

1 484-5. 'guardian of the precinct of the Hesperides, who both gave food to the dragon and kept safe the sacred branches on the tree, sprinkling liquid honey and sleep-bringing poppy'. The Hesperides ('daughters of the west') guarded the golden apples which Mother Earth had given to Juno when she married Jupiter; they were helped in their task by a dragon. The story has similarities with that of Medea and the Golden Fleece (guarded by a dragon, Ap. Rh. 4.127f.), and it is itself mentioned in Apollonius (4.1396f.). Difficulty has been felt from Servius onwards over the drowsy food apparently given to the sentinel dragon; it has been suggested that the honey and poppy is nothing to do with the dragon's food, but is an additional piece of magic for a different unspecified purpose, and this seems the best explanation. The alternative is that Virgil is following Apollonius' description of Medea putting the dragon to sleep by magic drugs (4.156f.) and has not properly accommodated it to his context. Mackail does not really solve it by saying 'Even a dragon had to be kept in good temper'. See further Pease's long note.

2 486. This is a very sleepy line, without any main caesura and with total coincidence of accent and ictus; cf. *Aen.* 5.856. Compare Shakespeare, *Othello,* 3.3.331. 'Not poppy, nor mandragora / Nor all the drowsy syrups of the world, / shall ever medicine thee to that sweet sleep / which thou ow'dst yesterday'.

3 487. **solvere mentes**: 'to release people's hearts' (from suffering, *duris . . . curis*), cf. 479. Hor. *Epod.* 5.71.

4 488. **aliis**: dative after *immittere,* supply *mentibus.*

5 489f. For this apparatus of magic cf. Ap. Rh. 3.532f., *Ecl.* 8.60f., 98f., Ov. *Met.* 7.199f., Tib. 1.2.43f. Pease ad loc. gives many additional references.

6 490. **mugire**: cf. *Aen.* 6.256.

7 493. **magicas . . . artis**: 'that I unwillingly arm myself with magic arts'; see note on 474f. To *invitam* supply *me,* cf. 383. For the archaic form of the infinitive *accingi* cf. *Aen.* 7.70, 8.493, 9.231, 11.242, and for the middle use of the passive see note on 137 and cf. especially 2.511.

8 494. **tecto interiore**: i.e. in a courtyard, cf. *Aen.* 2.512-13.

9 495-6. **arma viri. . . exuviasque**: cf. 507, where *arma* is specified by *ensis,* and 646; *exuviae* is a general word, no doubt including the *Iliacae vestes* of 648 (cf. 651, and *Ecl.* 8.91).

10 496. **impius**: the irony of the application of this epithet to *pius* Aeneas is enhanced by its position as a run-on word; in Dido's view he has broken all the ties of duty and responsibility which he owed to her. For *pietas* of love cf. Cat. 76.2, 26.

11 496-7. **lectumque iugalem quo perii**: 'the marriage bed which was my ruin'; cf. 648, and for Dido's belief that she was married cf. 172, 316.

12 497-8. 'it is my wish to rid myself of all the memories of this evil man, and the priestess shows me how'. The word *nefandus* echoes and enlarges *impius.*

13 500. **novis . . . sacris**: 'was using these strange rites to conceal suicide'; for *praetexere* cf. l 72.

germanam credit, ¹nec tantos mente furores
concipit aut graviora timet quam morte² Sychaei.
Ergo iussa parat.

*504-21. Dido now proceeds to perform magic rites, aided by
the priestess.*

At regina³ pyra penetrali in sede sub auras
erecta ingenti⁴ taedis atque ilice secta,   505
intenditque⁵ locum sertis et fronde coronat
funerea; super⁶ exuvias ensemque relictum
effigiemque⁷ toro locat haud ignara futuri.
Stant arae circum et crinis⁸ effusa sacerdos
ter centum tonat⁹ ore deos, Erebumque Chaosque   510
tergeminamque Hecaten, ¹⁰ tria virginis ora Dianae.
Sparserat et latices simulatos¹¹ fontis Averni,
falcibus¹² et messae ad lunam quaeruntur aenis
pubentes herbae nigri cum lacte veneni;
quaeritur et nascentis equi de fronte revulsus   515
et matri praereptus amor.
Ipsa mola¹³ manibusque piis altaria iuxta

---

1 501-2. Anna was unable to understand the deep emotions and frustrated pride of her sister (as Aeneas was, cf. 6.463f.).

2 502. **morte:** 'at the death', cf. 244, 436.

3 504. **At regina:** this is the third of the sections of this book which begins thus; cf. line 1 and line 296.

4 505. **ingenti . . . secta:** 'towering high with logs of pine and oak.'

5 506. **intenditque . . . sertis:** 'both hung the place with garlands and . . .'; the construction is unusual, cf. *Aen.* 5.403. Page well compares 'hang a wall with pictures'.

6 507. **super:** adverbial.

7 508. **effigiem:** the use of effigies in magic is very frequent, cf. *Ecl.* 8.75, Hor. *Sat.* 1.8.30.

8 509. **crinis effusa:** retained accusative with a passive verb, see note on 137. The hair is loosened in magic, see note on 518.

9 510. **tonat. . . deos**: for the accusative (*tonare* being equivalent to *vocat tonanti voce*) cf. Prop. 4.1.134.

10 511. 'and three-fold Hecate, the three faces of the maiden Diana'. Diana in the sky is the moon, on earth the huntress, and below the earth Hecate, a goddess associated with witchcraft and horror (cf. 6.247), also called Trivia, goddess of the crossroads which ghosts were supposed to haunt (cf. 609). She is shown in art with three faces.

11 512. **simulatos fontis Averni:** 'pretended to be from the fountain of Avernus', the entrance to the underworld (6.238f.).

12 513f. 'and herbs are brought, gathered by the light of the moon with bronze sickles, juicy with the milk of black poison, and the love charm too is brought, torn from the head of a colt at birth, snatched before the mother can get it.' For bronze sickles in magic (iron being taboo) cf. Ov. *Met.* 7.227. The oxymoron 'milk of black poison' is partly literal as the milk of plants can be dark, but mainly metaphorical, suggesting dark rituals, black magic. *Venenum* is cognate with *Venus* and often applied to love potions (cf. *Ecl.* 8.95, *Aen.* 7.190). The love charm is hippomanes, a fleshy growth on baby horses supposed to have magic significance: cf. Pliny *N.H.* 8.165 (in *Geo.* 3.280, Prop. 4.5.18, Tib. 2.458 the word has a different sense). This meaning of *amor* is a Virgilian innovation.

13 517. **mola manibusque piis:** 'with holy grain and pure hands'; the ablatives are rather different in kind, and some MSS have *molam,* which is without construction. The half-line in 516 perhaps suggests an unfinished passage, but the reading *mola* may stand.

unum exuta pedem vinclis, in veste recincta,[1]
testatur moritura deos et conscia fati
sidera; tum,[2] si quod non aequo foedere amantis   520
curae numen habet iustumque memorque, precatur.

> *522-52. Night falls and all the earth and its creatures enjoy*
> *sleep. But not Dido — her anguish keeps her awake and she*
> *turns over in her distracted mind all possibilities. Shall she*
> *go to the African suitors she has scorned? Or accompany*
> *the Trojans, alone or with an escort? Impossible: better to*
> *die; this is the proper atonement for her broken pledge to*
> *Sychaeus.*

[3]Nox[4] erat et placidum carpebant fessa soporem
corpora per terras, silvaeque et saeva quierant
aequora, cum medio volvuntur sidera lapsu,
cum tacet omnis ager, pecudes pictaeque[5] volucres,   525
quaeque[6] lacus late liquidos quaeque aspera dumis
rura tenent, somno positae sub nocte silenti.
[Lenibant curas et corda oblita laborum.][7]
at[8] non infelix animi Phoenissa, neque umquam
solvitur[9] in somnos oculisve aut pectore noctem   530

---

1 518. Magic demands the elimination of knots, cf. Ov. *Met.* 7.182-3. *Pedem* is governed by *exuta* in a middle sense ('having released'); see note on 137 and cf. *Aen.* 2.275. Pease gives references (especially from art) for 'one shoe off and one shoe on'; Servius says it is so that she may be freed, but not Aeneas.

2 520-1. 'then she prays to any divinity there may be, just and mindful, which cares for lovers joined in unequal alliance.' For the construction *aliquos curae* (predicative dative) *habere* cf. Cic. *Fam.* 8.8.10.

3 522f. The contrast between the peaceful slumber of the rest of the world and Dido's waking anguish (see next note) introduces a tormented soliloquy of mingled despair and reproach. All possible courses of action other than suicide are unacceptable to her pride (notice *inrisa* 534); there is here a most marked contrast with Catullus'Ariadne (notice on 537). The tone of bitter irony in which she rejects these courses is powerful, and the attempt at logical reasoning full of pathos: shall she go back to her African suitors? No. Well then, *igitur* (537), go with the Trojans? They wouldn't have me. But if they did, *quid tum?* (543); alone, or with an escort? So she brings herself to what she feels is an inevitable conclusion: *morere ut merita es.* She is too proud, too regally obdurate, to make the best of what is left to her; as she lists her possible courses she makes the worst of all of them. The prospect of trying to restore, for her people's sake, the situation as it was before Aeneas came does not ever occur to her; she is too deeply engulfed in her tragic frenzy.

4 522-32. This fine passage is inspired by an equally fine one in Apollonius (3.744f.), where a similar contrast is made between the sleeping world and the wakeful heroine. In Apollonius we see at first wakefulness at night, the sailors watching the stars, the wayfarer and the sentinel longing for repose; then sleep comes, the bereaved mother at last finds slumber, the sound of dogs barking in the city and men talking is stilled, but not on Medea came sweet sleep. Virgil has confined his picture to the stillness of the countryside (with some personification, 523) and its creatures, using his great powers of word music to convey rest and silence and to break it harshly in line 529. For further descriptions of sleeping nature see Pease's collection of passages ad loc; compare particularly *Aen.* 8.26f., 9.224f.

5 525. **pictaeque volucres**: 'gaily-coloured birds', cf. Milton, *P.L.* 7.434 'and spread their painted wings'.

6 526. 'both those that live all around the limpid lakes, and those that haunt the countryside with its tangled thickets'; compare Lucr. 2.344f. Notice the gentle alliteration of *l*.

7 528. This line (nearly the same as *Aen.* 9.225) is not in the best MSS and should certainly be omitted.

8 529f. The movement becomes dactylic and more disturbed, with harsh alliteration of *q,* then *s,* and the *r, -ur-* sounds at the end of 530.

9 530. **solvitur in somnos**: 'relax in sleep', cf. Ov. *Met.* 7.186 and *Aen.* 5.836. Compare line 695.

accipit: ingeminant curae rursusque resurgens
saevit amor magnoque irarum fluctuat aestu.[1]
Sic adeo insistit secumque ita corde volutat:
'en, quid ago?[2] Rursusne procos inrisa priores[3]
experiar, Nomadumque petam conubia supplex,   535
quos ego sim[4] totiens iam dedignata maritos?
Iliacas igitur classis atque ultima[5] Teucrum
iussa sequar? [6]Quiane auxilio iuvat ante levatos
et bene apud memores veteris stat gratia facti?
Quis me autem, fac[7] velle, sinet ratibusve superbis   540
invisam accipiet? [8]Nescis heu, perdita, necdum
Laomedonteae sentis periuria gentis?
Quid tum?[9] Sola fuga nautas comitabor ovantis?
An Tyriis omnique manu stipata meorum
inferar[10] et, quos Sidonia[11] vix urbe revelli,   545
rursus agam pelago et ventis dare vela iubebo?
Quin[12] morere ut merita es, ferroque averte dolorem.
Tu lacrimis evicta meis, tu prima furentem
his, germana, malis oneras[13] atque obicis hosti.[14]

---

1 532. Compare Ariadne in Cat. 64.62 *et magnis curarum fluctuat undis.*

2 534. **ago:** the indicative for the subjunctive of a deliberative question, cf. 368 and *Aen.* 3.88, 10.675, 12.637.

3 534-5. Compare Anna's words in 36f.

4 536. **sim:** concessive, 'when (although) I have . . .': cf. *Aen.* 2.248.

5 537. **ultima:** 'most extreme', i.e. whatever they may be. Dido's pride here contrasts very sharply with Ariadne's subservience (Cat. 64.158f.) where she is willing to be a servant to Theseus; Ovid's Dido is similarly subservient (*Her.* 7.168).

6 538f. 'Shall I do it because they are thankful for my previous help and their gratitude for my past deed lives firm in their memories?' The sentence is painfully sarcastic: to appeal now to to the grudging gratitude of the Trojans is utterly unacceptable. For *quiane* cf. *quemne* in Cat. 64.180.

7 540. **fac velle:** 'suppose I wished it', cf. Cic. *Phil.* 2.5 *fac potuisse.*

8 541-2. 'Wretched one, alas, do you not know, and do you not yet feel the treachery of the race of Laomedon?'; for the perjury of Laomedon see note on 3.248.

9 543. **quid tum?:** the argument is ... but suppose after all that the Trojans are willing to take me, should I go alone or try to persuade my Tyrians to escort me? Both ideas are impossible.

10 545. **inferar:** 'shall I set off after them?' The word here does not mean attack, but hasten to join; cf. 142 and *Aen.* 1.439.

11 **Sidonia . . . revelli:** cf. *Aen.* 1.360f. where however there is no mention of difficulty in persuading the Tyrians to leave.

12 547. 'No, die as you have deserved, and end your sorrow with the sword'; for *quin* with the imperative cf. *Aen.* 5.635.

13 549. **oneras . . . obicis:** for the idiomatic present (you are the one who did it) see note on 228.

14 548. The reproach against Anna (who is not present) has some justification; Dido, though blaming herself (*ut merita es*) clutches at excuses.

Non[1] licuit thalami expertem sine crimine vitam   550

degere more ferae, talis nec tangere curas;

non[2] servata fides cineri promissa Sychaeo.'

> *553-83- As Aeneas sleeps Mercury comes to him again in a vision, urging him to leave immediately for fear of attack. Aeneas immediately awakens his men, and the Trojans depart in hot haste.*

[3]Tantos illa suo rumpebat[4] pectore questus:

Aeneas celsa in puppi iam certus eundi

carpebat[5] somnos rebus iam rite paratis.   555

Huic se forma[6] dei vultu redeuntis eodem

obtulit in somnis rursusque ita visa monere est,

omnia[7] Mercurio similis, vocemque coloremque[8]

et crinis flavos et membra decora iuventa:[9]

'nate dea, potes hoc sub casu ducere somnos,   560

nec quae te circum stent deinde[10] pericula cernis,

demens,[11] nec Zephyros audis spirare secundos?

Illa dolos dirumque nefas in pectore versat

---

1 550-1. 'It was not allowed that I should in widowhood pass my life blamelessly like some wild creature without knowing such agonies of love'. This seems the best rending of this very difficult passage; by *thalami expertem* Dido means (as Servius says) 'without marrying again after the death of Sychaeus'; and by *more ferae* she refers to life free from social and personal relationships, like a deer on the mountains (the kind of life lived by a Camilla or a Harpalyce). Page quotes Ov. *Fast.* 2.291 *vita feris similis* of the happy, primitive, innocent life of the Arcadians. Others take *more ferae* to refer to sexual promiscuity (e.g. Hor. *Sat.* 1.3.109); the meaning would then be 'It was not allowed that I should live my life out of wedlock, in the fashion of a wild creature, without incurring blame; nor that I should experience love such as that'. But this is contrary to Dido's convinced view that she was not out of wedlock. For a very good full discussion see Austin ad loc.

2 552. 'I have not kept the faith which I promised to the ashes of Sychaeus'; this summarising line contains indeed the whole truth, as Dido well knows (cf. 15f., 28f.). *Sychaeo* is used as an adjective, see Page ad loc. and cf. *Aen.* 1.686; this seems preferable to accepting the reading *Sychaei* from *M* (which looks like a correction) or to understanding the Latin to mean 'I have not kept the faith to his ashes which I promised to Sychaeus'. Austin argues that the adjective would be too artificial in this context, but cf. *Aen.* 3.304.

3 553f. This passage, decisive as it is in the narrative, gives a relaxation of tension between the two speeches of Dido. The attention is focussed on Aeneas' obedience to his divine instructions, and for a brief while its tragic consequences are in the background.

4 553. **rumpebat ... questus**: cf. *Aen.* 2.129; we might say 'such were the lamentations that burst from her heart'.

5 555. **carpebat somnos**: a back reference to 522. Aeneas, like all nature but unlike Dido, was asleep. The phrases *iam certus eundi* and *rebus iam rite paratis* contrast the ordered purpose of Aeneas with the disordered distraction of the unhappy Dido. Critics are anxious to defend (or attack) Aeneas here on a charge of heartlessness; but the simple truth is that he has peaceful sleep because he has accepted the will of the gods.

6 556. **forma dei**: this is a dream, the previous appearance of Mercury had been a real visitation in daylight.

7 558. **omnia**: this and the following accusatives are Greek accusatives of respect, common in verse with parts of the body (see note on 1.320) and also found with *omnia, cetera, genus* (cf. 3.594, 9.650).

8 558. **coloremque**: for the hyper-metric elision cf. 629, and see Austin ad loc. and my note on 1.332.

9 559. **iuventa**: some MSS have *iuventae*, but cf. *Aen.* 2.473, 9.365.

10 561. **deinde**: 'from now on'; cf. *Aen.* 6.756, 890.

11 562. **demens**: strongly emphatic by position, see note on 185.

certa mori, variosque[1] irarum concitat aestus.

Non fugis hinc praeceps, dum praecipitare potestas?[2]   565

Iam mare[3] turbari trabibus saevasque videbis

conlucere faces, iam fervere litora flammis,

si te his attigerit terris Aurora morantem.

Heia age, rumpe moras. Varium[4] et mutabile semper

femina.' Sic fatus nocti se immiscuit atrae.   570

    Tum vero Aeneas subitis exterritus umbris[5]

corripit e somno corpus sociosque fatigat:[6]

'praecipites[7] vigilate, viri, et considite transtris;

solvite vela citi. Deus aethere missus ab alto

festinare fugam tortosque incidere funis   575

ecce[8] iterum instimulat. Sequimur te, sancte[9] deorum,

quisquis[10] es, imperioque iterum paremus ovantes.

Adsis o placidusque[11] iuves et sidera caelo

dextra feras.' Dixit vaginaque eripit ensem

fulmineum strictoque ferit retinacula ferro.   580

Idem[12] omnis simul ardor habet, rapiuntque ruuntque;

litora descruere,[13] latet sub classibus aequor,

adnixi torquent spumas et caerula verrunt.[14]

---

1 564. **variosque . . . aestus**: 'she arouses in her heart shifting tides of anger', cf. 531.

2 565. Mercury's alliteration is very strong as he comes to the point of his message.

3 566. **mare turbari trabibus**: 'the sea a turmoil of ships', i.e. Dido's ships preventing the Trojan departure. For *trabibus* cf. *Aen.* 3.191. These prophecies are vainly echoed in Dido's next speech (592f.).

4 569-70. **varium . . . femina**: 'a woman is always a fickle and changeable thing'; Mercury's phrase is made particularly contemptuous so that the use of the neuter. The commentators collect many parallels for this *sententia;* in its context, as uttered by Mercury, it serves well to suggest to Aeneas (particularly after *certa mori*) that the present tranquillity may not last. Dryden considered this 'the sharpest satire, in the fewest words, ever made on womankind', adding that if a god had not spoken these words Virgil would not have dared to write them nor he to translate them.

5 571. **umbris**: 'phantom', for the plural cf. *Aen.* 5.81, 6.510.

6 572. **fatigat**: 'arouses', *cum clamore increpat* (Servius); cf. *Aen.* 11.714.

7 573. **praecipites vigilate viri**: 'At it, men, wake up', equivalent (as Mackail says) to *praecipitate et vigilate.* Mynors and others punctuate so that *praecipites* goes with what precedes ('arouses them headlong') and the speech begins *vigilate viri*; but it is effective for Aeneas to echo Mercury's word (565), and the framing of the imperatives with the two adjectives *praecipites. . . citi* is forceful.

8 576. **ecce ... instimulat**: the elisions and conflict of accent with ictus give a breathless effect; for the infinitive after *instimulat* see note on 1.357.

9 576. **sancte deorum**: a Homeric turn (δια θεαων), used by Ennius (*sancta dearum*).

10 577. **quisquis es**: for the religious formula cf. *Aen.* 1.330, 9.22.

11 578. **placidusque**: 'graciously', cf. *Aen.* 3.266.

12 581. 'The same excitement seizes them all at once, they hurry and bustle'; notice the alliteration at the line ending.

13 582. **deseruere**: the perfect tense conveys the suddenness of departure, cf. 164, *Aen.* 1.84.

14 583. The same line occurs in *Aen.* 3.208, where see notes.

584-629. From her palace Dido sees the Trojans sailing away, and bursts into a soliloquy filled with anger, self-reproach, and longing for vengeance. She calls on the sun, the gods and the furies to avenge her, first on Aeneas personally and then on all his descendants.

[1]Et[2] iam prima novo spargebat lumine terras
Tithoni croceum linquens Aurora cubile.   585
Regina e[3] speculis ut primam albescere lucem
vidit et acquatis[4] classem procedere velis,
litoraque et vacuos sensit sine remige portus,
terque[5] quaterque manu pectus percussa decorum
flaventisque abscissa comas 'pro[6] Iuppiter! Ibit   590
hic,' ait 'et nostris inluserit[7] advena regnis?
Non arma expedient totaque ex urbe sequentur,[8]
diripientque[9] rates alii navalibus? Ite,[10]
ferte citi flammas, date tela, impellite remos!
Quid loquor? Aut ubi sum? Quae mentem insania mutat?   595

---

1 584f. This passage begins with a moving contrast between the serenity of the new dawn and the distracted and tormented emotions of the lonely queen (cf. 522f.). But pity is quickly replaced by horror. The speech she makes is a grandiloquent and formalised imprecation, arising from thwarted power, injured pride, and the uncontrollable passion for revenge.' Its great impact is due to the variety of ways in which her anger and hatred is conveyed: first a useless plea for action, then a moment of self blame followed by a violent and inhuman outburst dwelling on the horrors which she might have committed; then the recognition that she herself can do nothing, and the prayer to other powers to bring about the destruction which she cannot, the destruction first of Aeneas himself and his people, and then of his Roman descendants. Thus the particularised fury and despair of Dido turns into the generalised hostility and violence of two great peoples.

The speech is perhaps the most perfect example in the *Aeneid* of Virgil's ability to use words and metre to convey the tone and mood of an imagined situation at the highest possible point of intensity. I have endeavoured in the notes that follow to draw attention to some of the ways in which he achieves these effects.

2 584—5. 'And now first dawn was beginning to dapple the world with the new day's light as the goddess Aurora left the saffron bed of Tithonus'. These are calm and beautiful lines (used again in 9.459-60), describing dawn in phrases partly borrowed from Lucretius (2.144), and adding the distancing mythology of the goddess Aurora as bride of Tithonus (Hom. *Il.* 11.1, *Geo.* 1.447).Homer (e.g. *Il.* 8.1) uses the epithet κροκόπεπλος ('saffron-cloaked') of dawn; compare *lutea* in *Aen.* 7.26.

3 586. **e speculis**: 'from her high tower'; the remoteness of the queen and her isolation is impressed upon us; compare Amata in 12.595f., and Ariadne in Cat. 64.126f.

4 587. **aequatis . . . velis**: 'in ordered array', in formation with all their sails at the same angle; the smooth and organised departure of the Trojans contrasts with the wild disorder of Dido's thoughts and emotions.

5 589-90. 'three times and four times struck against her lovely breast and tore her fair hair'; for the middle use of *percussa* and *abscissa* see note on 137, and cf. 1.481, 7.503, 9.478, 11.877.

6 590. **pro**: the interjection, as in *pro di immortales.*

7 591. **inluserit**: for the use of the future perfect ('shall it be true that a stranger has mocked. . .?') cf. *Aen.* 2.581-2, 9.785. Dido here returns again to the thought that she has been slighted and mocked; cf. 534.

8 592. The indefinite unstated subject helps to convey the unreality of Dido's frantic appeals; there is no audience, and the commands she gives directly in the next two lines are inaudible.

9 593. **diripientque**: this is the reading of the MSS. Many editors have accepted Heinsius' conjecture *deripient,* but the more violent word is more appropriate.

10 593-4. 'Quick, off, bring fire, get weapons, drive on the oars'. These staccato outbursts are given added vehemence by the very unusual pause after the fifth foot in 593 (echoing 590) and the intense alliteration of *t.*

Infelix Dido,[1] nunc te facta impia tangunt?
Tum[2] decuit, cum sceptra dabas. En dextra[3] fidesque,
quem[4] secum patrios aiunt portare penatis,
quem subiisse[5] umeris confectum aetate parentem!
Non potui abreptum divellere corpus et undis   600
spargere? [6]Non socios, non ipsum absumere ferro
Ascanium patriisque epulandum ponere mensis?
Verum[7] anceps pugnae fuerat fortuna. Fuisset:
quem metui moritura? [8]Faces in castra[9] tulissem
implessemque foros flammis natumque patremque   605
cum genere exstinxem, memet[10] super ipsa dedissem.
Sol,[11] qui terrarum flammis opera omnia lustras,
tuque[12] harum interpres curarum et conscia Iuno,

---

1 596. The slow spondees and Dido's own use of the epithet *infelix* (used of her often in the narrative) convey the moment of realisation and self reproach for her *facta impia* in breaking her oath to Sychaeus, and perhaps also, as Austin suggests, in failing in her duties to her people. Some have argued that the reference is to the *facta impia* of Aeneas against her, but this is in appropriate to the context and the meaning of *tangunt*.

2 597. 'The proper time for that was when you were offering him a share in your power'; *cum* with the indicative stresses the point of time (= *eo tempore quo*), cf. Tib. 1.10.8.

3 **dextra**: 'honour', the keeping of pledges, cf. 307, 314.

4 598f. The omission of the antecedent (*eius*) to *quem* helps to convey the disjointed nature of Dido's phrases. The scornful alliteration of *p* in 598 is relaxed in 599 and then resumed in the last word. The sarcastic use of the vague *aiunt* to introduce the traditional qualities of Aeneas (guardian of his country's gods and rescuer of his father) gives a cold sense of distance as she ignores the fact that he had told her these things himself (2.707, 717).

5 599. **subiisse**: 'supported'; cf. *Aen.* 2.708, 12.899.

6 601-3. Both of these ghastly acts of vengeance which Dido says she could have performed are from Greek mythology. The first refers to the story of how Medea scattered on the sea the dismembered body of her brother Apsyrtus to delay the pursuit of her father (Cic. *Pro Lege Man.* 22); similarities between Medea and Dido have appeared in the course of the book (especially in Dido's use of magic; see note on 474f.). It is interesting that Apollonius used an alternative form of the legend which dispenses with this act of horror.
The second reference is to the story that Atreus served up to Thyestes the flesh of his sons (Aesch. *Agam.* 1.590f., Eur. *El.* 699f.). It is less likely that the reference is to Procne who killed Itys and served him up to his father Tereus (Ov. *Met.* 6.424f.). The horror and barbarity of Dido's thoughts reveal the depth of tragic madness to which she has come.

7 603. 'But the upshot of the battle would have been uncertain. Let it have been!' The imaginary objection of soliloquy is answered with violent force, with echoing alliteration of *f* (see note on 218) and a pause after the fifth trochee (a very unusual rhythm; see my note on *Aen.* 3.480, OUP Ed.). *Fuerat* is indicative replacing the expected past potential subjunctive; cf. *Aen.* 2.55. *Fuisset* is past jussive (in a concessive sense), a rare construction; cf. 678 for a different type of past jussive.

8 604-6. The long series of pluperfect subjunctives expresses with a kind of dinning insistence Dido's preoccupation with what might have been, what she could have done, and did not. *Exstinxem* is contracted for *exstinxissem* (a much rarer contraction than *implessem* in the previous line); cf. 1.201, 5.786, 6.57, 11.118 and line 682.

9 604. **castra**: i.e. the encampment by their ships, cf. *Aen.* 3.519, 9.69.

10 606. **memet ... dedissem**: 'I would have flung myself on top of all'; compare Ap. Rh. 4.391f. For the emphatic *memet* cf. *Aen.* 7.309.

11 607f. As Dido turns from the unfulfilled past to her prayers for the future the movement slows, becoming predominantly spondaic while in measured tones she invokes the powers that can bring aid. First she calls on the all-seeing Sun (cf. Hom. *Il.* 3.377), then her special goddess Juno, goddess of Carthage and of marriage, enemy of Aeneas; then the witch of the underworld, Medea's patron goddess Hecate (see note on 511), then the avenging furies (see note on 469, and cf. Cat. 64.192f.), and finally all gods, whoever they may be, sympathetic to her at her death (cf. 520-1).

12 608. 'and you Juno, mediator and witness of my suffering'; the word *interpres* suggests that Juno had, as *pronuba*, been personally involved in Dido's love.

184

nocturnisque Hecate triviis ululata[1] per urbes
et Dirae ultrices et di morientis Elissae,[2]   610
accipite haec, meritumque[3] malis advertite numen
et nostras audite preces. Si tangere portus
infandum caput[4] ac terris[5] adnare necesse est,
et sic fata Iovis poscunt, hic[6] terminus haeret,
at[7] bello audacis populi vexatus et armis,   615
finibus[8] extorris, complexu avulsus Iuli
auxilium imploret videatque indigna suorum
funera; nec, cum se sub leges pacis iniquae
tradiderit, regno aut optata[9] luce fruatur,
sed cadat ante diem mediaque inhumatus harena.   620
Haec precor, hanc vocem extremam cum sanguine fundo.
Tum[10] vos, o Tyrii, stirpem et genus omne futurum
exercete[11] odiis, cinerique haec mittite nostro
munera[12]. Nullus amor populis nec foedera sunto.[13]
Exoriare[14] aliquis nostris ex ossibus ultor   625
qui face Dardanios ferroque sequare colonos,

---

1 609. **ululata**: 'whose name is shrieked'; for the passive use cf. Stat. *Th.* 3.238 and compare *Aen.* 3.14; see further Austin ad loc. The association of Hecate with crossroads is reflected in her name Trivia (e.g. *Aen.* 6.13.).

2 610. **Elissae**: see note on 335.

3 611. **meritumque . . . numen**: 'turn towards my wrongs the divine power which I must deserve'; for *malis* cf. 169. Others take the meaning to be turn against evildoers (or evil behaviour) the divine power they deserve (cf. Hor. *Epod.* 5.54).

4 613. **caput**: for this contemptuous use cf. 640.

5 **terris adnare**: 'sail in to land', cf. *Aen.* 1.538.

6 614. **hic terminus haeret**: 'and if this outcome is firm-fixed', cf. Lucr. 1.77. Some punctuate so that this is the main clause, but it is better as another subordinate clause in asyndeton; for *at* ('yet') in the main clause after a *si* clause cf. *Aen.* 6.406, *Geo.* 4.241.

7 615f. These curses upon Aeneas (modelled in a general sense on Hom. *Od.* 9.532f., Polyphemus' curse on Odysseus) in one way or another all came true. He was harassed in warfare by Turnus and his Rutulians; he left the Trojan camp and the embrace of Iulus to seek help from Evander; he saw the death of many of his men (notably Pallas); he accepted peace terms more favourable to the Italians than the Trojans (12.834f.); and he did not rule his people for long (three years), but (according to one version of the legend) was drowned in the Numicus or (according to another) killed in battle and his body not recovered. These are the lines which confronted Charles I when he consulted the *sortes Vergilianae;* see Austin ad loc.

8 616. **finibus extorris**: 'exiled from his land', a rather exaggerated reference to Aeneas' departure from the Trojan camp site to seek help from Evander (*Aeneid* 8). Others take it to refer to his exile from Troy, but this was already a fact.

9 619. **optata**: a stock epithet, 'the lovely light'; cf. *Aen.* 6.363 *caeli iucundum lumen.*

10 622f. From her specific curse upon Aeneas Dido turns to the longer vista of history and undying hatred through the generations.

11 623. **exercete odiis**: 'harass with your hatred'; cf. *Aen.* 5.779, 6.739.

12 624. **munera**: the strong irony of this word is emphasised by the heavy sense-pause after it; Dido wants as a gift to her ashes not a tribute of affection, but a promise of never ending hatred.

13 **sunto**: the legalistic imperative, rare in verse, adds a feeling of solemn formality (cf. *Aen.* 6.153).

14 625f. 'Arise, some avenger from my bones, to pursue the Trojan settlers with fire and sword, now, one day, whenever strength offers. I call on shore to fight with shore, wave with sea, weapons with weapons; let the peoples fight, themselves and their children's children'. Dido's last appeal begins with hissing *s*'s, and the powerfully effective syntactical device of the third person *aliquis* as subject to the second person verb; then she asks her Carthaginians to use against her enemies that fire and steel which she herself might have used (604f.), but did not. The appeal to the Carthaginians is general, extending through all future time; but the specific *aliquis ultor* must have brought to Roman minds the thought of Hannibal.

nunc, olim, quocumque dabunt se tempore vires.
Litora litoribus contraria, fluctibus undas
imprecor, arma armis: pugnent ipsique nepotesque.'[1]

630-62. Dido sends Barce to fetch Anna for the pretended magic rites, and meanwhile climbs the pyre and prepares to kill herself. In her last words she speaks of her life's achievement and once more prays for vengeance on Aeneas.

[2]Haec ait, et partis animum versabat in omnis,   630
invisam quaerens quam primum abrumpere lucem.
Tum breviter Barcen nutricem adfata Sychaci,
namque[3] suam patria antiqua cinis ater habebat:
'Annam, cara mihi nutrix, huc siste sororem:
die[4] corpus properet fluviali spargere lympha,   635
et pecudes secum et monstrata piacula ducat.
Sic veniat, tuque ipsa pia tege tempora vitta.
Sacra Iovi[5] Stygio, quae rite incepta paravi,
perficere est animus finemque imponere curis
Dardaniique[6] rogum capitis permittere flammae.'   640
Sic ait. [7]Illa gradum studio celerabat[8] anili.
At trepida et coeptis immanibus effera Dido
sanguineam [9]volvens aciem, maculisque trementis
interfusa genas et pallida morte futura,

---

1 629. **nepotesque**: this is a most astonishing instance of hyper-metric *-que* (see note on 558); the elision has to be made not only over a full stop, but at the end of a speech. In a sense indeed the elision cannot be made at all; the never ending hatred of Dido is reflected in the un-ended rhythm of her final words.

2 630f. In these last scenes Dido is again seen as a tragic heroine, reminding us in the manner of her death of Ajax in Sophocles, and in her final speech of Euripides' *Alcestis* (175f.). Her last words are divided into two parts at line 659; in the first part Dido is once again the great queen of Carthage, as she bids farewell to her life and reviews its achievements; in the second she is again the fury of vengeance. At the moment of her death the beginning and the end of her tragedy are put before us in brief; under pressures which she could not resist she has moved from prosperity to tragedy, from an admirable and enviable personality to one consumed and destroyed by hate.

3 633. 'for the black ash of the pyre encompassed her own nurse in her onetime home'; i.e. in Tyre. Whether Virgil found this detail in the legend we do not know; but it is appropriate that Sychacus' old nurse should perform Dido's last errand, as she plans to expiate the wrong she had done to his memory. For the use of *situs* cf. *Aen.* 1.4.61; for *habebat* cf. perhaps *Aen.* 1.556, 6.362.

4 635. **die . . . properet**: jussive subjunctive in parataxis, cf. *Aen.* 5.550-1; for the purificatory ritual cf. 6.229-30.

5 638. **Iovi Stygio**: i.e. Pluto, cf. Hom. *Il.* 9.457; compare *Iuno inferna* (Proserpina) in *Aen.* 6.138.

6 640. 'and to commit to the flames the pyre of the Trojan wretch': Dido's proclaimed intention to light the pyre that has been built (504f.), with the possessions and effigy of Aeneas on it (507f.), continues to the last moment her pretence of magic rites directed against Aeneas. For *caput* cf. 613 and 11.399.

7 641. 'So she spoke. The other hastened her step with an old woman's eagerness'. Notice the momentary relief in this dactylic line, describing the agitated speed of the nurse as she bustles to obey her instructions.

8 **celerabat**: some MSS give *celebrabat,* but as Mackail points out this word is not used elsewhere by Virgil of a single person, 'nor could it properly be so used'.

9 643-4. 'rolling her bloodshot eyes, her trembling cheeks flecked with blotches of red, pale at the thought of imminent death'; the first phrase is used of Amata (7.399), the last is echoed in the description of Cleopatra in 8.709. For the retained accusative *genas* see note on 137.

interiora domus inrumpit limina[1] et altos   645
conscendit furibunda rogos[2] ensemque redudit[3]
Dardanium, non hos quaesitum munus in usus.
Hic,[4] postquam Iliacas[5] vestis notumque cubile
conspexit, paulum[6] lacrimis et mente morata
incubuitque[7] toro dixitque novissima verba: 650
'dulces exuviae, dum fata deusque sinebat,
accipite hanc animam meque his exsolvite curis.
Vixi[8] et quem dederat cursum Fortuna peregi,
et nunc magna[9] mei sub terras ibit imago.
Urbem praeclaram statui, mea moenia vidi,   655
ulta [10]virum poenas inimico a fratre recepi,
felix, heu nimium felix, si litora tantum
numquam[11] Dardaniae tetigissent nostra carinae.'
Dixit, et os[12] impressa toro 'moriemur inultae,
sed moriamur' ait. 'Sic,[13] sic iuvat ire sub umbras.   660
Hauriat[14] hunc oculis ignem crudelis ab alto
Dardanus, et nostrae secum ferat omina mortis.'

---

1 645. **limina**: the word is used here of an inner section of the palace; Austin compares the use of *moenia* to mean 'buildings' of a city (as in 74).

2 646. **rogos**: for the poetic plural cf. *Aen.* 11.66. *P* and Servius read *gradus,* which perhaps is a correction originating from 685.

3 646-7. This presumably refers to a gift which Dido had earlier sought from Aeneas, as a token of affection (Sil. 8.149), not a death weapon. Ovid elaborates the point in *Her.* 7.183f.

4 648. **hic**: 'next', cf. *Aen.* 2.122.

5 **Iliacas vestis notumque cubile**: this is a reference to her preparations in 496f., 507f.

6 649. **paulum . . . morata**: 'pausing a moment in tearful thought'.

7 650. **incubuitque . . . dixitque**: the use of -*que . . .* -*que* here ('both . . . and') gives a doubled trochaic lilt and a rhyme; it seems to contribute to the finality of the line.

8 653f. Dido's simple and noble statements of her life's achievements have a literary quality like the inscriptions on tombstones.

9 654. **magna**: the dominant meaning is the superhuman size of ghosts (cf. Creusa's ghost, 2.773 *nota maior imago*), but there is an undertone too of queenly majesty.

10 656. Cf. *Aen.* 1.343f. where Venus tells how Dido's husband Sychaeus was murdered by her brother Pygmalion, and how Dido took Pygmalion's treasures and ships and men away to Carthage.

11 657-8. 'Happy, alas too happy, if only the Trojan ships had never touched our shores'; the phrases are strongly reminiscent of Medea's thoughts in Ap. Rh. 3.774f., 4.32f., and Ariadne's in Cat. 64.171-2.

12 659. **os impressa**: for the middle use of the verb see note on 137.

13 660. **sic, sic**: Servius and many others have held that as Dido speaks these words she stabs herself twice; it is less melodramatic if we take the words at their face value: 'this shall be the manner of my dying' (Austin).

14 661-2. 'Let the cruel Trojan's eyes drink in these flames from over the ocean, and let him take with him the ill-omen of my death.' For *haurire oculis* cf. *Aen.* 12.945-6.

663-92. As Dido is seen to have stabbed herself wild lamentation spreads through the city. Anna rushes to the pyre and endeavours to staunch the blood, but Dido is past human aid.

¹Dixerat, atque illam media inter talia ferro²
conlapsam aspiciunt comites, ensemque cruore
spumantem sparsasque³ manus. It clamor ad alta   665
atria: concussam bacchatur⁴ Fama per urbem.
Lamentis gemituque et femineo ululatu⁵
tecta fremunt, resonat magnis plangoribus aether,
non aliter quam si immissis ruat⁶ hostibus omnis
Karthago aut antiqua Tyros, ⁷flammaeque furentes   670
culmina perque hominum volvantur perque deorum.
Audiit exanimis⁸ trepidoque exterrita cursu
unguibus ora soror foedans et pectora pugnis⁹
per medios ruit, ac morientem nomine clamat:
'hoc illud, germana, fuit?¹⁰ Me fraude petebas?   675
Hoc rogus iste mihi, hoc ignes araeque parabant?
Quid¹¹ primum deserta querar? Comitemne sororem
sprevisti moriens? ¹²Eadem me ad fata vocasses;
idem ambas ferro dolor atque eadem hora tulisset.
his etiam struxi¹³ manibus patriosque vocavi   680

---

1 663f. Only at the beginning and end of this scene does Virgil describe the dying queen; the greater part of the passage is taken up with the general grief of the people and the specific anguish of Anna. In this way the impact of lines 688-92 is made more striking.

2 663-5. Like a Greek tragedian, Virgil does not describe the death stroke (see note on 660), only the fact that it has occurred; cf. Soph. *Ajax* 828f.

3 665. **sparsasque manus**: 'her hands bespattered'. Austin agrees with Henry's view that *sparsas* means 'flung wide' (Servius gives both explanations), but there seem no grounds for rejecting the more normal meaning.

4 666. **bacchatur**: 'rushes wildly', as Dido herself had (301).

5 667. For the general scene cf. the fall of Troy, *Aen.* 2.487f. The line ends with a hiatus before a quadri-syllabic word (= 9.477); the effect is to reinforce the onomatopoeic sound of *ululatu*.

6 669. **ruat**: 'were falling', cf. *Aen.* 2.363 *urbs antiqua ruit*. For the comparison cf. Hom. *Il.* 22.410f., where the lamentation for Hector is as if all Troy were falling.

7 670-1. 'and the raging fire was eddying all around the rooves of the houses of men and the temples of gods'; for the position of *per* cf. 257, 5.663.

8 672. **exanimis**: 'distraught', out of her mind in panic. Virgil uses this form and the other (*exanimus*) equally.

9 673. This line is repeated (of Turnus' sister) in 12.871; cf. also 11.86.

10 675-6. 'Was this what it was, my sister? You sought me and deceived me? This was what your pyre was for, was it (*mihi*), and the fire and the altars?' Anna now realises that she has unwittingly been the accomplice in Dido's plans for suicide. For *hoc illud* cf. *Aen.* 3.558; *mihi* is ethic dative.

11 677. **quid ... querar?**: cf. 371, *quae quibus anteferam?*

12 678-9. 'You should have called me to the same fate; the same agony and the same hour should have taken off both of us with the sword together'. The subjunctives are past jussive (= *debuisti vocare, debuit ferre*); cf. *Aen.* 3.643, 10-854, 11.162 and (with a concessive force) line 603. For *ferre* = *auferre* cf. *Aen.* 2.555, 600.

13 680. **struxi**: understand *rogum*; the omission of the object shows that Anna is thinking of nothing else.

voce deos, sic te ut posita, crudelis,[1] abessem?
Exstinxti[2] te meque, soror, populumque patresque[3]
Sidonios urbemque tuam. Date[4] vulnera lymphis
abluam et, extremus si quis super halitus errat,
ore[5] legam.' Sic[6] fata gradus evaserat altos,   685
semianimemque[7] sinu germanam amplexa fovebat
cum gemitu atque atros siccabat veste cruores.
Illa gravis oculos conata attollere rursus
deficit; infixum stridit[8] sub pectore vulnus.
Ter[9] sese attollens cubitoque adnixa levavit,   690
ter revoluta toro est oculisque errantibus aho
quaesivit caelo lucem ingemuitque[10] reperta.

> *693-705. Because Dido's death was neither fated nor deserved Proserpina had not cut a lock of her hair to release her soul. Juno therefore sends Iris to perform the rite, and Dido's life departs into the winds.*

[11]Tum Iuno omnipotens longum miserata dolorem
difficilisque obitus Irim[12] demisit Olyrnpo
quae[13] luctantem animam nexosque resolveret artus.   695

---

1 681. **crudelis:** this is surely vocative, addressed to Dido, not nominative referring to Anna (as is often said); the second interpretation would be out of tune with the rest of Anna's words.

2 682. **exstinxti:** contracted for *exstinxisti,* see note on 606.

3 682-3. This is only too true; Dido's action, taken on entirely personal grounds, has repercussions upon all those towards whom she had responsibility. She has felt free to act purely as an individual; she has at the last disregarded all her obligations.

4 683-4. **date . . . abluam:** 'let me wash her wound with water'; *date* is addressed to the bystanders. For the parataxis cf. *Aen.* 6.883-4.

5 685. **ore legam:** 'let me catch it on my lips', cf.' Cic. *Verr. 2.5.118, Ov. Met. 12.424-5, and Pease's many illustrative citations.

6 **sic ... altos:** 'speaking thus she had already climbed the high steps'; notice the use of the pluperfect tense. For *evadere* with the accusative in this sense cf. Livy 2.65.3, and compare *Aen.* 2.458 (*evadere ad*).

7 686. **semianimemque:** the *i* of *semi-* is treated as a consonant (see note on 2.16); in some compounds it is omitted, cf. *Aen.* 3.578.

8 689. **stridit:** 'hissed'; the word refers to the sound of air in the wound; cf. Ov. *Met.* 4.123. There is no reason to take *vulnus* as equivalent to *ensis,* as many have done, rendering *stridit* as 'grated'. The line is reminiscent of the metaphorical wound of line 67 *taciturn vivit sub pectore vulnus.*

9 690-1. **ter . . . ter:** cf. Ap. *Rh.* 3.654-5.

10 692. **ingemuitque reperta:** 'and groaned when she found it'. To *reperta* supply *luce;* some MSS have *repertam,* probably through failure to understand the ablative absolute construction.

11 693f. The final scene is quiet and tranquil after the anguish and intensity of the preceding action. Its function is similar to that of the choral ode which closes a Greek tragedy on a calm note. The action passes from the turmoil of human suffering to the inevitable serenity of divine dispositions; and the goddess Iris, with her otherworldly beauty and colour, brings light at last to Dido's dark tragedy.

12 694. **Irim:** Iris is Juno's special messenger, cf. *Aen.* 5.606f., 9.2f.

13 695. 'to set free her struggling spirit from the fetters of her body'; the soul is imprisoned in the body (*Aen.* 6.734), and struggles to get away.

Nam[1] quia nec fato merita nec morte peribat,
sed misera ante diem subitoque accensa furore,
nondum[2] illi flavum Proserpina vertice crinem
abstulerat Stygioque caput damnaverat Orco.
Ergo[3] Iris croceis per caelum roscida pennis   700
mille trahens varios adverso sole colores
devolat et supra caput astitit. 'Hunc[4] ego Diti
sacrum iussa[5] fero teque isto corpore solvo.'
Sic[6] ait et dextra crinem secat; omnis et una
dilapsus calor atque in ventos vita recessit.   705

---

1 696-7. 'For because she was not dying by fate nor by a death she had deserved, but wretchedly before her time, set on fire by sudden frenzy . . .'. The meaning is that Dido dies only because she wished it; there was no other reason, she had not reached the end of her fated span, nor had she deserved death (e.g. by some criminal act leading to divine intervention; cf. Ov. *Fast.* 3.705f., where the phrase *morte iacent merita* is used of such people). These lines have been subjected from Servius onwards to severe metaphysical analysis; but their impact in the context is very very clear; Dido's death is self chosen. In *Aen.* 6.436f. Virgil comments on the fate in the underworld of those who chose suicide: *quam vellent aethere in alto / nunc et pauperiem et duros perferre labores.*

2 698-9. Macrobius (*Sat.* 5.19.2) refers to the view of Cornutus that Virgil invented this ritual, but refutes it by citing Euripides (*Alc.* 73f.) where Death plans to cut a lock of Alcestis' hair to make her sacred to the god of the underworld.

3 700-2. 'So Iris flew down from the sky on her saffron wings, dew bespangled, trailing a thousand changing colours as the sun shone on her'. The supernatural beauty of the rainbow goddess brings a calm serenity to these closing scenes; cf. *Aen.* 5.88f., 606f., Ov. *Met.* 11.589f., Stat. *Th.* 10.118f., and Ceres' words to Iris in Shakespeare, *The Tempest* 4.1.76f.
Hail, many colour'd messenger, that ne'er
Dost disobey the wife of Jupiter;
Who with thy saffron wings upon my flowers
Diffusest honey-drops, refreshing showers:
And with each end of thy blue bow dost crown
My bosky acres, and my unshrubb'd down,
Rich scarf to my proud earth. . . .

4 702. **hunc**: referring to *crinem* (698).

5 703. **iussa**: 'as instructed', by Juno; Iris does not perform this function on her own authority.

6 704-5. 'and with it all warmth left her, and her life departed into the winds'; cf. *Aen.* 10.819-20, 11.617. The final line is gentle and rhythmically conclusive with its fourth foot composed of a single word (see on 1.7), and its light alliteration. Page quotes Shakespeare, *Richard III*, 1.4.37f.
The envious flood
Kept in my soul, and would not let it forth
To seek the empty, vast and wandering air.

BOOK 5

Introductory Note

The fifth book provides a diminution of tension between the intensity of Book 4 and the majesty of Book 6; in this respect its structural function is not unlike that of Book 3. In order to maintain continuity Virgil leads into his description of the games by gradually lessening the emotional significance of the narrative, and leads out from them again by gradually increasing it. Thus the book starts with a last backward glance at Carthage and continues with an impressive description of the religious ceremonies and Aeneas' filial devotion to Anchises before the games themselves begin with the ship race. The tension is at its lowest for the boxing-match (see note on 362f.), and rises again with the omen after the archery contest and the spectacular cavalcade of the *lusus Troiae* with its optimistic and patriotic impact. Thus a serene mood is established, making the intervention of Juno all the more terrifying, as she attempts again to prevent the foundation of Rome by inciting the burning of the ships and the resultant despair of Aeneas. He is brought now to a point where he wonders whether to forget the fates, and is restored to confidence only by the intervention of the ghost of his father Anchises. This intervention motivates Aeneas' visit to the underworld, and the pathos of the story of Palinurus, with which the book ends, sets the tone for the mystery and awe of Book 6.

One way then in which continuity is achieved is by the subtle arrangements of mood and tension. Another is by the renewal of main themes of the poem; the religious aspect of the games is strongly stressed, and the future destiny of Rome is kept before our eyes by aetiological reference to famous Roman families (see note on 117f.) and to the contemporary pageant of the *lusus Troiae* (see note on 545f.). The importance of Anchises in guiding Aeneas, which had been illustrated during his lifetime in the account of the voyage (Book 3), is now further illustrated after his death; and the difficulties which beset Aeneas in fulfilling his mission are again seen to be almost overwhelming.

The description of the games themselves has as its literary source the account of the games for Patroclus in Hom. *Il.* 23, and there are frequent echoes. But in place of Homer's vivid and fast-moving narrative Virgil has substituted an elaborate and varied pattern, reducing the number of contests from eight to four, alternating the long accounts of the ship race and the boxing with the briefer footrace and archery, constantly changing his method of description and his way of interesting the reader in the characters and events (see Otis, *Virgil,* pp. 41f.). I have discussed the individual events in the notes at the beginning of each; for fuller details see E. N. Gardiner, *Athletics of the Ancient World,* and the introduction to my OUP Ed. of Book 5.

In addition to having a Homeric model Virgil was led to include an account of athletic games by the new popularity of festivals of the Greek type which Augustus fostered. The victory at Actium was celebrated by the inauguration of Actian games at Nicopolis in 28 B.C., and these took place subsequently every four years. Thus the description of the games represents an aspect of poetic creativity which is very characteristically Virgilian; the use of Homeric source material in such a way as to adapt it both to the more elaborately organised requirements of literary epic and to the traditions and interests of the contemporary Roman world.

1-7. As the Trojans sail away from Carthage, they look back and see a blaze in the city; although they do not know that it comes from Dido's Pyre, they feel presentiments of misfortune.

[1]Interea medium Aeneas iam classe tenebat

certus[2] iter fluctusque atros[3] Aquilone secabat

moenia respiciens, quae iam infelicis[4] Elissae

conlucent flammis.[5] Quae tantum accenderit ignem

causa latet;[6] [7]duri[8] magno sed amore dolores   5

polluto,[9] notumque[10] furens quid femina possit,

triste per augurium Teucrorum pectora ducunt.

8-41. When they reach the open sea, a violent storm comes upon them and Palinurus the helmsman tells Aeneas that it is impossible to hold their course for Italy, and suggests that they should run with the wind to Sicily. Aeneas agrees, and they land near the tomb of Anchises, and are welcomed by Acestes.

Ut pelagus tenuere rates nec iam amplius ulla[11]

occurrit tellus, maria undique et undique caelum,

---

1 1f. This is Virgil's transition from the tragic events of Book 4 to the resumption of the description of Aeneas' journey. It is brief and reticent and ends in slow phrases of sorrow (5-7) before Virgil suddenly returns (8f.) to lines of rapid narrative of a conventional kind which he had used before (3.192-5). The contrast in tone here is very abrupt as Virgil leaves at last a theme on which he could say no more, but on which he could never feel that enough had been said.

2 2. **certus**: 'resolute', cf. *Aen.* 4.554; Aeneas' decision has been taken and he cannot now be turned from his purpose.

3 **atros Aquilone**: 'darkened by the north wind', cf. Aul. Gell. 2.30.

4 3. **infelicis Elissae**: the adjective has frequently been applied to Dido in Books 1 and 4, and now it ends her story. It is used once more, by Aeneas to her ghost in the underworld, 6.456. For Elissa, the original Phoenician name of Dido, see note on 1.340 and 4.335.

5 4. **flammis**: i.e. the flames of the funeral pyre; we are reminded of Dido's last words in 4.661-2.

6 5. **latet**: 'is unknown to them'; the subject is the interrogative clause *quae . . . causa.*

7 5-7. 'but the thought of the bitter agony caused when a great love is desecrated, and the knowledge of what a woman in wild frenzy may do, led the hearts of the Trojans along paths of sad foreboding.' Notice the metrical art of these lines; the slow spondees, the alliteration of *d, f, t,* the assonance, of *u* and *-urn* and the coincidence of ictus and accent in the fourth foot in line 7, giving a finished effect; see further the note on this passage in my OUP Ed., and compare *Aen.* 1.7, 4.705.

8 5. **duri magno sed**: the postposition of the conjunction throws great emphasis on to the two adjectives.

9 6. **polluto**: a very strong word, given added weight by the enjambement before a pause; it denotes the breaking of a sacred tie (cf. *Aen.* 3.61, 7.467), and here (note its juxtaposition with *dolores*) reflects what the Trojans now realise Dido's feelings must have been.

10 **notumque**: the neuter of the participle is used as a noun, cf. 290, *Geo.* 3.348, Livy 27.375, Lucan 1.70.

11 8-11. These lines, modelled on Hom. *Od.* 12.403-6 (= 14.301-4) are almost exactly repeated in 3.192-5, where see notes.

olli[1] caeruleus supra caput astitit imber   10
noctem hiememque ferens et inhorruit unda tenebris.
Ipse gubernator puppi Palinurus ab alta:
'heu quianam[2] tanti cinxerunt aethera nimbi?
Quidve, pater Neptune, paras?' Sic[3] deinde locutus
colligere[4] arma iubet validisque incumbere remis,   15
obliquatque[5] sinus in ventum ac talia fatur:
'magnanime Aenea, non, si mihi Iuppiter auctor[6]
spondeat, hoc[7] sperem[8] Italiam contingere caelo.
Mutati [9]transversa[10] fremunt et vespere ab atro
consurgunt venti, atque in[11] nubem cogitur aer.   20
Nec[12] nos obniti contra nec tendere tantum
sufficimus. Superat quoniam Fortuna, sequamur,
quoque vocat vertamus iter. Nec litora longe[13]
fida reor fraterna[14] Erycis portusque Sicanos,
si[15] modo rite memor servata remetior astra.'   25
Tum pius[16] Aeneas: 'equidem sic poscere ventos
iamdudum et frustra cerno te tendere contra.
Flecte viam velis. [17]An sit mihi gratior ulla,

---

1 10. **olli**: archaic form for *illi,* cf. *Aen.* 1.254; this is varied from 3.194 *tum mihi caeruleus* etc., which perhaps explains the singular *olli* where we would expect *ollis,* referring to the Trojans.

2 13. **quianam**: 'why?', an archaic word used again in *Aen.* 10.6; see *Quint.* 8.3.24f.

3 14. **sic deinde**: for postponed *deinde* see note on 1.195, and cf. 321, 400.

4 15. **colligere arma**: 'to take in the tackle', i.e. to shorten sail (so Servius), not 'to get together their equipment', as some suggest; cf. Stat. *Th.* 7.88. For *arma* in a nautical sense cf. *Aen.* 4.290, 6.353.

5 16. **obliquatque . . . ventum:** 'he set the sails aslant into the wind', i.e. trimmed the sheets in order to luff, that is to sail nearer to the wind, now changed from north to west (19). Compare 828f., and Livy 26.39.19.

6 17-18. **auctor spondeat:** 'should pledge it with all his authority', a very emphatic phrase.

7 18. **hoc ... caelo:** 'in weather like this', cf. *Geo.* 1.51 ,*Aen*.4.53.

8 **sperem . . . contingere:** for *sperare* with the present infinitive cf. *Aen.* 4.337-8.

9 19f. The wind has now changed from north to west; it is not its direction which causes the trouble, but its violence, which means they cannot make way against it and must run before it.

10 19. **transversa:** adverbial accusative, cf. 381, 866, 869 and *Ecl.* 3.8.

11 20. **in nubem . . . aer:** 'the air thickens into cloud', cf. Cic. *Nat. De.* 2.101.

12 21-2. 'We cannot possibly battle against the storm, or make enough way against it'; for *tendere* cf. 286, and *Aen.* 1.205, 554. The infinitive with *sufficere* is uncommon, cf. Lucan 5.154.

13 23. **longe:** supply *abesse* or *esse* (*Aen.* 12.52).

14 24. **fraterna Erycis:** for *fraternus* (= *fratris*) cf. 630. Eryx, son of Venus and Butes, was Aeneas' half-brother; he gave his name to the well known mountain and town in Sicily (759).

15 25. 'if only I remember correctly as I plot our way back by the stars I watched before', i.e. when they set out from Sicily and were driven by a storm to Carthage (3.692f., 1.34f.). For *servare* cf. *Aen.* 6.338; for *remetiri* (calculating one's way back) cf. *Aen.* 2.181, 3.143.

16 26. **pius**: see note on 1.10; here the main reference of the word is to Aeneas' position of responsibility for his men.

17 28-30. The order is intricate, with *tellus* postponed from its adjective *ulla* — 'could any land be more welcome to me, or one to which (*quove* = *vel ad quam*) I would rather . . . than that land which. . . .'

quove magis fessas optem demittere[1] navis,
quam quae Dardanium tellus mihi servat Acesten[2]   30
et patris Anchisae[3] gremio complectitur ossa?'
Haec ubi dicta, petunt portus et vela secundi
intendunt Zephyri; fertur cita gurgite classis,
et tandem laeti notae advertuntur[4] harenae.

   At procul ex celso miratus vertice montis   35
adventum[5] sociasque rates occurrit Acestes,
horridus[6] in iaculis et pelle Libystidis[7] ursae,
Troia Criniso conceptum flumine mater[8]
quem genuit. Veterum[9] non immemor ille parentum
gratatur[10] reduces et gaza laetus agresti   40
excipit, ac fessos opibus solatur amicis.

---

1 29. **demittere:** 'bring to land'; for the nautical use of *de-* cf. 57, 212. The major MSS have *dimittere*, 'dismiss', i.e. 'disembark from', cf. *Aen.* 10.366, but as no confusion is commoner in MSS than that between *de-* and *di-* it seems better to accept the technical term.

2 30. Acestes, the Sicilian king of Trojan lineage, is mentioned in 1.195 and 550; see note on 38. He plays an important part in the *Aeneid*, foreshadowing in legend the very close historical bonds between Sicily and Rome.

3 31. The last incident of his journey which Aeneas related to Dido was the death of Anchises at Drepanum (3.709f.).

4 34. **advertuntur harenae:** the dative of motion towards is common in verse with compound verbs, cf. 93, 346, 434, 805.

5 36. **adventum sociasque rates:** 'the arrival of a friendly fleet', a good example of hendiadys, cf. *Aen.* 1.54, 61.

6 37 'a wild-looking figure carrying his javelins and wearing the skin of a Libyan she-bear'. This is a memorable and picturesque line which Tacitus recalled and imitated, *Hist.* 2.88 *tergis ferarum et ingentibus telis horrentes.* For *in iaculis* cf. 550 and Ennius' phrase (*Ann.* 506) *in hastis. Horridus* conveys its basic sense of 'bristling' (cf. *Aen.* 3.23) and also its wider meaning, 'rustic' (cf. *Aen.* 7.746).

7 **Libystidis:** the adjective *Libystis* (for *Libyca*) occurs only here and in *Aen.* 8.368.

8 38. Servius tells the story on *Aen.* 1550; Segesta (or Egesta) who gave her name to Acestes' town in Sicily was banished from Troy and in Sicily became the mother of Acestes (also called Egestus) by the god of the river Crimissus (near Segesta). Virgil's form *Crinisus* may be an error in the MSS or a variant of the name.

9 39. **Veterum . . . parentum:** i.e. his Trojan mother and her ancestors, this is a common meaning of *parens,* cf. *Aen.* 9.3.

10 40. **gratatur reduces:** 'showed his delight at their return'; *gratari* is an archaic form of *gratulari.* The construction is accusative and infinitive (*eos reduces esse*), cf. Tac. *Ann.* 6.21.

42-71. On the next day Aeneas summons an assembly and reminds the Trojans that it is the anniversary of the death of his father Anchises. He proclaims a solemn sacrifice at the tomb, which is to be followed on the ninth day by contests in rowing, running, boxing and archery.

¹Postera cum primo² stellas³ Oriente fugarat
clara dies, socios in coetum litore ab omni
advocat Aeneas tumulique⁴ ex aggere fatur:
'Dardanidae⁵ magni, genus alto a sanguine divum,   45
annuus⁶ exactis completur mensibus orbis,
ex quo reliquias divinique⁷ ossa parentis
condidimus terra maestasque sacravimus aras;
iamque dies, nisi fallor, adest, quem semper acerbum,
semper honoratum (sic di voluistis) habebo.   50
Hunc⁸ ego Gaetulis agerem si Syrtibus exsul,
Argolicove mari deprensus⁹ et urbe¹⁰ Mycenae,
annua vota tamen sollemnisque ordine pompas
exsequerer strueremque suis¹¹ altaria donis.
Nunc ultro¹² ad cineres ipsius¹³ et ossa parentis,   55
haud equidem sine mente reor sine numine divum,

---

1 42f. The detailed and colourful description of the honours paid at the tomb of Anchises gives a religious and patriotic setting to the account of the anniversary games. The games have their model in Homer (*Iliad* 23), but are also reminiscent of Roman *ludi funebres,* the games held after the funeral of important citizens (Livy 23.30.15, 28.21.10, etc.). Virgil mingles Greek and Roman traditions in the description of the religious ceremony; essentially Aeneas is celebrating the normal Roman ritual at the anniversary of a father's death (*parentatio,* see note on 59-60), but mystery and majesty is added by elements from the Greek hero cult (*divinus,* 47, *templa,* 60, *adyti,* 84). For further discussion see Bailey, *Religion in Virgil,* pp. 291f. Servius compares the 'deification' of Anchises here with that of Julius Caesar, but Virgil does not define the nature of Anchises' divinity very explicitly, and if there is allegory it is of a most indirect kind.

2 42. **primo . . . Oriente:** 'at first dawn', cf. *Aen.* 3.588. *Oriens* is a noun as in 739.

3 **stellas ... fugarat:** see note on *Aen.* 3.521. *Fugarat* is contracted for *fugaverat;* for Virgil's avoidance of the pluperfect subjunctive with *cum* see note on 1.36-7.

4 44. **tumulique ex aggere:** 'from a raised mound', as a Roman general would address his soldiers in camp; cf 113.

5 45. Dardanus, founder of the Trojan royal line, was a son of Jupiter, cf. *Aen.* 7.219f.

6 46. The passage of a year since Anchises' death is presumably to be accounted for by assuming that the Trojans stayed some months in Drepanum before spending the winter in Carthage.

7 47. **divini:** the word could be used of the *di parentes* in Roman religion, but may imply more than that; see note on 42f.

8 51f. 'If I were spending this day as an exile in the Gaetulian Syrtes, or caught in the Argolic sea and (held) in the city of Mycenae, yet I still would be fulfilling . . .', i.e. whether in desolate Africa or hostile Greece, whether at sea or on land. The Syrtes were the great sandbanks near Carthage, called Gaetulian by association with the Gaetuli of that area, cf. *Aen.* 4.40 and line 192. The Argolic sea could be a vague term for any part of the sea round Greece (cf. *Aen.* 3.283), but here perhaps refers to the *sinus Argolicus* near Mycenae.

9 52. **deprensus:** probably caught by a storm (*Geo.*4.421) rather than caught by the Greeks; certainly it does not mean caught (surprised) by the anniversary.

10 **urbe Mycenae:** Virgil does not elsewhere use the singular form of *Mycenae.* The genitive is appositional, cf. *Aen.* 1 247.

11 54. **suis:** 'due' (= *propriis*); cf. *Aen.* 1.461, 3.469, and line 832.

12 55. **ultro:** 'actually', 'unexpectedly', cf. *Aen.* 2.145 and line 446.

13 **ipsius et**: *et* is postponed, cf. *sed* in line 5.

adsumus et portus[1] delati intramus amicos.
Ergo agite et laetum[2] cuncti celebremus honorem:
poscamus[3] ventos, [4]atque haec me sacra quotannis
urbe velit posita templis sibi ferre dicatis.   60
Bina boum[5] vobis Troia generatus Acestes
dat numero capita in navis; adhibete penatis
et patrios epulis et quos colit hospes Acestes.
Praeterea, [6]si nona[7] diem mortalibus almum
Aurora extulerit radiisque[8] retexerit orbem,   65
prima citae[9] Teucris ponam certamina classis;
quique pedum cursu valet, et qui viribus[10] audax
aut iaculo incedit melior levibusque sagittis,
seu crudo fidit[11] pugnam committere caestu,[12]
cuncti adsint meritaeque exspectent praemia palmae[13]   70
Ore[14] favete omnes et cingite tempora ramis.'

---

1 57. **portus . . . amicos**: 'have reached land and come to a friendly haven'; the present tense *intramus* is influenced by *adsumus*.

2 58. **laetum . . . honorem**: 'our happy tribute'; *laetus* continues the idea built up in this passage (see note on 42f.) that the anniversary rites are to be performed not only in mourning for the dead, but also in joy for the evident concern of the gods for Anchises.

3 59. **poscamus ventos**: 'let us ask Anchises for favouring winds'; the point of this request at this moment seems at first obscure, but in the next line Aeneas shows how his thoughts are upon the foundation of his city at the end of his journey.

4 59-60. 'and may he grant me to pay these rites each year in a temple dedicated to him when my city is founded'. Virgil here looks forward to the Roman festival of the *Parentalia* described by Ovid (*Fast.* 2.543f.) as having been instituted by Aeneas in honour of Anchises.

5 61-2. **bourn . . . capita**: 'head of cattle', cf. *Aen.* 3.391.

6 64f. Two different explanations of Aeneas' meaning have been current since antiquity: 'when the ninth day brings its light', or 'if the ninth day is fine'. The first is much to be preferred; conjectures about the weather are inappropriate in epic. Further, *almus* is a permanent epithet for *dies,* cf. Hor. *Odes* 4.7.7, *Ecl.* 8.17, and its use with *lux* in *Aen.* 1.306, 3.311 etc. For the use of *si* cf. Cat. 14.17; the mode of expression may have been connected originally with superstitious fear.

7 64.-65. **nona . . . Aurora**: the solemnities at a Roman funeral lasted for nine days (Hor. *Epod.* 17.48, Apul. *Met.* 9.31).

8 65. **radiisque retexerit orbem**: 'reveals the world with his rays', cf. *Aen.* 4.119 (the same phrase).

9 66. **citae . . . classis**: 'a contest for swift ships'; the genitive is regularly used of the nature of the contest, cf. Livy 10.2.15 *sollemni certamine navium, Geo.* 2.530, Ov. *Met.* 10.177.

10 67. **viribus audax**: this goes with both the following lines: Aeneas proclaims a ship race, a foot race, and (for those who trust in their strength) a contest in javelin throwing and archery or boxing. In fact, no javelin contest is reported, but the formula in line 68 couples javelin throwing and archery as one type of activity, cf. *Aen.* 9.178.

11 69. **fidit. . . committere**: this is a marked extension of the normal use of *fidere;* it has the sense here of *audere,* hence the following infinitive.

12 **caestu**: see note on 364. The spondaic line is appropriate for the announcement of the heavyweight contest.

13 70. **palmae**: the palm as a prize for victory came late to Greece, not before 400 B.C.; according to Livy (10.47.3) it was introduced from Greece into the Roman world in 293 B.C.

14 71. **ore favete**: 'utter no ill-omened word', a religious formula tending to mean 'observe silence', cf. Hor. *Odes* 3.1.2.

*72-103. The Trojans proceed to the tomb of Anchises, where
Aeneas offers libations and addresses his father's shade.
Suddenly a huge snake comes forth from the tomb, tastes the
offerings, and then disappears. Aeneas recognizes that this
indicates the presence of Anchises' ghost at the ceremony,
and the sacrifice is renewed, and followed by a ritual feast.*

[1]Sic fatus velat materna[2] tempora myrto.
Hoc Heiymus facit, hoc aevi[3] maturus Acestes,[4]
hoc puer Ascanius, sequitur quos cetera pubes.
Ille e concilio [5]multis cum milibus ibat[6]   75
ad tumulum magna medius comitante caterva.
Hic[7] duo rite mero libans carchesia Baccho
fundit humi, duo lacte novo, duo sanguine sacro,
purpureosque iacit flores ac talia fatur:
'salve,[8] sancte parens, iterum salvete, recepti[9]   80
nequiquam cineres animaeque umbraeque paternae.
Non [10]licuit finis Italos fataliaque[11] arva
nec tecum Ausonium, quicumque[12] est, quaerere Thybrim.'
Dixerat haec,[13] adytis[14] cum lubricus anguis ab imis

---

1 72f. For the religious significance of this passage see note on 42f.

2 72. **materna . . . myrto**: the myrtle was sacred to Venus, Aeneas' mother (*Ecl.* 7.62, *Geo.* 1.28, *Aen.* 6.443);it was also sometimes associated with the dead.

3 73. **aevi maturus**: for the genitive of respect cf. *Aen.* 2.638 and note on 1.14.

4 73-4. Mackail points out how these lines indicate that the sports will be for all ages: Helymus, a young man, enters the foot race, the older Acestes is in the archery contest, and the boy Ascanius leads the *lusus Traiae*. Helymus' name is associated with the Sicilian people called the Elymi.

5 75-76. The alliteration of *m* and *c* is very marked, perhaps to give a tone of solemnity and archaic ritual at the beginning of the description of the ceremony.

6 75. **ibat**: 'set out', ingressive impeded.

7 77-78. 'Here in due libation he poured on the ground two goblets of unmixed wine, two of fresh milk, two of sacrificial blood'. The spirit of the departed was supposed to partake of such libations (cf. *Aen.* 3.66f., 301f.); for *libare* cf. *Aen.* 1.736. The ablatives are rather extended usages of the ablative of description. For *Bacchus = vinum*, a very common metonymy, cf. *Aen.* 1.215.

8 80. **salve . . . iterum salvete**: 'hail . . . , again I say hail', cf. Cat. 64.23. This meaning is preferable to the suggestion (so Servius) that Aeneas had first said *salve* at the time of burial.

9 80-1. **recepti . . . cineres**: 'ashes recovered in vain', a difficult phrase, meaning that the rescue of Anchises from Troy (*Aen.* 6.111 *eripui his umeris medioque ex hoste recepi*) was in vain because of his death before reaching Italy (82f. *non licuit*. . . .)

10 82. To this line supply *tecum quaerere* from the next clause, the postposition of *tecum* is unusual and puts emphasis on the word.

11 **fataliaque arva:** cf. *Aen.* 4.355.

12 83. **quicumque est:** Aeneas knows that the Tiber is his goal (2.782, 3.500), but it is still a vague and un-located goal. Page well draws attention to the contrast of this vague phrase with the Tiber's later fame.

13 84f. For the significance of the snake see note on 95; for other snake descriptions cf. lines 273f., *Aen.* 2.203f., 471f., *Geo.* 2.153f. The description here is one of exceptional colour and brilliance, without the note of fear in the other passages cited.

14 84. **adytis . . . ab imis**: Servius comments that Virgil in treating Anchises as a god makes his tomb a kind of temple; see note on 42f.

septem[1] ingens gyros, septena volumina traxit   85
amplexus placide tumulum lapsusque per aras,
caeruleae[2] cui terga notae maculosus et auro
squamam incendebat fulgor, ceu[3] nubibus arcus
mille iacit varios adverso sole colores.
Obstipuit visu Aeneas. Ille agmine[4] longo   90
tandem inter pateras et levia[5] pocula serpens[6]
libavitque[7] dapes rursusque innoxius imo
successit[8] tumulo et depasta[9] altaria liquit.
Hoc magis inceptos genitori instaurat honores,
incertus[10] geniumne[11] loci famulumne[12] parentis   95
esse putet; [13]caedit binas de more bidentis[14]
totque sues, totidem nigrantis terga[15] iuvencos,
vinaque fundebat pateris animamque vocabat
Anchisae magni manisque Acheronte[16] remissos.

---

1 85. 'drew along in mighty bulk its seven undulating coils'. *Septena volumina* is a variation on *septem gyros;* the meaning is not (as Henry, followed by Page, argues) that the snake made seven circuits of the tomb, progressing in seven coils. The figure seven is probably mystic (*Aen.* 6.38), rather than a reference, as Servius says, to the seven years of Aeneas' wanderings. The distributive *septena* is equivalent to the cardinal *septem,* as often in poetry; cf. 96 *binas,* 560 *terni.*

2 87-8. 'blue flecks mottled its back, and a sheen of golden markings lit up its scales'; to the nominative *notae* must be supplied from *incendebat* some verb like *distinguebant.*

3 88-9. 'like the rainbow when it catches the sun's rays and throws a thousand changing colours on the clouds'; cf. *Aen.* 4.701, almost the same words.

4 90. **agmine longo:** 'with its long sweep', cf. *Aen.* 2.212, 782.

5 91. **levia:** 'smooth', i.e. burnished, as in 558.

6 **serpens:** this is of course the participle, not the noun.

7 92. **libavitque:** 'tasted', cf. *Ecl.* 5.26, *Geo.* 4.54; the shade of meaning is different from that in 77. There is the same pattern of doubled -*que* ('both . . . and') in 177, 234.

8 93. **successit tumulo:** 'went into the tomb', cf. *Aen.* 1.627.

9 93. **depasta altaria:** 'the altars he had fed off', for *depascere* used actively cf. *Geo.* 4.539.
'Because of this he resumed all the more fervently the rites he had begun in honour of his father'; for *instaurare* cf. *Aen.* 2.451, 4.63.

10 95-6. **incertus . . . putet:** 'uncertain whether to think ... or'; for -*ne . . . -ne* cf. 702-3.

11 95. **geniumne loci:** according to the pantheistic view of the old Roman religion every natural feature, hill, spring, tree, river, had its *genius,* its local god; cf. *Aen.* 7.136 and Milton, *Lycidas* 182-3 'Now Lycidas the Shepherds weep no more; / Henceforth thou art the Genius of the shore . . .'

12 95. **famulumne parentis:** 'or the attendant spirit of his father'; cf. Val. Fl. 3.457f. The soul of the dead (like the *genius*) was often represented as a snake; see Conington ad loc. There is relatively little difference between these alternative views of the snake; it represents the spirit of Anchises appearing at his own tomb.

13 96f. The offerings of sheep, pigs and bullocks suggest the Roman sacrificial lustration *Suovetaurilia* (*sus, ovis, taurus*); cf. *Aen.* 11.197f.

14 96. **bidentis:** sheep in their second year, see note on 4.57.

15 97. **terga:** accusative of respect, see note on 1.320.

16 99. **Acheronte remissos:** 'released from Acheron', to visit the sacrifices, cf. *Aen.* 3.303f. Acheron was one of the rivers of the underworld (*Aen.* 6.295, Milton, *P.L.* 2.578 'Sad Acheron of sorrow, black and deep'), and was commonly used to mean the underworld itself: cf. *Aen.* 7.312.

Nec non et socii, quae[1] cuique est copia, laeti 100
dona ferunt, [2]onerant aras mactantque iuvencos;
ordine[3] aena locant alii fusique per herbam
subiciunt veribus prunas et viscera torrent.

> *104-113. The day of the games comes round, and the people*
> *assemble; the prizes are displayed, and the trumpet sounds*
> *for the beginning of the contests.*

[4]Exspectata dies aderat nonamque serena
Auroram Phaethontis[5] equi iam luce vehebant, 105
famaque finitimos et clari nomen Acestae
excierat: laeto complerant litora coetu
visuri Aeneadas, pars et certare parati.
Munera principio ante oculos circoque[6] locantur
in medio, [7]sacri tripodes viridesque coronae 110
et palmae pretium victoribus, armaque et ostro
perfusae vestes, argenti aurique talenta;
et tuba commissos medio canit aggere ludos.

---

1 100. **quae cuique est copia**: 'each according to his means', a 'detached' use of the relative, equivalent to *sicut cuique est copia;* cf. Plin. *Ep.* 8.8.7.

2 101-3. Notice the extreme simplicity of the construction of these lines with their short clauses each with its main verb; perhaps the style reflects the well known simple ritual acts performed one after the other.

3 102. **ordine**: 'in their due places', suggesting ritual correctness; cf. 53, 773.

4 104f. Virgil's long and elaborate description of the games is modelled, with variations, on the funeral games for Patroclus described in *Iliad* 23; in turn Statius (*Thebaid* 6) and Silius (*Punica* 16) imitated Virgil. In deciding to include an account of athletic contests in the *Aeneid* Virgil had a number of motives
apart from the Homeric precedent: to relieve the emotional tension between Books 4 and 6; to concentrate attention on Anchises and the religious honours paid to him by his son (see note on 42f.); and to serve as a prototype for current Roman customs and institutions, especially for the revival of interest in athletics fostered by Augustus.
In the description of the contests Virgil has aimed at an effect quite different from that of *Iliad* 23. Where Homer is direct and immediate in appeal, Virgil gives a more formally organised account, with a contrived balance and unity such as is appropriate for his kind of literary epic. There are many similarities of incident between Homer and Virgil, but the method and tone of the two differ completely. See further the introduction to this book.

5 105. **Phaethontis**: this is a name of the sun, the shining one (cf. Hom. *Il.* 11.735), not the Phaethon of mythology.

6 109. **circoque**: Virgil is probably thinking of a curving bank on the seashore, enclosing a space which could be called *circus;* cf. 289.

7 110f. The successful athletes are to receive prizes of material value as well as tokens of honour like garlands. This was the case in Homer, but not in the great Greek festivals like the Olympic games. In most Roman games prizes of value were given, but at his Actian games Augustus reverted to the practice of the Olympic games.

114-50. Four competitors enter for the ship race, Mnestheus in the Pristis, Gyas in the Chimaera, Sergestus in the Centaurus, and Cloanthus in the Scylla. The course is out to sea, round a rock and home again. The competitors draw lots for position; the starting signal is given, and the ships get under way amidst applause.

[1]Prima[2] pares ineunt gravibus certamina remis
quattuor ex omni delectae classe carinae.   115
Velocem[3] Mnestheus agit acri remige[4] Pristim,[5]
mox[6] Italus Mnestheus, genus[7] a quo nomine Memmi,
ingentemque[8] Gyas ingenti mole Chimaeram,[9]
urbis[10] opus, triplici[11] pubes quam Dardana versu
impellunt, terno consurgunt ordine remi;   120
Sergestusque, domus tenet a quo Sergia nomen,
Centauro invehitur magna,[12] Scyllaque Cloanthus
caerulea, genus unde tibi, Romane Cluenti.

---

1 114f. Virgil's ship race corresponds with the chariot race in Homer, both in being the first of the contests and in a number of details, especially at the turning point. Aeneas of course had no chariots, but in any case the maritime nature of much of the first half of the *Aeneid* makes a ship race particularly appropriate. Augustus' Actian games included a regatta, but a ship race was not an expected part of athletic contests. No other extant ancient epic contains one.

In the introductory section to the first contest (114-50) Virgil allows himself plenty of space to set the scene. Our interest is developed before the race by the descriptions of the competitors, the course, the waiting for the start, the excitement of the spectators.

2 114-15. 'For the first event four ships entered, well matched with their heavy oars, and especially chosen out of the whole fleet.' The ships are not of the same size, but they are of the same class (i.e. triremes) with an equal number of rowers. Triremes did not exist in Aeneas' time; these are contemporary Roman ships.

3 116f. The competitors have all been briefly introduced to us earlier in the poem (cf. 1.222, 510, 612, 4.288). Their characters are clearly revealed in the race, and directly influence the action. Sergestus is rash and impetuous, and runs aground; Gyas is hot tempered and foolish, and loses his chance of success through a fit of anger; Mnestheus is gallant and determined, and comes very near to victory; Cloanthus keeps going steadily and holds off the final challenge by a timely prayer to the deities of the sea.

4 116. **remige**: collective singular, cf. *Aen.* 4.588.

5 **Pristim**: 'Leviathan'. This is a word of vague meaning, indicating some kind of sea monster, cf. *Aen.* 10.211. There is also the form *pistrix* (*Aen.* 3.427). The ships would have figure-heads representing their names; cf. *Aen.* 10.195f.

6 117f. A considerable number of Roman families traced their origins back to the Trojans (cf. 568); Hyginus and Varro wrote works *De Familiis Troianis*. The Roman *gentes* whose ancestors figure here in the ship race were not among the most highly distinguished; the most famous of the Memmii was the propraetor of Bithynia whom Catullus accompanied, and to whom Lucretius dedicated his poem; the best known member of the *gens Sergia* was the infamous Catiline; and we know relatively little about the *Cluentii*, one of whom was defended by Cicero. Servius tells us that the *gens Gegania* (of whom a number appear in the pages of Livy) was descended from Gyas; perhaps Virgil omits mention of them because the family had died out by his time. Virgil's fondness for aetiological name associations was encouraged by the use made of them in Hellenistic poetry, but generally is directly related to the national theme of the *Aeneid*. Compare lines 568 and 718, *Aen.* 1.267 (Iulus), 6.234 (Misenus), 6.381 (Palinurus), 7.2 (Caieta), 10.145 (Capys), and the whole series in 8.337f. and in the catalogue (7.647f.).

7 117. **genus . . . Memmi**: 'from whose name comes the race of Memmius'; *Memmi* is the normal form of the genitive singular.

8 118. The repetition of *ingens* is reminiscent of Homer (*Il.* 16.776); cf. *Aen.* 10.842 (= 12.640). The phrase *ingenti mole* is ablative of description, 'with its mighty mass'.

9 118. **Chimaeram:** this fabulous tripartite dragon occurs first in Hom. *Il.* 6.179f., a lion in front, a serpent behind, and a she-goat in the middle; cf. *Aen.* 6.288, 7.785.

10 119. **urbis opus**: 'the size of a city', a most remarkable phrase imitated by Ovid (*Fast.* 6.641) and Statius (*Silv.* 2.2.30f., cf. *Th.* 6.86). For the idea cf. Cic. *Verr.* 2.5.89.

11 119. **triplici. . . versu**: 'with triple banks of oars , cf. Livy 33.30.5.

12 122. **magna**: as Centaurus is the name of a ship, it is feminine.

Est procul in pelago saxum spumantia contra
litora, quod tumidis summersum tunditur olim[1]   125
fluctibus, hiberni condunt ubi sidera Cauri;[2]
tranquillo[3] silet immotaque attollitur unda[4]
campus et apricis statio gratissima mergis.
Hic viridem Aeneas frondenti ex ilice metam[5]
constituit signum nautis pater,[6] unde [7]reverti   130
scirent et longos ubi circumflectere cursus.
Tum loca sorte legunt ipsique in puppibus auro[8]
ductores[9] longe effulgent ostroque decori;
cetera populea[10] velatur fronde iuventus
nudatosque umeros[11] oleo perfusa nitescit.   135
Considunt transtris, [12]intentaque[13] bracchia remis;
intenti exspectant signum, [14]exsultantiaque haurit
corda pavor pulsans laudumque arrecta cupido.
Inde ubi clara dedit sonitum tuba, finibus[15] omnes,
haud mora, prosiluere suis; ferit aethera clamor[16]   140
nauticus, adductis[17] spumant freta versa lacertis.

---

1 125. **olim**: 'at times', an archaic use (cf. *Aen.* 3.541).

2 126. **Cauri**: these are northwest winds bringing storms (Pliny *N.H.* 18.338); the word is sometimes spelled *Cori*.

3 127. **tranquillo**: 'in calm weather', ablative of time when (cf. Livy 31.23.4).

4 127-8. 'and rises up from the still waves as a level expanse, a favourite resort for cormorants basking in the sun'. *Campus* and *statio* are in apposition to the subject *saxum;* for *apricus* 'delighting in the sun' cf. Persius 5.179 *aprici. . . senes.*

5 129. **metam**: 'turning-point', see note on 3.714; presumably Aeneas has a leafy branch or young tree wedged into the flat rock to make it more easily visible.

6 130. **pater:** the order is unusual, and perhaps draws some attention to Aeneas' position of responsibility in making the proper arrangements.

7 130-1. 'so that they should know where to make the turn for home, where to come round in their long course'; cf. *Aen.* 3.430. The second phrase is a variation on the first.

8 132. For the drawing of lots for position cf. Hom. *Il.* 23.352f.

9 133. **ductores**: 'captains'. Each ship has its captain, its helmsman (*rector,* 161), and its rowers.

10 134. **populea . . . fronde**: the poplar was sacred to Hercules, patron of athletes; cf. *Aen.* 8.276.

11 135. **umeros . . . perfusa**: 'their shoulders anointed', retained accusative with a passive verb (here used in a middle sense); cf. 269, 309, 511, 774, 869 (and also 264, 608), and note on 1.228.

12 136-41. Notice how the spondaic movement of the first three lines conveys the pause and sense of waiting for action, and is released by the rapid movement of 139-41, where dactyls largely predominate.

13 136-7. **intentaque . . . intenti**: 'their arms are tensed on the oars, tensely they await the signal'; the word here is used in two slightly different senses.

14 137-8. 'and the throb of nervous excitement and their eager longing for glory clutch at their leaping hearts'. These powerfully pictorial phrases are repeated from *Geo.* 3.105f., and are an elaboration of Hom. *Il.* 23.370-1. *Pavor* does not mean 'fear', but the feeling akin to trembling experienced by an athlete in anticipation; *haurire* here literally means 'to drain of blood'.

15 139. **finibus**: 'starting-places', the *loco* of 132.

16 140-1. **clamor nauticus**: 'the shouts of the rowers', cf. *Aen.* 3.128.

17 141. **adductis . . . lacertis**: 'as they bring their arms right up to their chests', in the motion of rowing.

Infindunt pariter sulcos, totumque dehiscit[1]
convulsum remis rostrisque tridentibus aequor.[2]
Non[3] tam praecipites biiugo certamine campum
corripuere ruuntque effusi carcere[4] currus,   145
nec sic immissis aurigae undantia lora
concussere iugis[5] pronique in verbera pendent.
Tum plausu fremituque virum studiisque[6] faventum
consonat omne nemus, vocemque[7] inclusa volutant
litora, pulsati colles clamore resultant.[8]   150

151-82. Gyas gets the lead, followed by Cloanthus, with Mnestheus and Sergestus contending for third position. As they draw near the turning-point, Gyas urges his helmsman Menoetes to steer closer in; but in fear of fouling the rock he fails to do so, and Cloanthus' ship slips past on the inside. In a fury of anger Gyas throws Menoetes overboard; eventually he manages to clamber out on to the rock, while all the spectators are amused at the incident.

[9]Effugit ante alios primisque[10] elabitur undis
turbam inter fremitumque Gyas; quem deinde Cloanthus
consequitur, melior remis, sed pondere pinus[11]
tarda tenet. Post hos aequo[12] discrimine Pristis
Centaurusque locum[13] tendunt superare priorem;   155
et nunc Pristis habet, nunc victam praeterit ingens

---

1 142. **dehiscit**: 'is split open to its depth', cf. *Aen.* 1.106, 4.24. The long vowel of *de-* is shortened before the following vowel; cf. *dehinc* (722),*praeeunte* (186).

2 143. The same verse occurs in *Aen.* 8.690. *Tridentibus* refers to the three prongs on the prow of a ship.

3 144-7. 'Not with such headlong speed do chariots leap forward over the plain in a contest for paired horses, racing away as they come streaming out from the barriers; no, not when the charioteers shake out the rippling reins as they give free head to their teams, and lean right forward to use the whip.'
Virgil is influenced in his choice of simile by the fact that his ship race is modelled on Homer's chariot race; there are two images, the speed of the chariots, and the efforts of the charioteers to get more speed. Cf. also *Geo.* 3.103f.

4 145. **carcere**: this is the technical term for the starting pens or barriers on a race course; cf. *Geo.* 1.512.

5 147. **iugis**: the yokes, i.e. the yoked horses, are given free rein.

6 148. **studiisque faventum**: 'the rival cries of supporters', cf. 450.

7 149-50. **vocemque . . . litora**: 'the sheltered shores re-echo the noise'; the shores are *inclusa* by the foot-hills and cliffs. For *volutant* cf. *Aen.* 1.725.

8 150. **resultant**: 'reverberate'; cf. *Aen.* 8.305.

9 151f. The description of the race is full of incident, and all four of the competitors play important parts in it and leave a clear impression of their individuality (see note on 116f.).

10 151. **primisque . . . undis**: 'and sweeps ahead over the waves right at the beginning'.

11 153. **pinus**: his ship of pine, cf. *Aen.* 10.206. Notice the alliteration of *p* and *t* here, indicating heaviness.

12 154. **aequo discrimine**: 'equidistant'.

13 155. **locum ... priorem**: 'strive to get forward into a leading position', i.e. to be third rather than fourth; for *superare* cf. *Aen.* 2303.

Centaurus, nunc una[1] ambae iunctisque feruntur
frontibus et longa sulcant vada salsa carina.
Iamque propinquabant scopulo metamque tenebant
cum princeps medioque Gyas in gurgite victor   160
rectorem navis compellat voce Menoeten:
'quo[2] tantum mihi[3] dexter abis? Huc derige cursum;[4]
litus[5] ama et laeva[6] stringat sine palmula cautes;
altum alii teneant.' Dixit; sed caeca Menoetes
saxa timens proram pelagi[7] detorquet ad undas.   165
'quo diversus abis?' Iterum[8] 'pete saxa, Menoete!'[9]
Cum clamore Gyas revocabat, et ecce Cloanthum
respicit instantem tergo et propiora[10] tenentem.
Ille inter navemque Gyae scopulosque sonantis
radit[11] iter laevum interior subitoque priorem   170
praeterit et metis tenet aequora tuta[12] relictis.
Tum[13] vero exarsit iuveni dolor ossibus ingens
nec lacrimis caruere genae, segnemque[14] Menoeten
oblitus decorisque[15] sui sociumque salutis
in mare praecipitem puppi deturbat[16] ab alta;   175

---

1 157-8. **una ... frontibus:** 'together and prow to prow'.

2 162. **quo . . . abis:** 'Hey! Where are you going, so far off to the right?' The ships are making the turn in an anticlockwise direction, i.e. to the left, as in a Roman chariot race.

3 **mihi**: ethic dative, underlining the indignation of the speaker. Page drily says ' "Pray" and "Prithee" are accepted renderings, but a naval captain would perhaps put it otherwise'.

4 **cursum**: most MSS have *gressum*, for which there is much to be said (cf. Aul. Gell. 10.26), but it may have come in from *Aen.* 1.401 or 11.855 (non-naval contexts).

5 163. **litus una:** 'hug the edge of the island', cf. Hor. *Odes* 1.25.3f.

6 **laeva ... cautes:** 'let the oars on the left graze the rocks'; for *stringere* cf. Ov. *Am.* 3.2.12. For the parataxis *stringat sine* cf. line 717 and *Aen.* 2.669. *Palmula* is collective singular, cf. 116.

7 165. **pelagi. . . ad undas:** i.e. still outwards, instead of turning round the rock for home.

8 166. **Iterum:** with *revocabat*; Servius' suggestion (adopted by Mackail) of taking it with *abis* is possible, but the broken rhythm expresses well the anxiety of Gyas.

9 **Menoete**: Greek vocative, cf. 564, 843.

10 168. **propiora tenentem:** 'holding a course nearer in', i.e. nearer to the turning-point; for the adjective used as a noun cf. 194.

11 170. **radit ... interior:** 'grazed his way through (scraped through) inside on the left'; for *radere* cf. Ov. *Am.* 3.15.2 and *Aen.* 3.700, 7.10.

12 171. **tuta:** i.e. in contrast to the danger he had been in when he took the turn so fine.

13 172. 'Then indeed the young man blazed with furious indignation in every fibre of his being'; the headstrong Gyas is very vividly drawn, especially in contrast with his safety-first helmsman.

14 173. **segnem:** 'timid', 'unenterprising'; notice the emphasis given by the word order here: first the object, then a whole line in apposition to the subject before the verbal action is described.

15 174. **decorisque . . . salutis:** 'both of his own dignity and of his crew's safety'; *socium* is the archaic form of the genitive plural, see note on 1.4.

16 175. **deturbat:** 'pitches', a vivid and somewhat colloquial word, cf. *Aen.* 6.412 and Plaut. *Merc.* 116 *deturba in viam* ('kick him out').

ipse gubernaclo rector[1] subit,[2] ipse magister
hortaturque viros clavumque ad litora torquet.
At[3] gravis ut fundo vix tandem redditus imo est
iam senior madidaque fluens in veste Menoetes
summa petit scopuli siccaque in rupe resedit.[4]   180
Illum[5] et labentem Teucri et risere natantem
et salsos rident revomentem pectore fluctus.

> *183-226. Mnestheus and Sergestus now have new hope of passing Gyas. Sergestus gets slightly ahead and Mnestheus urges his men to put forward all their efforts to avoid the disgrace of coming in last. Sergestus goes in too near to the turning-point and runs aground, breaking his oars on one side. Mnestheus leaves him behind and soon overtakes Gyas too; then he sets out after Cloanthus.*

[6]Hic laeta extremis spes est accensa duobus,
Sergesto Mnestheique,[7] Gyan superare[8] morantem.
Sergestus capit[9] ante locum scopuloque propinquat,   185
nec tota tamen ille[10] prior praecunte[11] carina;
parte prior, partim[12] rostro premit aemula Pristis.
At media[13] socios incedens nave per ipsos
hortatur Mnestheus: [14]'nunc, nunc insurgite remis,

---

1 176. **rector . . . magister:** 'helmsman' and 'pilot'; the words are practically synonymous.

2 **subit**: in the sense of *succedit*, cf. *Aen.* 6.812.

3 178. 'But when at long last Menoetes in his sorry state was returned to the surface from the bottom of the sea. . .'. The picture of Menoetes' helplessness is built up by the epithet *gravis,* the exaggerated *fundo imo,* the adverbs *vix tandem,* and the passive *redditus* (he could do nothing himself, he was disgorged by the sea).

4 180. **resedit:**'sank down'.

5 181-2. Notice the similarity of participial endings, and the intricate word order. Virgil was perhaps thinking here (as he was in 357f.) of *Il.* 23.784, where all the Greeks laugh at Ajax covered in the slime in which he has slipped.

6 183f. Virgil now reverts to the two contestants for the third place, Sergestus in the *Centaurus* and Mnestheus in the *Pristis.* Sergestus is half a length ahead and on the inside when Mnestheus calls for a spurt; this causes Sergestus to try to hold him off by taking the turn too close in to the rocks, with unwished for consequences.

7 184. **Mnestheique:** Greek form of the dative; the *e* is slurred in pronunciation, cf. *Aen.* 1.41.

8 **superare**: for the infinitive dependent on a noun see note on 1.704.

9 185. **capit ante locum:** 'gets the lead', the adverb *ante* goes with the noun, cf. Lucr. 5.1371.

10 186. **ille:** for this pleonastic use of *ille* in the second of two clauses which have the same subject cf. lines 334 and 457 and see note on 1.3.
He is not a full length ahead; there is no daylight between.

11 **praeeunte**: the diphthong in *prae-* is shortened before the following vowel; cf. *Aen.* 7.524.

12 187. **partim ... premit:** *partim* is a form of the accusative, not the adverb. *Premit* means 'overlaps', 'is close upon', cf. *Aen.* 1.324, 467.

13 188. **media ... incedens nave:** 'pacing amidships', on the gangplank.

14 189f. Mnestheus' speech is like that of Antilochus to his horses in Hom. *Il.* 23.402f., where he tells them that they cannot defeat Diomedes but must beat Menelaus. Antilochus gets past Menelaus in a narrow place because Menelaus gives way; Virgil varies this by having Mnestheus get past because Sergestus rashly goes in too close.

Hectorei[1] socii, Troiae quos sorte suprema   190
delegi comites; nunc illas promite viris,
nunc animos, [2]quibus in Gaetulis Syrtibus usi[3]
Ionioque mari Maleaeque sequacibus[4] undis.
Non iam prima[5] peto Mnestheus[6] neque vincere certo
(quamquam[7] o! – sed superent quibus hoc, Neptune, dedisti);   195
extremos pudeat rediisse: hoc[8] vincite, cives,
et prohibete[9] nefas.' Olli certamine[10] summo
procumbunt: [11]vastis tremit ictibus aerea[12] puppis
subtrahiturque[13] solum, tum creber anhelitus artus
aridaque ora quatit, sudor fluit undique rivis.   200
Attulit ipse[14] viris optatum casus honorem:
namque furens animi dum proram ad saxa suburget
interior spatioque[15] subit Sergestus iniquo,
infelix saxis in procurrentibus haesit.
Concussae cautes et acuto in murice[16] remi   205
obnixi crepuere inlisaque[17] prora pependit.
Consurgunt nautae et magno[18] clamore morantur

---

1 190. **Hectorei socii**: 'my men, comrades of Hector'; the adjective is used with the emotional intention of calling for the utmost endeavours.

2 192f. These areas of sea through which Aeneas and his followers had come are in reverse chronological order. The storm at the Syrtes sandbank off Carthage is described in 1.102f., the storm in the Ionian sea in 3.192f.; Cape Malea (on the southern tip of the Peloponnese) was, like the Syrtes, proverbially dangerous, cf. Prop. 3.19.7-8.

3 192. **usi**: understand *estis;* the omission of the verb 'to be' in the second person (cf. 687) is not common.

4 193. **sequacibus**: 'pursuing'; cf. *Aen.* 8.432.

5 194. **prima**: 'victory'; for the neuter plural of the adjective used as a noun cf. 168, 335, 338.

6 **Mnestheus**: he uses his own name with some pathos in the humbling of his pride.

7 195. **quamquam o!**: the unfinished sentence (aposiopesis) continues the sense of pathos; the wish would have been something like *o si daretur superare* (cf. *Aen.* 11.415).

8 196. **hoc vincite**: 'win this victory', i.e. do not come in last. First place must go to those to whom Neptune has granted it; but not to come in last, let that be a victory. *Hoc* is cognate accusative.

9 197. **prohibete nefas**: 'save us from shame'; the exaggeratedly strong word *nefas* expresses Mnestheus' intense feelings.

10 **certamine**: 'effort', cf. *Aen.* 11.891.

11 198. The effort of the rowers as they get into their rhythm is reflected in the movement of this line, with conflict of ictus and accent in the first three feet and coincidence in the last three, each of which consists of a single word. For further discussion see my note ad loc. (OUP Ed.).

12 **aerea puppis**: 'the bronze-beaked ship', cf. *Aen.* 1.35.

13 199. **subtrahiturque solum**: 'and the surface of the water slips from under them'; cf. Ov. *Her.* 6.67. *Solum* is not used elsewhere of the sea; it occurs of the sky in Ov. *Met.* 1.73, cf. also *Aen.* 7.111.

14 201. **ipse ... casus**: 'mere chance', 'actually it was chance'.

15 203. **spatioque subit... iniquo**: 'and approached the danger area', by taking the turn dangerously close to the rocks.

16 205. **murice**: 'jagged edges'. The word means the purple shellfish with its jagged shell, and is here used of sharp rock.

17 206. **inlisaque prora pependit**: 'the prow, dashed against the rock, hung out of the water', cf. *Aen.* 10.303.

18 207. **magno clamore morantur**: 'hold her steady with loud shouts'. *Morantur* is explained by Servius as backing water, and this seems the correct sense; they try to stop the ship by reversing the oars to prevent further damage. Most commentators take the sense of the phrase to be 'clamouring loudly at the delay', but this seems improbable.

ferratasque trudes[1] et acuta cuspide contos
expediunt[2] fractosque legunt in gurgite remos.
At laetus Mnestheus successuque acrior ipso   210
agmine[3] remorum celeri ventisque vocatis
prona[4] petit maria et pelago decurrit aperto.
Qualis[5] spelunca subito commota columba,
cui [6]domus et dulces latebroso[7] in pumice nidi,[8]
fertur[9] in arva volans plausumque exterrita pennis   215
dat tecto ingentem, mox aere lapsa quieto
radit[10] iter liquidum celeris[11] neque commovet alas:
sic Mnestheus, sic ipsa[12] fuga secat ultima Pristis
aequora, sic illam fert impetus ipse volantem.
Et primum in scopulo luctantem deserit alto[13]   220
Sergestum brevibusque vadis frustraque vocantem
auxilia[14] et fractis discentem currere remis.
Inde Gyan ipsamque ingenti mole Chimaeram
consequitur; cedit, quoniam spoliata[15] magistro est.
Soliis iamque ipso superest[16] in fine Cloanthus,   225
quem petit et summis adnixus viribus urget.

---

1 208. **trudes:** 'poles', for pushing off (Tac. *Ann.* 3.46).

2 209. **expediunt:** 'get out', from where they were stored; cf. *Aen.* 1.178.

3 211. **agmine:** 'sweep', cf. 90; the word conveys the ordered progression of the series of strokes.

4 212. 'sets out for his shoreward course and speeds in over open water', i.e. rounds the rock and makes for home; *prona* combines its literal meaning of 'sloping downwards', i.e. 'down 'to shore from the high seas (*decurrit*), and its metaphorical meaning of 'easy'.

5 213f. The point of comparison in this remarkably pictorial simile is that Mnestheus' crew make rapid strokes at first and then speed onwards under the impetus gained, just as the dove flaps its wings furiously at the beginning of its flight, and then glides smoothly on through the sky. Cf. the comparison of the Argo with a hawk in Ap. Rh. 2.932f.

6 214. The spondaic line, together with the unusually long word in the second half of the line, represents rhythmically the sad end of Sergestus' hopes.

7 214. **latebroso in pumice:** 'in crannied rock'; there is the same phrase in *Aen.* 12.587.

8 **nidi:** 'nestlings', cf. *Geo.* 4.17, *Aen.* 12.475.

9 215f. Notice how the rhythm here corresponds with the sense: from *plausumque* to *ingentem* there is spondaic movement and alliteration of *p* and *t*; then the rhythm changes to dactyls, and there is smooth alliteration of *l* and *r*.

10 217. **radit iter liquidum:** 'skims her airy way'; for *liquidum* cf. 525.

11 **ceteris neque:** *neque* is postponed, and *ceteris* goes with *alas*.

12 218. **ipsa fuga:** 'speeding along on her own'; *ipsa* suggests that she has now no need of oars. Cf. Cic. *De Orat.* 1.153.

13 220. **alto:** 'projecting'.

14 222. 'taking a lesson in rowing with broken oars' (Day Lewis) which well renders the derisive humour.

15 224. **spoliata magistro:** 'deprived of her helmsman', cf. 176 and *Aen.* 6.353.

16 225. **superest:** 'is left' to overtake.

227-43. Mnestheus' final spurt to catch Cloanthus would perhaps have succeeded had not Cloanthus prayed to the gods of the sea. His prayers are heard, and he reaches harbour, the winner of the race.

Tum vero ingeminat clamor cunctique sequentem
instigant[1] studiis, resonatque fragoribus aether.
Hi [2]proprium decus et partum indignantur honorem
ni teneant, vitamque volunt pro laude pacisci;   230
hos successus alit: possunt,[3] quia posse videntur.
Et[4] fors aequatis cepissent praemia rostris,
ni palmas ponto tendens utrasque Cloanthus
fudissetque preces divosque in vota vocasset:
'di, quibus imperium est pelagi, [5]quorum aequora curro,   235
vobis laetus ego hoc candentem in litore taurum
constituam ante aras voti[6] reus, extaque salsos
porriciam[7] in fluctus et vina liquentia fundam.'
Aixit, [8]eumque imis sub fluctibus audiit omnis
Nereidum Phorcique chorus Panopeaque virgo,[9]   240
et pater ipse manu magna Portunus[10] euntem[11]
impulit: illa noto citius volucrique sagitta
ad terram fugit et portu se condidit alto.

---

1 228. **instigant**: 'urge on', cf. *Aen.* 11.730.

2 229-30. 'The leading crew think it shame not to hold on to the glory that is theirs, and the triumph already won'; *teneant* is semi-oblique (*putant indignum esse ni teneant*). For *pacisci* ('bargain') cf. *Aen.* 12.49.

3 231. **possunt . . . videntur:** 'they can do it, because they think they can'; cf. Livy 2.64.6 *dum se putant vincere, vicere,* and Dryden, *Ann. Mir.* 190 'And seeming to be stronger makes them so'.

4 232. 'And perhaps Mnestheus' crew, as they came up level, would have gone on to win the prize'; it is commonly thought that this line indicates that the result might have been a dead heat, but this implies an awkward change of subject to *utrique.* For *fors* used elliptically (= *forsitan*) cf. *Aen.* 2.139, 6.537; cf. Milton, *P.L.* 2.492 'If chance the radiant Sun. . . .'

5 235f. Compare Odysseus' prayer to Athena when he was just behind Ajax in the foot race (Hom. *Il.* 23.768f.).

6 237. **voti reus:** 'in discharge of my vow'; the man whose prayer is granted is under an obligation to pay what he has promised; he is a defendant in regard to it, liable for it.

7 238. **porriciam:** 'cast forth', a technical term in sacrifices (Livy 29.27.5); the MSS have *proiciam,* but Macrobius (*Sat.* 3.2.2) attests this orthography in religious contexts. Cf. 776.

8 239f. The description of the deities of the sea, who hear Cloanthus' prayer and give him victory, closes the long and exciting account of the race with a pictorial touch of a most attractive kind, a delightful glimpse of ancient pageantry.

9 240. Virgil is fond of this kind of descriptive line made up of sonorous names; compare 823f. Phorcus (an old man of the sea) and Panopea (one of the Nereids) occur again there in the description of Neptune's retinue.

10 241. **Portunus**: god of harbours, identified with Palaemon (Melicertes), cf. 823 and Ov. *Fast.* 6.547.

11 241. This line is closely modelled on Ennius *Ann.* 569 *atque manu magna Romanes inpulit amnis*; cf. Hom. *Il.* 15.694f. and Ap. Rh. 2.598f. (where Athena pushes the Argo through the Symplegades).

244-85. Aeneas distributes prizes to the crews of the three ships and their captains. When this is completed, Sergestus finally manages to bring home his disabled ship, moving slowly like a maimed snake; he duly receives his fourth prize.

Tum satus[1] Anchisa cunctis ex more vocatis
victorem magna praeconis voce Cloanthum   245
declarat viridique advelat tempora lauro,
muneraque in navis ternos optare[2] iuvencos[3]
vinaque et argenti magnum[4] dat ferre talentum.
Ipsis praecipuos ductoribus addit honores:
victori chlamydem[5] auratam, [6]quam plurima circum   250
purpura maeandro duplici Meliboea cucurrit,
intextusque puer frondosa regius Ida[7]
velocis iaculo cervos cursuque fatigat
acer, anhelanti[8] similis, quem praepes ab Ida[9]
sublimem pedibus rapuit Iovis armiger[10] uncis: 255
longaevi palmas nequiquam ad sidera tendunt
custodes, saevitque canum latratus in auras.
At qui deinde[11] locum tenuit virtute[12] secundum,
levibus [13]huic hamis consertam auroque trilicem
loricam, quam Demoleo[14] detraxerat ipse   260

---

1 244. **satus Anchisa**: a fairly frequent phrase for Aeneas (line 424, *Aen.* 6.331). *Satus* in this sense ('begotten from') is mainly poetic.

2 247. **optare . . . ferre**: for this use of the epexegetic infinitive after *dare* cf. 262, 307, 538, 572 and note on *Aen.* 1.66.

3 247-8. As prizes each crew is to have three bullocks of their choice (out of the herd), some wine and a talent of silver.

4 248. **magnum ... talentum**: i.e. the normal Attic talent (cf. *Aen.* 9.265).

5 250. **chlamydem**: a cloak of Greek type (cf. *Aen.* 4.137) here embroidered with gold.

6 250-1. 'round which ran a deep border of Meliboean purple with its double wavy line'. *Meliboeus* (from the town in Thessaly) is used of purple in Lucr. 2.500; for the formation of the adjective see note on 1.686. The river Macander was proverbial for its twists and turns (Ov. *Met.* 2.246, 8.162); it is used metaphorically in Cicero (*In Pis.* 53).

7 252f. Ganymede, the young and handsome son of the Trojan prince Tros was carried off from Mt. Ida by Jupiter's eagle to be cup-bearer to the gods (Hom. *Il.* 20.232f., Theoc. 15.123f. *Ov. Met.* 10.155f., and note on 1.28).

8 254. **anhelanti similis**: i.e. so life-like that you might forget it was a picture; cf. *Aen.* 8.649f.

9 254f. This is a second picture of Ganymede on the *chlamys*. For descriptions of works of art (ecphrasis) see note on 1.418f.

10 255. The eagle is Jupiter's *armiger* because it carries the thunderbolt, cf. *Aen.* 9.563f., Hor. *Odes* 4.4.1f. Pliny (*Nat. Hist.* 2.146) records the belief that eagles are not struck by thunderbolts.

11 258. **deinde:** for the position of this word see note on 14.

12 **virtute:** 'by his prowess'.

13 259. 'interwoven with burnished chain and triple-meshed in gold', i.e. a coat of mail; cf. *Aen.* 3.467.

14 260. Demoleos is not otherwise known; for the dative cf. 845.

victor apud rapidum Simoenta[1] sub Ilio[2] alto,
donat habere, viro decus et tutamen in armis.
Vix illam famuli Phegeus Sagarisque[3] ferebant
multiplicem conixi umeris; indutus[4] at olim
Demoleos cursu palantis Troas[5] agebat.   265
Tertia dona facit geminos ex aere lebetas
cymbiaque[6] argento perfecta atque aspera signis.
Iamque adeo donati omnes opibusque superbi
puniceis ibant evincti tempora[7] taenis,[8]
cum[9] saevo e scopulo multa vix arte revulsus[10]   270
amissis remis atque ordine debilis uno
inrisam sine honore ratem Sergestus agebat.
Qualis saepe viae[11] deprensus in aggere serpens,[12]
aerea quem obliquum[13] rota transiit aut gravis[14] ictu
seminecem liquit saxo[15] lacerumque viator;   275
nequiquam[16] longos fugiens dat corpore tortus
parte ferox ardensque oculis et sibila colla
arduus attollens; pars vulnere clauda retentat

---

1 261. **Simoenta:** Greek accusative, cf. 634, 536. For Simois, one of Troy's rivers, cf. *Aen.* 1.100.

2 **Ilio alto:** in this line of Homeric subject matter Virgil uses a line ending reminiscent of Greek rhythm, with the final syllable of *Ilio* shortened in hiatus; see note on 3.211.

3 263. Sagaris and Phegeus are both killed by Turnus (*Aen.* 9.575, 765).

4 264-5. **indutus . . . agebat:** 'but in days gone by Demoleos used to run wearing it, as he went in pursuit of Trojan stragglers'. *Indutus* has a middle sense, see notes on 135 and 2.275.

5 265. **Troas:** the Greek third declension form of the accusative plural, with short *-as*, cf. *lebetas* in the next line.

6 267. **cymbia:** small drinking cups, cf. *Aen.* 3.66, 9.263. *Aspera signis* means 'embossed', cf. 536.

7 269. **tempora:** for the retained accusative see note on 135.

8 **taenis:** 'ribbons', attached to their garlands (110). The ablative plural is here contracted (*taeniis*).

9 270-2. **cum ... agebat:** the imperfect is not common in an inverted *cum* clause. Here it pictorially represents the slowness and difficulty with which Sergestus got restarted: 'they were all parading with their prizes when, look, Sergestus began to bring back his ship'. Compare Cic. *Verr.* 2.2.89 and (slightly different) *Aen.* 3.301f. Notice how this sentence is built up with descriptive dependent clauses while the main verb and the subject are held up until 272.

10 270. **revulsus:** 'worked himself off'; the application of this word and of *debilis* in the next line to Sergestus himself rather than his ship has a vivid effect.

11 273. **viae . . . aggere:** 'on the causeway' rather than 'on the crown of the road'.

12 273f. For snake similes and descriptions see note on 84f. The point of comparison here is the maimed movement, but Virgil develops the picture of the snake beyond the point of comparison.

13 274. **obliquum . . . transiit:** 'has run over as it came from the side'; cf. Hor. *Odes* 3.27.6f.

14 274-5. **gravis ictu ... viator:** an unusual transference for *gravi ictu . . . viator,* emphasised by the fifth foot clash of word accent and ictus.

15 275. **saxo:** instrumental with *seminecem,* 'half-killed by a rock', rather than local 'half-dead on the road' (Henry, Page).

16 276f. 'In vain as it tries to get away does it writhe its body in great curves, part of it defiant, eyes blazing, hissing head raised high; but part is crippled by the wound and holds the snake back as it tries to struggle along in knots and keeps coiling back upon itself. The use of *dare* is a favourite Virgilian turn of diction, cf. 139, 435. For *arduus* adverbially with the participle cf. 567, 764, 838. Notice the assonance and rhyme in 278-9, and for the general picture cf. *Geo.* 3.420f., *Aen.* 2.381f., 475.

nixantem[1] nodis seque in sua membra plicantem:

tali remigio navis se tarda movebat; 280

vela facit tamen et velis subit ostia plenis.

Sergestum Aeneas promisso munere donat[2]

servatam ob navem laetus sociosque reductos.

Olli serva datur[3] operum haud ignara Minervae,[4]

Cressa genus,[5] Pholoe, geminique sub ubere nati. 285

> *286-314. Aeneas now leads the assembled company away from the shore to a grassy plain surrounded by hills, suitable for the remaining contests. He invites competitors for the foot race, and many Trojans and Sicilians enter for it. He promises gifts for all the runners, and announces the prizes which will be awarded to the first three.*

[6]Hoc pius Aeneas misso[7] certamine tendit

gramineum in campum, quem collibus undique curvis

cingebant silvae, mediaque in valle theatri[8]

circus erat; [9]quo se multis cum milibus heros

consessu medium tulit exstructoque resedit. 290

Hic, qui forte velint rapido contendere cursu,[10]

invitat pretiis animos, et praemia ponit.

Undique conveniunt Teucri mixtique Sicani,

Nisus et Euryalus primi,[11]

---

1 279. **nixantem:** frequentative form of *nitentem* ('struggling'), cf. Lucr. 3.1000, 4.506, 6.836. The less well attested variant *nexantem* (a most uncommon word) would mean 'twining (itself)'.

2 282f. This passage recalls Homer's account of how Achilles gave a prize to Eumelus who came in last in the chariot-race because of the accident which befell him (*Il.* 23.534f).

3 284. **datur:** the final syllable is lengthened in arsis; cf. 337, 521, 853, and *Aen.* 1.668.

4 **Minervae:** for Minerva as the patron of women's work cf. *Aen.* 7.805, 8.408f.

5 285. **genus:** accusative of respect; cf. *Aen.* 8.114 and notes on 97, 4.558.

6 286f. The foot race is modelled on *Il.* 23.740-97, but where Homer has only three competitors (Ajax, Odysseus, and Antilochus), Virgil has seven named and many unnamed runners. The main feature of the race, the fall of Nisus, is taken from *Il.* 23.773f., where Ajax slips in the dung left by sacrificed animals, and there are other reminiscences, (see notes on 324, 325). For the incidents of the race see note on 315-19.

7 286. **misso:** equivalent to *dimisso* (cf. 545), meaning that the prize giving and concluding arrangements of the ship race have been completed.

8 288-9. **theatri circus**: 'the circle of a theatre'; the hills surrounding this circular plain make it a natural theatre for the games. *Theatrum* is used here in its widest sense (place for watching), not in the technical sense in which it differs from *amphitheatrum* or *circus*.

9 289-90. 'To this the hero moved off accompanied by many thousand people, himself in the midst of the concourse, and took his seat on a platform'. *Consessu* is best taken as ablative ('the central figure in the assemblage') rather than dative ('went to the auditorium'), because the idea of motion has already been expressed by *quo*. *Exstructo* is a neuter noun made from the participle; cf. line 6 and the use by Cicero of *suggestum* (from *suggerere*) in the sense of 'platform'.

10 291-2. The sentence is somewhat loosely constructed; the addition of the word *animos*, stressing the spirit required of intending contestants, means that the antecedent to be supplied for *qui* is *eorum* rather than *eos*, which the run of the sentence had led the reader to expect.

11 294. For the half line see note on 1.534. The others in this book are 322, 574, 595, 653, 792, 815.

Euryalus forma insignis viridique iuventa,   295
Nisus[1] amore pio pueri; quos deinde secutus
regius egregia Priami de stirpe Diores;[2]
hunc Salius simul et Patron, quorum alter Acarnan,
alter ab Arcadio Tegeaeae sanguine gentis:
tum duo Trinacrii iuvenes, Helymus[3] Panopesque,   300
adsueti silvis, comites senioris Acestae;
multi praeterea, quos fama obscura recondit.
Aeneas quibus in mediis sic deinde locutus:
'accipite haec animis laetasque advertite mentes.
Nemo ex hoc numero mihi non donatus abibit.   305
Cnosia[4] bina dabo levato lucida ferro
spicula caelatamque argento ferre[5] bipennem;
omnibus hic erit unus[6] honos. Tres praemia primi
accipient flavaque caput[7] nectentur oliva.
Primus equum phaleris[8] insignem victor habeto,[9]   310
alter Amazoniam[10] pharetram plenamque sagittis
Threiciis, lato quam circum amplectitur auro[11]
balteus et tereti subnectit fibula gemma;
tertius Argolica hac galea contentus abito.'

---

1 296. The construction is *Nisus insignis amore pio pueri*. Nisus is portrayed as an older man; he calls Euryalus *puer* in *Aen.* 9.217.

2 297f. Diores, son of Priam, is killed by Turnus (*Aen.* 12.509). Salius and Patron, the two Greeks, presumably joined Aeneas when he was at Buthrotum (3.292f.). Dionysius (1.51) tells us that this was so of the Acarnanian Patron.

3 300. The Sicilian Helymus was mentioned in 73; Panopes is not elsewhere mentioned. For the epithet *Trinacrii* (from the triangular shape of Sicily) see note on 3.384.

4 306. **Cnosia**: Cretan, from its chief town Cnossos. The Cretans were famed for archery, cf. *Geo.* 3.345, *Aen.* 4.70, 11.773.

5 307. **ferre**: 'to take away', see note on 247-8.

6 308. **unus**: i.e. *idem*, cf. 616.

7 309. **caput**: retained accusative, see note on 135.

8 310. **phaleris**: 'trappings'; the word is used of the decorations worn by soldiers (*Aen.* 9.458) or of the trappings which adorned horses' heads (Livy 22.52.5).

9 **habeto**: this form of the imperative has a formal and legalistic ring about it, appropriate for a proclamation (cf. 314).

10 311. **Amazoniam ... Threiciis**: Penthesilea and her Amazons fought for the Trojans (*Aen.* 1.490f.), and the Thracians too were Trojan allies (*Aen.* 3.13f.).

11 312-13. The shoulder-belt (or baldric) which held the quiver was studded with gold (cf. Ov. *Met.* 9.190) and fastened with a buckle (*fibula*); cf. *Aen.* 12.273f.

315-39. Nisus gets well ahead in the foot race, but as he nears the finish he slips in a pool of blood. While lying on the ground he trips up Salius who was second, so that his friend Euryalus comes up from third place to win.

[1]Haec ubi dicta, locum capiunt signoque repente   315
corripiunt spatia audito limenque relinquunt,
effusi nimbo[2] similes. Simul ultima signant
primus abit longeque ante omnia corpora[3] Nisus
emicat et ventis et fulminis ocior alis;
proximus huic, longo[4] sed proximus intervallo,[5]   320
insequitur Salius; spatio post deinde relicto
tertius Euryalus;
Euryalumque Helymus sequitur; [6]quo deinde sub ipso
ecce volat calcemque[7] terit iam calce Diores
incumbens umero, [8]spatia et si plura supersint[9]   325
transeat elapsus prior ambiguumve[10] relinquat.

---

1 315-19. 'When he had said this, they took up their positions and as the signal was heard they immediately darted forward over the course, moving away from the starting-point, sweeping forward like a cloud; as soon as they came in sight of the finish Nisus went away in front.' The old punctuation of this passage, with a full stop after *signant,* gave a most abrupt picture of the race and no very clear meaning for *simul ultima signant.* With the punctuation printed, proposed by Sandbach and discussed in full in my note ad loc. (OUP Ed.) we have first a picture of the start and the massed runners, and then as they near the finish Nisus goes away in front, opening up a big gap (cf. Homer's chariot race in *Il.* 23.373f.). For the conjunction *simul* cf. *Aen.* 3.630f. For *ultima signant* Sandbach suggested 'began to trample the last stretch' (cf. Ov. *Am.* 2.11.15); I prefer to take *signare* in the sense of *discernere* (cf. *Aen.* 2.422f.), and to visualise the race as round a turning point.

2 317. **nimbo similes**: the picture is not of falling rain (Henry, Page), but of the rapidly moving mass of a storm-cloud coming across the sky; cf. *Aen.* 12.450f., 7.793f.

3 318. **corpora**: 'figures', the word is used to make us visualise the race.

4 320. **longo sed**: the postposition of *sed* emphasises *longo,* already emphatic because it repeats *longe* (318) in the same position of the line.

5 **intervallo**: the spondaic ending is very unusual (see note on 2.68), and is due partly to Lucretian precedent (Lucr. 2.295, 4.187), and partly perhaps (as Page suggests) to the desire to emphasise the long distance.

6 323-6. 'Then just behind him, look, Diores flies along, grazing his very heels now, right up to his shoulder; if there were more of the course left, he would shoot in front and pass him. . .'.

7 324. **calcemque terit iam calce**: the phrase is strange, not to say anatomically impossible. The idea is based on *Il.* 23.763f. where Odysseus, just behind, is treading in Ajax's footsteps before the dust had settled; the diction seems to be an extension of the expression *calcem terere* ('to tread on someone's heels') along the lines of phrases involving repetition like *manus manibus, pede pes.*

8 325. The phrase recalls Hom. *Il.* 23.765, where Ajax feels Odysseus' breath on his neck.

9 325-6. The present subjunctive used to express a past unfulfilled condition when the narrative is in the historic present occurs several times in Virgil; cf. *Aen.* 2.599f., 6.292f., 11.912f. The effect is 'graphic', i.e. it makes the reader feel that he is present.

10 326. **ambiguumve relinquat**: 'or leave the issue in doubt', i.e. leave Aeneas with a dilemma, a neck in neck which he could not resolve. I have argued at length in my OUP Ed. why I accept the emendation of Bentley and others for the MSS *ambiguumque;* it is much nearer to the Homeric parallels (*Il.* 23.382, 527), and no really satisfactory sense can be got from *ambiguumque,* which most modern editors accept in some sense like 'leave him behind doubtful' or 'outpace his close rival'. Recently McDevitt (*C.Q.,* 1967, 313) has suggested 'and leave the result in doubt', i.e. as to whether he had passed the others as well as Helymus; this is more possible than the other renderings, but gives a rather confused picture.

Iamque[1] fere spatio extremo fessique sub ipsam
finem adventabant, levi[2] cum sanguine Nisus
labitur infelix, caesis ut forte iuvencis
fusus humum viridisque super madefecerat herbas.   330
Hic iuvenis iam victor ovans vestigia presso[3]
haud tenuit titubata[4] solo, sed pronus in ipso
concidit immundoque[5] fimo sacroque cruore.
Non tamen Euryali, non ille oblitus amorum:
nam sese opposuit Salio per lubrica surgens,   335
ille autem spissa iacuit[6] revolutus harena;
emicat Euryalus[7] et munere victor amici
prima tenet, plausuque volat fremituque secundo.
Post Helymus subit et nun tertia[8] palma Diores.

> *340-61. An objection is now raised by Salius, Aeneas overrules it, but he presents Salius with a consolation prize ; Nisus too is given a special prize.*

Hic [9]totum caveae consessum ingentis et ora[10]   340
prima patrum magnis Salius clamoribus implet,
ereptumque dolo reddi sibi poscit honorem.
Tutatur favor Euryalum lacrimaeque[11] decorae,

---

1 327f. The unfortunate accident at the end of the race is modelled on Hom. *Il.* 23.774f., where Ajax slips and falls in the dung left by sacrificial animals. The subsequent disgraceful behaviour of Nisus has no parallel in Homer. It served as a model for Statius (*Th.* 6.914f.) and Silius (16.517f.) to go one better and have the leader held back by his flying locks while someone else shot past to win. Such departures from seemly behaviour were censured by Chrysippus, quoted in Cic. *De Off.* 3.42, where he says that just as in a race one must try one's best to win but must not trip up or pull back one's opponent, so in life it is right to want the good things but not to acquire them by foul means.

2 328. **levi**: 'slippery'.

3 331-2. **presso . . . solo**: 'as he trod on the spot', or possibly 'though he pressed against the ground' (in the hope of regaining his foothold).

4 332. **titubata**: 'tottering'; the past participle used in an active sense, cf. *iuratus, cretus,* etc.

5 333. **immundoque . . . sacroque**: the use of doubled *-que* ('both . . . and'), along with *ipso,* gives a fullscale picture of Nisus' immersion.

6 336. **iacuit revolutus**: 'went head over heels and there he lay'; the tense of *iacuit* portrays the suddenness of the whole thing.

7 337. **Euryalus**: the last syllable is lengthened in arsis; see note on 284.

8 339. **tertia palma**: a delightful use of metonymy: Diores is now 'third prize', cf. 498.

9 340-61. This passage is inspired by Hom. *Il.* 23.540f., where first Antilochus and then Menelaus object to the award of the prizes after the chariot race. Homer's account is much longer, and the indignation and subsequent magnanimity of Antilochus are superbly told. Virgil's brief description gives a lively picture of the chief persons involved in the dispute: Salius filled with excited indignation, Euryalus silent and winning sympathy, Diores vehemently opposing Salius in case he should lose his third prize, Aeneas benevolent and tactful, and finally Nisus urging with a theatrical gesture his own very doubtful claim.

10 340-1. 'At this Salius with loud objections appealed to the whole audience of the great stadium and to the watching fathers in the front'. *Cavea* and *consessus* are terms used of a Roman theatre or circus, cf. 288f., *Aen.* 8.636. The phrase *ora prima patrum* is no doubt inspired by the thought of Roman senators sitting in the allocated front seats at the theatre or the circus (Livy 1.35.8). The use of *implet* is colourful and unusual, extended from instances like *Aen.* 2.769, 9.480, so that it approximates here in meaning to 'constantly assails'.

11 343. **lacrimaeque decorae:** 'his modest tears';he does not make a scene, which would be *indecorum.* There is also a suggestion perhaps that his beauty (344) is enhanced.

gratior[1] et pulchro veniens[2] in corpore virtus.

Adiuvat[3] et magna proclamat voce Diores,   345

qui subiit palmae frustraque ad praemia venit

ultima, si primi Salio reddentur honores.

Tum pater Aeneas 'vestra' inquit 'munera vobis

certa manent, [4]pueri, et palmam movet ordine nemo;

me liceat casus[5] miserari insontis amici.'   350

Sic fatus tergum[6] Gaetuli immane leonis

dat Salio villis onerosum atque unguibus[7] aureis.

Hic Nisus[8] 'si tanta' inquit 'sunt praemia victis,

et te lapsorum miseret, quae munera Niso

digna dabis, primam merui qui laude[9] coronam[10]   355

ni me, quae Salium, fortuna inimica tulisset?'[11]

Et simul his dictis faciem ostentabat et udo

turpia membra fimo. Risit pater optimus olli

et clipeum efferri iussit, Didymaonis[12] artes,

Neptuni [13]sacro Danais de poste refixum.   360

Hoc iuvenem egregium praestanti munere donat.

---

1 344. **gratior et**: again' the postposition of the conjunction emphasises the word which precedes it (cf. 320).

2 **veniens**: an unexpected use, 'presenting itself'.

3 345. **Adiuvat**: 'backs him up'.

4 349. Hirtzel and Mynors punctuate so that *pueri* is genitive, but *pater Aeneas* is here addressing the runners as *pueri;* his opening words *vestra . . . vobis* almost demand a vocative.

5 350. **casus**: 'misfortunes', 'bad luck'. Nisus takes him up (354) on the more literal meaning ('fall'). By *insontis* Aeneas means that Salius was not to blame; if he implies that Nisus was, he could hardly have put it more mildly.

6 351. **tergum**: 'hide', 'skin', a common meaning, cf. 403.

7 352. **unguibus aureis**: for the custom of gilding the claws of a lion-skin cf. *Aen.* 8.552f.; for the synizesis of *aureis* (scanned as a spondee) cf. *Aen.* 1.698.

8 353f. 'Then Nisus said "If the losers get prizes like that, and you feel sorry for people who fall, what in all fairness are you going to award to Nisus ? Why, I earned first prize. . . ." '

9 355. **laude**: 'by my merits', a common use of *laus*, cf. *Aen.* 1.461, 9.252.

10 355-6. The true apodosis of this past unfulfilled condition is concealed in an ellipsis: 'I earned first prize (and would have got it) if. . .'. Cf. *Aen.* 6.358f.

11 356. **tulisset**: 'snatched me away', for *abstulisset.* This use of the word normally occurs in more important contexts (e.g. *Aen.* 2.555), so that the exaggerated diction conveys the cool audacity of Nisus in defending his case. He seems to have convinced Servius, who says 'bene dolum suum excusat'.

12 359. **Didymaonis artes**: Didymaon is not otherwise known. This meaning of *ars* ('a work of art') is not common, but cf. Cic. *De Leg.* 2.4, Hor. *Odes* 4.8.5; it is here used in the poetic plural.

13 360. 'taken down by the Greeks from the sacred portal of Neptune'. *Danais* is dative of agent, cf. 305, 610. We are not told how the Trojans came into possession of it. Servius suggests Helenus perhaps gave it to him, cf. *Aen.* 3.463 f., but the point is that this exceptionally fine shield, dedicated once to Neptune, was removed from its temple not by the Trojans but by the Greeks.

362-86. Aeneas now announces a boxing competition. Dares comes forward, but nobody is prepared to fight him. He claims the prize.

¹Post, ubi confecti cursus et dona peregit:
'nunc, ²si cui virtus animusque in pectore praesens,
adsit et evinctis³ attollat⁴ bracchia palmis.'
Sic ait, et geminum pugnae⁵ proponit honorem,   365
victori velatum⁶ auro vittisque iuvencum,
ensem atque insignem galeam solacia victo.
Nec mora; continuo vastis cum viribus effert⁷
ora Dares magnoque⁸ virum se murmure tollit,
solus qui Paridem⁹ solitus contendere contra,¹⁰   370
idemque ad tumulum quo maximus occubat Hector
victorem Buten immani corpore, ¹¹qui se
Bebrycia veniens Amyci de gente ferebat,
perculit et fulva moribundum extendit harena.
Talis prima Dares caput altum in proelia tollit,   375

---

1 362f. The boxing competition has a number of reminiscences of the shorter description in Hom. *Il.* 23.653f., and of Ap. Rh. 2.1 f. (Amycus and Polydeuces). With the Greeks boxing was a highly skilled art practised at the great festivals, but in Roman times the use of the *caestus* had transformed it into a far more dangerous contest requiring mainly brute force and unflinching courage. Virgil describes the Roman type of boxing, but having little liking for it in real life he has chosen to handle the narrative on a mythological plane, in a setting of the distant days of heroes and demigods; the contestants (unlike those in the other events) play no further part in the *Aeneid,* and are not associated with Roman families. They are characters drawn on a large scale and in an exaggerated manner, with the alliteration and assonance of the verse often exaggerated to match (see notes on 431-2, 481). The length of the boxing contest balances the ship race and contrasts with the briefer accounts of the foot race and the archery; but the method of description in the two long events is very different. The ship race is all excitement, with multiplication of incident involving the four competitors, while the boxing incident is at a minimum (contrast the boxing match in Theoc. 22). The interest is concentrated on the *mise-en-scene* and on the two contestants, enormous figures of almost more than mortal strength, figures of a distant world like Lapiths fighting Centaurs, or Titans from a legendary past.

2 363. 'if anyone has valour and ready courage in his heart', a passage referred to by Seneca, *Ep. Mor.* 92.29.

3 364. **evinctis . . . palm is**: the *caestus,* which Roman boxers wore on their hands, had an altogether different function from that of the modern boxing glove. It consisted of hard leather thongs, sometimes reinforced with pieces of metal (401-5), and its object was not protection (of one's own knuckles or the other man's face) but to cause greater damage. The soft leather strips used in Homer (*Il.* 23.684) and at the Greek games were intended to protect.

4 364. **attollat bracchia**: compare our 'put up your fists'.

5 365. **pugnae**: the original meaning of this word is a fight with fists (*pugnus*).

6 366. **velatum . . . vittisque**: 'crowned with gold and garlands'. The phrase is not a hendiadys, but refers to two separate forms of decoration, garlands and the overlaying of the horns of the bullock with gold (*Aen.* 9.627, cf. Hom. *Od.* 3.432f.).

7 368-9. **effert ora**: 'thrust out his jaw', an amusingly picturesque phrase conveying the arrogant defiance of Dares.

8 369. **magnoque . . . murmure**: 'amidst a buzz of excitement from the crowd', notice the strong alliteration of *m* here, with the *v* of *virum* picking up *vastis . . . viribus* in the previous line.

9 370. **Paridem . . . contra**: the preposition follows its case, cf. 435.

10 370. The origin of the tradition that Paris was an outstanding boxer was generally attributed to the cyclic poets.

11 372-3. 'the all-conquering Butes, a man of giant stature, who came to the games and boasted of his descent from the Bebrycian race of Amycus'; this Butes is not mentioned elsewhere. Amycus, savage king of the Bebrycian race, compelled all strangers to box with him for their lives; after many victories he was defeated by Polydeuces (Ap. Rh. 2.1f., Theoc. 22).

ostenditque ¹umeros latos alternaque iactat
bracchia protendens et verberat ictibus auras.
Quaeritur huic alius; nec quisquam ex agmine tanto
audet adire virum manibusque inducere caestus.²
Ergo atacris³ cunctosque putans excedere⁴ palma   380
Aeneae stetit ante pedes, nec plura moratus
tum laeva taurum cornu tenet atque ita fatur:
'nate dea, si nemo audet se credere pugnae,
quae finis standi? Quo⁵ me decet usque teneri?
Ducere dona iube.' Cuncti simul ore fremebant   385
Dardanidae reddique viro promissa iubebant.

387-423. Acestes now urges Entellus, who was trained by Eryx, to oppose Dares. He protests that he is now past the prime of his youth, but none the less accepts the challenge and hurls into the ring a pair of huge gauntlets with which Eryx once fought Hercules. The spectators are all shocked and amazed; Entellus makes a taunting speech, but agrees to fight with matched gauntlets.

Hic gravis⁶ Entellum⁷ dictis castigat Acestes,
proximus⁸ ut viridante toro consederat herbae:
'Entelle, heroum quondam fortissime frustra,⁹
tantane tam patiens nullo certamine tolli   390
dona sines? ¹⁰Ubi nunc nobis deus ille, magister
nequiquam memoratus, Eryx? Ubi fama per omnem
Trinacriam et spolia illa tuis pendentia tectis?'
Ille sub haec:¹¹ 'non laudis amor nec gloria¹² cessit

---

1 376-7. 'showed his left, then his right, shot each fist out and pounded the air with punches'; cf. *Aen.* 10.892f., 11.756. Observe how the coincidence of ictus and accent, and of words with feet, in the second half of the line helps to convey the idea of blow following blow.

2 379. **caestus**: see note on 364.

3 380. **alacris**: this archaic form of *alacer* occurs again in *Aen.* 6.685.

4 **excedere pugna**: 'were withdrawing from (a claim to) the prize', cf. *Aen.* 9.789.

5 384. **quo ... teneri?**: 'How long must I be kept waiting? *Quousque* is separated by tmesis into its component parts; cf. 603.

6 387. **gravis**: 'sternly'; the adjective is used adverbially.

7 **Entellum:** known only from this passage; it was a name associated with Sicily, as we see from the city Entella.

8 388. **proximus ut ... consederat:** 'sitting as he was next to him'. This usage of *ut* links the clause to its main verb in a very general way, sometimes causal, sometimes temporal, sometimes local. Cf. 329, 667 and *Aen.* 7.509.

9 389. **frustra:** the word conveys that the glories of the past are apparently of no avail now.

10 391f. 'Where now, tell us, is the divine Eryx whom you called your teacher, and all for this ?' *Nequiquam* has the same sense as *frustra* in 389. Many take *nequiquam memoratus* to mean 'idly famed' (Page, Fairclough) but this is a much rarer use of the word and the rebuke is directed at Entellus not Eryx.

11 394f. Entellus' words are strongly reminiscent of those of Nestor in *Il.* 23.626f.; cf. also *Aen.* 8.560f.

12 394. **gloria:** 'desire for glory', a frequent meaning of the word.

pulsa metu; sed[1] enim gelidus tardante senecta   395
sanguis[2] hebet, frigentque effetae in corpore vires.
Si mihi quae quondam fuerat[3] quaque improbus[4] iste
exsultat fidens, si nunc foret illa iuventas,
haud[5] equidem pretio inductus pulchroque iuvenco
venissem, nec dona moror.' Sic deinde locutus   400
in medium geminos immani pondere caestus
proiecit, quibus acer Eryx in proelia suetus
ferre manum duroque intendere[6] bracchia tergo.
Obstipuere animi: [7]tantorum ingentia septem
terga boum plumbo insuto ferroque rigebant.   405
Ante omnis stupet ipse Dares longeque[8] recusat,
magnanimusque Anchisiades et [9]pondus et ipsa
huc illuc vinclorum immensa volumina versat.
Tum senior[10] talis referebat pectore voces:
'quid, si quis caestus[11] ipsius et Herculis arma   410
vidisset tristemque hoc ipso in litore pugnam?[12]
Haec germanus Eryx quondam tuus arma gerebat
(sanguine cernis adhuc sparsoque infecta cerebro),
his magnum Alciden contra stetit, his ego suetus,
dum melior[13] viris sanguis dabat, [14]aemula necdum   415
temporibus geminis canebat sparsa senectus.

---

1 395. **sed enim**: 'but in fact', cf. *Aen.* 1.19.

2 396. 'my blood runs feebly, and the strength of my limbs is worn out and gone'. *Hebet* (literally, 'to be blunt') does not occur elsewhere in this sense before Val. Fl. 1.53 *ardor hebet*, 4.41 *corpus hebet somno*.

3 397. **fuerat**: this use of the pluperfect instead of the perfect or imperfect seems to have been a colloquialism which came into poetry while remaining rare in prose; cf. *Aen.* 10.613.

4 **improbus**: 'braggart'; the word is used of anything beyond normal bounds, see note on 2.79-80.

5 399f. 'I wouldn't have needed the lure of a fine young bull to bring me here, and I don't care about prizes'; the negative applies to *pretio inductus,* and the sentence is equivalent to *venissem sine pretii inductu.* For moror cf. Aen. 3.287, Hor. Epist. 1.15.16 *nam vina nihil moror illius orae.*

6 403. For this construction with *intendere* ('bind'), rather than the commoner *intendere terga bracchiis,* cf. 829 and *Aen.* 4.506.

7 404-5. 'so mighty were the seven huge ox-hides stiff with the lead and iron sewn on them'. Notice the elisions and the assonance of *-um* and *-o* in these heavy phrases. Virgil is clearly thinking of Ajax's shield of seven ox-hides, *Il.* 7.220f.

8 406. **longeque recusat**: an elliptical and vivid phrase equivalent to *longe refugit recusans certamen.*

9 407-8. 'turns the heavy enormous folds of the gauntlets over and over'; *et pondus et volumina* is a hendiadys.

10 409. **senior**: 'the veteran', Entellus.

11 410. **caestus . . . arma**: 'the gauntlets which Hercules himself wore'. *Et* is postponed; its meaning is epexegetic, i.e. *et arma* does not add a new idea, but explains *caestus.*

12 411. When Hercules was bringing back the cattle of Geryon (cf. *Aen.* 8.202), Eryx met and challenged him. In the resultant fight Eryx was killed.

13 415. **melior**: i.e. 'hotter', contrast *gelidus* in 395.

14 415-16. 'and jealous old age had not yet flecked both brows with white'; *aemula* means that old age is his 'rival', cf. *Aen.* 6.173.

Sed si nostra Dares haec Troius arma recusat
idque pio sedet[1] Aeneae, probat[2] auctor Acestes,
aequemus pugnas. Erycis tibi[3] terga remitto
(solve metus), et tu Troianos exue caestus.'   420
Haec fatus duplicem[4] ex umeris reiecit amictum[5]
et magnos membrorum[6] artus, magna ossa lacertosque[7]
exuit[8] atque ingens media consistit harena.

> *424-60. Aeneas brings out matching pairs of gauntlets, and
> the fight begins. After preliminary sparring Entellus aims a
> mighty blow which misses and causes him to fall flat on the
> ground. He is assisted to his feet, and in fury renews the
> fight, driving Dares all around the arena.*

Tum satus Anchisa caestus pater extulit[9] aequos
et paribus palmas amborum innexuit armis.   425
Constitit [10]in digitos extemplo arrectus uterque
bracchiaque ad superas interritus extulit[11] auras.
Abduxere[12] retro longe capita ardua ab ictu
immiscentque manus manibus pugnamque[13] lacessunt,[14]
ille pedum melior motu fretusque iuventa,   430
hic membris[15] et mole valens; [16]sed tarda trementi
genua[17] labant, vastos[18] quatit aeger anhelitus artus.

---

1 418. **sedet:** 'is the decision of', cf. *Aen.* 2.660, 4.15.

2 **probat ... Acestes:** 'if my sponsor Acestes agrees';Acestes is *auctor* because he urged Entellus to fight (387f.).

3 419. **tibi:** 'there you are, I forego the thongs of Eryx'; *tibi* is ethic dative, here conveying scorn.

4 421. **duplicem:** 'double-folded', a frequent Greek epithet for various forms of dress, here imitated from Ap. Rh. 2.32.

5 421f. Virgil here follows Homer *Il.* 23.685f., and Ap. Rh. 2.67f.

6 422. **membrorum artus:** 'joints of his limbs'.

7 **lacertosque:** for the hyper-metric elision see note on *Aen.* 1.332; here the effect is to help to convey enormous size, along with the spondaic movement, the other elisions, and the alliteration of *m*.

8 423. **exuit:** 'bared', cf. *Aen.* 2.153, 4.518.

9 424. **extulit:** 'brought out', 'produced', cf. *Aen.* 11.73.

10 426. 'Immediately each took up his stance, poised on his toes'; cf. Ap. Rh. 2.90.

11 427. **extulit:** 'raised', cf. Ap. Rh. 2.68, Hom. *Il.* 23.686.

12 428. 'They held their heads high, well back out of range of blows', i.e. not crouching, but leaning back. Greek and Roman boxers, unlike the moderns, adopted a stance to guard the head, not the head and body.

13 429. **pugnamque lacessunt:** 'sparring for an opening', cf. *Aen.* 7.165, 11.254.

14 429. Again Homer and Apollonius are imitated (*Il.* 23.687, Ap. Rh.2.78).

15 431. **membris et mole:** hendiadys, = *membrorum mole.*

16 431-2. Notice the strong alliteration of *t;* all through this passage the alliteration is deliberately more marked and violent than is usually Virgil's way; see especially 444-5.

17 432. **genua:** the *u* is treated as a consonant, cf. *Aen.* 12.905 (the same phrase) and *tenuia* as a dactyl (*Geo.* 1.397, 2.121); compare the consonantal *i* in 589 (*parietibus*), 663 (*abiete*).

18 **vastos . . . artus:** 'his laboured breathing shakes his huge frame'; cf. Ap. Rh. 2.85 and *Aen.* 9.814.

Multa[1] viri nequiquam inter se vulnera iactant,
multa cavo lateri ingeminant et pectore vastos
dant sonitus, erratque auris et tempora circum   435
crebra manus, duro crepitant sub vulnere malae.
Stat gravis Entellus[2] nisuque immotus eodem
corpore tela modo atque oculis vigilantibus exit.
Ille, velut celsam[3] oppugnat qui molibus urbem
aut montana sedet circum castella sub armis,   440
nunc hos, nunc illos aditus, omnemque pererrat[4]
arte locum et variis adsultibus[5] inritus urget.
Ostendit[6] dextram insurgens Entellus et alte
extulit; ille ictum venientem a vertice velox
praevidit celerique[7] elapsus corpore cessit;   445
Entellus viris in ventum effudit et ultro[8]
ipse gravis[9] graviterque ad terram pondere vasto
concidit, ut quondam[10] cava concidit aut[11] Erymantho[12]
aut Ida in magna radicibus eruta pinus.
Consurgunt studiis[13] Teucri et Trinacria pubes;   450

---

1 433-4. **multa . . . multa**: i.e. many of the punches miss, *but* many. . . . The words are in antithesis: Heyne and Conington are surely wrong in thinking that lines 434-6 elaborate 433 (*nequiquam* then meaning 'without decisive effect'). For *vulnera* (= blows) cf. *Aen.* 2.529, 7.533.

2 437-8. 'Entellus stands his ground, solid, unmoving, not changing his poised stance, just avoiding the blows with body sway, his eyes fixed on his opponent'. The word *nisus* well conveys the idea of tenseness; for *exire* cf. *Aen.* 11.750 and compare *evadere* (689). Notice the dactyls of 438, conveying the swift swaying of the body.

3 439. **celsam . . . urbem**: probably 'assails a city towering high with its massive walls' (cf. *Aen.* 9.711) rather than 'assails a lofty city with siege-works'.

4 441. **pererrat**: 'explores'; the line occurs in almost the same form in *Aen.* 11.766, with the same slight zeugma of *pererrare* with *aditus* as well as with *locum*.

5 442. **adsultibus**: an unusual word found otherwise only once in Tacitus (*Ann.* 2.21) before the fourth century.

6 443. **ostendit dextram**: 'showed his right'; the English phrase tends to refer to a feint, but that is not so here. For the whole line cf. Ap. Rh. 2.90f. The rhythm here imitates the meaning with its spondees, its fifth-foot pause to arouse expectation, its run-on verb to emphasise the action; this is followed by heavy alliteration, first of *v* and then of *c*. Notice too how line 446 has the same rhythmic effect as 443, and 448 echoes the run-on verb of 444.

7 445. **celerique . . . cessit**: 'side-stepped swiftly, and wasn't there'.

8 446. **ultro**: 'with his own impetus'.

9 447. **gravis graviterque**: this is reminiscent of Hom. *Il.* 16.776 κεῖτο μέγας μεγαλωστι, 'mighty and mightily fallen'. The redundant *-que* adds to the emphasis of the repetition, cf. *Aen.* 3.329, 12.289.

10 448. **quondam**; 'sometimes', cf. *Aen.* 2.367, 7.378.

11 448-9. **aut Erymantho aut Ida**: for the forest of Erymanthus (the chain of mountains in Arcadia where Hercules killed the boar) cf. Ov. *Met.* 2.499. For the forests of Ida (near Troy) cf. *Aen.* 2.696. Virgil uses the doubled geographical location in order to take advantage of the poetic suggestiveness of proper names; cf. 595.

12 448-9. For the simile cf. especially Cat. 64.105f.

13 450. **studiis**: 'with rival cries of support', cf. 148, 228. The ablative used without an adjective in an adverbial sense is typically Virgilian; cf. *Aen.* 12.131 and note on *Aen.* 2.51.

it clamor caelo[1] primusque accutrit Acestes
aequaevumque ab humo miserans attollit amicum.
At non tardatus casu neque territus heros
acrior ad pugnam redit ac vim[2] suscitat ira;
tum[3] pudor incendit viris et conscia virtus,   455
praecipitemque Daren ardens agit aequore[4] toto
nunc dextra ingeminans ictus, nunc ille[5] sinistra.
Nec mora nec requies: [6]quam multa grandine nimbi
culminibus crepitant, sic densis ictibus heros
creber utraque manu pulsat[7] versatque Dareta.   460

> *461-84. Aeneas intervenes and stops the fight. Dares is carried away by his friends back to the ships, and Entellus receives the ox as his prize. With a single blow he kills it as a sacrifice to Eryx, and announces his final retirement from boxing.*

Tum pater Aeneas procedere longius iras
et saevire animis Entellum haud passus acerbis,
sed finem[8] imposuit pugnae fessumque Dareta
eripuit mulcens dictis ac talia fatur:
'infelix, quae tanta animum dementia cepit?   465
Non viris[9] alias conversaque numina sentis?
Cede deo.' Dixitque et proelia voce diremit.
Ast illum fidi aequales genua aegra trahentem[10]
iactantemque utroque[11] caput crassumque cruorem
ore eiectantem mixtosque in sanguine dentes   470
ducunt ad navis; galeamque ensemque vocati[12]

---

1 451. **caelo:** dative of motion towards (= *ad caelum*), a poetic construction here seen in its most striking form; cf. *Aen.* 11.192 (the same phrase) and *Aen.* 2.186.

2 454. **vim suscitat ira:** 'grows violent in his anger', cf. *Aen.* 12.108.

3 455. 'then the thought of his honour fires his strength, and his confidence in his prowess'; cf. *Aen.* 12.666-8.

4 456. **aequore toto:** 'all over the arena'; in boxing in the ancient world the ring was not precisely defined as we know it.

5 457. **ille:** Servius says 'metri causa additum est', but perhaps it adds a little to the sense ('with left and right alike').

6 458f. 'thick as the hail which storm clouds send rattling on roof tops is the shower of blows . . .', cf. *Geo.* 1.449, *Aen.* 9.669f.

7 460. **pulsat versatque Dareta:** 'battered Dares and sent him spinning' (Jackson Knight). *Dareta* is a third-declension form of the Greek accusative; contrast *Daren* (456).

8 463. Like a modern referee Aeneas 'stops the fight', as Achilles stopped the wrestling match in Hom. *Il.* 23.734f.

9 466. **viris alias:** 'that this is strength of a different order' (Jackson Knight). The reference is to the increased strength of Entellus (454f.) which is attributed to divine aid.

10 468f. The whole of this passage is closely modelled on Hom. *Il.* 23.695f. Notice the very slow movement, and the deliberately harsh and excessive alliteration and assonance.

11 469. **utroque:** 'from side to side', adverb.

12 471. **vocati:** his friends are summoned by the herald to collect Entellus' second prize because he cannot collect it himself (so in Homer, *Il.* 23.699).

accipiunt, palmam Entello taurumque relinquunt.
Hic victor superans[1] animis tauroque superbus
'nate dea, vosque haec' inquit 'cognoscite, Teucri,
et mihi quae fuerint iuvenali in corpore vires   475
et qua servetis revocatum a morte Dareta.'
Dixit, et adversi contra stetit ora iuvenci
qui donum astabat pugnae, durosque reducta
libiavit dextra media inter cornua caestus
arduus, effractoque inlisit in ossa cerebro: 480
sternitur exanimisque tremens procumbit humi bos.[2]
Ille super talis effundit pectore voces:
'hanc tibi, Eryx, meliorem[3] animam pro morte Daretis
persolvo; hic victor caestus[4] artemque repono.'

> *485-518. Aeneas proclaims an archery contest, the target
> being a dove secured to a mast. Hippocoon hits the mast;
> Mnestheus' arrow cuts the cord; Eurytion then shoots down
> the bird as it flies away.*

Protinus Aeneas celeri certare sagitta[5]   485
invitat qui forte velint et praemia ponit,[6]
ingentique[7] manu malum de[8] nave Seresti
erigit et volucrem traiecto[9] in fune columbam,
quo tendant ferrum, malo suspendit ab alto.
Convenere viri deiectamque aerea sortem[10]   490

---

1 473. **superans animis**: 'overflowing with pride', a phrase from Ennius (*Ann.* 205).

2 481. Day Lewis renders the movement of the verse thus: 'sprawling, quivering, lifeless, down on the ground the brute fell'. This line is a well known example of the violent effect caused to the rhythm by ending a line with a single monosyllable, giving conflict of ictus and accent in the last two feet. The effect is intensified by the rare alliteration of *b*, and the postponement of the monosyllabic subject. We have seen that in many places in the account of the boxing match Virgil has permitted himself exaggerated effects of alliteration and assonance; here he concludes his series of pictures by painting with the whole palette. Some examples of monosyllabic endings of an imitative kind are line 638, *Aen.* 1.105, 6.346, 10.864; others are traditional and archaic (e.g. *Aen.* 1.65).

3 483. **meliorem animam**: 'more acceptable victim'; Servius explains *meliorem* as less cruel, others see a sarcastic and contemptuous reference to Dares. But Entellus simply uses the formula and leaves his implications ambiguous.

4 484. **caestus artemque repono**: 'I lay down my gloves and my skill', cf. Hor. *Epist.* 1.1.4f., *Odes* 3.26.3f. Entellus announces his retirement in the hour of victory; the slow spondees and the simple words are most effective.

5 485f. The archery contest is modelled, often quite closely, on Hom. *Il.* 23.850f. In Homer there are only two competitors: Teucer cuts the cord with his arrow, and Meriones kills the dove. Skill with the bow figures largely in the Homeric poems, but played no part in the great Greek games, nor in Roman *ludi*, and Virgil's reasons for including archery here are to recall Homer and especially to lead into the portent of Acestes' arrow (see note on 519f.).

6 486. **ponit**: so the majority of MSS (cf. 292): *P* has *dicit*.

7 487. **ingentique manu**: 'with his mighty hand', Homer's χειρι παχειη: cf. 241, *Aen.* 11.556. Aeneas sets up the mast as Achilles had done (*Il.* 23.852). Some follow Seivius and render 'with a large band of people', but this is most unnatural in the context.

8 **de nave**: i.e. the mast is removed from Serestus' ship and set up in the ground.

9 488. **traiecto in fune**: probably *traiectus* refers to the rope being passed round the mast, rather than round the bird's leg.

10 490. **sortem**: the singular is used to draw attention to the method of choice, where the plural would be more usual.

221

accepit galea; et primus clamore secundo
Hyrtacidae ante omnis exit[1] locus Hippocoontis;
quem modo[2] navali Mnestheus certamine victor
consequitur, viridi Mnestheus evinctus oliva.
Tertius Eurytion,[3] tuus, o clarissime, frater,   495
Pandare, qui quondam iussus confundere foedus
in medios telum torsisti primus Achivos.
Extremus galeaque ima subsedit Acestes,[4]
ausus et ipse manu iuvenum temptare laborem.
Tum validis flexos incurvant viribus arcus   500
pro se quisque viri et depromunt tela pharetris,
primaque per caelum nervo stridente sagitta
Hyrtacidae iuvenis volucris[5] diverberat auras,
et venit adversique infigitur arbore mali.
Intremuit[6] malus timuitque exterrita pennis   505
ales, et ingenti sonuerunt omnia plausu.[7]
Post acer Mnestheus adducto[8] constitit arcu
alta[9] petens, pariterque[10] oculos telumque tetendit.
Ast ipsam miserandus avem contingere ferro
non valuit; nodos et vincula linea rupit   510
quis[11] innexa[12] pedem malo pendebat ab alto;
illa[13] Notos atque atra volans in nubila fugit.
Tum rapidus, iamdudum arcu contenta parato

---

1 492. **exit locus Hippocoontis**: *locus* means 'the lot giving him first turn'; for *exire* cf. Hor. *Odes* 2.3.27. Hippocoon is not otherwise known; presumably he is the brother of Nisus, son of Hyrtacus (*Aen.* 9.406).

2 493. **modo ... victor**: 'recently a prize-winner'; he was actually second. His olive crown was not mentioned in the account of the ship race.

3 495. Eurytion is not mentioned elsewhere. Pandarus, who broke the truce at Athena's orders and wounded Menelaus (Hom. *Il.* 4.72f.), was an outstanding archer (*Il.* 2.827, 5.95f).

4 498. **Acestes**: metonymy for *sors Acestae*, like *Mnestheus* (493) and *Eurylion* (495); cf. 339 and *Aen.* 2.201, 312.

5 503. **volucris . .. auras**: 'cut through the winged breezes', cf. *Aen.* 6.294, 11.795.

6 505. 'terrified fluttered her wings in fright'; the word *timuit* is unusual with *pennis* where *tremuit* would have been normal. Slater conjectured *micuitque* (cf. *Geo.* 473), which Mynors accepts.

7 506. **plausu:** perhaps the noise of the dove's wings (Page), but much more likely the applause of the spectators (Hom. *Il.* 23.869).

8 507. **adducto:** 'brought to his chest', i.e. with the bowstring drawn back, cf. 141 and *Aen.* 9.632.

9 508. **alta**: 'the heavens', cf. *Aen.* 6.787, 9.564.

10 **pariterque ... tetendit**: 'took aim with eye and arrow together', a slight zeugma.

11 511. **quis:** an alternative form for *quibus,* cf. *Aen.* 1.95.

12 **innexa pedem:** for the retained accusative see note on 135, and cf. *Aen.* 6.281.

13 512. 'she was away in flight towards the south and the dark clouds'; *P* has *alta* for *atra,* but cf. 516. *Notos* is governed (like *nubila*) by *in*; for similar word order cf. *Aen.* 2.654, 6.416, 692.

tela[1] tenens, fratrem Euryton in[2] vota vocavit,
iam vacuo laetam caelo speculatus et alis   515
plaudentem nigra figit sub nube columbam.
Decidit exanimis vitamque reliquit in astris
aetheriis fixamque refert delapsa sagittam.

> *519-44. Acestes, left with no target to aim at, shoots his arrow high into the air. It catches fire, and disappears like a shooting star. Aeneas recognises this as a good omen and awards Acestes first prize.*

[3]Amissa solus palma superabat Acestes,[4]
qui tamen aerias telum[5] contorsit in auras   520
ostentans[6] artemque pater arcumque sonantem.
Hic oculis subitum obicitur [7]magnoque futurum
augurio monstrum; [8]docuit post exitus ingens
seraque terrifici[9] cecinerunt omina vates.
Namque volans liquidis[10] in nubibus arsit harundo   525
signavitque[11] viam flammis tenuisque recessit
consumpta in ventos, caelo ceu saepe refixa[12]
transcurrunt crinemque volantia sidera ducunt.[13]

---

1 514. **tela:** 'his arrow', a poetic plural of a somewhat striking kind, cf. *Aen.* 7.497, 10.731.

2 **in vota:** Pandarus had met his death at the hands of Diomedes: 517-18. Cf. *Geo.* 3.547; for this vague meaning of *astra* ('sky') cf. 838.

3 519f. In this sequel to the last contest of the games Virgil raises the level of significance of the events he has been describing, and emphasises the divine background to the action of the *Aeneid*. During the account of the games the tension of the poem has been relaxed; by concluding the archery with a miraculous portent Virgil restores the high epic tone so as to lead into the patriotic account of the *lusus Troiae* and the eventful narrative which follows.

4 519. 'Now only Acestes was left, with the prize lost' (i.e. already won by Euryton). For *superare = superesse* cf. 713.

5 520. **telum contorsit:** 'sent his arrow whirring', a more vivid phrase than with the reading *contendit* given by some MSS.

6 521. 'displaying both his veteran skill and his sounding bow'; for *pater* in apposition to the subject cf. 130, 424. Its second syllable is lengthened in arsis; see note on 284.

7 522-3. 'and destined to be of great portent'.

8 523-4. 'the great outcome proved it so in later days, when awe-inspiring prophets sang of the late-fulfilled omens'. There has been much debate about what is portended here; the most generally accepted explanation is that we have a reference to the comet of 44 B.C. and the deification of Caesar. But in its context the portent should be directly connected with Acestes; certainly Aeneas thinks so and says so. It seems best therefore to regard the star as portending the future greatness of Acestes, in particular the foundation and fame of his city Segesta (see note on 718), possibly with some forward reference to the part Segesta played in the First Punic War, when it immediately made common cause with Rome. I have discussed the question more fully in my note ad loc. in my OUP Ed.

9 524. **terrifici:** the word is poetic and rather rare. It does not imply, as some have thought, that the omen is interpreted as a bad one; there is no suggestion of that in anything which follows. It must be taken to refer to the natural feeling of dread and awe associated with supernatural happenings (cf. 529).

10 525. **liquidis:** 'thin', cf. *Aen.* 6.202, 7.699.

11 526. **signavitque viam flammis:** 'left the trace of its path in fire', not 'pointed out the way'; cf. *Aen.* 2.697.

12 527. **refixa:** 'unloosed', cf. Hor. *Epod.* 17.5. The stars are thought of as 'fixed' in the sky (Pliny, *Nat. Hist.* 2.28), so that shooting stars are *refixa*.

13 528. Compare Lucr. 2.206f., *Geo.* 1.365f, *Aen.* 2.693f. For the rhythm of the line cf. *Aen.* 2.9, 4.81.

Attonitis haesere animis superosque precati
Trinacrii Teucrique viri, nec[1] maximus omen   530
abnuit Aeneas, sed laetum amplexus Acesten
muneribus cumulat magnis ac talia fatur:
'sume[2] pater; nam te voluit rex magnus Olympi
talibus auspiciis exsortem ducere honores.
Ipsius Anchisae longaevi hoc munus habebis,   535
cratera[3] impressum signis, quem Thracius olim
Anchisae genitori in[4] magno munere Cisseus[5]
ferre sui[6] dederat monimentum et pignus amoris.'
Sic fatus cingit viridanti tempora lauro
et primum ante omnis victorem appellat Acesten.   540
Nec bonus Eurytion praelato[7] invidit honori,
quamvis[8] solus avem caelo deiecit ab alto.
Proximus ingreditur donis[9] qui vincula rupit,
extremus volucri qui fixit harundine malum.

---

1 530-1. **nec ... omen abnuit**: i.e. Aeneas accepted it as an omen, and acted accordingly, regarding it as favourable. Compare Anchises in *Aen.* 2.699f., and Tolumnius' words in 12.260.

2 533f. 'for the great king of Olympus, by giving auspices such as we have seen, intended that you should be especially distinguished in the winning of honours'. The phrase *exsortem ducere honores* is a most unusual one, including a number of implications.

The basic meaning of *exsors* is 'not drawn for by lot', i.e. especially set aside (cf. *Aen.* 8.552); when applied to persons it normally means 'not sharing in', e.g. *Aen.* 6.428. Virgil combines the two meanings in this line; Acestes was excluded by lot from sharing in the contest, and this is seen to be a mark of distinction.

3 536. **cratera impressum signis**: 'an embossed bowl', cf. 267. *Cratera* is Greek accusative, cf. 261, 839.

4 537. **in magna munere**: 'as a great gift'. The unusual use of *in* adds impressiveness, cf. *Aen.* 8.273.

5 **Cisseus**: in Virgil's version (cf. *Aen.* 7.320, 10.705) this Thracian king was father of Hecuba.

6 538. **sui**: objective genitive of *se* depending on *monimentum*, rather than genitive of *suus* agreeing with *amoris*. This line is almost exactly repeated at 572.

7 541. **praelato invidit honori**: 'grudge him his preferred position'; *praelato* agrees with *honori*; it is unnatural to regard it as a second dative (of the person) after *invidit*. *Invidere* often takes an accusative of the thing grudged (*Aen.* 8.509), but the dative is not uncommon, e.g. Cic. *De Leg. Agr.* 2.103 *qui honori inviderunt meo*.

8 542. **quamvis ... deiecit**: the indicative with *quamvis* (by analogy with *quamquam*) is quite common in verse, though Virgil has it only here and in *Ecl.* 3.84.

9 543. **donis**: ablative of respect with *proximus* (= *ordine donorum*) rather than, as Servius says, dative equivalent to *ad dona*.

545-603. The final event is an equestrian display by the Trojan boys. They procede in three companies, young Priam leading one, Atys another, and Iulus the third, and they give a brilliant display of intricate manoeuvres and mock battle. This is the ceremony which Iulus introduced to Alba Longa, and it was handed on to Rome and called the lusus Troiae.

[1]At pater Aeneas nondum[2] certamine misso   545
custodem ad sese comitemque impubis Iuli
Epytiden[3] vocat, et fidam sic fatur ad aurem:
'vade age et Ascanio, si iam puerile[4] paratum
agmen habet secum cursusque instruxit equorum,
ducat[5] avo turmas et sese ostendat in armis   550
dic' ait. Ipse omnem longo discedere circo
infusum populum et campos iubet esse patentis.
Incedunt pueri pariterque ante ora parentum
frenatis lucent in equis, quos[6] omnis euntis
Trinacriae mirata fremit Troiaeque iuventus.   555
Omnibus[7] in morem tonsa coma pressa corona;
cornea bina ferunt praefixa[8] hastilia ferro,
pars levis[9] umero pharetras; [10]it pectore summo
flexilis obtorti per collum circulus auri.

---

1 545f. The *lusus Troiae* brings the games to an end with the satisfying effect of a closing ceremony, and at the same time links the events of the remote past with Virgil's own days. We hear of these equestrian manoeuvres in the time of Sulla; they were revived by Julius Caesar, and established under Augustus as a regular institution, performed by boys of noble birth (Suet. *Aug.* 43). It seems most unlikely that the *lusus Troiae* was originally connected with Troy. The archaic verbs *amptruare, redamptruare* suggest a noun *troia* meaning 'movement', 'dancing', and the Etruscan word *Truia* found on a vase depicting horsemen and a labyrinth points in the same direction. When the legend of Rome's Trojan origins became widespread, the *lusus Troiae* could easily be associated with Troy.

The whole description of the ceremony is written with a verve which clearly reflects Virgil's enjoyment of such visual pageantry; and it is painted in the bright and joyful colours appropriate to the hopes that were placed in the promise and achievement of the younger generation, whether of Aeneas' day or Virgil's own.

2 545. **nondum certamine misso**: 'before the archery contest was duly concluded' (see note on 286). Servius finds difficulty with the tenses because the archery was already concluded, but the reference probably is to some final announcement or ceremony.

3 547. **Epytiden**: Periphas, son of Epytus, occurs in Hom. *Il.* 17.324.

4 548-9. **puerile . . . agmen**: Latin uses the adjective where we would say 'column of boys'.

5 550-1. **ducat avo turmas**: 'tell (Ascanius) to bring on the procession in his grandfather's honour'; *ducat* is jussive subjunctive in parataxis with *die,* of *Aen.* 4.635 and line 163. For the dative *avo* cf. 603.

6 554-5. **quos . . . mirata fremit**: 'murmurs its admiration for them'; the accusative is after *mirata*, not as Servius says after *fremit*.

7 556. 'Each has his hair bound in ceremonial style with a trimmed garland'. Later (673) Ascanius takes off his helmet, so we must assume that at some stage these garlands were taken off and helmets put on. *Tonsa* is generally taken to mean that the leaves were clipped to a uniform length; it is possible however that the meaning is simply a garland of 'cut' leaves.

8 557. **praefixa**: 'tipped', as in *Aen.* 10.479, 12.489.

9 558. **levis**: 'polished', 'burnished', as in 91.

10 558f. 'High on their chests and passing round their necks are pliant circlets of twisted gold'. The MSS vary (as often) between *it* and *et*, but the latter would give an intolerable construction here.

Tres equitum numero[1] turmae ternique vagantur[2]   560
ductores; pueri bis seni quemque secuti
agmine[3] partito fulgent paribusque[4] magistris.
Una acies iuvenum, ducit quam parvus ovantem[5]
nomen avi referens Priamus, tua clara, Polite,[6]
progenies, auctura Italos; [7]quem Thracius albis   565
portat equus bicolor[8] maculis, [9]vestigia primi
alba pedis frontemque ostentans arduus albam.
Alter Atys, genus unde Atii duxere Latini,[10]
parvus Atys pueroque puer dilectus Iulo.
Extremus formaque ante omnis pulcher Iulus[11]   570
Sidonio est invectus equo, quem candida[12] Dido
esse sui dederat monimentum et pignus amoris.[13]
Cetera Trinacriis pubes senioris Acestae
fertur equis.
Excipiunt plausu pavidos[14] gaudentque tuentes   575
Dardanidae, veterumque agnoscunt ora parentum.
Postquam[15] omnem laeti consessum oculosque suorum

---

1 560f. There are thirty-six boys plus three leaders (thirteen to each group). For *terni* as a variation on *tres* cf. 85. Each group is in two files of six, and each is accompanied by its trainer.

2 560. **vagantur**: 'weave their way', a colourful word for the wheeling movements of the ride-past.

3 562. **agmine partito**: 'in divided column', i.e. double file (*bis seni*).

4 **paribusque magistris**: 'each alike with its trainer'. *Paribus* suggests that the groups have their trainers stationed in corresponding positions (presumably at the side). Some argue that *magistri* are the same as *ductores,* but cf. 669.

5 563f. This sentence and the next are somewhat loosely constructed: *una acies iuvenum (est) ducit quam ...* is equivalent to *primam* aciem *iuvenum ducit; alter Atys* is very condensed for *alter ductor est ai itys,* i.e. *secundam aciem ducit Atys.* Other marks of incompleteness are the repetition of 572 from 538 and the unfinished line 574.

6 564. The death of Polites, son of Priam, is told in *Aen.* 2.526f. It was a common custom to name children after their grandfathers (cf. *Aen.* 12.348). For the Greek form of the vocative cf. 166.

7 565-70. This passage contains a number of different types of repetition: there is the threefold repetition of *albus,* a favourite turn of Virgilian diction; the repetition of the names Atys and (rather differently) Iulus; and the type common in Greek *pueroque puer* (cf. *Aen.* 1.684, 3.329).

8 566. **bicolor**: here 'dappled', cf. *Aen.* 8.276.

9 566-7. 'showing white pasterns and a white forehead held high'. *Vestigia* occurs in poetry with the meaning 'foot', cf. Cat. 64.162; here *vestigia pedis* is equivalent to *pedes,* cf. *Aen.* 7.689f. *Primus pes* refers to the front of the foot, not to the forefoot; cf. Cat. 2.3. Prop. 2.26.11.

10 568. Compare the association of the sea captains with Roman families (lines 116-23). Augustus' mother was a member of the *gens Atia;* hence there is a special point in the friendship of these two boys, founders of the *gens Iulia* and the *gens Atia.*

11 570. Notice how the spondees slow the movement to give emphasis and dignity.

12 571. **candida**: the word is nearly synonymous with *pulchra,* with the additional idea of radiance, cf. *Aen.* 8.138, 608.

13 472. This line is an almost exact repetition of 538; see note on 563f. We hear of gifts from Dido also on two later occasions, at points in the story where the tension is high, 9.266, 11.72f.

14 575. **pavidos**:'nervous', cf. 138.

15 577-8. 'After they had joyfully ridden round in front of the whole throng under the gaze of their families . . .'. For the zeugma cf. 340-1; for *lustrare* ('traverse') cf. 611.

lustravere in equis, signum[1] clamore paratis
Epytides longe dedit insonuitque flagello.
Olii discurrere pares atque agmina terni[2]   580
diductis solvere choris, rursusque vocati
convertere vias infestaque tela tulere.
Inde[3] alios incunt cursus aliosque recursus
adversi spatiis, alternosque orbibus orbis
impediunt pugnaeque[4] cient simulacra sub armis;   585
et nunc terga fuga nudant, nunc spicula vertunt
infensi, facta pariter nunc pace feruntur.
Ut quondam [5]Creta fertur Labyrinthus in alta[6]
parietibus textum caecis iter ancipitemque[7]
mille viis habuisse dolum, qua[8] signa sequendi   590
frangeret indeprensus et inremeabilis error:[9]
haud alio Teucrum nati vestigia[10] cursu
impediunt texuntque fugas et proelia ludo,

---

1 578-9. The signal was evidently given first with a shout, and then with the crack of a whip, like the spoken words 'On your marks, get set' before the starter's gun is fired.

2 580f. The boys are riding in a long double column down the centre, and at the word of command the right hand rider of each pair wheeled right and the left hand rider wheeled left (*discurrere pares*). The following two phrases explain the same movement: each of the groups breaks up its column formation (*agmina terni solvere*) as the files turn away from each other (*diductis choris*). Then at another word of command (*vocati*), they wheel about to face each other and charge. The *ductores* presumably remain in the centre of the field so that at the end of the charge the columns could be reformed as before.

3 583f. 'Then they enter upon other movements and counter movements, keeping corresponding positions, and they weave their circling patterns in and out, and wage phantom battles in their panoply'. In the previous sentence Virgil's account of the first manoeuvre was detailed and precise; now he describes the subsequent movements of the pageant in much more general terms, in order to convey the mood and colour of kaleidoscopic pattern. *Adversi spatiis* suggests that one half of the arena was a mirrored reflexion of the other. *Alternosque orbibus orbis impediunt* looks forward to the Labyrinth simile; cf. also *Aen.* 12.743.

4 585. **pugnaeque cient simulacra**: cf Lucr. 2.41 (= 324), and line 674.

5 588-91. 'It was like the Labyrinth in lofty Crete long ago, of which the story tells that it had a weaving path between blind walls and a bewildering riddle of a thousand ways, where the insoluble and ir-retraceable maze would break the tokens of the trail'. The Labyrinth at Cnossos was said to have been built by Daedalus for King Minos; the Athenians had to pay human sacrifice to the Minotaur which lived in the Labyrinth until Theseus killed it and returned out of the maze by means of the thread which Ariadne gave him. The story is told in Cat. 64 and in Ov. *Met.* 8.152f. Scenes from it are portrayed on the doors of Apollo's temple in *Aen.* 6.20f. The pattern of the Labyrinth is strongly associated with dancing movements (Hom.*Il.* 18.590f., Plut. *Thes.*21).

6 588f. Virgil uses two similes to illustrate his description of the *lusus Troiae;* the Labyrinth expresses the idea of complicated figures, and the dolphins convey the picture of swift and joyful movement.

7 589. **ancipitemque**: the polysyllabic ending, relatively rare in Virgil, rhythmically conveys a strangeness appropriate to the description of the maze.

8 590-1. **qua ... frangeret**: 'so that ... in it'. *Qua* is local, and the subjunctive *frangeret* final. The reading *falleret* in M probably originates from a gloss to explain the very difficult meaning.

9 591. This line is very closely modelled on Cat. 64.114-15 *ne labyrintheis e flexibus egredientem / tecti frustraretur inobservablis error.* Both Virgil's adjectives, which are not found earlier, are elaborations of Catullus' *inobservablis;* and the unusual rhythm of the line is very similar, with its total absence of strong caesurae and consequent total coincidence of ictus and accent (cf. 856). This conveys a strange feeling of monotony and sameness, and the long words help to convey an unforgettable impression of being lost in an interminable maze.

10 592-3. **vestigia ... impediunt**: 'weave a pattern of galloping movement', cf. 585 and Lucr. 1.240.

delphinum[1] similes qui per maria umida nando
Carpathium[2] Libycumque secant [luduntque[3] per undas].   595
Hunc[4] morem cursus atque haec certamina primus
Ascanius,[5] Longam muris cum cingeret Albam,
rettulit[6] et priscos docuit celebrare Latinos,
quo puer ipse modo, secum quo Troia pubes;
Albani docuere suos; hinc maxima porro[7]   600
accepit Roma et patrium servavit honorem;[8]
Troiaque[9] nunc pueri, Troianum dicitur agmen.
Hac[10] celebrata tenus sancto certamina patri.

604-63. While the games are being celebrated, Juno sends Iris down from heaven in order to incite the Trojan women to burn their ships. They are gathered on the shore weeping over Anchises' death and their endless wanderings; Iris takes on the appearance of Beroe and urges them to set fire to the ships so that they cannot wander any more. Pyrgo tells them that this is not Beroe, but a goddess; Iris reveals her divinity and driven on now by frenzy they set the ships ablaze.

[11]Hinc [12]primum Fortuna fidem mutata novavit.
Dum variis tumulo referunt sollemnia ludis,   605

---

1 594. **delphinum similes**: *similis* with the genitive occurs only here in Virgil, no doubt to avoid the dative plural of the Greek form *delphis* (which Virgil always uses in preference to *delphinus*). For the simile cf. Ap. Rh. 4.933f., and compare *Aen.*8.67 3f., Ov. *Met.* 3.683f.

2 595. **Carpathium Libycumque secant**: the Carpathian sea is around the island Carpathos, between Crete and Rhodes. For the geographical location in a simile cf. 448-9.

3 **luduntque per undas:** though these words are quite unobjectionable in themselves, they are omitted in two of the primary MSS and must be regarded as an interpolated completion of an unfinished line.

4 596. 'the tradition of this equestrian display and these mock battles'. Cf. *Aen.* 3.408. For the *lusus Troiae* at Rome see note on 545f.

5 597. Ascanius founded Alba Longa from Lavinium after the death of Aeneas, cf. *Aen.* 1.271.

6 598. **rettulit**: 'revived'.

7 600. **porro:** 'afterwards', 'in succession', a rather archaic use of the word, cf. the somewhat similar use in *Aen.* 6.711.

8 601. **honorem** : 'celebration', i.e. here 'tradition', cf. 58, 94.

9 602. **Troiaque nunc pueri:** 'the boys are now called Troy', rather an awkward phrase meaning that the performance is called Troy (we find the phrase *Troiam ludere* several times in Suetonius).

10 603. **hac ... tenus:** 'thus far', i.e. this was the conclusion of the games. For the tmesis of *hactenus* cf. *Aen* 6.62 and compare line 384.

11 604f. The episode of the burning of the ships figured early in the legend, but was generally localised in Italy. By placing it in Sicily Virgil stresses the association of Sicily with the early destiny of Rome (the foundation of Segesta now becoming the direct result of the loss of part of the fleet); and he also shows us Aeneas' fortunes and personal courage at their lowest ebb (687f., 700f.) at a time very shortly before the divine revelations of Book 6 give him the final certainty and strength to carry out his mission.

12 604. 'At this point for the first time Fortune changed and altered her allegiance'. *Primum* presumably means for the first time in Sicily; Fortune had been favourable at the landing and at the games.

Irim de caelo misit Saturnia Iuno[1]
Iliacam ad classem ventosque[2] aspirat eunti,
multa movens[3] necdum[4] antiquum saturata dolorem.
Illa viam celerans per[5] mille coloribus arcum[6]
nulli visa cito decurrit tramite virgo.   610
Conspicit ingentem concursum et litora[7] lustrat
desertosque videt portus classemque relictam.
At[8] procul in sola secretae Troades[9] [10]acta[11]
amissum Anchisen flebant, cunctaeque profundum
pontum aspectabant flentes. [12]Heu tot vada fessis   615
et tantum superesse maris, vox omnibus una:
urbem orant, taedet pelagi perferre laborem.
Ergo inter medias sese haud ignara nocendi
conicit et faciemque deae vestemque reponit;
fit[13] Beroe, Timarii coniunx longaeva Dorycli,   620
cui[14] genus et quondam nomen natique fuissent,
ac sic Dardanidum[15] mediam se matribus infert.
'O miserae, quas non manus' inquit 'Achaica bello
traxerit ad letum patriae sub moenibus! O gens
infelix, cui te[16] exitio Fortuna reservat?   625

---

1 606. This line occurs again in *Aen.* 9.2; cf. also 4.694f., and note on 4.700-2. The entry here of Juno into the narrative makes explicit the general statement in 604 about the change of fortune, and in a moment dims the gay mood on which the games had ended and introduces the sombre tone of the forthcoming setback for the Trojans.

2 607. **ventosque aspirat eunti:** 'breathes favouring winds upon her as she goes', cf. *Aen.* 4.223.

3 608. **movens:** 'plotting', cf. *Aen.* 3.34, 10.890.

4 **necdum ... dolorem:** cf. *Aen.* 1.25f. and Hor. *Odes* 3.3.30f. for Juno's long standing anger against the Trojans. *Saturate* is used in a middle sense, see note on 135.

5 609. **per mille coloribus arcum:** the preposition is separated from its noun by the ablative of description acting as a compound adjective (= *multicolor*).

6 609. For Iris journeying to earth on the rainbow cf. Ov. *Met.* 11.589f., 14.838.

7 611. **litora lustrat:** 'passes along the shore', cf. 578.

8 613f. The women have not been present at the games; they did not attend *ludi funebres* in Rome, and Suetonius (*Aug.* 44) relates that Augustus excluded women from watching athletic competitions.

9 613. **Troades:** notice the Greek scansion of the final short syllable; cf. *Aen.* 1.468.

10 **acta:** 'seashore', a transliteration of the Greek word which is not common in Latin.

11 613-15. The movement of these lines is very slow indeed with their heavy spondees and clash of ictus and accent; the very striking repetition of *flebant . . . flentes* in the same position in the line adds greatly to the effect.

12 615-16. The construction is accusative and infinitive of exclamation; cf. *Aen.* 1.97f.

13 620. **fit Beroe**: Iris chooses the form of Beroe because the latter was away ill (650f.), and because she was a woman of standing with the Trojans. Beroe is not otherwise known; a Doryclus, son of Priam, is mentioned in *Il.* 11.489, but it is difficult to see how he would be associated with Timarus, a mountain in Epirus.

14 621. 'who had been of noble birth and in days gone by had had sons and a famous name'; i.e. when Troy still stood. *Fuissent* is subjunctive because it expresses the thought in Iris' mind, the reason why she chose the form of Beroe.

15 622. **Dardanidum:** archaic form of *Dardanidarum*, cf. *Aeneadum* (1.565 etc.).

16 625. **te:** the use of the singular (rather than *vos*) emphasises the collective fortune of the *gens Troiana*.

VIRGIL

Septima¹ post Troiae excidium iam vertitur² aestas,
cum freta, cum³ terras omnis, tot inhospita saxa⁴
sideraque emensae ferimur, dum per mare magnum
Italiam⁵ sequimur fugientem et volvimur undis.
Hic Erycis⁶ fines fraterni atque hospes Acestes: 630
quis prohibet muros⁷ iacere et dare civibus⁸ urbem?
O patria et rapti⁹ nequiquam ex hoste penates,
nullane iam Troiae¹⁰ dicentur moenia? Nusquam
Hectoreos¹¹ amnis, Xanthum et Simoenta, videbo?
Quin agite et mecum infaustas exurite puppis.   635
Nam mihi Cassandrae¹² per somnum vatis imago
ardentis dare visa faces: "hic quaerite Troiam;
hic domus est" inquit "vobis." Iam tempus agi¹³ res,
nec¹⁴ tantis mora prodigiis. En quattuor arae
Neptuno; deus ipse faces animumque¹⁵ ministrat.'   640
Haec memorans prima infensum¹⁶ vi corripit ignem
sublataque¹⁷ procul dextra conixa coruscat
et iacit. Arrectae mentes stupefactaque corda
Iliadum. Hic una e multis, quae maxima natu,
Pyrgo, tot Priami natorum regia nutrix: 645

---

1 626. **septima ... aestas**: there is here an inconsistency with *Aen.* 1.755-6 where Dido used the same phrase; since then a winter has intervened. Probably in revision Virgil would have altered one place or the other.

2 **vertitur**: 'is passing', rather than 'is waning'.

3 627f. **cum ... ferimur**: 'while all the time we have been driven . . .', an unusual construction (more often introduced by *cum interea*); cf. *Aen.* 3645f., 10.665.

4 627-8. All four nouns are the object of *emensae* ('travelling through'). Servius interprets *sidera* as storms or climes; perhaps the second is better.

5 629. **Italiam ... fugientem**: 'an ever-receding Italy', cf. *Aen.* 3.496, 6.61.

6 630. **Erycis ... fraterni**: see note on 24.

7 631. **muros iacere**: 'found our city-walls'. The verb *iacere* is common with words like *fundamenta*, but not normal with *muros*; cf. however Prop. 2.34.64.

8 **civibus**: i.e. we shall then be citizens, not roaming exiles.

9 632. **rapti ... penates**: cf. *Aen.* 1.378, 2.293, 717, 3.148f.

10 633. **Troiae**: predicative; 'shall no walls ever again be called walls of Troy'?

11 634. **Hectoreos**: the adjective has an emotional effect, see on 190: Jackson Knight renders it 'to remind me of Hector'. For the use of the old names in the new city cf. 756 and especially *Aen.* 3.349f.; for these rivers of Troy cf. 261, 803.

12 636. **Cassandrae**: the fate of Cassandra, who was gifted with prophecy but never believed, is told in *Aen.* 2.403f.

13 638. **agi res**: the monosyllabic ending gives a most abrupt and emphatic ending; see on 481. Notice too the staccato short sentences, three in succession without a verb expressed.

14 639. **nec ... prodigiis**: understand *esto*; *tandis ... prodigiis* is ablative of attendant circumstances, 'in the face of. . . .'.

15 640. **animumque**: 'will', 'intent'; for the idea cf. *Aen.* 1.150.

16 641. **infensum**: 'deadly', 'destructive', cf. *Geo.* 4330., *Aen.* 9.793.

17 642f. 'and from where she stood, raising her right hand high, with all her might she brandished it and threw'. The emphasis on *iacit* is compelling because of the heavy pause after a first foot in which word accent conflicts with ictus; cf. *Aen.* 10.336, 12.730.

'non Beroe vobis,[1] non haec Rhoeteia,[2] matres,
est Dorycli coniunx; divini signa decoris
ardentisque notate oculos, qui[3] spiritus illi,
quis vultus vocisque sonus vel gressus eunti.
Ipsa egomet dudum Beroen digressa reliqui   650
aegram,[4] indignantem tali quod sola careret
munere nec meritos Anchisae inferret honores.'
Haec effata.
At[5] matres primo ancipites oculisque malignis
ambiguae spectare rates miserum inter amorem   655
praesentis terrae fatisque vocantia regna,
cum dea se paribus[6] per caelum sustulit alis[7]
ingentemque fuga secuit[8] sub nubibus arcum.
Tum vero attonitae monstris actaeque furore
conclamant, rapiuntque focis penetralibus ignem,[9]   660
pars spoliant aras, frondem[10] ac virgulta facesque
coniciunt. Furit[11] immissis[12] Volcanus habenis
transtra[13] per et remos et pictas[14] abiete puppis.

---

1 646. **vobis**: 'I tell you', ethic dative, cf. 162.

2 **Rhoeteia**: an epithet meaning Trojan, from the promontory Rhoeteum near Troy. cf. *Aen*. 3.108.

3 648f. **qui** ... **eunti**: these are indirect questions after *notate*. *Spiritus* is 'proud bearing', cf. Cic. *De Leg. Agr*. 2.93 *regio spiritu.*

4 651f. **aegram** . . . **munere**: 'sick and fretting because she was the only one not present at so important a ceremony'. The subjunctive represents the thought in Beroe's mind. *Tali* . . . *munere* refers to the funeral ceremonies and the lamentations of the women (613f.).

5 654f. 'But the matrons at first were uncertain, and gazed with angry eyes on the ships as they wavered between their wretched love for the land they had reached and the kingdoms which called them with the voice of fate'. *Spectare* is historic infinitive, cf. 685f. The word *miserum* indicates the sadness of their folly. For the causal ablative *fatis* cf. *Aen*. 10.109.

6 657. **paribus** . . . **alis**: 'on balanced wings', cf. *Aen*. 4.252.

7 657-8. Cf. *Aen*. 9.14-15, almost identical lines about Iris, and see note on 4.700-2. Mercury (4.276f.) and Apollo (9.656f.) take their departure from mortals by sudden disappearance, but Iris has her own path along the rainbow (see note on 609).

8 658. **secuit . . . arcum**: 'cut a rainbow', i.e. made a rainbow by cutting through the air (cf. *Geo*. 1.406, *Aen*. 6.899).

9 660f. The meaning is that some snatch fire from the hearths (of the Trojan encampment, cf. 668-9), while others despoil the four altars to Neptune (639-40).

10 661. **frondem**: common in the singular meaning 'foliage'.

11 662. **furit**: note the emphasis on the verb as it begins the sentence with strong conflict of ictus and accent; it picks up *furore* (659), and emphasises that the Trojan women (like Dido and Turnus) are victims of this madness which afflicts those who oppose the divine plan.

12 **immissis** . . . **habenis**: literally 'with the reins let loose', i.e. in full career, with unbridled frenzy, cf. Lucr. 5.787, *Aen*. 6.1.

13 663. **transtra per**: for *per* following its noun cf. *Geo*. 3.276, *Aen*. 4.671. This usage is generally confined to cases like this one where other nouns governed by *per* follow it.

14 663. **pictas abiete puppis**: 'painted ships of pine'. *Abiete* is ablative of description dependent on the noun *puppis*, an extended use of the ablative of which Virgil is fond, cf. 77-8, 609. For its scansion (as a dactyl) cf. 432.

664-99. The news reaches the Trojans. Ascanius immediately rides off and brings the women to a realisation of their crime. But the Trojans cannot put out the flames, and Aeneas prays to Jupiter either to send help or to bring final destruction upon them. Jupiter hears his prayer; the flames are quenched by a thunderstorm, and all the ships saved except four.

Nuntius Anchisae ad tumulum cuneosque[1] theatri
incensas perfert navis Eumelus, et ipsi 665
respiciunt[2] atram in nimbo volitare favillam.
Primus[3] et Ascanius, cursus ut laetus equestris
ducebat, sic acer equo turbata petivit
castra,[4] nec exanimes[5] possunt retinere magistri.
'Quis furor iste novus?[6] Quo nunc, quo tenditis,' inquit,[7] 670
'heu miserae cives? Non hostem inimicaque castra
Argivum, vestras spes uritis. En, ego vester
Ascanius!' — Galeam ante pedes proiecit inanem,[8]
qua[9] ludo indutus belli simulacra ciebat.
Accelerat simul Aeneas, simul agmina Teucrum. 675
Ast illae diversa metu per litora passim
diffugiunt, silvasque et sicubi[10] concava furtim
saxa petunt; piget[11] incepti lucisque, suosque
mutatae agnoscunt excussaque pectore Iuno est.
    Sed non ideirco flamma atque incendia viris 680
indomitas posuere;[12] udo sub robore vivit[13]
stuppa vomens tardum fumum, lentusque carinas

---

1 664. **cuneosque theatri**: these are the tiers, the wedge shaped blocks of seats in a Roman theatre or circus; the phrase is here applied to the natural 'theatre' used for the games.

2 666. **respiciunt ... volitare favillam**: 'look back and see ash eddying up'; the accusative and infinitive is used as if after *vident*.

3 667f. 'And first of them all Ascanius, just as he was as he gaily led his galloping troop, straight away set off in hot haste towards the confusion in the camp'. For *ut* cf. 388; the total effect is that of the phrase *sicut erat*.

4 669. **castra**; the encampment by the ships, cf. 660.

5 **exanimes**: 'breathless', cf. *Aen.* 4.672.

6 670. **novus**: 'strange', beyond belief; cf. *Aen.* 3.591.

7 670f. Notice the excited and staccato rhythm of the speech, where the mid-line pauses contribute greatly to the effect.

8 673. **inanem**: 'empty', conveying the clang of the helmet (Ov. *Fast.* 4.209), rather than 'sham' or 'useless'.

9 674. **qua ... indutus**: 'clad in which', cf. *Aen.* 10.775 and contrast the other construction of *induere* (e.g. *exuvias indutus, Aen.* 2.275). For the rest of the line cf. 585.

10 677. **sicubi**: 'any they could find', literally 'if there were any anywhere' (*si, alicubi*).

11 678. **piget ... lucisque**: 'they are ashamed of their deed and of the light of day', i.e. they want to hide in the darkness because of their shame.

12 681. **posuere**: equivalent to *deposuere*, cf. 286.

13 681-2. **vivit ... fumum**: 'the caulking was still alive, belching out a slow smoke'; the pictorial effect is enhanced by the comparatively unusual juxtaposition of noun and adjective with like endings, cf. 845.

est[1] vapor et toto descendit corpore pestis,[2]
nec vires heroum infusaque flumina prosunt.
Tum pius[3] Aeneas umeris abscindere[4] vestem   685
auxilioque vocare deos et tendere palmas:
'Iuppiter omnipotens, si nondum exosus[5] ad unum[6]
Troianos, si quid pietas[7] antiqua labores
respicit humanos, da[8] flammam evadere classi
nunc, pater, et tenuis Teucrum res eripe leto.   690
Vel tu,[9] quod superest, infesto fulmine morti,
si mereor, demitte tuaque hic obrue dextra.'
Vix haec ediderat cum effusis imbribus atra
tempestas sine[10] more furit tonitruque tremescunt[11]
ardua[12] terrarum et campi; ruit aethere toto   695
turbidus[13] imber aqua densisque nigerrimus Austris,
implenturque super[14] puppes, semusta madescunt
robora, restinctus donec vapor omnis et omnes
quattuor amissis servatae a peste carinae.

---

1 683. **est:** 'eats at', 'devours', cf. *Aen.* 4.66 and line 752.

2 **pestis:** i.e. the deadly fire, cf. *Aen.* 9.540.

3 685. **pius:** here the adjective has special reference to Aeneas' responsibility for his men his mission, and particularly force as Aeneas appeals to the *pietas* of Jupiter.

4 **abscindere:** historic infinitive, cf. 655.

5 687. **exosus:** active, cf. *Aen.* 11.436, 12.517, 818. For the omission of *es* cf. 19a.

6 687. For the form of the prayer cf. *Aen.* 2.689f. Aeneas' brief phrases are direct and urgent: this latest reverse, so soon after the short period of relaxation from toil, leaves him broken and weary in heart.

7 688. **pietas antiqua:** 'your loving-kindness of old', cf. *Aen.* 2.536f., 4.382.

8 689. **da . . . classi:** 'grant that the fleet may escape the flames'; for *evadere* cf. *Aen.* 3.282.

9 691f. 'If not, then do in your own person what is left to do, cast me down to destruction with your death-dealing thunderbolt if so I deserve, and overwhelm me here with your right hand'. I follow Servius in taking *quod superest* adverbially, with *me* or *nos* supplied as the object of the sentence. For the thought cf. *Aen* 12.643 *id rebus defuit unum*. There is another, perhaps less likely, interpretation according to which *quod superest* is the object, equivalent to *reliquias Troiae,* 'the remnants of Troy'. Cf. 796.

10 694. **sine more:** 'in wild fury', literally 'without restraint', cf. *Aen.* 7.377, 8.635.

11 694f. Notice the imitative alliteration of *t* and *r,* and later of *s;* compare the description of the storm in *Geo.* 1.322f.

12 695. **ardua terrarum:** 'the high places of the land'; for Virgil's fondness for the neuter of the adjective followed by a partitive genitive see note on 1.422, and cf. especially *Aen.* 8.221.

13 696. 'a downpour violent with torrential rain and deepest black on the misty south winds'; cf. *Geo.* 3.196, 278.

14 697. **super:** 'on top' (i.e. the decks were awash) rather than from above' or 'to overflowing'.

700-45. Aeneas in despair wonders whether to abandon his fated mission altogether. Nautes advises him to leave behind some of his company in Sicily, and take the rest onwards to Italy. As Aeneas is pondering this advice there appears to him in the night a vision of his father Anchises, who tells him to accept Nautes' advice; but before establishing his city in Italy he is to visit the underworld to meet his father and hear his destiny.

[1]At pater Aeneas casu concussus acerbo   700
nunc huc ingentis, nunc illuc pectore curas
mutabat versans, Siculisne resideret arvis[2]
oblitus[3] fatorum, Italasne capesseret oras.
Tum[4] senior Nautes, unum Tritonia Pallas
quem docuit multaque insignem reddidit arte   705
(haec[5] responsa dabat, vel quae portenderet ira
magna deum vel quae fatorum posceret ordo) —
isque his Aenean solatus vocibus infit:
'nate[6] dea, quo fata trahunt retrahuntque sequamur;
quidquid erit, superanda omnis fortuna ferendo est.   710
Est tibi Dardanius divinae stirpis Acestes:
hunc cape consiliis socium et coniunge volentem;
huic trade amissis superant qui navibus et quos[7]
pertaesum magni incepti rerumque tuarum est;
longaevosque senes ac fessas aequore matres   715

---

1 700f. In this passage we see very clearly the tension between Aeneas' duty towards his divine mission and the human weaknesses of character with which he has to struggle. He is aware that he is the chosen instrument of the will of the gods, but sometimes it seems that the task is almost too great for the frailty of a mortal man to achieve. At this stage in the poem his strength to continue is at its lowest ebb; and it is at this point that the vision of his father promises the inspiring revelations of Roman destiny which are given to Aeneas in the underworld (6.756f.). Thereafter Aeneas' strength and determination to fulfil his mission are no longer in doubt.

2 702-3. For -ne . . . -ne in an indirect question (here an indirect deliberative question) cf. 95. The jingling similarity of rhythm in the second halves of these two lines perhaps reproduces the insistent dinning of the problem in Aeneas' thoughts.

3 703. **oblitus fatorum**: see note on 700f.

4 704-5. 'whom above all Tritonian Pallas had taught, whom she had made renowned for great knowledge of her lore'. Varro tells us that the Nautii were priests of Pallas because Nautes was supposed to have bought back the Palladium (*Aen.* 2.166) to Italy. For *Tritonia* as Pallas' epithet see note on *Aen.* 2.171.

5 706-7. 'She it was who gave him replies about what the great anger of the gods was portending or what the march of the fates demanded'. These two lines are parenthetical and the subject of the main sentence (Nautes) is picked up by *isque* as if it were a new sentence (cf. *Aen.* 6.684, 9.549). *Haec* is Pallas; *quae* does not go with *responsa* but introduces the indirect question.

6 709f. Notice the slow oracular style of Nautes' speech. There is a marked absence of midline pauses; the first four lines are all end-stopped and self contained sentences which give a noticeable hortatory effect. Nautes' lack of emotion or excitement throws into clearer relief the anxiety of Aeneas, on whom rests the ultimate responsibility. The first two lines are *sentintiae* expressing Stoic ideas; notice the contrast between *fata* (destiny which we all must follow) and *fortuna* (circumstances which we may resist and overcome by endurance).

7 713. The word order is *huic trade (eos) qui amissis navibus superant; superant* means 'are left over', cf. 519.

et quidquid[1] tecum invalidum metuensque pericli est
delige, et his habeant terris sine moenia fessi;[2]
urbem appellabunt permisso[3] nomine Acestam.'[4]
    Talibus incensus dictis senioris amici
tum[5] vero in curas animo diducitur omnis.   720
Et Nox atra polum bigis[6] subvecta tenebat;
visa dehinc caelo facies[7] delapsa parentis
Anchisae subito talis effundere voces:
'nate, mihi vita quondam, dum vita manebat,
care magis, nate, Iliacis[8] exercite fatis,   725
imperio Iovis huc venio, qui classibus ignem
depulit, et caelo tandem miseratus ab alto est.
Consiliis pare quae nunc pulcherrima[9] Nautes
dat senior; lectos iuvenes, fortissima[10] corda,
defer in Italiam. Gens dura atque aspera[11] cultu   730
debellanda tibi Latio est. Ditis[12] tamen ante
infernas accede domos et Averna[13] per alta
congressus[14] pete, nate, meos. Non me impia namque[15]

---

1 716. **quidquid**: for the use of the neuter applied to people cf. *Aen.* 1.601, Hor. *Epod.* 5.1.

2 717. The word order again is complicated; the normal order would be *sine (ut) fessi moenia his terris habeant.* For the jussive subjunctive in parataxis with the imperative *sine* cf. 163.

3 718. **permisso nomine**: 'if the name be allowed', by Acestes, or by Aeneas.

4 **Acestam**: the town was called Egesta by the Greeks, Segesta by the Romans; for etymological associations of this kind see note on 117f. For the association of Trojans with Sicily cf. Thuc. 6.3.3, Cic. *Verr.* 2.4.72.

5 720. 'then indeed is he racked in mind with every kind of torment'; far from being comforted by Nautes Aeneas is made even more anxious, but at this point when his responsibilities press so heavily he receives through Anchises Jupiter's assurance (726f.).

6 721. **bigis**: Night (like Phoebus, line 739) drives across the sky in her chariot, and the stars follow in her train; cf. Enn. *Scen.* 112-13 (*sacra Nox*) *quae cava caeli / signitenentibus conficis bigis,* Tib. 2.1.87f., and Milton, *Comus* 553-4 'The drowsy frighted steeds / That draw the litter of close-curtain'd sleep'.

7 722. **facies**: the actual shade of Anchises is in Elysium (735). This is an apparition or vision sent by Jupiter; see note on 2.268f. (the apparition of Hector).

8 725. **Iliacis exercite fatis**: 'hard-pressed by Trojan destiny'; the same phrase occurs in *Aen.* 3.182. Its Stoic tenor is appropriate to Nautes' opening words (709-10).

9 728. **pulcherrima**: the placing of the adjective belonging to the antecedent (*consiliis*) in the relative clause is a common Latin usage, cf. *Aen.* 3.546.

10 729. **fortissima corda**: 'bravest hearts', cf. *Aen.* 2.348-9.

11 730. **aspera cultu**: 'rough in its way of life', cf. *Aen.* 1.263f., 9.603f.

12 731. **Ditis**: Virgil generally calls the king of the underworld Dis, but never uses the nominative; the sole occurrence of the name Pluton is where the nominative is needed (*Aen.* 7.327). The rhythm of the line ending here is striking; cf. *Geo.* 3.153 and my note on this passage (OUP Ed.).

13 732. **Averna**: sometimes the lake with its fabled entrance to the underworld (*Aen.* 3.442), sometimes the underworld itself (*Aen.* 7.91); here probably the latter. Virgil sometimes uses the neuter plural form, sometimes the masculine *Avernus* (813); cf. *Tartara* (734) and *Tartarus* (*Aen.* 6.577).

14 733. **congressus . . . meos**: 'seek a meeting with me'. The word is common in prose but unusual in poetry apart from its military meaning; Virgil has probably used the poetic plural here to avoid prosiness.

15 **namque**: the connexion of thought is that Aeneas would not be permitted to visit Tartarus (*Aen.* 6.563). The postposition of the colourless word to the end of the line is infrequent.

Tartara[1] habent, tristes[2] umbrae, sed amoena piorum
concilia Elysiumque colo.[3] Huc casta Sibylla[4]   735
nigrarum multo[5] pecudum te sanguine ducet.
Tum genus omne tuum et quae dentur moenia disces.[6]
Iamque vale; [7]torquet medios Nox umida cursus
et me saevus[8] equis Oriens adflavit anhelis.'
Dixerat et tenuis fugit ceu fumus in auras.   740
Aeneas 'quo deinde[9] ruis? Quo proripis?' Inquit,[10]
'quem fugis? Aut quis te nostris complexibus arcet?'
Haec memorans[11] cinerem et sopitos suscitat ignis,
Pergameumque Larem et canae penetralia Vestae[12]
farre[13] pio et plena[14] supplex veneratur acerra.   745

> 746-78. *Aeneas follows the new plan, and a city is founded
> under Acestes' rule for those staying behind; a temple is
> dedicated to Venus at Eryx, and Anchises' tomb has a priest
> and a sanctuary appointed for it. After nine days of
> celebration in honour of the new city the Trojans say their
> farewells to those staying behind; sacrifices are made, and
> they sail for Italy.*

Extemplo socios primumque accersit[15] Acesten
et Iovis imperium et cari praecepta parentis
edocet[16] et quae nunc animo sententia constet.
Haud mora consiliis, nec iussa recusat Acestes.

---

1 734-5. Tartarus and Elysium are described in *Aen.* 6.548f., 637f.

2 734. **tristes umbrae**: in apposition to *Tartara*, *umbrae* being used in its local sense ('grim region of darkness').

3 735. **colo. Huc**: there is hiatus between these two words, cf. *Aen.* 1.16.

4 **Sibylla**: the priestess of Apollo, cf. *Aen.* 3.441 f., 6.10f.

5 736. **multo . . . sanguine**: 'when you have paid rich sacrifice', ablative of price. The sacrifices are described in *Aen.* 6.243f.

6 737. This promise is fulfilled when Anchises describes the pageant of Roman heroes waiting to be born, *Aen.* 6.756f.

7 738. 'dewy Night is sweeping round past the mid-point of her course', i.e. her chariot has passed the midpoint of her orbit through the sky, cf. 721, 835.

8 739. **saevus**: because the dawn banishes ghosts. Cf. the Ghost in *Hamlet* (1.5.58f. 'But soft! Methinks I scent the morning air; / Brief let me be'. Compare *Geo.* 1.250.

9 741. **deinde**: apparently equivalent to *posthac*, in context implying 'so soon'; cf. 9.781 (= *posthac*).

10 741. Compare Hom. *Od.* 11.210, where Odysseus begs the phantom of his mother to stay. Notice the broken urgency of this line and the next, accentuated by the omission of the reflexive with *proripis* and the large number of short words.

11 743f. Sacrifices are made after supernatural appearances at *Aen.* 3.176f., 8.542f. Notice how the agitated excitement of Aeneas is calmed by the ritual performance of these religious ceremonies, described in the appropriate sonorous and formulary diction.

12 744. Vesta, goddess of the hearth, was closely associated with the Lar (more often plural, Lares) and Penates; cf. *Aen.* 8.542f., 9.258f.

13 745. **farre pio**: this is the *mola salsa* used in sacrifices, cf. *Aen.* 2.133, 4.517. For *pius* cf. also *Aen.* 4.637 *pia lege tempora villa;* in these contexts it means 'required by religion'.

14 **plena ... acerra**: cf. Hor. *Odes* 3.8.2f. *acerra turis / plena.*

15 746. **accersit**: variant spelling for *arcessit*.

16 748. 'the plan which now was firmly settled in his mind', cf. Cic. *Ad Att.* 8.11.1 *constitit consilium*, and *Aen.* 2.750 (*stat*).

Transcribunt[1] urbi matres populumque volentem   750
deponunt, animos nil magnae laudis egentis.
Ipsi transtra novant flammisque ambesa[2] reponunt
robora navigiis, aptant remosque rudentisque,[3]
exigui numero, sed[4] bello vivida virtus.
Interea Aeneas urbem designat aratro   755
sortiturque domos; hoc[5] Ilium et haec loca Troiam
esse iubet. Gaudet regno Troianus Acestes
indicitque[6] forum et patribus dat iura vocatis.
Tum vicina astris Erycino in vertice sedes[7]
fundatur Veneri Idaliae,[8] tumuloque sacerdos[9]   760
ac lucus late sacer additur Anchiseo.[10]

    Iamque [11]dies epulata novem gens omnis, et aris
factus honos: placidi straverunt aequora venti
creber[12] et aspirans rursus vocat Auster in altum.
Exoritur procurva[13] ingens per litora fletus;   765
complexi inter se noctemque[14] diemque morantur.
Ipsae iam matres, ipsi, quibus aspera quondam
visa maris facies et non tolerabile nomen,[15]
ire volunt omnemque fugae perferre laborem.

---

1 750. **transcribunt**: 'enrol', a technical term (according to Servius) like the much commoner *adscribere*.

2 752. **ambesa**: literally 'eaten round', (*Aen.* 3.257) hence here 'charred'.

3 753. **rudentisque**: for the hyper-metric *-que* cf. 422.

4 754. **sed . . . virtus**: 'but their valour in war never sleeps'; cf. Lucr. 1.72 (of Epicurus) *ergo vivida vis animi pervicit*, *Aen.* 11.386.

5 756-7. **hoc ... iubet**: 'this he bids be their Ilium, these lands their Troy'; see note on 634. The town is to be called Acesta; these are presumably the names of parts of it. Others take the meaning to be that Acesta is now to be metaphorically their Ilium and their Troy; this seems less likely in view of 633f.

6 758. **indicitque forum**: 'proclaims an assembly', cf. *comitia indicere* (Livy). Notice the very Roman terminology here, as in 750, 755.

7 759f. This temple of Venus on Mt. Eryx (see note on 24) was very famous in Greek and Roman times, cf. Thuc. 6.46.3, Tac. *Ann.* 4.43.5. There was a temple of Venus Erycina at Rome near the Colline Gate.

8 760. **Idaliae**: Idalium in Cyprus was one of Venus' most favoured abodes (*Aen.* 1.681) and as such is linked with Eryx in Theoc. 15.100f.

9 760-1. Compare Andromache's sacrifices at Hector's cenotaph, *Aen.* 3.300f. For the significance of this worship see note 42f.; the deification of Anchises is implied though not stated.

10 761. For the formation of the adjective cf. *stirpis Achilleae* (*Aen.* 3.326), *Cytherea* (line 800). For the spondaic ending (commoner with a Greek word than otherwise) see note on 2.68.

11 762. Aeneas had decreed for Anchises a religious ceremony of nine days with games on the ninth (64); this further period of nine days is to celebrate the foundation of the city.

12 764. **creber et aspirans**: 'and blowing steadily'; for the adverbial use of *creber* cf. 278 and *Aen.* 3.70.

13 765. **procurva**: an rare word not found elsewhere in classical Latin except for *Geo.* 2.421.

14 766. **noctemque diemque morantur**: probably 'they delay a night and a day' rather than 'they prolong night and day' by trying to make them last longer.

15 768. **nomen**: 'the very mention of it'; *P* has *numen* ('its power') which many editors accept, but *nomen* has better balance with *fades*, and gives more force to the sentence.

Quos bonus Aeneas[1] dictis solatur amicis   770
et consanguineo lacrimans commendat Acestae.
Tris Eryci[2] vitulos et Tempestatibus[3] agnam
caedere deinde iubet solvique ex[4] ordine funem.
Ipse caput tonsae foliis evinctus olivae[5]
stans procul in prora pateram tenet, extaque salsos   775
porricit in fluctus ac vina liquentia fundit.
Prosequitur surgens a puppi ventus euntis;
certatim socii feriunt mare et aequora verrunt.

> *779-826. Meanwhile Venus complains to Neptune of Juno's hostility to the Trojans, and asks for his engagement that the Trojans will safely cross the sea to Italy. Neptune gives his promise, but says that one life must be lost so that the others shall be safe. The seas are calmed as Neptune rides over them attended by his retinue.*

[6]At Venus interea Neptunum exercita curis
adloquitur talisque effundit pectore questus: 780
'Iunonis[7] gravis ira neque[8] exsaturabile pectus
cogunt me, Neptune, preces descendere in omnis;
quam nec longa dies pietas[9] nec mitigat ulla,
nec Iovis imperio fatisque infracta[10] quiescit.[11]

---

1 770f. Aeneas is now master of events again, consoling rather than consoled (708), calmly making all the necessary arrangements.

2 772. Eryx was the guardian deity of the place, cf. 24.

3 773. **Tempestatibus agnam**: cf. *Aen.* 3.120, Hor. *Epod.* 10.24. There was a temple to the *Tempestates* near the Porta Camena.

4 773. **ex ordine**: 'duly', cf. 102 and *Aen.* 7.139.

5 774-8. Almost the whole of this passage is made up of phrases and lines which occur elsewhere; cf. *Geo.* 3.21, lines 237-8, *Aen.* 3.130, 290. The familiar phrases give a calm ritualistic ending to this section of the poem. For the construction of *caput* see note on 135; for *tonsae* cf. 556; *procul* here is 'apart', away from the rest.

6 779f. At this critical moment in the narrative of the human events, as Aeneas sets out on the last phase of his long journey, the scene is elevated to the divine plane so that the events which follow are seen to be part of a larger context. The speech of Venus reflects her angry resentment against Juno, and expresses vividly and emotionally the insistent theme of Juno's disregard of the Fates, of Jupiter, of Neptune himself (792). Compare *Aen.* 1.229f., 10.18f.

7 781. Notice the emphatic position of *Iunonis,* the word which comes immediately to Venus' lips; we might translate 'Juno, with her fierce anger and implacable heart, forces me . . .'. The rhythm of the line is unusual; the absence of strong caesura in third and fourth foot gives coincidence of ictus and accent in the middle of the line which sharply contrasts with the conflict in the first two feet; compare *Aen.* 2.483, 12.619, both memorable lines.

8 **neque exsaturabile**: equivalent to *et inexsaturabile;* cf. Prop. 2.28.52, Ov. *Met.* 1.110. The word *exsaturabilis* does not occur elsewhere except for one instance in Statius (*Th.* 1.214); see note on 591.

9 783. **pietas nec:** the postposition of *nec* emphasises *pietas*, which refers both generally to Aeneas' quality (*Aen.* 1.10, 253) and specifically to his due worship of Juno (*Aen.* 3.547).

10 784. **infracta:** 'broken', cf. *Aen.* 7.332, 9.499, 10.731, 12.1. The adjective *infractus* = 'unbroken' occurs only in late Latin.

11 **quiescit:** cf. the ironical words of Juno in *Aen.* 7.297f. *at credo mea numina tandem / fessa iacent, odiis aut exsaturata quievi.*

Non[1] media de gente Phrygum exedisse nefandis   785
urbem odiis satis [2]est nec poenam traxe per omnem
reliquias[3] Troiae: cineres[4] atque ossa peremptae
insequitur. Causas tanti sciat[5] illa furoris.
Ipse mihi nuper Libycis tu testis in undis[6]
quam molem subito excierit: maria omnia caelo   790
miscuit Aeoliis nequiquam[7] freta procellis,
in regnis hoc ausa tuis.
Per[8] scelus ecce etiam Troianis matribus actis
exussit foede puppis et classe subegit[9]
amissa socios ignotae linquere terrae.   795
Quod[10] superest, oro, liceat dare[11] tuta per undas
vela tibi, liceat Laurentem[12] attingere Thybrim,
si concessa peto, si dant ea moenia Parcae.'
Tum Saturnius[13] haec domitor maris edidit alti:
'fas[14] omne est, Cytherea,[15] meis te fidere regnis,   800

---

1 785f. 'It is not enough that in her accursed acts of hatred she has devoured their city from the heart of Phrygia's people'. The language is harsh, perhaps partly in imitation of Homer (*Il.* 4.34f., where Zeus supposes that Hera will not be satisfied until she has eaten Priam and his children raw), but it is also appropriate to Venus' anger against Juno. Some of the most powerful language in the *Aeneid* issues from the mutual hatred of these two goddesses; cf. *Aen.* 10.16-95.

2 786f. 'nor that she has dragged the remnants of Troy through the utmost retribution'. The image is perhaps that of dragging captives off in chains, or even dragging a dead body (like Hector's) behind a chariot to satisfy the desire for vengeance. For *traxe* (syncope for *traxisse,* a mark of archaising style) cf. Lucr. 3.650, 5.1159 and *Aen.* 4.606, 682.

3 787. **reliquias:** cf. *Aen.* 1.30, 598, 3.87.

4 **cineres . . . peremptae:** 'the ashes and bones of the dead city'; Henry well points out that the suggestion of savage treatment of a dead body conveys the height of barbarism.

5 788. **sciat ipsa:** 'be it hers to know' (Fairclough); i.e. it is completely inexplicable to all right-minded people. The words which Venus uses here recall Virgil's question (*Aen.* 1.11) *tantaen e animis caelestibus irae*?

6 789f. Venus refers to the storm, aroused by Aeolus at Juno's instigation, with which the adventures of the Trojans begin in the *Aeneid* (1.84f.). Compare *molem* (790) with 1.134; *maria omnia caelo miscuit* with 1.133f.; *Aeoliis procellis* with 1.65f.; *in regnis hoc ausa tuis* with 1.138-9.

7 791. **nequiquam:** in vain because Neptune's intervention saved the Trojans.

8 793. **per scelus:** notice the emphatic position, in front of *ecce etiam* which would naturally begin a sentence. The phrase colours the whole sentence, but syntactically is to be linked with *actis* (drove them on a path of crime), cf. 786 and Hor. *Odes* 1.3.26.

9 794-5. The object to be supplied for *subegit* is Aenean. Venus' phrases are deliberately exaggerated; four ships (not the fleet) were lost, and Sicily was by now not wholly unknown.

10 796. **quod superest:** adverbial, 'for the rest', 'henceforward'; cf. 691 and *Aen.* 9.157, 11.15. As in 691, so here it could be equivalent to *reliquias* as object to *liceat* ('let what remains sail safely . . .'), but the balance of probability is against it.

11 796-7. **dare . . . tibi:** 'commit their sails to you over the waves in safety' rather than 'sail in safety over the waves through your help' which, while idiomatic for *dare vela* (*Aen.* 3.191), renders an impossible construction for *tibi*.

12 797. **Laurentem:** the *ager Laurens* evidently extended from the Tiber to Ardea (*Aen.* 7.650); the noun Laurentum was the name either of this region or of an ancient town within it, perhaps identical with Lavinium.

13 799. **Saturnius:** this epithet is normally applied to Juno (606); in using it of Neptune (who was of course also a child of Saturnus) Virgil is perhaps recalling the line of similar rhythm in *Aen.* 4.372.

14 800f. The tone and movement of Neptune's speech contrast markedly with the emotional excitement of Venus. It is calm and slow and reassuring; and the sentence beginning at 804 is unusually long and complex (dallying) compared with Virgil's usual style. It is the speech of a revered old counsellor.

15 800. **Cytherea:** for this epithet of Venus born from the sea (*unde genus ducis*) near Cythera cf. *Aen.* 1.257.

unde genus ducis. [1]Merui quoque; saepe furores
compressi et rabiem tantam caelique marisque.
Nec minor in terris, Xanthum[2] Simoentaque testor,
Aeneae mihi cura tui. Cum Troia Achilles
exanimata[3] sequens impingeret agmina muris,   805
milia multa daret[4] leto, gemerentque repleti
amnes nec reperire viam atque evolvere posset
in mare se Xanthus, Pelidae[5] tunc ego forti
congressum Aenean nec dis nec viribus aequis
nube[6] cava rapui, cuperem cum vertere ab imo   810
structa meis manibus periurae moenia Troiae.[7]
Nunc quoque mens eadem perstat mihi; pelle timores.
Tutus, quos optas, portus accedet Averni.[8]
Unus erit tantum amissum quem gurgite quaeres;[9]
unum pro multis dabitur caput.'   815
His ubi laeta deae permulsit pectora dictis,
iungit equos auro genitor,[10] spumantiaque addit[11]
frena feris manibusque omnis effundit habenas.
Caeruleo per summa levis volat aequora curru;
subsidunt undae tumidumque sub axe tonanti   820
sternitur aequor aquis, fugiunt vasto[12] aethere nimbi.

---

1 801-2. The storm aroused by Aeolus at the instigation of Juno (1.81f.) was calmed by Neptune; and we may believe that he was also responsible for the calming of the storms in 3.192f., 5.10f.

2 803. **Xanthum Simoentaque**: the rivers of Troy, cf. 634.

3 805. **exanimata**: 'breathless', 'panic-stricken', cf. *exanimes* (669).

4 806. **daret**: supply *et cum*. The phrases which follow are closely imitated from Hom. *Il*. 21.218f.

5 808. **Pelidae**: the meeting of Aeneas and Achilles, son of Peleus, is described in *Il*. 20.158f., and the rescue of Aeneas in *Il*. 20.318f. For the dative after *congressus* cf. *Aen*. 1.475.

6 810. **nube cava**: 'enfolding cloud', cf. *Aen*. 1.516, Hom. *Il*. 20.444.

7 811. Neptune and Apollo helped to build the walls of Troy, but were cheated of the agreed reward by Laomedon; cf. *Aen*. 4.542.

8 813. Notice the slow spondees to give due impressiveness to his promise. For *portus Averni* (Cumae) cf. *Aen*. 6.2, and *Geo*. 2.161f.

9 814-15. Palinurus (840f.) is to be the scapegoat for the successful completion of the voyage; the repetition of *unus* stresses the point. For *quaerere* (= 'look for in vain', 'miss') cf. *Aen*. 1.217, Prop. 1.17.18.

10 817-18. 'Father Neptune yoked his horses in their golden harness, then put the bit in their foaming mouths as they chafed to be away, and let all the reins run out free through his hands'. The word *feris* conveys the high spirits of the horses, cf. *Aen*. 4.135.

11 817f. The picture of Neptune driving over the waves in his chariot, attended by his retinue of creatures and deities of the sea, is painted in the most brilliant colours. It is based on Homer's memorable description of Poseidon's journey in *Il*. 13.23f., and it has points of similarity with Virgil's earlier description of Neptune in *Aen*. 1.142f., but it has a more sustained pictorial imagery than either of these passages.

12 821. **vasto**: 'savage', 'threatening', rather than 'vast'.

240

Tum[1] variae comitum facies, immania cete,[2]
et senior Glauci chorus Inousque Palaemon[3]
Tritonesque citi Phorcique exercitus omnis;
laeva tenent Thetis et Melite Panopeaque virgo,   825
Nisaee Spioque Thaliaque Cymodoceque.

> *827-71. The Trojans proceed on their voyage, Palinurus
> leading. During the night the god Sleep comes to Palinurus,
> disguised as Phorbas, and urges him to rest from his vigil.
> Palinurus refuses, and Sleep casts him into the sea. When
> the loss of the helmsman is discovered; Aeneas takes over
> the management of the ship and in deep sorrow speaks his
> farewell to Palinurus.*

[4]Hic patris Aeneae suspensam[5] blanda vicissim
gaudia pertemptant[6] mentem; iubet ocius omnis
attolli[7] malos, intendi[8] bracchia velis.
Una[9] omnes fecere[10] pedem pariterque sinistros,[11]   830

---

1 822. 'Then there come the manifold figures of his company'; for the absence of a main verb cf. *Aen.* 1.639f., 3.618f., 4.131. It has been suggested that this description of Neptune's retinue is based on a piece of sculpture by Scopas in the circus of Flaminius (Pliny, *Nat. Hist.* 36.26); at all events the passage has a most marked visual impact (cf. lines 240-1 and *Geo.* 4.334f.).

2 cete: 'sea-monsters'; a Greek neuter plural, cf. *Tempe* (*Geo.* 2.469).

3 823f. For these deities of the sea, compare Spenser, *F.Q.* 4.11.11f., and Milton, *Comus* 867f. Glaucus was a fisherman who became a sea-god (Ov. *Met.* 13.896f.); Palaemon, also called Melicertes, son of Ino, is identified with Portunus (241), cf. Ov. *Met.* 4.416f.; Triton was a son of Neptune whose skill at trumpeting with a seashell Misenus vainly tried to emulate (*Aen.* 6.171f.). Compare the final lines of Wordsworth's sonnet 'The world is too much with us. . . .'
So might I, standing on this pleasant lea,
Have glimpses that would make me less forlorn;
Have sight of Proteus rising from the sea
Or hear old Triton blow his wreathed Horn.
For the plural *Tritones* cf. Stat. *Ach.* 1.55. Phorcus was an old man of the sea (Hom. *Od.* 13.96); Thetis, the mother of Achilles, was the most famous of the Nereids; Melite and Panopea were also Nereids; the nymphs in line 826 are taken from Hom. *Il.* 18.39-40. The metrical pattern of this line of Greek names is also Greek (cf. *Geo.* 1.437, 4.336).

4 827f. The story of Palinurus with which the book ends leads into the atmosphere of Book 6; the liquid notes of pathos which are so marked a feature of the *Aeneid* are heard here at their clearest. As often in the poem, sorrow is to be endured at the moment of success. The sequel to Palinurus' death is told in *Aen.* 6.337f. (where see notes).
The origin of the legend of Palinurus, the helmsman who gave his name to Cape Palinurus in S. Italy, is a typical aetiological story to account for the foundation of a town (cf. *Aen.* 6.378f., and Servius' note). It seems likely that the legend can be traced back to Timaeus in the third century, and it probably came to Virgil through Varro; cf. also Dionysius 1.53.2.
The factual material of the legend has been transformed into poetry by the adaptation of a number of Homeric passages: the story of Elpenor in *Od.* 11, the death of Phrontis in *Od.* 3.278f., the god Sleep in *Il.* 14.231f. Fired by these sources Virgil's imagination worked on the prosaic material of the legend so as to produce an episode of haunting beauty and pathos.

5 827. **suspensam**: 'anxious'; cf. *Aen*.4.9.

6 828. **pertemptant**: 'came over', 'pervaded', a poetic use of the word, cf. *Aen.* 1.502.

7 829. **attolli malos**: the masts could be taken down when the ships were not being sailed (cf. 487).

8 **intendi bracchia velis**: 'the yardarms to be hung with their sails'; for *intendere* cf. 403. *Bracchia* in the sense of *antemnae* is not common; cf. Val. Fl. 1.126.

9 830f. Notice the emphasis on the regularity and precision of the manoeuvre given by the words *una, pariter, una*. The serene description of ordered progress heightens the pathos of the subsequent disaster

10 830. **fecere pedem**: 'set the sheets', i.e. fastened the ropes at the bottom of the sail to make the desired angle with the wind; cf. Cat. 4.21.

11 830-2. 'and together they let out their sails now to the left, now to the right; in unison they turn their lofty yard-arms now this way, now that'. *Cornua* is the technical term for the ends of the yardarms (cf. *Aen.* 3.549), here being adjusted for tacking.

241

nunc dextros solvere sinus; una ardua torquent
cornua detorquentque; ferunt sua[1] flamina classem.
Princeps ante omnis densum Palinurus[2] agebat
agmen; ad[3] hunc alii cursum contendere iussi.
Iamque fere mediam caeli Nox umida metam[4]   835
contigerat, placida laxabant membra quiete
sub remis fusi per dura sedilia nautae,
cum! Evis aetheriis delapsus Somnus[5] ab astris
aera [6]dimovit tenebrosum et dispulit umbras,
te, Palinure, petens, tibi somnia[7] tristia portans[8]   840
insonti; puppique deus[9] consedit in alta
Phorbanti[10] similis funditque has ore loquelas:[11]
Iaside[12] Palinure, ferunt ipsa aequora classem,
aequatae[13] spirant aurae, datur hora quieti.
Pone caput fessosque[14] oculos furare labori.   845
Ipse ego paulisper pro te tua munera inibo.'

---

1 832. **sua**: 'its own', i.e. favourable, cf. 54.

2 833f. Notice how the attention is concentrated on Palinurus before the fresh start in the narrative at 835.

3 834. **ad hunc . . . contendere**: 'direct their course towards him', i.e. mark their course by him.

4 835f. The new scene is set in peacefully descriptive verses, with alliteration of *m* and assonance of long vowel sounds. See note on 721 for Night's chariot; *meta* is here the halfway mark of her course through the sky, see note on 129.

5 838. **Somnus**: Homer tells in *Il.* 14.231f. how the god Sleep charmed the eyes of Zeus at Hera's request. There are fine descriptions of Somnus and his home in Ov. *Met.* 11.592f., Stat. *Th.* 10.84f.; cf. also Stat. *Silv.* 5.4 (where see Frère's introductory note in the Budé edition for a discussion of ancient concepts of the god and representations of him in art).

6 839. 'sundered the dusky air and parted the darkness'; the diction of this line conveys a strange other-worldly effect of midnight powers at work.

7 840. **somnia tristia**: a vague phrase of foreboding, where *somnia* does not mean specifically 'dreams', but rather 'the sleep that brings doom', cf. 854f.

8 840f. Here Virgil's art in giving emphasis by rhythmical and other means to an emotional part of the narrative can be very clearly seen. Line 840 is balanced with an effective simplicity by means of the repetition of *te . . . tibi* and the similar endings of *petens* and *portans;* there is very marked alliteration of *p* and *t*, and the insistent beat of the rhythm on the two dactylic words *somnia tristia* which fill the fourth and fifth feet is made all the more marked because they have similar grammatical endings. Finally *insonti* (the key word for the pathos of the whole passage) is given great emphasis by its position in the sentence (last word), by its position in the line (first word before a heavy pause), and by its spondaic slowness after the dactylic movement of the previous line.
For the use of the vocative to add to the feeling of personal involvement cf. *Aen.* 4.408.

9 841. **deus consedit**: 'alighted in his divine power'; *deus* has some predicative force, the subject still being *Somnus,* cf. *Aen.* 1.412, 692.

10 842. **Phorbanti similis:** compare Allecto in *Aen.* 7.406f., where she appears in disguise to Turnus, and, like Somnus, first tries persuasion and then uses her divine power.

11 **loquelas:** this is not a common word, and is employed here, as Page well says, to suggest the 'soft insinuating words he uses'; cf. Lucr. 139, 5.231.

12 843. **Iaside:** for Iasius, son of Jupiter, a founder of the Trojan race, cf. *Aen.* 3.168. The Greek vocative form ends in long *-e,* cf. *Aen.* 1.97.

13 844. **aequatae:** 'steadily', 'evenly', as opposed to gusty or veering winds.

14 845. **fessosque . . . labori:** 'steal your weary eyes from their vigil'. The metaphor is a vivid one, imitated in Stat. *Silv.* 4.4.29.
For the dative used with words meaning 'take away from' (*demere, eripere,* etc.) cf. 260, 726, *Aen.* 7.282-3. The juxtaposition of words with similar endings (*fessos, oculos*) is generally avoided by Virgil, and can therefore achieve a certain effect when used; cf. 682, *Aen.* 6.269-70, 469, 638-9.

Cui vix[1] attollens Palinurus lumina fatur:
'mene[2] salis placidi vultum fluctusque quietos
ignorare[3] iubes? Mene huic confidere monstro?[4]
Aenean[5] credam (quid[6] enim?) fallacibus auris   850
et[7] caelo, totiens[8] deceptus fraude sereni?'
Talia dicta dabat, clavumque adfixus et haerens
nusquam amittebat[9] oculosque sub astra tenebat.
Ecce[10] deus ramum Lethaeo rore madentem
vique soporatum Stygia super utraque quassat   855
tempora, cunctantique natantia lumina solvit.
Vix primos[11] inopina quies laxaverat artus,
et[12] super[13] incumbens cum puppis parte revulsa[14]
cumque gubernaclo liquidas proiecit in undas
praecipitem ac socios nequiquam saepe vocantem;   860
ipse volans tenuis se sustulit ales[15] ad auras.
Currit iter tutum non setius aequore classis
promissisque patris Neptuni interrita[16] fertur.

---

1 847. **vix attollens . . . lumina**: 'hardly lifting his eyes', (being intent on steering) rather than 'barely able to lift his eyes' (because of the power of the god).

2 848. **mene**: very emphatic: 'do you ask me of all men?' (Jackson Knight). Others may be tricked by the smiling face of the sea (cf. Lucr. 2.557f., 5.1002f.), but not so the helmsman of long experience.

3 849. **ignorare:** 'act as if I did not know', i.e. forget what I know.

4 **monstro**: 'demon'; the word in this usage conveys the idea of a vast and supernatural agent of evil. It is used of the wooden horse (*Aen.* 2.245), of the Harpies (3.214), of Polyphemus (3.658), of Fama (4.181), of Cacus (8.198).

5 850. **Aenean credam**: the pathos of this episode is greatly increased by the stress laid on Palinurus' loyalty as a helmsman, his sense of duty to the trust placed in him; cf. his words in the underworld to Aeneas (6.351f.).

6 **quid enim?:** it is perhaps best to take these words as parenthetical: 'for what then?'; cf. Hor. *Sat.* 1.1.7, 2.3.132. Others prefer to regard them as postponed from the beginning of the sentence 'for how could I entrust . . . ?'

7 851. **et caelo:** sc. *fallaci,* 'to the uncertainties of wind and weather'. Most MSS have *caeli* (a noun for *sereni*) but the first hand of P and Servius read *caelo. Serenum* then is a noun, cf. *Geo.* 1.393, Lucan 1.530, and compare *tranquillum* in line 127. The objection to the reading *caeli* is that *et* is then left without meaning.

8 **totiens . . . sereni**: 'when I have been so often cheated by the false promise of bright weather'.

9 853. **amittebat:** for the lengthened final syllable see note on 284. Notice the assonance of *dabat, amittebat, tenebat,* emphasising the steady monotonous determination of Palinurus.

10 854f. 'Then behold, the god shook over both his temples a branch dripping with the dew of Lethe, made sleepy with the power of Styx, and as he gradually yielded closed his swimming eyes.' These lovely lines were remembered and imitated by Valerius Flaccus (8.84) and by Silius (10.354f.). For Lethe, the river of forgetfulness, see note on 6.705. For the rhythm of line 856, where there is no strong caesura at all, cf. 591 and *Aen.* 4.486.

11 857. **primos**: the word conveys the idea of the gradual penetration of the body by sleep until finally the innermost being is subdued.

12 858. **et**: in the sense of inverted *cum,* cf. *Aen.* 2.692.

13 858. **super incumbens**: 'looming over him', cf. 325 and *Geo.* 2.377.

14 858-9. Palinurus even in sleep does not relax his hold, so that the helm and a part of the ship are torn away with him; cf. *Aen.* 6.349f.

15 861. **ales:** Sleep is often depicted in literature and art as winged; see note on 838 and cf. Prop. 1.3.45, Stat. *Th.* 10.137f.

16 863. **interrita:** 'without alarm', a slight personification of the fleet.

Iamque[1] adeo scopulos Sirenum[2] advecta subibat,
difficilis quondam multorumque ossibus albos   865
(tum rauca[3] adsiduo longe sale saxa sonabant),
cum pater amisso fluitantem[4] errare magistro
sensit, et ipse ratem nocturnis rexit in undis
multa gemens casuque animum[5] concussus amici:
'o nimium caelo et pelago confise sereno,   870
nudus in ignota, Palinure, iacebis harena.'

---

1 864f. 'And now the fleet voyaging on was approaching the cliffs of the Sirens, in former days perilous and white with the bones of many victims — at this time the rocks were re-echoing with roaring afar in the ceaseless surf, — when father Aeneas saw. . . .' The reference is to the legend that the Sirens killed themselves after Odysseus had got safely past them; when Aeneas reaches the rocks the enchanting voices are past history (*quondam*) and now (*tum*) only the harsh booming of the sea against the lonely rocks is to be heard.

2 864. **Sirenum**: the story is told in Hom. *Od.* 12.39f. The Alexandrians had established geographical locations for Homer's stories, and the Sirens were placed in the islands called Sirenusae near Capreae.

3 866. **rauca:** perhaps adverbial with *sonabant* rather than agreeing with *saxa*, cf. *Aen.* 9.125. Notice the alliteration of *s*, suggesting the seething surf.

4 867. **fluitantem:** 'drifting'; *ratem* is supplied from the following clause.

5 869. **animum concussus**: 'sick at heart'; for the construction see note on 135.

244

BOOK 6

Introductory note

The sixth book is the focal point of the *Aeneid*; much of what has gone before is resumed in it, and it provides the new impetus for the second half of the poem. In itself it offers some of Virgil's greatest poetry, and his deepest thought.

There are three particular aspects of the book which may be distinguished: firstly it provides Virgil with a setting for the exposition of his religious thought; secondly the final section of the book is the most outstanding patriotic expression of the whole poem; and thirdly the events in the underworld are a personal revelation for Aeneas, with a profound effect upon his character and resolution.

The structure of the book is tripartite: first the preparations for the descent (1.263); secondly the journey through the underworld to Elysium (264-678); thirdly (679-fin.) the meeting with Anchises and the exposition first of the nature of life beyond the grave and then of the greatness of Rome's future history.

1. *Preparation* (1-263).

In the long preliminaries to the actual descent to the underworld Virgil builds up a picture of religious ceremonies, of mystery and awe appropriate for the supernatural experiences in the rest of the book. The mysterious Labyrinth on the doors of Apollo's temple, the prophetic dementia of the Sibyl, the ritual prayers and formal request of Aeneas and the frightening oracular replies of the Sibyl lead to the two themes of the last part of this section, the death and funeral of Misenus and the discovery of the golden bough. The sudden unnecessary death of Misenus introduces a motif of the frailty of human life, and serves to emphasise still further the supernatural mystery of the experience Aeneas is about to undergo. Aeneas will visit the halls of Pluto, and return again; but one act of folly has blotted out Misenus' life for ever. This theme is interwoven structurally with the search for the golden bough, strange talisman of life and death, symbolising light in darkness, survival in destruction.

2. *The journey* (264-678).

For the background to Aeneas' experience Virgil has drawn on the rich heritage of Greco-Roman mythology and folklore; the eleventh book of Homer's *Odyssey* is several times recalled, and there are elements from Pindar and doubtless from many Orphic catabaseis of the kind which is parodied in Aristophanes' *Frogs,* and especially there are Orphic ideas from the myths of Plato, those of the *Phaedo,* the *Phaedrus,* the *Gorgias* and *Republic* 10. (Fuller information on these sources is given in the appropriate places in the commentary; see also my article in *Greece and Rome,* 1964, pp. 48f., and the introductions to the editions of Butler and Fletcher.)

Using this background of the traditional machinery of Hades, the rivers, the ferryman, the dog, the place of everlasting evildoers, Virgil describes the meeting of Aeneas with three of the ghosts of his past, Palinurus, Dido, Deiphobus. Palinurus had been swept overboard by the god Sleep near the very end of the journey, and Aeneas feels remorse and guilt that he was not able to save his faithful helmsman. When he encounters Dido he speaks to her in tones of sorrow and self blame. To Deiphobus he expresses his feelings of guilt at not having been able to find his body. In a sense Aeneas travels again through the sorrows and regrets of his past life (Palinurus and Dido have played very large parts in the poem, and Deiphobus recalls all the suffering of Book 2). He looks backwards with sorrow and self reproach; but he is taught that the past cannot now be altered, that no amount of brooding over what might have been can change the facts. This is made especially clear to him by Dido; as he had rejected her in life, now in death she rejects him. The hard lesson that Aeneas has to learn about the past is summarised when Deiphobus leaves him for the last time and tells him that he must go forward: *i, decus, i, nostrum; melioribus utere fatis* (546).

3. *The revelation* (679-fin.).

As the middle section of the book was concerned with the sorrow and gloom of the past, so now the last section is concerned with the hope and glory of the future. After learning something of evil and virtue from his vision of Tartarus and his first sight of Elysium, Aeneas now meets his father and learns how the good are rewarded after death (see note on 703f.). Anchises' first words are of joy that Aeneas' devotion to his mission has overcome the trials of the journey: *venisti tandem, tuaque exspectata parenti / vicit iter durum pietas?* (687-8). He wants to show him his future *quo magis Italia mecum laetere reperta* (718). And halfway through the pageant of Roman heroes, after the description of Augustus, Anchises breaks off to ask his son whether there is any more doubt: *et dubitamus adhuc virtutem extendere factis, aut metus Ausonia prohibet consistere terra?* (806-7). When the pageant is finished it has fired Aeneas with love for the glory to come: *incenditque animum famae venientis amore* (889). From the sorrowful encounters with ghosts of his past Aeneas moves forward to fulfil the destiny of his new nation. He leaves behind the history of Troy in order to start the history of Rome.

1-41. The Trojans arrive in Italy at Cumae; Aeneas goes to consult the Sibyl at Apollo's temple. He gazes in admiration at the pictures on the temple doors, and is called into the temple by the Sibyl.

[1]Sic[2] fatur lacrimans, classique[3] immittit habenas
et tandem Euboicis Cumarum[4] adlabitur oris.
Obvertunt[5] pelago proras; tum dente tenaci
ancora[6] fundabat navis et litora curvae
praetexunt puppes. Iuvenum manus emicat ardens   5
litus in Hesperium; quaerit pars semina[7] flammae
abstrusa in venis [8]silicis, pars densa ferarum
tecta rapit silvas inventaque flumina monstrat.
At pius[9] Aeneas arces[10] quibus altus Apollo
praesidet horrendaeque procul secreta Sibyllae,[11]   10
antrum immane, petit, [12]magnam cui mentem animumque
Delius inspirat vates aperitque futura.

---

1 1f. The final arrival of the Trojans in Italy after their seven years' wanderings is marked by excited activity, briefly described, and by Aeneas' immediate departure to consult the Sibyl in accordance with instructions given him by Helenus (3.441f.) and Anchises (5.728f.). The narrative is then suspended for a description of the pictures on the doors of Apollo's temple (an ecphrasis, see note on 1.418f.). The subject matter (Daedalus, the Minotaur, the Labyrinth) has links with the narrative in various ways, of which the most important is the symbolism of the Labyrinth for the maze like journey of Aeneas through the underworld. The Labyrinth suggests the mysterious paths of the hidden world which Aeneas must trace; it is a frequent visual symbol of death. It may also suggest the idea of the exclusion of all but those selected to enter; for a very full discussion see W. F. J. Knight, *Cumnean Gates,* Oxford, 1936. Other possible links between the ecphrasis and the narrative are the father-son relationship of Daedalus and Icarus compared with that of Aeneas and Ascanius, and the similarity of the complex of rooms and corridors in a Minoan palace with Aeneas' underworld journey (see Mackail, Appendix C, where he argues for a tradition of a Minoan settlement at Cumae). Above all the ecphrasis takes us back into the shadowy distances of ancient mythology and folklore, and thus helps to establish the atmosphere of awe and mystery which Virgil seeks.

2 1-2. These linking lines, referring to Aeneas' last farewell to his helmsman Palinurus and his arrival on the shores of Italy, were regarded by some scholars in antiquity as part of Book 5; but the opening phrase, *sic fatur,* is taken from the beginning of Hom. *Il.* 7 and *Od.* 13, and it is beyond reasonable doubt that Virgil wished Book 6 to begin thus.

3 **classique . . . habenas**: the metaphor from horses is common, cf. Lucr. 5.787, *Geo.* 2.364, *Aen.* 1.63, 5.662.

4 2. Cumae, ten miles west of Naples, was a famous and flourishing city during the first millennium B.C.; it was the first Greek colony in Italy and was founded by settlers from Chalcis (line 17) in Euboea (Livy 8.23.5) at a very early date (though long after the time of Aeneas of course), probably about 750 B.C. The area was well known to Virgil, who lived much of his life in this part of Italy. Augustus restored the temples and the Sibyl's worship at Cumae (after the completion of the major military works in this area, *Geo.* 2.161f.), but within a generation or two Cumae fell into decline.

5 3. **obvertunt . . . proras**: it was normal to beach ships with the prow seawards, doubtless in readiness for quick launching.

6 4. **ancora fundabat**: 'the anchors began to secure'; the imperfect expresses the continued activity of the sailors all along the shore as a variation from the instantaneous pictures conveyed by the present tenses.

7 6f. For the kindling of fire from flint cf. *Aen.* 1.174f.; for the notion of its being 'concealed' in flint cf. *Geo.* 1.135.

8 7-8. 'Some plunder the woods, tangled home of wild creatures'; *tecta* is in apposition to *silvas* (cf. 179). For *rapere* in this sense cf. *Aen.* 2.374. They are seeking timber for fuel, water and meat for food.

9 9. **pius**: Aeneas' epithet here refers primarily to his religious duties and the fulfilment of his mission to his father (cf. 403).

10 9-10. **arces . . . secreta**: the ruins of the temple of Apollo are still to be seen on the acropolis of Cumae; the cave of the Sibyl, some little way off (*procul*), cut into the west edge of the cliff, has been discovered and excavated in recent times, and may now be seen in all its eerie grandeur.

11 10. **Sibyllae**: the priestess of Apollo, see note on 3.443. Sibylla was a type-name for such oracular priestesses; this particular Sibyl was called Deiphobe (36).

12 11-12. 'into whom the prophetic god of Delos breathes his mighty purpose and will'; for Apollo of Delos see note on 3.75-6.

Iam subeunt Triviae[1] lucos atque aurea tecta.

    Daedalus,[2] ut fama est, fugiens Minoia regna

praepetibus[3] pennis ausus se credere caelo   15

insuetum[4] per iter gelidas enavit[5] ad Arctos,

Chalcidicaque[6] levis tandem super astitit arce.

Redditus his primum terris tibi, Phoebe, sacravit

remigium[7] alarum posuitque immania templa.

In[8] foribus letum Androgeo;[9] tum pendere[10] poenas   20

Cecropidae[11] iussi (miserum!) septena quotannis

corpora natorum; stat ductis sortibus urna.

Contra elata mari respondet[12] Cnosia tellus:

hic crudelis amor tauri suppostaque[13] furto[14]

Pasiphae mixtumque genus prolesque biformis   25

Minotaurus inest, Veneris monimenta nefandae;

hic[15] labor ille domus et inextricabilis error;

magnum reginae[16] sed[17] enim miseratus amorem

Daedalus ipse dolos tecti ambagesque resolvit,

caeca regens filo vestigia. Tu quoque magnam   30

---

1 13. **Triviae**: Diana is naturally associated with her brother Apollo: for her epithet as goddess of the crossroads, identifying her with Hecate, cf. 35, 69 and note on *Aen.* 4.511.

2 14f. Servius tells the story of how Daedalus helped Pasiphae, wife of Minos, king of Crete, to satisfy her love for the bull (lines 24f.), a love which Venus, angered, had implanted in her. As a result of this the hybrid monster called the Minotaur was born to her; it was kept in a labyrinth built by Daedalus, and fed on human sacrifices. After Daedalus had helped Theseus traverse the maze (28f.), he was imprisoned but escaped by making himself wings and flying north to Cumae (or in other versions Sardinia or Sicily); cf. Ov. *Met.* 8.183f., Hor. *Odes* 1.3.34-5.

3 15. **praepetibus**: 'swift', see note on 3.360-1.

4 16. **insuetum per iter**: 'by a novel route', i.e. by flying.

5 **enavit**: the verb is used of sailing or flying as well as swimming; cf. Enn. *Ann.* 21, Lucr. 3.591, *Aen.* 4.245 and lines 134, 369, 671.

6 17. **Chalcidica**: see note on 2.

7 19. **remigium alarum**: 'the oarage of his wings', i.e. the wings on which he had 'rowed' through the air; for the metaphor see note on 1.301.

8 20. **in foribus**: for the ecphrasis see note on 1f.

9 **Androgeo**: Greek genitive as in 2.392. Androgeos, a son of Minos, was killed by the Athenians, and as recompense Minos demanded the payment of seven youths and seven maidens each year as a sacrifice to the Minotaur; cf. Cat. 64.76f.

10 20-2. **pendere poenas**: 'to pay as recompense', *poenas* is in apposition to *septena . . . corpora.*

11 21. **Cecropidae**: Cecrops was a legendary king of Athens, cf. Cat. 64.79.

12 23. **respondet Cnosia tellus**: i.e. the pictures of Crete 'balance' the pictures of Athens. Cnossos was the chief town of Crete, cf. *Aen.* 3.115.

13 24. **suppostaque**: contracted for *suppositaque,* cf. 59 *repostas* and *Aen.* 1.26.

14 24f. For the story see note on 14f.

15 27. 'here is the famous toil, the insoluble maze, of the palace'; the reference is to the Labyrinth, see note on 5.588-91 and cf. Cat. 64.155.

16 28. **reginae**: the story switches from Pasiphae to her daughter Ariadne, whose love for Theseus is here referred to; he killed the Minotaur and found his way out of the maze by the thread which Ariadne at Daedalus' instigation gave him, cf. Cat. 64.113.

17 **sed enim**: 'but indeed', cf. *Aen.* 1.19.

partem opere in tanto, sineret[1] dolor, Icare, haberes.
Bis conatus erat casus effingere in auro,
bis patriae cecidere manus. Quin protinus[2] omnia[3]
perlegerent oculis, ni iam praemissus Achates
adforet atque una Phoebi Triviaeque sacerdos,   35
Deiphobe[4] Glauci, fatur quae talia regi:
'non[5] hoc ista sibi tempus spectacula poscit;
nunc grege de intacto septem mactare iuvencos
praestiterit,[6] totidem lectas de more bidentis.'[7]
Talibus adfata Aenean (nec sacra morantur   40
iussa viri) Teucros vocat alta in templa sacerdos.

*42-76. The Sibyl in her cave goes into a prophetic trance
and calls on Aeneas to make his prayer to Apollo. He does
so, asking to be allowed to enter into the kingdom granted to
him by fate, and promising a temple and a festival to the god
and a special shrine for the Sibyl.*

[8]Excisum[9] Euboicae latus ingens rupis in antrum,
quo lati ducunt aditus[10] centum, ostia centum,
unde ruunt totidem voces, responsa Sibyllae.
Ventum erat ad limen, cum virgo 'poscere fata   45
tempus' ait; 'deus ecce deus!' Cui talia fanti
ante fores subito non[11] vultus, non color unus,
non comptae mansere comae; sed pectus anhelum,
et[12] rabie fera corda tument, maiorque videri

---

1 31. **sineret . . . haberes**: 'You, Icarus, would have had a large part if grief had permitted it'; *sineret* is conditional (supply *si*), and the condition past unfulfilled, cf. 34-35. Daedalus' son Icarus flew too near the sun on the wings his father had made for him and fastened on with wax, so that the wax melted and he fell into the sea and was drowned.

2 33. **protinus**: 'one after the other', cf. *Geo.* 4.1.

3 **omnia**: scanned as a trochee by synizesis, or with consonantal 1, cf. *Aen.* 7.237 and notes on 1.41, 2.16.

4 36. **Deiphobe Glauci**: Deiphobe, daughter of Glaucus, is the name of the Sibyl (see note on 10).

5 37. 'The moment does not call for sight-seeing on your part'; the reading *poscunt* offered by some MSS is much inferior.

6 39. **praestiterit**: perfect subjunctive, expressing a potential idea, 'it would be better'.

7 **bidentis**: sheep in their second year, cf. *Aen.* 4.57.

8 42f. The prayer of Aeneas is closely linked with the special worship paid to Apollo (patron god of Actium, cf. *Aen.* 8.704, 720f.) by Augustus, and looks forward aetiologically to the marble temple built for Apollo on the Palatine in 28 B.C. and the transference to it of the Sibylline books.

9 42. 'The side of the cliff of Cumae is hollowed out into a huge cave'; for the cave of the Sibyl see note on 9-10; for the Euboean colonisation of Cumae cf. line 2.

10 43. **aditus . . . ostia**: these are slits or windows leading out from the cave laterally.

11 47. **non . . . unus**: i.e. the colour and expression of her face is transformed; cf. Lucan 5.165f. for an elaborate description of prophetic frenzy.

12 49-50. 'and she was bigger to look upon, and her voice of no mortal sound'; the infinitive is epexegetic (cf. Hor. *Odes* 4.2.59 *niveus videri*), and the accusative *mortale* adverbial, cf. *Aen.* 1.328, *Geo.* 3.149. Other examples in this book are 201, 288, 401, 467, 481. For the idea cf. *Aen.* 2.773.

nec mortale sonans, adflata est numine quando[1]   50

iam propiore dei. 'Cessas in vota precesque,

Tros' ait 'Aenea? Cessas? Neque enim[2] ante dehiscent

attonitae[3] magna ora domus.' Et talia fata

conticuit. Gelidus Teucris per dura cucurrit

ossa tremor, funditque preces rex pectore ab imo: 55

'Phoebe, gravis Troiae semper[4] miserate labores,

Dardana[5] qui Paridis derexti[6] tela[7] manusque

corpus[8] in Aeacidae, magnas obeuntia[9] terras

tot maria intravi duce te penitusque repostas[10]

Massylum gentis praetentaque[11] Syrtibus arva: 60

iam tandem Italiae fugientis[12] prendimus oras,

hac[13] Troiana[14] tenus fuerit[15] fortuna secuta.

Vos quoque Pergameae iam fas est parcere genti,

dique[16] deaeque omnes, quibus obstitit Ilium et ingens

gloria Dardaniae. tuque, o sanctissima vates,   65

praescia venturi, da (non[17] indebita posco

regna meis fatis) Latio considere[18] Teucros

errantisque deos agitataque numina Troiae.

---

1 50. **quando**: 'since'; the postposition of the conjunction to fourth place is very unusual; cf. *Aen.* 10.366.

2 52. **enim**: there is an ellipsis of meaning: 'are you slow? Hurry then, for. . . .'

3 53. **attonitae**: 'awestruck'; the temple is personified as if it were affected like a human at the god's presence.

4 56. **semper miserate**: 'you who have always felt pity for . . .'; Virgil is fond of the vocative of the past participle (cf. 83, 125).

5 57f. Paris (renowned for his archery) with Apollo's help killed Achilles (grandson of Aeacus) by shooting him in the heel, the only part of him not invulnerable; cf. Hom. *Il.* 22.359f., Ov. *Met.* 12.580f.

6 57. **derexti**: contracted perfect, see note on 4.604-6.

7 **tela manusque**: 'the weapons and the aim'.

8 58. **corpus in Aeacidae**: for the position of the preposition see note on 4.257.

9 **obeuntia**: 'bordering', cf. *Aen.* 10.483.

10 59. **repostas**: 'remote', contracted for *repositas*, cf. 24.

11 60. The references are to Carthage, cf. *Aen.* 1.111, 4.132; *praetenta* is 'fringing', cf. *Aen.* 3.692.

12 61. **fugientis . . . oras**: cf. *Aen.* 5.629.

13 62. **hac ... tenus**: 'thus far', cf. *Aen.* 5.603.

14 **Troiana ... fortuna**: the implication is that it has been unfavourable right up to this moment.

15 **fuerit**: 'let it have followed' (and follow no longer), perfect subjunctive of a wish.

16 64. **dique deaeque omnes**: Juno especially, and Pallas, and Neptune were deities whose ambitions and wishes were hindered by Troy's prosperity (cf. 2.610f.).

17 66-7. **non indebita . . . fatis**: a frequent theme of the *Aeneid*, cf. *Aen.* 1.382, 7.120.

18 67. **considere Teucros**: accusative and infinitive after *da*, cf. 697 and see note on 1.66.

Tum[1] Phoebo et Triviae solido de marmore templum
instituam festosque dies de nomine Phoebi.   70
Te quoque magna manent regnis penetralia nostris:
hic ego namque tuas sortis arcanaque fata
dicta meae genti ponam, lectosque sacrabo,
alma, viros. [2]Foliis tantum ne carmina manda,
ne turbata volent rapidis ludibria ventis: 75
ipsa[3] canas oro.' Finem dedit ore loquendi.

> *77-97. The Sibyl gives her prophetic reply, indicating the*
> *trials which still await Aeneas, but urging him to continue*
> *on in spite of all.*

[4]At Phoebi[5] nondum patiens immanis[6] in antro
bacchatur vates, magnum si[7] pectore possit
excussisse deum; [8]tanto magis ille fatigat
os rabidum, fera corda domans, fingitque premendo.   80
Ostia iamque domus patuere ingentia centum
sponte sua vatisque ferunt responsa per auras:
'o tandem magnis pelagi defuncte periclis
(sed terrae[9] graviora manent), in regna Lavini[10]
Dardanidae venient (mitte hanc de pectore curam),   85

---

1 69f. These promises relate to subsequent events in Roman history; the festal days for Phoebus predict the *Ludi Apollinares*, founded during the Second Punic war, while the marble temple refers to the new temple built in honour of Apollo by Augustus on the Palatine (cf. Suet. *Aug.* 29, Hor. *Odes* 1.31). The references to the Sibyl's oracular responses (see note on 3.443) are also especially relevant to Augustus' temple to Apollo, as the Sibylline books and the priests in charge of them (*lectos . . . viros*) were transferred to it (Suet. *Aug.* 31). Servius ad loc. tells the story of the origin of the books in the reign of Tarquinius Superbus; see also Page ad loc.

2 74. Aeneas' request is in fulfilment of Helenus' instructions (3.441f).

3 76. **ipsa canas oro**: 'I beg you to sing them yourself'; the paratactic jussive subjunctive is a reminiscence of Helenus (3.456-7 *poscas / ipsa canat*).

4 77f. The Sibyl's reply foretells in allusive terms the events of the second half of the poem. There will be fighting against Turnus, the new Achilles, because of his claim to Lavinia, the bride promised to Aeneas by Latinus; Juno's hostility will continue; but help will come from a Greek city, i.e. Pallanteum (see note on 97). The leading theme is the parallelism between the war just fought against the Greeks, and the new war: the rivers of Troy are equated with the Italian rivers, the Rutuli with the Greeks, and particularly Turnus with Achilles. This parallel, several times stressed in the second half (see note on 89) reaches its fulfilment in Book 12, where the final single combat between Aeneas and Turnus is a re-enactment of the combat of Hector and Achilles, this time with the opposite result.

5 77. **Phoebi . . . patiens**: 'able to endure', cf. *Aen.* 9.607, 10.610.

6 **immanis**: 'wildly', adverbial; cf. *Aen.* 7.510.

7 78. **si ... possit**: 'if thus she might'; for the form of the condition see note on 1.181-2. The perfect tense *excussisse*, as Fletcher well points out, conveys 'be rid of rather than 'get rid of.'

8 79-80. 'All the more he wearied her foaming mouth, taming her wild heart and moulding her to his will by his pressure'; the image is from taming a horse (cf. *excussisse*). *Fatigare* means to try to break down opposition through constant pressure, wearing out the victim; cf. *Aen.* 1.316, 5.253.

9 84. **terrae**: genitive (not locative) like *pelagi*, (sea dangers and land dangers').

10 **Lavini**: Lavinium was the first settlement of Aeneas in Italy, cf. *Aen.* 1.258 (where see note on the scansion of the word).

sed[1] non et venisse volent. Bella, horrida bella,
et Thybrim multo spumantem sanguine cerno.
Non Simois[2] tibi nec Xanthus nec Dorica castra
defuerint; alius[3] Latio iam partus Achilles,
natus et ipse dea; nec Teucris addita[4] Iuno   90
usquam aberit, cum[5] tu supplex in rebus egenis
quas gentis Italum aut quas non oraveris urbes!
Causa mali tanti coniunx[6] iterum hospita Teucris
externique iterum thalami.[7]
Tu ne cede malis, sed contra audentior ito   95
qua[8] tua te fortuna sinet. Via prima salutis,
quod minime reris, Graia[9] pandetur ab urbe.'

> *98-155. Aeneas in reply says that he is aware of the
> magnitude of his task; he asks to be allowed to visit his
> father in the underworld. The Sibyl describes the formidable
> nature of the journey, and states two prerequisites: the
> acquisition of the golden bough and the expiation of
> pollution incurred by the death of one of Aeneas'
> companions.*

Talibus[10] ex adyto dictis Cumaea Sibylla
horrendas canit ambages[11] antroque remugit,[12]
obscuris vera involvens: ea[13] frena furenti   100

---

1 86. **sed non ... volent**: 'but they will not also wish that they had come', i.e. they will wish that they had not come.

2 88f. Simois and Xanthus were rivers of Troy (cf. *Aen.* 1.100-1, 1.473), here equated with the Tiber and the Numicus, as the Greek camp is equated with that of the new enemy, Turnus and his Rutulians.

3 89. **alius ... Achilles**: i.e. Turnus, who is often compared with the Greeks in the second half of the poem, cf. *Aen.* 7.371f., 9.138f., 742. Turnus was born of the nymph Venilia, Achilles of the sea-goddess Thetis.

4 90. **addita**: 'to harass them'; Macrobius says *infesta*, quoting Lucilius *si mihi non praetor siet additus atque agitet me*. The word simply means 'present in addition', and derives its hostile meaning from the context. For Juno's opposition see note on 1.1f.

5 91. **cum**: equivalent to *cum interea*, 'while all the time you will be praying for help to every possible Italian tribe . . .'.

6 93-4. The first foreign bride was Helen, this one will be Lavinia.

7 94. For the half-line see note on 1.534; the only other in this book is 835.

8 96. **qua**: 'along the road on which . . .'. The MSS almost all have *quam* which may well be right (cf. *Aen.* 5.710, and Shakespeare, 3 *Henry* 6. 3.3.16-17 'Yield not thy neck to fortune's yoke'), but Seneca (*Ep. Mor.* 82.18) has *qua*, and on the whole the paradox with the reading *quam* seems awkward. The words *tua te* have better force with the reading *qua*.

9 97. **Graia ... ab urbe**: a reference to Evander's help (cf. *Aen.* 8.51f.).

10 98f. In this passage Virgil continues to develop the mood of awe and mystery preparatory to the descent to the underworld in three ways: firstly by emphasising the superhuman qualities required for a journey undertaken by only very few mortals (Orpheus, Pollux, Theseus, Hercules); secondly by introducing the mysterious talisman of the golden bough with its strange and magical associations; and thirdly by describing the unexpected disaster to Misenus and the need to expiate the pollution (see note on 156f.).

11 99. **ambages**: 'riddling responses', cf. Tac. *Ann.* 12.63.

12 **remugit**: 'boomed forth'; the word suggests the re-echoing and supernatural effect of the cave, cf. *Aen.* 3.92.

13 100-1. 'So violently did Apollo shake the reins as she raged, turning the goads in her heart'; the metaphor from horse-driving (79-80) is continued, cf. *Aen.* 5.147, 9.718. Ea has the sense of *talia* (= *tali modo*).

concutit et stimulos sub pectore vertit Apollo.
Ut primum cessit furor et rabida ora quierunt,
incipit Aeneas heros: [1]'non ulla laborum,
o virgo, nova mi[2] facies inopinave surgit;
omnia praecepi atque animo mecum ante peregi.   105
Unum oro: quando hic inferni ianua regis
dicitur et tenebrosa palus Acheronte[3] refuso,
ire ad conspectum cari genitoris et ora
contingat;[4] doceas iter et sacra ostia pandas.
Illum[5] ego per flammas et mille sequentia tela   110
eripui his umeris medioque ex hoste recepi;
ille meum comitatus iter maria omnia mecum
atque omnis pelagique minas caelique ferebat,
invalidus, viris ultra sortemque senectae.
Quin,[6] ut te supplex peterem et tua limina adirem,   115
idem orans mandata[7] dabat. Natique patrisque,
alma, precor, miserere, potes namque omnia, nec te
nequiquam lucis Hecate[8] praefecit Avernis:[9]
si potuit manis accersere coniugis Orpheus[10]
Threicia[11] fretus cithara fidibusque canoris,   120
si fratrem Pollux[12] alterna morte redemit

---

1 103-5. 'No aspect of toil, maiden, can rise before me as something new or unexpected; I have anticipated everything and considered it in advance silently in my heart'. These are Stoic terms, cf. Sen. *Ep. Mor.* 76.33f., where Virgil's lines are quoted to illustrate the Stoic attitude, and Cic. *DeOff.* 1.81f.

2 104. **mi**: *mihi*, cf. 123; these are the only two places in Virgil where the form (archaic and colloquial) occurs.

3 107. **Acheronte refuso**: 'where Acheron comes welling up', from the underworld (*Aen.* 5.99) into Lake Avernus (here called *palus*).

4 109. **contingat**: 'let it be permitted me', subjunctive of wish.

5 110f. Aeneas refers to his rescue of Anchises from Troy (*Aen.* 2.707f.), and their subsequent voyage together in quest of Italy (Book 3, *passim*).

6 115. **quin**: 'indeed', adding a new point like *quin etiam,* cf. *Aen.* 1.279.

7 116. **mandata dabat**: especially in *Aen.* 5.722f.

8 118. **Hecate**: Diana as goddess of the underworld (*Trivia*, line 13); cf. 247, 564 and note on 4.511.

9 **Avernis**: i.e. the woods around Lake Avernus, see note on 126.

10 119. The story of Orpheus' descent to the underworld to rescue his wife Eurydice, and how he lost her by looking back, is told in *Geo.* 4.467f. The monsters of Hades were charmed by his music (120); for *fides canorae* ('tuneful strings') cf. Hor. *Odes* 1.12.11 (again with reference to Orpheus).

11 120. **Threicia**: Orpheus came from Thrace, cf. 645, Ap. Rh. 1.23f.

12 121. When the mortal Castor died, his twin brother, the immortal Pollux, was allowed to die in his stead for six months each year (or on alternate days, Hom. *Od.* 11.303).

itque reditque viam totiens[1] — quid[2] Thesea[3] magnum,

quid memorem Alciden? Et mi[4] genus ab Iove summo.'

    Talibus orabat dictis arasque tenebat,

cum sic orsa loqui vates: 'sate[5] sanguine divum,   125

Tros Anchisiade,[6] facilis descensus Averno:[7]

noctes[8] atque dies patet atri[9] ianua Ditis;

sed revocare gradum superasque evadere ad auras,[10]

hoc opus, hic labor est. Pauci, quos aequus amavit

Iuppiter aut ardens evexit ad aethera virtus,   130

dis geniti potuere. Tenent media omnia silvae,

Cocytusque[11] sinu labens circumvenit atro.

Quod si tantus amor menti, si tanta cupido est

bis Stygios innare[12] lacus, bis[13] nigra videre

Tartara, et insano iuvat indulgere labori,   135

accipe quae peragenda prius. [14]Latet arbore opaca

aurcus et foliis et lento vimine ramus,

---

1 122-3. Theseus and Hercules (Alcides) are linked again in Charon's account of mortal visitors to Hades (392-3). Theseus (with Pirithous) attempted to carry off Proserpina (397) and was sentenced to eternal punishment, chained to a seat (618); one of Hercules' labours was to bring back the dog Cerberus (395). According to another version of the legend he also rescued Theseus; see note on 617-18.

2 122. **quid Thesea magnum**: the punctuation I have adopted means that the sentence takes a slight shift after the *si* clauses; this is far more natural than taking the *si* clauses with what precedes. It is also more natural to take *magnum* with *Thesea* rather than punctuate with a comma after *Thesea* so that *magnum* would go with *Alciden*.

3 **Thesea**: Greek accusative, cf. 393, 585.

4 123. **et mi — summo**: 'my ancestry too goes back to Jupiter' (through Venus).

5 125. **sate sanguine**: 'born of the blood', a mainly poetic phrase, cf. line 331 and *Aen*. 8.36.

6 126. **Anchisiade**: Greek vocative with long *e*, cf. 348 and *Aen*. 1.97.

7 **Averno**: 'by way of Avernus' rather than 'to Avernus', because in this context Avernus is more likely to mean the lake itself than the underworld. Some MSS have *Averni* ('the descent of Avernus', cf. Plin. *Nat. Hist*. 16.110 *descensus speluncae*), which may be right.

8 127. Cf. Spenser, *F.Q*. 2.3.41:
But easie is the way, and passage plaine
To pleasures pallace; it may soone be spide,
And day and night her dores to all stand open wide.

9 **atri ... Ditis**: Dis (Pluto) is black as befits the darkness of Hades; cf. Ov. *Met*. 4.438 *nigri Ditis*.

10 128-9. Cf. Milton, *P.L*. 3.18-21:
I sung of Chaos and Eternal Night,
Taught by the heav'nly Muse to venture down
The dark descent, and up to reascend,
Though hard and rare . . . .

11 132. **Cocytus**: one of the rivers of Hades, the river of lamentation (323, *Geo*. 3.38).

12 134. **innare**: for the poetic infinitive cf. *Aen*. 2.10; for the word in the sense of sailing cf. 369 and note on 16.

13 **bis**: instead of the normal once, cf. Hor. *Odes* 1.28.16 *et calcanda semel via leti*, Hom. *Od*. 12.21-2.

14 136-7. 'Hidden in a shady tree is a golden bough, its leaves and its pliant stem all golden'. Virgil's sources for the golden bough are not known: it is a mysterious talisman whose significance in folklore cannot be defined with precision. Sir James Frazer in his great work on comparative anthropology and folklore to which he gave the title *The Golden Bough* associates it with tree-magic, and particularly with the mistletoe, with which Virgil compares it in a simile (205f.). It is a symbol of mystery, a kind of light in darkness, a kind of life in death. See R. A. Brooks, *A.J.Ph*. 1953, pp. 260f., and C.P. Segal, *Arion* 1965, pp. 617f. and 1966, pp. 34f.

Iunoni[1] infernae dictus sacer; hunc tegit omnis
iucus et obscuris claudunt convallibus umbrae.
Sed[2] non ante datur telluris operta subire   140
auricomos quam quis decerpserit arbore fetus.
Hoc sibi pulchra suum[3] ferri Proserpina munus
instituit. Primo avulso non deficit alter
aureus, et simili frondescit virga metallo.
Ergo alte vestiga oculis et rite repertum   145
carpe manu; namque ipse volens facilisque sequetur,
si te fata vocant; aliter non viribus ullis
vincere nec duro poteris convellere ferro.
Praeterea[4] iacet exanimum tibi[5] corpus amici
(heu nescis) totamque incestat funere[6] classem,   150
dum consulta petis nostroque in limine pendes.
Sedibus[7] hunc refer ante suis et conde sepulcro.
Duc nigras[8] pecudes; ea prima piacula sunto.[9]
Sic demum lucos Stygis et regna invia vivis
aspicies.' dixit, pressoque obmutuit ore.   155

---

1 138. **Iunoni infernae**: Juno of the underworld is Proserpina (142); cf. *Aen.* 4.638 where Stygian Jupiter is Pluto.

2 140-1. 'But it is not permitted to enter the hidden places of earth till a man has plucked the golden-tressed growth from the tree'. *Quis* stands for *aliquis* (*M* has *qui*, which involves an awkward conflation of a temporal and a relative clause, equivalent in sense to 'except to the man who . . .'). For the lovely compound adjective *auricomus*, not found before Virgil, cf. Lucr. 6.152 *lauricomus* and see note on 3.544; cf. also Norden ad loc.

3 142-3. **suum . . . instituit**: 'has laid it down that it should be brought to her as her own special offering'; cf. line 632.

4 149. At first the reader perhaps thinks, wrongly, of Palinurus; but this idea is dispelled by the phrase *heu nescis,* and we realise that another death has occurred at the moment of the voyage's completion. See note on 156f.

5 **tibi**: 'I must tell you', ethic dative.

6 150. **funere**: 'dead body', cf. 510, *Aen.* 9.491.

7 152. **sedibus . . . suis**: 'first duly place him in his resting-place', cf. 328 and (for *suus*) 233.

8 153. **nigras**: appropriate, of course, for the underworld, cf. 243, 249.

9 **sunto**: this form of the imperative is legalistic and impressive, cf. *Aen.* 4.624.

156-82. Aeneas finds that the dead body referred to is that of Misenus, killed when he foolishly challenged Triton to a contest on the trumpet. He sets about organising funeral rites for Misenus.

[1]Aeneas maesto defixus lumina[2] vultu
ingreditur linquens antrum, caecosque volutat
eventus animo secum. Cui fidus Achates
it comes et paribus curis vestigia figit.
Multa[3] inter sese vario sermone serebant,   160
quem socium exanimum vates, quod corpus humandum
diceret. Atque[4] illi[5] Misenum in litore sicco,
ut venere, vident indigna morte peremptum,
Misenum[6] Aeoliden, quo non praestantior alter
aere ciere[7] viros Martemque accendere cantu.   165
Hectoris hic magni fuerat comes, Hectora[8] circum
et lituo pugnas insignis obibat et hasta.
Postquam illum[9] vita victor spoliavit Achilles,
Dardanio Aeneae sese fortissimus heros
addiderat socium, non[10] inferiora secutus.   170
Sed tum, forte cava dum personat[11] aequora concha,[12]
demens,[13] et cantu vocat in certamina divos,

---

1 156f. The episode of Misenus has similarities with that of Palinurus (see note on 149); both die near the very end of the voyage, both are modelled to some extent on Homer's Elpenor (*Od.* 11.51f.), and both have their names perpetuated in geographical place names (see note on 234-5). But they play different roles in the development of the story, and there is no reason to believe (as some commentators have) that Virgil would have eliminated one of the two stories in revision (see my OUP Ed. of Book 5, Intro, pp. xxviif.).
The main function played by the episode of Misenus in the structure of the narrative is to act as an indication of the nature of mortality. Aeneas, by his special qualities, is to be allowed to transcend the normal conditions, but for Misenus there is no return from the underworld. In a sense he represents a sacrifice for the success of the mission (as Palinurus certainly does); but more especially his unexpected fate conveys the feeling of the imminence of death in life, and the very elaborate description of the funeral rites (212f.) reinforces this feeling.

2 156. **lumina**: retained accusative with a passive verb, cf. 281, 470 and see note on *Aen.* 1.228.

3 160-1. 'They conversed much together with different suggestions, wondering what dead comrade. . .'. *Serebant* (from *serere*, 'join') is connected etymologically (Varro, *L.L.* 6.64) with *sermo;* the indirect question is loosely attached to the main sentence.

4 162. **atque**: 'and suddenly', cf. *Ecl.* 7.7, *Aen.* 1.227, 10.219.

5 **illi**: Fletcher rightly finds this very unnatural, there being no change of subject; he conjectures *illic*.

6 164. **Misenum Aeoliden**: perhaps son of the Trojan Aeolus (*Aen.* 12.542), but more likely son of the god of the winds (*Aen.* 1.52f.). Misenus was mentioned as a trumpeter in *Aen.* 3.239.

7 165. **ciere**: for the epexegetic infinitive after *praestantior* cf. *Ecl.* 5.1-2.

8 166. **Hectora circum**: 'in Hector's retinue'; *Hectora* is a Greek accusative governed by the postponed preposition *circum*.

9 168. **illum**: the death of Hector at the hands of Achilles was one of the scenes depicted on Dido's temple to Juno (1.483f.).

10 170. **non inferiora secutus**: 'following no lesser cause', cf. *Aen.* 11.291.

11 171. **personat aequora**: 'made the ocean resound', cf. 418.

12 **concha**: the seashells was the sea-god Triton's own special bugle (*Aen.* 10.209, *Ov. Met.* 1.333f.), so that Misenus' folly is highly provocative.

13 172. **demens**: notice the emphasis given by the pause after an initial spondee, cf. 590, *Aen.* 4.185, 562.

aemulus exceptum [1]Triton, si credere dignum est,
inter saxa virum spumosa immerserat unda.
Ergo omnes magno circum clamore fremebant,   175
praecipue pius Aeneas. Tum iussa Sibyllae,
haud mora, festinant flentes aramque[2] sepulcri
congerere arboribus caeloque[3] educere certant.
Itur[4] in antiquam silvam, stabula alta ferarum;
procumbunt piceae, sonat icta securibus ilex   180
fraxineaeque trabes cuneis et fissile robur
scinditur, advolvunt ingentis montibus ornos.

183-211. Aeneas is guided to the golden bough by two doves; he picks it and takes it to the Sibyl.

Nec non Aeneas opera inter talia primus
hortatur socios paribusque accingitur armis.
Atque haec ipse suo tristi cum corde volutat   185
aspectans silvam immensam, et sic forte[5] precatur:
'si[6] nunc se nobis ille aureus arbore ramus
ostendat nemore in tanto! Quando omnia vere
heu nimium de te vates, Misene, locuta est.'
Vix ea fatus erat geminae cum forte columbae[7]   190
ipsa sub ora viri caelo venere volantes,
et viridi sedere solo. Tum maximus heros
maternas agnovit avis laetusque precatur:
'este duces, o, si qua via est, cursumque per auras
derigite in lucos ubi pinguem[8] dives opacat   195
ramus humum. Tuque, o, dubiis ne defice rebus,

---

1 173-4. 'in jealousy Triton caught him, if it is right to believe it, and drowned the mortal in the foaming wave amidst the rocks'. For *excipere* cf. *Aen.* 3.332, 11.517; for *si credere dignum est* applied to a myth cf. *Geo.* 3.391.

2 177. **aramque sepulcri**: 'the altar of a tomb', i.e. a pyre, as a sacrifice to the powers of death, cf. *Aen.* 3.63.

3 178. **caelo**: dative of motion towards (= *ad caelum)*, cf. *Aen.* 2.186, 5.451.

4 179f. This passage is closely based on Ennius *Ann.* 187-91 (cf. also Hom. *Il.* 23.114f.):
Incedunt arbusta per alta, securibus caedunt:
percellunt magnas quercus, exciditur ilex,
fraxinus frangitur atque abies consternitur alta,
pinus proceras pervortunt; omne sonabat
arbustum fremitu silvai frondosai.

5 186. **forte**: Servius draws attention to the stopgap nature of the word; *R* has *voce,* but that seems to be a scribal improvement. The correlation with *forte* in 190 gives a heavy stress to the apparent coincidence, which Aeneas realises to be in fact a divine sign.

6 187. **si**: introducing a wish, cf. *Aen.* 8.560.

7 190. The dove is Venus' sacred bird (193, 197), cf. Ov. *Met.* 13.673-4.

8 195. **pinguem**: 'fertile', able to produce so rich a bough.

diva parens.' Sic effatus vestigia[1] pressit
observans quae signa ferant, quo tendere pergant.
Pascentes illae tantum prodire[2] volando
quantum acie[3] possent oculi servare sequentum.   200
Inde ubi venere ad fauces[4] grave olentis Averni,
tollunt se celeres liquidumque[5] per aera lapsae
sedibus[6] optatis gemina[7] super arbore sidunt,
discolor[8] unde auri per ramos aura refulsit.
Quale[9] solet silvis brumali frigore viscum   205
fronde virere nova, quod non sua seminat arbos,
et croceo fetu teretis circumdare truncos,
talis erat species auri frondentis opaca
ilice, sic[10] leni crepitabat brattea vento.
Corripit Aeneas extemplo avidusque refringit   210
cunctantem,[11] et vatis portat sub tecta Sibyllae.

212-35. The funeral rites for Misenus are performed.

[12]Nec minus interea Misenum in litore Teucri
flebant et cineri ingrato suprema ferebant.[13]

---

1 197. **vestigia pressit**: 'stopped', cf. 331, 389 *and Aen.* 2.378.

2 199. **prodire**: historic infinitive, cf. 256, 491-2, 557.

3 200. **acie**: 'with their gaze', cf. *Aen.* 12.558.

4 201. **fauces . . . Averni**: 'the jaws of evil-smelling Avernus'; the reference is to the sulphurous exhalations of this volcanic area, cf. 240-1, and (for *fauces*) also 273. Compare Spenser, *F.Q.* 1.5.31.

5 202. **liquidumque per aera**: 'through the yielding air', cf. *Aen.* 5.217, 525.

6 203. **sedibus optatis**: i.e. the place Aeneas was longing to find.

7 **gemina**: 'of twin nature' (= *biformis*), i.e. with leafy boughs and a golden bough, as explained in the next line; cf. Ov. *Met.* 2.630. *R* has *geminae* (the two doves) which is much weaker in the context.

8 204. 'from which the sheen of gold shone out with its contrast ing colour through the green branches'; for *discolor* cf. Ov. *Tr.* 5.5.8, for *aura* cf. Lucr. 4.252. Spenser imitates the use of *discolor* in *F.Q.* 3.11.47 (of Iris) 'when her discolourd bow she spreds through heaven bright'.

9 205f. 'Just like the mistletoe which often in the woods in the cold of winter puts out new leaves, nourished by a tree not its own, entwining the smooth trunk with its yellow growth'; see note on 136-7.

10 209. **sic . . . vento**: 'such was the foil tinkling in the gentle breeze'; *brattea* is thin metal, cf. Lucr. 4.727. The verb in this phrase is not relevant to the mistletoe comparison, only to the description of the bough.

11 211. **cunctantem**: this has seemed to many a contradiction with 147-8, but in fact refers quite appropriately to the natural resistance of a plant with pliant stem (137) to being picked off; for a not dissimilar usage cf. *Geo.* 2.236, and *Aen.* 5.856 ('slowly yielding').

12 212f. Virgil gives a long description of the funeral rites (cf. Pallas' funeral, *Aen.* 11.59f.); he is in any case fond of describing religious rites, being a poet interested in antiquity and tradition, and here the additional purpose is served of building up the mood for the entrance to the underworld (as also in the following episode, the preparatory sacrifices). The description is based on Patroclus' funeral (Hom. *Il.* 23.163f.), but it also contains Roman elements such as the averted faces, the *dapes,* the *lustratio* and the *novissima verba* (cf. *Aen.* 11.97f.). See Fletcher ad loc. and Bailey, *Religion in Virgil,* pp. 287f.

13 213. A mournful and sonorous line; notice the pause after the first foot spondee, and the rhyme of the verbs.

Principio pinguem[1] taedis et robore secto
ingentem struxere pyram, cui frondibus atris[2]   215
intexunt latera et feralis ante cupressos
constituunt, decorantque super fulgentibus armis.
Pars calidos latices et aëna undantia flammis
expediunt, corpusque lavant frigentis et unguunt.
Fit gemitus. Tum membra toro defleta[3] reponunt   220
purpureasque super vestis,[4] velamina nota,
coniciunt. Pars ingenti subiere feretro,
triste ministerium, et subiectam[5] more parentum
aversi tenuere facem. congesta cremantur
turea dona, dapes,[6] fuso[7] crateres olivo.   225
Postquam conlapsi cineres et flamma quievit,[8]
reliquias vino et bibulam lavere favillam,
ossaque[9] lecta cado texit Corynacus aeno.
Idem ter socios pura circumtulit[10] unda
spargens rore levi et ramo felicis[11] olivae,   230
lustravitque viros dixitque novissima verba.
At[12] pius Aeneas ingenti mole sepulcrum
imponit suaque arma viro remumque tubamque
monte sub aerio, qui nunc Misenus[13] ab illo

---

1 214. **pinguem**: 'rich' perhaps in the sense of resinous (Lucr. 5.296), in which case the word goes more closely with *taedis* than with *robore secto*. But it may simply mean that the huge pyre is amply provided with pine and oak; it is unlikely that *pinguem* goes with *taedis* and *ingentem* with *robore secto*.

2 215. **atris**: probably from the cypresses (216), cf. *Aen.* 3.64. The cypress with its dark foliage was the tree of death, cf. Hor. *Odes* 2.14.22f.

3 220. **defleta**: 'lamented', cf. *Aen.* 11.59, Lucr. 3.907.

4 221. The reference is probably to the tradition of purple shrouds for the burial of great men (cf. *Aen.* 11.72, Livy 34.7.2-3) rather than to well known purple garments which Misenus had worn in life (for which perhaps cf. *Aen.* 11.195).

5 223-4. **subiectam . . . facem**: 'with faces averted held the torch applied beneath according to the ancestral tradition'; cf. Lucr. 6.1285.

6 225. **dapes**: sacrificial offerings of food.

7 **fuso . . . olivo**: 'bowls of flowing olive oil'; notice the Greek nominative *crateres* with short final syllable, cf. 289.

8 226. Cf. Hom. *Il.* 23.250f., a passage which Virgil has very much in mind; see note on 212f.

9 228. 'and Corynaeus collected the bones and placed them in a bronze urn'; *lecta* is equivalent to *collecta*, cf. Ov. *Her.* 10.150.

10 229. **circumtulit**: 'circled'; a strange use of the word, apparently a traditional technical term in religion; Servius quotes Plautus *pro larvato te circumferam*.

11 230. **felicis**: fertile, as opposed to the wild olive (oleaster), cf. *Aen.* 7.751.

12 232-3. 'placed on top a tomb and the hero's own equipment, his oar and his trumpet'; above the burnt out pyre Aeneas has a tomb constructed, adorned with Misenus' oar (for the seven-years' voyage, cf. also Hom. *Od.* 12.15) and his special emblem, the trumpet (cf. 164f.). For the use of *suus — proprius* cf. *Aen.* 1.461. That *arma* does not here mean weapons is shown by 217 and Hom. *Od.* 12.13; the armour was placed on the pyre which was burnt and is now covered up by the mound. For *arma*, 'equipment', cf. *Aen.* 1.177.

13 234-5. It has indeed kept its name through the centuries; at the present day Punta di Miseno is a very prominent land-mark in the Cumae area, with its remarkable flat top; for the aetiology see note on 5.117f. and cf. 381.

dicitur aeternumque tenet per saecula nomen.   235

236-63. The preparatory sacrifices are made, and Aeneas and the Sibyl enter the underworld together.

His actis propere exsequitur praecepta Sibyllae.
Spelunca alta fuit vastoque immanis hiatu,
scrupea,[1] tuta lacu nigro nemorumque tenebris,
quam super haud ullae poterant impune volantes[2]
tendere iter pennis: talis sese halitus atris   240
faucibus effundens supera ad convexa ferebat.
[Unde locum Grai dixerunt nomine Aornum.][3]
Quattuor hic primum nigrantis terga[4] iuvencos
constituit frontique[5] invergit vina sacerdos,
et summas carpens[6] media inter cornua saetas   245
ignibus imponit sacris, libamina prima,
voce vocans Hecaten caeloque[7] Ereboque potentem.
Supponunt alii cultros tepidumque cruorem
suscipiunt pateris. [8]Ipse atri velleris agnam
Aeneas matri Eumenidum magnaeque sorori   250
ense ferit, sterilemque tibi, Proserpina, vaccam.
Tum Stygio[9] regi nocturnas incohat aras
et solida[10] imponit taurorum viscera flammis,
pingue super[11] oleum fundens ardentibus extis.
Ecce autem primi sub lumina[12] solis et ortus   255
sub pedibus mugire[13] solum et iuga coepta moveri

---

1 238. **scrupea**: a scarce word, used by Ennius, meaning 'jagged', made up of small pointed stones.

2 239. **volantes**: 'birds', cf. line 728 and Lucr. 2.1083; the participle is used as a noun. For the general description cf. Ap. Rh. 4.601f., Lucr. 6.740f., and note on 201.

3 242. This line is omitted by most of the major MSS, and is undoubtedly spurious, a gloss added by some learned scribe. It makes the derivation of Avernus from the Greek negative prefix α- and ορνις (bird).

4 243. **terga**: Greek accusative of respect, cf. 495-6 and *Aen.* 5-97.

5 244. **fronti**: 'on to their heads', = *in frontem;* for this ritual cf. *Aen.* 4.61.

6 245-6. For the plucking and burning of hairs from a sacrificial victim cf. Hom. *Od.* 3.446.

7 247. **caeloque Ereboque potentem**: 'powerful both in the upper world and in Erebus'; for Hecate see note on 118. *Caelum* is used several times in this book (e.g. 719) to mean the upper world; for Erebus cf. *Aen.* 4.26.

8 249f. The mother of the Furies (see note on 280) is Night (cf. *Aen.* 7.331, 12.860) and her sister is Earth; for the black lamb cf. Hom. *Od.* 11.32, *Il.* 3.103, and for the barren cow Hom. *Od.* 11.30.

9 252. **Stygio regi**: Pluto (*Iuppiter Stygius* in 4.638).

10 253. **solida . . . viscera**: 'whole carcasses'.

11 254. **super**: the last syllable is lengthened in arsis, cf. 768 and see note on 1.668. The MSS here (as there) have added *-que* to 'heal' the metre.

12 255. **lumina**: some MSS have *limina*, but the point here is the time (dawn; cf. Ap. Rh. 3.1223-4), not the place (east) as is the case in Cat. 64.271 *vagi sub limina solis.*

13 256. **mugire**: historic infinitive, cf. 199; for supernatural happenings of this kind cf. *Aen.* 3.90f., 4.490f.

silvarum, visaeque canes[1] ululare per umbram
adventante dea. 'Procul,[2] o procul este, profani,'
conclamat vates, 'totoque absistite luco;
tuque invade viam vaginaque eripe ferrum: 260
nunc animis opus, Aenea, nunc pectore firmo.'
Tantum effata furens antro[3] se immisit aperto;
ille ducem haud timidis vadentem passibus aequat.[4]

> *264-94. The poet invokes the gods of the underworld to*
> *permit him to tell of the journey. At the entrance Aeneas and*
> *the Sibyl are confronted by various horrible shapes of*
> *personified forms of suffering, and a host of monstrous and*
> *unnatural creatures of mythology.*

[5]Di, [6]quibus imperium est animarum, umbraeque silentes
et Chaos[7] et Phlegethon, loca nocte tacentia late,   265
sit[8] mihi fas audita loqui, sit numine vestro
pandere res alta terra et caligine mersas.

[9]Ibant obscuri sola sub nocte per umbram
perque domos Ditis vacuas et inania regna:
quale[10] per incertam lunam sub luce maligna   270
est iter in silvis, ubi caelum condidit umbra

---

1 257. For the dogs associated with Hecate cf. Ap. Rh. 3.1217 (Jason's invocation of Hecate, which Virgil clearly has in mind here).

2 258. **procul . . . profani**: a religious formula excluding the uninitiated, cf. Hor. *Odes* 3.1.1f.

3 262. **antro se immisit aperto**: 'rushed forward into the open cave'; *se immisit* is a strong phrase, often used in a military context, cf. Livy 9.4.10.

4 263. **aequat**: 'kept pace with', cf. *Aen.* 3.671.

5 264f. Virgil had many possible sources for personifications such as those presented here (273-81), e.g. Hesiod *Theog.* 211f., Lucr. 3.59f., Cic. *Nat. De.* 3.44; but we do not know of any previous writer who described them as being at the entrance to the underworld. On the other hand the monsters (285-9) are mostly associated with Hades, and are placed there e.g. in Aristophanes' *Frogs* (143, 278). Several of them are connected with Hercules, personifying an archaic barbarity of which he purged the world (cf. his encounter with Cacus, 8.184f.). The choice of the personifications is based partly on traditional folklore, but with special contemporary overtones (e.g. Discordia), and perhaps special reference to Aeneas himself (*ultrices Curae*). In particular there are echoes of Lucretius throughout (3.59f., 4.732, 5.22f., 5.890f.) as Virgil describes the horrors and fears from which Lucretius strove so hard to free men's minds. Virgil gives a kind of medieval iconography of Hades, but avoids the grosser and more ghastly features possible in such a description (see Butler's *Aeneid* 6, note on 285-9). Compare the different list in Spenser's imitation of this passage (*F.Q.* 2.7.21-3).

6 264-7. The new invocation draws special attention to the importance of the events about to be described (cf. *Aen.* 7.37f.); it is addressed not to the Muses but to the mysterious primordial deities of the underworld.

7 265. Chaos (cf. *Aen.* 4.510) was the parent of Night and Erebus; Phlegethon is the burning river of the underworld (cf. 551), Pyriphlegethon in Homer (*Od.* 10.513).

8 266. **sit numine vestro**: 'let it be permitted by your divine power'; understand *fas* from the previous clause, rather than taking *sit* in the sense of *liceat*.

9 268f. Observe the slow spondaic movement of these famous lines, and the juxtaposition of nouns and adjectives (a feature of normal usage generally avoided by Virgil, and thus available for special effect, cf. 638f., Norden's Appendix IV, and see note on 5.845).

10 270f. 'like people walking through the woods in the grudging light of a dim moon, when Jupiter has hidden the heavens in shadow and black night has taken the colour away from the world'. Page quotes Milton, *P.L.* 1.63 'no light, but rather darkness visible'.

Iuppiter, et rebus nox abstulit atra colorem.
Vestibulum[1] ante ipsum primis in faucibus Orci
Luctus et ultrices[2] posuere cubilia Curae,
pallentesque habitant Morbi[3] tristisque Senectus,   275
et Metus et malesuada Fames ac turpis Egestas,[4]
terribiles visu formae, Letumque Labosque;
tum consanguineus[5] Leti Sopor et mala[6] mentis
Gaudia, mortiferumque adverso in limine Bellum,
ferreique[7] Eumenidum[8] thalami et Discordia demens   280
vipereum crinem[9] vittis innexa cruentis.
    In[10] medio ramos annosaque bracchia pandit
ulmus[11] opaca, ingens, quam sedem Somnia vulgo[12]
vana tenere ferunt, foliisque sub omnibus haerent.
Multaque[13] praeterea variarum monstra ferarum,   285

---

1 273. 'In front of the porch itself, in the very jaws of Orcus ....'; Virgil visualised the end of the cave as a narrow passage (*fauces*) leading to a porch or forecourt outside the actual entrance to the palace of Dis. Orcus was a Latin deity identified with Pluto (Dis); the word is often used, as here, to mean the underworld (cf. *Aen.* 4.249).

2 274. **ultrices ... Curae**: 'the stings of guilty conscience' (so Servius); cf. *Juv.* 13.192f.

3 275. **Morbi tristisque Senectus**: the same words in *Geo.* 3.67, cf. Sen. *Ep. Mor.* 108.28 where the Virgil passage is quoted to illustrate the statement *senectus enim insanabilis morbus est.*

4 276. Virgil has in mind Lucr. 3.65f. *turpis enim ferme contemptus et acris egestas . . . videntur . . . quasi iam leti portas cunctarier ante. Malesuada* is a rare word (Plaut. *Most.* 213); Virgil may be thinking of Hom. *Od.* 17.286f.

5 278. **consanguineus Leti Sopor**: in Homer (*Il.* 14.231) Sleep is the brother of Death.

6 278-9. **mala mentis Gaudia**: again Virgil is probably thinking of the Lucretius passage (3.59f.) where *avarities* and *honorum caeca cupido* are the evil qualities which lead to misery. Seneca (*Ep. Mor.* 59.3) interprets *gaudia* as *voluptates.*

7 280. **ferreique**: the word scans as a spondee by synizesis; cf. line 412 and *Aen.* 1.698.

8 280. For the Eumenides cf. 250, 375, *Aen.* 4.469. Notice the alliteration of *d* in the last two words; Virgil gives to the hated Discordia (with all its connexions with civil war) the characteristic snaky hair of the Furies. For personified Discordia cf. *Aen.* 8.702, Ennius quoted in Hor. *Sat.* 1.4.60, and Homer's personified Eris (Strife), (*Il.* 20.48).

9 281. **crinem**: retained accusative, see note on 156.

10 282. **in medio**: this may mean, as Servius suggests, in the middle of the porch, but it is more likely that we are now in the courtyard inside the gates, as Virgil gradually phases out the notion of a palace and prepares to describe the large scale geography of underworld.

11 283-4. The elm has vain dreams clinging like bats beneath its boughs; these are the *falsa insomnia* of the ivory gate (896) waiting to attend and mislead sleeping mortals in the upper world. This is presumably a piece of ancient folklore (*vulgo . . . ferunt*) which Virgil has transformed into a pictorial tableau of remarkable visual impact.

12 283. **vulgo**: better with *ferunt* (a common tradition) than with *tenere* ('clinging everywhere', cf. *Aen.* 3.643).

13 285f. 'And in addition many monstrous shapes of different wild creatures have their dens at the doors, Centaurs and bipartite Scyllas. . .'. See note on 264f. and cf. Milton's description (*P.L.* 2.622f.):
'A Universe of death, which God by curse
Created sin, for sin only good,
Where all life dies, death lives, and nature breeds,
Perverse, all monstrous, all prodigious things,
Abominable, inutterable, and worse
Than Fables yet have feignd, or fear conceiv'd,
Gorgons and Hydras, and Chimeras dire.'

Centauri[1] in foribus stabulant Scyllaeque biformes
et centumgeminus Briareus[2] ac belua Lernae
horrendum stridens, flammisque armata Chimaera,[3]
Gorgones[4] Harpyiaeque[5] et forma[6] tricorporis umbrae.
Corripit hic subita trepidus formidine ferrum   290
Aeneas strictamque aciem[7] venientibus offert,
et[8] ni docta comes tenuis sine corpore vitas
admoneat volitare cava sub imagine formae,
inruat et frustra ferro diverberet umbras.

> *295-336. At the river Styx waits the ferryman Charon, a
> figure of horrid squalor. The shades flock to the river, and
> Charon ferries across those who have been buried, leaving
> the others to wail for a hundred years.*

[9]Hinc via Tartarei quae fert Acherontis[10] ad undas.   295
Turbidus[11] hic caeno vastaque voragine gurges
aestuat atque omnem Cocyto eructat harenam.
Portitor[12] has horrendus aquas et flumina servat
terribili squalore Charon, cui plurima mento

---

1 286. **Centauri ... Scyllaeque**: the Centaurs, composite figures of a human and a horse, occur in a more cheerful context in *Aen.* 7.675; for Scylla, a maiden above and sea monster below (*biformis*, cf. 25) see notes on 3.420f., 424f. Centaurs and Scyllas (as well as Chimaeras) are mentioned by Lucretius (5.890f., cf. 4.732) as creatures which cannot have existed. Scylla is plural (like Triton, 5.824); this is helped by confusion with the other Scylla (*Ecl.* 6.74-5).

2 287. **Briareus ... belua Lernae**: Briareus was a hundred-armed giant also called Aegaeon (*Aen.* 10.565). The beast of Lerna (a place in Argos) was the hydra killed by Hercules (*Aen.* 8.300); cf. Lucr. 5.26.

3 288. For the Chimaera, a tripartite dragon, cf. Lucr. 5.905 and see note on 5.118; cf. also *Aen.* 7.785 where Turnus has a fire breathing Chimaera as the emblem on his helmet.

4 289. **Gorgones**: Greek nominative plural with short *-es*, cf. 225; the most famous Gorgon was Medusa (see note on 2.616). Hercules was confronted by her phantom on his descent below.

5 **Harpyiaeque**: see note on 3.211-12.

6 **forma tricorporis umbrae**: i.e. Geryon, cf. 7.662, 8.202, Lucr. 5.28. It was one of Hercules' labours to deal with him.

7 291. **aciem**: 'blade', 'edge', cf. *Aen.* 2.333.

8 292-4. 'and if his wise companion had not warned him that they were unsubstantial bodiless creatures flitting about in the unreal semblance of shape, he would have rushed at them. . . .' The present subjunctives are used to make the past unfulfilled condition more vivid and immediate, cf. *Aen.* 2.599f., 5.325f.

9 295f. The ferryman Charon is perhaps the best known of all Pluto's people; he is a 'demon' of folk story, often portrayed (as Charun) on Etruscan tombs. In literature he has become less terrifying; he is a grumpy and rather humorous character in Aristophanes' *Frogs* (180f.), and Virgil's presentation of him is to some extent mock heroic (see note on 385f.), affording a contrast with the pathos of the other elements in the story.

10 295. **Acherontis**: Acheron was one of the rivers of the underworld (cf. line 107, *Aen.* 599, Hom. *Od.* 10.513f.; it is here identified with Styx (154, 385), traditionally the river which the unburied may not cross.

11 296-7. 'Here a whirlpool thick with mud and of unfathomed abyss boils up and belches all its sand out into Cocytus'; for Cocytus see note on 132.

12 298f. 'The grim ferryman who guards these waters and rivers is Charon, of horrible unkempt appearance with a mass of tangled white hair on his chin'. *Portitor* is strictly 'harbour-master' (*portus*), but as this harbour master was also the ferryman the traditional rendering may stand. Notice the interwoven order at the beginning and the jingling rhyme of *has ... aquas*. For Charon cf. *Geo.* 4.502 and note on 295f.

canities inculta iacet, stant[1] lumina flamma,   300
sordidus ex umeris nodo dependet amictus.
Ipse ratem conto subigit velisque ministrat
et ferruginea[2] subvectat corpora cumba,
iam senior, [3]sed cruda deo viridisque senectus.
Huc[4] omnis turba ad ripas effusa ruebat,   305
matres atque viri defunctaque corpora vita[5]
magnanimum heroum, pueri innuptaeque puellae,
impositique rogis iuvenes ante ora parentum:
quam[6] multa in silvis autumni frigore primo
lapsa cadunt folia, aut ad terram gurgite ab alto   310
quam multae glomerantur aves, ubi frigidus annus[7]
trans pontum fugat et terris immittit apricis.
Stabant[8] orantes[9] primi transmittere[10] cursum,
tendebantque manus ripae ulterioris amore.
Navita sed tristis nunc hos nunc accipit illos,   315
ast alios longe summotos arcet harena.
Aeneas miratus enim[11] motusque tumultu
'dic' ait, 'o virgo, quid vult concursus ad amnem?
Quidve petunt animae? Vel quo discrimine ripas
hae linquunt, illae remis vada livida verrunt?'   320
Olli sic breviter fata est longaeva sacerdos:
'Anchisa generate, deum certissima proles,

---

1 300. **stant lumina flamma**: 'his eyes are fixed and fiery', literally 'are fixed with flame', cf. *Aen.* 12.407f. *iam pulvere caelum stare vident,* and Hom. *Il.* 13.474. The reading *flammae,* whether genitive singular or nominative plural, would give very strange Latin.

2 303. **ferruginea**: 'rust-coloured', dull red, cf. Lucr. 4.76, *Geo.* 1.467, and Mackail ad loc. In 410 the boat is *caeruleus* ('greyish'); both words suggest a dusky colour.

3 304. 'aged now, but a god's old age is fresh and green'; for *crudus* cf. ωμογερων in Hom. *Il.* 23.791. The phrase is imitated in Tac. *Agr.* 29 *adfluebat omnis inventus et quibus cruda ac viridis senectus.*

4 305f. Compare Homer's description of the ghosts, *Od.* 11.36f.

5 306-8. These three lines are repeated from *Geo.* 4.475-7. For the form *magnanimum* see note on 3.704.

6 309f. The main point of the simile (for which cf. Hom. *Il.* 3.2f., 6.146, Ap. Rh. 4.216f., *Geo.* 4.473f.) is the large number of ghosts (*quam multa . . . quam multae);* a second point of similarity is the fluttering of the ghosts like leaves and birds; a third is that for the ghosts, as for the leaves and the migrating birds, the summer of their lives is past. Milton imitates Virgil in *P.L.* 1.302f. 'Thick as Autumnal Leaves that strow the Brooks / in Vallombrosa. . .'.

7 311. **annus**: 'season', cf. Hor. *Odes* 3.23.8.

8 313-14. These famous lines are especially memorable because the pathos of the thought is reinforced by a slow spondaic movement with most subtle assonance (notice especially *-an-,* and *-or-* at the close); for the thought cf. Milton, *P.L.* 2.606-7 'And wish and struggle, as they pass, to reach / the tempting stream . . .'.

9 313. **orantes primi transmittere**: this construction is a Grecism (= *ut primi transient,* Servius), cf. *Aen.* 9.231.

10 **transmittere cursum**: 'to make the crossing', cf. *Aen.* 4.154; here however the accusative is cognate.

11 317. **enim**: 'indeed', cf. 28.

Cocyti stagna alta vides Stygiamque paludem,

di cuius [1]iurare timent et fallere numen.

Haec omnis, quam cernis, inops inhumataque[2] turba est;   325

portitor ille Charon; hi, quos vehit unda, sepulti.

Nec ripas [3]datur horrendas et rauca fluenta

transportare prius quam sedibus ossa quierunt.

Centum errant annos volitantque haec litora circum;

tum demum admissi stagna exoptata revisunt.'[4]   330

Constitit Anchisa satus et vestigia pressit

multa putans sortemque animo miseratus iniquam.

Cernit ibi maestos et mortis[5] honore carentis

Leucaspim[6] et Lyciae ductorem classis Oronten,

quos simul a Troia ventosa per aequora vectos   335

obruit Auster, aqua involvens navemque virosque.

> *337-83. Aeneas meets the ghost of his helmsman Palinurus and hears the story of his death. Palinurus begs for burial, or to be taken across the Styx although unburied, but the Sibyl replies that this is impossible. She consoles him by telling him that the cape where he died will bear his name for ever.*

[7]Ecce gubernator sese[8] Palinurus agebat,

qui Libyco[9] nuper cursu, dum sidera servat,

---

1 324. 'by whose divinity the gods fear to swear and break their oath'; an oath by Styx was the most binding of all possible oaths, cf. Hom. *Il.* 15.37. *Numen* is cognate accusative, cf. 351.

2 325. **inhumataque**: the tradition that the unburied would not find rest is common throughout Greek and Latin literature, cf. Hom. *Il.* 23.70f., *Od.* 11.71f.

3 327-5. The construction is *non datur Charoni transportare eos trans ripas . . . .*

4 330. **revisunt**: i.e. they had been forced to wait some distance away, and then at last could come back; the spondees and elisions in this line contribute to the sonorous effect of the Sibyl's final sentence.

5 333. **mortis honore**: 'death's tribute', i.e. burial, cf. *Aen.* 10.493.

6 334. Leucaspis is not heard of elsewhere; the sinking of the ship of Orontes and his Lycians was described in *Aen.* 1.113f.

7 337f. For the story of Palinurus see note on 5.827f. There are certain inconsistencies between the account here and that in Book 5, for instance that the sea there was calm while here it is stormy, and that *Libyco cursu* (338) is a strange phrase for the last stage of the journey between Sicily and Italy (even allowing that the Trojans had come from Carthage before that). It is probable that Virgil would have made the necessary minor changes in revision. For fuller discussion see the Intro. to my OUP Ed. of *Aeneid* 5, pp. xxvf.

The facts of the legend of Palinurus probably came to Virgil through Varro. and he has conflated it with Homer's story of the unburied Elpenor, whose ghost is the first to appear to Odysseus in *Od.* 11. Virgil has added a pathos typical of his method of writing; the account of the death of Palinurus at the end of Book 5 is one of the most moving passages in the *Aeneid,* and here we see the sequel, the undeserved suffering of the faithful helmsman, and the deep sorrow of Aeneas at the irrevocable loss of his comrade, a scapegoat required by destiny for the safe arrival in Italy. It is the first of the events of the past which Aeneas must live through again in his passage through the underworld, and then leave behind for ever (see Otis, *Virgil,* pp. 290f.).

8 337. **sese . . . agebat**: 'was moving', cf. *Aen.* 8.465, 9.696.

9 338. **Libyco . . . cursu**: 'on the journey from Libya', cf. 5.833f. The phrase is strange in view of the long stop in Sicily during the voyage from Carthage to Italy.

exciderat[1] puppi mediis effusus in undis.
Hunc ubi vix multa maestum cognovit in umbra,   340
sic prior adloquitur: 'quis te, Palinure, deorum
eripuit nobis medioque sub aequore mersit?
Dic age. Namque mihi, fallax haud ante repertus,
hoc uno responso animum delusit Apollo,
qui fore te ponto incolumem finisque[2] canebat[3]   345
venturum Ausonios. [4]En haec promissa fides est?'
Ille autem: 'neque te Phoebi cortina[5] fefellit,
dux Anchisiade, nec[6] me deus aequore mersit.
Namque[7] gubernaclum multa vi forte revulsum,
cui datus haerebam custos cursusque regebam,   350
praecipitans traxi mecum. Maria[8] aspera iuro
non[9] ullum pro me tantum cepisse timorem,
quam tua ne spoliata armis, excussa magistro,
deficeret tantis navis surgentibus undis.
Tris[10] Notus hibernas immensa per aequora noctes   355
vexit me violentus aqua; vix[11] lumine quarto
prospexi Italiam summa sublimis ab unda.
Paulatim adnabam terrae; iam tuta tenebam,
ni gens crudelis madida cum veste gravatum[12]

---

1 339. 'had fallen from the ship, flung forth in mid-ocean'. The ablative after *effusus* draws attention to his plight after his fall rather than to his fall itself.

2 345-6. **finisque . . . Ausonios**: accusative of motion towards, cf. *Aen.* 1.2-3

3 345. There is no reference to this promise earlier in the *Aeneid.*

4 346. The unusual monosyllabic ending expresses excitement and indignation; see note on 5.481.

5 347. **cortina**: the cauldron of the oracular tripod, hence the oracle, cf. *Aen.* 3.92.

6 348. **nec . . . mersit**: i.e. I was not drowned, but did in fact reach Italy.

7 349 f. 'for the rudder was in fact ripped away by some mighty force (the rudder which I was holding firmly as its appointed guardian, directing the course of the ship), and as I went headlong I dragged it with me'. The connexion of thought is perhaps simply 'for the truth is as follows', or possibly (as Servius says) 'for I had the rudder which saved me from drowning'. For *praecipitans* intransitively used cf. *Aen.* 2.9.

8 351. **maria aspera iuro**: 'I swear by the rough seas', cf. 324.

9 352-4. 'that I did not feel any fear so much for myself as in case your ship, stripped of its steering-gear, deprived of its helmsman, might sink in those great surging billows'. For *capere timorem* cf. Livy 33.27.10; for the omission of the subject of the infinitive (*me*) cf. *Aen.* 2.432-3, 4.305-6. *Excussa magistro* is an innovation equivalent to *unde excussus erat magister* (*Aen.* 1.115).

10 355. **tris**: accusative plural (*tres*) cf. *Aen.* 3.203.

11 356. **vix**: i.e. the Italian coast was still far off. Virgil is here recalling the passage from Homer (*Od.* 5.392f.) where Odysseus reaches the coast of Phaeacia by swimming after his raft was destroyed; cf. also note on 360.

12 359. The unfulfilled condition depends on an ellipsis: 'was reaching safety (and would have reached it) had not' . . . , cf. *Aen.* 5.355f., 8.522f.

prensantemque[1] uncis manibus capita aspera montis   360
ferro invasisset praedamque[2] ignara putasset.
Nunc me fluctus habet versantque in litore venti.
Quod[3] te per caeli iucundum lumen et auras,
per genitorem oro, per[4] spes surgentis Iuli,
eripe me his, invicte, malis: aut[5] tu mihi terram   365
inice, namque potes, portusque[6] require Velinos;
aut tu, si qua via est, si quam tibi diva creatrix
ostendit (neque enim, credo, sine numine divum
flumina tanta paras Stygiamque innare[7] paludem),
da dextram misero et tecum me tolle per undas,   370
sedibus ut saltem[8] placidis in morte quiescam.'
Talia fatus erat coepit cum talia vates:
'unde haec, o Palinure, tibi tam dira cupido?
Tu Stygias inhumatus aquas amnemque severum[9]
Eumenidum aspicies, ripamve iniussus adibis?   375
Desine fata deum flecti sperare precando.
Sed cape dicta memor, duri solacia casus.
Nam tua finitimi, longe lateque per urbes
prodigiis[10] acti caelestibus, ossa piabunt[11]
et statuent tumulum et tumulo sollemnia mittent,   380
aeternumque locus Palinuri[12] nomen habebit.'
His dictis curae emotae pulsusque parumper

---

1 360. 'trying to grab with clutching fingers the jagged top of a high cliff', cf. Hom. *Od.* 5.428f. and for this use of *mons* cf. *Aen.* 12.687.

2 361. **praedamque . . . putasset**: 'and foolishly thought that I was booty worth having'.

3 363. **quod**: 'therefore', cf. *Aen.* 2.141.

4 364. **per spes . . . Iuli**: cf. *Aen.* 4.274.

5 365-7. **aut tu . . . aut tu**: notice the emphasis on the appeal to Aeneas personally in both cases (either to bury his body or take him over the Styx although unburied).

6 366. **portusque require Velinos**: notice the coordination, where in English we would say 'by returning to the harbour of Velia'; see note on 2.353 and Page on 6.361. Virgil was criticised in ancient times for this anachronism, as Velia (just north of Punta di Palinuro in Lucania) was not founded till long after Palinurus' day (Aul. Gell. 10.16).

7 369. **innare**: 'journey over', see note on 16.

8 371. **saltern**: with the whole sentence; if Palinurus could not share in the successful conclusion of the Trojan mission, at least he should find peace in death.

9 374. **severum**: 'grim', cf. *Geo.* 3.37 f. *Furias amnemque severum / Cocyti metuet.*

10 379f. Servius says this is based on history; when the people of Lucania were suffering from a plague the oracle told them to placate the ghost of Palinurus, and so they consecrated a grove and a tomb to him.

11 379. **piabunt**: 'appease', cf. Hor. *Ep.* 2.1.143,

12 381. It is still called Punta di Palinuro; for the aetiology see note on 234-5.

corde dolor tristi; gaudet cognomine[1] terrae.

384-416. Aeneas and the Sibyl are challenged by Charon; the Sibyl shows the golden bough and Charon ferries them across the Styx to the further shore.

[2]Ergo iter inceptum peragunt fluvioque propinquant.

Navita quos iam[3] inde ut Stygia prospexit ab unda   385

per tacitum nemus ire pedemque advertere ripae,

sic prior adgreditur dictis atque increpat ultro:

'quisquis es, armatus qui nostra ad flumina tendis,

fare age quid venias iam istinc, et comprime gressum.

Umbrarum hic locus est, somni noctisque soporae: 390

corpora viva nefas Stygia vectare carina.

Nec[4] vero Alciden[5] me sum laetatus euntem

accepisse lacu, nec Thesea[6] Pirithoumque,

dis quamquam geniti atque invicti viribus essent.[7]

Tartareum ille manu custodem in vincla petivit   395

ipsius a solio regis traxitque trementem;

hi dominam Ditis thalamo deducere adorti.'

Quae contra breviter fata est Amphrysia[8] vates:

'nullae hic insidiae tales (absiste moveri),

nec vim tela ferunt; licet ingens ianitor antro   400

aeternum latrans exsanguis terreat umbras,

---

1 383. **cognomine terrae**: 'in the name of the land', in the fact that the land would bear his name. The major MSS all read *terrae*; Servius read *terra* and explained *cognomine* as ablative of *cognominis* ('bearing the same name'), and many modern editors accept this. But Virgil nowhere else uses such an ablative form (for *cognomini*), although Ovid does (e.g. *Met.* 15.743); and it really seems that the testimony of the MSS should prevail.

2 384f. In the encounter with Charon (see note on 295f.) the epic tone is lowered to afford relief between the emotional tension of the encounters with Palinurus and with Dido. Charon's challenge (388f.) is blustering and bombastic (390-1), and he proceeds in a tone of indignation and complaint to inform the newcomers that he was made to suffer for it when he failed on previous occasions to keep the rules, adding (395-7) some gratuitous information about those occasions. The Sibyl replies coolly and sarcastically, urging Charon to keep calm (399) and ironically building up her description of Cerberus (400-1); she grandiloquently draws attention to Aeneas' qualities and mission (403-4), and pauses for her words to take effect. They have no effect, so peremptorily she tells him to take a look at the golden bough which she carries, and he is promptly deflated (*nec plura his,* 408). The scene ends with the half comic picture of the mighty figure of Aeneas among the weightless ghosts, very nearly sinking the ship.

3 385. **iam inde**: 'from where he was', cf. *iam istinc,* 389.

4 392. **nec ... sum laetatus**: Charon 'got no joy' from breaking the rules and according to Servius was chained up for a year as a punishment.

5 **Alciden**: Hercules went down to the underworld to bring back the dog Cerberus (*Tartareum . . . custodem* 395f., cf. 400f., and see note on 122-3).

6 393. **Thesea Pirithoumque**: they tried to steal Proserpina (*dominam Ditis* 397, cf. 402 and see note on 122-3).

7 394. **essent**: the subjunctive is sometimes used in poetry after *quamquam* by analogy with the use after *quamvis;* cf. Ov. *Met.* 14.465.

8 398. **Amphrysia**: this epithet of Apollo, whose priestess the Sibyl was, derives from his period of servitude to Admetus in Thessaly on the banks of the river Amphrysus (*Geo.* 3.2). Servius is justified in his comment *longe petitum epitheton.*

casta licet patrui[1] servet[2] Proserpina limen.
Troius Aeneas, pietate[3] insignis et armis,
ad genitorem imas Erebi descendit ad umbras.
Si te nulla[4] movet tantae pietatis imago,   405
at[5] ramum hunc' (aperit ramum qui veste latebat)
'agnoscas.' Tumida ex ira tum corda[6] residunt;
nec[7] plura his. Ille admirans venerabile donum
fatalis[8] virgae longo post tempore visum
caeruleam advertit puppim ripaeque propinquat.   410
Inde alias animas, quae per iuga[9] longa sedebant,
deturbat[10] laxatque[11] foros; simul accipit alveo[12]
ingentem[13] Aenean. Gemuit sub pondere cumba
sutilis et multam accepit rimosa paludem.
Tandem trans fluvium incolumis vatemque virumque   415
informi limo glaucaque exponit in ulva.

> *417-25. Cerberus guards the far bank of the Styx; the Sibyl throws a sop to him, and together with Aeneas enters the region of the untimely dead.*

[14]Cerberus haec[15] ingens latratu regna trifauci
personat adverso recubans immanis in antro.

---

1 402. **patrui**: Proserpina was daughter of Jupiter by Ceres; Pluto was Jupiter's brother.

2 **servet . . . limen**: 'look after the home', cf. *Aen.* 7.52, 8.412.

3 403. **pietate . . . et armis**: cf. *Aen.* 1.10, 545.

4 405. **nulla**: 'not at all', cf. *Aen.* 4.232 and Cat. 8.14.

5 406. **at**: introducing the main clause after a conditional clause, as in *Aen.* 4.615, *Geo.* 4.241. Notice the staccato narrative as the Sibyl produces her credentials (the subjunctive *agnoscas* is mockingly deferential) and Charon instantly yields.

6 407. **corda**: Charon's heart, poetic plural as often, cf. 49,80.

7 408. **nec plura his**: sc. *dicta sunt;* no more was said on either side.

8 409. **fatalis virgae**: 'the fateful bough'; the golden bough is *fatalis* because only those whom fate favours may have it (cf. 147). We do not know on what occasion Charon had last seen it, possibly when Orpheus descended to bring back Eurydice (obviously Hercules and Theseus had not had it).

9 411. **iuga**: 'benches', a rare use of the word in this sense, an imitation of the Greek ζυγα.

10 412. **deturbat**: 'pushes out of the way', cf. *Aen.* 5.175.

11 **laxatque foros**: 'and clears the gangways'.

12 **alveo**: 'in his hollow boat', cf. Prop. 3.7.16. The word is scanned as a spondee by synizesis, cf. 280 and *Aen.* 7.33.

13 413-14. 'the boat of skins groaned at the weight and took in a quantity of water through the seams'; *sutilis* is 'sewn', i.e. stitched together; *rimosa* ('chinky') means that the seams gaped apart. The boat was adequate for ghosts, but was put under most severe strain by a living warrior. Compare Hom. *Il.* 5.838f., where Athena mounts Diomedes' chariot and the axle groans at the weight.

14 417f. The dog of the underworld is mentioned in Homer (*Il.* 8.366f., *Od.* 11.623f.), but not by name; he is first named in Hesiod (*Theog.* 311), and thereafter is a favourite figure in poetic descriptions of Hades, with three or more heads and snakes for hair (cf. Hor. *Odes* 2.13.33f., 3.11.17f., Spenser *F.Q.* 1.5.34). Virgil does not dwell on frightening or repulsive aspects of Cerberus; like Charon he is part of the traditional machinery of Hades, stylised and unreal compared with the personal reality of the ghosts of Palinurus, Dido and Deiphobus.

15 417-18. 'the massive shape of Cerberus makes these realms re-echo with his barking from all three throats'. For *personare* cf. 171; *trifaux* does not occur elsewhere.

Cui vates horrere videns iam colla colubris[1]

melle soporatam et medicatis frugibus offam   420

obicit. Ille fame[2] rabida tria guttura pandens

corripit obiectam, [3]atque immania terga resolvit

fusus humi totoque ingens extenditur antro.

Occupat Aeneas aditum custode sepulto[4]

evaditque[5] celer ripam inremeabilis[6] undae.   425

> *426-93. The Sibyl and Aeneas now reach Limbo, the region of the untimely dead. Here are the souls of infants, the unjustly condemned, suicides and those who died from unhappy love. Here they meet the shade of Dido; Aeneas speaks to her in tones of deep affection and remorse, but she turns from him without a word.*

[7]Continuo auditae [8]voces vagitus et ingens

infantumque animae flentes in[9] limine primo,

quos dulcis vitae exsortis[10] et ab ubere raptos

abstulit atra dies et funere mersit acerbo.

---

1 420. 'a morsel made sleepy with honey and drugged meal'; the phrase 'a sop to Cerberus' is based on this line. Compare generally the drugging of the dragon in Ap. Rh. 4.140f.

2 421. **fame**: the final *e* is long, a survival of a fifth declension form, cf. Lucr. 3.732.

3 422-3. 'and promptly relaxed his mighty frame as he sank down on the ground and lay stretched out in all his bulk, covering the whole cave'. The tone is mock heroic and humorous; Disney would have done it justice.

4 424. **sepulto**: 'buried in sleep', cf. *Aen*. 2.265.

5 425. **evadit**: 'got away from', cf. *Aen*. 3.282.

6 425. **inremeabilis**: 'that permits no return', cf. *Aen*. 5.591 (of the Labyrinth).

7 426f. The area of Hades where the untimely dead are gathered was traditional, and Virgil uses it chiefly as a setting for the ghosts of Dido and Deiphobus. He does not define how long the ghosts remain here (one traditional version was that they stayed for the rest of their natural life, but the impression in Virgil is one of static permanence), nor endeavour to reconcile this feature of the traditional topography of Hades with the metaphysical speech of Anchises (724f.). For a discussion of these inconsistencies see Norden's edition, pp. 11f.; but it is more profitable to consider what Virgil has achieved poetically by his Limbo than to dwell on eschatological inconsistencies.

The first three classes (infants, the unjustly condemned, suicides) are briefly described without any specific references, and serve to build up the atmosphere of sorrow and bewilderment which becomes powerfully predominant at the appearance of Dido's ghost. In the Mourning Fields we meet first a series of traditional heroines who make no especial emotional impact (see note on 445f.), a crowd scene preparatory to the appearance of the most tragic figure of the whole *Aeneid*. Aeneas attempts to explain his conduct, and his reasons for sacrificing his personal feelings of love for her, just as he had in Book 4 (see notes on 460, 463), but this time *he* is pleading while *she* is unhearing. Echoes of Book 4 in his speech (456, 463, 466) increase the feeling of tragic irony, and when Dido finally rejects him he is still looking back, tormented with guilt and remorse, to the sorrows of the past, not yet turning (as at the end of his experiences in the underworld he learns he must) to a new future. He has to learn the hard lesson that he has caused Dido's death, that her ghost is implacably hostile to him, and that there is nothing he can now do about what has happened except to leave the past behind.

8 426. 'Straight away sounds could be heard, and a great noise of wailing'; the postponed *et* emphasises the imitative alliteration of the words beginning with *v.*

9 427. **in limine prima**: many editors punctuate so that this goes with what follows and refers to the threshold of life (cf. Lucr. 3.681, Lucan 2.106, Sil. 13.548), but in this topographical picture *in limine prima* (at the entrance to Limbo) balances *hos iuxta* (430).

10 428. **exsortis**: 'without having had a share in', equivalent to *expertes* (Servius), cf. Livy 23.10.3.

Hos iuxta falso damnati[1] crimine mortis.   430

Nec vero hae sine sorte datae, sine[2] iudice, sedes:

quaesitor Minos[3] urnam movet; ille silentum

consiliumque[4] vocat vitasque et crimina discit.

Proxima deinde tenent maesti loca, qui sibi letum

insontes peperere[5] manu lucemque perosi   435

proiecere animas. 'Quam vellent aethere[7] in alto

nunc et pauperiem et duros perferre labores!

Fas obstat, tristique[8] palus inamabilis unda[9]

alligat et novies Styx interfusa coercet.

Nec procul hinc partem fusi[10] monstrantur in omnem   440

Lugentes[11] Campi; sic illos nomine dicunt.

Hic quos durus amor crudeli tabe peredit

secreti celant calles et myrtea[12] circum

silva tegit; curae non ipsa in morte relinquunt.

---

1 430. **damnari . . . mortis**: 'condemned to death'; the genitive is similar to the prose phrase *damnari capitis*, cf. also Hor. *Odes* 2.14.19.

2 431. **sine sorte**: a reference to the Roman practice of appointing the jury by lot; they were presided over by a *quaesitor* (432) and would constitute a *consilium* (433).

3 432. **Minos**: he is a judge of the underworld in Homer (*Od.* 11.568f.); cf. Plato *Gorg.* 524a, Hor. *Odes* 4.7.21-22.

4 433. **consilium**: 'jury'; some MSS have *concilium* ('a gathering of the dead'), but the legal technical term is appropriate here.

5 435. **peperere**: perfect of *pario*, 'produced' death for themselves, i.e. committed suicide, a variant for *mortem sibi consciscere*.

6 436-7. 'How they would now wish, in the upper world high above, to endure both poverty and hard suffering'. Virgil's comment recalls Achilles' statement in the underworld (Hom. *Od.* 11.488f.); 'I would prefer to be a serf on earth serving a poor master rather than to be king of all the dead'. It runs counter to the contemporary Stoic attitude to suicide as an honourable escape from an intolerable position (Hor. *Odes* 1.12.35-6).

7 436. **aethere in alto**: compare the use of *caelum* for the upper world as viewed from the underworld (719) and cf. *ad superos* (481).

8 438. **tristique . . . unda**: the major MSS read *tristisque . . . undae*, which is accepted by modern editors, but the ablative (supported by Servius) gives a far more Virgilian ring, and it is hard to think that *palus undae* is possible Latin (*palus aquae* would be). Cf. *Geo.* 4.479 and Hor. *Odes* 2.14.8-9 *Geryonen Tityonque tristi / compescit unda*.

9 438-9. The second phrase repeats and emphasizes the first, the hateful waters hem them in, yes, Styx with its ninefold winding imprisons them; the lines are repeated almost exactly from *Geo.* 4.479-80. Cf. Milton, *P.L.* 2.434f.: 'our prison strong, this huge convex of Fire, / outrageous to devour, immures us round / ninefold, and gates of burning Adamant / Barrd over us prohibit all egress'.

10 440. **fusi**: 'extending', an unusual use of the word, cf. Lucan 4.670.

11 441. **Lugentes Campi**: 'the Mourning Fields'; we do not know from what source Virgil derived this name, or whether it is original with him. The personification of *campi* makes it remarkable and memorable.

12 443. **myrtea**: sacred to Venus, goddess of love, cf. *Aen.* 5.72.

His[1] Phaedram Procrimque locis maestamque Eriphylen   445
crudelis nati monstrantem vulnera cernit,
Euadnenque et Pasiphaen; his Laodamia
it comes et iuvenis quondam, nunc femina, Caeneus
rursus et in veterem fato revoluta figuram.
Inter quas Phoenissa recens a vulnere Dido   450
errabat silva in magna; quam Troius heros
ut primum iuxta stetit agnovitque per umbras
obscuram, [2]qualem primo qui surgere mense
aut videt aut vidisse putat per nubila lunam,
demisit lacrimas dulcique adfatus amore est:[3]   455
'infelix[4] Dido, verus[5] mihi nuntius ergo
venerat exstinctam ferroque extrema secutam?
Funeris heu tibi causa fui? Per sidera iuro,
per superos et si qua fides tellure sub ima est,
invitus,[6] regina, tuo de litore cessi.   460
Sed me iussa deum, quae nunc has ire per umbras,
per loca senta[7] situ cogunt noctemque profundam,
imperiis[8] egere suis; nec credere quivi
hunc tantum tibi me discessu ferre dolorem.
Siste gradum teque aspectu ne subtrahe nostro.   465

---

1 445f. This crowd scene of seven heroines irrelevant to the action of the *Aeneid* serves to focus the attention very sharply on the one who is not irrelevant, *inter quas Phoenissa*. . . . The scene is based on the long procession of heroines in Hom. *Od.* 11.225f.; cf. especially 11.321, 326. Phaedra's love for her stepson Hippolytus is well known from Euripides and Seneca; Procris (concealed and jealously watching her husband Cephalus) was accidentally killed by him (Ov. *Met.* 7.694f.); Eriphyle, bribed by a necklace, induced her husband Amphiaraus to join the Argive war against the Thebans in which he was killed, and his son Alcmaeon killed her in vengeance; Evadne, the wife of Capaneus, killed herself on his pyre; for Pasiphae's passion for the bull (which caused Minos to cast her into prison, where she died) cf. lines 25f.; Laodamia, the wife of Protesilaus, the first Greek to be killed at Troy (Cat. 68.73f., Ov. *Her.* 13), chose to accompany him back to the underworld after he had been permitted to visit her for a brief time; Caeneus was the maiden Caenis, changed by Neptune into a male and after death reverting to her original sex (Ov. *Met.* 12.172f.).

2 453-4. 'like the moon which a man sees or thinks he sees rising up through the clouds at the month's beginning', i.e. faint because (i) a crescent moon (ii) in a cloudy sky. For *aut videt aut vidisse putat* cf. Ap. Rh. 4.1479-80 and Milton, *P.L.* 1.783-4.

3 455. Notice the reiteration at this last moment of Aeneas' love for Dido, cf. *Aen.* 4.395.

4 456. **infelix Dido**: so Virgil has often called her, and so she called herself at the end (4.596).

5 **verus mihi nuntius**: cf. the beginning of Book 5 for the forebodings of the Trojans when they saw flames in Carthage.

6 460. For the sense cf. *Aen.* 4.361 *Italiam non sponte sequor.* The form of the line is very similar indeed to Cat. 66.39 where the lock of hair, snipped from Queen Berenice's head, says *invita o regina tuo de vertice cessi.* It is astonishing that Virgil has transferred a line from a mock heroic, indeed comic, context to this passage of intense emotional pathos. I do not find it satisfying to see in this, as many commentators do, a supreme example of Virgil's skill to do the near impossible successfully; I prefer to regard the line as a wholly unconscious reminiscence.

7 462. **senta situ**: 'rough with neglect', i.e. 'ragged and forlorn' (Page); *sentus* is a rare word indeed (cf. Ter. *Eun.* 236, Ov. *Met.* 4.436) meaning 'uncared for', and *situs* conveys absence of activity, a feeling of mould and decay (cf. *Geo.* 1.72). Compare Milton, *P.L.* 1.180-1 'Seest thou yon dreary Plain, forlorn and wild, / the seat of desolation ...?'.

8 463. **imperiis . . . suis**: cf. *Aen.* 4.237, 356f.

Quem[1] fugis? Extremum[2] fato quod te adloquor hoc est.'
Talibus[3] Aeneas ardentem et torva tuentem
lenibat dictis animum lacrimasque ciebat.
Illa[4] solo fixos oculos aversa tenebat
nec magis incepto vultum[5] sermone movetur   470
quam si dura silex aut stet Marpesia[6] cautes.[7]
Tandem corripuit sese atque inimica refugit
in nemus umbriferum, coniunx ubi pristinus illi
respondet[8] curis aequatque Sychaeus amorem.
Nec minus Aeneas casu concussus iniquo   475
prosequitur lacrimis longe et miseratur euntem.

> *477-93. Next they approach the final area of Limbo, home of
> the renowned in war. Here they meet the ghosts of various
> Argive warriors, and then of Trojan friends who welcome
> Aeneas with joy; finally the shades of the Greek warriors
> run from Aeneas in panic.*

[9]Inde datum molitur[10] iter. Iamque arva tenebant
ultima,[11] quae bello clari secreta frequentant.
Hic illi occurrit Tydeus,[12] hic inclutus armis
Parthenopaeus et Adrasti pallentis imago,   480

---

1 466. **quem fugis?**: an echo, the irony of which the reader easily catches, of Dido's *mene fugis* (*Aen.* 4.314); as Aeneas had turned from Dido, Dido now turns from Aeneas.

2 **extremum . . . hoc est**: 'this is the last word which fate allows me to speak to you'; notice the broken rhythm caused by the elision of the monosyllable *te* and by the two monosyllables in the sixth foot.

3 467-8. 'With these words Aeneas tried to soothe her fiery grim-eyed anger, shedding tears'. *Torva tuentem* would apply naturally to Dido herself, but is very striking with *animum*, deliberately reminiscent perhaps of this kind of phrase in Greek tragedy (Soph. *Ajax* 955, Aesch. *Choeph.* 854). For the adverbial accusative cf. Lucr. 5.33 *acerba tuens (= Aen.* 9.794). *Lacrimasque ciebat* might mean 'sought to arouse her tears', but cf. *Aen.* 3.344f.

4 469f. Dido's silence is modelled on that of Ajax in Hom. *Od.* 11.563f., on which Longinus (9.2) comments that the silence is more sublime than any words.

5 470. **vultum . . . movetur**: retained accusative, see note on 156.

6 **Marpesia cautes**: i.e. marble; Marpessos was a mountain in Paros, famous for its marble, cf. *Aen.* 1.593.

7 471. Notice the irony again by comparison with *Aen.* 4.366-7 where Dido reviled Aeneas as being born from no natural mother, but from the Caucasus mountains. For the simile cf. Eur. *Med.* 87f.

8 474. 'answers her sorrow and requites her love'; for Sychaeus cf. *Aen.* 1.343f. By strict logic Sychaeus has no place here in the *Lugentes Campi;* but logic is overridden by the poetic intention to show that Dido no longer needs Aeneas, indeed has resumed her deep devotion to her husband (4.457f., 552, 656).

9 477f. The ghosts in this last section of Limbo constitute a crowd scene preparatory to the meeting with Deiphobus (494f.). The first group, the Argives, are described objectively, but the other two (Trojans and then Greeks) are both brought into emotional relationship with Aeneas through their joy and their panic respectively; thus the way is prepared for Aeneas' deeply emotional meeting with Deiphobus.

10 477. **molitur**: 'he presses along', cf. *Aen.* 10.477.

11 478. **ultima**: i.e. the furthest fields of this particular area (Limbo).

12 479-80. These are three of the seven Argive leaders against Thebes.

hic multum fleti ad[1] superos belloque caduci[2]
Dardanidae, quos ille omnis longo ordine cernens
ingemuit, Glaucumque[3] Medontaque Thersilochumque,
tris Antenoridas Cererique sacrum Polyboeten,[4]
Idaeumque[5] etiam currus, etiam arma tenentem.   485
Circumstant animae dextra laevaque frequentes;
nec vidisse semel satis est: iuvat usque morari
et conferre gradum et veniendi discere causas.
At[6] Danaum proceres Agamemnoniaeque phalanges
ut videre virum fulgentiaque arma per umbras,   490
ingenti trepidare metu; pars vertere terga,
ceu quondam petiere rates, [7]pars tollere vocem[8]
exiguam: inceptus clamor frustratur hiantis.

494-547. Aeneas meets the ghost of his comrade-in-arms, Deiphobus, still bearing the marks of the cruel wounds inflicted upon him. In grief and remorse Aeneas asks what happened, explaining that he was not able to find Deiphobus' body for burial. Deiphobus replies that Helen, his wife, had betrayed him to the vengeance of Menelaus and Odysseus; in his turn he asks Aeneas for his story. The Sibyl interrupts to hasten Aeneas on and Deiphobus retires to his place among the shades, wishing Aeneas better fortune for his future.

[9]Atque hic Priamiden laniatum corpore toto

---

1 481. **ad superos**: 'in the world above', cf. 568, 680.

2 481. **caduci**: 'fallen', an unusual use of the word which generally means 'destined to fall', and is normally applied to inanimate things; cf. however Lucr. 5.1363, *Geo.* 1.368 (fallen leaves), and *Aen.* 10.622 (a warrior destined to die).

3 483f. The list of names is taken from Homer (*Il.* 17.216) and the rhythm (with no main caesura in third or fourth foot, and a polysyllabic ending) is also Greek. The three sons of Antenor are given in Hom. *Il.* 11.59f. as Polybus, Agenor, and Acamas.

4 484. Ceres' priest, Polyboetes, is not heard of elsewhere.

5 485. **Idaeumque**: Priam's charioteer, cf. Hom. *Il.* 24.325.

6 489f. The contrast of the panic stricken Greeks with the delighted Trojans is highly effective, underlined by the use of historic infinitives and the alliteration of *v* and *t*. Compare generally Hom. *Od.* 11.605f., where the ghosts are terrified of Hercules.

7 492. 'as when they ran for their ships in days gone by'; a reference to Trojan successes in the Trojan War which compelled the Greeks to retreat to the beach where their ships were anchored (e.g. Hom.*Il.* 15.320f.).

8 492-3. 'some raised a cry, but only a little one; the noise they tried to produce mocked their wide open mouths'; the ghosts can only squeak (cf. Hom. *Od.* 24.5), however loudly they try to shout.

9 494f. Aeneas' meeting with Deiphobus is modelled in a general way upon that of Odysseus with the ghost of Agamemnon (Hom. *Od.* 11.387f.), but Virgil has intensified the emotional mood by the sense of guilt which Aeneas feels for not having been able to pay the final rites to Deiphobus' dead body. This is the last of the three ghosts of his past encountered by Aeneas in the underworld; Deiphobus has not played a large part in the poem as Dido and Palinurus had, but he was mentioned in Book 2 in the account of Troy's last night (2.310), and his fate exemplifies the fate of all those comrades of Aeneas who did not survive the sack of Troy. Aeneas cannot tear himself away from conversation with his old friend, and after the Sibyl's intervention it is Deiphobus who ends the meeting, urging Aeneas to march on to the future. This is the point at which Aeneas is finally brought to realise that the past is dead.

Deiphobum vidit, lacerum crudeliter ora,[1]   495
ora[2] manusque ambas, [3]populataque tempora raptis
auribus et truncas inhonesto vulnere naris.
Vix adeo agnovit pavitantem ac dira tegentem
supplicia,[4] et notis compellat vocibus ultro:
'Deiphobe armipotens, genus alto a sanguine Teucri,   500
quis tam crudelis optavit sumere poenas?
cui[5] tantum de te licuit? Mihi fama suprema[6]
nocte tulit fessum vasta te caede[7] Pelasgum
procubuisse super confusae stragis acervum.
Tunc egomet tumulum[8] Rhoeteo[9] litore inanem   505
constitui et magna manis ter voce vocavi.
Nomen[10] et arma locum servant; te[11] amice, nequivi
conspicere et patria decedens ponere terra.'
Ad quae Priamides: 'nihil o tibi,[12] amice, relictum;
omnia Deiphobo solvisti et funeris[13] umbris.   510
Sed me fata mea et scelus exitiale Lacaenae[14]
his mersere malis; illa haec monimenta[15] reliquit.
Namque ut[16] supremam falsa[17] inter gaudia noctem
egerimus, nosti: et nimium meminisse necesse est.

---

1 495. **ora**: accusative of respect, like *manus, tempora, naris;* cf. 243 and see note on 1.320.

2 495-6. **ora . . . ora**: for this type of repetition, a method of increasing pathos, see note on *Aen.* 2.405-6.

3 496-7. 'and his temples disfigured, his ears ripped off, his nostrils torn with a shameful wound'; *inhonesto* implies moral condemnation (= *turpis*). For the idea of ghosts retaining their wounds cf. 450, *Aen.* 2.272f.

4 499. **supplicia**: 'punishment', i.e. the vengeance taken on him by the Greeks for marrying Helen after the death of Paris in the last year of the war.

5 502. **cui . . . licuit?**: 'who had such power over you?'; cf. Lucan 9.1025.

6 502-3. **suprema nocte**: 'on that last night' (of Troy's existence), cf. 513.

7 503. **caede Pelasgum**: 'slaughter of the Greeks'; for the word Pelasgi cf. *Aen.* 1.624.

8 505. **tumulum . . . inanem**: a cenotaph, cf. *Aen.* 3.300f. (Andromache's cenotaph for Hector, where she too calls on the *manes* of the dead man). For the three fold invocation cf. Hom. *Od.* 9.65.

9 505. **Rhoeteo litore**: i.e. the shore near Troy, cf. 3.108.

10 507. **nomen et arma**: i.e. an inscription, and a dedication of armour, not of course Deiphobus' own.

11 507. **te amice**: shortening in hiatus is extremely unusual; see note on 3.211. It does not occur elsewhere in the *Aeneid* with a monosyllable; cf. *Ecl.* 2.65, 8.108.

12 509. **tibi . . . relictum**: 'left undone by you', dative of agent.

13 510. **funeris**: 'corpse', cf. 150.

14 511. **Lacaenae**: Helen, the woman of Sparta, cf. *Aen.* 2.601, and see note on 499.

15 512. **monimenta**: 'memorials of her'; bitterly sarcastic.

16 513-14. **ut ... egerimus**: 'how we passed', perfect subjunctive (of *agere*) in an indirect question.

17 513. **falsa inter gaudia**: cf. *Aen.* 2.239 for the joy of the Trojans as they took in the wooden horse.

Cum fatalis[1] equus saltu super ardua venit[2]   515
Pergama et armatum peditem gravis attulit alvo,[3]
illa[4] chorum simulans euhantis[5] orgia circum
ducebat Phrygias; flammam media ipsa tenebat
ingentem et summa Danaos ex arce vocabat.
Tum me confectum curis somnoque gravatum   520
infelix[6] habuit thalamus, pressitque iacentem
dulcis et alta quies placidaeque similiima morti.
Egregia[7] interea coniunx arma omnia tectis
amovet — et[8] fidum capiti subduxerat ensem —;
intra tecta vocat Menelaum et limina pandit,   525
scilicet id magnum sperans fore munus amanti,
et famam exstingui veterum sic posse malorum.
Quid[9] moror? Inrumpunt thalamo, comes additus una
hortator scelerum Aeolides.[10] Di, talia Grais
instaurate,[11] pio si poenas ore reposco.   530
Sed te qui vivum casus age fare vicissim[12]
attulerint. Pelagine venis erroribus actus
an monitu divum? An quae te fortuna fatigat,[13]
ut tristis sine sole domos, loca turbida, adires?'

---

1 515. **fatalis**: 'sent by fate', cf. *Aen.* 2.237 *scandit fatalis machina muros. Saltu* gives a more exaggerated picture than *scandit;* it is a reminiscence of Ennius (*Scen.* 76-77) *nam maxima saltu superabit gravidus armatis equus, / qui suo partu ardua perdat Pergama.*

2 **venit**: the indicative is used after *cum* in its purely temporal sense, *eo tempore quo,* cf. 564.

3 516. For the imagery of the wooden horse pregnant with soldiers cf. *Aen.* 2.20, 243; this again goes back to Ennius, quoted on the previous line.

4 517f. 'she was leading the Trojan women, feigning a religious dance, as they celebrated Bacchic rites all around the city'. This account of Helen's activity on the last night, as she contrives by the feigned celebration to give torch signals to the Greek fleet, is somewhat at variance with Aeneas' meeting with her as she hid in panic in Vesta's temple (2.567f.). Doubtless the reason for this is the use of different sources and the incomplete state of revision of that part of *Aeneid* 2 (where see notes).

5 517. **euhantis orgia**: *euhare* (or *euare*) is to shout the Bacchic cry (cf. Cat. 64.391, *Aen.* 7.389), and here it is followed by an extended kind of cognate accusative (cf. 644).

6 521. **infelix . . . thalamus**: Deiphobus was now married to Helen, see note on 499.

7 523. **egregia**: bitterly ironical, cf. *Aen.* 493.

8 524. **et . . . ensem**: 'she had even removed my trusty sword from beside my head', i.e. before removing the armour from the rest of the house and calling in her former husband Menelaus (sarcastically called *amans* in line 526). For *capiti* cf. Tac. *Hist.* 2.49 (*pugionem*) *capiti subdidit.*

9 528. **quid moror?**: 'Why prolong the story?', cf. *Aen.* 2.102.

10 529. **Aeolides**: i.e. Ulysses, a reference to the version of his ancestry which made him the child of Anticleia not by Laertes, but illegitimately by the infamous Sisyphus, son of Aeolus; cf. Ov. *Met.* 13.31f. For the especial hostility of the Trojans to Ulysses see note on 2.7 and cf. 2.164.

11 530. **instaurate**: 'renew' (e.g. *Aen.* 5.94), here in the sense of 'repay'.

12 531-2. As Conington points out, Virgil here has given to the indirect question the word order of a direct question: *qui te casus, age fare, attulerunt?*

13 533-4. **fatigat ut . . . adires**: 'is dogging you so that you came. . . .': the imperfect denotes a past effect of the present situation.

276

Hac[1] vice sermonum roseis Aurora quadrigis   535
iam medium aetherio cursu traiecerat axem;
et[2] fors omne datum traherent per talia tempus,
sed comes admonuit breviterque adfata Sibylla est:
'nox ruit, Aenea; nos flendo ducimus horas.
Hic locus est, partis ubi se via findit in ambas:[3]   540
dextera quae Ditis magni sub moenia tendit,
hac iter Elysium[4] nobis; at laeva malorum
exercet[5] poenas et ad impia Tartara mittit.'
Deiphobus contra: 'ne saevi, magna sacerdos;
discedam, explebo[6] numerum reddarque tenebris.   545
I decus, i, nostrum; [7]melioribus utere fatis.'
Tantum effatus, et in verbo vestigia torsit.

> *548-627. Next they see Tartarus, the place of the worst evildoers, guarded by the Fury Tisiphone. The Sibyl tells Aeneas that he may not enter; she describes to him the evildoers and their punishments.*

[8]Respicit Aeneas subito et sub rupe sinistra
moenia lata videt triplici circumdata muro,
quae rapidus flammis ambit torrentibus amnis,   550
Tartareus Phlegethon,[9] torquetque sonantia saxa.

---

1 535f. Fletcher well points out the contrast of this description of bright sunlight with the 'sad sunless dwellings' of the underworld; cf. *Aen.* 7.26.

2 537. 'and perhaps they would have spent all the allotted time talking thus', i.e. all the time allotted to Aeneas in the underworld, probably thought of as a single day. For *fors* (= *forsitan*) cf. 2.139; for *traherent* (= *traxissent*, past potential) cf. 31, 34.

3 540. For the parting of the ways cf. Plato, *Gorg.* 524a.

4 542. **Elysium**: 'to Elysium'; for the accusative of motion towards after a verbal noun (*iter*) cf. *Aen.* 3.507.

5 543. **exercet poenas**: 'brings into effect the punishment', (cf. *Aen.* 4.100, Tac. *Ann.* 144) by sending them on to Tartarus, the lowest part of Hades.

6 545. **explebo numerum**: 'I will fill up the number' (i.e. resume my allotted place); cf. Sen. *Phaedr.* 1153.

7 546. 'Onwards, glory of our race, onwards; and enjoy better fate'. Deiphobus' words mark a crucial turning point in the development of the sixth book; Aeneas' encounters with his past are now over, and his thoughts must turn to the future.

8 548f. The description of the damned in Tartarus is firmly based on Greek tradition: the tortures of Tityos, Tantalus (see note on 601f.) and Sisyphus are described in Homer (*Od.* 11.576f.), and the existence of Tartarus as a place of punishment for great evildoers is an essential part of the underworld in Platonic myth (*Phaed.* 113e, *Gorg.* 526b). The visual impact of Virgil's passage is very great, and he may have based his writing partly on visual art, such as the painting by Polygnotus (Paus. 10.28f.). Interspersed with the individual evildoers are categories of evil (608f., 621f.). This again is in the Greek tradition (Plato, *Phaed.* 113e, Aristoph. *Frogs* 146f.), but Virgil has given his categories a special Roman relevance (see notes on 608f., 621f.). The selection of the traditional evildoers departs often from the orthodox. Salmoneus (585f.) is by no means a well known figure; and the punishments allotted to several of the famous evildoers differ from the usual version (see notes on 601f., 616-17, 617-18). Many commentators have seen in this a mark of incomplete revision by Virgil, as it may well be; but in scenes of this kind considerable variation may well be expected, and a rhetorical and grandiose impact is more significant than antiquarian accuracy.

9 551. **Phlegethon**: the burning river, cf. 265.

Porta adversa ingens solidoque adamante[1] columnae,
vis ut nulla virum, non ipsi exscindere bello
caelicolae valeant; stat ferrea turris ad auras,
Tisiphoneque[2] sedens palla succincta cruenta   555
vestibulum exsomnis servat noctesque diesque.
Hinc exaudiri[3] gemitus et saeva sonare
verbera, tum stridor[4] ferri tractaeque catenae.
Constitit Aeneas strepitumque[5] exterritus hausit.
'Quae scelerum facies? O virgo, effare; quibusve   560
urgentur poenis? Quis tantus plangor[6] ad auras?'
Tum vates sic orsa loqui: 'dux inclute Teucrum,
nulli[7] fas casto sceleratum insistere limen;
sed me cum lucis Hecate[8] praefecit Avernis,
ipsa deum[9] poenas docuit perque omnia duxit.   565
Cnosius[10] haec Rhadamanthus habet durissima regna
castigatque[11] auditque dolos subigitque fateri
quae quis apud superos furto laetatus inani
distulit in seram commissa piacula mortem.
Continuo sontis ultrix accincta flagello   570
Tisiphone quatit insultans,[12] torvosque sinistra
intentans anguis vocat agmina[13] saeva sororum.

---

1 552. **adamante**: a Greek word (e.g. Hes. *Theog.* 161) meaning the hardest kind of substance; cf. Milton, *P.L.* 2.645-6, 'And thrice threefold the Gates; three folds were Brass, / Three Iron, three of Adamantine Rock, / Impenetrable, impal'd with circling fire, / Yet unconsum'd.'

2 555. **Tisiphone**: one of the three Furies, cf. *Aen.* 10.761. The word in Greek means 'voice of vengeance', cf. *ultrix* in 570.

3 557. **exaudiri**: historic infinitive, cf. *Aen.* 4.460.

4 558. **stridor . . . catenae**: the second phrase explains the first. Notice the alliteration of *r*.

5 559. **strepitumque . . . hausit**: 'and, terrified, listened agog to the noise'; for *hausit* cf. *Aen.* 4.359. Some MSS have *strepituque . . . haesit* 'terrified by the noise, froze in his tracks' (cf. *Aen.* 3.597). There is little to choose between the readings.

6 561. **plangor ad auras**: 'lamentation rising to the breezes'; this is the reading of the majority of MSS, and there is not much to be said for the alternative *clangor ad auris* ('din reaching my ears').

7 563. 'it is not permitted for any innocent person to set foot on this threshold of crime'; for *insistere* with the accusative cf. *Geo.* 3.164.

8 564. **Hecate**: see note on 118.

9 565. **deum poenas**: 'the punishment inflicted by the gods', subjective genitive.

10 566. **Cnosius . . . Rhadamanthus**: like his brother Minos (432) the judge Rhadamanthus was from Crete (see note on 23); he is a judge of the dead in Plato *Gorg.* 523e.

11 567f. 'and he cross-examines them, hears their stories of falsehood, and compels them to admit those evils whose atonements any of them in the world above, rejoicing in his pointless deceit, had postponed till the late hour of death'. The phrase *commissa piacula* is condensed: 'atonements incurred' for evils committed.

12 571. **insultans**: 'leaping upon them', a vivid and terrifying picture; for Tisiphone's whip and snakes cf. *Geo.* 4.482, Stat. *Th* 1.112f., Val.Fl. 7.149.

13 572. **agmina saeva sororum**: i.e. Allecto and Megaera. For *agmina* cf. *Aen.* 4.469.

Tum demum horrisono[1] stridentes cardine sacrae
panduntur portae. Cernis custodia[2] qualis
vestibulo sedeat, facies quae limina servet?   575
Quinquaginta atris immanis hiatibus Hydra[3]
saevior intus habet sedem. Tum[4] Tartarus ipse
bis patet in praeceps tantum tenditque sub umbras
quantus ad aetherium caeli suspectus Olympum.
Hic genus antiquum Terrae, Titania[5] pubes,   580
fulmine deiecti fundo volvuntur in imo.
Hic et Aloidas[6] geminos immania[7] vidi
corpora, qui manibus magnum rescindere caelum
adgressi superisque Iovem detrudere regnis.
Vidi et crudelis dantem Salmonea[8] poenas,   585
dum flammas Iovis et sonitus imitatur Olympi.
Quattuor hic invectus equis et lampada quassans
per Graium populos mediaeque[9] per Elidis urbem
ibat ovans, divumque sibi poscebat honorem,
demens,[10] qui nimbos et non imitabile fulmen   590
aere et cornipedum pulsu simularet equorum.[11]
At pater omnipotens densa inter nubila telum
contorsit, non[12] ille faces nec fumea taedis
lumina, praecipitemque immani turbine adegit.

---

1 573. **horrisono**: a rare compound adjective, cf. *Aen.* 9.55; compare Milton, *P.L.* 2.879f. 'On a sudden open flie / With impetuous recoil and jarring sound / Th' infernal dores, and on thir hinges grate / Harsh Thunder'.

2 574. **custodia**: abstract for concrete (*custos*, cf. *Aen.* 9.166), referring to Tisiphone. The connexion of thought is: 'You see Tisiphone? — the Hydra is worse'.

3 576. The Hydra, with its fifty (or sometimes a hundred) heads, is one of the species of the Lernean Hydra killed by Hercules (line 287, *Aen.* 7.658).

4 577-9. 'Then Tartarus itself stretches open and extends sheer beneath the shades twice as far as is the upward gaze at the sky towards heavenly Olympus'. Cf. Hom. *Il.* 8.16, Lucr. 4.416-17, and Milton, *P.L.* 1.73f. 'As far remov'd from God and light of Heav'n / as from the Center thrice to th' utmost Pole'. *Caeli* is objective genitive after *suspectus*.

5 580. The Titans, sons of Mother Earth, rebelled against Jupiter and were destroyed; cf. *Geo.* 1.278f. and see note on 4.178.

6 582. The two sons of Aloeus were Otus and Ephialtes; they piled Ossa on Pelion and Mt. Olympus on top of both in order to reach heaven and attack Jupiter, cf. Hom. *Od.* 11.305f., *Geo.* 1.280f.

7 582-3. **immania . . . corpora**: in apposition to *Aloidas*.

8 585f. The story of Salmoneus and his punishment in Tartarus is a much less well known one than the others mentioned in this section; cf. Manil. 5.91f. *Saimonea* is Greek accusative, cf. 122, and *lampada* in 587, *Ixiona* in 601. *Dantem poenas dum . . .* means 'paying the penalty (incurred) while . . .', a strange ellipsis, but cf. Cicero's translation of Simonides (*Tusc.* 1.101) *Dic, hospes, Spartae nos te hic vidisse iacentes, / dum sanctis patriae legibus obsequimur.* There is a good deal to be said for a full stop after *poenas* and Havet's transposition of 586 and 587.

9 588. **mediaeque . . . urbem**: the city (called Salmone) in the middle of the region called Elis, which was specially associated with Jupiter Olympius.

10 590. **demens**: for the emphatic effect of a spondee filling the first foot cf. 172.

11 591. Salmoneus imitated thunder by driving horses over a bridge of bronze (Manil. 5.92).

12 593-4. **non ille . . . lumina**: 'not torches he, nor flames of smoky pine', cf. 587. For the use of *ille* cf. *Aen.* 1.3, 5.457.

Nec non et Tityon,[1] Terrae omniparentis alumnum,   595
cernere[2] erat, per tota novem cui iugera corpus
porrigitur, rostroque immanis vultur obunco
immortale[3] iecur tondens fecundaque poenis
viscera rimaturque[4] epulis habitatque sub alto
pectore, nec fibris requies datur ulla renatis.   600
quid[5] memorem Lapithas, Ixiona Pirithoumque?
Quos super atra silex iam iam lapsura cadentique[6]
imminet adsimilis;[7] lucent[8] genialibus altis
aurea fulcra toris, epulaeque ante ora paratae
regifico[9] luxu; Furiarum[10] maxima iuxta   605
accubat et manibus prohibet contingere mensas,
exsurgitque facem attollens atque intonat ore.
Hic, [11]quibus invisi fratres, dum vita manebat,
pulsatusve parens aut fraus innexa clienti,
aut qui divitiis soli incubuere repertis[12]   610
nec partem posuere suis (quae maxima turba est),
quique ob adulterium caesi, quique arma secuti

---

1 595. **Tityon**: the punishment of Tityos who assaulted the goddess Latona is told in Hom. *Od.* 11.576f.; cf. also Lucr. 3.984f., Hor. *Odes* 3.4.77f.

2 596. **cernere erat**: 'it was possible to see', a common construction of the verb 'to be' in Greek, apparently mainly colloquial in Latin.

3 598. **immortale**: this aspect of the story is stressed in the passage in Lucretius (3.984f.), and is reminiscent of the Prometheus legend (Hes. *Theog.* 523).

4 599. **rimaturque epulis habitatque**: 'both gropes for its feast and lives permanently . . . .'; for *rimari* cf. *Geo.* 1.384, for *-que . . . -que* cf. line 556.

5 601f. 'Why should I mention the Lapiths, Ixion and Pirithous, above whom a black rock looms, ever about to totter and most like to fall?' The punishment of the tottering rock and the forbidden food (603f.) is of course normally associated with Tantalus (hence our word 'tantalise'). Ixion (who assaulted Juno) is generally stretched out on a wheel (616-17) and Pirithous (see note on 122-3) confined in chains (Hor. *Odes* 3.4.79-80); they were two of the Lapiths, a Thessalian people best known for their battle against the Centaurs. The discrepancy with the normal legends has led to emendation of the text, with the postulation of a lacuna in which Tantalus was mentioned and the reading of *quo* (with R) for *quos*, or to the transposition of 616-20 after 601 (cf. Val. Fl. 2.192f., Stat. *Th.* 1.712f.). But it seems more likely that Virgil has varied the legends or accepted some unusual version.

6 602. **cadentique**: the hyper-metric elision helps to convey the overhang of the rock; see note on *Aen.* 1.332.

7 603. **adsimilis**: cf. *Aen.* 5.254 *anhelanti similis*, 12.754 *similisque tenenti*.

8 603-4. 'On high festive couches golden posts shine resplendent, and before his gaze banquets of regal luxury are displayed'. *Genialis torus* would normally be associated with marriage, but here is used in a very general sense (cf. *Geo.* 1.302).

9 605. **regifico**: a rare word meaning 'regal'; for the formation cf. *magnificus*.

10 **Furiarum maxima**: 'the oldest of the Furies', a vague phrase not intended to be identified. It was used of the Harpy Celaeno in *Aen.* 3.252, and Servius sees here a reference to *Fames*.

11 608f. This list of types of evildoers is partly based on Greek tradition but is also related to Roman ideas (cf. the corresponding list of the blessed in Elysium, 660f.). The ties of family life are emphasised in 608-9; the legal obligation of a *patronus* towards his *client* (one of the items of the Twelve Tables) in 609, the expectation of the unselfish use of riches (cf. *Geo.* 2.507, Hor. *Odes* 2.2) in 610-11; then the relationship with Roman history becomes closer with the reference to adultery in 612 (no doubt Augustus' moral reforms which culminated in the *Leges Iuliae* of 18 B.C. were already in the air), to civil war in 612-13 and to the arming of run-away slaves by Sextus Pompey (Hor. *Epod.* 9.9-10) in 613.

12 610. **repertis**: 'gained', cf. 718.

impia[1] nec veriti dominorum fallere dextras,
inclusi poenam exspectant. Ne quaere doceri
quam poenam, aut[2] quae forma viros fortunave mersit.   615
Saxum [3]ingens volvunt alii, radiisque rotarum
districti pendent; [4]sedet aeternumque sedebit
infelix Theseus, Phlegyasque[5] miserrimus omnis
admonet et magna testatur voce per umbras:
"discite iustitiam moniti et non temnere divos."   620
Vendidit[6] hic auro patriam dominumque potentem
imposuit; fixit leges pretio atque refixit;
hic thalamum invasit natae vetitosque hymenaeos:
ausi omnes immane nefas ausoque potiti.
Non,[7] mihi si linguae centum sint oraque centum,   625
ferrea vox, omnis scelerum comprendere formas,
omnia poenarum percurrere nomina possim.'

*628-36. Aeneas and the Sibyl turn away from Tartarus and
enter Elysium.*

Haec ubi dicta dedit Phoebi longaeva sacerdos,
'sed iam age, carpe[8] viam et susceptum perfice munus;
acceleremus' ait; 'Cyclopum[9] educta caminis   630
moenia conspicio atque adverso fornice portas,
haec[10] ubi nos praecepta iubent deponere dona.'

---

1 613. **impia**: a normal term for civil war, cf. *Aen.* 1.294, *Geo.* 1.511.

2 615. **aut quae ... mersit**: 'or the shape of punishment, the fortune which has overwhelmed them'. For *forma* cf. 626; the indicative is unusual in an indirect question, instances like 779 being rather easier; cf. Prop. 3.5.27f.

3 616-17. The punishment of for ever rolling a stone up a hill and seeing it come bounding back was traditional for Sisyphus. To be stretched out on a wheel is normally Ixion's fate, but unless we accept a transposition of lines or a lacuna (see note on 601f.) we must regard the wheel as here assigned to some other evildoer than Ixion.

4 617-18. Virgil has here departed from the normal legend, which was that Theseus, punished for attempting to carry off Proserpina (see note on 122, where the normal version is implied), was rescued by Hercules from the chair to which he was fixed. The passage is discussed by Hyginus in Aul. Gell. 10.16 as an error by Virgil. Servius' comment is 'frequenter variant fabulas poetae'.

5 618. Phlegyas, ancestor of the Lapiths, was punished for setting fire to Apollo's temple at Delphi.

6 621f. After the mythological figures of 616-20 Virgil returns to generalised crimes with possible application to the contemporary Roman world; various allegorical interpretations have been suggested from Servius' time onwards (621-2 Curio, Caesar's tribune, cf. Lucan 4.824; 622 Mark Antony) but Virgil is not in any way specific. Lines 621-2 are said by Macrobius to have been adapted by Virgil from a work of his friend Varius.

7 625-6. **non . . . vox**: repeated from *Geo.* 2.43-4, and based on Homer, *Il.* 2.488f., Ennius *Ann.* 561-2.

8 629. **carpe viam**: 'hasten along the way', cf. *Geo.* 3.347 and *corripere* in 634.

9 630-1. **Cyclopum . . . portas**: this is the entrance to Elysium, impassable to the living except with the talisman of the golden bough. It was constructed (*educta*, cf. *Aen.* 2.461, 12.674) by Vulcan and his Cyclopes in their forges (cf. *Aen.* 8.418f.).

10 632. 'where they bid us to place our appointed offerings', i.e. the bough. This is more natural than to take *praecepta* as the subject of *iubent*, 'where our instructions bid us. . .'.

Dixerat et pariter gressi per[1] opaca viarum
corripiunt spatium medium foribusque propinquant.
Occupat Aeneas aditum corpusque recenti   635
spargit aqua ramumque adverso in limine figit.

> *637-78. The Sibyl and Aeneas reach the Groves of the Blessed in Elysium, where idyllic scenes meet their eyes. They are directed to Anchises.*

[2]His demum exactis, perfecto[3] munere divae,
devenere locos laetos et amoena virceta[4]
fortunatorum nemorum sedesque beatas.
Largior[5] hic campos aether et lumine vestit   640
purpureo, solemque suum, sua sidera norunt.
Pars[6] in gramineis exercent membra palaestris,
contendunt ludo et fulva luctantur harena;[7]
pars pedibus[8] plaudunt chorcas ct carmina dicunt.
Nec non Threicius[9] longa cum veste sacerdos   645
obloquitur[10] numeris septem discrimina vocum,
iamque eadem digitis, iam pectine pulsat eburno.

---

1 633. **per opaca viarum**: 'through the darkness of the paths'; for the use of the neuter plural of the adjective as a noun see note on 1.422 and cf. *Aen.* 2.725.

2 637f. The description of Elysium is partly based on Homer (*Od.* 4.561f.), but there are also strong Orphic elements indicated by the presence of Orpheus himself and his disciple Musaeus, recalling passages in Pindar (e.g. *Od.* 2.61f.) and Plato (e.g. *Phaed.* 114b). As in the description of Tartarus the mention of specific individuals is varied with the enumeration of categories of people (660f.); the contrast between the gloom of Homer's underworld, to which all save those of divine descent must go, and the bright light of Virgil's Elysium, open to all whose virtue in life qualifies them, is very great indeed. Virgil has used all his skill in diction and metre to build up a picture of peace and serenity, contrasting very markedly with the gloom and sorrow of Aeneas' journey up to now.

3 637. **perfecto . . . divae**: 'when the offering to the goddess had been duly made', i.e. the golden bough to Proserpina.

4 638-9. Notice the juxtaposition of nouns and adjectives with similar endings, see note on 268f.

5 640. 'An atmosphere that is more bounteous and of brilliant radiance clothes these plains'; *et* links *largior* with the ablative of description (equivalent to a compound adjective) *lumine purpureo*. Virgil is recalling Homer's description of Olympus (*Od.* 6.44f.); cf. also Lucr. 3.18f. For *vestit* cf. Lucr. 2.148.

6 642f. Cf. Milton, *P.L.* 2.528f. (the fallen angels):
Part on the Plain, or in the Air sublime
Upon the wing, or in swift race contend,
As at th' Olympian Games or Pythian fields;
Part curb thir fierie steeds, or shun the Goal
With rapid wheels, or fronted Brigads form.

7 643. This line elaborates the wrestling (*palaestra*) of the previous line.

8 644. **pedibus ... choreas**: 'beat out the dances with their feet'; notice the imitative alliteration. *Choreas* is an extended cognate accusative (cf. 517); the *e* is generally long (*Aen.* 9.615, 10.224) but cf. Tib. 1.359. Compare Milton, *P.L.* 2.546f.:
Others more mild,
Retreated in a silent valley, sing
With notes Angelical to many a Harp...

9 645. The Thracian priest, Orpheus (see notes on 119, 120) is here in Elysium not only as the patron of music, but also as the legendary founder of the Orphic religious beliefs expounded by Anchises (724f.).

10 646-7. 'plays as accompaniment to the rhythm the seven distinct notes, plucking them now with his fingers, now with his ivory plectrum'. The ancient lyre had seven strings and Orpheus plays his lyre to accompany (*obloquitur*, cf. Lucr. 4.981) the songs.

Hic genus antiquum Teucri,[1] pulcherrima proles,
magnanimi heroes, nati[2] melioribus annis,
Ilusque[3] Assaracusque et Troiae Dardanus auctor.   650
Arma procul currusque virum miratur inanis.[4]
Stant terra defixae hastae passimque soluti
per campum pascuntur equi. Quae gratia currum[5]
armorumque fuit vivis, quae cura nitentis
pascere equos, eadem sequitur tellure repostos.   655
Conspicit, ecce, alios dextra laevaque per herbam
vescentis laetumque choro paeana[6] canentis
inter odoratum lauris[7] nemus, [8]unde superne
plurimus Eridani per silvam volvitur amnis.
hic [9]manus[10] ob patriam pugnando vulnera passi,   660
quique sacerdotes casti, dum vita manebat,
quique pii vates[11] et Phoebo digna locuti,
inventas [12]aut qui vitam excoluere per artis,
quique sui memores aliquos fecere merendo:
omnibus his nivea cinguntur tempora vitta.   665
Quos circumfusos sic est adfata Sibylla,
Musaeum[13] ante omnis (medium[14] nam plurima turba
hunc habet atque umeris exstantem suspicit altis):
'dicite, felices animae, tuque, optime vates,

---

1 648. **Teucri**: an early ancestor of the Trojans, like Dardanus (650); cf. 500 and see notes on 1.38, 3.167-8.

2 649. **nati melioribus annis**: cf. Cat. 64.22.

3 650. Ilus was grandfather of Priam and Assaracus of Anchises (Hom. *Il.* 20.232f.).

4 651. **inanis**: 'phantom' (969), rather than 'empty' (1.476).

5 653. **currum**: contracted for *curruum*.

6 657. **paeana**: a song of joy originally in honour of Apollo; the Greek loan word has the Greek form of the accusative; cf. *Aen.* 10.738.

7 658. **lauris**: the reading of *G*, preferable to the *lauri* of most MSS, cf. *Geo.* 3.334.

8 658-9. 'from which source the mighty river Eridanus flows up through the forest to the world above'. Eridanus is the river Padus (Po); cf. *Geo.* 1.482, 4.366f.

9 660f. This generalised list is parallel to those in Tartarus (612f., 621f.); it indicates the chief point of difference between Virgil's Elysium and Homer's (*Od.* 4.563f.), in that here the entrance is open not only to those of divine descent but to all those whose merits qualify them.

10 660. **manus . . . passi**: a rather striking example of *constructio ad sensum, manus* being equivalent to *viri*.

11 662. **vates**: here 'poets', under the patronage of Apollo, cf. 669.

12 663-4. 'or those who enriched life by finding new ways of living it, and those who made people remember them by their service'. These are very wide categories indeed, making Elysium potentially open to all mankind; cf. Aug. *Civ. Dei* 21.27. For *excolere* cf. Cic. *Tusc.* 1.62, *Rep.* 6.18; for *artes* (not 'skills' or 'arts' but the good way of life) cf. the common use of *bonae artes,* and Hor. *Odes* 4.15.12 *veteres . . . artes* ('the traditional way of life'). *Aliquos* has much stronger MSS support than the variant *alios.*

13 667. **Musaeum**: like Orpheus, a legendary poet and musician, cf. Plato *Apol.* 41a, *Rep.* 363c.

14 667-8. **medium . . . habet**: 'for a dense crowd had him in their midst', i.e. he was easily identifiable as someone of importance.

quae regio Anchisen, quis habet locus? Illius[1] ergo   670
venimus et magnos Erebi tranavimus[2] amnis.'
Atque huic responsum paucis ita reddidit heros:
'nulli certa domus; lucis habitamus opacis,
riparumque[3] toros et prata recentia rivis
incolimus. Sed vos, si fert ita corde voluntas,   675
hoc superate iugum, et facili iam tramite sistam.'
dixit, et ante tulit gressum camposque nitentis
desuper ostentat; dehinc summa cacumina linquunt.

>*679-702. Aeneas meets Anchises, who is surveying the unborn ghosts of his Roman descendants. Father and son welcome each other.*

[4]At pater Anchises penitus convalle virenti
inclusas animas[5] superumque ad lumen ituras   680
lustrabat studio[6] recolens, omnemque suorum
forte recensebat numerum, carosque nepotes
fataque fortunasque virum moresque manusque.[7]
Isque ubi tendentem adversum per gramina vidit
Aenean, alacris[8] palmas utrasque tetendit,   685
effusaeque genis lacrimae et vox excidit ore:
'venisti tandem, [9]tuaque exspectata parenti
vicit iter durum pietas? Datur ora tueri,
nate, tua[10] et notas audire et reddere voces?
Sic equidem ducebam animo rebarque futurum   690
tempora dinumerans, nec[11] me mea cura fefellit.
Quas[12] ego te terras et quanta per aequora vectum

---

1 670. **illius ergo**: 'for him'; the archaic preposition *ergo* (like *causa*) takes the genitive and follows its noun, cf. Lucr. 3.78.

2 671. **tranavimus**: see note on 16.

3 674. **riparumque toros**: 'river banks to recline on', cf. *Aen.* 5.388. In general cf. Spenser, *F.Q.* 4.10.24.

4 679f. Here Aeneas' journey through the underworld ends. He has travelled through the sorrows of his past in order to learn from Anchises of his future. As father and son face each other, Anchises rejoices in the triumph of *pietas;* Aeneas however is still bewildered and lonely, indeed in need of the full confidence and pride in his mission which his father is soon to give him.

5 680. These are the ghosts waiting by the river of Lethe for rebirth, cf. 703f., 748f.

6 681. **studio recolens**: 'eagerly surveying them', for *studio* cf. *Aen.* 5.450, 12.131.

7 683. **moresque manusque**: 'and their characters and feats'.

8 685. **alacris**: archaic form of *alacer*, cf. *Aen.* 5.380.

9 687-8. 'and has your devotion to duty, awaited by your father, overcome the hard toil of the journey?' This phrase summarises the first half of the *Aeneid;* it has indeed been *iter durum* and it has indeed been *pietas* that has prevailed.

10 689. 'to hear your familiar voice and make reply', cf. *Aen.* 1.409.

11 691. **nec . . . fefellit**: 'nor has my anxious hope misled me'.

12 692-3. 'Over what lands and what mighty seas have you travelled to reach my welcoming arms'; cf. Cat. 101.1. For the postponement of *per* (which governs *terras* as well as *aequora*) cf. *Aen.* 5.512.

accipio! Quantis iactatum, nate, periclis!

Quam[1] metui ne quid Libyae tibi regna nocerent!'

Ille autem: 'tua[2] me, genitor, tua tristis imago   695

saepius occurrens haec limina[3] tendere adegit;

stant sale [4]Tyrrheno classes. Da iungere dextram,

da, genitor, teque[5] amplexu ne subtrahe nostro.'

Sic memorans largo fletu simul ora rigabat.

Ter[6] conatus ibi collo dare bracchia circum;   700

ter frustra comprensa manus effugit imago,

par levibus ventis volucrique simillima somno.

703-51. Aeneas sees a great concourse of ghosts at the river Lethe, and asks Anchises what this means. Anchises explains that they are waiting for rebirth, and gives an account of the soul's relationship with the body, and what happens to it after death.

[7]Interea videt Aeneas in valle reducta

seclusum nemus et virgulta sonantia silvae,

Lethaeumque[8] domos placidas qui praenatat[9] amnem.   705

Hunc circum innumerae gentes populique volabant:

---

1 694. Anchises' fears about Aeneas' stay in Carthage with Dido were indeed justified: this was the hardest part of the journey for his *pietas* to overcome.

2 695. The ghost of Anchises appeared to Aeneas in sleep while he was in Carthage (4.351f.) and after the burning of the ships in Sicily (5.722f.).

3 696. **limina**: accusative of motion towards, cf. *Aen.* 1.553.

4 697. Aeneas says that his fleet is on the Tyrrhenian Sea (west of Italy) to explain that his voyage to Hesperia is complete.

5 698. **teque . . . nostro**: these are almost the same words (with *amplexu* for *aspectu*) which Aeneas had used to Dido's ghost (465).

6 700-2. These lines are repeated from *Aen.* 2.792-4 (see notes there), where they are used of Creusa's ghost. The loneliness of Aeneas is very strongly stressed in this passage.

7 703f. The famous account of the purification and transmigration of souls is presented in diction which often recalls Lucretius but offers a view of life after death directly opposed to the Epicurean view of the destruction of the soul at death. Anchises' speech is based largely on Orphic and Pythagorean ideas of purification and rebirth, especially as expressed by Plato (*Rep.* 10.614f., *Phaed.* 113f., *Phaedr.* 248f, *Gorg.* 493f.). Roman Stoicism had much in common with these Greek doctrines, and phraseology that is especially Stoic is sometimes used (*spiritus intus, igneus vigor;* we are reminded of the Stoic passage in *Geo.* 4.219f.).
The speech serves, as has often been pointed out, as a convenient piece of 'machinery' to introduce the pageant of Roman heroes waiting to be reborn; but its significance is far wider than that. It expresses a picture of hope after death, of virtue rewarded; it offers something of an explanation for the unexplained suffering of this life. With its emphasis on how the soul is defiled and tainted by the body (its tomb or prison) it reverses the Homeric attitude, and it brings Aeneas away from the heroic world to the spiritual climate of Virgil's own times.
For further discussion see Bailey, *Religion in Virgil,* pp. 275f., Guthrie, *Orpheus and Greek Religion,* pp. 157f., Otis, *Virgil,* pp. 300f.

8 705. Lethe is the river of forgetfulness (Plato, *Rep.* 621a); Virgil indicates the meaning of the Greek word with *oblivia* (715) and *immemores* in 750. Cf. Milton, *P.L.* 2.582f.
'Far off from these a slow and silent stream,
Lethe the River of Oblivion roules
Her watrie Labyrinth, whereof who drinks,
Forthwith his former state and being forgets . . .'

9 **praenatat**: 'flows past'; for *natare* cf. Enn. *Ann.* 596, Lucr. 5.488, and for the force of *prae* (= *praeter*) Hor. *Odes* 4.3.10.

ac[1] velut in pratis ubi apes[2] aestate serena
floribus insidunt variis et candida circum
lilia funduntur, strepit omnis murmure campus.
Horrescit visu subito causasque requirit   710
inscius Aeneas, quae sint ea flumina porro,[3]
quive viri tanto complerint agmine ripas.
Tum pater Anchises: 'animae,[4] quibus altera fato
corpora debentur, Lethaei ad fluminis undam
securos[5] latices et longa oblivia potant.   715
Has equidem memorare tibi atque ostendere coram,
iampridem hanc prolem cupio enumerare meorum,
quo[6] magis Italia mecum laetere reperta.'
'O pater, anne aliquas ad[7] caelum hinc ire putandum est
sublimis animas iterumque ad tarda reverti   720
corpora? Quae[8] lucis miseris tam dira cupido?'
'Dicam equidem nec te suspensum, nate, tenebo'
suscipit Anchises atque ordine singula pandit.
   [9]Principio[10] caelum ac terras camposque[11] liquentis
lucentemque globum lunae Titaniaque[12] astra   725
spiritus intus alit, [13]totamque infusa per artus
mens agitat molem et magno se corpore miscet.

---

1 707. **ac velut**: for this way of introducing a simile ('and it was as when') cf. *Aen.* 2.626f., 4.402f.

2 707f. For the bee simile cf. Hom. *Il.* 2.87f., Ap. Rh. 1.879f. and note on *Aen.* 1.430f.

3 711. **porro**: 'in the distance', an unusual and apparently archaic use, cf. Plaut. *Rud.* 1034; compare the somewhat similar usage in *Aen.* 5.600.

4 713. Anchises' explanation of the doctrine of transmigration of souls (*altera corpora*) is given more fully in 724f.; see note on 703f.

5 715. **securos latices**: 'the draught that takes away their cares'; cf. Plato *Rep.* 621a where Lethe is called Ameles, the river that removes cares.

6 718. 'so that you may rejoice the more with me now that you have found Italy'; so far Aeneas has had little cause for joy.

7 719-20. **ad. caelum ... sublimis**: 'aloft to the upper world', cf. 896.

8 721. Aeneas' sufferings during his mission are reflected in his astonished question: how could anyone possibly want to be back in the upper world?

9 724f. For Anchises' speech see note on 703f.

10 724. **principio**: a Lucretian way of introducing an explanation (cf. e.g. Lucr. 5.92).

11 **camposque liquentis**: a poetic periphrasis for the sea; cf. Lucr. 6.1142, *Geo.* 3.198.

12 725. **Titaniaque astra**: Titan's stars are the sun and the stars, cf. *Aen.* 4.119, where the sun is called Titan. Some think that the reference is to the sun alone, but the plural (though it can be paralleled, Ov. *Met.* 14.172) would be awkward.

13 726-7. 'and flowing through its members a mind sets the mass in motion and mingles with the mighty structure'; cf. Tennyson, *To Virgil*, 'Thou that seest Universal / Nature moved by Universal Mind'; Wordsworth, *Tintern Abbey*, 'A motion and a spirit, that impels / All thinking things, all objects of all thought, / And rolls through all things'; Pope, *Essay on Man* (1.267-8) 'All are but parts of one stupendous whole, / Whose body Nature is, and God the soul'.

Inde[1] hominum pecudumque genus vitaeque[2] volantum
et quae marmoreo fert monstra sub aequore pontus.
Igneus[3] est ollis vigor et caelestis origo   730
seminibus, quantum non noxia corpora tardant
terrenique hebetant artus moribundaque membra.
Hinc[4] metuunt cupiuntque, dolent gaudentque, neque auras[5]
dispiciunt clausae tenebris et carcere caeco.[6]
Quin et supremo cum[7] lumine vita reliquit,   735
non tamen omne malum miseris nec funditus omnes
corporeae excedunt pestes, [8]penitusque necesse est
multa diu concreta modis inolescere miris.
Ergo exercentur[9] poenis veterumque malorum
supplicia expendunt: aliae panduntur inanes   740
suspensae ad ventos, aliis sub gurgite vasto
infectum[10] eluitur scelus aut exuritur igni.
[11]Quisque[12] suos patimur manis. Exinde per amplum
mittimur Elysium et pauci laeta arva tenemus
donec longa dies perfecto temporis orbe   745
concretam exemit labem, [13]purumque relinquit

---

1 728. **inde**: i.e. from the *spiritus* and *mens*, cf. *Geo.* 4.221f.

2 **vitaeque volantum**: 'the lives of flying creatures', a poetic periphrasis (in the Lucretian style) for birds, cf. Lucr. 2.1083.

3 730-1. 'Those seeds have a fiery force and an origin in heaven, insofar as . . . .'; *igneus* is a Stoic term for the divine fire of the world soul, the *spiritus intus*, the *anima mundi*; cf. 747.

4 733. **hinc**: i.e. from the body, which causes mortal emotions far removed from things spiritual; cf. Cic. *Tusc.* 3.11, Hor. *Epist.* 1.6.12.

5 **auras**: the air of heaven.

6 734. The concept of the body as a prison (or a tomb) goes back to Orphic belief and is expressed by Plato; cf. Plato *Crat.* 400c, *Phaed.* 66b. Compare Wordsworth, *Intimations of Immortality*: 'Shades of the prison-house begin to close / Upon the growing Boy'.

7 735. **cum . . . reliquit**: = eo *tempore quo*, cf. 515.

8 737-8..'and it is necessary that many taints, long associated with the body, must be deeply ingrained in wondrous ways'; *penitus* goes with *inolescere*, *concreta* (cf. 746) means 'growing up with', hence 'associated with'. For *inolescere* cf. *Geo.* 2.77; *modis . . . miris* is a Lucretian phrase, see note on *Aen.* 1.354.

9 739. **exercentur**: 'they are disciplined', contrast the construction in 543. The lines which follow describe the three forms of discipline or purification, by air, water, and fire.

10 742. **infectum ... scelus**: 'the stain of crime', the crime with which they have been stained; cf. Cic. *Att.* 1.13.3.

11 743f. Many editors punctuate so that lines 743-4 are parenthetical, and *donec* in 745 depends on the verbs in 740-2. This gives a contorted sentence, and it is much preferable to take the passage in the order in which it is presented, with *donec* dependent on *tenemus*. The meaning is that those who are nearly spotless stay in Elysium until they are quite spotless and then depart for the ultimate heaven. The others pass through Elysium and then wait by the river for rebirth. Elysium, in the underworld, is the penultimate paradise, the real paradise is in heaven (cf. Plato, *Phaed.* 114c). I have argued this point in detail in *Greece and Rome*, 1964. 57f.

12 743. **quisque suos patimur manes**: 'we all endure our own ghosts', i.e. are guiltily aware of the imperfections of our souls, stained and blotched with earthly evils.

13 746-7. 'and has left unsullied the ethereal spirit and the fire of pure air', i.e. removed the blemishes so that the soul is the pure Stoic fire which can return to god.

aetherium sensum atque aurai[1] simplicis ignem.
Has omnis, ubi mille rotam[2] volvere per annos,[3]
Lethaeum ad fluvium deus evocat agmine magno,
scilicet immemores supera ut convexa revisant   750
rursus, et incipiant in corpora velle reverti.'

> *752-853. Anchises points out to Aeneas the famous Romans who are waiting their turn to be born: the Alban kings, Romulus, Augustus, the Roman kings and many heroes of the Roman Republic.*

[4]Dixerat Anchises natumque unaque Sibyllam
conventus trahit in medios turbamque sonantem,
et tumulum capit unde omnis longo ordine posset
adversos legere[5] et venientum discere vultus.   755
'Nunc age, Dardaniam prolem quae deinde[6] sequatur
gloria, qui maneant Itala de gente nepotes,
inlustris animas nostrumque in nomen ituras,
expediam dictis, et te tua fata docebo.

---

1 747. **aurai**: archaic genitive, common in Lucretius, used only four times in Virgil, cf. *Aen.* 3.354 (where see note), 7.464, 9.26.

2 748. **rotam**: the wheel of time, a phrase used in Orphic writings, said by Servius to occur in Ennius.

3 748. Cf. Plato *Rep.* 10.615a, *Phaedr.* 248e.

4 752f. The pageant of Roman heroes is the most sustained of all the patriotic passages in the *Aeneid:* it is comparable with *Aen.* 1.257f., 8.626f., 12.819f. (cf. also *Geo.* 2.149f.). It is a list of *exempla* familiar in rhetorical writing, owing something too to visual art, to friezes and groups of statues. But Virgil has transfigured these sources into majestic and sonorous poetry. His structural method is to interweave crowd scenes (the Alban kings, the Roman kings, the many heroes of the Republic) with descriptions where the spotlight is focussed on single individuals (Romulus, Augustus, Brutus, Caesar and Pompey); thus he has given form and shape to his emotional and intellectual presentation of the character of Rome.

The description begins quietly with the distant antiquarian interest of the Alban kings, and it rises to a crescendo for Romulus, founder of Rome, great mother of men; then the crescendo swells to its loudest for Augustus, restorer of the Golden Age. The chronological sequence so far followed is thus broken, so that the second founder of Rome may follow the first. At this point the description breaks off as Anchises asks his son whether he still feels doubts or fears about his mission; Aeneas does not reply, but the reader can answer for him. There can be no further hesitation now; this is the decisive moment of the whole poem.

The next section begins with a crowd scene of Roman kings, followed by the spotlit figure of Brutus. This is a very ambivalent passage: admiration for Brutus is muted by feelings of pathos (cf. Aug. *Civ. Dei.* 3.16), and in the *anima superba* of this early Brutus we surely feel an undertone of reference to his famous descendant, the assassin of Caesar. Virgil takes no political position, but he powerfully portrays the ambition as well as the idealism of such men, *laudumque immensa cupido*.

After another brief crowd scene the attention is focussed on Caesar and Pompey, and here again it is the tragedy of the situation that is stressed, not the rightness or wrongness of a cause. No attempt is made to blacken Pompey because of his association with the East (contrast Antony in *Aen.* 8.685f.).

Finally we have the densest crowd scene of all, preparatory to the famous passage outlining, with every justification, the contribution of Rome to world civilisation. It is interesting to compare the passage at the beginning of Cicero's *Tusculan Disputations* where Cicero concedes intellectual and literary dominance to the Greeks, but regards the Romans as superior in practical and ethical qualities (*mores, leges, res militaris, gravitas* etc.). These are proud claims which Anchises makes, first to conquer in war, and then to establish a peace in which the people are ruled with mercy and given the benefits of Roman civilisation and settled ways of life (cf. *Aen.* 4.229f.). Doubtless the Roman achievement of them was imperfect, but they constituted an ideal and a sense of calling which constantly illuminated the long centuries of the Roman Empire in the west.

5 755. **legere**: 'scan', cf. 34.

6 756. **deinde**: 'in the future', cf. 890.

Ille, vides, pura[1] iuvenis qui nititur hasta,   760
proxima[2] sorte tenet lucis loca, primus ad auras
aetherias Italo[3] commixtus sanguine surget,
Silvius,[4] Albanum nomen, tua postuma[5] proles,
quem tibi longaevo serum Lavinia coniunx
educet silvis regem regumque parentem,   765
unde genus Longa nostrum dominabitur Alba.
Proximus[6] ille Procas, Troianae gloria gentis,
et Capys et Numitor[7] et qui nomine reddet
Silvius Aeneas, pariter[8] pietate vel armis
egregius, [9]si umquam regnandam[10] accepcrit Albam.   770
Qui iuvenes! Quantas ostentant, aspice, viris
atque umbrata gerunt civili[11] tempora quercu!
Hi[12] tibi Nomentum et Gabios urbemque Fidenam,
hi Collatinas imponent montibus arces,
Pometios Castrumque Inui Bolamque Coramque.   775
Haec tum nomina erunt, nunc sunt sine nomine terrae.[13]
Quin et avo[14] comitem sese Mavortius[15] addet

---

1 760. **pura**: 'headless', with just the shaft; Servius quotes Varro to the effect that such a spear was given as a prize of valour to a young warrior for his first victory; it seems also to have been awarded for any special act of valour.

2 761. **proxima . . . loca**: 'has allocated to,him the next place in the world above', i.e. will be the first of the throng of ghosts to be reborn.

3 762. **Italo ... sanguine**: of Trojan descent 'mixed with Italian blood', i.e. son of the Trojan Aeneas and the Italian princess Lavinia (see note on 7.52f.).

4 763. **Silvius, Albanum nomen**: i.e. the kings of Alba Longa were all called Silvius (cf. 769, Livy 1.3) as their dynasty name, here derived by Virgil (765) from the circumstances of the birth of this son of Lavinia (cf. Ov. *Fast.* 4.41f., Livy 1.3.6). The tradition about him varied; according to Livy he was a son of Ascanius, according to Virgil and Dionysius a younger brother of Ascanius. In *Aen.* 1.267f. Ascanius is clearly designated as the first king of Alba Longa; he cannot be mentioned here because he is already on earth, so the list starts with his successor Silvius.

5 763. **postuma**: 'latest-born' (Aul. Gell. 2.16.5) not 'posthumous' (Servius).

6 767. **proximus . . . Procas**: i.e. he is standing next to Silvius, not next to be born (he was late in the order of the Alban kings, later than Capys).

7 768. **Numitor**: Numitor was the last Alban king, grandfather of Romulus (777). For the lengthening in arsis of the last syllable of *Numitor* cf. 254.

8 769. **pariter**: equally with Aeneas, rather than equally for devotion and valour.

9 770. Servius tells the story that the guardian of Silvius Aeneas usurped the throne from him for a long time.

10 **regnandam**: used transitively as in 793, *Aen.* 3.14.

11 772. **civili. . . quercu**: the 'civic crown' of oak, awarded to a Roman who had saved a fellow citizen's life in war. It had been voted to Augustus as a perpetual honour in 27 B.C., and adorned the portals of his palace (Ov. *Fast.* 1.614, *Trist.* 3.1.36).

12 773f. These are little towns near Rome, some of them deserted by Virgil's time; their impact on the Roman reader would be one of parochial affection. Fidena normally has a long *i* and the plural form *Fidenae*; *Collatinus* is the adjective of Collatia.

13 776. Cf. Milton, *P.L.* 12.140 (Michael's speech) 'Things by their names I call, though yet unnam'd.'

14 777. **avo**: Numitor (768), the father of Ilia, who had been deposed by his brother Amulius. His grandchildren Romulus and Remus were thrown into the Tiber, but survived and restored Numitor to his kingdom.

15 **Mavortius**: Romulus was son of Mars and Ilia; this is the archaic form of the adjective *Martius*, cf. 1.276, 3.13.

Romulus, Assaraci[1] quem sanguinis Ilia mater
educet. [2]Viden, ut geminae stant vertice cristae
et pater ipse suo superum iam signat honore?   780
En huius, nate, auspiciis illa incluta Roma
imperium terris, animos aequabit Olympo,[3]
septemque una sibi muro circumdabit arces,
felix prole virum: [4]qualis Berecyntia mater
invehitur curru Phrygias turrita per urbes   785
laeta deum partu, centum complexa nepotes,
omnis caelicolas, omnis supera alta tenentis.
Huc geminas nunc flecte acies, hanc aspice gentem
Romanosque tuos. Hic Caesar[5] et omnis Iuli
progenies magnum caeli ventura sub axem.   790
Hic[6] vir, hic est, tibi quem promitti saepius audis,
Augustus Caesar, divi[7] genus, aurea[8] condet
saecula qui rursus Latio regnata per arva
Saturno quondam, super et Garamantas[9] et Indos[10]
proferet imperium; iacet[11] extra sidera tellus,   795
extra anni solisque vias, ubi caelifer Atlas

---

1 778. **Assaraci . . . Ilia**: for Assaracus, a Trojan ancestor, cf. 650; Ilia is the Trojan name (cf. *Aen.* 1.274) of Rhea Silvia, the Vestal Virgin who was mother of the twins.

2 779-80. 'Do you see how the twin crests stand out from his head and the father of the gods himself marks him out already with his special emblem?' *Viden* is contracted for *videsne,* (note that the second syllable is short), and is followed by the indicative in parataxis, *viden ut* being equivalent to *ecce,* cf. Cat. 61.77-6, and lines 855f. *Superum* is archaic genitive, cf. *Aen.* 1.4; others following Servius take it as accusative, so that the meaning would be that Mars marks Romulus out as a god. But *superus* in the singular in this sense is not paralleled, and the *honos* is probably Jupiter's thunderbolt rather than any emblem of Mars. The phrase *geminae . . . cristae* perhaps signifies reconciliation with Remus.

3 782. Cf. *Aen.* 1.287 and Milton, *P.L.* 12.370-1 'and bound his Reign / With earths wide bounds, his glory with the Heav'ns'.

4 784f. Rome, the great mother of men (cf. *Geo.* 2.167f.), is compared with Cybele, the Great Mother of the gods, whose special worship was at Mt. Berecynthus in the Troad (*Phrygias . . . urbes*); see note on 3.111f., and cf. 2.788, 9.82, 10 252. The second point of comparison in the simile is the turret-like diadem of the goddess and the turreted defence walls of Rome (cf. Lucr. 2.606f.). Compare Spenser, *Ruines of Rome* 6: 'Such as the Berecynthian Goddesse bright / in her swift charret with high turrets crownde, / proud that so manie Gods she brought to light'.

5 789. **Caesar**: i.e. Augustus, picked up in *hic vir hic est* ('yes, this is indeed. . .'). It is impossible to maintain that this is Julius, because he occurs later in the pageant (826f.). Augustus is at first among the other descendants of Iulus (789-90), and then is picked out alone (791). His position next to Romulus breaks the chronology and emphasises his status as second founder of Rome (Suet. *Aug.* 7).

6 791. **hic vir hic est**: notice that the second *hic* is short, cf. *Aen.* 4.22.

7 792. **divi genus**: Julius Caesar was deified after his death, and Augustus, his adopted son, received the title *divi filius.*

8 792. Strong emphasis is put on *aurea* by its position at the head of the relative clause, with *qui* postponed to fourth place. The restored golden age is prophesied in *Ecl.* 4 (esp. 6f.), and in more general terms in *Aen.* 1.286f. For the original golden age under Saturnus cf. *Geo.* 2.538f., *Aen.* 8.319f., esp. 324.

9 794. **Garamantas**: Greek accusative with short final syllable. These were an African people (cf. *Aen.* 4.198, *Ecl.* 8.44) conquered by the Romans in 19 B.C., but this is no certain reason for dating this passage as late as that.

10 794. **Indos**: cf. Prop. 2.10.15, where India is mentioned with Parthia and Arabia as an area of Augustus' triumphs.

11 795. **iacet . . . tellus**: an elliptical and evocative phrase, *tellus* being logically equivalent to 'the land which he will rule', i.e. his empire will extend beyond the known world, beyond the path of the Zodiac.

axem umero torquet stellis ardentibus aptum.[1]
Huius[2] in adventum iam nunc et Caspia regna
responsis horrent divum et Maeotia tellus,
et septemgemini[3] turbant[4] trepida ostia Nili.   800
Nec vero[5] Alcides tantum telluris obivit,
fixerit[6] aeripedem cervam licet, aut Erymanthi
pacarit nemora et Lernam tremefecerit arcu;
nec[7] qui pampineis victor iuga flectit habenis
Liber, agens celso Nysae de vertice tigris.   805
Et[8] dubitamus adhuc virtutem extendere factis,
aut metus Ausonia prohibet consistere terra?
Quis[9] procul ille autem ramis insignis olivae
sacra ferens? Nosco crinis incanaque menta
regis Romani primam[10] qui legibus urbem   810
fundabit, Curibus[11] parvis et paupere terra
missus in imperium magnum. [12]Cui deinde subibit
otia qui rumpet patriae residesque movebit
Tullus in arma viros et iam desueta triumphis
agmina. Quem iuxta sequitur iactantior Ancus   815

---

1 797. This line, based on Ennius, is repeated from *Aen.* 4.482, where see notes.

2 798-9. 'At the prospect of his arrival even now the Caspian realms shudder because of oracular responses, and the Maeotian land too'; these are the areas of the Scythians and the Parthians, the north-eastern boundary of Rome's empire. There is possibly a reference to the recovery of the standards from the Parthians in 20 B.C.

3 800. **septemgemini . . . Nili**: the adjective refers to the Nile's delta, cf. Cat. 11.7; the whole line is particularly significant because of Augustus' victory over Egypt at the battle of Actium. Notice the emphasis given by alliteration of *t*.

4 **turbant**: intransitive, 'are in confusion', cf. Lucr. 2.126, Cic. *Fin.* 1.34.

5 801f. The point of comparing Augustus with Hercules (Alcides) and Bacchus (Liber) is (i) they all made their influence felt over very large areas; (ii) they were all connected with civilising activities; (iii) they were all mortals destined to become gods (Hor. *Odes* 3.3.9f.).

6 802. **fixerit ... licet**: 'although he transfixed the bronze footed stag'; this and the following two phrases refer to three of Hercules' labours, the stag of Gerynaia (Arcadia), the wild boar of Erymanthus (also Arcadia), and the hydra of Lerna in Argos.

7 804-5. 'nor he who victorious guides his yoked animals with reins of vine-shoots, Liber, driving his tigers from the lofty summit of Nysa'; for Bacchus' exploits see note on 801f. Mt. Nysa (in India) is where Bacchus' worship was said to have originated (the name Nysa was subsequently used of other centres of his cult). The yoking of tigers suggests the power of civilisation over wild nature (cf. Hor. *Odes* 3.3.13f.).

8 806-7. The interpolation by Anchises of this query is enormously significant: the vision of Augustus must surely dispel any lingering doubts or frailties. Some MSS have *virtute extendere vires* but cf. *Aen.* 10.468.

9 808f. The description of Numa Pompilius, second king of Rome, emphasises the peaceful (*ramis... olivae*) and religious (*sacra ferens*) aspect of this successor to Romulus, son of Mars, the war god. Cf. Livy 1.18f., Ov. *Met.* 15.482f. Numa is the embodiment of Jupiter's promise in *Aen.* 12.836-7 *morem ritusque sacrorum / adiciam.*

10 810-11. **primam . . . fundabit**: 'will establish the little city on the basis of laws', cf. *Aen.* 4.231, Livy 1.19.1.

11 811. **Curibus**: Cures was a little town of the Sabine territory, said to have given the Romans their name *Quirites*, cf. *Aen.* 7.710.

12 812f. The tradition about Tullus Hostilius, third king of Rome, was concentrated on military exploits (Livy 1.22, Juv. 5.57); nothing is known about why Ancus Marcius, the fourth king, should be called boastful and overfond of popularity.

nunc quoque iam nimium gaudens popularibus[1] auris.
Vis et Tarquinios[2] reges animamque[3] superbam
ultoris Bruti, fascisque[4] videre receptos?
Consulis imperium hic primus saevasque securis
accipiet, [5]natosque pater nova bella moventis   820
ad poenam pulchra pro libertate vocabit,
infelix, utcumque ferent[6] ea facta minores;
vincet amor patriae laudumque[7] immensa cupido.
Quin Decios[8] Drususque procul saevumque securi
aspice Torquatum et referentem signa Camillum.   825
Illae[9] autem paribus quas fuigere[10] cernis in armis,
concordes animae nunc et dum nocte prementur,
heu quantum inter se bellum, si lumina vitae
attigerint, quantas acies stragemque ciebunt,
aggeribus[11] socer Alpinis atque arce Monocci   830
descendens, gener adversis[12] instructus Eois!
Ne, pueri, ne[13] tanta animis adsuescite bella

---

1 816. **popularibus auris**: a common metaphor (= *favore*) in prose and verse.

2 817. **Tarquinios reges**: the fifth (Tarquinius Priscus) and seventh (Tarquinius Superbus) kings of Rome. Servius Tullius, the sixth king, is omitted because of the bracketing of the Tarquins; in a sense he is included in their dynasty.

3 **animamque . . . Bruti**: the first consul of Rome (509 B.C.), who expelled Tarquin the Proud and 'recovered authority' for the people. The story of the rape of Lucretia (which led to the expulsion) by Sextus, son of Tarquin the Proud, is told by Shakespeare, *Rape of Lucrece*. The transference of Tarquin's epithet (*superbus*) to Brutus, his avenger, is paradoxical and thought provoking (see note on 752f.). The punctuation of Norden and others (based on Servius), with a comma after *superbam,* so that the epithet goes with Tarquin, gives a quite impossible word order for the next line.

4 818. **fascesque**: the rods symbolising authority (*Geo.* 2.495, *Aen.* 7.173), wrapped round an axe (819), which were carried by the consul's lictors in the Roman Republic.

5 820f. The story of how Brutus' sons joined Tarquin in his efforts to return to Rome is told in Livy 2.5. Brutus as consul had to put them to death for their rebellion (notice the savage alliteration of *p* in 821), and Virgil reflects with compassion rather than pride on Brutus' devotion to duty.

6 822. **ferent**: 'will extol', as did Livy and Valerius Maximus (5.8), and doubtless many rhetorical declamations.

7 823. **laudumque . . . cupido**: an expansion of *amor patriae* couched in unexpectedly unfavourable terms. Virgil seems to suggest that the desire to show extreme devotion to duty may be activated by unworthy motives of a too inflexible kind. Servius comments: 'non extorquere vim naturae debet amor patriae'.

8 824-5. The Decii (father and son) devoted themselves to death on the battlefield (Livy 8.9, 10.28); the Drusi were one of the most famous Roman families of all (Augustus' wife Livia was one of their number); Torquatus, who won his *cognomen* from having killed a giant Gaul in combat (Livy 7.10) and stripped him of his necklace (*torques*), later put his sons to death for having fought out of line (Livy 8.7); Camillus recovered Rome from the Gauls after they had taken it, according to the Roman version (Livy 5.49f.), and regained the standards captured at the River Allia.

9 826f. The identity of Caesar and Pompey (opponents in the civil war, *paribus ... in armis,* both wearing Roman armour, cf. *Geo.* 1.489) is not specified until 830-1 by the words *socer . . . gener* (cf. Cat. 29.24); this refers to Pompey's marriage to Caesar's daughter Julia.

10 826. **fulgere**: for the unusual third conjugation form see on 4.409, and cf. Lucr. 5.1095.

11 830. **aggeribus . . . Alpinis**: Caesar invaded Italy from Gaul (i.e. past the Alps and Monaco) and across the Rubicon.

12 831. **adversis . . . Eois**: 'with Eastern troops to face his enemy'; Pompey had withdrawn to Greece to collect additional forces.

13 832. **ne . . . bella**: 'do not make such great wars habitual in your thoughts'; this is a rare variation of construction for *ne adsuescite animos bellis* (as in *Aen.* 9.201). Cf. Hor. *Sat.* 2.2.109.

neu patriae [1]validas in viscera vertite viris;
tuque prior, [2]tu parce, genus qui ducis Olympo,
proice tela manu, sanguis meus! —   835
[3]Ille[4] triumphata Capitolia ad alta Corintho
victor aget currum caesis insignis Achivis.
Eruet ille[5] Argos Agamemnoniasque Mycenas[6]
ipsumque Aeaciden, genus armipotentis Achilli,[7]
ultus avos Troiae templa[8] et temerata Minervae.   840
Quis te, magne[9] Cato, tacitum aut te, Cosse,[10] relinquat?
Quis Gracchi[11] genus aut geminos, [12]duo fulmina belli,
Scipiadas, cladem Libyae, parvoque potentem
Fabricium[13] vel te sulco, Serrane,[14] serentem?
Quo[15] fessum rapitis, Fabii? Tu Maximus ille es,   845
unus qui nobis cunctando restituis rem.

---

1 833. The alliteration of *v* to help to convey the notion of violence is overpowering here. For *viscera* we would say 'heart', 'guts'.

2 834-5. Anchises speaks to both Pompey and Caesar, but especially to Caesar, direct descendant of himself and the Olympian goddess Venus. The feeling of pathos is intensified by Anchises' personal appeal; this is the first time he has addressed the ghosts he is describing.

3 836f. This section concerns the conquerors of Greece, and the references are all relevant to Aeneas' own times (*Achivis, Argos, Agamemnoniasque Mycenas, Aeaciden, Achilli, Troiae templa*); the burning of Troy will ultimately be avenged. Compare *Aen.* 1.283-5.

4 836-7. 'That Roman over there will triumph over Corinth and victoriously drive his chariot to the lofty Capitol'. *Corinthus* is feminine, and *triumphatus* treated transitively (cf. *Geo.* 3.33). The reference is to Mummius who celebrated a triumph for his victory over Corinth in 146 B.C. (cf. Hor. *Epist.* 2.1.193).

5 838. **ille**: Aemilius Paullus, the Roman general who defeated King Perseus of Macedonia at the battle of Pydna in 168 B.C. Perseus claimed descent from Achilles (grandson of Aeacus); cf. Prop. 4.11.39.

6 **Mycenas**: Agamemnon's capital, cf. *Aen.* 1.284.

7 839. **Achilli**: for the form of the genitive see note on 1.30.

8 840. The reference is to the violation of Minerva's temple in Troy by Ajax, son of Oileus; see notes on 1.41 and 2.403f.

9 841. **magne Cato**: the elder Cato (the censor); his implacable hostility to Carthage begins the Carthaginian theme that occurs several times in the next few lines.

10 **Cossus**: one of the three Romans (see note on 855) who won the *spolia opima*; this was in 428 B.C. (Livy 4.19).

11 842. **Gracchi genus**: probably not merely the two famous brothers, but their immediate ancestors who achieved military glory in the Second Punic War and afterwards, and indeed their mother Cornelia (daughter of Scipio), proverbial model of a Roman matron.

12 842-3. Scipio Africanus the elder won the final battle of the Second Punic War at Zama in 202 B.C.; Scipio Africanus the younger (Aemilianus) destroyed Carthage in the Third Punic War. For *fulmina belli* cf. Cic. *Balb.* 34; Lucr. 3.1034.

13 844. **Fabricium**: the Roman general against Pyrrhus in the early third century B.C., a type of *iustitia* (the Roman Aristides) and *parsimonia* (Cic. *Tusc.* 3.56, Val. Max. 4.3.6).

14 Serranus was the cognomen of Regulus, famous Roman commander in the First Punic War who left his plough to become consul (like Cincinnatus); Virgil derives his cognomen from *serere* ('to sow').

15 845-6. 'Where do you hasten my weary gaze, you Fabii? You surely are the famous Fabius the Great, the one man who saved our state by delaying'. The *gens Fabia* was famous in early Republican times (Livy 2.48f.), and Quintus Fabius Maximus Cunctator was the Roman general who after the disasters at Trasimene and Cannae saved the Romans from Hannibal by his delaying tactics (Livy 22 *passim*). His position of honour at the end of the pageant is due to the fact that he saved Rome from the greatest enemy in all her history; he exorcises the memory of Dido's curse *exoriare aliquis nostris ex ossibus ultor* (4.625). Virgil presents his achievement in an adapted quotation from Ennius (*Ann.* 370) *unus homo nobis cunctando restituit rem*, thus reinforcing the mood of antiquity and history, and paying tribute to his great predecessor in Roman national poetry.

Excudent[1] alii[2] spirantia mollius aera
(credo equidem), vivos ducent de marmore vultus,
orabunt causas melius, caelique meatus
describent radio[3] et surgentia sidera dicent: 850
tu regere imperio populos, [4]Romane, memento
(hae tibi erunt artes[5]), pacique[6] imponere morem,
parcere subiectis et debellare superbos.'

> *854-92. Anchises now mentions one more Roman hero,*
> *Marcellus, famed in the Second Punic War. Aeneas enquires*
> *about a sad figure accompanying him, and is told that this is*
> *the young Marcellus, destined to an early death.*

[7]Sic pater Anchises, atque haec mirantibus addit:
'aspice,[8] ut insignis spoliis[9] Marcellus opimis   855
ingreditur victorque viros supereminet omnis.
Hic rem Romanam magno turbante tumultu
sistet[10] eques, sternet Poenos Gallumque rebellem,

---

1 847f. The 'others' referred to are the Greeks, and their achievements in sculpture (bronze or marble), oratory, and astronomy are conceded by the Romans. When one thinks of the Roman achievement in portraiture in stone, and in oratory (the most practical of the branches of literature, in which Cicero might well be pitted against Demosthenes), it seems that Anchises does less than justice in these matters to his own people, doubtless so that the impact of what the Romans do claim may be all the greater.

2 847. 'others will beat out bronze so that it breathes in softer lines'; for *spirantia* cf. *Geo.* 3.34, Hor. *A.P.* 33, and Addison's lines 'Where the smooth chisel all its force has shown / And soften'd into flesh the rugged stone'.

3 850. **radio**: the rod used for geometry, cf. *Ecl.* 3.41.

4 851. 'But, Romans, never forget that government is your medium' (Day Lewis). This proud claim was amply justified by Augustus and his long line of successors.

5 852. **artes**: i.e. in place of the 'fine arts' the Roman will practice the art of government.

6 **pacique imponere morem**: 'to add civilisation to peace', not (with Fletcher) 'to add tradition to peace', i.e. make it customary. The reading *pacisque*, adopted by many editors, has no manuscript authority of any importance, nor does Servius support it (as used to be thought from a misreading of Servius).
For the dative after *imponere* cf. *Aen.* 2.619; for the singular *mos* in the sense of *mores* (cf. *Aen.* 1.264) or *cultus* compare *Aen.* 8.316 *quis neque mos neque cultus erat*. In these famous lines the bipartite nature of Rome's mission is clearly stated; first to establish peace by taming the proud, and secondly to offer a settled and civilised way of life in which the people are ruled with mercy.

7 854f. In this passage the *Aeneid* comes into its closest contact with contemporary events. The death of Marcellus (see note on 861) in 23 B.C. was a deeply felt tragedy for the Roman world; it is very possible that Virgil himself attended the magnificent funeral ceremonies in the Campus Martius. The tribute to him by Anchises is filled with pathos, with Virgil's sense of sympathy for the waste of youthful death (as with Pallas, Lausus, Euryalus); and its position immediately following the trumpet notes of joyful pride in 851-3 presents the equipoise between triumph and disaster which the *Aeneid* so constantly explores. It is part of Virgil's special art to have given us, in Conway's words, 'this sudden gust of tragedy, when the sky at last seemed clear'. In the corresponding position at the end of the second half of the poem Virgil similarly mutes the long awaited triumph of Aeneas by concentrating our attention in the final lines of the poem not on the victor but on the vanquished. Because of this it seems unreasonable to suppose, as some do, that this passage was added to Book 6 after the pageant of heroes had already been composed; it is far more likely that these expressions of the joy and the sorrow of Rome's history were planned together.

8 855-6. **aspice ut . . . ingreditur**: for the parataxis see note on 779-80.

9 855. **spoliis . . . opimis**: the *spolia opima* ('rich spoils') were awarded to a Roman general who killed the enemy general in personal combat. They were first awarded to Romulus, and then to Cossus (line 841); the third recipient was Marcellus, who killed the general of the Insubrian Gauls (222 B.C.) and served with distinction against Hannibal in the Second Punic War. Cf. Prop. 4.10.

10 858. **sistet eques**: the battle against the Gauls was mainly a cavalry engagement (Plut. *Marcell.* 7).

tertiaque arma patri suspendet capta Quirino.'[1]
Atque hic Aeneas (una namque ire videbat   860
egregium forma iuvenem[2] et fulgentibus armis,
sed frons[3] laeta parum et deiceto lumina vultu)
'quis, pater, ille, virum qui sic comitatur euntem?
Filius, anne aliquis magna de stirpe nepotum?
Qui strepitus circa comitum! Quantum instar[4] in ipso!   865
Sed nox atra caput tristi circumvolat umbra.'
Tum pater Anchises lacrimis ingressus obortis:
'o nate, ingentem luctum ne quaere tuorum;
ostendent[5] terris hunc tantum fata nec ultra
esse sinent. Nimium vobis Romana propago   870
visa potens, superi, propria haec si dona fuissent.
Quantos[6] ille virum magnam Mavortis ad urbem
campus aget gemitus! Vel quae, Tiberine, videbis
funera, cum tumulum practerlabere[7] recentem!
Nec puer Iliaca quisquam de gente Latinos   875
in[8] tantum spe tollet avos, [9]nec Romula quondam
ullo se tantum tellus iactabit alumno.
Heu pietas, heu prisca fides invictaque bello
dextera! Non illi se quisquam impune tulisset
obvius armato, seu cum pedes iret in hostem   880
seu spumantis equi foderet calcaribus armos.

---

1 859. The normal version was that the captured spoils should be dedicated to Jupiter Feretrius; here Virgil follows a tradition that they were dedicated to the deified Romulus (Quirinus). The subject is discussed at length by Butler ad loc.

2 861. This is the Marcellus (son of Octavia, Augustus' sister) who married Augustus' daughter Julia and was marked out as his heir, but died at the age of 19 in 23 B.C. (cf. Prop. 3.18, Hor. *Odes* 1.12.45f.). Servius and Donatus tell how Octavia burst into tears when Virgil read this passage to her and Augustus.

3 862. 'but his expression was not happy and his eyes were downcast'; *deiecto vultu* (ablative of description) depends on *lumina.*

4 865. **instar**: probably 'presence', in the sense of impressiveness, greatness; or possibly 'resemblance' to his ancestor. For the word see note on 2.15; it occurs very rarely indeed without an accompanying genitive.

5 869-71. 'The fates will only give the world a glimpse of him and will not allow him to live longer than that. You gods above, you decided that the Roman stock would be powerful beyond bounds if this gift should be hers to keep '. *Fuissent* is reported future perfect: *'nimium potens erit si dona propria fuerint'*, so *visa est superis nimium potens fore si . . . fuissent.*

6 872-3. 'What deep lamentation from the people will the Campus Martius send echoing up to the mighty city of Mars!' Marcellus was buried with extraordinary funeral honours (*funera*, 874) in Augustus' Mausoleum on the Campus Martius, adjacent to the Tiber; the word *Mavortis* goes with *urbem* but also defines the meaning of *campus* (for the archaic form cf. 777).

7 874. **praeterlabere**: the long slow word gives a solemn, pictorial effect; cf. *Geo.* 2.157 *fluminaque antiquos subterlabentia muros.*

8 876. **in tantum spe tollet**: 'raise so high in hope'; it is however very possible that *spe* is an archaic form of the genitive, cf. *Geo.* 1.208.

9 876-7. 'nor will the land of Romulus ever in the future feel so proud of any of its sons'; for *quondam* cf. Hor. *Sat.* 2.2.82, and compare the similar use of *olim* (e.g. *Aen.* 1.289).

Heu, [1]miserande puer, si qua fata aspera rumpas!
Tu Marcellus eris. [2]Manibus date lilia plenis
purpureos spargam flores animamque nepotis
his saltem accumulem[3] donis, et fungar inani   885
munere.' sic tota passim regione vagantur
aeris in campis latis atque omnia lustrant.
Quae postquam Anchises natum per singula duxit
incenditque[4] animum famae venientis amore,
exim bella viro memorat quae deinde gerenda,   890
Laurentisque[5] docet populos urbemque Latini,
et quo quemque modo fugiatque feratque laborem.

> *893-901. There are two gates of Sleep leading out of the
> underworld, one of horn for true shades, and the other of
> ivory. Aeneas and the Sibyl leave by the ivory gate, and
> Aeneas rejoins his fleet and sails north to Caieta.*

[6]Sunt geminae Somni portae, quarum altera fertur
cornea, qua veris facilis datur exitus umbris,
altera candenti perfecta nitens elephanto,[7]   895

---

1 882-3. 'Alas, unhappy boy, if only somehow you could break through harsh fate! You will be Marcellus'. With this punctuation line 882 is a wish (cf. 187) and the next three words give the identity of the youth, not yet specified but of course guessed by every Roman, so that their impact is overwhelming in their simplicity. Most editors punctuate with a comma after *rumpas,* so that *eris* is the apodosis of a condition. This affords no satisfactory sense ('if you could break through fate, you most certainly will be a Marcellus, a true Marcellus'). Page has an excellent note on the subject.

2 883-4. Let me strew lilies, radiant blossoms, with unsparing hand'; the construction is *date spargam* (cf. *Aen.* 4.683-4), and *flores* is in apposition to *lilia.* The alternative explanation ('give me lilies, let me strew radiant blossoms') gives an unnatural construction to *spargam.*

3 885. **accumulem**: 'load', cf. *Aen.* 5.53a. Anchises, as Conington says, identifies himself with the mourners at the funeral on earth, long centuries hence.

4 889. 'fired his heart with love of the glory to come'; this line finely summarises the impetus given to Aeneas' resolution by the vision of his people's future.

5 891. **Laurentisque . . . populos**: the people in the area of King Latinus' settlement in Latium, see note on 5.797.

6 893f. The Gates of Sleep come from Homer: in *Odyssey* 19.562f. Penelope tells of the gates of dreams, one of horn for true dreams and one of ivory for false dreams (κερας, 'horn', being thought to be connected with 'fulfil', κραινω; and ελεφας, 'ivory', with 'deceive', ελεφαιρμαι). This image has been adopted by Virgil to serve as a way of exit from the underworld as the cave of Avernus provided an entrance.

Many views have been expressed on why Aeneas and the Sibyl leave by the gate of false dreams. (We may leave on one side the view that the false gate must be used because the time is before midnight, and true dreams appear after midnight; it is doubtful whether this was a common belief in Virgil's day, and in any case it has no relevance to Virgil's text). On one level it is fully adequate to say that as Aeneas and the Sibyl are not *verae umbrae* they do not qualify for the horn gate; but there are other levels to be considered. Particularly we may note how this imagery concentrates the attention of the reader on dreams, so that in a sense we may regard the underworld as a dream or vision of Aeneas, personal to him (see Otis, *T.A. Ph.A.* 1959, pp. 173f.). The book is thus a part of Aeneas' experience, a re-enactment of his past and a vision of his future; it profoundly affects his personality. Finally there is another level; possibly Virgil symbolises the uncertainty of his own religious vision, a dimly seen and groping concept, based on hope not faith, of virtue rewarded and suffering to some extent explained. This is far indeed from the gloom of Homer's ghosts, but far too from the certainty of religious conviction upon which Milton's *Paradise Lost* is based. Glover quotes 'The best in this kind are but shadows', and Fletcher 'We are such stuff as dreams are made on'.

7 895. **elephanto**: the quadri-syllabic ending-adds to the Greek atmosphere here, see note on 1.651.

sed falsa ad[1] caelum mittunt insomnia manes.
His[2] ibi tum natum Anchises unaque Sibyllam
prosequitur dictis portaque emittit eburna.
Ille viam[3] secat ad navis sociosque revisit.
    Tum se ad Caietae[4] recto[5] fert litore portum.   900
Ancora de prora iacitur; stant litore puppes.

---

1 896. **ad caelum**: i.e. to our world, cf. 719. For the false dreams cf. 283-4.

2 897-8. **his . . . dictis**: i.e. with the instructions he had been giving (890f.).

3 899. **viam secat**: cf. Lucr. 5.272, *Geo.* 1.238, *Aen.* 12.368, and (somewhat differently) 5.658.

4 900. **Caietae**: well north of Cumae, on the way to the Tiber. The name is derived (*Aen,* 7.2) from Aeneas' nurse who died on their arrival there.

5 **recto ... litore**: 'straight along the shore', ablative of route, cf. *recto flumine* (8.57). Some editors accept *limite* from inferior MSS, to avoid the repetition with 901, but the stopgap nature of 901 (repeated from 3.277) is sufficient explanation of this; see also note on 1.429.

BOOK 7

Introductory note

After the patriotic and religious vision of Book 6, a moving and mysterious climax to the voyage of Aeneas (the Odyssean half of the poem), Virgil turns to the second half of his theme, the Iliadic battles fought on Italian soil before the foundation of Aeneas' town could be achieved. But before the long descriptions of fighting begin the scene must be set, the opposing forces visualised and understood, the future glory anticipated; the war begins in the seventh book, but it is not until the ninth book that full scale battle is joined.

In his new invocation (37 - 45) Virgil concludes his appeal to the Muse with the words *maior rerum mihi nascitur ordo, / maius opus moveo*. To the modern reader, who finds the first half of the poem more immediate in its appeal and more universal, the statement seems perhaps surprising and the implied promise unfulfilled (see note on 37f.). Why should Virgil have felt that the subject of the second half offered a greater challenge? Partly perhaps because he comes now to the achievement of what was sought in the voyage; upon the prelude and the preliminaries follows the event of a new city's foundation; partly because the setting is now to be Virgil's own Italy, and a panorama of Roman history and traditions opens before him, a cavalcade of the national character and way of life symbolised in the dim past and stretching forward through a thousand years; and partly because the conflict of two peoples presented great dramatic possibilities, both of triumph and pathos, as in the *Iliad*. The battle scenes and the process of victory could indeed have been the triumphant climax of the spirit of adventure and endeavour in man, with conflict, defeat and death seen as part of a cosmic drama leading to a future worth all the sacrifices and suffering. This was the ultimate question which Virgil explored, but he did not find the answer he was seeking. Too often strength and bravery turn to hatred and violence. At the end there should have been some other way for Turnus.

The function of the seventh book in many ways balances with that of the first book: it provides a new impetus for action through the intervention of Juno. In the first book she persuades Aeolus to send a fierce storm upon the Trojans; in the seventh she calls on Allecto to summon the powers of Hades against them. In the first the friendly reception by Dido of the Trojans is the prelude to tragic events; in the seventh the friendly reception by Latinus is destroyed by the frenzy aroused by Allecto. The anger and hatred of this part of the book is the more striking after the serenity of the last part of Book 6 and before the idyllic setting of Book 8.

The seventh book is itself organised in three main sections: the arrival and welcome of the Trojans, the intervention of Juno and Allecto and the outbreak of war, the catalogue of the Italian forces. The first of these is joyful, the colours are bright, the undertones of impending tragedy kept in the background; friendship and chivalry are shown on both sides. The second is dark, terrifying, and daemonic, as the frenzy which Allecto can inspire is seen taking hold of Amata, Turnus, the shepherds; and the actual beginning of the war is motivated by the death of the pet stag, a passage of gentle sentiment

298

which contrasts poignantly with the violence and hatred aroused by Juno's minister. Finally the catalogue holds the action in suspense as it concentrates our attention on the lives and homes of those about to fight against the Trojans; Virgil is deeply involved emotionally in his 'gathering of the clans', the valiant ancestors of the Italian peoples of his own day.

The last two lines of Book 6 described the departure of the Trojans from Cumae, and their arrival at Caieta (modern Gaeta) some fifty miles north.

1 -4. Death of Aeneas' nurse, Caieta.

Tu quoque[1] litoribus nostris, Aeneia nutrix,

aeternam moriens famam, Caieta,[2] dedisti;

[3]et nunc servat honos sedem tuus, ossaque nomen

Hesperia in magna, si qua est ea gloria, signat.

5-24. The Trojans sail past the island of Circe.

[4]At pius[5] exsequiis Aeneas rite solutis,   5

aggere composito tumuli, postquam alta quierunt

aequora, tendit[6] iter velis portumque relinquit.

[7]Aspirant[8] aurae in noctem nec candida cursus

luna negat, splendet tremulo sub lumine pontus.

---

1 1. **Tu quoque**: Caieta also (like Misenus and Palinurus in Book 6; see notes on 6.234 and 381) gave her name to a part of the Italian coast. Ovid (*Met.* 14.443-4) records an epitaph for her tomb: *hic me Caietam notae pietatis alumnus / ereptam Argolico quo debuit igne cremavit.* For *Aeneia* ('of Aeneas') cf. 10.156.

2 2. The legend about Caieta varied greatly: Servius tells us that she was variously said to be nurse of Aeneas, Creusa, Ascanius. He also relates that according to a different legend Caieta was the place where the Trojan fleet was set on fire, and got its name from this (καιειν).

3 3-4. 'and now your glory marks the place, and the name commemorates your bones': i.e. her memorial in Virgil's time is the name of the town called after her, cf. *Aen.* 6.507 *nomen et arma locum servant.* The reading *signat* is preferable to *signant*, because the second phrase is a variant on the first, expressed in parallel fashion: cf. Tac. *Germ.* 28 *manet adhuc Boihaemi nomen, signatque loci veterem memoriam*

4 5f. This is the last part of the Trojan Odyssey before their arrival at their new home on the Tiber, and Virgil uses one of the stages in Odysseus' wanderings (Hom. *Od.* 10.133f., 203f.). Previous Odyssean episodes in Aeneas' journey have been Scylla and Charybdis, Polyphemus, the Sirens. Notice the brilliant descriptive colours of this episode, balancing the equally brilliant description of the Tiber which follows; but Circe's island is exotic, magical, frightening, while the Tiber is idyllic, calm, serene. The passage starts (lines 5-7) with matter-of-fact details of activity, subordinated with participial clauses and a temporal conjunction very much in the manner of Latin prose. The description begins (lines 8-9) with three short main clauses of colourful verbs and adjectives, with alliterative effects: it continues with patterned lines (10 and 14 are perfect Golden Lines, and 11 and 13 symmetrically interwoven) containing evocative imagery (*inaccessos lucos, odoratam cedrum, arguto pectine*); then suddenly shifting from the idyllic to the macabre it ends powerfully, with striking alliterative effects (*leonum . . . recusantum . . . rudentum, sera sub nocte . . . . saetigerique sues, magnorum . . . luporum*), reinforced by the abstract turns *iraeque leonum* and *formae . . . luporum*. Finally the last four lines (21-24) are quiet and simple

5 5. **pius**: this epithet, used a score of times of Aeneas (cf. 1.10 *insignem pietate virum*) conveys generally his role as man of destiny, his acceptance of his divine mission, his readiness to serve the gods in order to help to bring about their purpose for the world. It frequently has specific reference, as here and in 8.84, to his scrupulous observance of required religious rituals.

6 7. **tendit . . . velis**: 'directs his way under sail', cf. 6.240 *tendere iter pennis.*

7 8-9. Cf. Enn. *Scen.* 292 *lumine sic tremulo terra et cava caerula candent.*

8 8. 'the breezes blow on into the night'; Servius explains that at nightfall a change of wind might be expected. Cf. Horace's *dormiet in lucem* (*Epist.* 1.18.34), *in medios dormire dies* (*Epist.* 1.2.30), and Val. Fl. 2.59-60.

¹Proxima Circaeae raduntur² litora terrae,   10

³dives inaccessos ubi Solis filia lucos

adsiduo resonat cantu, tectisque superbis

urit odoratam nocturna in lumina cedrum

arguto⁴ tenuis percurrens pectine telas.

Hinc⁵ exaudiri gemitus⁶ iraeque leonum   15

vincla recusantum et sera sub nocte rudentum,⁷

saetigerique⁸ sues atque in praesepibus⁹ ursi

¹⁰saevire ac formae magnorum ululare luporum,

¹¹quos hominum ex facie dea saeva potentibus herbis¹²

induerat Circe in vultus ac terga ferarum.   20

Quae ne monstra¹³ pii¹⁴ paterentur talia Troes

delati in portus neu litora dira subirent,

Neptunus ventis implevit vela secundis,

atque fugam dedit et praeter vada fervida vexit.

25-36. The Trojans reach the mouth of the Tiber.

  ¹⁵Iamque rubescebat radiis mare et aethere ab alto   25

---

1 10-11. The island of Circe (3.386), halfway between Cumae and the mouth of the Tiber, had become in Virgil's time a promontory (cf. 799), as it is now (Monte Circeo). Circe is in Homer the sister of Acetes and the daughter of Helios, the sun; she is with Medea and Calypso among the sorceresses in Chaucer's *House of Fame* (3.182). Cf. Milton, *Comus* 50f.:
'Who knows not Circe
The daughter of the Sun, whose charmed Cup
Whoever tasted lost his upright shape,
And downward fell into a grov'ling swine?'

2 10. **raduntur**: in this nautical sense the word means 'to graze', 'sail close to', cf. 3.700.

3 11-12. 'where the rich daughter of the Sun makes the remote groves re-echo with her unending song': *inaccessus* is a scarce word, not found before Virgil (cf. 8.195, of the cave of Cacus); and *resonare* is not paralleled in this sense until Silius (14.30); cf. 451 *verbera insonuit*. In Hom. *Od.* 10.221 Circe is heard singing at her loom.

4 14. Cf. *Geo.* 1.294 *arguto coniunx percurrit pectine telas; argutus* refers to the shrill whirring sound of the shuttle running through the loom (cf. *Geo.* 1.143 *serra arguta*). It is worth reading Henry's note in favour of the meaning 'shuttle' for *pecten* rather than 'sley'.

5 15. For the historic infinitive of repeated action cf. line 78 and 6.557, 11.822.

6 **gemitus iraeque:** Servius explains as hendiadys, equivalent to *gemitus irascentium leonum*. Cf. Lucr. 3.297.

7 16. **rudentum**: 'roaring'; the word is used of Cacus (8.248) and of the groaning timbers of a ship (3.561).

8 17. **saetigeri**: a typically Lucretian adjective (5.969) used also in *Aen.* 11.198 and 12.170 of pigs.

9 **praesepibus**: 'pens', i.e. the bears are in captivity.

10 18. 'the shapes of huge wolves howled'; *formae* is very effective here, partly as an abstract word like *irae* in 15 and partly with the gruesome indication that these wolf shapes were really men.

11 19-20. **quos . . . induerat Circe in vultus**: 'whom Circe had clothed with the faces . . .'. Cf. *Geo.* 1.188, *Geo.* 4.143.

12 19. Cf. Milton, *Comus* 254 (of Circe and the Sirens) 'culling their potent herbs and baleful drugs'.

13 21. **monstra . . . paterentur**: 'should have to suffer such horrible plight'.

14 **pii**: Servius explains that Odysseus' companions, who suffered at Circe's hands the fate which the Trojans avoid, brought it upon themselves because they were *impii* (as they showed later by killing the cattle of the Sun).

15 25f. The description of the promised land is pastoral and idyllic. As the earliest part of Aeneas' story (the destruction of Troy in Book 2) was set in the darkness of night, so now the new chapter opens with the coming of dawn. The normal tradition put Aeneas' first landing south of the Tiber, but Virgil uses the poetic advantages offered by the great river with its mouth at Ostia.

¹Aurora in roseis fulgebat lutea bigis,
²cum venti posuere omnisque repente resedit
³flatus, et in lento luctantur marmore tonsae.
Atque hic Aeneas ingentem ex aequore lucum
prospicit. Hunc inter fluvio Tiberinus amoeno   30
⁴verticibus rapidis et multa flavus harena
in mare prorumpit. Variae circumque supraque
adsuetae⁵ ripis volucres et fluminis alveo⁶
aethera mulcebant⁷ cantu lucoque volabant.
Flectere⁸ iter sociis terraeque⁹ advertere proras   35
imperat et laetus fluvio succedit opaco.

37-45. Invocation to the Muse.

   ¹⁰Nunc age, qui reges, Erato,¹¹ quae tempora rerum,¹²
quis Latio antiquo fuerit status, advena¹³ classem
cum primum Ausoniis exercitus appulit oris,
expediam, et primae revocabo exordia pugnae.   40
Tu vatem, tu, diva, mone. Dicam horrida bella,

---

1 26. This description of dawn is especially highly coloured: *lutea* ('orange') recalls Homer's κροκόπεπλος, and *roseis* (cf. 6.535) his ροδοδάκτυλος.

2 27. This is an astonishingly serene line, reinforced by the trochaic lilt of *posuere* (with elision), *omnisque, repente,* and the assonance of *repente resedit. Posuere* ('abated') is an intransitive usage not paralleled before Virgil; cf. 10.103.

3 28. 'the oars toil in the sluggish sea': *marmor* is used for the unruffled surface of the sea as early as Ennius (*Ann.* 384); cf. 718 and 10.208. *Tonsae* is also an Ennian word.

4 30-1. *fluvio . . . amoeno* is ablative of description with *Tiberinus* (cf. 8.31); the ablatives in line 31 depend on *flavus.* This is a favourite adjective for the Tiber: cf. Hor. *Odes* 1.2.13.

5 33. **adsuetae ripis**: 'natives of the river's banks'.

6 **alveo**: the word scans as a spondee by synizesis or slurring of the *e*; cf. 190, 237, 249, 303, 609, 769 and *Aen.* 6.412.

7 34. **mulcebant**: 'caressed'; a bold usage based on phrases like *aera mulcentes motu* (Lucr. 4.136), *mulcens tremebundis aethera pinnis* (Cic. *Arat.* 88). It is imitated by Ovid, *Fast.* 1.155 *tepidum volucres concentibus aera mulcent.*

8 35-6. **flectere . . . imperat**: for the infinitive (mainly poetic) cf. Lucr. 5.672.

9 35. **terrae**: poetic dative of motion towards, common especially with compound verbs, cf. 36, 39.

10 37f. The new invocation prefaces the second half of the poem, the Iliadic books of war and battles. The emphasis is on the Italian setting, the peoples and places of Virgil's own country, destined to become a large part of the Trojan future. Virgil regards his task in the last six books as a greater one (lines 44-5) perhaps in three senses: firstly because from the promise of Aeneas' destiny he now comes to the fulfilment; secondly because the account of battles is in a way more decisive and dramatic than the Odyssean books (cf. Longinus' preference for the *Iliad, De Subl.* 9.13f.); and thirdly because he is now to portray the character and achievements of the early ancestors of his own Italians. Ironically the first six books have always been preferred by Virgil's readers; this is largely because of the greater variety of opportunity for character portrayal, mythology and imagery. For the contrast between the Homeric and Virgilian attitudes to warfare see the introductory note to Book 9.

11 37. **Erato**: the Muse of Love is invoked probably because the whole conflict about to be described arises from Turnus' refusal to give up his bride Lavinia to the Trojan stranger. Cf. Apollonius 3.1, and see Todd's excellent article about the Muses in *C.R.,* 1931) pp. 216f. Servius is probably wrong in explaining the word as unspecific (*pro qualicumque Musa*).

12 **tempora rerum**: 'historical situation', a vague phrase which led Peerlkamp (followed by Hirtzel and Mynors) to punctuate after *tempora,* so that *rerum* would go with *status.* But this is no improvement in sense, and is contrary to Virgil's metrical practice (see G. B. Townend, C.Q. 1969, pp. 330f.). Cf. Lucr. 5.1276, Cic. *Fam.* 2.18.3.

13 38-9. **advena . . . exercitus**: 'a foreign army . . .'; *advena* is adjectival, cf. *Ecl.* 9.2f. *advena . . . possessor agelli.*

dicam acies actosque animis[1] in funera reges,
Tyrrhenamque[2] manum totamque sub arma coactam
Hesperiam. Maior rerum mihi nascitur ordo,
maius opus moveo.

> *45-106. Latinus' daughter Lavinia was betrothed to Turnus,*
> *but portents confirmed by the oracle of Faunus indicate that*
> *she is destined to marry, a foreigner.*

[3]Rex[4] arva Latinus[5] et urbes   45
iam senior longa placidas in pace regebat.
[6]Hunc Fauno et nympha genitum Laurente[7] Marica
accipimus; Fauno Picus pater, isque parentem
te, Saturne, refert,[8] tu sanguinis ultimus auctor.
Filius huic fato divum[9] prolesque virilis   50
nulla fuit, primaque[10] oriens erepta iuventa est.

---

1 42. **animis:** 'with courage', 'with ardour', cf. 11.18.

2 **43. Tyrrhenamque manum**: the reference is to the Etruscans under Tarchon whose support for Aeneas is organised by Evander.

3 45f. Virgil's narrative of the situation existing at the time of Aeneas' arrival is rapid and incisive: first the peaceful state of the kingdom with the prospect of a prince to wed Lavinia; then the dark background of foreboding, with the portent of the bees swarming in the laurel tree, and the flame playing round Lavinia's person as she sacrifices; finally the oracular response of Faunus to Latinus that he must marry his daughter to a foreign stranger. From this marriage would come worldwide dominion. This was the talk of the kingdoms of Italy at the time of Aeneas' arrival (notice how the narrative is rejoined to the main thread, in a way rather reminiscent of Catullus' technique in his epyllion).

4 45-6. Notice the very interlaced order of this opening statement of the narrative: in prose it would be *rex Latinus iam senior arva et urbes placidas in longa pace regebat.*

5 45. **Latinus**: the tradition of the state of affairs in Italy on Aeneas' arrival varied greatly, and Virgil has felt able to adapt it freely for his own purposes. One version (Livy 1.1.5f.) said that Latinus and the Aborigines fought the Trojans and were defeated by them; another was that Latinus and Turnus fought against them and Latinus was killed (Cato, *ap. Serv.* 1.267). Virgil's main innovation is the emphasis on peace: Latinus' kingdom has been enjoying peace for a long time, and Latinus himself is a man of peace. The whole of the first part of the book, up to the intervention by Juno, is painted in joyful colours; there are tragic undertones and latent threats (see K. J. Reckford, *A.J. Ph.*, 1961, pp. 256f.), but the general mood is serene and optimistic.

6 47f. The early Greek legend about Latinus made him a son of Circe and Odysseus, or Circe and Telemachus. Virgil follows the Latin version (notice *accipimus* and *refert*), making him a king of the Aborigines (Sall. *Cat.* 6), son of the Italian god Faunus and the local Italian goddess, Marica. Circe figures in the Latin legend as wife of Picus, also an Italian god, the father of Faunus (lines 189-90). Saturnus, father of Picus and origin of the royal line, has of course the strongest associations with the Golden Age of primitive Italy (*Saturnia tellus*); cf. *Geo.* 2.538, *Aen.* 6.792f., and see note on 8.319f.

7 47. **Laurente**: the Laurentes lived roughly in the area between the Tiber and Ardea to the south. The noun Laurentum (which Virgil does not use) was the name either of this region or a town within it, perhaps identical with Lavinium (see Fairclough's Loeb edition of Virgil, vol. ii, p. 514).

8 49. **refert**: 'says that you were': cf. Ov. *Met.* 13.141.

9 50. **divum:** archaic genitive form used by Virgil with a limited number of words (*deum, virum, equum, iuvencum, famulum, socium, superum*), and often with proper nouns, e.g. *Lapithum*, 305, *Teucrum*, 344.

10 51. **primaque . . . iuventa est**: 'for they (his male progeny) were taken from him as they were growing up in their early years'. This phrase may well be regarded as a stopgap ('tibicen') which Virgil would have replaced: the construction with -*que* in a causal sense is harsh, and *oriens* is strange, apparently in the sense of our phrase 'the rising generation', cf. Hor. *Epist.* 2.1.130. Servius tells of a tradition that Latinus had two sons who were killed by Amata because they sided with their father over the question of Lavinia's marriage.

¹Sola domum et tantas servabat filia sedes
iam matura viro, iam plenis nubilis annis.
Multi² illam magno e Latio totaque petebant
Ausonia; petit ante alios pulcherrimus omnis   55
Turnus,³ avis atavisque potens, quem regia⁴ coniunx
adiungi generum miro properabat⁵ amore:
sed variis portenta deum terroribus obstant.
Laurus⁶ erat tecti medio in penetralibus altis
sacra⁷ comam multosque metu servata per annos,   60
quam pater inventam, primas cum conderet arces,
ipse ferebatur Phoebo⁸ sacrasse Latinus,
Laurentisque⁹ ab ea nomen posuisse colonis.
Huius¹⁰ apes summum¹¹ densae (mirabile dictu)
stridore ingenti liquidum trans aethera vectae   65
obsedere apicem, et pedibus¹² per mutua nexis
examen subitum ramo frondente pependit.
Continuo vates 'externum cernimus' inquit
'adventare¹³ virum et partis petere agmen easdem

---

1 52f. Lavinia is portrayed by Virgil as a gentle and dutiful princess of great filial devotion; she is not individualised at all. She is rarely mentioned in the *Aeneid*, and never speaks; she is important only as a part of the plot, a part of the destinies of Troy and Latium. She is quite remote from human passion, a distanced figure, simply a passive instrument of destiny in the hands of father or husband. No one could be more totally different from Dido. She gave her name to Aeneas' first settlement, Lavinium, and was the mother of Silvius Aeneas, successor to Ascanius and founder of the Alban line. For an excellent account of her character see D. C. Woodworth, *T.A. Ph.A.*, 1930, pp. 175f.

2 54. Cf. Cat. 62.55 (of the vine wedded to the elm) *multi illam agricolae, multi coluere iuvenci.*

3 56. Turnus, king of the Rutulians, was descended from Greek kings (371-2); he was the son of Daunus and brother of the nymph Juturna.

4 **regia coniunx:** Amata, a passionate and vehement queen whose reckless vigour contrasts markedly with the serenity and weakness of King Latinus and the self effacement of the shadowy Lavinia. The phrase *miro properabat amore* already prepares us for her easy victimisation by Allecto later in the book.

5 57. **properabat:** in the sense of *omni studio volebat.*

6 59. Notice how the flashback in time (which continues to line 105) is introduced by the ecphrasis *laurus erat . . . huius.* See note on 1.159f.

7 60. **sacra comam:** 'its foliage sacred'; the Greek accusative of respect is quite freely used by Virgil with parts of the body, cf. 74-5, 8.425 and notes on 1.320, 7.503. For a different type of accusative of respect see note on 8.114.

8 62. **Phoebo:** the laurel was Apollo's special emblem; see Ov. *Met.* 1.452f. for the story of Apollo and Daphne. When she was changed into a laurel tree Apollo said: 'at quoniam coniunx mea non potes esse, / arbor eris certe', dixit, 'mea'.

9 63. **Laurentisque:** in apposition to *nomen,* cf. 3.18.

10 64. The portent of a swarm of bees is frequent in Roman religion; cf. Livy 21.46.2 and Pease on Cic. *De Div.* 1.73. Bees were said to have swarmed on the standard of Pompey at Pharsalus and of Brutus at Philippi. Generally (but not invariably) such an occurrence was regarded as an unfavourable portent; here the meaning is that the foreign invasion will be successful.

11 64. **summum:** adjective agreeing with *apicem.*

12 66. **pedibus . . . nexis:** 'intertwining their legs with each other', cf. *Geo.* 4.257 *pedibus conexae.* Servius quotes Melissus: *duobus pedibus se tenent et duobus alias sustinent.*

13 69-70. 'a column of men making for the same parts from the same parts': a suitably oracular utterance, cryptic and with balanced repetition, meaning that the Trojans like the bees (*trans aethera*) have come from a distance and will seek the summit of power. There is point in *agmen* applied to the Trojans, for it is frequent of bees (cf. *exa(g)men*, 'swarm').

partibus ex isdem et summa dominarier[1] arce.'   70

[2]praeterea, castis adolet[3] dum altaria taedis,

et iuxta genitorem astat Lavinia virgo,

[4]visa (nefas) longis comprendere[5] crinibus ignem

atque[6] omnem ornatum flamma crepitante cremari,

regalisque accensa[7] comas, accensa coronam   75

insignem gemmis; tum fumida lumine fulvo

involvi ac totis Volcanum[8] spargere tectis.

Id vero horrendum ac visu mirabile ferri:[9]

namque fore inlustrem fama fatisque canebant

[10]ipsam, sed populo magnum portendere[11] bellum.   80

    At rex sollicitus monstris oracula Fauni,

fatidici[12] genitoris, adit lucosque sub alta

consulit Albunea,[13] nemorum quae maxima sacro

fonte sonat saevamque exhalat opaca mephitim.

Hinc Italae gentes omnisque Oenotria[14] tellus   85

in[15] dubiis responsa petunt; huc dona sacerdos

cum tulit et caesarum ovium sub nocte silenti

---

1 70. **dominarier:** deponent infinitive, archaic form; the other instances of this form in the *Aeneid* are 4.493, 8.493, 9.231, 11.242.

2 71f. This second portent is again a frequent one in Roman religion: cf. the story of Servius Tullius (Cic. *Rep.* 2.37), and the flame that played round Iulus' head (*Aen.* 2.682-4). Servius suggests that the addition of smoke and scattered sparks gives the otherwise favourable omen its unfavourable aspect.

3 71. It is best to take Lavinia rather than Latinus as the subject of *adolet*.

4 73f. Notice the pattern of alliteration and assonance in these vividly descriptive lines, reaching a climax in *fumida lumine fulvo*.

5 73. **comprendere . . . ignem:** 'to catch fire', cf. Caes. *B.G.* 5-43.

6 74. 'and all her apparel to be alight with cracking flames': the construction is *Lavinia visa est cremari omnem ornatum* (accusative of respect like *comas* and *coronam* in the next line; cf. 60).

7 75. The construction is *accensa regalisque comas et coronam;* *-que* meaning 'both' has its expected *'et'* replaced by the repeated *accensa;* cf. 327, 516.

8 77. **Volcanum spargere:** 'to scatter fire'; poetic usage of the god for his attribute, cf. 1.177.

9 78. **ferri:** 'spoken of as', historic infinitive, cf. 15.

10 81f. Virgil has here taken from the tradition the story of Latinus' dream (Dion. Hal. 1.57), and transferred it to the oracle of Faunus; this enhances the impressiveness of the revelation and associates it with the religious worship of the native Italian god Faunus. The oracular consultation is of the type called *incubatio* (cf. 88): i.e. the response comes in a dream to a person sleeping on the premises. Cf. Ov. *Fast.* 4.641f. and Bailey, *Religion in Virgil,* pp. 26f.

11 80. The subject of *portendere* is *id* (line 78), i.e. the omen.

12 82. **fatidici genitoris:** Faunus had very strong associations with oracular utterances and with the disembodied voice which is heard on mystic occasions: cf. Enn. *Ann.* 214, Cic. *De Div.* 1.101, *Nat. De.* 2.6, and Lucr. 4.581f. This is the reason for Servius' fanciful derivation of his name from φωνη, 'quod voce non signis ostendit futura'.

13 83. **Albunea:** this is the name of the grove and its fountain (modern Zolforata, near Lavinium); it should not be confused, as it has been since the time of Servius, with the Tiburtine Albunea of Hor. *Odes* 1.7.12. See B. Tilly, *Vergil's Latium,* ch. 6, and *J.R.S.* 1934, pp. 25f. The sulphurous fumes (*mephitim,* cf. Pers. 3.99 *sulpureas . . . mefites)* have given rise to the modern name, and presumably the ancient one too (*albus,* 'white', 'cloudy', water; Servius says *dicta est ab aquae qualitate).*

14 85. **Oenotria:** Italy, see note on 1.532.

15 86-7. 'whenever the priest brings gifts here . . .': *cum* is frequentative.

[1]pellibus incubuit stratis somnosque petivit,
multa[2] modis simulacra videt volitantia miris
et varias audit voces fruiturque deorum   90
conloquio atque imis[3] Acheronta adfatur Avernis.
Hic et tum pater ipse petens responsa Latinus
centum lanigeras mactabat rite bidentis,[4]
atque harum effultus tergo stratisque iacebat
velleribus: subita ex alto vox reddita luco est: 95
[5]'ne pete[6] conubiis[7] natam sociare Latinis,
o mea progenies, thalamis neu crede paratis;
externi venient generi, qui sanguine[8] nostrum
nomen in astra ferant, quorumque a stirpe nepotes
omnia sub pedibus, qua Sol utrumque[9] recurrens[10]   100
aspicit Oceanum, vertique[11] regique videbunt.'
Haec responsa patris Fauni monitusque silenti
nocte[12] datos non ipse suo premit ore Latinus,
sed circum late volitans iam Fama per urbes
Ausonias tulerat, cum[13] Laomedontia[14] pubes   105
gramineo ripae religavit ab aggere classem.

---

1 88f. The reference is to dreaming: see note on 81f.

2 89. An impressive line echoed from Lucr. 1.123; cf. Lucr. 6.789 and *Geo.* 1.477. Notice the alliteration of *m* and *v*, the latter continuing into the next line. The sentence concludes with marked assonance of *a*.

3 91. **imis . . . Avernis**: 'speak to Acheron in deepest Avernus', a vague phrase referring to the underworld (Avernus), with its river Acheron (Styx), as the place of dreams. *Acheronta* is Greek accusative, cf. 312.

4 93. **bidentis**: sheep in their second year, when they have two prominent teeth; see note on 4.57.

5 96f. The oracular response is confirmation of the interpretation of the bee portent (68f.), with a prophecy of Roman greatness, such as frequently was given to Aeneas during his journey. We are reminded, as so often in this book, of *Aeneid* 1: cf. Jupiter's prophecy, especially 287 *imperium Oceano, famam qui terminet astris . . . .*

6 96. **pete . . . sociare**: for the infinitive (mainly poetic) cf. 9.192-3.

7 **conubiis**: for the scansion (*conubiis* but *conubia*) see note on 1.73.

8 98. **sanguine**: i.e. by intermarriage with us.

9 100. **utrumque:** in the East and West; cf. *Culex* 103.

10 **recurrens:** 'in its daily journey'.

11 101. **vertique regique**: 'both overturned and ruled'. The doubled *-que* links very closely here the two aspects of the Roman mission; first conquest and secondly government.

12 103. As Servius explains, Latinus might have kept quiet in order to preserve the present arrangements for Lavinia, but he did not. *Premit responsa ore* is an unusual phrase varied from *premere os* (6.155); cf. Ov. *Met.* 14.779 *ore premunt voces*, Sil. 2.280, and line 119.

13 105. **tulerat cum:** 'had already published it at the time when . . .'. Notice how the pluperfect is used to bring us back from the historical digression to the narrative of present events.

14 **Laomedontia**: cf. 3.248. There is often a suggestion of treachery in this epithet (derived from the Trojan king Laomedon who defrauded Neptune and Apollo of their promised reward for building the walls of Troy), but here and in 8.18 there seem to be no overtones.

107-47. The Trojans land and at a banquet consume also the platters of bread on which the food is set out. Iulus exclaims 'We are eating our tables', and Aeneas recognizes the fulfilment of the oracle, and accepts that they have arrived at their destined home. He makes appropriate sacrifices and Jupiter thunders in confirmation of the omen.

[1]Aeneas primique duces et pulcher Iulus
corpora sub ramis deponunt arboris altae,
instituuntque dapes et adorea liba[2] per herbam
subiciunt epulis (sic Iuppiter ipse monebat)   110
et[3] Cereale solum pomis agrestibus augent.
[4]Consumptis hic forte aliis, ut vertere morsus
exiguam in Cererem penuria[5] adegit edendi,
et violare[6] manu malisque audacibus orbem
fatalis[7] crusti patulis[8] nec parcere quadris: 115
'heus, etiam mensas[9] consumimus' inquit Iulus,
nec plura, adludens. Ea vox audita laborum

---

1 107f. The fulfilment of the oracle about eating the tables is a balance for the portents and oracles given to Latinus, serving to emphasise the destiny of Aeneas to the Trojans as it has just been emphasised to the Latins. The oracle had been given to Aeneas by Celaeno the Harpy (3.250f.), who had told him that he would not found his city before hunger compelled the Trojans to eat their tables; he incorrectly attributes it to Anchises, an inconsistency due no doubt to the large part played by Anchises in the early stages of Aeneas' mission in advising and guiding his son. The episode is a strange piece of ancient folklore (comparable with the white sow and her thirty piglets) which had long figured in the Aeneas legend (Lycoph. 1250f., Varro quoted by Servius on 3.256, Dion Hal. 1.55.3). In Dionysius two versions of the 'tables' are given: one that they were thin platters of bread (as in Virgil), the other that they were parsley leaves on which the meal was spread.

2 109. **adorea liba:** 'spelt (wheat) wafers'. *Liba* were flat and thin, like pancakes, made of cereal, often used in sacrifices (*Geo.* 2.394). In the next lines Virgil uses four synonyms for these *liba*. There is the following account of a Turkish dinner in the introduction to the 1900 (Methuen) edition of Kinglake's *Eothen:* 'At first it looks somewhat mysterious when people apparently wrap up some pieces of string in brown paper, and eat the parcel with avidity. But the string is cheese drawn out like very attenuated vermicelli, and the brown paper sheets of very thin bread which serve as a tablecloth and napkin as well as for food.'

3 111. 'and they heap the wafer plates below with the produce of the countryside'; this line is a variation of *adorea liba . . . epulis.* For *solum* (= that which is below) cf. 5.199 (where it is used of the water beneath a ship) with Servius' sonorous comment: 'unicuique rei quod subiacet solum est ei cui subiacet'.

4 112f. 'Then, as it happened that everything else had been eaten, when the shortage of food made them begin to eat the thin wafers and to fall upon the circles of the fateful bread with rash hand and mouth, not sparing the outspread pieces, Iulus said "Look, we are even eating our tables"; just that, in jest.'
These are extraordinary lines of highflown epic vocabulary. It is of course Virgil's way to avoid ordinary terms in descriptions of ordinary events (as the eighteenth-century loved to speak of sheep as 'the fleecy breed', or of fish as 'the finny tribe'); here he has excelled himself, perhaps because he felt that the story, which Heyne called 'per se inepta et epici carminis maiestate indigna', needed dignifying.

5 113. **penuria . . . edendi:** *edendi* is here used very strangely in the sense of *cibi.*

6 114. **violare:** because the wafers were of religious significance (hence *parcere,* 115).

7 115. **fatalis:** because the oracle is fulfilled through the eating of the wafers, according to Jupiter's wish (110).

8 **patulis . . . quadris:** *patulis* refers to the large size of the thin wafers (like 'spreading' a table-cloth); *quadris,* according to Servius, means either 'table', because tables were square (Varro, *L.L.* 5.118); or 'pieces', because the Roman loaf was marked for dividing into quarters (Hor. *Epist.* 1.17.49, Juv. 5.2, Mart. 6.75.1) like a hot-cross bun. It seems probable that it means both, so that the ambiguity leads in to Iulus' comment.

9 116. **mensas:** Mackail *(C.R.,* 1914, p. 89) suggested that Iulus was making a pun on a word *mesa* (cake) and *mensa* (table); Enk *(Mnem.* 1913, pp. 386f.) suggested that the word *mensa* originally meant 'cake' and then came to mean 'table' (see P. Kretschmer, *Glotta,* 1917, pp. 79f.). The compound *adludens* suggests that Iulus 'played on' the word: cf. Cic. *De Orat.* 1.240.

prima[1] tulit[2] finem, primamque loquentis ab ore
eripuit[3] pater ac stupefactus numine pressit.
Continuo 'salve[4] fatis mihi debita tellus   120
vosque' ait 'o fidi Troiae salvete penates:
hic[5] domus, haec patria est. Genitor[6] mihi talia namque
(nunc repeto) Anchises fatorum arcana reliquit:
"cum te, nate, fames ignota ad litora vectum
accisis[7] coget dapibus consumere mensas,   125
tum sperare domos defessus, ibique memento
prima locare manu molirique aggere tecta."
Haec erat illa fames, haec nos suprema manebat
exsiliis[8] positura modum.
Quare agite et primo laeti cum lumine solis   130
quae loca, quive habeant homines, ubi moenia[9] gentis,
vestigemus et a portu[10] diversa petamus.
Nunc pateras libate Iovi precibusque vocate
Anchisen genitorem, et vina[11] reponite mensis.'
    Sic deinde effatus frondenti tempora ramo   135
implicat et geniumque[12] loci primamque deorum
Tellurem[13] Nymphasque et adhuc ignota precatur
flumina, tum Noctem Noctisque orientia signa

---

1 118. **prima . . . primamque:** a rhetorical repetition; *prima* refers to the first indication that they have really arrived at their goal; *primamque* is perhaps equivalent to *ut primum omen,* and may also convey the idea of rapidity.

2 **tulit**: equivalent to *attulit,* cf. 3.145.

3 119. 'His father seized upon it and astonished by the divine revelation stopped him from saying more.' Aeneas prevents any further speech (which might be ill-omened, cf. *favete lingua*) until he can say the appropriate formulae. For *premere vocem* cf. 9.324 and line 103; it is unusual here because the phrase is generally used of stopping one's own speech.

4 120-1. **salve . . . salvete:** religious formulae, cf. 5.80.

5 122. **hic domus, haec patria est:** 'here is our home, this is our country', cf. *Aen.* 4.347 *hic amor, haec patria est.*

6 122f. 'for these were the secrets of fate (now I recall it) which my father Anchises left me: "My son, when . . ." '. It was Celaeno, not Anchises, who made the prophecy (see note on 107f.), and the words which follow are quite different from her words.

7 125. **accisis:** a very strange usage; the word means 'cut away' (*Aen.* 2.627), and here presumably 'eaten up'. Celaeno had spoken of *ambesae mensae.*

8 129. **exsiliis:** most MSS have *exitiis.* I have given my reasons for preferring *exsiliis* in *C.R.* 1961, p. 195. Cf. 2.780 *longa tibi exsilia,* and Ov. *A.A.* 2.25 *sit modus exsilio.*
The half-line is an indication of the unrevised state of the *Aeneid;* see note on 1.534. The others in this book are 248, 439, 455, 702, 760.

9 131. **moenia gentis:** 'the city of the native inhabitants'.

10 132. **a portu diversa petamus:** 'let us set out in different directions from our landing place'.

11 134. **vina reponite mensis:** 'put wine again on the tables', i.e. renew the banquet in honour of the good news (cf. line 146, *Geo.* 3.527, *Aen.* 8.283).

12 136. **geniumque loci:** the guardian god of the locality, cf. 5.95.

13 137. **Tellurem:** 'Mother' Earth was the first of the gods; she is prayed to now, along with local deities like the *genius loci* and the nymphs and rivers, because this is to be Aeneas' land.

Idaeumque[1] Iovem Phrygiamque[2] ex ordine matrem
invocat,[3] et duplicis caeloque Ereboque parentis.   140
[4]Hic pater omnipotens ter caelo clarus ab alto
[5]intonuit, radiisque ardentem lucis et auro
ipse manu quatiens ostendit ab aethere nubem.
Diditur[6] hic subito Troiana per agmina rumor
advenisse diem quo debita moenia condant.   145
Certatim instaurant epulas atque omine magno
crateras laeti statuunt et vina[7] coronant.

148-69. The Trojans send an embassy to King Latinus.

[8]Postera cum prima lustrabat lampade terras
orta dies, urbem[9] et finis et litora gentis
[10]diversi explorant: haec fontis stagna Numici,[11]   150
hunc Thybrim fluvium, hic fortis habitare Latinos.
Tum satus[12] Anchisa delectos ordine ab omni
centum oratores augusta ad moenia regis
ire iubet, ramis velatos Palladis omnis,
donaque ferre viro pacemque exposcere Teucris.   155
Haud mora, festinant iussi rapidisque feruntur
passibus.[13] Ipse humili designat moenia fossa
moliturque locum, primasque[14] in litore sedes
castrorum in morem pinnis[15] atque aggere cingit.

---

1 139. **Idaeumque Iovem:** cf. 3.105 for Mt. Ida in Crete which gave its name to the Trojan Mount Ida.

2 **Phrygiam . . . matrem:** Cybele, the *magna mater,* associated with Mt. Ida; see note on 3.111f.

3 140. He prays to his father (Anchises in Erebus) and his mother (Venus in the heavens). *Duplicis* (= *duos*) has a ritual tone about it.

4 141f. Jupiter confirms the omen and shows his approval, as in 2.692f. For the omen of thunder in a clear sky cf. 9.630f., Hor. *Odes* 1.34.7f.

5 142f. 'himself striking with his hand revealed in the sky a cloud blazing with golden rays of light', i.e. the sky was cloudless (*clarus*) till Jupiter himself made a cloud with a blow of his hand. Cf. the prodigy in 8.524f.

6 144. **diditur:** 'was spread around', a word frequent in Lucretius; cf. *Aen.* 8.132 *tua terris didita fama.*

7 147. See note on 1.724, an almost identical line, where the phrase *vina coronant* 'puts garlands round the wine cups' is discussed.

8 148f. 'When the next dawn rose and was giving light to the world with its earliest rays'; cf. 4.6.

9 149-50. **urbem. . . explorant:** i.e. they locate Latinus' capital, some distance away.

10 150f. The accusative and infinitive construction depends on a leading verb understood; 'they learn' (presumably, as Servius says, from the inhabitants).

11 150. **Numici:** a river near the Tiber; cf. 797, Ov. *Met.* 14.598f.,Livy 1.2.6.

12 152. **satus Anchisa:** used also of Aeneas in 5.244, 424, 6.331. *Satus* in this sense ('born of') is mainly poetic, cf. 331, 656, 8.36, 10.563, 12.860.

13 157. Cf. *Aen.* 5.755 (of Segesta) *interea Aeneas urbem designat aratro* (where Servius in his note gives details about the procedure for marking out the site of a new town).

14 158. **primasque . . . sedes:** it was called Troia.

15 159. **pinnis:** 'battlements' (cf. Caes. *B.G.* 7.72), so called because of the similarity to the quills on a bird's wing.

Iamque iter emensi turris ac tecta Latinorum[1]   160
ardua cernebant iuvenes muroque subibant.
Ante urbem pueri et primaevo flore iuventus
exercentur equis domitantque[2] in pulvere currus,
aut acris[3] tendunt arcus aut lenta[4] lacertis
spicula contorquent, cursuque ictuque lacessunt: 165
cum praevectus equo longaevi regis ad auris
nuntius ingentis[5] ignota in veste reportat
advenisse viros. Ille intra tecta vocari
imperat et solio medius consedit avito.

170—91. Description of the palace in which King Latinus receives the Trojans.

[6]Tectum augustum, ingens, centum sublime columnis   170
urbe fuit summa, Laurentis regia[7] Pici,
horrendum silvis et religione[8] parentum.
hic sceptra accipere et primos attollere fascis[9]
regibus omen erat;[10] hoc illis curia templum,
hae sacris sedes epulis; hic ariete[11] caeso   175
perpetuis[12] soliti patres considere mensis.

---

1 160. **Latinorum:** hypermetric elision, cf. 470, 8.228, 9.650, 10.781, 895, 11.609, and see note on 1.332.

2 163. **domitantque . . . currus:** 'break in chariot-horses amidst clouds of dust', cf. 280, 12.287.

3 164. **acris:** only here and in 9.665 applied by Virgil to an inanimate object, so it is best to take it as a transferred epithet: 'they aim their fierce bows'.

4 164-5. **lenta . . . contorquent:** 'send the supple javelin whirling from their shoulders'; for *lenta* cf. 11.650, 12.489, and for *contorquent* 11.561, 676.

5 167. **ingentis:** a heroic touch; it is fitting that the Trojans should be 'mighty men'. Cf. Tacitus' *omne ignotum pro magnifico;* Servius says *ingentes enim esse quos primum videmus opinamur.*

6 170f. The contrast between this elaborate and highly wrought description of the palace and the simple fast moving narrative of the previous section is very marked. Virgil takes the opportunity (as so often elsewhere) of linking the ancient setting of his story with later Roman customs and institutions. The palace now described to us is, in Conington's phrase, 'a sort of museum of Roman antiquities'. It is almost wholly anachronistic *(fasces, curia, rostra)*, deliberately so: it is not intended as a piece of archaeological or historical research into origins but as an imaginative tableau of time-honoured Roman institutions. It is a palace which at the same time is a temple (see H. T. Rowell, *A.J.Ph.,* 1941, pp. 261f.); its impressive splendour would heighten in the Roman reader his awareness of the traditions which he had inherited and perhaps, as T. R. Glover says, 'remind him a little of a palace and a temple on the Palatine, where another and a greater ruler was gathering up the nation's traditions in himself, amidst surroundings as crowded with revivals of older memories'. Thus Servius on 170 (cf. also on 173, 175): 'domum in Palatio ab Augusto factam per transitum laudat'.

7 171. **regia Pici:** probably the building had been the palace of Picus (Latinus' grandfather), and had now been turned into a temple for the coronation of their kings (172), meetings of the Senate (174), religious banquets (175-6).

8 172. **religione:** the first syllable is lengthened, cf. 608 and *reliquias,* 244.

9 173. **fascis:** the bundle of rods symbolising authority, see note on 6.818.

10 174. **erat:** the final syllable is lengthened in arsis, i.e. by the ictus (beat) at the beginning of the foot; cf. 186 and 398, and see note on 1.308.

11 175. **ariete:** the word scans as a dactyl with consonantal *i*, cf. 8.599 *(abiete)* and 12.706.

12 176. **perpetuis . . . mensis:** 'at the long line of tables', i.e. they sat in unbroken rows, the tables were not spaced out, as opposed to the *triclinia* of Virgil's time. Cf. Ov. *Fast.* 6.305f *ante focos olim scamnis considere longis / mos erat.*

Quin[1] etiam veterum effigies ex ordine avorum
antiqua e cedro,[2] Italusque[3] paterque Sabinus[4]
vitisator[5] curvam[6] servans sub imagine falcem,
Saturnusque senex Ianique[7] bifrontis imago   180
vestibulo astabant, aliique ab[8] origine reges,
Martiaque[9] ob patriam pugnando vulnera passi.
[10]Multaque praeterea sacris in postibus arma,
captivi pendent currus curvaeque secures
et cristae capitum et portarum ingentia claustra   185
spiculaque[11] clipeique ereptaque[12] rostra carinis.
[13]Ipse Quirinali lituo parvaque sedebat
succinctus trabea laevaque ancile gerebat
Picus,[14] equum[15] domitor, quem capta cupidine coniunx[16]

---

1 177f. The list of ancestors which follows 'opens a vista of previous history far more extensive than what is sketched in 45f.' (Conington).

2 178. **cedro:** cedar is a long lasting wood; its oil was used by the Romans for preservation, cf. Pers. 1.42 *cedro digna locutus* (= 'worth preserving'). Notice the hiatus at the caesura; cf. 226.

3 **Italus:** for the legendary eponymous ancestor of the Italians see note on 1.532.

4 **Sabinus:** a shadowy Italian figure, cf. Dion. Hal. 2.49, clearly here mentioned as an eponym of the Sabines.

5 179. **vitisator:** an unusual word, first found in Accius (according to Macrobius).

6 **curvam . . . falcem:** 'still with his curved sickle represented', i.e. the statue does not hold a real sickle, but one carved in wood, cf. 6.293 *cava sub imagine formae.* This is certainly better than either of Servius' explanations: (1) beneath his face; (2) beneath its sheath, and perhaps better than 'beneath the statue'. The attributes of this line are commonly applied to Saturnus. *Servans* suggests that as in life, so in his image, he holds the sickle.

7 180. **Ianique bifrontis:** the two-headed god, said to have received Saturnus in Italy when he was expelled from Crete (Macr. *Sat.* 1.7.19f.). He is also called *anceps* and *geminus;* as god of entrances and beginnings he looks forwards and backwards.

8 181. **ab origine:** cf. 1.642; the notion of 'aboriginal' is strong here.

9 182. This line is almost a repetition of 6.660; it seems inappropriate here, and the *-que* is redundant. Heyne is perhaps right in regarding it as a marginal gloss which has crept into the text.

10 183f. For armour (spoils) fixed on the doors of temples cf. 3.287, 5.360. The passage is imitated by Statius (*Theb.* 7.55f., the temple of Mars). Ancient chariots were light (Hom. *Il.* 10.505); for the use of the axe in war cf. line 510, *Aen.* 11.696, 12.306.

11 186. **spiculaque:** for the lengthened *-que* see notes on 174 and 8.425.

12 **ereptaque . . . carinis:** the capturing of 'beaks' from enemy warships is perhaps the most striking anachronism of all in this passage.

13 187f. 'Picus himself sat there with the Quirinal staff, wearing a short cloak, holding the sacred shield in his left hand.' Aulus Gellius (5.8) discusses the construction of *lituo,* and considers it an ablative of description; it is more likely that there is a zeugma in the sentence with some verb like *ornatus* to be supplied from *succinctus.* The *lituus* was the augur's staff; the adjective *Quirinali* relates to early Rome. Like the noun Quirinus (1.296, 6.859) it often refers to Romulus but is also applied to Janus (line 612). *Trabea* is the robe of state worn by kings and augurs (cf. line 612 and Ov. *Fast.* 6.375 *lituo pulcher trabeaque Quirinus; Met.* 14.828); *ancile* is a small shield of the type which later was to become a Roman talisman associated with Numa (cf. 8.664).

14 189f. Picus so far has been presented as an Italian king, but now Virgil refers to the story of how Circe fell in love with him and when spurned turned him into a woodpecker (a bird associated by the Romans with augury). Ovid gives the tale at length, *Met.* 14.320f. The transition from legend and antiquarian history to mythology is strange and fascinating; notice how the second half of line 191 gives a serene sort of finality to the passage.

15 189. **equum domitor:** Ovid imitates this in *Met.* 14.320f. *Picus in Ausoniis proles Saturnia terris / rex fuit utilium bello studiosus equorum.*

16 189. **coniunx:** his would-be bride, cf. 2.344.

aurea[1] percussum virga versumque[2] venenis   190
fecit avem Circe sparsitque coloribus alas.

*192-248. Latinus welcomes the Trojans, asking them the
reason for their arrival. Ilioneus answers that fate has
brought them to Italy, and offers gifts.*

[3]Tali intus templo divum patriaque Latinus
sede sedens Teucros ad sese in tecta vocavit,
atque haec ingressis placido prior edidit ore:
dicite,[4] Dardanidae (neque enim nescimus et urbem   195
et genus, auditique advertitis aequore cursum),
quid petitis? Quae causa rates aut cuius[5] egentis
litus ad Ausonium tot per vada caerula vexit?
Sive[6] errore viae seu tempestatibus acti,
qualia[7] multa mari nautae patiuntur in alto,   200
fluminis intrastis ripas portuque sedetis,
ne fugite hospitium, neve ignorate Latinos
Saturni[8] gentem haud vinclo nec legibus aequam,
sponte sua veterisque dei se more tenentem.
Atque equidem memini (fama est obscurior annis)   205
Auruncos[9] ita ferre[10] senes, his ortus ut agris
Dardanus[11] Idaeas Phrygiae penetrarit ad urbes
Threiciamque Samum, quae nunc Samothracia fertur.

---

1 190. **aurea**: ablative, scanned as a spondee, cf. line 33 and 1.698. Servius and Donatus take it as nominative, but the wand needs an epithet and Circe does not.

2 **versumque venenis**: 'metamorphosed by drugs'.

3 192f. The interchange of speeches is in the true heroic style. Latinus speaks *placido ore,* paying full compliments to his Trojan visitors, and Ilioneus matches him in courtesy and dignity. We are reminded very strongly of the speeches between Dido and Ilioneus in Book 1, there as here friendly and peace loving preludes to the discordant events ahead

4 195f. Similarly Dido knows of the fame of the Trojans (*Dardanidae*) when they arrive (*Aen.* 1.565f.), but is uncertain of the reasons for their arrival.

5 197. The construction of *cuius egentis* is elliptical: 'what reason has brought your ships, what do you need from me?'

6 199. **sive**: 'or if'; the alternatives are: (i) what reason has brought you? (ii) or if you are here by chance. . . .

7 200. A rather banal line, characteristic of Latinus' desire to make an ample speech of welcome; cf. 208.

8 203-4. 'a race which is righteous not by compulsion or law but self-controlled voluntarily and according to the custom of the ancient god': there is antithesis between *vinclo* and *sponte sua,* and also (as Page points out) between *legibus* and *more.* The reference of course is to the Golden Age of Saturn: cf. 8.319f., Ov. *Met.* 1.89f. Compare Milton, *P.L.* 9.653-4: 'the rest, we live / Law to our selves, our Reason is our Law'.

9 206. **Auruncos**: cf. line 727; this is a name of the aboriginal inhabitants of Italy, cognate with *Ausonia.*

10 206f. **ferre . . . ut . . . penetrarit**: 'used to tell how he went . . .'. *Penetrarit* is perfect subjunctive in an indirect question; most MSS have *penetravit,* an indicative like 6.779, but the construction would be much harsher here and the corruption from the contracted form *penetrarit* to the far commoner indicative is an easy one.

11 207. Dardanus, son of Corythus (his mortal father, Zeus was his immortal father) and Electra, was said to have set out from Italy to Samothrace and Troy; see note on 3.167-8.

Hinc[1] illum Corythi[2] Tyrrhena ab sede profectum
aurea nunc solio stellantis regia caeli   210
accipit et numerum divorum altaribus auget.'[3]
     Dixerat, et dicta Ilioneus sic voce secutus:
rex,[4] genus egregium Fauni, nec fluctibus actos
atra subegit hiems vestris succedere terris,
nec sidus regione viae litusve fefellit:[5]   215
consilio hanc[6] omnes animisque volentibus urbem
adferimur[7] pulsi regnis, quae maxima quondam
extremo veniens sol aspiciebat Olympo.
Ab Iove principium generis, Iove Dardana pubes
gaudet avo,[8] rex ipse Iovis de gente suprema: 220
Troius Aeneas tua nos ad limina misit.
[9]Quanta per Idaeos saevis effusa Mycenis
tempestas ierit campos, quibus actus uterque
Europae atque Asiae fatis concurrerit orbis,
audiit et si quem tellus extrema refuso[10]   225
summovet[11] Oceano et si quem extenta plagarum
quattuor in medio dirimit plaga solis iniqui.
Diluvio[12] ex illo tot vasta per aequora vecti
dis sedem exiguam patriis litusque rogamus

---

1 209f. 'So it was from here that he set out, from the Etruscan home of Corythus, and now the golden palace of the starry sky welcomes him on his throne and he increases with his altars the number of the gods'.

2 209. **Corythi Tyrrhena ab sede**: the town in Etruria was called Corythus (3.170), after its founder, and later Cortona.

3 211. **auget**: much preferable to the reading *addit*, and read by the major MSS. Cf. Livy 1.7.10 (of Hercules) *te mihi mater aucturum caelestium numerum cecinit, tibique aram hic dicatum iri.*

4 213-15. Ilioneus replies to line 199: they have arrived not because of a tempest nor through an error of direction, but deliberately.

5 215. A highly ornate line for 'we did not lose our way': 'nor did constellation or shoreline deceive us in the direction of our journey'. For *regio* cf. Lucr. 2.249, *Aen.* 2.737, 9.385, Livy 21.31.9 *non recta regione iter instituit.* For *sidus* cf. 5.25; constellations and landmarks would be the two chief aids to navigation.

6 216. **hanc ... urbem**: accusative of motion towards, common without a preposition in verse, cf. 436, 8.136.

7 217f. 'from the kingdom which once was the greatest which the Sun looked upon as he came from the edge of the sky'. This means the greatest of all, as the Sun comes from the very edge and sees everything.

8 220. **avo**: 'ancestor', because he was the father of Dardanus, founder of Troy. The next phrase refers to Aeneas, son of Venus the daughter of Jupiter.

9 222f. The construction is *et is quem tellus . . . et is quem plaga . . . audiit quanta tempestas ierit . . .* (indirect question). The diction is very heightened, especially at the end of the sentence.

10 225-6. **refuso summovet Oceano**: 'separates from us where the Ocean rolls', i.e. on the edge of the land, next to encircling Ocean. Lucan (8.797-8) imitates the phrase, speaking of the extent of Pompey's glory: *qua terra extrema refuso / pendet in Oceano.* For *summovet* cf. 8.193. Notice the hiatus after *Oceano;* cf. 178.

11 226f. 'anyone whom the zone of the hostile sun (i.e. the tropics, torrid zone), stretching in the middle of the four zones (i.e. the temperate and arctic zones), sunders from us'; i.e. anyone who lives south of the torrid zone. Servius says 'significat Antipodas'. For the five zones cf. *Geo.* 1.233f., Ov. *Met.* 145f.

12 228. **diluvio ex illo**: 'escaping from that flood'; he takes up again the metaphor of *tempestas* (223).

innocuum[1] et cunctis[2] undamque auramque patentem.   230
Non erimus regno indecores, nec vestra feretur[3]
fama levis tantique[4] abolescet gratia facti,
nec Troiam Ausonios gremio excepisse pigebit.
Fata[5] per Aeneae iuro dextramque potentem,
sive[6] fide seu quis bello est expertus et armis: 235
multi nos populi, multae (ne temne, quod ultro
praeferimus manibus vittas ac verba precantia[7])
et petiere sibi et voluere adiungere gentes;
sed[8] nos fata deum vestras exquirere[9] terras
imperiis egere suis. Hinc[10] Dardanus ortus,   240
huc[11] repetit iussisque ingentibus urget Apollo
Tyrrhenum[12] ad Thybrim et fontis vada sacra Numici.
[13]Dat tibi praeterea fortunae parva prioris
munera, reliquias Troia ex ardente receptas.
Hoc pater[14] Anchises auro libabat ad aras,   245
hoc Priami gestamen[15] erat cum iura vocatis
more daret populis, sceptrumque sacerque tiaras[16]
[17]Iliadumque labor vestes'.

---

1 230. **innocuum:** 'harmless', which will not threaten anyone. Ilioneus puts what seems a very modest request: 'pia et verecunda petitio', says Servius.

2 **cunctis . . . patentem:** 'the water and air which are free for all', the 'general' air. 'Ista enim communia sunt', is Servius' comment.

3 231. **feretur:** 'be spoken of as . . .'.

4 232. **tantique:** = *neque tanti.* Not surprisingly one of the major MSS has *tantive,* which may well be right.

5 234. **fata per Aeneae:** for the position of the preposition cf. 9.643 and see note on 4.257.

6 235. Aeneas' right hand is mighty alike in peace or in war.

7 237. **precantia:** the last two vowels coalesce by synizesis, or consonantal *i*; cf. 33 and 175, and see note on 6.33.

8 239-40. A striking reminiscence of Aeneas' words to the ghost of Dido, 6.461-3 *sed me iussa deum . . . imperiis egere suis.*

9 **exquirere . . . egere:** for the infinitive of purpose cf. 393, and see note on 1.527-8.

10 240. **hinc Dardanus ortus:** the same words in 3.167, in Apollo's message conveyed to Aeneas by the Penates.

11 241. **huc repetit:** Dardanus is formally the subject; he is returning in the person of his descendants. *Huc* is used to supply the place of the expected object with *repetit,* influenced by the parallelism with *hinc.* Page's note is conclusive against those who wish to make Apollo the subject.

12 242. **Tyrrhenum ad Thybrim:** cf. *Geo.* 1.499 *Tuscum Tiberim.*

13 243f. The chivalrous speech ends with the heroic custom of the offering of gifts, modestly depreciated (*parva, fortunae prioris, reliquias*). Cf. 1.647f. *munera praeterea Iliacis erepta ruinis / ferre iubet.* For the scansion of *reliquias* cf. 172 and 8.356.

14 245. The reference is to a sacrificial goblet: cf. *Geo.* 2.192 *pateris libamus et auro.*

15 246. **gestamen:** 'accoutrement', cf. 3.286. Servius says that the meaning here is 'diadem', but it seems much more likely that *gestamen* refers to the sceptre, tiara, and robes.

16 247. **tiaras:** another form of the nominative of *tiara,* a turban.

17 248. The half-line (see note on 129) confirms the feeling that the last part of Ilioneus' speech lacked the *ultima manus* of revision.

249-85. Latinus realises that Aeneas is the stranger destined by the portents to become the husband of Lavinia, and after a joyful speech accepting the Trojan requests and offering them alliance, he sends princely gifts.

[1]Talibus Ilionei[2] dictis defixa[3] Latinus
obtutu tenet ora soloque immobilis haeret,   250
intentos volvens oculos. Nec purpura[4] regem
picta movet nec sceptra movent Priameia tantum
quantum in conubio natae thalamoque moratur,[5]
et veteris Fauni volvit sub pectore sortem:[6]
hunc illum[7] fatis externa ab sede profectum   255
portendi generum paribusque in regna vocari
auspiciis, huic progeniem virtute futuram
egregiam et totum quae viribus occupet orbem.
Tandem[8] laetus ait: 'di nostra[9] incepta secundent
auguriumque[10] suum! [11]Dabitur, Troiane, quod optas.   260
Munera nec sperno: non vobis rege Latino
divitis uber[12] agri Troiaeve opulentia deerit.[13]
Ipse modo Aeneas, nostri si tanta cupido est,
si iungi hospitio properat sociusque vocari,
adveniat, vultus[14] neve exhorrescat amicos: 265
pars[15] mihi pacis erit dextram tetigisse tyranni.

---

1 249f. This passage closes the first section of the book in a mood of optimism and rejoicing. It is true that there have been undertones of foreboding (see K. J. Reckford, *A.J.Ph.*, 1961, pp. 252f.), but they have not been allowed yet to come to the surface. No more complete picture of friendship and welcome could have been built up; it is indeed painted in the bright colours of radiant light, as opposed to the sombre darkness and gloom soon to descend with the intervention of Juno (286).

2 249. **Ilionei:** the last two vowels coalesce by synizesis, cf. 33 and 1.120.

3 249f. 'kept his gaze turned downwards and stared unmoving at the ground, shifting his eyes as he concentrated'; i.e. he does not look up, but his eyes move about as he listens. Cf. 12.939 for *volvens oculos,* where Aeneas pauses, deciding whether to spare Turnus.

4 251f. i.e. the gifts (*purpura* 248, *sceptra* 247) do not move him as much as his thoughts of Lavinia's marriage and the oracular response.

5 253. **moratur**: 'is absorbed', cf. 9.439 *in solo Volcente moratur.*

6 254. **sortem:** the oracular response of 96f.

7 255f. 'this was the man foretold by the fates as his daughter's husband, coming from a foreign home, called to share his rule with equal power'.

8 259. Notice the slow deliberate start to the line with the single spondaic word *tandem* filling the first foot.

9 **nostra incepta secundent**: 'prosper our plans', as he is about to outline them. Cf. 3.36 *rite secundarent visus.*

10 260. **auguriumque suum:** the portent of the bees, now fulfilled by the arrival of the Trojans.

11 260f. Latinus' reply is as generous as Dido's was in *Aen.* 1.569f.

12 262. **uber:** 'fruitfulness', a neuter noun frequently applied to the earth in the *Georgics.* Servius glosses it as 'ubertas'.

13 **deerit:** pronounced and sometimes spelled *derit;* cf. *Geo.* 2.200.

14 265. **vultus neve:** *neve* is postponed, cf. *munera nec sperno* above.

15 266. A strange line of compulsive alliteration; it sounds like a formulaic phrase. Servius and Donatus point out that *tyranni* is here used in the Greek sense without hostile overtones, as in line 342 where it is applied to Latinus himself.

Vos contra regi mea nunc mandata referte.
Est mihi nata, viro gentis quam iungere nostrae
non patrio ex adyto sortes, non plurima caelo
monstra[1] sinunt; generos[2] externis adfore ab oris,   270
hoc Latio restare canunt, qui[3] sanguine nostrum
nomen in astra ferant. Hunc[4] illum poscere fata
et reor et, si quid veri mens augurat, opto.'
Haec effatus equos numero pater eligit omni
(stabant ter centum nitidi in praesepibus altis):   275
omnibus extemplo Teucris iubet ordine duci
instratos ostro[5] alipedes[6] pictisque tapetis
(aurea pectoribus demissa monilia pendent,
tecti[7] auro fulvum mandunt sub dentibus aurum),
absenti Aeneae currum geminosque iugalis[8]   280
semine ab aetherio spirantis[9] naribus ignem,
illorum[10] de gente patri quos daedala[11] Circe
supposita de matre nothos furata creavit.
Talibus Aeneadae donis dictisque Latini
sublimes in equis redeunt pacemque reportant.   285

---

1 270. **monstra**: e.g. the swarm of bees (64f.), the flames that played round Lavinia as she sacrificed (71f.).

2 270f. 'the arrival of men from foreign lands to marry our daughters, this is what they prophesy awaits Latium'. The accusative and infinitive *generos adfore*, acting as a noun subject to *restare*, is picked up again by the neuter pronoun *hoc*; cf. 2.79.

3 271-2. **qui . . . ferant**: a quotation from the oracle's words of 98-9.

4 272. **hunc illum**: as in 255.

5 277. **ostro . . . pictisque tapetis**: 'embroidered purple horse-cloths' (housings); cf. Hom. *Il.* 24.230. *Tapetis* is here second declension; sometimes it is third (9.325), sometimes Greek (9.358).

6 **alipedes**: 'wing-footed' steeds, a rare and poetic word, suitable for the ornate and heightened style which Virgil here employs for the description of the splendid and sumptuous gifts; cf. 12.484 and note on 3.544.

7 279. **tecti auro**: 'caparisoned in gold' (i.e. with golden embroidery on the purple in addition to the golden trappings and bits). Cf. Dido's horse in 4.134 *ostroque insignis et auro*.

8 280. **iugalis**: 'chariot-horses', here used as a noun.

9 281. **spirantis naribus ignem**: cf. Lucr. 5.29, *Geo.* 2.140. F has *flagrantis* (which is adopted by Sabbadini and Durand), but there is no evidence at all for such a transitive usage.

10 282. The Sun-god had immortal horses, and Circe his daughter was able to mate a mortal mare (*mater*) with one of them, stealing the immortal strain from her father's stock (*patri . . . furata*: cf. *Aen.* 5.845 *fessosque oculos furare labori*). Hence arose a breed of mixed stock (*nothos*), two of which Latinus now presents. The story is like that in Hom. *Il.* 5.268f, in which Anchises stole from the stock (της γενεης εκλεψε) of Laomedon: λαθρη Λαομεδοντος υποσχων (cf. *supposita*) θηλεας ιππους.

11 **daedala**: here 'cunning'; as an enchantress she knew how to achieve her aims. Servius, rightly, gives *ingeniosa*; Ennius uses the word of Minerva, goddess of skills. The word (cf. the Greek δαιδαλεος) is of course connected with the mythical figure of Daedalus, the inventor (of the labyrinth, of wings); it is used several times by Lucretius in richly evocative phrases, *daedala tellus, naturaque daedala rerum, verborum daedala lingua*. Virgil has it also in *Geo.* 4.179 *daedala fingere tecta* (of the bees). Cf. Spenser (*F.Q.* 3 Prol. 2)

'All were it Zeuxis or Praxiteles —

His daedale hand would faile and greatly faynte.'

and Warton: 'Here ancient art her daedal fancies play'd.'

286-322. Juno observes the Trojans landing, and breaks out into an angry speech, culminating in her decision to arouse the powers of Hades on her side and exact a toll of bloodshed before the fated alliance takes place.

[1]Ecce autem Inachiis[2] sese referebat ab Argis

saeva Iovis coniunx aurasque[3] invecta tenebat,

et[4] laetum Aenean classemque ex aethere longe[5]

Dardaniam Siculo prospexit ab[6] usque Pachyno.[7]

Moliri iam tecta videt,[8] iam[9] fidere terrae,   290

deseruisse rates: stetit acri[10] fixa dolore.

Tum quassans[11] caput haec effundit pectore dicta:

[12]'heu stirpem invisam et fatis[13] contraria nostris

fata Phrygum! [14]Num Sigeis occumbere campis,

num capti potuere capi? Num incensa cremavit   295

---

1 286f. The change of mood from the optimism of the previous part of the book takes place violently and suddenly, rather as the happy finale of the games in Book 5 yields rapidly (604f.) to the plans of Juno resulting in the burning of the fleet. The whole situation is very closely parallel to the scene at the beginning of the poem (1.34f.): see Heinze pp. 182f., Pöschl pp. 24f., Otis pp. 320f. There are the same key words: there the Trojans were sailing joyfully onwards, *vela dabant laeti,* here Juno sees *laetum Aenean.* She is motivated here as there by angry resentment (*Aen.* 1.9 *quidve dolens regina deum,* 1.25 *saevique dolores;* cf. line 287 *saeva Iovis coniunx,* 291 *stetii acri fixa dolore*). Her speech is reminiscent in form and tone of the previous one — bitter rhetorical questions, sarcastic references to the fates, anger and resentment at the slight to her divinity (1.48, 7.297-8). In both speeches she refers to lesser deities who had their revenge on their enemies, Athena on Ajax in Book 1, Mars on the Lapiths and Diana on Calydon here. Yet she, the queen of heaven, is denied her vengeance: *ast ego, quae divum incedo regina Iovisque / et soror et coniunx . . .* (1.46-7); *ast ego, magna Iovis coniunx . . .* (7.308).

But these threats and complaints, so similar in their themes to those which she had used earlier, are expressed here more fully and more bitterly; and her plan this time is more terrible. Previously she had gone to Aeolus and urged him to create a storm; this time she turns to the powers of Hades. She recognizes that she cannot prevent the destined marriage, but she will encompass its fulfilment with bloodshed and disaster. The speech is rhetorical, forceful, laden with doom, comparable in some ways with Dido's final curse.

2 286. Juno has been visiting Argos, one of the seats of her special worship (*Aen.* 1.24), and is now returning to Carthage. For *Inachiis* cf. 372, 792.

3 287. 'in her chariot was journeying through the air': cf. 12.77.

4 288. **et:** here with the sense of inverted *cum;* cf. 5.858.

5 **longe:** so *FR,* against *M's longo* for which Sabbadini compares *Geo.* 3.223. But the sense of *longe* is required, and cf. 11.909; also it represents τηλοθεν, Hom. *Od.* 5.283, a passage which Virgil has in mind here.

6 289. **ab usque:** 'all the way from', cf. 11.262.

7 **Pachyno:** the S.E. promontory of Sicily, cf. 3.429.

8 290. The subject to the infinitives is *Troianos,* easily inferred from 288.

9 **iam fidere terrae**: in their many previous landfalls they had never had the same certainty that they had found the right place.

10 291. Notice the emphatic rhythm with the spondaic word *acri* filling the fourth foot; cf. 3.9, 5.116 with my notes (OUP Ed.), and Conway on *Aen.* 1.26.

11 292. **quassans caput:** very pictorial, cf. 12.894 of Turnus. Juno throughout the poem is presented in the most powerfully visual way, as a majestic and terrifying queen.

12 293. Juno's speech in 1.37f. also begins with accusative of exclamation and rhetorical questions; for similarities between the two speeches see note on 286f.

13 293-4. **fatis . . . Phrygum**: cf. Venus' words in 1.239 *fatis contraria fata rependens.*

14 294-5. 'So they couldn't fall dead on the Sigean plains? They couldn't, when captured, stay captured?' Sigeum (2.312) was a promontory near Troy. Virgil has closely followed and converted into irony the phraseology and rhetoric of Ennius (*Ann.* 358-9) *quae neque Dardaniis campis potuere perire / nec cum capta capi nec cum combusta cremari.* Cf. Hor. *Odes* 4.4.49f. (Hannibal's comments on the indestructibility of the Romans), esp. 65 *merses profundo, pulchrior evenit.*

Troia viros? ¹Medias acies mediosque per ignis
invenere viam. ²At, credo, mea numina tandem
fessa iacent, ³odiis aut exsaturata quievi.
quin etiam patria excussos infesta per undas
ausa⁴ sequi et profugis toto me opponere ponto.   300
Absumptae in Teucros vires caelique marisque.
⁵Quid Syrtes aut Scylla mihi, quid vasta Charybdis
profuit ? Optato conduntur Thybridis alveo⁶
securi⁷ pelagi atque mei. ⁸Mars perdere gentem⁹
immanem Lapithum¹⁰ valuit, concessit in iras   305
ipse deum antiquam genitor Calydona Dianae,
quod scelus aut Lapithis¹¹ tantum aut Calydone merente?
Ast ego, ¹²magna Iovis coniunx, nil¹³ linquere inausum
quae potui infelix, quae memet in omnia verti,
vincor ab Aenea. Quod si mea numina non sunt   310
magna satis, dubitem¹⁴ haud equidem implorare quod¹⁵ usquam est:
flectere si nequeo superos, ¹⁶Acheronta movebo.

---

1 296. For the preposition with the second of two nouns which it governs cf. 5.512.

2 297f This is heavily ironical: 'poor Juno'. she says, 'at long last your power is broken, or perhaps you've just given in'.

3 298. Cf. 5.781f. where Venus speaks of the insatiable and unresting hatred and opposition of Juno

4 300. **ausa sequi:** 'I brought myself to pursue them'; cf. 308 *nil linquere inausum* and 8.364. She means that she would have expected to achieve her will without so much trouble, let alone failing to achieve it altogether. For the omission of *sum* (not very common) cf. 2.792, 5.414.

5 302. The line is based on Catullus 64.156. Syrtes refers to the storm off Africa in *Aeneid* 1 (1.111); Scylla and Charybdis to *Aen.* 3.554f.

6 303. **alveo:** a spondee by synizesis, cf. line 33.

7 304. For the genitive with *securus* ('unconcerned about') cf. 1.350; it is found in the poets and in post-Augustan prose.

8 304f. For the theme cf. 1.39f., 242f.

9 304-5. Servius tells the story that Mars was not invited to the wedding feast of Pirithous, King of the Lapiths, at which the neighbouring people, the Centaurs, were present. In vengeance he caused them to fight each other. The more normal version is that Bacchus caused them to fight (*Geo.* 2.455f.). Scenes from the battle are depicted on the frieze of the Parthenon.

10 305-6. Notice the interwoven order: 'the father of the gods himself gave over the ancient town of Calydon to Diana's anger'. Again Servius gives the story: Oeneus King of Calydon omitted Diana from his sacrifices to the gods, in anger at which she sent a wild boar to ravage the land. It was finally killed by Meleager. The story is told in Hom. *Il.* 9.533f. and Ov. *Met.* 8.270f.

11 307. 'and what was the so very great crime for which the Lapiths or Calydon deserved punishment?' The ablative absolutes are preferable to the accusatives read by some MSS and some editors. Servius is correct when he says that the accusative would be ungrammatical. For *scelus merere* (a condensed phrase) cf. 2.229 *scelus expendisse* with Austin's note.

12 308. Cf. *Aen.* 1.46f. *ast ego quae divum incedo regina Iovisque / et soror et coniunx.*

13 308-9. **nil . . . potui:** 'who could not leave anything untried', i.e. everything she tried went wrong, and she had to keep trying something else. For *memet in omnia verti* cf. Cat. 75.4 *omnia si facias;* for the emphatic form *memet (me)* cf. *Aen.* 4.606.

14 311. Notice how the attention is compelled by the three elisions, *-em, -em, -am,* and the unusual caesurae.

15 **quod usquam est:** 'anything anywhere', an unusual use of *usquam,* cf. Ov. *Met.* 12.41.

16 312. A line of chilling simplicity and finality, aided in emphasis by the all-dactylic rhythm, and the chiastic order. *Acheronta* (Greek accusative of the river Acheron) is used to refer to the whole underworld; cf. 91, 569 and 5.99.

Non dabitur regnis, esto,[1] prohibere[2] Latinis,
atque immota manet fatis Lavinia[3] coniunx:
at trahere atque moras tantis licet[4] addere rebus,   315
at licet amborum populos exscindere regum.
[5]Hac gener atque socer coeant mercede suorum:
sanguine Troiano et Rutulo dotabere, virgo,
et Bellona[6] manet te pronuba. Nec face tantum
Cisseis praegnas ignis enixa iugalis;   320
quin idem Veneri partus suus et Paris alter,
funestaeque iterum recidiva in Pergama taedae.'

---

1 313. **esto:** 'let it be so', 'I accept it', see note on 10.67.

2 **prohibere:** the hated Trojans, object of *prohibere,* are not mentioned.

3 314. An unexpected turn of phrase: *Lavinia coniunx* is equivalent to 'Aeneas' marriage to Lavinia', so that *immota,* while grammatically agreeing with *Lavinia,* means that the marriage remained an unshakeable fact. Cf. *Aen.* 1.257.

4 315f. Fine rhetoric, with the repetition of *at* and of *licet,* and the staccato haste of *trahere.* For the concept that the fates can be hindered (though not changed) see note on 10.96f. In a way the essence of the conflict in the *Aeneid* between destiny on the one hand and the freewill of individuals for or against destiny on the other is that opposition or faint heartedness may cause the fated outcome to turn sour, to have been hardly worth it. The destiny of Aeneas is to found a great Empire, and this must happen; but the nature of the Empire will depend on what Aeneas and all other Romans have put into it, and on how far opponents can be successfully placated. That is why constant emphasis is put on the need to placate Juno (see especially 3.435f., 8.60f.), and why it is essential that the poem shall end, as it does, with her reconciliation.

5 317-19. Fine lines again: 'At this cost to their peoples let father and son-in-law make their alliance: your dowry, maiden, will be Trojan and Rutulian blood, and Bellona is waiting for you to conduct your marriage-ceremony.' Bellona (8.703) was sister of Mars; *pronuba* is the woman in charge of the marriage ceremony for the bride (*Aen.* 4.166, Cat. 61.179, Lucan 8.90 *bis nocui mundo, me pronuba ducit Erinys*).

6 319f. 'And the daughter of Cisseus was not the only woman who conceived a torch and brought forth fire to be a bridegroom: no, Venus' offspring will be just the same, a second Paris, and there are torches of death once more to consume reborn Troy.' Hecuba (daughter of Cisseus according to Euripides and the Roman writers; Homer makes her daughter of Dymas) dreamed that she was pregnant with a burning torch before giving birth to Paris (Enn. *Scen.* 35f., Cic. *Div.* 1.42); cf. 10.704f. The parallel between Aeneas and Paris in respect of Lavinia and Helen is made again by Amata (lines 363f). There is a double meaning in the torch imagery: the destructive fire of war and the marriage torches which in both cases cause war.

*323-405. Juno summons up Allecto to sow the seeds of war.
'The fiend hurls one of her snakes at Queen Amata. Amata,
after appealing in vain to Latinus not to give his daughter in
marriage to Aeneas, becomes frenzied, and pretending to be
filled by Bacchic inspiration she causes the women of the
city to follow her.*

[1]Haec ubi dicta dedit, terras horrenda petivit;

luctificam[2] Allecto dirarum ab sede dearum[3]

infernisque ciet tenebris, cui tristia bella   325

iraeque[4] insidiaeque et crimina noxia cordi.

Odit et ipse pater Pluton, odere sorores

Tartareae monstrum: tot sese vertit in ora,

tam saevae facies, [5]tot pullulat atra colubris.

Quam Iuno his acuit verbis ac talia fatur: 330

'hunc[6] mihi da proprium, virgo sata Nocte, laborem,

Hanc operam, ne[7] noster honos infractave cedat

fama loco, neu conubiis ambire[8] Latinum

Aeneadae possint Italosve obsidere[9] finis.

Tu potes unanimos armare in proelia fratres   335

---

1 323f. This is a passage of violence and daemonic terror as the imminent outbreak of hatred and bloodshed is portrayed in mythological terms. Juno's intention is to destroy the serenity of peace (*disice compositam pacem*), and the immediacy of the impact on us is due to Virgil's own experiences during the civil wars in Italy (*Ecl.* 1.71-2, *Geo.* 1.506-8). The fury and frenzy in human hearts, let loose by the powers of Hades, give Juno a more deadly weapon than the winds and waters of angry Nature. Allecto symbolises *furor*, the evil and uncontrolled quality which can dominate and consume a human personality. She does not create the passions which are let loose; the causation is not imposed externally, but arises from the perversion of existing human qualities. Psychologically both Amata and Turnus are, in their moods of anger and resentment, persons upon whom *furor* can work. On this see Otis, pp. 323f., Pöschl, pp. 28f.

In giving a shape to his personification of *furor*, in drawing the picture of Allecto, Virgil perhaps remembered Hesiod's Eris (Strife) (*Theog.* 225f.), and certainly was influenced by Ennius' Discordia (*Ann.* 266-7) *postquam Discordia taetra / Belli ferratos postes portasque refregit;* but above all she is the Greek Fury, the Erinys (447, 570), one of the *dirae deae* whose sisters are Tisiphone (6.555) and Megaera (12.846). Cf. *Aen.* 6.280-1 for Discordia and the Furies together in the list of grim shapes at the entrance to the underworld. It is very significant that neither Amata nor Turnus falls immediate victim to Allecto. The onset of *furor* is a gradual process as the qualities in a person which can oppose it are only slowly overcome. Amata uses gentle arguments at first (357); but when Latinus is unmoved, she yields to frenzy. The imagery reminds us of another of Juno's victims, Dido; Dido (4.301f.) is compared with a Bacchanal, but Amata actually pretends to become one. She allows herself to become the plaything of Allecto, and in one of Virgil's most memorable similes is compared with a top whipped on its whirling course by boys at play.

2 324. **luctificam Allecto:** for Allecto see previous note. The noun here is in the Greek accusative, cf. Hor. *Odes* 2.13.25 (*Sappho*).

3 **dirarum ... dearum:** observe the strong assonance in this phrase for the Furies.

4 326 Notice how the attention is compelled to the list of Allecto's pleasures by the relatively unusual rhythm with four of the words exactly fitting a metrical foot. For *cordi* cf. 9.615.

5 329. For the snakes of a Fury's head cf. Cat. 64.193f. and *Aen.* 6.280-1 *ferreique Eumenidum thalami et Discordia demens / vipereum crinem vittis innexa cruentis. Pullulat* (a term for plants shooting, *Geo.* 2.17) pictures the snakes growing from her head.

6 331. 'Do me this service', *dare proprium* is to give outright as opposed to *dare muluum* (to lend).

7 332-3. Notice the interwoven order: *ne noster honos famave infracta cedat loco.* The phraseology is military; cf. (for *infracta*) *Aen.* 5.784, 12.1, and for *loco cedere* 9.220.

8 333. **ambire:** 'cajole', cf. 4.283.

9 334. **obsidere**: 'settle in', 'occupy', cf. 9.159.

atque odiis versare[1] domos, tu[2] verbera tectis
funereasque inferre faces, tibi nomina[3] mille,
mille nocendi artes. Fecundum[4] concute pectus,
disice compositam pacem, sere crimina belli;
arma velit poscatque simul rapiatque iuventus.'   340
    Exim Gorgoneis[5] Allecto infecta venenis
principio Latium et Laurentis tecta tyranni
celsa petit, tacitumque[6] obsedit limen Amatae,
quam super[7] adventu Teucrum Turnique hymenaeis
femineae ardentem curaeque[8] iraeque coquebant.   345
Huic[9] dea caeruleis unum de crinibus anguem
conicit, inque sinum praecordia ad intima subdit,
quo[10] furibunda domum monstro permisceat[11] omnem.
Ille[12] inter vestis et levia pectora lapsus
volvitur attactu[13] nullo, fallitque furentem   350
vipeream[14] inspirans animam; fit tortile[15] collo
aurum ingens coluber, fit longae taenia vittae
innectitque comas et membris lubricus errat.

---

1 336. **versare:** for *evertere,* cf. Ov. *Am.* 2.2.29, and cf. *vertisse* in 407.

2 336-7. **tu ... faces:** 'you can bring scourges and deadly flames upon houses': *tectis* takes here something of the family meaning of the word *domos* which preceded it. *Verbera* and *faces* are attributes of the Fury, symbolising the madness and frenzy which she brings. Cf. lines 378, 451 and 456.

3 337. **nomina mille:** the Greek πολυώνυμος, e.g. Soph. *Ant.* 1115.

4 338. **fecundum concute pectus:** the metaphor is from shaking out in order to reveal what is hidden, cf. Hor. *Sat.* 1.3.34-35 *te ipsum concute.* In *Aen.* 11.451-2 *concussaque vulgi pectora* the meaning is 'shaken'; cf. also 5.147.

5 341. **Gorgoneis . . . venenis:** i.e. the poisonous snakes of her hair are like those of the Gorgon (cf. 6.289).

6 343. **tacitumque:** probably Servius is right in taking this as equivalent to *tacite.* The threshold of Amata's room is silent because the Fury's onset is silent; it is not a violent attack, but a secret stealthy incursion. There are other shades of meaning too, the silence of Amata's secret thoughts in the solitude of her room, the silence of the calm before storm.

7 344. For *super = propter* ('at'), quite common in Virgil, cf. 358.

8 345. The doubled -*que* here (added to the *c*'s and *q*'s in *curae* and *coquebant*) gives a startlingly harsh alliteration, reinforcing the metaphor of *ardentem . . . coquebant.* Cf. Enn. *Ann.* 336 (*cura*) *quae nunc te coquit et versat in pectore fixa.*

9 346f. This macabre picture is vivid indeed, and daemonic like the Fury in the shape of a bird that flutters in front of Turnus (12.861f.).

10 348. **quo furibunda . . . monstro:** 'so that, frenzied by this devilish thing . . .'; for *monstrum* cf. 376.

11 **permisceat:** 'bring to confusion'. *Miscere* in this meaning is a favourite Virgilian word; cf. 2.298, 10.721, 12.445.

12 349. For the sound of the line cf. the snake in 5.91 *tandem inter pateras et levia pocula serpens.*

13 350-1. 'slips unfelt, is not noticed by the frenzied queen as it breathes its snaky breath into her'. *Attactus* is an infrequent word, used in Ov. *Met.* 14.414 for the touch of Circe's wand. *Fallit* is like the Greek λανθάνειν, 'deceive' in the sense of not being noticed; cf. 12.634. *Furentem* is proleptic, as in 1.659f. *donisque furentem incendat reginam.* Mackail's 'insensibly maddens her' renders the sense. For the phraseology cf. Venus' instructions to the disguised Cupid to breathe love into Dido, 1.688 *occultum inspires ignem fallasque veneno.* The passage is imitated by Ovid, *Met.* 4.490f.

14 351f. The snake enters into her necklace or her ribbons (both snake like in appearance), or without shape glides over her. Ovid splendidly has (*Met.* 4.498-9) *inspirantque graves animos, nec vulnera membris / ulla ferunt, mens est quae diros sentiat ictus.*

15 351-2. **tortile ... aurum:** a golden necklace, literally 'twisted gold'. *Ingens coluber* is the subject; the snake is of variable size, but when it transforms itself into her necklace, it becomes huge like the regal necklace.

Ac[1] dum prima lues udo sublapsa veneno
pertemptat sensus atque ossibus implicat ignem   355
necdum animus toto percepit pectore flammam,
mollius et solito matrum de more locuta est,
multa super nata[2] lacrimans Phrygiisque hymenaeis:
'exsulibusne[3] datur ducenda Lavinia[4] Teucris,
o genitor,[5] nec te miseret nataeque tuique?   360
Nec matris miseret, quam primo[6] aquilone relinquet
perfidus[7] alta petens abducta virgine praedo?[8]
An non[9] sic Phrygius penetrat Lacedaemona pastor,
Ledaeamque Helenam Troianas vexit ad urbes?
Quid[10] tua sancta fides? Quid cura antiqua tuorum   365
et consanguineo[11] totiens data dextera Turno?
Si gener externa petitur de gente Latinis,
idque sedet, Faunique premunt te iussa parentis,
omnem[12] equidem sceptris terram quae libera nostris
dissidet[13] externam reor et sic dicere divos.   370
Et Turno, si prima domus repetatur origo,

---

1 354f. 'And while the plague in its early stages, stealing upon her with its moist poison, was assailing her senses and planting fire in her bones, and while her mind had not yet received the flames deep down in her heart, she spoke more gently . . .'. For the general sense cf. Cat. 64.92f., and *Aen.* 1.660. *Percepit* (*M*) is perhaps preferable to *concepit* (*R*); cf. Ov. *Met.* 14.700. *Locuta est* (*R*) is better than *locuta* (*M*); the main verb is necessary to make the emphasis.

2 358. **nata:** so *R*; *M* has *natae* which is far inferior in force. Amata is weeping for her daughter and her marriage.

3 **exulibusne:** notice the emphasis on the first word, put into the plural to generalise and convey contempt.

4 359. **Lavinia:** the scansion of the first vowel varies, contrast 72, 314; see note on 1.258.

5 360. **o genitor:** she calls Latinus by his relationship to Lavinia.

6 361. **primo aquilone:** 'as soon as the north wind blows', to take him back southwards, the way he had come, and to give him fair weather (cf. 5.2).

7 362. **perfidus:** the word in this context strongly reminds us of Dido's speech to Aeneas, *Aen.* 4.366.

8 **praedo:** 'pirate', applied twice again to Aeneas, in 10.774 by Mezentius and in 11.484 by the Latin women in their prayer to Athena.

9 363f. For the parallel between Aeneas and Paris see note on 319f. Paris is called *pastor* in Hor. *Odes* 1.15.1. Both *at non* (*R*) and *an non* (*M*) were known to Servius who preferred the former. But *an non* seems a better link with the previous lines, as well as being more vivid. In any case the sentence must be punctuated as a question. *Lacedaemona* is Greek accusative; Helen and her husband Menelaus lived in Sparta. *Ledaeamque* refers to the legend that Helen (like the twins Castor and Pollux) was a child of Leda by Jupiter in the guise of a swan (cf. *Aen.* 1.652).

10 365. For *quid* (= 'what about?') cf. 10.672.

11 366. **consanguineo:** Servius explains that Turnus' mother, Venilia was Amata's sister.

12 369f. 'then I myself think that all the world which is free and stands outside our authority is foreign, and that is what the gods are saying.' She means that Turnus is not a Latin, and therefore is foreign: anyway, she adds in the next lines, he has connexions of a more distant kind.

13 370. **dissidet:** in its original meaning, as here (= *distat*), the word is uncommon; cf. Prop. 1.12.4.

Inachus[1] Acrisiusque patres mediaeque[2] Mycenae.'
   His[3] ubi nequiquam dictis experta Latinum
contra stare videt, penitusque in viscera lapsum
serpentis furiale malum totamque pererrat,   375
tum vero infelix[4] ingentibus excita monstris[5]
immensam[6] sine more[7] furit lymphata[8] per urbem.
[9]Ceu quondam torto[10] volitans sub verbere turbo,
quem pueri magno in gyro vacua atria circum
intenti ludo exercent — ille actus habena   380
curvatis fertur spatiis; stupet inscia[11] supra
impubesque manus mirata volubile buxum;[12]
dant animos plagae: non cursu segnior illo
per medias urbes agitur populosque ferocis.

---

1 372. **Inachus Acrisiusque patres:** Servius gives the story that Danae, daughter of Acrisius (a king of Argos of which Inachus was the legendary founder), came to Italy and founded the city of Ardea, Turnus' capital; see 410. She was also said to have married Pilumnus, Turnus' ancestor.

2 **mediaeque Mycenae**: rather loosely attached to the sentence, for the sake of the emphatic proper name. *Mediaeque* means 'the heart of Mycenae'; cf. 9.738, and Juv. 3.80 *mediis sed natus Athenis*. There may be an echo of Homer's μεϲον Αργοϲ. Mycenae was said to have been founded by Perseus, Danae's son.

3 373f. Observe the long subordination of this sentence (*ubi . . . experta . . . videt penitusque . . . lapsum est . . . malum totamque pererrat*) concluded with emphasis by *tum vero;* thus strong stress is given to the eventual main verb *furit,* a key word both here (cf. *furiale* 375; *furorem* 386; *furiis* 392, *furores* 406; *furialia* 415) and in the poem generally.

4 376. **infelix**: the word reminds us, as so much in this passage does, of another victim of *furor,* Dido: cf. *Aen.* 1.749 and especially 4.68-9 *uritur infelix Dido totaque vagatur / urbe furens* and 4.450 *tum vero infelix fatis exterrita Dido . . .*

5 **monstris**: 'monstrous fantasies', with special reference to Allecto who inspired them (328, 348); cf. 3.307, 5.659 for the plural.

6 377. **immensam**: the word has caused difficulties, and *immensum* has been conjectured, but the meaning is that Amata, like the top with which she is compared (*magno in gyro,* 379), rushes all over the place; 'through the length and breadth of the city'. The line is reminiscent of the description of Dido in 4.300-1 *saevit inops animi totamque incensa per urbem / bacchatur.*

7 **sine more**: 'without restraint', cf. 5.694, 8.635.

8 **lymphata**: 'distracted', a very strong word, used only here in Virgil. Cf. Cat. 64.254f. *lymphata mente furebant / euhoe bacchantes,* Hor. *Odes* 1.37.14 (of Cleopatra) *mentemque lymphatam Mareotico.*

9 378f. 'Like a top sometimes, spinning under the impact of the whip, which boys intent on their sport send in a wide circle around empty courtyards; the top driven by the lash rushes in a curving course, while the ingenuous young lads look down on it in astonishment, marvelling at the flying boxwood to which the blows give impetus - no less wildly . . .'. This is one of the most memorable similes in Virgil; its point of comparison is not only the wild and agitated movement of Amata, but also the compulsion exercised; she has become the plaything of Allecto. Homer has a simile in which Ajax, striking Hector, spun him round like a top (*Il.* 14.413f.), and Virgil may also have been influenced by Callimachus' description of the boys and their tops (*Epigr.* 1.9f.), but he has applied his source material to a new context. Similes from ordinary human activities, quite common in Homer, are rare in Virgil, and this one is the more striking on that account. It may be that Virgil felt justified in using it, and in dressing it in ornate epic diction, partly because the top was a sacred emblem of Bacchus (as Dionysus the child god; see Hirst, *C.Q.,* 1937, p.65 andGuthrie, *Orpheus and Greek Religion,* pp. 120f.); its religious symbolism thus gave to the vivid and apt image the necessary high dignity. Certainly the association with Bacchus accords with the rest of the passage. There was a ceremony (*Liberalia*) in honour of Bacchus celebrated at Lavinium (Aug. *Civ.* 7.21).

10 378. **torto . . . sub verbere**: this image is especially appropriate in view of 336; the lashes which Allecto brings are here symbolically portrayed. Cf. *Geo.* 3.106 for *verbere torto* (= *flagello*); cf. also *Geo.* 1.309. Notice the patterned alliteration in this line.

11 381. **inscia**: the boys are captivated in their simple excitement; cf. *Geo.* 3.189 (of a young horse) *inscius aevi.* It is interesting that this word and *pererrat* (375) are both used of Dido, though in entirely different contexts (1.718, 4.363); cf. also line 393 and 4.581.

12 382. **buxum**: the top is called 'boxwood'; cf. our 'willow' for a cricket bat.

Quin[1] etiam in silvas simulato[2] numine Bacchi   385
maius adorta nefas maioremque orsa furorem
evolat et natam frondosis montibus abdit,
quo[3] thalamum eripiat Teucris taedasque moretur,
euhoe[4] Bacche fremens,[5] solum te virgine dignum
vociferans: [6]etenim mollis tibi sumere thyrsos,   390
te lustrare choro, sacrum tibi pascere crinem.
Fama volat, furiisque accensas pectore matres
idem omnis simul ardor agit[7] nova quaerere tecta;
deseruere[8] domos, ventis dant colla comasque;
ast[9] aliae tremulis ululatibus aethera complent   395
pampineasque gerunt incinctae pellibus[10] hastas.
Ipsa inter medias flagrantem[11] fervida pinum
sustinet ac natae Turnique canit[12] hymenaeos
sanguineam[13] torquens aciem, torvumque[14] repente
clamat: 'io matres, audite, ubi quaeque, Latinae: 400
si qua piis animis manet infelicis[15] Amatae

---

1 385. Dido is compared (*Aen.* 4.301f.) with a Bacchanal: Amata actually pretends to become one. Virgil has taken some phrases from Euripides' *Bacchae* and from Cat. 64.251f.; cf. also *Ecl.* 5.29f., *Geo.* 2.380f., *Aen.* 6.517f. The attitude of hostility towards Bacchic worship which we find in Virgil is similar to that of Livy's description in 39.13 (esp. *nihil ibi facinoris, nihil flagitii praetermissum*). For a through Bacchic description see Ov. *Met.* 3.511f., 4.1f.

2 **simulato numine Bacchi**: 'pretending that the power of Bacchus was upon her'. Cf. Ov. *Met.* 6.594f. *furiisque agitata doloris / Bacche tuas simulat.* The meaning seems to be that she knows she is frenzied, and pretends that it is Bacchic frenzy.

3 388. **quo . . . Teucris**: 'so that she might deprive the Trojans of their bride'; the metonymy of *thalamum* (= *conubium*, or *Laviniam coniugem*) is in the style which became excessively frequent in the Silver Age.

4 389. **euhoe**: this is the Greek Bacchic cry, from which Virgil has the verb *euhare* in *Aen.* 6.517; cf. Cat. 64.255 *euhoe bacchantes.*

5 389f. The strange mixture of direct and indirect speech seems designed to add to the feeling of uncontrolled emotional frenzy.

6 390f. 'for she is taking up the pliant wands in your honour, circling round you in the dance, growing her hair long as a sacred offering to you'. This is reported speech after *vociferans* with the subject *virginem* understood. The *thyrsus* is the Bacchic wand wreathed with vine and ivy leaves, called *mollis* partly literally ('leafy': cf. Ov. *Met.* 4.7 *frondentes thyrsos* and *Ecl.* 5.31 *et foliis lentas intexere mollibus hastas*), and partly metaphorically as the emblem of the women of Bacchus. *Lustrare,* a favourite word with Virgil, is here used in the sense of dancing round in worship (Bacchus being symbolised by his altar or emblems); cf. 10.224 *agnoscunt longe regem lustrantque choreis.*

7 393. **agit . . . quaerere**: infinitive of purpose, cf. 239-40.

8 394. **deseruere domos**: notice the vivid 'instantaneous' perfect; the picture is of the break-up of family life through irresponsible passion. Anarchy comes to Latinus' kingdom.

9 395. The dactylic line reinforces the wildness of the scene.

10 396. 'wearing skins and carrying stems of the vine'. For the wearing of fawn skins cf. Eur. *Bacch.* 24.

11 397. The burning pine-torch is an element of Bacchic worship, here used also as imagery for the marriage of Turnus and Lavinia.

12 398. **canit**: lengthened in arsis, cf. 174.

13 399. **sanguineam . . . aciem**: like Dido in 4.643, *sanguineam volvens aciem.*

14 **torvumque**: adverbial (cf. 510), 'stridently', i.e. in an unnatural voice.

15 401. **infelicis Amatae**: cf. *Aen.* 5.3 *infelicis Elissae;* this is the last and in some ways the most striking of the reminiscences of Dido in the description of Amata's frenzy.

gratia, si iuris materni cura remordet,[1]
solvite crinalis vittas,[2] capite orgia mecum.'
Talem[3] inter silvas, inter deserta ferarum
reginam Allecto stimulis agit undique Bacchi.　　　　405

> 406-74. *Allecto next goes to Turnus, and changing herself into the shape of an aged priestess, Calybe, urges Turnus to fight for his rights against the Trojans. He replies confidently and contemptuously that he is fully aware of what to do and needs no advice from old women. At this Allecto hurls twin snakes at him and rouses him to a mad desire for war.*

[4]Postquam visa satis primos acuisse furores
consiliumque omnemque domum[5] vertisse Latini,
protinus hinc fuscis tristis dea tollitur alis
audacis[6] Rutuli ad muros, quam dicitur urbem
Acrisionaeis[7] Danae fundasse colonis　　　　410
praecipiti delata Noto. Locus Ardea quondam
dictus avis, et nunc magnum manet Ardea nomen,
sed fortuna[8] fuit. Tectis hic Turnus in altis

---

1 402. 'If any thought of a mother's rights touches you'; for *remordet* cf. 1.261. There is a strong irony in the line, because Amata has abdicated her maternal and family responsibilities.

2 403. 'loosen the fastenings of your hair', i.e. the emblem of matrons; cf. Ov. *Met.* 4.6-7 (a passage closely similar to this) *pectora pelle tegi, crinales solvere vittas, / serta coma, manibus frondentes sumere thyrsos.* For *vittae* cf. Ov. *A.A.* 1.31 *este procul, vittae tenues, insigne pudoris*

3 404f 'Such was the queen in the forests, amidst the haunts of wild creatures, as Allecto from every direction hounded her with Bacchic torments.'

4 406f. This is the first appearance of Turnus in the poem, and the chief traits in his character are clearly defined. He is princely, handsome, and brave (473-4). He clearly has some justification for thinking that he is being wronged over Lavinia; but he is headstrong, impetuous, violent. We see this even before Allecto drives him to frenzy; he mocks her and derides her in youthful arrogance. We are prepared for his *audacia*, his *violentia* in the battles to come, for his boastfulness (470), his love of war and glory (460). He is to be a warrior of the type of the heroic age. He is bold, decisive, strong, skilful; but the allegiance which he owes is primarily to his own honour. He stands for individual prowess in contrast with the social responsibility of Aeneas.
We also see here the first seeds of the events of Book 12 of which Turnus is the tragic hero. His mind is twisted by Allecto, or by his own qualities perverted by events, so that he begins to follow the path which leads to madness and ruin. In a memorable simile his frenzied mind is compared with the seething and bubbling water in a boiling cauldron; the familiar visual image is used to explain what we cannot see, the thoughts and feelings of Turnus. With Amata, the less important of Allecto's victims, the simile of the top illustrates behaviour; with Turnus the simile goes deeper and reveals the mental and emotional attitude in which he will fight the war.
For discussion of the character of Turnus see especially Pöschl pp. 91f., Otis chs. 7 and 8, Putnam ch. 4, W. S. Anderson, *T.A.Ph.A.*, 1957, pp. 17f., S. G. P. Small, *T.A.Ph.A.*, 1959, pp. 243f.,G. E. Duckworth, *T.A.Ph.A.*, 1961, pp. 81f.

5 407. 'and to have overturned the intentions and the whole house of Latinus'; an echo of 335-6 *tu potes . . . odiis versare domos;* for *vertere* cf. 10.88. She has overturned Latinus' house in the sense of having started a family discord which is to lead to great losses.

6 409. **audacis Rutuli**: the adjective *audax* and words like *fiducia, violentia* are often associated in the rest of the poem with Turnus.

7 410. For the foundation of Ardea, the home of Turnus, by Danae, daughter of the Argive king Acrisius see note on 372. According to Servius she was shut up in a chest and thrown into the sea; hence *delata*, 'brought to land'.

8 413. **fortuna fuit**: 'its glory is gone': for *fuit* cf. 2.325-6 *fuimus Troes, fuit Ilium et ingens / gloria Teucrorum.* For Ardea's lost glory cf. Ov. *Met.* 14.573f: the heron (*ardea*) arose from its ashes, a bird characterised by *macies* and *pallor.*

iam mediam nigra carpebat nocte quietem.
Allecto torvam faciem et furialia membra   415
exuit, in vultus sese transformat anilis
et frontem[1] obscenam rugis arat, induit albos
cum vitta crinis,[2] tum ramum innectit olivae:
fit Calybe Iunonis[3] anus templique sacerdos,
et iuveni ante oculos his se cum vocibus offert: 420
'Turne, tot incassum fusos patiere labores,[4]
et tua Dardaniis transcribi[5] sceptra colonis?
Rex tibi coniugium et quaesitas sanguine dotes
abnegat, externusque in regnum quaeritur heres.
I nunc, ingratis offer te,[6] inrise, periclis;   425
Tyrrhenas, i, sterne acies, tege pace Latinos.
Haec adeo tibi me, placida cum nocte iaceres.
Ipsa palam fari omnipotens Saturnia[7] iussit.
Quare[8] age et armari pubem portisque moveri
laetus in arma para, et Phrygios qui flumine pulchro   430
consedere duces pictasque exure carinas.
Caelestum vis magna iubet. Rex ipse Latinus,
ni dare coniugium et dicto parere fatetur,[9]
sentiat[10] et 'andem Turnum experiatur in armis.'
    Hic iuvenis vatem inridens sic orsa[11] vicissim   435
ore refert: 'classis invectas Thybridis undam[12]
non, ut rere, meas effugit nuntius auris;

---

1 417. 'she furrowed her ugly forehead with wrinkles'. Cf. Hor. *Epod.* 8.3-4, and for *obscenus Aen.* 3.241 (of the Harpies).

2 418. The headband and olive branch in the hair are emblems of the priestess; cf. 751.

3 419. 'the aged priestess of Juno's temple', a double hendiadys. There was a cult of Juno at Ardea (Pliny, *Nat. Hist.* 35.115).

4 421. **labores:** here Virgil refers to a form of the legend according to which Turnus was helping the Latins in war against the Etruscans (423, 426): this version conflicts with Latinus' long peace (46).

5 422. **transcribi sceptra:** 'your expectation of rule should be transferred'; Servius says that *transcribi* is a financial metaphor.

6 425-6. Cf. the angry irony of Dido (4.381 i, *sequere Italiam ventis, pete regna per undas).*

7 428. **Saturnia:** a frequent epithet of Juno (cf. 560, 622).

8 429f. 'So into action, and jubilantly prepare the young men for arming themselves and moving out from the gates to arms, and consume in flames the Phrygian leaders who have established themselves by your lovely river, along with their painted ships'. *Iube,* the reading of *M,* seems likely to be an explanation of *para,* here used rather unusually ('get the young men ready for arming and moving', i.e. tell them such instructions will shortly be given). For the repetition of *armari . . . arma* (for which *arva* has been conjectured) see note on 11.173.

9 433. **fatetur:** 'agrees to', an unusual meaning and construction for *fateri;* cf. 12.568.

10 434. 'let him at last know and experience Turnus at war with him'; for *sentire* cf. Val. Fl. 4.745-6 *nos quoque nos Amycum . . . sensimus.*

11 435-6. **orsa . . . ore refert:** 'began to speak', cf. 11.122-3, and *exorsa* in 10. 111.

12 436. **undam:** for the accusative cf. 8.714-15 and see note on 216; it occurs with *invehi* in Livy (e.g. 35.8.9).

ne tantos mihi finge metus. Nec[1] regia Iuno
immemor est nostri.
Sed[2] te victa situ verique effeta senectus,   440
o mater, curis nequiquam exercet, et arma[3]
regum inter falsa vatem formidine ludit.
Cura tibi divum effigies et templa tueri;
bella viri[4] pacemque gerent quis bella gerenda.'
    Talibus Allecto dictis exarsit in iras.   445
At iuveni oranti[5] subitus tremor occupat artus,
deriguere oculi: tot Erinys[6] sibilat hydris
tantaque se facies aperit; tum flammea torquens
lumina cunctantem et quaerentem dicere plura
reppulit, et geminos erexit crinibus anguis,   450
verberaque[7] insonuit rabidoque haec addidit ore:
en[8] ego victa situ, quam veri effeta senectus
arma inter regum falsa formidine ludit.
Respice ad haec: adsum dirarum ab sede sororum,
bella manu letumque gero.'   455
Sic effata facem iuveni coniecit et atro[9]
lumine fumantis fixit sub pectore taedas.
Olli[10] somnum ingens rumpit pavor, ossaque et artus
perfundit toto proruptus corpore sudor.
Arma amens fremit, arma[11] toro[12] tectisque requirit: 460

---

1 438-9. 'Don't dream up all this panic, please! Queen Juno is not without thought for me.' By the latter comment he implies that he does not need an aged messenger to tell him of Juno's intentions for him.

2 440-1. 'But it's your dotage, feeble and decayed, past understanding of reality, madam, that is needlessly worrying you with these anxieties.' For *situs* ('decay') cf. *Aen.* 6.462; for the genitive with *effeta* cf. 10.630-1 *aut ego veri / vana feror. Mater* is a complimentary word, here used, as the context makes abundantly clear, with heavy irony.

3 441-2. **arma regum inter:** a striking postponement of the preposition, cf. 5.370.

4 444. 'Men will look after questions of war and peace, for they have to fight the wars.' Cf. Hom. *Il.* 6.492 πολεμος δ ανδρεςςι μελησει, where the future tense supports the reading *gerent* against *gerant* of M. For *quis* (= *quibus*) cf. 570, 742.

5 446. **oranti:** 'as he spoke'; Servius explains that the word *orator* conveys this meaning of *orare* (cf. Quint. 1.10.2 *orandi scientia* and *Aen.* 10.96) which in Classical times much more commonly means 'entreat'.

6 447f. The Fury resumes her natural shape, and 'reveals herself as so enormous an apparition'. For *Erinys* cf. 570, 2.337.

7 451. **verberaque insonuit:** 'made the sound of lashes'; the intransitive verb (cf. 5.579) is extended in meaning, cf. 12.529f. *sonantem nomina.* See note on lines 11-12.

8 452f. The almost exact repetition (cf. lines 440, 442) is unusual in Virgil, but here it is employed by Allecto for rhetorical emphasis.

9 456-7. **atro lumine:** an oxymoron: 'black light' is appropriate for torches from the underworld; cf. 4.384 *sequar atris ignibus absens.*

10 458. **olli:** archaic form for *illi*, quite frequent in Virgil.

11 460. **arma amens fremit:** cf. 2.314 *arma amens capio*, and for *fremit* used transitively cf. 11.453.

12 **toro:** cf. *Aen.* 6.523 for keeping the sword under the pillow.

¹saevit amor ferri et scelerata insania belli,

ira super: ²magno veluti cum flamma sonore

virgea suggeritur costis³ undantis aëni

exsultantque aestu latices, furit intus aquai⁴

fumidus atque alte spumis exuberat amnis,⁵   465

nec⁶ iam se capit unda, volat vapor ater ad auras.

Ergo iter ad regem polluta⁷ pace Latinum

indicit primis iuvenum et iubet arma parari,

tutari Italiam, detrudere finibus hostem;

se satis ambobus Teucrisque⁸ venire Latinisque.   470

Haec ubi dicta dedit divosque in vota vocavit,

certatim sese Rutuli exhortantur in arma.

Hunc decus egregium formae movet atque iuventae,

hunc atavi reges, hunc claris dextera factis.

> 475-510. *Allecto causes the war to begin by inciting the hunting hounds of Iulus to chase the pet stag of Silvia, sister of the chief herdsman of King Latinus' flocks. Iulus himself unaware that it is a pet, shoots it. The Latin herdsmen gather in anger for revenge.*

⁹Dum Turnus Rutulos animis audacibus implet.   475

---

1 461f. Notice these terms, *saevire, scelerata insania, ira:* the idea of violence and lack of control is powerfully expressed, reinforced by the simile, and summarised in *polluta pace* (467).

2 462f. 'As when a fire of twigs, roaring loudly, is heaped up under the sides of a foaming cauldron, and the water leaps in the heat, and a smoky river rages within and bubbles up in foam, and the water overflows and the dark steam shoots skywards.' The simile is based on a passage from Homer, *Il.* 21.362f., the boiling of the river Xanthus when attacked by the Fire-god; its application to mental agitation owes something to Lucretius (3.294f.). For its significance in portraying the character of Turnus see note on 406f.

3 463. **costis** . . . **aeni:** *costis* is dative, and means the sides of the cauldron, i.e. the fire extends around it. For *aenum* as a noun ('bronze vessel') cf. 1.213.

4 464. **aquai:** archaic genitive, cf. 3.354 with note, 6.747, 9.26. Some MSS have *aquae vis,* but this involves an unVirgilian postponement of *atque* in the next line. Servius says that Varro and Tucca were responsible for *aquai* instead of Virgil's own *aquae amnis,* but his story seems garbled.

5 465. **amnis:** in the high poetic style, for *aqua.*

6 466. **nec iam se capit unda:** literally 'does not contain itself', an extension of phrases like Lucr. 3.298 *nec capere irarum fluctus in pectore possunt;* cf. Ov. *Met.* 1.343. Notice the very short words in this line, reinforcing the idea of activity.

7 467. **polluta pace:** 'now that peace had been violated', cf. 3.61 *pollutum hospitium.* Allecto has introduced the poison which defiled the serene state of peace that existed.

8 470. A fine line indicating Turnus' boastful self-confidence; for the hyper-metric elision cf. 160.

9 475f. This is the last episode in the poem before the fighting begins, and it is one of tenderness and soft emotion, contrasting very sharply with the harsh sequel, the trumpet call of Allecto and the commencement of the war. We are back in the Arcadian world of the *Eclogues* as Virgil describes the affection of Silvia for her pet stag; there is an Alexandrian *mollities* of sentiment (especially lines 487-92, 500-2) presented with more poignancy than Virgil elsewhere permits himself in the *Aeneid.* The basis for this episode may have existed already in the Roman legend (Servius on *Aen.* 4.620 quotes Cato as saying that the battle began when Aeneas' party were hunting); but it is certain that Virgil developed it in his own way. Macrobius (*Sat.* 5.17.1f.) uses this passage as an indication of Virgil's difficulties when he had no Homeric source material; he regards it as *leve nimisque puerile.* But it is part of Virgil's structural art to have juxtaposed his nearest approach to sentimentality with the grim realism of the opening scenes of war.

Allecto in Teucros Stygiis se concitat alis,
arte[1] nova speculata locum, quo litore pulcher
insidiis cursuque feras agitabat Iulus.[2]
Hic subitam canibus rabiem Cocytia[3] virgo
obicit et noto naris contingit odore,   480
ut cervum ardentes agerent; quae prima laborum
causa fuit belloque animos accendit agrestis.
Cervus erat forma praestanti et cornibus ingens,
Tyrrhidae[4] pueri quem matris ab ubere raptum
nutribant Tyrrhusque pater, cui regia parent   485
armenta[5] et lati custodia credita campi.
Adsuetum[6] imperiis soror omni Silvia cura
mollibus intexens ornabat cornua sertis,
pectebatque ferum puroque in fonte lavabat.
Ille manum[7] patiens mensaeque adsuetus erili[8]   490
errabat silvis rursusque ad limina nota
ipse domum sera[9] quamvis se nocte ferebat.
Hunc procul errantem rabidae venantis Iuli
commovere[10] canes, [11]fluvio cum forte secundo
deflueret ripaque aestus viridante levaret.   495
Ipse etiam eximiae laudis succensus amore
Ascanius curvo derexit spicula cornu;

---

1 477. **arte nove:** 'in a new piece of trickery', additional to the devices already used against Amata and Turnus; cf. 1.657. As Conington says, it is the Homeric ενθ αυτ αλλ ενοησε.

2 478. Iulus' fondness for the hunt was described in 4.156f.

3 479. **Cocytia:** the river Cocytus gives Allecto another epithet from the underworld (cf. 562); cf. *Stygiis alis* in 476.

4 484. **Tyrrhidae pueri:** 'the sons of Tyrrhus who were young': for the long *i* cf. *Belïdae* from *Belus* (2.82).

5 486. Tyrrhus was the king's chief herdsman (*armentarius*) responsible for the whole domain. In one version of the legend (Servius on *Aen.* 6.760) Lavinia hid in his hut. Modern editors read *late* for *lati* (most MSS); there seems no reason for this.

6 487f. 'He knew his mistress's voice and Silvia, the boys' sister, used to love to deck out his antlers by winding soft garlands round them, and to comb the wild creature and bath him in a sparkling spring'. The movement of these lines is reminiscent of the *Eclogues:* notice especially the coincidence of ictus and accent in the fourth foot. The passage is imitated in Ov. *Met.* 10.109f. and Calpurnius Siculus, *Ecl.* 6.32f. On the name Silvia Servius says 'bonum puellae rusticae nomen formavit', but doubtless it has reference to the association of the name with the Silvii, kings of Alba Longa.

7 490. **manum patiens:** 'ready to be stroked'; Servius says *manum* is contracted for *manuum* (cf. 6.653) as genitive after the adjective *patiens*, but it is more likely that *patiens* here has its verbal force. Some MSS have *manu* (dative parallel to *mensae*). but this weakens the force of *patiens*.

8 **erili:** a word not common in the epic style, applied again to the 'master' of animals in 8.462.

9 492. **sera quamvis . . . nocte:** 'however late at night', i.e. he knew the way home in the dark.

10 494. **commovere:** 'roused' him, i.e. bayed the stag. Notice the pattern of alliteration in the line which portrays action after description.

11 494-5. These two phrases describe the quiet peace of the stag. now swimming, now resting on the bank.

nec dextrae erranti deus[1] afuit, actaque multo[2]
perque uterum sonitu perque ilia venit harundo.
Saucius at quadripes nota intra tecta refugit[3]   500
successitque gemens stabulis, questuque cruentus
atque[4] imploranti similis tectum omne replebat.
Silvia prima soror palmis percussa[5] lacertos
auxilium vocat et duros[6] conclamat agrestis.
Olli (pestis enim tacitis latet aspera silvis)   505
improvisi[7] adsunt, hic torre armatus obusto,
stipitis[8] hic gravidi nodis; [9]quod cuique repertum
rimanti telum ira facit. Vocat agmina Tyrrhus,
quadrifidam quercum cuneis ut forte coactis[10]
scindebat rapta[11] spirans[12] immane securi.   510

*511-71. Allecto now sounds the trumpet-note for war, and
Almo, Galaesus and many others are killed. Allecto reports
to Juno that her mission is completed; Juno contemptuously
orders her back to the underworld.*

[13]At saeva e speculis tempus dea nacta nocendi

---

1 498. 'The goddess (Allecto) guided his uncertain aim.' Servius explains that archers cannot always be certain of their aim, but it seems more likely that the meaning is that the young Ascanius was excited, and his hand unsteady. It is impossible to get out of the Latin the meaning which some wish to get - *non erravit nam deus non afuit.*

2 498-9. The word order is interwoven: *et harundo, acta multo sonitu, venit et per uterum et per ilia.*

3 500f. There is a faint reminiscence (no more of the simile in 4.69f. where Dido is compared with a wounded deer.

4 502. 'like someone asking for help': for the phrase cf. 5.254 *anhelanti similis. Gemens* and *questu* have prepared the way for the comparison of the wounded stag to a human.

5 503. **percussa lacertos**: 'beating her shoulders', retained accusative with a passive verb. This construction (for which see also note on 1.228 and Page on 9.478) is a favourite with Virgil and is influenced by one or both of two Greek constructions: (i) a middle verb governing a direct object (e.g. 640); (ii) the accusative of respect, common in Greek with parts of the body (see note on line 60). For the phrase cf. 1.481, 4.589, and for other examples of the construction in this book cf. 640, 669, 796, 806.

6 504. **duros conclamat agrestis**: 'called out to the hardy countryfolk'. *Conclamare* is very rare in this transitive sense (cf. Ov. *Met.* 13.73); it here something of its military meaning: *conclamare ad arma. Duros* suggests that the call to action will not be vain; cf. *indomiti* (521).

7 506. **improvisi**: 'all of a sudden', i.e. they were already preparing for trouble before Silvia called them, because Allecto (*pestis*, 505) was arousing them.

8 507. **stipitis hic gravidi nodis**: hendiadys, 'with a heavy knotted stake'.

9 507-8. 'what each found as he searched, anger converted into a weapon', i.e. they are too angry to wait to collect real weapons, anything that will serve will do. *Cuique* is dative of the agent after *repertum (est).*

10 509-10. 'as he chanced to be cutting an oak log into quarters with wedges forced into it'; for the use of *ut forte* cf. 5.388, 12.270. For *quadrifidus* cf. *Geo.* 2.25; the use here is predicative or proleptic. The alliteration in 509 and 510 is very exaggerated.

11 510. **rapta ... securi**: i.e. he drops his wedges and seizes his woodman's axe.

12 **spirans immane**: 'breathing fury'; *immane* is adverbial accusative, cf. 399.

13 511f. The outbreak of hostilities is harsh and pitiless, introduced by the trumpet note of Allecto, the panic of the women, the frenzy of the men. Virgil pauses on the death of Galaesus, an older man who tries to stop the fighting. He reveals a little of the past life (536-9) of one of the victims otherwise unknown to us, showing how all that a man has achieved and learned to do is gone for nothing as the sword drives home; so it was with Ripheus and Panthus (2.426f.), so it will be with Umbro (7.756f.) with Rhamnes (9.328) and many others (12.517f., 538f.). Finally the hatefulness of war is powerfully emphasised as even Juno, loathing her own agent of evil, sends her packing back to the underworld through its entrance at Amsanctus.

ardua tecta petit stabuli et de culmine summo[1]
pastorale[2] canit signum cornuque recurvo
Tartaream[3] intendit vocem, qua protinus omne
contremuit nemus et silvae insonuere profundae;   515
audiit et Triviae[4] longe lacus, audiit amnis
sulpurea Nar albus aqua fontesque Velini,
et trepidae matres pressere ad pectora natos.
Tum vero ad vocem celeres, qua bucina signum
dira dedit, raptis concurrunt undique telis   520
indomiti agricolae, nec non et Troia pubes
Ascanio auxilium[5] castris effundit apertis.
Derexere[6] acies. [7]Non iam certamine agresti
stipitibus duris agitur sudibusve praeustis,
sed ferro ancipiti[8] decernunt atraque[9] late   525
horrescit strictis seges ensibus, aeraque[10] fulgent
sole lacessita et lucem sub nubila iactant:
fluctus uti primo coepit cum[11] albescere ponto,
paulatim sese tollit mare et altius undas
erigit, inde imo consurgit ad aethera fundo.   530
Hic[12] iuvenis primam ante aciem stridente sagitta,
natorum Tyrrhi fuerat qui maximus, Almo,

---

1 512. Notice the pictorial imagery here of the goddess like a great evil bird alighting on a high roof: cf. Hor. *Odes* 3.24.5f.

2 513. **pastorale canit signum**: 'sounds the shepherd's alarm', a call-to-arms on the bugle.

3 514. **Tartaream intendit vocem**: 'sent forth a Tartarean blast'; for *vox* of a bugle cf. Ov. *Met.* 1.338. *Intendere* has its ballistic sense (cf. 9.590) used here in a musical context; cf. J. G. Landels, *C.Q.*, 1958, pp. 219f.

4 516f. Lake Trivia (Diana's Mirror) was near Aricia; for Diana's epithet Trivia cf. 774, 778 and note on 4.511. The river Nar, a tributary of the Tiber, was so called, according to Servius, from the Sabine word meaning sulphur. Cf. Enn. *Ann.* 260 *sulphureas posuit spiramina Naris ad undas*. Velinus was a lake in Sabine territory, cf. line 712. In this passage Virgil is following Ap. Rh. 4.127f. (the hiss of the dragon), where 'pathetic fallacy' is similarly employed; see note on 759-60.

5 522. **auxilium . . . effundit**: 'poured forth assistance', i.e. rushed out to help.

6 523. **derexere acies**: 'both sides have their formations ready', cf. *Geo.* 2.281.

7 523f. 'Not now in rustic contest do they fight with hard clubs or burnt stakes, but . . .' i.e. they have abandoned their chance weapons (506f.) ready for full-scale warfare. For the shortened diphthong in *praeustis* cf. 5.186 *praeeunte.*

8 525. **ancipiti**: 'two-edged', cf. Lucr. 6.168.

9 525-6. For *horrescit seges* cf. *Geo.* 2.142, *Aen.* 3.46, 12.663. The word *atra* conveys partly the darkness of a thick and dense mass, but its main impact is metaphorical, dark and deadly.

10 526-7. **aeraque . . . lacessita**: the bronze which is struck by the sunlight would be chiefly the helmets and shields. *Lacessere* is quite common in this sense (= 'strike') in Lucretius, e.g. 4.217.

11 528f. The specific point of the simile is the gradual development of the war from the shepherds' indignation to the full scale battle, but the idea of darkness and light is also present. *Primo* is probably an adverb, contrasting with *paulatim* and *inde*; *ponto* has much better MSS authority than *vento* (cf. *Geo.* 3.237). It is possible however that *primo . . . ponto* means 'on the sea's surface', in antithesis with *imo . . . fundo*, the final stage. Others take it as 'at the edge of the sea', comparing Hom. *Il.* 4.422.

12 531f. Both Servius and Donatus comment on the pathos of this first death, a young man, in the vanguard, eldest brother of Silvia, laid low by a cruel wound. His name is presumably taken by Virgil from the river of the same name, a tributary of the Tiber; Galaesus (535) is also called after a river.

sternitur; haesit enim sub gutture vulnus[1] et udae[2]
vocis iter tenuemque inclusit sanguine vitam.
Corpora multa virum[3] circa seniorque Galaesus,   535
Dum paci medium se offert, iustissimus[4] unus
qui fuit Ausoniisque olim ditissimus arvis:
quinque greges illi balantum, quina[5] redibant
armenta, et terram centum vertebat aratris.

Atque ea per campos aequo[6] dum Marte geruntur,   540
promissi[7] dea facta potens, ubi sanguine[8] bellum
imbuit et primae commisit funera pugnae,
deserit Hesperiam et caeli conversa[9] per auras
Iunonem victrix adfatur voce superba:
'en, perfecta tibi bello discordia tristi;   545
dic[10] in amicitiam coeant et foedera iungant.
Quandoquidem Ausonio respersi sanguine Teucros,
hoc[11] etiam his addam, tua si mihi certa voluntas:
finitimas in bella feram rumoribus urbes,
accendamque animos insani Martis amore   550
undique ut auxilio veniant; spargam[12] arma per agros.'
Tum contra Iuno: 'terrorum et fraudis abunde[13] est:

---

1 533. **vulnus:** a metonymy (= *vulniferum telum*) which became increasingly common in the Silver Age; cf. 2.529, 9.745, 10.140.

2 533-4. 'and choked with blood the path of his liquid voice and the frail breath of life'. *Udae vocis iter* conveys the idea of life and health, as opposed to parched dryness of the throat in sickness.

3 535. This line is harsh and abrupt: 'all around lay the many dead, among them old Galaesus'; from the slow, sad account of the first victim the narrative leaps violently onwards.

4 536. **iustissimus unus:** so was Ripheus among the Trojans (2.426), but the gods did not allow him to survive. See note on 511f.

5 538. **quina:** used as a variant for *quinque*, cf. 5.560.

6 540. **aequo:** this simply means that no decisive victory has yet occurred. Servius, troubled by the fact that Italians have fallen but not Trojans, finds the meaning 'open' warfare.

7 541. **promissi . . . facta potens:** 'having performed her promise', cf. *Aen.* 1.80, Ov. *Met.* 4.510. Servius explains that by her silent consent to Juno's request Allecto had made a promise.

8 541-2. **sanguine bellum imbuit:** 'had drenched the war in blood', a very startling phrase in which *bellum* is used as object to *imbuere* in the same sense as *arma* or *gladios imbuere* (cf. 554, Virgil's only other use of *imbuere*). The word also sometimes has the sense of 'initiate' (cf. Cat. 64.11), and Servius takes it thus here; no doubt this meaning is also present, but the other is primary.

9 543. **conversa per auras:** this is the reading of *M1;* the other MSS have *convexa,* which is a favourite word of Virgil's (e.g. 4.451), but has no construction here. Mackail suggests a lacuna, others emend *per auras* (*pererrans, peragrans, per ardua*). Servius reports a reading *convecta,* and it has been suggested that *convexa* is an adjective formed on the analogy of *devexa.* But it seems best to accept *conversa,* 'returning', in a sense somewhat extended from usages like 12.369, Livy 25.18.7.

10 546. **dic in amicitiam coeant:** 'now tell them to join in friendship', highly ironical. *Coeant* is jussive subjunctive in parataxis with *dic,* cf. 4.635, 5.550, 10.53-4, 258.

11 548. **hoc etiam his addam:** 'I will add to what is done this extra action', i.e. rousing the neighbouring cities. The second half of the line is the same as Juno's words to Venus in 4.125.

12 551. **spargam arma per agros:** a vivid metaphor, sowing the seeds from which weapons will spring up.

13 552. **abunde:** a rare use in the sense of *satis* with the genitive; cf. Suet. *Jul.* 86.

stant[1] belli causae, pugnatur comminus armis,
quae fors prima dedit sanguis[2] novus imbuit arma.
Talia coniugia et talis celebrent hymenaeos   555
egregium[3] Veneris genus et rex ipse Latinus.
Te super aetherias errare licentius auras
haud pater ille velit, summi regnator Olympi.
Cede locis. Ego, si[4] qua super fortuna laborum est,
ipsa regam.' Talis dederat Saturnia voces,   560
illa autem attollit stridentis[5] anguibus alas
Cocytique petit sedem supera[6] ardua linquens.
Est locus Italiae medio sub montibus altis,
nobilis et fama multis memoratus in oris,
Amsancti[7] valles;[8] densis hunc frondibus atrum   565
urget utrimque latus nemoris, medioque fragosus
dat sonitum saxis et torto vertice torrens.
Hic specus horrendum et saevi spiracula[9] Ditis
monstrantur, ruptoque ingens Acheronte vorago[10]
pestiferas aperit fauces, quis condita Erinys,   570
invisum numen, terras caelumque levavit.[11]

---

1 553. **stant:** 'are set up', cf. Hor. *Odes* 1.16.19.

2 554. 'Newly shed blood stains the weapons which chance offered them first'.

3 556. **egregium:** sarcastic as in 4.93 (Juno speaking to Venus).

4 559. **si qua . . . fortuna laborum est:** 'if there is any further occasion for action', 'if any further trouble occurs'.

5 561. **stridentis anguibus alas:** 'her wings hissing with their snakes', a very typically Virgilian ablative, cf. *Geo.* 4.310.

6 562. **supera ardua:** 'the lofty upper air'; *supera* (used as a noun) seems better than *super* of *M R:* cf. *Aen.* 6.787.

7 565. **Amsancti valles:** a valley containing a sulphurous lake in the territory of the Hirpini, said by Servius to be called the *umbilicus* of Italy (cf. 563, *Italiae medio*). It is the East-West centre that is referred to. Unlike Avernus it still today retains its dangerous exhalations; Cicero (*De Div.* 1.79) and Pliny (*Nat. Hist.* 2.208) say they were lethal. See J. A. S. Evans, *Vergilius,* 1964, pp. 12f., A. G. McKay, *Vergil's Italy,* pp. 240-1. Pliny mentions a temple of Mephitis there; see note on 83.

8 **valles:** nominative singular (for *vallis*); cf. 1 1.522.

9 568. **spiracula:** 'breathing-hole', cf. Lucr. 6.493. The word is very vividly used for the place where the underworld has an outlet to the air of our world. Pliny (*Nat. Hist.* 2.208) used the word in his discussion of places like Amsanctus.

10 569f. 'a great eddying abyss opens its deadly jaws where Acheron bursts through'; again the volcanic image. Acheron (one of the rivers of the underworld) is here used for the whole underworld; cf. 312.

11 571. **levavit:** 'relieved', by removing her hateful presence. Most editions follow *M* against *R* in reading *levabat,* but the instantaneous tense is far more appropriate.

572-640. *The Latin shepherds, Turnus, and the families of the women made frenzied by Amata beseech their king to declare war: he attempts to stand firm, but when he finds he cannot he withdraws from command and shuts himself in his palace. He refuses to open the Gates of War and Juno does so in his stead. The Latins arm themselves and prepare for battle.*

[1]Nec mirius interea extremam[2] Saturnia bello
imponit regina manum. Ruit omnis in urbem
pastorum ex acie numerus, caesosque reportant
Almonem puerum foedatique[3] ora Galaesi,   575
implorantque[4] deos obtestanturque Latinum.
Turnus adest medioque in crimine caedis et igni[5]
terrorem ingeminat: Teucros in regna vocari,
stirpem admisceri Phrygiam, se limine[6] pelli.
Tum[7] quorum attonitae Baccho nemora avia matres   580
insultant thiasis (neque enim leve nomen Amatae)

---

1 572f. Virgil now draws together (in reverse order) the events caused by the three interventions of Allecto: first the shepherds come to Latinus bringing the dead bodies of Almo and Galaesus; then Turnus appears; finally come the families of the women who had been roused by Amata to Bacchic frenzy. Against this pressure for unholy war (583-4) caused by Allecto Latinus for a while stands firm like a rock in a stormy sea, but he cannot prevail against the forces with which he has to contend, and with words of warning on the consequences of this wickedness he shuts himself up in his palace and lets lapse his authority. This present weakness at the hour of crisis contrasts markedly with his previous regal dignity and nobility of behaviour when all was going well: he now abdicates his power when he should have exercised it. He blames himself later on (11.302f.) for failing to take decisive action earlier. Latinus with his weakness and Turnus with his recklessness are foils for the controlled strength (*vis temperata*) of Aeneas. In Latinus' behaviour here, with its tragic consequences, we see emerging the justification for the harder and more ruthless actions of Aeneas in the later part of the poem.

There remains the formal ceremony of the declaration of war. The opening of the two Gates of War is closely related to the ceremonial of Virgil's own day for Roman wars against Getae or Arabs or Parthians. We are thus invited to relate war and peace in the times of Aeneas with the contemporary policies of Augustus: the gates had recently been closed by Augustus for the first time in two hundred years. We are also reminded once more of the first book of the *Aeneid,* when Jupiter had promised to Venus (294f.) that these gates would one day be closed, and *Furor impius* made a prisoner within. But the fulfilment of this promise is still far away, and the description of martial preparation is presented in staccato and breathless narrative (especially 623-5), broken by a sad reminiscence of the *Georgics* as the plough and the sickle yield to the sword (635-6). The peaceful beauty of the Italian countryside is now to be profaned, as it had been so often in Virgil's lifetime, by the sound of the bugle and the clashing of steel

2 572-3. **extremam . . . manum:** 'the final touches', a metaphor from art.

3 575. **foedatique ora Galaesi:** there is a slight shift in the structure of the sentence, when we would have expected *foedatum ore Galaesum*; this places extra emphasis on *ora.*

4 576. The spondaic movement of these long words focuses the attention on their pleas for vengeance.

5 577. 'in the midst of the charges of murder and the burning passions . . .'. *Igni* is striking, and this has given rise to an alternative *ignis* in some MSS; it is used with full metaphorical force, cf. *Geo.* 3.258, *Aen.* 2.575, 9.66, and for the general sense *Aen.* 11.225 *medio in flagrante tumultu.*

6 579. **limine:** here with the idea of the threshold as symbol of welcome and friendship; cf. 8.145.

7 580f. 'Then the families of the matrons who were in frenzy dancing for Bacchus in chorus through the pathless glades (for Amata's name was not lightly regarded) collected from all sides and gathered together, ceaselessly calling upon Mars.' *Nemora avia* is accusative of extent; cf. 1.67. *Thiasus* is the Bacchic dance; cf. *Ecl.* 5.30, Cat. 64.252. For *fatigant* cf. *Aen.* 4.572, Hor. *Odes* 1.2.26.

undique[1] collecti coeunt Martemque fatigant.
Ilicet infandum cuncti contra omina bellum,
contra fata deum perverso[2] numine poscunt.
Certatim regis circumstant tecta Latini;   585
Ille[3] velut pelagi rupes immota resistit,
ut pelagi rupes magno veniente fragore,
quae sese multis circum latrantibus undis[4]
mole[5] tenet; scopuli[6] nequiquam et spumea circum
saxa fremunt laterique inlisa refunditur alga.   590
Verum ubi nulla datur caecum exsuperare[7] potestas
consilium, et saevae nutu Iunonis eunt[8] res,
multa deos aurasque pater testatus inanis
'frangimur heu fatis'[9] inquit 'ferimurque procella!
Ipse has sacrilego pendetis sanguine poenas,   595
o miseri. Te,[10] Turne, nefas, te triste manebit
supplicium, votisque deos venerabere seris.
Nam mihi parta quies, omnisque in limine portus[11]
funere felici spolior.' Nec plura locutus
saepsit se tectis rerumque reliquit habenas.   600

---

1 583-4. These are strongly emphatic lines in which Virgil enters the narrative editorially to comment on the situation; the alliteration points the emphasis, and the fourfold repetition of the same idea in *infandum, contra omina, contra fata deum, perverso numine* hammers it home. There is a reversal of sympathy: the poet indicates that whatever the sympathy so far felt for the justice of the feelings of anger among the Latins it is nevertheless the case that what they are demanding is horrible.

2 584. **perverso numine:** 'under a malign influence', referring to Allecto and Juno; or possibly, as Page says, 'with misdirected impulse', *numen* being their own will, cf. Lucr. 4.179.

3 586f. For the simile cf. Hom. *Il.* 15.618f., and *Aen.* 10.693f. For the repetition of *pelagi rupes* cf. 9.774-5, 12.546-7, and see note on 2.405-6. Cf. Tennyson's *Will:*
'For him nor moves the loud world's random mock,
Nor all Calamity's hugest waves confound,
Who seems a promontory of rock,
That, compass'd round with turbulent sound,
In middle ocean meets the surging shock,
Tempest-buffeted, citadel-crown'd.'

4 588. Notice the spondaic movement with conflict of ictus and accent, suggesting the buffeting of the rock; in *latrantibus* Virgil may be thinking of Scylla's sea-dogs (Hom. *Od.* 12.85).

5 589. **mole:** cf. 10.771 *mole sua stat*, and 5.431 (of Entellus the boxer) *mole valens.*

6 589-90. The *scopuli* and *saxa* are parts of the rock; they 'groan in vain' in the sense that for all the roaring of the water around them they are not dislodged. *Refunditur* indicates that the seaweed is always flung back because the rock does not yield.

7 591. **exsuperare potestas:** for the infinitive with *potestas* cf. 3.670.

8 592. **eunt res:** the abrupt monosyllable (cf. 643, 790, 9.320) compels the attention.

9 594. Latinus' opening words continue the imagery of the simile: the rock is shattered and washed away by the tempest.

10 596. Notice the emphatic antithesis of the double *te* with *mihi* in 598. 'It is for you, Turnus, for you, that the sin and the awful punishment will be waiting'.

11 598-9. 'I have already won my repose, and being right on the edge of the haven I am robbed only of happiness in death.' This appears to be the sense of a difficult passage: *portus* means, as often, the haven of death (so Enn. *Scen.* 364, Cic. *T.D.* 1.118). *Limen* here is perhaps suggested by Homer's επι γηραος ουδω (*Il.* 22.60).

Mos[1] erat Hesperio in Latio, quem protinus[2] urbes
Albanae coluere sacrum, nunc maxima[3] rerum
Roma colit, cum prima movent in proelia Martem,
sive Getis inferre manu lacrimabile bellum[4]
Hyrcanisve Arabisve parant, seu tendere ad Indos   605
Auroramque sequi Parthosque reposcere signa:
sunt geminae Belli portae[5] (sic nomine dicunt)
religione sacrae et saevi formidine Martis;
centum aerei[6] claudunt vectes aeternaque ferri
robora, nec custos absistit limine Ianus: 610
has,[7] ubi certa sedet patribus sententia pugnae,
ipse Quirinali[8] trabea cinctuque[9] Gabino
insignis reserat stridentia[10] limina consul,
ipse vocat pugnas; sequitur tum cetera pubes,
aereaque adsensu conspirant cornua rauco.[11]   615
Hoc[12] et tum Aeneadis indicere bella Latinus
more iubebatur tristisque recludere portas.
Abstinuit tactu pater aversusque refugit
foeda ministeria, et caecis se condidit umbris.
Tum regina deum caelo delapsa morantis   620
impulit ipsa manu portas, et cardine verso

---

1 601f. Servius informs us that the custom in question (of opening the gates of war) was not in fact instituted until the time of Numa Pompilius; so Livy 1.19.2.

2 601. **protinus**: 'from then onwards', 'continually from then', cf. *Aen.* 6.33, 9.337, 10.340. For the theme of historical continuity cf. the *lusus Troiae* (5.596f.).

3 602. **maxima rerum**: 'greatest of states', cf. *Geo.* 2.534 *rerum facta est pulcherrima Roma*.

4 604f. These are places relevant to the foreign policy of Augustan Rome; cf. (of Augustus) *Aen.* 1.289 *spoliis Orientis onustum*, 6.798f., 8.725f. The Getae (cf. *Geo.* 2.497), north of the Danube, were checked in their raiding activities about 29 B.C.; an expedition into Arabia took place a few years later; the Hyrcani (near the Caspian Sea) fall under the general category of the eastern peoples against whom activity, diplomatic and otherwise, was constant. The standards lost by Crassus at Carrhae were eventually recovered by Augustus in 20 B.C.; cf. Hor. *Odes* 4.15.6f.

5 607f. The gates of war (cf. *Aen.* 1.294 and note on 622) were in a temple or archway sacred to Janus, the god of opening and closing. They were closed in 29 B.C. (for the first time since 235) and again in 25 B.C.

6 609. **aerei**: a spondee by synizesis, cf. line 33. For the sense compare 1.295.

7 611f. **has . . . stridentia limina**: both of these are objects of *reserat;* the sentence is a slight anacoluthon, cf. 2.438f.

8 612. **Quirinali trabea**: see note on 187. *Quirinali* here links with the god Janus, who sometimes has the epithet *Quirinus* (Suet. *Aug.* 22, cf. Hor. *Odes* 4.15.9).

9 **cinctuque Gabino**: Servius explains the reference; it was a particular way of wearing the toga during sacrifices, and when the Gabii, near neighbours of Rome, suddenly were attacked when they were sacrificing, they went out to battle thus clad in togas. It then became ritual costume for the declaration of war; cf. Livy 8.9.9.

10 613. **stridentia limina**: 'the creaking doors', cf. 2.480, and in general 1.449.

11 615. A fine golden line with forceful alliteration.

12 616. **hoc**: with *more* in the next line, rather unusually distant.

Belli[1] ferratos rumpit Saturnia postis.
[2]Ardet inexcita Ausonia atque immobilis ante;
pars[3] pedes ire parat campis, pars arduus altis
pulverulentus equis furit; omnes arma requirunt.   625
Pars levis[4] clipeos et spicula lucida tergent
arvina pingui subiguntque[5] in cote securis;
signaque ferre iuvat sonitusque audire tubarum.
Quinque adeo magnae positis incudibus urbes[6]
tela novant, Atina potens Tiburque superbum,   630
Ardea Crustumerique et turrigerae[7] Antemnae.
Tegmina tuta cavant capitum flectuntque salignas[8]
umbonum cratis; alii thoracas[9] aenos
aut levis ocreas lento ducunt argento;[10]
vomeris huc et falcis honos, huc omnis aratri[11]   635
cessit amor; recoquunt[12] patrios fornacibus ensis.
Classica iamque sonant, it[13] bello tessera signum.
Hic galeam tectis trepidus rapit, ille frementis

---

1 622. This line is virtually a quotation from Ennius, *Ann.* 267 *Belli ferratos postes portasque refregit.*

2 623. This is one of the most astonishing and unforgettable lines in the poem: all the words begin with a vowel, and the word division in the middle part of the line is infrequent. *Inexcitus* is not found elsewhere until Stat. *Ach.* 2.67; *immobilis* has an unusual meaning ('untroubled').

3 624f. The excitement continues with violent alliteration of *p*, remarkable syntax (*pars arduus furit*) and a line (625) divided exactly into two equal parts. There are many emendations proposed to heal the syntax, but it is probably deliberate: the justification for it is that *pars parat ire pedes* has preceded (= *alii parant ire pedites*), so that *pars arduus . . . equis furit* is equivalent to *pars arduus eques furit* (= *alii furunt ardui equites*). Translate 'some high up on their mighty horses tear wildly through the dust'.

4 626-7. **levis . . . pingui**: 'wipe their shields smooth and their javelins bright with thick fat'. This is preferable to 'cleanse them of their thick fat' (with which they had been covered for preservation) partly because the syntax of the ablative is easier, and partly because, according to Servius, *arvina* was a hard kind of fat.

5 627. **subigunt**: 'work on', i.e. sharpen.

6 629f. In fact five mighty cities were engaged in making new weapons, the anvils all ready in place . . .'. For *adeo* cf. 3.203. For Atina, a town in Latium, cf. Livy 9.28.6; Tibur (cf. 670) is the modern Tivoli (probably called 'proud' because of its high position); Ardea (411) was Turnus' capital; Crustumeri is Virgil's form for Crustumerium, a Sabine town; Antemnae too was Sabine, near the junction of the Anio and the Tiber.

7 631. **turrigerae Antemnae**: the rhythmic effect here is most unusual; a spondaic fifth foot with hiatus occurs only five times in the *Aeneid,* always with proper names (cf. 1.617, 3.74, 9.647, 11.31). See also note on 634.

8 632 f. 'They shape protective coverings for their heads, and interweave the willow wickerwork of their shields'; the first phrase is a very ornate description of helmets, reinforced by alliteration; the second refers to the ribs or framework supporting a metal shield.

9 633. **thoracas**: Greek accusative with short final syllable, used by Virgil with a few Greek common nouns (*crater, tapete*) and with Greek names (11.263); see note on 3.127.

10 634. The marking of the greaves by the shaping (beating out) of the silver metal is reflected in the slow spondees; a spondaic fifth foot is rare (35 instances altogether in Virgil, mostly with proper nouns; see note on 2.68 and cf. 8.167, 402) and it is rare indeed with a fourth foot spondee preceding (cf. 3.74).

11 635f. Cf. *Geo.* 1.506f. *non ullus aratro / dignus honos.*

12 636. **recoquunt**: 'forge afresh', i.e. the swords were not serviceable, and had to be hammered out again; cf. 8.624, and **Hor.** *Odes* 1.35.38f. *o utinam nova / incude diffingas retusum . . . ferrum.*

13 637. **it bello tessera signum**: 'the watchword, a sign of war, is passed round'. Servius gives *'symbolum bellicum'* for *tessera.*

ad[1] iuga cogit equos, clipeumque auroque trilicem[2]
loricam induitur[3] fidoque accingitur ense.   640

> 641-6. *Invocation to the Muse preparatory to the catalogue
> of Italian forces.*

[4]Pandite nunc Helicona, deae,[5] cantusque[6] movete,
qui bello exciti reges, quae quemque secutae
complerint campos acies, quibus Itala iam[7] tum
floruerit[8] terra alma viris, quibus arserit armis;
et meministis enim, divae, et memorare potestis;[9]   645
ad nos vix tenuis famae perlabitur aura.

> 647-54. *Mezentius, with his son Lausus, is first in the list.*

Primus[10] init bellum Tyrrhenis asper ab oris

---

1 639. **ad iuga cogit:** 'brings together under the yoke'; cf. Stat. *Th.* 7.136.

2 **trilicem:** cf. *Aen.* 3.467.

3 640. **induitur:** with a direct object (retained accusative), like the Greek middle voice; see note on line 503 and cf. 2.393. Notice how in the next phrase Virgil varies the construction (contrast 2.511).

4 641f. A 'catalogue', or list of military forces, was an expected part of the structure of epic poetry, established by Homer (*Il.* 2.484f., the catalogue of Greek ships followed by the list of Trojan forces) and used by his successors (Ap. Rh. 1.20f., Silius 3.222f., Stat. *Th.* 4.32f., Milton *P.L.* 1.376f.). The straight forward enumeration of Homer's catalogue (*divina illa simplicitas*, Macrobius calls it) would not be appropriate for the more sophisticated method of literary epic, and Virgil's list has elaborate aspects of function and structure.
The main function is to hold the attention for a time on the conflicting forces at the crucial moment, and for this purpose Virgil has placed his catalogue just after the beginning of the action which is to lead to the full scale outbreak of war. Every possible device is used for variety and vividness; the armies move, the men sweep over the plain, the scenes are like the edited shots of a ciné-camera. The reader's viewpoint constantly changes, the troops are seen departing, arriving, en route; in the final cameo of Camilla the emphasis on the visual aspect is very marked indeed (812f.). The soldiers and their commanders, their armour and their hometowns, are described with a lingering love of detail which recalls Virgil's love of Italy in the *Georgics;* there is an emotional patriotism which finds expression in sonorous lists of well-known names, glimpses of character and customs, aetiological references to the origins of Roman families. These Italians are the enemies of Aeneas, but it was through them as well as through him that Rome could grow to greatness (12.833f.). The long lists of names depend for their effect on the reader's familiarity with them (as does Milton's scriptural geography in his catalogue); the modern reader is here at a great disadvantage compared with Virgil's contemporaries. For a full account of the peoples and places see B. Tilly, *Vergil's Latium,* Oxford, 1947, A. G. McKay, *Vergil's Italy,* Bath, 1971.
The structure of the catalogue has been much discussed: it seems to me that it is constructed in three parts, the first and last balancing each other around a central section, with the Camilla episode as a concluding pendent. With Mezentius the great warrior corresponds Turnus, a greater; Aventinus and Virbius bring us into a world of mythology; Catillus and Coras, like Centaurs, balance with the supernatural Umbro. The six central episodes are very much concerned with the patriotic impact of Italian peoples and places. For a fuller discussion of this, and for bibliography on the catalogue, see my article in *C.Q.* 1961, pp. 146f.

5 641-6. Virgil bases his invocation to the Muses on Homer's invocation in *Il.* 2.484f., which precedes the catalogue of the ships. He asks them to open the gates of their mountain, Helicon, so that their song may come forth; cf. 10.163.

6 642f. The indirect questions depend on *cantusque movete,* 'raise your song, telling us what kings were roused to war . . .'.

7 643. **iam tum:** 'even then', i.e. before the Romans began; cf. 8.349, 350 (used of Evander's settlement on the future site of Rome). The phrase receives great emphasis here from its position at the line-ending.

8 644. **floruerit . . . viris:** the concept of Italy as the great mother recalls *Geo.* 2.173-4 *salve, magna parens frugum, Saturnia tellus, / magna virum.*

9 645-6. Mnemosyne (Memory) was the mother of the Muses; these two lines are closely modelled on Hom. *Il.* 2.485f.

10 647. **primus:** Virgil presents the catalogue as a kind of march-past. Servius points out that it is appropriate to begin with the godless Mezentius, set in opposition to Aeneas, *pietate insignis.*

contemptor[1] divum Mezentius agminaque armat.
Filius huic iuxta Lausus,[2] quo pulchrior alter
non fuit excepto[3] Laurentis corpore Turni,   650
Lausus, equum domitor debellatorque ferarum,
ducit Agyllina[4] nequiquam[5] ex urbe secutos
mille viros, dignus patriis qui laetior esset[6]
imperiis et cui pater haud Mezentius esset.

    655-69. *Next comes Aventinus, son of Hercules.*

Post hos insignem palma per gramina currum[7]   655
victoresque ostentat equos satus Hercule pulchro[8]
pulcher Aventinus, clipeoque insigne[9] paternum
centum anguis cinctamque gerit serpentibus[10] Hydram;
collis Aventini[11] silva quem Rhea sacerdos
furtivum[12] partu sub[13] luminis edidit oras,   660
mixta deo mulier, postquam Laurentia victor[14]
Geryone exstincto Tirynthius attigit arva,

---

1 648. **contemptor divum Mezentius:** Mezentius was a prominent figure in the various versions of the legend of Aeneas in Italy (Cato in Macrob. *Sat.* 3.5.10f., Livy 1.2.3, Dion. Hal. 1.64f.). In Virgil's account he was exiled by the Etruscans (8.481f.) who fight on Aeneas' side against their former tyrant; as far as we can tell this version was Virgil's own adaptation. Enough is said in Virgil's description of Mezentius' cruel and tyrannical behaviour (leading to his exile) to justify the phrase *contemptor divum;* in addition Macrobius (loc. cit.) cites a story from Cato that Mezentius demanded for himself the first fruits due to the gods. He is the most barbaric character in the *Aeneid,* yet even for him, at the moment of his death (Book 10, ad fin.), Virgil evokes sympathy.

2 649f. The death of Lausus, Mezentius' son, a young warrior comparable with Euryalus or Pallas, is described in moving terms in 10.809f. Virgil arouses our interest in him by the repetition of his name, each time with descriptive phraseology, spending three lines on him before the sentence begins to unroll at *ducit.*

3 650. **excepto . . . corpore Turni:** 'apart from the splendid physique of Turnus'. So in Hom. *Il.* 2.671f. Nireus is the fairest of all bar Achilles.

4 652. **Agyllina . . . urbe:** i.e. Caere in Etruria, cf. 8.479.

5 **nequiquam:** Virgil foreshadows for his reader the unhappy end of Lausus.

6 653f. 'worthy of being happier in the father whose authority he obeyed, worthy not to have had Mezentius as his father'. The repetition of *esset* gives an oddly lame paragraph ending.

7 655f. Virgil's Aventinus, son of Hercules, occurs nowhere else; according to Livy (1.3.9) and Dionysius (1.71) Aventinus was a king of the Albans, and according to Servius an Aborigine. The link with Hercules which Virgil gives him serves to prepare for the elaborate description of the festival of Hercules (who was especially associated with the Aventine Hill) in Book 8.

8 656-7. For the repetition of *pulcher* cf. Hor. *Odes* 1.16.1 *o matre pulchra filia pulchrior.*

9 657. For *insigne,* the pictorial emblem on a shield, cf. 2.392.

10 658. 'the hundred snakes of the Hydra enveloped with their writhing forms'; *centum anguis* and *serpentibus* refer to the same thing. The killing of the hundred-headed Hydra was Hercules' second labour; cf. Ov. *Met.* 9.68f. for the story, and Eur. *Phoen.* 1134f. for the Hydra as an emblem on the shield of Adrastus.

11 659. Virgil here gives Aventinus the distinction of having a mother of the same name as Romulus, and also alludes with the word *silva* to the cognomen Silvia of Romulus' mother.

12 660-1. **furtivum partu ... mixta deo mulier:** very Homeric phraseology, cf. *Il.* 6.161 κρυπταδιν φιλοτητι μιγηεναι, *Il.* 16.176 γυνη θεω ευνηθεισα.

13 660. **sub luminis edidit oras:** the phrase has a ring of Ennius and Lucretius, cf. *Geo.* 2.47.

14 661f. One of the labours of Hercules (*Tirynthius* also in 8.228, either because he was born at Tiryns, or because he served Eurystheus there) was to carry off the cattle from the giant Geryon in Spain (cf. 5.411). It was when returning from this labour that Hercules killed Cacus, as told in 8.185f.; cf. esp. 202f.

Tyrrhenoque boves in flumine[1] lavit Hiberas.
Pila[2] manu saevosque gerunt in bella dolones,
et tereti pugnant mucrone veruque Sabello. 665
Ipse[3] pedes, tegimen torquens immane leonis,
terribili impexum saeta, cum dentibus albis
indutus capiti, sic regia tecta subibat,
horridus Herculeoque umeros[4] innexus amictu.

670-7. The twins Catillus and Coras come from Tibur, like Centaurs from their mountain retreats in Thessaly.

Tum gemini fratres Tiburtia[5] moenia linquunt, 670
fratris Tiburti dictam cognomine gentem,
Catillusque acerque Coras, Argiva[6] iuventus,
et primam ante aciem densa inter tela feruntur:
ceu duo nubigenae[7] cum vertice montis ab alto
descendunt Centauri Homolen Othrymque nivalem 675
linquentes cursu rapido; dat euntibus ingens
silva locum et magno cedunt virgulta fragore.

678-90. Next comes Caeculus, founder of Praeneste, with his followers.

[8]Nec Praenestinae[9] fundator defuit urbis,

---

1 663. The Tiber is called Etruscan to give another forward link to Book 8.

2 664-5. These lines join rather abruptly with the preceding narrative but there is no adequate reason to suspect displacement. *Pila* are the well known Roman javelins, *dolones* probably poles with iron points. Servius comments that many link *tereti mucrone* with *dolones* (*teres* referring to the shaft, Livy 21.8.10) and *veru Sabello* with *pila* (thus giving antiquity to the *pilum*). This seems very possible.

3 666f. 'He himself was now on foot, swirling his enormous lion skin, matted, bristly, terrifying, wearing its head with its white teeth, this was the picture as he came to the palace, formidable, his shoulders adorned in the garment of Hercules.' This is an astonishing sentence, forceful, disjointed, vivid; the grammar and diction suit the subject matter. Notice *torquens* used as of the swishing movements made with a robe (cf. 8.460), the strange phrase *indutus capiti* (*capiti* is ablative, cf. *Ecl.* 6.16) on the analogy of *spoliis indutus,* the summarising *sic* and the final explicit connexion of the lion skin with Hercules.

4 669. **umeros innexus**: retained accusative, cf. 6.281 and see note on 503.

5 670f. The legend of the foundation of Tibur by Catillus, father of the twins Catillus and Coras and of their elder brother Tiburtus, goes back to Cato's *Origines* (Solinus 2.7). Servius simply relates that the three brothers came from Greece and founded Tibur. There was a hill Catillus or Catellus near Tibur (Hor. *Odes* 1.18.2), and a *civitas* called Cora (*Aen.* 6.775, Livy 2.16.8).

6 672. **Argiva iuventus:** Pliny (*N.H.* 16.237) tells that the family were connected with Amphiaraus of Argos.

7 674f. 'As when two cloud-born Centaurs descend from the high top of a mountain, speeding swiftly down from Homole and snowy Othrys; the mighty forest gives way for them as they go, and the undergrowth parts with deafening noise.' This splendid image varies the etymological and topographical interest of the passage by means of a touch of the world of fancy and mythology. For *nubigena* (not found before Virgil) cf. 8.293. Homole and Othrys are mountains in Thessaly, traditional home of the Centaurs.

8 678f. This episode begins with a strange piece of folklore; Caeculus was discovered near a temple fire by maidens going to fetch water (Cato's *Origines,* quoted by the Verona scholiast), and hence regarded as son of Vulcan. He was called Caeculus (the little blind boy) as his eyes were screwed-up because of the smoke; he was the eponymous founder of the *gens Caecilia.* Servius' version is that he was actually conceived from a spark, making him in a more real sense son of Vulcan. The interest quickly shifts from him to his followers, men from well known Italian places; from here on Virgil places more and more emphasis on the names of Italian peoples and districts and the archaic customs and armour of the warriors.

9 678. **Praenestinae . . . urbis**: Praeneste was one of the most famous towns of Latium; cf. *Aen.* 8.561, Hor. *Odes* 3.4.23.

Volcano[1] genitum pecora inter agrestia regem
inventumque focis omnis quem credidit aetas,   680
Caeculus. Hunc legio late comitatur agrestis:
quique altum Praeneste viri quique arva Gabinae[2]
Iunonis gelidumque Anienem et roscida rivis
Hernica saxa colunt, quos dives Anagnia pascis,[3]
quos Amasene pater. Non illis omnibus arma   685
nec clipei currusve sonant; pars maxima glandes[4]
liventis plumbi spargit, pars spicula gestat
bina manu, fulvosque lupi de pelle galeros[5]
tegmen habent capiti; vestigia nuda[6] sinistri
instituere pedis, crudus tegit altera pero.   690

> 691-705. *Messapus leads his contingent, who sing as they march.*

At Messapus,[7] equum domitor, Neptunia proles,
quem neque fas igni cuiquam nec sternere ferro,
iam pridem resides populos desuetaque bello
agmina in arma vocat subito ferrumque retractat.
Hi Fescenninas[8] acies Aequosque Faliscos,   695
hi Soractis habent arces Flaviniaque arva
et Cimini cum monte lacum lucosque Capenos.

---

1 679. 'born of Vulcan amidst the animals of the fields to be a king'; *Vulcano* is ablative of origin. Presumably his mother bore him in the fields and took him to the temple.

2 682f. Juno was called *Gabina* from her worship in the territory of Gabii, not far from Rome. The Anio (alternative nominative *Anien*)was a tributary of the Tiber; the Hernici lived a little further southeast, around the town Anagnia and the river Amasenus. Servius tells us that the Hernici were so called from the Sabine word *hernae* meaning 'rocks', so that Virgil's *Hernica saxa* has an etymological play; cf. 713, 740 and 3.693 with my note (OUP Ed.). Anagnia may owe its epithet *dives* simply to its fertility, or there may be a reference, as Servius says, to the mint there, perhaps established by Antony (H. Mattingly, *Numism. Chron.*, 1946, 91f.).

3 684. **pascis**: this reading of *V* is much preferable to *pascit* of the majority, because of the following vocative *Amasene pater.*

4 686. **glandes**: a technical term for the lead pellets shot by the slingers (*funditores*).

5 688. **galeros**: a type of cap like the *pilleus.*

6 689-90. 'They advance the left foot unshod, while a rough boot covers their right.' *Vestigia* occurs in poetry in the meaning of foot (Cat. 64.162), so that *vestigia pedis* here is equivalent to *pes;* cf. *Aen.* 5.566-7. The meaning seems to be that a better grip is achieved for throwing if the leading foot is unshod.

7 691f. Messapus is one of the chief Latin leaders, frequently mentioned in the poem. Virgil has given him characteristics of the eponymous hero of the Messapians in So. Italy, who was said to have come over the sea from Boeotia; the connexion here with Neptune suggests the sea as well as accounting for Messapus' excellence with horses. His invulnerability to fire or sword adds a supernatural element; nothing is known of the eventual method of his death.
According to Servius, Ennius claimed descent from Messapus, and it may well be that Virgil in making Messapus' contingent famous for song is paying an indirect tribute to his predecessor.

8 695f. These are places in South Etruria, not far north of the Tiber. *Acies* in its normal meaning is difficult with *habent.* and I accept Slater's suggestions (*C.R.* 1905, p.38 and 1919, p.144) of the meaning 'heights', 'Edge', not unlike *arces* in the next line (for which cf. *Geo.* 1.240, 4.461, *Aen.* 3.291). Heinsius' proposal that *Aequos* should be spelled with a capital, so that the town is called Acqui Falisci (Falisci-in-the-plain) seems likely. Falerii is the commoner prose name of the town, but for metrical reasons the poets use Falisci both for the people and the town (Ov. *Am.* 3.13.1).

Ibant aequati[1] numero regemque canebant:

ceu quondam nivei liquida inter nubila cycni[2]

cum sese e pastu referunt et longa canoros   700

dant per colla modos, sonat[3] amnis et Asia longe

pulsa palus.

Nec[4] quisquam aeratas acies ex[5] agmine tanto

misceri putet, aeriam sed gurgite ab alto

urgeri volucrum raucarum ad litora nubem.   705

> 706-22. *Clausus, founder of the gens Claudia, comes next with his followers from many small towns.*

Ecce Sabinorum[6] prisco de sanguine magnum

agmen agens Clausus magnique ipse agminis instar,[7]

Claudia nunc a quo diffunditur et[8] tribus et gens

per Latium, postquam in partem data Roma Sabinis.[9]

Una ingens Amiterna cohors[10] priscique Quirites,[11]   710

Ereti manus omnis oliviferaeque Mutuscae;

qui Nomentum[12] urbem, qui Rosea rura Velini,

---

1 698. **aequati numero:** 'formed up in equal groups'; as Servius says 'digesti in ordinem', cf. 11.599. The interpretation 'marching in measured time' is less natural, though it fits the context well.

2 699f. The simile is based on Hom. *Il.* 2.459f. and Ap. Rh. 4.1298f. For the song of swans cf. *Ecl.* 9.29, Hor. *Odes* 2.20.15-16. According to Servius, Pliny explained that the length of the swan's neck accounts for the beauty of its song. The location of the simile in Asia refers to the river Cayster famous for swans (Hom. *Il.* 2.461, *Geo.* 1.384).

3 701-2. **sonat . . . palus:** 'the river and the Asian pools re-echo the noise afar'; for *pulsa* referring to sound cf. *Ecl.* 6.84, *Aen.* 5.150. In Virgil the adjective *Asius* (unlike the noun *Asia*) has a long *a.*

4 703f. 'Nobody would think that bronze-armed battle-lines were massing from this great throng; but that a cloud of clamourous birds was sweeping through the air from the deep ocean to the shore.' This further elaboration of the simile is based on Ap. Rh. 4.238f., and it shifts the point of comparison from the song to the massed movement.

5 703. **ex agmine tanto:** a few late MSS read *examine,* and this is supported by Housman and accepted by Mackail and Mynors, but *exagmen* (*examen*) is not elsewhere used by Virgil of people; see note on 2.727.

6 706f. Servius regards this as an anachronism, because Clausus was a Sabine general who came to Rome after the expulsion of the kings, was given a part of the city, and founded the *gens Claudia* (cf. Livy 2.16). But Virgil refers to Rome in line 709 in such a way as to suggest that this Clausus was an ancestor of the later one. For the explicit derivation of one of the famous Roman *gentes,* cf. the ships' captains in 5.116f. The muster of Italian place names in this section is at its most dense; the Roman reader could identify himself with these little places, many of which he would know well, in a way quite impossible for the modern reader.

7 707. 'as good as a great army in himself; for *instar* cf. 2.15 *instar montis equum,* and Cic. *In Pis.* 52 *unus ille dies mihi immortalitatis instar fuit.* It is an oddly exaggerated phrase, referring to his courage and might.

8 708. **et tribus et gens:** some of the names of the 35 Roman tribes were the same as of the *gentes,* e.g. *Cornelia, Fabia, Horatia, Sergia.*

9 709. The reference is probably to the rape of the Sabines (as Servius says) as the point of time from which it was possible for Clausus to become ancestor of a Roman *gens,* but it might also be a reference to the actual Clausus who came to Rome in early Republican times (cf. note on 706f.).

10 710f. In the list of Sabine places which follows Virgil gives a wider area to Sabine territory than it had in later times.

11 710. **Quirites:** the use of this word here recalls its derivation from the Sabine town Cures (*Aen.* 6.811).

12 712. **Nomentum:** there is an inconsistency here with 6.773, where Nomentum is to be founded by Aeneas' descendants.

qui Tetricae[1] horrentis rupes montemque Severum
Casperiamque colunt Forulosque et flumen Himellae,
qui Tiberim Fabarimque bibunt, quos frigida misit   715
Nursia, et Ortinae[2] classes populique[3] Latini,
quosque[4] secans infaustum interluit Allia nomen:
quam multi Libyco volvuntur marmore fluctus
saevus ubi Orion[5] hibernis conditur undis,
vel cum sole novo densae torrentur aristae[6]   720
aut Hermi[7] campo aut Lyciae flaventibus arvis.
Scuta[8] sonant pulsuque pedum conterrita tellus.

    723-49. Next come Halaesus, Oebalus, Ufens.

⁹Hinc Agamemnonius,[10] Troiani nominis hostis,
curru iungit Halaesus equos Turnoque ferocis
mille rapit[11] populos, vertunt[12] felicia Baccho   725
Massica qui rastris, et quos de collibus altis
Aurunci misere patres Sidicinaque iuxta
aequora, quique Cales linquunt amnisque vadosi
accola Volturni,[13] pariterque Saticulus asper
Oscorumque manus. Teretes sunt aclydes[14] illis   730

---

1 713. **Tetricae horrentis rupes:** probably a piece of etymologising, where *horrentis* represents the meaning (from *taeter,* 'horrible') of the proper name Tetrica; see note on 682f.

2 716. **Ortinae classes:** 'troops', in its earlier meaning before it was specifically applied to the fleet. Servius says *equites,* which is likely. It is not known to which part of Sabine territory the adjective *Ortinus* refers.

3 **populique Latini:** presumably those on the borders of the Sabines, who joined the Sabine contingent.

4 717. 'and those in whose midst the Allia flows, cutting its course, that river of ill-omened name'. The reference is to the defeat of the Romans by Brennus the Gaul in 390 B.C., since which time the anniversary (July 18) was held accursed. The rhythm of the line and its alliteration of *in-* compels the attention for this climactic ending of the list of names.

5 719. Orion's winter setting, early in November, was often a stormy period; cf. Hor. *Odes* 3.27.17-18. and see note on 1.535.

6 720. The second part of the simile is introduced elliptically: the meaning is 'or as many as the thick corn-ears when . . .'. *Sole novo* seems to mean 'at the beginning of summer', as Servius says (*Geo.* 2.332); the impression of denseness is given as the corn comes to its maturity.

7 721. Hermus is in Lydia, a fertile area. Lycia is less fertile, but cf. Ov. *Met.* 6.317.

8 722. This final line, which is reminiscent of lines in Homer's catalogue, e.g. *Il.* 2.466, 784, has remarkably heavy and patterned alliteration.

9 723f. The interest in these three contingents is less maintained; they are treated briefly, and all in much the same way, with a short cameo of the leaders and a description of the armour and customs of their followers.

10 723-4. **Agamemnonius . . . Halaesus:** Servius reports that some said Halaesus was Agamemnon's son, others his companion; the former is inconsistent with 10.417f. On the theme of Greek origins for Aeneas' opponents see note on 372. Halaesus was the eponymous hero of the Falisci; Servius on 695 explains the shift of *h* to *f.* His followers come from the region of Campania.

11 725. **rapit:** 'marches at speed', cf. 10.178.

12 725-6. **vertunt . . . rastris:** 'who with their hoes cultivate Massica, a place fertile for the grape'; the postposition of *qui* is extreme for Virgil. Massic wine is frequently mentioned by Horace; cf. also *Geo.* 2.143.

13 729. The nominatives mark a change in the form of the sentence, which hitherto has been governed by *rapit.*

14 730. **aclydes:** long clubs, according to Servius, fitted with a thong so that they could be retrieved (731). Notice the Greek plural form, with short *-es*; cf. 8.51, 11.170, 660.

342

tela, sed haec lento mos est aptare flagello.
Laevas caetra tegit, falcati[1] comminus enses.
   Nec tu carminibus nostris indictus abibis,[2]
Oebale, quem generasse Telon Sebethide nympha
fertur, Teleboum[3] Capreas cum regna teneret,   735
iam senior; patriis sed non et filius arvis
contentus late iam tum dicione tenebat
Sarrastis[4] populos et quae rigat aequora Sarnus,
quique Rufras Batulumque tenent atque arva Celemnae,
et quos maliferae[5] despectant moenia Abellae,   740
Teutonico ritu soliti[6] torquere cateias;[7]
tegmina quis capitum[8] raptus de subere cortex
aerataeque micant peltae, micat aereus ensis.
   [9]Et te montosae misere in proelia Nersae,
Ufens, insignem fama et felicibus armis,   745
horrida praecipue cui gens adsuetaque multo
venatu nemorum, duris Aequicula glaebis.
Armati terram exercent semperque recentis
convectare iuvat praedas et vivere rapto.

---

1 732. **falcati comminus enses:** 'sickle-shaped swords (i.e. scimitars) are their weapons for close-fighting'. The phrase is remarkably abrupt, and some verb has to be supplied by zeugma from *tegit.*

2 733f. The contingent of Oebalus comes from the region of Naples, to the south and east of Halaesus' area. It is not known from what source Virgil has his story; it may well have been from Cato. The nymph Sebethis was a daughter of the river god of the river Sebethos, near Naples (Stat. *Silv.* 1.2.263).

3 735. 'when he ruled Capreae, kingdom of the Teleboae'; the father, Telon, was king of the isle of Capri, but his son extended the kingdom to the mainland.

4 738-9. The Sarrastes are called after the river Sarnus, between Naples and Salerno; the obscure names in the next line seem to be of places inland to the north.

5 740. **maliferae . . . Abellae:** again an etymological adjective (see note on 682), as the word *abella* meant a kind of fruit or nut. *Malifer,* 'apple-bearing', is not found elsewhere.

6 741. **soliti:** in strict grammar we would expect *solitos,* governed by *tenebat,* but the long series of relative clauses has caused the sentence to diverge from its original construction, as if these peoples were the subject of some verb like *aderant.*

7 **cateias:** a throwing weapon intended, like the *aclys* (730), to return to the thrower. Servius says this was done by a line attached; Isidore (*Orig.* 18.7.7) makes it a boomerang. The word, which is foreign, is not found before Virgil; presumably it entered the Latin language during the wars in and around Gaul.

8 742. 'whose heads were covered with bark taken from cork trees'; this would be very pliant when first cut, and could be shaped.

9 744f. Ufens and his people (the *gens Aequicula*) come from the foothills of the Apennines east of Rome. The sketch of their rugged way of life is reminiscent of Numanus' description of the simple life in 9.603f., esp. 609 and 612-13. Virgil takes the name for his Ufens (who is not heard of elsewhere, except that the name occurs in Silius) from the river of this area (802); his death is mentioned in 12.460.

750-60. *Umbro comes next, a priest with supernatural powers.*

[1]Quin et Marruvia[2] venit de gente sacerdos   750
fronde super galeam et felici comptus oliva
Archippi[3] regis missu, fortissimus Umbro,
vipereo generi et graviter spirantibus hydris[4]
spargere qui somnos cantuque manuque solebat,
mulcebatque iras et morsus arte levabat.   755
Sed non Dardaniae medicari cuspidis ictum[5]
evaluit neque eum iuvere in vulnere cantus
somniferi et Marsis quaesitae montibus herbae.
Te nemus Angitiae,[6] vitrea te Fucinus unda,
te liquidi flevere lacus.   760

761-82. *Virbius, son of Hippolytus, comes from Aricia.*

[7]Ibat et Hippolyti proles pulcherrima bello,
Virbius, insignem quem mater[8] Aricia misit,
eductum Egeriae lucis umentia circum
litora, pinguis ubi et placabilis[9] ara Dianae.
Namque[10] ferunt fama Hippolytum, postquam arte novercae   765

---

1 750f. The mood changes now: there is no reference in this section to Umbro's followers, or to types of armour. Instead we hear of a priest with strange powers, who yet could not save himself; pathos is strong at the end of the passage.

2 750. **Marruvia . . . de gente:** Servius tells us that Medea herself came from Colchis to Italy and taught the Maruvii remedies against serpents. Marruvium was a town on Lake Fucinus (759) in the Marsian territory (758), the Apennine foothills east of Rome.

3 752. Virgil probably has made up the name Archippus from a town Archippe (Plin. *Nat. Hist.* 3.108) on the borders of the Fucine Lake.

4 753-4. *qui* is very far postponed, cf. 726.

5 756. Cf. Rhamnes in 9.328, Panthus in 2.429.

6 759-60. The device of pathetic fallacy (cf. 516f., 8.91-2, 240) is particularly frequent in the *Eclogues,* e.g. 1.39, 10.13f. *Nemus Angitiae* was near Lake Fucinus: according to Servius Angitia was an epithet of Medea; others made her a sister of Medea. For the half-line, which here seems to enhance the effect of pathos. see note on 129.

7 761f. This episode is drawn in rich and vivid colours, with a mythological atmosphere of evocative imagination. The Roman deity Virbius, who was associated with Diana, was identified with Hippolytus miraculously restored to life after his fall from the chariot (Ov. *Met.* 15.497f, *Fast.* 6.737f.); Servius justifies this identification with the etymology of *Virbius = vir bis.* Virgil has invented a son of this deity, and can thus bring into his narrative not only the famous Greek story of Hippolytus, Phaedra and Theseus but also the revered features of Roman folklore and the religious associations connected with the sacred grove of Aricia, mystic home of Egeria, Diana of Nemi, and the Golden Bough. See H. J. Rose in *Myth or Legend,* ed. G. E. Daniel. ch. 12.

8 762-3. Mother Aricia (cf. 10.172) is the sacred grove where Virbius was born; Egeria was the mystic nymph by whom Numa, the second king of Rome, was said to have been instructed in religious truths.

9 764. 'where there was the rich shrine of Diana ready to be propitiated'; for the phraseology cf. 9.585, and for the meaning of *placabilis* cf. Ov. *Met.* 15.574 *placat odoratis herbosas ignibus aras.* The shrine of Diana by the lake (*Speculum Dianae*) at Nemi was the most famous of all her seats of worship, and was associated with the strange ritual of the *rex nemorensis* (see *O.C.D.*).

10 765f Theseus' wife Phaedra fell in love with her stepson Hippolytus and being repulsed committed suicide, leaving a letter accusing Hippolytus. Theseus wished him to be put to death, and at his request Poseidon caused a sea monster to frighten Hippolytus' horses, so that they reared and he was killed. The story is told in Euripides' *Hippolytus* and in Seneca's *Phaedra;* cf. also Spenser, *F.Q.* 1.5.36f.

occiderit patriasque explerit[1] sanguine poenas
turbatis distractus equis,[2] ad sidera rursus
aetheria et superas caeli venisse sub auras,
Paeoniis[3] revocatum herbis et amore Dianae.
Tum pater omnipotens aliquem indignatus ab umbris   770
mortalem infernis ad lumina surgere vitae,
ipse repertorem medicinae talis et artis
fulmine Phoebigenam[4] Stygias detrusit ad undas.
At Trivia Hippolytum secretis alma recondit
sedibus et nymphae Egeriae nemorique relegat,   775
solus[5] ubi in silvis Italis ignobilis aevum
exigeret versoque ubi nomine Virbius esset.
Unde etiam templo[6] Triviae lucisque sacratis
cornipedes arcentur equi, quod litore currum
et iuvenem monstris pavidi effudere marinis.   780
Filius ardentis haud[7] setius aequore campi
exercebat equos curruque in bella ruebat.

> 783-802. *Turnus himself, magnificently arrayed, comes in command of the Rutulians.*

Ipse inter primos praestanti[8] corpore Turnus
vertitur[9] arma tenens et toto vertice supra est.

---

1 766. 'paid with his life the penalty which his father demanded'.

2 767f. Hippolytus' restoration to life by Asclepius (Paeon) at Diana's instigation is told in both Ovid's versions (note on 761f.).

3 769. **Paeoniis**: the *o* is long, so the word scans as three long syllables by synizesis or consonantal *i*; cf. 12.401. and see notes on 33.175.

4 773. **Phoebigenam**: Paeon was son of Phoebus Apollo. There is a curious alternative reading *Poenigenam* which Servius knew, but he cites Probus' authority for *Phoebigenam*.

5 776f. 'so that solitary and unknown he might spend his life in the Italian woods. and have a different name. and be Virbius'. Cf. 10.52f.

6 778f. The story ends with a piece of aetiology; it has given the reason why horses are kept away from Diana s temple.

7 781. **haud setius**: 'none the less'; in spite of his father's tragedy, Virbius the son rides out to war.

8 783. **praestanti corpore**: we have already been prepared for this at the beginning of the catalogue (649), where we heard that Lausus was the most handsome figure of all except Turnus.

9 784. **vertitur**: an unexpected word, suggesting perhaps that he moves around among his men, not in formation with them, but always conspicuous because of his stature and splendour.

Cui[1] triplici crinita iuba galea alta Chimaeram   785
ustinet Aetnaeos efflantem faucibus ignis;
Tam[2] magis illa fremens et tristibus effera flammis
quam magis effuso crudescunt[3] sanguine pugnae.
At levem clipeum[4] sublatis cornibus Io
auro insignibat, iam[5] saetis obsita, iam bos,   790
argumentum[6] ingens, et custos virginis Argus,
caelataque amnem fundens pater[7] Inachus urna.
Insequitur nimbus[8] peditum clipeataque totis
agmina densentur campis, Argivaque[9] pubes
Auruncaeque manus, Rutuli veteresque[10] Sicani,   795
et Sacranae acies et picti[11] scuta Labici;
qui saltus, Tiberine, tuos sacrumque[12] Numici
litus arant Rutulosque exercent vomere collis
Circaeumque iugum,[13] quis Iuppiter Anxurus arvis
praesidet et viridi gaudens Feronia luco;   800

---

1 785f. 'His helmet bedecked with triple plume has high aloft an emblem of a chimaera, breathing Etna's flames from its jaws, roaring and spreading terror with its destructive breath more and more as the battles grow grimmer and the blood flows freer.' This is a splendid piece of imaginative symbolism; on one level it can be rationalised into the hot passion of Turnus in battle, but on another it deliberately defies the limitations of the inanimate. The buildup of anticipation as the reader has waited for Turnus enables the poet to require of him a 'willing suspension of disbelief'. The Chimaera was amongst the monsters in the jaws of Hades (6.288); for the flames cf. Lucr. 5.905f. Its significance as a symbol for Turnus is not only fierceness and strength, but also primitive and archaic violence; it is the kind of monster of which a Hercules would rid the world to everyone's benefit. The association with Etna, with volcanic violence, with the Giants, strengthens this concept; for a fine discussion of the symbolism see S. G. P. Small, *T.A.Ph.A.* 1959, pp. 243f. If Turnus could have learned to disown his emblem, the *Aeneid* could have ended without his death.

2 787-8. **tam magis . . . quam magis:** cited by Quintilian as an archaism. *Fremens* here is loosely used almost as a main verb.

3 788. **crudescunt:** cf. 11.833; the word is not found before Virgil.

4 789f. The emblem of the shield (Io daughter of the river god Inachus persecuted by Juno, turned into a cow and guarded by the hundred-eyed Argus) has a different function. Partly it reminds us of the power for harm which Juno, instigator of this war, possesses, and partly it turns our thoughts to Greece and the Greek connections of this new Achilles against whom Aeneas must fight (cf. 371-2).

5 790. **iam saetis obsita, iam bos:** 'already covered with hair, already a cow'; the monosyllabic ending emphasises the grotesque picture (Ovid's treatment of this story in *Met.* 1 is an astonishing mixture of comedy and pathos).

6 791. **argumentum ingens:** 'a huge picture'. *Argumentum* is a technical term for a composition (Quint. 5.10). and the meaning seems to be that the emblem on the shield is unusually large and elaborate.

7 792. 'and her father Inachus pouring a stream from an embossed urn'; this is a normal way of portraying a river-god.

8 793f. The 'cloud' of infantry come from places around the Rutulian territory, from the Tiber in the north to Anxur in the south. See B. Tilly, *Greece and Rome,* 1959, pp. 194f.

9 794. **Argivaque pubes:** probably from Ardea, Turnus' capital, founded by Danae; see note on 372.

10 795. **veteresque Sicani:** cf. 8.328f., 11.317, for the settlement of Sicani in Italy; *veteres* ('of old') suggests, as Servius says, that they did not stay in this area.

11 796. **picti scuta Labici:** 'the people of Labicum with their painted shields'; Labicum was one of the cities of the Latin league. For *scuta* (retained accusative) cf. 9.582, 11.777, and see note on 503. There may be another etymological play here, as Labici may mean 'shieldmen'.

12 797. For the Numicus, a small river near the Tiber, cf. 150; it is *sacrum* because Aeneas was said to have been buried there (Livy 1.2.6).

13 799. For the promontory of Circe see line 10; Anxur was a little further down the coast, and this grove of Feronia was nearby (Hor. *Sat.* 1.5.24f.).

qua Saturae[1] iacet atra palus gelidusque per imas
quaerit iter vallis atque in mare conditur Ufens.

803-17. *Last of all comes Camilla, the warrior princess of the Volsci.*

²Hos[3] super advenit Volsca de gente Camilla
agmen agens equitum et florentis[4] aere catervas,
bellatrix, non[5] illa colo[6] calathisve Minervae   805
femineas adsueta[7] manus, sed proelia virgo
dura pati cursuque pedum praevertere ventos.
Illa vel intactae[8] segetis per summa volaret[9]
gramina nec teneras cursu laesisset aristas,
vel mare per medium fluctu suspensa tumenti   810
ferret iter celeris nec tingeret aequore plantas.
Illam omnis tectis agrisque effusa iuventus
turbaque miratur matrum et prospectat euntem,
attonitis inhians animis ut regius ostro[10]
velet honos levis umeros, ut fibula crinem   815
auro internectat, Lyciam[11] ut gerat ipsa pharetram
et pastoralem[12] praefixa cuspide myrtum.

---

1 801. **Saturae . . . palus**: part of the Pomptine marshes of this area.

2 803f. The catalogue ends with the half-real, half-supernatural figure of the warrior princess Camilla. She is in one way real enough, a heroic figure worthy to fight beside the other Latin leaders (as indeed she shows by her deeds in Book 11); but she is also a fairy princess, able to move over growing corn or the waves of the sea, belonging to the beauty and unreality of the pastoral world.
She is Virgil's own creation, not heard of before him or again after him. Virgil's portrayal is built partly from mythological figures like Harpalyce (1.316f.) or the Amazon princess Penthesilea (1.490f.), and partly from Italian folklore. She was under Diana's special protection (11.532f.), and her name was evidently connected in Virgil's mind with the words *camillus, camilla,* cult names of youths and maidens in certain Roman religious ceremonies (Macrob. *Sat.* 3.8.6f.), as well as with the Roman family Camilli (*Geo.* 2.169, *Aen.* 6.825).

3 803. **hos super**: 'as well as these', *super* as in *alii super alios.*

4 804. **florentis aere**: 'brilliant with bronze armour', cf. Lucr. 4.450, 5.1442; the striking phrase is used again (11.433) of Camilla's troops.

5 805. **non illa**: cf. 5.457, 6.593.

6 **colo calathisve Minervae**: 'the distaff or work-baskets of Minerva (goddess of handicrafts)'; cf. Hor. *Odes* 3.12.4f, *Aen.* 8.409.

7 806f. **adsueta** is used in a middle sense with the accusative *manus* (cf. 12.224 and see note on 503); observe the change in construction, from the dative in line 805 to the infinitive in 807: 'not accustomed to the distaff . . . but to enduring stern battles'. Page takes *dura* with *virgo*: 'a maiden hardy to endure', but this spoils the balance of the sentence.

8 808. **intactae**: 'unreaped'.

9 808-9. Notice the variation of tense: 'she could fly (if she wished) . . . and would not have harmed (if she had done so)'. The passage is based on Hom. *Il.* 20.226f. (the horses of the North Wind). Cf. Ov. *Met.* 10.654-5, Milton, *Comus* 895f. 'Whilst from off the waters fleet / thus I set my printless feet / o'er the cowslip's velvet head, / that bends not as I tread', and Pope. *Essay on Criticism,* 370f. 'When Ajax strives some rocks vast weight to throw, / the line too labours, and the words move slow: / not so, when swift Camilla scours the plain. / flies o'er the unbending corn, and skims along the main'.

10 814-15. '(seeing) how royal splendour covers her smooth shoulders with purple', i.e. she wears a purple robe.

11 816. **Lyciam**: cf. 8.166, 11.773.

12 817. 'and the shepherds' myrtle staff with iron blade set in its head'; this last line brilliantly summarises the ambiguity of Camilla, carrying the myrtle staff from the idyllic pastoral world (cf. *Ecl.* 8.16) converted to military use by its iron point.

BOOK 8

Introductory note

The eighth book is a peaceful and serene interlude between the activity of the Furies and the outbreak of war in Book 7 and the long battle descriptions of Book 9. Its setting is Pallanteum, Evander's little town on the future site of Golden Rome, and in its central scene Evander introduces Aeneas to the hills and valleys which were to become famous throughout the world. The description of the places is balanced by the pictures of the people on the shield which Vulcan made for Aeneas. Thus the immortal city sees its beginning: Book 8 corresponds in its position in the poem (as the second book of the second half) with Book 2, in which Troy's history came to its end; Ilion falling, Rome arising'.

The structure of the book is based on two interwoven themes: Aeneas' visit to Evander (1.369, 454-607) and the making and description of armour (370-453, 608-731). These two themes present in different ways the same underlying concept, the defeat of violence and hostile powers by bravery, by avoidance of corrupting influences, above all by proper worship of the gods. Thus the monster Cacus is conquered by Hercules, the impious Mezentius destined to die at Aeneas' hands, the renegade Antony conquered by Augustus. The religious observances of Evander and Aeneas receive great emphasis throughout the book and are summarised on the shield as the gods save Rome from the Gauls, and Augustus defeats the powers of the East at Actium with the help of the Roman deities, drawn up in battle against the monstrous forms of Egyptian gods.

More than anywhere else in the poem Virgil employs here one of his best-loved narrative techniques, the interweaving of the story of Aeneas with thoughts and events from the past and (particularly) from the future. The mythology of Hercules' battle with Cacus (see note on 184f.) reaches back to the past to illustrate the qualities which lead to deification; the contemporary narrative of Aeneas and Evander has been very greatly re-cast from the mass of legend about early Italy available to Virgil, in order that the material could serve the main themes referred to above; and the anticipation of Roman history and particularly of Augustan Rome by prophetic pictures on the shield and aetiological references to customs and ceremonies and places gives a sense of destiny and achievement which make this the most optimistic book in the poem.

1-101. *Turnus gives the signal for war; the Latins prepare, and an embassy asking for help is sent to Diomedes. Aeneas is troubled at the turn of events, but a vision of the River-god Tiberinus appears to him, assuring him that he has reached his goal and urging him to seek help from Evander. He sees the omen of the white sow and rowing peacefully up the Tiber reaches Pallanteum, Evander's little settlement on the future site of Rome.*

[1]Ut belli[2] signum Laurenti Turnus ab arce
extulit et rauco strepuerunt cornua cantu,
utque acris concussit equos utque[3] impulit arma,
extemplo [4]turbati animi, simul omne tumultu
coniurat trepido Latium saevitque iuventus   5
effera. Ductores primi Messapus[5] et Ufens
contemptorque[6] deum Mezentius undique cogunt
auxilia et latos[7] vastant cultoribus agros.
Mittitur et magni Venulus[8] Diomedis ad urbem
qui petat auxilium, et[9] Latio consistere Teucros,   10
advectum Aenean classi victosque penatis
inferre et fatis regem se dicere posci,

---

1 1f. The book begins with a marked contrast between the eager vehemence of Turnus as he prepares for battle, and the worried anxiety of Aeneas who has no wish for war. The vision of Tiberinus is reminiscent of the appearance of the Penates to Aeneas in Book 3, and it serves at this crucial stage to reinforce the feeling of the divine intention working behind human affairs; Aeneas is reassured, given advice, and made to feel that he is right to continue his mission to establish his city even against the hostility which has been aroused among the inhabitants of Latium.

The idyllic picture of the old River-god takes us momentarily away from the harsh realities of impending battle (as does the transformation of the ships to Nymphs in Book 9), and the description of the journey from the mouth of the Tiber to Pallanteum (from Ostia to Rome as Virgil's readers would know it) is filled with a serene patriotic love of this scenery, brought to a climax by the first sighting of Evander's little settlement on the seven hills.

2 1. Immediately after the catalogue of Italian forces at the end of Book 7, the signal for war is given by Turnus (Latinus having abdicated his authority, 7.600 from the palace of Latinus in the Laurentian territory. For the adjective *Laurens* (the noun is never found) cf. 38, 371, and see note on 747.

3 3. **utque ... utque:** the doubling and trebling of subordinate clauses is very unusual in Virgil. Evidently here he wished to pause on the picture of Turnus, whipping up his horses. clashing his armour (cf. line 529. 12.332).

4 4f. 'immediately their passions were aroused, and straight away all Latium joined in excited uproar and the young men were all rage and frenzy'; notice the great emphasis on *effera,* first word in the line and last in the sentence.

5 6. Messapus and Ufens were described in the catalogue (7.691f.,744f.).

6 7. **contemptorque deum Mezentius:** the exiled Etruscan tyrant Mezentius, *contemptor divum* (7.648), came first in the catalogue; see note on 7.648.

7 8. **latos ... agros:** 'despoil the wide fields of their farmers'; *cultoribus* is ablative of separation after *vastant,* cf. Stat. *Th.* 3.576. The thought reminds us of the poet of the *Georgics* (e.g. 1.507 *squalent abductis arva colonis*).

8 9. **Venulus Diomedis ad urbem:** the return of Venulus and his party from Argyripa (Arpi), Diomedes' city in Daunia, reporting Diomedes' refusal to help, is described at length in 11.225f. Venulus was from Tibur (11.757), said to be an Argive colony: he is therefore appropriately chosen to approach Diomedes, who was said to have fled from Argos (where he was king) to Italy after the Trojan war.

9 10f. **et Latio ... edoceat:** 'and tell him that the Teucrians were settling in Latium, that Aeneas had arrived by sea and was bringing in his conquered gods and saying that he was called by fate to be king'. With *advectum* understand *esse; classi* is a less frequent form of the ablative (cf. Cat. 64.212 and compare *amni* in 473, *capiti* in 7.668); for the emphasis on *penates* see note on 1.6.

edoceat, multasque viro se adiungere gentis
Dardanio et late Latio increbrescere nomen:
quid struat his coeptis, quem, si fortuna sequatur,[1]   15
eventum pugnae cupiat, manifestius ipsi
quam Turno regi aut regi apparere Latino.[2]
    Talia per Latium. Quae Laomedontius[3] heros
cuncta videns magno curarum fluctuat aestu,
atque animum nunc huc celerem nunc dividit illuc   20
in partisque rapit varias perque omnia versat,
sicut[4] aquae tremulum labris[5] ubi lumen aenis
sole repercussum[6] aut radiantis imagine lunae
omnia pervolitat late loca, iamque sub auras
Tigitur summique ferit laquearia[7] tecti.   25
Nox erat et terras animalia fessa per omnis[8]
alituum[9] pecudumque genus sopor altus habebat,
cum pater in ripa gelidique sub aetheris axe
Aeneas, tristi turbatus[10] pectora bello,
procubuit seramque dedit per membra quietem.   30
Huic[11] deus ipse loci fluvio Tiberinus amoeno[12]
populeas inter senior se attollere frondes

---

1 15f. This is still part of the message Venulus is to carry: Turnus means that Diomedes (*ipsi*) knows Aeneas better and will better read his aggressive intentions, and know that he may be next on the list. It is possible that *ipsi* refers to Aeneas, in the sense that he may know what he hopes to gain, but Turnus and Latinus cannot imagine : cf. 5.788.

2 17. A prosaic line, a piece of formal language for the envoys to get their tongues round.

3 18. **Laomedontius heros**: for Laomedon, father of Priam (158, 162), cf. 3.248, 7.105 (with note).
20-1. These lines are repeated from 4.285-6, where see notes.

4 22f. 'Like flickering light. reflected off the water in bronze vessels from the sun or the form of the shining moon, when it flits all around everywhere, rising up now to the heights and catching the gilt panels in the high ceiling.' The simile is based on Ap. Rh. 3.756f, where the fluttering heart of Medea is compared with light reflected from water; it has some similarity to the comparison in *Aen*. 7.462f. of Turnus' anger with water boiling over.

5 22. **labris**: cf. *Geo.* 2.6, *Aen.* 12.417. The *a* in this word is long by nature; in *labrum* (lip) it is short.

6 23. **repercussum**: 'thrown back', used of sounds (echoes) as well as light. The reference here is to the reflection of the sun not on the water but thrown off from the water on to other objects in the form of a dancing blob of light.

7 25. **laquearia**: cf. 1.726.

8 26f. For the description of night cf. *Aen.* 4.322f., 3147f.

9 27. **alituum pecudumque genus**: in apposition to *animalia. Alituum* is a lengthened form of the genitive plural of *ales*, found in Lucretius (e.g. 5.801).

10 29. **turbatus pectora**: retained accusative. cf. lines 265, 286, 457, 662, *Aen.* 1.579, and see note on 7.503.

11 31-4. 'To him there appeared the god of the place himself, old Tiber, rising up from his lovely stream amidst the poplar leaves; the transparent material of a grey robe enfolded him, and shady reeds hid his locks.' The ghostly picture of the River-god is superbly done in misty phrases; cf. the river Mincius in 10.205-6. Page quotes Milton, *Lycidas* 103-4
'Next Camus, reverend Sire, went footing slow,
His mantle hairy, and his bonnet sedge'.

12 31f. Observe how the descriptive narrative of night and Aeneas' anxieties has prepared the way for the vision and the prophecies of the River-god Tiber.

visus (eum tenuis glauco velabat amictu
carbasus, et crinis umbrosa tegebat harundo),
tum sic adfari et curas his demere dictis:[1]   35
    'O sate[2] gente deum, Troianam ex hostibus urbem
qui revehis[3] nobis aeternaque Pergama servas,
exspectate[4] solo Laurenti arvisque Latinis,
hic[5] tibi certa domus, certi (ne absiste) penates.
Neu belli terrere minis; [6]tumor[7] omnis et irae   40
concessere deum.[8]
Iamque tibi,[9] ne vana putes haec fingere somnum,
litoreis ingens inventa sub ilicibus sus[10]
triginta capitum fetus enixa iacebit,
alba solo recubans, albi circum ubera nati.   45
[Hic locus urbis erit, requies ea certa laborum,][11]
ex quo ter denis urbem redeuntibus annis[12]
Ascanius clari condet cognominis Albam.
Haud incerta cano. Nunc qua ratione quod instat[13]
expedias victor, paucis (adverte) docebo.   50
Arcades[14] his oris, genus a Pallante[15] profectum,
qui regem Euandrum comites, qui signa secuti,[16]

---

1 35. The same line occurs in 2.775 (the vision of Creusa) and 3.153 (the vision of the Penates which Aeneas sees in sleep). The prophecies given there are now fulfilled. *Adfari* and *demere* depend on *visus* (*est*).

2 36. **sate gente**: for *satus* ('born of') see note on 7.152.

3 37. **revehis**: because Dardanus originally came from Italy, cf. 3.167, 7.240.

4 38. **expectate**: for the vocative of the past participle cf. 2.282-3 *quibus Hector ab oris / expectate venis?*

5 39. **hic tibi certa domus**: Tiber confirms Aeneas' words in 7.122 (after the omen of eating the table) *hic domus haec patria est.*

6 40. 'and do not be frightened by the threats of war', the clause is parallel to the parenthetical *ne absiste. Terrere* is the passive imperative.

7 40-1. **tumor . . . deum**: Servius points out that this is not true (cf. angry Juno in 60), and concludes therefore that the half-line is deficient in sense like 3.340), quoting as a supplement *profugis nova moenia Teucris*. As it stands *concessere* means 'have departed' (cf. 2.91) and may stand as a rhetorical exaggeration to encourage Aeneas, prophetic rather than actual in meaning.

8 41. For the half-line see notes on 1.534, 7.129. The others in this book are 469, 536.

9 42. **tibi**: ethic dative, 'I can tell you'.

10 43-6. These verses are repeated from *Aen.* 3.390f. (where see notes), the prophecy of Helenus. The white sow with its thirty young marks the site of Lavinium from which after thirty years the Trojans were to move to Alba Longa.

11 46. This verse (= 3.393, except *hic locus* for *is locus*) is in only one of the three chief MSS, and is not commented on by Servius; it should therefore be omitted and *ex quo* in the next line taken to mean 'and in accordance with this (portent)'.

12 47. The period of thirty years at Lavinium before moving to Alba was prophesied by Jupiter, *Aen.* 1.269f. Notice that Virgil does not use the version of the legend according to which the sow marked the site of Alba Longa.

13 49-50. Cf. *Aen.* 4.115-16 (Juno to Venus).

14 51. **Arcades**: a dactyl, with the Greek declension of short *-es;* cf. *Cyclopes* (424).

15 **Pallante**: Servius tells us that this Pallas was the grandfather of Evander; there was a city Pallanteum in Arcadia (Livy 1.5) and this was also the name of Evander's settlement on the site of Rome (54). The Palatine hill was connected with this verbal root in antiquity; cf. *Aen.* 9.9.

16 52. **secuti**: understand *sunt,* cf. line 4.

delegere locum et posuere in[1] montibus urbem
Pallantis proavi de nomine Pallanteum.[2]
Hi bellum adsidue ducunt cum gente Latina;   55
hos castris adhibe socios et foedera iunge.
Ipse [3]ego te ripis et recto flumine ducam,
adversum remis superes subvectus ut amnem.
Surge age, nate dea, primisque[4] cadentibus astris
Iunoni fer rite preces, iramque minasque   60
supplicibus supera votis. Mihi victor honorem
persolves. Ego[5] sum pleno quem flumine cernis
stringentem ripas et pinguia culta secantem,
caeruleus[6] Thybris, caelo gratissimus amnis.
hic[7] mihi magna domus, celsis caput urbibus exit.'   65
    Dixit, deinde lacu fluvius[8] se condidit alto
ima petens; nox Aenean somnusque reliquit.
Surgit et aetherii spectans orientia solis
lumina rite cavis undam de flumine palmis
sustinet ac talis effundit ad aethera voces: 70
'nymphae, Laurentes nymphae, genus[9] amnibus unde est,
tuque, o Thybri tuo genitor cum flumine sancto,[10]
accipite Aenean et tandem arcete periclis.

---

1 53. **in montibus** : i.e. the site of Rome, city of seven hills.

2 54. For the spondaic fifth foot cf. 167, 341, 345, 402 and see note on 7.634.

3 57. 'I will myself lead you on between my banks, straight up my stream, so that as you journey inland you may conquer the current against you by rowing.' The ablatives *ripis* and *recto flumine* are ablative of route, like *ibam forte Via Sacra;* cf. also *recto litore* (6.900).

4 59. **primisque cadentibus astris**: this appears to refer to the paling of stars in the sky as dawn first comes: cf. 2.9.

5 62f. Tiber's revelation of his identity is very impressive; the slow descriptive clauses of 63-4 follow majestically upon the rapid phrases of 59-61. His words are not unlike those which Aeneas first heard about him (in 2.781f.). from Creusa.

6 64. **caeruleus:** the normal epithet of deities of sea or river; the god is green, though the river is yellow (*flavus*).

7 65. 'Here is my mighty palace; my fountainhead springs from a region of lofty cities.' By *domus* he means the mouth of his river or perhaps more specifically the bend near the mouth called *Tiberina atria* (Ov. *Fast.* 4.329f.); for *caput* cf. *Geo.* 4.368f., Lucr. 5.270; *celsis urbibus* refers to the hill towns of Etruria. For *exit* cf. 75. Cf. Milton, *Comus* 933-6 (of the river Sabrina):
'May thy lofty head be crowned
With many a tower and terrace round.
And here and there thy banks upon
With groves of myrrh and cinnamon'.
Others punctuate so that *domus* is the subject of *exit* with *celsis caput urbibus* (which they refer to Rome) in apposition to it. but see Semple in *C.R.* 1936, p.112.

8 66. **fluvius:** here the River-god, disappearing into his subaqueous palace.

9 71. **genus amnibus unde est**: 'from whom comes the birth of rivers', i.e. the nymphs of the mountains give birth to rivers. For *genus unde* cf. 1.6.

10 72. Cf. Enn. *Ann.* 54 *teque pater Tiberine tuo cum flumine sancto. Thybri* (with short final *i*) is a Greek vocative, cf. 540.

Quo [1]te cumque lacus miserantem incommoda nostra
fonte tenet, quocumque solo pulcherrimus exis,   75
semper honore meo, semper celebrabere donis
corniger[2] Hesperidum[3] fluvius regnator aquarum.
Adsis[4] o tantum et propius[5] tua numina firmes.'
Sic memorat, geminasque legit de classe biremis
remigioque [6]aptat, socios simul instruit armis.   80
   Ecce autem subitum atque oculis mirabile monstrum,
candida [7]per silvam cum fetu concolor albo
procubuit viridique in litore conspicitur sus:
quam pius[8] Aeneas tibi enim,[9] tibi, maxima Iuno,
maetat[10] sacra ferens et cum grege sistit ad aram.   85
Thybris[11] ea fluvium, quam longa est, nocte tumentem
leniit, et tacita refluens ita substitit unda,
mitis ut in morem stagni placidaeque paludis
sterneret aequor aquis, remo ut luctamen abesset.
Ergo iter inceptum celerant rumore[12] secundo: 90
labitur uncta vadis abies; [13]mirantur et undae,[14]
miratur [15]nemus insuetum fulgentia longe

---

1 74-5. 'Wherever the spring is where your waters encompass you as you pity our distress, wherever the ground from which you gush forth in all your glory.' The second phrase paraphrases the first: *quicumque* or *quisquis* is a common formula in prayers. See Pliny, *Epp.* 8.8, for a description of the worship of the Clitumnus at its source.

2 77. **corniger**: river-gods are frequently portrayed with horns, cf. 727, Ov. *Met.* 14.602, and *Geo.* 4.371.

3 **Hesperidum . . . aquarum**: 'of Western waters'; the feminine form *Hesperis* here acts as an adjective.

4 78. **adsis o tantum**: 'only be with me'; for *tantum* cf. 9.636.

5 **propius**: 'yet more favourably', cf. 1.526, and for the request for confirmation of a divine sign cf. 2.691.

6 80. 'he fits them out with their complement of oarsmen, and also provides the men with their equipment': 3.471, where *remigium* is (as here) abstract for concrete.

7 82-3. 'a white sow, with her offspring, all white as well, was seen through the wood, lying there on the green bank'; cf. lines 43-4. *Per silvam* is curiously placed; its sense is dependent on *conspicitur*, though it is helped by *candida* ('gleaming white through the wood'). The tense of *procubuit* indicates that the sow 'has lain down' and is visible.

8 84. **pius**: here with particular reference to the fulfilment of religious obligations in appeasing the hostility of Juno (60f., 3.435f.).

9 **enim**: in its archaic sense, 'indeed', cf. 1.19, 6.317, 10.874.

10 85. 'offered to you, making a sacrifice, and set it with its offspring at the altar'. We need not regard this as an inversion of clauses (hysteron proteron), because *mactat* car mean 'offer as a sacrifice' as well as 'perform a sacrifice'.

11 86-9. 'The Tiber made its swollen waters calm for all the length of that night, and checking its current was so still with silent stream that it smoothed the surface of its waters like a placid swamp or a stagnant marsh, so that there was no need to toil hard at the oars'. For *quam longa est* cf. 4.193; for *sterneret aequor aquis* cf. 5.821. Evidently the sacrifices and preparations have occupied the day: the Trojans set out at the end of the day and row through the night till noon on the next day.

12 90. **rumore secundo**: 'with cheerful noise'. cf. 3.128, 5.140, 5.338, 10.266, Enn. *Ann.* 255. The punctuation after *celerant*, so that *rumore secundo* goes with *labitur* and refers to the noise of the water (cf. Aus. *Mos.* 22) gives a less natural sense. The reading *Rumone* (an old name for the Tiber), known to Servius, is not at all likely.

13 91-2. For the pathetic fallacy (the attribution of feeling to inanimate objects) cf. 240, 7.759-60.

14 91. Cf. Enn. *Ann.* 386 *labitur uncta carina, volat super impetus undas,* and 478.

15 92-3. 'the surprised grove marvels that far-flashing shields of warriors and painted ships are moving on the river'; for *innare* cf. 6.369.

scuta virum fluvio pictasque innare carinas.
Olli remigio noctemque[1] diemque fatigant
et longos superant flexus, variisque teguntur   95
arboribus, viridisque secant[2] placido aequore silvas.
Sol medium caeli conscenderat igneus orbem
cum muros arcemque procul[3] ac rara domorum
tecta vident, quae nunc Romana potentia caelo[4]
aequavit, tum res[5] inopes Euandrus[6] habebat.   100
Ocius advertunt proras urbique propinquant.

> 102-83. *The Arcadians are celebrating a festival for Hercules when they see Aeneas and his men approaching along the river. Pallas challenges them, and Aeneas replies that they are Trojans. They are welcomed, and Aeneas tells Evander that in the name of their common ancestry he asks for help against Turnus. Evander remembers meeting Anchises and promises help; they feast together.*

⁊Forte die sollemnem illo rex Arcas honorem
Amphitryoniadae[8] magno divisque[9] ferebat[10]
ante urbem in luco. Pallas[11] huic filius una,
una omnes iuvenum primi pauperque[12] senatus   105
tura dabant, tepidusque cruor fumabat ad aras.

---

1 94. **noctemque diemque fatigant**: outlast night and day', i.e. continue on right through without weariness; cf. 1.316.

2 96. **secant**: 'cut through', probably in the sense in which a river cuts through land (7.717), but Servius may be right with his suggestion that the ships cut through the reflections in the still water. Henry in a splendid passage finds Servius' interpretation 'wholly unsuitable to a great epic'.

3 98. **procul**: the second syllable is lengthened in arsis, cf. 363, 425 and see note on 7.174.

4 99-100. For the theme of Evander's 'little Rome' cf. Prop. 4.1, Tib. 2.5.23f, Ov. *Fast.* 5.91f., and cf. 347f., 364f.

5 100. **res inopes**: the rhyme emphasises the phrase, his 'little empire'.

6 **Euandrus**: this is Virgil's preferred form of the nominative, but *Evander* occurs in 10.515.

7 102f. The mood of optimism and serenity continues. The speeches of Aeneas and Evander are filled with chivalry and dignified compliment; the scene is reminiscent of the welcome given to the Trojans in Book 1 by Dido and her Carthaginians. The anticipation aroused in the reader by Aeneas' arrival at the site of Rome is held in suspense during these slow moving scenes as we wait to hear more about the first inhabitants of the Palatine.

8 103. **Amphitryoniadae**: Hercules' mortal father was Amphitryo (his real father was Jupiter); cf. Cat. 68.112 *falsiparens Amphitryoniades*. For the Roman festival in honour of Hercules at the *Ara Maxima* of which this was the origin see note on 271-2.

9 **divisque**: 'and the other gods', cf. 3.19 and the Greek ω Ζευ και θεοι. Servius says 'nam cuivis deo sacrificaretur, necesse erat post ipsum etiam reliquos invocari'. On the other hand Plutarch (*Quaest. Rom.* 90) cites Varro as saying that no other god is mentioned during a sacrifice to Hercules.

10 103f. The arrival of Aeneas is based on Hom. *Od.* 3.4f., Telemachus' visit to Nestor at Pylos, where a sacrifice is taking place and Nestor's son greets him.

11 104. This is the first appearance in the poem of Evander's son Pallas; he is, like Euryalus and Lausus, a young warrior destined to an early death, and it is because of Turnus' arrogance when he kills Pallas that Turnus himself is not spared by Aeneas at the end of the poem. His part in the plot is not unlike that of Patroclus in the *Iliad.*

12 105. **pauperque senatus**: 'the senators strangers to riches'. cf. line 100 and Prop. 4.1.12 (*curia*) *pellitos habuit, rustica corda, patres.* Servius mentions that *pauper* might mean 'few in number', but also gives the correct interpretation: *parsimonia pro laude tunc habita.*

Ut[1] celsas videre rates atque inter opacum
adlabi nemus et tacitos incumbere remis,
terrentur visu subito cunctique relictis
consurgunt mensis. Audax quos rumpere Pallas   110
sacra vetat raptoque volat telo obvius ipse,
et procul e tumulo: 'iuvenes, quae causa subegit
ignotas temptare vias? Quo tenditis?' Inquit.
'qui genus?[2] Unde domo? Pacemne huc iertis an arma?'
tum pater Aeneas puppi sic fatur ab alta   115
paciferaeque manu ramum praetendit olivae:
'Troiugenas[3] ac tela vides inimica Latinis,
quos[4] illi bello profugos egere superbo.
Euandrum petimus. Ferte[5] haec et dicite lectos
Dardaniae venisse duces socia arma rogantis.'   120
obstipuit tanto[6] percussus nomine Pallas:
'egredere o quicumque es,' ait 'coramque parentem
adloquere ac nostris succede penatibus hospes.'
Excepitque manu dextramque amplexus inhaesit.
Progressi subeunt luco fluviumque relinquunt.   125

    Tum regem Aeneas dictis adfatur amicis:
'optime Graiugenum,[7] cui[8] me Fortuna precari
et vitta comptos voluit praetendere ramos,[9]
non equidem extimui Danaum[10] quod ductor et Arcas

---

1 107-8. 'When they saw the lofty ships, and men silently gliding along through the shady grove and bending to the oars . . .'. all the chief MSS have *tacitos,* and in spite of Servius' support for *tacitis* it is hard to see why some recent editors have preferred it; an accusative is badly needed as subject of *adlabi* and *incumbere,* and to supply *rates* to the second of these seems impossible. There is little point in calling the oars silent, while it is the silence of the Trojans which makes their unexpected approach seem all the more sinister to the Etruscans.

2 114. **genus**: accusative of respect, a Grecism, cf. 5.285, 12.25; it is quite common in Virgil with parts of the body (e.g. line 425) but otherwise rare.

3 117. **Troiugenas**: a dignified form, cf. 3.359, 12.626 and compare *Graiugenae* in 127.

4 118. 'whom they have attacked, exiles though we are, with arrogant warfare', a somewhat exaggerated statement designed to win support for the Trojans against the common enemy. Some take *profugos egere* to mean 'have put to flight, but the Trojans are already *profugi.* Henry's brief note reads: 'The wolf and the lamb! Is it not, reader?'

5 119. **ferte haec:** 'report these words to him' (cf. 1.645), rather than (as Servius) 'take this offering to him' (the olive branch).

6 121. **tanto . . . nomine**: i.e. Dardania.

7 127. **Graiugenum**: the archaic form for *Graiugenarum,* cf. 3.550, and the forms *Aeneadum:* (e.g. 9.180), *Dardanidum* (10.4), *Ausonidum* (10.564).

8 **cui**: this dative (praying to) is not found elsewhere with *precari.* It is normal with *supplicare,* and here helped by its function in the next clause with *praetendere.*

9 128. The olive-branch was decked with the suppliant's chaplet (*supplice vitta,* Hor. *Odes* 3.14.8, cf. *Aen.* 7.237). For *comptus* cf. 7.751.

10 129. **Danaum . . . Arcas:** supply *fores* from the next line, an alternative form for *esses.* The subjunctive conveys that *quod* means 'because of the thought that'. The Greeks are frequently called *Danai,* cf. 9.154, 12.349.

quodque a stirpe fores geminis coniunctus Atridis;[1]   130
sed mea[2] me virtus et sancta[3] oracula divum
cognatique[4] patres, tua terris didita fama,
coniunxere tibi et fatis[5] egere volentem.
Dardanus,[6] Iliacae primus pater urbis et auctor,
Electra, ut Grai perhibent, Atlantide cretus,[7]   135
advehitur Teucros;[8] Electram maximus Atlas
edidit, aetherios umero qui sustinet orbis.[9]
Vobis Mercurius[10] pater est, quem candida Maia
Cyllenae gelido conceptum vertice fudit;
at Maiam, auditis si quicquam credimus, Atlas,[11]   140
idem Atlas generat[12] caeli qui sidera tollit.
Sic genus amborum scindit[13] se sanguine ab uno.
His [14]fretus non legatos neque prima per artem
temptamenta tui pepigi; me, me ipse meumque
obieci caput et supplex ad limina veni.   145
Gens eadem, quae te, crudeli Daunia[15] bello
insequitur; nos si pellant nihil afore[16] credunt
quin omnem Hesperiam penitus sua sub iuga mittant,

---

1 130. Evander's relationship to the sons of Atreus (Agamemnon and Menelaus) is traced in various complicated ways by Servius.

2 131. **mea . . . virtus:** open statements of one's qualities were characteristic of heroic society; cf. 1.378f., based on *Od.* 9.19f.

3 **sancta oracula divum:** most recently Tiberinus, but also the Sibyl in 6.96-7 *via prima salutis, / quod minime reris, Graia pandetur ab urbe.*

4 132. **cognatique patres:** as explained in the following lines.

5 133. **fatis egere volentem:** 'have brought me gladly here by destiny'. The phrase has a Stoic ring, cf. Sen. *Ep. Mor.* 107.11 (translating Cleanthes) *ducunt volentem fata, nolentem trahunt.*

6 134f. Dardanus, the founder of Troy (3.167f, 7.207f.) was the son of Jupiter and Electra; Electra was one of the seven daughters of Atlas (Atlantides. who made up the constellation of the Pleiades (*Geo.* 1.221). If the description of genealogy seems frigid to modern taste. we must remember that in Virgil's time great interest was taken in it generally and in Trojan origins in particular.

7 135. For *cretus* ('born from', passive participle of *cresco* with an active meaning) with the ablative of origin cf. 2.74, 9.672.

8 136. **Teucros:** accusative of motion towards, cf. 1.2, 7.216. and line 715.

9 137. For this description of Atlas cf. 4.247, 482 (= 6.798).

10 138-9. Evander was said to be the son of Mercury and Carmentis (see note on 335-6); Maia, Mercury's mother (1.297), was like Electra one of the seven Pleiades. Mercury is sometimes called after Cyllene in Arcadia where he was born; cf. 4.258. He had a cult at Pheneus (see note on 165 and cf. Cic. *N.D.* 3.56 *Mercurius quem colunt Pheneatae*) and appeared on coins of the city.

11 140-1. **Atlas, idem Atlas:** the repetition (cf. 135-6) is very overpowering; Aeneas does not want his point to be missed.

12 141. **generat:** like the Greek τικτει, an idiomatic use of the present ('is father of'); cf. 10. 518, *Geo.* 1.279.

13 142. **scindit se:** 'divides off', like a family tree.

14 143-4. 'Putting my trust in this I did not send envoys or arrange my first approaches to you by diplomacy'; it is better to regard *legatos* as the object of a verb supplied from *pepigi* (zeugma), rather than as governed by *per;* see note on 9.427. The metaphor in *pepigi* (*pactus sum* is also used) is from fixing.

15 146. **Daunia:** Turnus' father was Daunus king of Daunia (part of Apulia ; Turnus is *Daunius heros* (12.723); the meaning here is the people of Turnus, the Rutulians.

16 147. **afore:** the MSS vary, and Servius seems to have read *obfore,* but the common prose formula *non multum abest quin* is appropriate here in the diplomatic language.

et mare [1]quod supra teneant quodque adluit infra.
Accipe[2] daque fidem. Sunt nobis fortia bello   150
nectora, sunt animi et rebus spectata iuventus.'

   Dixerat Aeneas.[3] Ille os oculosque loquentis
iamdudum et totum lustrabat lumine corpus.
Tum sic pauca refert: 'ut[4] te, fortissime Teucrum.
Accipio agnoscoque libens! Ut verba parentis   155
et vocem Anchisae magni vultumque recordor!
Nam memini Hesionae[5] visentem regna sororis
Laomedontiaden Priamum Salamina[6] petentem
protinus[7] Arcadiae gelidos invisere finis.
Tum mihi prima genas vestibat flore iuventas,   160
mirabarque duces Teucros, mirabar et ipsum
Laomedontiaden; sed cunctis altior ibat
Anchises. Mihi mens iuvenali ardebat amore[8]
compellare virum et dextrae coniungere dextram;
accessi et cupidus Phenei[9] sub moenia duxi.   165
Ille mihi insignem pharetram Lyciasque[10] sagittas
discedens chlamydemque auro dedit intertextam, [11]
frenaque bina meus[12] quae nunc habet aurea Pallas.
Ergo et quam petitis iuncta[13] est mihi foedere dextra,
et lux cum primum terris se crastina reddet,   170
auxilio laetos dimittam opibusque iuvabo.[14]

---

1 149. 'and take possession of the sea which washes the shores to the north and south', i.e. hold Italy from coast to coast. The Adriatic and Tyrrhenian seas were called *mare superum* and *mare inferum;* cf. also *Geo.* 2.158.

2 150. **accipe daque fidem**: cf. Enn. *Ann.* 31 *accipe daque fidem, foedusque feri bene firmum.*

3 152-3. Aeneas has not actually said who he is; Evander has gradually been becoming more and more sure that he could be the son of his old friend Anchises. Cf. Hom. *Od.* 4.140f.

4 154. **ut**:'how', cf. 2.283.

5 157. Hesione the daughter of Laomedon married Telamon, father of Ajax and Teucer; Priam (with Anchises in his entourage) on his way to visit her in the island of Salamis apparently passed through Arcadia. This recognition scene is not unlike that between Dido and Aeneas in 1.619f.

6 158. **Salamina**: Greek accusative, cf. 354, 438.

7 159. **protinus . . . invisere**: 'went on and visited': Arcadia was not *en route* but he went on (*porro, tenus*) to take it in.

8 163-4. Cf. *Aen.* 3.298-9 *incensum pectus amore / compellare virum.*

9 165. Pheneus is on the north side of Lake Stymphalus not far from Mt. Cyllene; cf. Hom. *Il.* 2.605, Cat. 68.109 *Pheneum prope Cylleneum,* and see note on 138-9.

10 166. **Lyciasque sagittas**: cf. 7.816: the Lycians were famous archers.

11 167. For the spondaic fifth foot see note on 54.

12 168. Notice the interwoven clauses. with *meus* taken outside the relative clause and *aurea* put into it.

13 169. **iuncta est mihi**: *mihi* is dative of agent or perhaps ethic: the perfect tense indicates that it is done.

14 171. Cf. *Aen.* 1.571 (Dido to Ilioneus).

Interea sacra¹ haec, quando huc venistis amici,
annua, quae differre nefas, celebrate faventes²
nobiscum, et iam nunc sociorum adsuescite mensis.'

    Haec ubi dicta, dapes iubet et sublata reponi³   175
pocula gramineoque⁴ viros locat ipse sedili,
praecipuumque⁵ toro et villosi pelle leonis
accipit Aenean solioque invitat acerno.
Tum lecti iuvenes certatim araeque sacerdos
viscera tosta ferunt taurorum, onerantque canistris   180
dona⁶ laboratae Cereris, Bacchumque ministrant.
Vescitur Aeneas simul et Troiana iuventus
perpetui⁷ tergo bovis et lustralibus⁸ extis.

> 184-279. *Evander tells the story of how the monster Cacus used to terrify the neighbourhood from his cave on the Aventine. One day when Hercules was returning from one of his labours in Spain with the cattle of Geryon, Cacus stole some of them and hid them in his cave. Hercules discovered them, and after a mighty battle with the fire-breathing monster killed him and delivered the people from their fear. Since then Hercules has been honoured on his annual festival at the Ara Maxima.*

⁹Postquam exempta fames et amor compressus edendi,¹⁰
rex Euandrus ait: 'non haec sollemnia nobis,   185
has ex more dapes, hanc tanti numinis aram

---

1 172-3. **sacra haec ... annua**: see note on 271-2.

2 173. Again a reminiscence of Dido's welcome to the Trojans (1.735).

3 175. The banquet had been interrupted by the Trojan arrival (109).

4 176. **gramineo ... sedili**: 'a seat on the grass', cf. 1.167 for this sense of *sedile*. Servius and Macrobius tell us that the worshippers did not recline but were seated at the feast of Hercules.

5 177-8. Aeneas as chief guest (*praecipuum*) sits on a maple throne covered with a cushion (*torus*) over which was spread the skin of a lion (Hercules' special emblem. cf. 7.669). The ablatives are instrumental, 'welcomes and entertains him with', as is regular with *accipere* and *invitare*.

6 181. **dona laboratae Cereris**: 'the gifts of Ceres which they had prepared'. i.e. bread; for Ceres - corn cf. 1.177, 1.701, for *laboratae* 1.639 *arte laboratae vestes*, for Bacchus (= wine) 1.215.

7 183. **perpetui tergo bovis**: the Homeric νωτοισι διηνεκέεσσι, the whole chine of an ox; for *perpetuus* cf. 7.176.

8 **lustralibus**: 'sacrificial' (Livy 1.28), or perhaps the ox was a ritual five years old (*lustrum*).

9 184f. This wholly self-contained story (see note on 194) may be regarded as a piece of inset narrative of the kind familiar in Homer. As is appropriate for the demands of literary epic, it is highly finished and economical in method, and it has immediate relevance to the chief themes of the poem: firstly as an aetiological story of religious significance, explaining the origins of the well known ceremony of Virgil's time in Hercules' honour, and secondly as a mythological parallel to the task of Aeneas (and Augustus) of ridding the world of barbaric and archaic violence. Hercules was a prototype of the Roman hero, an important paradigm in the Stoic philosophy, and an example of a mortal deified (like Aeneas, Romulus. and, still in the future, Augustus) for his great achievements. His strength and his endurance furnished an example which Aeneas, less well endowed physically, was called upon to emulate in order to found Rome.

10 184. A Homeric line: cf. Hom. *Od.* 3.67, *Aen.* 1 216, 723.

vana superstitio veterumque ignara deorum[1]
imposuit: saevis, hospes Troiane, periclis
servati facimus meritosque novamus honores.
Iam primum saxis[2] suspensam hanc aspice rupem,　　　　190
disiectae [3]procul ut moles desertaque montis
stat domus et scopuli ingentem traxere ruinam.
Hic spelunca fuit vasto summota recessu,
semihominis[4] Caci facies quam dira tenebat[5]
solis inaccessam[6] radiis; semperque recenti　　　　195
caede tepebat humus, foribusque adfixa superbis
ora virum tristi pendebant pallida tabo.
Huic[7] monstro Volcanus erat pater: illius atros
ore vomens ignis magna se mole ferebat.
Attulit et[8] nobis aliquando[9] optantibus aetas　　　　200
auxilium adventumque dei. Nam maximus ultor
tergemini nece Geryonae[10] spoliisque superbus
Alcides aderat taurosque hac victor agebat
ingentis, vallemque boves amnemque tenebant.
At furiis[11] Caci mens effera, ne quid inausum　　　　205
aut intractatum scelerisve dolive fuisset,

---

1 187. Evander says that this new worship is not an empty superstition or due to lack of respect for the old gods. Livy (1.7.15) says that the Greek ritual of the worship of Hercules at the Ara Maxima in the Forum Boarium was the only foreign ceremony introduced by Romulus. There is doubtless here a reflection of the dislike in Augustus' time for new foreign cults (Prop. 4.1.17, Suet. *Aug.* 93, which slighted the old gods whose cults Augustus was busily reviving and often seemed to conservative Roman opinion to be empty (*vana*) of real religious content. See also notes on 271-2, 698-700.

2 190. **saxis suspensam . . . rupem**: 'this cliff with its over-hanging rocks'. cf. 1.166. The remains of caves in the Aventine (231) are still to be seen.

3 191-2. 'how there are far-scattered boulders, and an abandoned mountain dwelling remains. where the rocks have crashed down in a great avalanche'; cf. 2.608f. *Ut* follows *aspice* in parataxis, cf. 6.855-6 *aspice ut . . . ingreditur.*

4 194. **semihominis Caci facies**: the story, which Virgil has adapted to his own purposes. making Cacus a more formidable figure, is in Livy 1.7.4f., Prop. 4.9, Ov. *Fast.* 1.543f., Dion. Hal. 1.39. For the scansion of *semihominis* 'the first *i* treated as a consonant or not pronounced at all) cf. *sem* (*i)esus* (297), *semianimis* (12.356), *sem(i)ustus* (11.200. The postposition of the relative *quam* to fourth word gives strong emphasis to the words which precede it. For the periphrasis *Caci facies* cf. 7.18 *formae . . . luporum.*

5 **tenebat**: 'lived in' is natural, and should be accepted in preference to *tegebat* of most MSS, out of which it is almost impossible to extract a meaning.

6 195. **inaccessam**: cf. 7.11 (of Circe's grove).

7 198-9. 'it was his black fires (Vulcan's) that he belched forth as he moved around in all his massive bulk'; for the last phrase cf. 3.656 *vasta se mole moventem* and 1.503 *se . . . ferebat.*

8 200. **et nobis**: i.e. time brought a response to prayers (in the person of Hercules) for us as it does for so many others; this seems perhaps preferable to the meaning 'a god to help us too' (as Cacus had Vulcan to help him).

9 **aliquando**: 'at long last', as in *tandem aliquando* (Cic. *Cat.* 2.1).

10 202-3. Hercules (Alcides) came back via Rome from Spain where he had killed the three-bodied monster Geryon (Lucr. 5.28). and taken his cattle (*spolia*); see note on 7.661f. For Geryon cf. *Aen.* 6.289 and Hes. *Theog.* 287f.

11 205. **furiis**: *M* and Servius offer *furis* ('of the bandit Cacus'), and some modern editors accept it, but it is not an epic word (as Servius recognises).

quattuor a stabulis[1] praestanti corpore tauros
avertit, totidem forma superante iuvencas.
Atque hos, [2]ne qua forent pedibus vestigia rectis,
cauda in speluncam tractos versisque viarum   210
indiciis raptos[3] saxo occultabat opaco;
quaerenti[4] nulla ad speluncam signa ferebant.
Interea, cum iam stabulis saturata moveret
Amphitryoniades[5] armenta abitumque pararet,
discessu mugire[6] boves atque omne querelis   215
impleri nemus et colles[7] clamore relinqui.
Reddidit una boum vocem vastoque sub antro
mugiit et Caci spem[8] custodita fefellit.
Hic[9] vero Alcidae furiis exarserat atro
felle dolor, rapit arma manu nodisque gravatum[10]   220
robur, et aerii cursu petit ardua montis.
Tum primum nostri Cacum videre timentem
turbatumque oculi;[11] fugit ilicet ocior Euro
speluncamque petit, pedibus timor addidit alas.
Ut sese inclusit ruptisque immane catenis   225
deiecit saxum,[12] ferro quod et arte paterna
pendebat, [13]fultosque emuniit obice postis,

---

1 207. **stabulis:** the word seems to mean their pasturage, cf. 213.

2 209. 'so that there should not be any traces of their hooves pointing in the right direction'; the trick (not a very subtle one) is taken from the Homeric hymn to Hermes, 75f., where Hermes steals Apollo's cattle.

3 211. **raptos:** Ribbeck and Mynors accept Wakefield's attractive conjecture *raptor,* but the MSS reading can stand.

4 212. **quaerenti:** 'for anyone searching', a kind of ethic dative, cf. *Geo.* 4.272.

5 214. **Amphitryoniades:** see note on 103.

6 215. **mugire:** this and the following verbs are historic infinitives.

7 216. **colles clamore relinqui:** 'they moved off from the hills with a great uproar'; Servius quotes *Aen.* 1.519 *templum clamore petebant,* and possibly 5.207 is parallel *magno clamore morantur.* Some see a reference to the echo 'leaving' the hills, cf. 5.150, but this seems less likely.

8 218. **spem custodita fefellit:** the unusual relationship between the word meanings which constitute the phrase is typically Virgilian, 'the cow kept captive frustrated his hope', i.e. the captive cow frustrated his hope of keeping her so.

9 219f. 'At this the anger of Alcides had indeed blazed out furiously with black rage'; the pluperfect shoots the narrative forward, as this part of it is gone by before we reach it. Cf. 12.430f. *Fel* in this metaphorical sense is like the Greek χολος.

10 220-1. Hercules' club is of knotted oak; cf. 7.507. For *ardua* as a noun cf. 5.695.

11 223. The reading of the major MSS *oculis* is weak, and *oculi* is as old as Servius.

12 226-7. 'which was suspended above by means of steel and his father's skill', i.e. steel chains had been forged by Vulcan and attached to the rock to make a kind of portcullis.

13 227. 'and he strengthened the support of the doorposts with the obstacle'; the rock is wedged between the edges of the entrance. *Obice* scans as a dactyl by the pronunciation of *j* after the *b,* cf. 10.377.

ecce furens animis aderat Tirynthius[1] omnemque[2]
accessum lustrans huc ora ferebat et illuc,
dentibus infrendens. Ter totum fervidus ira   230
lustrat Aventini montem, ter saxea temptat
limina nequiquam, ter fessus valle resedit.
Stabat acuta silex praecisis undique saxis
speluncae dorso insurgens, altissima visu,
dirarum[3] nidis domus opportuna volucrum.   235
Hanc, ut prona[4] iugo laevum incumbebat ad amnem,
dexter[5] in adversum nitens concussit et imis
avulsam solvit radicibus, inde repente
impulit; impulsu quo maximus intonat aether,[6]
dissultant[7] ripae refluitque exterritus amnis.   240
At specus et Caci detecta apparuit ingens
regia, et umbrosae penitus patuere cavernae,
non secus ac si qua penitus vi terra dehiscens[8]
infernas reseret sedes et regna recludat
pallida, dis invisa, superque[9] immane barathrum[10]   245
cernatur, trepident immisso lumine Manes.[11]
Ergo insperata[12] deprensum luce repente
inclusumque cavo saxo atque insueta[13] rudentem
desuper Alcides telis premit, omniaque arma
advocat et ramis vastisque molaribus[14] instat.   250

---

1 228. **Tirynthius:** for Hercules' connexion with Tiryns cf. 7.662.

2 **omnemque:** for the hyper-metric elision see note on 7.160. The line has been predominately dactylic as Hercules comes rushing up, now it trips and slows with the next line's spondees.

3 235. **dirarum . . . volucrum:** i.e. vultures, waiting for their prey.

4 236. **prona iugo:** 'leaning away from the ridge'.

5 237. **dexter . . . nitens:** 'pushing full against it from the right': he first dislodges it, then heaves it into the river.

6 239. Rhythm and assonance echo Hercules' efforts: the caesura, the initial *i*'s, the *p*'s and *t*'s, the pause after the first dactyl with repetition of the word involved (achieved by dislocation of *quo*), *impulit, impulsu*. For such repetition cf. Lucr. 6.289f.

7 240. 'the banks leap apart, and the terrified river flows backwards'. The banks become further apart from each other as the rock sends a wave both ways across, and the river flows back as the wave goes upstream. For *exterritus* see note on 91-2.

8 243f. The simile takes an idea from Hom. *Il.* 20.61f. where the king of the underworld fears that Poseidon's earthquake will open up his realms to the sky. Notice how the viewpoint shifts, first from above and then from below, as the ghosts tremble at the light let in (like Cacus).

9 245. **super:** 'from above'.

10 **barathrum:** 'abyss' cf. *Cat.* 68.108, *Aen.* 3.421.

11 246. Dryden, *Ann. Mir.* 514, has 'dreadful as day let in to shades below'.

12 247. **insperata:** 'unexpected', quite frequent without the idea of hoping for something.

13 248. **insueta rudentem:** 'bellowing as never before'; *rudere* is a word generally used of animals, *insueta* is adverbial accusative, cf. 489 and *acerba fremens* (12.398).

14 250. **molaribus:** properly 'mill-stones', used here of large lumps of rock the size of mill-stones.

Ille autem, neque enim fuga iam super[1] ulla pericli,
faucibus ingentem fumum (mirabile dictu)
evomit involvitque domum caligine caeca
prospectum[2] eripiens oculis, glomeratque sub antro
fumiferam noctem commixtis igne tenebris.   255
Non tulit Alcides animis,[3] seque ipse per ignem
praecipiti[4] iecit saltu, qua plurimus undam
fumus agit nebulaque ingens specus aestuat atra.
Hic Cacum in tenebris incendia vana vomentem
corripit[5] in nodum complexus, et angit inhaerens   260
elisos oculos et siccum sanguine guttur.
Panditur extemplo foribus domus atra revulsis
abstractaeque boves abiurataeque[6] rapinae
caelo ostenduntur, pedibusque informe cadaver
protrahitur. Nequeunt expleri[7] corda tuendo   265
terribilis oculos, vultum villosaque saetis
pectora semiferi atque exstinctos[8] faucibus ignis.
Ex[9] illo celebratus honos laetique minores[10]
servavere diem, primusque Potitius[11] auctor
et domus Herculei custos Pinaria sacri.   270

---

1 251. **super:** = *superest;* some MSS add *est* after *pericli.*

2 254-5. 'and masses a cloud of smoky night in the cave, interrupting the darkness with fire'. The bravura of highflown rhetoric is less frequent in Virgil than in Ovid or Lucan, but is one of the styles which he occasionally enjoyed using; cf. the description of Etna in 3.571f.

3 256. **animis** : 'in his fierce courage', cf. 7.42.

4 257-8. 'where the thickest smoke was billowing forth. and the huge cave seething with black clouds of it'.

5 260-1. 'knotting his arms about him and holding on he throttled him, till his eyes started from his head and his throat had no blood left'. *Angit* is used in its original archaic sense, cf. *Geo.* 3.497; this was how Hercules killed the snakes (289) and Antaeus. It applies, as Servius says, to *guttur* rather than *oculos.*

6 263. **abiurataeque rapinae:** 'the theft which he had denied'. In Dionysius (1.39.3) Cacus told Hercules that he had nothing to do with it; cf. Hermes in the Hermes-Apollo story. Virgil here introduces a detail which does not cohere with his story. Sometimes such a detail can be inferred from the previous narrative, but the pursuit of Hercules and flight of Cacus has been told in such a way as to preclude the possibility of any conversations. It is possible that Servius' suggestion 'contra ius retentas intellegamus' is right, i.e. illegal plunder.

7 265. **expleri:** middle, cf. 1.713, with *corda* retained accusative (see note on 29).

8 267. **exstinctos faucibus ignis:** 'that mouth whose fires have been put out for ever'.

9 268-72. These five lines are disjointed: Virgil obviously had the Hercules-Cacus story as he wanted it, but was not yet happy with his transition from it.

10 268-9. Compare 5.600-1, on the continuance of the tradition of the *lusus Troiae. Minores* is apparently spoken in Virgil's person rather than Evander's (who seems to have been a contemporary of Hercules, 363), unless we think it refers to Evander's younger contemporaries.

11 269-70. The *gens Politia* and the *gens Pinaria,* here called *domus Pinaria,* were originally associated with this worship of Hercules (Livy 1.7.12f., 9.29.9f.).

Hanc aram luco statuit,[1] quae maxima semper
dicetur nobis et erit quae maxima semper.
Quare agite, o iuvenes, tantarum in munere laudum
cingite fronde comas et pocula porgite[2] dextris,
communemque[3] vocate deum et date vina volentes.'   275
Dixerat,[4] Herculea bicolor cum populus umbra
velavitque comas foliisque innexa pependit,
et sacer implevit dextram scyphus.[5] Ocius omnes
in mensam laeti libant divosque precantur.[6]

> *280-369. The celebrations in Hercules' honour are continued, and a hymn of praise is sung. Evander next tells Aeneas of the early history of Latium, and the golden age under Saturnus, and takes him on a tour of his little city, showing him places destined to be famous in Roman history.*

[7]Devexo[8] interea propior fit Vesper Olympo.   280
iamque sacerdotes primusque Potitius ibant
pellibus in[9] morem cincti, fiammasque ferebant.
Instaurant[10] epulas et mensae grata secundae

---

1 271-2. Presumably the subject of *statuit* is Potitius: other traditions make Evander or Hercules himself the founder of the Ara Maxima (here given its specific adjective) where the ceremony took place each year on August 12th; cf. Ov. *Fast.* 1.581. The point of the rather weak line 272 (which some have wished to delete is that the fame of the altar is true to its name *Maxima*.

2 274. **porgite**. contracted for *porrigite.* said by Servius to be an Ennian form.

3 275. **communem:** the two peoples are united and so the Trojans can share in the Etruscan ceremony, cf. Prop. 1.11.16. Others take it to mean 'call on the gods to share in the banquet'.

4 276f. 'He had spoken; then double-hued poplar leaves were placed on his hair, like those which shaded Hercules, and they hung down in garland form.' These are highly pictorial lines of most unusual diction: the inverted *cum* is strange (the nearest parallel is 5.84); the doubled *-que* (a feature of epic style) is more usually attached to similar parts of speech; *Herculea . . . umbra* is characteristic of the style of Statius rather than of Virgil. The poplar was sacred to Hercules (*Ecl.* 7.61, *Geo.* 2.66. *Aen.* 5.134) because he was said to have worn it on his way to the underworld; it is *bicolor* in nature from the different colour of the two sides of its leaves (silvery and dark green), and in mythology according to Servius because the underside of the leaves on his crown absorbed the sweat of his brow, while the outside remained dark dark the underworld.

5 278. **scyphus:** Servius and Macrobius tell us that this kind of cup was especially associated with Hercules: cf. also Sen. *Ep. Mor.* 83.23.

6 279. Cf. *Aen.* 1.736 *in mensam laticum libavit honorem.*

7 280f. This is one of the most dense passages in the *Aeneid,* thick with religious and national associations of a patriotic and emotional kind. In place, though not yet in time, Aeneas sees the city of his descendants. Following his usual aetiological method Virgil quite often speaks in his own person, adding comments and information which Evander could not know, and linking the legendary past with the Rome of history and the age of Augustus. Something of the tremendous impact of this conducted tour through a city not yet built is conveyed by the warm enthusiasm of Warde Fowler's *Aeneas at the Site of Rome;* see also Camps, pp. 98f.

With the topographical and aetiological theme Virgil interweaves a moral theme of simplicity of behaviour, sincerity of religious worship. The Greek aspects of Hercules in mythology are presented alongside the Roman concept of the Stoic hero; Aeneas is invited to enter, as Hercules had done. the simple home of a rustic ruler, to recognise that greatness can be humble; the concluding phrases of Evander are twice quoted by the Stoic Seneca (see note on 364-5).

8 280. **devexo . . . Olympo:** 'as the sky moved down towards night'; Olympus, the heavens, is thought of as revolving like the sun, cf. 2.250, 11.202.

9 282. **in morem:** like *ex more,* 'in the traditional way', cf. 5.556.

10 283-4. 'They renew the banquet and bring the pleasing gifts of the second part of the meal'; the banquet starts again at its next stage. *Secunda mensa* was a technical Roman term for wine and dessert; cf. 7.134, *Geo.* 2.101.

dona ferunt cumulantque oneratis lancibus aras.
Tum Salii[1] ad[2] cantus incensa altaria circum   285
populeis adsunt evincti tempora[3] ramis,
hic iuvenum chorus, ille senum, qui carmine laudes
Herculeas[4] et facta ferunt: ut prima novercae
monstra manu geminosque premens eliserit anguis,
ut bello egregias idem disiecerit urbes,   290
Troiamque[5] Oechaliamque, ut duros mille labores[6]
rege sub Eurystheo fatis Iunonis iniquae
pertulerit. 'Tu nubigenas,[7] invicte, bimembris
Hylaeumque[8] Pholumque manu,[9] tu Cresia mactas[10]
prodigia et vastum Nemeae sub rupe leonem.   295
Te Stygii tremuere lacus, te ianitor Orci[11]
ossa super recubans antro semesa[12] cruento;
nec te ullae facies, non terruit ipse Typhoeus[13]

---

1 285. The Salii are depicted on the shield of Aeneas (8.663); they were the dancing priests (*salire*) who turned away danger and malign influences, and were particularly responsible for safeguarding the sacred shield upon the preservation of which Rome's continued existence depended. They were especially associated with Mars, and here join the celebration for Hercules' warlike exploits; Macrobius (*Sat.* 3.12.7) tells us that they took part in the worship of Hercules at Tibur.

2 285-6. **ad cantus . . . adsunt**: 'are present to sing'. The song of praise is based on the hymn to Apollo in Ap. Rh. 2.704f., where there is a similar change from indirect narrative to direct apostrophe.

3 286. **tempora**: retained accusative after the middle use of *evincti*, cf. 5.269, and see note on 29.

4 288-9. 'how he squeezed and strangled with his hands his first monsters, sent by his stepmother, the two snakes'; they were sent by Juno in her anger against Jupiter and Alcmena in order to kill their baby child Hercules (Theoc. *Idyll* 24). The line affords a particularly clear example of epexegetic -*que, the angues* being the *monstra*; cf. 11.207.

5 291. **Troiamque Oechaliamque**: in apposition to *urbes,* 'both Troy and Oechalia'. The reference is to the sack of Troy by Hercules to take vengeance on Laomedon (Hom. *Il.* 5.640f.); cf. 2.643, 11.402. The city of Oechalia (probably the one in Euboea) was destroyed by Hercules when its king refused him the promised hand of his daughter.

6 291-2. It was for Eurystheus, king of Mycenae, that Hercules was forced by Juno to perform his twelve labours (on *mille* Servius comments *pro 'multis'*). *Eurystheo* scans as three syllables by synizesis of the last two vowels; cf. lines 372, 383, 553 and see note on 7.33. *Fatis* is a rather extended use of the causal ablative, because of the fate which Juno imposed on him.

7 293. **nubigenas . . . bimembris**: for the epithet *nubigena* of the Centaurs (born of Ixion and a cloud: cf. 7.674; *bimembris* (half-man, half-horse) is said by Macrobius to have been first used by Cornificius. The compound epithets reinforce the Greek flavour of the hymn, as do the two occurrences of doubled -*que* (291, 294).

8 294. **Hylaeumque Pholumque**: the same kind of apposition ('both . . . and') as in 291; cf. *Geo.* 2.456-7 for a reference to these Centaurs killed in the battle with the Lapiths; here Virgil is following a different tradition.

9 294-5. The Cretan prodigy is the bull sent by Poseidon from the sea (Hom. *Il.* 20.145f.) which according to other versions Hercules brought back alive to Eurystheus. The Nemean lion was Hercules' first labour, hence his lion-skin; after his victory he founded the Nemean games in the Argolid.

10 294. **mactas**: the present tense is used unexpectedly; see note on 9.266 and cf. 141.

11 296. One of Hercules' labours was to bring up Cerberus, the watchdog of Hades (cf. Hom. *Il.* 8.366f., *Aen.* 6.395f. and Hor. *Odes* 3.11.16) to his master Eurystheus, and then to take him back again. For Cerberus see note on 6.417f.; Virgil's description here of his ferocity and of the bones in his cave is imitated by Statius (*Th.* 2.26f.). Henry has a good note on the question of Cerberus' diet.

12 297. **semesa**: see note on *semihominis,* 194, and cf. 3.244.

13 298. **Typhoeus**: cf. 1.665 for the giant Typhoeus; Hercules fought on the side of the gods against the Giants and Titans (Pind. *Nem.* 1.67f., Eur. *H.F.* 178f.). It is much less likely that the reference here is to the shades at the entrance of the underworld (6.285f.) which terrified Aeneas.

arduus[1] arma tenens; [2]non te rationis egentem
Lernaeus turba capitum circumstetit anguis.   300
Salve, vera Iovis proles, decus addite divis,
et nos et tua dexter adi pede sacra secundo.'
Talia carminibus celebrant; super[3] omnia Caci
speluncam adiciunt spirantemque ignibus ipsum.
Consonat omne nemus strepitu collesque resultant.[4]   305
   [5]Exim se cuncti divinis rebus ad urbem
perfectis referunt. Ibat rex obsitus[6] aevo,
et comitem Aenean iuxta natumque tenebat
ingrediens varioque viam sermone levabat.
Miratur facilisque[7] oculos fert omnia circum   310
Aeneas, capiturque[8] locis et singula laetus
exquiritque auditque virum monimenta priorum.
Tum rex Euandrus Romanae[9] conditor arcis:
'haec nemora indigenae[10] Fauni[11] Nymphaeque tenebant[12]
gensque virum truncis et duro robore nata,[13]   315
quis[14] neque mos[15] neque cultus erat, nec iungere tauros
aut componere opes norant aut parcere[16] parto,

---

1 299. **arduus:** the adverbial use of the adjective with a participle is poetic, cf. 559, 683 and 5.278.

2 299-300. 'nor did you lack resource when the Lernaean serpent encompassed you with the multitude of its heads'. The hydra of Lerna (near Argos) had nine heads. each in the form of a snake; every time it was decapitated it grew two more heads. It formed the trial for Hercules' second labour, and was defeated by fire.

3 303-4. **super omnia . . . adiciunt:** 'to crown it all, they round off with (a song of) the cave of Cacus'. Notice how as the hymn ends we are brought back to the main theme of the section.

4 305. **resultant:** 'reverberate', 5.150.

5 306f. For the topography of Evander's tour see Warde Fowler. *Aeneas at the Site of Rome,* A. G. McKay. *Vergil's Italy,* pp. 122f.

6 307. **obsitus aevo:** literally, 'covered over with old age', i.e. 'full of years'; cf. Ter. *Eun.* 236 *pannis annisque obsitum.*

7 310. **facilisque oculos:** 'his obedient eyes', i.e. he showed quick interest in what Evander pointed out.

8 311. **capiturque:** 'and is entranced'; *delectatur, uno loco diutius retinetur* (Servius).

9 313. **Romanae . . . arcis:** i.e. his city Pallanteum on the Palatine, the earliest *arx* of Rome.

10 314. **indigenae:**'aboriginal, autochthonous', cf. 12.823.

11 **Fauni:** cf. Lucr. 4.580f. The ancient Roman god Faunus became plural under the influence of Greek mythology, and associated with local deities like Nymphs and Satyrs; cf. *Geo.* 1.10-11. In 7.48 Virgil follows a different version which puts Faunus later.

12 314f. The passage is reminiscent of Lucretius' description of primitive man in 5.837f. (esp. 925f.) as well as of Hesiod (*Works and Days,* 319f.), and its anthropology is interwoven with the rich colours of Roman legend and tradition. See M. E. Taylor. *A.J.Ph.,* 1955, 276f.

13 315. The line is based on Hom. *Od.* 19.163 ου γαρ απο δρυος εσσι παλαιφατου αυδ απο πετρης. Cf. also Juv. 6.12 *rupto robore nati,* and compare the Deucalion myth (Ov. *Met.* 1.313f., cf. *Geo.* 2.340f.).

14 316. **quis:** dative, alternative for *quibus,* cf. 7.444.

15 **mos:** the word is much commoner in the plural in this meaning ('way of behaviour', 'civilised life'), but cf. 6.852 *pacique imponere morem.*

16 317. **parcere parto:** 'husband what they had produced'.

sed rami[1] atque asper[2] victu venatus alebat.
Primus ab aetherio venit Saturnus Olympo[3]
arma Iovis fugiens et regnis exsul ademptis.   320
Is genus indocile ac dispersum montibus altis
composuit legesque dedit, [4]Latiumque vocari
maluit, his quoniam latuisset tutus in oris.
Aurea quae perhibent illo sub rege fuere
saecula: sic placida populos in pace regebat,[5]   325
deterior donec paulatim ac decolor[6] aetas
et belli rabies et amor successit habendi.
Tum manus Ausonia et gentes venere Sicanae,[7]
saepius et nomen posuit Saturnia[8] tellus;
tum reges asperque immani corpore Thybris,[9]   330
a[10] quo post Itali fluvium cognomine Thybrim
diximus; amisit verum vetus Albula[11] nomen.
Me pulsum patria pelagique[12] extrema sequentem[13]
Fortuna omnipotens et ineluctabile[14] fatum
his posuere locis, [15]matrisque egere tremenda   335

---

1 318. **rami:** i.e. oak branches fed them with acorns, cf. Lucr. 5.939.

2 **asper victu venatus:** 'the rough livelihood of hunting', contrast *facilis victu* in 1.445.

3 319f. In Hesiod (*Works and Days.* 111f.), the golden age was during the rule of Cronos (Saturnus), before he was deposed by his son Zeus. In the Italian version of the legend Saturnus took refuge in Latium and was received into the kingdom by Janus; he taught the Latins agriculture and his name was connected with sowing (*satus*). Under his rule Latium had its golden age; cf. *Geo.* 2.538, *Aen.* 6.792f., 7.202f.

4 322-3. 'chose that it should be called Latium, because he had found a safe hiding-place in these regions'; for Virgil's fondness for etymologies cf. 340, 343, 425 and see note on 7.632f. Servius says that Varro also derived Latium from *latere*, but for a different reason, that Italy is hidden between the Alps and the Apennines.

5 325-6. Cf. Ov. *Met.* 1.113f.; notice the remarkable alliteration of *p* and *d.*

6 326. **decolor:** the word normally means 'faded', here 'of a less bright colour' than gold; cf. Ov. *Her.* 9.4.

7 328. For the Ausonians (cognate with the Aurunci) see note on 7.206. For the Sicani (apparently identified with the Siculi, see Thuc. 6.2.5) see note on 7.795, and cf. 11.317.

8 329. 'and Saturnus' land often changed its name', i.e. was called Ausonia, Hesperia, Oenotria, Italia: Virgil is here thinking of Italy generally rather than Latium in particular.

9 330. Servius has a number of stories about Thybris, king of the Tusci, a man of violence; he draws attention to the impossibility of Livy's version (1.3) according to which the river was so called from Tiberinus, an Alban king.

10 331-2. 'from whom we Italians have since called the river by the name Thybris'; Evander now regards himself as an Italian.

11 332. **Albula:** Servius says 'antiquum hoc nomen a colore habuit'.

12 333. **pelagique extrema sequentem:** seeking the utmost edges of the ocean', a naturally exaggerated phrase for an exile to use. This is more likely than 'putting all to the hazard on the sea', which is suggested by some.

13 333.The cause for Evander's exile is not known; Ovid (*Fast.* 1.481) tells us he had committed some crime. Servius speaks of parricide or the orders of an oracle.

14 334. **ineluctabile:** a sonorous word, cf. 2.324.

15 335-6. 'and the fearful warnings of my mother, the nymph Carmentis, and the authority of the god Apollo acted as compulsions upon me', i.e. Evander was under the same sort of divine compulsion as Aeneas, to leave his home and found a new city in a preordained place. His mother Carmentis (connected with *Camenae, carmen* and *cano,* 340) gave him instructions (340f.) which she got from Apollo (god of the founding of cities, the guide of Aeneas in his wanderings in Book 3).

Carmentis nymphae monita et deus auctor Apollo.'

   Vix ea dicta, dehinc[1] progressus monstrat et[2] aram

et Carmentalem Romani nomine portam

quam memorant, nymphae priscum Carmentis honorem.

Vatis fatidicae, cecinit quae prima[3] futuros   340

Aeneadas magnos et nobile Pallanteum.[4]

Hinc lucum ingentem, quem Romulus acer Asylum[5]

rettulit, et gelida monstrat sub rupe Lupercal[6]

Parrhasio [7]dictum Panos de more Lycaei.

Nec non et sacri monstrat nemus [8]Argileti[9]   345

testaturque[10] locum et letum docet hospitis Argi.

Hinc ad Tarpeiam sedem et Capitolia ducit[11]

aurea nunc, olim silvestribus horrida dumis.

Iam tum religio[12] pavidos terrebat agrestis

dira loci, iam tum silvam saxumque tremebant.   350

'Hoc nemus, hunc' inquit 'frondoso vertice collem

(quis deus incertum est) habitat deus; Arcades ipsum

---

1 337. Notice the paratactic form of the sentence, cf. 520; *dehinc* is sometimes a dissyllable (as here, cf. 12.87), and sometimes a single syllable by synizesis (cf. 9.480).

2 337-9. **et aram . . . memorant**: 'the altar and the gate which the Romans call by the name Carmental'. The altar of Carmentis (Dion. Hal. 1.32) was close to the famous gate near the Tiber which took the name *Scelerata* after the death of the Fabii who went forth to battle from it (Ov. *Fast.* 2.195f.).

3 340. **prima**: i.e. before the oracles which came to Aeneas from Apollo (Book 3), the Sibyl (Book 6), Faunus (Book 7).

4 341. **Pallanteum**: cf. 54.

5 342-3. **Asylum rettulit**: brought back into use as the Asylum', the place of refuge for runaways and exiles opened by Romulus to increase the population of his tiny city. *Rettulit* is unusual; it seems to mean restored in the sense of 'made use of again'; cf. 5.598. 11.426. Servius sees a reference to the Asylum or Altar of Mercy at Athens which was connected with Hercules, so that the meaning would be 'founded in imitation of', but this seems improbable.

6 343-4 The Lupercal, the grotto of Faunus-Lupercus, was at the foot of the Palatine; it was restored by Augustus (Suet. *Aug.* 31). Here the Arcadian origins are indicated by mention of Pan, the Greek equivalent of Faunus, and his epithet Lycaeus (Greek λυκος, wolf. Latin *lupus*). The *Lupercalia* in February was one of Rome's chief festivals; cf. Livy 1.5.2, Ov. *Fast.* 2.271f. The wolf-mother of Romulus and Remus was said to have had her home in the Lupercal (Ov. *Fast.* 2.380f.).

7 344. 'named from the Arcadian tradition of Lycaean Pan'. *Parrhasius* (cf. 11.31) is from the town Parrhasia near Mt. Lycaeus in Arcadia; *Panos* is a Greek genitive form.

8 345-6. Virgil is here explicit about the derivation of Argiletum, 'the death of Argus'. Argus was a guest of Evander who plotted against him and was killed by Evander or by his friends. The place Argiletum was near the forum; it is really so called from the clay (*argilla*) used by the potters in that quarter.

9 345. For the fifth foot spondee cf. 341.

10 346. **testaturque locum:** probably 'called on the place as his witness', that he had been justified in killing Argus. Possibly the meaning may simply be 'bore witness of the place' indicated that here was the place'.

11 347f. The Capitol was also called *mons Tarpeius* after the treacherous Tarpeia, daughter of one of Romulus' generals. who gave her name to the Tarpeian rock, a cliff on the SW of the Capitol; cf. 652. It was in Evander's time without buildings, but already inspired awe and was thought to be Jupiter's home: cf. Prop. 4.1.7 *Tarpeiusque pater nuda de rupe tonabat.* For the theme of the original simplicity of golden Rome see note on 99-100; the temple of Jupiter Optimus Maximus on the Capitoline Hill had been magnificently restored in 83 B.C., and again by Augustus in 26 B.C., and a new temple to Jupiter Tonans was dedicated in 22 B.C.

12 349. **religio:** the first syllable is scanned long, as in *reliquiae* (356);cf. 7.172, 244.

credunt se vidisse Iovem, cum saepe nigrantem[1]
aegida concuteret dextra nimbosque cieret.
Haec duo praeterea disiectis[2] oppida muris,   355
reliquias veterumque vides monimenta virorum.
Hanc Ianus pater, hanc Saturnus condidit arcem;
Ianiculum huic, illi fuerat[3] Saturnia nomen.'
Talibus inter se dictis ad tecta subibant
pauperis[4] Euandri, [5]passimque armenta videbant   360
Romanoque foro et lautis mugire Carinis.
Ut ventum ad sedes, 'haec' inquit 'limina victor
Alcides subiit,[6] haec illum regia cepit.[7]
Aude, hospes, contemnere opes et te quoque dignum[8]
finge deo, rebusque veni non asper egenis.'   365
Dixit, et angusti subter fastigia tecti
ingentem Aenean duxit stratisque locavit
effultum foliis et pelle[9] Libystidis ursae:
nox ruit et fuscis[10] tellurem amplectitur alis.

---

1 353-4. **nigrantem aegida:** the *aegis* (here in the Greek accusative, cf. 158) was the divine shield of Jupiter or Pallas (435). It is called *nigrantem* because it summons the clouds and storms; cf. Hom. *Il.* 4.166f.

2 355f. Evander now speaks of the ruined remains (*disiectis . . . muris*) of the ancient towns of Janus (Janiculum) and Saturnus (Saturnia). See notes on 319f. and 7.180. Saturnia was on the Capitol (Varro, *L.L.* 5.42); the town of Janiculum was presumably on the Janiculum Hill on the other side of the Tiber (but see P. Grimal, *Rev. Arch.* 1945, 56f. where he argues that it also was on the Capitol).

3 358. **fuerat:** the tense is strange. intended to indicate perhaps that these towns and their names were now past history; cf. 10.613.

4 360. **pauperis:** see note on 99-100.

5 360-1. 'and everywhere they saw cattle lowing, both in the Roman forum and in the elegant quarter of Carinae'; in Virgil's time Carinae, on the west of the Esquiline, was a very fashionable area; cf. Hor. *Epist.* 1.7.48. Compare Prop. 4.1.1f.

6 363. **subiit:** the last syllable is lengthened in arsis (it was originally long); see note on 98.

7 **cepit:** 'was big enough for him', cf. 9.644, Juv. 10.148.

8 364-5. These are famous lines, twice quoted by Seneca to support his Stoic arguments (*Ep. Mor.* 18.12, 31.11): 'Be brave enough, my friend, to despise riches, and make yourself also (like Hercules) worthy of divinity, and come not disdainful to my humble realm.' *Deo* is deliberately very ambiguous: it can mean 'of heaven' or 'of Jupiter' (his ancestor and Hercules'), and it also suggests that Aeneas like Hercules will become a god. There may be an implied reference to Jupiter visiting the humble home of Baucis and Philemon (Ov. *Met.* 8.637f.), and we think perhaps of the studied simplicity of Augustus' own house (Suet. *Aug.* 72).

9 368. **pelle . . . ursae:** cf. 537. the same phrase.

10 369. **fuscis . . . alis:** cf. Milton, *P.R.* 1.499f.: 'For now began / Night with her sullen wing to double-shade / the Desert'.

370-453. *Venus asks her husband Vulcan to make new armour for her son; he is easily persuaded by her rhetoric and her charms. Within his workshop beneath the earth the Cyclopes set to the task.*

[1]At Venus haud[2] animo nequiquam exterrita[3] mater   370
Laurentumque[4] minis et duro mota tumultu
Volcanum adloquitur, thalamoque haec coniugis aureo[5]
incipit et dictis divinum aspirat amorem:
'dum bello Argolici vastabant Pergama reges[6]
debita[7] casurasque inimicis ignibus arces,   375
non ullum auxilium miseris, non arma[8] rogavi
artis opisque tuae, nec te, carissime coniunx.
Incassumve[9] tuos volui exercere labores,
quamvis et Priami deberem plurima natis,[10]
et durum Aeneae flevissem saepe laborem.   380
Nunc Iovis imperiis Rutulorum constitit oris:

---

1 370f. The mood and tone of this section is entirely different from what has preceded. It is set in the fabulous world of anthropomorphic deities and semi-divine giants. The rhetoric of Venus' speech and the detached half-irony of her blandishments affect the reader with literary pleasure without involving his emotions; it is an ornate. almost baroque interlude, far removed from the human relationships of the scenes between Aeneas, Evander and Pallas. Similarly the brilliant and exaggerated description of the forgers of thunderbolts, of fire and molten steel and massive toil in the deep caverns of rock, strikes the reader with the glittering impact of a rhetorical display. The poet takes holiday from the human themes and problems of the poem. and parades his verbal and pictorial skill.

This episode is based on Hom. *Il.* 18.428f. where Thetis beseeches Hephaestus to make armour for Achilles. He consents, and there is a brief description (468f.) of his smithy (cf. *Aen.* 8.424f). There are also elements from Hera's beguiling of Zeus (*Il.* 14.292f.).

2 370. **haud . . . nequiquam**: 'by no means without reason', cf. *Geo.* 4.353 *non frustra exterrita.*

3 **exterrita mater:** 'ideo territa quia mater' (Servius).

4 371. **Laurentumque**: see note on line 1.

5 372. Cerda points out that Venus has chosen *mollissima tempora* for her request, when she and her husband Vulcan have retired to their golden bedroom. The oblique cases of *aureus* are quite often scanned as a spondee by synizesis of the *e;* cf. 553 and note on 291-2.

6 374f. Servius points out how this passage is a *rhetorica suasio,* beginning with a plea that she had not before made such a request, but now must do so, passing to *exempla* of others who had successfully asked, and ending with *pathos,* an appeal to save her and hers from disaster.

7 375. **debita**: owed to them by fate, further explained by *casuras.*

8 376-7. **arma . . . artis opisque tuae:** 'the weapons of your skill and power', i.e. provided by your unique ability in the manufacture of armour.

9 378. **incassumve:** the word applies to the preceding clause as well: 'to call on you or your trouble in vain'.

10 379. Aphrodite was one of Troy's goddesses in Homer, and doubtless she felt particularly well disposed to Paris after the judgment in her favour.

ergo eadem[1] supplex venio et sanctum[2] mihi numen
arma rogo, genetrix nato. [3]Te filia Nerei,[4]
te potuit lacrimis Tithonia flectere coniunx.
Aspice qui coeant populi, quae moenia clausis[5]   385
ferrum acuant portis in me excidiumque meorum.'
Dixerat et niveis hinc atque hinc diva lacertis
cunctantem[6] amplexu molli fovet. Ille repente
accepit [7]solitam flammam, notusque medullas
intravit calor et labefacta per ossa cucurrit,   390
non [8]secus atque olim tonitru cum rupta corusco
ignea rima micans percurrit lumine nimbos.
Sensit laeta dolis et formae conscia coniunx.
Tum pater[9] aeterno fatur devinctus amore:[10]
'quid causas petis ex[11] alto? Fiducia[12] cessit   395
quo tibi, diva, mei? Similis[13] si cura fuisset,
tum quoque fas nobis Teucros armare fuisset;
nec pater omnipotens Troiam nec fata vetabant[14]
stare decemque alios Priamum superesse per annos.
Et nunc, si bellare paras atque haec tibi mens est,   400

---

1 382. **eadem . . . venio**: 'I now *do* come'; *eadem* means that she who did not come before, now under these changed circumstances does come.

2 382-3. **sanctum . . . nato**: 'and I ask your divine power, sacred to me, for armour, a mother asking for her son'; for *numen rogo* cf. 1.666 *supplex tua numina posco,* said by Venus to Cupid; for *rogo* with double accusative cf. Hor. *Odes* 2.16.1 *otium divos rogat.* The unusual rhythm of the line ending *sanctum mihi numen* (see note on 10.440) gives emphasis; so too does the juxtaposition after the verb of *genetrix nato;* this is made more noticeable by the rhyme of *-o.* Servius prefers to punctuate so that *genetrix nato* begins the next sentence, in order to save Venus from tactlessness, her son Aeneas not being also the son of her husband Vulcan. Evangelus in Macrobius (*Sat.* 1.24.6-7) regards this piece of immorality as one of the reasons why Virgil wanted to burn the *Aeneid*!

3 3 383f. The daughter of Nereus was Thetis, who persuaded Hephaestus (Vulcan) to make new armour for Achilles (*Il.* 18.428f.); the wife of Tithonus was Aurora, who obtained armour for her son Memnon.

4 383. **Nerei**: for the scansion as a spondee by synizesis cf. 372.

5 385-6. **clausis . . . portis**: an indication of preparation for war, cf. 2.27, Hor. *Odes* 3.5.23.

6 388. **cunctantem:** 'hesitating' whether to grant her request; cf. Hom. *Il.* 1.511-12 where Zeus considers Thetis' request in silence for a long time.

7 389-90. 'the desire he knew so well entered deep into him and throbbed within his enamoured heart'; English permits the freezing, but not the heating, of the marrow of one's bones. Servius unanswerably asks: *si ossa labefecit, quanto magis animum?*

8 391-2. 'Just as sometimes happens when a streak of fire, torn out by thunder, flashes and shoots through the clouds with its brilliant light.' Virgil is following Lucretius' account of lightning. 6.282f. *Olim* is used like *quondam* in a simile, cf. 9.710.

9 394. **pater**: a general epithet of gods (454), like *genitor.*

10 394. Virgil is thinking of Lucretius' phrase in his praises of Venus at the beginning of Book 1 where he speaks of her power over Mars (33f.) *in gremium qui saepe tuum se / reicit aeterno devictus vulnere amoris.*

11 395. **ex alto**: 'far-fetched', cf. *Geo.* 4.285.

12 395-6. **fiducia . . . mei**: 'what has become, goddess, of your trust in me?', literally 'where has it gone?' Compare the favourable reply given to Venus by Neptune in 5.800f.

13 396. **similis . . . fuisset**: 'if you had wanted it then'. For the repetition of *fuisset* cf. 7.653-4.

14 398-9. The intervention of individual deities cannot alter, but might possibly postpone, the fates; cf. 7.315.

quidquid in arte mea possum promittere curae,
quod fieri ferro liquidove potest electro,[1]
quantum ignes animaeque[2] valent, absiste[3] precando
viribus indubitare tuis.' Ea verba locutus
optatos dedit amplexus placidumque petivit[4]   405
coniugis[5] infusus gremio per membra soporem.

    Inde ubi prima quies medio iam noctis[6] abactae
curriculo expulerat somnum, cum femina primum,[7]
cui[8] tolerare colo vitam tenuique Minerva
impositum, cinerem et sopitos suscitat ignis   410
noctem addens operi, famulasque[9] ad lumina longo
exercet[10] penso, castum ut servare cubile
coniugis et possit parvos educere natos:
haud secus ignipotens[11] nec tempore segnior illo
mollibus e stratis opera ad fabrilia surgit.   415
Insula[12] Sicanium iuxta latus Aeoliamque
erigitur Liparen fumantibus ardua saxis,

---

1 402. **electro:** sometimes amber (*Geo.* 3.522), here (and in 624) the metal compounded of gold and silver. For the spondaic ending see note on 54.

2 403. **animaeque:** 'and blasts of air', to operate the bellows (449f.).

3 403-4. **absiste . . . tuis:** 'cease to show lack of confidence in your power by using entreaties'. Vulcan very effectively changes the direction of the sentence; he was going to say 'whatever I can do, I will', but the shift adds greatly to the rhetorical impact. *Indubitare* is not found before Virgil, nor afterwards except once in Statius; its construction is by analogy with *diffidere.*

4 405-6. Again reminiscent of Venus in Lucr. 1.33f., 38f.

5 406. **coniugis infusus gremio:** 'lying relaxed in his wife's embrace', cf. Ov. *Her.* 2.93.

6 407-8. Night (like the Sun) drives across the sky in her chariot. cf. 5.721; here she is in the midst of the completion of her course (*abactae* like *curriculo* is a metaphor from driving. cf. 3.512, *Nox Horis acta*), when 'first repose had driven out sleep'. i.e. the first period of deepest sleep is over (cf. 2.268). The subordinate clauses *ubi. . . cum primum . . .* are very loosely connected with the main sentence beginning at *haud secus* (414).

7 408f. This is one of the most memorable of Virgil's similes: it is based in part on Hom. *Il.* 12.433f. (a woman weighing wool in the course of her work to win a poor livelihood for her children), and on Ap. Rh. 4.1062f. (a widow working at her spindle through the night), 3.291f. (a woman making a fire early in the morning to keep her warm as she spins her wool). It has an element of sympathy and pathos which extends its impact far beyond its immediate point of comparison.

8 409-10. 'whose burden it is to make life bearable by spinning and simple crafts'; for *tolerare vitam* cf. Lucr. 2.1171. Minerva, the goddess of handicrafts, is here used by metonymy for what she presides over, cf. Ceres (bread), Bacchus (wine). The epithet *tenuis* means humble, just adequate for supporting life: Servius mentions and rightly rejects the possibility that it might mean 'fine' work.

9 411-12. **famulasque . . . penso:** 'keeps her women at their long task by the firelight'; cf. 7.13.

10 412-13. 'so that she can keep her husband's bed unsullied, and bring up her little children'. For *servare* in a similar context cf. the formula on women's tombstones *domum servavit, lanam fecit.* The picture is of a young wife or widow struggling to make ends meet, but determined to remain *univira.* Compare the imitation in Val. Fl. 2.137-8.

11 414. **ignipotens:** used of Vulcan several times by Virgil (lines 628, 710), but not found earlier.

12 416. The island in question is one of the volcanic Aeolian islands to the north of Sicily, in ancient times called Hiera ('sacred' to Vulcan, hence 'bearing his name', 422; its modern name is Vulcano). Lipare was identified with the home of Aeolus, king of the winds (Hom. *Od.* 10.1f.).

quam ¹subter specus et Cyclopum exesa caminis
antra Aetnaea tonant, validique incudibus ictus
auditi² referunt gemitus, striduntque cavernis   420
stricturae³ Chalybum et fornacibus ignis anhelat,
Volcani domus et Volcania nomine tellus.
Hoc⁴ tunc ignipotens caelo descendit ab alto.
    Ferrum exercebant vasto Cyclopes in antro,
Brontesque⁵ Steropesque et nudus membra⁶ Pyracmon.   425
His informatum⁷ manibus iam parte polita
fulmen⁸ erat, toto genitor quae plurima caelo
deicit in terras, pars imperfecta manebat.
Tris⁹ imbris torti radios, tris nubis aquosae
addiderant, rutuli tris ignis et alitis Austri.   430
Fulgores¹⁰ nunc terrificos sonitumque metumque
miscebant operi flammisque¹¹ sequacibus iras.
Parte alia Marti currumque¹² rotasque voluens
instabant, quibus ille viros, quibus excitat urbes;

---

1 418-19. 'beneath which a cavern and Aetnaean caves hollowed out for the workshops of the Cyclopes thunderously resound'; Virgil located the Cyclopes at Etna in *Geo.* 4.170f, *Aen.* 3.569f., and here preserves a hint of that tradition. The caves are thought to be linked with Mt. Etna under the sea (cf. *Aetna* 445f.) or *Aetnaea* might simply mean. as Servius says, 'like those of Etna' (but *Aetnaei Cyclopes,* 440, is against this). The Cyclopes are shepherds in Homer: the first mention of their workshops is in Hes. *Theog.* 139f.; cf. *Geo.* 4.17 of, *Aen.* 6.630f. Callimachus (*Hymn. Art.* 46f.) locates their workshops in Lipare.

2 420. **auditi referunt gemitus:** 'are heard re-echoing and booming'; for *gemitus* of inanimate sound see note on 3.555 and Ov. *Met.* 12.487 *plaga facit gemitus.*

3 421. **stricturae Chalybum:** 'the iron bars of the Chalybes'; *strictura* is iron compressed into a mass. cf. Cat. 66.50 *ferri stringere duritiem.* The Chalybes of the Pontus are associated with iron (*Geo.* 1.58, *Aen.* 10.174, Cat. 66.48), and the word *chalybs* is used for iron (446).

4 423. **hoc:** archaic for *huc,* cf. Plaut. *Amph.* 164.

5 425. 'Thunder and Lightning and Fire-Anvil.' The first half of the line is from Hes. *Theog.* 140 Βροντην τε Στεροπην τε, and Virgil has retained the lengthening in arsis at the beginning of the second foot, a Greek device which he uses with doubled *-que* sixteen times altogether; cf. 3.91 with my note (OUP Ed.), and see notes on 7.174, 8.98. Pyracmon is not found before Virgil; Hesiod's third Cyclops is Arges.

6 **membra:** Greek accusative of respect, see note on 7.60.

7 426. **informatum:** 'made', cf. 447; the word is more frequent in its metaphorical sense, 'sketch'.

8 427. **fulmen erat. . . quae plurima:** 'there was a thunder-bolt (partly made) such as those which very often . . .'; cf. Hom. *Od.* 5.422 κητος . . . οια τε πολλα . . . The passage is reminiscent of Ap. Rh. 1.730f. (the picture on Jason's cloak of the Cyclopes finishing the forging of a thunderbolt).

9 429-30. 'They had given it three rays of twisted rain (hail), three of watery cloud, three of red fire and three of the winged south 'wind'; Servius' explanation of 'twisted rain' (= *grando*) seems correct, as also does Conington's comment that these rays represent the component parts of a thunderstorm.

10 431-2. These are very heightened lines. and the effect of intermingling real elements (fire, lightning, etc.) with abstract conceptions like fear and anger is most striking.

11 432. **flammisque sequacibus iras:** 'and anger with its pursuing flames'; for *sequacibus* cf. 5.193.

12 433-4. **currumque . . . quibus:** 'they were vigorously making a chariot for Mars with those flying wheels with which . . .'. *Instare* with the accusative is very unusual ('nova locutio', says Servius), but an example is preserved from the dramatist Novius, *instant mercaturam.* For the chariot of Mars cf. 12.331f.

aegidaque[1] horriferam, turbatae[2] Palladis arma.   435
Certatim squamis[3] serpentum auroque polibant
conexosque anguis ipsamque in pectore divae[4]
Gorgona desecto vertentem lumina collo.
'Tollite cuncta' inquit 'coeptosque auferte labores,
Aetnaei Cyclopes, et huc advertite mentem: 440
arma acri facienda viro. Nunc viribus usus,[5]
nunc manibus rapidis, omni nunc arte magistra.
Praecipitate[6] moras.' Nec plura effatus, at illi
ocius incubuere omnes pariterque laborem
sortiti. Fluit aes rivis aurique metallum   445
vulnificusque[7] chalybs vasta fornace liquescit.
Ingentem clipeum informant, unum omnia contra
tela Latinorum, [8]septenosque orbibus orbis
impediunt. Alii ventosis follibus auras[9]
accipiunt redduntque, [10]alii stridentia tingunt   450
aera lacu; gemit impositis[11] incudibus antrum.
Illi inter sese multa vi bracchia tollunt[12]
in numerum versantque tenaci forcipe massam.[13]

---

1 435. **aegida:** cf. 354 for Jupiter's *aegis* (shield). Here Athena's *aegis* with its Gorgon-device (cf. 2.616, Hom. *Il.* 5.738f.) is visualised as a breastplate (*in pectore,* 437).

2 **turbatae:** 'when roused'.

3 436. **squamis . . . polibant:** 'they were adorning it with golden serpent scales', i.e. putting the finish on it; *polire* has a wide range of meanings, cf. Enn. *Ann.* 319-20 *causa poliendi / agri.*

4 437-8. The intertwining snakes are the hair of Medusa the Gorgon; her head was cut off, and her gaze (*vertentem lumina*) still had the power to turn those she looked on to stone. *Gorgona* is Greek accusative, like *aegida* in 435.

5 441. **usus:** an archaic equivalent for *opus est,* 'now there is occasion for . . .', cf. Plaut. *Most.* 250.

6 443. **praecipitate moras** : 'throw off all hesitation', cf. 12.699.

7 446. **vulnificusque chalybs:** 'the death-dealing steel', see note on 421.

8 448-9. 'they fix together layers upon layers, seven of them'. Virgil is clearly thinking of Ajax's shield in Hom. *Il.* 7.245; cf. also Turnus' shield in 12.925. The force of *impediunt* is the connection of the circles of metal to each other, perhaps especially at their rims.

9 449-53. These lines are taken, with small variations, from *Geo.* 4.171-5; they are imitated by Spenser, *F.Q.,* 2.7.36.

10 449-50. 'Some suck in and blow out the air with their puffing bellows'; Spenser (*F.Q.* 4.5.38) has the phrase 'breathful bellows'.

11 451. **impositis:** 'set in position on its floor'.

12 452. A famous line, where the rhythm echoes the sense. The spondees and the conflict of ictus and accent convey heavy and difficult movement — cf. 1.118, 10.146, 12.720. *Inter sese* means alternating, each striking on the anvil in turn.

13 453. Again there is a rhythmical effect, this time of an opposite kind with coincidence of ictus and accent in the third and fourth foot (there being no main caesura in either foot, cf. 549). The work gets into an easier rhythm.

454-607. *Aeneas and Evander meet again the next morning. Evander tells Aeneas about the tyrannical deeds of Mezentius which led to his exile from Caere and his alliance with Turnus in war against the Etruscans. An oracle required a foreign leader for the Etruscans in this war, and Evander asks Aeneas to undertake this with the assistance of his son Pallas. A sign from heaven is given, and Aeneas agrees to do so; arrangements are made for him to set out to meet Tarchon with his Etruscan forces. Evander says goodbye to Pallas, beseeching the gods for his safety; in a splendid array they set off and join Tarchon.*

[1]Haec pater[2] Aeoliis properat dum Lemnius oris,
Euandrum[3] ex humili tecto lux suscitat alma   455
et matutini volucrum sub culmine cantus.
Consurgit senior tunicaque induciturⁿ[4] artus
et Tyrrhena[5] pedum circumdat vincula plantis.
Tum lateri atque umeris Tegeaeum[6] subligat ensem
demissa ab[7] laeva pantherae terga retorquens.   460
Nec non et gemini[8] custodes limine ab alto
praecedunt gressumque canes comitantur erilem.
Hospitis Aeneae sedem et secreta petebat
sermonum[9] memor et promissi muneris heros.
Nec minus Aeneas se[10] matutinus agebat.   465

---

1 454f. The resumption of the human story, set between the scene where Vulcan begins to make armour for Aeneas and the final scene of the book where it is presented and described, is given in quite rapid narrative interspersed with three speeches. In the first, Evander outlines the situation and makes his request. in the second Aeneas agrees but with regret for the bloodshed which must result; and in the third the note of tragic irony is very strong, as Evander begs Jupiter to keep Pallas safe. The mood of pathos is established here, but not yet developed; it is preparatory to the doom of Pallas at Turnus' hands in Book 10, and the distraught lamentation of Evander when he hears the news (11.139f.).
The final result of this chain of events is the scene which ends the poem, when Aeneas sees the belt of Pallas which Turnus is then wearing, and in anger at having failed to defend Evander's young son takes vengeance on Turnus.

2 454. **pater . . . Lemnius:** Vulcan has the epithet *Lemnius* because when he was hurled by Zeus out of Olympus he fell to earth on the isle of Lemnos (Hom. *Il.* 1.593). It became his favourite haunt (Hom. *Od.* 8.283f.). For *Aeoliis* see note on 416.

3 455-6. The idyllic picture of Evander's humble simplicity here reaches its climax; cf. 100, 364f. It is reinforced in the following few lines by the Homeric style of detailed narrative of everyday events; cf. *Il.* 2.42-5, *Od.* 2.1f. For *matutini. . . cantus* cf. Milton, *P.L.* 5.7-8 'the shrill Mattin Song / of Birds on every bough'.

4 457. **inducitur artus:** for the retained accusative see note on 29; probably there is some middle force in the verb on the analogy of (e.g.) 12.416 *faciem circumdata nimbo,* or 2.392-3 *galeam . . . induitur.*

5 458. **Tyrrhena . . . vincula:** 'Etruscan sandals'; the Roman *calceus* was of Etruscan origin; cf. 526.

6 459. **Tegeaeum . . . ensem:** an Arcadian sword, cf. 5.299; it would be suspended from the right shoulder by a sword belt, and hung along the left thigh.

7 460. 'swirling the panther skin which hung on his left side', cf. 7.666.

8 461-2. **gemini custodes . . . canes:** 'two watch-dogs'; cf. Hom. *Od.* 2.11, where Telemachus has two dogs with him as he goes out in the morning. *Erilis* is not common in epic, and contributes here to the domestic tone of the passage; cf. 7.490.

9 464. 'mindful, as befitted a hero, of their talk together when he had promised assistance'; *heros* has strong emphasis from its position, cf. 1.196. The reference is to Evander's promise in lines 170-1.

10 465. **se matutinus agebat:** 'was astir early', a very poetic use (helped by Greek influence) of the adjective used adverbially; cf. Hom. *Il.* 8.530, *Geo.* 3.538 *nocturnus obambulat,* and my note on 5.868 (OUP Ed.).

Filius huic Pallas, illi comes ibat Achates.
Congressi iungunt dextras mediisque[1] residunt
aedibus et licito[2] tandem sermone fruuntur.
Rex prior haec:
'maxime Teucrorum ductor, quo sospite numquam   470
res equidem Troiae victas aut regna fatebor,
nobis ad belli auxilium pro[3] nomine tanto
exiguae vires; hinc Tusco[4] claudimur amni,
hinc Rutulus premit et murum circumsonat armis.
Sed tibi ego ingentis populos opulentaque regnis   475
iungere castra paro, quam[5] fors inopina salutem
ostentat: fatis huc te poscentibus adfers.[6]
Haud procul hinc saxo incolitur fundata vetusto
urbis[7] Agyllinae sedes, ubi Lydia[8] quondam
gens, bello praeclara, iugis insedit Etruscis.   480
Hanc multos florentem annos rex deinde superbo
imperio et saevis tenuit Mezentius[9] armis.
Quid memorem infandas caedes, quid facta tyranni
effera? Di[10] capiti ipsius generique reservent!
Mortua quin etiam iungebat corpora vivis[11]   485
componens manibusque manus atque oribus ora,
tormenti[12] genus, et sanie taboque fluentis
complexu in misero longa sic morte necabat.
At fessi tandem cives infanda[13] furentem

---

1 467-8. **mediisque . . . aedibus:** 'in the centre of the buildings', i.e. in the enclosed courtyard.

2 468. **licito tandem . . . fruuntur:** i.e. the festival on the previous day had not permitted discussion of public business.

3 472. **pro nomine tanto:** 'to match the glory of your name'; some take the meaning to be 'to match our name', i.e. we are Arcadians but lacking in present resources.

4 473. **Tusco . . . amni:** the Tiber, the western and northern boundary of Evander's kingdom; cf. Juv. 8.265, *Geo.* 1.499. *Amni* is a form of the ablative; cf. 549 and *classi* (11).

5 476. **quam . . . salutem:** 'a way of salvation which . . .'; *salutem,* in apposition to the previous sentence, is put within the relative clause to which it is the antecedent.

6 477. Cf. 7.272 *hunc illum poscere fata,* and lines 512, 533.

7 479. **urbis Agyllinae sedes:** i.e. Caere, cf. line 597 and 7.652.

8 **Lydia:** for the supposed Lydian origin of the Etruscans, established in Italy by the Lydian king Tyrsenus, cf. 2.781-2 and Herod. 1.94, Cat. 31.13.

9 482. For Mezentius see note on 7.648; there were many variants of the legend, and Virgil's version involving his exile is not found earlier.

10 484 **di . . . reservent:** understand *talia facta;* for the formula cf. 2.190-1.

11 485. This form of torture is attributed to Etruscan pirates by Cicero in his *Hortensius,* as Servius tells us; the fragment is preserved in August. *Cont. Jul.* 4.15.

12 487. **tormenti genus:** 'his method of torture', *genus* is accusative in apposition to the sentence, cf. 10.311.

13 489. **infanda:** adverbial, cf. 248.

armati circumsistunt ipsumque domumque,   490
obtruncant socios, ignem ad fastigia iactant.
Ille inter caedem Rutulorum elapsus in agros
confugere[1] et Turni defendier hospitis armis.
Ergo omnis furiis surrexit Etruria iustis,
regem ad supplicium praesenti[2] Marte reposcunt.   495
His ego te, Aenea, ductorem milibus addam.
Toto namque fremunt condensae[3] litore puppes
signaque ferre iubent, retinet longaevus haruspex
fata canens: "o Maeoniae[4] delecta iuventus,[5]
flos[6] veterum virtusque virum, quos iustus in hostem   500
fert dolor et merita accendit Mezentius ira,
nulli fas Italo tantam subiungere gentem:
externos optate duces." [7]Tum Etrusca resedit
hoc acies campo monitis exterrita divum.
Ipse oratores ad[8] me regnique coronam   505
cum sceptro misit mandatque insignia Tarchon,[9]
succedam castris Tyrrhenaque regna capessam.[10]
Sed[11] mihi tarda gelu saeclisque effeta senectus
invidet imperium seraeque ad fortia vires.
Natum exhortarer, ni mixtus[12] matre Sabella   510
hunc partem patriae traheret. [13]Tu, cuius et annis
et generi fata indulgent, quem numina poscunt,
ingredere, o Teucrum atque Italum fortissime ductor.

---

1 493. **confugere . . . defendier**: historic infinitives. For the archaic *defendier* see note on 7.70.

2 495. **praesenti Marte:** 'under threat of immediate attack'.

3 497. **condensae:** a Lucretian adjective, used also in *Aen.* 2.517.

4 499. **Maeoniae:** an area of Asia Minor associated with the Lydians (cf. 4.216) and hence with the Etruscans (11.759).

5 499f. The fates require a foreign leader, as in the oracle in 7.96f.

6 500. **flos . . . virum:** 'the brave flower of an ancient stock of warriors'; notice the alliteration emphasising this remarkable phrase, which Servius tells us is from Ennius.

7 503-4. 'Then the Etruscan battle-line stayed inactive on this field'; *hoc* means the one where they had so promptly assembled ready for action.

8 505. **ad me:** Evander was a foreigner in one sense, having recently arrived in Italy, and could have been general had he been younger; his son Pallas (as he explains in 510-11) is not eligible.

9 506. **Tarchon:** the story is told in Strabo (5.2.1) that Tarchon was the founder of the Etruscan town Tarquinii.

10 507. The jussive subjunctives depend on an understood verb of asking;cf. 1.645.

11 508-9. 'But old age is upon me, sluggish, cold, feeble with the passing of the years, and it forbids command; my strength for deeds of daring is slow to respond.' The words are reminiscent of Entellus, the old boxer, in 5.395-6.

12 510. **mixtus matre Sabella:** he is of mixed nationality, Arcadian from Evander and Sabine from his mother.

13 511-13. 'You are he whose age and descent the fates approve, whom the gods require; enter on the task. bravest leader of the Teucrians and now of the Italians too.'

Hinc tibi praeterea, spes[1] et solacia nostri,
Pallanta adiungam; sub te tolerare magistro   515
militiam et grave Martis opus, tua cernere facta
adsuescat, primis et te miretur ab annis.
Arcadas huic equites bis centum, robora pubis
lecta dabo, totidemque[2] suo tibi nomine Pallas.'
   Vix[3] ea fatus erat, defixique ora tenebant   520
Aeneas Anchisiades[4] et fidus Achates,
multaque dura suo tristi cum corde putabant,[5]
ni signum caelo Cytherea[6] dedisset aperto.
Namque improviso vibratus ab aethere fulgor[7]
cum sonitu venit et ruere[8] omnia visa repente,   525
Tyrrhenusque[9] tubae mugire per aethera clangor.
Suspiciunt, iterum atque iterum fragor increpat ingens.
Arma inter[10] nubem caeli in regione serena
per sudum rutilare vident et pulsa tonare.
Obstipuere[11] animis alii, sed Troius heros   530
agnovit sonitum et divae promissa[12] parentis.
Tum memorat: 'ne vero, hospes, ne quaere profecto[13]

---

1 514. **spes et solacia nostri:** the alliteration of *s* draws attention to this phrase, so fraught with tragedy for the future.

2 519. **totidemque . . . Pallas:** 'and Pallas will give you the same number in his own name'; Evander wishes to associate Pallas with his provision of troops for Aeneas. Some MSS have *munere*, i.e. 'in his own gift'.

3 520. **Vix . . . defixique:** for the paratactic construction, cf. 337 and 2.692. For *defixique ora tenebant* cf. 2.1.

4 521. **Anchisiades:** the patronymic is used with special effect, drawing attention to Aeneas' understanding of the father-son relationship of Evander and Pallas; cf. 10.822, and see Warde Fowler ad loc.

5 522-3. **putabant ni . . . dedisset:** 'they were thinking (and would have long continued) if she had not given . . .'; for the elliptical condition cf. 6.358f.

6 523. **Cytherea:** a frequent epithet of Venus (cf. 615) from the island Cythera, just south of Greece. one of her most famous places of worship (cf. 10.51).

7 524f. For the sign of lightning and thunder in a clear sky cf. Hor. *Odes* 1.34.5f. The word *vibratus* suggests the action of gods behind the natural phenomena.

8 525. **ruere . . . repente:** 'the heavens suddenly seemed to fall', cf. *caelique ruina,* 1.129; notice the dactylic movement of this line.

9 526. **Tyrrhenus:** the trumpet (*tuba*) was said to have been invented by the Etruscans, cf. 458.

10 528f. For visions of battles in the sky cf. *Geo.* 1.474f. The meaning of *inter nubem* is that a cloud surrounds the vision of the armour (as a kind of setting) in a sky otherwise cloudless.

11 529. 'flashing red in the clear sky, and clashing like thunder'; for *sudum* (*se, udus,* 'not damp') cf. *Geo.* 4.77. Here it is used in the neuter as a noun.

12 531. **promissa:** what Venus had promised is explained in 534f.; the occasion of this promise has not been narrated, but may be inferred from the Homeric source (*Il.* 18.134f.), where Thetis promised armour to Achilles.

13 532. **profecto:** a stronger repetition of the sense of *vero.* The word *profecto* is not found elsewhere in Virgil, nor often in verse, and adverbs rarely end Virgilian hexameters. This has led to the suggestion that it should be taken (as the participle of *proficiscor*) with what follows; but this gives wholly inferior sense. Aeneas' anxiety to convince Evander that all is well leads him to an over-reliance on emphatic particles which is very common in such a situation.

quem casum portenta ferant: ego[1] poscor Olympo.
Hoc signum cecinit missuram[2] diva creatrix,
si bellum ingrueret,[3] Volcaniaque arma per auras   535
laturam auxilio.
Heu quantae miseris caedes Laurentibus instant!
Quas poenas mihi, Turne, dabis! Quam[4] multa sub undas
scuta virum galeasque et fortia corpora volves,
Thybri pater! Poscant acies et foedera rumpant.'[5]   540
    Haec ubi dicta dedit, solio se tollit ab alto
et primum Herculeis[6] sopitas ignibus aras[7]
excitat, hesternumque[8] larem parvosque penatis
laetus adit; mactat lectas de more bidentis
Euandrus pariter, pariter Troiana iuventus.   545
Post hinc ad navis graditur sociosque revisit,
quorum de numero qui sese in bella sequantur
praestantis virtute legit; pars cetera prona[9]
fertur aqua segnisque[10] secundo defluit amni,
nuntia ventura Ascanio rerumque patrisque.   550
Dantur equi Teucris Tyrrhena petentibus arva;
ducunt exsortem[11] Aeneae, quem fulva leonis
pellis obit totum praefulgens unguibus aureis.[12]
    Fama volat parvam subito vulgata per urbem
ocius ire equites Tyrrheni ad limina regis.   555

---

1 533. **ego poscor Olympo:** the suggestion, first mentioned in Servius, and accepted by Hirtzel, that *Olympo* should go with what follows, not with *poscor,* gives an unthinkable abruptness of rhythm and a totally un-Virgilian word order; it should not be entertained for a moment. *Olympo* is instrumental ablative, like *fatis posci* in line 12.

2 534. **missuram:** for the omission of *se* cf. 12.655, 762.

3 535. **ingrueret:** 'should threaten', cf. 2.301. The word was uncommon before Virgil, and became a favourite with Tacitus.

4 538-9. **quam multa . . . volves:** very similar words were used by Aeneas of the river Simois in 1.100-1; the slaughter of the Trojan war must now be re-enacted. For Aeneas' reluctance to fight the war which he must fight cf. 11.108f.

5 540. The treaties are those made by Latinus with the Trojans (7.259f).

6 542-3. **Herculeis . . . excitat:** 'he re-kindles the smouldering altars with Hercules' flames'; i.e. renews the flames on Hercules' altars.

7 542f. For the sacrifice after a supernatural event cf. 3.176f., 5.743f.

8 543-4. **hesternumque . . . adit:** 'joyfully approaches the household god and the humble penates which he had worshipped the day before'; some MSS have *externumque,* which Servius knew but rightly rejected, cf. Ov. *Met.* 8.642.

9 548. **prona**: 'down-stream', cf. *Geo.* 1.203.

10 549. **segnisque . . . amni:** 'and without exertion float along with the current'; the absence of a main caesura in third or fourth foot conveys speed and ease, cf. 453 and *Geo.* 3.447.

11 552. **exsortem:** 'special', not drawn by lot. cf 5.534, 9.270f.

12 553. **aureis:** scanned as a spondee by synizesis. cf. 372. For gilded claws on a lion skin cf. 5.352.

Vota metu duplicant matres, propiusque[1] periclo
it timor et maior Martis iam apparet imago.
Tum pater Euandrus dextram complexus euntis
haeret inexpletus[2] lacrimans ac talia fatur:
'o[3] mihi praeteritos referat si Iuppiter annos,   560
qualis eram cum primam aciem Praeneste[4] sub ipsa
stravi scutorumque incendi victor acervos[5]
et regem hac Erulum dextra sub Tartara misi.
Nascenti cui tris animas Feronia[6] mater
(horrendum dictu) dederat, terna[7] arma movenda   565
(ter leto sternendus erat; cui tunc tamen omnis
abstulit haec animas dextra et totidem exuit armis):
non ego nunc dulci amplexu divellerer usquam.
Nate, tuo, neque finitimo[8] Mezentius umquam
huic capiti insultans tot ferro saeva dedisset   570
funera, tam multis viduasset civibus urbem.[9]
At vos, o superi, et divum tu maxime rector[10]
Iuppiter, Arcadii, quaeso, miserescite regis
et patrias audite preces. Si numina vestra
incolumem Pallanta mihi, si fata reservant,   575
si visurus eum vivo et venturus in unum,
vitam oro, patior quemvis durare laborem.
Sin aliquem infandum casum, Fortuna, minaris,

---

1 556-7. **propiusque . . . timor**: 'fear goes closer to the danger' (than they really are); some take *periclo* as ablative, but this is unnatural after *propius*. and involves taking *it* as if it were *venit*.

2 559. **inexpletus lacrimans**: some MSS have *inexpletum* (adverbial), which Servius prefers, but the nominative adjective used adverbially is in Virgil's manner, cf. 299.

3 560f. 'Oh if only Jupiter would give back to me the years gone by, as I was when . . .'. The ellipsis is natural ('so that I might now be as I was'); for *si* introducing a wish cf. 6.187, for its postposition cf. 2.110 *fecissentque utinam*. The speech is reminiscent of that of Nestor in Hom. *Il.* 7.132f. (cf. 11.670f.). The pathos is expressed in highly developed rhetoric, with elaborately organised clauses and frequent parallelism of phrases.

4 561f. The story of Erulus of Praeneste (a doublet of Geryon) is known only from this passage. *Praeneste* is normally a neuter word, here feminine through the influence of *urbs* understood.

5 562. The burning of enemy shields as an offering to Vulcan was originated, according to Servius, by Tarquinius Priscus; cf. Livy 1.37.5.

6 564. For the rural deity Feronia cf. 7.800.

7 565. **terna arma movenda**: 'and three sets of weapons for attack'; the phrase is better taken as the object of *dederat* than with what follows, because of the parallel with 567.

8 569-70. **finitimo . . . huic capiti**: me, his neighbour'; for *caput* cf. 4.640 and the common use of κάρα in periphrasis in Greek tragedy (e.g. Soph. *Ant.* 1).

9 571. **urbem**: presumably Pallenteum, Evander's city, against which we must suppose Mezentius had made incursions. Many take it to mean Caere, Mezentius' own city, but this hardly fits with the rest of the sentence.

10 572f. The change of tone from angry indignation to the measured movement of a prayer is reminiscent of Dido's speech in 4.603-14, and the phraseology of 574 recalls 4.612. The end of the passage (584) also recalls 4.391-2.

nunc, nunc o liceat crudelem abrumpere vitam,

dum curae ambiguae, dum spes incerta futuri, 580

dum te, care puer, mea sola et sera voluptas,

complexu teneo, gravior neu[1] nuntius auris

vulneret.' Haec genitor digressu dicta supremo

fundebat; famuli conlapsum in tecta ferebant.

    Iamque[2] adeo exierat portis equitatus apertis 585

Aeneas inter primos et fidus Achates,

inde alii Troiae proceres, ipse agmine Pallas

in[3] medio, chlamyde et pictis conspectus in armis,

qualis ubi Oceani perfusus Lucifer[4] unda,

quem Venus ante alios astrorum diligit ignis, 590

extulit os sacrum caelo tenebrasque resolvit.

Stant pavidae in muris matres oculisque sequuntur

pulveream nubem et fulgentis aere catervas.

Olli per dumos, qua[5] proxima meta viarum,

armati tendunt; it clamor, et agmine facto 595

quadripedante putrem sonitu quatit ungula campum.[6]

Est ingens gelidum lucus prope Caeritis[7] amnem,

religione patrum late sacer; undique colles

inclusere cavi[8] et nigra nemus abiete[9] cingunt.

Silvano[10] fama est veteres sacrasse Pelasgos, 600

arvorum peconsque deo, lucumque[11] diemque,

---

1 582-3. **neu . . . vulneret**: 'and let not any more terrible tidings assail my ears'; *neu* links *vulneret* with *liceat*. For the speech ending after the first dactyl cf. 6.886, 9.250, 10.495.

2 585. **iamque adeo**: 'and now indeed'; *adeo* intensifies *iamque*, cf. 5.268. Henry well compares the brilliance before tragedy of *Aen.* 4.129f.

3 588. **in medio**: Mynors accepts Markland's conjecture *it,* which is attractive but not essential.

4 589f. Lucifer, the morning star, i.e. the planet Venus, rises from the bath of Ocean before any other star; cf. 2.801f., Hom. *Il.* 5.5-6, 22.318, Spenser, *F.Q.* 1.12.21:
'As bright as doth the morning star appeare
Out of the East, with flaming locks bedight,
To tell that dawning day is drawing neare,
And to the world does bring long wished light'.

5 594. **qua . . . viarum**: 'by the path by which the end of their journey is reached most quickly', i.e. they go cross country.

6 596. A famous example of imitative rhythm, where the dactyls and harsh consonants convey the sound of galloping; cf. Enn. *Ann.* 277 *summo sonitu quatit ungula terram,* and *Aen.* 11.875.

7 597. **Caeritis**: genitive of *Caere,* see note on 479.

8 599. **cavi**: 'encircling', so as to make a hollow between them.

9 **abiete**: for the scansion as a dactyl with consonantal *i* see note on 2.16 and cf. 5.663, 9.674, 11.667.

10 600. Silvanus was a Roman god of the woods, resembling the Greek Pan; cf. *Ecl.* 10.24, *Geo.* 1.20, 2.494. The Pelasgi were very early inhabitants of Greece; here they are the Greek predecessors of the Etruscans, who once (*aliquando*) lived in those parts.

11 601. **lucumque diemque**: 'a grove and a festival'; *dies* is a sacred day to be celebrated in his honour each year.

qui primi finis aliquando habuere Latinos.

Haud procul hinc Tarcho[1] et Tyrrheni tuta tenebant

castra locis, celsoque omnis de colle videri

iam poterat legio et latis tendebat in arvis.   605

Huc pater Aeneas et bello lecta iuventus

succedunt, fessique et equos et corpora curant.

> 608-731. *Venus brings to Aeneas the armour which Vulcan has made. The pictures on the shield are described, scenes from early Roman history around the outside, and in the centre the battle of Actium and Augustus' triumph over the forces of the East. Aeneas takes upon himself the pictured destiny of his people.*

[2]At Venus aetherios inter dea candida nimbos

dona ferens aderat; natumque in valle reducta

ut[3] procul egelido secretum flumine vidit,   610

talibus adfata est dictis seque obtulit ultro:

'en perfecta mei promissa coniugis arte

---

1 603f. Tarchon and his Etruscan soldiers are mobilised and encamped (*tendebat*, cf. 2.29) in the grove of Silvanus, and Aeneas and his party come in sight of them as they mount a hill. These forces of Tarchon and Aeneas do not reappear again in the narrative until 10.146.

2 608f. Virgil's precedent for this description (ecphrasis is the shield made by Hephaestus for Achilles (Hom. *Il.* 18.478f.); he may also have used Hesiod's description of Heracles' shield *(Scut.* 139f.). The motivation for the making of a new shield is much more immediate in Homer than in Virgil (Achilles' shield has been captured), and the pictures described on Achilles' shield (a series of general scenes of Greek life) do not have particular reference to the situation in the poem. In Virgil the description of the shield is functional, thematically vital at this point; before the beginning of the long battle-scenes he wishes to reiterate the nature of the destiny for which Aeneas is fighting, to present again in a different way the future history of the Romans as it had been presented at the end of Book 6. Other descriptions in Virgil are similarly made integral with the themes of the poem; see note on 1.418f. (the pictures on Juno's temple), 6.1f. (the pictures on the doors of Apollo's temple).

The choice of subjects for description is partly based on critical moments in Roman history (see Warde Fowler, *Aeneas at the Site of Rome*, and J. R. Bacon, *C.R.* 1939, pp. 97f.), but two other aspects are very prominent; first the visual possibilities of the scenes, and secondly the presentation of Roman virtues, of *exempla* of the Roman character (see Otis, pp. 341f. and D. L. Drew, *The Allegory of the Aeneid*, 1927, pp. 26f.). The twins suckled by the she-wolf give an introductory symbol of Rome's power of survival; the story of the Sabine women illustrates the grafting of religious and social ideals on to the hard valour of Romulus' men; the story of Mettius illustrates the punishment for breaking faith *(fides)*; the invasion by Porsena shows Roman resistance to tyranny *(pro libertate)*, achieved by *fortitudo* (Cocles and Cloelia); the defence of the Capitol against the Gauls is given the strongest possible religious emphasis, the gods look after a righteous people; the scenes in Elysium and Tartarus illustrate punishment for rebellion (Catiline) and the triumph of justice (Cato). All these illustrations of the character of Rome are preliminary to the victory over alien ways of life which is depicted in the centre of the shield, where Augustus' triumph at Actium over Antony and Cleopatra is presented as a triumph of West over East.

Finally the relationship of Virgil's narrative to the visual art of a metal-worker is a fascinating one to explore. Virgil wishes us to be constantly aware that he is describing pictures; throughout his narrative he interweaves comments like *addiderat, extuderat, cernere erat, fecerat ignipotens,* and indications of position like *in summo, hinc procul, in medio, parte alia, hic, hinc, desuper.* Throughout the *Aeneid* we see Virgil's love for pictorial presentation, and here he is in his element. The main pattern of the pictures on the shield is clear; in the centre are three pictures of Actium and its consequences, separated from the scenes round the circumference by the spirals of the sea. At the top of the outside section is the Capitol, at the bottom the underworld, and round the outside between them are the first four scenes described, two on each side. Virgil does not profess to describe everything Vulcan put on the shield, but the scenes which he selects for description do correspond with a symmetrical pattern of design. He does not make his pattern obtrusive, but he invites us, while we read his words, to visualise his pictures on the shield.

3 610. 'when she saw her son some way off, alone by a cool stream'; *secretum* is the participle of *secerno; egelidus* sometimes means 'warm' with the privative e- (Cat. 46.1), but here the prefix e- is intensifying, 'very cold'; Servius compares *Geo.* 4.145 *eduramque pirum,* cf. also Manil. 5.131 and Auson. *Caes.* 21.1. There is strong MSS support for *et gelido,* but *M* has *egelido* and it was the only reading known to Servius.

munera: ne mox aut Laurentis, nate, superbos
aut acrem dubites in proelia poscere Turnum.'
Dixit, et amplexus nati Cytherea petivit,   615
arma sub adversa posuit radiantia quercu.
Ille deae donis et tanto laetus honore
expleri nequit atque oculos per singula volvit,
miraturque interque manus et bracchia versat
terribilem cristis galeam flammasque[1] vomentem,   620
fatiferumque[2] ensem, loricam ex aere rigentem,
sanguineam, ingentem, qualis cum caerula nubes[3]
solis inardescit radiis longeque refulget;
tum levis ocreas electro auroque recocto,
hastamque et clipei non[4] enarrabile textum.   625
Illic res Italas Romanorumque triumphos[5]
haud [6]vatum ignarus venturique inscius aevi
fecerat ignipotens, illic genus omne futurae[7]
stirpis ab Ascanio pugnataque in ordine bella.
Fecerat et viridi fetam Mavortis in antro[8]   630
procubuisse[9] lupam, geminos huic ubera circum
ludere pendentis pueros et lambere matrem
impavidos, illam tereti cervice reflexa
mulcere alternos[10] et corpora[11] fingere lingua.

---

1 620. **flammasque vomentem:** cf. Hom. *Il.* 5.4 where Athena makes Diomedes' helmet and shield glow with fire; *Aen.* 7.785f., where Turnus' helmet has an emblem of a Chimaera breathing flames; *Aen.* 10.270, where Aeneas' armour shoots out flames and fire. *P* has *minantem*, but cf. 681 and 10.271 for *vomentem*.

2 621. **fatiferum:** 'death-dealing', as in 9.631, perhaps here with an overtone of the idea that the fates decree that Aeneas shall conquer Turnus.

3 622f. The simile recalls Ap. Rh. 4.125f. where the golden fleece is like a cloud from which the sun's rays are brilliantly reflected.

4 625. **non enarrabile textum:** 'the indescribable texture', i.e. the way that the various layers were made into a unity (cf. 449f.); compare for *textum* Cat. 64.10, Lucr. 6.1054. Servius is wrong in relating *non enarrabile* to the pictures; it refers to the workmanship.

5 626. Notice the association of Italy and Rome, cf. 678.

6 627. 'not unaware of the prophecies. not without knowledge of the ages to come'; Vulcan has learned of the future of Rome from prophets (e.g. Apollo and those inspired by him).

7 628-9. The shield contains, we are told, all the race of Ascanius and the wars fought; the actual description, very naturally, concentrates on a few. Hence *et* in 630, 'in particular'.

8 630f. The she-wolf who nurtured Romulus and Remus cf. 1.275) was the most famous of all Rome's pictorial emblems. and was constantly depicted on coins, with her head turned round to watch her foster-children (633). According to Servius the description is based on Ennius. The 'green grotto of Mars' is the Lupercal; see note on 343-4. *Mavors* is an archaic form of *Mars*. cf. 700.

9 631. **procubuisse:** the perfect tense is natural; she has lain down (and is lying down). The infinitive rather than the participle after *fecerat* (both are possible) begins the description with a vivid effect, the artist has caused what he depicts.

10 634. **alternos:** this could not be portrayed pictorially, and is an extension of the visual art towards narrative, cf. 695, 708 and cf. 1.483.

11 **corpora fingere lingua:** we are reminded of how Virgil was reported (Aul. Gell. 17.10.3) to have said that he licked his verses into shape, as a she-bear her cubs. Cf. Ov. *Fast.* 2.418 *et fingit lingua corpora bina sua.*

Nec procul hinc Romam et raptas sine more Sabinas[1]   635
consessu[2] caveae, magnis[3] Circensibus actis,
addiderat, subitoque novum consurgere bellum
Romulidis[4] Tatioque seni Curibusque severis.
Post idem inter se posito[5] certamine reges
armati Iovis ante aram paterasque tenentes   640
stabant et caesa iungebant foedera porca.[6]
Haud procul inde citae Mettum[7] in diversa quadrigae
distulerant[8] (at tu dictis, Albane, maneres![9]),
raptabatque viri mendacis viscera Tullus
per silvam, et sparsi rorabant sanguine vepres.   645
Nec[10] non Tarquinium eiectum Porsenna[11] iubebat[12]
accipere ingentique urbem obsidione premebat:
Aeneadae in ferrum pro libertate ruebant.

---

1 635f. The rape of the Sabines is portrayed in two pictures: the scene of violence at the games, and the subsequent reconciliation. The subject is chosen partly for its pictorial impact, and partly because it symbolises the addition of religion and law; with which Numa Pompilius, the Sabine successor of Romulus was always associated) to the rough valour of Romulus' reign: *sine more,* 'without restraint' (cf. 7.377) here means 'outrageously', cf. 316 and Ov. *A.A.* 1.119 (of the Sabine women) *sic illae timuere viros sine more ruentes.*

2 636. **consessu caveae:** 'in the midst of the audience in the circus', cf. 5.340, Lucr. 4.78.

3 **magnis Circensibus actis:** the *ludi Circenses* (*ludi magni*) seem to be here referred to, but the rape of the Sabine women is said by Servius and Livy (1.9) to have occurred at the *Consualia,* and Virgil is perhaps using the term very generally for any games held in a *circus. Actis* is equivalent in time indication to a present participle (as is not infrequent with deponent past participles); cf. 407.

4 638. *Romulidae* (Lucr. 4.683) means 'the people of Romulus', compare *Aeneadae.* Titus Tatius was king of the Sabines before Numa (Livy 1.10); his capital was Cures (6.811), where the way of life was simple and severe (*Geo.* 2.532f.). For *Cures* = *Curenses* cf. *Ov.Fast.* 3.201.

5 639. **posito:** 'laid aside', cf. 1.302.

6 641. For the sacrifice of a pig on the occasion of a treaty cf. 12.170 and Livy 1.24.8.

7 642f. Mettus (or Mettius) Fufetius of Alba promised to help Rome under her third king Tullus Hostilius in her war against the people of Fidenae, but defected to the enemy. For this he was torn to pieces by being tied to chariots which were driven (*citae,* participle of *cieo,* cf. Lucr. 1.997) in opposite directions (*in diversa*) as a punishment for *fides violata* (as Virgil emphasises in his apostrophe to him). Cf. Livy 1.27f., esp. 1.28.10 *in diversum iter equi concitati.*

8 643. **distulerant:** the pluperfect indicates that this had taken place before the scene depicted, cf. 1.483.

9 **maneres:** past jussive, 'you ought to have . . .', cf. 4.678, 10.854, 11.118, 162. The construction occurs in prose, but the more normal construction is with *debere;* cf. Cic *Verr.* 3.195 *quid facere debuisti? . . . retulisses . . .* As with potential sentences (650, *aspiceres* = *aspexisses)* the imperfect subjunctive can have the same meaning as the pluperfect.

10 646f. The famous story of the attack on Rome by Lars Porsena of Clusium in order to restore the exiled Tarquin is told in Livy 2.10f. and by Macaulay in his *Lays of Ancient Rome.* Horatius Cocles held the bridge (Pons Sublicius) against them till it could be cut down (Virgil represents him as actually cutting it down), and then plunged into the Tiber and swam to safety:
'O Tiber, father Tiber,
To whom the Romans pray,
A Roman's life, a Roman's arms
Take thou in charge this day . . .'
After peace had been made, Porsena took hostages from Rome, one of whom was Cloelia. She escaped and swam the Tiber to safety; the Romans sent her back, but Porsena was so impressed by her bravery that he freed her and other captives (Livy 2.13.6-11). In Valerius Maximus (3.2) Cocles and Cloelia head the list of *exempla* of *fortitudo.*

11 646. **Porsenna:** Servius points out that the word is generally in Latin spelled *Porsena* and scanned as a dactyl.

12 **iubebat:** the object of this and subject of *accipere* is *Romanos* understood.

Illum[1] indignanti similem similemque minanti
aspiceres, pontem auderet quia vellere Cocles   650
et fluvium[2] vinclis innaret Cloelia ruptis.
In[3] summo custos Tarpeiae Manlius arcis
stabat pro templo et Capitolia celsa tenebat,
Romuleoque[4] recens horrebat regia culmo.
Atque hic auratis volitans argenteus[5] anser   655
porticibus Gallos in limine adesse canebat;
Galli per dumos aderant arcemque[6] tenebant
defensi tenebris et dono noctis opacae:
aurea caesaries ollis atque aurea vestis,
virgatis [7]lucent sagulis, tum lactea colla   660
auro innectuntur, duo quisque Alpina coruscant
gaesa manu, scutis protecti corpora[8] longis.
Hic exsultantis[9] Salios nudosque[10] Lupercos
lanigerosque apices et lapsa ancilia caelo
extuderat, castae ducebant sacra per urbem   665

---

1 649-50. 'You could have seen him looking exactly like a man angered, like a man threatening', i.e. the picture represents his likeness so well that emotions can be seen, cf. 5.254.

2 651. **fluvium . . . innaret**: cf. 6.369 for the accusative with *innare*.

3 652f. The picture on the top of the shield is a composite one; in the middle is the Capitol, on one side (655) the Gauls attacking, on the other side the religious celebrations of the delivered city. The story of the sacred geese, which in 390 B.C. warned Manlius, the Roman general, of the attack of the Gauls under Brennus against the Capitol on its steepest side, the Tarpeian rock (see note on 347f.), is very suitable for visual art, the Gauls in their gold, the white geese shown in silver. The story is told in Livy 5.47 with emphasis on how the god-fearing Romans had refrained in a time of famine from supplementing their rations with the sacred geese, *quae res saluti fuit*. The religious orders which Virgil mentions had both figured in Evander's description of early Rome (281f.); the Salii were the priests most particularly associated with Rome's safety, and the Luperci celebrated a rite of great antiquity designed to ward off evil. The matrons in their carriages are mentioned here because at the time of the Gallic crisis they gave up their gold to the state (Diod. 14.116, Livy 5.25.9, 550.7), and were as a reward accorded the privilege of riding in carriages.

4 654. 'and Romulus' palace shone new with its rough covering of thatch'. The thatched house of Romulus was one of the historical monuments on the Capitol (Vitr. 2.1, Sen. *Cont.* 2.1.4); *recens* refers to the constant renovation of the thatch (Dion. Hal. 1.79). Some commentators have objected to this line as otiose, as it might be in narrative, but we are here concerned with pictorial vividness. Others have transposed it to follow 642, on the grounds that some authorities put the *regia* of Romulus on the Palatine, and that *recens* is difficult here. But there is no sufficient reason for deserting the MSS.

5 655. **argenteus anser**: the silver contrasts with the gold of the other figures and of the colonnade; also, Servius tells us, a silver model of a goose was set up on the Capitol to commemorate the event.

6 657. **arcemque tenebant**: 'were reaching the citadel', were on the point of success.

7 660. 'they shine in their striped cloaks and their white necks are circled with golden necklaces'; *virgatis* is literally 'of wicker-work', cf. Cat. 64.319; *auro innectuntur* refers to the famous Gallic *torques*, the necklace from which Manlius' son got his cognomen Torquatus.

8 662. **corpora**: retained accusative after the middle sense of *protecti*, see note on 29.

9 663. **exsultantis Salios**: for the dancing priests, the Salii. see note on 285; they wore woollen caps (664) and were the guardians of the sacred shield (which was thought to have fallen from the sky in the reign of Numa) on which Rome's safety depended (Livy 1.20.4. Ov. *Fast.* 3.373f.).

10 **nudosque Lupercos**: see note on 343 4.

pilentis[1] matres in mollibus. Hinc procul addit[2]
Tartareas etiam sedes, alta ostia Ditis,
et scelerum poenas, et te, Catilina,[3] minaci[4]
pendentem scopulo Furiarumque ora trementem,
secretosque pios, his dantem iura Catonem.[5]   670
Haec[6] inter tumidi late maris ibat imago
aurea, sed fluctu spumabant caerula[7] cano,
et circum argento clari delphines[8] in orbem
aequora verrebant caudis aestumque secabant.
In medio[9] classis aeratas, Actia[10] bella,   675
cernere[11] erat, totumque instructo Marte videres
fervere[12] Leucaten[13] auroque effulgere fluctus.
Hinc Augustus[14] agens Italos in proelia Caesar
cum patribus populoque, penatibus et magnis dis,[15]
stans celsa in puppi, geminas cui tempora flammas[16]   680
laeta vomunt patriumque aperitur vertice sidus.

---

1 666. **pilentis** : see note on 652f.

2 666f. The scenes of Tartarus and Elysium are at the bottom (*hinc procul*) of the shield.

3 668f. Cf. 6.580f. for some mythological examples of retribution ; the punishment of Catiline (the conspirator whom Cicero defeated in 63 B.C.) is like that of Ajax impaled on a rock in 1.42f., and the presence of the Furies is reminiscent of 6.605 Servius suggests that the mention of Catiline here is intended as a tribute to Cicero, who is not elsewhere referred to in the *Aeneid*.

4 668. **minaci**: threatening in the sense of huge and awe inspiring (1.162), not threatening to fall.

5 670. **Catonem:** i.e. Cato the younger, of Utica, here thought of not in his capacity as a republican opponent of Caesar, but as the Stoic type of justice and virtue; cf. Hor. *Odes* 1.12.35, 2.1.24, Sen. *Ep. Mor.* 11.9f.

6 671. **haec inter:** 'all in among these scenes', i.e. separating them off, partly from one another, but particularly from the centre piece described in 675f.

7 672. **caerula:** used in the neuter plural as a noun (cf. 3.208), meaning simply 'the sea', apparently without reference here to its colour, which on the shield is gold and white. The major MSS have *spumabat caerula,* in which case *caerula* would be an adjective agreeing with *imago,* but this would make an awkward sentence.

8 673. Dolphins are depicted on the shield of Hercules in Hes. *Scut.* 209f.; *in orbem* means that a circle of dolphins encloses the centrepiece.

9 675f. The centrepiece is in three sections, each illustrating an aspect of the battle of Actium, the naval battle at which Augustus defeated Antony and Cleopatra in 31 B.C. The first (675-703) is a picture of the battle about to begin, the second (704-13) shows the defeat of Cleopatra, the third shows the subsequent triumph of Augustus in Rome. See also note on 608f.

10 675. **Actia bella:** for descriptions of the battle which inaugurated the Roman Empire cf. Hor. *Odes* 1.37, *Epod.* 9, Prop. 3.11, 4.6. This is the passage to which Propertius specifically refers when he says *nescio quid maius nascitur Iliade* (2.34.59f.).

11 676. **cernere erat:** 'it was possible to see', cf. 6.596.

12 677. **fervere:** for the archaic third conjugation form cf. 4.409, 9.693, and Quint. 1.6.7.

13 **Leucaten:** the battle of Actium took place some distance north of this promontory on the island of Leucas, off western Greece; cf. *Aen.* 3.274.

14 678. **Augustus . . . Italos**: notice the emphasis on how the Italians, now Aeneas' enemies, contributed a great part to Rome's destiny; cf. 626, 714-15, and 12.827 *sit Romana potens Itala virtute propago.*

15 679. See note on *Aen.* 312, a line of very similar rhythm and diction; Virgil is recalling Ennius (*Ann.* 201) *dono, ducite, doque volentibus cum magnis dis.* The *magni di* probably include the *penates.* and allied deities like Vesta and the Lares.

16 680-1. The twin flames are partly associated with his helmet (cf. 620 and the twin crests of Romulus, 6.779), but also give an element of the supernatural to Augustus himself; cf. the flames round Iulus' head in 2.682f., and those around Lavinia (7.73f.). The star of his father Julius Caesar which shines at the top of the helmet is a reference to the comet which appeared shortly after Caesar's death; cf. 10.272f., *Ecl.* 9.47, Hor. *Odes* 1.12.47.

Parte alia ventis et dis Agrippa[1] secundis
arduus agmen agens; cui, belli insigne superbum,
tempora [2]navali fulgent rostrata corona.
Hinc[3] ope barbarica variisque Antonius armis,   685
victor ab Aurorae populis et litore rubro,[4]
Aegyptum virisque Orientis et ultima secum
Bactra vehit, sequiturque (nefas[5]) Aegyptia[6] coniunx.
Una omnes ruere ac totum spumare reductis[7]
convulsum remis rostrisque tridentibus aequor.   690
Alta[8] petunt; pelago credas innare revulsas
Cycladas aut montis concurrere montibus altos.
Tanta mole viri turritis puppibus instant.
Stuppea flamma[9] manu telisque volatile ferrum
spargitur, arva nova Neptunia[10] caede rubescunt   695
regina in mediis patrio[11] vocat agmina sistro,
necdum etiam geminos a tergo respicit anguis.[12]

---

1 682. **Agrippa:** one of Augustus' leading generals and ministers, at one time marked out for the succession. It is only in this passage (and in 6.863f., the ghost of Marcellus) that Virgil refers to contemporaries of Augustus.

2 684. 'his head is brilliantly adorned with the figure-heads of a naval crown'; the reference is to the emblem of distinction, a crown decorated with golden images of the 'beaks' of ships, awarded for Agrippa's victory against the fleet of Sextus Pompeius (36 B.C.); cf. Aul. Gell. 5.6. The rhythmical symmetry of the 'golden' line reinforces the description.

3 685. 'On the other side Antony with his foreign wealth and medley of troops . . .'; cf. Enn. *Scen.* 94 (of Priam's palace) *vidi ego te adstantem ope barbarica.* The conflict between Eastern and Western types of civilisation is emphasised al) through Virgil's description (cf. esp. 698f.).

4 686f. The reference is to Antony's campaigns against the Parthians (41-36 B.C.) ; the Red Sea is linked with the distant east in Hor. *Odes* 1.35.30f. For Bactra (in Turkestan) cf. *Geo.* 2.138.

5 **nefas:** parenthetical, 'the sin of it', cf. 7.73, 10.673. For the Roman hostility to marriage with Eastern races see the sustained scorn of Hor. *Odes* 3.5.5f.

6 688. For other hostile descriptions of Cleopatra see note on 675; Hor. *Odes* 1.37 is remarkable in its reversal of mood from hatred to sympathy.

7 689. The historic infinitives help to give the impression of action, of narrative added to the visual art.
For *tridentibus* (the three prongs on the prow of a ship) cf. 5.143. the same line.

8 691f. 'They are making for the open sea ; you would think that the Cyclades had been uprooted and were floating on the sea, or that mighty mountains were clashing against mountains, so huge were the towered ships in which the warriors moved to battle.' The comparison is one of size and hence it is better to take *tanta mole* with *puppibus,* rather than with *instant* ('with such mighty force did they move'). The ships of Antony were unusually large (Dio 50.23, Plut. *Ant.* 64), and according to Dio had towers, which was not without precedent at that time Caes. *B.G.* 3.14). Servius says Agrippa invented a collapsible type. Dryden imitates this passage in *Annus Mirabilis* 227-8:
So vast the noise, as if not Fleets did join,
But Lands unfixed and floating Nations strove.

9 694-5. 'Flames of tow, flying iron weapons are hurled on all sides'; *manu* goes with *spaigitur, telis* with *volatile* (literally 'iron made winged on weapons'). Both phrases refer to the weapon known as *malleolus,* a bunch of flax smeared with pitch and fixed to an iron shaft.

10 695. For the fields of Neptune (the sea) cf. 10.214 *campos salis. Nova caede rubescunt* means that the sea seems to be turning red with the fresh spilled blood; the artist's skill is such that it almost portrays continuous action.

11 696. **patrio . . . sistro:** the Egyptian 'rattle' which was used in the worship of Isis; cf. Prop. 3.11.43.

12 697. The asp with which she finally killed herself is symbolically portrayed by Vulcan behind the figure of Cleopatra in a tableau of two serpents; in itself such an emblem would be sinister (e.g. 7.450), and when applied to Cleopatra it becomes more specific.

Omnigenumque[1] deum[2] monstra et latrator Anubis
contra Neptunum et Venerem contraque Minervam
tela tenent. Saevit medio in certamine Mavors[3]   700
caelatus[4] ferro, tristesque ex aethere Dirae,
et scissa gaudens vadit Discordia palla,
quam cum sanguineo sequitur Bellona flagello.
Actius[5] haec cernens arcum intendebat Apollo
desuper: omnis eo terrore Aegyptus et Indi,   705
omnis Arabs, omnes vertebant terga Sabaei.[6]
Ipsa videbatur[7] ventis regina vocatis
vela dare et[8] laxos iam iamque immittere funis.
Illam inter caedes pallentem morte futura
fecerat ignipotens undis[9] et Iapyge ferri,   710
contra autem magno maerentem corpore Nilum[10]
pandentemque sinus et tota veste vocantem
caeruleum in gremium latebrosaque flumina victos.
At[11] Caesar, triplici invectus Romana triumpho
moenia,[12] dis Italis votum immortale sacrabat,   715

---

1 698. **omnigenum:** archaic genitive, used in Virgil with an adjective only with this word and with *magnanimus* (3.704, 6.307). Priscian however regards it as genitive of a noun *omnigena* in apposition to *deum*.

2 698-700. The conflict of religious attitudes between East and West is here very clearly seen: Anubis was the Egyptian dog-headed deity (Prop. 3.11.41) who exemplifies the various monstrous shapes in which their gods were visualised (cf. Juv. 15.1f.). The worship of Egyptian gods was disapproved by Augustus (Suet. *Aug.* 93). The line which follows achieves a remarkable sonorous simplicity; Neptune is the Roman god of the sea where the battle takes place, Venus the mother of the Roman race, Minerva the goddess of wisdom, and one of the Capitoline triad.

3 701-3. The Furies (cf. 12.845) are hovering above the battle, Discord (cf. 6.280) rejoices at the civil war, and her torn clothing symbolises disorder; for Bellona (goddess of war) cf. 7.319.

4 701. **caelatus ferro:** Mars is appropriately depicted in iron, rather than gold.

5 704. **Actius . . . Apollo:** the temple of Apollo at Actium was restored by Augustus in honour of his victory; see note on 3.274f. The god is here depicted in his role as avenging archer, cf. Hor. *Odes* 2.10.19-20.

6 706. **Sabaei:** from Arabia (Sheba), cf. *Geo.* 1.57.

7 707. **videbatur:** 'was depicted', 'was to be seen'. This second scene is in two parts, Cleopatra on the point of flight, and (709) in flight to the Nile.

8 708. **et laxos . . . funis:** 'and on the very point of slackening and releasing the ropes', so as to give full sail, with nothing hauled in (cf. 10.229). *Iam iamque* is an indication of the vividness of the visual art, so that what she is preparing to do practically is happening (cf. 649).

9 710. **undis . . . ferri:** 'being swept on by the waves and the northwest wind'; for Iapyx cf. 11.678, Hor. *Odes* 1.3.4, Aul. Gell. 2.22.23.

10 711f. The personification of the mighty River-god Nile is splendidly pictorial; the mystery of his size and origin is summarised in *latebrosa* — he has room for all to hide; cf. Hor. *Odes* 1.37.23f.

11 714f. The last scene (in two parts) shows (i) Augustus' triumph in Rome, a triple triumph (lasting three days) which he celebrated in 29 B.C. for the battle of Actium, the Dalmatian war and the Alexandrian war (Suet. *Aug.* 22); (ii) Augustus at Apollo's temple (720f.). The passage generally may be compared with the temple of song for Augustus which Virgil visualises in *Geo.* 3.16f.

12 715. **moenia:** accusative of motion towards without a preposition, helped by the compound *invectus;* cf. 7.436.

maxima ter centum totam delubra per urbem.[1]
Laetitia ludisque viae[2] plausuque fremebant;
omnibus in templis matrum chorus, omnibus arae;[3]
ante aras terram caesi stravere iuvenci.
Ipse sedens niveo candentis limine Phoebi[4]   720
dona recognoscit populorum aptatque superbis[5]
postibus; incedunt victae longo ordine gentes,
quam variae linguis, habitu tam vestis et armis.
Hic Nomadum genus et discinctos Mulciber[6] Afros,
hic Lelegas Carasque sagittiferosque Gelonos   725
finxerat; Euphrates[7] ibat iam mollior undis,
extremique hominum Morini,[8] Rhenusque[9] bicornis,
indomitique Dahae,[10] et pontem indignatus Araxes.

    Talia per clipeum Volcani, dona parentis,
miratur [11]rerumque ignarus imagine gaudet   730
attollens umero famamque et fata nepotum.

---

1 716. This line is in apposition to *votum;* his offering was to be 300 shrines. Three hundred is an indefinite large number (cf. 4.510); in his *Res Gestae* Augustus claimed to have restored 82, and names also twelve new ones which he built, including Apollo's (720); cf. Hor. *Odes* 3.6.1f., Ov. *Fast.* 2.63.

2 717. 'The highways echoed with joy, revelry and applause.'

3 718. It goes without saying that there were altars in all the temples; but what Virgil means is that Vulcan had portrayed them on the shield.

4 720. In the second part of this scene Augustus sits by the white marble temple of Apollo on the Palatine. which he dedicated in 28 B.C. (cf. Hor. *Odes* 1.31.1, Prop. 2.31, and note on *Aen.* 6.69f.).

5 721-2. Cf. *Aen.* 3.287 for the hanging up of votive offerings.

6 724f. Vulcan is called Mulciber already in Accius (Macr. *Sat.* 6.5.2). Nomades are the wandering tribes of Africa (*Geo.* 3.339, *Aen.* 4.320); the Afri are *discincti* because they wore flowing robes without girdles (Livy 35.11.7); the Leleges and Cares are from Asia Minor, and the Geloni (quiver-bearing also in Hor. *Odes* 3.4.35) from Scythia. Line 725 is without main caesura in third or fourth foot; Virgil often uses lists of proper names to produce variations on his normal rhythm.

7 726. **Euphrates:** cf. *Geo.* 4.561 for Augustus' activities in Parthia, and for the humbling of the river cf. Hor. *Odes* 2.9.21f. *Medumque flumen gentibus additum / victis minores volvere vertices.* The rivers appear in the procession as river gods; cf. the Danube on Trajan's column.

8 727. **Morini:** a people of northern Gaul, 'qui Britanniam spectant, proximi Oceano' (Servius).

9 **Rhenusque bicornis**: the Rhine has two horns because river-gods were frequently depicted with the heads of bulls; cf. 77 and *Geo.* 4.371-2 *et gemina auratus taurino cornua vultu / Eridanus.* Servius however explains it of the two main estuaries of the river, the Rhine and the Waal; for this use of *cornua* cf. Ov. *Met.* 9.774.

10 728. The Dahae are Scythian nomads; according to Servius the river Araxes in Armenia had broken the bridge which Alexander put over it, and Augustus built a new bridge to tame the resentful river.

11 730-1. 'and knowing nothing of the events he rejoiced in the pictures of them as he raised high on his shoulder the glory and destiny of his children's children'. The last line is most memorable, with its dignified cadence and diction and its symbolism behind the literal meaning; Aeneas has on his shoulders in actuality the pictured shield of Vulcan, but metaphorically the future destiny of Rome.

BOOK 9

Introductory note

The ninth book falls naturally into three sections: the Rutulian attack on the Trojan ships and their transformation into nymphs; the story of Nisus and Euryalus; the battle scenes and the victories of Turnus. Here at last Virgil comes to the description of fighting of which he spoke in the invocation in Book 7: *dicam horrida bella / dicam acies actosque animis in funera reges.* The seventh book set the scene for war, the eighth held the action static, in the ninth the battles begin.

Virgil's attitude to war was quite different from that of Homer; in Homer war is an accepted part of the heroic world, bringing its triumphs and its tragedies as a part of the human condition; it is the framework within which society worked. In Virgil's early years war had been frequent, but of a kind which did not seem inevitable, which indeed caused deep guilt feelings in the Romans; and at the time when the *Aeneid* was being written there seemed some prospect of universal peace, based on Roman military might. Virgil's problem is whether it is possible and, if possible, acceptable that peace should be imposed by means of war. His personal hatred for violence, conflict and war is obvious from the *Eclogues* and the *Georgics;* and as a result there is a strange tension between the epic form with its requirement for deeds of prowess, death and bloodshed, and Virgil's personal reaction to his material. This shows itself in two contrasting ways: sometimes by intensely felt pity for the victims ,'as for Euryalus and for his mother), sometimes by a deliberate and almost reckless intensification of the horror (as in the slaughter of the sleeping Rutulians, or some of the detail of Turnus' triumphs). Because this tension is so far from any resolution, many have felt that Virgil's battle scenes are unsuccessful; it seems better to say that they are deliberately incoherent, lacking unity of tone but preserving integrity. Virgil was not prepared to falsify them in order to make them less grim; he could have stood much further away from the detail, but he would not. In a way we could say that Virgil's battle scenes present his own self in the scenes of pathos and an 'anti-self', a 'mask', in the scenes of horror.

The first episode describes the beginning of the Rutulian attack in terrifying phrases of violence unleashed, but miraculously the ships are saved from the threat of fire and we enter for a brief moment into the pastoral world of dreams and visions. Against this is set in stark contrast the realism and horror of the story of Nisus and Euryalus; Virgil involves us very closely in the tragedy of their story, and with the lament of Euryalus' mother makes a poignant protest against the futility of war. There is a softness of sentiment here alien to the heroic world. But in the last section, introduced by a line from Ennius and often closely modelled on Ennius and Homer, the tone is far less emotional, and the excitement of the narrative moves rapidly onward.

1-76. Juno sends Iris to Turnus, in order to tell him that Aeneas is away and that the moment for attack has arrived. Turnus accepts the divine call to arms. The Trojans, in accordance with Aeneas' instructions, stay within their camp, and Turnus, wild for blood like a wolf at a sheepfold, prepares to set fire to the Trojan fleet.

Atque ea diversa[1] penitus dum parte geruntur,
Irim[2] de caelo misit Saturnia Iuno
audacem[3] ad Turnum. Luco tum forte parentis
Pilumni[4] Turnus sacrata valle sedebat.
Ad quem sic roseo[5] Thaumantias[6] ore locuta est: 5
'Turne,[7] quod optanti divum promittere nemo[8]
auderet, volvenda[9] dies en attulit ultro.
Aeneas urbe[10] et sociis et classe relicta
sceptra[11] Palatini sedemque petit Euandri.
Nec satis: extremas Corythi penetravit ad urbes[12] 10
Lydorumque manum,[13] collectos armat agrestis.
Quid dubitas? Nunc tempus equos, nunc poscere currus.
Rumpe moras omnis et turbata[14] arripe castra.'

---

1 1. **diversa penitus**: 'far distant', i.e. at Pallanteum, Evander's city, and in Etruria where Aeneas met Tarchon (8.597f.). The separate actions (Aeneas' journey in Book 8, the events at the Trojan camp in Book 9) are brought together at Aeneas' return in 10.260f.

2 2. Iris is in Virgil the special messenger of Juno. The same line occurs in 5.606, in a similar context: after the peaceful atmosphere of the funeral games Juno causes the burning of the ships by the Trojan women through the agency of Iris. Observe the slow spondees of this and the next two lines, suggesting the imminent threat of action, the menacing hush before the storm.

3 3. **audacem**: notice the immediate reference to the character of Turnus upon his re-introduction into the action after his absence since the opening scene of Book 8: for his character see note on 7.406f.

4 4. **Pilumni**: Pilumnus was father (or grandfather, 10.619) of Daunus, the father of Turnus. He was a Roman deity associated with agriculture: see Servius ad loc.

5 5. **roseo**: often of the gods (*Aen.* 2.593), perhaps here specially appropriate for the goddess of the rainbow.

6 **Thaumantias**: an epithet of Iris, daughter of Thaumas (Hes. *Theog.* 265f.).

7 6-7. 'Turnus, look, time in its passage has brought to you unasked a thing which none of the gods would dare to promise to a man's hope'.

8 6. **nemo**: a rare word in epic, occurring elsewhere in Virgil only three times, all within a hundred lines in Book 5. For details see my note on 5.305 (OUP Ed.).

9 7. **volvenda:** the gerundive supplies the need of the present participle passive; cf. 1.269.

10 8. **urbe**: rather grandiloquently for what was still a camp, the first place of landing (later known as Troia): cf. 48.

11 9. 'has sought the kingly power and home of Palatine Evander'; *Palatini* is an adjective, referring to Evander's town Pallanteum on the site of Rome and the Palatine Hill. *Petit* is perfect, contracted for *petiit* (cf. Lucan 10.64); the final syllable is therefore long by nature. For the spondaic ending cf. 196, 241, 647, and see note on 7.634. *Sceptra . . . sedemque* is virtually a hendiadys for 'palace'.

12 10-11. The reference is to 8.585f. where Aeneas sets off with Pallas from Evander's city to meet Tarchon and his Etruscans. For Corythus and his connexions with Etruria see notes on 3.170, 7.209; for *Lydorum* of the Etruscans cf. 8.479. Iris exaggerates the distance of Aeneas' journey (he met Tarchon near Caere) to convince Turnus that this is the moment for attack.

13 11. It is better to take *manum* in apposition to *agrestis* ('he arms a band of Lydians, countryfolk he has mustered'); to regard it as parallel with *urbes,* governed by *ad,* is not appropriate with the verb *penetravit*.

14 13. **turbata arripe castra**: 'strike confusion into their camp and capture it'; in the absence of Aeneas, Turnus will be able *turbare et arripere castra*.

Dixit, et in caelum paribus se sustulit alis[1]
ingentemque fuga secuit sub nubibus arcum.   15
Agnovit iuvenis duplicisque[2] ad sidera palmas
sustulit ac tali fugientem est voce secutus:
'Iri,[3] decus caeli, quis te mihi nubibus[4] actam
detulit in terras? [5]Unde haec tam clara repente
tempestas? Medium video discedere caelum   20
palantisque polo stellas. Sequor omina tanta,
quisquis[6] in arma vocas.' Et sic effatus ad undam
processit summoque hausit[7] de gurgite lymphas
multa deos orans, oneravitque[8] aethera votis.

    Iamque omnis campis exercitus ibat apertis   25
dives equum, dives[9] pictai[10] vestis et auri;
Messapus[11] primas acies, postrema coercent
Tyrrhidae[12] iuvenes, medio dux agmine Turnus:
[vertitur arma tenens et toto vertice supra est.]
Ceu[13] septem surgens sedatis amnibus altus   30
per tacitum Ganges aut pingui flumine Nilus

---

1 14-15. These lines occur (of Iris) in nearly the same form in 5.657-8. *Paribus . . . alis* is 'on balanced wings', cf. 4.252; *secuit . . . arcum* means that by cutting her way through the air (*secare aethera, Geo.* 1.406, *secare viam, Aen.* 6.899), she makes a rainbow.

2 16. **duplicis:** poetic and formulaic for *ambas,* cf. 1.93.

3 18. **Iri:** Greek vocative, scanning as a trochee; cf. 8.72 and Hom. *Il.* 18.182.

4 **nubibus actam:** 'coming by way of the clouds', cf. 10.38, the same phrase; *actam* has a reflexive sense, cf. 9.696. Iris journeys to and from earth on her rainbow, which is brought into being by clouds and sun.

5 19f. The imagery of the radiant glow of the rainbow is powerfully expressed here: Turnus sees it as brilliant light suddenly parting the veil of heaven, like a curtain drawn back to reveal the stars moving in their courses. Cf. Cic. *De Div.* 1.97 (in a list of portents) *caelum discessisse visum est atque in eo animadversi globi.* For *tempestas* (= weather) cf. Lucr. 2.32 *tempestas arridet*; the whole image is not unlike *nova lux oculis offulsit* in line 110 (Cybele's supernatural appearance). For *palantes stellas* cf. Lucr. 2.1031.

6 22. **quisquis:** he knows that it is Iris who has appeared to him; he does not know who sent her to convey the call to arms.

7 23. **hausit:** 'drew', as part of the purification before his ceremonial prayers; cf. 8.69.

8 24. **oneravit:** a metaphorical variant of phrases like *onerant aras* (5.101), *cumulatque altaria donis* (11.50), the basic idea being the constant repetition of the prayers.

9 26. **dives equum:** 'rich in horses', genitive of respect, cf. 1.14, *dives opum,* and lines 246, 255.

10 **pictai:** archaic form of the genitive; see note on 7.464.

11 27 **Messapus:** described in the catalogue, 7.691f.

12 28. **Tyrrhidae:** the brothers of Silvia, whose pet stag was shot by Ascanius, thus causing the outbreak of the war; cf. 7.484. This line, repeated from 7.784, is not found in the good MSS, and interrupts the movement of the sentence.

13 30f. 'like the Ganges silently rising, fed by its seven placid tributaries, or the Nile with its rich stream when it has flowed back from the plains and has now confined itself within its banks'.
The movement of the line of soldiers is compared with (i) the steady forward movement of the Ganges after receiving its seven tributaries; (ii) the Nile when it has returned after flooding to its own channel. Thus there are two points of comparison: the first is with the now steady flow of a great river (notice the reinforcing alliteration in lines 30 and 32), and the second is with the previously scattered and dispersed waters. The number seven for the tributaries of the Ganges may be influenced by the Nile's seven channels in its delta (*Aen.* 6.800). The word *alius* is the past participle of *alere* ('nourish'), cf. Hor. *Odes* 4.2.5-6, Cic. *Brut.* 39, and my note in *C.Ph.* 1968, 143; it is generally taken to mean 'deep', but this does not fit well into the sentence.

cum refluit campis et iam se condidit alveo.[1]
Hic subitam nigro glomerari[2] pulvere nubem
prospiciunt Teucri ac tenebras insurgere campis.
Primus ab adversa conclamat mole Caicus:[3]   35
'quis globus, o cives, caligine volvitur atra?
Ferte citi ferrum, date tela, ascendite muros,[4]
hostis adest, heia!' ingenti clamore per omnis
condunt[5] se Teucri portas et moenia complent.
Namque ita discedens praeceperat optimus armis[6]   40
Aeneas: [7]si qua interea fortuna fuisset,
neu struere auderent aciem neu credere campo;
castra modo et tutos servarent aggere muros.
Ergo etsi conferre manum pudor iraque monstrat,[8]
obiciunt portas tamen et praecepta facessunt,   45
armatique cavis exspectant turribus hostem.
  [9]Turnus, ut ante volans tardum praecesserat agmen
viginti lectis equitum comitatus et urbi
improvisus adest, maculis quem Thracius albis[10]
portat equus cristaque tegit galea[11] aurea rubra,   50
'ecquis erit mecum, iuvenes, qui[12] primus in hostem — ?
En,' ait et iaculum attorquens[13] emittit in auras,

---

1 32. **alveo:** scanned as a spondee, see note on 7.33, and cf. 480.

2 33-4. **glomerari . . . insurgere:** they see a dense mass of dust spreading upwards (*glomerari* is a favourite Virgilian word; cf. *globus* in 36).

3 35. **Caicus:** a Trojan mentioned in 1.183.

4 37. Compare 4.594 *ferte citi flammas, date tela, impellite remos.*

5 39. **condunt se:** 'seek shelter', cf. 5.243. Some of the Trojans had been outside the camp walls before danger threatened.

6 40f. Notice the emphasis on the forethought and military care of Aeneas; it is the basic feature of the concept of Roman leadership that the general should act not as a brilliant individual in the heroic style, but as one responsible for those under his command. Contrast the 'heroic' style behaviour of the wild, impetuous Aeneas of Book 2.

7 41f. 'If in the meantime anything should happen they were not to risk drawing up their line of battle or entrusting themselves to open combat; they were simply to defend their camp and their walls protected by the rampart.' *Fortuna* is a neutral word, here used euphemistically for bad fortune (like our 'anything'); cf. 7.559. *Fuisset* is reported future perfect (cf. 2.94), and *neu auderent* reported prohibition: Aeneas' words were *si qua fortuna fuerit, ne audete.* For the *agger* cf. 7.159.

8 44. **monstrat:** with the infinitive on the analogy of *iubet* (prose) or *suadet* (poetry).

9 47f. Turnus had been in the middle of the column (28); he now rides to the front and actually (*et*) reaches the city (the Trojan camp, cf. line 8) sooner than they could have expected (though they knew the enemy was approaching). *Et* (= *etiam*) is a little strange here; some therefore regard it as linking *improvisus* with *comitatus*, and others take *ut* with *ante volans* (= *ut qui ante volaret*) so that *et* would link the main verbs *praecesserat* and *adest.*

10 49-50. Cf. 5.565-7 (of Ascanius' horse).

11 50. **galea aurea** is nominative, *crista rubra* ablative; Servius oddly comments: 'sane huiusmodi versus pessimi sunt'.

12 51. **qui primus:** understand *ibit;* Turnus is deliberately abrupt here, and again in ending his speech with *en* in the next line.

13 52. **attorquens:** the compound occurs only here in Classical Latin; cf. *advelat* (5.246).

principium[1] pugnae, et campo sese arduus infert.
Clamorem excipiunt socii fremituque sequuntur[2]
horrisono; Teucrum mirantur inertia corda,   55
non aequo dare se campo, non obvia ferre[3]
arma viros, sed castra[4] fovere. Huc turbidus atque huc
lustrat equo muros aditumque per avia quaerit.
Ac[5] veluti pleno lupus insidiatus ovili
cum fremit ad caulas[6] ventos perpessus et imbris   60
nocte[7] super media; tuti sub matribus agni
balatum[8] exercent, ille asper et improbus[9] ira
saevit[10] in absentis, collecta fatigat edendi
ex longo rabies et siccae sanguine fauces:
haud aliter Rutulo muros et castra tuenti   65
ignescunt irae; duris dolor[11] ossibus ardet.
Qua temptet ratione aditus, et quae[12] via clausos
excutiat Teucros vallo atque effundat in aequum?[13]
Classem,[14] quae lateri castrorum adiuncta iatebat,

---

1 53. **principium pugnae:** in apposition to the previous clause, cf. 6.223, 10.311. The ancient Roman method of declaring war was for the *pater patratus* to hurl a spear from the frontier into enemy territory.

2 54f. The beginning of full-scale violence and bloodshed is here described in chilling terms, developed by the wolf simile of 59f. and the fierce battle cry of the Rutulians, 71f. The Lucretian type epithet *horrisono,* used also in 6.573 of the gates of Tartarus, adds power to the picture.

3 56f. The construction after *mirantur* changes from the simple accusative to the accusative and infinitive.

4 57. The trochaic movement of *castra fovere,* with elision over the caesura at a full stop, conveys the excitement of the moment, and so does the monosyllable at the line ending. *Fovere* is used contemptuously, as appropriate to domestic scenes but not to warfare; cf. *Geo.* 4.43, *Aen.* 4.193.

5 59f. This is one of the most terrifying similes in the *Aeneid,* having about it a realism which transcends its literary models in Homer (e.g. *Od.* 6.130f.) and Apollonius (1.124.3f.);this is partly because of its echo of the actual situation in the *Georgics* (3-537f. *non lupus insidias explorat ovilia circum, / nec gregibus nocturnus obambulat.*) The other three wolf similes in the *Aeneid* are at 2.355f (Aeneas and the Trojans), 9.565f. (Turnus again), 11.809f. (Arruns).

6 60. **caulas:** 'chinks'. The word, which is associated with *cavus,* is used by Lucretius to mean openings, and is otherwise rare. Here it refers to narrow gaps in the fence through which the wolf cannot get.

7 61 **nocte super media:** 'upon the middle of the night', 'at midnight', an unusual use of *super.* It would be still more unusual if the meaning were (as Servius suggests) 'after midnight'.

8 62. **balatum exercent:** 'raise a bleat'; cf. *Geo.* 1.403 *exercet noctua cantus.*

9 **improbus:** 'beside himself, used of anything that passes normal bounds; cf. 10.727, 11.767. It is used of a wolf in the simile in 2.356.

10 63f. 'savages them in imagination; his craving for food, long unsatisfied, torments him, and his fangs are starved of blood'. *Sanguine* is ablative of separation, *siccae* being equivalent to *carentes;* cf. 8.261, Prop. 4.10.12, and for the idea cf. the wolf cubs in 2.358 waiting *faucibus siccis.*

11 66. **dolor:** 'angry frustration', cf. 5.172. The point of *duris . . . ossibus* is that indignation penetrates to the very core of his being; cf. 6.54.

12 67. The deliberative questions represent the thought in his mind. *Quae via* gives an unexpected change of subject: 'what approach would dislodge . . . ?' Some MSS read *qua via,* which is more abrupt still; suggested emendations are *qua vi, qua vice.*

13 68. **aequum:** cf. 56. This is far better than *aequor,* read by some MSS, which would give a kind of pun with *effundat.*

14 69. **classem:** notice the great emphasis on this word, filling the initial spondee, followed by a pause and separated by two lines from the verb governing it.

aggeribus saeptam circum et fluvialibus undis,   70
invadit sociosque incendia poscit ovantis
atque manum pinu flagranti fervidus implet.
Tum vero incumbunt (urget praesentia Turni),
atque omnis facibus[1] pubes accingitur atris.
Diripuere[2] focos: piceum fert fumida lumen   75
taeda et commixtam Volcanus[3] ad astra favillam.

> 77-122. *The Trojan ships, which had been made from the sacred pine trees of the goddess Cybele, are saved from burning by being transformed into nymphs.*

[4]Quis deus,[5] o Musae, tam saeva incendia Teucris
avertit? Tantos ratibus quis depulit ignis?
Dicite: prisca fides facto, sed fama perennis.
Tempore quo primum Phrygia formabat in Ida[6]   80
Aeneas classem et pelagi[7] petere alta parabat,
ipsa deum fertur genetrix Berecyntia[8] magnum
vocibus his adfata Iovem: 'da, nate, petenti,
quod tua cara parens domito[9] te poscit Olympo.

---

1 74. **facibus ... accingitur atris**: 'arm themselves with smoking torches', perhaps with a touch of metaphorical meaning in *atris,* as in 4.384, 10.77, 11.186. *Accingitur* is middle, cf. 7.188.

2 75. **diripuere focos**: the 'instantaneous' perfect adds to the rapidity of the narrative. For the phrase cf. 5.660, the burning of the fleet by the Trojan women, *rapiuntque focis penetralibus ignem.* The description here is more powerful and terrifying; notice the astonishing alliteration and assonance, especially of *-um,* in the second half of this line; cf. 7.76-7.

3 76. **Volcanus**: as in 5.662, the fire-god is present in person. The order of these two clauses is interlaced, *fert* being the verb for both.

4 77f. This is the most incongruous episode in the whole *Aeneid,* and has been censured by the critics from the time of Servius onwards (on 82, *notatur a criticis*); Page finds the subject 'somewhat ludicrous', and Heyne says it is easy to censure it as 'absurdam et epica gravitate indignant'. The story is told in Ov. *Met.* 14-530f., where it easily and naturally belongs. It does not seem to have figured in the normal version of the Aeneas legend.
There were of course precedents in epic for this kind of magical story: in Apollonius (4.580f.) the good ship Argo can talk, and in Homer (*Od.* 8-557f.) the Phaeacian ships steer themselves; but the Argo and the Phaeacians belong wholly to a heroic world, in contrast with Aeneas' fleet which is entering a proto-Roman world. Virgil is aware of this incongruity when he says (line 79) *prisca fides facto, sed fama perennis.* Why then did he introduce the story?
We may understand his motives best if we consider the context. The passage which has just preceded (47-76) has given a chilling and terrible picture of violence unleashed: irresistibly, it seems, the Rutulians fall in wild frenzy upon the ships, and yet they *are* resisted, supernaturally. Virgil snatches us away from the awful inevitability of unopposed military might into the pastoral world, where violence and destruction is avoided by supernatural power, where fire cannot burn nor brute force prevail, where at the moment of annihilation there is intervention, escape, transformation from the mortal world.

5 77-9. The new invocation to the Muses draws particular attention to the shift from the mortal world to the supernatural, and this is reiterated in 79; the story is such that only in olden times could it be accepted literally, but in Virgil's time its value lives on in a symbolic or mythological way. Cf. Livy 7.6.6 *fama rerum standum est ubi certam derogat vetustas fidem,* and see previous note.

6 80f. This refers to the events at the beginning of Book 3; cf. 3.5-6 *classemque sub ipsa / Antandro et Phrygiae molimur montibus Idae.*

7 81. **pelagi ... alta**: 'the deeps of the sea', cf. 8.691.

8 82. **Berecyntia**: an epithet of Cybele, the *Magna Mater,* the mother of the gods, cf. 619 and 6.784.

9 84. **domito ... Olympo**: the ablative absolute has a causal sense, 'in return for your power in Olympus'. Cybele saved Jupiter by rescuing him when Saturnus decided to consume his children (Ov. *Fast.* 4.199f.), and again by her help when the Titans rebelled.

Pinea[1] silva mihi multos dilecta per annos,   85
lucus in arce fuit summa, quo sacra ferebant,
nigranti picea trabibusque obscurus acernis:
has ego Dardanio iuveni, cum classis egeret,
laeta dedi; nunc sollicitam timor anxius[2] angit.
Solve [3]metus atque hoc precibus sine posse parentem,   90
ne cursu quassatae ullo neu turbine venti
vincantur: prosit[4] nostris in montibus ortas.'
Filius huic contra, torquet qui sidera mundi:
'o[5] genetrix, quo fata vocas? Aut quid petis istis?
Mortaline manu factae immortale carinae   95
fas habeant? Certusque[6] incerta pericula lustret
Aeneas? Cui tanta deo permissa potestas?
Immo, ubi defunctae[7] finem portusque tenebunt
Ausonios olim, quaecumque evaserit undis[8]
Dardaniumque ducem Laurentia[9] vexerit arva,   100
mortalem eripiam formam magnique iubebo
aequoris esse deas, [10]qualis Nereia Doto
et Galatea secant spumantem pectore pontum.'
Dixerat idque ratum Stygii[11] per flumina fratris,

---

1 85f. 'I had a pine-wood, a grove on the top of the mountain . . .'; the words *silva* and *lucus* are in apposition, and there is no reason to suspect interpolation, as Heyne and Ribbeck and others have done. The pinewood has pitch pines in it (*picea*), with some maple interspersed. Servius is uneasy about the use of *trabes* for living timber, but this is frequent in the poets (cf. 6.181).

2 89. **anxius angit**: a Lucretian assonance, cf. Lucr. 3.993 *anxius angor.*

3 90f. 'Dispel my fear and permit your mother to achieve this with her pleas, namely that they be not shattered and sunk on any voyage or by whirlwinds.' *Hoc* points forward to the final clause, and *neu* joins the two ablatives. This is better than regarding *quassatae* as a finite verb.

4 92. **prosit . . . ortas**: Met it benefit them that they were born on our mountains'; the full construction would be, as Servius says, *prosit his ortas esse in montibus nostris.*

5 94. 'Mother, to what end are you trying to turn the fates? What do you seek with such a request?' He means that the fates cannot be directly diverted in this way, though a method can be found in another way; Servius well says *ostendit fata posse aliquatenus trahi, non tamen usquequaque.* The unusual rhythm of the line ending emphasises the verb *petis*. *Istis* might be dative (*navibus*), but it is better understood as ablative (*precibus*).

6 96. **certusque incerta**: there is a strong irony in this rhetorical antithesis: indeed Aeneas was not able in full certainty to traverse the uncertain dangers of the long voyage.

7 98. **defunctae**: absolute, 'having completed their task'; cf. the fuller phrase in 6.83 *defuncte peridis.*

8 99f. There is some disjunction here between singular and plural: 'whatever ship has escaped . . . (from that ship) I will remove its mortal shape, and I will bid them all be goddesses'. Some ships were lost, one sunk in the storm off Carthage, and four burnt in Sicily.

9 100. **Laurentia . . . arva**: accusative of motion towards, cf. 474, 601 and 1.2, 8.136.

10 102f. 'like Doto, daughter of Nereus, and Galatea cutting through the waves'; again singular and plural are interwoven, but there is no occasion to change *qualis* to *quales* or *et . . . secant* to *aut . . . secat.* These two Nereids are linked in Homer, *Il.* 18.39f.

11 104f. The words *Stygii . . . Olympum* are repeated in 10.113-15. For the solemn oath sworn by the Styx, river of Pluto (Jupiter's brother), cf. 6.323f. *Ratum* is predicative: he indicated that it was certain.

per[1] pice torrentis atraque voragine ripas   105
adnuit, et totum nutu tremefecit Olympum.
   Ergo aderat promissa dies et tempora Parcae
debita complerant, cum Turni iniuria Matrem
admonuit ratibus sacris depellere taedas.
Hic[2] primum nova[3] lux oculis offulsit et ingens   110
visus ab Aurora caelum transcurrere nimbus[4]
Idaeique chori; tum vox horrenda per auras
excidit et Troum Rutulorumque agmina[5] complet:
'ne[6] trepidate meas, Teucri, defendere navis
neve armate manus; maria ante exurere Turno[7]   115
quam sacras dabitur pinus. Vos ite solutae,
ite deae pelagi: genetrix iubet.' Et sua quaeque
continuo puppes abrumpunt vincula ripis
delphinumque modo demersis aequora rostris[8]
ima petunt. Hinc virgineae (mirabile monstrum)   120
[quot prius aeratae steterant ad litora prorae][9]
reddunt[10] se totidem facies pontoque[11] feruntur.

---

1 105. 'by those banks which seethe with pitch-black water and dark whirlpools'; for *torrentis* cf. 10.603.

2 110. **hic primum:** these words are used idiomatically to express the suddenness of a change of situation, cf. 1.450-1 (Aeneas sees the pictures of the Trojan war in Dido's temple) *hoc primum in luco nova res oblata timorem / leniit, hic primum Aeneas sperare salutem / ausus* ... It is possible however that *primum* looks forward to *tum* (line 112).

3 **nova lux oculis offulsit:** 'a strange light shone on their eyes' — contrast line 731 *nova lux oculis effulsit* 'a strange light shone in his eyes'. Here the reference is to the supernatural light accompanying the presence of the goddess; it is rather like the description of Iris (lines 19f.) except that here the imagery is more powerful still.

4 111-12. The cloud and the bands of Cybele's votaries (Corybantes, 3.111) come across the sky from Cybele's home on Mount Ida in the East; compare the heavenly apparitions in 8.524f. In Ovid's version of the story (*Met.* 14.530f.) Cybele rides through the heavens in her chariot drawn by tame lions, accompanied by Eastern music, hail, thunder, and storm winds.

5 113. **agmina complet:** 'dins into the ears of the troops', a very extended use of *complet,* cf. 11.140 and 4.189.

6 114. **ne trepidate ... defendere:** for the infinitive with *trepidare* cf. Hor. *Odes* 2.4.23; the sense is *ne nimia trepidatione festinetis defendere.*

7 115-16. 'Turnus will be permitted to burn up the ocean itself sooner than my ships. Away you go, you are released, away you go, you are goddesses of the ocean; your mother speaks'.

8 119. **rostris:** the normal word for a ship's beak, and also, it appears (Plin. *N.H.* 9.20), for a dolphin's head. Compare the dolphin simile in 5.594f., and the depiction of dolphins on Aeneas' shield, 8.673f.

9 121. This line (= 10.223) is not in the best MSS, and is clearly spurious.

10 122. **reddunt se:** 'return to view' (in a changed form, as sea-nymphs); cf. 5.178.

11 **pontoque feruntur:** 'and move over the ocean'; after the transformation we are invited for a moment to visualise the nymphs at play. Virgil is perhaps thinking of Thetis and her sister Nereids appearing to the Argonauts (Cat. 64.12f.).

123-175. *The Rutulians are shaken by this, but Turnus rallies them with a confident speech, saying that this portent is directed against the Trojans who cannot now escape. They will find the Rutulians more formidable enemies than the Greeks. He urges his men to get ready for battle; they place sentries, and the Trojans for their part prepare defences.*

[1]Obstipuere animis Rutuli, conterritus ipse
turbatis Messapus[2] equis, [3]cunctatur et amnis
rauca sonans revocatque pedem Tiberinus ab alto.   125
At non audaci Turno[4] fiducia cessit;
ultro animos tollit dictis atque increpat ultro:
'Troianos[5] haec monstra petunt, his Iuppiter ipse
auxilium solitum eripuit, non tela neque ignis
exspectans Rutulos. Ergo maria invia Teucris,   130
nec spes ulla fugae: rerum[6] pars altera adempta est,
terra autem in nostris manibus, [7]tot milia gentis
arma ferunt Italae. Nil me fatalia[8] terrent,
si qua Phryges prae se iactant, responsa deorum:
sat fatis Venerique datum, tetigere quod arva[9]   135
fertilis[10] Ausoniae Troes. Sunt et mea contra[11]

---

1 123f. Virgil powerfully illustrates the boastful self-confidence of Turnus, *audaci Turno fiducia,* in a highly rhetorical and forthright speech, delivered in abrupt phrases; the theme is that the Trojans are now destined to pay again for a similar crime to the one which caused the Greeks to attack them, and this time they will find a far stronger enemy. The points which Turnus makes are cumulative: Lavinia is compared with Helen, the Trojan camp with the walls of Troy, the Greek armada and divine armour with his simpler methods, Greek strategy with his direct and open plans, the ten year duration with his confidence in immediate victory. His speech concludes with simple words of dismissal, and the narrative continues with two plain passages describing the preparations on each side.

2 124. **Messapus:** Turnus' second-in-command, cf. 27.

3 124-5. 'the river too checked its flow, roaring turbulently, and the river-god Tiberinus retreated back from the sea'; cf. 8.240 *refluitque exterritus amnis.* For *rauca* (adverbial) cf. 5.866 and line 794.

4 126. The build-up for Turnus' unconcern has been threefold: the Rutulians were amazed, Messapus terrified, even the river god recoils, but not Turnus. Observe how the spondees give emphasis and solidity. The line occurs again at 10.276.

5 128f. 'These portents are aimed at the Trojans; from them Jupiter himself has snatched their usual support, not waiting for Rutulian weapons and fire'. *Auxilium solitum* is a gibe: Turnus suggests that the normal recourse of the Trojans is flight. *Exspectans* is the reading of the first hand of *M*; the other MSS and *M*'s correcting hand have *exspectant,* which most editors adopt. Whether we supply *Troiani* or *naves* as the subject, *exspectant* is very harsh; *exspectans* fits well with *ipse.*

6 131. **rerum pars altera:** 'one element of the world', i.e. the sea.

7 132-3. 'So many thousands of the Italian race are bearing arms': this is preferable to reading *gentes* and taking *tot milia* in apposition to it, cf. 6.757 and *Catal.* 9.51 *periurae milia gentis.* The main MSS are equally divided.

8 133-4. **fatalia ... responsa deorum:** he means the prophecy to Latinus about a foreign son-in-law (7.96f.), but he refers to it contemptuously in a vague plural, with a conditional qualification ('Any oracular prophecies of fate which the Phrygians bandy about frighten me not in the slightest.') But in the end it is the opposition of heaven which he cannot face; he says to Aeneas (12.894f.) *non me tua fervida terrent / dicta, ferox: di me terrent et Iuppiter hostis.*

9 135. Turnus means that the part of the prophecy which said that the Trojans should reach Italy has now been fulfilled, and he will allow no more.

10 136. **fertilis:** a patriotic touch, our bountiful land.

11 136-7. Cf. Venus in 1.239 *fatis contraria fata rependens,* Juno in 7.293f. *fatis contraria nostris / fata Phrygum.*

fata mihi, ferro sceleratam[1] exscindere gentem
coniuge[2] praerepta; nec solos tangit Atridas
iste dolor, solisque licet capere arma Mycenis.
"Sed[3] periisse semel satis est": peccare fuisset   140
ante satis, penitus modo non genus omne perosos
femineum. [4]Quibus haec medii fiducia valli
fossarumque morae, leti discrimina parva,
dant animos; at non viderunt moenia Troiae
Neptuni[5] fabricata manu considere in ignis?   145
Sed vos, o lecti, ferro qui[6] scindere vallum
apparat et mecum invadit trepidantia castra?
Non armis[7] mihi Volcani, non mille carinis
est opus in Teucros. Addant se protinus omnes
Etrusci socios. Tenebras et inertia furta[8]   150
[Palladii caesis summae custodibus arcis]
ne timeant, nec equi caeca condemur in alvo:
luce[9] palam certum est igni circumdare muros.

---

1 137. A sudden burst of anger comes over him, expressed in the harsh words *sceleratam exscindere,* and the abrupt construction of *exscindere* in a kind of apposition with *fata.*

2 138. **coniuge praerepta**: 'now that my bride has been stolen from me.' He regards his loss of Lavinia to a Trojan as similar to the rape of Helen by the Trojan Paris, which caused Greece (Mycenae was its chief city) to sail to Troy in vengeance. The sons of Atreus are Menelaus, Helen's husband, and Agamemnon.

3 140-2. 'But to have been destroyed once is enough. Their previous crime would have been enough if only they didn't deeply despise the whole female sex.' This is an obscure sentence with a doubtful meaning; Turnus imagines someone saying 'But they have paid for their crime against Helen', and he replies, 'Yes, they wouldn't have to pay again if they hadn't shown their contempt for the rights of women by doing the same thing again.' *Genus omne femineum* is a rhetorical exaggeration suggesting that no woman is safe against the caveman methods of the Trojans. Others render 'their previous sin ought to have been enough (*fuisset: debebat esse*) to make them hate (i.e. want nothing to do with) practically (*modo non omne*) the whole female sex'. This seems even more difficult.

4 142-4. The disjointed nature of Turnus' speech reflects his indignation: '(Here we have) people to whom courage is given by their trust in this mound of earth between us, the barriers of these ditches — what a tiny gap from death!' There is something to be said for the reading of Servius and the old editors which begins the next sentence with *an non,* so that we could remove the punctuation after *animos,* and get the construction *ei quibus . . . an non viderunt?* For the phrase *leti discrimina parva* cf. 3.685 *leti discrimine parvo;* some MSS have the ablative here. For the sense cf. Juv. 12.58-9 *digitis a morte remotus / quattuor:* 'four fingers from death'.

5 145. Neptune and Apollo built Troy, cf. 2.625.

6 146. **qui**: interrogative, used instead of *quis* for reasons of euphony (before the *s* of *scindere*); see my note on 3.608, OUP Ed. Many editors alter to *quis,* against the consensus of the MSS.

7 148. For the arms of Achilles made by Hephaestus (Vulcan) see Hom. *Il.* 18.478f.; for the 'thousand ships' which the Greeks sent against Troy cf. *Aen.* 2.198.

8 150-1. Line 151, which is almost the same as *Aen.* 2.166, should be regarded as an interpolation not only because of the un-contracted genitive *Palladii* but because it is quite unsuitable in the context here; there is no reason at all for Turnus to speak of the theft of the statue of Pallas by Diomedes and Ulysses (see note on 2.166), or to add that the guardians of the citadel were slain on that occasion. It probably arises from a gloss on *furta:* but the meaning of *inertia furta* is very general ('unwarlike trickery'), and a specific example (the wooden horse) is given in the next line.

9 153. **luce palam**: in antithesis to *tenebras, caeca.* This is a fine forceful line.

Haud[1] sibi cum Danais rem faxo et pube Pelasga
esse ferant, decimum quos distulit Hector in annum.   155
Nunc adeo,[2] melior quoniam pars acta diei,
quod superest, laeti[3] bene gestis corpora[4] rebus
procurate, viri, et pugnam sperate parari.'
Interea vigilum[5] excubiis obsidere portas
cura datur Messapo et moenia cingere flammis.   160
Bis septem Rutuli muros qui milite servent[6]
deiecti, ast illos centeni quemque sequuntur
purpurei[7] cristis iuvenes auroque corusci.
Discurrunt variantque[8] vices, fusique per herbam
indulgent vino et vertunt[9] crateras aenos.   165
Conlucent[10] ignes, noctem custodia ducit
insomnem ludo.[11]

    Haec[12] super e vallo prospectant Troes et armis
alta tenent, nec non trepidi formidine portas
explorant[13] pontisque et propugnacula iungunt,   170
tela gerunt. Instat Mnestheus acerque Serestus,
quos pater Aeneas, si[14] quando adversa vocarent,
rectores iuvenum et rerum dedit[15] esse magistros.

---

1 154-5. 'I'll see to it that they don't reckon they have to deal with Danaans and Pelasgian warriors, whom Hector held off till the tenth year': Turnus promises that the Rutulians will deal with the Trojans much more quickly than the Greeks did. The Greeks are often called Danai (from Danaus, founder of Argos); for the term Pelasgi applied to them cf. 8.600. *Faxo* is an archaic future of *facere;* cf. 12.316, and 11.467 (*iusso*). *Ferant* is jussive subjunctive in parataxis; the verb is rather strangely used (an extension of the sense of *ferunt, 'they* say'), and some MSS have *putent,* which is plainly a gloss or a simplification.

2 156. **adeo:** a favourite emphasising word with Virgil, cf. 8.585, 11.314.

3 157. **laeti bene gestis . . . rebus:** 'contented because things have gone well', he presumably refers to the loss of the Trojan fleet, and the fact that the Trojans have retreated into their camp.

4 157-8. **corpora . . . procurate:** 'look after your physical welfare', i.e. rest and eat (cf. *Geo.* 4.187).

5 159. **vigilum excubiis:** 'with pickets of sentries', to prevent a breakout; they light watchfires round the walls, a different operation from the threat of setting fire to the walls which Turnus made in 153.

6 161. Virgil is recalling Hom. *Il.* 9.85 where seven Greek chieftains, each with 100 men, guard the camp.

7 163. 'young men with purple plumes, resplendent with gold', i.e. with golden decoration on their helmets and armour. The use of the ablative is typical of Virgilian style; see note on 2.51.

8 164. **variantque** vices: 'take up their various duties', while those not yet on duty relax with wine and gambling.

9 165. **vertunt crateras aenos:** 'uptilt the bronze bowls', a phrase from Ennius (according to Servius). Notice the Greek accusative plural with short *-as;* cf. 358.

10 166-7. 'the watch (i.e. the men on guard) prolongs the sleepless night with gambling', an elaboration of *Geo.* 3.379 *hic noctem ludo ducunt.* For the abstract *custodia* cf. 6.574.

11 167. For the half-line see notes on 1.534, 7.129; others in this book are 295, 467, 520, 721, 761.

12 168. **haec super e vallo prospectant:** 'look out at all this from the rampart above'.

13 170. 'build joining gangways and bastions', i.e. add further strongpoints and improve access.

14 172. **si quando adversa vocarent:** cf. line 41. This is a reported future condition: Aeneas said 'My instructions are that if at any time a crisis shall require it, Mnestheus and Serestus shall take command.'

15 173. **dedit esse:** for the infinitive with *dare* cf. 362, and see note on 1.66.

Omnis per muros legio sortita periclum

excubat[1] exercetque vices, quod cuique tuendum est. 175

> 176-313. *Nisus and Euryalus plan to break out through the enemy lines in order to reach Aeneas. They seek an audience with the Trojan leaders, and present their plan. Aletes and Ascanius accept it with great gratitude and admiration, offering lavish rewards. Euryalus asks that in the event of his death his aged mother should be cared for ; Ascanius promises that this shall be so. The two warriors arm for their exploit.*

[2]Nisus erat portae custos, acerrimus armis,

Hyrtacides,[3] comitem Aeneae quem miserat Ida[4]

venatrix iaculo celerem levibusque sagittis;

et iuxta comes Euryalus, quo pulchrior alter

non fuit Aeneadum[5] Troiana[6] neque induit arma, 180

ora [7]puer prima signans intonsa iuventa.

His amor unus erat pariterque in bella ruebant;

tum quoque communi portam statione tenebant.

Nisus ait: [8]'dine hunc ardorem mentibus addunt,

Euryale, an sua cuique deus fit dira cupido? 185

---

1 175. 'is on guard, taking turns of duty, each defending what he is required to defend': the last phrase is very loosely attached to the sentence, in apposition to *vices*.

2 176f. The story of Nisus and Euryalus is based on the exploits of Odysseus and Diomedes in Homer, *Iliad* 10, often with quite close verbal similarities. Virgil had added another aspect to it, that of the older warrior and his younger friend; we think of Achilles and Patroclus, Hopleus and Dymas (in Statius), Roland and Oliver.
The friendship of Nisus and Euryalus has already been set before us in Book 5, where in the lighthearted atmosphere of the games Nisus shows his devotion to Euryalus by tripping up the man who would have beaten him in the footrace. There are many similarities of phraseology with *Aeneid* 5 in this episode, suggesting that Virgil had the previous appearance of Nisus and Euryalus very much in mind as he wrote the last chapter to their story.
The episode is constructed in two parts of almost equal length: the long-drawn-out preparation and speeches (176-313) and the fast moving narrative (314-449). The first half is remarkably direct and straightforward in diction, quite without the usual density of Virgilian imagery and overtone; the speeches are simple in phraseology, on occasion naive. Ascanius and Euryalus speak their thoughts ingenuously; the Homeric atmosphere of chivalry and bravery and princely behaviour is not modified or adorned in Virgil's usual manner, but directly transplanted. The episode is made to depend on its immediacy and its content; it is less sophisticated than any other part of the poem. It does not really fit the style and method of the *Aeneid*; consequently critics have singled it out, either for praise or (much more rarely) for blame. Heyne shall speak for all: 'Pervenimus nunc ad episodium Aeneidis omnium facile nobilissimum . . . suavitas summa . . . quem vero ne huius quidem loci dulcedine tactum <magistri> videant iuvenem, eum omni liberali disciplina indignum iudicent'.

3 177. **Hyrtacides:** Nisus (like Hippocoon, 5.492) was a son of Hyrtacus (406).

4 177-8. **Ida venatrix:** Ida is an eponymous nymph of the Trojan Mt. Ida on which Nisus used to hunt, or perhaps the mountain itself (cf. 7.744, *Geo.* 3.44).

5 180. **Aeneadum:** archaic form of the genitive, see note on 8.127.

6 **Troiana neque induit arraa**: a condensed construction meaning 'nor did any more handsome warrior don Trojan armour'.

7 181. 'a boy whose unshaven cheeks were showing the first signs of maturity', i.e. the first down of the young man; cf. Hom. *Od.* 10.278-9.

8 184-5. 'It is the gods who put this passion in men's minds, Euryalus, or does each person's fierce desire become his god?' A good deal of the divine symbolism in the *Aeneid* revolves around this question, e.g., did Allecto drive Turnus to frenzy, or is his frenzy symbolised in Allecto?

Aut pugnam aut aliquid iamdudum invadere magnum
mens[1] agitat mihi, nec[2] placida contenta quiete est.
Cernis quae Rutulos habeat fiducia rerum:
lumina rara micant, somno vinoque soluti[3]
procubuere, silent late loca. Percipe porro   190
quid[4] dubitem et quae nunc animo sententia surgat.
Aenean[5] acciri omnes, populusque patresque,
exposcunt, mittique viros qui certa reportent.[6]
Si tibi quae posco promittunt (nam mihi facti[7]
fama sat est), tumulo videor[8] reperire sub illo   195
posse viam ad muros et moenia Pallantea.'[9]
Obstipuit magno laudum percussus amore
Euryalus, simul his ardentem adfatur amicum:
'mene igitur socium summis adiungere rebus,
Nise, fugis?[10] Solum te in tanta pericula mittam?   200
Non ita me genitor, bellis adsuetus Opheltes,
Argolicum[11] terrorem inter Troiaeque labores
sublatum erudiit, nec[12] tecum talia gessi
magnanimum Aenean et fata extrema secutus:
est[13] hic, est animus lucis contemptor et istum   205
qui vita bene credat emi, quo tendis, honorem.'
Nisus ad haec: 'equidem de te nil tale verebar,

---

1 187. **mens agitat mihi**: 'my mind is planning'; the infinitive with *agitat* (Nep. *Ham.* 1.4) is on the analogy of *cupere*.

2 **nec placida contenta quiete est**: a phrase reminiscent of the Epicurean philosophy: Nisus is the man of action, not the contemplative type. The style of his speech is extremely direct; notice in the following lines the brevity of the sentences, packed with main verbs.

3 189. **soluti**:'relaxed', cf. 4.530.

4 191, **quid dubitem**: 'what I am wondering about'; Servius says *cogitem;* cf. Juv. 13.200.

5 192-3 **Aenean acciri . . . exposcunt:** for the poetic construction cf. 4.78-9.

6 193. **reportent:** 'report' (cf. 7.167), i.e. report the present situation to Aeneas.

7 194. Gifts and glory are the expected reward of the heroic age (*Il.* 10.204f., 303f.): Nisus will be content with the glory and will give Euryalus the gifts.

8 195-6. **videor . . . posse:** 'I think I can'.

9 196. **Pallantea:** cf. line 9 and 8.54 for the spondaic fifth foot. *Pallenteum* is the name of Evander's city; *Pallenteus* its adjective (cf. 241).

10 200. **fugis:** with the infinitive = 'refuse', cf. Lucr. 1.1052.

11 202-3. 'brought up as I was during the Greek terror and the suffering of Troy'; for *sublatum* cf. 547.

12 203. **nec tecum talia gessi:** 'I have not behaved like this (i.e. staying out of danger) while I've been with you.'

13 205-6. 'There is here — I tell you there is — a heart ready to sacrifice the light of day, which reckons the glory to which you are going well bought at the price of life itself; cf. 5.230 *vitamque volunt pro laude pacisci*, 12.49, Hor. *Odes* 1.12.37f. *animaeque magnae / prodigum.* These lines splendidly express the attitude of the heroic warrior.

nec[1] fas; non ita me referat tibi magnus ovantem
Iuppiter aut quicumque oculis haec aspicit aequis.
Sed si quis (quae[2] multa vides discrimine tali)   210
si quis in adversum rapiat casusve deusve,
te superesse velim, tua vita dignior aetas.
Sit qui me raptum[3] pugna pretiove redemptum
mandet humo, solita[4] aut si qua Fortuna vetabit,
absenti ferat inferias decoretque sepulcro.[5]   215
Neu matri miserae tanti sim causa doloris,
quae te sola, puer, multis e matribus ausa
persequitur, magni nec moenia curat Acestae.'[6]
Ille autem: 'causas nequiquam nectis inanis
nec mea iam mutata loco sententia cedit.   220
Acceleremus' ait, vigiles simul excitat. Illi
succedunt[7] servantque vices; statione relicta
ipse comes Niso graditur regemque[8] requirunt.

   Cetera per terras omnis animalia somno[9]
laxabant curas et corda oblita laborum: 225
ductores Teucrum primi, delecta iuventus,
consilium summis regni de rebus habebant,
quid facerent quisve Aeneae iam nuntius esset.
Stant longis adnixi hastis et scuta tenentes
castrorum[10] et campi medio. Tum Nisus et una   230
Euryalus confestim alacres admittier[11] orant;

---

1 208. **nec fas; non ita me referat:** Nisus swears by his hope of safe return that he had not entertained such a thought. This is a difficult use of *non ita*. Servius proposed to punctuate after *non,* and many have followed him ('it wouldn't be right, no: so may ...'), but such a usage would be highly colloquial, and unepic.

2 210. **quae multa:** 'as you often see', loosely in apposition to the whole sentence.

3 213. **raptum pugna:** 'snatched from the battle', i.e. if his corpse can be rescued during the fighting (or, if not, ransomed).

4 214. **solita . . . vetabit:** 'or if Fortune perchance makes impossible the normal rites'. I have followed Mackay (*C.J.* 1938, p.171) in deleting *id,* which causes an awkward rhythm, and might well have been a gloss arising from a misunderstanding of the text. The alternatives seem unacceptable: to take *solita* with *humo* gives an impossible ablative after *mandet;* to take it with *Fortuna* seems senseless, and contradicts *qua.* Possible emendations include Powell's *aut solitas* (*Phil.,* 1934, p.386), or Henry's *saltem.*

5 215. Compare the cenotaph for Deiphobus (6.505) and Hector (3.304).

6 218. The other mothers were left behind in Acesta (5.767f.).

7 222. **succedunt servantque vices:** 'take over and maintain the watch'.

8 223. **regem:** the prince Ascanius.

9 224f. For description of the sleeping world cf. *Aen.* 4.522f., 8.26f.

10 230. **castrorum et campi medio:** 'in the middle of the camp and its open space', i.e. a space in the middle of the camp corresponding to the Roman praetorium (so Servius).

11 231. **admittier orant:** for the archaic form of the passive infinitive see note on 7.70; for *orare* with the infinitive cf. 6.313.

rem[1] magnam pretiumque morae fore. Primus Iulus
accepit trepidos[2] ac Nisum dicere iussit.
Tum sic Hyrtacides: 'audite o mentibus aequis,
Aeneadae, [3]neve haec nostris spectentur ab annis   235
quae ferimus. Rutuli somno vinoque soluti
conticuere; locum insidiis conspeximus ipsi,
qui patet in[4] bivio portae quae proxima ponto.
Interrupti ignes aterque ad sidera fumus[5]
erigitur; si fortuna permittitis[6] uti   240
quaesitum[7] Aenean et moenia Pallantea,
mox hic cum spoliis ingenti caede peracta
adfore[8] cernetis. Nec nos via fallet[9] euntis:
vidimus obscuris primam sub vallibus urbem[10]
venatu adsiduo et totum cognovimus amnem.'   245
Hic annis gravis atque animi maturus Aletes:[11]
'di patrii, quorum semper sub numine Troia est,
non tamen[12] omnino Teucros delere paratis,
cum[13] talis animos iuvenum[14] et tam certa tulistis
pectora.' Sic memorans umeros dextrasque tenebat   250
amborum et vultum lacrimis atque ora rigabat.
'Quae vobis, quae digna, viri, pro laudibus[15] istis

---

1 232. 'they said it was a matter of importance, and would be worth their while': Servius reports a curious view that *pretium morae* means that they would have to pay dear for delay.

2 233. **trepidos**:'excited'.

3 235-6. 'do not judge our proposals from our youth'; presumably Nisus was younger than the Trojan leaders; certainly Euryalus was.

4 238. **in bivio portae:** 'in the forked road leading to the gate'. Nisus refers to the gate at which he had been on watch with Euryalus.

5 239. i.e. there is a gap in the watchfires, and in addition the smoke from the others makes it darker still.

6 240. **permittitis uti:** for the construction with the infinitive (mainly poetic) cf. *Ecl.* 1.10.

7 241. **quaesitum:** the supine depends on an ellipsis, 'if you let us use this piece of good fortune to go to find . . .'. For the line ending cf. 196.

8 243. **adfore cernetis:** the subject of *adfore* (*nos*) is omitted; the future infinitive is very vivid, the construction being really a mixture of *nos adesse mox cernetis* and *nos mox adfore exspectate*.

9 **fallet:** so *M*; most editors prefer *fallit* of *P* and *R*, but this seems harsh with *euntis*.

10 244-5. During their frequent hunting expeditions in the few days since they arrived they have explored the Tiber far enough to have seen glimpses of the outskirts of the city of Pallanteum, looking up at it from hidden valleys.

11 246. Aletes was mentioned during the storm in *Aen.* 1.121 *grandaevus Aletes.* For *animi* ('in mind', genitive of respect or sphere in which, not locative) cf. 685, 10.686, 11.417, 12.19 and see note on 2.61; compare also 255.

12 248. **tamen:** in spite of our present plight.

13 249. **cum . . . tulistis:** 'when you have given'; *cum* in this virtually causal sense with the indicative has an archaic flavour, cf. Ter. *Andr.* 488, Lucr. 1.566. For *tulistis* cf. 1.605.

14 **iuvenum:** we should say 'in our young men'.

15 252. **laudibus:** 'deeds of glory', cf. 10.825.

praemia posse rear solvi? Pulcherrima[1] primum
di moresque dabunt vestri: tum cetera reddet
actutum pius Aeneas atque integer[2] aevi   255
Ascanius meriti tanti non immemor umquam.'
'Immo ego vos, cui sola salus genitore reducto,'
excipit Ascanius 'per magnos, Nise, penatis
Assaracique [3]larem et canae penetralia Vestae
obtestor, [4]quaecumque mihi fortuna fidesque est,   260
in vestris pono gremiis; revocate parentem,
reddite conspectum: nihil illo triste recepto.
Bina dabo argento perfecta atque aspera signis[5]
pocula, devicta[6] genitor quae cepit Arisba,
et tripodas geminos, auri duo magna[7] talenta,   265
cratera antiquum quem dat[8] Sidonia Dido.
Si vero capere Italiam sceptrisque potiri
contigerit victori et praedae dicere[9] sortem,
vidisti, quo Turnus equo, quibus ibat in armis[10]
aureus; ipsum[11] illum, clipeum cristasque rubentis   270
excipiam[12] sorti, iam nunc tua praemia, Nise.[13]
praeterea bis sex genitor lectissima matrum
corpora captivosque dabit suaque omnibus arma,

---

1 253. **pulcherrima**: i.e. the fairest reward will be your own knowledge that you have done well in the sight of the gods; cf. Cic. *Phil.* 2.114.

2 255. **integer aevi**: for the phrase cf. 2.638, and for the genitive of respect cf. 5.73 *aevi maturus,* and lines 26, 246. The point of mentioning Ascanius' youth is that the memory of their exploit will be long-lived with their rulers.

3 259. 'the household god of Assaracus and the innermost shrines of hoary Vesta', cf. 5.744. Assaracus was a Trojan ancestor.

4 260-1. 'all my fortune and hope I commit to your care'.

5 263-4. For embossed silver cups cf. 5.267.

6 264. **devicta . . . Arisba:** nothing is known of this exploit of Aeneas (Arisbe, a town in the Troad, is mentioned in Hom. *Il.* 2.836.)

7 265. **magna talenta:** cf. 5.248; the phrase means the normal Attic talent.

8 266. **dat:** this is an idiomatic use of the present tense, meaning that the gift which Dido gave 'comes' from Dido; Virgil has it several times, 8.141, 10.518, 11.172 and line 361. On a later occasion (11.74, at the funeral of Pallas) we hear of a gift from Dido, then too linking Dido's tragedy with the death of a young warrior.

9 268. **dicere sortem:** 'apportion', 'proclaim the distribution', cf. 11.353. Some MSS have *ducere,* which gives an inappropriate meaning (suggesting chance distribution): the same is true of the reading *deicere,* reported by Servius.

10 269f. In *Il.* 10.322 Dolon asks to be given the horses of Achilles.

11 270. **ipsum ilium:** i.e. Turnus' horse; his horse and his red-plumed helmet were described in 49-50.

12 271. **excipiam sorti:** cf. 5.534; these items would then be *exsortes,* specially set aside. *Sorti* is probably ablative, cf. *Geo.* 4.165 and *capiti* (7.668).

13 272f. The offer of captured women and men and armour, and Latinus' personal estate, continues the mood of Homeric gift giving.

insuper his campi[1] quod rex habet ipse Latinus.
Te vero, mea quem spatiis propioribus aetas   275
insequitur, venerande[2] puer, iam pectore toto
accipio et comitem casus complector in omnis.
Nulla meis sine te quaeretur gloria rebus:
seu pacem seu bella geram, tibi maxima rerum
verborumque fides.' Contra quem talia fatur   280
Euryalus: [3]'me nulla dies tam fortibus ausis
dissimilem[4] arguerit; tantum fortuna secunda
haud adversa cadat. Sed te super omnia dona
unum oro: genetrix Priami de gente vetusta
est mihi, quam miseram tenuit non Ilia tellus   285
mecum excedentem, non moenia regis Acestae.[5]
Hanc ego nunc ignaram huius[6] quodcumque pericli
inque[7] salutatam linquo (nox et tua testis
dextera) quod nequeam[8] lacrimas perferre parentis.
At tu, oro, solare inopem et succurre relictae.   290
Hanc sine me spem[9] ferre tui, audentior ibo
in casus omnis.' Percussa mente dedere
Dardanidae lacrimas, ante omnis pulcher Iulus,
atque animum patriae[10] strinxit pietatis imago.
tum sic effatur: 295
'sponde[11] digna tuis ingentibus omnia coeptis.

---

1 274. **campi quod . . . habet:** literally 'what Latinus has of land', his private estate; for the neuter followed by a partitive genitive cf. 1.78 *quodcumque hoc regni,* 12.678 *quidquid acerbi est.*

2 276. **venerande puer:** Euryalus is said to have achieved already by his bravery that quality of distinction which would normally be applied to older men. Throughout this speech of Ascanius Virgil aims to convey an impression of youthful sentiment and ingenuousness.

3 282-3. 'only let good fortune not turn hostile', a flat statement which is not improved by punctuating after *tantum* ('that's all') and reading *aut* for *haud.* The best suggestion is Madvig's *aut . . . cadet,* so that the meaning would be: 'only fortune will turn out good or bad', i.e. I shall be constant. But this is ingenious rather than convincing.

4 282. **dissimilem:** 'unequal', an unexpected word equivalent to *imparem.*

5 286. See note on 218.

6 287. **huius quodcumque pericli:** 'of this peril, whatever its nature'.

7 288. **inque salutatam:** 'and ungreeted', a remarkable instance of the tmesis of *insalutatam,* paralleled only in Virgil by 10.794 *inque ligatus;* it is not uncommon in Lucretius (e.g. 1.452).

8 289. **nequeam:** potential, 'I could not'.

9 291. **spem . . . tui:** *tui* is objective genitive ('this expectation of you'), cf. 12.29 *amore tui.*
For the hiatus between *tui* and *audentior* cf. 7.178, 226.

10 294. **patriae . . . pietatis imago:** 'the thought of his love for his father'; cf. 10.824 (Aeneas' pity for Lausus for this reason).

11 296. **sponde:** 'promise yourself', 'be assured of', an unusual meaning of the word, but cf. Livy 28.38.9 *spondebantque animis* ('they promised themselves in their hearts'). Some inferior MSS have *spondeo;* this makes clearer sense, and many editors before Ribbeck read it, but Virgil does not shorten the final *-o* of verbs (other than *scio, nescio*), and the synizesis (see note on 7.33) of such a verbal form would be contrary to his practice.

Namque erit ista mihi genetrix nomenque Creusae[1]
solum defuerit, nec partum[2] gratia talem
parva manet. Casus factum quicumque sequentur,
per caput hoc iuro, per quod pater ante solebat[3]:　　　　　　300
quae tibi polliceor reduci rebusque secundis,
haec eadem matrique tuae generique manebunt.'
Sic ait inlacrimans; umero[4] simul exuit ensem[5]
auratum, mira quem fecerat arte Lycaon
Cnosius[6] atque habilem[7] vagina aptarat eburna.　　　　　　305
Dat Niso Mnestheus [8]pellem horrentisque leonis
exuvias, galeam fidus permutat[9] Aletes.
Protinus armati incedunt; quos omnis euntis
primorum manus ad portas, iuvenumque senumque,
prosequitur votis. Nec non et pulcher Iulus,　　　　　　310
ante[10] annos animumque gerens curamque virilem,
multa patri mandata dabat portanda; sed aurae[11]
omnia discerpunt et nubibus inrita donant.

---

1 297. Creusa, Ascanius' mother, was lost during the sack of Troy(2.738f.).

2 298. **partum . . . talem**: 'such motherhood', i.e. (apparently) her having produced such a son.

3 300. He seems to mean that the oath will be as binding as if Aeneas himself had sworn it; there is an element of pathos in *ante*.

4 303. **umero:** cf. 8.459; the sword belt passes over the shoulder.

5 303f. The presentation of armour before the exploit is modelled on Hom. *Il.* 10.255f.

6 305. Cnosius: the Cretans (Cnossos was their main town) were famous for craftsmanship; cf. 5.306. Daedalus the master craftsman came from Crete.

7 **habilem:** cf. 1.318 *habilem suspenderat arcum;* the meaning is 'so that it could be readily used'; here translate 'to hold it'.

8 306-7. 'a skin, the shaggy spoils taken from a lion'; hendiadys.

9 307. **permutat:** 'exchanges' his helmet for that of Nisus.

10 311. 'taking thought and showing responsibility beyond his years, like a grown man'.

11 312-13 This prolepsis of the narrative (cf. 10.438, 503) recalls the pathos of Cat. 64.142 (Ariadne's prayers) *quae cuncta aerii discerpunt inrita venti.*

314-449. *Nisus and Euryalus fall upon the sleeping Rutulians, and kill many of them. As they start off on their journey to Aeneas, the light flashing on the helmet which Euryalus has taken as part of the spoils reveals their presence to a band of Latin cavalry. Nisus gets away, but Euryalus is caught; Nisus returns but cannot save his friend; when Euryalus is killed by Volcens Nisus rushes in to exact vengeance, kills Volcens and himself meets his death.*

[1]Egressi superant fossas noctisque per umbram
castra inimica petunt, multis tamen[2] ante futuri   315
exitio. Passim somno vinoque per herbam
corpora fusa vident, arrectos[3] litore currus,
inter lora rotasque viros, [4]simul arma iacere,
vina simul. Prior Hyrtacides sic ore locutus:
'Euryale, audendum dextra: nunc ipsa vocat res.[5]   320
Hac iter est, tu, ne qua manus se attoilere nobis
a tergo possit, custodi et consule[6] longe;
haec ego vasta[7] dabo et lato[8] te limite ducam.'
Sic memorat vocemque premit, simul ense superbum
Rhamnetem[9] adgreditur, qui forte tapetibus[10] altis   325
exstructus toto[11] proflabat pectore somnum,
rex idem et regi Turno gratissimus augur,[12]

---

1 314f. The concluding episode of the night sally is modelled, like the earlier part, on *Iliad* 10, the account of the night raid of Odysseus and Diomedes upon Rhesus and the Thracian allies of Troy. Virgil's treatment is different from Homer's; the scenes of violence are more horrible, and the episode ends tragically, affording one of the outstanding examples of Virgilian pathos in the whole poem. Although our sympathy has been alienated from the two Trojans by the exultation they show in butchering the sleeping Rutulians, it is evoked again when they are overwhelmed by numbers, and particularly so in the scene where Nisus desperately dies to revenge his friend.

Virgil's presentation of the action is as rapid and vivid as his introduction to the action was slow and formalised. Sentences are brief, the narrative is elliptical and selective, the events proceed in a series of flashes. There is all the speed of Ovid's narrative power, but the movement is more vigorous, more compelling.

2 315. **tamen ante**: this is very elliptical indeed (= although they were fated to die, yet destined first . . .), and Sabbadini suspected a lacuna. But line 313 has prepared us for the idea that all will not be well; cf. 4.329, 10.509.

3 317. **arrectos**: 'up-tilted', 'parked'.

4 318-19. 'and by them their armour lying around, and jars of wine as well'.

5 320. The abrupt monosyllable expresses immediacy, action: cf. 5.638, 7.592 and line 723.

6 322. **consule longe**: 'lookout all round'.

7 323. **vasta dabo**:'will devastate', cf. 12.437.

8 **lato . . . limite**: i.e. he will cut a broad path through the enemy ranks, cf. *Aen.* 10.514.

9 325. **Rhamnetem**: a name connected with the ancient Roman tribes.

10 325-6. **tapetibus . . . exstructus**: 'raised high (propped up) on pillows'; both *tapetibus* (third, cf. 358) and *tapetis* (second declension, cf. 7.277) occur.

11 326. **toto . . . somnum**: Servius remarks that this periphrasis is to avoid the vulgar word 'snoring'.

12 327. Rhamnes was probably a *rex sacrificiorum*; the reflexion in the next line is of a kind fairly frequent in the *Aeneid* (cf. 2.429), based in this case on Hom. *Il.* 2.859. It is typical of Virgil to begin the scene of bloody slaughter with irony and pathos of this kind.

sed non augurio potuit depellere pestem.
Tris iuxta famulos temere inter tela iacentis
armigerumque Remi[1] premit aurigamque sub ipsis   330
nactus [2]equis ferroque secat pendentia colla;
tum caput ipsi aufert domino truncumque relinquit
sanguine singultantem; atro tepefacta cruore[3]
terra torique madent. Nec non Lamyrumque Lamumque
et iuvenem Serranum, illa qui plurima nocle   335
luserat, insignis facie, multoque iacebat
membra[4] deo[5] victus; [6]felix, si protinus illum
aequasset nocti ludum in lucemque tulisset:
impastus[7] ceu plena leo per ovilia turbans[8]
(suadet enim vesana fames) manditque trahitque[9]   340
molle pecus mutumque metu, fremit ore cruento.
Nec minor Euryali caedes; incensus et ipse
perfurit ac multam in medio sine nomine plebem,
Fadumque Herbesumque subit Rhoetumque Abarimque
ignaros;[10] Rhoetum vigilantem et cuncta videntem,   345
sed magnum metuens se post cratera[11] tegebat.
Pectore in adverso totum cui comminus ensem
condidit adsurgenti et multa[12] morte recepit.
Purpuream vomit ille animam et cum sanguine mixta

---

1 330. **Remi:** the development of the narrative is that Nisus kills (*premit* for *opprimit*, cf. Tac. *Hist.* 4.2) first the three attendants of Remus, then his armour-bearer and charioteer, then Remus himself (*dominus*).

2 331. 'severing with the sword their drooping heads': as Servius says, the word *pendentia* draws attention to the disorderly scene of drunken sleep.

3 333. This gruesome line is accentuated by the unusual elision, and the alliteration of *s* and *t*, carrying on into the next line.

4 337. **membra:** retained accusative, cf. 478, 543-4, 582 and see note on 7.503.

5 **deo:** = 'wine', the god Bacchus (rather than Somnus); cf. Stat. *Silv.* 3.1.41 (of Hercules) *multo fratre* (= *Baccho*) *madentem.*

6 337-8. 'Happy would he have been if he had made his game go on as long as the night, and continued it till dawn'. For *protinus* cf. 7.601; *tulisset* is in the sense of *pertulisset*, cf. Hor. *Odes* 3.8.14f. *vigiles lucernas perfer in lucem.*

7 339f. The simile is based, like much else in this passage, on the slaughter of Rhesus and the Thracians in *Il.* 10; cf. *Il.* 10.485f.

8 339. **turbans:** 'raging', intransitive as in 6.800; Servius suggests that Virgil has used tmesis for *perturbans ovilia,* but this seems less likely.

9 340. The two verbs with doubled *-que* ('both . . . and') give energy to the description of the lion, contrasting with the mournful alliteration of *m* in the picture of the sheep which follows.

10 345. **ignaros; Rhoetum vigilantem:** if *Rhoetum* is the right reading, Virgil corrects himself strangely after saying that Rhoetus was among those asleep. It seems possible that we should read some different name in one place or the other.

11 346. **cratera:** Greek accusative, cf. 535.

12 348. **multa morte recepit:** 'withdrew it dripping with death', a very strange and powerful phrase. Some read *purpureum* in the next line to agree with *ensem* and give the ablative phrase *multa morte* a better construction: this reading was known to Servius. The MSS however are against it, and *purpurea anima* may have been influenced by Homer's πορφύρεος θάνατος (*Il.* 5.83).

vina refert moriens, hic furto[1] fervidus instat.   350
Iamque ad Messapi socios tendebat; [2]ibi ignem
deficere extremum et religatos rite videbat
carpere gramen equos, breviter cum talia Nisus
(sensit enim nimia caede atque cupidine ferri[3])
'absistamus' ait, 'nam lux inimica propinquat.   355
Poenarum[4] exhaustum satis est, via facta per hostis.'
Multa[5] virum solido argento perfecta relinquunt
armaque craterasque simul pulchrosque tapetas.
Euryalus phaleras[6] Rhamnetis et aurea bullis
cingula, [7]Tiburti Remulo ditissimus olim   360
quae mittit dona, hospitio cum iungeret absens,
Caedicus; ille suo moriens dat habere nepoti;
post mortem bello Rutuli pugnaque potiti;
haec rapit atque umeris nequiquam fortibus aptat.
Tum[8] galeam Messapi habilem cristisque decoram   365
induit. Excedunt castris et tuta capessunt.

    [9]Interea praemissi equites ex urbe Latina,
cetera dum legio campis instructa moratur,
ibant et Turno[10] regi responsa ferebant,
ter centum, scutati omnes, Volcente magistro.   370
Iamque propinquabant castris murosque subibant

---

1 350. **furto fervidus instat**: 'eagerly continues the massacre'; *furto* refers to the attack on those off their guard; it is dative with *instat* rather than ablative with *fervidus*.

2 351-3. 'that was where he could see the outer campfires burning dim and the horses securely tethered grazing on the grass', i.e. he knew it was Messapus, leader of the cavalry. This part of the story reminds us again of *Iliad* 10, where Odysseus and Diomedes steal the Thracian horses of Rhesus.

3 354. **ferri**: 'that he (Euryalus) was being carried away by . . .'. This use of *ferri* is Ciceronian.

4 356. 'enough vengeance has been inflicted', cf. *Geo.* 2.398.

5 357-8. The construction is loose, 'they leave behind much enemy (*virum*) booty wrought of solid silver, armour and mixing-bowls too — as well as gorgeous coverlets'. *Crateras* and *tapetas* are Greek accusatives of the third declension; cf. 165.

6 359-60. **phaleras . . . cingula**: the accusatives are summarised in *haec* (364) as object to *rapit*. *Phalerae* are ornamental metal discs (cf. Juv. 16.60); the next phrase means 'his belt with golden studs'.

7 360f. 'which the rich Gaedicus once sent to Remulus of Tibur as gifts when he wanted to join with him in friendship although they had not met; Remulus when dying gave them to his grandson to have; after his death the Rutulians got them in war and battle'. The account of the provenance of these spoils is complicated, and Servius regarded 363 as one of the twelve 'insoluble' passages in Virgil. But though complicated the account is quite comprehensible as it stands, Rhamnes the Rutulian got them as spoils in a war in which Remulus' grandson was killed. For *mittit* and *dat* (present tense) see note on 266; for *habere* (epexegetic) see note on 173; *iungeret* is intransitive with a reflexive sense.

8 365. 'the well-fitting helmet of Messapus, distinguished by its plumes' he presumably picks this up from near the sleeping Messapus just as they leave. For *habilem* cf. 305.

9 367f. We have not previously been told of a message sent by Turnus to Latinus, to which the three hundred cavalry now bring a reply, while the rest of the Latin forces (*cetera legio*) wait at a distance.

10 369. **Turno regi**: so the MSS; the scholiasts report a reading *regis* which some modern editors adopt, but King Latinus had withdrawn from all active participation in the war.

cum procul hos laevo flectentis[1] limite cernunt,
et galea[2] Euryalum sublustri noctis in umbra
prodidit immemorem radiisque adversa refulsit.
Haud[3] temere est visum. Conclamat ab agmine Volcens: 375
'state, viri. Quae causa viae? Quive estis in armis?
Quove tenetis iter?' Nihil[4] illi tendere contra,
sed celerare fugam in silvas et fidere nocti.
Obiciunt equites sese ad divortia[5] nota
hinc atque hinc, omnemque abitum custode coronant.[6] 380
Silva fuit late dumis atque ilice nigra
horrida, quam densi complerant undique sentes;
rara[7] per occultos lucebat semita callis.
Euryalum tenebrae ramorum onerosaque praeda
impediunt, [8]fallitque timor regione viarum. 385
Nisus abit; [9]iamque imprudens evaserat hostis
atque locos qui post Albae de nomine dicti
Albani (tum rex stabula alta Latinus habebat),
ut stetit et frustra absentem respexit amicum:
'Euryale infelix, qua te regione reliqui? 390
Quave sequar?' Rursus perplexum iter omne revolvens
fallacis silvae simul et vestigia retro[10]
observata legit dumisque silentibus errat.
Audit equos, audit strepitus et signa sequentum.
Nec longum in medio tempus, cum clamor ad auris 395
pervenit ac videt Euryalum, [11]quem iam manus omnis

---

1 372. **flectentis:** 'turning their steps', cf. Livy. 28.16 *ad Oceanum flectit*.

2 373-4. **galea . . . refulsit:** ironically it is the helmet which he has just taken from Messapus that causes Euryalus' death. *Sublustri* refers to the half-light of a clear night (Hor. Odes 3.27.31): *radiis* presumably to the moon.

3 375. **haud temere est visum:** 'the glimpse they got was not disregarded'.

4 377. **nihil illi tendere contra:** 'they offered no reply'; historic infinitive, cf. 789.

5 379. **divortia:** 'side roads', 'byways', which are familiar to them (*nota*), but not to the Trojans.

6 380. **coronant:** 'surround', with a *corona*, a military term for an encircling force (508).

7 383. 'only occasionally was a path discernible through concealed clearings'.

8 385. 'and fear gives him false directions' (literally 'makes him go wrong with regard to the direction of the paths'); cf. 7.215.

9 386f. 'and now without thinking he had got away from the enemy and the area later called Alban (from Alba), at that time King Latinus had his great cattle enclosures there, when he stopped . . .'. *Imprudens* means that he did not realise he had left Euryalus behind: nothing is known of the *loci Albani*, and some editors read *lacus Albani*, but the lake was too far away from the Trojan camp to make sense here. The point is that he had thrown off the enemy and also got safely past the farm buildings where he might have been seen. *Ut* in the sense of inverted *cum* is most unusual, and various other ways of punctuating this passage have been suggested, but none is convincing.

10 392-3. Cf. 2.753f. *vestigia retro / observata sequor*, of Aeneas going back to look for Creusa in Troy.

11 396f. 'The whole crowd of them were now getting hold of him, overwhelmed as he was by the disadvantages of the place, the darkness, the sudden confused onrush'.

fraude loci et noctis, subito turbante tumultu,
oppressum rapit et conantem plurima frustra.
Quid faciat? Qua vi iuvenem, quibus audeat armis
eripere? An sese medios moriturus in ensis   400
inferat et pulchram properet per vulnera mortem?
Ocius adducto torquet[1] hastile lacerto
suspiciens altam Lunam[2] et sic voce precatur:
'tu, dea, tu praesens nostro succurre labori,
astrorum decus et nemorum Latonia custos.[3]   405
Si qua tuis umquam pro me pater Hyrtacus aris
dona tulit, si qua ipse meis venatibus auxi
suspendive tholo[4] aut sacra ad fastigia fixi,
hunc sine me turbare globum et rege tela per auras.'
Dixerat et toto conixus corpore ferrum   410
conicit. Hasta volans noctis diverberat umbras
et venit aversi in tergum[5] Sulmonis ibique
frangitur, ac fisso transit praecordia ligno.
Volvitur ille vomens calidum de pectore flumen
frigidus et longis singultibus ilia pulsat.   415
diversi circumspiciunt. Hoc acrior idem
ecce aliud summa[6] telum librabat ab aure.
Dum trepidant, it[7] hasta Tago per tempus utrumque
stridens[8] traiectoque haesit tepefacta cerebro.
Saevit atrox Volcens nec teli conspicit usquam   420
auctorem nec quo se ardens immittere possit.
'Tu tamen interea calido mihi sanguine poenas
persolves amborum' inquit; simul ense recluso
ibat in Euryalum. Tum vero exterritus, amens,
conclamat Nisus nec se celare tenebris   425
amplius aut tantum potuit perferre dolorem:

---

1 402. **torquet:** this is Ribbeck's conjecture for *torquens* of the MSS (if we keep *torquens* then *et* in the next line is redundant). The final syllable of *torquet* has to be lengthened in arsis (see note on 7.174), and this could have led a scribe to change it.

2 403. Nisus prays to the moon especially as the goddess of hunting, but also as present in the sky in the night scene.

3 405. Cf. Spenser, *F.Q.* 7.6.38 (of Cynthia the moon) 'that is soveraine Queene profest / of woods and forrests'.

4 408. **tholo:** the dome of the temple in which votive offerings were hung.

5 412. **tergum:** 'back', hence *aversi* must be read for the MSS *adversi*. *Tergum* can of course mean an animal's hide which might be used for a shield, but *venit in tergum Sulmonis* cannot but mean 'pierced Sulmo's back'.

6 417. **summa . . . ab aure:** 'from high up, by his ear'.

7 418. **it:** perfect, a long syllable contracted from *iit*.

8 419. **stridens:** emphasis is gained by the unusual rhythm of a spondee filling the first foot, cf. 4.185, 12.859.

'me,[1] me, adsum qui feci, in me convertite ferrum,
o Rutuli! Mea fraus omnis, nihil[2] iste nec ausus
nec potuit; caelum hoc et conscia sidera testor;
tantum infelicem nimium dilexit amicum'.[3]   430
Talia dicta dabat, sed viribus ensis adactus[4]
transabiit[5] costas et candida pectora rumpit.
Volvitur Euryalus leto, pulchrosque per artus
it cruor inque umeros cervix conlapsa recumbit:
purpureus veluti cum flos succisus aratro[6]   435
languescit moriens, lassove papavera collo
demisere caput pluvia cum forte gravantur.
At Nisus ruit in medios solumque per omnis
Volcentem petit, in solo Volcente moratur.[7]
Quem circum glomerati hostes hinc comminus atque hinc[8]   440
proturbant. Instat non setius ac rotat ensem
fulmineum, donec Rutuli clamantis in ore
condidit adverso et moriens animam abstulit hosti.
Tum super exanimum sese proiecit amicum
confossus, placidaque ibi demum morte quievit.   445

　　　[9]Fortunati ambo! Si quid mea carmina possunt,
nulla dies umquam memori vos eximet aevo,

---

1 427. **me, me:** exclamatory and absolute, with no construction; certainly not to be taken as governed by in.

2 428. **nihil. . . nec:** for the doubled negative of. 12.189-90.

3 430. This line must be regarded as part of Nisus' speech; he says Euryalus was too young to have achieved anything, and to the imaginary objection (as Servius says) 'then why did he come?' Nisus replies that it just was that he loved his unhappy friend too much.

4 431-2. Notice the effect of inevitable finality given by the metrical movement, with the fourth foot in both lines made up of a single dactyl.

5 432. **transabiit:** *M2* and *P* have *transadigit* (cf. 12.276, 508), but the imitation by Statius (*Th.* 2.9 *transabiit animam . . . ensis*) supports *R's* reading.

6 435f. The simile is based on Hom. *Il.* 8.306f., and particularly on Catullus 11.21f. *nec meum respectet ut ante amorem, / qui illius culpa cecidit velut prati / ultimi flos praetereunte postquam / tactus aratro est*; cf. also Cat. 62.39f. Compare the flower simile at the death of Pallas, 11.68f., and for Virgil's use of Catullan echoes at moments when the emotion is intense see note on 11.1f.

7 439. **moratur:** 'is concerned with', cf. 7.253.

8 440f. In this rapid narrative, urgency is added by the unusual line endings of 440 (double monosyllable) and 441 (double disyllable) and the elision before the fifth foot in 443. A very evident finality is given by the fourth foot coincidence on the word *demum* in 445.

9 446f. The invocation of the ghosts of the two warriors comes naturally after an episode in which Virgil has particularly sought to involve the reader in sympathy for the pathos of youthful death; cf. 10.507f. (the death of Pallas). Statius invokes Hopleus and Dymas similarly in *Thebaid* 10 (an episode based on Virgil's story) and adds that perhaps the ghosts of Nisus and Euryalus will not spurn their company.

dum domus Aeneae Capitoli immobile saxum[1]
accolet imperiumque pater Romanus habebit.

> 450-502. *The Rutulians discover the slaughter in their camp. Next day they march forth to battle, carrying the heads of Nisus and Euryalus impaled on spears. Euryalus' mother learns the truth and laments her young son.*

[2]Victores praeda Rutuli spoliisque potiti   450
Volcentem exanimum flentes in castra ferebant.
Nec minor in castris luctus Rhamnete reperto
exsangui et primis una tot caede peremptis,
Serranoque[3] Numaque. Ingens concursus ad ipsa
corpora seminecisque viros, [4]tepidaque recentem   455
caede locum et plenos spumanti sanguine rivos.
Agnoscunt[5] spolia inter se galeamque nitentem
Messapi et multo phaleras sudore receptas.

Et iam prima novo spargebat lumine terras[6]
Tithoni croceum linquens Aurora cubile.   460
Iam sole infuso, iam rebus[7] luce retectis
Turnus in arma viros armis circumdatus ipse
suscitat, aeratasque acies in proelia cogit
quisque suos,[8] variisque acuunt rumoribus iras.
Quin[9] ipsa arrectis (visu miserabile) in hastis   465

---

1 448-9. Cf. Hor. *Odes* 3.30.8f. *dum Capitolium / scandet cum tacita virgine pontifex. Pater Romanus* refers to Jupiter of the Capitol; cf. Hor. *Odes* 3.5.12 *incolumi Iove et urbe Roma*, Prop. 4.1.7 *pater Tarpeius;* it might however mean the emperors of Rome (Hor. *Odes* 3.24.27), with reference to Aeneas' epithet *pater;* or possibly the Roman senate (*patres*).

2 450f. The events leading to the lamentation of Euryalus' mother are briefly narrated; the lamentation itself aims at and achieves a high degree of pathos. It is rhetorically constructed (like the speeches of Dido in Book 4) and Servius draws attention to the fact that it contains almost all the features mentioned by Cicero in the section of his rhetorical works *de misericordia commovenda* (cf. *De Inv.* 1.107-9). But it achieves a high degree of immediacy, an impression of personal involvement which is largely due to Virgil's special sympathy (often shown in the *Aeneid*) for youthful death. Its appeal to the emotions is made denser and enriched by the reminiscences of Andromache's lamentation for Hector in *Iliad* 22, and of the plight of forsaken Dido in *Aeneid* 4; Virgil here describes one special occasion of sorrow, but he does not leave it isolated, he relates it to other occasions of tragic loss and death.

3 454. **Serranoque Numaque**: 'including Serranus and Numa'. Numa was not mentioned before, and a Rutulian of that name appears in *Aen.* 10.562. Hence the emendation *Lamoque* (cf. 334); but it is more likely that the inconsistency is Virgil's (rather than that of the MSS) and would have been removed in revision.

4 455-6. 'the field fresh with warm blood'; some MSS have *tepidumque recenti,* but cf. 6.674 *prata recentia rivis,* and 6.450 *recens a vulnere Dido.* In the next phrase too the MSS vary between *plenos spumanti* and *pleno spumantis,* but *pleno . . sanguine* would be strange.

5 457. **agnoscunt spolia inter se**: 'they identify the spoils to one another', i.e. the spoils now recovered from Nisus and Euryalus, including the shining helmet of Messapus which was Euryalus' downfall, and the *phalerae* of Rhamnes (359).

6 459-60. The same lines occur in 4.584-5, where see notes. Tithonus was the mortal husband of Aurora, the dawn-goddess.

7 461. **rebus luce retectis**: 'as the world was revealed again by the daylight', cf. 4.119 (5.65), 6.272.

8 464. **suos**: object of *cogit,* with *acies* in apposition, 'each leader marshals his men for battle, squadrons in bronze armour'. This is the reading of most MSS and of Servius; *suas* looks like a scribe's assimilation to *acies.*

9 465. **quin**: like *quin etiam,* adding a further point; cf. 10.23.

praefigunt capita et multo clamore sequuntur
Euryali et Nisi.[1]
Aeneadae duri murorum in parte sinistra
opposuere aciem (nam dextera cingitur amni[2]),
ingentisque tenent fossas et turribus altis   470
stant maesti; simul[3] ora virum praefixa movebant
nota nimis miseris atroque fluentia tabo.
    [4]Interea pavidam volitans pennata per urbem[5]
nuntia Fama ruit matrisque adlabitur[6] auris
Euryali. At subitus miserae calor ossa reliquit,   475
excussi manibus radii revolutaque pensa.[7]
Evolat infelix et femineo ululatu
scissa[8] comam muros amens atque agmina cursu
prima petit, non illa virum, non[9] illa pericli
telorumque memor, caelum dehinc[10] questibus implet: 480
'hunc[11] ego te, Euryale, aspicio? Tune ille senectae
sera meae requies, potuisti linquere solam,
crudelis? Nec te[12] sub tanta pericula missum
adfari extremum miserae data copia matri?
Heu, terra ignota canibus data praeda Latinis   485
alitibusque iaces! Nec[13] te tua funere mater
produxi pressive oculos aut vulnera lavi,

---

1 467. The proper names in the half-line are given a strange emphasis by the insertion of the words *et multo clamore sequuntur,* which has led the reader to think that the sentence ended at *sequuntur.*

2 469. **amni:** ablative, cf. 8.473.

3 471. **simul:** the word adds the extra reason for their despondency, in addition to the siege and the absence of Aeneas.

4 473-4. For the wings of Rumour cf. the full scale personified description in 4.173f. (esp. 180

5 473. **urbem:** the Trojan camp, cf. 48.

6 474. **adlabitur auris:** for the accusative cf. *Ciris* 476 and see note on 100; the dative is much more common.

7 476-7. We are reminded first of Andromache hearing the news of Hector's death (*Il.* 22.448), where she swoons and the shuttle falls from her hand; and then of Anna rushing to Dido (*Aen.* 4.672f.). For the unusual rhythm *femineo ululatu* (quadri-syllabic ending and hiatus) cf. 4.667.

8 478. **scissa comam:** 'tearing her hair', retained accusative after the passive participle in a middle sense; cf. 4.590 *flaventisque abscissa comas,* and see note on 337.

9 479. **non ilia . . . non ilia:** cf. 6.593. *Virum* refers to the expectation that women would keep out of the way; Servius tersely says *unum pudoris est, aliud* (i.e. *pericli*) *salutis.*

10 480. **dehinc:** one syllable, cf. 6.678, and contrast 8.337.

11 481. 'Is it thus, Euryalus, that I see you?' *Hunc* is equivalent in meaning to *talem* but more forceful. Notice the tremendous effect achieved by the initial pronouns, an effect reinforced by the three elisions in the line.

12 483-4. **te . . . adfari extremum:** 'to say my last farewell to you', cf. 2.644 *sic o sic positum adfati discedite corpus. Extremum* is adverbial accusative, see note on 630-1.

13 486-7. **nec te tua funere mater produxi:** 'nor did I, your mother, escort you at your funeral procession'. *Funere* is an emendation of Bembus for *funera* of the MSS, which would give a frigid rephrasing of *te:* 'you — your body, that is'. The corruption could have been caused by *vulnera* in the next line.

veste[1] tegens tibi quam noctes festina diesque
urgebam, et tela curas solabar anilis.
quo sequar? Aut quae nunc artus avulsaque membra   490
et funus[2] lacerum tellus habet? Hoc[3] mihi de te,
nate, refers? Hoc sum terraque marique secuta?
Figite me, si qua est pietas, in me omnia tela
conicite, o Rutuli, me primam absumite ferro;
aut tu, magne pater divum, miserere, tuoque[4]   495
invisum hoc detrude caput sub Tartara telo,
quando aliter nequeo crudelem abrumpere vitam.'
Hoc fletu concussi animi, maestusque per omnis
it gemitus, torpent infractae[5] ad proelia vires.
Illam incendentem luctus Idaeus et Actor   500
Ilionei[6] monitu et multum lacrimantis Iuli
corripiunt interque[7] manus sub tecta reponunt.

503-89. *The full scale attack on the Trojan camp begins.*
Virgil invokes the Muse to tell of the slaughter dealt by
Turnus; he kills Helenor and Lycus and in the general
fighting many fall on both sides.

[8]At [9]tuba terribilem sonitum[10] procul aere canoro
increpuit, sequitur clamor caelumque remugit.

---

1 488. She means that the fine garment she has been making for him to wear might at least have been used as a shroud (cf. Hom. *Il.* 22.510f.).

2 491. **funus**: 'corpse', cf. 6.150, Prop. 1.17.8; this is a very frequent meaning in Silver Latin.

3 **hoc mihi de te**: observe again the use of pronouns, as at the beginning of the speech, here in a very broken rhythm at the line end. Of *hoc* Servius says 'caput intuens ait'.

4 495-7. She ends with an appeal to Jupiter to kill her with his thunderbolt (cf. 5.691f.), using phrases reminiscent of Dido's decision to leave the light she hated (4.631).

5 499. **infractae**: 'broken', cf. *Aen.* 12.1.

6 501. **Ilionei**: the last two vowels coalesce by synizesis, cf. 7.249.

7 502. **interque manus**: 'supported on their arms', cf. Cic. *Verr.* 2.5.28. The passage ends with one more reminiscence of Dido, cf. 4.391f.

8 503f. Virgil's description of the battle at the walls begins with a general account of the scene of fighting (503-24), not particularised except for the mention at the end of two of Turnus' most powerful lieutenants, Mezentius and Messapus. Then the invocation focuses the attention on Turnus, and his αριστεια begins with the deaths at his hands of Helenor and Lycus, each illustrated with a simile and the first with a brief glimpse of biography. Then the viewpoint is enlarged with the summary description of the deaths of many warriors of both sides, in lines filled with names and little else, and finally it is concentrated again on the deaths of Privernus and the son of Arcens; with Privernus Virgil tells us only the details of the manner of his death, with the son of Arcens he gives us first a little vignette about his appearance and his past life. Echoes of Homer and Ennius give some density to a passage which is mainly transitional and preparatory.

9 503. Virgil here recalls and modifies Ennius' line (*Ann.* 140) *at tuba terribili sonitu taratantara dixit*, in which the alliteration and the onomatopoeic word *taratantara* were insufficiently sophisticated for the tone of the *Aeneid.*

10 **sonitum**: cognate accusative, 'sounded its terrifying call', cf. Prop. 1.17.6.

Accelerant acta[1] pariter testudine Volsci[2]   505
et fossas implere parant ac vellere vallum.
Quaerunt[3] pars aditum et scalis ascendere muros,
qua rara est acies interlucetque[4] corona
non tam spissa viris. Telorum effundere[5] contra
omne genus Teucri ac duris detrudere contis,   510
adsueti longo muros defendere bello.[6]
Saxa quoque infesto volvebant pondere, si qua
possent tectam aciem perrumpere, [7]cum tamen omnis
ferre iuvat subter densa testudine casus.
Nec iam sufficiunt. [8]Nam qua globus imminet ingens,   515
immanem Teucri molem volvuntque ruuntque,
quae stravit Rutulos late armorumque resolvit
tegmina. Nec curant caeco[9] contendere Marte
amplius audaces Rutuli, sed pellere vallo
missilibus certant.   520
Parte alia horrendus visu quassabat Etruscam[10]
pinum et fumiferos infert Mezentius ignis;
at Messapus equum domitor, Neptunia proles,[11]
rescindit vallum et scalas in moenia poscit.

    Vos, o Calliope,[12] precor, aspirate canenti   525
quas ibi tum ferro strages, quae funera Turnus
ediderit, quem quisque virum demiserit Orco,
et mecum ingentis oras evolvite belli.[13]

---

1 505. **acta pariter testudine:** 'bringing up their shield-roof in even line', cf. 2.441 and line 513 *tectam aciem;* it is certain that Virgil refers to the use of shields to achieve cover rather than to the siege engine which later performed the same function, cf. 517-18.

2 **Volsci:** allies of the Rutilians, led by Camilla.

3 507. Notice the variation of construction with *quaerunt,* first the accusative as object and then the infinitive; cf. *Geo.* 1.25.

4 508. **interlucetque corona:** 'and the line of defenders shows gaps', a scarce meaning of the verb; for *corona* cf. 10.122.

5 509-10. **effundere . . . detrudere:** historic infinitives.

6 511. The weariness of the ten years' defence of Troy is reflected in the spondaic line.

7 513-14. 'while none the less the enemy are glad to endure under their thick shelter all that comes'; for the rather strange connexion of the subordinate clause to the main clause cf. 10.509.

8 515. 'And now they cannot hold out any more; for where the huge enemy throng threatens . . .', i.e. the besiegers under their *testudo* are overwhelmed by the mass of wall dislodged on them (cf. 2.460f.).

9 518. **caeco . . . Marte:** i.e. covered by a *testudo.*

10 521-2. **Etruscam pinum:** Mezentius' firebrand (cf. 72) is called Etruscan because he came *Tyrrhenis . . . ab oris* (7.647).

11 523. The same line is used of Messapus in the catalogue (7.691).

12 525f. In the new invocation to the Muses, Calliope (Muse of epic) is particularised to stand for all the Muses (the pronoun and verb are plural; cf. *Aen.* 1.140) of which she was the chief.

13 528. Another very noticeable reminiscence of Ennius: *quis potis ingentis oras evolvere belli? (Ann.* 174). The metaphor in *evolvere* is of unrolling a mighty book, in *oras* of the extent and confines of the subject.

[et meministis enim, divae, et memorare potestis.][1]
Turris erat vasto[2] suspectu et pontibus[3] altis.   530
Opportuna loco, summis quam viribus omnes
expugnare Itali summaque[4] evertere opum vi
certabant, Troes contra defendere saxis
perque cavas densi tela intorquere fenestras.
Princeps ardentem coniecit lampada[5] Turnus   535
et flammam adfixit lateri, quae plurima[6] vento
corripuit tabulas et postibus haesit adesis.[7]
Turbati trepidare[8] intus frustraque malorum
velle fugam. Dum se glomerant retroque residunt
in partem quae peste[9] caret, tum pondere turris   540
procubuit subito et caelum tonat omne fragore.
Semineces ad terram immani mole secuta
confixique suis telis et pectora[10] duro
transfossi ligno veniunt. Vix unus Helenor
et Lycus elapsi; quorum primaevus Helenor,   545
Maeonio regi quem serva Licymnia furtim[11]
sustulerat vetitisque ad Troiam miserat armis.
Ense[12] levis nudo parmaque inglorius alba.
Isque ubi se Turni media inter milia vidit,
hinc acies atque hinc[13] acies astare Latinas,   550

---

1 529. This line occurs in the invocation at 7.645, and is omitted in most of the MSS; it is probably interpolated here.

2 530. **vasto suspectu:** 'formidable to look up at', ablative of description.

3 **pontibus**: see note on 170.

4 532. **summaque . . . opum vi:** cf. Ennius (*Ann.* 161) *summa nituntur opum vi* (cf. *Aen.* 12.552). The archaic rhythm makes the reminiscence very obvious.

5 535. **lampada:** Greek accusative, cf. 346.

6 536. **plurima vento:** 'fanned by the wind' ('gliscens et magna facta', Servius).

7 537. **adesis:** 'consumed', cf. Prop. 4.7.9; i.e. it clung to the doorways as it burnt them up, a vivid personification of fire as a giant shape which will not be shaken off from its prey.

8 538. **trepidare**: historic infinitive, like *velle* in the next line.

9 540. **peste:** of fire in 5.683.

10 543-4. **pectora . . . transfossi:** 'their chests pierced', retained accusative with a passive verb, much influenced by the accusative of respect construction; cf. 2.57 *mantis . . . post terga revinctum,* and see note on 337.

11 546-7. i.e. he was the illegitimate son of the King of Maeonia (Hom. *Il.* 2.864f.) by the slave-girl Licymnia: he came to Troy although he had been forbidden to be a soldier, presumably by his father (*Il.* 2.832), perhaps because he was too young (*primaevus*), or because of his birth, or both.

12 548. 'a light-armed soldier with drawn sword, undistinguished, with white shield', i.e. a new recruit having as yet no emblazoned armour.

13 550. **hinc acies atque hinc acies**: the repetition conveys the inevitability of his situation; cf. 11.766 *hos aditus iamque hos aditus.*

ut fera, quae densa venantum saepta corona[1]
contra tela furit seseque haud nescia morti
inicit et saltu supra venabula fertur —
haud aliter iuvenis medios moriturus in hostis
inruit et qua tela videt densissima tendit.   555
At pedibus[2] longe melior Lycus inter et hostis
inter et arma fuga muros[3] tenet, altaque certat
prendere tecta manu sociumque[4] attingere dextras.
Quem Turnus [5]pariter cursu teloque secutus
increpat his victor: 'nostrasne evadere, demens,   560
sperasti te posse manus?' Simul arripit ipsum
pendentem et magna muri cum parte revellit:
qualis[6] ubi aut leporem aut candenti corpore cycnum
sustulit alta petens pedibus Iovis armiger uncis,
quaesitum aut matri multis balatibus agnum   565
Martius a stabulis rapuit lupus. Undique clamor
tollitur: invadunt et fossas aggere[7] complent,
ardentis taedas alii ad fastigia iactant.
Ilioneus saxo atque ingenti fragmine montis[8]
Lucetium portae subeuntem ignisque ferentem,[9]   570
Emathiona Liger, Corynaeum sternit Asilas,
hic iaculo bonus, hic longe fallente sagitta,
Ortygium Caeneus,[10] victorem Caenea Turnus,
Turnus Ityn Cloniumque, Dioxippum Promolumque
et Sagarim et summis stantem pro turribus Idan,   575
Privernum Capys. Hunc primo levis hasta Themillae

---

1 551f. This simile of an animal at bay leaping on to the spears of its attackers is brief and economical in expression. For this it is censured by Macrobius (*Sat.* 5.1325) in comparison with Hom. *Il.* 20.164f. (which it does not greatly resemble).

2 556. **pedibus longe melior**: 'much better at running' (than at fighting); cf. Drances in 11.338 *lingua melior.*

3 557. **muros tenet**: 'keeps close to the walls', like Hector in *Iliad* 22.

4 558. **sociumque**: archaic genitive plural, cf. 609, 10.410 and note on 7.50.

5 559. 'catching him and stabbing him at the same moment', cf. 12.775.

6 563f. 'like the armour bearer of Jupiter when it has carried off in its hooked claws soaring aloft a hare or a white swan, or the wolf of Mars when it has snatched from the fold a lamb which it's mother seeks in vain with loud bleating'. *Iovis armiger* is the eagle, cf. 5.255; for the simile cf. lines 59f. and Hom. *Il.* 15.690f., 22.308f. The wolf is sacred to Mars because Romulus and Remus, his sons, were suckled by a she-wolf.

7 567. **aggere**:'with earth'.

8 569. An example of hendiadys; the effect is something like this: 'with a rock, a huge piece of a mountain it was'.

9 570-6. The victims are successively Rutulian, Trojan, Trojan, Rutulian, and then all Trojan till Privernus the Rutulian.

10 573-4. Notice how the repetition of Caeneus as victor and then victim attracts our attention to the repetition of Turnus, always victor. The rhythm of line 574 is Greek, as often in Virgil with lists of names.

strinxerat, ille manum proiecto tegmine demens
ad vulnus tulit; [1]ergo alis adlapsa sagitta
et laevo infixa est alte lateri, abditaque intus
spiramenta[2] animae letali vulnere rupit. 580
Stabat in egregiis Arcentis[3] filius armis
pictus[4] acu chlamydem et ferrugine clarus Hibera,
insignis facie, genitor quem miserat Arcens
eductum Martis[5] luco Symaethia circum
flumina, pinguis ubi et placabilis ara Palici:[6] 585
stridentem fundam positis Mezentius hastis
ipse ter adducta[7] circum caput egit habena
et media adversi liquefacto[8] tempora plumbo
diffidit ac multa porrectum extendit harena.

> 590-671. *Numanus makes a taunting speech, contrasting the hard vigour of the Italians with the oriental effeminacy of the Trojans: Ascanius kills him with an arrow. Apollo appears to Ascanius and prophesies a glorious future, but warns him that from now on he must keep out of the fighting until he is mature.*

[9]Tum primum bello celerem intendisse sagittam 590

---

1 578-80. 'so an arrow in its winged flight deeply penetrated his left side, and hidden within destroyed the path of breath with its deadly wound'. I have accepted Housman's conjecture of *alte lateri* for *lateri manus;* his argument is that *alte* fell out and *manus* was added to fill up the scansion. The manuscript reading is intolerable with its change of subject from *sagitta* to *manus* and back again to *sagitta;* also *ergo* does not make good sense and the co-ordination *adlapsa* (*est*) *et infixa est* is very awkward. With the emendation *et . . . que* is 'both . . . and'.

2 580. **spiramenta animae:** a fine phrase, cf. *Geo.* 1.90, 4.39.

3 581. The son of Arcens evidently joined Aeneas in Sicily; Symaethus was a river and town on the East coast of Sicily. The lines describing him are remarkably like *Aen.* 7.761-4.

4 582. **pictus acu chlamydem:** 'his tunic brightly embroidered', the same construction (retained accusative, see note on 337) occurs with *pictus* in 7.796 and 11.777. For *ferrugo* ('brown', 'purplish-brown'; Servius says *vicinus purpuras subnigrae*) as a colour of distinction, cf. 11.772; for Spanish purple cf. Cat. 64.227 with Fordyce's note.

5 584. **Martis:** nothing is known of a grove of Mars near Symaethus. Many editors read *matris,* with Macrobius, a reference to the nymph of the region as his mother; some read *Matris,* i.e. the Mother of the gods.

6 585. **Palici:** the Palici were Sicilian deities; for the singular cf. Ov. *Pont.* 2.10.25. For *placabilis* (= gentle, easily appeased) cf. 7.764.

7 587. **adducta . . . habena:** 'pulling the thong inwards', holding it tight, counteracting the tendency of the sling to fly outwards; cf. 632.

8 588. **liquefacto:** for the idea that a lead pellet melted in its swift flight cf. Lucr. 6.177f.

9 590f. The speech of Numanus is the outstanding exposition of a theme which occurs elsewhere, the view of Troy's opponents that the Trojans are effeminate and decadent. Iarbas had spoken thus in his prayers to Jupiter (4.215f.); Turnus had rallied the Rutulians by elaborating this idea (9.128f.); cf. also 12.99f. Here the point is made particularly strongly by contrast with the simple virtues of the primitive Italians in phrases which recall the *Georgics* and the early books of Livy, and win our sympathy for the losing cause, the men of Italy destined to contribute so much to the civilisation established by their conquerors.

The reaction of Ascanius and the vengeance taken on Numanus is particularly effective because it is his first and only participation in the fighting. The divine intervention by Apollo, first as a voice from heaven prophesying greatness for Troy (as he had several times in Book 3), and then in mortal guise to warn Ascanius not to try to repeat his prowess, adds a special note of impressiveness to this little episode set amidst the account of the triumphs of Turnus.

dicitur ante feras solitus terrere fugacis
Ascanius, fortemque manu fudisse Numanum,
cui Remulo cognomen erat, Turnique minorem
germanam nuper thalamo sociatus habebat.
Is primam ante aciem digna[1] atque indigna relatu   595
vociferans tumidusque[2] novo praecordia regno[3]
ibat [4]et ingentem sese clamore ferebat:
'non pudet obsidione iterum valloque teneri.[5]
Bis[6] capti Phryges, et morti[7] praetendere muros?
En qui nostra sibi bello conubia poscunt!   600
Quis[8] deus Italiam, quae vos dementia adegit?
Non hic Atridae[9] nec fandi[10] fictor Ulixes:
durum[11] a stirpe genus natos ad flumina primum
deferimus saevoque[12] gelu duramus et undis;
venatu[13] invigilant pueri silvasque fatigant,[14]   605
flectere[15] ludus equos et spicula tendere cornu.
At [16]patiens operum parvoque adsueta iuventus
aut rastris terram domat aut quatit oppida bello.
Omne aevum ferro teritur, [17]versaque iuvencum
terga fatigamus hasta, nec tarda senectus   610

---

1 595. **digna atque indigna:** cf. *dicenda tacenda, fanda infanda;* the meaning is 'indiscriminate insults'.

2 596. **tumidusque . . . praecordia:** 'arrogant in heart', accusative of respect, cf. lines 650, 678 and see note on 7.60.

3 **regno:** because he had married into the royal house of Turnus.

4 597. 'and loudly boasted his mighty prowess'; for *sese ferebat* cf. 5.372-3.

5 598f. Compare Turnus'taunting speech, 144f.

6 599. **bis capti Phryges:** once by the Greeks, once now (rather than once by Hercules, once by the Greeks as in 11.402; *iterum* proves the point).

7 **morti praetendere muros:** 'to have city walls to shelter you from death'; cf. *Geo.* 1.270 *segeti praetendere saepem.*

8 601. 'what god — what madness rather — brought you to Italy?' For the accusative of motion towards cf. 100.

9 602. **Atridae:** see note on 138.

10 **fandi fictor:** 'fashioner of speech'; for the trickery and villainy of Ulysses see notes on 2.7, 44. Numanus' point (like that of Turnus, 150f.) is that the Greeks prevailed by trickery, the Rutulians will prevail by valour.

11 603. **durum a stirpe genus:** in apposition to the subject *deferimus:* 'we are a hard race by heritage, and we begin by taking . . .'. *A stirpe* is 'from the beginning', 'as taught by our elders'.

12 604. **saevoque gelu . . . et undis:** 'in the bitterly cold water', hendiadys.

13 605. **venatu invigilant pueri:** 'when they grow to boyhood their passion is hunting'; *venatu* is dative, cf. *Geo.* 4.158 *victu invigilant.*

14 **fatigant:** 'scour', cf. *Aen.* 1.280.

15 606. **flectere ludus equos:** 'their fun is taming horses and archery'; i.e. they do not play childish games. Contrast the complaints in Hor. *Odes* 3.24.54f. about hoops and dice being preferred to horse-riding and hunting.

16 607-8. 'But when they grow up they are accustomed to work and used to poverty, and they conquer the soil with hoes or shake towns in warfare.' Servius comments *hoc et in Georgicis laudat.* Notice the unusual symmetry of the bipartite line 608.

17 609-10. 'All our life is lived out with weapons, and we goad our bullock's backs with a reversed spear', i.e. they always have military weapons in their hands even when ploughing and use the spear for a goad. *Iuvencum* is genitive plural; cf. 558. The last syllable of *fatigamus* is lengthened in arsis; cf. 767 and see note on 7.174.

debilitat viris animi mutatque vigorem:
canitiem galea premimus, semperque recentis
comportare iuvat praedas et vivere rapto.
vobis picta croco et fulgenti murice vestis,[1]
desidiae[2] cordi, iuvat indulgere[3] choreis,   615
et tunicae manicas[4] et habent redimicula mitrae.
o vere Phrygiae, neque enim Phryges, ite per alta[5]
Dindyma, ubi adsuetis[6] biforem dat tibia cantum.[7]
tympana vos buxusque vocat Berecyntia Matris
Idaeae; sinite arma viris et cedite ferro.'   620
    Talia iactantem dictis ac dira[8] canentem
non tulit Ascanius, [9]nervoque obversus equino
intendit telum diversaque bracchia ducens
constitit, ante Iovem supplex per vota precatus:
'Iuppiter omnipotens, audacibus adnue coeptis.   625
Ipse tibi ad tua templa feram sollemnia dona,
et statuam ante aras aurata fronte iuvencum
candentem[10] pariterque caput cum matre ferentem,
iam cornu petat et pedibus qui spargat harenam.'
Audiit et caeli genitor de[11] parte serena   630
intonuit laevum, sonat una fatifer arcus.
Effugit horrendum stridens adducta sagitta
perque caput Remuli venit et cava tempora ferro

---

1 614f. For the effeminacy of the Trojans (called *Phryges* in this connexion because of the later reputation of the Phrygians: *phrygio* was the Latin for an embroiderer in gold) cf. Iarbas' taunts in 4.215f., and Turnus' in 12.99-100.

2 615. **desidiae cordi:** 'idleness your delight'; *cordi* is predicative dative, cf. 776.

3 **indulgere choreis:** for disapproval of dancing cf. Cic. *Mur.* 13, Hor. *Odes* 3.6.21f.

4 616. Tunics with sleeves were regarded as effeminate by the Romans (Aul. Gell. 7.12, Cic. *Cat.* 2.22; for ribboned bonnets cf. 4.216.

5 617. Cf. Hom. *Il.* 2.235, where Thersites calls the Greeks Achaean women, not men: 'Αχαιιδεσ, ουκετ' Αχαιοι. The bucolic diaeresis here adds emphasis to the vocative phrase.

6 618. **adsuetis:** 'her devotees'.

7 618f. The references recall Catullus 63 and Lucr. 2.611f. Dindyma (10.252) and Berecynthus (line 82) were mountains close to Mt. Ida sacred to the Great Mother Cybele. The flute and the cymbals and the boxwood pipe were accompaniments in her wild orgiastic worship; *biforem* refers to the Phrygian flute with double pipe, which sounded two different notes simultaneously: i.e. the adjective refers to the double bore of the pipe, not to finger holes.

8 621. **dira canentem:** 'proclaiming awful threats'; for *canere* in the sense of solemn utterance cf. 11.399.

9 622f. 'turning towards him he tautened the arrow on the horse-gut, and pulling his arms wide apart stood there, first invoking Jupiter in prayer and entreaty'.

10 628-9. 'holding its head on high as its mother does, one ready to butt with its horns and scatter the sand with its hooves', i.e. of the appropriate age for sacrifice. Line 629 is repeated from *Ecl.* 3.87; the long postposition of *qui* is unusual.

11 630-1. **de parte serena intonuit laevum:** for thunder in a clear sky as an omen cf. *Geo.* 1.487f. Hor. *Odes* 1.34; for the left as a good omen cf. *Aen.* 2.693. Servius subtly says that if it is on our left it is on Jupiter's right; in Roman religion left was lucky in certain contexts. *Laevum* is adverbial accusative, like *horrendum* in the next line; see Page on 632 for lists.

traicit. 'i,[1] verbis virtutem inlude superbis!
Bis capti Phryges haec Rutulis responsa remittunt':   635
hoc tantum Ascanius. Teucri clamore sequuntur
laetitiaque fremunt animosque ad sidera tollunt.
    Aetheria tum forte plaga crinitus Apollo
desuper Ausonias acies urbemque videbat
nube sedens, atque his victorem adfatur Iulum: 640
'macte[2] nova virtute, puer, sic itur ad astra,
dis[3] genite et geniture deos. [4]Iure omnia bella
gente sub Assaraci fato ventura resident,
nec te Troia capit.' Simul haec effatus ab alto
aethere se mittit, spirantis dimovet auras   645
Ascaniumque petit; forma[5] tum vertitur oris[6]
antiquum in Buten. Hic Dardanio[7] Anchisae
armiger ante fuit fidusque ad limina custos;
tum comitem Ascanio pater addidit. Ibat Apollo
omni longaevo similis vocemque coloremque[8]   650
et crinis albos et saeva sonoribus arma,
atque his ardentem dictis adfatur Iulum:[9]
'sit satis, Aenide,[10] telis impune Numanum
oppetiisse tuis; primam hanc tibi magnus Apollo
concedit laudem et paribus[11] non invidet armis;   655
cetera[12] parce, puer, bello.' Sic orsus Apollo

---

1 634. **i verbis virtutem inlude superbis**: 'come on now, mock our valour with your arrogant words'; for *i* used sarcastically with a following imperative cf. 7.425. Notice the rhyme of *verbis . . . superbis*, and the alliteration of *r* in the next line.

2 641. **macte nova virtute**: 'a blessing on your first act of prowess'; *macte* is vocative by attraction, equivalent as Servius says to *mactus esto*. It became a formulaic phrase in the vocative, especially with *virtute* as a means of congratulation; cf. Cic. *Tusc.* 1.40, Livy 2.12.14.

3 642. **dis genite et geniture deos**: Servius refers the first to Venus and the second to Julius Caesar and Augustus.

4 642f. 'With justice shall all the wars which are destined by fate to occur eventually cease beneath the sway of the race of Assaracus, and Troy cannot hold you.' For the prophecy of Roman peace cf. *Aen.* 1.291f. Assaracus was a Trojan ancestor (line 259), but his descendants will reach far beyond the bounds of Troy (*nec te Troia capit*). Cf. Philip to Alexander (Plut. *Alex.* 6) 'Macedonia cannot hold you.'

5 646. **forma . . . vertitur**: a middle use of the verb, cf. line 74; *forma* is ablative of respect. Some MSS have *formam*, retained accusative.

6 646f. Compare Iris in 5.620, taking the form of Beroe; in Hom. *Il.* 17.322f. Apollo appears in mortal form to Aeneas.

7 647. **Dardanio Anchisae**: hiatus and spondaic ending, cf. 1.617 (the same phrase) and see note on 7.631.

8 650-1. Cf. 4.558-9 *omnia Mercurio similis vocemque coloremque / et crinis flavos et membra decora iuventa*, and see notes there on the hyper-metric elision and the accusatives of respect; cf. also 8.228 and line 596.

9 657f. Compare the disappearance of Mercury, expressed in almost identical lines, in 4.277-8.

10 653. **Aenide**: this form of the patronymic occurs only here; the usual form is *Aeneades*. The vocative is Greek in form, with a long *e*.

11 655. **paribus**: equal on this occasion to Apollo's nonpareil skill as an archer.

12 656. **cetera**: accusative of respect, cf. 650 and 3.594.

mortalis medio aspectus sermone reliquit
et procul in tenuem ex oculis evanuit auram.
Agnovere deum proceres divinaque tela[1]
Dardanidae pharetramque fuga sensere sonantem.   660
Ergo avidum pugnae dictis ac numine Phoebi
Ascanium prohibent, ipsi in certamina rursus
succedunt animasque in aperta pericula mittunt.
It clamor totis per propugnacula muris,
intendunt acris arcus amentaque[2] torquent.   665
Sternitur omne solum telis, tum scuta cavaeque
dant sonitum flictu[3] galeae, pugna aspera surgit:
quantus [4]ab occasu veniens pluvialibus Haedis
verberat imber humum, quam multa grandine nimbi
in vada praecipitant, cum Iuppiter horridus Austris   670
torquet aquosam hiemem et caelo cava nubila rumpit.

672-818. *Pandarus and Bitias throw open the Trojan gates;
the Rutulians by the gates are defeated until Turnus comes
to their help. He kills Bitias; Pandarus shuts the gates
again, but Turnus is inside. Pandarus challenges Turnus
with a taunt, and Turnus kills him. Turnus could now have
opened the gates again and introduced the rest of his army,
but he is intent on personal triumphs, and kills many
Trojans. At last they rally, led by Mnestheus, and Turnus is
compelled to give way. He plunges into the Tiber and rejoins
his army.*

[5]Pandarus[6] et Bitias, Idaeo Alcanore creti,[7]

---

1 659-60. As he departs, Apollo becomes the god again; cf. Venus in 1.402f.

2 665. **amenta:** the thongs attached to throwing weapons so that greater impetus could be imparted. Notice the strong alliteration in this and the following lines, as the description of battle is resumed.

3 667. **flictu:** 'with the impact', a rare word; Servius rightly regards it as archaic, and quotes Pacuvius *flictus navium*. The only other author to use it is Virgil's faithful imitator, Silius Italicus.

4 668f. 'as mighty as the storm which, when the Kids rise portending rain, comes from the west and lashes against the ground, as dense as the hailstones which the clouds spatter on the sea when Jupiter threatens with his south winds and sends rainstorms in whirls, shattering the arching clouds in the sky'. *Pluvialibus Haedis* is ablative of time; cf. Hor. *Odes* 3.1.28, *Geo.* 1.205.

5 672f. This is one of the most vivid pieces of battle description in the *Aeneid*. The giant figures of the brothers Pandarus and Bitias compel our interest, and the irresistible might of Turnus is portrayed in thickly packed narrative of action. The final tableau of his retreat is presented in powerful and exaggerated rhetoric, with reminiscences of the slow retreat of Ajax in *Iliad* 15 and 16. Other echoes of Homer (notably the beginning of the battle at the ships in *Iliad* 12) and of Ennius add density; the impetus of the movement is very rapid and the frequent similes are directly illustrative of action, giving an extra dimension to the event (as Homer's do) rather than looking forward and backward, as is sometimes Virgil's way with similes. All the action is centred upon Pandarus, Bitias, and Turnus; the many others who meet their deaths are mostly mere names, though occasionally we are permitted to know just a little about them, as for example with Amycus and his poisoned darts, and Cretheus the war poet. Above all an impression is built up in Aeneas' absence of the formidable foe awaiting him.

6 672-90. The passage is based on Homer, *Il.* 12.127f., where Polypoetes and Leonteus defend the gate of the Greek camp; Macrobius tells us that there was a similar passage in Ennius, *Ann.* 15.

7 672. **creti:** 'born from', cf. 8.135.

quos Iovis eduxit luco silvestris Iaera[1]
abietibus[2] iuvenes[3] patriis et montibus aequos,
portam,[4] quae ducis imperio commissa, recludunt   675
freti armis, ultroque invitant moenibus hostem.
Ipsi intus dextra ac laeva pro turribus astant
armati ferro et [5]cristis capita alta corusci:
quales aeriae Liquetia[6] flumina circum[7]
sive [8]Padi ripis Athesim seu propter amoenum   680
consurgunt geminae quercus intonsaque caelo
attollunt capita et sublimi vertice nutant.
Inrumpunt aditus Rutuli ut videre patentis.[9]
Continuo Quercens et pulcher Aquiculus armis
et praeceps animi[10] Tmarus et Mavortius Haemon   685
agminibus[11] totis aut versi terga dedere
aut ipso portae posuere in limine vitam.
Tum magis increscunt animis discordibus irae,
et iam collecti Troes glomerantur eodem
et conferre manum et procurrere longius audent.   690
    Ductori Turno diversa in parte furenti
turbantique viros perfertur nuntius, hostem
fervere[12] caede nova et portas praebere patentis.
Deserit inceptum atque immani concitus ira

---

1 673. Iaera was a wood-nymph in the grove of Jupiter on Mt. Ida: in Homer (*Il.* 18.42) she was a Nereid.

2 **abietibus**: for the scansion with consonantal *i* see note on 8.599.

3 674. 'young men like the pine trees and mountains of their fatherland', a very striking phrase indeed. In the background of Virgil's picture are Homeric phrases like *Il.* 12.132 (the passage he is here following) 'they stood there like high oaks on the mountains'. *Il.* 5.560 two warriors fall 'like lofty pines', *Il.* 17.747 the two Ajaxes 'like a mountain ridge holding back a flood', *Od.* 9.191 Polyphemus like 'the peak of a mountain ridge'. The image is of giant stature and unyielding resistance, but its two parts do not quite cohere. The conjecture of Bryant (*in* for *et*) is very attractive, especially because of *Il.* 12.132 (cited above).

4 675. **portam**: the structure of this sentence is very striking; after the three lines describing the subject of the sentence there is a single word filling the first foot of the line as the object, followed by a relative clause before the verb finally completes the syntax.

5 678. 'their plumes waving high on their heads'; *capita* is Greek accusative of respect, see note on 596. For *corusci* = waving, cf. 1.164, 12.701; the point of comparison in the simile with the waving tops of trees (682) shows that this is the meaning, rather than 'glittering', describing their helmets.

6 679. **Liquetia flumina circum**: we have the testimony of Servius and late manuscripts for this reading, rather than the *liquentia* of the best manuscripts. This river (Livenza) flows into the Adriatic near Venice; it is also spelled *Liquentia*. For the adjectival form (*Liquetius* from the noun *Liquetia*) cf. *Lyaeus, Sychaeus* etc.

7 679f. For the simile compare 3.679f. (the Cyclopes fringing the shores like *aeriae quercus*), and Hom. *Il.* 12.131f.

8 680. 'or on the banks of the Po or by lovely Athesis'; Athesis (Adige) is north of the Po. Virgil, like Milton, is fond of geographical localisation of his similes, cf. line 710 and 7.674f., 10.708f.

9 683f. The names which follow are all Rutulian leaders, thrown back or killed by the Trojans.

10 685. **animi**: 'in mind', see note on 246.

11 686. **agminibus totis**: 'with all their followers'.

12 693. **fervere**: see note on 8.677.

Dardaniam ruit ad portam fratresque superbos.   695
Et primum Antiphaten (is enim se[1] primus agebat),
Thebana de matre nothum Sarpedonis alti,[2]
comecto sternit iaculo: volat Itala[3] cornus
aera[4] per tenerum stomachoque infixa sub altum
pectus abit; reddit specus[5] atri vulneris undam   700
spumantem, et fixo ferrum in pulmone tepescit.
Tum Meropem atque Erymanta manu, tum sternit Aphidnum,
tum Bitian ardentem oculis animisque frementem,
non iaculo (neque enim iaculo vitam ille dedisset),[6]
sed magnum[7] stridens contorta phalarica[8] venit   705
fulminis acta modo, quam nec duo taurea[9] terga
nec duplici squama lorica fidelis et auro
sustinuit; conlapsa ruunt immania membra,
dat tellus gemitum et clipeum super intonat ingens.[10]
Talis[11] in Euboico[12] Baiarum litore quondam[13]   710
saxea pila cadit, magnis quam molibus ante
constructam ponto[14] iaciunt, [15]sic illa ruinam
prona trahit penitusque vadis inlisa recumbit;
miscent se maria et nigrae attolluntur harenae,

---

1 696. **se primus agebat:** 'he was coming in front', cf. 6.337.

2 697. i.e. Antiphates was the illegitimate son of the famous Trojan Sarpedon by a woman from Thebe in Asia Minor.

3 698. **Itala cornus:** 'the Italian cornel-shaft', a more precise description of *iaculo*, cf. 12.267.

4 699. **aera per tenerum:** 'through the yielding air', cf. Lucr. 1.207.

5 700. **specus atri vulneris:** 'the black wound's chasm', a phrase of vivid horror.

6 704. Compare Hom. *Il.* 9.545 (of the Calydonian boar overwhelmed by men and dogs from many cities, for he would not have yielded to less) ου μην γαπ κε δαμη παυροισι βροτοισιν.

7 705. **magnum:** adverbial, cf. 631, 632.

8 **phalarica:** the massive spear used by the Saguntines with a three-foot blade (Livy 21.8.10); in Lucan it is propelled by a machine.

9 706. **taurea terga:** i.e. his shield of double oxhide. The next line refers to his coat of mail with small overlapping golden plates like scales. *Duplici squama . . . et auro* is hendiadys.

10 709. A fine line, with personification of Mother Earth and reminiscence of Homer's αραβησε δε τευχε επ αυτω (e.g. *Il.* 542). *Clipeum* (neuter) is a scarcer form than *clipeus*.

11 710f. The simile refers to the construction of piers or moles out in the sea; cf. Hor. *Odes* 3.1.34 *iactis in altum molibus*, Suet. *Claud.* 20, Vitr. 5.12. This kind of activity whether for private pleasure or military defence works was especially frequent in the area around Naples, Baiae and Cumae (which Virgil knew well); cf. *Geo.* 2.161, and A. G. McKay, *Vergil's Italy,* pp. 220f. The point of the simile is the crash caused by toppling a piece of masonry already constructed (*ante constructam*) of rocks and cement into the sea to provide a foundation for breakwaters or other buildings.

12 710. **Euboico:** a reference to the tradition that Cumae was founded by settlers from Euboea, cf. *Aen.* 6.2.

13 **quondam:**'sometimes', cf. 12.863.

14 712. **ponto:** dative (= *in pontum*), cf. 10.683.

15 712-13. 'so it leans and then crashes down, and hurled completely into the shallows lies at the bottom'.

tum sonitu Prochyta[1] alta tremit durumque cubile   715
Inarime[2] Iovis imperiis imposta Typhoeo.
   Hic Mars armipotens animum virisque Latinis
addidit et stimulos acris sub pectore vertit,
immisitque Fugam[3] Teucris atrumque Timorem.
undique conveniunt, quoniam data copia pugnae,   720
bellatorque animo[4] deus incidit.
Pandarus, ut fuso germanum corpore cernit
et quo sit fortuna loco, qui casus agat res,[5]
portam vi magna converso cardine torquet[6]
obnixus latis umeris, multosque suorum   725
moenibus exclusos duro in certamine linquit;
ast alios secum includit recipitque ruentis,
demens, qui Rutulum in medio non agmine regem
viderit[7] inrumpentem ultroque incluserit urbi,
immanem veluti pecora inter inertia tigrim.   730
Continuo nova lux oculis effulsit et arma[8]
horrendum sonuere, tremunt in vertice cristae
sanguineae[9] clipeoque micantia fulmina mittit.[10]
Agnoscunt faciem invisam atque immania membra[11]
turbati subito Aeneadae. Tum Pandarus ingens   735
emicat et mortis fraternae fervidus ira
effatur: [12]'non haec dotalis regia Amatae,

---

1 715. **Prochyta alta:** a nearby island, now Procida.

2 716. **Inarime:** also nearby, modern Ischia (cf. Hom. *Il.* 2.783). The tradition about the burial of the Giant Typhoeus varied: sometimes he was placed under Etna, and Enceladus under Inarime; see my note on 3.578f. (OUP Ed.).

3 719. For Fuga and Timor as part of the retinue of Mars. cf. Hom. *Il.* 4.440 Δειμος τ ηδε Φοβος; compare *Il.* 13.299 where Fear is a son of Mars, and *Aen.* 12.335f.

4 721. **animo:** dative, cf. *Geo.* 2.107.

5 723. For the rhythm cf. 320.

6 724. Notice the very heavy spondaic rhythm, beginning with the key word *portam* filling the first foot, and re-emphasised with *demens* (728).

7 729. **viderit . . . incluserit:** causal subjunctives, cf. 6.590-1. Notice the effect of the great word *inrumpentem* elided across the caesura.

8 731f. Turnus is a terrifying figure, like a Homeric hero (e.g. *Il.* 5.4f., 22.131f.). For *horrendum* adverbially cf. 632 and *Aen.* 12.700 *horrendumque intonat armis.*

9 733. Notice the trochaic caesura, characteristic of Greek and unusual in Latin, and here adding to the Homeric mood.

10 733. **mittit:** *P* and *R* have *mittunt,* which makes little sense; Nettleship conjectured *nictant* ('shine'), but *mittit* keeps the attention on Turnus.

11 734. Again a metrically emphatic line, with three elisions clustering around the caesurae.

12 737f. 'This is not the palace of Amata, her wedding present to you; and it's not the stronghold of Ardea protecting its Turnus with its ancestral walls. You have before you the camp of your enemy, and you cannot get out.' These are splendidly ironic and confident phrases, but they leave Turnus entirely unmoved, as we see in the slow spondees (740) describing his reaction.

nec muris cohibet patriis media Ardea Turnum.
Castra inimica vides, nulla hinc exire potestas.'
Olli subridens sedato pectore Turnus: 740
'incipe, si qua animo virtus, et consere dextram,
hic[1] etiam inventum Priamo narrabis Achillem.'
Dixerat. Ille rudem[2] nodis et cortice crudo
intorquet summis adnixus viribus hastam;
excepere aurae, vulnus Saturnia Iuno[3]   745
detorsit veniens,[4] portaeque infigitur hasta.
'At non hoc telum, mea quod vi dextera versat,[5]
effugies, neque enim is teli nec vulneris auctor':
sic ait, et sublatum alte consurgit[6] in ensem
et mediam ferro gemina inter tempora frontem   750
dividit impubisque immani vulnere malas.
Fit sonus, ingenti concussa est pondere tellus;
conlapsos artus atque arma cruenta cerebro
sternit humi moriens, atque illi partibus aequis
huc caput atque illuc umero ex utroque pependit.   755
    Diffugiunt versi trepida formidine Troes,
et[7] si continuo victorem ea cura subisset,
rumpere claustra manu sociosque immittere portis,
ultimus ille dies bello gentique fuisset.
Sed furor ardentem caedisque insana cupido   760
egit in adversos.
Principio Phalerim et succiso poplite Gygen
excipit, hinc[8] raptas fugientibus ingerit hastas
in tergus, Iuno viris animumque ministrat.

---

1 742. 'You will be able to tell Priam that you found another Achilles here', i.e. in the underworld you will meet your dead king again. Cf. Pyrrhus' words in 2.547f. Turnus himself confirms the words of the Sibyl in 6.89 *alius Latio iam partus Achilles*.

2 743. **rudem . . . crudo**: 'unpolished and knotted, with green bark', i.e. the spear has a rustic looking shaft.

3 745f. This kind of divine intervention is frequent in Homer, e.g. *Il.* 20.438f., where Athena turns aside Hector's spear.

4 746. **veniens:** with *vulnus,* not with *Iuno;* cf. 412.

5 747-8. Turnus' speech is abruptly introduced, and the final phrase is cryptic, apparently meaning that the man (i.e. himself) who wields the weapon (in this case a sword) and inflicts the wound is not one from whom escape is possible. For *auctor* cf. line 421.

6 749. **consurgit in ensem**: cf. 10.797, 12.729.

7 757f. ' and if the thought had immediately come to him in his moment of victory to break the bolts forcibly and let his friends in through the gates, that would have been the last day of the war and of the Trojan people, but frenzy and mad lust for slaughter drove him on in his hot passion against the foe'. Here the failing of Turnus is clearly pinpointed: all his ambition could have been realised had it not been for the evil qualities of frenzy and bloodlust. These are the qualities which Aeneas tries throughout the poem to control in himself, with more success than Turnus, but still only very imperfectly.

8 763. **hinc raptas . . . hastas**: 'the spears which he snatched from them,' cf. 12.330.

Addit Halyn comitem et confixa Phegea[1] parma,   765
ignaros deinde in muris Martemque cientis
Alcandrumque[2] Haliumque Noemonaque Prytanimque.
Lyncea tendentem contra sociosque vocantem
vibranti gladio conixus ab[3] aggere dexter
occupat, huic uno deiectum comminus ictu   770
cum galea longe iacuit caput. Inde ferarum
vastatorem Amycum, quo non felicior[4] alter
unguere tela manu ferrumque armare veneno,
et Clytium Aeoliden et amicum[5] Crethea Musis,
Crethea[6] Musarum comitem, cui carmina semper   775
et citharae cordi[7] numerosque[8] intendere nervis,
semper equos atque arma virum pugnasque canebat.[9]

    Tandem ductores audita caede suorum
conveniunt Teucri, Mnestheus acerque Serestus,
palantisque vident socios hostemque receptum.   780
Et Mnestheus: [10]'quo deinde fugam, quo tenditis?' Inquit.
'quos alios muros, quae iam ultra moenia habetis?[11]
Unus homo et vestris, o cives, undique saepius
aggeribus tantas strages impune per urbem
ediderit?[12] Iuvenum primos tot miserit Orco?   785
Non infelicis patriae veterumque deorum
et magni Aeneae, segnes, miseretque[13] pudetque?"
Talibus accensi firmantur et agmine denso

---

1 765. **Phegea:** Greek accusative of *Phegeus;* cf. *Lyncea* (768), *Crethea* (774).

2 767. The Homeric list of names (*Il.* 5.678) keeps its Greek rhythm, with trochaic caesura, lengthening of a short *e* (see note on 8.425), and polysyllabic ending.

3 769-70. **ab aggere dexter occupat:** 'attacked him from the rampart on the right'; Turnus has climbed on to the walls (766), and thrusts with his sword at Lynceus from the right.

4 772-3. **felicior . . . unguere:** 'more successful at smearing'; for the epexegetic infinitive cf. 6.165; for poisoned arrows cf. Hom. *Od.* 1.261f., *Aen.* 10.140.

5 774. **amicum . . . Musis:** cf. Hor. *Odes* 1.26.1 (of himself) *Musis amicus.*

6 775. For the repetition of the words *Cretheus* and *Musae* cf. 10.180-1, and see note on 7.586f.

7 776. **cordi:** 'his delight', see note on 615.

8 **numerosque intendere nervis:** 'to set tunes for the strings'.

9 777. Notice the irony of this line: war poetry is different from war.

10 781. 'Where are you directing your flight after this then?' For *deinde* cf. 5.741.

11 782. Cf. Hom. *Il.* 15.735f. (Ajax to the Greeks), and Scipio's speech to the Romans in Livy 21.41.15.

12 785. **ediderit . . . miserit:** for this use of the future perfect ('is it going to be true that he has ...?') cf. 2.581-2, 4.591.

13 787. **miseretque pudetque:** 'are you not both sorry and ashamed when you think of . . . ?' The genitive is natural with *miseret* and this makes clear its meaning with *pudet*, 'ashamed before . . .'. The rhyme of fifth and sixth foot is rhetorically impressive.

consistunt. Turnus paulatim excedere[1] pugnae
et fluvium petere ac partem quae cingitur anda.   790
Acrius hoc Teucri clamore incumbere magno
et[2] glomerare manum, ceu saevum turba leonem
cum telis premit infensis: at territus ille,
asper,[3] acerba tuens, retro[4] redit et neque terga
ira dare aut virtus patitur, nec tendere contra   795
ille[5] quidem hoc cupiens potis[6] est per tela virosque.
Haud aliter retro dubius[7] vestigia Turnus
improperata[8] refert et mens exaestuat ira.
Quin etiam bis tum medios invaserat[9] hostis,
bis confusa fuga per muros agmina vertit;   800
sed manus e castris propere coit omnis in unum
nec contra[10] viris audet Saturnia Iuno
sufficere;[11] aeriam caelo nam Iuppiter Irim[12]
demisit germanae haud mollia iussa ferentem,[13]
ni Turnus cedat Teucrorum moenibus altis.   805
Ergo[14] nec clipeo iuvenis subsistere tantum[15]
nec dextra valet, iniectis sic undique telis
obruitur. [16]Strepit adsiduo cava tempora circum

---

1 789. **excedere pugnae:** 'began to withdraw from the fight'; *excedere* is historic infinitive, and *pugnae* probably genitive of separation (rather than dative), in imitation of the Greek construction, cf. Hor. *Odes* 2.9.17, 3.27.70, 3.29.5, and see note on 10.441. Many editors read *pugna* with *M*, but *pugnae* (*P, R*) would be more likely to be corrupted into *pugna* than *vice versa*.

2 792f. 'As when a crowd of huntsmen with their deadly weapons closely pursue a fierce lion'; for *premere* cf. 1.324, 8.249; for the simile cf. Hom. *Il*. 11.544f. (Ajax in retreat), and *Il*. 17.108f., 657f.

3 794. **asper, acerba tuens:** from Lucr. 5.33; *acerba* is adverbial, cf. 125, 632.

4 **retro redit:** 'backs away'.

5 796. **ille quidem hoc cupiens:** 'though he longed to', cf. 10.385 *ille quidem hoc sperans.*

6 **potis est:** an archaic turn of phrase for *potest,* cf. 3.671, 11.148.

7 797. **dubius:** like the lion, he does not want to back away, and keeps wondering whether there is anything else he can do.

8 798. **improperata:** 'unhurried'; the word occurs only here.

9 799. **invaserat:** the pluperfect, strangely used here, gives the feeling that his two attacks were over and done with; we know from the tense that they were vain before we are told so (801).

10 802. **contra:** adverbial; Juno dare not give him strength to deal with them.

11 803. **sufficere:** mostly poetic in this transitive sense, cf. 2.618. Contrast 810, where it is intransitive.

12 **Irim:** Jupiter sends Juno's own messenger down to her; Juno seems to be pictured as in some sense present on the battlefield.

13 804-5. The construction is elliptical: Iris carries severe commands: if Turnus does not withdraw, i.e. she says what will happen if he does not.

14 806f. The picture of Turnus under pressure is based on *Il*. 16.102f. (Ajax) and Ennius (*Ann*. 401-8: a soldier in the Histrian war). Compare also Capaneus at the end of Stat. *Th*. 10.

15 806. **tantum:** 'enough', *tantum quantum opus est,* cf. 5.21.

16 808f. 'His helmet around his curving brows rang all the time with the clash of blows, the solid bronze was cracked by rocks, the plumes were knocked off his head, his shield could not withstand the battering.' Hirtzel and Mynors punctuate after *iubae,* but *capiti* surely goes with *discussae.* It is probably dative (cf. 10.462) rather than ablative (7.668).

tinnitu galea et saxis solida aera fatiscunt
discussaeque iubae capiti nec sufficit umbo   810
ictibus; ingeminant[1] hastis et Troes et ipse
fulmineus[2] Mnestheus. [3]Tum toto corpore sudor
liquitur et piceum (nec respirare potestas)
flumen agit, [4]fessos quatit aeger anhelitus artus.
Tum demum praeceps saltu sese omnibus armis[5]   815
in fluvium dedit. Ille suo cum gurgite flavo
accepit venientem ac mollibus extulit undis
et laetum sociis abluta caede remisit.

---

1 811. **ingeminant hastis:** 'they redouble their efforts with their spears', for *ingerminant* intransitive cf. 1.747.

2 812. **fulmineus:** like the lightning, cf. 442.

3 812f. 'The sweat poured down all his limbs and formed a river of pitch', i.e. it was black from the dust and dirt of battle.

4 814. 'his heavy breathing shook his weary body', cf. 5.432.

5 815f. The Tiber saves Turnus and lifts him up on its gentle wave because it was his river before it became Trojan. The reader cannot help thinking of Horatius Cocles leaping into the river after holding the bridge against Lars Porsena; Livy 2.10.11 *tum Cocles 'Tiberine pater' inquit, 'te sancte precor, haec arma et hunc militem propitio flumine accipias'. Ita sic armatus in Tiberim desiluit multisque superincidentibus telis incolumis ad suos tranavit.*

BOOK 10

Introductory note

The tenth book, like the ninth, is very largely taken up with battle scenes; only in the two scenes in Olympus (1.117, 606-32) and in the description of the return of Aeneas (146-307) are we away from the fighting. (On Virgil's battle scenes see the introductory note to Book 9.) A central part is played by the account of the death of Pallas, an event which proves so crucial later, since it motivates the final scene in which Aeneas kills Turnus because he is wearing the spoils he stripped from Pallas.

The account of Pallas' death (see note on 439f.) is coloured with that sense of pathos which Virgil expresses more poignantly than any other Roman poet (cf. Euryalus' death, 9.433f.), and the pathos is resumed in the description of his funeral at the beginning of Book 11. Similarly the death of Lausus (see note on 769f.) expresses Virgil's intense feeling of the futility and waste of the death in war of those whose qualities might have been used for the benefit of humanity. This is not so with Mezentius, whose death at Aeneas' hands closes the book; his cruelty and wickedness make his death a reason for rejoicing among those who had suffered at his hands. Yet even here Virgil succeeds in arousing a certain pathos, a certain grudging admiration for the way he meets his end.

Turnus and Aeneas play very large parts in this book; Turnus' behaviour is characteristic of what we expect of him, while that of Aeneas is not. In his combat with Pallas Turnus shows all the arrogant self-confidence of the Homeric hero, confident in his valour and jealous of his honour, making no concessions (see note on 439f.). He knows he can win, and he sets about doing so. In the process he alienates the reader's sympathy by his cruel and boastful behaviour, and Virgil comments on the narrative to reflect how Turnus' failure to show moderation in victory will lead to his downfall (501f). The reader is made to feel that vengeance must come.

When Aeneas learns of the death of Pallas he gives way to reckless frenzy, and kills all who cross his path on the battlefield. We seem to be back again in the wild scenes of the second book, when Aeneas showed all the savage bravery of the heroic warrior. All the lessons of the subsequent years, as Aeneas strove to find a better way, a more controlled and rational approach to crisis and danger, are now forgotten as he kills indiscriminately, taunts his defeated enemies, shows himself to have all the qualities which in Turnus caused the reader deep disquiet.

When the youthful Lausus encounters Aeneas to try to save his father's life, Aeneas still shows the same savage attitude (*furit,* 802, *saevae . . . irae,* 813). But at the moment of killing Lausus suddenly a revulsion comes over Aeneas, and a sense of pity and sorrow as he speaks gently to his victim and picks him up in his arms. Now he is different indeed from Turnus when he killed Pallas; now indeed we can see the qualities in Aeneas which can lead to the advancement of human civilisation, as those of Turnus could not. This is the aspect of Aeneas which harmonises with the theme of the *Aeneid;* here is *misericordia, dementia, humanitas;* here is the warrior who must oppose violence with violence, yet hesitates in doing so. But this is in victory; after the defeat of Pallas, beset by guilt and fury, Aeneas could not show these qualities. It would have been easier for Virgil to pretend that even in wild grief his hero would show the self-control and humanity that we all admire; but it was truer to what Virgil knew of real human behaviour to present Aeneas otherwise.

1-15. *Jupiter calls a council of the gods in Olympus, and urges them to cease from stirring up warfare between the Trojans and Italians; the time for strife will be when Juno's Carthage attacks Venus' Rome.*

¹Panditur² interea domus omnipotentis³ Olympi
conciliumque vocat divum⁴ pater atque hominum rex
sideream in sedem, terras unde arduus omnis
castraque Dardanidum⁵ aspectat populosque Latinos.
Considunt tectis⁶ bipatentibus, incipit ipse: 5
'caelicolae magni, quianam⁷ sententia vobis
versa retro tantumque animis certatis iniquis?
Abnueram⁸ bello Italiam concurrere Teucris.
Quae contra⁹ vetitum discordia? Quis metus aut¹⁰ hos
aut hos arma sequi ferrumque lacessere suasit?   10
Adveniet iustum pugnae, ne arcessite, tempus,
cum¹¹ fera Karthago Romanis arcibus olim

---

1 1f. The council in Heaven (the only one in the *Aeneid*) is based especially on Hom. *Il.* 8.1f. (cf. also *Il.* 4.1f., 15.1f., 20.1f.). It was a feature of epic which Ennius used (*Ann.* 1.60f., *Ann.* 8), and Virgil has several echoes of Ennian style (2, 5, 6) to help to achieve a formal and sonorous opening to the scene.

2 1. 'Meanwhile the house of all-powerful Olympus is opened', i.e. a new day dawns and the gates of heaven are opened; cf. 1.374 (of sunset) *ante diem clauso componat Vesper Olympo,* and Hom. *Il.* 5.749f., Ov. *Met.* 1.112-13 *rutilo palefecit ab ortu / purpureas Aurora fores.*

3 **omnipotentis Olympi**: the same phrase in 12.791, Jupiter's epithet *omnipotens* is transferred to heaven, visualised here as his palace.

4 2. **divum pater atque hominum rex**: the phrase is from Ennius, and occurs also in line 743 and 1.65; the monosyllabic ending gives an archaic and formal ring. See Page ad loc, and cf. 107, 361, 9.532.

5 4. **Dardanidum**: archaic for *Dardanidarum;* see note on 8.127.

6 5. **tectis bipatentibus:** 'in the palace with its gates at each end', i.e., as Servius explains, to symbolise that it stretches from east to west. The rare word *bipatens* (taken from Ennius) is used once elsewhere by Virgil (2.330, of double gates).

7 6. **quianam**: 'why?', again an Ennian word, cited by Quintilian as an archaism; cf. 5.13.

8 8. **abnueram:** 'I had forbidden',for the construction cf. Lucr. 3.641.

9 9. **contra vetitum:** 'in defiance of my ban'.

10 9-10. **aut hos . . . suasit:** *hi . . . hi* are the Trojans and Italians; Jupiter implies that they have been caused to fear by the intervention of some of the gods.For the accusative and infinitive with *suadere* cf. 366-7, 12.813, Lucr. 1.140f., and see note on 1.357. Notice the jerky rhythm of the ending of line 9, helping perhaps to reflect Jupiter's indignation.

11 12-13. 'when fierce Carthage will one day bring upon Roman strongholds great destruction, breaching the Alps'. The construction is very condensed, with a marked zeugma of the verb *immittet.* The reference is to the invasion of Italy through the Alps by Hannibal in 218 B.C.; cf. 6.842f. for the Roman answer to Hannibal.

exitium magnum atque Alpis immittet apertas:
tum certare odiis, tum res[1] rapuisse licebit.
Nunc sinite[2] et placitum[3] laeti componite foedus.'   15

> 16-95. *Venus makes an indignant speech, bitterly complaining at Juno's interventions and the Trojan setbacks, and ironically suggesting that as all else is lost Jupiter should at least save the life of little Ascanius, Juno angrily replies, maintaining that the Trojan disasters have not been caused by her, and that any assistance she may give to the Rutulians is justified.*

[4]Iuppiter haec paucis; at non Venus aurea[5] contra
pauca refert:[6]
'o pater, o hominum[7] rerumque aeterna potestas
(namque aliud quid sit quod iam implorare queamus?),
Cernis ut insultent Rutuli, Turnusque feratur[8]   20
per medios insignis equis tumidusque secundo
Marte ruat? Non clausa tegunt iam moenia Teucros;
quin[9] intra portas atque ipsis proelia miscent
aggeribus murorum et inundant[10] sanguine fossae.
Aeneas[11] ignarus abest. Numquamne levari   25
obsidione sines? Muris iterum imminet rostis[12]
nascentis Troiae nec non exercitus alter,

---

1 14. **res rapuisse:** 'plunder each other'; the infinitive is 'timeless', cf. 625.

2 15. **sinite:** used absolutely, 'refrain', 'leave it'.

3 **placitum:** 'that I have decreed', cf. 1.283.

4 16f. The interchange of angry speeches between the two goddesses is in marked contrast with the serenity of the previous scene and Jupiter's opening speech. The rhetorical power is comparable with the interchanges between Drances and Turnus (11.343f.), and the two speeches contain, as Servius points out, many of the devices of formal rhetoric; he tells us that rhetorical theorists used them as examples of *controversiae.* Particularly noticeable is the irony used heavily by both goddesses (29-30, 42-3) 53-5, 61-2, 75, 89), and the reply of Juno is built largely on the repetition of Venus' phraseology and arguments either to refute them or merely contemptuously to quote them as she makes her own points (65, 74, 75, 76, 85, 86, 89). The main feature of this passage is that the rhetoric is not used, as it is,for example, in Dido's speeches in Book 4, in order to involve the reader deeply with the speaker, but in order to produce an intellectually satisfying display of verbal dexterity.

5 16. **aurea:** a Homeric epithet of Aphrodite.

6 17. For the half line see note on 7.129; others in this book are 284, 490, 580, 728, 876.

7 18. **hominum:** for hiatus after *o* cf. *Geo.* 2.486.

8 20f. The deeds of Turnus outside and inside the Trojan camp were told at length in the second half of Book 9; they were in fact done on foot, not on horseback, but Venus is more concerned with rhetorical effect than with factual accuracy.

9 23. **quin:** 'infact', like *quin etiam,* cf. 470, 570 and 9.465.

10 24. **inundant ...fossae:** 'the ditches overflow', cf. 11.382, the same phrase. Some MSS have *fossas* ('they flood the ditches'), but in the only other place where Virgil has the word (12.280) it is intransitive.

11 25. Throughout Books 8 and 9 Aeneas has been away from the Trojan camp, getting assistance from Evander and assuming the command of the forces entrusted to him; his return is described at 147f.

12 26f. The theme of another siege of the new Troy by the Rutulians (like the ten year siege of the old city by the Greeks) is emphasised by Turnus in 9.142f.

atque iterum in Teucros Aetolis surgit ab Arpis[1]
Tydides. [2]Equidem credo, mea vulnera restant
et tua progenies mortalia demoror arma.   30
Si sine pace tua atque invito numine Troes
Italiam petiere, luant peccata neque illos
iuveris auxilio; sin tot responsa secuti[3]
quae superi manesque dabant, cur nunc tua quisquam[4]
vertere iussa potest aut cur nova condere fata?   35
Quid repetam exustas Erycino in litore classis,[5]
quid tempestatum[6] regem ventosque furentis
Aeolia excitos aut actam[7] nubibus Irim?
Nunc etiam manis[8] (haec intemptata manebat
sors[9] rerum) movet et superis immissa repente   40
Allecto medias Italum bacchata per urbes.
Nil super imperio moveor; speravimus ista,[10]
dum fortuna fuit; vincant, quos vincere mavis.
Si nulla est regio Teucris quam det tua coniunx[11]
dura, per eversae, genitor, fumantia Troiae   45
excidia obtestor: liceat dimittere ab armis
incolumem Ascanium, liceat superesse nepotem.

---

1 28f. The son of Tydeus, Diomedes, the Aetolian, one of the leading Greek warriors who fought against Troy, had settled in Arpi in S. Italy, and an embassy was sent by Turnus asking for help (8-9f.). The refusal of Diomedes is told in 11.225f.

2 29-30. 'I do indeed believe that wounds are still in store for me, and that I your offspring am delaying the attack of a mortal'. Venus alludes to the attack made upon her, and her wound at the hands of Diomedes, as told in Hom. *Il.* 5.336f. Sarcastically she suggests that Jupiter is prepared to allow the same thing to happen again, and that by not being on the battlefield she is keeping Diomedes waiting.

3 33-4. Throughout the *Aeneid* Aeneas has received prophecies and visions telling him to seek Italy, particularly from Apollo and Mercury (*superi*) and the ghosts of Hector and Anchises (*manes*).

4 34. **quisquam**: notice the rhetorical impact of this pronoun which is used in negative sentences, implying 'surely nobody can'; cf. line 65, 1.48, 11.392.

5 36. Cf. 5.606f., the description of the firing of the ships near Mt. Eryx in Sicily by the Trojan women, involving the destruction of four of them.

6 37f. This refers to the storm aroused at Juno's instigation by Aeolus, king of the winds, which are imprisoned on his island Aeolia (1.50f.).

7 38. **actam . . . Irim**: 'Iris, coming by way of the clouds'; the same phrase in 9.18, where see note. Iris was Juno's special messenger and intervened to cause the burning of the ships (5.607f.) and to arouse Turnus to attack the Trojan camp (9.2f.).

8 39f. **manis . . . movet**: in 7.312 Juno had threatened *flectere si nequeo superos, Acheronta movebo,* and had summoned the fiend Allecto from the underworld to the world above (*superis*) to arouse Turnus and Amata to frenzy. The image of *bacchata* had been applied to Amata under Allecto's influence (7.385, 405). Supply *est* to *immissa* rather than to *bacchata.*

9 40. **sors rerum**: 'province of the universe'; *sors* means 'allocated part', i.e. the realm of Pluto.

10 42-3. The irony of these brief clauses is very powerful indeed; Jupiter had said to Venus (1.279) *imperium sine fine dedi;* now she states that she has given up hope of the great promises, and only wants to plead for her little grandson Ascanius to be saved from the wreck of all her hopes. She does not, of course, mean a word of what she says.

11 44f. Cf. 1.233 where Venus complains to Jupiter *cunctus ob Italiam terrarum clauditur orbis,* because (251) of the wrath of one goddess Juno of course.

Aeneas sane ignotis iactetur in undis[1]
et quacumque viam dederit Fortuna sequatur:
hunc tegere [2]et dirae valeam subducere pugnae.   50
Est Amathus, est celsa mihi Paphus atque Cythera[3]
Idaliaeque domus: positis inglorius armis
exigat hic aevum. [4]Magna dicione iubeto
Karthago premat Ausoniam: nihil urbibus inde
obstabit Tyriis. [5]Quid pestem evadere belli   55
iuvit et Argolicos medium fugisse per ignis
totque maris vastaeque exhausta pericula terrae,
dum Latium Teucri recidivaque[6] Pergama quaerunt?
Non[7] satius cineres patriae insedisse supremos
atque solum quo Troia fuit? Xanthum[8] et Simoenta   60
redde, oro, [9]miseris iterumque revolvere[10] casus
da, pater, Iliacos Teucris.' Tum regia Iuno
acta furore gravi: 'quid me alta silentia cogis
rumpere et obductum[11] verbis vulgare dolorem?
Aenean hominum quisquam[12] divumque subegit   65

---

1 48-9. Venus seems to suggest that Aeneas may again have to undertake the kind of perilous voyage which has been already his fortune; or possibly she refers with rhetorical exaggeration to his journey up the Tiber; this at all events is how Juno understands her (69).

2 50. 'but grant me the power to protect this my grandson and save him from the grim battle'; *valeam* is subjunctive of a prayer; *pugnae* is dative, cf. 615, 12.157.

3 51-2. These seats of Venus' worship are in Cyprus, except for Cythera, an island off the south of Greece from which she has her frequent epithet *Cytherea* (8.523, 615). *Amathus* is a third declension word with long final syllable for Paphus cf. 1.415, for Idalia (sometimes Idalium) cf. 1.693.

4 53-5. 'Be sure to give orders for Carthage to overwhelm Ausonia beneath her mighty sway; there shall be no opposition from that quarter to the cities of Tyre'. This is the most bitterly ironic part of all Venus' speech, that Rome should yield to Carthage (founded by Dido from Tyre, 1.340) without opposition is an unthinkable travesty of history. Notice the irony of the emphatic imperative *iubeto* (cf. 3.388); for the jussive subjunctive following it in parataxis cf. 258, 7.546.

5 55-6. 'What has been the use of their having escaped the plague of war . . .?'for *evadere* in this sense cf. 5.689. Venus refers in this phrase and the next to the burning of Troy by the Greeks, and then in the next line to the long wanderings described in Book 3.

6 58. **recidivaque Pergama:** 'a reborn Troy', cf. 1.206, 4.344, 7.322, 8.36f.

7 59f. 'Would it not have been better for them to have stayed in the burnt wreckage of their fatherland, in the place where Troy once stood?'for *satius* cf. *Ecl.* 2.14.

8 60. **Xanthum et Simoenta:** the rivers of Troy, cf. 1.473, 618. The quadri-syllabic ending as well as the form of the accusative *Simoenta* gives a Greek form to the phrase.

9 61-2. 'grant,father, to the Trojans, that they may again endure the whole cycle of the fortunes in Ilium'. Dryden conveys the meaning well:
'To Simois' banks the fugitives restore,
And give them back to war and all the woes before'.
Venus' angry irony is based on the thought that after all their sufferings the Trojans are supposed to be destined for a glorious future; if this is not so, they might as well return home and endure all over again the miseries of Troy's destruction.

10 **revolvere . . . da:** for *dare* with the infinitive cf.235 and 9.173.

11 64. **obductum . . . dolorem:** 'reveal in words the anger I have kept hidden'; Servius says that the metaphor in *obductum* is from the scar over a wound; cf. Cic. *Leg. Agr.* 3.4 *ne refricare obductam iam reipublicae cicatricem viderer.*

12 65. **quisquam:** picking up Venus' words in 34.

bella sequi aut hostem regi se inferre Latino?
Italiam petiit fatis auctoribus (esto[1])
Cassandrae impulsus furiis: num linquere castra[2]
hortati sumus aut vitam committere ventis?
Num puero summam belli, num credere muros, 70
Tyrrhenamque[3] fidem aut gentis agitare quietas?
Quis deus in fraudem,[4] quae dura potentia nostra[5]
egit? Ubi hic Iuno demissave nubibus Iris?
Indignum[6] est Italos Troiam circumdare flammis
nascentem[7] et patria Turnum consistere[8] terra, 75
cui Pilumnus avus, cui diva Venilia mater:[9]
quid face[10] Troianos atra vim ferre Latinis,
arva aliena iugo[11] premere atque avertere praedas?
Quid[12] soceros legere et gremiis abducere pactas,
pacem orare manu,[13] praefigere[14] puppibus arma? 80
Tu potes Aenean manibus subducere Graium[15]
proque viro nebulam et ventos obtendere inanis,
et potes in totidem classem convertere nymphas:[16]
nos aliquid[17] Rutulos contra iuvisse nefandum est?

---

1 67. **esto:** 'let it be so', i.e. 'I grant it', a rhetorical device (*concessio,* Quint, 9.2.51) used by Juno also in 7.313, 12.821. Juno cannot deny that the fates authorised Aeneas to seek Italy, but she ridicules the importance of the mission by associating it with the mad prophecies of the Trojan priestess Cassandra (cf. 2.246, 3.183).

2 68-9. Juno suggests that the difficulties Aeneas has now put the Trojans in, by leaving them leaderless while he went to Evander on a risky voyage, are none of her doing; for the infinitive with *hortari* cf. 2.33; *hortati sumus* is the regal plural in which the masculine, not the feminine, is used.

3 71. 'or to tamper with Etruscan loyalty and peaceful tribes?' Juno exaggerates again: the Etruscans had no reason for loyalty towards their exiled king Mezentius who was on Turnus' side.

4 72. **fraudem:** 'harm', cf. 11.708.

5 **nostra:** preferable to *nostri,* the reading of the first hand of *M.*

6 74. **indignum est:** i.e. you say it's wrong for your side to suffer; then what about, *a fortiori,* the greater wrong we are suffering (77f.)?

7 75. **nascentem:** your newborn Troy, ironically picking up Venus' words (27).

8 **consistere:** 'standfirm', refuse to withdraw from his rights.

9 76. If Venus claims that Aeneas' ancestry is impressive, then Turnus equally has a goddess mother (cf. 6.90 *natus et ipse dea*), the sea-nymph Venilia, and his grandfather (or great-grandfather, line 619), was Pilumnus (9.4), a Roman agricultural deity.

10 77. 'what of the Trojans attacking the Latins with black torches?' *Face atra* is highly pictorial, cf. 9.74.

11 78. **iugo premere:** 'to oppress with their yoke', i.e. rule; cf. 8.148.

12 79. 'what about their choosing whose daughters they will marry and wrenching pledged brides from their husbands' embraces?' The plurals are rhetorical; only Aeneas so far is guilty of the charge. *Legere* suggests an arrogant confidence, 'taking their pick'; normally the future father in law would do the picking from would-be sons-in-law.

13 80. **manu:** 'with outstretched hands', cf. 8.116, 11.332.

14 **praefigere . . . arma:** 'yet displaying weapons on their ships', cf. 8.92f.

15 81f. Cf. 1.39f., 242f. for similar arguments about what was permitted to others. The reference here is to the story told in Homer (*Il.* 5.315f.) of how Aphrodite saved Aeneas from Diomedes and Apollo concealed him in a cloud.

16 83. This was done by Cybele, 9.80f., Juno presumably assumes that Venus was behind the deed.

17 84. **aliquid . . . contra:** 'in some way in return', both words are adverbial.

"Aeneas ignarus abest": ignarus et absit.[1]   85

Est Paphus Idaliumque tibi, sunt alta Cythera:[2]

quid gravidam bellis urbem et corda aspera temptas?

Nosne tibi fluxas[3] Phrygiae res vertere fundo

conamur? Nos? An miseros[4] qui[5] Troas Achivis

obiecit? [6]Quae causa fuit consurgere in arma   90

Europamque Asiamque et foedera solvere furto?

Me duce Dardanius Spartam expugnavit[7] adulter,[8]

aut ego tela dedi fovive Cupidine bella?

Tum decuit metuisse tuis: nunc sera querelis

haud iustis adsurgis et inrita iurgia iactas.'[9]   95

96-117. Jupiter refuses to side with either of the goddesses and says he will remain impartial, allowing the fates to find a way.

[10]Talibus orabat Iuno, cunctique fremebant

caelicolae adsensu[11] vario, [12]ceu flamina prima

cum deprensa fremunt silvis et caeca volutant

murmura venturos nautis prodentia ventos.

Tum pater omnipotens, rerum cui prima potestas,   100

---

1 85. Again Juno echoes Venus' words (25); this time she makes no counter-argument, contenting herself with the hope that Venus' grounds for complaint may continue to exist.

2 86. This echoes 51-2, and Juno turns the point of Venus' words to a contemptuous suggestion that she would be better staying in her own area rather than meddling in wars; cf. Diomedes' taunt to Aphrodite in Hom. *Il.* 5.348f.

3 88. **fluxas**: 'frail', not uncommon in prose, but unusual in verse.

4 89. **miseros**: another ironic echo of Venus' speech (61).

5 89-90. **qui . . . obiecit**: i.e. Paris (*Dardanius adulter,* 92). *Troas* is Greek accusative with short final syllable, cf. 11.263.

6 90-1. 'What caused Europe and Asia to rise up for battle and by trickery to break the laws of hospitality?' The last phrase refers to Asia alone, Juno is stressing the guilt of Asia, and here as in the next line strongly hinting that the cause behind Paris's rape of Helen from Sparta was Venus herself. For *causa . . . consurgere* (= *consurgendi*) cf. Lucan 5.464.

7 92. **expugnavit**: 'laid siege to', rhetorically exaggerating the deeds of Paris.

8 92-3. Notice the emphasis on *me* and *ego,* implying that the truth requires *te* and *tu.* The implication becomes crystal clear with the word *Cupidine* in 93.

9 95. The absence of strong caesura in the third or fourth foot gives a line of unusual rhythm for Juno's final words.

10 96f. The relationship between Jupiter, the fates, and the human actors is here more explicit than elsewhere in the poem. The longterm fate cannot be destroyed by human or divine opposition, and Jupiter must see that it comes true, but the way it comes about, the time of its achievement, indeed its very nature is dependent upon the conflicting forces in heaven and, in particular, on the mortal actors who are the essential agents of heaven. See notes on 106, 111-13, Otis, pp. 353-4, Camps, pp. 42f. ('the texture, so to speak, of the ordinances of fate is loose').

11 97. **adsensu vario**: i.e. in support either of Juno or of Venus, cf. 11.296.

12 97-9. 'like the first rustlings of wind caught in woodland, sending forth unseen murmurs, revealing to sailors the gales that are imminent'; cf. *Geo.* 1.356f. For *caeca* cf. 12.591; for *volutant* 5.149. Compare Milton, *P.L.* 2.284f. (where the comparison is with the end, not the beginning, of a storm):

'He scarce had finished, when such murmur filled

Th'Assembly, as when hollow Rocks retain

The sound of blustring winds, which all night long

Had rous'd the Sea, now with hoarse cadence lull

Seafaring men o'erwatched . . .'

437

infit (eo dicente deum domus alta silescit
et tremefacta solo tellus, silet arduus aether,
tum Zephyri posuere,[1] premit placida aequora pontus):
'accipite ergo animis atque haec mea figite dicta.
Quandoquidem Ausonios coniungi foedere Teucris   105
haud[2] licitum, nec vestra capit discordia finem,
quae[3] cuique est fortuna hodie, quam quisque secat spem,
Tros Rutulusne fuat, nullo discrimine habebo,
seu fatis Italum castra obsidione tenentur
sive errore malo Troiae monitisque sinistris.   110
nec[4] Rutulos solvo. Sua cuique exorsa laborem
fortunamque ferent. Rex Iuppiter omnibus idem.
fata viam invenient.' Stygii per flumina fratris,[5]
per pice torrentis [6]atraque voragine ripas
adnuit et totum nutu tremefecit Olympum.   115
Hic finis fandi. Solio tum Iuppiter aureo[7]
surgit, caelicolae medium quem ad limina ducunt.

---

1 103. **posuere:** *se posuerunt,* cf. 7.27. Notice the strong alliteration of *p* in this line. *Placida* is predicative, 'controls and calms'.

2 106. **haud licitum:** cf. 344. Jupiter means that in view of the attitudes of Juno and Venus he cannot insist on his request for peace (15). But, he goes on to say, he will not be moved by either of the goddesses, he will leave fate to decide. It is of course fated that Aeneas is in the end to prevail, but the time and the methods are always open to change through either mortal or divine activity.

3 107-8. 'I will make no distinction whether he be Trojan or Rutulian in the fortune which each man will have today, or the hope which each pursues'. For *secare* ('carve out') cf. 6.899, 12.368, but Servius may be right in regarding the word as an old form of *sequi.* Notice how the monosyllabic ending with alliteration conveys an archaic and impressive effect (see note on line 2), like the old form *fuat* (= *sit*) which is not uncommon in Plautus and Terence; it occurs once in Lucretius (4.637), and only here in Virgil.

4 111-13. 'Nor do I exempt the Rutulians. Each man's endeavours will bring him his suffering and his success. King Jupiter is impartial: the fates will find a way'. As the Trojans have already been shown to be in the worse position, Jupiter now states that he is not favouring the Rutulians. The final phrases are reminiscent of Hom. *Il.* 8.10f., but are more striking in Virgil because of the more positive part played by Jupiter in the destiny of man. Here they convey that the will of the fates, which Jupiter will not permit to be made void, is nevertheless dependent on the human actors; Aeneas and the Trojans receive help from Jupiter when most in need, but they must themselves achieve their destiny.

5 113-15. The words from *Stygii . . . Olympum* are repeated from g.104-6, where see notes.

6 109-10. 'whether the camp is blockaded because of the fates of the Italians or because of a foolish mistake by the Trojans and misleading advice'; Jupiter is not prepared to reveal whether the Italian success is due to fate temporarily supporting them, or the human folly of the Trojans.

7 116. **aureo:** a spondee by synizesis, cf. 129, 378, 487, 496, 764 and see note on 7.33. For the ending of the council cf. Milton, *P.L.* 2.506f.
'The Stygian Council thus dissolved, and forth
In order came the grand infernal Peers;
Midst came their mighty Paramount . . .'

118-45. The Rutulians continue to attack the Trojan camp.

[1]Interea Rutuli portis[2] circum omnibus instant
sterne re caede viros et moenia cingere flammis.
At legio Aeneadum[3] vallis[4] obsessa tenetur   120
nec spes ulla fugae. Miseri stant turribus altis
nequiquam et rara[5] muros cinxere corona:
Asius[6] Imbrasides Hicetaoniusque Thymoetes
Assaracique duo et senior cum Castore Thymbris,
prima acies; hos germani Sarpedonis ambo[7]   125
et Clarus et Thaemon Lycia comitantur ab alta.
Fert ingens toto conixus corpore saxum,
haud partem exiguam montis, Lyrnesius[8] Acmon,
nec Clytio genitore minor nec fratre Menestheo.
Hi iaculis, illi certant defendere saxis   130
molirique[9] ignem nervoque aptare sagittas.
Ipse inter medios, Veneris iustissima[10] cura,
Dardanius caput, [11]ecce, puer detectus honestum.
Qualis[12] gemma micat fulvum quae dividit aurum,
aut collo decus aut capiti, vel quale per artem   135
inclusum buxo aut Oricia terebintho

---

1 118f. The narrative now resumes from the end of Book 9, when in Aeneas' absence Turnus' exploits had brought the besieged Trojan camp under extreme pressure.

2 118-19. **portis ... viros:** 'all around at every gate press forwards to kill their enemies'; for the infinitive with *instare* cf. 2.627, and cf. line 130.

3 120. **Aeneadum:** for the form of the genitive cf. lines 4 and 564.

4 **vallis:** 'within their ramparts', cf. 9.142, 598.

5 122. **rara ... corona:** 'ring the walls with a thin line'; for *corona* cf. 9.508, 11.475.

6 123. These names are taken from Homer (*Il.* 3.146, 147, 12.96); in the next line the two Assaraci are called after Assaracus, grandfather of Anchises (9.259).

7 125-6. Clarus and Thaemon are brothers of Sarpedon, the famous warrior from the mountainous land of Lycia (cf. 471 and 1.100). *Comitantur* suggests that they form a second line behind the warriors named in 123-4 as being *prima acies*.

8 128-9. Again the names are Homeric; Lyrnesus was in the Troad. Menestheus is different from Mnestheus (143); notice the scansion of *-eo* as one syllable by synizesis, cf. 116.

9 131. **molirique ignem:** 'and to wield fire', i.e. to hurl blazing brands; cf. *Geo.* 1.329.

10 132. **iustissima cura:** Ascanius was Venus' proper care as her grandson (cf. 1.678) and also because of his destiny ('de quo merito curet, quia ei debebatur imperium', Servius).

11 133. 'behold the Trojan boy, his handsome head uncovered'; for the retained accusative cf. 157, 838, and see note on 7.503. The meaning is that Ascanius is un-helmeted because he is not taking part in the fighting, Apollo had forbidden him to do so (9.656).For *honestum = pulchrum*, a mainly poetic use, cf. *Geo.* 2.392.

12 134f. 'like a shining jewel set in yellow gold, an ornament for a necklace or a diadem, or like ivory glistening when skilfully inset in boxwood or Orician terebinth-wood'. Compare for the image the beautification of Aeneas in 1.592f., and for ivory 12.67f. Terebinth is a black wood (Pliny, *N. H.*, 13.54); Oricum is a town in N. Greece, cf. Prop. 1.8.20, 3.7.49. Notice the hiatus at the caesura of 136 (cf. 141, 156) and the quadri-syllabic ending, giving a Greek rhythm appropriate to the subject matter.

lucet ebur; [1]fusos cervix cui lactea crinis
accipit et molli subnectens circulus auro.
Te quoque magnanimae[2] viderunt, Ismare, gentes
vulnera[3] derigere et calamos armare veneno,[4]   140
Maeonia generose domo,[5] ubi[6] pinguia culta
exercentque viri Pactolusque inrigat auro.
Adfuit et Mnestheus,[7] quem pulsi pristina Turni
aggere murorum sublimem gloria tollit,
et Capys:[8] hinc nomen Campanae ducitur urbi.   145

> *146-62. Aeneas returns by sea with a contingent of Etruscan forces; with him are the Etruscan king, Tarchon, and Evander's young son, Pallas.*

[9]Illi inter sese duri certamina belli
contulerant:[10] media[11] Aeneas freta nocte secabat.
Namque[12] ut ab Euandro castris ingressus Etruscis
regem adit et regi memorat nomenque genusque
quidve petat quidve ipse ferat, [13]Mezentius arma   150
quae sibi conciliet, violentaque[14] pectora Turni

---

1 137-8. 'His flowing locks fell over his milk-white neck, and a circlet of pliant gold encompassed them'; cf. 5.559.

2 139. **magnanimae:** a strange epithet here, perhaps linked with *generose* (141) and referring to the noble followers of Ismarus of Maeonia (cf. 9.546).

3 140. **vulnera derigere:** 'directing blows', cf. 7.533, 9.745.

4 **veneno:** cf. 9.773.

5 141. There is hiatus at the caesura after *domo*; cf. 136.

6 141-2. 'where men work the fertile fields and Pactolus waters them with gold'; Servius tells the story of King Midas washing away his 'golden touch' in this Lydian river.

7 143. Mnestheus' part in checking Turnus' successes was told in 9.779f.

8 145. Capys has already been mentioned several times; here Virgil pauses to link him etymologically with the famous Campanian town of Capua. For Virgil's fondness for etymological links of this kind cf. especially 5.117f., and notes on 7.1, 682f.

9 146f. This is the first mention of Aeneas' actions since 8.606, when we heard of his leaving Evander in company with Pallas and making a rendezvous with Tarchon near Caere. Throughout the whole of Book 9 the besieged Trojans were managing as well as they could without him. Now he returns by sea, sailing south to the mouth of the Tiber.

10 147. **contulerant:** the tense indicates that the battles described had finished before the narrative turns to Aeneas.

11 **media . . .freta:** 'the midst of the waters', i.e. the sea between Caere and Ostia. Servius mentions the possibility of taking *media* with *nocte,* which is much less likely; cf. 5.1.

12 148-9. 'For when after leaving Evander and entering the Etruscan camp he approached the king . . .'. The main verbs to this sentence are *fit, iungit,ferit* (153-4). The Etruscan camp is that of King Tarchon; for the dative with *ingressus,* a rare use, cf. 763.

13 150-1. 'and what he was seeking and offering, what armed forces Mezentius was winning to his side . . .'. The doubled *-ve* is used instead of *-que* to avoid repetition with the doubled *-que* of the previous line. For Mezentius, the exiled Etruscan, see note on 7.648; the reference is to his alliance with Turnus (8.492-3).

14 151. **violentaque:** the adjective *violentus* and the noun *violentia* are used of no one but Turnus in the *Aeneid;* see notes on 7.406f., 12.9.

edocet, humanis[1] quae sit fiducia rebus
admonet immiscetque preces, haud fit mora, Tarchon
iungit opes foedusque ferit; tum libera[2] fati
classem conscendit iussis gens Lydia divum   155
externo commissa duci. Aeneia puppis[3]
prima[4] tenet rostro[5] Phrygios subiuncta[6] leones,
imminet [7]Ida super, profugis gratissima Teucris.
Hic magnus sedet Aeneas secumque volutat
eventus belli varios, Pallasque[8] sinistro   160
adfixus[9] lateri iam quaerit sidera, opacae
noctis iter,[10] iam quae passus terraque marique.

163-214. Virgil makes a new invocation to the Muse and then gives a list of the Etruscan allies of Aeneas as they sail south with him to join the war against Mezentius and Turnus.

[11]Pandite nunc Helicona, deae, cantusque movete,[12]

---

1 152-3. **humanis . . . admonet**: 'while he warned him of what men must rely on in mortal affairs', i.e. their own resolution and actions and foresight;for the phrase cf. 2.75.

2 154. **libera fati**: the Lydian people (i.e. the Etruscans under Tarchon, cf. 8.479) are 'free from fate' in the sense that they have met their obligations to the demands of fate that they should choose a foreign leader (8.503). The genitive *fati* is in imitation of the Greek construction after ελευθερος, cf. Eur. *Phoen.* 999; compare Hor. *A.P.* 212 *liberque laborum*, Livy 5.28.1 *voti liberari*.

3 156. Notice the hiatus at the caesura, cf. 136, 141.

4 157. **prima tenet**: 'leads', cf. 5.338.

5 **rostro . . . leones**: 'with Phrygian lions attached to its beak', i.e. as the lower part of the figure-head, Mt. Ida being the upper part. The lions (cf. 253) are those of Cybele, the *Magna Mater* of Mt. Ida near Troy (cf. 3.113); the Trojan fleet was made of pinewood from Mt. Ida and was sacred to Cybele. This ship is surely thought of as Aeneas' original Trojan ship (the main fleet having been turned into nymphs during Aeneas' absence to save it from being burnt by Turnus, 9.80f.). We may guess (though Virgil has not told us) that it was sent to Caere to meet Aeneas in response to a message (8.546f).

6 **subiuncta leones**: retained accusative with a passive verb, see note on 133.

7 158. The image of Mt. Ida, looming over the lions as part of the figurehead, is *gratissima* because it reminds the Trojans of home.

8 160. **Pallas**: Evander's son, sent by him to aid Aeneas (8.514f.).

9 161. **adfixus**: 'keeping close to' (cf. 5.852), in order to question Aeneas about the stars and the adventures (*quae passus sit*) of his voyage.

10 162. **iter**: in apposition to *sidera;* the stars are said to be the pathway of Aeneas through the night because they guide his path; this is more likely than that the stars are the route of the night through the sky.

11 163f. The first line of the invocation is the same as that used (7.641) to introduce Virgil's previous catalogue, that of the Italian forces under Turnus. The use of the catalogue as a traditional piece of epic machinery has been discussed in the note on 7.641f.; this second catalogue, a naval one, is closer inform to the Homeric original (*Il.* 2.484f, which is in the main a catalogue of Greek ships before it passes to a briefer list of the Trojan land forces.
The structure of this catalogue is closely analysed by Mackail ad loc.: the thirty ships (213) are divided into five groups of six: six with Massicus, six with Abas, six with Asilas, six with Astyr and Cunarus and Cupavo, six with Ocnus and Aulestes. For these Etruscan peoples see A. G. McKay, *Vergil's Italy,* pp. 86f. Three aspects of the presentation command special interest as varying the subject matter; firstly the glimpse of a supernatural world in the story of the metamorphosis of Cycnus; secondly the ambiguity of the Centaur (195) and the Triton (209), where the phraseology suggests sometimes a ship, sometimes its figurehead, sometimes the mythological creature itself (compare the description of Atlas, mountain and man, in 4.246f. and see Quinn, pp. 216f.); and thirdly the personal note introduced by the description of the contingent from Virgil's home-town, Mantua, with the reference to its mixed population and the beauty of the river Mincius flowing out of Lake Benacus.

12 163. The same verse in 7.641, where it is also followed by indirect questions ('telling what company ...'). *Helicona* is the Greek accusative form of Helicon, mountain of the Muses.

quae manus interea Tuscis comitetur ab oris
Aenean armetque[1] rates pelagoque vehatur.   165
Massicus[2] aerata[3] princeps secat aequora Tigri,
sub quo mille manus iuvenum, qui moenia Clusi[4]
quique urbem liquere Cosas,[5] quis[6] tela sagittae
gorytique[7] leves umeris et letifer arcus.
Una torvus Abas: huic[8] totum insignibus armis   170
agmen et aurato fulgebat Apolline puppis.
Sescentos illi dederat Populonia[9] mater
expertos[10] belli iuvenes, ast Ilva[11] trecentos
insula inexhaustis Chalybum generosa metallis.
Tertius ille hominum divumque interpres Asilas,[12]   175
cui pecudum fibrae, caeli cui sidera parent[13]
et linguae volucrum et praesagi fulminis ignes,
mille rapit[14] densos acie atque horrentibus hastis.
Hos[15] parere iubent Alpheae ab origine Pisae,
urbs Etrusca solo. Sequitur pulcherrimus Astyr,   180
Astyr equo fidens et versicoloribus[16] armis.
Ter centum adiciunt[17] (mens omnibus una sequendi)

---

1 165. **armetque rates:** 'mans the ships', cf. 4.299.

2 166. Massicus is a name taken from Mt. Massicus in Campania. Servius says 'Sane sciendum amare Vergilium ducibus Italis dare nomina vel fluviorum vel montium', and cites Almo and Aventinus as other examples; Conington adds Sulmo, Clarus and Anxur as names taken from towns.

3 **aerata . . . Tigri:** for ship names cf. 5.116f.; doubtless the Tigris would have a tiger as its figurehead.

4 167. **Clusi:** Clusium (town of Lars Porsena) was a very famous Etruscan city (Livy 5.35) near Lake Trasimene; cf. 655.

5 168. **Cosas:** Cosae (more often called Cosa) was on the coast north of Graviscae (184).

6 **quis:** = *quibus*, cf. 435.

7 169. **goryti:**'quivers', cf. Ov. *Trist.* 5.7.15.

8 170-1. **huic . . . puppis:** 'his whole company were resplendent in conspicuous armour and his ship shone with its gold figure of Apollo'; the reference is to the image of the ship's tutelary deity, cf. Ov. *Trist.* 1.10.1.

9 172. **Populonia mater:** his 'motherland' Populonium was on the coast just opposite Ilva (Elba).

10 173. **expertos belli:** genitive of respect (cf. 225, 563, 630-1, 666), not common with *expertus*, cf. Tac. *Hist.* 4.76.

11 173-4. Ilva is mentioned twice by Pliny as rich in iron; for the Chalybes (blacksmiths) see note on 8.421.

12 175. For the prophetic skill of the Etruscan Asilas compare generally Helenus in 3.359f.; the reference here is to divination from inspection of entrails, from astrology, auspices and lightning.

13 176. **parent:** 'obey', an exaggerated word because Asilas is master not of the events but only of their interpretation. Servius' suggestion, supported by Mackail, that the word is equivalent to *apparent*, 'are clear', is unlikely.

14 178. **rapit:** 'hastens along with him', cf. 308, 574, 660, 7.725.

15 179-80. **hos . . . solo:** 'Pisae, an Etruscan city in situation, Alphean in origin, orders these to obey him'. The Etruscan city of Pisae (Pisa) was founded by settlers from the city of the same name in Elis, near the river Alpheus.

16 181. **versicoloribus:** 'flashing', of changing colours.

17 182. **adiciunt:** the subject is vague, 'they' being the whole expedition; we might say 'in addition there were 300 . . .'.

qui Caerete[1] domo, qui sunt Minionis in arvis,
et Pyrgi veteres intempestaeque[2] Graviscae.
Non ego te, Ligurum ductor fortissime bello,   185
transierim, Cunare[3], et paucis[4] comitate Cupavo,
cuius olorinae surgunt de vertice pennae,
crimen,[5] Amor, vestrum formaeque[6] insigne paternae.
Namque ferunt luctu Cycnum Phaethontis amati,
populeas inter frondes umbramque sororum[7]   190
dum canit et maestum musa solatur amorem,
canentem [8]molli pluma duxisse senectam
linquentem terras et sidera voce sequentem.
Filius[9] aequalis comitatus[10] classe catervas
ingentem remis Centaurum[11] promovet: ille   195
instat aquae saxumque undis immane minatur
arduus, et longa sulcat maria alta carina.
Ille etiam patriis agmen ciet Ocnus[12] ab oris,
fatidicae Mantus[13] et Tusci filius amnis,
qui muros matrisque dedit tibi, Mantua, nomen,   200

---

1 183. **Caerete domo**: 'from their homes in Caere', cf. 8.114 *unde domo?* There was also a contingent from this important Etruscan town fighting for the other side, under Lausus (7.652); the river Minio and the towns Pyrgi and Graviscae were in the region of Caere, to the north.

2 184. **intempestaeque Graviscae**: 'unhealthy Graviscae', an etymological epithet, as Servius says, quoting Cato: 'ideo Graviscae dictae sunt, quod gravem aerem sustinent'. Day Lewis probably rightly translates 'malarial'.

3 186. Cunarus (the form of the spelling is very doubtful) and Cupavo were leaders of the Ligurians (to the north of Etruria) with which area the legend of Cycnus and Phaethon was associated (Ov. *Met.* 2.370; the story of the metamorphosis of Cycnus into a swan is told there). For the addition of Cupavo after the singular *te* referring to Cunarus cf. *Geo.* 2.101f.

4 **paucis comitate**: 'accompanied by few', cf. 1.312 *comitatus Achate;* for the use of the vocative cf. 327 and 8.38.

5 188. **crimen, Amor, vestrum**: it was the fault of Love (a 'reproach' to Love, cf. Prop. 1.11.30), that Cycnus could not bear the loss of his beloved friend Phaethon (consumed by fire as he drove the sun's chariot) and so was changed into a swan; for the plural *vestrum* cf. 1.140, 9.525.

6 **formaeque insigne paternae**: 'the emblem of his father's metamorphosis'; the swan feathers on his helmet are the emblem (- *que* is explanatory).

7 190. The sisters of Phaethon, mourning inconsolably for his death, were turned into poplar trees and their tears into amber (Ov. *Met.* 2.340f.).

8 192-3. 'took on the whiteness of old age with his soft plumage as he left the earth and sought the stars with his song'.

9 194. **filius**: i.e. Cupavo.

10 **comitatus**: here 'accompanying' (contrast 186, 'accompanied by'). Both usages are common.

11 195. **Centaurum**: this was the name of one of the ships in the games in 5.155. *Ille* refers to the Centaur figurehead of the ship, brandishing a rock which threatens the waves (for the construction cf. 11.348); at *sulcat* the ship itself becomes the subject.

12 198. Servius identifies Ocnus, founder of Mantua (the town near which Virgil himself was born), with Bianor (*Ecl.* 9.60). He is the son of Manto (probably an Italian borrowing of Manto the daughter of the Theban seer Teiresias) and the Tuscan river, i.e. the Tiber (8.473). Servius comments on the fact that this is the only contingent from the Transpadine area, much further north than any of the others: 'putetur poeta in favorem patriae suae hoc locutus'.

13 199. **Mantus**: Greek third-declension genitive, cf. *Clius* (from *Clio*),Ov. *A.A.* 1.27.

Mantua[1] dives avis, sed non genus omnibus unum:
gens illi triplex, populi sub gente quaterni,
ipsa caput populis, Tusco de sanguine vires.
Hinc quoque quingentos in se Mezentius[2] armat,
quos[3] patre Benaco velatus harundine glauca   205
Mincius infesta ducebat in aequora pinu.
It gravis Aulestes centenaque arbore fluctum[4]
verberat adsurgens, spumant vada marmore verso.
Hunc vehit immanis[5] Triton et caerula concha
exterrens freta, [6]cui laterum tenus hispida nanti   210
frons hominem praefert, in pristim desinit alvus,
spumea semifero sub pectore murmurat unda.
    Tot lecti proceres ter denis navibus ibant
subsidio Troiae et campos[7] salis aere secabant.

> *215-59. Aeneas on his return is met by the nymphs into whom the Trojan fleet had been changed. One of them, Cymodocea, tells him of Turnus' attack on his camp, and warns him to be ready for battle. Aeneas, with a prayer to Cybele, prepares for action.*

[8]Iamque dies caelo concesserat almaque[9] curru   215
noctivago Phoebe medium pulsabat Olympum:
Aeneas (neque enim membris dat cura quietem)

---

1 201f. The three races of Mantua are probably Etruscans, Gauls, Veneti; each had four peoples so that Virgil refers to a group like the twelve Etruscan cities mentioned in Livy 5.33.9, making Mantua itself head of them. In Virgil's time Etruscan influence was still strong in Mantua, though not elsewhere so far north.

2 204. **Mezentius armat**: i.e. causes them to go to war because of their hatred of him.

3 205-6. 'whom the river Mincius coming from father Benacus veiled in grey reeds led down to the sea in their fighting ships'; the river Mincius flows out of the southeast corner of Lake Garda (Benacus, *Geo.* 2.160) into the Po. We had better not ask how these ships reached the other side of Italy. For the imagery of Mincius veiled in reeds cf. the Tiber in 8.33f.

4 207. The transition to Aulestes (brother of Ocnus) in his ship Triton is abrupt. *Gravis* means something like 'mighty', having reference to his enormous ship with its hundred tree trunks for oars; with the verb *adsurgens* he is identified with his crew.

5 209-10. **immanis Triton et . . . exterrens**: 'the Triton, huge and terrifying . . .'; *et* links *immanis* with *exterrens*. Again the reference is to the figurehead depicting the sea god Triton, Neptune's trumpeter (cf. 6.171f.).

6 210-12. 'whose shaggy front as he swam was of human appearance to the waist, but his body ended in the form of a whale, and the foaming wave splashed beneath his half-human shape'. This bipartite Triton (cf. Ap. Rh. 4.1610f.) is reminiscent of Scylla (3.426f.); for *pristis (pistrix)*, a kind of sea-monster, cf. also the ship in the games in 5.154.for the phrase cf. Hor. *A.P.* 4 *desinat in piscem mulier formosa superne.* Notice the imitative alliteration of *s* in 212 and the predominantly dactylic rhythm.

7 214. **campos salis**: 'the fields of sea', cf. 8.695, *Geo.* 3.198.

8 215f. The resumption of the story of how Cybele turned the Trojan fleet into nymphs (see note on 9.77f.) briefly re-introduces the mythical fairytale world of Ovid's *Metamorphoses* into the hard reality of the battle scenes. It affords an attractive glimpse of supernatural powers intervening in the mortal world before Virgil returns again to the description of fighting which fills the rest of this book.

9 215-16. **almaque . . . Olympum**: 'and the kindly moon was riding in her night-wandering chariot through the middle of the sky'; a night and a day have passed since the first mention of the voyage of Aeneas and his Etruscan allies (147). The moon, like the sun (5.739) and like night (3.512, 5.721, where see note), drives through the sky in her chariot; for *noctivagus* cf. Lucr. 5.1191,for the phrase *pulsabat Olympum* cf. Enn. *Ann.* 1 *Musae quae pedibus magnum pulsatis Olympum.*

ipse sedens clavumque regit velisque ministi at.
Atque[1] illi medio in spatio chorus, ecce, suarum
occurrit comitum: nymphae, quas alma Cybebe[2]   220
numen[3] habere maris nymphasque e navibus esse
iusserat, innabant pariter fluctusque secabant,
quot prius aeratae steterant ad litora prorae.
Agnoscunt longe regem lustrantque[4] choreis.
Quarum quae fandi doctissima Cymodocea[5]   225
pone sequens dextra puppim tenet ipsaque[6] dorso
eminet ac laeva tacitis subremigat[7] undis.
Tum sic ignarum adloquitur: 'vigilasne, deum[8] gens,
Aenea? Vigila et velis[9] immitte rudentis.
Nos sumus, Idaeae sacro de vertice pinus,[10]   230
nunc pelagi nymphae, classis tua. Perfidus[11] ut nos
praecipitis ferro Rutulus flammaque premebat,
rupimus[12] invitae tua vincula teque per aequor
quaerimus. Hanc[13] genetrix faciem miserata refecit
et dedit[14] esse deas aevumque agitare sub undis.   235
At puer Ascanius muro fossisque tenetur
tela inter media atque horrentis Marte Latinos.
Iam loca iussa tenet forti[15] permixtus Etrusco

---

1 219. **atque:** 'and suddenly', cf. 572 and 6.162.

2 220f. The story of how the goddess Cybele (here, as often, called Cybebe), turned the Trojan ships into nymphs to save them from being burnt by Turnus is told in 9.77f., where see note.

3 221. **numen habere maris:** 'to have power over the sea', to be sea-deities.

4 224. **lustrantque choreis:** 'and circle him in dance', cf. 7.391.

5 225. For the nymph Cymodocea cf. 5.826 and Spenser, *F.Q.* 4.11.50: 'And she, that with her least word can assuage / The surging seas, when they do sorest rage, / Cymodoce . . .'. The phrase *quae fandi doctissima* has an Ovidian ring which seems strange in Virgil; *fandi* is genitive of respect, cf. 173.

6 226-7. **ipsaque dorso eminet:** 'emerging waist-high', cf. Cat. 64.14f., which Virgil surely has in mind (cf. line 230 with Cat. 64.1).

7 227. **subremigat:** 'paddles', literally 'rows', rather attractively reminding us that the nymph had recently been a ship.

8 228. **deum gens:** the monosyllabic ending is abrupt, attracting the attention.

9 229. **velis immitte rudentis:** 'let out the ropes on the sails', i.e. the sheets, to secure full speed, cf. 8.708 and for *rudentis* 3.267.

10 230. Aeneas' ships were made of trees sacred to Cybele which grew on Mt. Ida near Troy (252); cf. 9.80f.

11 231-2. **perfidus . . . premebat:** 'when the treacherous Rutulian attacked us headlong with sword and fire'; notice the indignant alliteration of *p*, and the emphasis on *perfidus* preceding the conjunction *ut*. The line ending again is abrupt (cf. 228).

12 233. **rupimus . . . vincula:** cf. 9.118 *continue puppes abrumpunt vincula ripis.*

13 234. **hanc . . .faciem . . . refecit:** 'refashioned us into this shape', cf. 9.122. *Genetrix* is Cybele, the Great Mother (cf. 9.82).

14 235. **dedit esse:** for the infinitive with *dare* cf. line 61.

15 238. **forti . . . Etrusco:** singular for plural, like *eques* in the next line.

Arcas[1] eques; medias illis opponere turmas,
ne[2] castris iungant, certa est sententia Turno.   240
Surge age et Aurora socios veniente vocari
primus[3] in arma iube, et [4]clipeum cape quem dedit ipse
invictum ignipotens atque oras ambiit auro.
Crastina lux, mea[5] si non inrita dicta putaris,
ingentis Rutulae spectabit[6] caedis acervos.'   245
Dixerat et dextra discedens impulit altam[7]
haud[8] ignara modi puppim: fugit illa per undas
ocior et iaculo et ventos aequante sagitta.
inde aliae celerant cursus. Stupet inscius ipse
Tros Anchisiades,[9] animos tamen omine tollit.   250
Tum breviter supera aspectans convexa precatur:
'alma parens Idaea deum, cui[10] Dindyma cordi[11]
turrigeraeque urbes biiugique[12] ad frena leones,
tu mihi nunc pugnae princeps, tu rite propinques[13]
augurium Phrygibusque adsis pede, diva, secundo.'   255
Tantum effatus, et interea revoluta[14] ruebat
matura iam luce dies noctemque fugarat;
principio sociis[15] edicit signa sequantur
atque animos aptent armis pugnaeque parent se.

---

1 239. **Areas eques:** presumably a contingent of Evander's forces (8.518) joined Tarchon's Etruscans (8.603) and were sent by land while Pallas and others accompanied Aeneas by sea.

2 240. **ne castris iungant:** 'so that they cannot link up with the Trojan camp'; *iungant* here is intransitive, equivalent to *iungant se* (cf. 362 and 1.104).

3 242. **primus:**'straight away'.

4 242-3. Cymodoce refers to the shield which Vulcan (*ignipotens*) had made for Aeneas (8.625f.).

5 244. **mea . . . putaris:** a rather strange equivalent for 'if you follow my instructions'. *Putaris* is contracted future perfect.

6 245. **spectabit:** most of the good MSS have *spectabis,* which may well be right, giving an archaic and colloquial construction to *crastina lux* ('come tomorrow, you will see . . .'). Servius quotes Lucilius *hinc media remis Palinurum pervenio nox,* but prefers to read *spectabit.*

7 246-8. The passage is reminiscent of the push given to Cloanthus by the sea-god Portunus at the end of the boat-race (5.241f.); cf. also Ap. Rh. 2.598f.

8 247. **haud ignara modi:** she had been a ship herself, and knew how this ship would respond.

9 250. **Anchisiades:** cf. 822, where Aeneas' patronymic is used with particular force. Here there is no special effect.

10 252. **cui Dindyma cordi:** 'whose delight Mt. Dindyma is'; *cordi* is predicative dative, cf. 9.615.

11 252f. For these attributes of Cybele cf. 230 (*Idaea*), 9.618f. (*Dindyma*), 6.784f. (*turrigerae*), and line 157 (*leones*); see also Lucr. 2.604f.

12 253. **biiugique adfrena leones:** 'and twin lions yoked together in harness', cf. Lucr. 2.601.

13 254-5. **propinques augurium**: 'hasten the fulfilment of your prophecy', literally 'make it close'; cf. the use of *propius* in 8.78 *adsis o tantum et propius tua numina firmes.* This transitive use of *propinquare* is rare; cf. Sil. 2.281.

14 256-7. **revoluta . . .fugarat:** 'the day in its revolving course was now hastening onwards in its full brightness, and had put night to flight', cf. 2.250, 3.508, 6.539.

15 258. **sociis edicit signa sequantur:** 'he ordered the crews to follow out instructions'; for the jussive subjunctive in parataxis cf. 3.234f., *sociis tunc arma capessant / edico.* Observe the pattern of alliteration in this and the following line.

260-86. Aeneas as he approaches lifts high his shield and the Trojans shout in joy at his return. Light flashes from his armour, like a comet or Sirius, but Turnus is not dismayed and urges his troops to be ready for battle.

[1]Iamque in conspectu Teucros habet et sua castra   260
stans celsa in puppi, clipeum cum[2] deinde sinistra
extulit ardentem. Ciamorem ad sidera tollunt
Dardanidae e muris, spes addita suscitat iras,
tela manu iaciunt, quales sub nubibus atris[3]
Strymoniae dant[4] signa grues atque aethera[5] tranant   265
cum sonitu, fugiuntque Notos clamore[6] secundo.
At Rutulo regi ducibusque ea mira videri[7]
Ausoniis, donec versas ad litora puppis
respiciunt totumque[8] adlabi classibus aequor.
Ardet[9] apex capiti cristisque[10] a vertice flamma   270
funditur et vastos umbo vomit aureus ignis:

---

1 260f. The confrontation of the two leaders is presented powerfully; Aeneas with his shining armour and the shield Vulcan made for him, a resplendent and terrifying sight like Augustus at Actium (see note on 261); Turnus undaunted as ever, showing the *fiducia* and *audacia* (276) which marks him out as the leader of his men.

2 261. **cum deinde:** 'when promptly'; inverted *cum* is here strengthened by *deinde* (like *tum deinde*); he waited till he could see his camp, *then* he raised his shield. The pictorial impact of this sentence is most vivid; Aeneas himself is now like the picture of Augustus at Actium depicted on his shield (8.680, *stans celsa in puppi,* cf. 261; with his head surrounded by light, cf. 270f.).

3 264f. The simile of the cranes is based on Hom. *Il.* 3.2f., where the noise of the Trojans moving to battle is compared with that of cranes attacking the Pygmies. Cf. also Lucr. 4.181f. *ille gruum . . . clamor in aetheriis dispersus nubibus austri.* The epithet *Strymoniae* (from Thrace) is used of cranes also in *Geo.* 1.120, *Aen.* 11.580.

4 265. **dant signa:** probably 'call to each other', rather than 'give indications' of a storm.

5 **aethera tranant:** 'fly across the sky', cf. 4.245.

6 266. **clamore secundo:** 'with glad sounds', cf. 5.491, the same phrase, and 8.90 *rumore secundo,* and note there. This is Servius' interpretation and seems better than 'with the noise following them'.

7 267. **videri:** historic infinitive, conveying suddenness, cf. 288, 299.

8 269. **totumque . . . aequor:** 'and the whole sea rolling in upon them with ships', a most extraordinary phrase, to their startled eyes the sea rolls in not as usual with waves, but with ships. To explain the phrase as hypallage for 'ships rolling in from the whole sea' is not merely an impossibly mechanical way of treating language, but also a way of destroying the remarkable boldness of the phrase.

9 270. **ardet apex capiti:** a rather abrupt resumption of the description of Aeneas (from 262). *Apex* (properly the cone of the helmet into which the plume is set) here means generally 'his helmet'. *Capiti* could be dative, or local ablative (cf. 7.668).

10 270-1. **cristisque . . .funditur:** 'and from the plume at the top flames pour forth'; the exaggeration of brightness into actual fire prepares for the simile. Notice the heavy alliteration in the next phrase.

non secus [1]ac liquida si quando nocte cometae
sanguinei lugubre[2] rubent, aut Sirius[3] ardor
ille sitim morbosque ferens mortalibus aegris
nascitur et laevo[4] contristat[5] lumine caelum.   275
Haud tamen audaci Turno fiducia cessit[6]
litora praecipere et venientis pellere terra.[7]
[ultro animos tollit dictis atque increpat ultro:][8]
'Quod votis optastis adest, perfringere[9] dextra.
In[10] manibus Mars ipse viris. Nunc coniugis esto[11]   280
quisque suae tectique memor, nunc[12] magna referto
facta, patrum laudes. Ultro occurramus ad uadam
dum[13] trepidi egressisque labant vestigia prima.
Audentis Fortuna iuvat.'[14]
Haec ait, et secum versat quos ducere contra   285

---

1 272f. 'Just as when sometimes blood-red comets blaze ill-omened in the clear night, or the burning dog-star rises, bringing as he does drought and disease to unhappy mortals, making the sky mournful with his inauspicious light'. The second part of the simile is based on Hom. *Il.* 22.26f. where Achilles' armour gleams like the dog-star of Orion, 'brightest of the stars, yet a sign of evil bringing much fever on wretched mortals' — . . .κακον δε τε σημα τετυκται, / και τε φερει πολλον πυρετον δειλοισι βροτοισιν. The effect of Aeneas' return to the scene of battle is to bring as certain disaster on his enemies as Achilles' return did. Compare also *Il.* 5.4f. where Diomedes' armour shines like the autumn star, brightest of all, i.e. the dog star; and Ap. Rh. 3.956f., where Jason is like Sirius. The first half of the simile has a historical rather than a literary reference, and recalls the comet that appeared shortly after Julius Caesar's death (cf. 8.680-1 and *Geo.* 1.488 *diri . . . arsere cometae*). Compare Milton, *P.L.* 2.706f.

On th' other side
Incenst with indignation Satan stood
Unterrifi'd, and like a Comet burnd,
That fires the length of Ophiucus huge
In th' Arctic Sky, and from his horrid hair
Shakes Pestilence and Warr.

2 273. **lugubre:** adverbial accusative, cf. *Ecl.* 3.63 *suave rubens hyacinthus;* compare 572, 664, 726.

3 **Sirius ardor:** the noun form *Sirius* is used as an adjective, cf. 1.686.for Sirius cf. 3.141 (the plague in Crete).

4 275. **laevo:** cf. *Aen.* 2.54.

5 **contristat ... caelum:** cf. *Geo.* 3279 (of the storm wind) *pluvio contristat frigore caelum.* Here however the use of *contristat* is much more striking, almost an oxymoron, when used of a bright object.

6 276. Cf. 9.126, almost the same line describing Turnus' reaction to the metamorphosis of the ships into nymphs.

7 277. For the infinitive after *fiducia* cf. 712, 715 and see note on 1.704.

8 278. This line (= 9.127) is omitted by *M* and *P* and should be regarded as spurious.

9 279. **perfringere dextra:** 'to crush them by force'; the infinitive is in apposition to the clause *quod votis optastis.*

10 280. **in manibus . . . viris:** 'Mars himself is in the hands (i.e. deeds) of brave men', cf. Hom. *Il.* 16.630 and contrast Turnus' taunt to Drances (11.389f.) *an tibi Mavors / ventosa in lingua pedibusque . . .* (Mars is in his tongue and feet). *R* has *viri,* vocative, which is less forceful.

11 280-1. Cf. Hom. *Il.* 15.662, Livy 21.41.16.

12 281-2. **nunc . . . laudes:** 'now let each perform again the mighty deeds that brought glory to our fathers'; *referto* is third person with *quisque* (*P* has *referte*).

13 283. 'while they are anxious, and immediately after disembarking their tread is uncertain'; i.e. before they have their land legs. *Egressique* is read by some MSS and older editors, but gives an extraordinary construction for *vestigia* (accusative of respect).

14 284. This famous proverb occurs in Latin as early as Ennius (*Ann.* 257 *fortibus est fortuna viris data*) and Terence (*Phorm.* 203 *fortes fortuna adiuvat*).

vel quibus obsessos¹ possit concredere muros.

287-307. Aeneas' men disembark; Tarchon runs his ship at the shore, and it breaks its back on a sandbank.

²Interea Aeneas socios de puppibus altis
pontibus³ exponit. ⁴Multi servare recursus
languentis pelagi et brevibus⁵ se credere saltu,
per remos alii. Speculatus litora Tarchon,   290
qua⁶ vada non sperat nec⁷ fracta remurmurat unda,
sed mare inoffensum⁸ crescenti adlabitur aestu,
advertit subito proram sociosque precatur:
'nunc, o lecta manus, validis incumbite remis;
tollite,⁹ ferte rates, inimicam findite rostris   295
hanc terram, sulcumque sibi premat ipsa carina.
Frangere ¹⁰nec tali puppim statione recuso
arrepta tellure semel.' Quae talia postquam
effatus Tarchon, socii consurgere¹¹ tonsis
spumantisque rates arvis inferre Latinis,   300
donec rostra tenent siccum et sedere¹² carinae
omnes innocuae. Sed non puppis tua, Tarchon:¹³
namque inflicta vadis, ¹⁴dorso dum pendet iniquo
anceps sustentata diu fluctusque fatigat,
solvitur atque viros mediis exponit in undis,   305
fragmina remorum quos et fluitantia transtra

---

1 286. **obsessos . . . muros:** i.e. the continuation of the blockade of the Trojan camp.

2 287f. The wild impetuosity of Tarchon, in his deep and bitter hatred for Mezentius, stands in marked contrast with the purposeful and calm leadership of Aeneas.

3 288. **pontibus:**'gangways', cf. 654.

4 288-9. 'many watched for the ebb of the spent sea'; *servare* (like *credere*) is historic infinitive.

5 289. **brevibus:** *brevia* is used as a noun ('shallows', cf. 1.111).

6 291. **qua . . . sperat:** 'where he did not expect shallow water'. An alternative reading *spirant* is offered by *M* and known by Servius: 'where the shallows did not heave', cf. *Geo.* 1.327.

7 **nec fracta . . . unda:** 'and no breaking waves boomed'; for *fracta* cf. 1.161.

8 292. **inoffensum:** 'placid'; the word has an active meaning as in Ov. *Am.* 1.6.8 *inoffensos dirigit ille pedes.*

9 295. **tollite,ferte rates:** 'life up your ships, drive them on'; the effect of urgency is strengthened by the alliteration of *t*.

10 297. 'and I do not hesitate to wreck my ship in such an anchorage once it has touched land'; he means that he will not want it again for retreat.

11 299. **consurgere:** historic infinitive, like *inferre* in the next line.

12 301-2. **sedere . . . innocuae:** 'all the ships were beached unharmed'; the passive use of *innocuus* is rare.

13 302. Emphasis is here added by the use of the vocative and the rare rhythm of the hexameter ending, see note on 440.

14 303-5. 'as it hung on a projecting sandbank, held balanced for a long time and defying the waves, suddenly it broke up . . .'. *Fatigare* is 'giving no rest to', i.e. not yielding to; cf. 9.605.

449

impediunt retrahitque[1] pedes simul unda relabens.

> *308-61. The battle begins, and the first victories are won by Aeneas himself. Elsewhere however the Italians are successful, and the struggle is equally poised.*

[2]Nec Turnum segnis retinet mora, sed rapit acer
totam aciem in Teucros et contra in litore sistit.
Signa[3] canunt. Primus turmas invasit agrestis[4]   310
Aeneas, omen[5] pugnae, stravitque Latinos
occiso Therone,[6] virum qui maximus ultro
Aenean petit. [7]Huic gladio perque aerea suta,
per tunicam squalentem auro latus haurit apertum.
Inde Lichan ferit exsectum iam matre perempta[8]   315
et tibi, Phoebe, sacrum casus[9] evadere ferri
quod licuit parvo. Nec[10] longe Cissea[11] durum
immanemque Gyan sternentis agmina clava[12]
deiecit leto; nihil illos Herculis arma
nec validae iuvere manus genitorque Melampus,   320
Alcidae comes[13] usque gravis dum terra labores

---

1 307. **retrahitque pedes**: 'sucked back their feet', with its undertow.

2 308f. The account of the outbreak of fighting, in which Virgil describes first the successes of Aeneas and then those of the Italians, uses phrases and techniques from the battle scenes of Homer and Ennius. The method of narrative is direct and severe, but it obtains variety from Virgil's brief descriptions or 'vignettes' of warriors otherwise unknown to us: Lichas, sacred to Phoebus (315f.); Gyas, companion of Hercules (318f.); Cydon, lover of Clytius (324f.); the seven sons of Phorcus (328f.). See notes on 362f., 12.500f. At the end of this section, just prior to the introduction of Pallas, the narrative slows as Virgil emphasises with a simile the equipoise of the decisive struggle *limine in ipso Ausoniae*.

3 310. **signa canunt**: 'the battle-notes ring out', cf. Livy 27.47.3.

4 **agrestis**: the Latins are called *legio agrestis* in 7.681; the rural folk who rallied to Turnus' side are described in the catalogue from 7.641 onwards.

5 311. **omen pugnae**: 'a prophecy of the battle's outcome', cf. 9.53 *principium pugnae,* and Livy 21.29.4 *hoc principium simul omenque belli . . . victoriam Romanis portendit.* The phrase is in apposition to the previous clause; that Aeneas fights and wins the first contests is an omen of the ultimate result.

6 312. **Therone**: Theron and the following eight Italians who fall victim to Aeneas (up to 344) are not known except for what Virgil tells us here.

7 313-14. 'both through the bronze fastenings of his mail and then through his tunic with its golden scales he stabbed with his sword and pierced his side';for *perque . . . per* ('both . . . and', the repetition replacing the second *-que*) cf. 11.171, 12.548; for *squalere* cf. 12.87 and for the idea cf. 9.707, 11.487, 770 and Aul. Gell. 2.6.19f.; for *haurire* cf. 2.600.

8 315-16. Servius tells us that all children born by Caesarean operation after the death of their mothers were consecrated to Apollo, god of medicine.

9 316-17. **casus . . . parvo**: 'because when a baby he had been allowed to escape the dangers of the knife'. Some modern editors (including Sabbadini and Mynors) read *quo* with the correcting hand of *P* (*M* and *P1* have *quod*, *R* has *cui*), making the sentence a question with the meaning 'to what end did he . . .?', 'what was the use that he did ...?'. This is strained and abrupt, and Heyne is right in calling it unVirgilian.

10 317. **nec longe**: 'and not far off', cf. 5.406; not, as Servius says, 'not long afterwards'.

11 **Cissea**: Greek accusative of *Cisseus,* cf. 399.

12 318. **clava**: the club was the famous weapon of Hercules (319) son of Alceus (321).

13 321. **comes usque ... dum**: 'his companion all the time while . . .'. The earth is said to have provided Hercules with his twelve labours in the sense that he had to travel the whole world to complete them.

praebuit. Ecce Pharo,[1] voces dum iactat inertis,[2]
intorquens iaculum clamanti sistit in ore.
Tu quoque, flaventem[3] prima lanugine malas
dum sequeris Clytium infelix, nova[4] gaudia, Cydon,   325
Dardania stratus dextra, securus[5] amorum
qui iuvenum tibi semper erant, miserande[6] iaceres,
ni fratrum stipata cohors foret obvia, Phorci
progenies, septem numero, septenaque[7] tela
coniciunt; partim galea clipeoque resultant   330
inrita, deflexit partim stringentia corpus
alma Venus. Fidum Aeneas adfatur Achaten:[8]
'suggere tela mihi, non[9] ullum dextera frustra
torserit in Rutulos, steterunt quae in corpore Graium
Iliacis campis.' Tum magnam corripit hastam   335
et[10] iacit: illa volans clipei transverberat aera
Maeonis et thoraca[11] simul cum pectore rumpit.
Huic frater subit Alcanor fratremque ruentem
sustentat dextra: [12]traiecto missa lacerto
protinus hasta fugit servatque cruenta tenorem,   340
dexteraque ex umero nervis moribunda pependit.
Tum Numitor iaculo fratris de corpore rapto
Aenean petiit: sed non et figere contra
est licitum, magnique femur perstrinxit Achatae.

---

1 322. **Pharo**: dative with *clamanti*, cf. 1.102.

2 **inertis**: 'empty'; Servius says 'ubi pugnari oportet, loqui inertis est'.

3 324. **flaventem . . . malas**: 'his chin covered with the first fair down of youth', cf. 8.160. *Malas* is accusative of respect ('fair as to his cheeks'), cf. 699, 711, 869 and see note on 7.60.

4 325. **nova gaudia**: 'your newest delight'.

5 326. **securus amorum**: 'forgetful of his love', cf. 1.350, the same phrase in a somewhat different sense.

6 327. **miserande iaceres**: i.e. he would have been killed, laid low by Aeneas, had not the sons of Phorcus saved him. The predicate *miserande* is attracted into the vocative, cf. 186.

7 329. **septenaque**: the distributive is used for the cardinal number, as often (cf. 207, 566); the seven brothers each throw one spear.

8 332. **Achaten**: Aeneas' closest companion, cf. 8.466.

9 333-4. **non ullum . . . steterunt quae**: 'not one of those weapons shall my right hand have sent whirling against the Rutuli in vain, not one of those which found their mark . . .'. Notice the short *e* in the perfect form *steterunt*; see note on 2.774.

10 336. **et iacit**: observe the emphasis secured by the pause after the first dactyl and the word accent on its second syllable.

11 337. **thoraca**: Greek accusative, cf. 163, 413.

12 339-41. 'the spear flung by Aeneas pierced his arm and winged its way straight on and dripping blood kept on its course and Alcanor's right hand hung useless from his shoulder by the sinews'. Servius says *traiecto . . . lacerto* means 'as Aeneas drew his arm back', but this is unlikely in the context. For *protinus* cf. 9.337.

451

Hic Curibus fidens primaevo corpore Clausus[1]   345
advenit et rigida Dryopem ferit eminus hasta
sub [2]mentum graviter pressa, pariterque loquentis
vocem animamque rapit traiecto gutture; at ille
fronte ferit terram et crassum vomit ore cruorem.
Tris quoque Threicios Boreae[3] de gente suprema   350
et tris quos Idas pater et patria Ismara mittit,
per varios sternit casus. Accurrit Halaesus
Auruncaeque manus, subit et Neptunia proles,
insignis Messapus equis. Expellere tendunt
nunc hi, nunc illi: certatur limine in ipso   355
Ausoniae. Magno discordes aethere venti[4]
proelia ceu tollunt animis et viribus aequis;
non ipsi inter se, non nubila, non mare cedit;
anceps pugna diu, stant[5] obnixa omnia contra:
haud aliter Troianae acies aciesque Latinae   360
concurrunt, haeret[6] pede pes densusque viro vir.

*362-438. Pallas encourages his Arcadians and kills many of
the enemy; Halaesus rallies the Italians but is killed by
Pallas. Lausus then moves to attack Pallas, but fate prevents
their meeting.*

[7]At parte ex alia, qua[8] saxa rotantia late

---

1 345f. The scene now shifts from Trojan successes to Italian successes: Clausus the Sabine from Cures (6.811) was mentioned in the catalogue (7.707); Halaesus with his Italians (*Auruncaeque manus,* 353) was also in the catalogue (7.723f., 727); Messapus (354) was one of the outstanding Latin leaders (cf. 7.691, where he is also called *Neptunia proles*). Nothing else is known of the Trojan victims, Dryops (346) and the six Thracians, three sons of the North Wind and three of Idas (350-1).

2 347-8. 'and transfixing his throat, he ended the words Dryops was uttering and his life at the same moment'.

3 350. **Boreae de gente suprema:** 'of the exalted lineage of Boreas', cf. 7.220. The Thracians were allies of Troy in Homer; Ismara was a mountain in Thrace.

4 356f. The point of the simile is the stalemate produced by equal forces in conflict: as the Trojans and Italians cannot move each other so the conflicting winds cause the clouds (cf. Lucr. 6.96f.) and the sea (cf. Lucan 5.602) to be motionless under the impact of contrary forces. For the simile of conflicting winds cf. *Aen.* 2.416f., Hom. *Il.* 16.765f; here however the emphasis is on the moment of stillness.

5 359. **stant obnixa omnia contra:** 'all the world locked in conflict hangs motionless'.

6 361. **haeret ... vir:** 'foot to foot they hold their position, man to man in dense array'; cf. Hom. *Il.* 13.131 (= 16.215), Enn. *Ann.* 572 *pes premitur pede* and Furius quoted by Macrobius (*Sat.* 6.3.5) *pressatur pede pes, macro mucrone, viro vir.* The monosyllabic ending to Virgil's line reflects the archaic mood; see note on line 2.

7 362f. The description of the valour of Pallas and then of Lausus builds up the expectation for the major part which each plays later in the book. The young Pallas is cast altogether in the heroic mould, encouraging his men with a speech (369f.) reminiscent both of Homer's Ajax (*Il.* 15.733f.) and of a typical Roman commander leading his men into battle.
As in the previous section, Virgil diversifies the long lists of those killed in battle by touches of personal description: the evil act of Anchemolus (389); the striking similarity of the twin sons of Daucus (390-6), a poignant passage (see note on 393) emphasised by apostrophe; and especially the pathetic efforts of the father of Halaesus to save his son from the death in battle which he had foreseen (417f.).

8 362-3. **qua . . . ripis:** 'where the rushing river had brought rolling rocks over a wide area and bushes torn up from the banks'; i.e. in a river-bed now dried up. *Rotantia* is used intransitively, cf. 240.

intulerat torrens arbustaque diruta ripis,
Arcadas insuetos acies inferre pedestris
ut vidit Pallas Latio[1] dare terga sequaci,   365
aspera[2] aquis natura loci dimittere quando
suasit equos, unum[3] quod rebus restat egenis,
nunc prece, nunc dictis virtutem accendit amaris:
'quo fugitis, socii? Per[4] vos et fortia facta,
per ducis Euandri nomen devictaque bella   370
spemque meam, patriae quae nunc subit aemula laudi,
fidite[5] ne pedibus. Ferro rumpenda per hostis
est via. Qua globus ille virum densissimus urget,
hac vos et Pallanta ducem patria alta[6] reposcit.
Numina nulla premunt, mortali urgemur ab hoste   375
mortales; totidem nobis animaeque manusque.
Ecce maris magna claudit nos obice[7] pontus,
deest[8] iam terra fugae: pelagus[9] Troiamne petamus?'
haec ait, et medius densos prorumpit in hostis.
Obvius huic primum fatis adductus iniquis   380
fit Lagus.[10] Hunc, vellit[11] magno dum pondere saxum,
intorto figit telo, discrimina[12] costis
per medium qua spina dabat, hastamque receptat
ossibus haerentem. Quem[13] non super occupat Hisbo,

---

1 365. **Latio . . . sequaci:** 'the pursuing Latins', the country (*Latium*) is put for the people (*Latini*).

2 366-7. **aspera . . . equos:** 'since the nature of the ground rugged with rocks had persuaded them to abandon their horses'. I accept Madvig's conjecture *aquis* for *quis* of the MSS; the latter gives an intolerable double subordination of this clause, both by *quando* and by *quis*, unless we take *quando* as equivalent to *aliquando* ('at last'), which is most unlikely. *Quando* is unusually postponed to the sixth word of its clause; Virgil does not often end a line with so weak a word (cf. 11.509). For *suadere* with the infinitive cf.9-10.

3 367. **unum . . . egenis:** this clause is in apposition with the next line.

4 369. **per vos . . . facta:** 'by yourselves individually and by your brave deeds'. *Vos* is governed by *per*, not by an understood verb *precor* with misplaced object; cf. Sall. *Jug.* 14.25, and line 597.

5 372.**fidite ne:** the conjunction is postponed, and the construction (*ne* with imperative) poetic.

6 374. **alta:**'glorious', cf. 11.797.

7 377. **obice:** the word scans as a dactyl (*objice*), cf. 8.227, 11.890.

8 378. **deest:** scanned as a single syllable by synizesis, cf. *dehinc* (9.480), and note on 116.

9 **pelagus Troiamne petamus?:** 'are we to make for the sea or Troy (i.e. the Trojan camp)?'. Pallas, who came with Aeneas by sea, has evidently joined his Arcadians who came by land, and their object now is to join their forces with the beleaguered Trojans, cf. 238-40. For the use of *-ne* (= *an*) cf. 11.126, Hor. *Epist.* 1.11.3 *maiora minorane fama*, Livy 5.28.5.

10 381f. The victims of Pallas: Lagus, Hisbo, Sthenius, Anchemolus, Larides, Thymber, Rhoeteus, are not elsewhere heard of.

11 381. **vellit . . . dum:** 'while he was trying to pick up', cf. 11.566.

12 382-3. **discrimina . . . dabat:** 'right through where the spine separated his ribs'. Notice the lengthening of the final syllable of *dabat*, cf. 394, 433, 487, 720 and note on 7.174.

13 384. **quem . . . Hisbo:** 'but Hisbo did not catch Pallas as he bent over his victim'; for *occupat* cf. 699, 9.770.

ille quidem hoc sperans; nam Pallas ante[1] ruentem, 385
dum furit, incautum crudeli morte sodalis
excipit atque ensem tumido in pulmone recondit.
Hinc Sthenium petit et Rhoeti de gente vetusta
Anchemolum[2] thalamos ausum incestare novercae.
Vos etiam, gemini, Rutulis cecidistis in arvis, 390
Daucia,[3] Laride Thymberque, simillima[4] proles,
indiscreta suis gratusque parentibus error;
at nunc dura dedit vobis discrimina Pallas.[5]
Nam tibi, Thymbre, caput[6] Euandrius[7] abstulit ensis;
te[8] decisa suum, Laride, dextera quaerit 395
semianimesque micant [9]digiti ferrumque retractant.
Arcadas accensos monitu et praeclara tuentis
facta viri mixtus[10] dolor et pudor armat in hostis.
Tum Pallas biiugis fugientem Rhoetea[11] praeter[12]
traicit. Hoc spatium[13] tantumque morae fuit Ilo; 400
Ilo namque procul validam derexerat hastam,
quam medius Rhoeteus[14] intercipit, optime Teuthra,
te fugiens fratremque Tyren, curruque volutus
caedit[15] semianimis[16] Rutulorum calcibus arva.

---

1 385. **ante:** adverbial with the verb *excipit* (387).

2 389. Servius tells how Anchemolus, having seduced his stepmother, fled from his father's anger to Daunus, Turnus' father, hence his presence here among Turnus' allies.

3 391. **Daucia:** vocative agreeing with *proles,* 'offspring of Daucus'. *Laride* is Greek vocative; cf. 461.

4 392. 'offspring indistinguishable to their own parents, a happy confusion'; the change from *vos* to *suis,* where *vestris* would be expected, generalises the picture, cf. 3.494.

5 393. 'but now Pallas gave you grim differentiation', a fine line, typical of Virgil's brief vignettes of warriors otherwise unknown and un-described, cf. 9.328, 12.542f., and see notes on 308f., 362f.

6 394. **caput:** the final syllable is lengthened in arsis at the caesura, cf. 383.

7 **Euandrius . . . ensis:** i.e. the sword of Pallas, son of Evander, cf. 420.

8 395. **te . . . suum:** 'you, its owner'. This kind of gruesome exaggeration in battle scenes becomes very frequent in Silver Age epic, especially in Lucan and Statius; cf. also Ov. *Met.* 6.560.

9 396. 'his dying fingers quiver and tighten again on the sword'; cf. Hom. *Il.* 5.79f., Enn. *Ann.* 472-3 and Lucr. 3.642f. For the scansion of *semi-* as a single long syllable cf. 8.194.

10 398. **mixtus dolor et pudor:** 'a mixture of anger and shame', i.e. their shame makes them angry.

11 399. **Rhoetea:** Greek accusative, cf. 317; this victim of Pallas, like the more fortunate Ilus, is not otherwise known.

12 **praeter:** adverbial with *fugientem.*

13 400. **spatium tantumque morae:** 'a respite and that much of delay'.

14 402-3. Rhoeteus was trying to escape from the Trojan brothers Teuthras and Tyres when he was struck down by Pallas.

15 404. **caedit:** 'scored', contrast *tundit* in 731.

16 **semianimis:**for the scansion see note on 396; the word is probably third declension nominative in apposition to the subject rather than ablative plural with *calcibus* from *semianimus,* a form which Virgil does not use.

454

Ac velut optato[1] ventis aestate coortis[2]   405
dispersa[3] immittit silvis incendia pastor,
correptis subito mediis extenditur una[4]
horrida[5] per latos acies Volcania campos,
ille sedens victor flammas despectat ovantis:
non aliter socium[6] virtus coit omnis in unum   410
teque iuvat, Palla. Sed bellis acer Halaesus[7]
tendit in adversos seque[8] in sua colligit arma.
Hic mactat Ladona Pheretaque Demodocumque,[9]
Strymonio dextram fulgenti deripit ense
elatam[10] in iugulum, saxo ferit ora Thoantis   415
ossaque dispersit cerebro permixta cruento.
Fata canens silvis genitor celarat Halaesum;[11]
ut senior leto canentia[12] lumina solvit,
iniecere manum Parcae telisque sacrarunt
Euandri.[13] Quem sic Pallas petit ante precatus: 420
'da nunc, Thybri[14] pater, ferro, quod missile libro,
fortunam atque viam duri per pectus Halaesi.
Haec arma exuviasque viri tua quercus habebit.'[15]
Audiit illa deus; dum texit Imaona[16] Halaesus,

---

1 405. **optato**: 'in accordance with his prayers', an impersonal use of the ablative absolute giving an adverbial sense equivalent to *ex voto* (Servius). Cf. 1.737 *libato*. Winds in summer might not be very common, and the shepherd wishing to burn waste shrub-land (cf. 12.521f.) has been praying for them.

2 405f. The simile of fire for martial ardour is of course very common indeed, but Virgil's application of it here is original; the little flames suddenly unite into one as the deeds of valour of various Etruscans unite into one brilliant scene of success.

3 406. **dispersa immittit silvis incendia**: 'starts scattered fires in the woods'.

4 407. **una**: adverb, 'in an unbroken stretch'.

5 408. **horrida . . . acies Volcania**: 'a terrifying line of fire'; *acies* refers to the long thin line of the blaze.

6 410. **socium**: genitive plural, cf. 9.558.

7 411. **Halaesus**: cf. 352.

8 412. **seque . . . arma**: 'covering himself behind his shield', cf. 12.491.

9 413. As often in Virgil (cf. 9.767) the list of names is given a Greek rhythm (no masculine caesura in third or fourth foot and a polysyllabic ending). *Ladona* and *Phereta* are Greek accusatives of *Ladon* and *Pheres*. None of these Trojans (nor Strymonius, 414, or Thoas, 415) is heard of elsewhere.

10 415. **elatam in iugulum**: 'as Strymonius raised it to attack his throat'.

11 417f. Halaesus' father had foreseen the future (*fata canens*) and the death in battle of his son and had kept him apart in the forests (cf. Hom. *Il.* 2.831f.), but when the old man died the fates proceeded to bring his son to his destined end.

12 418. **canentia lumina**: Servius says this is either a transferred epithet (*ipse canens*) or refers to the whitening of the pupils at death. The first is surely true, perhaps with reference to the white hair of the eyebrows.

13 420. **Euandri**: i.e. Pallas' weapons, cf. 394.

14 421. **Thybri**: Greek vocative, cf. 8.72.

15 423. For spoils hung on an oak tree, cf. 11.5f.

16 424. **Imaona**: Greek accusative. Imaon the Italian is not heard of elsewhere.

Arcadio infelix telo dat pectus inermum.[1]   425
At non[2] caede viri tanta perterrita Lausus,[3]
pars[4] ingens belli, sinit agmina: primus Abantem[5]
oppositum interimit, pugnae[6] nodumque moramque.
Sternitur Arcadiae proles, sternuntur Etrusci[7]
et vos, o Grais[8] imperdita corpora, Teucri.   430
Agmina concurrunt ducibusque et viribus aequis;
extremi[9] addensent acies nec turba moveri
tela manusque sinit.[10] Hinc Pallas instat et urget,
hinc contra Lausus, nec multum discrepat aetas,
egregii forma, sed quis[11] Fortuna negarat   435
in patriam reditus. Ipsos concurrere passus
haud tamen inter se magni regnator Olympi;
mox illos sua fata manent maiore sub hoste.[12]

---

1 425. **inermum:** second declension, as in 12.131; it is more usually third.

2 426-7. **non . . . perterrita . . . sinit agmina:** 'did not desert his troops, terrified as they were'; for *sinere* cf. 598, 12.316. Others supply *esse to perterrita,* 'did not let them be frightened'.

3 426f. Lausus, the young son of Mezentius, was described at the beginning of the catalogue (7.649f.) as worthy of a better father.

4 427. **pars ingens belli:** cf. 2.6 (of Aeneas) *quorum pars magna fui,* and line 737 (of Orodes) *pars belli haud temnenda.*

5 **Abantem:** cf. 170, the arrival by sea of the Etruscan Abas.

6 428. **pugnae nodumque moramque:** 'the knot and bulwark of the battle'; for the second phrase cf. Apronius (quoted in Sen. *Suas.* 2) *belli mora concidit Hector.* The first phrase is unparalleled (except for an imitation by Florus, 4.9) and seems to mean 'the hardest, toughest point'.

7 429f. The three sets of allies are Pallas' Arcadians, Tarchon's Etruscans and Aeneas' Trojans.

8 430. **Grais imperdita:** 'un-destroyed by the Greeks', i.e. those who survived the Greeks; *Grais* is dative of agent after the verbal notion in the very rare adjective *imperditus.*

9 432. **extremi . . . acies:** 'the rearguard (pressing forward) makes the battle lines thickly packed'; *addensere* is a rarity.

10 433. **sinit:** the last syllable is lengthened in arsis at the caesura, cf. 383.

11 435. **quis:** = *quibus,* cf. 168.

12 438. i.e. Turnus (for Pallas), 442f.; Aeneas (for Lausus), 809f.

439-509. Turnus and Pallas meet in single combat. Pallas is killed and Turnus strips off his sword-belt as spoils of battle. The poet reflects that a day will come when he will bitterly regret this deed.

[1]Interea soror[2] alma monet[3] succedere Lauso
Turnum, qui[4] volucri curru medium secat agmen.   440
Ut vidit socios: 'tempus desistere pugnae;[5]
solus ego in[6] Pallanta feror, soli mihi Pallas
debetur; cuperem[7] ipse parens spectator adesset.'
Haec ait, et socii cesserunt aequore[8] iusso.
At Rutulum abscessu iuvenis tum iussa superba   445
miratus stupet[9] in Turno corpusque per ingens
lumina volvit obitque[10] truci procul omnia visu,
talibus et dictis it contra dicta tyranni:
'aut spoliis[11] ego iam raptis laudabor opimis

---

1 439f. This episode is crucial in the *Aeneid* as it provides the motivation for the final scene, in which Aeneas refuses Turnus' plea for mercy because he catches sight of the belt which Turnus had stripped from Pallas. Structurally it can be compared with the death of Patroclus at the hands of Hector in Homer's *Iliad*, which in turn costs Hector his life at the hands of Achilles. In treatment and tone it alienates the reader's sympathy from Turnus, and this feeling is reinforced by Virgil's interventions into the narrative (501-2, 503-5, 507f.). Turnus is depicted as arrogant in his superior military qualities (441f., his wish that Evander were present to watch; 445 *iussa superba;* 491f., his boast over the dead body; 495f., his stripping of the belt; 500f., his excessive delight in his triumph). It is true that the actions of Turnus as such are within the conventions of Homer's battle scenes: the arrogant speech, the bestriding of the dead, the stripping of spoils are normal in the heroic way of battle, and Pallas too acts within this convention and would have stripped Turnus (449, 462). But many will agree with Otis (p. 356) when he says that the episode reveals Turnus' *culpa* and character rather than with Camps (p. 39); 'the effect (of the death of Turnus) is one of poetic justice, not moral retribution', or Quinn (p. 327); 'Turnus' death is no *punishment,* it is merely the way things worked out'.

It is sometimes argued that the action of Turnus which causes him to deserve his death is the stripping of the spoils for his own use; a captured enemy helmet cost Euryalus his life (9.373), and Aeneas for his part dedicates to the gods the spoils that he has taken (11.7f.). But there is no real ground for this view. Pallas after all intended the same (462), and the heroic convention seems to justify Turnus' action. What cannot be justified is his arrogant attitude.

2 439. **soror alma:** the nymph Juturna, not mentioned by name till 12.146.

3 439-40. **monet succedere . . . Turnum**:for the construction cf. *Geo.* 1.457.

4 440. **qui . . . secat**: 'and he then cut his way through . . .'. The use of *qui* is rather abrupt. The rhythm of the line ending is unusual, cf. 302, 400, 442, 471, 772, 849; Page points out that such a rhythm does not occur in the first six books.

5 441. **pugnae:** some MSS have *pugna,* but cf. 9.789. The construction is probably Greek genitive of separation (cf. Hor. *Odes.* 2.9.17), but may be dative like *subducere pugnae* (lines 50, 615), *decedere . . . calori* (*Geo.* 4.23).

6 442. **in Pallanta feror:** 'I am going after Pallas'; *Pallanta* is Greek accusative, cf. 480. The double repetition in this line gives an arrogant emphasis.

7 443. **cuperem . . . adesset:** 'I could wish his father were here in person to see it'; Servius comments *aspere et amare dictum,* and compares the barbaric behaviour of Pyrrhus in Book 2 in killing Polites before his father Priam's eyes. This remark is savage in the extreme, and like other aspects of Turnus' behaviour in this episode (see note on 439f.) alienates the reader's sympathy.

8 444. **aequore iusso:** an unusual phrase, equivalent to *ab aequore ut iussi sunt;* cf. the much easier phrase in 238 *loca iussa.*

9 446. **stupet in Turno:** cf. Hor. *Sat.* 1.6.17 *stupet in titulis et imaginibus.*

10 447. **obitque . . . visu:** 'and surveyed Turnus' every aspect from where he stood with unflinching gaze'; cf. 8.618 *oculos per singula volvit.*

11 449. **spoliis . . . opimis:** the 'rich spoils' awarded for killing the enemy general; see note on 6.855.

aut leto insigni: sorti[1] pater aequus utrique est.   450
Tolle minas.' Fatus medium procedit in aequor;
frigidus Arcadibus coit in praecordia sanguis.
Desiluit Turnus biiugis, pedes apparat ire
comminus; utque leo, specula[2] cum vidit ab alta[3]
stare procul campis meditantem[4] in proelia taurum,   455
advolat, haud alia est Turni venientis imago.
Hunc ubi contiguum[5] missae fore credidit hastae,
ire[6] prior Pallas, si[7] qua fors adiuvet ausum[8]
viribus imparibus, magnumque ita ad aethera fatur:
'per [9]patris hospitium et mensas, quas advena adisti,   460
te precor, Alcide, [10]coeptis ingentibus adsis.
Cernat semineci sibi[11] me rapere arma cruenta
victoremque[12] ferant morientia lumina Turni.'
Audiit Alcides iuvenem magnumque sub imo
corde premit gemitum lacrimasque[13] effundit inanis.   465
Tum genitor[14] natum dictis adfatur amicis:
'stat sua[15] cuique dies, breve et inreparabile[16] tempus
omnibus est vitae; sed famam[17] extendere factis,

---

1 450. **sorti . . . est:** 'my father (Evander) is ready for either outcome'; this reply to Turnus' taunt (443) is rhetorically effective rather than true, cf. Evander's farewell speech in 8.578f.

2 454. **specula:** as the lion leaps down from his high watch-point, so Turnus leaps from his chariot.

3 454f. The simile is based on Hom. *Il.* 16.823f. where Hector is compared with a lion defeating a wild boar. Hector's victim was Patroclus, with whom in the development of the plot Pallas has many similarities; as Hector met his death at Achilles' hands for having killed and stripped Patroclus, so Turnus meets his death (12.940f.)for having killed Pallas and taken and worn his sword-belt.

4 455. **meditantem in proelia:** 'rehearsing for battle', the phrase is imitated by Silius, 17.438; its more normal construction is as in Juv. 4.112 *meditatus proelia*. Compare the description of the bull in *Geo.* 3.232f.

5 457. **contiguum missae . . . hastae:** 'within range of a spear cast'; this is an unusual use of *contiguus* which normally means 'bordering upon'.

6 458. **ire:** historic infinitive, cf. 288-9.

7 **si qua:** 'if in some way', and so 'in the hope that', an elliptical construction of the type often introduced by *si forte;* cf. 2.136.

8 458-9. **ausum viribus imparibus:** 'as he ventured against the odds'; cf. Troilus in 1.475 *impar congressus Achilli.*

9 460. Pallas refers to the hospitality which his father Evander showed to Hercules (Alcides) when the latter was returning from Spain; cf. 8.362-3.

10 461. **Alcide:** cf. 321;for the Greek vocative cf. 391.

11 462. **sibi:** 'from him', a frequent use of the dative after verbs of taking away like *eripere, adimere,* etc., cf. 12.157.

12 463. **victoremque ferant:** 'endure the sight of his conqueror' ;for the attitude of Pallas to war see note on 439f.

13 465. **lacrimas . . . inanis:** cf. 4.449 and *Geo.* 4.375; Hercules knows before Jupiter tells him that because of fate he cannot help Pallas. The passage recalls Jupiter's tears of blood for Sarpedon (*Il.* 16.459f.) ;cf. 471.

14 466. **genitor natum:** Hercules was the son of Jupiter and Alcmene.

15 467. **sua:** as in 471 used to refer emphatically to a word which is not the subject.

16 **inreparabile:** 'irretrievable', the same phrase is used in *Geo.* 3.284.

17 468. **famam . . . factis:** cf. 6.806, Anchises' words to Aeneas. Compare Dryden, *Troilus and Cressida,* 5.1:
'Our life is short, but to extend that span
To vast eternity, is Virtue's work'.

hoc virtutis opus. Troiae sub moenibus altis
tot nati cecidere deum, quin[1] occidit una   470
Sarpedon,[2] mea progenies; etiam sua Turnum
fata vocant metasque dati pervenit ad aevi.'
Sic ait, atque oculos Rutulorum reicit[3] arvis.
At Pallas magnis emittit viribus hastam
vaginaque cava fulgentem deripit ensem.   475
Illa[4] volans umeri surgunt qua tegmina summa
incidit, atque viam clipei molita per oras
tandem etiam magno strinxit de corpore Turni.
Hic Turnus ferro praefixum robur[5] acuto
in Pallanta diu librans iacit[6] atque ita fatur: 480
'aspice num mage[7] sit nostrum penetrabile telum.'
Dixerat; [8]at clipeum, tot ferri terga,[9] tot aeris,
quem pellis totiens obeat[10] circumdata tauri,
vibranti cuspis medium transverberat ictu
loricaeque[11] moras et pectus perforat ingens.   485
Ille rapit calidum frustra de vulnere telum:
una eademque[12] via sanguis[13] animusque sequuntur.[14]

---

1 470. **quin:** = *quin etiam*, cf. 23.

2 472. **Sarpedon:** the famous Trojan warrior, son of Jupiter and Europa, who was killed by Patroclus; see notes on 125-6 and 465.

3 473. **reicit:** 'turned away'; cf. Hom. *Il*. 13.3. Notice the scansion as a dactyl, cf. 11.619.

4 476-8. 'In its flight it struck where the top covering of the shoulder projects upwards, and forcing its way through the layers of the shield in the end it actually grazed the mighty frame of Turnus'. *Umeri . . . tegmina summa* refers to the top of the breastplate;for *molitur* cf. 6.477; *strinxit de corpore* is an unusual variation for *strinxit corpus,* drawing attention to the actual fact of contact. In Homer (*Il.* 16.477) Sarpedon's spear flies just over the shoulder of Patroclus.

5 479. **robur:** shaft of the spear; the periphrasis is Homeric (e.g.*Il*. 10.351).

6 480. **iacit:** notice the energy of the rhythm, with word accent conflicting with ictus, a conflict echoed in the fifth foot with *ita.*

7 481. **mage . . . penetrabile:** *mage* is an archaic form of *magis,* cf. Lucr. 4.81. *Penetrabilis* more often means 'able to be pierced', but for the active meaning 'able to pierce' cf. *Geo.* 1.93, Ov. *Met.* 13.857.

8 482-4. The sentence order is very involved, beginning with the object, phrases in apposition to it, the adjective for *ictu* before the subject *cuspis* and then a reiteration of the object with *medium*: 'There was Pallas' shield, countless layers of iron and bronze, with the hide of a bull enveloping and encircling it with countless folds - yet with quivering impact the spear pierced right through the middle of it . . .'.

9 482. **terga:** the word means 'back', hence skin or hide, and is common in the meaning layers of leather; it is a remarkable transference to use it of layers of iron; compare line 784.

10 483. **obeat:** cf. 8.553. The subjunctive is concessive.

11 485. **loricaeque moras:** 'the barrier of his breastplate', cf. 12.541.

12 **eademque:** the ablative *eadem* is scanned as a spondee by synizesis of the *e;* cf. 116 and 12.847 *uno eodemque.*

13 **sanguis:** the final syllable is lengthened in arsis; cf. 383, and compare *pulvis* in 1.478. In a number of instances of lengthening in arsis, including this one, the syllable involved originally was long.

14 487. The line is based on Hom. *Il*. 16.505.

Corruit in vulnus (sonitum[1] super arma dedere)
et terram hostilem moriens petit ore cruento.
Quem Turnus super adsistens: 490
'Arcades, haec' inquit 'memores mea dicta referte
Euandro: qualem[2] meruit,[3] Pallanta remitto.
Quisquis honos tumuli, quidquid solamen humandi est,
largior. [4]Haud illi stabunt Aeneia parvo
hospitia.' Et laevo pressit pede talia fatus[5]   495
exanimem rapiens immania pondera baltei[6]
impressumque[7] nefas: una sub nocte iugali
caesa manus iuvenum foede thalamique cruenti,
quae Clonus[8] Eurytides multo caelaverat auro;
quo nunc Turnus ovat spolio gaudetque potitus.   500
Nescia[9] mens hominum fati sortisque futurae
et servare modum rebus sublata secundis!
Turno[10] tempus erit magno cum optaverit emptum
intactum Pallanta, et cum spolia ista diemque

---

1 488. **sonitum . . . dedere:** again a Homeric phrase (see note on 9.709) translated by Ennius (*Ann.* 415 *concidit et sonitum simul insuper arma dederunt*). Similarly *terram petit ore* is reminiscent of Homer's οδαξ ελον ουδας ('bit the ground'), e.g. *Il.* 11.479; cf. *Aen.* 11.418.

2 492. **qualem . . . remitto:** I send him back Pallas as he has deserved to have him', i.e. dead. These are harsh and heartless words; Turnus means that Evander has only himself to blame for the death of his son. The phrases which follow are contemptuous, as is shown by the arrogant *largior* and the taunt with which he finishes.

3 **meruit:** Page very properly demolishes the view of some that Pallas (not Evander) is subject.

4 494-5. 'His hospitality to Aeneas will cost him dear'; *parvo* is ablative of price (an idiomatic construction with *stare*), cf. 503. For *Aeneia* (adjective) cf. 156. The use of the word *hospitium* recalls Dido's hospitality (1.299 etc.) to the Trojans; Aeneas seems destined to bring mischief to his hosts.

5 495-6. This is normal battle behaviour in Homer, cf. *Il.* 13.618; see note on 439f.

6 496. **baltei:** it is because Turnus is wearing this sword-belt that his plea for mercy at the end is rejected; cf. line 504 and *Aen.* 12.941f. The word scans as a spondee by synizesis, cf. 116.

7 497. **impressumque nefas:** 'and the tale of sin embossed upon it'. The picture described is the occasion of the marriage of the 50 sons of Aegyptus to the 50 daughters of Danaus; the brides, at their father's instigation (because of an oracle that he would be killed by his son-in-law) all killed their husbands except Hypermnestra, who spared her husband Lynceus, cf. Hor. *Odes* 3.11. It is a tale of violence suitable for Pallas on the battlefield, and even more suitable for Turnus, its new owner.

8 499. **Clonus Eurytides:** nothing is known of the artist who made the picture.

9 501-2. 'How ignorant are men's hearts of fate and destiny to come, and of how to keep within bounds when uplifted by success!' The generalised comment of the poet breaks the narrative and compels the attention; compare 4.65-6, 412, also passages of high emotional impact. The thought is typical of Greek tragedy where υβρις (arrogance) leads to νεμεσις (retribution).

10 503-4. 'A time will come for Turnus when he would give anything not to have touched Pallas', literally 'when he would wish Pallas untouched bought at a high price'. Virgil follows the generalised comment of 501-2 with a foreshadowing of the narrative (as he did several times in the story of Dido, e.g. 1.712, 4.169f.). Compare Milton's apostrophe to Adam and Eve (*P.L.* 4.366f.)
'Ah gentle pair, ye little think how nigh
Your change approaches, when all these delights
Will vanish and deliver ye to woe,
More woe, the more your taste is now of joy'.

oderit. At socii multo gemitu lacrimisque[1]   505
impositum scuto referunt Pallanta frequentes.
O[2] dolor atque decus magnum rediture parenti,
haec[3] te prima dies bello dedit, haec eadem aufert,
cum[4] tamen ingentis Rutulorum linquis acervos!

> *510-605. Aeneas rages in mad anger over the battlefield,*
> *seeking vengeance for Pallas and killing many of the enemy*
> *violently and ruthlessly.*

[5]Nec iam fama mali[6] tanti, sed certior[7] auctor   510
advolat Aeneae tenui[8] discrimine leti
esse[9] suos, tempus versis succurrere Teucris.
Proxima quaeque metit[10] gladio latumque[11] per agmen
ardens[12] limitem agit ferro, te, Turne, superbum[13]
caede nova quaerens. Pallas, Euander,[14] in ipsis[15]   515
omnia sunt oculis, mensae quas advena primas

---

1 505. The quadri-syllabic ending is unusual and is intended (as Page says) to suggest discordant sounds; cf. 4.667 *latnentis gemituque et femineo ululatu.*

2 507. 'O you who are destined to return to your father bringing him (literally 'as') great grief and yet great glory'. Again Virgil intervenes in his narrative, this time to apostrophise Pallas: cf. 4.408f., 9.446f.

3 508. **haec eadem aufert:** the line ending again is unusual, with the elision after the fifth foot; cf. 3.581 (with my note, OUP Ed.), 12.26.

4 509. **cum tamen:** 'yet in spite of it', i.e. in spite of the fact that his first day on the battlefield was also his last.

5 510f. In this passage Aeneas totally loses that selfcontrol which he has been striving to achieve all through the poem. In mad anger at the death of Pallas he acts savagely and relentlessly against all whom he meets on the battlefield. The phraseology used is of the most powerful kind (*proximo quaeque metit gladio*, 513; *limitem agit ferro*, 514; *Dardanides contra furit*, 545; *caput orantis . . . deturbat terrae*, 554-5; *truncumque tepentem provolvens*, 555-6; *Aegaeon qualis . . . desaevit . . . ut semel intepuit mucro*, 565-70; *torrentis aquae vel turbinis atri more furens*, 603-4). The boastful words with which he taunts his victims are heartless and cruel (531f., 557f., 592f., especially 600, *morere et fratrem ne desere frater*). Most striking and terrible of all is his intention (fulfilled later) to sacrifice alive eight captives at the tomb of Pallas (517f., see note there). The motivation for Aeneas' frenzied behaviour is his feeling of guilt at having failed to protect Pallas from Turnus, and his need to expiate it by deeds of vengeance; this perhaps is the reason for the striking use of *pius* in line 591 (his duty to Euander can now only be expressed by acts of revenge). Whatever the motive, Aeneas now behaves in as unrestrained a fashion as Turnus or any Homeric hero (many of these episodes are based on Homer); and we are prepared for his later outburst in 12.441f. and for his final refusal to show mercy to his defeated adversary (12.930f.). See further Camps pp. 28, 142, and Quinn, pp. 223f.

6 510. **mali tanti:** i.e. the death of Pallas and the consequent rout of the Trojans and their allies (512).

7 **certior auctor:** presumably a messenger Aeneas can trust.

8 511. **tenui discrimine leti:** 'a hairbreadth from death', cf. 3.685, 9.143.

9 512. **esse suos:** the accusative and infinitive follows the reported idea in *advolat.*

10 513. **metit:** the metaphor is from cutting down standing corn, cf. Hor. *Odes* 4.14.31.for the frenzy of Aeneas in his passion for vengeance see note on 510f.

11 **latumque:** with *limitem*, not with *agmen.*

12 514. **ardens limitem agit:** notice the metrical effect with a spondee filling the first foot (cf. 842 and see note on 9.419) and the elision of the quasi cretic word *limitem* before a short syllable.

13 514-15. **superbum caede nova:** cf. 445 and see note on 439f.

14 515. **Euander**: elsewhere Virgil uses the form *Euandrus.*

15 515-17. for the hospitality (*mensae*) of Evander and Pallas cf. 8.121-4, 308f. Servius draws attention to the broken structure of this sentence, reflecting the agitation of Aeneas.

tunc adiit, dextraeque datae. Sulmone[1] creatos
quattuor hic iuvenes, totidem quos educat[2] Ufens,
viventis rapit, inferias[3] quos immolet umbris
captivoque rogi perfundat sanguine flammas.   520
Inde Mago[4] procul infensam contenderat hastam.[5]
Ille astu[6] subit, at tremibunda supervolat hasta,
et genua amplectens effatur talia supplex:
'per patrios manis et spes surgentis Iuli[7]
te precor, hanc animam serves natoque patrique.   525
Est domus alta, iacent penitus defossa talenta
caelati argenti, sunt auri pondera facti[8]
infectique mihi. Non hic victoria Teucrum
vertitur aut anima una dabit discrimina tanta.'
Dixerat. Aeneas contra cui talia reddit: 530
'argenti atque auri memoras quae multa[9] talenta
natis parce tuis. [10]Belli commercia Turnus
sustulit ista prior iam tum Pallante perempto.
Hoc patris Anchisae manes, hoc sentit Iulus.'
Sic fatus galeam laeva tenet atque reflexa   535
cervice orantis capulo[11] tenus applicat ensem.
Nec procul Haemonides, [12]Phoebi Triviaeque[13] sacerdos,

---

1 517-18. Sulmo the Rutulian is mentioned in 9.412; Ufens was in the catalogue of Italian forces (7.745). Mackail however, perhaps rightly, maintains that Sulmo is the town and Ufens the river in the Volscian territory.

2 518. **educat**: for the idiomatic use of the present tense cf. 8.141 (*generat*).

3 519. **inferias . . . umbris**: 'to sacrifice them as offerings to the shades'. The human sacrifice at Pallas' funeral is prepared in 11.81f. The passage is based on Hom. *Il.* 21.27f., 23.175f., where the human sacrifice is a horrifying act of barbarity; in the gentle Virgil it seems worse still. Nothing would have been easier than for Virgil to omit this ghastly act of Achilles in his reworking of the story; therefore the fact that he has included it must be accorded its full significance. The anger and passion for vengeance which overwhelms Aeneas is terrible enough to cause even such an act of savagery as this. We may also compare the report in Suetonius (*Aug.* 15) that Octavian (Augustus) offered human sacrifice to the shade of Julius Caesar. See further note on 510f.

4 521. **Mago**: the dative is a poetic variant of *in Magum* (cf. 401). Magus is not mentioned elsewhere.

5 521f. This episode too is Homeric; it is closely based on Achilles' refusal to spare Lycaon (*Il.* 21.64f.).

6 522. **astu subit**: 'skilfully ducked under it'.

7 524. The appeal is by the dead Anchises (cf. 534), and the young Iulus (6.364); cf. Hom. *Il.* 6.46f., 10.378f.

8 527-8. **facti infectique**: 'worked and unworked', cf. Livy 34.10.4.

9 531. The phrase *multa talenta* is taken into the relative clause: the prose order would be *talenta argenti atque auri quae multa memoras*.

10 532-3. 'This kind of trading in war Turnus has eliminated already, at the time when Pallas was killed'. Compare the well known phrase of Ennius *cauponantes bellum* (*Ann.* 195), and the words of Achilles to Lycaon (*Il.* 21.99f.); cf. also Tac. *Hist.* 3.81 *dirempta belli commercia.*

11 536. **capulo tenus**: 'to the hilt';for *tenus* following its noun cf. line 210 (with the genitive), 2.553.

12 537. **Haemonides**: this priest is not mentioned elsewhere. A verb such as *abest* is to be supplied. The slaughter of a priest is a further indication of the wild frenzy of Aeneas in his grief for Pallas.

13 **Triviae**: Diana, goddess of the crossroads, cf. 11.566, 836 and see note on 7.516f.

infula cui sacra redimibat tempora vitta,
totus conlucens veste atque insignibus albis.[1]
Quem congressus agit campo,[2] lapsumque superstans   540
immolat[3] ingentique[4] umbra tegit; arma Serestus[5]
lecta refert umeris tibi, rex Gradive, tropaeum.
Instaurant[6] acies Volcani stirpe creatus
Caeculus[7] et veniens Marsorum montibus Umbro.
Dardanides[8] contra furit. Anxuris[9] ense sinistram   545
et totum clipei ferro deiecerat orbem
(dixerat ille aliquid magnum vimque adfore verbo
crediderat, caeloque[10] animum fortasse ferebat
canitiemque sibi et longos promiserat annos);
Tarquitus exsultans contra fulgentibus armis,   550
silvicolae[11] Fauno Dryope[12] quem nympha crearat,
obvius ardenti sese obtulit. [13]Ille reducta
loricam clipeique ingens onus impedit hasta,
tum caput orantis nequiquam et multa parantis
dicere deturbat[14] terrae, truncumque tepentem   555
provolvens super[15] haec inimico pectore fatur:

---

1 539. **albis:** the reading of Probus, reported by Servius, is much to be preferred to *armis* of the MSS; cf. Stat. *Th.* 6.330-1.

2 540. **campo:** ablative, 'over the plain', cf. 5.456, 12.501.

3 541. **immolat:** again the religious word (cf. 519, 12.949) which suggests the offering of a victim.

4 **ingentique umbra tegit:** 'obscuring his body with his great shadow', a vividly pictorial phrase. Some take the meaning to be 'covered him in the deep night of death' (cf. Hom. *Il.* 13.425), but this seems less appropriate for *ingens.*

5 **Serestus:** cf. 9.171, 779. The offering to Mars (Gradivus) of the spoils may be compared with 11.7f.; it contrasts with the personal possession by Turnus of Pallas' belt.

6 543. **instaurant acies:** 'renew the fighting' (cf. 2.669), i.e. rally to meet Aeneas' onslaught.

7 544. Caeculus, son of Vulcan, was described in the catalogue (7.678f., and so was the Marsian Umbro (7.750f.).

8 545. **Dardanides:** used of Aeneas only once elsewhere (12.775); in the plural it is of course very commonly used of the Trojans.

9 545f. Aeneas cuts off the left hand of Anxur which is holding his shield. Anxur is not heard of elsewhere, nor are most of the other victims of Aeneas (Tarquitus, Antaeus, Lucas, Numa, Niphaeus, Lucagus); Camers (562) is mentioned again in 12.224 and Liger was referred to in 9.571.

10 548. **caeloque . . .ferebat:** 'was perhaps hoping for immortal glory', literally 'was raising his spirit to the heavens'; *caelo* is dative of place to which, cf. line 555, 5.451, 11.192, 12.256 (with Page's note).

11 **silvicolae:** Macrobius tells us that Naevius and Attius used this compound; Propertius and Ovid have it once each. Compare *silvicultrix* (Cat. 63.72).

12 551. Dryope was a wood-nymph (connected with δρθς, oak), and Faunus one of the many rural deities so named (not Faunus himself, father of Latinus). Cf. Spenser, *F.Q,.* 1.6.15 (of Silvanus) 'his own faire Dryope now he thinks not faire'.

13 552-3. 'Aeneas with a cast of his spear put out of action his breastplate and the mighty weight of his shield'. The diction is strange; *reducta* has to combine the notion of throwing with that of drawing back, and *impedit* is more appropriate with *clipeus* (the shield is made useless when transfixed) than with *lorica.*

14 555. **deturbat terrae:** 'dashed to the ground', for *delurbat* see note on 5.175; *terrae* is dative for *ad terram,* cf. 548. Notice the very heavy alliteration of *d* and *t* in this gruesome line; for comment on Aeneas' savage behaviour see note on 510f. His actions are in the Homeric tradition, cf. *Il.* 10.454f.

15 556. **super:** adverbial, 'over him'.

'istic[1] nunc, metuende, iace. Non te optima mater
condet humi patrioque onerabit[2] membra sepulcro:
alitibus linquere[3] feris, aut gurgite mersum
unda feret piscesque[4] impasti vulnera[5] lambent.'   560
Protinus Antaeum et Lucam, prima agmina Turni,
persequitur, fortemque Numam[6] fulvumque Camertem,
magnanimo Volcente[7] satum, ditissimus agri[8]
qui fuit Ausonidum[9] et tacitis[10] regnavit Amyclis.
Aegaeon[11] qualis, centum[12] cui bracchia dicunt   565
centenasque manus, quinquaginta[13] oribus ignem
pectoribusque arsisse, Iovis cum fulmina contra
tot paribus[14] streperet clipeis, tot stringeret ensis:
sic toto Aeneas desaevit in aequore[15] victor
ut[16] semel intepuit mucro. Quin[17] ecce Niphaei   570

---

1 557f. Aeneas' arrogant and sarcastic (*metuende*) speech is also Homeric; cf. *Il.* 11.452f., 21.122f. In the former passage Odysseus says to Socus 'Your father and mother will not close your eyes but ravening vultures will tear you'; in the latter Achilles says to Lycaon, whom he has thrown into the river, 'Lie there with the fishes who will lick your blood, and your mother shall not place you on a bier and weep for you'.

2 558. **onerabit**: 'cover', 'pile high', so that the earth lies heavy.

3 559. **linquere:** for *linqueris*, 'you will be left'.

4 560. **piscesque impasti**: 'ravening fishes'; Virgil has transferred to fishes the Homeric word ωμησται used of vultures (*Il.* 11.454).

5 **vulnera lambent**: a rendering of *Il.* 21.122-3 μετ ιχθυσιν οι σ ωτειλην / αιμ απολιχμσονται ακηδεες.

6 562. **Numam:** another warrior of this name was killed by Nisus (9.454).

7 563. Volcens figured largely in Book 9 (370f.) as leader of the band of Latins who caught Nisus and Euryalus; he was killed by Nisus (442f.).

8 **agri:** genitive of respect, cf. 173, 225 and 1.14, 343.

9 564. **Ausonidum:** the Italians are called *Ausonidae* also in 11.297, 12.121. for the archaic form of the genitive (for *Ausonidarum*) cf. 4 (*Dardanidum*), 120 *Aeneadum*.

10 **tacitis . . . Amyclis**: Amyclae was well to the south, not far from Caieta. Its silence is referred to several times (Afranius, *Amyclas tacendo periisse audio; Pervig. Ven.* 92 *sic Amyclas, cum tacerent, perdidit silentium*; Sil. 8.528 *quasque evertere silentia Amyclae*). Presumably therefore Servius' story is to be accepted, that because of false alarms it was decreed that nobody was allowed to announce an enemy approach. Just possibly the epithet might mean 'deserted', cf. Plin. *Nat. Hist.* 3.59.

11 565f. Aegaeon is another name of the hundred-armed giant Briareus, mentioned among the shapes at the entrance to the underworld in 6.287 and called *centumgeminus*. It is very significant that Aeneas, given over as he now is to rage and frenzy, should be compared with a barbaric figure symbolising violence and brutality. The second part of Horace's fourth ode of the third book is taken up with depicting the violence (*vis consili expers*) of the Giants in contrast with the control (*vis temperata*) which the gods favour. Normally it is Turnus rather than Aeneas who shows the qualities of unrestrained violence; see note on 510f.

12 565-6. **centum . . . centenasque:** notice the variation between the cardinal and distributive numbers, with no distinction of meaning, cf. 329. The verb *fuisse* is to be supplied after *dicunt*.

13 566-7. **quinquaginta . . . arsisse:** 'fire flashed forth from his fifty mouths and chests', i.e. he breathed forth fire from his lungs and through all his throats.

14 568. **paribus:** 'matching each other', not 'matching Jupiter' For the battle of the Giants and Titans against Jupiter on the fields of Phlegra cf. Hor. *Odes* 3.4.

15 569. **aequore**: 'the field', as often, cf. 444.

16 570. **ut semel intepuit mucro:** 'when once his sword blade grew warm', with the blood of his opponents. The phrase, along with *desaevit* in the previous line, conveys starkly the violent blood-lust of Aeneas' revenge.

17 **quin**: = *quin etiam*, cf. 23.

quadriiugis[1] in equos adversaque pectora tendit.
Atque illi[2] longe[3] gradientem et dira[4] frementem
ut videre, metu versi retroque ruentes
effunduntque[5] ducem rapiuntque ad litora currus.
Interea biiugis infert se Lucagus albis   575
in medios fraterque Liger; sed frater habenis
flectit equos, strictum rotat acer Lucagus ensem.
Haud tulit Aeneas tanto fervore furentis;
inruit adversaque ingens apparuit hasta.
Cui Liger: 580
'Non [6]Diomedis equos nec currum cernis Achilli[7]
aut Phrygiae campos: nunc belli finis et aevi
his dabitur terris.' Vesano talia late
dicta volant Ligeri.[8] Sed non et Troius heros
dicta parat contra, iaculum nam torquet in hostis.   585
Lucagus ut pronus pendens[9] in verbera telo
admonuit biiugos, proiecto dum pede laevo
aptat se pugnae, subit oras[10] hasta per imas
fulgentis clipei, tum laevum perforat inguen:
excussus curru moribundus volvitur arvis.   590
Quem pius[11] Aeneas dictis adfatur amaris:
'Lucage, nulla tuos currus fuga segnis equorum[12]
prodidit aut vanae vertere ex hostibus umbrae:
ipse rotis saliens iuga deseris.' Haec ita fatus

---

1 571. **quadriiugis**: accusative plural; elsewhere Virgil uses the second declension form of the word.

2 572. **illi**: i.e. the horses.

3 **longe gradientem**: 'coming from afar' not 'taking mighty steps' as some commentators say, comparing Hom. *Il.* 7.213 μακρα βιβας.

4 **dira**: adverbial, cf. 12.398 *acerba fremens* (of Aeneas). Notice the emphasis of the rhyme *-entem*.

5 574. **effundtque ... rapiuntque**: for doubled *-que* cf. 687, 692, 749; for *rapere* ('whirl') cf. 178.

6 581f. for the taunt, that Aeneas will not escape as he did from the Greeks on the plains of Troy, cf. 9.148f., 602f. Aeneas was rescued from Diomedes by Aphrodite and Apollo (Hom. *Il.* 5.311f., 446f.), and from Achilles by Poseidon (*Il.* 20.290f.);cf. 1.96f., 752.

7 581. **Achilli**:for this fifth declension form of the genitive cf. 12.352, and compare *Oronti* (1.220) and *Ulixi* (2.7).

8 584. **Ligeri**: dative, cf. the very similar expression in 11.381 (*verba*) *quae tuto tibi magna volant* ('the grand words which pour forth from your lips when you are safe').

9 586. **pendens in verbera**: 'leaning forward to slap them', cf. 5.147; Lucagus uses the flat of his sword to urge the horses on faster (cf. Hom. *Il.* 10.513f. where Odysseus uses his bow for the same purpose).

10 588. **oras ... per imas**: 'through the innermost layers'; for *oras* cf. 477.

11 591. **pius**: here with reference perhaps mainly to his responsibility to Evander for Pallas; Aeneas feels that revenge is his bitter duty.

12 592f. The sarcastic taunt is in the heroic tradition: cf. Patroclus in *Il.* 16.744f. Aeneas means that the horses are not to blame, either through cowardice or fright; the warrior has deserted his horses, not vice versa as with Niphaeus (572-4).

arripuit biiugos; frater tendebat inertis[1]   595
infelix palmas curru delapsus eodem:
'per[2] te, per qui te[3] talem genuere parentes,
vir Troiane, sine[4] hanc animam et miserere precantis.'
Pluribus oranti Aeneas: 'haud talia dudum
dicta dabas. Morere et fratrem ne desere frater.'   600
Tum latebras[5] animae pectus mucrone recludit.
Talia per campos edebat funera ductor
Dardanius, torrentis aquae vel turbinis atri
more furens.[6] Tandem erumpunt et castra relinquunt[7]
Ascanius puer et nequiquam obsessa iuventus.   605

606-88. Meanwhile in Olympus Juno obtains permission from Jupiter to save Turnus, but only temporarily. She makes a phantom of Aeneas: Turnus pursues it on to a ship, and Juno then sets the ship loose. Turnus, bitterly chafing at his enforced absence from the battle, is carried away to his home at Ardea.

[8]Iunonem interea compellat Iuppiter ultro:
'o germana mihi atque eadem gratissima coniunx[9]
ut[10] rebare, Venus (nec te sententia fallit)
Troianas sustentat opes, non vivida[11] bello
dextra viris animusque ferox patiensque pericli.'   610
Cui Iuno summissa: 'quid, o pulcherrime coniunx,

---

1 595. **inertis**: 'powerless', cf. 11.414.

2 597. **per te, per:** it is just possible that *per* in both cases governs *parentes,* and *te* is the object of an understood verb like *oro* (cf. 4.314); but it is preferable (cf. 369) to take the meaning to be 'by your own self and by your parents I beseech you'.

3 **te talem genuere parentes:** cf. 1.606.

4 598. **sine**: 'leave alone', i.e. 'spare', cf. 427.

5 601. **latebras animae:** 'the hiding-place of his life-breath', in apposition to *pectus.*

6 604. **furens:** again the keyword for loss of control, cf. 545.

7 604-5. The Trojans had been besieged in their camp ever since Aeneas' departure in Book 8. *Nequiquam* means that the siege was in the end unsuccessful.

8 606f. This episode acts as a brief interlude in the violent fighting. The scene in heaven indicates once more Juno's ultimate helplessness, while the deception of Turnus affords another glimpse of his strong sense of obligation to his honour and of shame when he cannot fulfil it (notice *conscia fama,* 679). The episode of the phantom is close to Hom. *Il.* 5.449f., when Apollo makes a phantom of Aeneas so that he shall escape Diomedes; but it is nearer still in the part it plays in the structure of the poem to *Il.* 20.443f. where Apollo saves Hector from Achilles by shrouding him in mist. There as here the escape of the lesser warrior postpones but cannot change the ultimate issue.

9 607. For Juno as sister and wife of Jupiter cf. Hom. *Il.* 18.356, *Aen.* 1.47.

10 608. **ut rebare:** 'as you thought', cf. lines 81f. The words of Jupiter should be taken ironically; the deeds of Aeneas have shown that it really is *vivida bello dextra viris* which upholds the Trojan fortunes. Cf. Hom. *Il.* 4.5f. (Zeus mocks Hera).

11 609-10. **vivida . . . dextra**: cf. 5.754 *bello vivida virtus.*

sollicitas¹ aegram et tua² tristia dicta timentem?
Si mihi, quae quondam fuerat quamque esse decebat,³
vis in amore foret, non⁴ hoc mihi namque⁵ negares,
omnipotens, quin et pugnae⁶ subducere Turnum   615
et Dauno⁷ possem incolumem servare parenti.
Nunc⁸ pereat Teucrisque pio det sanguine poenas.
Ille tamen nostra⁹ deducit origine nomen¹⁰
Pilumnusque illi quartus pater, et tua larga
saepe manu multisque oneravit limina donis.'   620
Cui rex aetherii breviter sic fatur Olympi:
'si mora¹¹ praesentis leti tempusque caduco
oratur iuveni meque¹² hoc ita ponere sentis,
tolle fuga Turnum atque instantibus eripe fatis:
hactenus indulsisse vacat.¹³ Sin altior¹⁴ istis   625
sub precibus venia ulla latet totumque moveri
mutarive putas bellum, spes pascis inanis.'
Et Iuno adlacrimans: ¹⁵'quid si, quae voce gravaris,
mente dares atque haec Turno rata vita maneret?
Nunc manet insontem gravis exitus, aut¹⁶ ego veri   630

---

1 612. **sollicitas**: 'taunt'; Juno recognises the irony.

2 **tua . . . timentem**: the alliteration of *t* helps to convey her aggrieved tone.

3 613f. Compare Entellus' lament for his lost youth, 5.397f. *si mihi quae quondam fuerat . . . si nunc foret ilia iuventas.* The pluperfect *fuerat* is used there as here somewhat colloquially; cf. Ov. *Trist.* 3.11.25 *non sum ego quod fueram.*

4 614-16 **non hoc . . . negares . . . quin . . . possem**: 'you would not refuse me the power to . . .'; the *quin* clause is explanatory of *hoc*, the object of *negares.*

5 614. **namque**: 'indeed', in the archaic sense of *enim*, cf. 874 and see note on 8.84. This is probably preferable to regarding the *si* clause as a wish and taking *namque* in its normal sense, 'for'.

6 615. **pugnae subducere**: *pugnae* is dative, see note on 50.

7 616. **Dauno**: Turnus'father Daunus (see note on 8.146) lived in Ardea (688).

8 617. **nunc pereat**: angrily sarcastic, like Venus in 42f., 48f. *Pio . . . sanguine,* as Servius points out, gives a hint of comparison with *pius Aeneas.*

9 618. **nostra**: i.e. divine.

10 618f. Juno made this point also in 74f.; for Pilumnus see note on 76 (there he is grandfather of Turnus, here great-grandfather).

11 622. **mora praesentis leti**: 'a respite from immediate death', cf. 12.74 *neque enim Turno mora libera mortis.*

12 623. **meque . . . sentis**: 'and you realise that I am laying it down on these terms', i.e. purely temporarily.

13 625. **vacat**: 'there is room to grant that much indulgence'; for *vacare* impersonally cf. 1.373 (in a different sense). For the 'timeless' use of the perfect infinitive cf. 14.

14 625-6. **altior . . . venia ulla**: 'any greater favour'.

15 628f. 'What if you were granting in your purpose what you grudge in your words, and Turnus' survival were fixed and firmly decided?' *Quid si* is equivalent in meaning here to *utinam.*

16 630-1. **aut ego veri vana feror**: 'or else I am carried away, mistaken about the truth'; for *feror* cf. 4.110 *sed fatis incerta feror,* and for the genitive of respect cf. 7.440 *veri effeta* and Sil. 12.261 *voti vanus.*

vana feror. Quod[1] ut o potius formidine falsa
ludar, et in[2] melius tua, qui potes, orsa reflectas!'
    Haec ubi dicta dedit, caelo se protinus alto
misit agens hiemem nimbo succincta per auras,
Iliacamque aciem et Laurentia[3] castra petivit.   635
Tum dea nube[4] cava tenuem sine viribus umbram[5]
in faciem Aeneae (visu mirabile monstrum)
Dardaniis ornat telis, clipeumque[6] iubasque
divini adsimulat capitis, dat inania verba,
dat sine[7] mente sonum gressusque[8] effingit euntis: 640
morte[9] obita qualis fama est volitare figuras
aut quae sopitos deludunt somnia sensus.
At primas laeta ante acies exsultat imago
inritatque virum[10] telis et voce lacessit.
Instat cui Turnus stridentemque eminus hastam   645
conicit; illa dato vertit vestigia tergo.
Tum vero Aenean aversum ut cedere Turnus
credidit atque[11] animo spem turbidus hausit inanem:
'quo fugis, Aenea? Thalamos ne desere pactos;
hac[12] dabitur dextra tellus quaesita per undas.'   650
Talia vociferans sequitur strictumque coruscat
mucronem, nec ferre[13] videt sua gaudia ventos.

---

1 631-2. **quod ut o . . . ludar**: 'but oh let me be deceived'; *quod* is accusative of respect ('with regard to which', as in *quod si*) *ut* is for *utinam*, introducing a wish.

2 632. **in melius . . . reflectas**: 'and may you, for you can, change your plans for the better'; the phrase is reminiscent of Jupiter's prophecy about Juno (1.281) *consilia in melius referet.*

3 635. **Laurentia**: Latin, see note on 7.47 and cf. 671.

4 636. **nube cava:** 'of unsubstantial cloud', ablative of description with *umbram.*

5 636f. This passage is based on Hom. *Il.* 5.449f., where Apollo takes Aeneas out of the battle and makes a phantom of him, thus deceiving Diomedes.

6 638-9. **clipeumque . . . capitis:** 'and makes an imitation of his shield and the plume of his immortal head'; *divini* refers to Aeneas' divine parentage, and perhaps too to the special armour made for him by Vulcan at Venus' instigation.

7 640. **sine mente sonum**: 'sound without intelligence', elaborating *inania.* As Page says, 'it speaks as an automaton might'.

8 **gressusque . . . euntis:** 'and reproduced the gait of Aeneas' movements' (literally 'of Aeneas going').

9 641-2. The phraseology here is Lucretian, cf. Lucr. 1.135 *morte obita* (after death), and 4.749f. *figurae* means 'ghosts', the Greek εἰδωλον, contrasted with the phantoms of sleep in the next line.

10 644. **virum:** i.e. Turnus.

11 648. **atque . . . hausit:** understand *ut* to this second subordinate clause; the main clause is 'he said', supplied from 649-50. For *hausit*, literally 'drank in' (perhaps translate 'conceived'), cf. the use with *oculis* (4.661, 12.946), with *auribus* (4.359) and especially 12.26 *simul hoc animo hauri.*

12 650. Turnus plays on the thought that Aeneas is seeking a land, and promises him six feet of it; cf. 741 and 12.359-60 *en agros et quam bello Troiane petisti / Hesperiam metire iacens.*

13 652. **ferre:** equivalent to *auferre*, cf. Cat. 30.10. Servius says *venti ferunt gaudia* was a proverb.

Forte ratis[1] celsi coniuncta crepidine saxi
expositis stabat scalis et ponte parato,
qua rex Clusinis advectus Osinius[2] oris.   655
Huc sese trepida Aeneae fugientis imago
conicit in latebras, nec[3] Turnus segnior instat
exsuperatque moras[4] et pontis transilit altos.
Vix proram attigerat,[5] rumpit Saturnia[6] funem
avulsamque[7] rapit revoluta per aequora navem.   660
Illum autem Aeneas[8] absentem in proelia poscit,[9]
obvia multa virum demittit corpora morti.
Tum levis haud ultra latebras iam quaerit imago,
sed sublime[10] volans nubi[11] se immiscuit atrae,
cum[12] Turnum medio interea fert aequore turbo.[13]   665
Respicit ignarus rerum[14] ingratusque salutis
et duplicis cum voce manus ad sidera tendit:
'omnipotens genitor, tanton[15] me crimine dignum
duxisti et talis voluisti expendere[16] poenas?
Quo[17] feror? Unde abii? Quae[18] me fuga quemve reducit?   670

---

1 653. **ratis . . . saxi:** 'a ship attached to the side of a great rock', i.e. with a mooring-rope (659) and gangways and scaling-ladders down (654).

2 655. Presumably Osinius came in the contingent of Massicus (166f.).

3 657. **nec . . . segnior:** 'but just as determinedly', i.e. not hesitating to board the ship; cf. 12.525.

4 658. **moras:** 'everything in his way'.

5 659. **attigerat, rumpit:** notice the paratactic use of the two main verbs, equivalent to *et rumpit* or *cum rumpit;* cf. 3.512f. with my note (OUP Ed.), 12.113f.

6 **Saturnia:** a frequent epithet of Juno, cf. 760.

7 660. 'and whirled the ship away and sent it speeding through the retreating waters'; for *rapit* cf. 178. *Revoluta* refers to the sea striking the rock and flowing back again: cf. *sinus . . . reductos* in 1.161.

8 661-2. Meanwhile the real Aeneas is searching on the battlefield for the absent Turnus and killing all who came his way.

9 661-4. The narrative is somewhat disjointed; it is not greatly improved by the transposition, accepted by Hirtzel and Mynors, of 661-2 after 663-4 or by Mackail's suggestion of 665 after 662. If transposition of 661-2 is necessary, the lines would go best after 688. That difficulty was felt already in early times is shown by the reading of some MSS (and Urbanus) of *ille . . . Aenean.*

10 664. **sublime:** adverbial, cf. *Geo.* 3.108.

11 **nubi:** dative for *in nubem,* cf. 678.

12 665. **cum . . . interea:** 'while all the time . . .', cf. 5.627f. with my note (OUP Ed.).

13 **turbo:** the blast of wind which Juno had aroused to set the ship moving (660).

14 666. **rerum . . . salutis:** genitives of respect (see note on 173), similar in phrases like this to an objective genitive, cf. 12.227. The second phrase is very unusual, but is made easier by the first.

15 668. **tanton:** for *tantone,* cf. 12.503 and compare 3.319 *Pyrrhin,* 6.779 *viden,* 12.797 *mortalin,* 12.874 to *talin.*

16 669. **expendere:** supply the subject *me* from the previous clause.

17 670. **quo feror? unde abii?:** the second phrase is rhetorical rather than logical, cf. Hor. *Odes* 3.27.37 *unde quo veni?* It is based on the Greek fondness for a doubled interrogative, (as in τισ ποθεν εις ανδρων).

18 **quae . . . reducit?:** 'what flight is this that takes me away; what has happened to me?' *Quemve* is again an idiomatic second interrogative, equivalent to *vel qui* (or *qualis*) *sum?*

Laurentisne iterum muros aut castra videbo?
Quid[1] manus illa virum, qui me meaque arma secuti?
Quosne[2] (nefas) omnis infanda in morte reliqui
et nunc palantis video, gemitumque cadentum
accipio? Quid[3] ago? Aut quae[4] iam satis ima dehiscat   675
terra mihi? Vos o potius miserescite, venti;
in rupes, in saxa (volens[5] vos Turnus adoro)
ferte[6] ratem saevisque vadis immittite syrtis,
quo neque me Rutuli nec conscia[7] fama sequatur.'
Haec memorans animo nunc huc, nunc fluctuat illuc,   680
an sese[8] mucrone ob tantum dedecus amens
induat et crudum[9] per costas exigat ensem,
fluctibus an iaciat[10] mediis et litora nando
curva petat Teucrumque iterum se reddat in arma.
Ter conatus utramque viam, ter maxima Iuno   685
continuit iuvenemque animi[11] miserata repressit.
Labitur alta secans fluctuque[12] aestuque secundo
et patris antiquam Dauni defertur ad urbem.[13]

---

1 672. **quid manus:** 'What of my men?' Again this is a rhetorical construction, cf. 7.365.

2 673. **quosne:** the main MSS have *quosve* or *quosque* (which Mackail and Mynors prefer), but Servius reports that Asper read *quosne.* Cf. Cat. 64.180 *an patris auxilium sperem? quemne ipsa reliqui . . .?*, Cat. 68.91-2 *(Troia) quaene etiam nostro letum miserabile fratri / attulit* (with Fordyce's note).

3 675. **quid ago?:** 'what am I to do?', the indicative is used vividly for the deliberative subjunctive, cf. 4.534, 12.637.

4 675-6. **quae . . . terra mihi?:** cf. 12.883-4 (Juturna's words) and 4.24 (Dido's words).

5 677. **volens . . . adoro:** 'I beg you with all my heart'; for *adoro* (= *oro*) cf. Prop. 1.4.27 *maneat sic semper adoro.*

6 678. 'drive me into the deadly shallows of a quicksand'; the word *syrtis* (more normally plural, but cf. 4.41) is usually applied to the sandbanks off Carthage, but here is general.

7 679. **conscia fama:** 'the report of my guilt', i.e. anyone knowing of his guilt.

8 681-2. **sese mucrone . . . induat:** 'should throw himself on his sword', indirect deliberative question. It is a strange use of *induere* ('clothe oneself'), but cf. Ov. *Am.* 2.10.31-2 *induat adversis contraria pectora telis / miles.* Some MSS have *mucroni,* but Servius and Priscian attest the ablative, and either construction is possible.

9 682. **crudum:** 'cruel', cf. 12.507-8 (the same phrase) and 5.69 (*crudus caestus*).

10 683. **iaciat:** supply *sese* from 681; *fluctibus* is dative (= *in fluctus*), cf. 9.712.

11 686. **animi miserata:** 'pitying him in her heart', for the genitive *animi* see note on 9.246.

12 687. **fluctuque aestuque:** for the doubled -*que* ('both . . . and') cf. 574.

13 688. Ardea, Turnus' home, was on the coast to the south.

470

689-768. Mezentius enters the battle and performs mighty deeds.

[1]At Iovis[2] interea monitis Mezentius ardens
succedit[3] pugnae Teucrosque invadit ovantis.   690
Concurrunt Tyrrhenae[4] acies [5]atque omnibus uni,
uni odiisque viro telisque frequentibus instant.
Ille (velut rupes vastum quae prodit in aequor,[6]
obvia ventorum furiis expostaque[7] ponto,
vim cunctam atque minas perfert caelique marisque   695
ipsa immota manens) prolem[8] Dolichaonis Hebrum
sternit humi, cum quo Latagum Palmumque fugacem.
Sed Latagum saxo[9] atque ingenti fragmine montis
occupat os[10] faciemque adversam, poplite Palmum
succiso volvi[11] segnem sinit, armaque Lauso   700
donat[12] habere umeris et vertice figere cristas.
Nec non Euanthen[13] Phrygium Paridisque Mimanta
aequalem comitemque. Una[14] quem nocte Theano[15]

---

1 689f. This account of the aristeia of Mezentius, the ally of Turnus who despises the gods (see note on 150-1), is built up carefully to make him a worthy adversary of Aeneas. It is based very largely on Homeric battle scenes, and indeed Mezentius in his ruthless valour shows all the qualities of a warrior of the heroic age. The victims of Mezentius are sometimes simply listed (696f.), sometimes given a touch of personality (719f.), and the scene ends (747f.) with a general list of those killed in the battle and a glimpse of the gods watching before it finally focuses once again on Mezentius.

The passage is made particularly Homeric by the frequency of similes (the *Iliad* has more similes than any other ancient epic). There are four extended similes in seventy lines (693f., 707f., 723f., 763f., the latter a double simile), and the first three are very largely based on Homeric originals. Virgil is closer to Homer here than almost anywhere else in the poem; this is deliberately done to portray the archaic nature of Mezentius' qualities as compared with those of Aeneas.

2 689. **Iovis . . . monitis:** this seems strange in view of 104f., especially 112, but presumably Jupiter intervenes to balance the situation after Juno's removal of Turnus.

3 690. **succedit pugnae:** 'came to help the battle', i.e. his side in the battle; cf. 11.826, the same phrase.

4 691. **Tyrrhenae acies:** the Etruscans, now Aeneas' allies, had special hatred towards Mezentius as the despot who had oppressed them and been deposed; cf. 8.481f.

5 691-2. 'and with all their hatred, their thronging weapons, they turn to attack him alone, their single target'. The construction is *et omnibus odiis et telis frequentibus uni viro instant;* notice the doubled *-que* ('both . . . and', cf. 695) placed after the adjective *omnibus,* and the elision of a long syllable before a short twice (*Tyrrhenae* and *uni*).For the repetition of *uni* cf. 180-1 and 821-2.

6 693f. For the simile of a rock cf. Hom. *Il.* 15.618f., and *Aen.* 7.586f. (with note).

7 694. **expostaque:** syncope for *expositaque,* cf *repostus* (1.26, 11.149), *suppostus* (6.24).

8 696. **prolem Dolichaonis Hebrum:** this victim of Mezentius, like those who follow (Latagus, Palmus, Euanthes, Mimas), is not heard of elsewhere in the *Aeneid.*

9 698. **saxo . . . montis:** the same phrase in 9.569, where see note.

10 699. **os faciemque:** accusatives of respect, see note on 324. In this instance the construction is like the Homeric 'partial apposition', e.g.*Il.* 7.14-16; cf. 12.275-6.

11 700. **volvi . . . sinit:** 'left him helplessly writhing', a savage phrase.

12 701. **donat habere . . . et . . . figere:** epexegetic infinitives, cf. 5.262, 12. 211.

13 702. **Euanthen . . . Mimanta:** Greek accusatives.

14 703-4. **una . . . nocte . . . et:** 'in the same night as . . .', cf. 12.846-7.

15 **Theano . . . Amyco:** the father and mother of Mimas are not heard of elsewhere; the names occur elsewhere, referring to different persons.

471

in lucem genitore[1] Amyco dedit et face praegnas
Cisseis[2] regina Parim; Paris[3] urbe paterna   705
occubat, ignarum[4] Laurens habet ora Mimanta.
Ac velut ille[5] canum morsu de montibus altis[6]
actus aper, multos Vesulus[7] quem pinifer annos
defendit multosque[8] palus Laurentia silva
pascit harundinea, postquam inter retia ventum[9] est,   710
substitit infremuitque ferox et inhorruit[10] armos,
nec[11] cuiquam irasci propiusve accedere virtus,
sed iaculis tutisque procul clamoribus instant;
[12]ille autem impavidus partis[13] cunctatur in omnis   717
dentibus infrendens et tergo decutit hastas: 718
haud aliter, iustae quibus[14] est Mezentius irae, [15]   714
non ulli est animus stricto concurrere ferro,   715

---

1 704. **genitore**: this is Bentley's probable conjecture for *genitori* of the MSS (only Mynors of recent editors accepts it). *Genitore* could have been changed by a scribe to the dative because of *dedit*, but in fact *in lucem* has the function of the in direct object.

2 705. **Cisseis**: i.e. Hecuba; for the story see note on 7.319f.

3 **Paris**: this is Bentley's conjecture (accepted almost universally) for *creat*, which is the wrong tense to balance with *dedit*; also a subject is needed for *occubat*. Servius, who read *creat*, saw the second point and says the omission is due to metrical compulsion. The word *Paris* would have dropped out after the previous word *Parim*, and *creat* have been inserted to heal the metre. For this type of repetition cf. 751 ... *peditem. pedes* ... , 753 *Salius Saliumque* ...

4 706. **ignarum ... Mimanta:** the phrase is in strong anti thesis to the previous one; 'Paris lies in the city of his fathers, *but* ... *Ignarum* here has a passive sense ('unknown'), as Gellius (9.12.22) points out; cf. Ov. *Met.* 7.404 *proles ignara parenti.* For the pathos of death far away from home cf. 12.546-7.

5 707. **ille**: a nice touch (making it 'the boar' rather than 'a boar'); cf. 11.809, 12.5. It is evident from the two geographical locations, which are far apart, that Virgil is not referring to one particular boar.

6 707f. Wild boar similes occur in Homer, *Il.* 11.414f., 13.471f.; Virgil has emphasised the local setting (*Vesulus, palus Laurentia*).

7 708. **Vesulus**: a mountain in Liguria, where the river Po has its source.

8 709-10. **multosque palus ... harundinea**: 'or one that the Laurentian marsh has nurtured for many years in its thickets of reeds'; *Laurentius* is an unusual variant for *Laurens* (706). The construction is strange: *multosve* is read by P, but would be equally difficult. *Pascit* is an emendation of Bentley for *pastus* of the MSS, which is ungrammatical.

9 710. **ventum est**: impersonal, = *venit aper.*

10 711. **inhorruit armos**: 'bristles all along its back', like Homer's φρισσει δε τε νωτον (*Il.* 13.473); *armos* means the shoulders or fore parts of an animal, cf. 768, 894. Its construction is accusative of respect, see note on 324.

11 712. 'and no-one has the courage to pluck up anger or go any nearer'; for the infinitive after the noun *virtus* cf. 277 and 715. *Irasci* is very striking of the hunter (it is the expected word for the boar); it is picked up by *irae* in 714.

12 717-18. Scaliger's transposition of these lines so that they apply to the boar and not to Mezentius seems essential. *Dentibus infrendens* could be applied to a human (3.664, Polyphemus; 8.230, Hercules); and *tergo* could presumably refer to Mezentius' shield (cf. 482, 784). But both phrases are so natural of a boar (cf. Homer's κομπος οδοντων, *Il.* 11.417) that it would be comical to metamorphose Mezentius thus. Cf. Lucan 6.208-9 where Virgil's phrase *tergo decutit hastas* is applied to an elephant.

13 717. **partis cunctatur in omnis**: 'hesitates which of all ways to go', a colourful use of *cunctatur;* he is ready to charge but being surrounded on all sides cannot decide which direction to choose for an attack.

14 714. **quibus**: the antecedent to be supplied is *eorum (non animus est ulli eorum quibus ...).*

15 **irae**: predicative dative, an unusual usage, especially with the adjective *iustae*; Macrobius (*Sal.* 6.6.9) says *odio esse aliquem usitatum, irae esse inventum Maronis est.* The phrase has been taken as genitive of quality, but cf. Sil. 11.604 *Hannibal est irae tibi.*

missilibus longe et vasto clamore lacessunt.   *716*

    Venerat antiquis Corythi de finibus Acron,[1]   *719*

Graius homo, infectos linquens profugus[2] hymenaeos;   *720*

hunc ubi miscentem[3] longe media agmina vidit,

purpureum[4] pennis et pactae coniugis ostro,

impastus stabula[5] alta leo[6] ceu saepe[7] peragrans

(suadet enim vesana fames), si forte fugacem

conspexit capream aut surgentem[8] in cornua cervum,   *725*

gaudet hians[9] immane comasque arrexit et haeret

visceribus super incumbens; lavit[10] improba[11] taeter

ora cruor —

sic ruit in densos alacer Mezentius hostis.

Sternitur infelix Acron et calcibus atram   *730*

tundit humum exspirans infractaque[12] tela cruentat.

Atque idem fugientem haud est dignatus Oroden[13]

sternere nec iacta caecum dare cuspide vulnus;

obvius adversoque[14] occurrit seque viro[15] vir

contulit, haud furto melior sed fortibus armis.   *735*

Tum[16] super abiectum posito pede nixus et hasta:

---

1 719. Acron is not mentioned elsewhere in the *Aeneid*; for the Etruscan town Corythus see notes on 7.209, 9.10-11 (where its Greek connexions are mentioned).

2 720. **profugus hymenaeos:** notice the quadri-syllabic ending and the lengthening in arsis of the last syllable of *profugus;* cf. 7.398, 11.69, *Geo.* 4.137.

3 721. **miscentem ... vidit:** the subject is Mezentius for *miscere* ('throw into confusion') cf. 7.348, 12.445.

4 722. 'gleaming purple on his crest, and with the heliotrope of his promised bride'; Acron is wearing the colour of Love, cf. Ov. *Am.* 2.1.38, 2.9.34 *purpuras Amor.* Conington quotes Milton: 'Celestial rosy red, Love's proper hue'. For the phraseology cf. 9.163.

5 723. **stabula alta:** 'the deep hiding places', cf. 6.179, 9.388.

6 723f. The lion simile (for which cf. 9.339f. and *Il.* 3.23f., 12.299f., 17.61f.),following so soon upon the wild boar simile (707f.), is very much in the Iliadic tradition of wild animal similes, and stresses the heroic and Homeric nature of Mezentius' aristeia (see note on 689f.).

7 **saepe:** 'as often happens', cf. 1.148.

8 725. **surgentem in cornua cervum:** 'a stag towering high to its antlers'; for *in cornua* cf. Ov. *Met.* 10.538.

9 726. **hians immane:** 'opening its jaws in terrifying fashion'; for *immane* (adverbial accusative) cf. 7.510, 12.535. The trochaic diaereses in this line add to the impression of speed and action.

10 727. **lavit:** for this form of the present indicative of *lavare* cf. 3.663.

11 **improba:** 'relentless', cf. 9.62.

12 731. **infracta:** 'broken', by wounding him, cf. 12.387.

13 732. Orodes is not mentioned elsewhere.

14 734. **adversoque:** the redundant *-que* adds emphasis, cf. 12.289 and 5.447 with my note (OUP Ed.).

15 **viro vir:** for the phrase and the monosyllabic ending cf. 361.

16 736. 'Then putting his foot on him as he pushed him away and pulling on the spear, he said . . .'; literally 'striving with planted foot and spear', i.e. pressing with his foot so as to pull out the spear. The line is closely based on Hom. *Il.* 16.862-3; *abiectum* is a rendering of τον δ υπτιον ωσ απο δουρος.

'pars belli haud temnenda, viri, iacet altus Orodes.'[1]
Conclamant socii laetum paeana[2] secuti.
Ille autem exspirans: 'non me, quicumque es, inulto,[3]
victor, nec[4] longum laetabere; te quoque fata   740
prospectant paria atque eadem mox arva tenebis.'
Ad quae subridens mixta Mezentius ira:
'nunc morere. Ast de me divum[5] pater atque hominum rex[6]
viderit.'[7] Hoc dicens eduxit corpore telum.
Olli dura quies oculos et ferreus[8] urget   745
somnus, in aeternam clauduntur lumina noctem.

    Caedicus Alcathoum obtruncat, Sacrator Hydaspen[9]
Partheniumque Rapo et praedurum viribus Orsen,
Messapus Cloniumque[10] Lycaoniumque Erichaeten,
illum infrenis[11] equi lapsu tellure iacentem,   750
hunc peditem. Pedes et Lycius processerat Agis,
quem tamen haud expers Valerus virtutis avitae
deicit; at Thronium Salius Saliumque Nealces[12]
insignis[13] iaculo et longe fallente sagitta.

    Iam[14] gravis aequabat luctus et mutua Mavors[15]   755
funera; caedebant pariter pariterque ruebant
victores victique, neque his fuga nota neque illis.

---

1 737. Compare 427, where see note.

2 738. **paeana:** Greek accusative; so Achilles tells the Greeks to sing a paean after he has killed Hector (*Il.* 22.391f.).

3 739f. The sentiment is Homeric; cf. the dying Patroclus to Hector (*Il.* 16.852f.), and Hector to Achilles (*Il.* 22.359f.).

4 740. **nec longum:** 'nor for long'; *nec* links *longum* with *me inulto*.

5 743. **divum . . . rex:** the same phrase (based on Ennius) as was used in line 2, where see note.

6 743f. Again the sentiment is from Achilles' speech to the dying Hector, *Il.* 22.365f.

7 744. **viderit:** 'let him see to it', suggesting indifference, cf. Cic. *Tusc.* 2.42, Ov. *A.A.* 2.371.

8 745-6. **ferreus . . . somnus:** an adaptation of Homer's 'sleep of bronze' (χαλκεος υπνος, *Il.* 11.241); cf. 12.309-10, the same two lines. Dryden (*Thren. Aug.* 70) has (of Charles II) 'An iron slumber sate on his majestic eyes'.

9 747f. This account of Italian successes against the Trojans is rather abruptly introduced. These warriors are not heard of elsewhere in the *Aeneid* (though the names Caedicus and Clonius have been used of others) except for Messapus, the prominent Latin leader (354, 7.691 etc.).

10 749. **Cloniumque Lycaoniumque Erichaeten:** the list of names is given in a line of Greek rhythm, with no main caesura in third or fourth foot and a quadri-syllabic ending; cf. 413. The doubled -*que* ('both . . . and') reinforces the Greek feeling (τε . . . τε is very frequent in Homer). *Lycaonius* means 'son of Lycaon', cf. 123.

11 750. **infrenis:** in 4.41 Virgil uses the other form, *infrenus*.

12 753. The vengeance of Nealces on Salius is the only Trojan success in this section.

13 754. **insignis:** this is the reading of *M1*; the other main MSS have *insidiis*. It is obviously improbable that Virgil means that Nealces killed him with a javelin and an arrow, so it would be necessary (if we read *insidiis*) to accept Servius' view that *iaculo et. . . sagitta* means (by hendiadys) 'with the shooting of an arrow', a most unlikely suggestion. For the linking of prowess with *iaculum* and *sagitta* cf. 5.68, 9.178.

14 755f. This passage is based on Hom. *Il.* 11.70f. (the battle equally poised, neither side giving ground, the gods watching from Olympus).

15 755. **Mavors:** the archaic form of Mars, cf. 8.630, 9.685.

Di Iovis in tectis iram miserantur inanem
amborum et tantos mortalibus esse labores;
hinc Venus, hinc contra spectat Saturnia Iuno.   760
Pallida Tisiphone[1] media inter milia saevit.
At vero ingentem quatiens Mezentius hastam
turbidus ingreditur campo.[2] Quam magnus Orion,[3]
cum pedes incedit medii[4] per maxima Nerei
stagna viam scindens, umero supereminet[5] undas,   765
aut[6] summis referens annosam montibus ornum
ingrediturque solo et caput inter nubila condit:
talis[7] se vastis infert Mezentius armis.[8]

*769-832. Aeneas and Mezentius meet in single combat.
Mezentius is wounded and his son Lausus intervenes to save
him. Aeneas kills Lausus and in profound sorrow at what he
has had to do lifts up his body and restores it to his
comrades.*

[9]Huic contra Aeneas speculatus in agmine longo
obvius ire parat. Manet imperterritus[10] ille   770

---

1 761. Tisiphone is the fury who guards Tartarus in the underworld, cf. 6.555: here, like Allecto in 7.323f. (where see note), she personifies *furor*, mad frenzy on the battlefield. Compare also Eris in Homer (*Il.* 11.73, 18.535).

2 763. **campo:** dative, equivalent to *in campum* (cf. 148). The meaning is that he resumes his attacks, this time in the part of the battlefield where Aeneas is fighting.

3 763f. This is the fourth full scale simile about Mezentius in sixty lines; see note on 689f. Orion, the hunter, is called huge in Hom. *Od.* 11.572; there is a reference to the constellation Orion setting his feet on the sea in Theoc. 7.54, and we are reminded of the giant Polyphemus (3.664-5).

4 764-5. **medii . . . stagna:** 'through the great expanses of the middle of the sea'; for *medium* cf. 3.665, for Nereus (god of the sea, used by metonymy for the sea, like Bacchus = wine, Ceres = corn) cf. 8.383; there the word is scanned, as here, as a spondee by synizesis.

5 765. **supereminet:** 'towers above', transitive as in 1.501, 6.856.

6 766-7. 'or as when he brings back an aged ash from the mountain heights he treads on the ground yet hides his head among the clouds'; the second line is repeated from 4.177 (applied to Fama). This is a second picture of Orion, showing his giant stature by the fact that he carries an uprooted tree (cf. Polyphemus in 3.659) and towers as high as the clouds.

7 768. Notice the heavy spondaic line, with the first foot diaeresis emphasising *talis*.

8 **armis:** probably here 'shoulders' (cf. 765) from *armus*, rather than 'weapons'; cf. 711, 11.644.

9 769f. The final encounter between Aeneas and Mezentius is interrupted by the intervention of Lausus and his vain attempt to save his father. It is doubtful whether this was in the tradition of the Aeneas legend: Dionysius (1.65) mentions the death of Lausus but does not connect it with Mezentius. Possibly the idea is based on the death of Antilochus, Nestor's son, when he tried to save Nestor from Memnon (Pind. *Pyth.* 6.27f.; the story was told in the lost *Aethiopis*); but it is certain that Virgil has used whatever sources he may have had (see also note on 789) in order to make something quite new, and specially relevant to the development of his story. The pathos of the death of the youthful Lausus repeats a theme often found in the *Aeneid* (Polites, Euryalus, Pallas and many of lesser fame), and has a profound effect upon Aeneas. His battle-fury gives way to sorrow and revulsion, and he becomes more himself again. But in particular the episode makes a sharp contrast with the death of Pallas at the hands of Turnus. Virgil does not explicitly make any comparison, but it is implicit from lines 821-32 and the more effective because we are left to realise it for ourselves. In place of the arrogant and boastful joy of Turnus as he strips Pallas' spoils, Aeneas bitterly regrets what he has had to do, and speaks in tones of sorrow, almost of remorse, to the dying man (see note on 827-8).

10 770. **imperterritus:** 'utterly unafraid', a strange and rare word, not found before Virgil, commented on by Quintilian (1.5.65) because *im-* and *per-* are mutually contradictory.

hostem magnanimum opperiens, et mole[1] sua stat
atque oculis spatium emensus quantum[2] satis hastae:
'dextra[3] mihi deus et telum, quod missile libro,
nunc adsint! [4]Voveo praedonis corpore raptis
indutum spoliis ipsum te, Lause, tropaeum   775
Aeneae.' Dixit, stridentemque eminus hastam
iecit. At illa volans clipeo est excussa proculque
egregium Antoren[5] latus inter et ilia figit,
Herculis Antoren comitem, qui missus ab Argis
haeserat Euandro[6] atque Itala consederat urbe.   780
Sternitur infelix alieno[7] vulnere, caelumque
aspicit et dulcis moriens reminiscitur Argos.
Tum pius[8] Aeneas hastam iacit; illa[9] per orbem
aere cavum triplici, per linea terga tribusque
transiit intextum tauris opus, imaque sedit   785
inguine, sed viris[10] haud pertulit. Ocius ensem

---

1 771. **mole sua stat**: 'stands firm in all his might', the monosyllabic ending gives an abrupt and emphatic ending (cf. 734);for *mole sua* cf. 5.431 *mole valens* (Entellus the boxer) and 7.589; for *stat* cf. Stat. *Th.* 10.935 (of Capaneus) *stat tamen . . .* ('he still stands firm').

2 772. **quantum satis hastae**: again an unusual line ending, cf. 440.

3 773-4. 'Now let my right hand, for that is the god I worship, and this weapon which I poise for its throw be favourable to me'. Mezentius does not worship the accepted gods (he is *contemptor divum*, 7.648); his own valour is the deity he acknowledges. The phrase is imitated by Statius (*Th.* 9.548f. *ades o mihi, dextera, . . . te voco, te solam superum contemptor adoro*) in a speech by Capaneus, who is modelled on Virgil's Mezentius; cf. also *Th.* 3.615 (said by Capaneus) *virtus mihi numen et ensis*. Compare Spenser's Sarazin (*F.Q.* 1.2.12):
In whose great shield was writ with letters gay
Sans foy: full large of limb and every joint
He was, and cared not for God or man a point.

4 774-6. 'I vow you yourself, Lausus, as a trophy of Aeneas, decked as you shall be in the spoils snatched from that pirate's body'; this strange promise reflects the blasphemy of Mezentius, as a trophy would normally consist of a trunk of a tree decked with the enemy's spoils and vowed to a deity (such as Aeneas' trophy of triumph over Mezentius himself, 11.5f.). Mezentius offers no trophy to the gods, but 'dedicates' his spoils to his son. *Praedonis* is used contemptuously of Aeneas also by Amata (7.362) and by the Latin women (11.484); *Aeneae* in 776 is genitive after *tropaeum*.

5 778. **Antoren**: nothing is known of Antores elsewhere.

6 780. Evander came from Arcadia to Pallanteum on the Tiber (8.51f.), and presumably Antores has joined him from Argos (in Virgil *Argi*) before he left Greece for Italy.

7 781. **alieno**: 'meant for someone else'.
Notice the hypermetric elision of *caelumque*; cf. 895 and see note on 7.160.

8 783. **pius**: here the epithet concentrates our attention on the contrast between the godless Mezentius (773f.) and the god fearing Aeneas.

9 783-5. **illa per orbem . . . opus**: 'it went through the shield's circle, convex with three layers of bronze, through the layers of linen and the texture made of the hide of three bulls'; the description is based on Hom. *Il.* 3.357f. for *terga* (properly hide) used of linen cf. 482 with note.

10 786. **viris haud pertulit**: 'did not drive its force right home', cf. 12.907 (the stone which Turnus throws) *neque pertulit ictum*. The frequency of bucolic diaeresis (word ending and pause after the fourth dactyl) is striking here (783, 785, 786). There is a diaeresis after the fourth foot in all six lines from 783-8.

Aeneas viso Tyrrheni[1] sanguine laetus[2]
eripit a femine et trepidanti fervidus instat.
Ingemuit cari graviter genitoris amore,[3]
ut vidit, Lausus, lacrimaeque per ora volutae.   790

    Hic mortis durae casum tuaque optima facta,[4]
si qua fidem tanto est operi latura vetustas,[5]
non equidem nec[6] te, iuvenis memorande, silebo.

    Ille pedem referens et inutilis inque[7] ligatus
cedebat clipeoque inimicum hastile trahebat.   795
Proripuit[8] iuvenis seseque immiscuit armis,
iamque adsurgentis dextra plagamque ferentis[9]
Aeneae subiit[10] mucronem ipsumque morando
sustinuit; socii magno clamore sequuntur,
dum[11] genitor nati parma protectus abiret,   800
telaque coniciunt perturbantque eminus hostem
missilibus. Furit[12] Aeneas tectusque tenet se.
Ac velut effusa si quando grandine nimbi
praecipitant, omnis campis diffugit arator
omnis et agricola, et tuta latet arce[13] viator   805
aut amnis[14] ripis aut alti fornice saxi,
dum pluit in terris, ut possint sole reducto
exercere[15] diem: sic obrutus undique telis

---

1 787. **Tyrrheni:** the epithet is used again of Mezentius the Etruscan in 898.

2 787-8. **laetus . . . fervidus:** in battle against the fierce Mezentius Aeneas rejoices in his success; he does not do so when he kills Mezentius' young son Lausus (821f.).

3 789. The pathos of Lausus, devoted to his unlovable father (cf. 7.653-4), is introduced in a line made memorable by the strong alliteration of *g* and the rhyme of *-or-*. Conington compares the story of the young Scipio defending his father in Livy 21.46.

4 791f. The invocation concentrates the sympathy of the reader; cf. 9.446f. and the apostrophe to Pallas in 507f. The emphasis is increased by the word order, with accusatives in 791, and a subordinate clause in 792 before the subject and the verb in 793.

5 792. **vetustas:** 'antiquity', cf. 3.415, 12.686, Ov. *Met.* 1.400 *quis hoc credat, nisi sit pro teste vetustas?, Fast.* 4.203-4 *pro magno teste vetustas / creditur.*

6 793. **nec te:** *nec* links *te* with *casum* and *facta* (791).

7 794. **inque ligatus:** = *et inligatus* ('hampered'), by the spear sticking in his shield. The only other example of such tmesis in Virgil is 9.288 *inque salutatam.* It is common in Lucretius (e.g. 3.484 *inque pediri*).

8 796. **proripuit:** 'dashed forward', supply *sese* from the following clause; some MSS have *prorupit,* which may be right.

9 797. Page draws attention to the assonance of *-entis* to suggest awe, cf. 572.

10 798-9. **subiit . . . sustinuit:** 'parried his sword and checked Aeneas and held him off'.

11 800. **dum . . . abiret:** for the idea of purpose expressed by the subjunctive cf. 809, *Aen.* 1.5, *Geo.* 4.457f.

12 802. Aeneas' frustration is emphasised by the short sentence with its two main verbs, the alliteration of *t,* and the monosyllabic ending. *Tectus* means under cover of his shield.

13 805. **arce:** 'retreat', defined by *aut . . . aut* in the next line; the MSS have *arte,* which makes no real sense.

14 806. **amnis ripis:** presumably high banks under which he can shelter.

15 808. **exercere diem:** 'get on with the day's work', cf. 8.94.

Aeneas nubem[1] belli, dum[2] detonet omnis,

sustinet et Lausum increpitat Lausoque minatur: 810

'quo moriture ruis maioraque viribus audes?

Fallit[3] te incautum pietas tua.' Nec minus ille

exsultat demens, saevae[4] iamque altius irae

Dardanio surgunt ductori, extremaque Lauso

Parcae[5] fila legunt: validum namque exigit ensem   815

per medium Aeneas iuvenem totumque recondit.

Transiit et parmam mucro, levia[6] arma minacis,

et tunicam molli mater quam neverat auro,

implevitque sinum[7] sanguis; tum vita per auras

concessit maesta ad manis corpusque reliquit.   820

At vero ut vultum vidit morientis et ora,[8]

ora modis Anchisiades pallentia miris,

ingemuit miserans graviter dextramque tetendit,

et[9] mentem patriae subiit pietatis imago.

'Quid tibi nunc, miserande puer, pro laudibus[10] istis,   825

quid pius[11] Aeneas tanta dabit indole dignum?

Arma, quibus laetatus,[12] habe tua; teque parentum[13]

manibus et cineri, si qua est ea cura, remitto.

Hoc tamen infelix miseram solabere mortem:

---

1 809. **nubem belli:** cf. Hom. *Il.* 17.243. Here it very precisely picks up the simile.

2 **dum detonet:** 'waiting for it to spend its fury'; for the subjunctive cf. 800.

3 812. 'Your love for your father is leading you astray, into folly'. It is very ironical for Aeneas to chide Lausus for too much *pietas;* it is in the end his appreciation of Lausus' *pietas* (824) that causes his intense sorrow at having killed him.

4 813. Notice the emphasis on *saevae,* placed before *iamque,* and in juxtaposition with *demens;* war-frenzy possesses both men.

5 815. **Parcae fila legunt:** the three fates (Parcae, 419) 'gather' the threads of Lausus' life prior to cutting them.

6 817. **levia arma minacis:** 'frail defence for one so threatening'; the *parma* (800) was a small shield.

7 819. **sinum:** the folds of his tunic, cf. Hom. *Il.* 20.471.

8 821-2. The transition in Aeneas from savage anger (813) to pity is presented in slow spondees with strong alliteration of *v,* with the repetition of *ora* (cf. 2.405-6 with note, 6.495-6), with the evocative Lucretian phrase (1.123) *modis . . . pallentia miris* (cf. *Aen.* 1.354), and with the long sonorous word *Anchisiades,* here indicating that Aeneas as son of Anchises is moved by the gallantry Lausus displays on behalf of his father (cf. 824).

9 824. 'and the picture of his own love for his father came into his thoughts'; cf. 9.294.

10 825. **laudibus:** 'deeds worthy of praise', hence 'glory', as often (e.g. 282, 9.252).

11 826. **pius Aeneas:** with, of course, reference to *pietas* in 824.

12 827. **laetatus:** supply *es,* cf. 1.237.

13 827-8. Aeneas returns Lausus' armour for burial with his corpse; Turnus had stripped Pallas of his (495f.). In addition the tone of each man's words is entirely different: Turnus was contemptuous and arrogant (491f.), Aeneas is deeply moved.for the pathos of *si qua est ea cura* cf. 7.4.

Aeneae magni dextra cadis.[1] Increpat ultro[2]   830
cunctantis socios et terra sublevat ipsum[3]
sanguine turpantem comptos de more capillos.

> *833-908. Mezentius hears of the death of his son Lausus,*
> *and prepares to give up his own life by confronting Aeneas.*
> *In the ensuing contest he is mortally wounded, and meets his*
> *death with the dignity of the heroic warrior.*

[4]Interea genitor Tiberini ad fluminis undam
vulnera siccabat[5] lymphis corpusque levabat[6]
arboris acclinis trunco. Procul aerea ramis   835
dependet galea et prato gravia[7] arma quiescunt.
Stant lecti circum iuvenes; [8]ipse aeger anhelans
colla fovet fusus propexam in pectore barbam;
multa super Lauso rogitat, multumque[9] remittit
qui revocent maestique ferant mandata[10] parentis.   840
At Lausum socii exanimem super[11] arma ferebant[12]
flentes, ingentem atque ingenti vulnere victum.
Agnovit longe gemitum praesaga mali mens. [13]
Canitiem multo deformat pulvere et ambas
ad caelum tendit palmas et corpore inhaeret.   845

---

1 830. The sentiment is (in Page's words) 'in the epic vein'; cf. *Aen.* 11.689 and Achilles in Ov. *Met.* 12.80f. Notice how the speech ends at the bucolic diaeresis, cf. 812, 827 and note on 786.

2 830. **ultro:** before they (Lausus' companions, 799, 841) took any action.

3 831. Aeneas himself picks up Lausus' body; by contrast Turnus had put his foot on Pallas' body to despoil him.

4 833f. Mezentius has been depicted in the *Aeneid* as the most hateful of all the characters (cf. especially 8.481f.), yet at these last moments of his life Virgil evokes a kind of sympathy even for him. There is about him a certain astringent realism, what Quinn calls 'his icy, contemptuous acceptance of the calculated risks of war' (p. 16). Quinn rightly describes this passage as a 'masterpiece of unsentimental pathos' (p. 232) and contrasts Mezentius' 'final unflinching acceptance of the realities of war' with the protests of Camilla and Turnus. There is a fine simplicity about lines 855-6, 861-2, 865-6, 881-2, 900-1; in the vicious tyrant Mezentius we see at the last the full heroic acceptance of death when it comes.

5 834. **siccabat:** 'staunched', cf. 4.687.

6 **levabat:** 'relaxed', 'eased'; all the major MSS have *lavabat,* but Servius read *levabat,* and cf. Ov. *Fast.* 6.328 *gramine membra levat.*

7 836. **gravia arma quiescunt:** 'his heavy armour lies silent', away for the moment from the clash of war.

8 837-8. 'he himself, weak and gasping, bathes his head, his long combed beard hanging forward and spreading over his chest', i.e. because of the inclination of his head. For *fovere* in this medical sense (it can also mean, more generally, 'relieve') cf. 12.420, *Geo.* 4.230; for *propexa barba* cf. Ov. *Fast.* 1.259; for the retained accusative *barbam* after *fusus* ('spreading his beard') see note on 133.

9 839. **multumque:** adverbial, equivalent to *saepe* (as Servius says).

10 840. **mandata**: i.e. that he should withdraw from battle (*qui revocent*).

11 841. **super arma**: i.e. on his shield, cf. *impositum scuto* (of Pallas) in 506.

12 841-2. The diction and metre here are designed to emphasise the pathos of the situation; notice how the accusative *Lausum* is brought forward, how stress is put on *flentes* filling the first spondee of the spondaic line 842 (cf. 514, *Ecl.* 5.21), and how the memorable Homeric phrase (used again in 12.640) 'a mighty warrior laid low by a mighty wound' (*Il.* 16.776), rounds off the description.

13 843. The monosyllabic ending, with alliteration of *m*, metrically emphasises Mezentius' forebodings.

'Tantane me tenuit vivendi, nate, voluptas,[1]
ut pro me hostili paterer succedere dextrae,[2]
quem genui? Tuane haec genitor per vulnera servor
morte tua vivens? Heu, nunc misero mihi demum[3]
exsilium[4] infelix, nunc alte vulnus adactum!   850
Idem ego, nate, tuum maculavi crimine nomen,
pulsus ob invidiam solio sceptrisque paternis.
Debueram patriae poenas odiisque meorum:
omnis per mortis animam sontem ipse dedissem![5]
Nunc vivo neque adhuc homines lucemque relinquo.   855
Sed[6] linquam.' Simul hoc dicens attollit in aegrum
se femur et, quamquam vis[7] alto vulnere tardat,
haud deiectus[8] equum duci iubet. Hoc[9] decus illi,
hoc solamen erat, bellis hoc victor abibat
omnibus. [10]Adloquitur maerentem et talibus infit: 860
'Rhaebe,[11] diu, res si qua diu mortalibus ulla est,
viximus. Aut hodie victor spolia[12] illa cruenta
et caput Aeneae referes Lausique dolorum
ultor eris mecum, aut aperit si nulla viam[13] vis,
occumbes pariter; neque enim, fortissime, credo,   865
iussa[14] aliena pati et dominos dignabere Teucros.'

---

1 846. In this line of bitter self-reproach Mezentius blames himself more than he need — cowardice was not one of his vices. Cerda compares Cassius' words in Plut. *Brut.* 43 (φιλοψυχουντες ανεμειναμεν . . .). Notice the pattern of alliteration, *t* and then *v*.

2 847. As the object of *paterer* supply *eum*, antecedent to *quem genui*.

3 849. Virgil again (as often in this book, see note on 440) has the relatively rare line ending of a double dissyllable.

4 850. **exsilium:** the major MSS have *exitium*, but Servius read *exsilium* and this makes far better sense; Mezentius could endure his exile (852, cf. 8.481f.) as long as he had the companionship of his son. I have argued the point in detail in *C.R.* 1961, pp. 195f.

5 854. **dedissem:** 'I ought to have yielded up', past jussive subjunctive equivalent to *debueram dare*, cf. 8.643, 11.162.

6 856. **sed linquam:** a fine heroic style ending to his self-torturing speech.

7 857. **vis alto vulnere tardat:** 'his strength fails because of his deep wound', a very strange phrase which may be corrupt (the MSS vary, and Peerlkamp ingeniously conjectured *quamvis dolor alto vulnere tardet*); as it stands *tardat* is used intransitively, like *tarda est* (which Schaper conjectured); cf. Cic. *Ad Att.* 6.7.2, *Ad Brut.* 1.18.1.

8 858. **deiectus:** 'downcast', sc. *animo* (as Servius says).

9 **hoc:** referring to the horse, and attracted to the gender of its predicate, cf. 3.660, 12.572.

10 860. Hector talks to his horse in Homer, *Il.* 8.184f., and Achilles does so in *Il.* 19.400f.; for the idea that horses sorrow for their masters cf. *Aen.* 11.89f., and Hom. *Il.* 17.426f. Only here in the *Aeneid* does a warrior address his horse, and it is appropriate that Mezentius should do so, whose only good quality is courage on the battlefield. Heyne rightly says of Mezentius' opening words 'gravis sententia et affectus plena'.

11 861. **Rhaebe:** the Greek word means 'bandy-legs'.

12 862. **spolia illa cruenta:** i.e. the arms of Aeneas stained with his blood.

13 864. **viam vis:** for the monosyllabic ending cf. 9.532, 11.373.

14 866. 'you will not be prepared to endure the commands of another and the Trojans as your masters'; *Teucros* (like *iussa*) is governed by *pati*. This is a fine heroic sentiment, simply and splendidly expressed.

Dixit, et exceptus[1] tergo consueta locavit
membra manusque ambas iaculis oneravit acutis,
aere caput[2] fulgens cristaque hirsutus equina.
Sic cursum in medios rapidus dedit. Aestuat ingens[3]   870
uno in corde pudor mixtoque insania luctu.
[Et furiis agitatus amor et conscia virtus.]
    Atque hic Aenean magna ter voce vocavit.
Aeneas agnovit enim[4] laetusque precatur:
'sic pater ille deum faciat, sic altus Apollo![5]   875
Incipias conferre manum.'
Tantum effatus et infesta subit obvius hasta.
Ille autem: 'quid me erepto, saevissime, nato
terres? Haec[6] via sola fuit qua perdere posses:
nec mortem horremus nec[7] divum parcimus ulli.   880
Desine, nam venio moriturus et haec tibi porto[8]
dona prius.' Dixit, telumque intorsit in hostem;
inde aliud super atque aliud figitque[9] volatque
ingenti gyro, sed sustinet aureus umbo.
Ter circum astantem laevos[10] equitavit in orbis   885
tela manu iaciens, [11]ter secum Troms heros
immanem aerato circumfert tegmine silvam.
Inde ubi tot[12] traxisse moras, tot spicula taedet

---

1 867. **exceptus tergo**: 'received on its back'; *exceptus* suggests the willingness of the horse to accept the weight of its well-known rider.

2 869. **caput**: accusative of respect, see note on 324.

3 870-1. These lines are used of Turnus (12.666-7); line 872 (= 12.668) is omitted in the major MSS, and is certainly spurious here.

4 874. **enim**: 'indeed', an archaic sense of the word; cf. 6.317, 8.84, and *namque* in 614.

5 875. The wish is defined by the next line; may Jupiter and Apollo bring it about that you come to meet me. Apollo, Aeneas' main guide in Book 3, was Augustus' patron deity; see note on 8.704.

6 879. **haec via**: i.e. through his son, who is now dead.

7 880. **nec divum parcimus ulli**: 'nor do I concede anything to any of the gods', a reference (as Servius saw) to Aeneas' invocation in 875; Mezentius does not care if Jupiter and Apollo answer Aeneas' prayer. Conington quotes Sall. *Cat*. 52.33 *parcite dignitati Lentuli si ipse . . . dis aut hominibus umquam ullis pepercit*; cf. also *Geo.* 4.239.

8 881. The rhythm of the second half of the line is very unusual with its two dissyllables at the line end (cf. 849) and especially the pause after the fourth trochee, a most unusual pause (see my note on 5.166-7, OUP Ed.).

9 883. **figitque volatque**: a strange coordination by doubled -*que* ('both ... and'); we would say 'another and another javelin he implants (in Aeneas' shield) as he speeds round him in a great circle'.

10 885. **laevos**: so that he was protected by his shield in his left hand.

11 886-7. 'three times the Trojan hero turned right around, and turned with him in his brazen shield a terrifying forest'. For *silva* of a thick mass of spears cf. Stat. *Th.* 5.533, Lucan 6.205. Aeneas' shield had brass as well as gold (8.445) in it.

12 888. **tot . . . moras**: for *tantum morae*. to balance (as Conington points out) with *tot spicula*.

vellere, et urgetur[1] pugna congressus iniqua,
multa movens animo iam tandem erumpit et inter   890
bellatoris equi cava tempora conicit hastam.
Tollit se arrectum quadripes et calcibus auras[2]
verberat, [3]effusumque equitem super ipse secutus
implicat eiectoque incumbit cernuus armo.
Clamore[4] incendunt caelum Troesque[5] Latinique.   895
Advolat Aeneas vaginaque eripit ensem
et super haec: 'ubi nunc Mezentius acer et illa
effera vis animi?' Contra Tyrrhenus, ut auras
suspiciens hausit[6] caelum mentemque recepit:
'hostis amare, quid increpitas mortemque minaris?[7]   900
Nullum[8] in caede nefas, nec sic ad proelia veni,
nec tecum meus haec pepigit mihi foedera Lausus.
Unum hoc per si qua est victis venia hostibus oro:
corpus humo patiare[9] tegi. Scio acerba meorum
circumstare odia: hunc, oro, defende furorem[10]   905
et me consortem nati concede sepulcro.'
Haec loquitur, iuguloque haud[11] inscius accipit ensem

---

1 889. **urgetur . . . iniqua:** 'he is hard-pressed because he is meeting his opponent under unfavourable conditions', i.e. by remaining on the defensive and allowing Mezentius to use the advantage of being on horseback.

2 892-3. i.e. the horse reared up and pawed the air.

3 893-5. 'and threw off its rider and then fell itself on top in a tangled heap, pinning him as it collapsed headfirst upon him, dislocating its shoulder'. Some have argued that *eiecto* is dative ('upon the unseated rider') and *armo* ablative; but it would be unusual for Virgil to have rhyme at the caesura and line ending with words not in agreement. Conington quotes a number of parallels for this use of *eicere*. *Cernuus* is a rare word, explained by Servius thus: *'cernuus dicitur equus qui cadit in faciem* and by Nonius as *inclinatus, quasi quod terram cernat;* Silius (10.255) imitates the passage, *cernuus inflexo sonipes effuderat armo.*

4 895. **clamore incendunt caelum:** 'they light up the sky with their shouts', an extraordinary and very vivid use of the verb; cf. 11.147 *incendunt clamoribus urbem,* and 9.500 for another vivid but rather different use of *incendere.* Heyne quotes Aesch. *Pers.* 395 σαλπιγξ δ αυτη παντ εκειν επεφλεγεν, 'the trumpet with its blare set all the place alight'. Servius comments 'abusive dixit'; certainly Virgil's phrase seems to be a bold innovation.

5 **Troesque Latinique:** doubled *-que* ('both ... and'); the second *-que* is elided hyper-metrically, see note on 781 and cf. 4.629.

6 899. **hausit caelum:** 'drew in breath'; *caelum* here is in the sense of *aera* (as Servius says), cf. Lucr. 4.132 and Juvenal's imitation (3.84-5) *nostra infantia caelum / hausit.* That this is the meaning (and not something like 'sought the light') is reinforced by the original in Homer (*Il.* 22.475) η δ επει ουν εμπνυτο και εσ φρενα θυμος αγερθη ('when she got breath again and her senses returned').

7 900. This splendid line, in which Mezentius tells Aeneas that no words are called for, because he knows and accepts that death is a condition of battle, is made memorable by the unusually large number of trochaic breaks (first foot, second foot, fifth foot) and the striking word *amarus* (echoed by assonance in *minaris*) which is not applied to people by Virgil elsewhere.

8 901. **nullum. . . . nefas:** Mezentius was ready to kill or be killed, he has no complaint. *Nec sic* refers back to this phrase; he did not come to battle under any illusion that he would receive mercy if defeated, nor (he says in the next line) did his son make any such pleas on his behalf.

9 904. **patiare:** jussive subjunctive, dependent on *oro.*

10 905. **furorem:** he fears that his body may be found and maltreated by those he had caused to hate him. Virgil does not tell us whether Mezentius' request was granted.

11 907. **haud inscius:** 'deliberately', cf. 9.552.

undantique animam diffundit in arma cruore.[1]

---

1 908. Compare 487. Servius points out that *in arma* goes with *undantique*, not with *diffundit*.

BOOK 11

Introductory note

This book begins in a tone of pathos and pity of the kind which is specially associated with Virgil's poetry. The sorrow and guilt which Aeneas feels for the death of Pallas, the young son of Evander, who had been particularly entrusted to his care, is expressed in a long, drawn out account if the funeral ceremonies (see note on 1f.); the pathos is deepened by the mention of Dido (72f.), and by reminiscences of Catullus (68f., 96f.).

This tone of pathos is continued during the description of the truce, with Aeneas' outburst against the horrors of war, and the lamentation of Evander; it begins to change during the factual report by Venulus of the failure of the embassy to Diomedes and the reply by King Latinus. Here the interest is intellectual, and it leads up to the rhetorical vigour of the altercation between Drance and Turnus. This is distanced and detached writing (see note on 336f.), and forms a complete contrast with the opening scenes of the book and also with the subsequent description of the deeds and death of Camilla. The rhetoric is strong and sinewy: the reader is not personally involved in this clash of personalities and can take a detached intellectual pleasure in the violent cut-and-thrust of debate.

For the remainder of the book the tone changes again for the half pastoral half military description of the aristeia of the warrior-maid Camilla (notes on 532f., 648f.). In many respects she is a figure from a magic world, under the protection of Diana (532f.), able to skim over fields of growing corn without bruising the shoots (7.808f.); but she is also a full scale heroic warrior in her own right, with very strong resemblances in her bravery and impetuosity to Turnus himself (cf. especially 502, 507, 648, 664, 709, 762). The story of her valiant deeds is in outline very like those of the Homeric warriors in the *Iliad;* but a special sympathy is aroused for her by the blackening of the character of Arruns, the cunning and cowardly Ligurian who kills her without ever having faced her in battle. Like Turnus, she seemed well able to look after herself; like Turnus however she was fighting against fate and the oracles of the gods, and could not survive into the new order destined to be founded by the Trojans; like Turnus she wins our sympathy in defeat, and the line which describes her death — *vitaque cum gemitu fugit indignata sub umbras* (831) — is repeated as the last line of the *Aeneid* (12.952) to describe Turnus' death.

1-99. Aeneas dedicates the spoils of Mezentius as a trophy to Mars, and then arranges for the funeral procession to escort Pallas' body back to his father Evander. He speaks to the dead youth in terms of the most extreme sorrow.

¹Oceanum interea surgens Aurora reliquit:²
Aeneas, quamquam et sociis dare³ tempus humandis
praecipitant curae turbataque funere mens est,
vota⁴ deum primo victor solvebat Eoo.⁵
Ingentem quercum decisis undique ramis   5
constituit tumulo fulgentiaque induit arma,
Mezenti ducis exuvias, tibi, magne, tropaeum,⁶
bellipotens; aptat rorantis sanguine cristas
telaque trunca⁷ viri, ⁸et bis sex thoraca petitum
perfossumque locis, clipeumque ex aere sinistrae⁹   10
subligat atque ensem collo suspendit eburnum.¹⁰
Tum socios (namque omnis eum stipata tegebat¹¹
turba ducum) sic incipiens hortatur ovantis:
'maxima res effecta, viri; timor omnis abesto,
quod¹² superest; haec sunt spolia et de rege superbo   15

---

1 1f. The long description of the funeral rites for Pallas is laden with sorrow, and is in sharp contrast with the harder tones of the end of Book 10 where the death of Mezentius was described in realistic acceptance of the harshness of war. The pathos is achieved partly by the knowledge of Aeneas' feelings which have already been revealed in Book 10 (e.g. 515f.), and partly by the long build-up in the description of Aeneas' arrival and first speech (36f.) and his arrangements for the funeral procession (see note on 59f.) before his final words of farewell (96f.). Two aspects in particular may be stressed, the reference to Dido's gift (see note on 74), and the imitations of Catullus. Virgil recalls Catullus much less often than his more immediate models like Homer and Ennius, but when he does it is often in moments of great pathos (as for example Dido's speech to Aeneas in 4.305f., or the description of Euryalus' death, 9.435f. Here Catullus is recalled by the flower simile (68f.) and by Aeneas' final words to Pallas. With Aeneas' feelings of sorrow are linked his feelings of guilt. In 8.514f. Evander had entrusted Pallas, *spes et solacia nostri,* to Aeneas to be taught the lessons of battle; in 10.515f. after the death of Pallas, Aeneas grimly reflects on the hospitality he had been shown by Evander; and in this passage his self blame is often evident (45-6, 49, 55). These lines indeed are crucial to an appreciation of the last scene of the poem, when Aeneas kills Turnus in vengeance for Pallas.

2 1. A formulaic line (cf. 4.129) conveying the passing of a night since the death of Mezentius at Aeneas' hands at the end of Book 10.

3 2-3. **dare ... praecipitant:** 'are eager (i.e. urge him) to give'; for the infinitive, analogous to that after *properare,* cf. Stat. *Th.* 1.679. Aeneas wants to bury the dead, and is deeply distressed at Pallas' death in particular, but nevertheless he first pays his thank offerings for his victory over Mezentius.

4 4. **vota deum:** 'vows to the gods', probably a possessive genitive, as the vows made to the gods in a sense belong to them.

5 **Eoo:** 'dawn'; the adjective *Eous* is used in the neuter as a noun, cf. 3. 588.

6 7. **tropaeum:** the trophy, a trunk of a tree (cf. 83), generally an oak (cf. 10.423), is decked with the armour and spoils of the vanquished, and dedicated to a god (here Mars, the god of war); cf. Stat. *Th.* 2.704f. an imitation of this passage, Suet. *Cal.* 45 *truncatis arboribus et in modum tropaeorum adornatis.*

7 9. **trunca:** 'broken', as was normal on trophies, cf. Juv. 10.134-5.

8 9-10. 'and his breastplate attacked and penetrated in twelve places'; *thoraca* is Greek accusative, cf. 487 and 141, 270, 675.

9 10-11. **sinistrae ... collo:** the trunk of the tree is now thought of as the body of a man, with the shield on the left side, and the sword hanging from the shoulder by a sword-belt.

10 11. **eburnum:** probably the hilt was of ivory, or perhaps the sheath (9.305).

11 12. **tegebat:** 'covered' him in the sense of 'encircled' him.

12 15. **quod superest:** the phrase is used adverbially, 'for the future', cf. 9.157.

primitiae[1] manibusque[2] meis Mezentius hic est.
Nunc iter[3] ad regem nobis murosque Latinos.
Arma parate animis[4] et spe[5] praesumite bellum,
ne qua mora ignaros,[6] ubi primum vellere[7] signa
adnuerint[8] superi pubemque educere castris.   20
Impediat segnisve[9] metu sententia tardet.
Interea socios[10] inhumataque corpora terrae
mandemus, qui solus honos Acheronte[11] sub imo est.
Ite' ait, 'egregias animas, quae sanguine nobis[12]
hanc patriam peperere suo, decorate supremis   25
muneribus, maestamque Euandri primus ad urbem
mittatur Pallas, quem[13] non virtutis egentem
abstulit[14] atra dies et funere mersit acerbo.'
  Sic ait inlacrimans, recipitque ad limina gressum
corpus ubi exanimi positum[15] Pallantis Acoetes   30
servabat senior, qui Parrhasio[16] Euandro
armiger ante fuit, sed non felicibus aeque
tum comes auspiciis caro datus ibat alumno.
Circum omnis famulumque[17] manus Troianaque turba
et maestum[18] Iliades crinem[19] de more solutae.   35

---

1 16. **primitiae**: 'first offerings' of the war, defining *spolia*.

2 **manibusque . . . est**: 'and by my efforts in war here we have Mezentius', i.e. the trophy is all that is left of the proud enemy.

3 17. **iter**: supply *faciendum est*, cf. 6.542.

4 18. **animis**: this goes with *parate* ('with courage prepare for war'), not with *et spe* (as Servius, followed by Hirtzel and Mynors); cf. 438.

5 **spe praesumite bellum**: 'anticipate the war in your hopes', cf. 9.158 *pugnam sperate parari*, and line 491.

6 19. **ignaros**: 'unready'.

7 **vellere signa**: battle was begun by pulling up the standards from the ground and carrying them forward (cf. *Geo.* 4.108).

8 20. **adnuerint**: followed by the infinitive ('allow') as in Enn. *Ann.* 133, Livy 28.17.8.

9 21. **segnisve . . . sententia**: 'or feelings of cowardice'.

10 22. **socios inhumataque corpora**: hendiadys, 'the unburied bodies of our comrades'; cf. 64 and see Page's note on this line.

11 23. **Acheronte**: Acheron was a river of the underworld, often used (as here) to mean the underworld itself; cf. 7.312.

12 24-5. **nobis . . . peperere**: 'have won for us this land to be our own' (i.e. Italy).

13 27. **quem non virtutis egentem**: 'a warrior not lacking in valour', an example of litotes (understatement), taken (according to Servius)from Ennius.

14 28. This line is repeated from 6.429.

15 30. **positum**: 'laid out', cf. 2.644.

16 31. **Parrhasio Euandro**: the rhythm is Homeric, with a spondee and hiatus in the fifth foot; see note on 7.631. Parrhasia was a town of Arcadia; cf. 8.344.

17 34. **famulumque**: archaic form of the genitive, as with *deum, superum, socium* etc.; see note on 7.50. The doubled *-que* ('both. . . and') links *manus* with *turba*; the main verb (*erant* or *stabant*) is to be supplied.

18 35. **maestum**: the epithet is rather strikingly transferred from the women to their hair.

19 **crinem . . . solutae**: retained accusative with a passive verb, cf. 3.65 (the same phrase), lines 480, 487, 507, 596, 649, 777, 877, and see note on 7.503.

Ut vero Aeneas foribus sese intulit altis
ingentem gemitum tunsis ad sidera tollunt
pectoribus, maestoque immugit[1] regia[2] luctu.
Ipse caput nivei fultum[3] Pallantis et ora
ut vidit levique patens in pectore vulnus   40
cuspidis Ausoniae, lacrimis ita fatur obortis:
'tene'[4] inquit, 'miserande puer, cum laeta veniret,
invidit Fortuna mihi, ne regna videres
nostra neque ad sedes victor veherere[5] paternas?
Non haec Euandro de te promissa parenti[6]   45
discedens dederam, cum me complexus euntem
mitteret in magnum imperium metuensque moneret[7]
acris esse viros, cum dura proelia gente.[8]
Et nunc ille quidem spe multum[9] captus inani
fors[10] et vota facit cumulatque altaria donis,   50
nos[11] iuvenem exanimum et nil[12] iam caelestibus ullis
debentem vano maesti comitamur honore.
Infelix, nati funus crudele videbis!
Hi nostri reditus exspectatique triumphi?
Haec mea magna fides?[13] At non, Euandre,[14] pudendis   55
vulneribus pulsum aspicies, nec sospite dirurn
optabis nato funus pater. Hei mihi, quantum

---

1 38. **immugit**: 'groaned', a very strong word, cf. 3.674 (of the volcano Etna), and *mugire* of the earth in 4.490, 6.256.

2 **regia**: this word (like *foribus altis* in 36) seems over-elaborate in the context of a camp, but as Mackail well points out Virgil is obsessed with the idea that the temporary Roman camp is already a city (he calls it *Troia* and *urbs*).

3 39. **fultum**: 'propped up', cf. *positum* in 30.

4 42-3. 'Was it you', he said, 'unhappy boy, that fortune begrudged me when she came smiling on me ...?', i.e. when everything else went well the only reverse was of the worst possible kind.

5 44. **veherere**: 'ride back', imperfect subjunctive passive of *veho* (= *vehereris*).

6 45-6. Compare Evander's words in 152. Aeneas' feeling of guilt in his failure to protect Pallas is here and elsewhere (e.g. 55) very strong.

7 47. The alliteration in this speech (*v* in 44, *p* in 45, *d* in 46) now becomes very powerful indeed with the mournful *m's*.

8 48. Here the metrical effects add emphasis and slowness, as both the first foot and the fourth foot are composed of single spondaic words, adjectives describing the enemy. See notes on 7.291, 10.514. The effect is continued in the next line.

9 49. **multum**: adverbial, 'utterly'; the metre (see previous note) adds emphasis to the sorrowful word.

10 50. **fors et**: equivalent to *forsitan*, 'perhaps'; see note on 2.139, and cf. 12.183.

11 51. **nos**: in strong antithesis; 'while we . . .'.

12 51-2. **nil iam . . . debentem**: 'not now owing a debt to any of the gods above', i.e. unlike Evander and Aeneas, who survive him, Pallas has no obligations to fulfil any more. From this point for the next three lines the metre is almost wholly spondaic.

13 55. **fides**: cf. *promissa* (45).

14 55f. The only consolation Aeneas can offer Evander is that Pallas died heroically, not in flight with wounds in the back which would have made Evander long for death out of shame.

praesidium, Ausonia, et quantum tu perdis, Iule!'[1]

    [2]Haec ubi deflevit, tolli miserabile corpus

imperat, et toto lectos ex agmine mittit[3]   60

mille viros qui supremum comitentur honorem

intersintque patris lacrimis, solacia luctus

exigua ingentis, misero sed debita patri.

Haud segnes alii cratis[4] et molle feretrum

arbuteis texunt virgis et vimine querno   65

exstructosque toros[5] obtentu frondis inumbrant.

Hic iuvenem agresti[6] sublimem stramine ponunt:

qualem[7] virgineo demessum pollice florem

seu mollis violae seu languentis[8] hyacinthi,

cui neque fulgor adhuc nec dum sua forma recessit.   70

Non iam mater alit tellus virisque ministrat.

tum geminas vestis auroque[9] ostroque rigentis[10]

extulit Aeneas, quas illi laeta[11] laborum

ipsa suis quondam manibus Sidonia[12] Dido

fecerat et tenui telas[13] discreverat auro.   75

Harum unam iuveni supremum[14] maestus honorem

induit arsurasque comas obnubit amictu,

---

1 58. Aeneas ends by linking Pallas with his own son Iulus, a further indication of his feelings of guilt for having failed to protect Pallas.

2 59f. Notice the dense build-up here of words of sorrow: *deflevit, miserabile, supremum honorem, lacrimis, solacia exigua, luctus ingentis, misero patri.*

3 60f. Aeneas sends a thousand men to accompany the funeral procession back to Evander and share in (*intersint*) the lamentations of the father.

4 64. **cratis et molle feretrum:** 'a soft bier of wicker-work', hendiadys. For *feretrum* cf. 6.222 (Misenus' funeral).

5 66. **toros:** poetic plural; the couch is the bier (*feretrum*).

6 67. **agresti . . . stramine:** 'on his rustic bed'; *stramen* refers to the bier and the foliage generally, it does not have its specific meaning of 'straw'.

7 68f. 'Like a blossom plucked by a maiden's hand, of the gentle violet or the drooping hyacinth; its brightness and beauty have not yet left it, but mother earth no longer nourishes it and gives it life'. The flower simile is reminiscent of Catullus (62.43f, 11.22f.); compare also the flower simile at the death of Euryalus (9.435f.). See note on 1f.

8 69. **languentis hyacinthi:** the rhythm is Greek to suit the Greek word, a quadri-syllabic ending with lengthening in arsis of the last syllable of *languentis;* compare 111, see note on 10.720, and cf. *Ecl.* 6.53 *molli fultus hyacintho.*

9 72. **auroque ostroque:** doubled -*que* ('both . . . and') is particularly frequent with juxtaposed nouns or verbs, cf. 150, 178.

10 72. Purple coverings are laid over Misenus' body at his funeral (6.221).

11 73. **laeta laborum:** poetic genitive of cause, cf. 126 and see note on 1.178 *fessi rerum.* It is somewhat different from (though influenced by) the genitive of respect as in 416-17; see note on 1.441 *laetissimus umbrae.*

12 74. **Sidonia Dido:** gifts from Dido are mentioned in 5.571f. (Iulus rides a horse which Dido had given as a token of her love) and 9.266 (where Iulus promises to Nisus a bowl which Dido had given). Here the effect is strongly to link the tragedy of Pallas' death with the tragic events of Book 4, especially as line 75 is repeated from 4.264, where it is used of a cloak which Dido had made for Aeneas.

13 75. **telas discreverat:** 'had interwoven (literally 'separated') the texture'.

14 76. **supremum ... honorem:** in apposition to *unam;* Aeneas takes out the two robes, and chooses one as a shroud.

multaque praeterea Laurentis[1] praemia pugnae
aggerat et longo praedam iubet ordine duci;
addit equos et tela quibus spoliaverat hostem. 80
Vinxerat[2] et post terga manus, quos mitteret umbris[3]
inferias, caeso sparsurus sanguine flammas.
Indutosque[4] iubet truncos hostilibus armis
ipsos ferre duces inimicaque nomina figi.
Ducitur[5] infelix aevo confectus Acoetes, 85
pectora nunc foedans pugnis, nunc unguibus ora.
Sternitur[6] et toto proiectus corpore terrae.
Ducunt et Rutulo perfusos sanguine currus.
Post bellator equus positis[7] insignibus Aethon[8]
it lacrimans guttisque[9] umectat grandibus ora. 90
Hastam alii galeamque ferunt, nam cetera Turnus
victor habet. [10]Tum maesta phalanx Teucrique sequuntur
Tyrrhenique omnes et versis[11] Arcades armis.
Postquam omnis longe comitum praecesserat ordo,
substitit Aeneas gemituque haec addidit alto: 95
'nos[12] alias hinc ad lacrimas eadem horrida belli

---

1 78. **Laurentis . . . pugnae**: the battle in the Laurentian fields; the adjective *Laurens* is used to refer to the area just south of the Tiber where the fighting has been taking place; see note on 7.47.

2 81-2. 'He had also bound behind their backs the hands of those whom he intended to send as funeral offerings to the world below'. The antecedent to *quos* (*eorum*) has to be supplied; *mitteret* is final subjunctive.

3 81f. Aeneas' intention to offer human sacrifice at Pallas' funeral was stated in 10.519, where see note.

4 83-4. 'and he gave instructions for the leaders themselves to carry the trophies adorned with enemy weapons, and for the names of the foemen to be inscribed on them'. These are Pallas' trophies, which the leaders of the procession are to carry, like the one Aeneas made for his victory over Mezentius (sf., where see note). The last phrase refers to the titles (*tituli*) normal for trophies and memorial statues etc.; cf. Tac. *Ann.* 2.18 *in modum tropaeorum arma subscriptis victarum gentium nominibus imposuit.*

5 85. **ducitur . . . Acoetes**: Pallas' old squire (cf. 30f.) has to be helped along.

6 87. 'and he falls collapsing full-length on the ground'; postponed. *Terrae* is dative (= *ad terram*). The line does not link very well with the previous lines, the sense must be that as he is led along he keeps falling to the ground.

7 89. **positis insignibus Aethon**: the *insignia* would be the *phalerae*, 'trappings', which are discarded to show grief; Aethon ('Blazing') was also the name of one of the horses of the Sun.

8 89f. The idea of the horse weeping is taken from the fine passage in Homer where Patroclus' horses weep for him and are consoled by Zeus (*Il.* 17.426f. Cf. Suet. *Jul.* 81 (Caesar's horses weep at the prospect of his death), Pliny *Nat. Hist.* 8.157 (of horses) *amissos lugent dominos, lacrimasque interdum desiderio fundunt.* Some critics have regarded this passage as frigid, as indeed it could be, but the powerful accumulation of sorrow and pathos for some thirty lines produces a context in which many readers will accept the sentiment.

9 90. **guttisque . . . grandibus**: 'big tears', reminiscent of the frequent phrase in Homer θαλερον οαλρυ.

10 92. 'Then follows a sad troop — both Trojans and . . .'; the nominative plurals are in apposition to *phalanx;* they refer to Aeneas' Trojans, Tarchon's Etruscans, Evander's Arcadians.

11 93. **versis . . . armis**: a sign of mourning, cf. Tac. *Ann.* 3.2 (of Germanicus' funeral) *versi fasces.*

12 96-7. These words epitomise the attitude of Aeneas in his normal frame of mind (as opposed to his frenzy immediately after Pallas' death): *lacrimae,* but *fata vocant.* The relatively unusual rhyme between the first syllable of the second and the first syllable of the fourth foot emphasises the phrase.

fata vocant: salve aeternum mihi, maxime Palla,[1]
aeternumque vale.' Nec plura effatus ad altos
tendebat muros gressumque in castra ferebat.

> *100-38. Spokesmen arrive from the Latin camp asking for a truce to bury the dead; Aeneas grants it most willingly. Drances thanks Aeneas and inveighs against Turnus. A twelve-day truce is arranged.*

[2]Iamque oratores aderant ex[3] urbe Latina   100
velati ramis oleae veniamque[4] rogantes:
corpora, per campos ferro quae fusa iacebant,
redderet[5] ac tumulo[6] sineret succedere terrae:
nullum[7] cum victis certamen et aethere[8] cassis;
parceret hospitibus quondam socerisque vocatis.[9]   105
Quos bonus Aeneas haud[10] aspernanda precantis
prosequitur venia et verbis haec insuper addit:
'quaenam vos tanto fortuna indigna, Latini,
implicuit bello, qui[11] nos fugiatis amicos?
Pacem me exanimis et Martis sorte peremptis[12]   110
oratis?[13] Equidem[14] et vivis concedere vellem.

---

1 97-8. The formulaic lines (the phrases recall sepulchral inscriptions) are strongly reminiscent of Catullus' well known lament at his brother's tomb (101.10 *atque in perpetuum frater ave atque vale*). See note on 1f. *Aeternum* is adverbial, cf. 64.01, 617; *mihi* is ethic dative, cf. Hom. *Il.* 23.19 (Achilles to the dead Patroclus) χαιρε μοι ω Πατροκλε, και ειν Αοδαο δομοιαιν.

2 100f. The passage in which Aeneas grants a truce to the Latins expresses very powerfully indeed his hatred of the war which he is forced to fight, and in his speech (108-19) he very clearly shows how different he is from Turnus in this respect. It is true that in Book 10 we saw him driven to extreme savagery and ruthlessness on the battlefield, but it is also true that here we see him as he really is.
The reply of the orator Drances serves to show that he, and presumably many more, are against the war; but in his rhetorical display he alienates our sympathies (see further note on 336f.) and serves to bring out by his unpleasantness the simpler, more noble, qualities of Turnus. As Quinn well points out, he is on the right side for the wrong reasons.

3 100. **ex urbe Latina**: i.e. From King Latinus' capital.

4 101. **veniamque rogantes**: 'seeking favour for their plea'; *venia* does not always mean pardon, cf. 358, 1.519.

5 103. **redderet . . . sineret**: reported imperatives, representing their request (*redde . . . ac sine*); so *parceret* (105).

6 **tumulo . . . succedere terrae**: 'be placed under a mound of earth'; for *succedere* (literally 'enter under') cf. 5.93.

7 104. **nullum . . . certamen**: supply *esse;* the line is part of the oratio obliqua which extends from 102-105.

8 **aethere cassis**: 'bereft of the light', cf. 2.85 *cassum lumine,* and for *aether* in this sense cf. 1.546-7 *si vescitur aura / aetheria.*

9 105. A reference to Latinus' welcome to Aeneas and his offer of his daughter Lavinia in marriage (7.263f.). The plural *soceris* is used because other Latins would follow the example of their king in marrying their daughters to the Trojans, cf. 7.98.

10 106-7. **haud aspernanda . . . venia**: 'as what they sought could not be refused Aeneas sent them on their way with their request granted'.

11 109. **qui nos fugiatis**: 'that you flee from us', the subjunctive is consecutive.

12 110-11. These phrases sum up the spirit in which Aeneas tries to conduct the war; his general reluctance to fight (but see note on 10.510f.) contrasts with the eager enthusiasm of Turnus. Conington quotes Scaliger on these lines: 'vivi et caelestes'.

13 111. **oratis**: the final syllable is lengthened in arsis; cf. 69, 323, 469, and see note on 7.174.

14 **equidem . . . vellem**: 'for my part I would have wished to grant it to the living as well'; *vellem* is past potential.

Nec [1]veni, nisi fata locum sedemque dedissent,
nec bellum cum gente gero; rex nostra reliquit[2]
hospitia et Turni potius se credidit armis.
Aequius [3]huic Turnum fuerat se opponere morti.   115
Si bellum finire manu, si pellere Teucros
apparat, his[4] mecum decuit concurrere telis:
vixet[5] cui vitam deus aut sua dextra dedisset.
Nunc ite et miseris supponite civibus ignem.'[6]
Dixerat Aeneas. Illi obstipuere silentes   120
conversique[7] oculos inter se atque ora tenebart.
    [8]Tum senior semperque odiis et crimine Drances
infensus iuveni Turno sic ore[9] vicissim
orsa refert: 'o fama ingens, ingentior armis,[10]
vir Troiane, quibus caelo te laudibus aequem?   125
Iustitiaene[11] prius mirer belline[12] laborum?
Nos vero haec patriam grati referemus ad urbem
et te, si qua viam dederit Fortuna, Latino
iungemus regi. Quaerat sibi foedera Turnus.

---

1 112. 'And I would not have come except that fate had granted me this place to settle in'; cf. 7.239 and 8.39 (where the god Tiber says *hic tibi certa domus*). The condition is very extraordinary with the substitution of *veni* for *venissem;* cf. 2.54f. *si mens non laeva fuisset / impulerat,* where however the more natural pluperfect tense is used. There is no question of an ellipsis of the true apodosis, as in 6.358f.; it is rather a conflation of two ideas: 'I have not come except to fulfil my destiny', and 'I would not have come unless destiny had called'.

2 113f. Aeneas says (in curiously modern phrases) that it is King Latinus, and more particularly Turnus, not the Latin people, who are responsible for the hostility to the Trojans. Compare his similar sentiments in 12.190f. For Latinus' reluctant acceptance of the war against Aeneas cf. 7.586f.; before Juno aroused hostility in Amata and Turnus he had welcomed him (see note on 105).

3 115. 'It would have been more just for Turnus to expose himself to this death' i.e. to which the Latins have just fallen victims. Servius explains *huic* as deictic, i.e. he points to the dead. The indicative is normal (the perfect tense is commoner than the pluperfect) in phrases like *melius fuit, aequius fuit, decuit* (117), *potuit* etc. Cf. *melius fuerat,* 303.

4 117. **his . . . telis:** 'with these weapons', i.e. his and mine in single combat.

5 118. **vixet:** contractedfor *vixisset,* past jussive; cf. 162-3, 8.643, 10.854.

6 119. For the lighting of the pyre from beneath cf. 6.223-4.

7 121. 'and turning to each other kept their eyes and their gaze still'; cf. 2.1, 7.250, 8.520.

8 122-3. 'Then Drances, an older man, always hostile to the young Turnus with accusations showing his hatred for him . . .'; the cunning politician, Drances, is set up as a foil to the impetuous Turnus in a large section of the book (336f., where see note).

9 123-4. **ore . . . orsa refert:** 'began to speak', cf. 7.435-6.

10 124f. The speech of Drances is very strongly in the mode of an orator; he begins with flattery and praise (Servius says 'est oratorium non invenire paria verba virtutibus') which he expresses in chiastic order with repetition, then in rhetorical questions; grateful acceptance of Aeneas' kindness is followed by indignant rejection of Turnus and then reinforced by extravagant promise of help.

11 126. **iustitiaene . . . laborum:** the genitives are very striking, being imitations of the Greek genitive of cause after words meaning 'wonder', 'envy' (e.g. θαυμαζειν). Latin would normally use a preposition (like *propter*). The commentators compare line 280, but there the verb *memini* greatly helps the genitive. For the causal genitive after an adjective cf. 73.

12 **belline:** this is not locative, but genitive of definition (war-toils) ; *-ne* is used for *an,* cf. 10.378.

Quin[1] et fatalis[2] murorum attollere moles   130
saxaque subvectare umeris Troiana iuvabit.'
Dixerat haec unoque omnes eadem ore fremebant.
Bis[3] senos pepigere dies, et pace[4] sequestra
per silvas Teucri mixtique impune Latini[5]
erravere iugis. Ferro sonat alta bipenni[6]   135
fraxinus, evertunt actas[7] ad sidera pinus,
robora nec cuneis et olentem scindere cedrum[8]
nec plaustris cessant vectare gementibus ornos.

> *139-81. Pallas' funeral procession arrives at Pallanteum ;*
> *the citizens are deeply grief stricken and his father Evander,*
> *in a speech of lamentation, ends by asking Aeneas to take*
> *vengeance on Turnus.*

[9]Et iam Fama volans, tanti praenuntia luctus,
Euandrum Euandrique domos et moenia replet,[10]   140
quae modo victorem Latio Pallanta ferebat.
Arcades ad portas ruere[11] et de more vetusto
funereas rapuere faces; lucet[12] via longo
ordine flammarum et late discriminat[13] agros.

---

1 130. **quin et**: = *quin etiam* (cf. 169), adding the further point that so far from continuing to be enemies, they will now become positive and active friends.

2 **fatalis**: 'decreed by fate'; Drances refers to Aeneas' words in 112.

3 133. **bis . . . dies**: 'they made a pact for twelve days'.

4 **pace sequestra**: 'in the peace which intervened'. *Sequester* is a technical term meaning the person with whom two parties deposited money, a trustee; here peace is the intermediary between the two parties (not, as Servius says, between the two periods of hostilities).

5 134-5. These simple phrases, with the slow spondees and the rhyme of final -*i,* convey very memorably the joy of peace after war.

6 135f. The scene of wood cutting for the funeral pyres is reminiscent of that in *Aen.* 6.179f. (for Misenus' pyre); both passages recall Ennius (*Ann.* 187f.) as well as Homer (*Il.* 23.114f.). *Bipennis* (generally used as a noun, meaning 'a double headed axe', cf. 2.627) is here an adjective.

7 136. **actas**: 'that had soared up'; there is a touch of personification about the tree driving itself upwards, cf. *Geo.* 2.363-4 *dum se laetus ad auras / palmes agit.*

8 137-8. The word order is *nec robora et cedrum scindere cessant nec . . . Robora* here is specific, 'oaks', not general 'hard wood'.

9 139f. After the interlude of the description of the truce in the previous section the narrative returns for the last time to Pallas' funeral. The long speech of Evander is more conventional and rhetorical than that of Aeneas had been (41f.), and is therefore less moving. Its main impact is in the demand for vengeance which Evander sends to Aeneas; Virgil invites the reader to consider whether Evander is justified in making this demand, and whether Aeneas is justified in satisfying it when he kills the suppliant Turnus at the end of the poem.

10 140. **replet**: for the use with persons (*Euandrum*), we might say 'filled his ears', cf. 896 and 4.189 (*Fama*) *populos sermone replebat.*

11 142. **ruere**: historic infinitive; the construction changes at *rapuere* to the perfect tense.

12 143. **lucet via longo**: notice the double dissyllable at the line end, dislocating the normal rhythm; cf. 170, 442, 562 and see note on 10.440.

13 144. **discriminat**: 'picks out', i.e. the lights on the road shine on to the surrounds.

Contra turba[1] Phrygum veniens plangentia iungit   145
agmina. Quae postquam matres succedere tectis
viderunt, maestam incendunt[2] clamoribus urbem.
At non Euandrum potis[3] est vis ulla tenere,
sed venit in medios. Feretro[4] Pallante reposto
procubuit super atque haeret lacrimansque gemensque,   150
et via vix tandem voci laxata dolore est:[5]
'non[6] haec, o Palla, dederas promissa petenti[7]
cautius ut saevo velles te credere Marti.
Haud[8] ignarus eram quantum nova gloria in armis
et praedulce decus primo certamine posset.   155
Primitiae[9] iuvenis miserae bellique propinqui[10]
dura rudimenta, et nulli exaudita deorum
vota precesque meae! Tuque, o sanctissima[11] coniunx,
felix morte tua neque in hunc servata dolorem!
Contra[12] ego vivendo vici mea fata, superstes   160
restarem ut genitor. Troum socia arma secutum
obruerent[13] Rutuli telis! Animam ipse dedissem
atque haec pompa domum me, non Pallanta, referret!
Nec[14] vos arguerim, Teucri, nec foedera nec quas

---

1 145. **turba Phrygum**: i.e. the escort of a thousand Trojans sent by Aeneas (60f.).

2 147. **incendunt**: for the metaphor cf. 10.895 with note.

3 148. **potis est**: archaic for *potest*, cf. 3.671, 9.796.

4 149. **feretro . . . reposto**: 'when Pallas had been laid on the bier'; the two separate ablative constructions are a little awkward and *M2* may be right with *Pallanta* (governed by *super*). *Reposto* is contracted for *reposito*, see note on 10.694.

5 151. Notice the alliteration of *v* and the spondaic movement, emphasising the pathos of Evander's speechlessness at first.

6 152f. The passage is imitated by Spenser, *F. Q.* 6.3.4f.

7 152. **petenti**: the *MSS* all have *parenti*, but Servius knew the reading *petenti*, which makes perfect sense of the next line; 'to me when I asked that you should be willing to entrust yourself with some caution to fierce warfare', and combines very well with 154-5. If we read *parenti*, then *ut velles* depends on *promissa* ('promises that you would'), a strange Latin construction; or else a full stop may be put after *parenti* and *ut velles* taken as a past unfulfilled wish ('if only you had been willing'), cf. 10.631, this would be very abrupt.

8 154-5. 'I knew very well how far new found triumph in war and the sweets of glory could lead in the first contest', i.e. they could lead to excessive boldness and disaster.

9 156-8. The nouns *primitiae, rudimenta, vota, preces* are vocatives (like *coniunx*, 158): 'Oh unhappy first-fruits . . .'.

10 156. **propinqui**: 'so near', 'nimium vicini, quo Pallas mitti posset' (Servius). Page well says 'the lesson he has learned was cruel, and he had not to go far to learn it'.

11 158. **sanctissima**: 'of blessed memory'; Virgil does not elsewhere mention Evander's dead wife.

12 160-1. 'But I outlived my fate, so that I, his father, was left surviving'. The phrases compel the attention, with the alliteration of *v*, the fifth foot pause, the most unusual position of *ut*. The words *vivendo vici mea fata* recall Lucr. 1.202 *multaque vivendo vitalia vincere saecla* (cf. *Geo.* 2.295); the point of *mea fata* is. that, as Page says, 'according to the law of nature he should have died before his son', cf. Cic. *N.D.* 2.72, Eur. *Alc.* 695, 939.

13 162. **obruerent**: 'should have overwhelmed me', past jussive (or past unfulfilled wish), like *dedissem* and *referret;* see note on 118. The imperfect is often used interchangeably with the pluperfect, but here *referret* may convey the present unfulfilled idea of 'would now be bringing me back'.

14 164. **nec vos arguerim**: 'nor would I blame you'; the potential subjunctive (cf. 10.186) here conveys the gentleness of Evander.

iunximus hospitio dextras: sors ista senectae   165

debita[1] erat nostrae. Quod si immatura manebat

mors natum, caesis Volscorum[2] milibus ante[3]

ducentem[4] in Latium Teucros cecidisse iuvabit.

Quin[5] ego non alio digner te funere, Palla,

quam pius Aeneas et quam magni[6] Phryges et quam   170

Tyrrhenique duces, Tyrrhenum[7] exercitus omnis.

Magna tropaea ferunt quos[8] dat[9] tua dextera leto;

tu[10] quoque nunc stares immanis truncus[11] in armis,[12]

esset[13] par aetas et idem si robur ab annis,

Turne.[14] Sed infelix Teucros quid demoror armis?[15]   175

vadite et haec memores regi mandata referte:

quod vitam moror invisam Pallante perempto[16]

dextera causa tua est, Turnum[17] natoque patrique

---

1 166. **debita:** Evander now accepts that destiny wished it thus.

2 167. **Volscorum:** the Volsci were among Turnus' allies (line 463, 9.505).

3 **ante:** adverbial, 'first', i.e. before his death.

4 168. **ducentem . . . Teucros:** Pallas actually had his own contingent of Arcadians, but as an ally of the Trojans he was helping to lead them to their destined home in Latium.

5 169-70. **quin . . . Aeneas:** 'indeed I would not honour you with any different funeral, Pallas, than the one with which the good Aeneas . . .'. *Quin* is equivalent to *quin etiam* (cf. 130) and *digner* is potential; after *quam* supply *quo dignatur*. *Pius* here mainly refers to the religious obligations which Aeneas is fulfilling.

6 170. **magni Phryges et quam:** for the line ending see note on 143; *Phryges* is Greek nominative plural with a short final syllable, like *Arcades* (93, 142).

7 171. **Tyrrhenique . . . Tyrrhenum:** the -*que* means 'both', and the -*que* which would follow to mean 'and' is here replaced by the repetition; see note on 10.313-14. The three forces allied against Turnus are Aeneas' Trojans (*Phryges*), Tarchon's Etruscans (*Tyrrheni*) and Pallas' Arcadians.

8 172. **quos:** supply *ei* as the antecedent; the warriors whom Pallas has killed 'bring' him great trophies in the sense of being his trophies. Others take the subject of *ferunt* to be the men in the funeral procession bringing trophies of those whom Pallas has killed.

9 **dat:** idiomatic use of the present, see note on 9.266.

10 173. **tu:** the sight of the trophies turns Evander's thoughts to what would have been the most glorious trophy of all, that of Turnus whom he now apostrophises.

11 **truncus:** the trophy would be a tree trunk decked in Turnus' spoils, see notes on 7 and 83-4. *Truncus* is in apposition to *stares*, Turnus being identified with the imaginary trophy of him.

12 **armis:** Mynors accepts Bentley's conjecture *arvis* to avoid the repetition with 175, but the Romans were less sensitive to this kind of repetition than we are; cf. 1.429, 6.901, 7.430 and see Austin on 2.505.

13 174. 'if his age had been the same and the strength of his years the same'; the sentence is a present unfulfilled condition. Servius is uncertain whether Evander means 'if Pallas had been older' or 'if I were younger', but the first is much more likely.

14 175. **Turne:** the holding up of the vocative to the end of the sentence, and the very unusual heavy pause after a trochee in the first foot gives enormous emphasis to the hated word.

15 **armis:** for *ab armis*.

16 177f. The message to Aeneas is that Evander only lives now for vengeance; this is the reason why Aeneas does not spare Turnus at the end of the poem (12.948-9).

17 178-9. **Turnum . . . vides:** 'which you see owes Turnus to son and father'; Aeneas' right hand is to be the instrument of the vengeance that he surely sees is due.

quam debere vides. Meritis[1] vacat hic tibi solus
fortunaeque locus. [2]Non vitae gaudia quaero,   180
nec fas, sed nato manis perferre sub imos.'

> *182-224. The Trojans and their allies bury their dead; in*
> *another part of the field the Latins do likewise. Resentment*
> *against Turnus grows in the Latin capital, but he has strong*
> *support too.*

[3]Aurora interea miseris[4] mortalibus almam
extulerat lucem referens opera atque labores:
iam pater Aeneas, iam curvo in litore Tarchon[5]
constituere pyras. Huc corpora quisque suorum[6]   185
more tulere patrum, subiectisque[7] ignibus atris[8]
conditur in tenebras altum caligine caelum.
Ter[9] circum accensos cincti fulgentibus armis
decurrere[10] rogos, ter maestum funeris ignem
lustravere[11] in equis ululatusque ore dedere.   190
Spargitur et tellus lacrimis, sparguntur et arma.
It caelo[12] clamorque virum clangorque tubarum.
Hic alii spolia occisis derepta Latinis[13]
coniciunt igni, galeas ensisque decoros

---

1 179-80. **meritis ... locus:** 'this is the only field open for your valour and fortune'; *merita* and *fortuna* are, as Servius points out, the two constituent parts of victory.

2 180-1. 'I do not seek joy in life, nor would it be right, but to take the news to my son in the underworld below'. Evander means that he cannot take any more pleasure in life after his son's death, not even from Turnus' death; but he does ask that he may after death be able to meet his son and tell him that vengeance has been taken. *Perferre* is used absolutely ('make a report', 'take the news'), not with *gaudia* as its object, as some suggest. *Quaero* is used first with a direct object, then with an infinitive (cf. 6.614f.).

3 182f. The scene changes back again to the battlefield and the preparations for burial, left at line 138. The passage describing the Trojan funeral rites is elaborate, with detailed description of ritual and a sort of muted and stylised sorrow; by contrast the Latin lamentations are much starker, with some of Virgil's most memorable phrases to convey the pathos of the unnumbered dead and the sorrow of the living: *cetera confusaeque ingentem caedis acervum nec numero nec honore cremant* (207-8); *hic matres miseraeque nurus . . . dirum exsecrantur bellum* (215-17).

4 182-3. **miseris . . . labores:** compare 10.759; *miseris mortalibus* (cf. 10.274, 12.850 *mortalibus aegris*) is a rendering of Homer's δειλοῖσι βροτοῖσιν.

5 184. **Tarchon:** the leader of the Etruscan contingent which came to help Aeneas, cf. 8.603f.

6 185. **suorum:** with *corpora*, not with *patrum*.

7 186. The torch was applied to the base of the pyre, cf. 6.223f.

8 186. **atris:** partly literal, 'smoky' (cf. the next line), but partly metaphorical (as Servius says), 'funereal', cf. 4.384, 10.77.

9 188f. The ritual is similar to that at Patroclus' funeral (*Il.* 23.13f.) where the Greeks ride round three times on their horses, while the sand and their armour are sprinkled with tears (191). Compare also Ap. Rh. 4.1535.

10 189. **decurrere:** a technical word for ritual procession, cf. Livy 25.17.5, Tac. *Ann.* 2.7.

11 190. **lustravere:** 'circled around', cf. 5.578, here (as often) with the additional idea of religious ritual.

12 192. **caelo:** cf. 10.548 with the note there on this very poetic usage of the dative of place to which.

13 193-4. Burning the spoils on the pyre was a Roman custom; see note on 8.562.

frenaque ferventisque[1] rotas; [2]pars munera nota,   195
ipsorum clipeos et non felicia tela.
Multa boum circa mactantur corpora Morti,[3]
saetigerosque[4] sues raptasque ex omnibus agris
in flammam iugulant pecudes. Tum litore toto
ardentis spectant socios semustaque[5] servant[6]   200
busta, neque avelli possunt, nox umida donec[7]
invertit[8] caelum stellis[9] ardentibus aptum.
    Nec minus et miseri diversa in parte Latini
innumeras struxere pyras, et corpora partim
multa virum terrae[10] infodiunt, avectaque partim[11]   205
finitimos tollunt in agros urbique remittunt.
Cetera confusaeque[12] ingentem caedis acervum[13]
nec numero nec honore cremant; tunc undique vasti[14]
certatim crebris conlucent ignibus agri.
Tertia lux gelidam caelo dimoverat umbram: 210
maerentes altum cinerem et confusa ruebant[15]
ossa focis tepidoque onerabant aggere terrae.
Iam vero in[16] tectis, praedivitis urbe Latini,

---

1 195. **ferventisque:** the epithet is applied to chariot wheels glowing hot from their speed (cf. *Geo.* 3.107, Hor. *Odes* 1.1.4-5), and is a standing epithet not applicable here, as Servius says: 'non modo, sed quae soleant fervere'.

2 195-6. 'some fling on well known offerings, the shields of the dead and their weapons which brought them no fortune'; compare 6.221 (with note) where there is the same doubt whether *nota* means 'well known', as often having been seen by their friends, or 'traditional'.

3 197. **Morti:** for the personification of Death cf. Stat. *Th.* 4.528 *in scopulis Mors atra sedet*. Mackail and others take the word as an ordinary noun in the ablative (archaic form, see note on 9.271), 'are sacrificed in death'.

4 198. **saetigerosque sues:** cf. 7.17.

5 200. **semusta:** sometimes spelled *semiusta*, see note on 8.194.

6 **servant:** 'stay by', defined in the next line.

7 201. **donec:** the postposition of a conjunction is quite common in poetry, but not normal in the sixth foot; cf. 509 and 3.212 with my note (OUP Ed.).

8 202. **invertit caelum:** cf. 2.250 *vertitur interea caelum*.

9 **stellis . . . aptum:** the same phrase, based on Ennius, is used in 4.482, 6.797. Compare Milton, *P.L.* 4.604-5 'Now glow'd the firmament / with living sapphires'.

10 205. **terrae:** = *in terram*, cf. 192, 194, 206 (*urbi*).

11 205-6. i.e. in these cases the bodies are returned to their homes, as opposed to being buried on the battlefield.

12 207. **confusaeque:** -*que* is epexegetic or explanatory, i.e. it does not add something new but explains and amplifies *cetera;* cf. 8.289, 12.945_6, and my note (OUP Ed.) on 5.410-11.

13 207-9. These lines vividly expressing Virgil's horror of war, and especially his sympathy for the unnumbered and unhonoured dead, are very carefully patterned with powerful alliteration of *c* and spondaic movement in 207 and 209 varied by the dactyls of 208.

14 208. **vasti:** here as often the word includes the idea of desolation or devastation.

15 211-12. **ruebant . . . Focis:** 'levelled on the pyre'; for *ruere* cf. *Geo.* 1.105 *cumulosque ruit male pinguis harenae, Aen.* 12.453-4. The deep ash where the fire had been (*focis*) and the bones are raked over and buried beneath a funeral mound.

16 213. **in tectis:** 'in the town', defined by the following *urbe,* and contrasted with the *vasti . . . agri* (208-9). For Latinus' capital cf. 100.

praecipuus fragor et longi pars maxima luctus.
Hic matres miseraeque nurus, hic cara[1] sororum   215
pectora maerentum puerique parentibus orbi
dirum exsecrantur bellum Turnique hymenaeos;[2]
ipsum armis ipsumque iubent decernere ferro.
Qui regnum Italiae et primos sibi poscat honores.
Ingravat[3] haec saevus Drances solumque vocari   220
testatur, solum posci in certamina Turnum.
Multa[4] simul contra variis sententia dictis
pro Turno, et magnum reginae nomen obumbrat,[5]
multa[6] virum meritis sustentat fama tropaeis.

> *225-295. The embassy sent to ask Diomedes for help returns
> with an unfavourable answer. Diomedes had said that he
> would not fight against the Trojans again on any account,
> particularly not against so great a warrior as Aeneas. He
> advised them to make peace.*

[7]Hos inter motus, medio in flagrante tumultu,   225
ecce super[8] maesti magna Diomedis ab urbe[9]
legati responsa ferunt: nihil omnibus actum[10]
tantorum impensis operum, nil dona neque aurum
nec magnas valuisse preces, alia arma Latinis

---

1 215-16. **cara ... maerentum**: 'sorrowing sisters with their loving hearts'; this periphrasis for *sorores unanimae* is strangely out of balance with the other subjects of *exsecrantur*. For *carus* = loving cf. 1.646.

2 217. Again spondees are used to emphasise the line, cf. 209. For the sentiment cf. Hor. *Odes* 1.1.24-5 *bellaque matribus detestata.*

3 220. **ingravat ... Drances**: Drances, leader of the recent embassy to Aeneas (cf. 122f.), plays on Italian resentment against Turnus by recalling Aeneas' insistence (115f.) that single combat between himself and Turnus was the proper way to settle the issue. *Ingravat* is unusual and mainly poetic; cf. Ov. *Trist.* 3.4.60.

4 222. **multa ... sententia**: 'much opinion', i.e. the views of many.

5 223. The support of Queen Amata (cf. 7.343f.) 'shelters' Turnus; for *obumbrat* Servius says *tuetur, defendit.* Cf. Livy 7.30.18 *itaque umbra vestri auxilii, Romani, tegi possumus.*

6 224. 'and his great fame with all the trophies he had won gains the hero support'.

7 225f. The next two hundred lines are taken up with four speeches at the council which King Latinus calls: the report of Diomedes' reply to the envoys, the proposals of Latinus, and then the angry invective of Drances against Turnus and Turnus' reply. The mood of the first two is quiet and factual; that of the second two violent and rhetorical.
The main features of Diomedes' reply are firstly his praises of Aeneas' great ability in war (282-93, a picture much more impressive than is given in the *Iliad,* where the deeds of Hector far outshine those of Aeneas); and secondly his constant indications that the Greek attack was wicked and rightly punished by the disasters which befell their leading warriors. This slant is of course quite contrary to the Greek traditions which would be well known to the Roman readers, and serves to stress the virtue of the Trojans (cf. especially 255 *violavimus,* 258 *scelerum poenas,* 260 *ultor,* 277 *violavi*). This praise in the mouth of an enemy causes Latinus to wish once again that he was not involved in a war contrary to the decrees of destiny.

8 226. **super**: to add to the sorrow and confusion: *ad cumulationem malorum* (Servius).

9 226f. These are the ambassadors who were sent to Argyripa (246), also called Arpi (250), to ask for help from Diomedes against Aeneas (8.9, l0.28f., where see notes).

10 227. **actum**: sc. *esse,* as with *quaerenda* and *petendum* in 230; the accusative and infinitive construction reports their reply.

quaerenda, aut pacem Troiano ab rege petendum.[1]   230
Deficit[2] ingenti luctu rex ipse Latinus.
fatalem [3]Aenean manifesto numine ferri
admonet ira deum tumulique ante ora recentes.[4]
Ergo concilium magnum primosque suorum
imperio[5] accitos alta intra limina cogit.   235
Olli[6] convenere fluuntque[7] ad regia plenis
tecta viis. Sedet in mediis et[8] maximus aevo
et primus sceptris haud laeta fronte Latinus.
Atque hic legatos Aetola[9] ex urbe remissos
quae referant fari iubet, et responsa reposcit   240
ordine cuncta suo. Tum facta silentia linguis,
et Venulus[10] dicto parens ita farier[11] infit:

'Vidimus, o cives, Diomedem Argivaque[12] castra,
atque iter emensi casus superavimus omnis,
contigimusque manum qua concidit Ilia tellus.[13]   245
Ille urbem Argyripam[14] patriae cognomine gentis
victor Gargani[15] condebat Iapygis agris.
Postquam introgressi et coram data copia fandi,
munera praeferimus, nomen patriamque docernus,
qui bellum intulerint, quae causa attraxerit Arpos.[16]   250
Auditis ille haec placido sic reddidit ore:

---

1 230. **petendum:** this use of the gerund with a direct object is scarce and archaic (cf. Lucr. 1.111 *poenas . . . timendum*) and most MSS have *petendam,* but Servius attests the rarer form.

2 231. **deficit:** 'was overcome', i.e. Failed to face up to the situation.

3 232. 'That Aeneas was brought to them as a man of destiny by the clear divine will . . .'; for *fatalis* cf. 130, 7.272, for *ferre* cf. 2.34 *sic fata ferebant.*

4 233. The second phrase is explanatory of the first, the wrath of the gods being indicated by the many Latin deaths.

5 235. **imperio accitos . . . cogit:** 'he summoned by his decree and assembled . . .'; cf. 304, 460.

6 236. **olli:** the archaic form of *illi* is appropriate here in the formal situation.

7 **fluuntque:** for the metaphor, we might say 'flock', cf. 12.444.

8 237-8. **et . . . sceptris:** 'both oldest and first in authority', a common use of *sceptra,* cf. 9.9, 10.852.

9 239. **Aetola:** Diomedes' city is called Aetolian because Diomedes lived in Aetolia before becoming king of Argos (243 *Argivaque castra*) and then, after the Trojan war, moving to Italy; cf. 10.28.

10 242. **Venulus:** the leader of the embassy to Diomedes, cf. 8.9.

11 **farier:** archaic form of the infinitive *fari;* see note on 7.70.

12 243. **Argivaque castra:** see note on 239.

13 245. Diomedes was one of the foremost Greek warriors in the destruction of Troy; cf. 1.96f., 752.

14 246. **Argyripam:** see notes on 226, 239; the name is connected with Argos, Diomedes' homeland. The legend says that Diomedes joined Daunus in a war against the Messapians, and received some of their land when the war was won.

15 247. **Gargani . . . Iapygis:** *Iapyx* is here an adjective (cf. 678) referring to the area of Iapyx (Iapygia) in Apulia in (or near) which Mt. Garganus was situated.

16 250. The indirect questions are dependent on *docemus:* 'we told him our names and country and who had attacked us and what reason had brought us to Arpi'.

"o fortunatae gentes, Saturnia[1] regna,
antiqui Ausonii,[2] quae vos fortuna quietos
sollicitat suadetque[3] ignota[4] lacessere bella?
Quicumque Iliacos ferro violavimus agros   255
(mitto[5] ea quae muris bellando exhausta[6] sub altis,
quos Simois[7] premat ille viros) infanda per orbem
supplicia et scelerum poenas expendimus omnes,
vel[8] Priamo[9] miseranda manus; scit triste Minervae
sidus et Euboicae cautes ultorque Caphereus.   260
Militia ex illa diversum ad litus abacti[10]
Atrides Protei[11] Menelaus adusque columnas
exsulat, Aetnaeos vidit Cyclopas[12] Ulixes.
Regna[13] Neoptolemi referam versosque penatis
Idomenei? Libycone habitantis litore Locros?   265
Ipse Mycenaeus magnorum ductor Achivum[14]
coniugis infandae prima inter limina dextra

---

1 252. **Saturaia regna:** 'where Saturn once ruled', cf. 1.569 and 8.319f. (where see note).

2 253. **Ausonii:** this word is commonly used by the poets to mean Italian; it has legendary links with Auson, a son of Ulysses and Calypso.

3 254. **suadetque . . . lacessere:** the infinitive with *suadere* is common in poetry, cf. 10.9-10.

4 **ignota . . . bella:** 'wars of which you know nothing', referring to their peacefulness, (*quietos,* 253), and also to their ignorance of the formidable nature of their enemy.

5 256. **mitto:** 'I say nothing of' Diomedes' point is that quite apart from the many Greeks who died at Troy those who survived have been harassed by ill fortune ever since. Compare Hom. *Od.* 3.86f.

6 **exhausta:** 'endured to the end', cf. 4.14, 10.57.

7 257. Simois was one of the rivers of Troy (10.60). In using the verb *premat* Diomedes identifies the river with the land of Troy (cf. 1.100-1); the river presses on the dead as the earth does.

8 259. **vel . . . manus:** 'a company that would win pity even from Priam'; the phrase is in apposition to *nos,* subject of *expendimus.*

9 259-60. 'the baleful star of Minerva is witness, and the Euboean rocks and Caphereus that took vengeance'. The reference is to the storm and shipwreck of the returning Greeks off Euboea (Caphereus is a promontory of Euboea); this was caused by Minerva (Pallas Athena) because of the violation of her priestess Cassandra by Ajax, son of Oileus, cf. 1.39f., Hom. *Od.* 3.132f. Hor. *Epod.* 10. *Triste . . . sidus* refers to the storm, as weather conditions were thought to be influenced by the rising and settings of constellations.

10 261-3. Further examples follow of Greek disasters on the return from Troy: Menelaus, son of Atreus, was driven to Egypt, where Proteus was king (Hom. *Od.* 4.351f., Eur. *Helen* passim); and Ulysses (Odysseus) during his ten years' wanderings came to the land of the Cyclops near Mt. Etna (Hom. *Od.* 9.105, *Aen.* 3.613f.).

11 262. **Protei . . . columnas:** Servius explains that this is by analogy with the columns of Hercules (Gibraltar). *Protei* scans as two syllables by synizesis; cf. *Idomenei* (265), *proinde* (383) and see note on 7.33. For *adusque* (right up to) cf. Hor. *Sat.* 1.5.96-7 *adusque / Bari moenia,* and compare *ab usque* (7.289), *super usque* (317).

12 263. **Cyclopas:** Greek accusative with short final syllable, cf. 395 *Arcadas* and 10.89 *Troas.*

13 264-5. Diomedes cites three more examples of Greek disasters: Neoptolemus (Pyrrhus) died after a brief rule in Epirus (3.333f.); Idomeneus of Crete was driven out of his kingdom (3.121f.); the Locri were followers of Ajax, son of Oileus, and it seems that after his death some became exiles in N. Africa.

14 266. The final example is the most impressive of all, the murder of Agamemnon, king of Mycenae and leader of the Greeks (*Achivi*), by his wife Clytemnestra and her lover Aegistheus.

oppetiit,[1] devictam[2] Asiam subsedit adulter.

Invidisse[3] deos, patriis ut redditus aris

coniugium optatum et pulchram Calydona[4] viderem?   270

Nunc etiam horribili visu portenta sequuntur[5]

et socii amissi[6] petierunt aethera pennis

fluminibusque vagantur aves (heu, dira meorum

supplicia!) et scopulos lacrimosis vocibus implent.

Haec[7] adeo ex illo mihi iam speranda fuerunt[8]   275

tempore cum ferro caelestia corpora demens[9]

appetii et Veneris violavi vulnere dextram.

Ne vero, ne me ad talis impellite pugnas.

Nec mihi cum Teucris ullum post[10] eruta bellum

Pergama nec[11] veterum memini laetorve malorum.   280

Munera quae patriis ad me portatis ab oris

vertite ad Aenean. Stetimus tela[12] aspera contra

contulimusque manus: experto[13] credite quantus

---

1 268. **oppetiit:** 'died', poetic variant for the prose *oppetere mortem,* cf. 1.96.

2 **devictam . . . adulter:** 'an adulterer lay in wait for conquered Asia', i.e. For the conqueror of Asia at the moment of his conquest. This use of *subsidere* is rare and poetic, cf. Sil. 13.221 *subsidere saepe leonem.* It is possible that the phrase might mean 'came in to avenge conquered Asia' (like the Greek εφεδρπς, a third person who takes on the victor of a duel), but this would be an unparalleled use of *subsidere.* It is best to accept the remarkable phrase as, in Quinn's words, 'a concentrated, ironical expression of the cliche "How are the mighty fallen".'

3 269. **invidisse deos:** this phrase comes in very abruptly, perhaps expressing Diomedes' emotion: 'to think that the gods grudged that . . .'. The construction is accusative and infinitive of exclamation, cf. 1.37f., 97f. Some editors transpose 269-70 to follow 265, so that *invidisse deos* is governed by *referam;* but the list must end with Agamemnon, not with the Locri. Others take it as governed by *referam* without transposition; this is possible but harsh.

4 270. **Calydona:** Greek accusative, cf. 272 *aethera* and 675. It is a town in Aetolia, where Diomedes originally lived.

5 271f. This strange story about the companions of Diomedes being changed into birds occurs in Lycophron (597) and is fully treated by Ovid (*Met.* 14.497f., where he too is telling the story of Venulus' embassy to Diomedes); he says the birds were similar to swans, and the reason for the metamorphosis was an insult to Venus. There was an island off Apulia called *Diomedea insula* and the birds on it were called *Diomedeae aves* (Plin. *Nat. Hist.* 10.126); they have been identified by Warde Fowler as shearwaters (see Thompson, *C.R.* 1918, pp. 92f.).

6 272. **amissi:** 'lost' in the sense of metamorphosed into birds; Servius knew of a reading *admissis* ('taking to themselves wings').

7 275-6. 'Indeed I had to expect this kind of disaster ever since . . .'; for *adeo* cf. 314, 487.

8 275f. Diomedes feels that these portents indicate that the wrath of the gods confronts him too (like his companions in the war against Troy), and therefore he will not oppose the Trojans any more.

9 276-7. Notice the pattern of alliteration of *c* and *v;* the wounding of Venus (Aphrodite) in the hand by Diomedes is described in Hom. *Il.* 5-334f.

10 279-80. **post eruta . . . Pergama:** 'after the destruction of Troy', a favourite Latin idiom with the participle, as in *post urbem conditam;* cf. 308.

11 280. **nec . . . malorum:** 'nor do I think upon or rejoice over those old unhappy days'; the genitives are governed, according to the normal construction, by *memini* and there is no question here of a Greek genitive of cause with *laetor,* as in 73.

12 282. **tela aspera contra:** the anastrophe of a dissyllabic preposition is very common in Virgil; for the phrase cf. 5.414 *Alciden contra stetit.*

13 283-4. **experto . . . hastam:** 'believe one who knows from experience how mighty he towers with his shield outstretched, with what force he whirls his spear'; for *in clipeum* cf. 9.749 *consurgit in ensem,* 10.725 *surgentem in cornua cervum.* The shield could be used as an offensive weapon for thrusting, cf. 12.712, 724. The meeting of Aeneas and Diomedes is described in Hom. *Il.* 5.239f.

in clipeum adsurgat, quo turbine torqueat hastam.

Si duo praeterea talis Idaea[1] tulisset[2]   285

terra viros, ultro Inachias[3] venisset ad urbes

Dardanus,[4] et versis lugeret Graecia fatis.

Quidquid[5] apud durae cessatum est moenia Troiae,

Hectoris Aeneaeque manu victoria Graium

haesit et in decimum vestigia rettulit annum.   290

Ambo animis, ambo insignes praestantibus armis,[6]

hic pietate prior. Coeant in foedera dextrae,

qua[7] datur; ast armis concurrant[8] arma cavete."

Et responsa simul quae sint, rex optime, regis[9]

audisti et[10] quae sit magno sententia bello.'   295

> *296-335. Latinus makes a speech in which he says that the Latin situation is hopeless: he proposes to make peace with the Trojans either by ceding them land or by providing them with ships to find land elsewhere.*

[11]Vix[12] ea legati, variusque per ora cucurrit

Ausonidum turbata fremor: ceu[13] saxa morantur

cum rapidos amnis, fit clauso gurgite murmur

---

1 285-6. **Idaea . . . terra:** Troy is so-called from Mt. Ida, cf. 7.222.

2 285f. The thought is from Hom. *Il.* 2.371f.; *praeterea* is 'in addition to him'.

3 286. **Inachias:** a general word for Greek,from Inachus, king of Argos, but here with some special reference to Diomedes' connexions with Argos.

4 287. **Dardanus:** 'the Trojans', collective singular, cf. 10.238-9.

5 288f. 'During all the long wait outside the walls of stubborn Troy the Greek victory hung fire and receded until the tenth year only because of the valour of Hector and Aeneas'. The *quidquid* clause is equivalent to duration of time; for *vestigia rettulit* cf. 2.169-70 *retro sublapsa referri* / *spes Danaum.*

6 291-2. Hector and Aeneas are linked in Homer as the bravest of the Trojans (*Il.* 6.77f., 17.513); notice how the proto-Roman aspect of Aeneas is emphasised by *hic pietate prior.* Conington well says 'it may be doubted whether the Homeric Diomed would have made any such distinction as that here expressed'.

7 293. **qua datur:** 'as is permitted', literally 'in the way which is permitted', i.e. it is possible to make peace with Aeneas. Almost all commentators and translators follow Servius and take the meaning to be 'in whatever way is offered'; but Page is probably right in saying that this cannot be got out of the Latin.

8 **concurrant . . . cavete:** the jussive subjunctive in parataxis with *cavere,* without *ne* added, occurs sometimes in prose too.

9 294-5. The transition from the end of Diomedes' reply to the end of Venulus' speech is made informal and stiff phrases.

10 295. **et quae . . . bello:** 'and also his opinion in view of the magnitude of the war'; i.e. as well as giving a negative response to their requests Diomedes has expressed his views about the best thing for them to do when confronted by so formidable an enemy. The phrase *magno . . . bello* is ablative of attendant circumstances.

11 296f. The speech of Latinus reflects his general unwillingness to continue a war which he had never wished to start (7.259f., 594f.). He takes advantage of the adverse reply from the envoys to stress the hopelessness of the war (309-11) in spite of all their efforts (312). The speech is reasoned and moderate and tries to disarm opposition (especially that of Turnus); it is in very marked contrast with the fireworks of the succeeding speech by Drances.

12 296-7. **Vix ea . . . Fremor:** 'Scarcely had the envoys spoken thus, and (when) a murmuring of conflicting opinions rippled from lip to lip through the anxious ranks of the Italians'; notice the paratactic use of -*que,* equivalent to an inverted *cum* clause, cf. 2.692 and note on 10.659. For *Ausonidum,* archaic for *Ausonidarum,* cf. 503 and 10.564.

13 297-8. **ceu . . . amnis:** 'as when rocks check swift rivers . . .'; the construction is *ceu fit . . . cum saxa morantur amnis;* notice the alliteration of *r* all through lines 297-99.

vicinaeque fremunt ripae crepitantibus undis.

ut primum placati animi et trepida ora quierunt,   300

praefatus[1] divos solio rex infit ab alto:

  'Ante equidem summa[2] de re statuisse, Latini,

et[3] vellem et fuerat melius, non tempore tali

cogere concilium, cum muros adsidet hostis.

Bellum importunum,[4] cives, cum gente[5] deorum   305

invictisque viris gerimus, quos nulla fatigant

proelia nec victi possunt absistere ferro.

Spem si quam ascitis[6] Aetolum habuistis in armis,

ponite.[7] Spes sibi quisque; sed haec quam angusta videtis.

Cetera qua rerum iaceant perculsa ruina,[8]   310

ante[9] oculos interque manus sunt omnia vestras.

Nec quemquam incuso: potuit[10] quae plurima virtus

esse, fuit; toto certatum est corpore regni.

Nunc adeo quae sit dubiae sententia menti,

expediam et paucis (animos adhibete) docebo.   315

Est antiquus[11] ager Tusco[12] mihi proximus amni,

longus[13] in occasum, finis super usque Sicanos;

---

1 301. **praefatus divos**: 'after first praying to the gods'; for the accusative cf. Cato, *Agr.* 141.2 *Ianum Iovemque vino praefamino.*

2 302. **summa de re**: 'on this crisis', cf. 2.322.

3 303. **et vellem et fuerat melius**: 'I could have wished, and it would have been better'; for *vellem* cf. 111, for *fuerat melius* cf. 115.

4 305. **importunum**: 'ill-omened'. The word basically means 'untimely', 'inappropriate', hence 'horrible', 'monstrous'; on the other two occasions where Virgil uses it (*Geo.* 1.470, *Aen.* 12.864) it is applied to ill-omened, horrible birds.

5 305-6. **gente deorum invictisque viris**: the first phrase refers to Aeneas' divine descent through his mother Venus; the second is paradoxically explained in 307; they are unconquerable because when conquered they fight on. Servius quotes Ennius (*Ann.* 493) *qui vincit non est victor nisi victus fatetur*; cf. also Ennius, *Ann.* 359 (of Troy) *nec cum capta capi*, imitated in *Aen.* 7.295. For the general sentiment cf. Hor. *Odes* 4.4.50f., Livy 27.14.1 (Hannibal's comment on the Romans: *seu victus est, instaurat cum victoribus certamen*).

6 308. **ascitis Aetolum ... in armis**: 'in winning the armed support of the Aetolians'; for this use of the participle cf. 279. Diomedes' people are called Aetoli because Diomedes was originally from Aetolia, cf. 239.

7 309. **ponite**: 'lay it down' (Servius says *deponite*), i.e. give it up; cf. 366 and 8.329. The final vowel of *ponite* is left short before the double consonant *sp-*; this is the only instance in the *Aeneid* except 3.270 *nemorosa Zacynthos,* where the word *Zacynthos* could not otherwise be used in a hexameter. The full stop of course makes the abnormality easier. Lucretius is rather freer in this licence, see Bailey's edition, *Proleg.* p. 126. The line generally is staccato, with three heavy stops (including the unusual one after the third foot trochee) and verbs to be understood, *spes sibi quisque (sit); sed haec quam angusta (sit) videtis.* The words from *spes . . . videtis* are parenthetical to the train of thought continued in 310 ('if you had hopes of the Aetolians, give them up, and you see how all other aspects of our cause are in ruins').

8 310-11. There is a slight shift of construction; instead of the indirect question being governed by *est* (*ante oculos*) the more emphatic *sunt omnia* is substituted.

9 311. **ante oculos interque maims**: 'in seeing and touching distance'; Servius compares the Greek προχειροσ ('at hand').

10 312-13. **potuit . . . Fuit**: 'the very most which valour could have done has been done'.

11 316. **antiquus**: 'long in my possession'; the land in question is presumably part of Latinus' own royal domains.

12 **Tusco . . . amni**: the Tiber, cf. 8.473.

13 317. 'stretching far to the west, even beyond the Sicanian territory'. The Sicani are mentioned as an Italian people of this area in 7.795 (where they are also linked with the Aurunci and Rutuli) and 8.328.

Aurunci Rutulique serunt, et vomere duros
exercent collis atque horum[1] asperrima pascunt.
Haec omnis regio et celsi plaga pinea montis   320
cedat[2] amicitiae Teucrorum, et foederis aequas[3]
dicamus leges sociosque in regna vocemus:
considant, si tantus amor,[4] et moenia condant.
Sin alios finis aliamque capessere gentem
est animus possuntque[5] solo decedere nostro.   325
Bis denas Italo texamus[6] robore navis;
seu pluris complere valent, iacet omnis ad undam
materies: ipsi numerumque[7] modumque carinis
praecipiant, nos aera,[8] manus, navalia demus.
Praeterea, qui dicta ferant et foedera firment   330
centum oratores prima de gente Latinos
ire placet pacisque manu praetendere ramos,
munera[9] portantis aurique eborisque talenta
et[10] sellam regni trabeamque insignia nostri.
Consulite in[11] medium et rebus succurrite fessis.'   335

---

1 319. **horum asperrima pascunt:** 'and use as pasture the roughest parts of them'; this is a very rare use of *pascere,* not unlike *depascere* in *Geo.* 1.112. Compare our use of 'graze'.

2 321. **cedat . . . Teucrorum:** 'be given over to the friendship of the Trojans', i.e. be used to win their friendship.

3 321f. Latinus' proposals here are ironically very like what Aeneas promises he will do if he wins the single combat (12.189f.).

4 323. **amor:** the last syllable is lengthened in arsis, see note on 111.

5 325. **possuntque:** i.e. if, in addition to wanting to depart (*est animus*), they feel they are allowed by fate to do so (as Latinus knows well they are not). This alternative proposal is introduced simply out of a desire to placate Turnus; and for the same reason there is no further reference here to Lavinia, as Drances is quick to see(354f.).

6 326. **texamus:** the metaphor is of 'weaving' the planks together for the hulls of ships (cf. the wooden horse, 2.16). Servius quotes *textrinum* from Ennius, 'shipyard'.

7 328. **numerumque modumque:** 'the number and type'; for the linking of adjacent nouns by doubled -*que* ('both . . . and') cf. 333.

8 329. **aera, manus, navalia:** 'bronze, labour, dockyards'; Conington follows Servius in taking *navalia* to mean *res navales,* i.e. sails, pitch, etc., but cf. 4.593 for the commoner use of the word.

9 333. **munera:** in apposition to *talenta, sellam, trabeam; insignia* is in apposition to the last two.

10 334. 'and the throne and robe that are emblems of my kingdom'; Livy tells us (27.4.8) that the Romans sent a toga, a purple tunic, an ivory throne, and a golden bowl, as gifts to Syphax as a mark of honour.

11 335. **in medium:** 'for the common good', or perhaps simply 'together'.

336-75. Drances supports Latinus' proposals for peace in a highly rhetorical speech directed against Turnus.

[1]Tum Drances idem infensus, quem gloria Turni
obliqua[2] invidia stimulisque agitabat amaris,
largus[3] opum et lingua[4] melior, sed frigida bello
dextera, consiliis habitus non futtilis auctor,
seditione potens (genus huic materna superbum   340
nobilitas dabat, incertum[5] de patre ferebat),
surgit et his[6] onerat dictis atque aggerat iras:
'rem nulli obscuram nostrae nec vocis egentem
consulis,[7] o bone rex: cuncti se scire fatentur
quid fortuna ferat populi, sed dicere[8] mussant.   345
Det libertatem fandi flatusque[9] remittat,
cuius ob[10] auspicium infaustum moresque sinistros
(dicam equidem, licet arma mihi mortemque minetur)
lumina[11] tot cecidisse ducum totamque videmus
consedisse urbem luctu, dum Troia temptat   350

---

1 336f. The speech of Drances (like the reply of Turnus, 378f.) is a piece of scintillating and unscrupulous rhetoric; it arouses in the reader a pleasurable sense of horrified expectation; Turnus is not the kind of man to accept these taunts with equanimity. The tone of the passage is distanced and intellectual; the reader is not emotionally involved in the rights or wrongs of this personal quarrel; indeed Virgil has gone out of his way to avoid involving us in sympathy for either character. Drances, although he is urging the right course, is self-seeking and malicious and if anything sometimes inclines our support towards Turnus; but there is enough truth in what he says to alienate us from Turnus too. We feel that we are in the audience listening to a debate, not in any way identified with either party; it is a performance in which our emotions are not involved, and we are free to enjoy the intellectual fireworks. Cicero would have enjoyed listening to this manipulation of rhetorical devices. See further Quinn, pp. 240f. In some respects Drances reminds us of the sour Thersites in Hom. *Il.* 2.212f.; the content of his speech (but not the manner) is reminiscent of Polydamas' attempt to persuade Hector (*Il.* 18.240f.) to withdraw within the walls of Troy. But essentially he is Virgil's own creation and his function is to provide an opportunity or rhetorical and highflown writing of a kind which Virgil and his readers enjoyed and which could add another dimension to the narrative of battle and pathos in the last books of the *Aeneid.*

2 337. 'stung with jealousy half-hidden and goaded with bitter torments'; cf. 122f., where Drances' hostility to Turnus is indicated before his first speech.

3 338. **largus opum:** 'unsparing of his money'; for the genitive of respect cf. 416-17, 9.26 and Lucan 9.608 *largus aquae.* The phrase is used to discredit Drances.

4 **lingua melior:** cf. Milton's description of Belial, *P.L.* 2.112f. 'His tongue / dropped Manna, and could make the worse appear / the better reason ... to vice industrious, but to nobler deeds / timorous and slothful.'

5 341. **incertum ... Ferebat:** 'he had dubious ancestry on his father's side'; *ferebat* is awkward here, and some MSS have *ferebant* ('men said . . .'), but this does not cohere well with *incertum.*

6 342. **his onerat ... iras:** 'with these words heaped up and stoked the fires of their anger'; for *onerat* in this sense cf. Tac. *Hist.* 2.52.

7 344. **consulis:** 'discuss', *consulere de* is commoner, but for the transitive usage cf. Livy 2.28.2.

8 345. **dicere mussant:** 'they hesitate to say'; the infinitive is used on the analogy of *nolunt, dubitant.*

9 346. **flatusque remittat:** 'let him (i.e. Turnus, defined in the next line) stop his fire-breathing'; this metaphorical use of *flatus* is equivalent to *superbia.*

10 347. **ob auspicium infaustum:** 'because of his unholy instigation'; the word *auspicium* has a religious connotation: Turnus' leadership is unblessed.

11 349. **lumina:** 'shining lights'; Conington quotes Cic. *Cat.* 3.24 *clarissimis viris interfectis lumina civitatis exstincta sunt.*

castra fugae[1] fidens et caelum[2] territat armis.
Unum etiam donis istis, quae plurima mitti[3]
Dardanidis dicique iubes, unum, optime regum,
adicias,[4] nec te ullius[5] violentia vincat[6]
quin natam egregio genero dignisque hymenaeis   355
des, pater, et pacem hanc aeterno foedere iungas.
Quod si tantus habet mentes et pectora terror,[7]
ipsum obtestemur veniamque[8] oremus ab ipso:
cedat,[9] ius[10] proprium regi patriaeque remittat.
Quid miseros totiens in aperta pericula civis   360
proicis, o Latio caput[11] horum et causa malorum?
Nulla salus bello, pacem te poscimus omnes,
Turne, simul pacis[12] solum inviolabile pignus.
Primus ego, invisum[13] quem tu tibi fingis (et[14] esse
nil moror), en supplex venio. Miserere tuorum,   365
pone[15] animos et pulsus abi. Sat funera fusi
vidimus ingentis[16] et desolavimus agros.
Aut, si fama movet, si[17] tantum pectore robur

---

1 351. **fugae fidens:** probably a reference to Turnus' pursuit of the phantom of Aeneas (10.645f.), and perhaps also to 9.815f.; the pattern of alliteration hereabouts (*t, c, f*) helps Drances' rhetoric.

2 **caelum territat armis:** a suggestion of arrogance and vanity, and of folly too.

3 352-3. **mitti . . . dicique:** Latinus had proposed to send gifts (gold etc.) and to make verbal offers (land, ships, etc.).

4 354. **adicias:** jussive subjunctive, more deferential than the imperative.

5 **ullius violentia:** Drances does not mention Turnus, but he uses the word associated with him and with no one else (376, 12.9, 45).

6 354-5. **vincat quin:** 'intimidate you from . . .'; *vincat* is used in the sense *vi impediat*.

7 357. **terror:** i.e. of Turnus, who is pointedly not named and ironically referred to by the mock-deferential *ipse* in the next line (invidiose repetitum pronomen, Servius).

8 358. **veniamque:** 'a favour', cf. 101.

9 359. **cedat:** used absolutely, 'let him give in'; the pause after the first foot spondee adds emphasis, cf. 48, 804.

10 **ius . . . remittat:** 'let him give back to his king and country their proper rights', i.e. to give Lavinia in marriage to whomsoever Latinus desires and the people of the country approve; Drances implies that the people also are in favour of Aeneas and hostile to Turnus. It is possible, as Page urges, that *ius proprium* means 'his own proper rights', with sarcastic deference.

11 361. **caput:** 'source', a metaphor from rivers, cf. 8.65. Notice the very jingling rhyme of *horum . . . malorum*, a device to achieve rhetorical emphasis.

12 363. **pacis . . . pignus:** i.e. the giving up of Lavinia.

13 364. **invisum:** 'hostile', the active sense is very unusual, cf. Lucan 1.9.

14 364-5. **et esse nil moror:** 'and I don't care if I am'; as Servius says, this explains *fingis:* Turnus thinks it and Drances does not deny it.

15 366. **pone . . . abi:** 'lay aside your pride, and withdraw defeated'; for *pone* (= *depone*) cf. 309. The second phrase is a military metaphor (cf. *Geo.* 3.225), and chosen to inflame Turnus.

16 367. **ingentis ... agros:** 'and we have made great tracts of our countryside desolate', by causing the absence and death of the farmers; cf. 8.8 *latos vastant cultoribus agros.*

17 368-9. **si tantum . . . concipis:** 'if you feel such great strength in your heart', i.e. put it to good use by fighting Aeneas yourself.

concipis et si adeo dotalis[1] regia cordi[2] est,
aude atque adversum fidens[3] fer pectus in hostem.   370
Scilicet ut Turno contingat regia coniunx,[4]
nos animae viles, inhumata infletaque turba,
sternamur campis? [5]Etiam tu, si qua tibi vis,
si patrii quid Martis habes, illum aspice contra
qui vocat.'[6]   375

> 376-444. *Turnus in reply angrily reviles Drances with taunts of cowardice; then more calmly he replies to Latinus' proposals, saying that there is no need to despair of their situation. Finally he says that he is ready to face Aeneas in single combat.*

[7]Talibus exarsit dictis violentia[8] Turni.
Dat gemitum rumpitque[9] has imo pectore voces:
'larga quidem semper, Drance,[10] tibi copia fandi
tum cum bella manus poscunt, patribusque[11] vocatis
primus ades. Sed non replenda est curia verbis,   380
quae[12] tuto tibi magna volant, dum distinet hostem
agger murorum nec inundant sanguine fossae.
Proinde[13] tona eloquio (solitum tibi) meque timoris
argue tu, Drance, quando tot stragis acervos

---

1 369. **dotalis regia:** 'a palace as your dowry', by marrying the princess; cf. 9.737. Page points out the sneer: 'it is not for Lavinia but her dower that he cares'.

2 **cordi est:** predicative dative, cf. 10.252.

3 370. **fidens fer:** the alliteration emphasises the tiny verb which has so much meaning.

4 371f. The heavy irony of this sentence is indicated by the opening word *scilicet* and the rhetorical exaggeration of 372; cf. 2.577f.

5 373f. 'And you too, if you have any strength, if you have anything of your father's valour, look face to face at the opponent who calls you'. *Etiam tu* sarcastically contrasts with *nos* (we are fighting and dying, you too might do something about your own war). The line ending of 373 is abrupt with the monosyllabic ending (cf. 10.864) and the relatively rare scansion of *tibi* with long final syllable. For *Mars* in the sense of 'valour', cf. 389.

6 375. For the half-line see notes on 1.534, 7.129. There is only one other in this book (391).

7 376f. The final speech of the four delivered at Latinus' council is the longest, and it reflects both the impetuous anger and the military courage of Turnus. In dealing with Drances he is violent, sarcastic, uncontrolled; he has been stung by Drances' taunts and he replies without finesse or subtlety, in terms of forthright abuse, exaggerating his own achievements (393-5, 396-8), and making no reference to the recent disasters that have befallen the Latins.
When he turns (410f.) to Latinus' proposals his tone becomes much calmer and his advocacy of death or glory is in parts very impressive, a fine expression of heroic tradition (415-18, 428-31). Finally he says that, if it is the general wish, he will indeed meet Aeneas in single combat; here a certain unease seems to lurk behind the bold phrases, almost a presentiment of having met his match (cf. 12.219f., 643f.).

8 376. **violentia:** the word is used only of Turnus in the *Aeneid;* see note on 354.

9 377. **rumpitque has . . . voces:** 'burst into speech with these words', cf. 2.129 (with note there).

10 378. **Drance:** Greek vocative with long *-e* (as in 384), cf. 10.461.

11 379. **patribusque vocatis:** the Roman technical phrase for a meeting of the senate in the Senate House (*curia*, 380).

12 381. **quae ... volant:** 'which fly so splendidly from your lips as long as you are safe'; for the dative cf. 10.583-4.

13 383. **proinde:** 'so', 'therefore' (cf. 400), ironically used. The word scans as two syllables by synizesis (like *deinde*).

Teucrorum tua dextra dedit, passimque tropaeis   385
insignis[1] agros. Possit[2] quid vivida virtus
experiare licet, nec longe scilicet hostes
quaerendi nobis; circumstant undique muros.
Imus in adversos — quid cessas? An[3] tibi Mavors
ventosa in lingua pedibusque fugacibus istis   390
semper erit?
Pulsus[4] ego? Aut[5] quisquam merito, foedissime, pulsum
arguet, Iliaco tumidum qui crescere Thybrim
sanguine et Euandri totam cum stirpe videbit[6]
procubuisse[7] domum atque exutos Arcadas[8] armis?   395
haud ita me experti Bitias et Pandarus[9] ingens
et quos mille die victor sub Tartara misi,
inclusus muris hostilique aggere saeptus.
Nulla[10] salus bello? Capiti[11] cane talia, demens,
Dardanio rebusque tuis. Proinde omnia magno   400
ne cessa turbare metu atque extollere viris
gentis bis[12] victae, contra premere[13] arma Latini.

---

1 386. **insignis:** from *insignire*, 'you adorn', cf. 7.790.

2 **possit . . . virtus:** 'what shining valour can do', cf. 5.754.

3 389-91. **an tibi . . . erit?:** 'will your martial spirit always be in your windy words and your flying feet?' For *Mavors* (archaic for *Mars*) in this sense cf. 374; for *ventosus* cf. 708, where (as here) the sense is 'puffed up'. Cf. Beaumont and Fletcher, *The Maid's Tragedy*, 4.2. 231-2 'You cannot blast me with your tongue, and that's / the strongest part you have about you'.

4 392. **pulsus ego?:** Turnus picks up Drances' word (366).

5 **aut quisquam:** the pronoun is used to indicate a negative answer, cf. 10.34.

6 394. **videbit:** 'will take the trouble to look at'; the infinitives governed by *videbit* describe not so much future prospects as the present situation as Turnus sees it.

7 395. **procubuisse:** 'flattened to the ground', the perfect expresses the completed fact; Turnus refers to the death of Pallas.

8 **Arcadas:** Greek accusative with short final syllable, cf. 263; we are not told of the other Arcadians (besides Pallas) whom Turnus killed.

9 396. Pandarus and Bitias, guardians of the Trojan camp, were killed by Turnus (9.703f., 722f.); Turnus entered the Trojan camp and dealt destruction around him before escaping by diving into the Tiber (9.815f.).

10 399. **nulla . . . bello:** again Turnus picks up Drances' words (362).

11 399-400. **capiti . . . tuis:** 'intone these gloomy chants to that Trojan creature, you madman, and apply them to your own fortunes'; for *caput* in a derogatory sense (applied to Aeneas by Dido) cf. 4.640.

12 402. **bis victae:** once by Hercules and once by the Greeks, cf. 2.642f., 8.290f.

13 **premere:** 'disparage' (in contrast to *extollere*, 'exalt'); *cf.* Livy 22.12.12, Tac. *Ann.* 1549, Hor. *Epist.* 1.19.36.

Nunc¹ et Myrmidonum proceres Phrygia arma tremescunt,

[nunc et Tydides et Larisaeus Achilles,]

amnis et Hadriacas retro fugit Aufidus² undas.   405

Vel cum se pavidum contra mea iurgia fingit,

artificis³ scelus, et formidine crimen acerbat.

Numquam animam talem dextra hac (absiste moveri)

amittes: habitet tecum et sit pectore in isto.

Nunc ad te et tua magna, pater, consulta⁴ revertor.   410

Si nullam nostris ultra spem ponis in armis,

si tam deserti sumus et semel agmine verso

funditus occidimus neque habet Fortuna regressum,

oremus pacem et dextras tendamus inertis.

Quamquam o si solitae quicquam virtutis adesset!⁵   415

Ille⁶ mihi ante alios fortunatusque laborum

egregiusque animi, qui, ne quid tale videret,

procubuit moriens et humum semel⁷ ore momordit.

Sin et opes nobis et adhuc intacta iuventus

auxilioque urbes Italae populique supersunt,   420

sin et Troianis cum⁸ multo gloria venit

sanguine (sunt illis sua funera, parque⁹ per omnis

tempestas), cur indecores in limine primo

---

1 403-7. 'Now indeed the chieftains of the Myrmidons are afraid of Trojan might and the river Aufidus is in full flight upstream away from the waves of the Adriatic. Or what about when he pretends that he is frightened of my taunts, the low trick of a cunning schemer, and strengthens his accusation against me by appearing frightened?'

This is a very difficult passage, which I have discussed in full in *C.P.* 1966, pp. 184f. The first sentence sarcastically rejects Drances' allegations about Trojan strength; the second rejects Drances' feigned fear of violence at Turnus' hands. The use of *vel cum* (the ellipsis is not unlike that in *quid quod? quid cum?*) is cited by Quintilian (9.3.14) as an archaism; it is used here very abruptly as Turnus stops addressing Drances directly and turns to the audience to refer to him in the third person.

Line 404 is given by all the MSS, but there are very strong reasons for regarding it as an interpolation (as suggested by Kloucek, but only Hirtzel of modern editors has followed him). It is nearly the same as 2.197, and could have been inserted by a scribe with a good memory triggered off by *Myrmidonum* (Achilles' special followers); it is very unsuitable here, as Turnus would be saying: 'You'll be telling me next that Achilles and Diomedes are afraid of the Trojans!' Of these, one is dead and the other is in fact afraid of the Trojans, as has been reported at length (282f.).

2 405. **Aufidus**: a violent river (cf. Hor. *Odes* 3.30.10) mentioned here because it was in the territory of Daunus, Turnus' father. (For this idea of nature reversed, a figure called αδυνατον, cf. *Ecl.* 1.59f.,Ov. *Trist.* 1.8.1 and Gow on Theoc. 1.132).

3 407. **artificis scelus**: *scelus* is in apposition to the sentence, the sort of construction which Virgil uses with *nefas!, miserum!* etc.; cf. also 6.223. Some commentators regard the phrase as the subject of *fingit*, equivalent to *scelestus artifex*, but this would be unVirgilian.

4 410. **consulta**: the proposals Latinus put forward for discussion, cf. 335 *consulite in medium*.

5 415. The form of the wish begins like 5.195; compare also 8.560f. To *virtutis* supply *nostrae*.

6 416-17. 'The man who to me is both happy in his toil and most noble in heart is he who . . .' *Laborum* and *animi* are genitives of respect, cf. 338 and 9.246.

7 418. **semel**: most MSS have *simul*, but Servius attests *semel*, which makes better sense ('once and for all', cf. Ov. *Her.* 5.104).

8 421-2. **cum multo . . . sanguine**: 'at a price of much bloodshed', cf. Lucan 1.670 *cum domino pax ista venit*.

9 422-3. **parque ... tempestas**: 'a similar storm has swept through their ranks'; for the metaphorical use of *tempestas* cf. 7.223, Livy 31.10.6.

deficimus? Cur ante tubam tremor occupat artus?
Multa[1] dies variique labor mutabilis aevi   425
rettulit in melius, multos alterna revisens
lusit et in solido rursus Fortuna locavit.
Non erit auxilio nobis Aetolus et Arpi:[2]
at Messapus erit felixque Tolumnius et quos[3]
tot[4] populi misere duces, nec parva sequetur   430
gloria delectos Latio et Laurentibus agris.
Est et Volscorum egregia de gente Camilla[5]
agmen agens equitum et florentis aere catervas.
Quod si me solum Teucri in certamina poscunt
idque placet tantumque[6] bonis communibus obsto,   435
non[7] adeo has exosa manus Victoria fugit
ut tanta quicquam pro spe temptare recusem.
Ibo animis[8] contra, [9]vel magnum praestet Achillem
factaque Volcani manibus paria induat arma
ille licet. Vobis animam hanc soceroque Latino[10]   440
Turnus ego, haud ulli veterum virtute secundus,
devovi. Solum[11] Aeneas vocat? Et[12] vocet oro;
nec[13] Drances potius, sive est haec ira deorum,

---

1 425-7. 'The passage of the days and the changing toil of shifting time has often altered things for the better: often changeable fortune has mocked people and then put them back again on firm ground'. This is a fine series of impressively phrased commonplaces: cf. Enn. *Ann.* 287-9 *multa dies in bello conficit unus: / et rursus multae fortunae forte recumbunt: / haudquaquam quemquam semper fortuna secuta est.*

2 428. This line refers to Diomedes' refusal to help; see notes on 226f. and 239.

3 429. A splendid line, where the repetition, in strong antithesis, of the simple verb *erit* is extremely moving. Messapus is in the catalogue in 7.691f., and is frequently mentioned as one of the Latin leaders (cf. 464); Tolumnius the augur occurs again in 12.258f. *Felix* is a frequent epithet of successful warriors. The abrupt line ending *et quos* helps to suggest Turnus' emotion.

4 430. **tot . . . duces:** as listed in the long catalogue, 7.647f.

5 432f. The Volscian warrior-maid Camilla had the final place of honour in the catalogue (7.803f., where see note); the mention of her now foreshadows the large part she is to play in the second half of this book (498f.). Line 433 is repeated from 7.804, where see note.

6 435. **tantumque:** 'so much' (in tantum, Servius).

7 436. **non adeo . . . Fugit:** 'Victory has not so spurned and rejected these hands of mine . . .'; a fine understatement of his past bravery.

8 438. **animis:** 'with courage', cf. 18.

9 438-40. 'though he should surpass even mighty Achilles and put on armour like his, made by the handiwork of Vulcan'; the order is intricate with *ille licet* postponed to the end. Both Achilles and Aeneas had armour made by Vulcan; see note on 8.608f.

10 440f. Turnus solemnly devotes himself to the cause on behalf of his (hoped-for)father-in-law Latinus and all the Latins; for the anticipatory use of *socer* cf. 9.138 (*coniunx*).

11 442. **solum . . . vocat:** a reference to Drances' final words, 375.

12 **et vocet oro:** 'I pray that he does challenge me', the parataxis (jussive subjunctive) with *oro* is common, cf. 6.76 *ipsa canas oro.* The repetition of *vocet* is given extra emphasis by the rhythm of a double dissyllabic ending; see note on 143.

13 443-4. 'and I do not want Drances instead of me to pay with death for the anger of the gods, if that is the situation, or win the praise, if it's a case of valour and glory'. Turnus means that Drances need not think he is involved at all; Turnus will handle it himself, for good or ill.

morte luat, sive est virtus et gloria, tollat.'

*445-97. While the debate in the Latin headquarters
continues Aeneas moves to the attack. Turnus hearing of this
gives instructions for action, and fiercely arms himself for
battle.*

[1]Illi haec inter se dubiis de rebus agebant   445
certantes: castra Aeneas aciemque movebat.[2]
Nuntius ingenti per regia tecta tumultu
ecce ruit magnisque urbem terroribus implet:
instructos acie Tiberino a flumine Teucros
Tyrrhenamque[3] manum totis descendere campis.   450
Extemplo turbati animi concussaque vulgi
pectora et arrectae stimulis haud mollibus irae.
Arma[4] manu trepidi poscunt, fremit[5] arma iuventus,
flent maesti mussantque patres. Hic undique clamor
dissensu vario magnus se tollit in auras,   455
haud secus atque alto in luco cum forte catervae[6]
consedere avium, piscosove amne Padusae
dant sonitum rauci per stagna loquacia[7] cycni.
'Immo,'[8] ait 'o cives,' arrepto tempore Turnus,
'cogite concilium et pacem laudate sedentes;   460
illi armis in regna ruunt.' Nec plura locutus
corripuit sese et tectis citus extulit[9] altis.
'Tu, Voluse,[10] armari[11] Volscorum edice maniplis,

---

1 445f. This passage clearly reflects the impetuous bravery of Turnus. His reaction to the news of the attack is to prepare immediately for full scale battle, forgetful of his promise to meet Aeneas in single combat. He sarcastically taunts the peace party (459f.), rapidly gives his instructions (463f.) and arms wildly for battle (486f.) like a horse at last freed from captivity. As a foil to Turnus' exultation Virgil describes the gloomy misery of Latinus (470f.) and the frightened supplication of the matrons (482f.).

2 446. **Aeneas**: in strong antithesis to *illi;* we would say 'while they were discussing . . . , Aeneas began to move his men out of the camp'; (*castra movebat* would normally mean that he was 'breaking' camp, but the addition of *aciem* conveys the meaning that he set the men in the camp moving into action). The truce for the burial of the dead (133f.) is now ended, and Aeneas sets out to attack Latinus' capital.

3 450. **Tyrrhenamque manum**: the Etruscan allies of Aeneas led by Tarchon (184).

4 453. **arma . . . poscunt**: 'excitedly brandishing their fists they call for their weapons'; manu (as Servius says) refers to their gesticulations, adding a pictorial image to the noise expressed in *fremit.*

5 **fremit arma**: the transitive use of *fremere* ('shout for') occurs also in 7.460, the same phrase; cf. also line 132.

6 456f. for bird similes cf. Hom. *Il.* 2.459f., and *Aen.* 7.699f.; Padusa is near the mouth of the Po (for the adjective *piscosus* cf. 4.255, 12.518, Hom. *Il.* 20.392).

7 458. **loquacia**: 'sounding', i.e. with the noise of the swans, cf. 12.475.

8 459. **immo**: ironical, 'all right then'.

9 462. **extulit**: supply *sese,* 'departed', cf. 12.441.

10 463. **Voluse**: Volusus the Volscian is not heard of elsewhere.

11 **armari**: for the infinitive after *edicere* cf. 7.35-6 (after *imperare*). 464-5.

duc' ait 'et Rutulos. Equitem[1] Messapus in armis,
et cum fratre Coras latis diffundite campis.   465
Pars[2] aditus urbis firmet turrisque capessat;[3]
cetera, qua iusso,[4] mecum manus inferat arma.'
   Ilicet in muros tota discurritur[5] urbe.
Concilium ipse pater[6] et magna incepta Latinus
deserit ac tristi turbatus tempore differt,[7]   470
multaque se incusat qui[8] non acceperit ultro
Dardanium Aenean generumque[9] asciverit urbi.
Praefodiunt[10] alii portas aut saxa sudesque
subvectant. Bello dat signum[11] rauca cruentum
bucina. Tum muros varia[12] cinxere corona   475
matronae puerique, vocat labor[13] ultimus omnis.
Nec non ad templum summasque ad Palladis arces[14]
subvehitur[15] magna matrum regina[16] caterva
dona ferens, iuxtaque comes Lavinia[17] virgo,
causa mali tanti, oculos[18] deiecta decoros.[19]   480
Succedunt matres et templum ture vaporant
et maestas alto fundunt de limine voces:[20]

---

1 464-5. **equitem . . . campis:** 'You Messapus, and you Coras with your brother, deploy the cavalry under arms over the wide plains'; Messapus was mentioned (as an outstanding Latin leader) in 429, and Coras and his twin brother Catillus in 7.672 (cf. 604, 640).

2 466-7. **pars . . . cetera . . . mairas:** this refers to the Latin infantry.

3 466. **capessat:** 'man', literally 'take possession of.'

4 467. **iusso:** archaic form of the future, cf. 9.154 (*faxo*); cf. Sen. *Ep. Mor.* 58.4.

5 468. **discurritur:** impersonal passive, 'there was a rush'.

6 469. **pater:** the last syllable is lengthened in arsis, cf. 323.

7 470. **differt:** 'postponed it', the object is *concilium;* notice how the alliteration of (in this line is rounded off by the last letter of *differt.*

8 471. **qui non acceperit:** causal subjunctive. Latinus did in fact accept Aeneas, but was caused by the pressure of Amata and Turnus (inspired by Juno) to withdraw his acceptance (cf. 231f. and 7.591f.); for his weakness of character see note on 7.572f.

9 472. **generumque asciverit urbi:** 'and join him to his city as his son-in-law', cf. line 105 and 7.367,

10 473. **praefodiunt . . . portas:** id est, ante portas fossas faciunt (Servius).

11 474. **signum . . . cruentum:** the epithet is transferred; warfare being bloody, the signal for it is called bloody.

12 475. **varia ... corona:** 'in a motley circle', for *corona* cf. 10.122.

13 476. **labor ultimus:** 'the call of crisis'; Servius says *omnes ad laborem ultima necessitas convocat.*

14 477f. The supplication to Pallas Athena (Minerva) is closely based on Hom. *Il.* 6.297f.; cf. also *Aen.* 1.479f.

15 478. **subvehitur:** 'rides up'; Servius points out that Roman matrons rode in carriages to such supplications, cf. 8.665-6.

16 **regina:** Latinus' wife Amata, see note on 7.56.

17 479. **Lavinia:** Latinus' daughter, see note on 7.52f.

18 **oculos:** retained accusative, cf. 487, 507 and see note on 35.

19 480. For the hiatus at the caesura cf. 10.136.

20 482. The spondaic movement of 481 is repeated here and compels the attention, reflecting the sorrow of the matrons.

'armipotens, praeses belli, Tritonia virgo,[1]
frange manu telum Phrygii[2] praedonis, et ipsum
pronum sterne solo portisque effunde sub altis.'   485
Cingitur[3] ipse furens certatim in proelia Turnus.[4]
iamque adeo rutilum thoraca[5] indutus aenis
horrebat[6] squamis surasque[7] incluserat auro,
tempora[8] nudus adhuc, laterique accinxerat ensem,
fulgebatque alta decurrens aureus arce   490
exsultatque animis et spe iam praecipit[9] hostem:
qualis ubi abruptis fugit praesepia vinclis[10]
tandem liber equus, campoque potitus aperto
aut ille[11] in pastus armentaque tendit equarum[12]
aut adsuetus aquae perfundi flumine noto   495
emicat, arrectisque fremit cervicibus alte
luxurians[13] luduntque iubae per colla, per armos.

> *498-531. The warrior-queen Camilla offers help to Turnus:*
> *he gratefully accepts and asks her to engage the enemy*
> *cavalry while he lays an ambush for Aeneas and his*
> *infantry.*

[14]Obvia cui Volscorum acie comitante Camilla[15]

---

1 483-5. These lines are very closely based on Hom. *Il.* 6.305-7 (see note on 477f.); the compound adjective *armipotens* is used of Athena also in 2.425. For her epithet *Tritonia* (from a lake in Libya where she was said to have been born) cf. 2.171,615.

2 484. **Phrygii praedonis:** this description of Aeneas occurs also in 7.362, 10.774.

3 486. **cingitur:** 'arms himself; cf. 536.

4 486f. The description of Turnus' excited preparation for battle reflects the impetuous nature of the man, cf. 12.81f. Notice the brilliant colours (*rutilum, fulgebat, aureus*). The word *furens* is characteristic of him (e.g. 9.691), and *certatim* suggests that he could not bear not to be first into battle.

5 487. **thoraca indutus:** *thoraca* is Greek accusative as in line 9 (cf. *aethera,* 556); it is a retained accusative after the passive verb *indutus* which has middle force (see note on 35 and cf. 7.640).

6 488. **horrebat squamis:** for the 'scales' of the breastplate cf. 9.707, 10.314. The verb refers partly to the roughness of the surface, partly to the formidable appearance.

7 **surasque ... auro:** the same phrase in 12.430 of Aeneas putting on his greaves.

8 489. **tempora:** Greek accusative of respect, cf. 8.425 and see note on 7.60.

9 491. **praecipit:** 'anticipates', cf. line 18 and 6.105.

10 492f. The simile of the horse, freed at last from restraint, is very appropriate for the character of Turnus charging into battle, the activity in which he is most completely himself. It is very closely based on Homer's simile (*Il.* 6.506f.) which was translated by Ennius as follows (*Ann.* 514-18): *et tum sicut equus qui de praesepibus fartus / vincla suis magnis animis abrupit et inde / fert sese campi per caerula laetaque prata, / celso pectore saepe iubam quassat simul altam, / spiritus ex anima calida spumas agit albas.*

11 494. **ille:** resumptive of the subject, cf. 9.796. 497.

12 494-6. The meaning is that he rushes away either to the mares or to the river where he loved to bathe before he was captured.

13 497. **luxurians:** 'in the pride of his strength', cf. *Geo.* 3.81 and Homer's κυδιόων (*Il.* 6.509).

14 498f. The first appearance of Camilla in the book (she had been mentioned by Turnus in 432) prepares the way for her deeds of valour, her aristeia (see note on 648f.). She shows a bravery and a self-confidence (502) very similar to that of Turnus, and he treats her as an equal on the field of battle. This picture of her is very much softened in the next section (532f.).

15 498-9. The marked alliteration of *c* emphasises the first appearance of Camilla whose exploits dominate the rest of the book.

occurrit portisque ab equo regina sub ipsis
desiluit, quam tota cohors imitata relictis   500
ad terram defluxit[1] equis; tum talia fatur:
'Turne, sui[2] merito si qua est fiducia forti,
audeo[3] et Aeneadum[4] promitto[5] occurrere turmae
solaque Tyrrhenos equites[6] ire obvia contra.
Me sine prima manu temptare pericula belli,   505
tu pedes ad muros subsiste et moenia serva.'
Turnus ad haec oculos[7] horrenda[8] in virgine fixus:
'o decus Italiae virgo, quas[9] dicere grates
quasve referre parem? Sed nunc, est[10] omnia quando
iste animus supra, mecum partire[11] laborem.   510
Aeneas, ut[12] fama fidem missique reportant
exploratores, equitum levia improbus[13] arma
praemisit, quaterent[14] campos; ipse[15] ardua montis
per deserta iugo superans adventat ad urbem.
Furta[16] paro belli convexo[17] in tramite silvae,   515
ut bivias[18] armato obsidam milite fauces.
Tu Tyrrhenum equitem conlatis excipe signis;

---

1 501. **defluxit:** a pictorial word, 'swept down from their horses', drawing attention (as Servius says) to the grace and uniformity of their method of dismounting.

2 502. **sui . . . Forti:** 'if the brave may rightly feel some confidence in themselves'; *sui* is objective genitive of *se*. The phrase *sui fiducia* is one which would commend itself to Turnus, cf. 9.126, 10.276.

3 503. **audeo:** the word is emphasised by the elision of the long *o* before the short syllable *et*.

4 **Aeneadum:** archaic form of the genitive, cf. 297.

5 **promitto occurrere:** for the construction (poetic for *promitto me occursurum esse*) cf. 4.337-8 *neque ego hanc abscondere furto speravi (ne finge) fugam.* Here it is influenced by *audeo*, which of course also governs *occurrere*.

6 504. **equites . . . contra:** the preposition is postponed as in lines 509-10 (*omnia . . . supra*).

7 507. **oculos . . . Fixus:** retained accusative with a passive verb, see note on 35.

8 **horrenda:** 'awe-inspiring'.

9 508-9. **quas . . . parem:** 'what thanks can I prepare to say, let alone show in deeds?'

10 509-10. **est . . . supra:** 'since your courage surpasses all bounds'; for the postponement of the weak word *quando* to the line ending cf. 201 and 10.366; for the postposition of the preposition cf. 504.

11 510. **partire:** 'share' (imperative), replying to her offer of going alone (504).

12 511-12. **ut . . . exploratores:** 'as the report of the scouts I have sent out reliably informs me'; *fama* and *missi exploratores* constitute a hendiadys.

13 512. **improbus:** 'that evil man'; this is used as Turnus' epithet for Aeneas rather than with special reference to the context; cf. 12.261 (of Aeneas) *improbus advena.* See also note on 9.62.

14 513. **quaterent:** 'ordering them to scour'; the oblique jussive subjunctive reports Aeneas' instructions to his cavalry; for *quatere* cf. 9.608.

15 513-14. **ipse . . . superans:** 'he himself traversing the heights of the mountain along the ridge over desolate areas'; for *ardua* as a noun followed by the partitive genitive cf. 882 and 8.221.

16 515. **furta . . . belli:** 'an ambush'.

17 **convexo:** probably 'over-arched' (cf. 1.310) rather than 'sloping'.

18 516. **bivias . . . fauces:** 'the passage at both ends'.

tecum acer Messapus[1] erit turmaeque Latinae
Tiburtique[2] manus, ducis[3] et tu concipe curam.'
Sic ait, et paribus Messapum in proelia dictis 520
hortatur sociosque duces et pergit in hostem.

 Est curvo[4] anfractu valles, accommoda fraudi
armorumque dolis, quam[5] densis frondibus atrum
urget utrimque latus, tenuis quo semita ducit
angustaeque ferunt fauces aditusque maligni. 525
Hanc super in speculis summoque in vertice montis
planities[6] ignota iacet tutique receptus,
seu dextra laevaque velis occurrere pugnae
sive instare iugis et grandia volvere saxa.
Huc iuvenis nota fertur regione[7] viarum 530
arripuitque locum et silvis insedit iniquis.[8]

> 532-96. *Diana speaks to her nymph Opis, lamenting the impending fate of Camilla, and telling the story of her escape as a baby and her subsequent devotion to the goddess. She tells Opis to lake vengeance on the man who kills Camilla.*

[9]Velocem[10] interea superis in sedibus Opim,[11]
unam ex virginibus sociis sacraque caterva,
compellabat et has tristis Latonia[12] voces
ore dabat: 'graditur bellum ad crudele Camilla, 535

---

1 518. **Messapus:** cf. 464.

2 519. **Tiburtique manus:** Tibertus was the brother (he gave his name to Tibur, 7.671) of the twins Catillus and Coras (465).

3 **ducis . . . curam:** 'you too are to undertake the responsibility of leader', i.e. with me (as Servius says).

4 522. **curvo anfractu valles:** 'a valley with winding recesses', cf. Livy 33.1.4 *anfractus viarum;* for the nominative form *valles* (*vallis*) cf. 7.565.

5 523-4. **quam . . . latus:** 'bounded on both sides by slopes dark with dense undergrowth; a tiny path leads that way and a narrow pass and a forbidding approach bring you into it'. The passage is reminiscent of Livy's description of the Caudine forks (g.2.6f.); the words from *densis . . . latus* are repeated from 7.565-6.

6 527. **planities ignota:** 'a hidden plateau'; *ignota* means unknown to the Trojans, not being visible (to Turnus it is *notus,* 530).

7 530. **regione:** 'direction', cf. 2.737.

8 531. **iniquis:** 'treacherous', cf. 5.203.

9 532f. The larger part of Diana's speech is taken up with a digression about the childhood of Camilla. It is of epyllion type (cf. the story of Hercules and Cacus in Book 8) and serves to focus our attention still more on Camilla. It is not perfectly fitted to the context, in that Diana's use of her own name and epithet (566, 582) is slightly strange and the story is not of particular relevance to Opis, to whom it is addressed. But it contains some very fine writing, and serves Virgil's purposes admirably at this point in arousing our interest in Camilla and giving a pastoral prelude to the scenes of battle shortly to be described.

10 532. **velocem . . . Opim:** the epithet indicates that she is a huntress, like Camilla and Diana. Opis sometimes was an epithet of Diana herself (Callim. *Hymn.* 3.204), but it also occurs as the name of an attendant of Diana (Callim. *Hymn.* 4.292); cf. *Geo.* 4.343.

11 532-4. The change of scene is abrupt, with the word order throwing unexpected emphasis on Opis.

12 534. **Latonia:** Diana, daughter of Latona (Leto), cf. 9.405.

o virgo, et nostris[1] nequiquam[2] cingitur armis,
cara mihi ante alias. Neque[3] enim novus iste Dianae
venit amor subitaque animum dulcedine movit.
Pulsus[4] ob invidiam regno virisque superbas
Priverno antiqua Metabus cum excederet urbe,   540
infantem fugiens media inter proelia belli
sustulit exsilio comitem, matrisque vocavit
nomine Casmillae[5] mutata parte Camillam.
Ipse sinu prae se portans[6] iuga longa petebat
solorum nemorum: tela undique saeva premebant   545
et circumfuso volitabant milite Volsci.
Ecce fugae medio summis Amasenus[7] abundans
spumabat ripis, tantus se nubibus imber
ruperat. Ille innare parans infantis amore
tardatur caroque oneri timet. [8]Omnia secum   550
versanti subito vix haec sententia sedit:
telum[9] immane manu valida quod forte gerebat
bellator, solidum nodis et robore cocto,
huic natam libro et silvestri subere clausam
implicat atque habilem mediae circumligat hastae;   555
quam dextra ingenti librans ita ad aethera fatur:
'alma, tibi hanc, nemorum[10] cultrix, Latonia virgo,

---

1 536. **nostris . . . armis:** i.e. as a huntress (652, 844), especially with bow and quiver.

2 **nequiquam:** Diana foresees Camilla's death.

3 537-8. **neque . . . movit:** 'for Diana's love for her which you know well (*iste*) is not new; it has not come on my heart with a passion that is sudden'; the phrases serve to introduce the story of Camilla's devotion to Diana long ago. For Diana's use of her own name (*Dianae = mihi*) cf. 582.

4 539-40. 'When Metabus, driven out of his kingdom because of the hatred aroused by his arrogant power, was departing from the ancient city of Privernum . . .'. The story of Metabus and his daughter Camilla is not known before Virgil, and is probably his own invention. Privernum was a town of Latium, some 40 miles S.E. of Rome.

5 543. **Casmillae ... Camillam:** for the morphology cf. Casmena, the old form of Camena (Muse); for the name Camilla see note on 7.803f.

6 544. **portans:** supply *eam*.

7 547. **Amasenus:** a river near Privernum, cf. 7.685.

8 550-1. 'As he turned over every possibility in his thoughts he came reluctantly to this sudden decision'; for the dative *versanti* cf. 12.919. *Subito* and *vix* are rather awkward together in the same phrase; Day Lewis renders 'this desperate remedy'. For *sedit* cf. 7.611; notice the strong alliteration of *s*.

9 552-5. 'The huge spear which the warrior chanced to be carrying in his mighty hand, tough with knots and hardened oak — to this he tied his daughter, wrapped up in the bark of cork from the woods and fastened her neatly to the middle of the lance'. The sentence is an anacoluthon, that is to say the initial word *telum* has no construction, but is resumed by the dative *huic*. *Coctus* means 'seasoned' by being dried in smoke, cf. *Geo.* 1.175; *libro et silvestri subere* is a hendiadys (cf. 571); *habilem* refers partly to the protection of the cork and partly to her position in the middle of the shaft; *hastae* is dative equivalent to *ad hastam*.

10 557. **nemorum cultrix:** 'guardian of the groves'; for *cultrix* cf. 3.111, for Diana as goddess of the groves cf. 9.405 *nemorum Latonia custos*.

ipse pater famulam voveo; tua[1] prima per auras
tela tenens supplex hostem fugit. Accipe, testor,
diva tuam, quae nunc dubiis committitur auris.'   560
dixit, et adducto[2] contortum hastile lacerto
immittit: sonuere[3] undae, rapidum[4] super amnem
infelix[5] fugit in iaculo stridente Camilla.
At Metabus magna propius iam urgente caterva
dat sese fluvio, atque hastam cum virgine victor   565
gramineo, donum Triviae,[6] de caespite vellit.
Non[7] illum tectis ullae, non moenibus urbes
accepere (neque ipse manus feritate dedisset).
Pastorum et[8] solis exegit montibus aevum.
Hic natam in dumis interque horrentia lustra[9]   570
armentalis[10] equae mammis et lacte ferino
nutribat teneris immulgens[11] ubera labris.
Utque[12] pedum primis infans vestigia plantis
institerat, iaculo palmas armavit acuto
spiculaque ex umero parvae suspendit et arcum.   575
Pro[13] crinali auro, pro longae tegmine pallae
tigridis exuviae per dorsum a vertice pendent.
Tela manu iam tum tenera puerilia torsit
et fundam[14] tereti circum caput egit habena

---

1 558-9. **tua . . . fugit**: 'it was your weapon which first she held as she fled from the enemy through the breezes as your suppliant'; Metabus dedicates his spear to Diana (566).

2 561-2. **adducto . . . immittit**: 'drawing his arm back to his chest he sent the spear whirring'; for *adducto lacerto* cf. 9.402; for *contortum* cf. line 676, 5.520 and *torquere* in 9.402.

3 562. **sonuere undae**: for the perfect tense cf. 12.283; the image could be rendered in English thus 'as the waves roared Camilla went soaring . . .'

4 **rapidum super amnem:** the line ending is very unusual, with the conflict of ictus and accent in fourth and fifth foot (see note on 143), and helps to reflect the drama of the moment.

5 563. **infelix:** the outcome was successful, but the moment of transit far from enviable.

6 566. **Triviae:** an epithet of Diana, goddess of the crossroads, cf. 836 and see note on 7.516f.

7 567-8. 'No cities received him within their houses or boundaries, nor would he in any case have consented, because of his wild nature'; the ablative *feritate* is very abrupt, and best taken as causal equivalent to *ob feritatem* or *prae feritate*.

8 569. **et:** postponed from the head of its clause; it links *accepere* with *exegit*.

9 570. **lustra:** 'dens of wild animals', cf. 3.647, 4.151.

10 571. **armentalis:** 'of the herd', an extremely rare word meaning that it was a brood mare.

11 572. **immulgens ubera labris:** 'pressing its milky udders to her lips'; literally 'milking its udders into . . .'

12 573-4. **utque . . . institerat:** 'and as soon as the infant had set her feet in their first steps'; for *vestigia pedum* cf. 7.689-90.

13 576. **pro crinali auro:** 'instead of a golden headband', i.e. she wore the tiger skin so that it covered her head as well as her body.

14 579. **fundam . . . egit:** 'whirled a sling'; for the sling (catapult) as a weapon of hunters cf. *Geo.* 1.309.

Strymoniamque[1] gruem aut album deiecit olorem.   580
Multae illam frustra Tyrrhena per oppida matres[2]
optavere nurum; sola contenta Diana
aeternum telorum et virginitatis amorem
intemerata colit. Vellem[3] haud correpta fuisset
militia tali conata lacessere Teucros: 585
cara mihi comitumque foret[4] nunc una mearum.
Verum age, quandoquidem fatis urgetur acerbis,
labere, nympha, polo finisque invise Latinos,
tristis ubi infausto[5] committitur omine pugna.
Haec[6] cape et ultricem pharetra deprome sagittam: 590
hac, quicumque sacrum violarit vulnere corpus,
Tros Italusque,[7] mihi pariter det sanguine poenas.
Post ego nube cava miserandae corpus et arma
inspoliata feram tumulo[8] patriaeque reponam.'
Dixit, at illa levis caeli delapsa per auras   595
insonuit[9] nigro circumdata[10] turbine corpus.

> *597-647. The cavalry battle outside the walls develops on a
> large scale; first one side prevails and then the other.*

[11]At manus[12] interea muris Troiana propinquat,
Etruscique duces equitumque exercitus omnis
compositi numero in turmas. Fremit aequore[13] tolo
insultans sonipes et pressis[14] pugnat habenis   600

---

1 580. **Strymoniamque gruem**: the epithet is ornate, referring to the famous cranes of the river Strymon in Thrace, cf. *Geo.* 1.120, *Aen.* 10.265 and compare line 773.

2 581. The line is based on Cat. 62.42; cf. also *Aen.* 7.54. *Tyrrhena per oppida* suggests that Etruscan dominion extended south to the area of the Volsci.

3 584. **vellem . . . fuisset**: 'I could have wished that she had not been caught up . . .'; *vellem* is past potential and *fuisset*, a past unfulfilled wish, in parataxis with it.

4 586. **foret nunc**: 'and that she were now . . .', a present unfulfilled wish.

5 589. **infausto . . . omine**: because Diana knows Camilla's fate, cf. 536.

6 590. **haec**: i.e. *tela*, the bow and arrows.

7 592. **Italusque**: i.e. one of the Etruscan or Arcadian allies of Aeneas.

8 594. **tumulo**: = *ad tumulum*, like *patriae* (= *in patriam*). For the idea compare Zeus' promise about Sarpedon (Hom. *Il.* 16.667f.).

9 596. **insonuit**: 'went whirring on her way', probably referring to the sound of movement through the air, but perhaps also to her bow and arrows clashing (4.149, 9.732, Hom. *Il.* 1.46).

10 **circumdata . . . corpus**: retained accusative, see note on 35.

11 597f. This narrative of general warfare acts as an interlude between the description of Camilla's childhood and the account of her deeds in battle (648f.).

12 597. **manus ... Troiana**: i.e. the cavalry (defined in the next line) who were mostly Etruscan allies of the Trojans.

13 599-600. **aequore ... sonipes**: 'the war-horses prancing over the whole area'; singular for plural (cf. 464).

14 600. **pressis ... habenis**: 'fight against their tight reins', *habenis* is dative after *pugnare*, cf. 4.38, 12.678.

huc conversus et huc; tum late[1] ferreus hastis
horret ager campique armis sublimibus ardent.
Nec non Messapus contra celeresque Latini[2]
et cum fratre Coras et virginis ala Camillae
adversi campo apparent, hastasque reductis   605
protendunt longe dextris et spicula vibrant,
adventusque[3] virum fremitusque ardescit equorum.
Iamque intra iactum teli progressus uterque[4]
substiterat: subito erumpunt[5] clamore furentisque[6]
exhortantur equos, fundunt simul undique tela   610
crebra nivis[7] ritu, caelumque[8] obtexitur umbra.
Continuo adversis Tyrrhenus[9] et acer Aconteus
conixi incurrunt hastis primique[10] ruinam
dant sonitu ingenti perfractaque[11] quadripedantum
pectora pectoribus rumpunt; excussus Aconteus   615
fulminis in[12] morem aut[13] tormento ponderis acti
praecipitat[14] longe et vitam dispergit in auras.
    Extemplo turbatae acies, versique Latini
reiciunt[15] parmas et equos ad moenia vertunt.
Troes agunt, princeps turmas inducit Asilas.[16]   620

---

1 601-2. **late . . . ardent:** 'the battlefield was a bristling mass of iron spears and the plains shone with weapons raised high'; for the imagery cf. 7.526 with note and Hom. *Il.* 13.339 εφριξεν δε μαχη φθισιμβροτος εγχειησιν, Enn. *Ann.* 393 *horrescit telis exercitus asper utrimque.*

2 603-4. For the Latin cavalry and its leaders cf. 464-5, 517-19.

3 607. 'the approach of warriors and the neighing of horses grew hotter'; the use of *adventus* is strange as it is not the kind of word to balance with *fremitus* and is a much less appropriate subject for *ardescit.* Conington compares Milton, *P.L.* 6.768 'Far off his coming shone'.

4 608. **uterque:** i.e. each of the opposing groups of cavalry.

5 609. **erumpunt:** 'burst forth' from the positions in which they had halted (*substiterat*), cf. 10.890.

6 **furentisque:** hypermetric elision, cf. 10.895 and see note on 7.160.

7 611. **nivis ritu:** the simile of missiles falling like snowflakes occurs in Hom. *Il.* 12.156.

8 **caelumque . . . umbra:** for the general idea cf. 12.578; the image here is the texture of a veil or curtain, perhaps as Mackail suggests with the notion of the network of crossing spears. The commentators cite the famous story (Herod. 7.226) about the Spartan who, when told that the Persian arrows would blot out the sun, replied 'Then we can fight in the shade'.

9 612. Tyrrhenus is the name of one of the Etruscans; Aconteus is a Latin.

10 613-14. **primique . . . ingenti:** 'and are the first to fall, crashing to the ground with terrific impact'; for *dare ruinam* cf. 2.310.

11 614-15. **perfractaque . . . rumpunt:** 'and burst open and break the ribs of their chargers as they crashed into each other'; the excessive consonants here and the unusual polysyllabic line ending emphasise the gruesome image.

12 616. **in morem:** 'in the manner of', 'like', cf. 8.88.

13 **aut tormento ponderis acti:** 'or a weight hurled by a siege engine', cf. 8.487, 12.921-2.

14 617. **praecipitat longe:** 'falls headlong far from his horse'; the verb is intransitive (cf. line 3, 10.804) or transitive (cf. 12.699) in Virgil.

15 619. **reiciunt:** the syllable *re-* is long (cf. 630 and 10.473). The meaning is that the Latins ride away holding their shields behind them to cover their backs.

16 620. Asilas the Etruscan was mentioned in 10.175.

Iamque propinquabant portis rursusque Latini
clamorem tollunt et mollia[1] colla reflectunt;
hi[2] fugiunt penitusque[3] datis referuntur habenis:
qualis[4] ubi alterno procurrens gurgite pontus
nunc ruit ad terram scopulosque superiacit[5] unda   625
spumeus extremamque[6] sinu perfundit harenam,
nunc[7] rapidus retro atque aestu revoluta resorbens
saxa fugit litusque vado labente relinquit.
Bis Tusci Rutulos egere ad moenia versos,
bis reiecti armis respectant[8] terga tegentes.   630
Tertia sed postquam congressi in proelia totas
implicuere inter se acies legitque virum vir,[9]
tum vero et gemitus morientum et sanguine in alto[10]
armaque[11] corporaque et permixti caede virorum
semianimes[12] volvuntur equi, pugna aspera surgit.   635
Orsilochus[13] Remuli, quando ipsum horrebat adire,
hastam intorsit equo[14] ferrumque sub aure reliquit;
quo sonipes ictu furit[15] arduus altaque iactat
vulneris impatiens arrecto pectore crura,
volvitur ille excussus humi. Catillus[16] Iollan   640

---

1 622. **mollia colla reflectunt:** 'turn the supple necks of their horses round again'; for *mollia colla* of horses cf. *Geo.* 3.204.

2 623. **hi**: i.e. the Trojans.

3 **penitusque datis . . . habenis**: 'with the reins let completely free'. cf. 1.63.

4 624f. 'Like the ocean as it rolls in with waves ebbing and flowing'; the simile is perhaps inspired by Hom. *Il.* 11.305f. (the waves rolling on driven by the wind), but the idea of the ebb and flow of battle is not in the Homeric passage.

5 625. **superiacit:** 'flows over', transitive, a very rare use. The alliteration of *s* hereabouts reflects the hissing of the waves, and there is also a marked pattern of *r* and *l* in the following lines.

6 626. **extremamque . . . harenam:** 'floods the sand at the land's edge with its curling wave'.

7 627-8. **nunc . . . fugit:** 'now it ebbs rapidly in retreat (and) sucking back again the stones sent spinning by its tide'; *atque* joins *rapidus* and *resorbens*.

8 630. **respectant:** intransitive, 'look backwards', while riding away in retreat.

9 632. The rhythm is imitative of the sense, with the two elisions intertwining the words and the monosyllabic ending (cf. 10.361) expressing energy and action.

10 633-4. Supply the verb *erant*, as not infrequently in descriptive passages, cf. 642, 655.

11 634. **armaque corporaque:** an unusual rhythm, cf. Stat. *Th.* 10.275 *tergaque pectoraque*. Notice the large number of conjunctions *(et, -que)* in 633-4.

12 635. **semianimes:** for the scansion (the *i* of *semi-* is treated as a consonant) cf. 10.396.

13 636. Orsilochus was a Trojan; his death is described at 690f. The name Remulus is used several times of Italian warriors. Notice how the juxtaposition of the names in different cases (*Remuli* depends on *equo*) indicates the confrontation.

14 637. **equo:** = *in equum.*

15 638. **furit arduus:** 'madly reared high'; the rhythm reflects agitation, with each of the last three feet composed of a single word; cf. 5.198 *vastis tremit ictibus aerea puppis* (with my note, OUP Ed.), and compare the various effects of this rhythm in 746, 756, 810.

16 640. Turnus' ally Catillus was mentioned in 7.672 and in lines 465, 604 as the brother of Coras; his Trojan victims Iollas and Herminius are not heard of elsewhere.

ingentemque animis, ingentem corpore et armis[1]
deicit Herminium,[2] nudo cui vertice fulva
caesaries nudique umeri; nec vulnera terrent,
tantus[3] in arma patet. Latos huic hasta per armos
acta tremit duplicatque virum transfixa[4] dolore.   645
Funditur ater ubique cruor; dant funera ferro
certantes pulchramque petunt per vulnera mortem.

*648-724. Camilla, like an Amazon warrior-maiden,
performs mighty deeds on the battlefield, killing twelve of
the enemy.*

[5]At medias inter caedes exsultat Amazon[6]
unum[7] exserta latus pugnae,[8] pharetrata[9] Camilla,
et[10] nunc lenta manu spargens hastilia denset,   650
nunc validam dextra rapit indefessa bipennem;
aureus ex umero sonat[11] arcus et arma Dianae.
Illa etiam, si quando in tergum pulsa recessit,
spicula converso[12] fugientia derigit arcu.

---

1 641. **armis**: 'shoulders', from *armus*, as is evident from 644.

2 642f. Herminius evidently fought without helmet or breastplate, presenting a terrifying figure with his mighty stature and long blond hair.

3 644. **tantus in arma patet**: the connexion of thought seems to be that he is so confident in his enormous physique as not to entertain any fear of wounds.

4 645. **transfixa**: 'driven through him', an extremely rare use of *transfigere* (which normally means 'to pierce', e.g. *transfigere pectus,* 1.44); here *transfigere hastam* is to drive the spear through. Compare Lucan 9.138 *transfixo pilo.*

5 648f. This first section of the aristeia of Camilla is very Homeric in tone, and emphasises the violent aspects of heroism on the battlefield. In a number of important respects Camilla is like Turnus; her bravery is simple, direct, unreflecting; she exults in battle (648) as Turnus had done (491); she is frenzied (*furens,* 709) as Turnus was (486); in a previous section (502) we have seen her with the same self-confidence in her bravery as Turnus had; and later the end of her life is described (831) in the same phrases as those describing Turnus' death (12.952).

There are also some similarities in her simplicity, her inexperience, her devotion to deeds of courage with the character of Euryalus in Book 9; both meet their ends through unthinking love for plunder, Euryalus for a helmet as his spoils (9.365, 373), Camilla for purple and gold (772-82 - *femineo praedae et spoliorum ardebat amore*).

Virgil's sources for Camilla, who is his own creation, were the Amazon queen Penthesilea (648) and pastoral huntresses like Harpalyce (1.317); see further note on 7.803f. (the description of Camilla in the catalogue). He has created in her a strange and memorable mixture of the idyllic pastoral world (see note on 532f.) and the heroic world of insensitive cruelty (cf. the epithet *aspera,* 664, the violence of the description of the death of her victims, e.g. 668-9, 698, and the simile of the falcon and the dove, 721-4).

6 648. **Amazon**: 'like an Amazon'. Camilla is like Penthesilea, Queen of the Amazons (662, 1.490); cf. 660 and see note on 648f. The warrior maidens called Amazons are mentioned in Homer (e.g. *Il.* 3.189).

7 649. **unum . . .latus**: 'one breast exposed', cf. 803 and 1.492. For the retained accusative see note on 35.

8 **pugnae**: = *ad pugnam.*

9 **pharetrata**: i.e. like Diana (652), cf. Ov. *Am.* 1.1.10.

10 650. 'and now she hurls volley on volley of vibrating spears'; for *lenta* (literally 'flexible') cf. 7.164; for *densere* (here, as Servius says, dense tacit) cf. 7.794.

11 652. **sonat arcus**: cf. 4.149 (of Apollo) *tela sonant umeris.*

12 654. **converso . . . arcu**: 'reversing her bow', i.e. turning round on horseback so as to shoot backwards (like the Parthians, *Geo.* 3.31).

At circum lectae comites, Larinaque virgo[1]   655
Tullaque et aeratam quatiens Tarpeia securim,
Italides, quas ipsa decus[2] sibi dia[3] Camilla
delegit pacisque[4] bonas bellique ministras:
quales[5] Threiciae cum fiumina Thermodontis
pulsant et pictis bellantur[6] Amazones armis,   660
seu circum Hippolyten[7] seu cum se[8] Martia curru
Penthesilea refert, magnoque ululante tumultu
feminea exsultant lunatis agmina peltis.[9]

    Quem telo primum,[10] quem postremum, aspera virgo,
deicis? Aut quot humi morientia corpora fundis?   665
Eunaeum Clytio primum patre, [11]cuius apertum[12]
adversi longa transverberat abiete pectus.
Sanguinis ille vomens rivos cadit atque cruentam
mandit humum moriensque suo[13] se in vulnere versat.
Tum Lirim Pagasumque super, quorum alter[14] habenas   670
suffuso revolutus equo dum colligit, alter
dum subit ac dextram labenti tendit inermem,[15]
praecipites pariterque ruunt. His addit Amastrum

---

1 655. The verb 'to be' is omitted in the descriptive list of Camilla's Italian attendants (cf. 633).

2 657. **decus**: *'ornamentum', id est, 'ad ornamentum'* (Servius).

3 **dia**: an archaic form of *diva*, used only here by Virgil, cf. Enn. *Ann.* 22 *dia dearum*.

4 658. **pacisque ... bellique**: 'of both peace and war', cf. *-que ... -que* in 655-6, 675, 696.

5 659-60. 'Like the Amazons of Thrace when they gallop on the streams of Thermodon and fight with their painted armour'; Thermodon was a river in the area of the Black Sea, often associated with the Amazons (Ov. *Met.* 2.249). The adjective *Threicius* is here used loosely for the area of the frozen north. *Pulsant* refers to the beat of the horses' hooves on the frozen river. For the spondaic fifth foot in 659 cf. 31 and see note on 7.634; for the short final syllable of *Amazones* cf. *Arcades* (93), *Phryges* (170).

6 660. **bellantur**: a much rarer form than *bellant*.

7 661-2. Hippolyte and Penthesilea were legendary queens of the Amazons; Hippolyte fell in love with Theseus when he made his expedition against the Amazons (cf. Shakespeare's *Midsummer Night's Dream*); for Penthesilea see note on 648. Hippolyte was a daughter of Mars; according to some versions Penthesilea was her sister.

8 **se ... refert**: 'returns from battle'.

9 663. The crescent shields are mentioned also in 1.490.

10 664f. The apostrophe (based on Hom. *Il.* 5.703, 16.692) concentrates the attention on Camilla, and this is reinforced by the strong word *aspera* ('ferocious'), making an oxymoron with *virgo*.

11 666-7. 'whose unprotected breast as he faced her she pierced with the long shaft of pine'; *abiete* scans as a dactyl with consonantal *i*, cf. 890 and 8.599; for *apertum* cf. line 748.

12 666f. The Trojan and Etruscan victims of Camilla (666-689) are not heard of elsewhere.

13 669. **suo ... versat**: 'doubled up over his wound', cf. 5.279 (of a wounded snake) *seque in sua membra plicantem*.

14 670-1. **alter ... colligit**: 'the former while he was recovering the reins after being thrown off his horse as it went sprawling under him'; the use of *suffuso* ('laid low under him') is very strange, and some MSS, perhaps rightly, have the much easier *suffosso* ('stabbed under him', cf. Tac. *Ann.* 1.65).

15 672. Pagasus cannot use his weapon hand as he is trying to help his friend, cf. 10.338f., 425f.

Hippotaden, sequiturque incumbens[1] eminus hasta
Tereaque Harpalycumque et Demophoonta Chromimque;[2] 675
quotque emissa manu contorsit[3] spicula virgo,
tot Phrygii cecidere viri. Procul Ornytus armis[4]
ignotis et equo venator Iapyge[5] fertur,
cui[6] pellis latos umeros erepta iuvenco
pugnatori operit, caput ingens oris hiatus 680
et malae texere lupi cum dentibus albis,
agrestisque manus armat sparus; ipse catervis
vertitur in mediis et toto vertice supra est.
Hunc illa exceptum (neque enim labor agmine verso)[7]
traicit et super haec inimico pectore fatur:[8] 685
'silvis te, Tyrrhene,[9] feras agitare putasti?
Advenit[10] qui vestra[11] dies muliebribus armis
verba redargueret. Nomen[12] tamen haud leve patrum
manibus hoc referes, telo[13] cecidisse Camillae.'
     Protinus Orsilochum[14] et Buten, duo maxima Teucrum 690
corpora, sed Buten aversum cuspide fixit
loricam galeamque inter, qua[15] colla sedentis

---

1 674. **incumbens eminus:** almost an oxymoron 'looming over them from a distance'; so formidable is she that at the distance of a spear cast she appears to be right upon them. It is unlikely that *incumbens* means 'leaning forward to throw her spear'; it has more force than that.

2 675. The list of names is in the Homeric style, cf. 10.413, 749. *Terea* and *Demophoonta* are Greek accusatives; the first *-que* means 'both'(655, 658, 696).

3 676. **contorsit:** cf. 561.

4 677-8. **armis ignotis:** 'with novel armour'; he was a hunter and was not properly equipped for battle, as Camilla says in her taunt (686).

5 678. **Iapyge:** from S. Italy, cf. 8.710.

6 679-82. **cui . . . sparus:** 'as he went into battle a skin from a bullock covered his broad shoulders, the huge gaping mouth and the jaws of a wolf with their white teeth veiled his head, and a rustic hunting spear was his weapon'. The word *pugnatori* is emphatic; this hunter has not (as Camilla has) made the necessary adjustments to his equipment in order to go to war. Some take *pugnatori* with *iuvenco* ('a fighting steer', i.e. a wild bull), comparing *bellator equus* (89), but the contrast between Ornytus as *venator* and as *pugnator* is vital to the context.

7 684. The meaning seems to be that Camilla picked him out as a victim (because of his conspicuous appearance), and could easily catch him because he was impeded by the confusion of the retreat.

8 685. The words introducing the taunt are repeated from 10.556 (Aeneas' taunt over Tarquitus).

9 686. **Tyrrhene:** Ornytus was an Etruscan.

10 687-8. **advenit . . . redargueret:** 'a day came to refute your words by means of the weapons of a woman'; the subject (*dies*) of *advenit* is taken into the relative clause. Many editors accept *redarguerit* from Priscian, but the reading of the MSS can stand.

11 687. **vestra:** referring to the Etruscans generally and the threats they have made against their enemies.

12 688. **nomen:** 'glory', cf. line 846, 2.89 *nomenque decusque;* the glory is defined by the words *telo cecidisse Camillae.*

13 689. **telo cecidisse Camillae:** these words are reminiscent of what Aeneas said to Lausus (10.829-30).

14 690. Orsilochus was mentioned in 636f.; this Butes is not otherwise heard of. The accusatives are governed by a word like *necavit* which can be supplied from the context generally, and also from the following verbs *fixit,* (*securim*) *congeminat.*

15 692-3. **qua colla sedentis lucent:** 'where the rider's neck was visible'; for *lucent* cf. 9.383.

lucent et laevo[1] dependet parma lacerto;
Orsilochum fugiens magnumque[2] agitata per orbem
eludit gyro interior sequiturque sequentem;   695
tum validam perque arma viro perque ossa securim[3]
altior exsurgens oranti et multa precanti
congeminat; vulnus calido rigat ora cerebro.
Incidit huic subitoque aspectu territus haesit
Appenninicolae bellator filius[4] Auni,   700
haud Ligurum extremus, dum fallere fata sinebant.[5]
Isque ubi se nullo iam cursu evadere pugnae[6]
posse neque instantem reginam avertere cernit,
consilio[7] versare dolos ingressus et astu
incipit haec: 'quid tam egregium, si femina[8] forti   705
fidis equo? Dimitte fugam et te comminus aequo
mecum crede solo pugnaeque[9] accinge pedestri:
iam[10] nosces ventosa ferat cui gloria fraudem.'
Dixit, at illa furens acrique accensa dolore[11]
tradit equum comiti paribusque resistit in armis   710
ense pedes nudo puraque[12] interrita parma.
At iuvenis vicisse[13] dolo ratus avolat ipse
(haud mora), conversisque fugax aufertur habenis
quadripedemque citum ferrata calce fatigat.[14]

---

1 693. **laevo . . . lacerto:** i.e. his shield was dangling down, not in the on-guard position.

2 694-5. **magnumque . . . sequentem:** 'riding in a great circle she outmanoeuvres him by curving inside him and now the pursued is the pursuer'. For *interior* cf. Cloanthus' ship in the boat race (5.170) *radit iter laevum interior.*

3 696-8. **securim . . . congeminat:** 'brought the axe down again and again', an extension of a phrase like *ictus congeminant* (12.713-14).

4 700. We are not told the name of the warrior son of Aunus who lived in the northern Apennines in Liguria. Servius assumes that his name was Aunus too. The long sonorous word *Appenninicolae* is imitated by Ovid (*Met.* 15.432 *Appenninigenae*).

5 701. The meaning is that he was not the least of the Ligurians in guile (704) while the fates allowed the use of guile; Conington quotes a number of passages to illustrate the bad reputation of the Ligurians, e.g. Cic. *Cluent.* 72; cf. *patrias . . . artis,* 716.

6 702. **pugnae:** dative, see notes on 10.50, 10.462.

7 704. 'starting to concoct a stratagem by trickery and guile'; the use of the three nearly synonymous nouns leaves no doubt about this slippery character.

8 705-6. **femina forti fidis:** the alliteration of *f* strongly underlines the sarcasm. The point of the sarcasm is that to be a woman warrior is doubtless a remarkable thing, but not if you leave it all to your horse.

9 707. **pugnaeque . . . pedestri:** supply *te* again as the object of *accinge; pugnae = ad pugnam.*

10 708. 'You'll soon find out whose empty vainglory is going to cheat them'; i.e. Camilla shows *ventosa gloria* and will find herself undeceived. For this use of *gloria* cf. 10.144,for *ventosus* cf. 390. Some MSS have *laudem* ('to which of the two of us fickle fortune will bring glory') but *fraudem* is much more likely to have been changed by a scribe into *laudem* than vice versa.

11 709. **dolore:** 'anger', 'resentment' at his gibe.

12 711. **puraque:** 'plain', 'undecorated', cf. 9.548.

13 712. **vicisse . . . ratus:** supply *se,* cf. 8.534.

14 714. **fatigat:** 'spurs on', cf. 9.610.

'Vane[1] Ligus frustraque animis elate superbis,[2] 715
nequiquam patrias[3] temptasti lubricus artis,
nec fraus te incolumem fallaci perferet[4] Auno.'
Haec fatur virgo, et pernicibus ignea[5] plantis
transit[6] equum cursu frenisque adversa prehensis
congreditur poenasque inimico ex sanguine sumit: 720
quam facile accipiter saxo sacer[7] ales ab alto[8]
consequitur pennis sublimem in nube columbam
comprensamque tenet pedibusque eviscerat uncis;
tum cruor et vulsae labuntur ab aethere plumae.

725-67. Jupiter intervenes to send Tarchon to rally the Etruscan allies of the Trojans. Tarchon upbraids them and leads them into battle, capturing the Latin Venulus. Meanwhile Arruns shadows Camilla, preparing to attack her.

[9]At non[10] haec nullis hominum[11] sator atque deorum 725
observans oculis summo sedet altus Olympo.
Tyrrhenum genitor Tarchonem[12] in proelia saeva
suscitat et stimulis haud mollibus inicit iras.
Ergo inter caedes cedentiaque agmina Tarchon
fertur equo variisque instigat vocibus alas[13] 730
nomine quemque vocans, reficitque[14] in proelia pulsos.

---

1 **vane Ligus . . . elate:** 'Foolish Ligurian, puffed up . . .'; the doubled vocative increases the emphasis of Camilla's words.

2 715. The direct speech immediately following the narrative without an introductory phrase adds to the drama of the action.

3 716. **patrias:** 'of your country', see note on 701.

4 717. **perferet:** 'take you home', cf. 1.389.

5 718. **ignea:** 'swift as fire', cf. 746 and Cat. 64.341 *flammea . . . vestigia cervae.*

6 719. **transit equum cursu:** 'outruns his horse'; for Camilla's speed cf. 7.807.

7 721. **sacer:** in Hom. *Od.* 15.526 the falcon is called the 'swift messenger of Apollo'.

8 721f. The image of the falcon and the dove is from Hom. *Il.* 22.139f. (cf. also Hor. *Odes* 1.37.17f.); the last two lines are from Hom. *Od.* 15.525f.

9 725f. This episode serves to slow down the story of Camilla by concentrating attention on the Etruscan recovery led by Tarchon, and his remarkable feat in sweeping his enemy Venulus off his horse and on to his own. But it returns at the end to Camilla as we see the sinister Arruns shadowing her every movement and watching for his chance to kill her.

10 725-6. **non . . . nullis . . . oculis:** Servius explains as 'non neglegentibus', i.e. with not inattentive eyes, not indifferently. It is based on the Homeric ουδ αλαοσκοπιην ειχεν (e.g. *Il.* 10.515), 'not blind was the watch he kept'.

11 725. **hominum . . . deorum:** the phrase is used of Jupiter also in 1.254.

12 727. **Tarchonem:** Tarchon was the leader of the Etruscan allies of Aeneas, cf. 184.

13 730. **alas:** it has been a cavalry engagement, cf. 598f.

14 731. **reficitque in proelia pulsos:** 'heartens the defeated to enter battle again'; Macrobius (*Sat.* 6.1.34) quotes a passage from Furius as Virgil's model here, ending with the phrase *reficitque ad proelia mentes.*

'Quis metus, o[1] numquam dolituri, o semper inertes

Tyrrheni, quae tanta animis ignavia venit?

Femina palantis agit atque haec agmina vertit'

quo[2] ferrum quidve haec gerimus tela inrita dextris?   735

At[3] non in Venerem segnes nocturnaque bella,

aut ubi curva choros indixit tibia Bacchi.

Exspectate[4] dapes et plenae pocula mensae

(hic amor, hoc studium) dum sacra secundus haruspex

nuntiet ac lucos vocet hostia pinguis in altos!'   740

Haec effatus equum in medios moriturus[5] et ipse

concitat, et Venulo[6] adversum se turbidus infert

dereptumque ab equo dextra complectitur hostem[7]

et[8] gremium ante suum multa vi concitus aufert.

Tollitur in caelum clamor cunctique Latini   745

convertere oculos. Volat[9] igneus aequore Tarchon

arma[10] virumque ferens; tum summa ipsius ab hasta

defringit ferrum et partis rimatur apertas, [11]

qua vulnus letale ferat; contra ille repugnans

sustinet a iugulo dextram et vim[12] viribus exit.   750

---

1 732. **o numquam dolituri:** 'you who it seems never will feel shame'. They should feel anger and resentment (cf. *dolor* in 709) at being driven in rout by a woman. The speech may be compared with Agamemnon's angry speech to the Greeks in Hom. *Il.* 338f.

2 735. 'What's the use of having swords? Why are we carrying weapons and not using them?' For *quo ferrum,* literally 'to what purpose (do we have) steel', cf. Hor. *Epist.* 1.5.12 *quo mihi fortunam, si non conceditur uti?* It is less forceful to take *ferrum* as governed by *gerimus.*

3 736-7. 'But you are not slow for love and battles by night, not slow when the curving flute proclaims Bacchus' dances'. Supply the main verb *estis. Nocturna bella* is reminiscent of the language of the elegists, cf. Prop. 2.1.45, 3.8.32. The taunt is similar generally to Numanus' remarks in 9.617f., where the Trojans are said to be better at celebrating the wild orgies of Cybele than at fighting. Here the orgies of Bacchus have the same implication, and the idea is picked up in the next line with reference to the wine of Bacchus (*plenae pocula mensae*).

4 738-40. 'Wait for your feasts and wine-goblets at a sumptuous banquet, this is what you love and crave for, until the soothsayer at the hour of success announces the religious celebrations and the rich victim calls you into the deep groves'. These sarcastic lines convey that battle comes first, and only after success can there be thank offerings linked with celebration.

5 741. **moriturus et ipse:** 'ready to die himself too'; as far as we know he was not in fact killed. *Et* means that as well as dealing death, he was himself prepared to die.

6 742. **Venulo:** the Latin spokesman (from Tibur, 757) of the embassy to Diomedes (242f.).

7 743. Tarchon sweeps Venulus off his horse on to his own horse; Servius tells a story that the same feat was performed by Caesar in Gaul.

8 744. 'and with all his might carried him off holding him in front of his own body as he rode speedily away'. *Gremium ante suum* is a very vivid description of how a rider might hold another man in front of him on his horse: *gremium* conveys his seated posture.

9 746. **volat . . . Tarchon:** the rhythm helps to convey speed, cf. 756, 810 and 638 with note; for *igneus* cf. 718, and for *aequore* ('over the plain') cf. 599.

10 747. **arma virumque:** 'the man and his weapons', as we hear in a moment he uses Venulus' own spear (*ipsius,* 747) to kill him.

11 748. **apertas:** 'unprotected', cf. 666.

12 750. **vim viribus exit:** 'avoids the violent onslaught with all his strength'; for the use of *exit* (= *evitat)* cf. 5.438.

Utque volans alte raptum cum fulva draconem[1]
fert aquila implicuitque pedes atque unguibus haesit,
saucius at serpens sinuosa volumina versat[2]
arrectisque[3] horret squamis et sibilat[4] ore
arduus insurgens, illa haud minus urget obunco   755
luctantem rostro, [5]simul aethera verberat alis:
haud aliter praedam Tiburtum ex agmine Tarchon
portat ovans. Ducis exemplum eventumque[6] secuti
Maeonidae[7] incurrunt. Tum fatis[8] debitus Arruns
velocem[9] iaculo et multa prior arte Camillam   760
circuit, et quae sit fortuna[10] facillima temptat.
Qua se cumque furens medio tulit agmine virgo,
hac Arruns subit et tacitus vestigia lustrat;[11]
qua victrix redit illa pedemque ex hoste reportat,
hac iuvenis furtim celeris detorquet habenas.   765
Hos aditus iamque hos aditus omnemque pererrat[12]
undique circuitum et certam quatit improbus[13] hastam.

---

1 751f. The simile of the eagle and the snake is based on the description (not a simile) in Hom. *Il.* 12.200f.; Cicero used the Homeric passage (in which the snake is ultimately released) in his *Marius* (quoted in *De Div.* 1.106). The application of the passage as a simile is extremely apt here; the closeness of the comparison greatly intensifies the impact of the narrative.

2 753f. Virgil is fond of descriptions of snakes; cf. 2.203f., 5.84f., 273f., *Geo.* 2.153f. Notice the heavy alliteration of *s*.

3 754. **arrectisque horret squamis:** 'stiffens, its scales protruding', cf. *Geo.* 3.545 (of snakes) *squamis astantibus.*

4 754-5. **sibilat . . . insurgens:** cf. 5.277-8 *sibila colla arduus attollens.*

5 755-6. 'but the eagle just the same attacks it as it struggles with hooked beak, beating the air with its wings'; for the rhythm of the last phrase cf. 746.

6 758. **eventumque:** 'achievement', 'felicitatem' (Servius).

7 759. **Maeonidae:** the Etruscans were supposed to have originated in Lydia or Maeonia in Asia Minor; cf. 8.479, 499.

8 **fatis debitus Arruns**: Arruns the Etruscan is first mentioned here; he is 'owed to fate' because of Diana's vow that the killer of Camilla would himself be killed (590f.).

9 760-1. 'first circled, spear in hand, around the swift Camilla, using all his cunning'. Others take *prior* to mean' superior in cunning', and others 'anticipating her movements'.

10 761. **Fortuna:** 'opportunity', cf. 7.559.

11 763. **lustrat:**'watches', cf. 2.754.

12 766. This line is nearly the same as 5.441, where it is used of a boxer; there is a slight zeugma with the verb *pererrat,* he tries every approach and keeps circling around her.

13 767. **improbus:** partly with its meaning of 'evil', cf. 512, and partly 'relentless', cf. 9.62.

768-835. Camilla's attention is caught by a gorgeously attired Trojan priest, and as she tracks him to capture spoils from him Arruns shoots her. As he turns away Camilla falls dead — in her last words she sends a message to Turnus telling him to take her place in the battle.

[1]Forte sacer[2] Cybelo[3] Chloreus[4] olimque[5] sacerdos
insignis longe Phrygiis fulgebat in armis
spumantemque agitabat equum, quem[6] pellis aenis 770
in plumam squamis auro conserta tegebat.
Ipse peregrina[7] ferrugine clarus et ostro
spicula [8]torquebat Lycio Gortynia cornu;
aureus ex umeris erat arcus et aurea vati
cassida;[9] tum[10] croceam chlamydemque sinusque crepantis 775
carbaseos fulvo in nodum collegerat auro,
pictus[11] acu tunicas et barbara tegmina crurum.
Hunc virgo, sive ut templis praefigeret arma
Troia, captivo sive ut se[12] ferret in auro
venatrix,[13] unum ex omni certamine pugnae 780
caeca sequebatur totumque incauta per agmen

---

1 768f. The death of Camilla, brought about by her rash desire (781)for glorious spoils, is described by Virgil in the liquid tones of sorrow (818f., 827f.) which are so especially associated with him. The pathos is increased by the wholly unsympathetic portrayal of Arruns, her killer (889f.). See note on 648f.

2 768. **sacer Cybelo**: 'sacred to Mt. Cybelus', the mountain of the goddess Cybele, cf. 3.111.

3 768-77. The description of the splendid appearance of Chloreus, which lures Camilla to her death, is long-drawn-out (up to line 777) in order to increase the suspense.

4 **Chloreus:** we hear of his death in 12.363.

5 **olimque sacerdos**: 'long time a priest', i.e. already when he was in Troy.

6 770-1. **quem pellis . . . tegebat**: 'which was caparisoned with a cloth of bronze scales interlinked with gold to form a plume', i.e. the horse wore a kind of coat of mail whose adornments gave an impression of plumage (cf. Stat. *Th.* 11.543). Servius explains that the word *cataphractus* was used for cavalry so equipped (Livy 37.40.5).

7 772. **peregrina . . . ostro**: 'glorious with exotic browns and purples'; *peregrina* refers to his Eastern (Trojan) colours (cf. *barbara*, 777); for *ferrugo* cf. 9.582.

8 773. 'shot Gortynian shafts from his Lycian bow'; both the epithets are 'ornate' (cf. 580); Gortyna was a city of Crete,famous for archery (cf. 4.70), and similarly Lycia was associated with bows (7.816, 8.166).

9 775. **cassida:** an alternative form (cf. Prop. 3.11.15)for *cassis.*

10 775f. 'then he had fastened his saffron tunic with its rustling linen folds into a knot with a brooch of yellow gold'. These are very ornate lines; the alliteration off *c* and *q* conveys something of the tinkle of his splendid garb; the postposition of the first *-que* is unusual (cf. *Geo.* 2.119) and so is the use of both a participle *crepantis* and an adjective *carbaseos* with the noun *sinus* (cf. 6.603).

11 777. 'his tunic and his foreign trousers decorated with embroidery'; for the retained accusative ('decorated as to . . .') see notes on 35, 9.582. For *tegmina crurum* cf. Valerius Flaccus' imitation of this passage (6.225f.). At the end of the description of this gloriously accoutred warrior Servius rightly comments 'sane armorum longa descriptio illuc spectat ut in eorum cupiditatem merito Camilla videatur esse succensa'.

12 779. **se ferret**: 'flaunt herself', cf. 9.597.

13 780. **venatrix**: 'when she went hunting'.

femineo[1] praedae et spoliorum ardebat amore,
telum [2]ex insidiis cum tandem tempore capto
concitat et superos Arruns sic voce precatur:
'summe[3] deum, sancti custos Soractis[4] Apollo,   785
quem primi[5] colimus, cui pineus[6] ardor acervo
pascitur, et medium freti pietate per ignem
cultores multa premimus vestigia pruna,
da,[7] pater, hoc nostris aboleri dedecus armis,
omnipotens. Non exuvias pulsaeve tropaeum   790
virginis aut spolia ulla peto, mihi cetera laudem
facta ferent; haec dira meo dum vulnere pestis[8]
pulsa cadat, patrias remeabo inglorius urbes.'
   [9]Audiit et voti Phoebus succedere partem
mente[10] dedit, partem volucris dispersit in auras: 795
sterneret ut subita turbatam[11] morte Camillam
adnuit oranti; reducem[12] ut patria alta videret
non dedit, inque Notos vocem vertere procellae.
Ergo ut missa manu sonitum dedit hasta per auras.
Convertere animos acris[13] oculosque tulere   800
cuncti ad reginam Volsci. Nihil ipsa nec aurae[14]
nec sonitus memor[15] aut venientis ab aethere teli,
hasta sub exsertam donec perlata papillam

---

1 782. 'burned with a woman's love for booty and spoils' (she wanted to win these fineries whether to dedicate them, 778, or possess them, 779). We are reminded of how Euryalus' desire for spoils led to his wearing the helmet which betrayed him (9.365f., 373). Servius glosses *femineus* as *impatiens, irrationabilis*, quoting 7.345.

2 783-4. 'when at last, seizing his moment, Arruns poised his spear from where he was lurking'; the inverted *cum* here is very effective after the long introduction of the sentence, and *tandem* filling the fourth foot has a special emphasis (see note on 7.291), especially with the alliteration of *t* in line 783.

3 785. **summe deum**: cf. 4.576 *sancte deorum*.

4 785. **Soractis Apollo**: Apollo had a temple on the top of Mt. Soracte (Hor. *Odes* 1.9), in Etruria, twenty miles north of Rome.

5 786. **primi**: he means that the Etruscans more than all others worship Apollo.

6 786-8. **pineus . . . pruna**: 'in whose honour a fire of pinewood feeds on its heaped-up pile, and we your worshippers sure in our faith plant our footsteps on the deep ashes in the fire'. This custom of fire walking is mentioned by Pliny (*Nat. Hist.* 7.19); cf. also Sil. 5. 175f.

7 789. **da . . . aboleri**: the infinitive with *dare* is frequent in Virgil, cf. 794 and 9.173, 10.61, 12.97.

8 792. **pestis**: a very violent word, cf. 3.215 (of the Harpies).

9 794f. These lines are based on Hom. *Il.* 16.250f.

10 795. **mente**: 'in his decision', cf. 10.629.

11 796. **turbatam**: 'surprised', an unusual use of the word. 797-8.

12 797-8. **reducem . . . non dedit**: 'he did not grant that his lofty fatherland should see him return'; *alia* because of Mt. Soracte (785).

13 800. **acris**: with *animos* in an adverbial sense, 'intently'.

14 801. **aurae**: the wind of the approaching spear.

15 802. **memor**: 'conscious', supply *erat*, cf. 633.

haesit[1] virgineumque alte[2] bibit acta cruorem.
Concurrunt trepidae comites dominamque ruentem 805
suscipiunt. Fugit ante omnis exterritus Arruns
laetitia mixtoque metu, nec iam amplius hastae
credere nec telis occurrere virginis audet.
Ac velut ille,[3] prius quam tela inimica sequantur,[4]
continuo in montis sese avius[5] abdidit altos 810
occiso pastore lupus magnove iuvenco,
conscius audacis facti, caudamque[6] remulcens
subiecit pavitantem utero silvasque petivit:
haud secus ex oculis se turbidus abstulit Arruns
contentusque[7] fuga mediis se immiscuit armis. 815
Illa manu moriens telum trahit, ossa sed inter[8]
ferreus ad[9] costas alto stat vulnere mucro.
Labitur exsanguis, labuntur frigida leto[10]
lumina, purpureus quondam color ora reliquit.
Tum sic exspirans Accam ex aequalibus unam 820
adloquitur, fida[11] ante alias quae sola Camillae
quicum partiri curas, atque haec ita fatur:
'hactenus, Acca soror, potui: nunc vulnus acerbum[12]
conficit, et tenebris nigrescunt omnia circum.
Effuge et haec Turno mandata novissima peifer: 825
succedat[13] pugnae Troianosque arceat urbe.

---

1 804. **haesit**: the single word filling a spondaic first foot gives metrical emphasis, cf. 48, 359.

2 **alte . . . acta**: 'driven deep', cf. 10.850.

3 809. **ille**: see note on 10.707.

4 809f. The simile is somewhat reminiscent of Hom. *Il.* 15.586f., where Antilochus flees from the battle like an animal running away. Virgil has three other wolf similes (2.355f., 9.59f., 565f.), but all stress savagery, not slinking cowardice.

5 810. **avius abdidit altos**: for the rhythm, here emphasised by alliteration, see note on 638 and cf. 814. For *avius*, 'out of the way', cf. 12.480.

6 812-13. **caudamque . . . utero**: 'drooping his tail he tucks it in panic between his legs'; *remulcens* is a rare word, and *pavitantem* a boldly transferred epithet.

7 815. **contentusque fuga**: Page and others give 'straining every nerve to fly', but the meaning must be 'content with flight' (cf. Ov. *Met.* 5.169) because this exactly fits what we have been told of Arruns' attitude (791-2); he seeks no booty from his victim.

8 816. In this decisive line Virgil uses patterned alliteration (*m* and *t*), bucolic diaeresis (the pause after *trahit*), and postponed *sed* and *inter*.

9 817. **ad costas . . . stat**: 'is fixed in her ribs'.

10 818-19. The pattern of alliteration of initial *l* is picked up in the closing words *color, reliquit*.

11 821-2. **fida . . . curas**: 'faithful before all the others, who was the only one with whom Camilla shared her cares'; some MSS have *fidam*, but this gives an inferior run to the sentence. To *quae sola* supply *erat*; *quicum* is archaic, *qui* being the ablative of all genders; *partiri* is historic infinitive of repeated action, cf. 4.422, 7.15, 12.216.

12 823f. The last words of Camilla are impressive in their simplicity: notice the pathos of *hactenus potui,* followed by her last thoughts (*novissima,* 825), not for herself, but for the battle.

13 826. **succedat pugnae**: 'he must take over the battle', cf. 10.690.

Iamque vale.' Simul his dictis linquebat habenas[1]
ad terram non[2] sponte fluens. [3]Tum frigida toto
paulatim exsolvit se corpore, lentaque colla
et captum leto posuit caput, arma relinquens,[4]   830
vitaque cum gemitu fugit indignata sub umbras.[5]
Tum vero immensus surgens ferit aurea clamor
sidera: deiecta crudescit[6] pugna Camilla;
incurrunt densi simul omnis copia Teucrum
Tyrrhenique duces Euandrique Arcades alae.[7]   835

> *836-915. Opis avenges the death of Camilla by shooting down Arruns. The Latins are driven in flight, and their city is besieged. Turnus is told of Camilla's death, and he abandons his plan for an ambush and returns to the capital. Nightfall ends the battle.*

[8]At Triviae custos iamdudum in montibus Opis[9]
alta sedet summis spectatque interrita[10] pugnas.
Utque procul medio iuvenum in clamore furentum
prospexit tristi mulcatam[11] morte Camillam,
ingemuitque deditque[12] has imo pectore voces: 840
'heu nimium, virgo, nimium crudele luisti
supplicium Teucros conata lacessere bello!
Nec tibi desertae[13] in dumis coluisse Dianam
profuit aut nostras umero gessisse pharetras.

---

1 827f. Macrobius (*Sat.* 6.4.10) quotes a passage from Furius which Virgil probably used here: *ille gravi subito devinctus vulnere habenas / misit equi, lapsusque in humum defluxit et armis / reddidit aeratis sonitum.*

2 828. **non sponte**: litotes, 'in spite of all her efforts'.

3 828-30. 'Then slowly she grew cold and was wholly set free from her body, and she laid down her drooping neck and her head, subdued in death'; for *exsolvit se* cf. 4.703, Lucr. 3.576. Notice the alliteration of the gentle letter *l* in these lines (cf. 818-19).

4 830. **relinquens:** some MSS have *reliquit* or *relinquit,* and Servius mentions a reading *relinquunt* which Hirtzel adopts.

5 831. The line describing Camilla's death is also the last line of the *Aeneid,* describing Turnus' death. *Indignata* means 'complaining', and is based on the Homeric phrase ον ποτμον γοωωσα (*Il.* 16.857, 22.363).

6 833. **crudescit:** 'intensifies', 'crudelior fit' (Servius), cf. 7.788.

7 835. The Etruscans (under Tarchon) and the Arcadians (whom Evander had sent) are the allied forces of the Trojans. *Arcades* is here in apposition to *alae* and is virtually adjectival (cf. 12.551).

8 836f. The book ends, now that its climax (the death of Camilla) is past, with rapid narrative. The vengeance of Diana on Arruns is quickly accomplished; the scene of confusion in the Latin capital is vividly described; and the book ends with the return of Turnus who impetuously abandons all his plans when he receives the news of Camilla's death. The word *furens* (901), applied to him yet again, indicates his inability to organise his campaign rationally (he could presumably still have continued his plan to ambush Aeneas), and underlines the rash individual prowess which is his characteristic throughout the poem.

9 836. Opis had been told by Diana (Trivia, see note on 566) to watch the battle and avenge the death of Camilla (532f., 587f.).

10 837. **interrita:** conveying that she is immortal, above and beyond the usual hopes and fears of battle.

11 839. **mulcatam:** 'stricken', cf. Cic. *Verr.* 2.4.94.

12 840. The doubled *-que* gives a lilting effect.

13 843. **desertae:** 'living a lonely life', having dedicated herself to the service of Diana in the woodlands.

Non tamen indecorem tua te regina reliquit   845
extrema iam in morte, neque hoc sine nomine letum
per gentis erit aut famam[1] patieris inultae.
Nam quicumque tuum violavit vulnere corpus
morte luet merita.' Fuit ingens monte sub alto
regis Dercenni[2] terreno ex aggere bustum   850
antiqui Laurentis opacaque[3] ilice tectum;
hic dea se primum rapido pulcherrima nisu
sistit et Arruntem tumulo speculatur ab alto.
Ut vidit fulgentem armis ac vana[4] tumentem,
'cur' inquit 'diversus abis? Huc derige gressum,   855
huc[5] periture veni, capias ut digna Camillae
praemia. Tune[6] etiam telis moriere Dianae?'
Dixit, et aurata volucrem Threissa[7] sagittam
deprompsit pharetra cornuque infensa tetendit
et duxit longe, donec curvata coirent   860
inter se capita[8] et manibus iam tangeret aequis,[9]
laeva aciem ferri, dextra nervoque papillam.
Extemplo teli stridorem aurasque sonantis
audiit una[10] Arruns haesitque in corpore ferrum.
Illum exspirantem socii atque extrema gementem   865
obliti[11] ignoto camporum in pulvere linquunt;
Opis ad aetherium pennis aufertur Olympum.
      Prima fugit domina amissa levis ala Camillae,
turbati fugiunt Rutuli, fugit acer Atinas,[12]

---

1 847. **Famam ... inultae:** 'nor will you suffer the report of being unavenged', i.e. nobody shall say that you were not avenged.

2 850. Nothing is known of Dercennus, the king of Laurentum in times gone by.

3 851. **opacaque:** -*que* links *tectum* with *terreno ex aggere*. The caesura in this line is unusual, the trochaic break in the third foot not being followed by a main caesura in the fourth foot (cf. 8.549).

4 854. **vana:** adverbial, cf. 865.

5 856. **huc periture veni:** 'come here, to die'.

6 857. **tune etiam:** as Servius says, spoken with bitterness; better people die at the hands of Diana.

7 858. **Threissa:** cf. 659 (the Amazons from Thrace), and *Threissa Harpalyce* in 1.316-17.

8 861. **capita:** the ends of the bow.

9 **aequis:** equidistant from the ground, one hand advanced holding the arrow and one retracted, holding the bowstring against the breast, cf. Hom. *Il.* 4.122-3.

10 864. **una ... haesitque:** i.e. he heard the sound at the same time as he was struck (not before); cf. 10.703f.

11 866. **obliti:** Servius reports a view that this means 'neglegentes', 'ignoring him', but it is more likely that his companions, unaware of his activities, simply forgot him and did not know that he was dead.

12 869. Atinas has not been mentioned before, but in 12.661 we hear of him holding out along with Messapus against the Trojans.

disiectique duces desolatique manipli[1]   870
tuta petunt et equis aversi ad moenia tendunt.
Nec quisquam instantis Teucros letumque ferentis
sustentare valet telis aut sistere contra,
sed laxos referunt umeris languentibus arcus,
quadripedumque putrem cursu quatit ungula campum.[2]   875
Volvitur ad muros caligine turbidus atra
pulvis, et e speculis percussae[3] pectora matres[4]
femineum clamorem ad caeli sidera tollunt.
Qui cursu portas primi inrupere patentis,
hos inimica super mixto[5] premit agmine turba,   880
nec miseram effugiunt mortem, sed limine in ipso,
moenibus in patriis atque inter tuta[6] domorum
confixi exspirant animas. Pars claudere[7] portas,
nec sociis aperire viam nec moenibus audent
accipere orantis, oriturque miserrima caedes   885
defendentum armis aditus inque arma ruentum.
Exclusi ante oculos lacrimantumque ora parentum
pars in praecipitis fossas urgente[8] ruina
volvitur, immissis pars caeca et concita frenis
arietat[9] in portas et duros[10] obice postis.   890
Ipsae de muris summo certamine matres
(monstrat amor verus patriae, ut videre Camillam)[11]
tela manu trepidae iaciunt ac[12] robore duro
stipitibus ferrum sudibusque imitantur obustis
praecipites, primaeque mori pro moenibus ardent.   895

---

1 870. The alliteration of *d* is extremely marked in this line of only four words.

2 875. The line conveys onomatopoeically, by the dactyls and harsh consonants, the sound of galloping horses; cf. 8.596.

3 877. **percussae pectora**: retained accusative, cf. 4.589 and note on 35.

4 The alliteration of *p*, to convey the violence of their retreat, is very marked.

5 880. **mixto . . . agmine**: 'intermingling with their own troops'.

6 882. **tuta domorum**: 'the safety of their houses'; *tuta* is used as a noun (cf. 871)followed by a possessive genitive; cf. 513-14 and see note on 1.422 *strata viarum*.

7 883. **claudere**: historic infinitive of sudden action, rather unusual when used (as here) once only without repetition.

8 888. **urgente ruina**: 'under the pressure of the rout'; *ruina* picks up *ruentum* (886).

9 890. **arietat**: the word scans as a dactyl, the *i* being consonantal, cf. 667.

10 **duros obice postis**: 'the unyielding barriers of the gates', literally 'the gates unyielding with their barrier', a typically Virgilian ablative, cf. 5.663 *pictas abiete puppis*. *Obice* scans as a dactyl by the pronunciation of *j* after the *b*; cf. 8.227.

11 892. The punctuation of this line is disputed; some prefer to end the parenthesis at *patriae*, but *ut videre Camillam* explains the previous phrase.

12 893-4. **ac robore . . . obustis**: 'and with stakes of tough oak and poles hardened in the fire they do the work of steel'; *robore duro* is ablative of description dependent on *stipitibus*.

Interea Turnum[1] in silvis saevissimus implet
nuntius et iuveni ingentem[2] fert Acca tumultum:
deletas Volscorum acies, cecidisse Camillam,
ingruere[3] infensos hostis et Marte secundo
omnia corripuisse, metum iam ad moenia ferri.   900
Ille furens[4] (et saeva Iovis sic numina poscunt[5])
deserit obsessos collis, nemora aspera linquit.[6]
Vix e[7] conspectu exierat campumque tenebat,
cum pater Aeneas saltus ingressus apertos
exsuperatque iugum silvaque evadit opaca[8].   905
Sic ambo ad muros rapidi totoque feruntur
agmine nec longis inter se passibus absunt;
ac simul Aeneas fumantis pulvere campos
prospexit longe Laurentiaque[9] agmina vidit,
et saevum Aenean agnovit Turnus in armis   910
adventumque pedum flatusque audivit equorum.
Continuoque ineant pugnas et proelia temptent,[10]
ni roseus fessos iam gurgite[11] Phoebus Hibero
tingat equos noctemque die labente reducat.
Considunt castris ante urbem et moenia vallant.[12]   915

---

1 896. **Turnum ... implet**: 'came in all its force to Turnus' ears', a very colourful use of *implet*, cf. 5.341 (with my note, OUP Ed.) and *replere* in line 140, 4.189.

2 897. **ingentem fert Acca tumultum**: 'Acca reports the terrible disaster'. Her report (898-900) is in very simple dramatic phrases.

3 899. **ingruere**: 'were sweeping on', cf. 8.535.

4 901. **furens**: 'in wild frenzy', the expected reaction of the impetuous Turnus.

5 **poscunt**: *R* has *pellunt* which is much inferior; cf. 4.614.

6 902. This line refers to the ambush which Turnus had laid (522f.) and which now seems to him useless.

7 903. **e conspectu**: i.e. of the position he was occupying; he was only just out of sight of it when Aeneas came through it, finding no obstruction now (*apertos*, 904).

8 905. The doubled *-que* emphasises the ease with which Aeneas gets through the unfavourable but now undefended terrain; for the ridge cf. 514.

9 909. **Laurentiaque**: the word is here used for the Latins and Rutulians under Turnus.

10 912f. For the past unfulfilled condition put into the graphic present subjunctive, involving the reader in the narrative as if he were there, cf. 5.325f., 6.292f., 12.733. Notice the idyllic description of nightfall, closing a book of bloodshed and horror on a quiet and gentle note.

11 913-14. **gurgite ... Hibero**: 'in the western ocean'; the idea of the sun sinking into the ocean in the west is common from Homer onwards (e.g. *Il.* 8.485), cf. *Aen.* 1.745.

12 915. Probably the meaning is that the Trojans pitch camp outside the Latin capital, while the Latins withdraw into the town and man the walls; at the beginning of Book 12 Turnus is within the town. This seems more likely than that both parties pitch camp outside the town.

BOOK 12

Introductory note

The twelfth book is rich in character and incident and develops steadily towards the tragic intensity and inevitability of the final defeat of Turnus. It has close similarities with the tone of Greek tragedy (note on 614f.), and this is highlighted by similarities with the tragic doom of Dido, another opponent of the Roman destiny (note on 843f.). It uses the poems of Homer for its martial effects in narrative, and is especially close to *Iliad* 22 at the end (note on 697f.); but we also see, particularly in the reconciliation scene between Jupiter and Juno (791f.), the great non-Homeric theme of the *Aeneid*, namely the sense of destiny working towards the history of mankind's future.

The book begins with an extremely vivid portrayal of the impetuous courage of Turnus as he prepares for single combat (note on 1f.); this is contrasted with the calmer mood of Aeneas and his moderate and reasonable attitude seen in the oath he swears before battle (note on 189-91). As the combat becomes imminent we see Turnus suddenly lose his self confidence (note on 210f.), and the intervention of Juturna postpones his hour of reckoning as she persuades the Italians to break the truce and resume large-scale fighting. Aeneas is wounded; his wound is healed by the intervention of Venus and he now enters battle in a mood of passion and anger, causing destruction around him with the same violent fury which he had shown after the death of Pallas (10.513f.). In the scenes which follow Aeneas and Turnus deal death indiscriminately, and there is hardly any difference between them (note on 500f.). We see once more that Aeneas is reluctant to enter battle, but when he does enter it he can fight ruthlessly and savagely.

Events now follow fast: the Trojans attack the Latin capital, and Amata in despair hangs herself; Turnus, who has been kept by his divine sister Juturna in a distant part of the battlefield, hears news of misfortune, and in deep shame at his failure hastens to face the single combat which he thought he had avoided (note on 614f.). In its early stages the combat is indecisive, as there are divine interventions on both sides. At this point the narrative leaves the mortal combatants, and in Olympus Jupiter and Juno resolve the conflict on the divine plane. Juno agrees to give up her hostility to the Trojans on condition that the Italians become the dominant partners in the alliance between the two peoples (note on 791f.). The Italian peoples thus gain all they could wish for, but there is no reprieve for Turnus.

Jupiter sends down a Fury in the shape of an owl, bewildering and terrifying Turnus and forcing his sister Juturna to withdraw from the battle. Here reminiscences of the tragic helplessness of Dido deepen the sympathy for the victim of forces which have now become irresistible (note on 843f.). The wounding of the bemused Turnus follows quickly, and as he begs for mercy the reader may well anticipate that Aeneas is the sort of man who will grant it (note on 887f.). He is indeed on the point of doing so, but the sight of Pallas' belt causes in him an upsurge of hot fury and in vengeance he kills his enemy. Should he have done so? Virgil has posed this question not in order to give an easy answer, but to make his contemporaries ponder its implications.

> 1-106. *In the moment of their defeat Turnus feels the eyes of all the Latins are upon him; he tells King Latinus that he will fight Aeneas in single combat. Latinus tries to dissuade him, but Turnus is all the more fiercely determined. Amata beseeches him not to go and Turnus replies that he is not free to refuse. He arms himself in rehearsal for the next day's combat.*

¹Turnus ut infractos² adverso Marte Latinos
defecisse videt, sua³ nunc promissa reposci,
se⁴ signari oculis, ultro⁵ implacabilis ardet
attollitque animos. Poenorum⁶ qualis in arvis⁷
saucius ille⁸ gravi venantum vulnere pectus⁹   5
tum¹⁰ demum movet¹¹ arma leo, gaudetque¹² comantis

---

1 1f. The opening scenes of Book 12 concentrate on Turnus, and present a fully developed picture of his character and present mood; a hundred lines are taken up with speeches to and by Turnus and with descriptions of his warlike attitude. The situation is based on that of *Iliad* 22 (as also are the final phases of this book); the attempts of Latinus and Amata to dissuade Turnus from facing Aeneas are similar to those of Priam and Hecuba when Hector goes to meet Achilles. But the differences are significant; Hector does not answer, but Turnus replies both to Latinus and Amata, reiterating what he originally said to Latinus and revealing increasingly his unshakeable determination to show his heroic courage now that the supreme moment has come. Hector was quieter, facing the inevitable with a brave resignation and soliloquising (22.99f.) rather than seeking to impose his qualities on an audience.

The impetuous violence, the irrationality of Turnus' display of courage, most clearly seen in the wild animal similes which begin and end this passage, is emphasised throughout (notes on 3, 8, 45, 71, 82) and in particular the scene in which he rehearses his preparations for battle (82f.) that show him as a man who realises himself most completely in warfare. This is what he is best at and he arms himself for it with pleasure even though he must know that he is not likely to win this time. There is a certain heroic splendour about his display, but essentially he shows himself to be a victim of *furor*, a man concerned only with his own reputation and unable and unwilling to control his violent passions. Heinze (p. 211f.) compares Aeneas' *vis temperata* with Turnus' *vis consili expers* (Hor. *Odes* 3.4.65-6), and quotes Cicero (*De Off.* 1.62) *sed ea animi elatio, quae cernitur in periculis et laboribus, si iustitia vacat, pugnatque non pro salute communi sed pro suis commodis, in vitio est; non modo enim id virtutis non est, sed est potius immanitatis omnem humanitatem repellentis.*

2 1. **infractos ad verso Marte:** 'broken by defeat on the battlefield', as described in 11.868f. after the death of Camilla. For *infractus* cf. 387 and 9.499.

3 2. **sua nunc promissa reposci:** he had promised to meet Aeneas in single combat to decide the war (11.434f.); this pledge now has to be redeemed.

4 3. **se signari oculis:** 'that he was the target of everyone's gaze'. Observe how *se* emphatically repeats *sua;* it is Turnus himself and no other now.

5 **ultro:** i.e. he reacted before any words were spoken. The description of Turnus which follows conveys a most powerful picture of his impetuosity and eagerness for battle (*ardet, attollitque animos, gaudet, impavidus, accenso, gliscit violentia, turbidus*).

6 4. **Poenorum:** Virgil gives a geographical localisation to the simile, cf. 67, 715 and 10.708f.

7 4f. The simile of the wounded lion is reminiscent of Hom. *Il.* 5.134f., 20.164f., but Virgil has greatly developed and enlarged the imagery, relating it closely to the mood of the narrative (see previous note). Turnus is compared with a lion in 9.792f., 10.454f; cf. also 9.339f. (Euryalus), 10.723f. (Mezentius). See note on 8, and Pöschl, pp. 109f.

8 5. **ille:** 'the' lion rather than 'a' lion, cf. 10.707, 11.809; the effect is emphasised by the long postponement of the subject *leo*.

9 **pectus:** accusative of respect, cf. 25, 224, 276, 386, 652, and see note on 7.60.

10 6. **tum demum:** i.e. not until he was wounded.

11 **movet arma:** 'goes into battle', a frequent military phrase applied to humans (Livy 7.29.1), here personifying the' lion, as Servius saw, quoting *Geo.* 3.236 (of a bull) *signa movet.*

12 6-7. **gaudetque . . . toros:** 'and rejoices as he tosses his rippling mane (literally "his hairy muscles") on his neck', cf. Cat. 63.83 (Cybele speaking to one of her lions) *rutilam ferox torosa cervice quate iubam.*

excutiens cervice toros fixumque latronis[1]
impavidus frangit telum et fremit[2] ore cruento:
haud secus accenso gliscit[3] violentia[4] Turno.
Tum sic adfatur regem atque ita turbidus infit: 10
'nulla mora in Turno; nihil est quod dicta retractent[5]
ignavi Aeneadae, nec quae pepigere recusent.
Congredior. Fer sacra, pater,[6] et concipe[7] foedus.
Aut hac Dardanium[8] dextra sub Tartara mittam,
desertorem[9] Asiae (sedeant spectentque Latini),   15
et solus ferro crimen[10] commune refellam,
aut habeat victos, cedat Lavinia[11] coniunx.'
    Olli[12] sedato respondit corde Latinus:
'o praestans animi[13] iuvenis, quantum ipse feroci
virtute exsuperas,[14] tanto me impensius aequum est   20
consulere atque omnis metuentem[15] expendere casus.
Sunt tibi regna patris Dauni,[16] sunt oppida capta[17]
multa manu, nec non aurumque[18] animusque Latino est;
sunt aliae innuptae Latio[19] et Laurentibus agris,

1 7. **latronis:** 'the huntsman', an unusual sense of the word, which normally means 'brigand'.

2 8. **fremit ore cruento:** also of a lion in 9.341, and of imprisoned *Furor* in 1.296; the lion-like Turnus represents the violent forces which must be conquered before Rome's era of ultimate peace can be achieved.

3 9. **gliscit:** 'began to burn'; Servius glosses with crescit latenter. The word is a favourite with Tacitus, e.g. *gliscit saevitia (Ann.* 6.19).

4 **violentia:** the word is used only of Turnus in the *Aeneid,* cf. line 45 and 11.376. See note on 3.

5 11. **retractent:** 'withdraw', a reference to Aeneas' words in 11.116f.

6 13. **pater:** the last syllable is lengthened in arsis, cf. 11.469 and 68, 422, 550, 648, 668, 772, 883.

7 **concipe:** 'draw up', cf. 158. Servius tells us that concepta verba was a formula in taking oaths.

8 14. **Dardanium:** 'the Trojan', contemptuous.

9 15. **desertorem Asiae:** a reference to the legend that Aeneas had acted in a cowardly fashion in leaving Troy, cf. Aeneas' denials of this in 2.431f.

10 16. **crimen commune refellam:** 'I will refute the charge brought against all of us', i.e. the charge of fear and cowardice (line 2 *defecisse*).

11 17. **Lavinia:** the princess whom Turnus hoped to marry before Latinus, in deference to the oracle, gave her hand to Aeneas; cf. 64f.

12 18. The archaic *olli (= illi)* and the spondaic movement suggest the calm dignity of Latinus.

13 19. **animi:** 'in courage', genitive of respect, cf. 11.417.

14 20. **exsuperas:** 'stand out', intransitive as in 46.

15 21. **metuentem expendere:** 'anxiously to weigh up'; *expendere* picks up *impensius* in the previous line, emphasising Latinus' anxiety to consider all possibilities before giving his answer.

16 22. **Dauni:** Turnus' father (10.616, 688) who lived in Ardea, cf. 44, 90.

17 22f. Latinus suggests to Turnus that if he withdraws his claim to Lavinia and the succession he still has much power left and could be given more.

18 23. **aurumque animusque:** 'both gold and willingness to give it'.

19 24. **Latio et Laurentibus agris:** the second phrase means the same as the first; for the Laurentes, a name of the inhabitants of Latium, cf. 137, 240, 280.

nec genus[1] indecores. Sine me haec[2] haud[3] mollia fatu   25
sublatis aperire dolis, simul hoc[4] animo hauri:
me natam nulli veterum sociare procorum[5]
fas erat, idque omnes divique hominesque canebant.
Victus amore[6] tui, cognato[7] sanguine victus
coniugis et maestae lacrimis, vincla[8] omnia rupi: 30
promissam eripui genero,[9] arma impia[10] sumpsi.
Ex illo[11] qui me casus, quae, Turne, sequantur
bella, vides, quantos primus patiare labores.
bis[12] magna victi pugna vix urbe[13] tuemur
spes Italas; recalent[14] nostro Thybrina[15] fluenta   35
sanguine adhuc campique ingentes ossibus albent.
Quo[16] referor totiens? Quae mentem insania mutat?
Si Turno exstincto socios sum ascire paratus,[17]
cur non incolumi potius certamina tollo?
Quid consanguinei Rutuli, quid cetera dicet   40
Italia, ad mortem si te (fors dicta refutet!)
prodiderim, natam[18] et conubia nostra petentem?
Respice res bello varias, miserere parentis

---

1 25. **genus:** accusative of respect (cf. 5); compare 8.114 *qui genus?*

2 **haec:** this must refer to what he has already said; he apologises for having had to speak frankly (*sublatis . . . dolis*). *Simul hoc* refers to what follows.

3 **haud mollia fatu:** 'not easy to say'; *fatu* is the ablative (of respect) of the supine, as in *mirabile dictu.*

4 26. **hoc animo hauri:** the rhythm of the line-ending is very unusual, with the elision before the sixth foot and the conflict of ictus and the accent in the fifth; see note on 10.508 *haec eadem aufert.*

5 27-8. Latinus refers to the oracle that he must marry his daughter to a foreigner (7.96f.); the prophecy came from Faunus and was then reported by Rumour all through Latium (7.102f.). *Homines* (as Page says) means soothsayers and the like.

6 29. **amore tui:** 'my love for you', objective genitive of the pronoun *tu,* cf. 659 and 9.291 *hanc sine me spem ferre tui.*

7 29-30. **cognato . . . lacrimis:** 'prevailed upon by your being a kinsman and by the tears of my sorrowing wife'; Turnus' mother Venilia was the sister of Queen Amata, who strongly supported Turnus.

8 30. **vincla omnia rupi:** 'I broke all my obligations'.

9 31. **genero:** i.e. Aeneas, son-in-law to be (cf. 55). Notice the hiatus at the caesura, cf. 535, 648, 10.141.

10 **impia:** because against the wishes of the gods, with some undertone of his fighting against *pius Aeneas.*

11 32-33. 'Since that time you see, Turnus, what disasters and wars dog me, what toils you yourself first and foremost are suffering'.

12 34. **bis:** first when Mezentius was killed (10.833f.) and then after Camilla's death (11.868f.). The spondaic movement and the clash of accent and ictus emphasise the grim situation.

13 **urbe:** 'in the capital', where they are now besieged.

14 35. **recalent:** a rare verb, meaning 'grow warm again and again'.

15 **Thybrina:** the Greek form of *Tiberina* (cf. the noun *Thybris,* e.g. 11.393, Virgil's preferred form for *Tiberis*).

16 37. 'Why do I keep retreating from my decision? What madness alters my purpose?' *Quo* is literally 'to what end'; the second phrase is repeated from 4.595.

17 38f. The logic of this would not be accepted by Turnus, as it ignores the possibility of his victory. *Socios* is predicative, the object *Troianos* being understood.

18 42. **natam et conubia nostra:** a good example of hendiadys: 'marriage to my daughter'.

longaevi, quem nunc maestum patria[1] Ardea longe
dividit.' Haudquaquam dictis violentia[2] Turni   45
flectitur; exsuperat[3] magis aegrescitque medendo.
Ut primum fari potuit, sic institit[4] ore:
'quam[5] pro me curam geris, hanc precor, optime, pro me
deponas letumque[6] sinas pro laude pacisci.
Et[7] nos tela, pater, ferrumque haud debile dextra   50
spargimus, et nostro sequitur de vulnere sanguis.
Longe[8] illi dea mater erit, quae nube fugacem
feminea[9] tegat et[10] vanis sese occulat umbris.'
   At regina[11] nova[12] pugnae conterrita sorte
flebat et ardentem generum moritura[13] tenebat: 55
'Turne, per[14] has ego te lacrimas. Per[15] si quis Amatae
tangit honos animum (spes tu nunc una, senectae
tu requies miserae, decus imperiumque Latini
te penes, in te omnis domus inclinata recumbit),
unum oro: desiste manum committere Teucris.   60
Qui te cumque manent isto certamine casus
et me, Turne, manent; simul haec invisa relinquam
lumina nec generum Aenean captiva videbo.'

---

1 44. **patria Ardea:** Daunus' home, cf. 22; compare Turnus' final plea (934) *Dauni miserere senectae*.

2 45. **violentia Turni:** cf. line 9. The emotional reaction of Turnus is emphasised by the dactyls of 46, his speechlessness in 47, and the extraordinary rhythm of his first words (48), with no less than ten words in the line and the highly rhetorical repetition of *pro me*.

3 46. **exsuperat:** the subject is *violentia*, his violence rises up all the more; cf. line 20, and 2.759.

4 47. **institit:** 'breaks into speech', cf. 4.533.

5 48. 'The anxiety you have on my behalf, I beg you, your highness, put it away on my behalf; see note on 45.

6 49. **letumque . . . pacisci:** 'let me bargain death for glory', cf. 5.230.

7 50. **et nos:** as well as Aeneas; cf. Hector in Hom. *Il.* 20.437 (to Achilles) 'my spear too is sharp'.

8 52. **longe . . . erit:** = *longe aberit*, cf. Ov. *Her.* 12.53-4, Caes. *B.C.* 1.36.5. The reference is to the rescue of Aeneas by his mother in Hom. *Il.* 5.311f., and subsequently by Apollo in a cloud, *Il.* 5.344f. Compare *Aen.* 10.82.

9 53. **feminea:** 'contrived by a woman', contemptuously said.

10 **et vanis . . . umbris:** 'and conceal herself in unreal shadows', while achieving the protection of Aeneas (cf. line 416). For *vanae umbrae* cf. 10.593. The coordination *tegat et occulat* is typically Virgilian for *tegat occulendo* (cf. 2.353 *moriamur et in media arma ruamus*).

11 54. **regina:** King Latinus' wife, Amata, who wanted Turnus to be her son-in-law (*generum*, 55).

12 **nova . . . sorte:** 'new turn', i.e. the proposal for single combat.

13 55. **moritura:** 'determined to die', if Turnus died (62f.); cf. 11.741.

14 56. **per has ego te lacrimas:** this is the normal idiomatic Latin word order in oaths, cf. 4.314.

15 56-7. **per si quis . . . animum:** 'by any regard for Amata which you have in your heart'; the noun for *per* is taken into the conditional clause; *per honorem tuum Amatae, si quis honos tangit animum*, cf. 2.142. Notice the emotional use of her own name, cf. 11 and see Austin on *Aen.* 1.48.

Accepit vocem lacrimis[1] Lavinia[2] matris
flagrantis[3] perfusa genas, cui plurimus ignem   65
subiecit rubor et calefacta per ora cucurrit.
Indum[4] sanguineo veluti violaverit ostro
si quis ebur,[5] aut mixta rubent ubi lilia multa
alba rosa, talis virgo dabat ore colores.
Illum[6] turbat amor figitque in virgine vultus.   70
Ardet in arma magis paucisque adfatur Amatam:[7]
'ne, quaeso, ne me lacrimis neve[8] omine tanto[9]
prosequere in duri certamina Martis euntem,
o mater;[10] neque[11] enim Turno mora libera mortis.
Nuntius haec, Idmon,[12] Phrygio[13] mea dicta tyranno   75
haud placitura refer: Cum primum crastina caelo[14]
puniceis invecta rotis Aurora rubebit,
non[15] Teucros agat in Rutulos; Teucrum arma quiescant

---

1 64-5. **lacrimis . . . flagrantis perfusa genas**: 'her burning cheeks bathed in tears', retained accusative after a passive verb; cf. 120, 172, 416, 468, 599, 605, 606, and see note on 7.503 and Maguinness' note on this passage.

2 64. **Lavinia**: the daughter of Amata and Latinus is not strongly characterised by Virgil; she never speaks and is merely a part of the plot; see note on 7.52f.

3 65-6. 'a deep blush revealed its fires, and suffused her hot face'; the passage is recalled by Statius (*Silv.* 1.2.244f.).

4 67-9. 'As it is when someone stains Indian ivory with blood-red dye, or when many white lilies shine red with the roses among them; such were the colours the maiden showed in her cheeks'. The simile is based on Hom. *Il.* 4.141f., where the blood from Menelaus' wound on his skin is compared with the staining of ivory with red dye; Virgil has applied this image to a quite different situation. Spenser imitates the first part of the simile in *F.Q.*. 2.9.41
'And ever and anone with rosie red
The bashfull bloud her snowy cheeks did dye,
That her became, as polisht yvory,
Which cunning craftsmans hand hath overlaid
With faire vermilion or pure castory'.
and the second part in *F.Q.* 2.3.22 'and in her cheeks the vermeill red did shew / like roses in a bed of lilies shed' (cf. *F.Q.* 5.3.23).

5 68. **ebur**: the final syllable is lengthened in arsis, cf. 13.

6 70. **illum**: notice how Turnus' reaction is emphasised by the single word filling the first spondaic foot; cf. 661, 674, 788, 819, 859, 927.

7 71. The impetuosity of Turnus is underlined by the assonance of initial *a* (picking up the alliteration of *v* at the end of 70).

8 72. **neve omine tanto**: defining *lacrimis,* a bad omen, cf. Ap. Rh. 1.303f., Sil. 3.133.

9 72f. The speech of Turnus is reminiscent of Hector's to Andromache in Hom. *Il.* 6.486f.

10 74. **mater**: Turnus calls her by the title he hopes for (cf. *generum,* 55).

11 **neque enim Turno . . . mortis**: 'for Turnus is not free to delay his death', i.e. he has obligations which as chief warrior of his people he must always meet; he cannot avoid them just because risk of death is involved. This is more likely in the context of Turnus' present mood than Servius' alternative explanation (supported by Hom. *Il.* 6.487f.) that when his hour has come he cannot avoid it, whether he goes to war or not. Notice the emotional use of his own name (cf. 56).

12 75. **Idmon**: a Rutulian not mentioned elsewhere.

13 **Phrygio**: used contemptuously, cf. 99 and 11.484.

14 76-7. Turnus uses serene and beautiful phrases for dawn to hold the suspense until his announcement of his message. For the chariot of Aurora cf. 7.26.

15 78. **non Teucros**: *non* is used rather than *ne* to emphasise that it is not the Trojans but Aeneas himself alone who is to come forward to battle.

et Rutuli; nostro dirimamus[1] sanguine bellum;
illo quaeratur coniunx Lavinia campo.'[2]   80
  Haec ubi dicta dedit rapidusque in tecta recessit,
poscit equos gaudetque[3] tuens ante ora frementis,
Pilumno[4] quos ipsa decus[5] dedit Orithyia,[6]
qui candore nives anteirent,[7] cursibus auras.
Circumstant properi aurigae manibusque[8] lacessunt 85
pectora plausa cavis et colla comantia pectunt.
Ipse dehinc[9] auro squalentem[10] alboque orichalco[11]
circumdat loricam umeris, simul aptat habendo[12]
ensemque[13] clipeumque et rubrae cornua[14] cristae,
ensern quem Dauno ignipotens[15] deus ipse parenti 90
fecerat et Stygia[16] candentem tinxerat unda.
exim quae[17] mediis ingenti adnixa columnae
aedibus astabat, validam vi corripit hastam,
Actoris[18] Aurunci spolium, quassatque[19] trementem

---

1 79. **dirimamus**: 'end', cf. 5.467, Livy 27.30.4.

2 80. Observe how the slow spondaic movement gives finality to his statement.

3 82. **gaudetque**: the joy of Turnus in his preparations for war is presented with great power in this section; it contrasts very sharply with the brief preparations of the peace loving Aeneas (107f.). It should be noted that these long preparations are in one sense inappropriate, as the duel cannot take place till the next day; but in another more important sense they are vital to the portrayal of the mood of Turnus in his time of crisis.

4 83. **Pilumno**: Turnus' grandfather (or great-grandfather), a Roman agricultural deity, cf. 9.4.

5 **decus**: 'to honour him', in apposition with *quos;* cf. 11.657.

6 **Orithyia**: wife of the North Wind, Boreas; cf. *Geo.* 4.463, and Hom. *Il.* 16.150f., 20.223f. for speedy horses associated with gods of the winds. The fifth foot is spondaic (*-yi-* is a Greek diphthong), as is not infrequent with Greek words, cf. 9.196; see also note on 863.

7 84. **anteirent**: 'could surpass' (if the comparison were made), present potential. The *e* of *ante* is slurred in pronunciation by synizesis, cf. 847 and see note on 7.33. For the image cf. Hom. *Il.* 10.437.

8 85-6. **manibusque . . . cavis**: 'slap their chests with their cupped hands and make them resound'; cf. *Geo.* 3.186 for the horse's pleasure in being thus patted. The use of the verb *lacessunt* (literally 'arouse') with *pectora* (chest or heart) probably introduces an overtone of arousing the spirits of the horses; see Quinn, P. 397. The alliteration of *p* and *c* in line 86 is very marked.

9 87. **dehinc**: scanned sometimes as an iambus (as here, cf. 8.337), sometimes as a single syllable (9.480).

10 **squalentem**: for the 'scales' on a coat of mail cf. 10.314.

11 **orichalco**: a Greek word (hence the Greek rhythm of a polysyllabic ending), originally meaning an undefined brilliant metal, and later coming to mean 'bronze', cf. Hor. *A.P.* 202; *albus* suggests that it is lighter in colour than gold.

12 88. **habendo**: 'for use', dative of the gerund; cf. *habilis* in 432.

13 89. **ensemque clipeumque**: the first *-que* of the double *-que . . . que* ('both . . . and') is lengthened in arsis in imitation of the Homeric τε … τε; cf. 181, 363, 443, and see note on 8.425.

14 **cornua**: the two sockets of the crest on the helmet, cf. Livy 27.33.2.

15 90. **ignipotens deus**: i.e. Vulcan, cf. 8.628.

16 91. **Stygia . . . unda**: for the 'dipping' of the metal cf. 8.450; to dip it in the Styx would add a special supernatural quality.

17 92-3. **quae ... corripit hastam**: the relative clause precedes its antecedent *hastam.*

18 94. Actor is not heard of elsewhere; the Aurunci were from Campania (7.206).

19 94. **quassatque trementem**: 'brandished the quivering spear'; cf. 11.645.

vociferans: 'nunc, o numquam frustrata vocatus[1]   95

hasta meos, nunc tempus adest: te[2] maximus Actor,

te Turni nunc dextra gerit; da[3] sternere corpus

loricamque [4]manu valida lacerare revulsam

semiviri Phrygis et foedare in pulvere crinis

vibratos[5] calido ferro murraque madentis.'   100

His[6] agitur furiis, totoque ardentis ab ore

scintillae absistunt, oculis micat acribus ignis,

mugitus veluti cum prima in proelia taurus[7]

terrificos ciet atque irasci in cornua temptat

arboris obnixus trunco, ventosque lacessit   105

ictibus aut sparsa ad pugnam proludit harena.

107-12. Aeneas also prepares for the coming single combat.

[8]Nec minus interea maternis[9] saevus in armis

Aeneas acuit[10] Martem et se suscitat ira,

oblato[11] gaudens componi foedere bellum.

Tum socios maestique metum solatus Iuli   110

fata[12] docens, regique iubet responsa Latino

certa referre viros et pacis dicere leges.

---

1 95. **vocatus**: 'my appeal', a rare fourth declension noun; the 'dialogue' between Turnus and his spear adds to the gusto of the scene.

2 96. **te maximus Actor**: understand *quondam gerebat*.

3 97. **da sternere**: for the infinitive cf. 211 and 9.173.

4 98-9. 'and to tear off and rend in pieces with the strength of my right hand the breastplate of the effeminate Phrygian'; for *semivir* cf. 4.215 (Iarbas' words about Aeneas as a second Paris).

5 100. **vibratos . . . ferro**: 'crimped with hot curling irons', highly sarcastic, cf. again Iarbas' taunts (4.216) and Cic. *Sest.* 18.

6 101f. This describes the heroic impulse, the angry reaction of the proud warrior to any challenge to his honour. For the vivid metaphor of his eyes sparkling with excitement and rage cf. Plaut. *Men.* 830 *ut oculi scintillant vide,* and Lucr. 3.289 *ex oculis micat acribus ardor;* Virgil's phrase however ('the sparks fly off') is much bolder than either.

7 103f. 'Just as when a bull gives terrifying bellows as he goes into the beginning of a battle, and tries to vent his rage on his horns as he crashes against the trunk of a tree, and challenges the breezes with his charges or plays a prelude to the fight as he paws the flying sand'. For the simile of a bull cf. 715f.; for the description of the bull cf. the very similar lines in *Geo.* 3.232-4; for *irasci in cornua* cf. Eur. *Bacch.* 743 (of bulls) εισ κερας θυμουμενοι.

8 107f. The brief mention of Aeneas' preparations contrasts very markedly with the long account of Turnus' rehearsal for battle; Aeneas is calm, in control and ready to face what must be faced.

9 107. **maternis ... in armis**: 'in the armour given by his mother'; the making of Aeneas' armour by Vulcan at the instigation of his mother Venus (cf. 167) is described in 8.370f., cf. 8.608f.

10 108. **acuit Martem**: 'sharpened his warlike spirit'; cf. 590.

11 109. **oblato**: 'offered' by Turnus, referring to the agreement for single combat which has evidently been conveyed to him (cf. *responsa,* 111).

12 111. **fata docens:** Warde Fowler well comments: 'If this divine assurance seems to any reader to detract from the interest or from the heroism of Aeneas, let him spend an hour or two in reading the Book of Joshua. We do not usually complain of the divine assurance of that great leader of an invading army in a strange land'.

VIRGIL

113-215. *The troops on both sides take up their positions to watch the single combat. Juno tells Juturna that she herself can do no more; if Juturna can do anything, then she has authority from Juno to act. The two parties proceed to the battle area, and oaths are sworn, first by Aeneas, and then by Latinus on behalf of Turnus.*

[1]Postera vix summos spargebat lumine montis
orta dies, cum[2] primum alto se gurgite tollunt
Solis equi lucemque elatis[3] naribus effiant: 115
campum ad certamen magnae sub moenibus urbis
dimensi [4]Rutulique viri Teucrique parabant
in medioque focos et dis communibus aras[5]
gramineas. Alii fontemque[6] ignemque ferebant
velati limo[7] et verbena[8] tempora[9] vincti.   120
Procedit legio Ausonidum,[10] pilataque[11] plenis
agmina se fundunt portis. Hinc Troius[12] omnis
Tyrrhenusque ruit variis exercitus armis,
haud secus instructi ferro quam si aspera Martis
pugna vocet. Nec non mediis in milibus ipsi[13]   125
ductores auro volitant ostroque superbi,

---

1 113f. The brief scene in Olympus, in which Juno tells Juturna that she has done all she can for Turnus and must now withdraw, casts its shadow over the events which follow; the inevitability of Turnus' defeat is presented against an increasingly stark background. The oaths sworn by Aeneas and Latinus serve to accentuate this; both are moderate and conciliatory in their attitudes, speaking in quite a different way from Turnus' normal mode of speech. Aeneas' promises in the case of victory are reasonable in the highest degree (note on 189-91), while Latinus for his part also looks forward to peace and reconciliation. The isolation of Turnus, the tragic impasse into which he has forced himself, becomes ever more clear.

2 114-15. **cum primum ... equi:** 'at the time when the Sun's horses first rise up from the deep flood', i.e. from the Ocean, cf. 11.1.

3 115. **elatis naribus:** 'from their upturned nostrils', an extraordinarily vivid image taken from Enn. *Ann.* 600 *funduntque elatis naribus lucem:* cf. also Pind. *Ol.* 7.70-1. Henry quotes Marlowe (*Tamb.* 2.4.3):
'The horses that guide the golden eye of heaven,
And blow the morning from their nosterils'.

4 117. 'the Rutulians and Trojans were measuring and preparing . . .'; for the doubled *-que* ('both . .. and') cf. 119; the conglomeration of words ending in *-i* is not in accordance with Virgil's usual practice.

5 118-19. The accusatives are governed by *parabant; communibus* means 'worshipped by both sides'; cf. the oaths of Aeneas and Latinus (176f., 197f.).

6 119. **fontemque:** = *aquam,* very much in poetic style, cf. 417.

7 120. **limo:** Servius tells us that this word, meaning a kind of cloak (cf. Aul. Gell. 12.3), was attested by Hyginus and Caper; the MSS all have *lino* ('linen').

8 **verbena:** 'sacred foliage'; the word has a general meaning, though Servius tells us that it can also specifically mean 'rosemary'.

9 **tempora vincti:** retained accusative with a passive verb, see note on 64-5.

10 121. **Ausonidum:** archaic for *Ausonidarum,* cf. 11.297; *Ausonii* and *Ausonidae* are commonly used for the Italians.

11 121-2. **pilataque ... portis:** 'the troops closely massed pour forth from the packed gates'; *pilata* is a rare and archaic word which Servius explains as 'dense', quoting *inter alia* Ennius (*Sat.* 3-4) *contemplor inde loci liquidas pilatasque aetheris oras.* It is also possible that it means 'carrying their javelins', cf. Mart. 10.48.2.

12 122-3. **Troius ... Tyrrhenusque:** i.e. Aeneas' Trojans with their Etruscan allies under Tarchon.

13 125-6. Compare the description of the splendid appearance of the sea captains in 5.132-3.

542

et[1] genus Assaraci Mnestheus et fortis Asilas[2]
et Messapus equum domitor, Neptunia proles;[3]
utque dato signo spatia in sua quisque recessit,
defigunt tellure hastas et scuta reclinant.   130
Tum studio[4] effusae matres et vulgus inermum[5]
invalidique senes turris ac tecta domorum
obsedere, alii portis sublimibus astant.
    At Iuno e summo, qui nunc Albanus habetur[6]
(tum neque nomen erat neque honos aut gloria monti),[7]   135
prospiciens tumulo campum aspectabat et ambas
Laurentum[8] Troumque acies urbemque Latini.
Extemplo Turni[9] sic est adfata sororem
diva deam, stagnis quae fluminibusque sonoris
praesidet (hunc illi rex aetheris altus honorem   140
Iuppiter erepta pro virginitate sacravit):
'nympha, decus fluviorum, animo gratissima nostro,
scis ut te cunctis unam, quaecumque Latinae[10]
magnanimi Iovis ingratum ascendere cubile,[11]
praetulerim caelique libens in parte locarim:[12]   145
disce tuum, ne me incuses, Iuturna, dolorem.
Qua[13] visa est Fortuna pati Parcaeque sinebant
cedere[14] res Latio, Turnum et tua moenia texi:

---

1 127. **et ... Mnestheus et:** 'both Mnestheus, descendant of Assaracus and . . .'. Mnestheus is frequently mentioned in the *Aeneid*, and was one of the captains in the boat race (5.116f.); Assaracus was a Trojan ancestor, cf. 9.259.

2 **Asilas:** an Etruscan, cf. line 550 and 11.620.

3 128. This line about Messapus, a prominent Italian leader, is repeated from 7.691 (where see note) and 9.523.

4 131. **studio:** 'eagerly', cf. 5.450.

5 **inermum:** second declension (the third declension form *inermis* is more usual); cf. 10.425.

6 134. The Alban Mount (site of Alba Longa) was to the southeast of the site of Rome; in later times its *honos* and *gloria* was reflected in the great temple to Jupiter built upon it and the festival (*feriae Latinae*) celebrated there.

7 135. Compare 6.776 *haec tum nomina erunt, nunc sunt sine nomine terrae.*

8 137. **Laurentum:** the Italians, cf. 24.

9 138. **Turni . . . sororem:** this is the first mention of Juturna (146) the sister of Turnus ravished by Jupiter (Ov. *Fast.* 2.583f.) and made a river nymph and granted immortality as a reward (878f.). There was a lake called Juturna formed by a stream flowing from the Alban mount, and a temple to her in Rome (Ov. *Fast.* 1.463f.) and a festival in her honour.

10 143. **Latinae:** the antecedent is placed in the relative clause (*cunctis Latinis quaecumque . . .*). Servius drily says 'quae sint Latinae cum quibus Iuppiter concubuerit incertum est'.

11 144. The line has no caesura in third or fourth foot, other than the semblance of one made by the elided syllable of *ingratum*. *Magnanimi* is a standing epithet of Jupiter, here used with irony; *ingratum* ('ungrateful') means that Jupiter's gifts for favours received were not real, as Juturna herself complains (878f.).

12 145. Juno means that she did not oppose Jupiter's offer of immortality to Juturna.

13 147. **qua:** 'in whatever way', i.e. to the permitted extent.

14 148. **cedere:** in the context equivalent to *succedere*, 'feliciter procedere' (Servius), cf. Ov. *Met.* 8.862 *bene cedere.*

nunc iuvenem imparibus video concurrere fatis,

Parcarumque[1] dies et vis inimica propinquat.   150

Non pugnam aspicere hanc oculis, non foedera possum.[2]

Tu pro germano si quid praesentius[3] audes,

perge; decet. Forsan miseros meliora sequentur.'

Vix ea, cum lacrimas oculis Iuturna profudit

terque quaterque manu pectus percussit honestum.[4]   155

'Non lacrimis hoc tempus' ait Saturnia[5] Iuno;

'accelera et fratrem, si quis modus, eripe morti;[6]

aut[7] tu bella cie conceptumque[8] excute foedus.

Auctor[9] ego audendi.' Sic exhortata reliquit

incertam et tristi[10] turbatam vulnere mentis.   160

    Interea[11] reges, ingenti[12] mole Latinus

quadriiugo vehitur curru (cui[13] tempora circum

aurati bis sex radii fulgentia cingunt,

Solis avi specimen), bigis[14] it Turnus in albis,

bina manu lato crispans hastilia ferro.[15]   165

Hinc pater Aeneas, Romanae stirpis origo,[16]

---

1 150. **Parcarumque dies:** 'the (last) day which the Fates have decreed'.

2 151. Servius comments that the gods withdraw when their proteges are destined to die; cf. Hom. *Il.* 22.213, where Apollo leaves Hector.

3 152. **praesentius:** 'more immediate', 'more effective', cf. 245.

4 155. The line is nearly the same as that used of Dido (4.589 *terque quaterque manu pectus percussa decorum*); for *honestum* ('beautiful') cf. 10.133.

5 156. **Saturnia:** a frequent epithet (cf. 178, 807) of Juno, daughter of Saturnus.

6 157. **morti:** dative, cf. 31, 948 and 2.134.

7 158. **aut tu:** for the use of the pronoun in the second of two alternatives cf. 6.367 and Hor. *Odes* 1.9.15-16.

8 **conceptumque excute foedus:** 'destroy the agreed treaty', cf. line 13.

9 159. **auctor:** i .e. Juno takes the responsibility.

10 160. **tristi . . . mentis:** 'distraught at the cruel wound to her heart'; this metaphorical use of *vulnus* is quite common, cf. 1.36 (of Juno) *aeternum servans sub pectore vulnus*.

11 161. **Interea reges:** this sentence is clearly unrevised; as it stands the construction of *Latinus* and *Turnus* in apposition to *reges* is not in Virgil's style, and probably extra phrases would have been added after *reges*.

12 **ingenti mole:** 'with a huge retinue' (as Servius says, glossing with *pompa, ambitu*) rather than ablative of description with *curru* ('a chariot of huge size', cf. 5.223) or with *Latinus* ('of mighty stature').

13 162-4. **cui . . . specimen:** 'whose shining temples twelve golden rays encircle, the emblem of his ancestor the Sun'; *circum* is adverbial; for *specimen* (visual proof) cf. *Geo.* 2.241. The reference is to the version of the legend according to which Latinus was son (or grandson) of Circe, daughter of the Sun (Hes. *Theog.* 1011f.); see note on 7.47f., where Virgil follows a different version. For the emblem cf. Suet. *Aug.* 94.6 where he says that Augustus' father dreamed that his son appeared to him with the thunderbolt and insignia of Jupiter, wearing a *radiata corona*.

14 164. **bigis . . . albis:** 'a chariot drawn by two white horses', cf. 7.26.

15 165. The same line occurs in 1.313; *crispans* means 'grasping'.

16 166. The line is made impressive by the long syllables after the first foot, and the direct association at this moment of Aeneas (and Ascanius in 168) with the origins of Rome.

sidereo flagrans clipeo et caelestibus armis[1]
et iuxta Ascanius, magnae spes altera Romae,
procedunt castris, puraque in veste sacerdos
saetigeri [2]fetum suis intonsamque bidentem   170
attulit admovitque pecus flagrantibus aris.
Illi ad surgentem conversi[3] lumina solem
dant fruges manibus salsas et tempora ferro
summa notant[4] pecudum, paterisque altaria libant.[5]

    Tum pius[6] Aeneas stricto sic ense precatur: 175
'esto nunc Sol testis et haec[7] mihi terra vocanti,
quam propter tantos potui perferre labores,
et pater omnipotens et tu Saturnia coniunx,
iam[8] melior, iam, diva, precor; tuque inclute Mavors,[9]
cuncta tuo qui bella, pater, sub numine torques;   180
fontisque[10] fluviosque voco, [11]quaeque aetheris alti
religio[12] et quae caeruleo sunt numina ponto:
cesserit[13] Ausonio si fors victoria Turno,
convenit[14] Euandri victos discedere ad urbem,

---

1 167. Compare the radiant appearance of Aeneas in 10.270f., and of Augustus in 8.680f. For the shield made for Aeneas at Venus' instigation cf. 107.

2 170. 'the offspring of a bristling boar, and an un-dipped sheep'; they are first brought (*attulit*), then taken to the altar (*admovitque*). The sacrifice of a pig was normal in Roman treaties (cf. 8.641); Servius says that the sheep (for *bidens* see note on 7.93) is taken from Greek ceremonial.

3 172. **conversi lumina**: retained accusative, see note on 64-5.

4 174. **notant**: i.e. by cutting off some hair, cf. 6.245.

5 **libant**: 'sprinkle', an unusual use which Servius explains by saying that *altaria* is equivalent to 'offerings paid at an altar', cf. 4.207. Normal usage would be *in altaria*.

6 175. **pius**: Aeneas' adjective is here used with full emphasis; the single combat against Turnus is the final act required of him by his duty to his divine mission and his human followers; see note on 7.5.

7 176. **haec . . . terra**: specifically the land of Italy, as is shown by the next line (cf. 7.136-7), though there is also some of the impact of the Homeric passage (*Il.* 3.276f.) where Agamemnon invokes Zeus, the Sun, the Rivers and the Earth. Cf. also *Il.* 19.258f.

8 179. **iam melior**: Juno is not yet reconciled, but is soon to be (818f.).

9 **Mavors**: the archaic form of *Mars* (cf. 332), especially appropriate in an oath.

10 181. **fontisque fluviosque**: so Agamemnon (*Il.* 3.276f.) had invoked the rivers; it is especially appropriate for Aeneas to appeal to the local deities (cf. 7.137-8). The first *-que* is lengthened in arsis; see note on 89.

11 181-2. 'and the sanctity of the high heavens and the divinities in the blue sea'; *religio* and *numina* are the objects of *voco* taken into their relative clauses. The first phrase refers (as Page says) to 'the great elemental powers of the sky' (rather than the Olympian gods specifically), balancing the reference to those of the sea; compare Latinus' invocation of *sidera* (197).

12 182. **religio**: the first syllable is scanned long, as in *reliquiae;* cf. 7.172, 244.

13 183. 'if perchance victory falls to Ausonian Turnus'; for *cedere* cf. 3.333, for *fors* adverbially used cf. 11.50.

14 184. 'it is agreed that we the defeated depart to Evander's city', i.e. Pallanteum where Aeneas had been hospitably received when he went there for help (8.154f.).

cedet[1] Iulus agris, nec[2] post arma ulla rebelles   185
Aeneadae referent ferrove haec regna lacessent.
Sin nostrum adnuerit[3] nobis Victoria Martem
(ut potius reor et potius di numine firment),
non[4] ego nec Teucris Italos parere iubebo[5]
nec mihi regna peto: paribus se legibus ambae   190
invictae gentes aeterna in foedera mittant.
Sacra[6] deosque dabo; socer[7] arma Latinus habeto,
imperium sollemne socer; mihi moenia Teucri
constituent urbique dabit[8] Lavinia nomen.'

    Sic prior Aeneas, sequitur sic deinde Latinus   195
suspiciens caelum, tenditque ad sidera dextram:
'haec[9] eadem, Aenea, terram, mare, sidera, iuro
Latonaeque[10] genus duplex Ianumque[11] bifrontem,
vimque deum infernam et duri[12] sacraria Ditis;
audiat haec genitor qui foedera[13] fulmine sancit.   200
Tango aras, medios[14] ignis et numina testor:
nulla dies pacem hanc Italis nec foedera rumpet,
quo res cumque cadent; nec me vis ulla volentem

---

1 185. **cedet Iulus**: for this use of *cedere* ('withdraw from') cf. 9.805. Iulus is mentioned here because in the case of defeat Aeneas will have been killed.

2 185-6. **nec . . . referent**: 'nor after that will the people of Aeneas rebel and bear arms again'; *post* is adverbial (= *postea*); *Aeneadae* is fairly frequent for the Trojans generally (cf. 779).

3 187. **adnuerit nobis**: 'grants us', cf. 1.250, Hor. *Odes* 4.6.22f.; *nostrum* is predicative, 'that Mars is favourable'.

4 189-90. **non . . . nec . . . nec**: the first negative is redundant and adds a strong emphasis; cf. *Ecl.* 4.55-6, 5.25, *Aen.* 9.428.

5 189-91. These statements of Aeneas' non-aggressive intentions are finely presented, and represent the justification of the battles he has to fight; cf. 11.110f.

6 192. **sacra deosque dabo**: this was the mission entrusted to Aeneas by Hector's ghost (2.293) *sacra suosque tibi commendat Troia Penates*.

7 192-3. **socer . . . sollemne socer**: 'my father-in-law Latinus is to keep his army, my father-in-law is to keep his traditional authority'; the repetition of *socer* in chiastic order adds a powerful emphasis to Aeneas' insistence that they will be kinsfolk, made specific by the mention of Lavinia in 194. For *habeto* (third person imperative) cf. *facito*, 438.

8 194. **dabit Lavinia nomen**: the first settlement was called Lavinium, cf. 1.258, 6.84.

9 197. **haec eadem**: cognate accusative after *iuro* ('swear by'), cf. 816 and 6.324, 351; the following nouns are in apposition. It has been argued that *iurare* here governs two different kinds of accusative: 'I swear to these same terms by the earth etc. . . .', but this seems forced. Latinus' list of the powers by which he swears is differently phrased from Aeneas', but broadly similar.

10 198. **Latonaeque. . . duplex**: i.e. Apollo and Diana, children of Latona, the Sun and the Moon. Latinus thus continues the appeal to elemental powers which he began in the previous line.

11 **Ianumque bifrontem**: the same epithet is used of the two-headed god Janus in 7.180, where see note. He is especially associated with treaties, representing originally (according to Servius) the treaty between the two hostile parties after the rape of the Sabine women by the Romans. See also note on 7.607f. (the gates of war in the temple of Janus).

12 199. **duri sacraria Ditis**: 'the shrine of grim Dis', god of the underworld (Virgil uses the Roman name Dis in preference to the Greek Pluto, which he has only once).

13 200. **foedera fulmine sancit**: 'enforces treaties with his thunderbolt'; Jupiter punishes the violators of treaties.

14 201. **medios**: partly 'that are between us', but also 'mediating' (= *sequestres*).

avertet, non[1] si tellurem effundat in undas

diluvio miscens caelumque in Tartara solvat,   205

ut[2] sceptrum hoc' — dextra sceptrum nam forte gerebat —

'numquam fronde[3] levi fundet virgulta nec umbras,

cum[4] semel in silvis imo de stirpe recisum

matre caret posuitque comas[5] et bracchia ferre

olim arbos, nunc[6] artificis manus aere decoro   210

inclusit patribusque dedit[7] gestare Latinis.'

Talibus inter se firmabant foedera dictis

conspectu in medio procerum. Tum rite sacratas

in flammam iugulant pecudes et viscera vivis

eripiunt, cumulantque oneratis lancibus aras.   215

> *216-310. The Rutulians are uneasy about the single combat, and Juturna, disguised as Camers, intervenes to urge them to break the truce. An omen of an eagle forced by a mass attack of other birds to release a swan is interpreted by Tolumnius to mean that the Rutulians must attack to save Turnus. Fighting breaks out.*

[8]At vero Rutulis impar ea pugna videri[9]

iamdudum et vario[10] misceri pectora motu,

tum magis ut propius cernunt non[11] viribus aequis.

---

1 204-5. **non si . . . solvat:** 'not if it should cast forth the land into the waves, confusing all in flood, or send the sky smashing into the underworld'; cf. Lucr. 3.842, Hor. *Epod.* 5.79-80.

2 206. **ut:** 'just as surely as'; the following phrases are based very closely indeed on Achilles' oath in Hom. *Il.* 1.234f.

3 207. **fronde levi . . . virgulta:** 'shoots of light foliage', ablative of description.

4 208-9. **cum semel . . . matre caret:** 'once it is away from mother earth', i.e. now that it is away from. . . . Servius mentions the possibility of taking *mater* as the mother tree, but *imo de stirpe* refutes this.

5 209. **comas et bracchia:** a quite frequent metaphor of trees, *comae* being the leaves and *bracchia* the branches (cf. 6.282, 7.60).

6 210-11. **nunc . . . inclusit:** 'now the hand of the craftsman has overlaid it with fine bronze'; for *inclusit* cf. 10.136

7 211. **dedit gestare:** cf. 97.

8 216f. This passage begins with a quite different picture of Turnus from the normal one of arrogant and impetuous bravery; at the supreme moment his self-confidence is drained from him (see note on 219f.) and our sympathy for him is increased. The intervention of Juturna and the omen of the eagle and the swan prepare the way for the resumption of the fighting, and the description of the renewed battle is violent and cruel (282f., 290f., 301f.). The warriors on both sides easily yield to the heroic impulse and the onset of *furor.*

9 216. **videri:** historic infinitive (like *misceri* in the next line), here denoting continuous action, cf. 2.98, 3.141, 11.822.

10 217. **vario . . . motu:** 'and their hearts had long been troubled with conflicting emotions'.

11 218. **non viribus aequis:** this is unsatisfactory as it stands, and some such phrase as *eos dimicaturos esse* has to be supplied; it is probable that Virgil would have added a line giving a fuller construction to *non viribus aequis*. On the other hand Schrader's conjecture *aequos*, accepted by Mynors, may be right. Others take *cernunt* in the sense of *decernunt* ('fight'), but this is out of the question; Turnus and Aeneas are not yet fighting. Others again bracket the phrase as an interpolation, regarding the line as an incomplete one.

Adiuvat[1] incessu tacito progressus et aram[2]
suppliciter venerans demisso lumine Turnus   220
pubentesque[3] genae et iuvenali in corpore pallor.
Quem[4] simul ac Iuturna soror crebrescere vidit
sermonem et vulgi[5] variare labantia corda,
in medias acies formam[6] adsimulata Camerti
(cui genus a proavis ingens clarumque paternae   225
nomen erat virtutis, et ipse acerrimus armis) —
in[7] medias dat sese acies haud[8] nescia rerum
rumoresque serit varios ac talia fatur:
'non pudet, o Rutuli, pro cunctis talibus[9] unam
obiectare animam? Numerone an viribus aequi   230
non sumus? [10]En, omnes et Troes et Arcades hi sunt,
fatalesque manus, infensa Etruria Turno:
vix hostem, alterni si congrediamur, habemus.
Ille[11] quidem ad superos, quorum se devovet aris,
succedet fama vivusque[12] per ora feretur;   235
nos patria amissa dominis[13] parere superbis

---

1 219. **adiuvat:** 'increases their anxiety'.

2 219f. This description of Turnus' fear contrasts very markedly with the impression of him given at the start of the book; Virgil has brilliantly portrayed the psychology of the young impetuous warrior who at the moment of crisis turns pale and loses his dash, but still knows he must go on. Later he recovers his confidence (325, 331f.). See Heinze, p. 212f.

3 221. **pubentesque genae:** 'his youthful face'; some inferior MSS have *tabentesque* ('ashen'), but there is no reason whatever to abandon the well attested reading, especially as the only other use of *tabentes* in Virgil (*Aen.* 1.173) is rather different.

4 222-3. **quem . . . sermonem:** 'talk of this kind', i.e. that it was an unfair combat.

5 223. **vulgi . . . corda:** 'and that the feelings of the people were shaken and confused', cf. 217.

6 224. **formam . . . Camerti:** 'assuming the appearance of Camers', literally 'making herself like Camers in appearance'. For *adsimulata* with the dative cf. Lucr. 6.189, Tac. *Ann.* 11.11; *formam* is accusative of respect, see note on line 5. Camers was mentioned in 10.562. Compare generally the intervention of Iris in the person of Beroe (5.620f.), where there is the same explanation (nobility of race) to indicate why the goddess chooses that particular person. The divine intervention is based on Hom. *Il.* 4.75f. where Athena comes down from Olympus to break the treaty for single combat between Menelaus and Paris.

7 227. Observe the emphatic repetition of *in medias acies* from 224.

8 227. **haud nescia rerum:** 'well aware of the situation', i.e. what she could do and what were the limits imposed on her, cf. 149f.

9 229. **talibus:** i.e. able-bodied and young and able to fight for themselves (*viribus aequi,* 230).

10 231-3. 'Look, these are all the Trojans and Arcadians there are; yes, and these are all there are of the bands of Etruria, sent by fate to be enemies of Turnus; if only half of us went to battle, we would scarcely find an opponent each'. The three components of Aeneas' forces are mentioned and dismissed as paltry; the Arcadians were sent by Evander and the Etruscans came to help under the leadership of Tarchon. *Fatales* is heavily ironical ('omen-ridden', Jackson Knight), conveying disbelief in the oracles (8.499f.) which told the Etruscans to wait for foreign leaders; Etruria (= Etrusci) is rather awkwardly in apposition to *manus,* and the second half of the line reads like a stopgap. Some MSS have *fatalisque manus* (singular), which involves lengthening in arsis at the caesura, cf. 13.

11 234. **ille:** Turnus, in strong antithesis to *nos* (236).

12 235. **vivusque . . . feretur:** 'will live for ever, praised on the lips of men', cf. Ennius' epitaph (V. 18) *volito vivus per ora virum, Geo.* 3.9 *victorque virum volitare per ora.*

13 236. **dominis parere superbis:** this is the complete opposite of what Aeneas had promised in the event of victory (189f.).

cogemur, qui nunc lenti[1] consedimus arvis.'

Talibus incensa est iuvenum sententia dictis
iam magis atque magis, serpitque per agmina murmur:
ipsi Laurentes mutati ipsique Latini.[2]   240
Qui sibi iam requiem pugnae[3] rebusque salutem
sperabant, nunc arma volunt foedusque precantur
infectum[4] et Turni sortem miserantur iniquam.
His[5] aliud[6] maius Iuturna adiungit et alto
dat signum caelo, [7]quo non praesentius ullum   245
turbavit mentes Italas monstroque fefellit.
Namque volans rubra[8] fulvus Iovis ales in aethra[9]
litoreas[10] agitabat avis turbamque sonantem
agminis [11]aligeri, subito cum lapsus ad undas
cycnum excellentem[12] pedibus rapit improbus[13] uncis.   250
Arrexere[14] animos Itali, cunctaeque volucres
convertunt[15] clamore fugam (mirabile visu),
aetheraque obscurant pennis hostemque per auras
facta[16] nube premunt, donec vi victus et ipso
pondere defecit praedamque ex unguibus ales   255
proiecit[17] fluvio, penitusque in nubila fugit.

---

1 237. **lenti**: 'idle', otiosi (Servius).

2 240. The Laurentians and Latins (as well as the Rutulians to whom Juturna's words had been addressed) now change their minds about the single combat.

3 241. **pugnae**: genitive, cf. 3.393 *requies ea certa laborum.*

4 243. **infectum**: predicative, 'cancelled', cf. Livy 9.11.3 *omnia pro infecto sint.*

5 244. **his:** 'to these thoughts', dative with *adiungit.*

6 **aliud maius**: the same phrase is used of the Laocoon portent (2.199).

7 245-6. 'than which no other more powerfully confused the thoughts of the Italians, deceiving them with its portent'. For *praesentius* cf. 152.

8 247. **rubra** ... in **aethra:** 'in the rosy heavens', cf. Enn. *Ann.* 434-5 *interea fax / occidit oceanumque rubra tractim obruit aethra.*

9 247f. The portent is somewhat similar to that in Hom. *Il.* 12.200f. (translated by Cicero in *De Div.* 1.106); cf. also Hom. *Od.* 2.147f., and the eagle (*Iovis ales*) and twelve swans in *Aen.* 1.393f. Compare too the simile of Hector like an eagle attacking geese and swans by a riverbank in Hom. *Il.* 15.690f.

10 248. **litoreas . . . avis**: 'river birds' (Servius says *palustres*). For *litus* of riverbanks cf. 8.83.

11 248-9. 'a shrieking mass in winged column'; *-que* is epexegetic, i.e. elaborates the previous phrase; *sonantem* refers in this context to their cries of fear; for the military metaphor *agmen* cf. 1.393. *Aliger* is a highly poetic word; cf. 1.663 and see my note on 5.452 (OUP Ed.). The assonance of *a* in *agminis aligeri* echoes that of the previous line, *agitabat avis.*

12 250. **excellentem**: 'conspicuous', 'outstanding', as Turnus was among the Rutulians.

13 **improbus**: 'ruthlessly', cf. *Geo.* 3.431 (of a snake with its prey).

14 251. **arrexere animos**: 'riveted their attention on it'.

15 252. **convertunt clamore fugam.** 'reversed their flight with loud cries', i.e. turned to the attack.

16 254. **facta nube:** 'forming a cloud', cf. 7.705 *volucrum . . . nubem.*

17 256. **proiecit fluvio:** 'cast away from him into the river'; *fluvio* is poetic dative for *in fluvium,* see Page's note ad loc. and cf. 292, 303.

Tum vero augurium Rutuli clamore salutant
expediuntque[1] manus, primusque Tolumnius[2] augur
'hoc[3] erat, hoc, votis' inquit 'quod saepe petivi.
Accipio agnoscoque deos; me, me duce ferrum   260
corripite, o miseri, quos improbus[4] advena bello
territat invalidas[5] ut avis, et litora vestra
vi populat. Petet ille fugam penitusque profundo
vela dabit. Vos unanimi densete[6] catervas
et[7] regem vobis pugna defendite raptum.'   265
Dixit, et adversos telum contorsit in hostis
procurrens; sonitum dat stridula[8] cornus et auras
certa[9] secat. Simul[10] hoc, simul ingens clamor et omnes
turbati cunei[11] calefactaque corda tumultu.
Hasta volans, ut[12] forte novem[13] pulcherrima fratrum   270
corpora constiterant contra, quos fida crearat
una[14] tot Arcadio coniunx Tyrrhena Gylippo,[15]
horum unum ad[16] medium, [17]teritur qua sutilis alvo
balteus et laterum iuncturas fibula mordet,
egregium forma iuvenem et fulgentibus armis,   275

---

1 258. **expediuntque manus:** 'prepare to fight', literally 'make ready their hands'.

2 **Tolumnius:** the Rutulian augur was mentioned in 11.429 as one of Turnus' strongest supporters.

3 259. 'This, this I tell you, was what I so often sought in my prayers', i.e. a favourable omen such as he takes this to be.

4 261. **improbus advena:** 'that criminal intruder'; for this use of *improbus* cf. 11.512 where it is used by Turnus of Aeneas, it picks up *improbus* used of the eagle in 250.

5 262. **invalidas ut avis:** 'like feeble birds', as they were (248) against the eagle until aroused to retaliate *en masse;* the word *litora* also picks up the phraseology of the omen (248), and so does *penitusque profundo* (263, cf. 256).

6 264. **densete catervas:** 'mass your troops', cf. 7.794 *agmina densentur campis.*

7 265. 'and defend in battle the king snatched from you', i.e. Turnus has been isolated from their support by the agreement for single combat, again an echo of the omen (*rapit,* 250).

8 267. **stridula cornus:** 'the whistling shaft'; the word *stridulus* is itself onomatopoeic, and is here reinforced by other *s*'s in the line. For *cornus* cf. 9.698 and *Geo.* 2.447-8 *bona bello / cornus.*

9 268. **certa:** 'with sure aim', anticipating the narrative of 270f.

10 **simul . . . simul:** cf. 758; the effect is abrupt and emphatic, combining with the omission of the main verbs and the dactylic rhythm.

11 269. **cunei:** 'ranks', cf. 457, 575.

12 270. **ut forte:** 'where by chance', cf. 7.509, and rather differently 488-90.

13 270-1. **novem pulcherrima fratrum corpora:** 'nine brothers of splendid physique'; for the periphrasis Conington quotes Enn. *Ann.* 93-4 *ter quattuor corpora sancta / avium* and *Aen.* 9.272.

14 272. **una tot:** rhetorical antithesis, the one woman had so many children.

15 **Gylippo:** Gylippus evidently came with Evander's expedition from Arcadia to Pallanteum and there married an Etruscan wife.

16 273. **ad medium:** 'in the waist', for *medium* as a noun cf. 11.547.

17 273-4. 'where the stitched belt is rubbed against the stomach, and the buckle secures the ends of the side-straps'; *sutilis* suggests that the belt was of leather with metal sewn on; *laterum iuncturas* refers to the belt, not as some say to the ribs of the warrior (cf. Hom. *Il.* 4.132-3).

transadigit[1] costas fulvaque effundit harena.
At fratres, animosa phalanx accensaque luctu,
pars[2] gladios stringunt manibus, pars missile ferrum
corripiunt caecique ruunt. Quos[3] agmina contra
procurrunt Laurentum, hinc densi rursus[4] inundant[5]   280
Troes Agyllinique[6] et pictis Arcades armis:
sic omnis amor unus habet decernere[7] ferro.
Diripuere[8] aras, it toto[9] turbida caelo
tempestas telorum ac ferreus ingruit imber,
craterasque[10] focosque ferunt. Fugit ipse Latinus   285
pulsatos referens infecto foedere divos.
Infrenant alii currus[11] aut corpora[12] saltu
subiciunt in equos et strictis ensibus adsunt.
Messapus[13] regem[14] regisque insigne gerentem
Tyrrhenum Aulesten,[15] avidus[16] confundere foedus,   290
adverso proterret equo; ruit ille recedens
et[17] miser oppositis a tergo involvitur aris
in caput inque umeros. At fervidus[18] advolat hasta
Messapus teloque orantem multa trabali[19]
desuper altus equo graviter ferit atque ita fatur: 295

---

1 276. **transadigit costas:** 'pierced through the ribs', cf. line 508, and for the construction of *costas* (accusative of respect, or perhaps partial apposition) see note on 10.699.

2 278. **pars . . . pars:** a very natural apposition to *fratres* (= *fratrumpars stringit*).

3 279. **quos . . . contra:** the postponement of the dissyllabic preposition is frequent in poetry (cf. 177) but the intrusion of the subject (*agmina*) is rather unusual.

4 280. **rursus:** probably here meaning 'in reply'.

5 **inundant:** 'stream out against them', intransitive here as in 11.382.

6 281. **Agyllinique:** Etruscans from Agylla (7.652, 8.479).

7 282. **decernere:** for the poetic infinitive with *amor* cf. 2.10, and compare line 290.

8 283. **diripuere:** the interposed perfect among present tenses conveys a vividness: 'they have dismantled . . .'; cf. 1.84, 9.75.

9 283-4. **toto . . . telorum:** the alliteration of *t* is violent, matching the vivid metaphors *tempestas* and *imber* (cf. Enn. *Ann.* 284 *hastati spargunt hastas, fit ferreus imber*). For *ingruit*, 'becomes fiercer', cf. 11.899.

10 285. **craterasque . . . ferunt:** 'and they carry away the sacrificial bowls and the sacred fires'; *ferunt* is equivalent to *auferunt*, cf. 493.

11 287. **currus:** i.e. their horses, an easy metonymy for which Servius quotes *Geo.* 1.514 *neque audit currus habenas*.

12 287-8. **corpora saltu subiciunt:** 'leap on to', literally 'heave up their bodies with a leap', cf. *Geo.* 2.19.

13 289. **Messapus:** cf. 128.

14 **regem regisque:** the *-que* is redundant and so adds emphasis to the repetition; see note on 10.734.

15 290. **Aulesten:** the Etruscan Aulestes is mentioned in 10.207.

16 **avidus confundere:** poetic infinitive, cf. 282.

17 292-3. 'and the poor wretch crashed head and shoulders into the altars standing behind him'. *Aris* is poetic dative for *in aras*, cf. 256.

18 293. **fervidus advolat hasta:** notice the emphatic pattern of words, each filling a foot, cf. 328, 422, 923 and note on 11.638.

19 294. **trabali:** 'massive', like a beam. Servius quotes *teloque trabali* from Ennius; cf. Stat. *Th.* 4.6-7 *trabalem / hastam*.

'hoc[1] habet, haec melior[2] magnis data victima divis.'
concurrunt Itali spoliantque calentia membra.
Obvius ambustum torrem Corynaeus[3] ab ara
corripit et venienti Ebyso plagamque ferenti[4]
occupat[5] os flammis: olli ingens barba reluxit   300
nidoremque[6] ambusta dedit. Super ipse secutus
caesariem[7] laeva turbati corripit hostis
impressoque genu nitens terrae[8] applicat ipsum;
sic rigido latus ense ferit. Podalirius[9] Alsum
pastorem primaque[10] acie per tela ruentem   305
ense sequens nudo superimminet; ille[11] securi
adversi frontem mediam mentumque reducta
disicit et sparso late rigat arma cruore.
olli dura quies oculos et ferreus urget[12]
somnus, in aeternam clauduntur lumina noctem.   310

311-82. Aeneas attempts to prevent his men from breaking the treaty, but is wounded by an arrow from an unknown source. Thereupon Turnus excitedly leads his men into battle, and the fighting is resumed.

[13]At pius[14] Aeneas dextram tendebat inermem
nudato capite atque suos clamore vocabat:

---

1 296. **hoc habet:** 'he's got it', a colloquial expression used at the deathblow of a gladiator; cf. Plaut. *Most.* 715, Ter. *Andr.* 83. Servius explains correctly with id est, letali percussus est vulnere.

2 **melior . . . victima:** ironical, a 'better' victim than the proposed sacrificial animals, cf. 5.483.

3 298-9. Corynaeus the Trojan and Ebysus the Latin have not been mentioned before; it is a different Corynaeus in 6.228, 9.571.

4 299. **ferenti:** 'aiming', literally 'bringing'; Servius says '*pro inferenti*'.

5 300. **occupat os:** 'hit him in the face', cf. 10.699.

6 301. **nidoremque ambusta dedit:** 'was singed and gave off a smell of burning'.

7 302. 'he seized the hair of his dazed foe with his left hand'; cf. the death of Priam in 2.552f. *implicuitque comam laeva . . .*

8 303. **terrae applicat ipsum:** 'forced him to the ground'; *terrae* is poetic dative for *ad terram*, cf. 256.

9 304. Neither Podalirius the Trojan nor Alsus the Rutulian is heard of before.

10 305. **primaque:** the redundant *-que* is less effective here than in 289.

11 306. **ille:** i.e. Alsus turns the tables on his pursuer.

12 309-10. These lines are repeated from 10.745-6 where see notes.

13 311f. The beginning of this passage shows clearly the difference between Aeneas and Turnus; Aeneas here stands for order and peace and is prepared to risk his own life to achieve it (*inermem,* 311, *nudato,* 312.) Turnus on the other hand welcomes the outbreak of battle, and his bravery and military skill are described in the full heroic style, with frequent imitations of Homer. He rushes into the fight with impetus and enthusiasm (325f.), with pride in his known ability (*superbus,* 326); he is compared with the war-god Mars himself (331f.) and with the wild winds from Thrace (365f.); in the hurly-burly of general slaughter he is most truly himself.

14 311. **pius:** cf. 175. Here attention is drawn particularly to Aeneas' feelings of religious obligation to the sworn treaty and also to his responsibility for preventing further bloodshed among his troops.

'quo¹ ruitis? Quaeve ista repens discordia surgit?
O² cohibete iras! Ictum iam foedus et omnes
compositae leges, mihi ius concurrere soli,   315
me³ sinite atque auferte metus; ego foedera⁴ faxo
firma manu, Turnum debent haec⁵ iam mihi sacra.'
Has inter voces, media inter talia verba⁶
ecce viro stridens alis⁷ adlapsa sagitta est,
incertum⁸ qua pulsa manu, quo turbine adacta,   320
quis tantam Rutulis laudem, casusne deusne,
attulerit; pressa⁹ est insignis gloria facti,
nec sese Aeneae iactavit vulnere quisquam.
Turnus ut Aenean cedentem ex agmine vidit¹⁰
turbatosque duces, subita spe fervidus ardet;   325
poscit equos atque arma simul, saltuque superbus
emicat in currum et manibus molitur¹¹ habenas.
Multa virum volitans¹² dat fortia corpora leto,
seminecis volvit¹³ multos aut agmina curru
proterit aut raptas¹⁴ fugientibus ingerit hastas.   330

---

1 313. **quo ruitis:** an unmistakable echo of Horace's great poem (*Epode* 7) which expresses unforgettably the guilt and horror of the civil wars: *quo quo scelesti ruitis . . .?* The connexion with civil war is made clearer still with the word *discordia*, personified by Virgil as the last of the shapes at the entrance to the underworld, 6.280-1 *et Discordia demens / vipereum crinem vittis innexa cruentis*. In a sense this incident is a foreshadowing of civil war, as it breaks the treaty which had been made between the two partners in Italy's future greatness (189f.).

2 314. **o cohibete iras:** this is the theme of the *Aeneid*, expressed in Jupiter's prophecy that in the Golden Age *Furor impius* will be enchained (1.294). Seneca says that *ira is brevis furor;* but it is realised in the poem by the human actors only very intermittently and imperfectly.

3 316. **me sinite:** 'let me' (understand *concurrere*), staccato like the rest of his speech, which contains ten main verbs in five lines.

4 316-17. **foedera faxo firma:** notice the heavy alliteration of *f; faxo* is an archaic form of the future of *facere*, cf. 9.154.

5 317. **haec iam mihi sacra:** the rhythm is abrupt (cf. 406, 532, 646) and emphasis is put on *mihi* by the clash of ictus and accent in the fifth foot.

6 318f. This scene is based on the breaking of the truce in Hom. *Il.* 4.104f., where Pandarus shoots an arrow at Menelaus and wounds him.

7 319. **alis adlapsa:** 'winged its way', cf. 9.578, the same phrase of an arrow, and 5.319 *fulminis ocior alis*.

8 320-2. 'no one ever knew by whose hand it was propelled, by whose effort it was sent whirring on its course, what chance or divine guidance brought such glory to the Rutulians'. *Turbo* refers to the whirring motion (cf. 531, 11.284 and *contorquere* in 266, 490); *quo turbine* is equivalent to *cuius turbine*, parallel to *qua manu* (= *cuius manu*).

9 322. **pressa:** 'suppressa' (Servius).

10 324f. Turnus now again becomes the proud and confident warrior, very different from the pale young man preparing to face Aeneas (219f.). Notice the strong word *superbus*, the alliteration of *s* and *m*, and the vivid picture of *emicat*; cf. 11.496 where the word is used of the warhorse with which Turnus is compared as he leaps forth to battle.

11 327. **molitur:** 'tugs at'; the word suggests his frenzied activity.

12 328. **volitans:** 'darting about', a rather unexpected word of a warrior in battle, again stressing (like *emicat*) the impetuous energy and excitement of Turnus. The rhythm of the second half of the line (see note on 293) reinforces the idea of rapid action.

13 329. **volvit:** 'throws down', cf. 9.433.

14 330. **raptas:** the spears that he snatches from his victims he throws at others who are trying to get away; cf. 9.763.

Qualis [1]apud gelidi cum flumina concitus Hebri
sanguineus Mavors clipeo increpat atque furentis
bella movens immittit equos, illi aequore aperto
ante Notos Zephyrumque volant, gemit ultima pulsu
Thraca[2] [3]pedum circumque atrae Formidinis ora   335
Iraeque Insidiaeque, dei comitatus, aguntur:
talis equos alacer media inter proelia Turnus
fumantis sudore quatit, miserabile[4] caesis
hostibus insultans; spargit rapida ungula rores[5]
sanguineos mixtaque cruor calcatur harena.   340
Iamque neci Sthenelumque dedit Thamyrumque Pholumque,[6]
hunc congressus[7] et hunc, illum eminus; eminus ambo
Imbrasidas[8], Glaucum atque Laden, quos Imbrasus ipse
nutrierat Lycia paribusque ornaverat armis
vel conferre manum vel equo praevertere ventos.   345
    Parte alia media Eumedes[9] in proelia fertur,
antiqui proles bello praeclara Dolonis,[10]
nomine avum referens, animo manibusque parentem,
qui quondam, castra ut[11] Danaum speculator adiret,
ausus Pelidae pretium sibi poscere currus;   350
illum Tydides alio[12] pro talibus ausis

---

1 331f. 'Like the blood spattered figure of Mars, when roused to fury alongside the streams of the frozen Hebrus he clashes his shield and purposing war drives on his wild horses . . .'. The simile is based on the passage comparing Idomeneus with Ares in Hom. *Il.* 13.298f. The river Hebrus (1.317) was in Thrace (335), an area especially associated with Mars, cf. 3.13; Mavors is an archaic form for Mars (179). For *increpat* some MSS have *intonat,* but cf. Sil. 12.685.

2 335. **Thraca:** a Latinised form of the Greek word *Thrace,* the normal Latin being *Thracia.*

3 335-6. 'and around him the figure of black Fear, and Anger and Ambush, the god's retinue, rush onwards'. The personification of abstract qualities as attendants of Mars is from Homer (*Il.* 4.440-1: 'Terror and Fear, and Strife, raging wildly, the sister and companion of man-slaying Ares', cf. also *Il.* 13.298f.; compare the elaborate imitation in Stat. *Th.* 7.47f., and Spenser, *F.Q.* 1.4.33f. The phrase *atrae Formidinis ora* (which does not balance with the nominatives *Iraeque Insidiaeque)* is from Lucr. 4.173.

4 338. **miserabile caesis:** 'piteously slain', adverbial accusative, cf. 535; it is less natural to take *miserabile* with *insultans.*

5 339-40. **rores sanguineos:** 'dew of blood', a very poetic use of *ros,* cf. Stat. *Th.* 2.674 and line 512, *rorantia sanguine.*

6 341. The enumeration of names (cf. 363) is in the Homeric style, and the repeated *-que* (the first meaning 'both') recalls the Homeric τε. None of these warriors, nor those in 343, is heard of elsewhere.

7 342. **congressus:** in the context equivalent to *comminus,* as opposed to *eminus.*

8 343-5. 'whom Imbrasus had himself brought up in Lycia, fitting them out with matching armour, teaching them to meet the enemy in close combat or to outstrip the winds on horseback'. The infinitives depend on *nutrierat* (not on *paribus,* as some maintain) in the sense of 'had brought them up to . . .' (*nutrierat docens . . .*).

9 346. **Eumedes:** Dolon is the son of Eumedes in Homer (*Il.* 10.314); this Eumedes, son of Dolon, is called after his grandfather (348).

10 347f. The story of Dolon the Trojan is told in detail in Homer (*Il.* 10.299f.), with much less sympathy for him. Dolon was promised the horses and chariot of Achilles (son of Peleus, 350) if he would spy out the Greek camp; in the course of his explorations he encountered Odysseus and Diomedes (son of Tydeus, 351) and was killed.

11 349. **ut . . . adiret:** 'as the price of going . . .'; Servius finds difficulty over this quite natural use of a final clause.

12 351-2. **alio . . . adfecit pretio:** 'paid him quite a different reward'; an ironical variant on *adficere aliquem poena.*

adfecit pretio nec¹ equis aspirat Achilli.
Hunc² procul ut campo Turnus prospexit aperto,
ante³ levi iaculo longum per inane secutus
sistit equos⁴ biiugis et⁵ curru desilit atque   355
semianimi⁶ lapsoque supervenit, et pede collo⁷
impresso dextrae⁸ mucronem extorquet et alto
fulgentem tingit iugulo atque haec insuper addit:
'en⁹ agros et, quam bello, Troiane, petisti,
Hesperiam metire iacens: haec praemia, qui me   360
ferro ausi temptare, ferunt, sic moenia condunt.'
Huic comitem Asbyten coniecta cuspide mittit¹⁰
Chloreaque Sybarimque Daretaque Thersilochumque
et sternacis¹¹ equi lapsum cervice Thymoeten.
Ac¹² velut Edoni Boreae cum spiritus alto   365
insonat Aegaeo sequiturque ad litora fluctus;
qua venti incubuere,¹³ fugam dant nubila caelo:
sic Turno, quacumque viam secat, agmina cedunt
conversaeque ruunt acies; fert impetus ipsum

---

1 352. **nec equis aspirat Achilli**: 'and now he does not aspire to the horses of Achilles', i.e. his death has eliminated his vainglorious aspirations. *Aspirare* in this sense is frequent in Cicero (e.g. *aspirare in curiam*); *Achilli* is a fifth-declension form of the genitive used several times by Virgil (see note on 10.581).

2 353. **hunc**: i.e. Eumedes, resuming the narrative from 346.

3 354. 'after having first hit him with his light javelin from a long distance off'; *inane* ('space') is frequent as a noun in Lucretius, cf. also line 906. *Secutus* is equivalent to *consecutus*, cf. line 775, 893.

4 355. **equos biiugis**: 'the horses of his two-yoked chariot'; *biiugis* is best taken as accusative plural of the third declension (cf. *Geo.* 3.91) rather than ablative of the second declension ('in the two-yoked chariot'), cf. 10.453.

5 355-8. **et . . . atque**: the conjunctions here (five in four lines) give an impression of rapid action; Mackail calls it 'the calculated *reduction* of a complex craftsmanship', and associates it with Virgil's later style. See also Warde Fowler, *The Death of Turnus*, pp. 3-5. The position of *atque* at the line ending of 355 is most unusual, cf. 615 and 11.509.

6 356. **semianimi**: dative; Virgil always uses the form *semianimis* in preference to *semianimus*. For the scansion, with the *i* of *semi-* treated as a consonant, cf. 401, 706, and compare 8.194 *semihominis*.

7 **collo** = *in collum*.

8 357. **dextrae**: 'from Eumedes' hand'; the dative after *extorquere* is as with *eripere* (31, 157, 539, 948).

9 359-60. 'There you are, Trojan, measure out with your length the fields and the Italy which you sought in war'. The taunt is like that of 10.650, where see note; he is to measure with his body the fields he had intended to measure out for the buildings of the new city.

10 362-4. Of the warriors named only Chloreus (11.768), Dares (5.369), Thymoetes (10.123) are heard of elsewhere. Line 363 is Greek in rhythm with its absence of main caesura in the third or fourth foot, its polysyllabic ending, and the lengthening in arsis of the first *-que* (see note on 89). *Asbyten, Chlorea, Dareta, Thymoeten* are all Greek accusative forms.

11 364. **sternacis**: 'bucking', liable to throw off (*sternere*) its rider. The word is rare and not found elsewhere except in imitations of this passage (e.g. Sil. 1.261).

12 365-6. 'Just as when the blast of the Edonian north wind whistles over mid ocean in the Aegean Sea, and pursues the waves to the shore'. The simile is based on Hom. *Il.* 11.305f. where Hector cuts his way through the Greeks like the west wind driving the clouds and the waves. *Edonus* is from Mt. Edon in Thrace (cf. Hor. *Odes* 2.7.26); it agrees with the masculine word *Boreae*; *alto* means 'out to sea' rather than simply 'deep', as is shown by the next clause; *fluctus* might be nominative singular (Servius says some people so took it), but a far better image results if it is taken as the accusative plural, object of *seguitur*.

13 367. **incubuere**: 'have swooped down', cf. 1.84.

et cristam adverso curru quatit aura volantem.　370
Non tulit instantem Phegeus[1] animisque frementem;
obiecit [2]sese ad currum et spumantia frenis
ora citatorum dextra detorsit equorum.
Dum [3]trahitur pendetque iugis, hunc lata retectum
lancea consequitur rumpitque infixa bilicem[4]　375
loricam et summum degustat vulnere corpus.
Ille tamen clipeo obiecto conversus in hostem
ibat et auxilium[5] ducto mucrone petebat,
cum[6] rota praecipitem et procursu concitus axis
impulit effunditque solo, Turnusque secutus　380
imam inter galeam summi[7] thoracis et oras
abstulit ense caput truncumque reliquit harenae.[8]

383-440. The wounded Aeneas is helped back to camp. The physician Iapyx cannot remove the arrow-head, but Venus intervenes and with supernatural potions causes the arrowhead to come out and the wound to heal. Aeneas immediately rearms for battle.

[9]Atque ea dum campis victor dat[10] funera Turnus,
interea Aenean Mnestheus[11] et fidus Achates
Ascaniusque[12] comes castris statuere cruentum　385

1 371. **Phegeus**: another Trojan of the same name was killed by Turnus (9.765).

2 372-3. 'and with his right hand pulled at the mouths of the galloping horses as they foamed on the bit'.

3 374-5. 'a broad spear struck his exposed body'; he is unable to use his shield. For *retectus* cf. 9.461.

4 375. **bilicem**: 'double-meshed', cf. *trilix* in 7.639.

5 378. **auxilium . . . petebat:** i.e. tried to help himself.

6 379-80. 'when the wheel and the axle, whirling round as the chariot sped on, knocked him headlong and laid him low on the ground'. For *procursus* Servius says *impetus;* cf. 711.

7 381. **summi . . . oras:** 'and the top edge of his breastplate'; *et* is postponed.

8 382. **harenae:** dative of indirect object, personifying the sand as the recipient of the corpse. Some explain as locative, but this is very unlikely.

9 383f. This scene provides a relaxation in intensity between the fierce battles of Turnus which have preceded and those of Aeneas which follow. The picture of the doctor Iapyx, devoted to his art but unable to succeed in this instance till divine aid is given, is a very attractive one; and the intervention of Venus is described in rich and exotic terms. Finally we see Aeneas ready to return to battle, anxious to confront Turnus and quietly confident of his ability to do so (436f.). His words to Ascanius as he prepares to depart (435-6) very fairly summarise his actions in the *Aeneid*; he has indeed shown valour (*virtus*) and endured toil (*labor*), and has experienced the constant hostility of *fortuna* (see note on 436). He wishes his son an easier passage through life than he has had himself, and the reader accepts the justice of Aeneas' words and admires the qualities which have enabled him to see his task through to the end.

10 383. **dat funera:** 'deals death', see Page ad loc. and cf. 8.570-1.

11 384. For Aeneas' lieutenants, Mnestheus and Achates, see notes on 127 and 10.332.

12 385. Aeneas' son Ascanius (called Iulus in 399) had accompanied him to the altars (168) when he went to swear the oath before single combat.

alternos[1] longa nitentem cuspide gressus.
Saevit[2] et infracta[3] luctatur[4] harundine telum
eripere auxihoque[5] viam, quae proxima, poscit:
ense secent lato vulnus telique latebram
rescindant penitus, seseque in bella remittant.   390
Iamque aderat Phoebo ante alios dilectus Iapyx[6]
Iasides, acri quondam cui captus amore
ipse suas artis, sua munera, laetus Apollo
augurium citharamque dabat celerisque sagittas.[7]
Ille, ut depositi[8] proferret[9] fata parentis,   395
scire potestates herbarum usumque medendi[10]
maluit et mutas[11] agitare inglorius artis.
Stabat acerba[12] fremens ingentem nixus in hastam
Aeneas magno[13] iuvenum et maerentis Iuli
concursu, lacrimis immobilis. Ille[14] retorto   400
Paeonium in morem senior succinctus amictu

---

1 386. 'supporting every other step on his long spear'; literally 'leaning on his long spear with regard to every other step'. *Gressus* is probably accusative of respect, cf. line 5, rather than accusative of extent of space.

2 387. **saevit:** the reaction of Aeneas is that of the Homeric warrior, fierce anger at being prevented temporarily from leading his men, and impatience to get into battle (388).

3 **infracta:** the shaft of the arrow has broken, leaving the head embedded; cf. Spenser, *F.Q.* 4.3.10.

4 387-8. **luctatur . . . eripere:** the infinitive after *luctari* is a poetic usage, cf. Ov. *Met.* 15.300, and compare *certare* with the infinitive (9.520, 10.130).

5 388-9. **auxilioque . . . secent:** 'demands the quickest possible method of treatment: they must cut with the sword . . .'. The jussive subjunctive *secent* (like *rescindant* and *remittant* in 390) expresses obliquely the imperative of Aeneas' actual words.

6 391-2. **Iapyx Iasides:** the name of Iapyx's father suggests the Greek word ιασθαι ('to heal'). The passage is based on the healing of Menelaus by Machaon in *Il.* 4.210f., but Virgil has added the divine intervention of Venus.

7 394f. Apollo offered him (*dabat,* the imperfect indicates 'he was ready to give') the most highly valued attributes he could give (prophecy, music, skills as an archer).

8 395. **depositi:** 'despaired of '(Servius, quoting Cicero *Verr.* 2.1.5 aegram et prope depositam reipublicae partem suscepisse; cf. also Ov. *Trist.* 3.3.40). The reference is to the custom of placing the dying outside the doors of their house, either (says Servius) so that their last breath might be received by Mother Earth or in case a passerby who had had a similar illness might be able to cure them.

9 **proferret fata:** 'postpone the death', cf. Hor. *Odes* 1.15.33 *diem proferet Ilio.*

10 396. The practice of healing was also one of Apollo's attributes, in his capacity as Paean (the healer, cf. 401), father of Aesculapius, god of medicine.

11 397. **mutas . . . inglorius:** in comparison, as Servius says, with the attributes offered in 394. Cf. Virgil's use of *inglorius* applied to himself in *Geo.* 2.486. The phrase in Gray's *Elegy* 'mute inglorious Milton' is reminiscent of Virgil's diction, though the context is quite different.

12 398. **acerba fremens:** 'chafing furiously'; *acerba* is adverbial accusative (compare 338, 535), cf. 9.794 *acerba tuens* and 10.572 *dira frementem.*

13 399-400. **magno . . . immobilis:** 'surrounded by a great throng of warriors including the grief-stricken Iulus, unmoved by their tears', i.e. making no concessions to their concern, anxious only to get into battle. For *immobilis* in this sense cf. 7.250.

14 400-1. **ille ... amictu:** 'the old doctor, wearing his robe tied back in the Paeonian fashion . . .'; Paeon (or Paean) was an epithet of Apollo and the adjective is used to mean 'like a doctor'. The word scans as three long syllables with consonantal t, see note on 7.769 and cf. 356. *Retorto . . . amictu* refers to leaving the limbs free for movement, cf. Stat. *Silv.* 1.4.107-8.

557

multa¹ manu medica Phoebique potentibus herbis
nequiquam trepidat, nequiquam spicula dextra
sollicitat² prensatque³ tenaci forcipe ferrum.
Nulla⁴ viam fortuna regit, nihil auctor Apollo   405
subvenit, et saevus campis magis ac magis⁵ horror
crebrescit propiusque malum est. Iam pulvere⁶ caelum
stare vident: subeunt equites et spicula castris
densa cadunt mediis. It tristis ad aethera clamor
bellantum iuvenum et duro sub Marte cadentum.⁷   410

    Hic Venus indigno nati concussa dolore
dictamnum⁸ genetrix⁹ Cretaea carpit ab Ida,¹⁰
puberibus¹¹ caulem foliis et flore comantem
purpureo; non illa feris incognita capris
gramina, cum tergo volucres haesere sagittae.¹²   415
Hoc¹³ Venus obscuro faciem¹⁴ circumdata nimbo
detulit, ¹⁵hoc fusum labris splendentibus amnem
inficit occulte medicans, spargitque salubris
ambrosiae¹⁶ sucos et odoriferam panaceam.

---

1 402-3. **multa . . . trepidat**: 'anxiously tries many remedies'; *trepidat,* as Servius says, is used in the sense of *trepidanter facit,* cf. *properare* in 425.

2 404. **sollicitat**: 'tugs at'.

3 **prensatque . . . ferrum**: cf. *Geo.* 4.175 *versantque tenaci forcipe ferrum,* where there is the same absence of main caesura in third and fourth foot.

4 405-6. **nulla . . . subvenit**: 'no good luck guided any of his approaches, his patron Apollo gave no help'; for *auctor* cf. 5.418, 8.336.

5 406. **magis ac magis horror**: the unusual rhythm of the fifth foot (cf. 317) emphasises the drama of the situation. *Horror* here suggests the noise of war, cf. 2.301 *armorumque ingruit horror.*

6 407-8. **pulvere caelum stare**: 'the heavens thick with dust', a memorable use of *stare* taken from Ennius *Ann.* 608 *stant pulvere campi,* itself imitated from Hom. *Il.* 23.365-6, κονιη / ιϲτατ αειρομενη. The image seems to be of a pillar or a wall of dust rising high and dense. The usage is linked in Aul. Gell. 8.5 with the phrase *pectus sentibus stat* from Lucilius.

7 410. The assonance of *-antum, -num., -entum* gives a strong emphasis to the description of battle and death.

8 412. **dictamnum**: a herb with healing properties especially associated with Crete (Theophr. *H.P.* 9.16); the story of goats looking for it when wounded (414-15) is told in Cic. *N.D.* 2.126 (following Aristotle, *H.A.* 9.6.1).

9 **genetrix**: 'with a mother's care', the separation of this word from *Venus,* with which it agrees, gives it emphasis; cf. 871 (*soror*).

10 412. Mt. Ida in Crete is said to have given its name to Mt. Ida near Troy (3.105).

11 413-14. 'a plant with fresh leaves, tressed with purple flowers'; for *puberibus* cf. 4.514 *pubentes herbae,* for the metaphor in *comans* cf. *Geo.* 4.122-3 *sera comantem narcissum,* and compare line 209. *Caulem* is literally a stalk and is here in apposition to *dictamnum,* referring to the particular plant which Venus picked.

12 415. Cicero (see note on 412) says that dittany was supposed to make the arrows fall out of the goats' bodies.

13 416-17. **hoc . . . hoc**: the first *hoc* is accusative, the second ablative.

14 416. **faciem circumdata**: 'covering her form', retained accusative (see note on 64-5).

15 417-18. 'with this she impregnated the water which they had poured into a sparkling basin, secretly treating it'; notice the highflown poetic diction where *amnis* is used for *aqua* (cf. *fons* in 119) and *labrum* (cf. 8.22) in the poetic plural for *vas.*

16 419. **ambrosiae . . . panaceam**: ambrosia is a mythical food or unguent (*Geo.* 4.415) associated (like nectar) with the immortals. *Panacea* (cf. Lucr. 4.124, Spenser *F.Q.* 3.5.32) is a Greek word ('all-curing'); the rhythm too, with the quadri-syllabic ending, is Greek.

Fovit[1] ea vulnus lympha longaevus Iapyx   420
ignorans,[2] subitoque omnis de corpore fugit
quippe[3] dolor,[4] omnis stetit[5] imo vulnere sanguis.
Iamque secuta manum nullo[6] cogente sagitta
excidit, atque novae[7] rediere in pristina vires.
'Arma citi properate viro! Quid statis?' Iapyx[8]   425
conclamat primusque animos accendit in hostem.
'Non haec humanis opibus, non arte[9] magistra
proveniunt, neque te, Aenea, mea dextera servat:
maior[10] agit deus atque opera ad maiora remittit.'
Ille avidus pugnae suras incluserat auro[11]   430
hinc atque hinc oditque moras hastamque coruscat.
Postquam habilis[12] lateri clipeus loricaque tergo est,
Ascanium fusis[13] circum complectitur armis
summaque[14] per galeam delibans oscula fatur:
'disce, puer, virtutem ex me verumque laborem,[15]   435
fortunam[16] ex aliis. Nunc te mea dextera bello

---

1 420. **fovit:** 'bathed', cf. 10.838.

2 421. **ignorans:** unaware that it had been medicated.

3 422. **quippe:** like *scilicet* (cf. 1.59), here emphasising the fact that the apparently impossible did indeed happen.

4 **dolor:** the final syllable is lengthened in arsis, see note on 13.

5 **stetit:** 'was congealed', 'stopped flowing', cf. 10.834 (of Mezentius) *vulnera siccabat lymphis*. Notice the rhythm of the second half of the line, with the last three feet each composed of a single word; see note on 293.

6 423. **nullo cogente:** i.e. without any force applied.

7 424. **novae ... vires:** 'his strength was renewed and returned to him as it was before'; *pristina* is used as a noun, literally 'to its previous state'.

8 425. The excitement of Iapyx is reflected by the staccato metre, with the two mid-line pauses; the fifth foot pause is a rare one.

9 427. **arte magistra:** 'from the guidance of my skill', cf. 8.442.

10 429. **maior agit deus:** 'a greater one is active, a god'; Iapyx recognises that the cure is supernatural.

11 430. Aeneas' golden greaves had been made by Vulcan and given to him by his mother (8.624); for the phrase cf. 11.488. The pluperfect suggests the rapidity with which the action had already been taken.

12 432. **habilis:** 'fitted comfortably', cf. 9.305, 365, 11.555.

13 433. **fusis circum complectitur armis:** 'fully armed as he now was spread his arms wide and embraced him'; Day Lewis has 'folded his son in a mailed embrace'. *Armis* is from *arma* ('weapons'), not from *armus* ('shoulder').

14 434. **summaque ... delibans oscula:** 'lightly kissing him', cf. 1.256 *oscula libavit*.

15 435f. The situation is reminiscent of Hector's prayer for his son Astyanax (Hom. *Il.* 6.476f.) before he goes to battle, and the words Aeneas uses are very strongly reminiscent of Ajax's to his son in Sophocles' *Ajax* 550-1 ('My son, may you be luckier than your father, but otherwise the same'). Macrobius (*Sat.* 6.1.58) quotes Accius' imitation of Sophocles *virtuti sis par, dispar fortunis patris*. *Virtus* is the *summum bonum* of the Stoics; here it mainly has its martial meaning, cf. 4.3 (Dido constantly thinks of Aeneas' *virtus*), 6.806 (Anchises' message to Aeneas, *virtutem extendere factis*). The phrase *verumque laborem* also has a Stoic ring, 'true endurance of hardship'.

16 436. **fortunam ex aliis:** we are reminded of Aeneas' speech to Venus in 1.372f. where he laments the ill fortune which dogs him, and of his words in 6.62 *hac Troiana tenus fuerit fortuna secuta*. It was part of the Stoic creed to rise superior to the blows of fortune (cf. 5.710), and throughout the *Aeneid* Aeneas has been constantly exposed to these blows.

defensum[1] dabit et magna inter praemia ducet.
Tu[2] facito, mox cum matura adoleverit aetas,
sis memor[3] et te[4] animo repetentem exempla[5] tuorum
et pater Aeneas et avunculus[6] excitet Hector.'[7]   440

> *441-99. The Rutulians are terrified as Aeneas rushes into battle. He pursues Turnus and Turnus only. Juturna intervenes in the guise of Metiscus, Turnus' charioteer, and keeps Turnus away from Aeneas. Messapus attacks Aeneas and realising that Turnus will not meet him Aeneas begins to attack his enemies indiscriminately.*

[8]Haec ubi dicta dedit, portis sese extulit ingens
telum immane manu quatiens; simul agmine denso
Antheusque[9] Mnestheusque ruunt, omnisque relictis
turba fluit[10] castris. Tum caeco pulvere campus
miscetur[11] pulsuque[12] pedum tremit excita tellus.   445
Vidit ab adverso venientis aggere Turnus,
videre Ausonii, gelidusque per ima cucurrit
ossa tremor; prima ante omnis Iuturna Latinos
audiit agnovitque sonum et tremefacta refugit.
Ille volat campoque atrum[13] rapit agmen aperto.   450

---

1 437. **defensum dabit**: 'defendet' (Servius). Virgil is very fond indeed of periphrases with *dare* (cf. 383 and see Maguinness on 12.69), and this is a particularly striking example (cf. 9.323).

2 438-9- **tu facito … sis**: the jussive subjunctive *sis* is in parataxis with the leading verb (*facito*, 'see to it') without the insertion of the subordinating *ut. Facito* is the emphatic form of the imperative, cf. 10.53.

3 439. **memor**: 'subaudiendum meorum factorum' (Servius).

4 **te animo**: the elision of a long monosyllable before a short vowel is very rare in Virgil. There is another example at 657.

5 **exempla**: 'models to imitate', a favourite word with the Romans in relation to the deeds of their ancestors; cf. Cic. *Off.* 3.47 *plena exemplorum est nostra respublica.*

6 440. **avunculus**: Creusa, Aeneas' wife, was a sister of Hector.

7 440. This line is repeated (with *excitet* for *excitat*) from Andromache's tearful enquiry about Ascanius, a passage which also includes the word *virtus* (3.342-3) *ecquid in antiquam virtutem animosque virilis / et pater Aeneas et avunculus excitat Hector?*

8 441f. The picture of Aeneas' entry into battle, like a storm-cloud approaching the land, is vivid and terrifying; but at first Aeneas refrains from fighting as he searches out Turnus, so that the single combat may in fact take place even if in the midst of general fighting. But when he realises that he cannot catch Turnus, and in addition a spear from Messapus narrowly misses him, he gives way to battle fury (497f., where see note), and in Quinn's words 'we are back where we were at 10.513-14'.

9 443. **Antheusque Mnestheusque**: the first *-que* is lengthened in arsis, see note on 89. Of these two Trojans Antheus is mentioned in 1.181, 510 and Mnestheus (see note on 127) frequently.

10 444. **fluit**: 'rolled forward', like a great wave, cf. 11.236.

11 445. **miscetur**: a favourite word of Virgil's to express confusion and turmoil, cf. 2.298, 4.160, 10.721.

12 **pulsuque … tellus**: the sound of these words, with the predominantly dactylic rhythm and the alliteration of the harsh consonants *p* and *t,* is clearly intended to reflect the sense. The personification of *tellus* with the verbs *tremit* and *excita* adds to the intensity; cf. 3.581 *intremere omnem . . . Trinacriam,* 3.673f. *exterrita tellus Italiae* (with my note, OUP Ed.), 7.722.

13 450. **atrum rapit agmen**: 'led his dark column at high speed'; *atrum* conveys an idea of black menace, linked with the blinding dust of 444 and the simile of a storm cloud which follows. For *rapit* cf. 10.178.

Qualis ubi ad terras abrupto[1] sidere nimbus[2]
it mare per medium (miseris, heu, praescia longe
horrescunt corda agricolis: dabit[3] ille ruinas
arboribus stragemque satis, ruet omnia late),
ante volant sonitumque ferunt ad litora venti: 455
talis in adversos ductor Rhoeteius[4] hostis
agmen agit, densi cuneis[5] se quisque coactis
adglomerant. Ferit ense gravem[6] Thymbraeus Osirim,[7]
Arcetium Mnestheus, Epulonem obtruncat Achates
Ufentemque Gyas; cadit ipse Tolumnius augur,   460
primus in adversos telum qui torserat hostis.
Tollitur in caelum clamor, versique vicissim
pulverulenta fuga Rutuli dant terga per agros.
Ipse[8] neque aversos dignatur sternere[9] morti
nec[10] pede congressos aequo, nec[11] tela ferentis   465
insequitur: solum densa in caligine Turnum
vestigat[12] lustrans, solum in certamina poscit.

---

1 451. **abrupto sidere**: 'cutting off the sun's light', cf. Stat. *Th.* 1.325 *abrupto sole,* and for *sidus = sol* cf. Ov. *Met.* 1.424. I have argued for this interpretation (which picks up the idea in *atrum,* 450) in *C.R.* 1956, p. 104. The traditional interpretation is 'when a storm breaks out', but this kind of metonymy of *sidus* for *tempestas* is surely impossible.

2 451f. The simile of the advancing storm cloud is closely based on Hom. *Il.* 4.275f., where advancing warriors are compared with a storm approaching from the sea, sighted by a goat herd who in fear drives his goats to safety; Virgil has varied the image to farmers in fear for their crops, adding, as Conington points out, an element of personal involvement by means of the adjective *miseris.* The comparison is discussed by Pöschl, pp. 121-2, with reference to the destruction imminent for Turnus as for the farmers.

3 453-4. **dabit . . . late**: 'it will uproot the trees and destroy the crops, it will flatten everything far and wide'; for *ruere* in this sense cf. 11.211.

4 456. **Rhoeteius**: i.e. Trojan, from the promontory near Troy, cf. 3.108, 5.646.

5 457. **cuneis . . . coactis**: 'in serried ranks', cf. 269, 575.

6 458. **gravem**: 'formidable' ('fortem', Servius).

7 458-60. Of the victorious Trojans Thymbraeus is not heard of elsewhere, Mnestheus and Achates appear frequently in the *Aeneid,* Gyas is a contestant in the ship race (5.118f.). Of the Italians Osiris, Arcetius and Epulo are not otherwise heard of, Ufens is mentioned several times (e.g. 7.745f.), and Tolumnius has figured largely in this book (258f., cf. especially 266).

8 464. **ipse**: Aeneas himself is looking only for Turnus.

9 **sternere morti**: 'to cast down to death', for the dative (*ad mortem*) cf. line 513, 8.566, 10.319. It is also possible that *morti* is an archaic form of the ablative, cf. 11.197 and 9.271 *sorti.*

10 465-6. 'nor those who meet him foot to foot', governed by *sternere morti,* contrasted with those who run away: *pede . . . aequo* is an unusual phrase, made clear by the contrast with *aversos,* meaning that they stood their ground ready to match Aeneas in battle.

11 465-6. **nec . . . insequitur**: 'nor does he pursue those wielding spears', i.e. threatening him from a distance, as opposed to those in his path.

12 467. **vestigat lustrans**: 'tracks down as he circles round him', cf. 481-2; the image is from hunting. For *lustrari* cf. 474 of the swift's circling flight.

Hoc¹ concussa² metu mentem Iuturna virago³
aurigam Turni media⁴ inter lora Metiscum
excutit et longe lapsum temone relinquit;   470
ipsa subit⁵ manibusque undantis flectit habenas,
cuncta⁶ gerens vocemque et corpus et arma Metisci.
Nigra⁷ velut magnas domini cum divitis aedes⁸
pervolat et pennis alta atria lustrat hirundo
pabula parva legens nidisque⁹ loquacibus escas,   475
et nunc porticibus vacuis, nunc umida circum
stagna sonat: similis medios Iuturna per hostis
fertur equis rapidoque volans obit¹⁰ omnia curru,
iamque hic germanum iamque hic ostentat ovantem
nec conferre manum patitur, volat avia longe.   480
Haud minus Aeneas tortos¹¹ legit obvius orbis,
vestigatque virum et disiecta¹² per agmina magna¹³
voce vocat. Quotiens oculos coniecit in hostem
alipedumque¹⁴ fugam cursu temptavit equorum,
aversos totiens currus Iuturna retorsit.   485
Heu, quid agat? Vario nequiquam fluctuat aestu,¹⁵
diversaeque vocant animum in contraria curae.

---

1 468. **hoc ... metu**: 'with fear of this', literally 'with this fear', a normal Latin idiom.

2 **concussa ... mentem**: retained accusative, see note on 64-5.

3 **virago**: 'warrior-maid', only here in Virgil; the word was used by Ennius (*Ann.* 521 *Paluda virago*), cf. also Ov. *Met.* 2.765. The sense is like that of *bellatrix*, used of Camilla in 7.805.

4 469. **media inter lora**: 'from between the reins', i.e. as he held them on each side of him.

5 471. **subit**: 'took over', cf. 5.176. Compare Hom. *Il.* 5.835f. where Athena takes over from Sthenelus, Diomedes' charioteer.

6 472. 'having everything that was Metiscus's, his voice, his appearance, his weapons'; for *gerens* cf. 1.315.

7 473f. The point of resemblance in this simile is the darting circular flight of the swift with the rapid swerving course of Juturna driving Turnus' chariot. There is an unusually large proportion of non-similar elements in the simile, the palace, the seeking of food for the baby birds, the noise of the swift. Notice how the simile takes us away momentarily from the battle to a scene of peace and normality. As far as we can tell the simile is original; the setting is like a Roman villa with its *atrium* and *porticus* and ponds in the grounds (*stagna*).

8 473-4. **aedes pervolat**: the accusative is governed by the preposition in the verb, cf. 8.24 *omnia pervolitat late loca*.

9 475. **nidisque loquacibus**: 'her noisy babies'; *nidi* ('nests') is used by metonymy for 'nestlings', cf. *Geo.* 4.17, *Aen.* 5.214.

10 478. **obit omnia**: 'ranged over the whole area', cf. 10.447.

11 481. **tortos ... orbis**: 'followed his twists and turns all round about, trying to confront him'; for *legit* cf. 9.393.

12 482. **disiecta**: 'scattered', by his approach.

13 482-3. **magna voce**: these two words go together; notice how the alliteration of *voce vocat* picks up the *v*'s of the previous line.

14 484. 'and tried to match with his speed the flight of Turnus' wing-footed horses'; for the sonorous compound adjective *alipes* see note on 7.277.

15 486-7. For the phraseology and general sense cf. 8.19-21. The meaning of *aestu* there is defined by *curarum* ('seething tide of anxiety'); here the same sense is understood from the next line.

Huic[1] Messapus, uti[2] laeva duo forte gerebat
lenta, levis[3] cursu, praefixa hastilia ferro,
horum unum certo contorquens derigit ictu.   490
Substitit Aeneas et se[4] collegit in arma
poplite subsidens; apicem tamen incita[5] summum
hasta tulit[6] summasque excussit vertice cristas.
Tum vero adsurgunt[7] irae, insidiisque[8] subactus,
diversos ubi sensit equos currumque referri,   495
multa[9] Iovem et laesi testatus foederis aras
iam[10] tandem invadit medios et Marte secundo
terribilis saevam nullo discrimine caedem
suscitat, irarumque omnis effundit habenas.

*500-53. In the general battle which ensues both Aeneas and
Turnus deal death all around them.*

[11]Quis mihi nunc tot acerba[12] deus, quis carmine caedes[13]   500
diversas obitumque ducum, quos aequore toto
inque vicem nunc Turnus agit, nunc Troius heros,
expediat? Tanton[14] placuit concurrere motu,

---

1 488. **huic:** *in hunc* (i.e. Aeneas), cf. 10.401.

2 **uti . . . gerebat:** 'carrying as he was', cf. 270, 623, and 5.388, 7.509.

3 489. **levis cursu:** 'lightly running along'; the word order here is unusual, with this phrase in apposition to the subject placed between the adjective *lenta* and its noun *hastilia.*

4 491. **se collegit in arma:** 'crouched behind his shield', cf. 10.412, 802.

5 492. **incita:** 'as it sped', 'cum impetu veniens', Servius.

6 493. **tulit:** 'took away', = *abstulit*, as in Enn. *Ann.* 416; cf. also 285.

7 494. **adsurgunt irae:** Aeneas' battle frenzy is like that which he showed in Book 10 (513f., 613f.).

8 **insidiisque subactus:** 'impelled by their treachery', in attacking him when he was not fighting them (464f.) but only seeking Turnus.

9 496. **multa:** adverbial, 'often', cf. 294, 7.593.

10 497. **iam tandem:** for a long time Aeneas has been trying to observe the spirit of the treaty for single combat by attacking only Turnus; but now he yields to battle-fury and attacks indiscriminately (498). Lines 498-9 are terrifying in their description of how Aeneas finally throws off all restraint (*terribilis, nulla discrimine,* summarised in *irarumque omnis effundit habenas*).

11 500f. Here Virgil places side by side the violent achievements on the battlefield of Aeneas and Turnus. He has arranged the structure of his narrative so that it switches constantly from the one to the other (505, 509, 513, 516, 529, 535, 539, 540). The reader realises (as he did in 10.513-604) that the qualities of Aeneas as a warrior are in every way as formidable as those of Turnus, and that although he is reluctant to fight and slow to be roused he does in fact fight violently and savagely once he is on the battlefield. The similarity between the two is explicitly indicated when Virgil uses a doubled simile applied to both of them (521f.). Generally speaking then Aeneas and Turnus are similar in this scene (contrast 311f., where see note); but there is one significant point of difference, namely the barbaric behaviour of Turnus in his first contest when he cuts off the heads of his victims and attaches them to his chariot (compare 9.465f.).

The terse recital of the names of the victims is varied with some brief characterisation (529, 535, 539) and with two longer descriptive passages, both of great pathos; the one (517f.) tells of Menoetes who had been a simple fisherman before he was sucked into war, and the other (542f.) invokes the Trojan Aeolus who had survived the ten year siege only to come to his final resting-place in Laurentian soil. See notes on 10.308f., 362f.

12 500. **acerba:** 'bitter suffering', used as a noun, cf. 678.

13 500-4. The new invocation is reminiscent of 9.525f.

14 503. **tanton:** for *tantone*, cf. 797 *mortalin*, 874 *talin* and note on 10.668 *tanton.*

Iuppiter, aeterna gentis in pace futuras?[1]
Aeneas Rutulum Sucronem[2] (ea[3] prima ruentis   505
pugna loco statuit Teucros) haud multa morantem
excipit in latus et, qua fata celerrima, crudum[4]
transadigit[5] costas et cratis pectoris ensem.
Turnus equo deiectum Amycum[6] fratremque Dioren,
congressus pedes, hunc venientem cuspide longa,   510
hunc mucrone ferit, curruque abscisa duorum[7]
suspendit capita et rorantia sanguine portat.
Ille[8] Talon Tanaimque neci fortemque Cethegum,
tris uno congressu, et maestum mittit Oniten,
nomen[9] Echionium matrisque genus Peridiae;   515
hic fratres Lycia missos et Apollinis agris[10]
et iuvenem exosum nequiquam bella Menoeten,[11]
Arcada, piscosae cui circum flumina Lernae
ars fuerat pauperque domus nec[12] nota potentum
munera, conductaque pater teliure serebat.   520

---

1 504. The alliance of Trojans and Italians is finally conceded by Juno in 821f.

2 505. **Sucronem:** this Rutulian is not heard of before.

3 505-6. **ea prima . . . Teucros:** 'this was the first battle which held up the Trojans as they rushed forward'; cf. 458f. for the Trojan successes. It was only however a brief check (*haud multa morantem*).

4 507. **crudum:** 'cruel', 'pitiless', cf. 10.682.

5 508. **transadigit . . . ensem:** 'drove his sword through his ribs, through the fence of his chest'; the words *costas* and *cratis* are governed by *trans* in the verb (cf. 276 and *transportare*, 6.328). *Cratis* is explanatory of *costas* (cf. 516 for this use of *et* and compare 531): the ribs are the 'fence' of the chest, cf. Ov. *Met.* 12.370.

6 509. Amycus and Diores are unhorsed by Turnus and then killed on foot (*pedes*, 510); a Trojan Amycus is mentioned several times in the poem (e.g. 1.221) but without characterisation; the Trojan Diores competed in the foot-race (5.297f.).

7 511-12. For all the similarity between Aeneas and Turnus in these violent battle scenes, Aeneas does not behave with this kind of barbarity.

8 513. **ille:** Aeneas (in 516 *hic* is Turnus). The four victims of Aeneas mentioned here are not heard of elsewhere.

9 515. 'an Echionian name, son of Peridia', i.e. Theban; for *nomen* cf. 1.288, for *genus* (which implies nobility) 7.213. The quadri-syllabic ending in the Greek style reflects the Greek subject-matter.

10 516. The brothers are not named, but may be those mentioned in 10.126; one of Apollo's most famous centres of worship was at Patara in Lycia (Hor. *Odes* 3.4.64).

11 517f. This is one of the most memorable of Virgil's brief descriptions of otherwise unknown warriors. The pathos is immediately aroused by the phrase *exosum nequiquam bella*, and elaborated and deepened by the description of how he loved to fish in the waters of Lerna (in Argolis) near his humble home in Arcadia while his father ploughed in his rented farm.

12 519-20. **nec nota potentum munera:** 'knowing nothing of attendance on men of power' (Jackson Knight), i.e. he had been happy with his simple life and had not wished to be dependent on any patron or to seek power and ambition that way. The phrase recalls the famous praise of the farmer's life in *Geo.* 2.495f. *illum non populi fasces, non purpura regum flexit . . .* For *munera* M has *limina*, cf. Hor. *Epod.* 2.8, but this is probably a substitution for the more difficult *munera* (here equivalent to *obsequia*, as Servius says). Others take *munera* to mean the responsibilities which great men bear, or the gifts given by the powerful to their poor dependants.

Ac velut immissi diversis partibus ignes[1]
arentem in silvam et virgulta[2] sonantia lauro,
aut ubi decursu rapido de montibus altis
dant sonitum spumosi amnes et in[3] aequora currunt
quisque suum populatus[4] iter: non[5] segnius ambo   525
Aeneas Turnusque ruunt per proelia; nunc,[6] nunc
fluctuat ira intus, rumpuntur[7] nescia vinci
pectora, nunc totis in[8] vulnera viribus itur.

    Murranum[9] hic,[10] atavos et avorum antiqua sonantem[11]
nomina per[12] regesque actum genus omne Latinos,   530
praecipitem scopulo[13] atque ingentis turbine saxi
excutit effunditque solo; hunc lora et iuga subter[14]
provolvere[15] rotae, crebro super ungula pulsu
incita nec domini memorum proculcat equorum.
Ille[16] ruenti Hyllo[17] animisque immane[18] frementi   535
occurrit telumque aurata[19] ad tempora torquet:

---

1 521f. The doubled simile compares Aeneas and Turnus first with two separate forest fires burning in the same area, and then with two great rivers close to one another rushing down from the mountains. Both similes have parallels in Homer; cf. *Il.* 11.155f., 20.490f., and *Il*.4.452f., 11.492f., 16.389f. Compare also *Aen.* 2.304f. where the destruction of Troy is compared with fire burning a cornfield or a river spreading destruction, and for the general phraseology cf. *Aen.* 10.405f. (fire), Lucr. 1.283f. (water).

2 522. **virgulta sonantia lauro**: cf. 3.442 *Averna sonantia silvis,* 6.704 *virgulta sonantia silvae;* the meaning here (as there) is 'rustling', not 'crackling' in the fire (which most commentators give, following Servius). Compare *Ecl.* 8.82 *fragilis incende . . . lauros,* where *fragiles* (like *sonantia* here) explains why the laurel will burn well.

3 524. **in aequora**: perhaps 'plains', as often in Virgil, but more likely 'sea', cf. Hom. *Il.* 16.391.

4 525. **populatus iter**: 'carving out its course', with the idea of leaving devastation in its wake.

5 **non segnius**: 'with no less vehemence', also after a simile in 4.149, 7.383, 8.414. 10.657.

6 526. **nunc, nunc**: the metrical effect here is very violent, with the rare sense pause after the fifth foot and the highly rhetorical monosyllabic ending with repetition.

7 527-8. **rumpuntur . . . pectora**: 'their unconquerable hearts are at bursting-point', i.e. the waves of fury can hardly be contained; cf. Lucr. 3.297-8 (describing lions) *pectora qui fremitu rumpunt plerumque gementes, nec capere irarum fluctus in pectore possunt. Nescia* with the infinitive occurs in *Geo.* 2.467, 4.470; cf. especially Hor. *Odes* 1.6.6 *Pelidae stomachum cedere nescii.*

8 528. **in vulnera . . . itur**: 'they move to deadly combat', *itur* is impersonal, cf. 6.179, 9.641, and line 739.

9 529. **Murranum**: this Latin warrior was evidently a close friend of Turnus (639).

10 **hic**: again Aeneas and Turnus (535) are compared with *hic* and *ille* (cf. 513, 516).

11 **sonantem**: 'loudly boasting of, cf. *iactare avos* in Prop. 2.13.10, and see note on 7.451.

12 530. **per regesque . . . Latinos**: 'and all his race descended through Latin kings'; cf. Hor. *Odes* 3.17.3-4. *Actum* has the sense of *ductum.*

13 531. **scopulo atque . . . saxi**: 'with a rock, with the whirling impact of a mighty boulder'; *atque* is used in an explanatory sense (a sort of hendiadys), cf. 508, 516, and especially 9.569.

14 532. The rhythm of the second half of the line is very abrupt (representing the violence of Murranus' fall) with the elisions at the fourth foot caesura, over a heavy pause, and at the end of the fourth foot, and the double dissyllable at the line end.

15 533-4. 'the rapid hooves above him, with their repeated impact, the hooves of the horses that did not think of their master trampled him down'; *nec* is archaic for *non,* cf. *Ecl.* 9.6 *quod nec vertat bene.*

16 535. **ille**: Turnus (see note on 529). His Trojan victim Hyllus is not heard of before.

17 **Hyllo animisque**: there is hiatus at the caesura, cf. 31.

18 **immane**: adverbial, cf. 10.726 *hians immane,* and line 398 *acerba fremens.*

19 536. **aurata ad tempora**: i.e. his helmet was of gold, cf. 9.50. Notice the alliteration of *t.*

olli per galeam fixo stetit hasta cerebro.
Dextera nec tua te. Graiurn fortissime Cretheu,[1]
eripuit Turno, nec di texere Cupencum
Aenea veniente sui:[2] dedit obvia ferro   540
pectora, nec misero clipei[3] mora profuit aeris.
Te[4] quoque Laurentes viderunt, Aeole, campi
oppetere et late terram consternere tergo:
occidis, Argivae quem non potuere phalanges[5]
sternere nec Priami regnorum eversor Achilles;   545
hic[6] tibi mortis erant metae, domus alta sub Ida,
Lyrnesi[7] domus alta, solo Laurente sepulcrum.
Totae adeo conversae[8] acies omnesque[9] Latini,
omnes Dardanidae, Mnestheus[10] acerque Serestus
et Messapus[11] equum domitor[12] et fortis Asilas   550
Tuscorumque phalanx Euandrique Arcades alae,[13]
pro se quisque viri summa[14] nituntur opum vi;
nec mora nec requies, vasto certamine tendunt.[15]

---

1 538. **Cretheu**: this Cretheus, a Greek presumably from Evander's city, is not mentioned before (which is the case also with Cupencus and Aeolus). The use of the vocative (apostrophe) adds a variety to the list of victims, but is not developed here as it is with Aeolus (542f.).

2 540. **sui**: Servius tells us that Cupencus was a Sabine word for a priest.

3 541. **clipei mora . . . aeris**: 'the defence of the bronze of his shield'; for *mora* cf. 10.485. *Aeris* is the reading of all the MSS; almost all editors accept a sixteenth-century emendation *aerei* (scanned as a spondee by synizesis, see note on 84), but 10.336 *clipei transverberat aera* seems a sufficient parallel.

4 542. **te quoque**: after the rapid switch from a victim from Aeneas' side (538) to one from Turnus' side (539) we return again to a Trojan death.

5 544-5. The survival of Aeolus through all the perils of the Greek siege of Troy is described in phrases somewhat reminiscent of Aeneas' words in 2.196f.

6 546-7. 'Here was the end of your life's course; your proud home was beneath Mt. Ida, at Lyrnesus your proud home, but your tomb was in Laurentian soil'. Here the pathos, already potentially invoked by the extended use of apostrophe (542-7), is strengthened by the metaphor in *metae* (the end of the course, cf. 3.714, 10.472) and especially by the repetition of *domus alta;* cf. 2.405-6 (with Austin's note), 6.495-6, 7.586-7, 10.821-2. The thought of these two lines is based on Hom. *Il.* 20.389f.

7 547. **Lyrnesi**: locative. For Lyrnesus in the Troad cf. 10.128.

8 548. **conversae**: 'engaged', turned to face each other.

9 omnesque: *-que* here means 'both', and its corresponding *-que* ('and') is replaced by the repetition of *omnes*; see note on 10.313-14.

10 549. The Trojan Mnestheus has been frequently mentioned in this book; he is linked with Serestus in 9.171.

11 550. Messapus the Latin is frequently mentioned (128); for the Etruscan Asilas, ally of Aeneas, cf. line 127.

12 **domitor:** the last syllable is lengthened in arsis, see note on 13.

13 551. These are Aeneas' allies, the Etruscans under Tarchon and the Arcadians sent by Evander under the leadership of his son Pallas; cf. 11.835.

14 552. **summa nituntur opum vi**: the phrase is taken from Ennius (*Ann.* 161, 412). Compare also *Aen.* 9.532 *summaque evertere opum vi,* where the same archaic effect is achieved by the imitation of the monosyllabic ending.

15 553. **tendunt**: 'press on', cf. 917.

554-92. Venus puts into Aeneas' mind the idea of attacking the Latin capital itself. He urges on his men, and they move in to the attack. There is panic within the city.

¹Hic mentem² Aeneae genetrix pulcherrima misit

iret ut ad muros urbique adverteret agmen   555

ocius et subita turbaret clade Latinos.

ille³ ut vestigans diversa per agmina Turnum

huc atque huc acies⁴ circumtulit, aspicit urbem

immunem⁵ tanti belli atque impune quietam.

Continuo pugnae accendit maioris imago: 560

Mnesthea⁶ Sergestumque vocat fortemque Serestum

ductores, tumulumque capit quo⁷ cetera Teucrum

concurrit legio, nec⁸ scuta aut spicula densi

deponunt. Celso medius stans aggere fatur:

'ne⁹ qua meis esto dictis mora, Iuppiter¹⁰ hac stat,   565

neu quis ob inceptum subitum mihi¹¹ segnior ito.

Urbem¹² hodie, causam belli, regna ipsa Latini,

ni¹³ frenum accipere et victi parere fatentur,

eruam et aequa solo fumantia culmina ponam.

Scilicet exspectem libeat dum proelia Turno   570

nostra pati rursusque velit concurrere victus?¹⁴

---

1 554f. We see here a very different Aeneas from the man who swore the oaths before single combat (175f.). He is angry at the breaking of the treaty, and frustrated by being unable to catch Turnus. His speech is brusque and cruel (see note on 568), and though he justifies himself as he moves to the attack (579f.) there is here an element of ruthlessness, accentuated by the simile of the smoked-out bees (587f.).

2 554. **mentem:** 'intention', 'idea', cf. 8.400; the phrase *mentem misit* is followed by a final clause.

3 557. **ille:** Aeneas responds to the plan Venus has put in his mind, to make a sudden direct attack on Latinus' capital.

4 558. **acies circumtulit:** 'turned his gaze', cf. 6.788 *huc geminas nunc flecte acies.*

5 559. 'free of all the war, at peace and undisturbed'; for *immunis* cf. Ov. *Met.* 8.690, 9.253; the adverb *impune* qualifies the adjective *quietam.*

6 561. Mnestheus (*Mnesthea* is Greek accusative) and Serestus were mentioned in line 549; Sergestus was one of the competitors in the ship-race (5.121f.). The same line occurs in 4.288.

7 562. **quo:** 'to which' ('whither').

8 563-4. **nec scuta … deponunt:** Roman soldiers remained in full battle-array when being addressed by their commander.

9 565. **ne … esto:** 'let there not be'; *ne* with the imperative is poetic.

10 **Iuppiter hac stat:** the line ending is taken from Ennius (*Ann.* 258); the rhythm is unusual for Virgil, and adds a powerful emphasis.

11 566. **mihi:** ethic dative, 'I urge you'.

12 567f. Observe how the accusative *urbem* is thrown to the front of the sentence and held in tension by two appositional phrases in this line, then by two conditional clauses in the next line, before the verb is finally offered; this is itself a violent word and its metrical shape is such that it can only be used by means of an elision of-am before a short syllable, a rare type of elision.

13 568. 'unless they agree to accept the yoke and as conquered people to obey us'; (*or fateri* in this unusual sense cf. 7.433; the metaphorical use of *frenum* (literally 'bridle') is common, though the word is much more frequent in the plural. Aeneas' conditions here contrast very strongly with his previous statement in the oaths before the single combat (189f.), that he would not impose obedience on his enemy; then he was composed and calm, now he is angry.

14 571. **victus:** 'already defeated as he is'; Aeneas interprets Turnus' avoidance of the single combat as a defeat.

Hoc caput, [1]o cives, haec belli summa nefandi.
ferte faces propere foedusque reposcite flammis.'[2]
dixerat, atque animis pariter certantibus omnes
dant[3] cuneum densaque ad muros mole feruntur.   575
Scalae improviso subitusque apparuit ignis.
Discurrunt alii ad portas primosque trucidant,
ferrum alii torquent et obumbrant[4] aethera telis.
Ipse inter primos dextram sub moenia tendit[5]
Aeneas, magnaque incusat voce Latinum   580
testaturque deos iterum se ad proelia cogi,
bis[6] iam Italos hostis, haec altera foedera rumpi.
Exoritur trepidos inter discordia civis:
urbem alii reserare iubent et pandere portas
Dardanidis ipsumque trahunt[7] in moenia regem;   585
arma ferunt alii et pergunt defendere muros.
Inclusas ut cum latebroso[8] in pumice pastor[9]
vestigavit apes fumoque[10] implevit amaro:
illae intus trepidae[11] rerum per cerea[12] castra
discurrunt magnisque acuunt stridoribus iras;   590
volvitur ater[13] odor tectis, tum murmure caeco
intus saxa sonant, vacuas it fumus ad auras.

---

1 572. 'this city, my citizens, is the capital and the centre of this wicked war'; *hoc* is attracted into the gender of its predicate *caput*, as is normal in Latin, cf. 10.858.

2 573. Notice the very violent alliteration of *f* in this final violent line; the phrase *foedus reposcite flammis* means that they are to require the restoration of the broken treaty by fire and sword.

3 575. **dant cuneum:** 'they form ranks', in attacking wedge-formation, cf. 269, 457. Notice the pattern of alliteration of *d* and *m*.

4 578. **obumbrant . . . telis:** cf. 11.611, with note.

5 579f. This is a fine picture of Aeneas standing before the walls, his right hand outstretched, rebuking Latinus and proclaiming his reluctance to be driven to further acts of war.

6 582. 'that the Italians were now his enemies for the second time, this was the second treaty to be broken'; the first occasion was described in Book 7, where Latinus accepts the Trojans' peaceful overtures (259f., 284-5), but is before long brushed aside by his own people as they rush to arms (591f.).

7 585. **trahunt:** *trahere volunt* (Servius); they are for forcing Latinus to go to the walls to negotiate or surrender.

8 587f. Virgil uses bee similes also at 1.430f., 6.707f on both occasions to illustrate busy activity and movement; here the point is anger and panic as the bees are smoked out. Cf. Ap. Rh. 2.130f., whom Virgil follows closely here, and compare Virgil's own phrase in *Geo.* 4.230 *fumosque manu praetende sequacis.*

9 587. **latebroso in pumice:** 'in crannied rock', cf. 5.214, the same phrase, *Geo.* 4.44 *pumicibusque cavis.*

10 588. **fumoque implevit amaro:** 'has enveloped them in acrid smoke'.

11 589. **trepidae rerum:** 'terrified at what is happening'. *Rerum* is an extension of the objective genitive, cf. Livy 5.11.4 *trepidi rerum suarum,* Ov. *Her.* 20.198 *anxia sunt vitae pectora nostra tuae;* it is very like the genitive of cause in 1.178 *fessi rerum.*

12 **cerea castra:** the personification of the bees (they are trying to defend their 'camp' or their 'home', *tectis,* 591) is reminiscent of *Georgics* 4 (cf. especially *cerea regna, Geo.* 4.202, and the use of *castris* of the bees in *Geo.* 4.108).

13 591. **ater odor:** Servius points out the unusual phrase, as the colour really applies to the visual aspect not to the smell.

593-613. Queen Amata is driven to utter despair by the sight of the Trojans attacking, and blaming herself for the imminent disaster commits suicide by hanging herself.

Accidit haec fessis etiam fortuna Latinis,[1]

quae totam luctu concussit funditus urbem.

Regina[2] ut tectis[3] venientem prospicit hostem,   595

incessi[4] muros, ignis ad tecta volare,

nusquam acies contra[5] Rutulas, nulla agmina Turni,

infelix[6] pugnae iuvenem in certamine credit

exstinctum et subito[7] mentem[8] turbata dolore

se causam clamat crimenque caputque malorum,[9]   600

multaque [10]per maestum demens effata furorem[11]

purpureos moritura manu discindit amictus

et[12] nodum informis leti trabe nectit ab alta.

Quam cladem miserae postquam accepere Latinae,

filia prima manu floros[13] Lavinia crinis   605

et roseas laniata genas, tum cetera circum

turba furit[14], resonant late plangoribus aedes.

Hinc totam infelix vulgatur[15] fama per urbem;

demittunt mentes, it scissa veste Latinus

---

1 593f. The suicide of Amata is very reminiscent of the tone of Greek tragedy (see note on 603), and in this and other aspects recalls the death of Dido. Both look out on misfortune from their watchtowers (see note on 595), both are *infelix* (598), both act on a sudden impulse (599); *moritura* is used of both (602, 4.519); above all both are victims of *furor* (601, 4.697).

2 595. **regina:** notice the emphasis on the first word, and the way in which suspense is held by the build-up of subordinate clauses (595-7) and the series of main verbs (598-603) describing Amata's thoughts, words, and finally deeds.

3 **tectis:** 'from the roof of her palace', with *prospicit;* cf. Dido in 4.586.

4 596. **incessi:** passive infinitive of *incessere* ('attack'), cf. Stat. *Th.* 1 1.361 *tecta incessentem.*

5 597. **contra:** adverbial, 'Rutulian lines nowhere in opposition'.

6 598. **infelix:** the special epithet of Dido in Book 4; cf. also 7.376 with note.

7 599. **subito . . . dolore:** cf. 4.697 (Dido) *subitoque accensa furore.*

8 **mentem turbata:** retained accusative, see note on 64-5.

9 600. The violence of Amata's outburst is emphasised by the fierce alliteration of *c* and *q* as well as by the unusual trochaic break in both fourth and fifth feet (see my note on 5.52, OUP Ed.) and the vivid use of *crimen* ('the guilty one') and *caput* ('source', cf. 11.361). Amata recognises that her opposition to Lavinia's marriage with Aeneas was the cause of the disastrous war.

10 601-3. The pattern of alliteration becomes subtler as the mournful narrative is resumed after Amata's outburst, observe the pairs of *m*'s, *f*'s, *m*'s again, interwoven with the *d* sounds, and finally the *n*'s, *l*'s and *t* 's of 603.

11 601. **furorem:** cf. 4.697, quoted above on 599.

12 603. 'and she secured a noose, instrument of a hideous death, from a high beam'. We are reminded here very strongly indeed of Greek tragedy, especially perhaps of Sophocles' Jocasta and Euripides' Phaedra; this method of death (described here as *informis*) was regarded by the Romans as particularly degrading, and draws attention to Amata's wild and uncontrolled character (see notes on 7.56, 323f.).

13 605. **floros . . . crinis:** the construction is retained accusative (so also *genas* in the next line), see note on 64-5. The MSS all have *flavos,* but Servius attests *floras* as read by Probus; it is a rare and archaic word meaning 'flower-like', 'shining', found in Naevius, Ennius, Accius, and Pacuvius.

14 607. **furit:** 'became frenzied in their grief, a very strong word.

15 608. **vulgatur fama per urbem:** cf. 4.666 (after Dido's death) *bacchatur Fama per urbem.*

coniugis attonitus[1] fatis urbisque ruina,   610

canitiem[2] immundo perfusam pulvere turpans.

[[3]Multaque se incusat, qui non acceperit ante

Dardanium Aenean generumque asciverit ultro].

> *614-96. Turnus hears the noise of lamentation from the capital; Juturna tries to persuade him to stay away from Aeneas, but he now insists that he must go to face him. News is brought of the siege of the city and the death of Amata. Turnus at first is rooted to the ground, bewildered and confused; then he rushes to the capital and calls on his friends to cease fighting and leave him to single combat with Aeneas.*

[4]Interea extremo bellator in aequore Turnus

palantis sequitur paucos iam segnior atque[5]   615

iam minus atque minus successu laetus equorum.

Attulit[6] hunc illi caecis terroribus aura

commixtum clamorem, arrectasque impulit auris

confusae sonus urbis et inlaetabile murmur.

'Hei mihi! quid tanto turbantur moenia luctu?   620

Quisve ruit tantus diversa[7] clamor ab urbe?'

Sic ait, adductisque amens subsistit habenis.

Atque [8]huic, in faciem soror ut conversa Metisci

aurigae currumque et equos et lora regebat,

---

1 610. **attonitus:** 'thunderstruck', 'dazed'.

2 611. 'defiling his white hair by covering it with filth and dust', cf. Cat. 64.224 *canitiem terra atque infuso pulvere foedans.*

3 612-13. These lines (almost the same as 11.471-2) are not in the major MSS and are clearly spurious.

4 614f. It is in this passage that Turnus is seen in his full tragic stature. We are often reminded of Greek tragedy (notes on 650, 665-8) as we see the disintegration of Turnus' strength under the pressure of calamity and reverses. All of his confidence crumbles in the realisation that doom is near, and a new aspect of his character emerges as he brings himself to face the destruction of all he has fought for and his own imminent death. He forces himself to throw off delusion, to accept (what he knew all along, 632f.) that Juturna was shielding him and that he cannot permit this to continue; he becomes honest with himself and acquires a new heroic stature in so doing. He faces death with courage and pride (646f., 676f., 693f.), and as the fragments of his world fall around his head he is, in the midst of catastrophe, still unbowed.

5 615. **atque:** the weak line ending (cf. 355) seems here to convey a sense of weariness, especially as it is picked up with another *atque* in the next line.

6 617-19. 'The breeze bore to him, bringing hidden terrors, this confused noise, and there struck upon his listening ears the sound of the city in tumult, the murmur that portended nothing happy'.
The pattern of alliteration in 618 (first *c*, then initial vowels) prepares the expectation for the memorable rhythm and diction of 619, a rhythm used by Virgil elsewhere very rarely and always in places of high emotional tension, e.g. 2.483 (Priam's palace) *apparet domus intus et atria longa patescunt*, 3.707 (death of Anchises) *hinc Drepani me portus et inlaetabilis ora . . .* , 5.781 (Venus' anger) *Iunonis gravis ira neque exsaturabile pectus* (where see my note, OUP Ed.).

7 621. **diversa:** 'distant', cf. 3.4 *diversa exilia*, 9.1, Ov. *Trist.* 1.3.19. The point is that the noise is so great although the city is a long way off.

8 623-5. 'And his sister, changed as she was into the appearance of his charioteer Metiscus, and controlling chariot, horses, and reins, confronted him with these words'. Turnus has taken the reins from his charioteer (his sister Juturna disguised as Metiscus, cf. 468f.), and she opposes the implication of his words and actions by trying to persuade him to continue to fight on the outskirts of the battlefield. For the construction of *ut* cf. 488 with note.

talibus occurrit dictis: 'hac, Turne, sequamur   625
Troiugenas,[1] qua prima viam victoria pandit;
sunt alii qui tecta manu defendere possint.
Ingruit[2] Aeneas Italis et proelia miscet;
et nos saeva manu mittamus funera Teucris.
Nec numero[3] inferior pugnae neque honore recedes.'   630
Turnus ad haec:[4]
'o soror, et dudum[5] agnovi, cum prima per artem
foedera turbasti teque haec in bella dedisti,
et nunc nequiquam[6] fallis dea. Sed quis Olympo
demissam tantos voluit te ferre labores?   635
An fratris miseri letum ut crudele videres?
Nam quid[7] ago? Aut quae iam spondet fortuna salutem?
Vidi oculos ante ipse meos me voce[8] vocantem
Murranum,[9] quo non superat[10] mihi carior alter,
oppetere ingentem[11] atque ingenti vulnere victum.   640
Occidit infelix ne nostrum dedecus Ufens[12]
aspiceret; Teucri potiuntur corpore et armis.
Exscindine domos (id rebus defuit unum)
perpetiar, dextra[13] nec Drancis dicta refellam?
Terga dabo et Turnum[14] fugientem haec terra videbit?   645

---

1 626. **Troiugenas:** cf. 8.117, and compare *Graiugenae* (8.127).

2 628. **ingruit:** 'is sweeping down on', cf. 11.899. This sentence is in the form of an imagined objection (such as is introduced in prose by *at enim*), and it is answered by *et nos;* we can do as well here as he is doing there.

3 630. **numero:** understand *funerum* from the previous line; *pugnae* goes with *honore*.

4 631. This is the only incomplete line in Book 12 (unless 218 is considered incomplete); see notes on 1.534, 7.129.

5 632-4. **et dudum ... et nunc:** Turnus says he recognised Juturna before when she was disguised as Camers (222f.) and urged the Rutulians to fight, and he recognises her now, disguised as Metiscus though she is. Compare Diomedes' recognition of Athena in Hom. *Il.* 5.815.

6 634. **nequiquam fallis dea:** 'in vain you try to hide your divinity', literally 'try to deceive me, goddess as you are'; the construction of *fallere* is like that of the Greek λανθάνειν, cf. 7.350.

7 637. **quid ago:** 'what am I to do?' The present indicative is used vividly for the deliberative subjunctive, cf. 10.675.

8 638. **voce vocantem:** the repetition (cf. 483) reinforces the emphasis already given by *ipse meos* on the guilt felt by Turnus at his personal failure to heed the appeal which he saw and heard.

9 639. **Murranum:** cf. 529f.

10 **superat:** Turnus means no living person is dearer to him than Murranus was. For *superat* (= *superest*) cf. 873.

11 640. **ingentem ... victum:** a Homeric phrase (*Il.* 16.776) repeated from 10.842.

12 641. **Ufens:** cf. 460; the rhetorical statement that Ufens died to avoid seeing Turnus' shame is very effective.

13 644. **dextra ... refellam:** emphasis is put on *dextra* by its position before *nec;* notice the very heavy alliteration of *d* in this line (and of *t* in the next, and *m* in the next). Turnus refers to Drances' taunt in 11.370f.

14 645. **Turnum:** the use of his own name adds to the indignation of his feelings, cf. 74.

Usque[1] adeone mori miserum est? Vos[2] o mihi, Manes,[3]
este boni, quoniam superis[4] aversa voluntas.
Sancta[5] ad vos anima[6] atque istius inscia culpae
descendam magnorum haud umquam indignus avorum'.
   Vix[7] ea fatus erat, medios volat ecce per hostis   650
vectus equo spumante Saces,[8] adversa sagitta
saucius ora, ruitque implorans nomine Turnum:
'Turne, in te suprema salus, miserere tuorum.
Fulminat Aeneas armis summasque minatur[9]
deiecturum arces Italum[10] excidioque daturum,   655
iamque faces ad tecta volant. In te ora Latini,
in te oculos referunt; mussat[11] rex ipse Latinus
quos generos[12] vocet aut quae sese ad foedera flectat.
Praeterea regina, tui[13] fidissima, dextra
occidit ipsa sua lucemque exterrita fugit.   660

---

1 646. **usque . . . miserum est?:** compare the speech of Mezentius, when he recognises his death is imminent and goes forth to meet it, 10.846-56.

2 **vos o mihi, Manes:** the rhythm is unusual with the double dissyllabic ending and the pause after the fifth foot; this — along with the alliteration — puts strong stress on the word *Manes* which is in antithesis with *superis*.

3 **Manes:** gods of the underworld, of death, as opposed to the *di superi*. Warde Fowler (ad loc.) mentions Antigone's wish to find favour with 'those below' (οι κατω), Soph. *Ant.* 75, but rightly says that the main reference is a Roman one, an appeal to the spirits of Turnus' ancestors.

4 647. **superis:** dative with *voluntas,* equivalent to *superorum voluntas.*

5 648-9. 'I shall descend to you as a guiltless soul, without knowledge of any such sin, never unworthy of my great ancestors'. By *istius culpae* he means 'flight' (645). These are splendid heroic sentiments, sonorously rounded with the elisions and striking rhyme of *-orum* at the speech's end, particularly noticeable as the genitive with *dignus* is rare and with *indignus* unparalleled except for the imitation in Sil. 8.383. Turnus' words are faintly reminiscent of what Dido had said just before she died (4.654) *et nunc magna mei sub terras ibit imago.*

6 648. **anima atque istius inscia:** the reading and scansion here are much disputed. The scansion can be restored by accepting the reading *nescia* from a few late MSS, but it would be hard to explain the corruption. If we keep *inscia* we may regard *istius* as scanning with three long syllables (the lengthening in thesis of the final syllable would be unparalleled); or we may regard the final syllable of *anima* as lengthened in arsis (see note on 13) and hiatus (again unparalleled). Thus the choice is between

$\mathsf{anim(a)\ atqu(e)\ istius}$ or $\mathsf{anima\ atqu(e)\ istius}$; the latter is on the whole to be preferred because the metrical innovation is more startling and more likely to have been done for deliberate effect than the other. Emendations carry no conviction (*anima ah, anima hic, anima atque anima*). Housman's conjecture (*C.Q.*, 1927, p. 10) *sancta atque istius ad vos anima inscia* is based on convincing paleographical arguments, but does not produce a good line.

7 650. **Vix ea . . . volat ecce**: the dramatic suddenness is portrayed by the parataxic sentence (= *vix fatus erat cum volat*) and by the present tense following a pluperfect (cf. 574) as well as by *ecce.* The speech which follows, with its message of disaster and death, is reminiscent of one of the structural features of Greek tragedy, the messenger's speech.

8 651-2. **Saces . . . ora**: 'Saces, wounded by an arrow full in the face'; Saces has not been mentioned before. *Ora* is accusative of respect, see note on 5.

9 654-5. **minatur deiecturum**: the reflexive *se* is omitted as in 762, 8.534.

10 655. **Italum**: genitive; Virgil never uses the form *Italorum.*

11 657. **mussat**: 'mutters to himself in doubt'; the word is followed by an indirect deliberative question as in 718; cf. Enn. *Ann.* 344-5 *expectans si mussaret quae denique causa pugnandi fieret.*

12 658. **generos**: the plural is used to imply that if Latinus gave his daughter to Aeneas other marriages between Latins and Trojans would follow; see note on 11.105.

13 659. **tui fidissima**: 'whose trust was all in you'; for the objective genitive *tui* cf. 29, and compare the use after *amantissimus.*

Soli[1] pro portis Messapus et acer Atinas
sustentant acies. Circum hos utrimque phalanges
stant densae strictisque seges[2] mucronibus horret
ferrea; tu currum deserto in gramine versas.'
Obstipuit[3] varia confusus imagine rerum   665
Turnus et obtutu tacito stetit; aestuat ingens
uno in corde pudor mixtoque insania luctu
et furiis agitatus amor[4] et conscia virtus.
Ut primum discussae umbrae et lux reddita menti.
Ardentis oculorum orbis ad moenia torsit   670
turbidus[5] eque[6] rotis magnam respexit ad urbem.
    Ecce autem flammis inter tabulata[7] volutus
ad caelum undabat vertex[8] turrimque tenebat,
turrim[9] compactis trabibus quam eduxerat ipse
subdideratque rotas pontisque instraverat altos.[10]   675
'Iam[11] iam fata, soror, superant, absiste morari;
quo deus et quo dura vocat Fortuna sequamur.

---

1 661. **soli:** 'all alone'; the spondaic word filling the first foot gains emphasis, cf. 70, 674. Messapus and Asilas were mentioned together in 550.

2 663-4. **seges . . . ferrea:** for the metaphor cf. 7.525-6 and compare 11.601-2.

3 665-8. 'Turnus was thunderstruck, thrown into confusion by the shifting picture of events, and stood there staring and speechless; in that one heart there surged intense shame, madness mingling with misery, love tormented by frenzy, and the knowledge of his personal valour'. This is a memorable description of the utter confusion of the tragic hero about whose ears the world falls in fragments; nothing could more vividly suggest the nemesis sent by the gods on those who disobey them. We now see that Turnus is in the process of that inexorable movement towards tragedy which characterises the heroes of the Greek stage. The aspects of his mental turmoil are clearly presented: first and foremost shame and humiliation (*pudor*), because he has failed his people and his queen; then intense grief driving him to madness, arising from the horrible consequences of his failure; then his love for Lavinia, inflamed by the Furies (for it was contrary to the wishes of heaven); and finally his sense of personal honour, his knowledge of his prowess which prevents him from seeking a way of escape (for *conscia virtus* cf. 5.455). The words from *aestuat . . . luctu* were used of Mezentius (10.870-1) as he went to meet his death, and the reminiscence deepens the certainty that this must be Turnus' fate too (compare the reminiscence of Mezentius in 646, where see note).

4 668. **amor:** the final syllable is lengthened in arsis at the caesura, see note on 13.

5 671. **turbidus:** the run-on dactylic adjective is given metrical emphasis, cf. 951 and my note on 5.480 (OUP Ed.).

6 **eque rotis:** 'from his chariot'; for the metonymy cf. *Geo.* 3.114.

7 672. **tabulata:** the 'stories' of the tower, the different levels; cf. 2.464.

8 673. **vertex:** 'a tongue of fire' (cf. Lucr. 6.298, Hor. *Odes* 4.11.12), defined in meaning by *flammis* in the previous line.

9 674. **turrim:** the emphasis given by the repetition of the word is made stronger by the alliteration of *t* and the diaeresis after the first spondee; cf. 70, 661. The reason for the emphasis is to bring out the symbolism: the destruction of the tower which Turnus has built suggests his own imminent destruction, and the fire which destroys it takes our thoughts back to the fire planted in Turnus by Allecto (7.456-7).

10 675. Compare 9.530f. for a similar description of a mobile tower with connecting gangways (*pontes*) which when used by the defenders of a city could be moved to any point of the walls where danger threatened, thus presenting them with an advantage of height and easier reinforcement.

11 676. 'Now, I see it now, sister, the fates are too strong; hold me not back'. Turnus' realisation that his hour has come, confirmed by the destruction of the tower he himself had built, is expressed in a fine line of simple phraseology.

Stat conferre manum Aeneae,[1] stat,[2] quidquid[3] acerbi est,
morte pati, neque me indecorem, germana, videbis
amplius. Hunc,[4] oro, sine me furere ante furorem.'   680
Dixit, et e curru saltum dedit ocius arvis
perque hostis, per tela ruit maestamque sororem
deserit ac rapido cursu media agmina rumpit.
Ac veluti montis saxum de vertice praeceps[5]
cum ruit avulsum[6] vento, seu turbidus imber   685
proluit aut annis solvit sublapsa vetustas;
fertur in[7] abruptum magno mons[8] improbus actu[9]
exsultatque[10] solo, silvas armenta virosque
involvens secum: disiecta per agmina Turnus
sic urbis ruit ad muros, ubi plurima[11] fuso   690
sanguine terra madet striduntque hastilibus aurae,
significatque[12] manu et magno[13] simul incipit ore:
'parcite iam, Rutuli, et vos tela inhibete, Latini;
quaecumque est fortuna, mea est; me[14] verius unum[15]
pro vobis foedus luere et decernere ferro.'   695
Discessere omnes medii spatiumque dedere.

---

1 **Aeneae**: poetic dative with verbs of fighting against, cf. *congredi* (1.475), *concurrere* (1.493),*pugnare* (4.38, 11.600).

2 678. **stat**: 'it is my fixed purpose', cf. 2.750 *stat casus renovare omnis*.

3 678-9. **quidquid . . . pati**: 'to suffer in death all its bitterness'; for the partitive genitive with the neuter of the pronoun cf. Cat. 31.14 *quidquid est domi cachinnorum*, and *Aen.* 9.274.

4 680. **hunc ... furorem**: 'let me, I beg, show this last madness before the end'; *ante* is adverbial. The repetition of the idea of *furere* by its cognate accusative *furorem* puts enormous emphasis, at this last moment, on the characteristic quality of Turnus.

5 684f. The simile compares the uncontrolled impetus and power of Turnus with that of a rock scattering all in its path (*disiecta per agmina*); compare Hom. *Il.* 13.137f. (of Hector), Spenser, *F.Q.* 1.11.54.

6 685-6. **avulsum . . . vetustas**: 'torn up by the wind, or by a storm of rain washing it away, or by the long passage of the years undermining and loosening it'; for the construction cf. Hor. *Odes* 3.4.21f. *Sublapsa* means partly that time with its years imperceptibly had 'stolen up on' the rock (cf. 7.354), and partly that time had 'undermined' its foundations.

7 687. **in abruptum**: 'headlong'; *abruptum* is used as a noun as in 3.422; cf. Milton *P.L.* 2.409 'over the vast abrupt'.

8 **mons improbus**: 'the uncontrollable mass'; *improbus* here is a reminiscence of Homer's αναιδής πέτρη ('ruthless rock'), *Il.* 13.139, in the simile Virgil is imitating; it personifies the inanimate object, and its overtones apply to Turnus as well as to the rock.

9 **actu**: *impetu* (Servius); this is an uncommon use of the word, cf. Lucr. 3.192.

10 688. **exsultatque solo**: 'and bounds over the ground'; there is probably an overtone of rejoicing, again personifying the inanimate object.

11 690-1. **plurima . . . terra madet**: 'the earth is soaked deep', cf. *Geo.* 2.166 *auro plurima fluxit*.

12 692. **significatque manu**: 'and he made a sign with his hand', calling for silence so that he could make his announcement.

13 **magno . . . ore**: 'with a loud cry', more vivid than *magna voce*.

14 694-5. **me verius . . . luere**: 'it is more proper for me alone to atone for the (broken) treaty on your behalf; *verius* is equivalent to *aequius, iustius* (cf. Hor. *Sat.* 2.3.312); *foedus luere* conveys *ruptum foedus luere* (266f.). Others, perhaps rightly, take the meaning to be simply 'to atone for the treaty' in the sense that Turnus considers the making of a treaty with an enemy to be a stain on his countrymen.

15 694f. Turnus' words now are remarkably like those of Aeneas when the truce was broken (315f.).

697-790. Aeneas moves to fight with Turnus and the combat begins. They throw their spears without effect and then join in close combat. Turnus strikes Aeneas with his sword, but it shatters in fragments — Turnus had in his hurry taken his charioteer's sword by mistake. Aeneas chases Turnus, and as they pass the stump of an oleaster sacred to Faunus Aeneas tries to regain his spear which is sticking in the root. Faunus prevents him from pulling it out, and meanwhile Juturna gives Turnus his own sword. Venus promptly restores Aeneas' spear to him, and they stand again facing each other poised for battle.

¹At pater² Aeneas audito nomine Turni

~~deserit et muros et summas deserit arces~~

praecipitatque³ moras omnis, opera omnia rumpit

laetitia exsultans horrendumque⁴ intonat armis: 700

quantus⁵ Athos⁶ aut quantus Eryx aut ipse⁷ coruscis

cum fremit⁸ ilicibus quantus gaudetque nivali

---

1 697f. This is a section of rapid and eventful narrative, finishing without advantage to either contestant; at the end of it the action is held in suspense as the narrative moves to Olympus before the final decisive scenes on earth (887f.). In Homeric fashion Virgil intersperses similes to illustrate the action (701f., Aeneas like a mountain; 715, Aeneas and Turnus like two bulls; 749f., Aeneas pursues Turnus like a hunting hound pursuing a stag). The similarity of the narrative itself with Homer, both here and in the final section of this book, is extremely marked, as Virgil reenacts the famous and familiar scenes of *Iliad* 22 (the pursuit of Hector by Achilles); see notes on 725f., 749f., 761, 763-5, 784-5, 887f.

The overall effect of this is not merely to enrich the narrative with literary reminiscence, but also to add a new chapter to the Homeric story; this time the Trojan is the pursuer and will be the victor. Already in Book 6 Turnus had been called 'a second Achilles' (6.89), and on other occasions in the poem we have been reminded of this (e.g. 7.371-2, 9.136f., 9.742); now the new Achilles is in the losing position, and Aeneas, leader of the *gens Hectorea,* will win the contest for the future of his people. It is the Trojan war over again, but this time *versis fatis* (11.287).

2 697. **pater:** this epithet (rather than *pius*) is chosen at this decisive stage because the father of Rome now faces his last enemy for the last time.

The sentence is prolonged by the repetition of *et . . . et* ('both . . . and') and of *deserit* to emphasise how Aeneas leaves everything else when he hears the name of Turnus.

3 699-700. 'and thrust aside all impediments, broke off all other operations exulting in his joy, thundering fearfully in his armour'; the delight of Aeneas at having at last forced his enemy to battle is portrayed very strongly. For *praecipitare moras* cf. 8.443; for *intonat* (clashing his sword on his shield) cf. 332 *clipeo increpat.*

4 700. **horrendumque**: adverbial accusative; cf. 338 and g.632 *horrendum stridens,* 9.732 (*arma*) *horrendum sonuere.*

5 701f. 'As huge as Athos, as huge as Eryx, or as huge as Father Appenninus himself when he roars amidst his waving oak trees and rejoices as he towers high with snow white summit up to the breezes of heaven'. This simile gives a statuesque picture of Aeneas, massive as a mountain; contrast the simile of Turnus like a rock crashing down a mountain (684f.). The main point of comparison is size, but subsidiary comparisons are made with the roar of the forests (cf. *intonat*) and the joy of Appenninus (cf. *laetitia*); notice too how the epithet of the father of Italy's mountains (*pater*) echoes *pater Aeneas* (697). Compare the brief simile in Hom. *Il.* 13.754 where Hector sets out to battle 'like a snowy mountain'; Conington quotes Milton, *P.L.* 4.985f.:

On the other side Satan alarmed
Collecting all his might dilated stood,
Like Teneriff or Atlas unremoved:
His stature reached the Skie . . .

6 701. **Athos . . . Eryx:** Mt. Athos is in Northern Greece, on the Chalcidice peninsula (its final syllable is long, the Greek Ἄθως, cf. Juv. 10.174; in *Geo.* 1.332 Virgil uses the form *Athos*). Eryx is the mountain in N.W. Sicily, cf. 10.36.

7 701-3. **ipse** . . . **auras:** the order is very interwoven, with *quantus* postponed by five words from the head of its clause, and *ipse* far divided from its noun *pater.* Notice how Virgil lingers on the description of the Appennines after passing over Athos and Eryx with a mere mention.

8 702. **fremit**:cf. 10.98 (*flamina*) *fremunt silvis.*

vertice se attollens pater[1] Appenninus ad auras.
Iam vero et Rutuli certatim et Troes et omnes
convertere oculos Itali, quique[2] alta tenebant   705
moenia quique imos pulsabant ariete[3] muros,
armaque deposuere umeris. Stupet ipse Latinus[4]
ingentis, genitos diversis partibus orbis,
inter se colisse viros et cernere[5] ferro.
Atque[6] illi, ut vacuo patuerunt aequore campi,   710
procursu rapido coniectis eminus hastis
invadunt[7] Martem clipeis atque aere sonoro.
Dat[8] gemitum tellus; tum crebros ensibus ictus
congeminant, fors[9] et virtus miscentur in unum
ac velut ingenti Sila[10] summove Taburno[11]   715
cum duo conversis inimica in proelia tauri
frontibus incurrunt, pavidi cessere magistri,[12]
stat pecus omne metu mutum, mussantque[13] iuvencae
quis nemori imperitet, quem tota armenta sequantur;
illi inter sese multa vi vulnera miscent[14]   720

---

1 703. **pater Appenninus:** the Appennines, as the main mountain range in Italy, are personified and receive the title *pater* as the River Tiber does (*Geo.* 4.369). Mackail suggests that the reference is to the central mountain in the chain, now called Gran Sasso d'Italia; see also Warde Fowler, ad loc.

2 705-6. **quique ... quique:** 'both those who ... and those', referring first to the besieged Rutuli, then to the attacking Trojans.

3 706. **ariete:** scanned as a dactyl with consonantal *i*, cf. 356, 401 and 11.890 *arietat.*

4 707-9. By presenting the situation as seen through the eyes of Latinus Virgil achieves a momentary detachment from the personality of the two main contestants, giving a sense of history and of the universal importance of the event.

5 709. **cernere ferro:** *cernere* is here used in its archaic sense for *decernere* (cf. 695); compare Enn. *Ann.* 196, 555. The main MSS have the unmetrical *et decernere,* but *cernere* is attested by Seneca (*Ep. Mor.* 58.3) and by Servius, and is far preferable to reading *decernere* without *et.*

6 710. **atque illi:** the narrative returns from the spectators to the two contestants.

7 712. **invadunt Martem:** 'rush to battle', a highly poetic variant for *ineunt pugnam;* for *invadere* in this sense cf. 9.186, for the full scale metonymy *of Mars = pugna* cf. 790.

8 713. **dat gemitum tellus:** cf. Hom. *Il.* 2.784 των υπο ποσσι μεγα στεναχιζετο γαια, *Aen.* 9.709, Milton, *P.L.* 9.782f.

9 714. **fors ... unum:** 'chance and valour mingle together', not (as Servius says) the *fors* of Turnus and the *virtus* of Aeneas, but the *fors* and *virtus* of each: *fors* refers to the opportunities which each man's *virtus* gives him in the course of the battle.

10 715. **Sila ... Taburno:** as is often his way (cf. 4, 331, 701, 857) Virgil gives geographical location to his simile. Both these mountains (the Sila range in Bruttium, S. Italy, and Taburnus in the Samnite territory) were mentioned in the *Georgics* (3.219, 2.38).

11 715f. The simile is based on a brief comparison in Apollonius (2.88-9, two bulls fight for a heifer). Virgil has greatly developed it, emphasising the conflict for leadership, the isolation of the two contestants as the cowmen and the herds stand off, the noise and violence of the clash. He has used much of the material of *Geo.* 3.220f., a description of two bulls fighting. Turnus was compared with a bull earlier in the book (103f.): now Aeneas matches him. Cf. Spenser *F.Q.* 4.4.18.

12 717. **magistri:** 'cowmen', cf. *Geo.* 3.445.

13 718. **mussantque iuvencae:** for the construction of *mussare* governing an indirect deliberative question cf. 657; the alliteration of *m* adds to the effect.

14 720. The slow spondaic line with clash of accent and ictus conveys the struggle; cf. 8.452 (the Cyclopes at work in their smithy) *illi inter sese multa vi bracchia tollunt, Geo.* 3.220 (two bulls fighting) *illi alternantes multa vi proelia miscent.*

cornuaque obnixi infigunt et sanguine largo
colla armosque lavant, gemitu nemus omne remugit:
non aliter Tros Aeneas et Daunius[1] heros
concurrunt clipeis, ingens fragor aethera complet.
Iuppiter ipse duas aequato examine lances[2]   725
sustinet et fata imponit diversa duorum,
quem[3] damnet labor et quo vergat pondere letum.

    Emicat hic[4] impune[5] putans et corpore toto
alte sublatum consurgit[6] Turnus in ensem
et[7] ferit; exclamant Troes trepidique[8] Latini,   730
arrectaeque[9] amborum acies. At perfidus ensis
frangitur in medioque ardentem deserit ictu,
ni[10] fuga subsidio subeat. Fugit ocior Euro
ut capulum ignotum[11] dextramque aspexit inermem.
Fama[12] est praecipitem, cum prima in proelia iunctos   735

---

1 723. **Daunius heros:** Turnus is so called from his father Daunus, cf. 22 and compare 785.

2 725f. This image is very closely based on Hom. *Il.* 22.209f. (cf. also *Il.* 8.68f.), and is the first of many reminiscences during the single combat of the final contest between Achilles and Hector, recounted in *Iliad* 22. In the passage in Homer Zeus takes his golden scales, puts in two 'fates' of death, one of Achilles and one of Hector, holds the scales at the point of balance, and Hector's day of doom sinks down. Virgil uses *lances* for the pans of the scales, *examen* for the 'tongue' (a somewhat more specific description than Homer's), and *fata* for the Greek κηρε; the noticeable difference between the two is that Virgil does not indicate the result of the weighing.
The concept of the weighing of a man's fate in the scales is quite frequent in Greek literature (cf. Aesch. *Agam.* 439, *Pers.* 346, *Supp.* 822); cf. also Suet. *Vesp.* 25 and Milton *P.L.* 4.1010f.

3 727. 'to see whom the struggle would condemn to destruction and on which side death would sink down with its weight'. The indirect question is loosely attached to the previous sentence; there is an ellipsis of something like *ut indicaret*. The idea of the loser sinking (as also in Homer; contrast Milton, quoted above, where Satan's scale rises) is linked with the idea of death and the underworld. Both of the clauses in this line refer to the loser (cf. 719, where both clauses refer to the same bull); Servius and some of the old grammarians read *aut,* and maintained that *damnet* meant 'set free' (cf. *Ecl.* 5.80); this is followed by some modern commentators and translators, but seems unlikely in the highest degree. *Quo . . . pondere* is very difficult: it may mean *cuius pondere* ('with the weight of which warrior'), or Maguinness may be right in taking it as the adverb *quo* ('whither', i.e. upon which warrior).

4 728. **hic:** 'at this moment', 'next', a rather abrupt introduction of the first individual action of the duel.

5 **impune putans:** 'thinking it safe', i.e. seeing his opportunity.

6 729. **consurgit ... in ensem:** the same phrase in g.749; the warrior is pictured as lifting his sword high above him at full stretch; cf. 11.284 *in clipeum adsurgat.*

7 730. **et ferit:** the conflict of accent and ictus on the pyrrhic word and the heavy pause add great dramatic emphasis after the slow spondees of the previous line; cf. 5.643, 10.336.

8 **trepidique:** the Latins are 'excited' at the decisive move, anxiously hoping that it will be successful.

9 731. **arrectaeque ... acies:** 'the gaze of both sides was riveted on them'; notice the assonance of initial *a*. Servius says for *acies* 'aut exercitus, aut oculi'; if we take it as *exercitus* the meaning is 'the battle lines were on tiptoe with excitement', but the other explanation is preferable, cf. 558 and 2.173, 7.399.

10 733. **ni ... subeat:** there is an ellipsis before the conditional sentence of something like *et inermis relictus Turnus periisset* (Heyne). This gives a very abrupt effect, which led Ribbeck to postulate a lacuna, not without good reason; examples like 8.522f. are much easier. Another possibility would be to punctuate with a full stop after *ictu* and an aposiopesis after *subeat: nifuga subsidio subeat, fugit* etc. For the use of the present subjunctive to portray a past unfulfilled condition vividly cf. 6.292f., 11.912f.

11 734. **ignotum:** i.e. not his own, contrast *notum* in 759.

12 735. **fama est praecipitem:** 'the story is that in his hurry . . .'; *fama* is used simply to add an explanation of past events to the present narrative.

conscendebat equos, patrio[1] mucrone relicto,
dum[2] trepidat, ferrum aurigae rapuisse Metisci;
idque diu, dum terga dabant palantia Teucri,
suffecit; postquam arma[3] dei ad Volcania ventum[4] est,
Mortalis[5] mucro glacies ceu futtilis[6] ictu   740
dissiluit; fulva[7] resplendent fragmina harena.
Ergo amens diversa fuga petit aequora Turnus
et nunc huc, inde huc incertos[8] implicat orbis;
undique enim densa Teucri inclusere corona[9]
atque hinc vasta palus, hinc ardua moenia cingunt.   745
    Nec minus Aeneas, quamquam tardata[10] sagitta
interdum genua impediunt cursumque recusant,
insequitur trepidique[11] pedem pede fervidus urget:
inclusum[12] veluti [13]si quando flumine nactus
cervum aut puniceae saeptum formidine[14] pennae[15]   750
venator cursu canis et latratibus instat;

---

1 736. **patrio mucrone:** 'his father's sword', cf. 90, where Turnus puts it on when rehearsing for the battle; evidently he took the wrong sword on the next day, when after the wounding of Aeneas he rushed to battle (326f. *poscit equos atque arma simul, . . . emicat*), cf. *dum trepidat* (737).

2 737. **dum trepidat:** idiomatic use of *dum* with the present indicative (contrast 738 where *dum*, *'as* long as'), here kept even in oratio obliqua, like *cum conscendebat* (= *eo ipso tempore quo*).

3 739. **arma . . . Volcania:** the weapons made for Aeneas by Vulcan at the instigation of Venus (cf. 107, 167).

4 **ventum est:** the impersonal passive (cf. 528, 803) has particular point here; 'when it was a question of facing . . .'; the effect would have been the same with any mortal weapons.

5 740. **mortalis:** Turnus' *patrius mucro,* which he left behind, had also been made by Vulcan (90-1).

6 **futtilis:** 'useless', used metaphorically in 11.339.

7 741. **fulva . . . harena:** a vivid pictorial image, picking up the simile of 740.

8 743. **incertos implicat orbis:** 'wound his erratic course in many a circle', cf. 5.584-5 *alternosque orbibus orbis impediunt.*

9 744. **corona:** 'ring', the encircling crowd of the onlookers, cf. 11.475.

10 746. **tardata sagitta**: the reference is to Aeneas' arrow wound, cf. 319f.

11 748. **trepidique . . . urget:** 'fiercely presses hard on the track, step for step, of his frightened opponent'. The dactylic rhythm of the line helps to represent the speed of the chase.

12 749. **inclusum . . . nactus:** the word order of the simile is unusual; emphasis is put on *inclusum* (Turnus is trapped) by its position before the conjunctions which introduce the clause; and the subject *canis* is held up and strangely placed between *cursu* and *et latratibus.* This has led some commentators to take *venator* as the subject ('huntsman') with *canis* as genitive; but this is highly unlikely. The adjectival use of *venator* is like that of *bellator* (*equus*) in 10.891, 11.89.

13 749f. 'As when sometimes a hunting dog finds a stag hemmed in by a river or trapped by the ropes with their brilliant feathers and pursues it hotly, chasing after it and barking . . .' The simile is mainly based on Hom. *Il.* 22.188f. (Achilles pursuing Hector like a hound pursuing a stag); cf. also Hom. *Il.* 10.360f., Ap. Rh. 2.278f. But Virgil has adapted and enlarged the image; in Homer there is no emphasis on how the stag is trapped, and there is an Italian atmosphere in the present passage, with the use of the technical word *formido* and the geographical epithet *Umber.* The passage recalls to mind the simile comparing Dido with a hunted deer (*Aen.* 4.69f.).

14 750. **formidine:** this is a technical word for a frightening device used in hunting, made of brilliant feathers attached to a rope; cf. *Geo.* 3.372 *puniceaeve agitant pavidos formidine pennae.* There is a full description of it in Nemesianus (*Cyn.* 303f.); cf. also Sen. *De Ira* 2.12.

15 **pennae**: rather a striking instance of the singular used for the plural.

ille autem insidiis[1] et ripa territus alta
mille fugit refugitque vias, at vividus Umber[2]
haeret[3] hians, iam[4] iamque tenet similisque tenenti
increpuit malis morsuque elusus inani est;   755
tum vero exoritur clamor ripaeque lacusque[5]
responsant circa et caelum tonat omne tumultu.
Ille simul[6] fugiens Rutulos simul increpat omnis
nomine quemque vocans notumque[7] efflagitat ensem.
Aeneas mortem contra praesensque[8] minatur   760
exitium, si quisquam adeat, terretque trementis[9]
excisurum[10] urbem minitans et saucius[11] instat.
Quinque[12] orbis explent cursu totidemque retexunt
huc illuc; neque enim levia aut ludicra[13] petuntur[14]
praemia, sed Turni de vita et sanguine certant.   765
    Forte sacer Fauno[15] foliis oleaster amaris[16]
hic steterat, nautis olim[17] venerabile lignum,

---

1 752. **insidiis:** i.e. by the *formido*.

2 753. **Umber**: the geographical noun conveys the excellence of the hound (cf. Gratt. *Cyn.* 172) as well as adding an Italian atmosphere. Umbria was to the north of Rome, east of Etruria.

3 754. **haeret:** 'hangs on the trail', *haerere* is metaphorical, not literal, as the following phrases show.

4 754-5. **iam iamque . . . malis**: 'and is ever on the point of seizing him, and snaps with his jaws as if actually seizing him'; for *iam iamque* and *similis* cf. 6.602-3 *atra silex iam iam lapsura cadentique imminet adsimilis* (cf. also 2.530, 5.254 and line 940). These lines are closely modelled on the simile in Apollonius (2.280-1); Ovid in his turn imitates Virgil (*Met.* 1.533f., esp. 535-6 (*canis*) . . . *inhaesuro similis iam iamque tenere sperat*).

5 756-7. Servius reports that there was some uncertainty whether these lines should be included in the simile, but he rightly concludes that they should not. It is true that the simile ends rather abruptly without a clause (introduced by *non aliter* or the like) to resume the narrative.

6 758. **simul . . . simul:** very emphatic, 'at every moment as he fled', cf. 268.

7 759. **notumque:** his own sword that he knew so well, *patrius mucro* (736); contrast *ignotum* in 734.

8 760. **praesensque:** neuter, agreeing with *exitium*.

9 761. The situation is reminiscent (with a different application) of Hom. *Il.* 22.205, where Achilles stops any intervention from his own side.

10 762. **excisurum:** supply *se*, cf. 655.

11 **saucius:** 'wounded though he was', cf. 746-7.

12 763-4. 'They run five full circles, and as many again in the opposite direction'. The diction is highly ornate, reminiscent of Virgil's description of the cavalcade of the *lusus Troiae*; cf. especially 5.583 *inde alios ineunt cursus aliosque recursus*. In Homer, *Iliad* 22, Achilles chased Hector three times round the walls (208).

13 764. **ludicra:** such as would be given in games, *digna ludo* (Servius).

14 764-5. Again Virgil recalls Homer, *Iliad* 22, this time very closely imitating lines 159f.: επει ουχ ιερηιον ουδε βοειην αρνυσθην α τε ποσσιν αεθλια γιγνεται ανδων, αλλα περι ψυχης θεον Εκτορος ιπποδαμοιο ('for they were not striving for a beast of sacrifice or an oxhide, such as are men's prizes for speed of foot, but their race was for the life of Hector, tamer of horses').

15 766. **Fauno:** King Latinus was the son of the Italian country deity Faunus; see note on 7.47f.

16 766. The wild olive tree again recalls a detail from *Iliad* 22, where Achilles and Hector speed past 'the wind swept fig tree' (145).

17 767. **olim:** 'from early times', cf. *Geo.* 4.421.

servati ex undis ubi figere dona solebant[1]
Laurenti divo et votas suspendere vestis;
sed stirpem Teucri nullo[2] discrimine sacrum   770
sustulerant, puro[3] ut possent concurrere campo.
Hic hasta Aeneae stabat,[4] huc impetus illam
detulerat fixam[5] et lenta[6] radice tenebat.
Incubuit voluitque manu convellere ferrum
Dardanides,[7] teloque sequi quem prendere cursu   775
non poterat. Tum vero amens formidine Turnus
'Faune, precor, miserere' inquit, 'tuque optima ferrum
Terra tene, colui vestros si semper honores,
quos contra[8] Aeneadae bello fecere[9] profanos.'
Dixit, opemque dei non[10] cassa in vota vocavit.   780
Namque diu luctans lentoque in stirpe moratus
viribus haud ullis valuit discludere[11] morsus
roboris Aeneas. Dum nititur acer et instat,
rursus in aurigae faciem mutata Metisci[12]
procurrit fratrique ensem dea Daunia reddit.   785
Quod Venus audaci nymphae indignata licere
accessit telumque alta ab radice revellit.
Olli sublimes armis animisque refecti,[13]
hic gladio fidens, hic acer et arduus hasta,

---

1 768-9. The custom was for sailors who were saved from shipwreck to dedicate their clothing as a thank offering to Neptune (Hor. *Odes* 1.5.13f.); in this case they make the dedication to the Laurentian deity (Faunus) to whose guardianship they had safely returned.

2 770. **nullo discrimine**: not making an exception of this sacred tree when they were cutting down the other trees.

3 771. **puro**: 'open', cf. Livy 24.14.6 *dimicaturum puro ac patenti campo.*

4 772. **stabat**: 'was sticking'; this is the spear Aeneas had unsuccessfully thrown at Turnus (711). For the lengthening in arsis of the second syllable of *stabat* see note on 13.

5 773. **fixam et ... tenebat**: 'and was holding it fast', *et* is postponed; the subject is *impetus* extended to mean the penetration caused by the impetus. Compare Achilles' spear in Hom. *Il.* 21.171f.

6 **lenta**: 'tough', cf. 781.

7 775. **Dardanides**: used of Aeneas also in 10.545.

8 779. **contra**: 'in contrast', adverbial.

9 **fecere profanos**: 'have profaned', by destroying Faunus' sacred tree which was growing in Mother Earth.

10 780. **non cassa**: 'not vain', equivalent to *non incassum* (8.378).

11 782-3. **discludere morsus roboris**: 'to loosen the bite of the tree'; this is highly ornate diction; for *morsus* cf. 1.169 (of the anchor's bite).

12 784-5. Juturna, *dea Daunia* (daughter of Daunus, cf. 723), again assumes the disguise of Turnus' charioteer Metiscus (cf. 468f.). The return of the sword recalls the passage in Homer *Il.* 22.276f. where Athena restores to Achilles the spear he has thrown at Hector.

13 788-90. After the two divine interventions, which cancel each other out, Virgil halts the narrative with a static picture prior to leaving the mortal scene in order to describe the events in Olympus (791f.). The archaic *olli*, filling the first foot (see note on 70), serves to slow the movement for this summarising picture of the two contestants facing each other.

adsistunt[1] contra certamina Martis anheli.   790

> *791-842. In Olympus Jupiter orders Juno to cease from interference against the Trojans. She yields, but begs that the Latins may keep their language and dress, and not become Trojans; that Rome may be great because of Italian virtues. Jupiter agrees to this, and promises that the Romans will above all other peoples pay worship to Juno.*

[2]Iunonem interea rex omnipotentis Olympi
adloquitur fulva[3] pugnas de nube tuentem:
'quae iam finis erit, coniunx? Quid[4] denique restat?
Indigetem[5] Aenean scis ipsa et scire[6] fateris
deberi caelo fatisque ad sidera tolli.[7]   795
Quid struis? Aut qua spe gelidis in nubibus haeres?[8]
Mortalin[9] decuit[10] violari vulnere divum?
Aut ensem (quid enim sine te Iuturna valeret?[11])
Ereptum[12] reddi Turno et vim crescere victis?
Desine iam tandem precibusque inflectere[13] nostris,   800

---

1 790. 'stand facing the contest of breathless Mars'; Servius knew of a reading *certamine,* in which case *contra* would be adverbial. *Anheli* might be nominative plural, referring to Aeneas and Turnus, but the run of the line makes it perhaps preferable to take it with *Martis.* The line is a variation on 12.73 *in duri certamina Martis euntem;* for the remarkable phrase *Martis anheli* cf. Sil. 2.430 *certamina anhela movere.*

2 791f. In this episode the conflict is resolved on the divine plane. The hostility of Juno to the Trojans has been a major theme throughout the poem; it was powerfully stated in the invocation to the poem (1.8f.), and in the introduction to the start of the narrative (1.12-33), and now at last it is overcome, as Jupiter had prophesied it would be (1.279f.). But it is overcome largely on Juno's own conditions, that Troy should become a city of the past and that the new people from which the Romans will spring should be Latins in language and way of life (see notes on 823-5, 827, 828). 'Let the Roman race be strong because of Italian virtues', she says (827), and in this she reflects the admiration for the Italians that has been evident often in the second half of the *Aeneid.* Instead of an enemy she now becomes one of Rome's great guardian deities: *mecumque fovebit Romanos, rerum dominos gentemque togatam* (Jupiter's words in 1.281-2). Her enmity, so often perplexing and frightening as the poem has unrolled, is now seen to have achieved a beneficial outcome in the long aspect of history; for the Romans as civilisers of the world were indeed Italians and not Trojans.

3 792. **fulva . . . de nube:** compare Apollo in 9.640, watching the battle from his position in the clouds. *Fulva* is 'golden', cf. 7.76.

4 793. **quid denique restat:** 'what is left for you now at the last?'; cf. 2.70. Jupiter asks Juno to realise that she has no resources left.

5 794. **indigetem**: 'as native hero of the land', cf. *Geo.* 1.498 where the Indigetes are invoked. The word is used of a national hero who is deified; it is applied to Aeneas in Livy 1.2.6 *Iovem indigetem appellant,* and in Tib. 2.5.44, *Ov. Met.* 14.608.

6 **scire fateris:** for the construction (in prose it would be *scire te fateris*) cf. 3.603, 7.433, and compare 568.

7 795. The deification of Aeneas was promised explicitly by Jupiter in 1.259-60 (to Venus) *sublimemque feres ad sidera caeli magnanimum Aenean.*

8 796. The first half of this line is similar to Jupiter's message of disapproval in 4.235.

9 797. **mortalin:** = *mortaline,* see note on 503.

10 **decuit:** 'was it right?', that Aeneas (destined to be a god) should have been wounded by a mortal (319f.).

11 798. **valeret:** past potential, 'what could she have done?'

12 799. **ereptum:** this is a strange word, as his sword was restored (*reddit,* 785) to Turnus because he had not brought it to battle, having taken Metiscus' by mistake. Day Lewis renders 'missing'. Perhaps Lejay is right in suggesting that Jupiter means that fate snatched Turnus' sword away by making him forget it.

13 800. **inflectere:** 'be moved by', imperative passive.

ne[1] te tantus edit tacitam dolor et[2] mihi curae
saepe tuo dulci tristes ex ore recursent.
Ventum[3] ad supremum est. Terris[4] agitare vel undis
Troianos potuisti, infandum accendere bellum,
deformare[5] domum et luctu miscere hymenaeos: 805
ulterius temptare veto.' Sic Iuppiter orsus;
sic dea summisso contra Saturnia vultu:
'ista[6] quidem quia nota mihi tua, magne, voluntas,
Iuppiter, et Turnum et terras invita reliqui;
nec[7] tu me aeria solam nunc sede videres   810
digna[8] indigna pati, sed[9] flammis cincta sub ipsa
starem acie traheremque inimica in proelia Teucros.
Iuturnam misero (fateor) succurrere[10] fratri[11]
suasi et pro vita maiora audere[12] probavi,
non ut tela tamen, non ut contenderet arcum;   815
adiuro [13]Stygii caput implacabile fontis,
una[14] superstitio superis quae reddita divis.
Et nunc cedo equidem pugnasque exosa[15] relinquo.

---

1 801. **ne ... edit:** the *ne* clause is dependent on the idea of praying in the previous line. *Edit* is an archaic form of the subjunctive of *edere* ('eat', 'consume'), cf. Plaut. *Capt.* 461, Hor. *Epod.* 3.3; most MSS have the normal subjunctive form *edat*, but *P1* has *edit* and it is attested by Acron and Diomedes.

2 801-2. **et mihi ... recursent:** 'and that sad anxieties coming from your sweet lips may not keep visiting me'; compare 1.662 *sub noctem cura recursat. Mihi* is emphatic by its antithesis with *te* and its position in the fifth foot, causing conflict of accent and ictus. Jupiter urges reconciliation for Juno's sake (*te*) and for his own (*mihi*), tactfully softening the point about having to listen to his wife's perpetual complaints by the phrase *tuo dulci ex ore.*

3 803. **ventum ad supremum est:** the use of the impersonal passive here conveys the inevitability of the situation.

4 803-4. **terris ... potuisti:** cf. 1.3-4 *et terris iactatus et alto vi superum, saevae memorem Iunonis ob iram.*

5 805. **deformare domum:** 'to mar their home', elaborated in the next phrase, meaning that Juno's schemes have caused the marriage between Aeneas and Lavinia to have a background of dissension and death (especially that of Amata, Lavinia's mother).

6 808. **ista:** notice the emphatic position of the second person pronoun, soon to be reinforced by *tua.*

7 810. **nec ... videres:** 'nor would you now be seeing me', if it was not for my knowledge of your wishes.

8 811. **digna indigna:** cf. 9.595 *digna atque indigna relatu:* Servius says 'id est omnia, et proverbialiter dictum est'. Compare *fanda nefanda* (Cat. 64.405).

9 811-12. **sed flammis ... Teucros:** 'but encircled in fire I would have my place right by the battle line, and I would be dragging the Trojans into deadly combat'. These are resounding phrases, similar to those used by Juno in Hor. *Odes* 3.3.61f.

10 813. **succurrere:** the infinitive with *suadere* is common in verse, cf. 10.10.

11 813-14. **fratri ... pro vita:** notice how sympathy is sought for Turnus by Juno's rhetoric (Juturna is not portrayed as helping an enemy general, but as trying to save her poor brother's life).

12 814. **audere probavi:** the subject of *audere* is *Iuturnam.*

13 816. An oath by the Styx was the strongest asseveration that could be made by an immortal; cf. 6.323f., 9.104, 10.113, Hom. *Il.* 15.37-8, *Od.* 5.185-6, and Warde Fowler ad loc. The construction after *adiuro* is cognate accusative ('swear by'), cf. 6.324 *iurare ... numen (Stygiae paludis)*, and line 197.

14 817. 'which is the one religious sanction granted to the gods above'. The construction is *quae una superstitio est reddita; quae* refers to the whole previous line and is attracted to the gender of its predicate *superstitio.*

15 818. **exosa:** 'in hatred', cf. 5.687. The word is very strong: Juno is not prevailed upon to withdraw, but in a positive spirit of revulsion because of her ultimate helplessness she abandons her part in the war.

Illud¹ te, nulla fati quod lege tenetur,²
pro Latio obtestor, pro maiestate tuorum:³   820
cum iam conubiis pacem felicibus (esto⁴)
component, cum iam leges et foedera iungent,
ne⁵ vetus indigenas nomen mutare Latinos
neu Troas fieri iubeas Teucrosque vocari
aut vocem mutare viros aut vertere vestem.   825
Sit Latium, sint Albani⁶ per saecula reges,
sit Romana potens Itala virtute propago:⁷
occidit, ⁸occideritque⁹ sinas cum nomine Troia.'
Olli subridens hominum rerumque repertor:¹⁰
'es¹¹ germana Iovis Saturnique altera proles,   830
irarum tantos volvis sub pectore fluctus.
Verum age et inceptum frustra summitte furorem:

---

1 819. This line is slow and deliberate, spondaic in movement (note *illud* filling the first foot, cf. 70, 661); the spondaic rhythm continues in the next three lines as Juno holds the suspense before coming to her request.

2 **tenetur**: 'is stopped', in the sense of 'is forbidden', cf. 2.159.

3 820. **tuorum**: because Latinus was descended from Jupiter's father Saturnus, 7.47f.

4 821. **esto**: 'so be it', cf. 7.313, 10.67, where Juno uses the same rhetorical phrase. Here as in 10.67 special emphasis is put, by the rare pause after the fifth foot, on what precedes, especially on *felicibus,* an adjective which Juno hates to have to use of her enemies.

5 823-5. 'Do not order the Latins, who were born here, to change their old name, or become Trojans, or be called Teucri, or that the people should change their language or alter their dress'. At this point the sympathy turns towards Juno, as she puts the emphasis on her love for the Italians and the Latin language and way of life (emphasised very heavily here with alliteration of *v.*) Throughout the *Aeneid* the Latins have been shown as ancient inhabitants of Italy; contrast Livy 1.2, Dion. Hal. 1.60, where a people called Aborigines were the older inhabitants, and the name Latins used only in Aeneas' time.

6 826. **Albani . . . reges:** the reader's thoughts go back to the great pageant of unborn Roman heroes at the end of Book 6, starting (760f.) with the kings of Alba Longa. According to Jupiter's prophecy (1.266f.) Ascanius founded Alba Longa and his successors ruled there for three hundred years before Romulus founded Rome.

7 827. This line magnificently summarises the general feeling of the second half of the *Aeneid* (cf. especially the loving description of the Italian peoples in the catalogue, 7.641f.). It also expresses the feelings of Virgil's own time, as indicated in the description of the battle of Actium on Aeneas' shield (8.678 *hinc Augustus agens Italos inproelia Caesar*).

8 828. 'Troy has fallen, and let her stay fallen, name and all'. This final line, like much else in Juno's speech, is very closely similar to her speech, to the gods in council, in Hor. *Odes* 3.3, especially 57f., *sed bellicosis fata Quiritibus / hac lege dico, ne nimium pii / rebusque fidentes avitae / tecta velint reparare Troiae*. One of the most fascinating tensions in the *Aeneid* centres on the image of Troy; on the one hand the glorious home from which came the hero of the poem and through him the Julian *gens;* and on the other hand a barbaric Eastern city lacking the robust virtues of the simple Italians (cf. Numanus' speech in 9.598f., and the taunts levelled at Aeneas by Turnus, 99-100). Many have linked this passage, the ode of Horace (3.3), and the speech of Camillus in Livy 5.51f. with a statement in Suetonius (*Jul.* 79) of a rumour that Caesar intended to transfer the capital from Rome to Troy or Alexandria, suggesting that Augustus may have had a similar idea. It seems unlikely in the highest degree that Augustus had any such intention, but it is possible that gossip on the subject was heard from time to time in Rome.

9 828. **occideritque . . . sinas:** both verbs are jussive subjunctive, with *occiderit* in parataxis instead of being subordinated: *sinas (Troiam) occidisse.* Compare 2.669 *sinite . . . revisam,* 5.163 *stringat sine,* 5.717 *habeant . . . sine moenia.*

10 829. Jupiter replies serenely, as he had done to Venus' complaints in 1.254f. *olli subridens hominum sator atque deorum . . . Repertor* is here rather striking in the sense of 'creator'.

11 830-1. 'You are indeed the sister of Jupiter and second child of Saturnus, such tides of passion do you allow to surge in your heart'. Jupiter's opening words are ironic and homely in the fashion of the speech of Homer's Olympians (cf. *Il.* 5.892-3); he means that Juno is similarly liable to the violent passions of their father Saturnus.

do quod vis, et me[1] victusque volensque remitto.[2]
Sermonem Ausonii patrium moresque tenebunt,[3]
utque[4] est nomen erit; commixti[5] corpore tantum   835
subsident Teucri. Morem[6] ritusque sacrorum
adiciam faciamque omnis uno ore Latinos.
Hinc[7] genus Ausonio mixtum quod sanguine surget,
supra homines, supra[8] ire deos pietate videbis,
nec gens ulla tuos aeque celebrabit honores.'[9]   840
Adnuit his Iuno et mentem laetata retorsit.[10]
Interea excedit caelo nubemque relinquit.

---

1 **me** . . . **remitto**: 'I give in', 'I unbend', cf. 11.346, *Geo.* 4.536.

2 833. Notice the extreme deliberateness of Jupiter's concession, slow moving with its spondees and five consecutive mono syllables.

3 834. This concedes more than Juno had asked in 825; *mores* ('way of life') is the fullest concession that could be made, and reiterates strongly the surpassing importance of the Italian contribution to the union of the two people.

4 835. **utque est nomen erit:** i.e. they will still be called Latini (823). The word Ausonii, which Jupiter used in the previous line, is a name of wider application (Italians, cf. 121); this particular subdivision of the Ausonians will keep the name Latini.

5 835-6. **commixti . . . Teucri:** 'mingling in stock only, the Trojans will sink into lesser importance'; i.e. they will become the recessive partners, the only contribution they will make is to be united physically with the Italian race, but they will not impose their language or way of life. For *corpore* cf. 11.313, *Geo.* 2.327. *Subsidere* here means that they will subside from leadership, cf. 5.498. Jupiter here perhaps somewhat overstates the case in order to placate Juno.

6 836-7. **morem . . . adiciam:** I will add the custom and method of worship', i.e. Jupiter here takes responsibility for the mingling with the original Italian religion of the Trojan worship which was a vital aspect of Aeneas' mission (line 192, cf. 1.6 *inferretque deos Latio*, 2.293 *sacra suosque tibi commendat Troia penatis*).

7 838. **hinc:** i.e. from the Trojans (mingling with Ausonian blood, cf. 6.757).

8 839. **supra ire deos pietate:** a rhetorical exaggeration of a paradoxical kind appropriate to the concessive tone of the speech. The emphasis on *pietas* (here in its sense of religious worship) summarises the theme of the mission of *pius Aeneas,* and chimes in with Augustus' restoration of the temples and the old Roman religion (Hor. *Odes* 3.6). Maguinness quotes, to illustrate Roman admiration for *pietas,* Livy 44.1.11 *favere pietati fideique deos, per quae populus Romanus ad tantum fastigii venerit*; Cic. *Harusp. Resp.* 19 *pietate ac religione . . . omnis gentis nationesque superavimus,* Cic. *Nat. De.* 2.8. Compare also the memorable line which Horace addresses to the Roman people (*Odes* 3.6.5) *dis te minorem quod geris imperas.*

9 840. This is the final metamorphosis of Juno, the inveterate enemy of the Trojans, into Juno the goddess (with Jupiter and Minerva) of the Capitoline triad, queen of heaven in the Roman hierarchy. Her temple on the Aventine was restored by Augustus (*Res. Gest.* 19.2). See note on 791f.

10 841. **retorsit:** 'changed'; the word is strange and striking in this context.

843-86. Jupiter sends one of the Furies down to the battlefield, in the shape of an owl, in order to terrify Turnus by flitting in front of his face, and to convince Juturna that she must withdraw. Juturna laments her helplessness, and finally leaves the battlefield.

[1]His actis aliud genitor secum ipse volutat

Iuturnamque parat fratris dimittere ab armis.[2]

Dicuntur[3] geminae pestes cognomine Dirae,   845

quas et Tartaream Nox intempesta[4] Megaeram

uno eodemque[5] tulit partu, paribusque revinxit[6]

serpentum spiris[7] ventosasque addidit alas.

Hae Iovis ad solium saevique[8] in limine regis

apparent acuuntque metum mortalibus aegris,   850

si quando letum[9] horrificum morbosque deum[10] rex

molitur,[11] meritas aut bello territat urbes.

Harum unam celerem demisit ab aethere summo

Iuppiter inque[12] omen Iuturnae occurrere iussit:

illa volat celerique ad terram turbine fertur.   855

Non secus ac nervo per nubem impulsa sagitta.

Armatam[13] saevi Parthus quam felle veneni,

---

1 843f. This is a daemonic scene, terrifying in its weird and supernatural aspect; the transformation of the Fury into a bird fluttering in front of Turnus' face conveys with chilling certainty the tragic and total helplessness of the brave Rutulian warrior. We are powerfully reminded of the scene in *Aeneid* 4 where Dido, another tragic victim of the events of the poem, visits her dead husband's grave and is terrified by omens, voices, and the hooting of owls by night (4.452f.).

There are other deliberate reminiscences of the story of Dido; Juturna's position as a sister who cannot help is similar to that of Anna, and the repetition (871) of the line describing Anna's grief (4.673) takes the thoughts back to that other tragedy. The complaint of Juturna that she cannot accompany her brother in death (880-1) recalls Anna's words to Dido (see note on 880-1), and her wish to be swallowed up in the depths of the earth (883) is reminiscent of Dido's words in 4.24f. In the sympathy it evokes this final tragic death in the poem is thus deliberately made parallel with the death of Dido, the other great opponent of the mission of Aeneas.

2 844. Notice that the task of withdrawing Juturna from the battle is not left to Juno, but performed by Jupiter himself.

3 845. 'There are twin fiends called by name the Dread Ones'; these are Allecto (7.324) and Tisiphone (6.555, 10.761), sisters of Megaera. For *Tartareus* used of them cf. 7.328. The Dirae, daughters of Night, are identified with the Furies; see notes on 7.323f., 8.701-3.

4 846. **intempesta**: 'timeless', emphasising the deep dead aspect of night when time seems to stand still, cf. 3.587.

5 847. **eodemque**: the *e* is slurred out in scansion by synizesis; see note on 84 and cf. especially 10.487 *una eademque via*.

6 **revinxit**: 'wreathed', cf. 4.459.

7 848. **spiris**: 'coils', cf. *Geo.* 2.154, *Aen.* 2.217; for the snaky hair of the Furies cf. 7.329, *Geo.* 4.482.

8 849. **saevique . . . regis**: i.e. Jupiter in his angry mood, as explained in 851f.

9 851. **letum horrificum morbosque**: cf. *Geo.* 3.552, where Tisiphone brings pestilence to the world.

10 **deum rex**: the monosyllabic ending is traditional and archaic in this phrase, cf. Enn. *Ann.* 175, *Aen.* 10.2.

11 852. **molitur**: 'is wreaking', a favourite word of Virgil's, cf. line 327, 7.127, 10.477.

12 854. **inque omen**: 'to be an omen'; for the use of in cf. 7.13 *in lumina* ('to be a light'), 11.771 *in plumam* ('to form a plume').

13 857-8. 'which a Parthian shoots, a Parthian or a Cydonian, an arrow armed with the gall of cruel poison, a weapon against which there is no remedy'. The Parthians were famous for their archery, cf. *Geo.* 4.313-14; so were the Cydonians from Crete, who are linked with the Parthians in *Ecl.* 10.59. The repetition *Parthus . . . Parthus* is very much in Virgil's manner, e.g. 5.116-17, 9.774-5, 10.200-1, 778-9, and lines 896-7.

Parthus sive Cydon, telum immedicabile, torsit,
stridens[1] et celeris incognita transilit umbras:
talis se sata Nocte tulit terrasque petivit.　　　　　　　860
Postquam acies videt Iliacas atque agmina Turni,
alitis[2] in parvae subitam collecta figuram,
quae quondam[3] in bustis aut culminibus desertis[4]
nocte sedens serum[5] canit importuna per umbras —
hanc versa in faciem Turni se[6] pestis ob ora　　　　　865
fertque refertque sonans clipeumque everberat alis.
Olli membra novus[7] solvit formidine torpor,
arrectaeque horrore comae et vox faucibus haesit.
　　　At procul ut Dirae stridorem[8] agnovit et alas,
infelix[9] crinis scindit Iuturna solutos　　　　　　　870
unguibus ora soror foedans et pectora pugnis:[10]
'quid[11] nunc te[12] tua, Turne, potest germana iuvare?
Aut quid iam durae[13] superat mihi? Qua tibi lucem[14]
arte morer? Talin[15] possum me opponere monstro?[16]

---

1 859. 'whistling and unperceived cuts through the swift shadows'; the line is governed by *non secus ac* ('just as an arrow . . .'). The spondaic word *stridens* filling the first foot attracts attention to itself; cf. 4.185, 9.419, and note on 70. The epithet *celeris* is transferred from the arrow to the shadows through which it swiftly wings its way; cf. *celeris . . . per auras* (4.226).

2 862. 'suddenly shrinking into the shape of a small bird'; this use of *subitus* is one which became commoner in the Silver Age, e.g. Tac. *Hist.* 4.76 *subitus miles*. P has *subito*, which may be right. *Collecta* (cf. line 491, *Geo.* 2.154) is much more vivid than *M's conversa*.

3 863. **quondam:** 'sometimes', cf. 9.710.

4 863f. These lines make it evident that the bird is an owl, a bird ever and always associated with mystery and weirdness; cf. *Geo.* 1.402-3, and the owl that haunted Dido at her husband's tomb (4.462f.), and Shakespeare, *Macbeth* 2.2.4-5 'it was the owl that shriek'd, the fatal bellman, which gives the stern'st goodnight'. The spondaic movement and especially the spondaic fifth foot help to convey the strangeness: such a fifth-foot rhythm is very rare indeed in Virgil except with Greek words (see note on 83); compare 2.68 *Phrygia agmina circumspexit* and see note on 7.634.

5 864. **serum canit importuna:** 'sings its ill-omened song late at night'; *importuna* (see note on 11.305) is in agreement with the subject, and *serum* is adverbial accusative.

6 865-6. **se pestis . . . alis:** 'the fiend flew and flew again against Turnus' face, flapping and beating his shield with its wings'; *ob* is vividly used to express hostility; for *fertque refertque* cf. 6.122 *itque reditque*. Cerda cites the story from Livy 7.26 of Valerius Corvus who was enabled to kill his Gallic opponent because of a crow which attacked his enemy by flying around his head.

7 867. **novus . . . torpor:** 'a strange numbness'.

8 869. **stridorem . . . et alas:** 'the whirring wings', a good example of hendiadys.

9 870. **infelix:** see note on 598; notice the spondaic movement to reflect the wretchedness of Juturna.

10 871. This line occurs in 4.673, also of a sister's grief, as Anna rushes to Dido's side when she lies dying. Virgil very deliberately recalls the tragedy of Dido in this passage; see note on 843f.

11 872. **quid:** 'how', adverbial.

12 **te tua . . . germana:** notice the effect achieved by the juxtaposition and the alliteration.

13 873. **durae:** a difficult word, perhaps meaning 'hard-hearted as I must be'; others give 'long-enduring', 'much-tried'.

14 873-4. **lucem . . . morer?:** 'am I to prolong your life?'

15 874. **talin:** = *taline*, cf. 503.

16 **monstro:** 'portent'; she recognises the supernatural element in the apparition of the bird.

Iam iam linquo acies. Ne me terrete[1] timentem,   875
obscenae volucres: alarum verbera nosco
letalemque sonum, nec fallunt iussa superba
magnanimi[2] Iovis. Haec[3] pro virginitate reponit?
Quo[4] vitam dedit aeternam? Cur mortis adempta est
condicio? Possem[5] tantos finire dolores   880
nunc certe, et misero fratri comes ire per umbras!
Immortalis ego? Aut quicquam mihi dulce meorum
te sine, frater, erit?[6] O[7] quae satis ima dehiscat
terra mihi, manisque deam demittat ad imos?'
Tantum effata caput glauco[8] contexit amictu   885
multa gemens et se fluvio[9] dea condidit alto.

---

1 875. **terrete timentem**: 'do not intimidate your frightened victim further'; the rhetorical play on words is emphasised very heavily indeed by the alliteration of *t* (cf. 761).

2 878. **magnanimi Iovis**: the standing epithet is used here with ironical effect, cf. 144.

3 **haec . . . reponit**: 'is this his payment for my virginity?'; cf. lines 140-1 and note on 138.

4 879. **quo**: = *in quem usum*.

5 880-1. **possem . . . umbras**: i.e. otherwise I would have been able, past potential. Compare Anna's words to Dido, 4.677-9 *comitemne sororem sprevisti moriens? eadem me ad fata vocasses; idem ambas ferro dolor atque eadem hora tulisset*.

6 883. **erit**: the final syllable is lengthened in arsis, see note on 13.

7 **o quae . . . mihi**: 'what ravine could gape deep enough for me'; these words were used by Turnus (10.675-6); cf. also Dido's words in 4.24 *sed mihi vel tellus optem prius ima dehiscat*.

8 885. **glauco . . . amictu**: 'in a green veil', the colour that befits a river deity; cf. 8.33-4 (of the river-god Tiber) *eum tenuis glauco velabat amictu carbasus;* 10.205 ('he Mincius) *velatus harundine glauca*.

9 886. **fluvio**: her own river, the Juturna, see note on 138.

887-952. Aeneas threatens Turnus; Turnus replies that he is not afraid of Aeneas, only of the gods. He tries to throw a huge rock at Aeneas, but his strength fails him; he is like a man in a dream. Aeneas hurls his spear and wounds Turnus in the thigh. Turnus begs for mercy, and Aeneas is on the point of granting it when he catches sight of the belt of Pallas which Turnus is wearing. In fury and anger he kills his suppliant enemy.

[1]Aeneas instat contra telumque coruscat

ingens[2] arboreum, et saevo sic pectore fatur:

'quae nunc deinde mora est? Aut quid iam, Turne, retractas?[3]

Non cursu, saevis certandum est comminus armis. 890

Verte[4] omnis tete[5] in facies et contrahe[6] quidquid

sive animis sive arte vales; opta ardua pennis

astra sequi clausumve cava te condere terra.'

ille[7] caput quassans: 'non me tua fervida terrent

dicta, ferox; di me terrent et Iuppiter hostis.' 895

---

1 887f. The impact of the final scene of the *Aeneid* is complex and has been interpreted in very different ways by different critics; this is because Virgil has most deliberately avoided any specious simplification of the issues in order to compel the reader's attention to the dilemmas involved in victory and defeat. Nothing could have been simpler than to end the poem in such a way as to concentrate attention on the final triumph of Aeneas, making the way clear at last for the fulfilment of Rome's world mission; but in fact the attention is concentrated on Turnus in defeat, and the last line of the poem focuses not on Rome but on the pathos of Turnus' death. Similarly the behaviour of Aeneas, as he kills his enemy in a fit of fury (*furiis accensus et ira terribilis*, 946-7), goes counter to all his efforts in the poem to overcome the evil effects of *furor* in himself and in others.

There are reasons why Turnus must die: Otis, with some justification, strongly stresses that Turnus is a survival of an outdated social order, an individual who is quite unable to sink his individual desires in consideration for the common good. We need not necessarily think that his death is a moral retribution, but rather an inevitable consequence of the progress of history. But it should be noted that this aspect is not the one stressed by Virgil in the final scene; one reason and one reason only is dominant in the mind of Aeneas, and that is the desire for vengeance (948-9). When Turnus killed Pallas (10.439f., see note on 941-4) poetic justice demanded that he should pay for his arrogant cruelty, and now indeed he pays. The ethical justification of Aeneas is his sense of *pietas* towards Pallas and his father Evander who had entrusted the young man to him, and who, upon the news of his death, had one last request to make of Aeneas, vengeance (11.177f.). But the fact remains that the reader expects Aeneas to show mercy (notes on 933, 938, 938-9) and is disquieted when he does not. Virgil's contemporaries would have been well aware of the relevance to their own times of this dilemma between mercy and vengeance. The reconciliation in heaven between Jupiter and Juno had come about peacefully; in the human world of Aeneas and Turnus it has not done so.

For further discussion of this passage see Otis, pp. 378f., Quinn pp. 270f., Pöschl pp. 133f., Putnam, *The Poetry of the Aeneid*, ch. iv, R. Beare, 'Invidious Success', *Proc. Virgil Soc.*, 1964-5, pp. 18f., and my summary in *Virgil (Greece and Rome, New Surveys in the Classics*, 1967), pp. 31-8, where additional bibliography is given.

2 888. **ingens arboreum:** 'huge, like a tree', an exaggerated picture of the spear designed to build up the impression of the overwhelming might of Aeneas. Page compares Milton, *P.L.* 1.292f. and Hom. *Il.* 5.746. For the doubled adjective cf. 8.622 (*loricam*) *sanguineam, ingentem.*

3 889. **retractas:** 'draw back', intransitive, cf. Livy 3.52.4.

4 891. **verte . . . facies:** Aeneas ironically suggests that Turnus should rival Proteus (*Geo.* 4.440f.) in transforming himself into some creature such as a bird or a mole, to try to escape his fate; it would still be of no avail.

5 **tete:** emphatic form of *te* (cf. *Ecl.* 3.35, *tute*), like *temet.*

6 **contrahe:** 'summon up', 'collige' (Servius).

7 894-5. 'Shaking his head he replied: "It is not your hot words that frighten me, proud man; it is the gods that frighten me, and Jupiter my foe".' These are stirring phrases (adapted from Hom. *Il.* 22.297); Turnus in full realisation of his imminent death (made clear to him by the supernatural omen) is unbowed to the last. For *caput quassans* cf. 7.292 and Lucr. 2.1164 *iamque caput quassans grandis suspirat arator.* See Warde Fowler's excellent appreciation of this passage (*The Death of Turnus*, p. 153).

Nec plura effatus saxum circumspicit ingens,[1]
saxum[2] antiquum ingens, campo quod forte iacebat,
limes[3] agro positus litem ut discerneret arvis.
Vix illud lecti bis sex cervice subirent,
qualia[4] nunc hominum producit corpora tellus; 900
ille manu raptum trepida torquebat in hostem
altior[5] insurgens et cursu concitus heros.
Sed neque currentem se nec cognoscit euntem[6]
tollentemve manus saxumve immane moventem;
genua[7] labant, gelidus concrevit frigore sanguis. 905
Tum lapis ipse viri vacuum per inane[8] volutus
nec[9] spatium evasit totum neque pertulit ictum.
Ac velut in somnis, oculos ubi languida pressit[10]
nocte quies, nequiquam avidos[11] extendere cursus
velle videmur et in mediis conatibus aegri[12] 910
succidimus — non lingua valet, non corpore notae[13]
sufficiunt vires nec vox aut verba sequuntur:

---

1 896f. The image of a man lifting a huge stone which normal men could not lift is based on Hom. *Il.* 12.445f. (Hector); cf. also *Il.* 5.302f., and compare Spenser *F.Q.* 2.11.35-6.

2 897. **saxum . . . ingens**: for repetition from the previous line see note on 857-8, and cf. 546-7, 673-4.

3 898. 'set up as a boundary stone on the land to resolve disagreement about the fields'; cf. Hom. *Il.* 21.405 where Athena picks up a stone which had been set up as a boundary mark.

4 900. **qualia . . . tellus**: 'men of such physique as the earth now brings forth'; *qualia . . . hominum . . . corpora* is in apposition to *lecti* (*homines*). Compare Hom. *Il.* 12.447-9.

5 902. **altior . . . heros**: 'stretching up high, and speeding along in all his heroic stature'; the word *heros,* in apposition to the subject *ille,* reinforces the Homeric atmosphere of these final scenes.

6 903-4. These lines, describing how Turnus does not 'know himself (i.e. no longer feels his usual strength of limb, cf. Patroclus in Hom. *Il.* 16.805f.) contain a most astonishing quadruple rhyme of *-entem, -untem,* conveying the sameness of his inability in all his attempted activities. See Austin on *Aen.* 4.55.

7 905. **genua**: the *u* is treated as a consonant, so that the word scans as a trochee; cf. 5.432 (the same phrase), and *tenuia* as a dactyl in *Geo.* 1.397, 2.121. Compare the consonantal treatment oft (note on 356).

8 906. **inane**: 'space', used as a noun as in 354.

9 907. 'did not cover the whole distance between them, or drive its blow home'; for *evasit* cf. 2.730-1 *omnemgue videbar evasisse viam;* for *pertulit* cf. 10.786 *viris haud pertulit.*

10 908f. This simile is yet another recollection of a famous passage in *Iliad* 22 (199f.; 'As in a dream the man pursuing cannot catch the man running away; the one cannot escape, nor the other catch him: so Achilles could not catch Hector, nor Hector escape'). Virgil has changed the application, so that the reference is not to both men but to Turnus alone; but he has retained the eerie impression of an unreal world and strengthened it by applying it personally with the use of the first person verbs *videmur, succidimus.* Dreams in Virgil are rarely psychological portrayals of character, as this one is (much more often they are divine revelations which further the plot); the closest parallel to this passage is Dido's dream in 4.465f., where she is all alone on a long desolate road.

11 909. **avidos extendere cursus**: 'eagerly run on further', i.e. continue running from the point at which we visualise ourselves in our dreams; cf. Lucr. 5.631.

12 910. The rhythm is haunting with its trochaic lilt in the first and second feet, and the absence of third foot caesura, it is a reminiscence of Lucr. 4.456, a passage about dreams, (*membra movere*) *nostra videmur et in noctis caligine caeca . . .* Notice too the alliteration of *v* which is echoed in the following lines, especially 912 and 913.

13 911-12. **notae ... vires**: this element in the simile picks up the description of Turnus in 903 *se nec cognoscit euntem.*

sic Turno, quacumque viam virtute petivit,
successum dea[1] dira negat. Tum[2] pectore sensus
vertuntur varii; Rutulos aspectat et urbem   915
cunctaturque metu letumque[3] instare tremescit,
nec quo se eripiat, nec qua vi tendat in hostem,[4]
nec currus usquam videt aurigamve sororem.

    Cunctanti[5] telum Aeneas fatale[6] coruscat,
sortitus[7] fortunam oculis, et corpore toto   920
eminus intorquet. [8]Murali concita numquam
tormento sic saxa fremunt nec fulmine tanti
dissultant crepitus. Volat atri[9] turbinis instar[10]
exitium dirum hasta ferens orasque[11] recludit
loricae et clipei extremos septemplicis orbis;   925
per medium stridens transit femur. Incidit[12] ictus
ingens ad terram duplicato[13] poplite Turnus.
Consurgunt[14] gemitu Rutuli totusque remugit[15]
mons circum et vocem late nemora alta remittunt.

---

1 914. **dea dira:** i.e. the Fury, one of the *Dirae* (845).

2 914-18. **tum pectore . . . sororem:** notice how after the long simile, which held the action in suspense, the attention is now concentrated upon the feelings of Turnus himself in a series of rapid clauses with many finite verbs (*vertuntur, aspectat, cunctatur, tremescit, eripiat, tendat, videt*). His helpless plight is reminiscent of that of Hector in *Iliad* 22.293f., where Hector in his helplessness calls on his brother Deiphobus, in vain.

3 916. **letumque instare tremescit:** the accusative and infinitive following *tremescere* is not found before Virgil. For *letum,* (read by *P*) *M* and *R* have *telum;* this would be much less effective in the context.

4 917. The indirect questions depend on *videt,* as do the accusatives in 918. For *tendere* cf. 553.

5 919. **cunctanti:** 'as Turnus hesitated'; for the dative cf. 1.102, 8.212, 11.551.

6 **fatale:** the word has its main overtones in the meaning of 'guided by fate', i.e. the *fata* of the Trojans now at last are to be fulfilled by Aeneas' spear. But it also contains the notion of 'fatal' to Turnus, bringing his fate of death.

7 920. **sortitus fortunam oculis:** 'seeing a favourable chance'; cf. Hom. *Il.* 22.321.

8 921f. 'Never do stones hurled by a siege engine attacking city walls make such a mighty roar, nor do such shattering cracks come from thunderbolts'. It is rare for Virgil to end a line with an adverb, and consequently *numquam* has great emphasis. *Murale tormentum* is a siege engine for attacking walls by hurling lumps of rock against them; the simile relates to the sound through the air of Aeneas' spear, not to its impact.

9 923. **atri turbinis instar:** notice how the word division corresponds with the feet; cf. 293, 328, 422. The effect generally is a certain deliberateness of rhythm, and often an emphasis on the word filling the fourth foot.

10 **instar:** 'like', 'as mighty as', literally 'the size of'; cf. 7.707, and see note on 2.15 *instar montis equum.*

11 924-5. **orasque . . . orbis:** 'and pierced the edge of his breastplate and the outside of the circles of his seven-layered shield', i.e. the spear struck the lowest part of the armour protecting Turnus' body, and hit him in the thigh. The shield made by Vulcan for Aeneas was of seven layers (8.448); cf. also Ajax's shield in Hom. *Il.* 7.245.

12 926-7. **incidit . . . ingens:** the rhythm here again helps the effect, and is strongly stressed with the assonance of initial *i.* The pause after the first spondee is emphatic; see note on 70.

13 927. **duplicato poplite:** 'on bended knee', for the verb cf. 11.645.

14 928. **consurgunt gemitu:** 'start up with a groan', a use of the ablative that is characteristic of Virgil, cf. lines 131 and 252.

15 928-9. The echo of the groans from mountain and forest has a suggestion of the involvement of inanimate nature in the human tragedy; notice the predominance of a sounds.

Ille humilis¹ supplexque oculos² dextramque precantem   930
protendens 'equidem³ merui nec deprecor' inquit;
'utere⁴ sorte tua. Miseri te si qua parentis
tangere cura potest, oro (fuit et tibi talis
Anchises genitor) Dauni⁵ miserere senectae
et me, seu corpus spoliatum lumine mavis,   935
redde meis. Vicisti et victum tendere palmas
Ausonii videre; tua est Lavinia coniunx,
ulterius ne tende odiis.' Stetit acer in armis
Aeneas volvens oculos dextramque repressit;
et iam iamque magis cunctantem flectere sermo   940
coeperat, infelix umero cum apparuit alto
balteus et notis fulserunt cingula bullis
Pallantis pueri, victum quem vulnere Turnus
straverat atque umeris inimicum insigne gerebat.
Ille, oculis postquam saevi monimenta doloris   945
exuviasque hausit, furiis accensus et ira
terribilis: 'tune hinc spoliis indute meorum
eripiare mihi? Pallas te hoc vulnere, Pallas
immolat et poenam scelerato ex sanguine sumit.'
Hoc dicens ferrum adverso sub pectore condit   950
fervidus. Ast illi solvuntur frigore membra
vitaque cum gemitu fugit indignata sub umbras.
Dissultant crepitus. Volat atri turbinis instar
exitium dirum hasta ferens orasque recludit
loricae et clipei extremos septemplicis orbis;   925
per medium stridens transit femur. Incidit ictus
ingens ad terram duplicato poplite Turnus.

---

1 930. **humilis:** thus is the proud Turnus brought low. It was the purpose of Rome *debellare superbos* (6.853); the purpose has now in this instance been achieved, and the reader may expect Rome's mercy to come into play (*parcere subiectis*). Some MSS read *supplex* for *supplexque*, in which case *humilis* would go with *oculos* rather than with *ille* in asyndeton with *supplex*.

2 930-1. **oculos . . . protendens:** there is a slight zeugma here in the use of the verb; it is appropriate literally with *dextram* but somewhat extended to convey the meaning of *tollens* with *oculos*. Catullus (64.127) has *aciem protendere* in the rather different sense of gazing at a distant object; cf. also *Aen.* 2.405 *ad caelum tendens ardentia lumina.*

3 931. **equidem . . . deprecor:** 'I have earned it, and I do not complain'; at this last moment Turnus achieves full heroic stature, like Mezentius in 10.900f. The phrase *merui* does not acknowledge moral guilt (*pace* Pöschl and others); it simply means (as Mezentius too said) that he chose to go into battle and he has been defeated, and so he accepts the condition of the loser in warfare. Scaliger finely commented 'Dignus profecto Turnus qui aut vinceret aut divinis tantum armis neque aliis vinceretur'.

4 932. **utere sorte tua:** cf. Spenser, *F.Q.* 2.8.52 'But use thy fortune, as it doth befall'.

5 934. **Dauni miserere senectae:** the phrase echoes Latinus' plea to Turnus to pity his old father Daunus and to refrain from battle; *miserere parentis longaevi* (43-4).

Consurgunt gemitu Rutuli totusque remugit
mons circum et vocem late nemora alta remittunt.
Ille humilis supplexque oculos dextramque precantem   930
protendens 'equidem merui nec deprecor' inquit;
'utere sorte tua. Miseri te si qua parentis
tangere cura potest, oro (fuit et tibi talis[1]
Anchises genitor) Dauni miserere senectae
et[2] me, seu corpus spoliatum lumine mavis,   935
redde meis. Vicisti et victum tendere palmas
Ausonii[3] videre; tua est Lavinia coniunx,
ulterius[4] ne tende odiis.' [5]Stetit acer in armis
Aeneas volvens oculos dextramque repressit;
et iam iamque magis cunctantem flectere sermo   940
coeperat, [6]infelix[7] umero cum apparuit alto
balteus et notis fulserunt cingula bullis[8]
Pallantis pueri, victum quem vulnere Turnus
straverat atque[9] umeris inimicum[10] insigne gerebat.
Ille,[11] oculis postquam saevi monimenta doloris   945
exuviasque hausit, furiis[12] accensus et ira

---

1 933. **talis:** i.e. *senex* (looking forward to *senectae* in the next line); the phrase is based on Hom. *Il*. 22.420, cf. also *Il*. 24.486. The appeal to filial piety deepens the expectation that Aeneas will in fact spare Turnus.

2 935-6. 'and give me, or if you wish it so, give my dead body back to my people'; the appeal for mercy is based on Hom. *Il*. 22.338f., where Hector begs Achilles that his dead body may be returned to his people.

3 937. **Ausonii videre:** his own people have seen him acknowledge defeat; this is the worst that could happen to Turnus.

4 938. **ulterius . . . odiis:** 'go no further in hatred'; the implication that to kill Turnus would be an act of hate (because all Aeneas' objectives have been achieved) again arouses the expectation that Aeneas will not kill him.

5 938-9. 'Aeneas, fierce in full panoply, stood still, shifting his gaze, and restrained his hand'. Servius comments that this whole passage reflects glory on Aeneas, because he shows his *pietas* by thinking of sparing Turnus, and then his *pietas* again by killing him to avenge Pallas in accordance with his obligations to Evander. See note on 887f.

6 941-4. 'when the ill-starred belt high on Turnus' shoulder met his gaze, and the baldric with its familiar studs shone out, the baldric of young Pallas whom Turnus had overcome and laid low with a fatal wound; and now he was wearing his enemy's insignia on his shoulders'. The story of the death of Pallas at the hands of Turnus was told in 10.439-509, including an account (496f.) of how Turnus stripped from him the sword-belt (*balteus, cingula,* the two words refer to the same thing), and with an anticipatory comment inset into the narrative: 'there will come a time for Turnus when he would have given anything to have left Pallas untouched, and when he will hate this day and these spoils' (503-5). The description of Turnus' ruthless cruelty to Pallas (see note on 10.439f.) should be in the reader's mind now.

7 941. **infelix:** i.e. *infelix* for Turnus, see previous note, or possibly, as Servius says, *nulli domino felix*.

8 942. **bullis:** the mention of the decoration (cf. 9.359) adds a further vivid image to the picture, and recalls the engraving on the belt of the violent story of the Danaids (10.497-8).

9 944. **atque . . . gerebat:** this clause is loosely attached to the preceding relative clause, returning the attention from the past to the present narrative.

10 944. **inimicum:** 'of his foe' (cf. 10.295, 11.84), with an overtone of the meaning 'fatal', cf. 10.795.

11 945-6. 'after he had gazed on the sight of those spoils, the memorials of his savage grief; for *haurire oculis* (literally 'drink in with the eyes') cf. 4.661, and compare line 26. The *-que* is epexegetic, the spoils being the memorials; cf. 248. The description of how the memories come flooding back to Aeneas prepares the reader for the sequel.

12 946-7. **furiis . . . terribilis:** at the last Aeneas falls a victim to the violent passions (*furor* and *ira*) against which he has so long been struggling with partial success. See note on 887f.

terribilis: 'tune hinc spoliis[1] indute meorum
eripiare[2] mihi? Pallas[3] te hoc vulnere, Pallas
immolat et poenam scelerato ex sanguine sumit.'
Hoc dicens ferrum adverso sub pectore condit   950
fervidus.[4] Ast[5] illi solvuntur frigore membra
vitaque cum gemitu fugit indignata sub umbras.

---

1 947. **spoliis indute meorum:** 'clad in the spoils of one of my people'; *indute* is vocative of the past participle, a favourite construction of Virgil's, cf. 8.38, 10.186.

2 948. **eripiare mihi:** 'are you to be snatched from me?' *Eripiare* is deliberative subjunctive (cf. 486), alternative form for *eripiaris;* the dative is common after such words, cf. 31.

3 948. **Pallas ... Pallas:** the repetition leaves (or should leave) no doubt in the reader's mind that Aeneas' motive is vengeance, and this is stressed again in the next line with *poenam sumit,* and presented as a religious duty with the verb *immolat,* a word used of sacrificial victims (cf. 10.519). Other reasons also may be advanced for the necessity of Turnus' death, but the reason which Virgil presents is the need to take vengeance. Whether this is justified or not constitutes the dilemma of the ending of the poem (see note on 887f.).

4 951. **fervidus:** the emphasis on the run-on adjective before the full stop is very strong indeed. Aeneas' action is not taken coldly or rationally, but in the heat of emotion and anger.

5 951-2. 'but his enemy's limbs were loosened in the chill of death, and his soul with a groan fled complaining to the shades below'. The phrase *solvuntur membra* is closely reminiscent of Homer's words γυτο γουνατα, linking Turnus once again with the warriors of the heroic age. The last line has occurred earlier in the poem describing Camilla's death (11.831). Two points may be noted here: firstly it recalls the Homeric formula ον ποτμον γοοωσα, used of Patroclus (*Il.* 16.857) and Hector (*Il.* 22.363); and secondly it closes the *Aeneid* with a feeling of sorrow and bewilderment, as the emphasis centres not on the triumphs of Aeneas but on the tragedy of Turnus' death.

Index to the Notes

Reference is given to the main note or notes on each subject, where further references will often be found. There are separate sub-headings under 'metre' and 'prosody'.

A full index of proper names is to be found in Mynors's Oxford Text, and there is a complete word-index of Virgil's works by M. N. Wetmore *Index Verborem Vergilianus* (New Haven, v.d.).

ablative

(description), 2.333; 5.663; 9.630-1
(instrumental), 2.51
(separation), 1.38
(form in -*i*), 1.174; 8.10f.; 12.464

accusative

(adverbial), 2.630; 5.19; 6.49-50; 9.630-1
(cognate), 1.328; 6.517; 12.197
(extent), 1.67
(motion), 1.2; 3.507; 7.126
(respect), 1.320; 4.558; 5.285; 6.243; 7.60; 8.114; 9.596; 10.324; 11.489; 12.5
(retained), 1.228; 2.210; 3.47; 4.137; 5.135; 6.156; 7.503; 8.29; 9.337; 10.133; 11.35; 12.64-5

Acestes, 1.195; 5.30
Achaemenides, 3.588f.
Achates, 1.120
Acheron, 5.99; 6.295; 7.91
Achilles, 1.483f.; 12.697f.
Achivi, 6.836f.
acies, 7.695; 12.731
Acrisius, 7.372
Actium, 3274f.; 278f.; 6.800; 8.675f.

adjectives

(compound), 3.544
(used in neuter as noun), 1.422; 3.208

Aeacides, descendant of Aeacus
(= Achilles), 1.99
(= Pyrrhus), 3.296
(= Perseus), 6.838
Aeneadae, 1.157
Aeneas, 1.81f.; 8.1f.; 10.510f., 769f.; 11.100f.; 12.311f., 887f. *et passim*
Aeolus, 1.52f.

aetiology, 1.267-8; 3.18; 5.117f.; 6.69f.; 8.280f.
Aetoli, 11.308
Agamemnon, 1.458
Agrippa, 8.682
Ajax (son of Oileus), 1.41
Alba Longa, 1.7, 269; 6.763
Albani, 12.826
Albunea, 7.83
Alcides (Hercules), 6.122-3; 8.202-3
alipedes, 7.277
Allecto, 7.323f.
Aloidae (Otus and Ephialtes), 6.582
Amata, 7.323f.; 12.593f.
Amazon, 11.648
Amsanctus, 7.565
Anchises, 2.634f.; 3.1f., 708f.; 6.679f.
ancile, 7.187f.
Andromache, 2.453-5; 3-294f.
animi, 2.61; 9.246
Anna, 4.1f., 8,421f.
Antenor, 1.242f.
Antony, 8.686f.
Anubis, 8.698-700
Apollo, 3.84f., 4.143f., 6.69f.; 8.704; 9.590f.
Apollonius Rhodius, 1.657f.; 4.1f., 166f, 522-32; 5.362f.
apostrophe, 3.710; 4.408; 5.840f.; 10.507; 12.538
Ara Maxima, 8.271-2
Ardea, 7.372
Argi, 1.24
Argiletum, 8.345-6
arma (nautical), 4.290
armus, 10.768
Arruns, 11.759
Ascanius (Iulus), 1.267-8; 9.590f.
Assaracus, 1.284; 10.123

594

ast, 1.46

Astyanax, 2.457

at (resumptive), 4.614

ater, 11.186

Atlas, 4.247

Atridae (Agamemnon and Menelaus), 2.104; 9.138-9

Augustus, 1.267-8, 286; 3.280; 6.42f, 789, 801f.; 7.170f, 572f., 604f.; 8.187, 675f., 680-1, 714f., 716

Ausonius, 3.171

Ausonia, 8.328

Ausonii, 12.835

Aventinus, 7.655f.

Averna (Avernus), 3.441f.; 6.126; 7.91

Bacchanal, 7.385

Bacchante, 4.301f.

Bacchus, 6.801f.

Barcaei, 4.42

Belli portae, 7.572f., 607f.

Berecynthia, 6.784f.

bidens, 4.57

Brutus, 6.817f.

bubo, 4.462f.

Buthrotum, 3.294f.

Cacus, 8.194

Caere, 7.652

Caesar, 1.286; 6.789, 826f.

caestus, 5.364

Caieta, 7.2

Camilla, 7.803f.; 11.648f.

caput, 8.569-70; 11.399-400

cardo, 1.671-2

Carmentis, 8.335-6, 337-8

carpere, 4.2

Carthage, 1.13, 15-16, 297f.

Cassandra, 1.41; 2.246-7

catalogue, 7.641f.

Catiline, 8.668f.

Cato, 8.670

Catullus, 4.1f., 296f. *et passim;* 11.1f.

Celaeno, 3.211-12

Centaurs, 7.674f.; 8.293

Cerberus, 6.417f.; 8.296

Ceres, 1.177; 4.58

Chalybes, 8.420

Charon, 6.295f., 384f.

Charybdis, 3.420f., 421-3

Chimaera, 5.118; 6.288; 7.785f.

Circe, 3.386; 7.10-11, 47f.

Circenses (ludi), 8.636

Cisseis (Hecuba), 7.319f.

Claudia (gens), 7.706f.

Cleopatra, 8.688

Cloelia, 8.646f.

Cnosius, 3.115; 9.305

Cocytus, 6.132

cometae, 10.272f.

conditional sentences, 8.522-3; 11.112, 912f.; 12.733
    (indicative in unfulfilled condition), 2.54f.
    (present for past), 2.599-600
    (reported future perfect), 2.94
    (*si forte*), 1.181-2; 2.136
    (with ellipsis), 5.355-6

contracted forms, see syncope

cordi, 9.615

corona, 10.122

coronare, 1.724

corripere, 1.418

Corybants, 3.111f.

Corythus, 7.209

Crete, 3.121f.; 4.70

cretus, 2.74; 8.135

Creusa, 2.730f.

crudus, 10.682

culpa, 4.19, 172

cum (*interea*), 3.645-7; 10.665

cum (inverted), 1.36-7; 5.270-2

cum (with indicative), 9.249

Cumae, 3.441f.; 6.2

Cupid, 1.663, 664-5

cura, 4.1

Cures, 6.811

Cybele, 2.788; 3.111f.; 6.784f.; 7.139; 9.11-12, 618f.; 10.157

Cyclops, 3.617; 8.418-19

Cyllenius (Mercury), 4.252; 8.138-9

Cynthus, 1.498-502

Cytherea (Venus), 1.257; 8.523

Daedalus, 6.14f.; 7.282

Danae, 7.372

Danai (Greeks), 1.30; 8.129

Danaids, 10.497

Dardanidae (Trojans), 1.38; 10.545

Dardanides (Aeneas), 10.545

Dardanus, 1.28; 3.167-8; 7.207; 8.134f.

dare, 12.437

dative

    (agent), 1.440; 7.507-8

    (ethic), 1.102-3; 8.212; 12.566

    (motion), 1.6; 2.19, 186; 7.35; 10.548; 12.256

    (predicative), 9.615; 10.714

    (purpose), 1.22

    (*with eripere*), 12.157

    (with *subducere*), 10.50

    (form in *-u*), 1.156; 9.605

    (Greek form), 5.184

Daunia, 8.146

Daunius heros (Turnus), 12.723

Daunus, 12.22

deinde, 1.195; 2.691

Deiphobus, 6.494f.

Delos, 3.75-6

depositus, 12.395

Diana, 4.511; 7.516f., 761f.

Dido, 1.494f., 695f.; 4 *passim*; 5.572; 6.426f.; 7.323f .; 11.74; 12.593f., 843f.

diminutive adjective, 4.327f.

Dindyma, 9.618f.

Diomedes, 1.97; 8.9; 10.28f.; 11.225f.

Dirae, 4.469; 7.323f.; 12.845

Dis (Pluto), 5.73; 12.199

Discordia, 6.280; 12.313

Dolon, 12.347f.

Dolopes, 2.7

Drances, 11.124f., 336f.

dreams, 2.268 f.; 4.465f.; 12.908f.

dum (with present indicative), 12.737; (with subjunctive), 1.5; 2.136; 10.800

ecphrasis, 7.59; 8.608f.

edit (subjunctive), 12.801

Elissa (Dido), 1.340; 4.335

Elysium, 6.637f.

enim (archaic), 1.19; 2.100; 8.84

Ennius, 6.845-6; 9.503, 528; 11.492f. *et passim*

Epicureanism, 4.379f.

equus Troianus, 2.15f., 235f.

Erato, 7.37

Erinys, 2.337; 7.323f.

erubescere, 2.541-2

erumpere, 1.580

Eryx, 1.570; 5.24

est (= *edit*), 4.66

esto, 10.67

Etna, 3.571f.; 8.418-19

etymology, 1.267-8; 3.693; 5.117f.; 7.682f.; 8.322-3; 10.145 (see also aetiology)

Eumenides, 4.469

Euphrates, 8.726

evadere, 2.731; 3.282; 4.685

Evander, 7.43; 8.152f.; 11.139f.

exanimis, 4.672

exosus, 5.687

exsors, 5.533f.; 8.552

Fabius, 6.845-6

fallere, 2.744; 7.350-1

Fama, 4.173f.

fata, 7.315f.; 10.96f., 111-13

fatalis, 11.232; 12.919

fateri, 7.433

fatum, 1.2, 39; 4.225

Faunus, 7.47f., 81, 82

ferre, 4.678-9; (= *auferre*), 10.652; 12.285

Fides, 1.292

florus, 12.605

formido, 12.750

fors, 2.139; 11.50

fortuna, 5.709f.

fremere (transitive), 7.460

funus, 6.150; 10.491

Furiae, 3.252

Furies, 12.845

furor, 1.148f; 294; 2.314f.; 5.662; 7.323f., 373f.; 12.593f., 680, 946-7

future, 9.154-5 (*faxo*); 11.467 (*iusso*)

future perfect, 2.581-2

Gaetuli, 5.51f.

Galaesus, 7.511f.

Ganymede, 1.28; 5.252f.

Garamantes, 6.794

gemitus, 3.555

genitive

(causal), 1.178; 11.73, 126

(objective), 1.461-2; 12.589

(respect), 1.14; 2.61; 7.440-1; 9.26, 246 (*animi*)

(separation), 9.789; 10.441

(in *-ai*), 3.354; 7.464

(in *-um*), 1.4; 3.21,704; 6.653; 7.50; 8.127, 698

(form *Achilli, Ulixi*), 1.30; 2.7; 10.581

(form *Androgeo*), 2.392

(form *dii*), 1.636

(form *Mantus*), 10.199

(form *Panos*), 8.344

(form *spe*?), 6.876

genius, 5.95

gerund, 11.230

golden age, 6.792; 7.47f.; 8.319f.

golden bough, 6.136-7

Gorgon, 6.289

Gracchi, 6.842

Gradivus (Mars), 3.35

Greek tragedy, 12.614f., 843f.

Harpies, 3.211-12

haurire, 4.359; 10.648; 12.946

Hecate, 4.511; 6.118

Hector, 1.483 f.; 2.268f.; 11.291-2

Hecuba, 7.319f.

Helen, 2.567f.; 6.517f.

Helenus, 3.295, 296

hendiadys, 1.54, 61; 7.15

Hercules, 3.551; 5.411; 6.122-3, 801f.; 7.655f.; 8.184

Hermione, 3.328

Hesperia, 1.530-3

Hesperides, 4.484-5

Hippolyte, 11.661-2

Homer, 1.1f., 34f.; 10.689f.; 12.697f. *et passim*

Horae, 3.512

Horatius Codes, 8.646f.

horridus, 3.22-3

Hydra, 7.658

hysteron proteron, 2.353

Iarbas, 4.36

Ida, 7.139; 10.157

Idomeneus, 3.122

igneus, 10.718

ignipotens, 8.414

Ilia (Rhea Silvia), 1.273-7

Ilioneus, 1.120; 7.192f.

ille (resumptive), 1.3; 6.593-4; 10.707; 11.494

imbuere, 7.541-2

immugire, 11.38

imperterritus, 10.770

imperative, 3.388; 4.624

impius, 1.294; 6.613

implere, 11.896

importunus, 11.305

improbus, 2.79-80; 4.412; 9.62; 11.512; 12.687

inaccessus, 7.11

Inachius, 11.286

Inachus, 7.372

incendere, 10.895

indicative

(in deliberative question), 4.368; 10.675

(in indirect question), 6.615

infinitive

(epexegetic), 6.49-50, 165

(historic), 2.98

(purpose), 1.527-8

(after noun). 1.704

(after *ardere*), 1.514-15

(after *dare*), 1.66

(after *exposcere*), 4.78-9

(after *hortari*), 2.33

(after *insequi*), 3.31-2

(after *instimulare*), 4.576

(after *orare*), 6.313

(after *suadere*), 1.357

(present after *sperare*), 4.306

(archaic form in *-ier*), 4.493

indiges, 12.794

induere, 10.681

infelix, 7.376; 12.598

infinitive

(historic), 7.15

(purpose), 7.239-40

(after *dare*), 9.173

(after *imperare*), 7.35-6

(after *luctari*), 12.387-8

(after *suadere*), 10.9-10

(archaic form), 7.70

ingeminare, 1.747

instar, 2.15; 6.865; 7.707

instaurare, 4.63

intempesta (nox), 3.587

intendere, 7.514

inundare, 10.24

invadere, 12.712

Io, 7.789f.

Iris, 4.700-2; 9.2

is, 4.479

Italians, 7.641f.; 8.678; 12.791f.

Italus, 1.532

Ithaca, 3.270-1

Ithacus (Ulysses), 2.104

Iulus, 1.267-8

Ixion, 6.601f.

iamdudum, 2.103

Janiculum, 8.355f.

Janus, 7.180, 607f.; 12.198

Iulia (gens), 1.267-8

Juno, 1.1f., 4.34 f.; 7.286f.; 12.791f. *et passim*

Jupiter, 1.223f.; 4.219f.

jussive subjunctive, 2.669; 4.678-9; 5.550-1; 8.643; 10.53-5

Juturna, 12.138

Labyrinth, 5.588-91; 6.1f, 27

Laocoon, 2.41f., 119f., 201

Laomedon, 3.248; 7.105

Lapiths, 7.304-5

Lares, 5.744

Latini, 12.823-5

Latinus, 7.45, 572f.; 11.296f.

Latium, 1.569; 6.792; 8.319f., 323-3

Latona, 12.198

Laurens, 5.797; 7.47

Lausus, 7.649f; 10.769f.

lavere, 3.663

Lavinia, 7.52f.; 12.64

Lavinium, 1.2; 7.52f.; 12.194

Lethe, 6.705

Leucate, 8.677

libare, 5.92; 12.174

Ligurians, 11.701

Liber (Bacchus), 6.801f.

Liquetia, 9.679

litare, 2.118-19

Lucifer, 8.589f.

Lucretius, 1.742f.; 6.264f, 703f. *et passim*

Lupercal, 8.343-4

lusus Troiae, 5545f.

Lyaeus (Bacchus), 1.686; 8.343-4

Lydia, 8.479

Lydius, 2.781-2

lymphata, 7.377

machina, 4.88-9

macte, 9.641

Maeonia, 8.499

mage, 10.481

magic, 4.474f., 489f.

Manes, 12.646

Manlius, 8.652f.

Mantua, 10.198

Marcellus, 6.854f.

marmor, 7.28

Mars (Mavors), 1.276; 10.755; 11.373f.; 12.712

Massyli, 4.132

Medea, 4.1f., 296f., 474f., 601-3

mensa, 7.116

Mercury, 4.219f., 238f.; 8.138-9

Messapus, 7.691f.

meta, 3.714; 12.546-7

metonymy, 2.311, 312; 3.275; 7.77; 10.764-5

metre (see also prosody)

    caesura, 2.9, 483-4; 3.12, 269, 549, 707; 4.486; 5.591, 781; 7.623; 8.453; 10.413; 12.617-19

    diaeresis, 1.81f.; 4.372; 10.786; 11.638; 12.293

    elision, 1.332, 599; 10.508, 514, 691-2, 904; 12.439

    elision, hypermetric, 1.332; 4.558, 629; 5.422, 753; 6.602; 7.160

    fourth foot (single word), 1.7, 296; 2.266-7; 4.384f.; 7.291; 9.431-2

    half lines, 1.534; 2.65-6; 3.218; 4.44; 5.294; 6.94; 7.129; 8.41; 9.167; 10.17; 11.375; 12.631

    hiatus, 1.16, 402f., 617; 3.74. 464. 606; 4.235, 667; 7.178, 631; 10.18; 12.648

hiatus with shortening, 3.211; 5.261; 6.507

lengthening in arsis, 1.308; 2.369; 3.91 ;4.64; 5.284; 6.254; 7.174; 8.98; 9.609-10; 10.382-3; 11.69; 12.13, 89

monosyllabic ending, 1.65, 105; 2.170, 250, 355; 3.12, 390; 4.132; 5.481; 6.346, 466; 7.592; 8.679; 9.320, 532; 10.2; 11.373f.; 12.552

polysyllabic ending, 1.651; 2.68; 5.589; 9.767; 10.505; 11.69

two dissyllables ending, 10.440; 11.143; 12.317

spondaic fifth foot, 1.617; 2.68; 3.12, 74, 517, 549; 5.320; 7.631, 634; 8.54; 9.9; 11.31; 12.863f.

spondaic word at line beginning, 4.185; 6.172; 9.69; 10.514; 11.48; 12.70

Mettus, 8.642f.

Mezentius, 7.648; 10.689f., 773-4, 833f.

middle voice (see also accusative, retained), 2.383; 3.279; 5.264-5; 7.806; 9.74

Mincius, 10.205-6

Minerva — (see Pallas); 7.805; 8.409-10

Minos, 6.432

Minotaur, 6.14f.

misceri, 1.124; 2.298; 4.160; 7.348

Misenus, 6.156f.

moles, 7.589

moliri, 1.424; 4.309; 12.852

monstra, 7.376

monstrum, 3.214-15; 5.849

morari, 5.207

mos, 6.852; 8.316

Mulciber, 8.724f.

Musaeus, 6.667

mussare, 11.345; 12.657

Mycenae, 1 284-5

Myrmidons, 2.7

myrtus, 5.72

namque, 1.65; 10.614

nare, 6.16

-ne, 10.378, 673

-ne (tanton for *tantone),* 10.668

nec (= *non*), 12.533

negare, 3.201; 4.428

nemo, 9.6

Neoptolemus — see Pyrrhus

Neptune, 1.144f.; 2.610

nemo, 9.6

Nereus, 10.764-5

Nile, 8.711f.

nodum, 10.428

nubigena, 7.674

Numa Pompilius, 6.808f.

Numanus, 9.590f.

Numicus, 7.150

Numitor, 6.777

Oenotri, 1.532

olim, 1.20:3.541

olli, 1.254; 11.236

omission of main verb, 3.22-3; 4.131; 5.822

omission of pronoun in accusative and infinitive, 4.383; 6.352-4

omission of reflexive, 8.534

Opis, 11.532

orare, 7.446

Orcus, 6.273

Orestes, 3.331; 4.469f.

Orion, 1.535; 7.719; 10.763f.

Orpheus, 6.119, 645

Paeon, 12.400-1

Palinurus, 3.202; 5.827f.; 6.337f.

Palladium, 2.166; 9.150-1

Pallanteum, 8.51

Pallas, 8.51, 104; 10.362f., 439f.; 11.1f.; 12.887f.

Pallas Athena (Minerva), 1.41; 2.615; 3.544

palma, 5.70

parataxis, 2.172, 669; 4.683-4; 5.550-1; 6.779-80; 8.191-2, 520; 11.296-7; 12.828

Parcae, 1.22; 10.815

Parentalia, 5.59-60

Paris, 4.215f.; 7.319f.

Paros, 1.593

Parrhasius, 8.344

Parthi, 12.857-8

partial apposition, 10.699

participle (used in neuter as noun), 3.422; 5.6

parvulus, 4.327f.

pascere, 11.319

pathetic fallacy, 7.759-60; 8.91-2
Patroclus, 10.454f.
Pelasgi, 8.600
Pelides (Achilles), 2.547-8; 5.808
(Neoptolemus), 2.263
Penates, 1.6; 3.12, 148
Penthesilea, 11.648f.
perfect tense, 1.84; 2.325
Pergama, 1.466
personification, 12.335-6
pestis, 4.90; 5.683
Phlegethon, 6.265
Phrygius, 12.75
Picus, 7.47f., 171, 188f.
pietas, 1.10, 148f.; 2.536f.; 12.839
pilatus, 12.121-2
Pilumnus, 9.4
pius, 1.220, 378; 4.393; 7.5; 8.84;
10.783; 12.175
pluperfect, 5.397
Pluto (Dis), 4.638
Polydorus, 3.19f.
Polyphemus, 3.617
ponere, 7.27; 11.309
populus (poplar), 8.276f.
porgere, 8.274
porro, 5.600
Porsena, 8.646f.
postponed conjunctions, 1.453; 3.25
postponed prepositions, 1.13-14; 4.257;
5.512, 663; 7.234, 296, 441-2
potis, 3.671; 9.796
praepes, 3.360-1
praecipitare, 11.617
praedo, 7.362
Praeneste, 7.678
premere (vocem), 7.119
present tense, 2.275; 4.228; 8.141; 9.266
Priam, 2.506f., 554f.
pronuba, 7.317-19
Proserpina, 6.138
prosody (see also metre)
consonantal *i,* 2.16; 4.686; 6.33;
7.175, 237; 12.356
conubium, 1.73; 7.96
dehinc, 1.131; 8.337
disice, 1.70
fame, 6.421

fevere, 4.409; 8.677
fulgere, 6.826
genua, 5.432; 12.905
Greek scansion, 1.172; 3.127; 7.633,
730
hic, 6.791
hoc, 2.660
obice, 8.227
perfect in *-erunt,* 2.774; 10.333-4
reicit, 10.473
religio, 2.151; 7.172
reliquiae, 1.30; 7.243f.
scio, 3.602
semianimis, 12.356
semihominis, 8.194
shortened diphthong or long vowel,
5.142, 186; 7.523f.
synizesis, 1.41, 697f.; 6.280; 7.33;
8.291-2; 9.32; 10.116; 11.262; 12.84
variation of vowel length, 1.258; 2.663;
3.647; 7.359
protinus, 3.416-17; 6.33; 7.601
pudor 4.27, 322-3
Pyrrhus, 2.263, 453f.

quamquam, 6.394
quamvis, 5.542
quando, 10.366-7
-que epexegetic, 11.207
-que redundant, 10.734
-que . . . -que, 1.43; 10.749
-que redundant, 5.447
quianam, 5.13
quicum, 11.821-2
quin, 1.279; 4.99-100; 10.23
quippe, 1.39
Quirinus, 1.292; 7.187f.
quis (adj.), 1.459
quis (= *quibus*), 1.95-6; 7.444
quisquam, 10.34
quod superest, 5.691f.
quondam, 2.367; 6.876-7; 9.710

radere, 3.700; 7.10
rapere, 1.175-6; 6.7-8; 10.178
rarescere, 3.411
reddere, 3.333
repetition, 1.684; 2.405-6; 7.586f.;
10.705; 11.173; 12.546-7, 857-8

replere, 11.140
Rhadamanthus, 6.566
Rhea Silvia (Ilia), 6.778
Rhesus, 1.469f.
Rhoeteum, 3.108
Romulus, 1.275, 292; 6.779-80; 8.630f.,
    654
ros, 12.339-40
rotate, 10.362-3
ruere, 1.35; 11.211-12
rumpere, 2.129

Sabines, 7.178; 8.635f.
sacer, 3.57
Salii, 8.285, 652f., 663
Salmoneus, 6.585f.
Sarpedon, 10.471
Saturnia (Juno), 1.23; 7.426
Saturnius (Jupiter), 4.372
Saturnius (Neptune), 5.799
Saturnus, 1.569; 6.792; 7.47f.; 8.319f.
satus, 5.244; 7.152
Scaeae portae, 2.612
sceptra, 11.238
Scylla, 3.420f., 424f.
secare, 10.107-8
secundus, 10.266
Segesta, 5523-4
sequester, 11.133
seu, 1.218
si (= *num*), 4.110
si (= *utinam*), 6.882; 8.560f.
Sibylla, 3.443; 6.9-10
Sicani, 7.795
Sicily, 3.692f.; 5.30, 604f.
Sidonia (Dido), 1.446
sidus, 12.451
Silvius, 6.753
Silvia, 7.475f., 487
Simois, 1.100-1; 10.60
simul (= *simul ac*), 3.630; 5.315-19
sinere, 10.426-7; 12.828
singular for plural, 1.564; 5.116; 10.238;
    11.599-600
Sinon, 2.57f.
Sirens, 5.864f.
Sirius, 10.273
sistrum, 8.696
snakes, 2.209-11, 471f.; 11.753f.

Somnus, 5.838
spolia opima, 6.855; 10.449
squalere, 10.313-14
stare, 6.300; 12.407-8
Stoicism, 1.305f., 384-5; 2.428; 3.182;
    4.396; 5.709f.; 6.103-5, 703 f.;
    8.133, 280f.; 12.435f., 436.
Strymonius, 11.580
Styx, 6.295; 9.104f.; 12.816
subjunctive (of purpose), 1.5, 193
subjunctive (past jussive), 8.643
subsidere, 11.268
supine, 2.786
suus, 1.461-2; 10.467
Sychaeus, 1.343; 4.17; 6.474
syncope, 1.26, 201; 2.379; 3.143;
    4.604-6; 5.786f.; 8.274; 10.694;
    11.118
Syrtes, 1.111

Tantalus, 6.601f.
tapete, 7.277
Tarchon, 8.506
tardare, 10.857
Tarpeia, 8.347f.
Tartara (Tartarus), 6.548f.
tenus, 2.553; 10.536
terga, 10.482
Teucer (Greek), 1.619
Teucer or Teucrus (Trojan ancestor),
    1.38; 3.108
Teucri (Trojans), 1.38
Theseus, 6.122-3
Thybrinus, 12.35
thyrsus, 7.390f.
Tiber, 2.781-2; 3.500; 7.25f.
Tirynthius (Hercules), 7.661f.
Tisiphone, 6.555; 10.761
Titans, 4119; 6.580, 725
tmesis, 1.411f.; 5.384, 603; 9.288
transfigere, 11.645
transitive usages, 1.580; 2.541-2; 314;
    7.451, 504
Trinacria, 3.384
Triones, 1.744
Triton, 5.823f.
Tritonia or Tritonis (Pallas), 2.171;
    11.483-5
Trivia, 6.13; (Diana), 7.516f.

Troilus, 1.474f.

tropaeum, 10.774-6; 11.7

Turnus, 6.77f., 89; 7.406f, 785f.; 10.151;
    11.445f.; 12.1f., 614f., 887f. *et*
    passim

Tydides (Diomedes), 1.97, 469f.; 2.163-4

Tyndaris (Helen), 2.601

tyrannus, 7.266

Tyrii, 1.13

Tyrrhus, 7.486

ultra, 2.145

Ulysses (Odysseus), 2.7; 3.588f.; 6.529;
    9.602

ut (= *utinam*), 10.631-2

ut forte, 7.509-10

venia, 11.101

Venilia, 10.76

ventosus, 11.389-91

Venulus, 8.9

Venus, 1.223f., 382, 657f.; 4.90f.;
    5.779f.; 8.370f.; 10.16f. *et passim*

Vesta, 1.292; 2.296-7

vestigia, 7.689-90

vetustas, 10.792

viden, 6.779-80

violentia, 11.354; 12.9

violentus, 10.151

virago, 12.468

virtus, 12.435f.

vocative, predicative, 2.283

vocative (of past participle), 10.186;
    12.947

Vulcanus, 7.77; 8.370f.

vulnus, 7.533

Xanthus, 1.473; 10.60

GLOSSARY

ad loc. - *ad locum*, at the place

aetiology *or* etiology - study of causation, finding a reason for
anacoluthon - change of syntax in a sentence
anapest - two unstressed syllables followed by one stressed (e.g. compre**hend** com-pre-**hend**)
antithesis - setting opposite, a counter proposition
apodosis - the main clause in a conditional statement
apophasis - mention by not mentioning
aposiopesis - a incomplete thought whose ending is left to the imagination
arsis - the up, or weak beat of the metrical foot
asyndeton - the omission of conjunctions
caesurae - a complete pause

cf. - *confer*, compare
chiasmus - the second part is in the reverse order of the first
cretic - a metrical foot of the form long, short, long
dactyl - a stressed syllable followed by two unstressed (e.g.**an**notate **an**-no-tate)
deictic (deixis) - meaning depends on context
diaeresis - one syllable pronounced as two; division when the end of a foot is also a line end

e.g. - *exempli gratia*, for example
ecphrasis - a word description of beauty
elisions - omission of one or more sounds
ellipsis - omission of a word or sound
enclitic - suffix dependant on its host word
epexegesis - word(s) added to elucidate
epyllion - very short epic or biography
f. - forward

gloss - *glossa*, marginal explanation
gnomic - *sententia* in verse

hendiadys - one by means of two (words) for emphasis
hiatus - a line break when a vowel is not elided before a following vowel
iamb - an unstressed syllable followed by a stressed syllable (e.g. des**cribe**, In**clude**, re**tract**)
hypallage - reversed order of two parts of a proposition
iambus - a metrical foot with a short followed by a long syllable
ictus - the stress on a given syllable
litotes - understatement for effect
metonymy - a related noun is substituted for the exact noun
onomatopoeia - a word's sound suggests something other
parataxis - side by side without connectives, *veni, vidi, vici*

passim - scattered
prolepsis - an object described by what it will be but is not yet
protasis - a proposition
pyrrhic - two unstressed syllables together (rare, usually used to end dactylic hexameter)
sc. - scilicet
scansion - metrical analysis of poetry into long and short feet
spondee - two stressed syllables together (e.g. **e-nough)**
syncope - loss of one or more sounds from a word
synizesis - two sounds pronounced as one, slurring
thesis - the down, or strong beat of the metrical foot
tmesis - two parts of a word separated by other words
tricolon - a sentence in three parts
trochee - one stressed syllable followed by an unstressed syllable (e.g. **pic**ture, **flow**er)
zeugma - two or more parts of a sentence joined by a common verb or noun

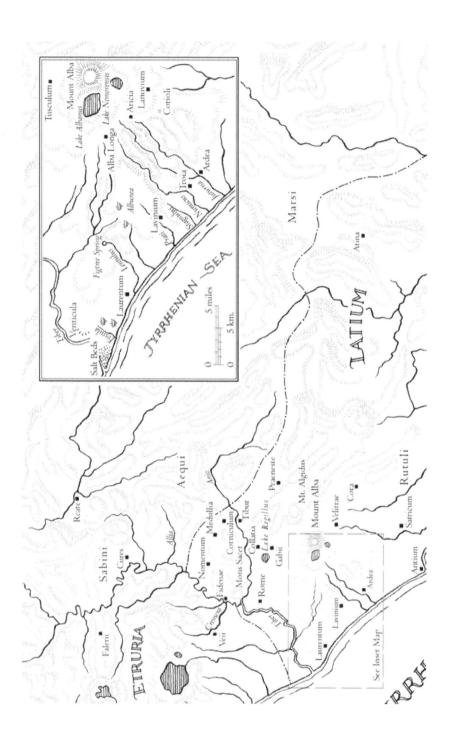

Tusculum
Mount Alba
Lake Albanus
Lake Nemorensis
Aricia
Lanuvium
Corioli
Alba Longa
Ardea
Troia
Laurentum
Numicus
Albunea
Stagnum
Padusa
Lavinium
Figure Spring
Stagnum
Laurentum
Numicius
Lily
Venticula
Salt Beds
TYRRHENIAN SEA
5 miles
5 km.
0
0

Marsi

LATIUM

Acqui
Anio
Reate
Alba
Sabini
Cures
Nomentum Medullia
Corniculum
Collatia
Mons Sacer
Crustumerium
Veii
Caenina
Ficulnea
Tiber
Rome
Gabii
Lake Regillus
Mt. Algidus
Mount Alba
Praeneste
Velitrae
Cora
Satricum
Rutuli
Faleri
ETRURIA
Antium
Laurentum
Lavinium
Ardea
See Inset Map
TRRH

604

Made in the USA
Charleston, SC
27 September 2012